THE THIRTIES

By the same author

The History Today *Companion to British History*
(editor, with Neil Wenborn)
From the Bomb to the Beatles
Who's Who in British History (editor)
The Penguin Dictionary of British History (editor)
The 1940s House
The Edwardian Country House
'Over Here': GIs in Wartime Britain
D-Day: Those Who Were There
Wartime: Britain 1939–45
The Children's War: The Second World War Through
the Eyes of the Children of Britain
The Animals' War: Animals in Wartime from
the First World War to the Present Day
War on the Home Front: Experience
Life in Britain During the Second World War

JULIET GARDINER

The Thirties

An Intimate History

Harper
Press

HarperPress
An imprint of HarperCollins*Publishers*
77–85 Fulham Palace Road,
Hammersmith, London W6 8JB

www.harpercollins.com

Published by HarperPress in 2010

Copyright © Juliet Gardiner 2010
1

A catalogue record for this book is
available from the British Library

ISBN 978 0 00 724076 0

Set in Minion by Palimpsest Book Production Limited,
Grangemouth, Stirlingshire

Printed and bound in Great Britain by
Clays Ltd, St Ives plc

This book is proudly printed on paper which contains wood
from well managed forests, certified in accordance with
the rules of the Forest Stewardship Council.
For more information about FSC,
please visit www.fsc-uk.org

 Mixed Sources
Product group from well-managed
forests and other controlled sources
www.fsc.org Cert no. SW-COC-1806
© 1996 Forest Stewardship Council
FSC

FSC is a non-profit international organisation established to promote the
responsible management of the world's forests. Products carrying the FSC
label are independently certified to assure consumers that they come
from forests that are managed to meet the social, economic and
ecological needs of present and future generations.

Find out more about HarperCollins and the environment at
www.harpercollins.co.uk/green

For Joseph

CONTENTS

ILLUSTRATIONS

Neighbours outside a block of flats in London's East End. Photograph by Wolf Suschitzky, c.1935. *(© Wolfgang Suschitzky/Museum of London)*
The funeral cortège for some of the seventy-one child victims of the Glen cinema disaster passes through the streets of Paisley on 4 January 1930. *(© Newsquest (Herald & Times). Licensor www.scran.ac.uk)*
The Hatry Crash: a newspaper vendor outside Charing Cross station in January 1930. *(© Getty Images)*
Brushes for sale in London's Caledonian Market in 1935. Photograph by Cyril Arapoff. *(© Museum of London)*
A column of men on a hunger march trudge through the rain on their way to London. *(© Getty Images)*
Hunger marchers climb the railings of Hyde Park during a protest rally against the Means Test on 27 October 1932. *(© Topfoto)*
The vicar of St Luke's, Kew Gardens, posts a notice inviting his parishioners to vote in favour of cinemas opening on Sundays. *(© Topfoto)*

Passengers at Victoria Coach Station in 1939. Photograph by Wolf Suschitzky. *(W. Suschitzky/Lebrecht Music & Arts)*
British Union of Fascists couple T. Naylor and Edith Taylor leave the Free Catholic Church, Edmonton, after their wedding on 5 February 1934. *(© Getty Images)*
Children playing at a nursery school on the site of the old Foundling Hospital in Bloomsbury, March 1936. *(© Getty Images)*
Ramblers and hikers demonstrate on 1 January 1932 in support of the

Open Air Charter for the preservation of public rights on roads and foot-paths. (© *Getty Images*)

Twenty-nine-year-old Richard Crossman calls on the Robbins family during his unsuccessful by-election campaign to become Labour MP for West Birmingham in April 1937. (© *National Portrait Gallery, London*)

Famous tipster Ras Prince Monololu (real name Peter Carl Mackay) at Epsom racecourse on 28 May 1933. (*Daily Herald Archive/NMeM/Science & Society Picture Library*)

Edward VIII visiting Abertillery during his tour of Welsh mining areas in November 1936. (© *Getty Images*)

A London family taking a midday break during a hop-picking holiday in the Kent countryside. Photograph by Cyril Arapoff. (© *Museum of London*)

The inauguration of Weston-Super-Mare's magnificent concrete cantilevered diving tower in July 1937. (*By kind permission of the North Somerset Museum and Gallery*)

Dolls being distributed in June 1937 to Basque children, refugees from the Spanish Civil War, at Watermillock, Bolton. (© *Getty Images*)

Eric Gill and his nearly-complete monumental sculpture *Creation*, destined for the League of Nations Building in Geneva, in 1937. (© *National Portrait Gallery, London*)

A family enjoying a day on the beach at Blackpool on 1 July 1939. (© *Getty Images*)

The roof gardens of Selfridges in Oxford Street, decorated to celebrate the Silver Jubilee of George V in May 1935. (© *Getty Images*)

Members of the royal family at the service of thanksgiving for George V's Silver Jubilee at St Paul's Cathedral on 6 May 1935. (© *Getty Images*)

Local residents crowd round the gates of Sandringham, Norfolk, to read the bulletin about the illness of George V on 19 January 1936. (© *Getty Images*)

Swastika flying at half-mast over the German Embassy in London on 21 January 1936 as a mark of respect for the death of George V. (© *Getty Images*)

The Duke of Windsor, formerly Edward VIII, with his mother, Queen Mary, in the grounds of Marlborough House on 6 October 1945. It was the first time they had met since Edward's abdication nine years before. *(© Getty Images)*

Guests at a Buckingham Palace garden party in the summer of 1936 scurry for shelter from a sudden downpour. *(© Topfoto)*

Prime Minister Neville Chamberlain and his wife Anne walk across Horse Guards Parade on 7 September 1939, four days after the outbreak of the Second World War. *(© Getty Images)*

PREFACE

There will be time to audit
The accounts later, there will be sunlight later
And the equation will come out at last.

Louis MacNeice, 'Autumn Journal' (1939)

The thirties is a statement as well as a decade. And it is one that is frequently heard today, because while those years are gradually slipping from our grasp, what they have come to represent is ever more present: confusion, financial crises, rising unemployment, scepticism about politicians, questions about the proper reach of Britain's role in the world.

Famously, to W.H. Auden, sitting on a bar stool in 'one of the dives on Fifty-Second Street' in New York in September 1939, the thirties were a 'low, dishonest decade'. Looking back later, others followed him, labelling it 'the devil's decade', 'a dark tunnel', 'the locust years', a 'morbid age', a time tainted by the dolorous spectres of intractable unemployment, the Means Test and appeasement, that ended inexorably in the most terrible war the world has ever known. But others claimed that this was a partial picture. It ignored those areas of Britain largely unaffected by the 'Great Depression', where the symbols of prosperity were the growth of home ownership, new light industries, a consumer society – evidenced by rapidly multiplying acres of suburban semis, the hope of a Baby Austin in the garage, a branch of Woolworths in every town, roadhouses on every arterial road, lidos, cinemas, paid holidays, dance halls, greyhound racing, football pools, plate glass, the modernist and the 'moderne'. In sum, J.B. Priestley's new 'third England' to set alongside two old Englands – one 'byways England', slow, rural and benign, the other harsh, ugly and industrial.

'There ain't no universals in this man's town,' wrote Louis MacNeice in 1939. This book recognises the claims of all of these Englands (or rather Britains) to tell the story of the thirties. Its aim is to explore all three, to uncover the 'intimate history' of what it was like to live through the decade.

It is not one story; it is not three stories: it is hundreds of interwoven stories, from that of the Prime Minister(s) to a discontented North London schoolteacher, from three Kings to one rather anxious Oxford vicar's wife, from the economist J.M. Keynes and the novelist Virginia Woolf to the intermittently unemployed gardener Frank Forster and the astute Hull journalist Cyril Dunn. Lives, events, aspirations, plans and the tireless search for solutions by people who felt that after the trauma of the First World War it must be possible to reorder society better, and those for whom this disastrously failed. All fitting into a panorama of Britain in the thirties, a decade that haunts us today with the magnitude of its problems, the paucity of its solutions, the dreadfulness of its ending, while snaring us with the boldness of its political and social experiments, the earnestness of its blueprints, the yearnings of its young, and the sheer glamour of its design, art, architecture, fashion, dream palaces, dance halls, and obsession with speed.

The story begins on the last day of 1929; it has no conclusion other than the outbreak of the Second World War on 3 September 1939, which, while not formally ending the decade, definitively foreclosed thirties Britain.

Juliet Gardiner
November 2009

A NOTE ON MONEY

Translating the value of money is fraught with difficulties. As Adam Smith wrote in *The Wealth of Nations* (1776): 'The real price of every thing, what every thing really costs to the man who wants to acquire it, is the toil and trouble of acquiring it . . . but it is not that by which their value is estimated . . . Every commodity is more frequently exchanged for, and thereby compared with other commodities.'

www.measuringworth.com/ukcompare suggests that there are five indices that can be used to compare monetary values in different eras. I have generally chosen the lowest (the retail price index), which multiplies a sum by roughly fifty – so that £100 in the 1930s would equal almost £5,000 today. But perhaps a more useful guide is to remember that in 1935 a working man would earn between £3 and £4 a week, and that an average semi-detached suburban house would have cost between £500 and £750.

PART ONE

How it was Then

The Eve of the Decade

'Wi' ye nae git out fra under ma feet,' seven-year-old Robert Pope's mother, wielding a mop and a bucket, scolded as she shooed him out of the house. The string bag full of jam jars he was clutching banged against his shins as he ran along Maxwell Street in Paisley to meet his friends. It was Hogmanay, the last day of the year 1929: the day that Scottish housewives busied themselves 'redding' (readying) their homes in a frenzy of mopping, sweeping, scrubbing, polishing, dusting, all to make sure that they were as clean as the proverbial new pin to welcome the New Year in through the front door as the Old Year slipped out by the back. The tallyman should have been paid off too, and any goods 'on tick' settled, since it was considered bad luck to start the New Year in debt. But that wouldn't be so easy.

By midday a queue of almost a thousand children, some clutching the hands of smaller siblings, others with bairns little more than babies in their arms, were waiting outside the Glen cinema in the centre of town. Admission was a penny for the stalls, tuppence for the balcony, and those children whose fathers were maybe out of work, or had been killed in the Great War that had ended just over a decade earlier, and whose mothers hadn't been able to spare the necessary coins, had scoured their tenement homes for empty bottles or jam jars to take back to the shop with the promise that the returned deposit could be used for the cinema.

The Glen, with its ornate façade and stained-glass windows, was one of six cinemas in Paisley, a town lying in Glasgow's southern shadow. If cinema-going was popular with adults – and it was, with some eighteen to nineteen million attendances every week in the 1930s – it was even more so for children. And if that was true of the South, it was more so in the North: in 1933 it was reported that seven out of ten children in Edinburgh went to the pictures at least once a week, most to the special Saturday-afternoon shows that cinema managers laid on for children, filling the seats by showing usually old films at cheap prices. 'Most children spend longer at the cinema than they do at many school subjects,' wrote Richard Ford, who organised cinema clubs for children for the Odeon cinema chain, and reckoned that by 1939 some 4,600,000 children went to the cinema every week all over Britain.

In Paisley the Glen had started life as accommodation for a crypto-Masonic sect called the Good Templars, a temperance movement founded in 1850 to encourage moderation in, or preferably total abstinence from, the consumption of alcohol. As an encouragement to the sober life, the Templars organised various non-alcoholic entertainments, including tea concerts which were held on Saturday afternoons and were known as 'Bursts', since those attending were handed a paper bag containing an apple and an orange and at some point were encouraged to blow up their paper bags and burst them simultaneously. In homage to this innocent way of passing a dull afternoon, those watching silent films once the Glen had been converted into a cinema in 1910 (since lack of enthusiasm for temperance had by then reduced the Templars to holding their meetings in the basement) would burst a paper bag at appropriate moments in a film, such as a gunshot; and even when the introduction of the 'talkies' in the late 1920s rendered this unnecessary, there were children who were gamely prepared to uphold the tradition.

Over a thousand children were packed into the Glen that Hogmanay afternoon. Most found seats, but the cinema could accommodate an additional 140 standing in the gangways both downstairs and in the more expensive balcony, where children were not allowed, though some slipped in regardless. The main feature was a silent film, *The Crowd*, but this was preceded by a short western which starred the ever-popular Tom Mix as a bareback-riding, lasso-twirling cowboy in one of the last silent films Mix made on his self-constructed film-set ranch, 'a complete frontier town . . . typical of the early Western era', Mixville in California.

At 2 p.m. the lights dimmed and a cheer went up as the children settled down to watch the film, with loud cheers or catcalls as the action unfolded. But about halfway through the second reel (which had to be changed manually) dense, sulphurous carbon-monoxide-laden smoke began to fill the auditorium, and the children started to panic. 'Fire!' one shouted – though there wasn't – prompting a mass stampede for the exits. Most of the children made for a side door that led to a narrow staircase down into an alleyway. But when they reached the bottom they found that the exit was barred by an iron trellis gate that was firmly padlocked in place. However much they pushed and screamed, the gate would not yield, as more and more frightened children continued to push down the stairs, stumbling, falling, fainting, crushed underfoot.

Others ran into the lavatories, where they smashed the windows to get out, cutting their arms and legs on the jagged shards as they did so. Those in the balcony jumped down into the auditorium, adding to the panic, and a heavy swing door was wrenched off its hinges by small boys finding a superhuman strength in their desperation. Some children lost precious minutes frantically searching for a mislaid shoe, a discarded scarf, fearing that with money so tight, they would get in trouble if they came home having lost an item of clothing.

By now smoke was swirling into the street, and anxious passers-by tried to get into the building. Driven back by the dense smoke, they summoned the police, who smashed all the windows of the cinema with their batons to let the noxious fumes escape. Within minutes the fire brigade had arrived. 'Several people cried out "For God's sake get your smoke helmets: we can't get through the smoke. The cinema's full of children,"' the Deputy-Chief Fire Marshal reported. 'As soon as my men heard about the children there was no holding them back. Smoke helmets or no smoke helmets we were off the engine into the cinema with no delay.' The firemen were followed by members of the public clutching handkerchiefs over their mouths to try to protect themselves from inhaling the smoke.

A terrible sight met their eyes: sweets, comics, torn clothes lay scattered in disarray all over the floor, seats were upturned, there were pools of blood near the doorways and windows where children had tried to claw their way out. And there were the children: heaps of contorted bodies, most dead, some unconscious, piled up in nightmarish heaps, still and grotesque. 'Behind the screen,' reported Deputy-Chief Fire Marshal Wilson, 'the space was packed with children huddled together in every conceivable attitude. They were as tightly packed as a wall of cement bags. Some still moved, others were motionless, blue in the face . . . some were able to scream . . . Legs and arms were intertwined in the most appalling tangle. In some cases it took two of us working very gradually to extricate one child.' The oldest victim was thirteen, the youngest a toddler of eighteen months, and there were all ages in between, siblings, friends, neighbours, all dead or mortally injured, trapped in a 'pleasure palace' on the last day of the decade.

Those children who could walk were led out, shocked, shaken and in some cases hysterical; others were carried to ambulances, private cars and buses to be taken to the Royal Alexandra Infirmary, suffering from carbon-monoxide poisoning or injuries sustained in the crush to get out. A tramway Inspector turned the passengers off a couple of trams and requisitioned them to convey the injured to hospital, while the workers at a nearby print factory downed tools and hurried to the Glen to carry twenty children to the safety of their works. Again and again the firemen went back, sometimes accompanied by desperate parents searching for their offspring. 'Two small bodies were found huddled together in the orchestra pit. It appeared as if two children had crept there for safety after finding the passage to the door blocked by the bodies of their young friends,' and several more bodies were found under upturned seats. A father staggered out carrying his small son, blue in the face, his head lolling lifelessly.

By 4 p.m. the cinema had been cleared: two hours after the matinee had started, fifty-nine children had been pronounced dead on arrival at the Infirmary. Many had barely a mark on them, suffocated by the weight of others frantically trying to get out, while others 'bore scratches on their face, hands and knees, eloquent testimony to the desperation with which they had struggled to get out of the death trap . . . So rapidly were the victims brought in that, in order to make room for those who were alive, the bodies were hurried to a lift and conveyed to the basement. Here they were placed on trolleys by twos and threes and rushed along a tunnel to the mortuary. Numbers grew so rapidly that the mortuary was soon full and other rooms [including the hospital chapel] had to be used to accommodate the bodies.' That night ten more children died from their injuries: the final death toll in the Glen cinema disaster was seventy-one. One family lost all three children, another four families lost two children each. Robert Pope's name was not among the list of the dead, but many of his schoolfriends' were. A BBC New Year programme from Scotland was pulled and a four-minute silence broadcast instead. And the streets of Paisley, usually packed with revellers at Hogmanay, were eerily empty and silent.

The King, George V, and Queen Mary sent messages of sympathy, so did the Prime Minister, Ramsay MacDonald, and another Scot, the music-hall star Sir Harry Lauder. Condolences, money and offers of help poured in from all over the world, as did offers to adopt the survivors – something no one wanted even to consider.

The funerals of sixty of the victims were held on 4 January 1930. It was a bleak, grey day, with intermittent flurries of sleet as the funeral processions started out. Flags on public buildings flew at half-mast, and as services in Paisley Abbey and the four Roman Catholic churches in the town started at 11 a.m., shops shut their doors and drew their blinds as a mark of respect. Crowds lined the route, everyone wearing black or a black armband, many hurriedly made from crêpe paper; the only relief came from the wreaths atop the coffins and from the flash of white on the uniforms of the Boys' Brigade band as they followed the white coffin of one of their members, twelve-year-old Robert Wingate, playing the heartbreaking lament 'Flowers o' the Forest' as the coffin was carried up the nave of Paisley Abbey. Journalists came too, compelled by their own headlines – 'Scotland's Worst ever Cinema Disaster' – and cinema operators from all over Britain joined the mourners, hats in hands, heads bowed.

Paisley Council, mindful that many families would not be able to afford the cost of burying their dead children, offered a free burial ground at Hawkhead Municipal Cemetery for those who could not afford a plot, and the town's team of ten gravediggers was trebled to thirty. Tragically, some of this swollen workforce found themselves digging the final resting place of their own child.

Two days earlier, on 2 January, the Glen cinema manager Charles Dorward had been arrested and charged with culpable homicide. The charge hung on whether the metal trellis gate that had trapped so many of the dead had been padlocked rather than left unlocked during the performance, as it should have been according to health and safety regulations. Dorward was released on bail of £750, and hastily packed and left his home in the town where so many families had been touched by the disaster.

The case was heard before the Lord Advocate, Craigie Aitchison KC, in Edinburgh on 29 April 1930. During the proceedings it came out that on the morning of the fire the cinema had been inspected by members of the Paisley Fire Brigade, who had pronounced it safe. The Glen's owner, James Graham, agreed that there were insufficient exits, and claimed that he had repeatedly reminded Dorward that under no circumstances were the gates to be shut during matinee performances. The manager replied that they were locked on occasions to stop children who hadn't bought tickets from slipping in for free during the film. Graham replied that 'he didn't care if the whole of Paisley slipped in; the gates must be kept open'. A policeman gave evidence that when he arrived on the scene the gates were padlocked, but Dorward was adamant that he had opened them himself before the start of the matinee on 31 December 1929. The cinema chocolate girl, Isla Muir, confirmed that she had seen him open the gates. She was unable to say how they came to be closed subsequently, but suggested that two boys she had seen hanging about outside might have been responsible. After a trial lasting only two days, Charles Dorward was found not guilty by the un-animous verdict of the jury. It was concluded that although cigarette butts, spent matches and an empty cigarette box had been found in the projection room – where smoking was not permitted – these were not the cause of the film combusting: rather it was the carelessness of a fifteen-year-old assistant, James McVey, who had put a metal canister containing the first reel of nitrate on top of a battery, causing a short circuit, that was to blame, though once the film started to smoke, the limited number of exits, the shortage of attendants and the excessive number of children packed into the cinema that afternoon had all contributed materially to the tragedy.

Lessons were learned from the Glen cinema disaster. In the new decade many municipal authorities – Glasgow included – ordered an inspection of all theatres and cinemas under their jurisdiction. Licences were scrutinised and the fitness of those holding them checked, legislation was introduced to check the 'tuppenny rush' at children's matinees, those under seven must be accompanied by an adult, there had to be a higher ratio of attendants to children, and the Cinematograph Act of 1909 was updated to extend local authorities' powers to ensure that all cinemas had a greater number of exits, that doors opened outwards and were fitted with push bars, and that seating capacity was limited, among other safety stipulations.

There was no counselling offered to the traumatised survivors. They were advised to forget about the terrible experience, and in an effort to help this healing process Paisley Town Council offered injured children and bereaved parents a week at the seaside. Small parties left Paisley a fortnight after the tragedy for West Kilbride and Dunoon. The relief fund was closed: it had raised £5,300.

It was a welcome sum. Paisley was a poor town. Although men such as the thread manufacturers Peter and James Coats, who were both worth more than £2 million (around £100 million in today's prices) when they died in 1913, had made their fortunes in Paisley, by 1929 the town was the victim of the industrial depression that swept the West of Scotland, the Valleys of Wales, and the manufacturing North and other pockets of England. Unemployment was high and rising, and wages were low for those in work in Paisley.

Yet even before the Glen cinema disaster brought the town unwanted publicity, Paisley's name was known throughout the English-speaking world. It was synonymous with soft woollen shawls bearing distinctive teardrop or tadpole patterns (probably representing the growing shoot of the date palm), usually in muted, smudged colours that had been greatly prized since the East India Company had first brought such shawls, woven of goatsdown, from Kashmir in the eighteenth century. Desirable these might have been, but they were fabulously expensive, so around 1780 weavers in Norwich and Edinburgh began to produce shawls 'in imitation of the Indian', using a new technique that reduced the cost of production by three-quarters. Paisley had a workforce of skilled weavers, but its silk industry had been hit badly by the Napoleonic Continental blockade. It seized on this new fashion accessory, and by the 1840s was effectively a one-industry town, with a monopoly of such shawl production, with the so-called 'big corks' of Paisley buying the yarn and the designs and distributing them to cottage-industry handloom weavers. Shawl-making brought new prosperity to the town – though not to the weavers, who were now outworkers rather than creative artisans, and gradually, with the introduction of the Jacquard loom, factory hands. But since by definition fashion items are just that, there were slumps and booms throughout the nineteenth century, and by the twentieth coats and jackets had replaced shawls as outer wear. The weavers of Paisley persevered and adapted to making any new products that might sell, but by 1930 only vestiges remained of the weaving industry that had made the town's name go around the world. In mid-nineteenth-century Scotland the textile industry had employed over 20 per cent of the population; by 1931 the figure was less than 7 per cent, and those who could find work found it in thread manufacture, starching and dyeing.

Those who couldn't would take a train to nearby Glasgow, with a population in 1931 of over a million and still claiming to be the 'second city of the Empire'. But Glasgow had also been hard hit, with a large proportion of its resources tied up in what would become irredeemably depressed heavy industries: shipbuilding on the Clyde, where one-fifth of the world's tonnage of ships had been launched by the start of the First World War, coalmining in Lanarkshire, and jute and linen manufacture on Tayside. By 1930, while 16.1 per cent of the population of the United Kingdom was unemployed, in Scotland the figure was 18.5 per cent, and by 1933 it had soared to 26.1 per cent compared to the overall UK figure of 19.9 per cent. And for those in work, wages were low: less than 92 per cent of those earned in England. By 1931–32 that had fallen further, to 87 per cent. The thirties were always going to be a difficult decade for Paisley: now it had tragedy layered over hardship.

ONE

Goodbye to All That

We have magneto trouble. How, then, can we start up again?
John Maynard Keynes, December 1930

'It is difficult to see the wood for the trees,' mused Gerald Barry, then editor of Lord Beaverbrook's *Saturday Review*, though soon to resign on a question of principle and start the *Week-End Review*, and something of a connoisseur of English eccentricities and oddities, in a BBC broadcast on the final day of the 1920s. He rounded off his talk in much the same vein. 'We cannot put the jigsaw puzzle of the present together, because we are sitting on the pieces.' In between he surveyed the year that had passed, commenting on the progress of the R100 and the R101 airships, and on the 'thirst for speed . . . one of the significant tendencies of our time', which had been partially slaked by Sir Henry Segrave's 'remarkable motor-car record at Daytona Beach of 231 m.p.h.', and on the extraordinary weather, which 'began with extreme and prolonged cold which those of us with burst water pipes will not forget in a hurry . . . followed by a superb summer and a drought which caused many towns and villages great anxiety and stopped many of us watering our gardens and washing our cars', and ending with 'disastrous floods and record gales'. The number of motorists had continued to increase, and with them the number of accidents, as had what Barry called the 'continued uglification of the countryside'. On the credit side Stonehenge, Friday Street, Runnymede and many more 'notable spots' had been saved, and in Barry's mind the fierce controversies over Sir Gilbert Scott's design for a new power station at Battersea, the erection of pylons across the South Downs as part of the new electrical grid system and proposals for the new Charing Cross Bridge were evidence that 'in 1929 we have become more conscious of the need of beauty and orderliness in our midst'.

Barry's notion of sitting on a jigsaw, knowing that there were crucial pieces to be fitted together, but unable to see how they could coalesce, nonplussed by the odd shapes and irregularities of the pieces, the intransigent way one

11

could not be locked with what seemed to be its natural partner to make a satisfying whole, could be a metaphor that would carry all the way from the turn of the decade when he conjured up the image, through the 1930s. It would be a decade of despair and frustration for many, of confusion and stasis, and sometimes, in what seemed a purblind refusal to recognise the true nature of economic and social problems, of government inaction and public despair. Yet paradoxically, this decline would co-exist alongside rising wages and falling prices, a steady increase in living standards, a housing boom and unprecedented growth in domestic consumption. While abroad the thirties would be a decade of escalating tension and the rise of fascism – again met with uncertainty, irresolution, self-deception, misread signals, anxious hopes and missed opportunities – they were also years of experimentation, of hope, of resolution, of a confident belief that modernity had provided the tools with which to fashion a better future, above all a *planned* future, that mobilised politics, economics, science and the arts to build a brave new world (Aldous Huxley's novel – albeit a dystopia – was written in 1931 and published the following year). But while, of course, no one could be certain of the picture that would emerge from the disparate pieces at the start of 1930, there was the feeling that the coming decade would be significant. That the thirties would be very different from the twenties. As indeed they would.

The *Lady*, a magazine for women who lived a leisurely life in society, thought that 1930 'somehow assumes an added importance because it is a round number'. The magazine's columnist was 'curious' that given this 'added importance . . . most girls do not choose New Year's Day for their wedding instead of hastening to the altar in December. It seems such a very appropriate day for the beginning of a new life – or, at any rate a new enterprise.' One society girl did buck the trend in 1930 – though not entirely of her own volition: the wedding of Miss Zelia Hambro, daughter of Sir Percival Hambro of the merchant banking family, had to be rushed as the groom, Lieutenant Patrick Humphreys of the Royal Navy, was about to sail for China at short notice. For the wedding in Holy Trinity church, Sloane Street, Chelsea, the bride chose 'a really lovely dress, far too good for any festivities on the China station', and her mother, who was 'rather keen on politics and belongs to the Ladies Imperial Club' no doubt enlivened proceedings on the day by being 'one of the few women in London who smokes cigars – real ones, and not the little affairs provided for women who prefer something stronger'.

There was, however, a more serious investment in marking the end of the 1920s, ten years stained by the memory of the Great War, in which

5.7 million British men had joined the armed forces, of whom three-quarters of a million had been killed and more than one and a half million seriously wounded. Proportionately this was less than the French and German losses, but there was an overwhelming feeling of a 'lost generation', as perhaps more than 30 per cent of all men aged between twenty and twenty-four in 1914 were killed in the war, and 28 per cent of those aged thirteen to nineteen. Many of those seriously wounded – physically or mentally – never recovered, and certainly never worked again: the sight of a blind or maimed ex-serviceman trying to scrape a living by selling matches or bootlaces in the street, or simply by begging, was commonplace throughout the 1920s and 1930s. Two and a half million men were sufficiently disabled to qualify for a state pension, which was calculated on a harsh sliding scale: those suffering from the loss of two or more limbs, or major facial disfigurement, qualified for a full pension (27s.6d a week); the loss of a whole right arm brought 90 per cent of that; if the arm was intact below the shoulder but had been amputated above the elbow, or the veteran was totally deaf, that netted 70 per cent, falling to fourteen shillings a week if the amputation was below the elbow or knee, or the sight of one eye had been lost. On the assumption that most men were right-handed, the award was a shilling a week less in each category if it was the left arm that was involved, though if 'only' two fingers on either hand had been blown away, a man would receive 5s.6d a week. More than that, the war had come to the Home Front, with air raids claiming some 1,400 civilian lives and leaving 3,400 wounded.

The reminders of the war were material in so many ways. Within months of the Armistice on the eleventh hour of the eleventh day of the eleventh month of 1918, war memorials to commemorate the dead were being built in cities, towns and villages all over Britain, and plaques were being screwed on the walls of railway stations, police stations, depots, schools and factories in honour of 'the fallen'. On many of them it was difficult to find space to carve the litany of the dead: in Lancashire, for example, the Chorley Pals (which became Y Company of the 11th Battalion, the East Lancashire Regiment) lost 758 officers and men. The architect of Imperial Delhi, Sir Edwin Lutyens, designed a simple concrete altar to those slaughtered in the war to stand in the middle of Whitehall: it would stand like a reproach on an axis that crossed from the Prime Minister's residence to the War Office. A nameless corpse was selected from those buried as 'unknown' near the trench-riddled wastelands of northern France, transported by boat and train in a coffin made from an oak felled at Hampton Court and lowered into a grave just inside the west entrance of Westminster Abbey. Covered with sandbags filled with sand from the Western Front, it was topped with a slab of black Tournai marble from Belgium bearing an inscription that included the words 'a British warrior unknown by name or rank'. King George V, finding himself – after a slow start – much affected by the notion, attended the funeral service for this poignant representative of Britain's lost generation on Armistice Day 1920 before unveiling Lutyens's stark concrete memorial. The ceremony concluded with a haunting rendition of the 'Last Post' that seemed to hang in the air.

Within five days over a million people had visited the grave and left hillocks of flowers at the cenotaph, and from that day forward Armistice Day has been commemorated throughout Britain by a two-minute silence as the eleventh hour strikes, those who fought and survived, and those who remembered, bowing their heads, in their buttonholes a fabric replica of the fragile, ubiquitous Flanders poppy adopted by the British Legion as the symbol of the debt owed to those whose blood seeped into the mud of the Western Front.

The new decade had a new government: David Lloyd George's wartime coalition had ended in 1922 when the Conservatives under Andrew Bonar Law withdrew their support, wishing to re-establish the old party system. Only it wasn't the old system: no longer was there a Conservative/Liberal duopoly alternating in power as it had throughout most of the nineteenth century, up until the First World War. Henceforth the Labour Party, which had only been founded in 1900, would provide the main opposition to the Conservatives. The Liberal Party had split during the war between those who were loyal to the former leader Herbert Asquith – known as 'Asquithian Liberals' – and those who grouped around Lloyd George – the 'National Liberals'.

After the 1922 election each faction claimed roughly the same number of MPs – between fifty and sixty – but the electoral system, which the Liberals had failed to reform when they had the opportunity, meant that with their support spread thinly across the country and the classes, they were increasingly doomed to be runners-up to Labour in industrial and urban seats, and to the Conservatives in wealthy and rural ones. Labour enjoyed its first taste of government – albeit a brief one – between January and November 1924. On taking power, the Labour Prime Minister Ramsay MacDonald had two objectives. One was to dispose of the Liberal Party, the other to prove that Labour was fit to govern. In both he succeeded, although the Liberal Party's decline was slow. However, by 1929 although the Liberals polled over five million votes, this translated into only fifty-nine MPs, mainly returned from Celtic fringe constituencies around the edge of Britain. By comparison the Conservatives won 260 seats and Labour 287.

The electorate that voted in the second Labour government that year had increased since 1918 by almost 30 per cent to nearly twenty-nine million – 91 per cent of the adult population were now eligible to vote, with women given the vote at the same age as men – twenty-one – rather than thirty, as had been the case when women's suffrage had first been granted in 1918.

The second Labour government had a small majority and a massive problem: unemployment. The Conservatives had narrowly lost the election campaigning under the slogan 'Safety First', copied from a campaign to reduce the number of road accidents. But it seemed that what was needed was less caution, and more action and imagination. The economy was out of balance, with more than a million workers unemployed on average throughout most of the 1920s.

The causes were complex: the war of course was partly to blame. The four years of conflict had cost – in monetary terms – £11,325 million, including loans to allies to help them fight the war; many of these, including those to Russia, would never be repaid. The war was paid for partly out of taxation, partly by liquidating foreign investment, but mainly by loans both from home and overseas. The national debt, which had stood at £620 million in 1914, had risen to £8,000 million by 1924 – the largest slice of it owed to the United States. This led to a vicious spiral: something approaching half the country's annual expenditure of £800 million went on servicing this debt, meaning that of the revenue raised by income tax, which had risen to an unprecedented five shillings in the pound by 1924, a quarter went towards debt repayment.

Stanley Baldwin, essentially Prime Minister when Ramsay MacDonald was not, that is three times between 1923 and 1937, was a Worcestershire ironmaster whose companies had profited from wartime munitions contracts. Baldwin made an honourable (and discreet) gesture by sending a personal cheque for £120,000 to the Treasury, and there was talk of a national levy. But the problem was not solely debt. The requirements of peace were very different from those of war, and the heavy industries that had expanded to fulfil military needs now found themselves with spare capacity and an export market cut by half, with American and Japanese manufacturers moving into former British markets.

Before the war Britain had been one of the most prosperous countries in the world. After a century and a half of economic growth, expanding trade and shrewd overseas investment, Britain could claim to be among the major industrialised nations and the undisputed hub of international trade and finance. Lancashire cotton mills produced sufficient yarn and textiles to clothe half the world, the shipbuilders of the North-East alone produced a third of the world's output, Britain was the second largest producer of coal in the world; its merchant fleet accounted for almost half the world's tonnage, while Britain was a major international creditor with a large inflow of invisible earnings from investments, shipping and insurance.

However, there were serious long-term structural problems that exacerbated the consequences of war. Britain's prosperity had depended largely on 'old staples' – coal, iron, steel, textiles and shipbuilding – which had provided three-quarters of the country's exports and employed almost a quarter of the working population. At the turn of the century more recently industrialised countries such as Germany and the United States had challenged Britain's position as the 'workshop of the world', and were developing new industries such as chemicals, electrical goods and engineering more rapidly than Britain. The appeal of overseas investment, and a dependence on the Empire as the market for British goods, had led to a neglect of the domestic market and the opportunities offered by these new industries. By 1913 Britain's economic growth was little more than half what it had been in 1900, and its share of world trade had dropped from a third in 1870 to a seventh by 1914.

The necessities of war boosted Britain's traditional heavy industries – particularly those linked to the production of munitions and textiles, such as the Scottish jute industry, which was kept at full stretch manufacturing sandbags – and provided a stimulus to accelerate the development of newer ones such as electrical goods, aircraft and motor construction, precision engineering, radio and pharmaceuticals. A post-war boom fuelled by rising prices and the speculative investment of wartime profits lulled people into thinking that the normal rhythms of trade and production would soon be reasserted, and Britain would regain her pre-war markets. Indeed, there was a 'craze of speculation' in Lancashire, where old textile mills were bought and sold and new ones constructed in eager anticipation of an export boom, and shipyard owners shared a similar confidence. In 1920 coal still made up 9 per cent of Britain's exports – only 1 per cent less than in 1913. But the boom was short-lived: by 1921 increases in interest rates and a fall in prices on the world market hit exports, which in turn hit production, and by the winter of 1921–22 more than two million British men and women were unemployed. Cotton textile exports fell to less than half the 1913 figure by 1929, and would never again reach pre-war levels, while coal represented less than 7 per cent of exports: down from 287 million tons in 1913 to forty million by 1922.

It wasn't only the 'old staples' that were in decline: London was losing its pre-war position as the financial capital of the world as the City lost its exclusive authority over monetary policy at home. During the war financial exigencies had forced Britain off the Gold Standard, with the issue of paper £1 and ten-shilling notes that could no longer be converted directly into gold. Financial orthodoxy regarded a return to the Gold Standard as a prerequisite for economic stability: it was essential that the 'pound should look the dollar in the face'. As far as Lord Bradbury (a former head of the Treasury who chaired a committee appointed in 1924 to advise the newly appointed Conservative Chancellor of the Exchequer, Winston Churchill, on the matter) was concerned, it was not so much a question of whether the pound was overvalued in relation to the dollar, as of removing monetary policy from political influence: in his eyes the Gold Standard was 'knave-proof'. The Governor of the Bank of England, Montagu Norman, agreed: the Gold Standard was the best 'Governor' a fallibly human world could have. It was ominously portentous that the notion of the government 'meddling' in economic matters was regarded with suspicion and distaste. On the whole gold occupied the same iconic position for the Labour Party, and it was left to the economist John Maynard Keynes, who in *The Economic Consequences of Winston Churchill* (a title resonant of his Cassandra-like warnings of the effects of harsh reparation payments imposed on Germany in 1919, *The Economic Consequences of the Peace*), published in 1925, to put the case against, or rather to point out the consequences if the Gold Standard was re-embraced. These included rising unemployment as the bank rate rose and cheap money was denied for industrial investment. In 1925 Britain went back onto the Gold Standard: the bank rate averaged 5 per cent for the rest of the decade, making the country uncompetitive in the world market, particularly against the United States, which was enjoying boom conditions at the time.

How far and how deep would the pernicious stain of unemployment, which throughout the 1920s had never been less than a million, spread? How could men earn a living when the great staples on which Britain's industrial might had been built over nearly two centuries – iron, steel, textiles, coal, shipbuilding – were losing out to competition from Europe and the United States?

In coalmining areas such as South Wales, the Lowlands of Scotland and Lancashire, the future was bleak. Men had no work in the pits; women were laid off from the textile mills. British exports were no longer competitive in the world market. Labour costs were high – nearly double what they had been in 1914 – whereas the cost of living had only risen by 75 per cent, and the average working week had been reduced by ten hours. In crude terms, those in work were being paid more for working less. Hence the tensions between employers and their workforces – particularly in the mining industry – when international competition undercut prices and eroded markets.

How would Britain be governed, now that the old duopoly of Conservative and Liberal had been definitively replaced by new sparring partners: Labour and Conservative, alternating in power since neither seemed to have satisfactory answers to the country's economic and social ills. Would the bitter legacy of the 1926 General Strike be gradually softened, even though its collapse had brought no resolution to the fundamental problems that had caused it?

On 24 October 1929 on the floor of the New York Stock Exchange, '12,894,650 shares changed hands, many of them at prices that shattered the dreams and hopes of those who had owned them', wrote the economist J.K. Galbraith in his book *The Great Crash*. Prices on the US market went into freefall, and financial companies as well as individual men and women who had speculated on the over-buoyant American economy lost their fortunes, or their modest savings, overnight. On that 'Black Thursday' (which would be followed by 'Black Monday' and 'Black Tuesday') a record 12.9 million shares were traded: the press reported losses of $30 billion over four days, and there were rumours that eleven speculators had already committed suicide. Watching the 'wild turmoil' on the floor from the public gallery of the New York Stock Exchange was Winston Churchill, former British Chancellor of the Exchequer, 'he who in 1925 had returned Britain to the Gold Standard and the overvalued pound. Accordingly he was responsible for the strain that sent Montagu Norman to plead in New York for easier money, which caused credit to be eased at that fatal time, which, in this academy view, in turn caused the boom. Now Churchill, it could be imagined, was viewing his awful handiwork.' However, there is no record of anyone having reproached him. Economics was never his strong point, so (and wisely) it seems most unlikely that he reproached himself. But, having invested heavily in the market, he himself lost a large percentage of his savings when it crashed, though he waxed philosophical: 'No one who has gazed on such a scene could doubt that this financial disaster, huge as it is, cruel as it is to thousands, is only a passing episode.'

The US market continued to decline, reaching its lowest point in July 1932, when it had fallen 89 per cent from its peak in 1929. Unemployment went from 1.5 million in 1929 to 12.8 million, or 24.75 per cent of the workforce, by 1933. 'Liquidate labor, liquidate stocks, liquidate the farmers, liquidate real estate,' the Secretary of the Treasury, Andrew Mellon, had advised. 'It will purge the rottenness out of the system . . . People will work harder, live a more moral life. Values will be adjusted and enterprising people will pick up the wrecks from less competent people.'

The Great Depression bit deeper in America (as it did in Germany) than it did in Britain, and lasted much longer, but although J.M. Keynes couldn't help 'heaving a big sigh of relief at what seemed like the removal of an incubus which has been lying heavily on the business life of the whole world outside America', the effect of the Wall Street Crash on trade world-wide would prove deleterious in the next few years. The US government initially raised tariffs against foreign imports and its overseas investment all but dried up, forcing Europe to pay for imports and pay off debts in gold which was sucked into the vaults of America (and France, which had somehow managed to stand aside from the economic crisis). This had serious long-term consequences for the international circulation of money, and led to a collapse in commodity prices and an economic slowdown. 'Almost throughout the world, gold has been withdrawn from circulation. It no longer passes from hand to hand, and the touch of metal has been taken from men's greedy palms' Keynes noted.

Yet, speaking only a matter of weeks after that cacophony of black days in New York and growing anxiety about their effect on Britain's already ailing, out-of-joint economy, Gerald Barry thought he saw some scattered green shoots, a few straws in the wind that he might clutch at: the summer of 1929 had witnessed a lockout in the cotton industry which was solved, he said, 'on the principle of rough justice whereby Solomon cut the baby in half', meaning that each side agreed to accept 50 per cent of what it wanted. He was optimistic that the *rapprochement* between capital and labour begun in 1929 by the Melchett–Turner conversations (tentative corporatist interchanges between Lord Melchett – or Sir Alfred Mond, as he had been until 1928 – chairman of the recently amalgamated giant chemical firm ICI, and the trade union leader Ben Turner, which ultimately led nowhere) had been 'further cemented'. And he also saw signs of co-operation paying dividends in agriculture, 'that Cinderella of home industries', with initiatives from the Ministry of Agriculture for a series of marketing schemes for foodstuffs such as flour, fruit, eggs and meat.

The shadow of the Great War had darkened the 1920s; in the 1930s men and women would grow to maturity who had no memory of that terrible carnage, and on the cusp of the decades international peace and accommodation seemed assured, with the Labour Foreign Secretary Arthur Henderson's agreement to withdraw the last British troops from the Rhine.

Confrontations between the incorruptible Labour Chancellor of the Exchequer Philip Snowden and the ever-rotating French Finance Ministers showed, however, that tensions over the peace treaty of 1919 were by no means entirely relaxed, and the issue of war debts to the United States continued to be a live and fractious issue. Even so, perhaps Barry's optimism was justified. Perhaps Britain's economic and social ills really could still be put down to the working out of the dislocations of war, the turbulence could be expected to fade away, the normal rhythms of trade and production would reassert themselves, and British society would return to an equilibrium that it had, in fact, never really known.

TWO

A Great Clearance

... An utterly lost and daft
System that gives a few at fancy prices
Their fancy lives
While ninety-nine in the hundred who never attend the banquet
Must wash the grease of ages off the knives ...

Louis MacNeice, 'Autumn Journal' (1939)

The post of Poet Laureate, official versifier, has had a chequered history. Originating with John Dryden in 1670, it has had its peaks – Wordsworth, Tennyson – and its troughs – possibly Colley Cibber, possibly Robert Southey (who only got the laurel wreath because Sir Walter Scott declined), certainly Alfred Austin (who was wheeled on because William Morris refused). When the scholarly, pantheistic Robert Bridges (who was only in post because Rudyard Kipling had said no) died on 21 April 1930, the honorary position as a member of the royal household (ranking between the Gentleman Usher of the Black Rod and the Marine Painter in the arcane hierarchy), carrying a nugatory stipend, was offered to John Masefield. He had his doubts: 'I can write verse only in moments of deep feeling ... this may perhaps be a disqualification,' he wrote on 30 April to Ramsay MacDonald, who had offered to submit his name for royal approval – a mere formality, particularly since it was rumoured that Masefield was George V's favourite poet. The Prime Minister must have had many more pressing matters on his mind, but he took time out to reply to the havering fifty-one-year-old poet, reassuring him that should the spirit move him, he could 'write odes and such things' on occasions of national import, but if it did not, he could keep quiet. Masefield accepted, but made it clear that as a writer committed to the cause of 'the man with too weighty a burden, too heavy a load', he would *not* define his task as being to acclaim 'The princes and prelates with periwigged charioteers/Riding triumphantly laurelled to lap the fat of the years'. He would hold the post for thirty-seven years until his death in 1967, a longer tenure than any of his predecessors except Tennyson.

John Masefield had long hymned the sea and the men who went down to the sea in ships (although he himself was an indifferent sailor who failed in his first choice of career in the Merchant Navy, and on one occasion had to be shipped home from Chile as a DBS – Distressed British Seaman). In 1934 the perfect opportunity to fuse his maritime yearnings with the gravitas of a national event presented itself. Masefield rose to the challenge with a seven-stanza poem entitled, rather unpromisingly, 'Number 534'. '. . . Man in all the marvel of his thought/Smithied you into form of leap and curve,' he wrote, 'And took you so, and bent you to his vast/Intense great world of passionate design/Curve after changing curving, bracing and mast/To stand all tumult that can tumble brine.' Far from being one of Masefield's best-known 'dirty British coaster[s] with a salt-caked smoke stack . . . With a cargo of Tyne coal/Road-rail, pig-lead/Firewood, iron-ware, and cheap tin trays', 'Number 534' was the largest ocean-going liner ever built, the *Queen Mary*, and the occasion of his tribute was the ship's launch, when in pouring rain on 26 September 1934 in front of a crowd of 200,000 mostly umbrella-holding spectators, the consort whose name the vessel carried, the wife of George V, dressed in powder blue, smashed a bottle of Australian wine over her bows, pressed a button, and the massive 81,000-ton Cunard liner, 'long as a street and lofty as a tower' and looking like a 'great white cliff', slipped into the Clyde.

The *Queen Mary* represented many things. It was a gamble that despite a world depression this luxury liner, this super ship, would enable Britain to recapture its prestige on the seas, would win the coveted Blue Riband for the fastest crossing of the Atlantic, and would rekindle a glamorous and moneyed lifestyle that seemed lost. And yet, though its elaborate and luxurious interiors, its fabulous menus, its non-stop programme of entertainment seemed to hold out such a promise, the construction of the *Queen Mary* could be seen as an unfolding metaphor for the ambitious intentions, the rigid yet muddled thinking, the collective misery and dashed hopes of British industrial production in the early 1930s.

British shipbuilding had suffered a similar fate to other heavy industries in the 1920s: a sharp decline from the First World War, when orders had flooded in for battleships, the big yards on the Clyde had expanded their capacity and their workforce to cope with military orders. When the war ended it seemed natural that the requirement for warships would be replaced by the need for a steady supply of merchant vessels, many of them to replace those lost at sea during hostilities. Indeed, foreseeing a boom in merchant orders John Brown & Co. had injected a huge capital sum of £316,000 into the facilities at their Clydebank yard, and shipbuilding companies merged and acquired control of the majority of Scotland's steel industry. For the first two years after the war it looked as if this would pay off: between December 1918 and December 1920 Clydebank received orders for twelve merchant ships, including seven for the Royal Mail, two large passenger liners, the *Franconia* and the *Alaunia* for the Cunard line, and another two, the *Montcalm* and the *Montclare*, for Canadian Pacific.

But in fact the industry was facing a series of problems, the most pressing of which was a decline in world trade. Added to this were technical innovations that had improved speeds and shipping capacity, meaning that what trade there was could be carried in fewer ships, fierce overseas competition, and at home overmanning, fractious industrial relations, underinvestment in new technologies – particularly the switch from steam to diesel – unprofitable credit arrangements, cut-to-the-bone profit margins and a high rate of emigration of skilled workers, mainly to Canada. As a result, by 1930, when almost no new orders were coming in, the shipyards had already been in deep trouble for some years. The only hope on the horizon was the announcement in May 1930 of an order from Cunard for an ocean-going liner. Without it, John Brown's yard would probably have had to close, with the loss of thousands of jobs. The insurance liability for the liner while she was being built and when she put to sea was reckoned at £4 million, but the commercial marine insurance market was only prepared to cover £2.7 million. The whole project was at risk, but eventually the government, only too aware of the political as well as the economic and social implications of thousands of shipworkers being thrown out of work, agreed to cover the shortfall of £1.3 million itself, though *The Times* had sounded a cautionary note: 'Is it wise that Parliament should be asked to lend a hand on a project planned on so colossal a scale that private enterprise could not find the means to carry it through?'

On 1 December 1930 the contract was finally signed, and on the day after Boxing Day, 'a particularly raw, foggy winter's day [when] the electric lights under the cranes of the building berth had to be put on soon after three in the afternoon', the hull plate was laid and named Job No. 534. It would mean three to four years' work, and 'so strong was the grim enthusiasm of managers, foremen and workers in their determination to have something to show at the end of that first day after all the months of waiting that work continued in the wet and the darkness well into the night'.

By the end of January 1931 the whole of the keel had been laid, and the lower ribs and frame were in position. With three shifts working round the clock the skeleton of the hull had been completed by late spring. By November 80 per cent of the hull plating had been riveted into place and the great liner loomed above Clydebank, its graceful bows dwarfing men and machines. There was a general feeling of optimism that ship No. 534 would be launched in May or June 1932, ready to vie with France's pride, the *Normandie*, currently under construction in Saint-Nazaire, for the Atlantic crown.

But that crown was already tarnished. Fewer passengers were making the crossing, about half as many as had done so in 1926, and those who did were less lavish in their spending: British earnings from passenger ships had been over £9 million in 1928; by 1931 they had fallen to less than £4 million, and foreign competition for fewer passengers was fierce.

On Thursday, 10 December 1931, the directors of Cunard in Liverpool decided that the Clydebank project was no longer viable: the plug was pulled on ship No. 534. At seven o'clock the next morning a notice was nailed up in John Brown's shipyard. 'The services of all employees . . . will terminate at noon today.' Three thousand men directly employed on building the ship were sacked, and 10,000 men and women at work on subsidiary contracts for electrical equipment and all the other parts needed to build and equip such a liner were also affected, either losing their jobs or put onto short-time working.

The directors blamed 'world conditions'. The *Daily Telegraph* reported that while the announcement 'proved somewhat of a shock in the City . . . the wisdom of the decision was not questioned', though the newspaper recognised that the cessation of the project was 'an industrial catastrophe', and suggested that 'Even as an emergency measure for the prevention of un-employment a government loan or guarantee of cheap money would be a far sounder business proposition than most of the "unemployment schemes" in which public money has been sunk . . . here is an obvious case for government help.'

But the government did not see it like that. Speaking in the House of Commons that same afternoon, the President of the Board of Trade, Walter Runciman, rejected the idea: 'I am afraid that any idea of direct govern-ment financial assistance is out of the question.' Offers poured into the Cunard Company from individuals willing to lend money to see the ship completed, and Will Thorne MP, General Secretary to the National Union of General and Municipal Workers, tirelessly lobbied the government to 'supply the necessary money needed to complete the work at a reasonable rate of interest'. The Labour MP for Clydebank and Dumbarton, David Kirkwood, a trade unionist who had himself worked at John Brown's shipyard, 'had "534" engraved on his heart', and for two years he 'outdid the importunate widow . . . I had written, spoken, pleaded, cajoled, threatened men and masters, shipbuilders and ship owners, Cabinet Ministers and financiers.' But no help was forthcoming. By the beginning of 1932 the Clyde was building fewer ships than at any time since 1860. Almost the only people still employed in the shipyards were 'black-coated' workers such as foremen and draughtsmen. Other shipyards were as badly hit as John Brown's and had either chained their gates shut or kept only a skeleton staff. Since the only other source of employment was the Singer sewing-machine factory, from which half the workforce had been laid off, Clydebank became a town of the unemployed, and the vast, gaunt hulk of the unfinished liner a daily reminder of that fact. And the symbol resonated beyond the banks of the Clyde. 'I believe that as long as No. 534 lies like a skeleton in my constituency so long will the depression last in this country,' David Kirkwood told the Commons. 'To me it seems to shout "Failure! Failure!" to the whole of Britain.'

By 1933 almost 75 per cent of shipbuilding workers in Scotland were unemployed. Edwin Muir, a poet and novelist born on Orkney whose family had moved to Glasgow, where he had worked as a clerk in a shipyard office, found when he revisited his former workmates that half had been laid off, and those who were still at their desks were on half time (and half pay). All were sunburned, an unwelcome mark then of the un- and under-employed who spent too many hours outside, hanging around, digging allotments, scavenging for coal and wood. 'The dead on leave' was how Muir described Britain's unemployed, borrowing the phrase ('*die Toten auf Urlaub*') from the German socialist Rosa Luxembourg.

It was not until 3 April 1934 that work resumed on No. 534. With a slow upturn in the economy, and concerned for British maritime prestige, particularly with the spectre of the *Normandie*, the government finally agreed to advance £3 million to complete the work, plus a further £5 million if it was decided to build a sister ship, as had been the original plan. A skirl of bagpipes accompanied the three hundred workers who marched through the gates of John Brown's shipyard to scour off the tons of accumulated rust on the hulk, displace the colonies of birds nesting there, and resume building. Soon some one thousand men from all over the country were supplying what was needed to complete the liner later that summer.

One of the conditions of the government loan had been that Cunard should merge with White Star Lines, creating a strong British firm to compete for the North Atlantic trade. So-called 'rationalisation' was seen as the key to increasing efficiency and productivity, and allaying schemes of nationalisation which would cut a swathe through Britain's staple industries. It was an *au courant* term even if no one was quite sure what it meant, and it invariably meant the merger of larger companies, with smaller ones left on the sidelines. The Labour MP for Jarrow, Ellen Wilkinson, wrote of this tendency in the Tyneside shipyards: 'If the lambs would not lie down with the lions, the lions were ready to co-operate together to make certain of their victims later.' Such mergers meant that by 1937 twenty-eight British shipyards, with a total capacity of over a million tons, had been put out of business. The men thus displaced were unlikely to be absorbed into other industries. Until 1938 the highest rates of unemployment in any British industry were in shipbuilding: not just along the Clyde, but in Belfast, the North-East of England and on Merseyside too. When Palmer's shipyard closed in 1932, 'Jarrow was utterly stagnant. There was no work. No one had a job except a few railway officials, and workers in the co-operative stores, and the few clerks and craftsmen who went out of town to their jobs each day.' Across the country 60 per cent of those who had worked building or repairing ships were unemployed, compared to an average unemployment rate of around 22 per cent.

But the decay of Britain's staple traditional industries, on which the country's nineteenth-century prosperity had been based, was not confined to shipbuilding. Coal, iron, steel, heavy engineering and cotton accounted for more than 40 per cent of total unemployment, and in areas where they were concentrated – Teesside, South Wales and Monmouthshire, Tyneside, Cumberland, Lowland Scotland and Lancashire – the unemployment figure was much higher than the average: in some cases staggeringly high. In July 1931 Jarrow's employment exchange reported that 72.6 per cent of its workforce was unemployed, and in Ferndale in the Rhondda Valleys, 96.5 of those in jobs covered by insurance contributions from workers, employers and the government were out of work. In the worst of times – 1932 – nearly a third of all coalminers were unemployed, and even in 1936, when the economy was in upswing, a quarter of all coalminers were still without work, as were almost a third of iron and steelworkers.

'Everybody knows that there are at present in England prosperous districts and "depressed areas"', explained *Men Without Work*, a report from the Pilgrim Trust, which had been established in 1930 under the chairmanship of Stanley Baldwin with a £2 million gift from Edward Harkness, an American philanthropist who had inherited a vast oil fortune and who, proud that his ancestors came from Dumfries, took a most munificent interest in Britain, its society and culture, at a time when his own country was also in the throes of a deep depression.

The 'prosperous districts' were to be found mainly in the Midlands and the South of England: 'a line from the Severn to the Wash' was generally recognised as roughly delineating the areas of prosperity from those of 'distress'. Although the Yorkshire novelist and playwright J.B. Priestley famously came across three rather than two 'Englands' in his 'rambling but truthful account of what one man saw and heard and felt and thought during a journey through England during the autumn of the year 1933', he reported finding prosperity in only two of these. It was apparent in much of the first, 'Old England, the country of cathedrals and minsters, of manor houses and inns, of Parson and Squire; guide-book and quaint highways and by ways England', the Cotswolds, parts of rural 'middle England', most of Southern England, and also in the third, 'the new post-war England . . . of arterial and by-pass roads, of filling stations and factories that look like exhibition buildings . . . all glass and white tiles and chromium plate . . . of giant dance-halls and cafés, bungalows with tiny garages'. It was largely in 'new post-war England' around London and in the Midlands – Leicester 'claims to be the most prosperous city in England' – that the new industries were located. Indeed, they and the lifestyles they engendered defined Priestley's somewhat scornful characterisation, since he did not much care for the 'third England' he had happened across, with its 'depressing monotony', its 'trumpery imitation of something not very good in the original' (that is, 'American influence') and its general 'Woolworths culture' of cheapness – and, he admitted, accessibility – defined by money.

Such recently established and expanding industries as light engineering, artificial-textile and motor-vehicle manufacture, electrical goods (the national grid, which was completed in 1933, provided a stimulus for the manufacture of electrically-powered domestic appliances such as radios, cookers, vacuum cleaners, gramophones and electric irons) were invariably smaller-scale than the old industrial giants, and often a number of diverse enterprises were located in one place, each employing fewer people, but less vulnerable to the vagaries of world trade, particularly as many were producing goods primarily for the home market, and were concentrated where that market was dense.

However, in the depressed regions the most deeply disquieting fact was not just the number of unwilling conscripts into the army of the un-employed – an estimated nearly three and a half million in total in 1932, at the deepest trough of the Depression – and their concentration in certain areas: it was the length of time some of them had been without a job. Long-term unemployment was defined as having been out of work for more than a year. In September 1929 about 45,000 were in that category; by August

1932 the number had risen to 400,000, or over 16 per cent of the unemployed workforce. In Crook, in County Durham, 71 per cent of the unemployed had been without a job for five years or more, while the figure for the Rhondda Valley in South Wales was 41 per cent, and for Liverpool 23 per cent. Even in a generally prosperous city such as York, where the overall rate of unemployment was relatively low, Seebohm Rowntree's 1935 survey found that 21.9 per cent of unemployed heads of families had been out of work for between two and four years, 23.6 per cent for four to six years, and 17.9 per cent for over six.

Moreover, the numbers proved obdurate. The Pilgrim Trust reported that while there had been optimism that with industrial recovery growing rapidly after 1935, labour would start to resemble 'a fairly rapidly moving stream with only small stagnant pools here and there'. But the murky water that the long-term unemployed represented proved deep and still. While the total number of those without work fell, the proportion of those idle for longer than a year stayed roughly the same. 'Recovery had failed to solve the problem. On the contrary, as the unemployment figures fell, the seriousness [of the matter of the long-term unemployed] became more and more obvious.' Indeed, in the month before Britain declared war on Germany on 3 September 1939 there were still nearly a quarter of a million long-term unemployed, men with little chance of ever working again – at least in peacetime.

The problem of the long-term unemployed particularly exercised politicians, economists and social scientists – either for the insight the phenomenon might provide into the nature of industrial decline, the prospects for recovery and the seemingly unstoppable rise in the cost of unemployment insurance and relief, or to help them discover if the problem was 'industrial' (that is, the long-term unemployed would get work if there was work to be got) or 'residual' (that is, was there a 'type' who were in some way 'inadequate', physically, psychologically or morally for the world of work?). Sir William Beveridge, later to garner for himself the accolade 'father of the Welfare State', had written and lectured on the subject extensively, and had suggested to the Pilgrim Trust that this was 'the crux of the matter', and worthy of extensive investigation.

What were the effects of such unemployment, particularly in single-industry towns where the decay of the staple industry polluted not only the lives of those thrown out of work with little hope of a job, but impoverished the whole community? As the Pilgrim Trust put it: 'Beyond the man in the queue we should always be aware of those two or three at home whom he has to support.' It calculated that the 250,000 long-term unemployed were responsible for 170,000 wives and 270,000 young children, 'whose burden is perhaps the heaviest of all'.

'Attention has been repeatedly drawn by the Minister of Labour . . . and many others, to the extent to which unemployment is "an old man's problem",' reported the Pilgrim Trust. Men in their middle years were less likely to remain without work for long: across the country 13 per cent of men between the ages of twenty-five and forty-four were unemployed, but for those between fifty-five and sixty-four the percentage was 22.6 – though of course this number was much higher in areas with the highest levels of unemployment. Men over fifty were noticeably less likely to find another job in times of high unemployment, since employers tended to regard such old-stagers as less flexible, less able to 'adjust' to modern working methods and technologies. This was seen as a particular problem in the Welsh coalfields, where life in the pits began early: 'When he is 35 a man has already been at work for more than twenty years underground, and above that age adjustment [to new methods of coal cutting and other forms of mechanised production] begins to get harder.'

In addition, years cutting coal underground, often with scant concern for health or safety, made relatively young men old. A feature of life in the coalmines was the high incidence of disabling industrial diseases such as nystagmus and silicosis among the older miners with a (shortened) lifetime of breathing in coal dust. 'The Coal Mines Act was flagrantly broken day in, day out, year in year out,' remembers Kenneth Maher, who started work in the Bedwas colliery near Newport in Monmouthshire aged fourteen in January 1930, earning 12s.4d a week for six eight-hour shifts. Apart from the danger of explosion from the methane gas that collected in the underground passages, or the couplings breaking on the heavy metal tubs that conveyed the coal, 'the coal-cutting machines cut out the seams, raising clouds of dust. When the compressed air exhaust caught it, when the colliers shovelled it on to the conveyors, when it tipped into the tubs, it was like black fog travelling into the ventilation. A miner in South Wales who is free from dust is called a wet lung. There is a difference between silicosis and pneumoconiosis. The stone dust [found in the stones at the bottom of pits] sets like cement [in the lungs] but coal doesn't. Particles of silica cut into the lungs and kill the tissue. I remember taking my wife to my brother's home. We saw a man leaning over a low wall. My wife said, "Whatever is the matter with that man?" "That," I said, "is what dust does to a man." He was gasping and coughing his lungs up. He was dying on his feet. He was 45 years old.'

Furthermore, older men were less likely to be offered the opportunity of learning a new trade, or of relocating to find work, and thus were forced into what was in effect early retirement whether they wanted – or could afford – it or not. And usually they couldn't afford it, since with no older children still living at home who could have contributed to the family budget, the older unemployed worker was likely to be living on an income which was only half what it would have been if he was in work.

At the other end of the age range, young, untrained men often found similar difficulties in getting steady work. The school leaving age was fourteen, and only those whose family could afford to send them to grammar school, or who had won a scholarship, had any hope of secondary education. Most working-class children left elementary school at fourteen and, like Jim Wolveridge from Stepney in the East End of London, found themselves at a disadvantage. 'I went into a dead end job . . . Not many kids in the neighbourhood did get good jobs . . . I spent a few weeks calling at the juvenile exchange at Toynbee Hall, but the few vacancies that were available were for boys who'd had secondary or grammar school education. That left me, and a good many more like me, out in the cold.'

Charles Graham was born in South Shields on the north-east coast of England, 'a beautiful place. There's beautiful scenery there' – but little work. When he left school at fourteen in 1930 he 'went round the quay trying to get to sea because this was the dream in that area. But after a year I got a job as a lather boy at a barber's. Five shillings a week. I was there for about eight months. I knew I wasn't going to learn how to cut hair because he didn't want to teach me because he was afraid for his job. This was general. People were afraid of letting you know their little secrets. It was only short back and sides after all . . . Then I got a job as an errand boy in a grocer's shop. Trade was really competitive. One grocer's shop next to another . . . I used to have to fill these seven or fourteen pound bags of flour and deliver the orders . . . I used to have a sack barrow for deliveries and I had to walk about five miles [there] and five miles back . . . When I was seventeen I managed to get work from a lady who owned two hardware shops and a wholesale grocery business . . . My take home pay was 13/6d [minus five shillings a week deducted to repay his employer for driving lessons] (I would have had 14/- on the dole).'

Graham started work sweeping out the shop at 6 a.m., and 'very often did not finish work until eight or nine p.m. (but there was no overtime pay) . . . I got a job as a driver for a biscuit factory. I was only 17 then and I had a huge van . . . You had to go at 60 miles an hour to get round . . . I managed to get a job with Wall's ice cream once. With a tricycle. I was getting about 32/- a week. A fortune for me.' But that came to an end too, and Graham got a job on a building site. 'My stepfather knew the builder. That's why I got the job . . . A lot of apprentices were used as cheap labour on the building site. They'd be signed on as apprentices and work for about four hours on the site and all they'd be doing was wheeling a barrow and stacking bricks like I was doing. And then when the building was completed the apprentices would be out before they'd even started laying bricks. Anyway, that lasted about eighteen months. Then I was unemployed again looking for work . . . During the slump you couldn't join the Army because there were so many. There was such a great demand to get into the forces, to get away from it, although the wages were only 14/- a week, with stoppages out of that. But they were so selective, just like the police. The police could say six foot, and that was your lot, and so much chest because they had anyone to choose from.' Eventually, when war broke out in 1939, Charles Graham was able to join the army. 'I don't suppose 90 per cent of the men in the army with me would have been able to get in two years before because of malnutrition. But when war broke out, they were all fit.'

Many others, taken on as cheap labour when they left school at fourteen, might find that once they reached eighteen, when by law their employer had to contribute towards their unemployment insurance, they were sacked. Being both less experienced than older men (and often untrained), and more expensive than the next wave of school leavers, a long period of unemployment followed in those regions where jobs were scarce anyway.

Donald Kear lost his job a fortnight before his twentieth birthday in 1933: 'I was a machine attendant at a small factory [in the Forest of Dean, where coalmining was the predominant industry] and it was the custom of my employer to discharge employees when they became older and more expensive to him and employ younger lads in their place. There was plenty of labour available. Young lads were hanging around the factory gates every day looking for work.'

Jack Shaw 'went butchering' when he left school in Ashton-under-Lyne, just outside Manchester. 'The idea in my dad's mind was that I was going to learn a trade. But there was a lot of butchers and he picked the wrong one. He was probably only making enough to keep his self. He gave me five shillings a week. Then I got seven and sixpence. When I got [to] about eighteen I come to ten shillings a week and he couldn't pay me any more. He said "I'll give you a reference, and that's about all I can do. I just hope you can get a job." So that's when I had my first experience of the dole.'

'I am glad that I haven't a son,' said an unemployed Welsh miner vehemently. 'It must be a heartbreaking business to watch your boy grow into manhood and then see him deteriorate because there is no work for him.

And yet there are scores of young men in the Valley who have never worked since the age of sixteen . . . at sixteen they become insurable, and the employers sack them rather than face the extra expense. So we have young men who have never had a day's work since. They have nothing to hope for but aimless drift. I'm glad no son of mine is in that position.'

Even those signing up for apprenticeships in industries such as engineering or shipbuilding might be no better off, since when they had completed their training the depressed state of the industry could mean there were no jobs. Around 4 per cent of juveniles (those aged fourteen to eighteen) were unemployed, but again this varied from area to area. In 1933, 10 per cent of boys and 9 per cent of girls available for work in Sheffield, a depressed city, were unemployed. The true figure of young people without work was undoubtedly much higher, as these statistics relate only to sixteen-to-eighteen-year-olds: those under sixteen did not qualify for unemployment benefit, and therefore were not registered at the Labour Exchange. The implications for the future of large numbers of young people without skills, proper training or any real prospect of regular employment was bleak, not only for the individuals but for the national economy. 'They tell me I haven't the experience and they'll not give me the chance of getting it,' one young man reported in a Carnegie Trust survey complained, while others felt fed up with being 'messed around'. The Pilgrim Trust was disquieted to discover that in Liverpool there were 'large numbers of young men to be found who "don't want work"'.

During the 1930s employers in depressed areas knew that they could take their pick from a large pool of the workless, and tended to shun those in shabby clothes or exhibiting tendencies to demoralisation and apathy, the inevitable consequences of long months stretching into years searching for work. The Unemployment Assistance Board stressed problems that arose from 'loss of industrial efficiency' in the long-term unemployed. E. Wight Bakke, a young American who came to Britain in 1931 on a Yale fellowship to study the problem of unemployment, was not alone in concluding that 'even a short period of unemployment handicapped a man in his efforts to market his labour . . . The handicap increased with the length of time out of work . . . [long-term unemployment leads] to the slow death of all that makes a man ambitious, industrious and glad to be alive.'

So the dreary spiral was perpetuated: no work increasingly seen as a disqualification for work. The Pilgrim Trust also found that anyone with a minor physical defect such as a speech impediment, a slight limp, or even being short of stature, might be discriminated against, regardless of whether this was in any way relevant to the sort of work he was likely to be required to do, when there was an embarrassment of 'perfect specimens' for hire.

Disconsolate groups of the long-term unemployed, shabbily dressed, hanging round street corners slicked black by rain against a background of boarded-up shops, lounging against lamp-posts, playing desultory games in the gutter, kicking a tin around in lieu of a football, watched by ragged, grimy-faced urchins, have become a familiar image of the 1930s, captured in grainy *Picture Post*-like photographs in the years before *Picture Post* existed. The young Canadian writer George Woodcock described a typical scene when he took a free holiday from his 'wretchedly paid' job in London with a Welsh aunt in a small town in Glamorgan:

> One day I decided to take a bus and visit the Rhondda area, the heart of the South Wales mining district . . . It was the worst of times in the Rhondda, though it probably looked little better than the best of times, since most of the mines were not working, and the smoke that would normally have given a dark, satanic aspect to the landscape was less evident than in more prosperous times. Still it was dismal enough . . . it had the feeling of occupied territory. Many of the shops had gone out of business, the mines had slowed down years ago, and the General Strike of 1926 –disastrous for workers – had delivered the coup de grace to the local economy. The people were shabby and resentful. Groups of ragged men squatted on their haunches, as miners do, and played pitch-and-toss with buttons, they had no halfpennies to venture. A man came strolling down the street, deject-edly whistling 'The Red Flag' in slow time as if it were a dirge.

Caught in a downpour of rain, Woodcock was

> a sad, sodden object . . . as I came down into the valley beside a slag heap where fifty or so men and women were industriously picking over the ground. I caught up with a man walking along the overgrown road from the mine to the village, whose damp slate roofs I could see glistening about half a mile away. He was pushing a rusty old bicycle that had no saddle and no tires, but it served to transport the dirty gunnysack he had tied onto the handle-bars. He had been picking up coal from the slag heap. 'No bigger nor walnuts, man,' he explained. The big coal had been taken years ago, so long ago was it that work had been seen in the village. I asked him how long he had been unemployed. 'Ach y fi, man, it's nine years I've been wasting and wasted.' . . . He apologetically remarked that these days nobody had a fire in the village except to cook the mid-day dinner, if there was anything to cook, so I'd find it difficult to dry my clothes. Then he suddenly brightened. 'Try the Brachi

shop, man. They'll have a fire, sure to goodness. And it's glad they'll be for a couple of pence to dry your clothes.'

Long ago an Italian named Brachi had found his way into one of the Welsh mining villages and had established a modest café. Others had followed him, but his name had clung, and Italian cafés in the Rhondda were generically called Brachi shops. The Brachi shop in Rhondda Fach was a melancholy place, its front in need of a paint, a sheet of old cardboard filling the broken part of the window in which stood a few dummy packets of tea and biscuits. A dejected girl came from the back. Her black hair and olive complexion were Mediterranean, but her voice had the lilt of Wales. She looked at me hostilely when I talked about a fire, and I think I was humiliating her into admitting that they, too, lit the fire only at mealtimes. Nobody came for meals anymore. So I spent my tuppence on a cup of tea, which she languidly made on a primus stove. She thawed a little as the kettle warmed up, and talked of her longing to go to London. I hope she got there.

The Orcadian poet Edwin Muir witnessed the state of the unemployed in Scotland when he took a journey there in 1934 at the request of the publishers of J.B. Priestley's *English Journey*:

It was a warm, overcast summer day: groups of idle, sullen-looking young men stood at the street corners; smaller groups were wandering among the blue black ranges of pit-dumps which in that region are a substitute for nature; the houses looked empty and unemployed like their tenants; and the road along which the car stumbled was pitted and rent, as if it had recently been under shell-fire. Everything had the look of a Sunday that had lasted for many years, during which the bells had forgotten to ring and the Salvation Army, with its accordions and concertinas had gone into seclusion, so that one did not even bother to put on one's best clothes: a disused, slovenly, everlasting Sunday. The open shops had an unconvincing yet illicit look, and the few black-dusted miners whom I saw trudging home seemed hardly to believe in their own existence . . . A century ago there was a great clearance from the Highlands, which still rouses the anger of the people living there. At present, on a far bigger scale, a silent clearance is going on in industrial Scotland, a clearance not of human beings, but of what they depend on for life.

THREE

Dole Country

This word dole has two meanings. It means a charitable distribution, especially a rather niggardly one. It also means, or did mean, in its archaic use,
a man's lot or destiny. We have contrived most artfully to combine these two
meanings. As I looked back on it, the England of the dole did not seem to
me to be a pleasant place. We could not be proud of its creation. We could
not really afford to be complacent about it, although we often are. It's a poor
shuffling job, and one of our worst compromises.

J.B. Priestley, English Journey (1934)

'At the present time I am out of work,' recorded Frank Forster in his diary
on Saturday, 14 December 1935. 'I have been out for 3 or 4 weeks. I am safe
for 6 months on the Labour and for this period will receive each week 17/-
. But what is to happen after that if I do not get a job, I just don't know.'
Forster, who was in his mid-twenties and of strongly left-leaning persuasions,
lived at home in Saltney in Cheshire with his father, who worked in the sanitation department of the local rural district council, his mother and one of
his two sisters (the other was married). 'During the past few years my life
has consisted of a series of periods of unemployment spaced out with periods
of employment' – as a fitter's mate, in horticulture and as a casual labourer.

Life at home was not easy:

Our family at the present time is in rather straitened financial circumstances.
From father's side came only 9/- Union benefit. [Forster's father was in hospital
with 'the old stomach trouble'.] Mother gets 10/- from cleaning at a public
house in the village. Hilda [his sister] gives in about 8/- or 9/- from her wages.
She is working on a stall in Chester market. I give 8/- out of the 17/- which
I get from the Labour Exchange. We have had to cut down considerably on
various things and are able to buy only necessities. We are helped a great deal
by our various relatives who now and again give us food or money . . . There

is at times talk of me getting a job somewhere no matter what it is or what the money being paid is. I do not relish making small money. [I] would sooner die fighting and starving than live cringing and in slavery. The thrill which I get out of the situation is the thought of what might happen when my point of view clashes with the law or with authority when our family is bought to the point of starvation, to Poor Law level. Then, at that time, I would be able to come into my own and express my opinion against this damnable society.

The Forsters' pared-down family income would not have been unusual in an area where there was little regular work to be had – nor would Frank's feelings of frustration as a youngish man with apparently no prospects. The money he received was unemployment insurance benefit, since at some point he had worked in the building trade, which was covered by the government insurance scheme that had been in existence since before the First World War.

An unemployed married man with two children still at school who was covered by the insurance scheme would receive thirty shillings per week, or half the national average wage of £3. This benefit was paid at a flat rate regardless of previous earnings, and the scheme was intended to insure the worker against unemployment, *not* against poverty. As the author of an informative if briskly upbeat coda, 'The State Services for the Unemployed', to *Time to Spare*, a book of a BBC series of talks published in 1935 which gave the unemployed 'a chance to speak out freely, according to one of them', explained: 'Although the rates of insurance benefit may . . . have provided the subsistence of millions of persons, on and off, during recent years, they still have nothing to do with maintenance. No British Government, as yet, has ever accepted such a liability.' This was not entirely true, since an Out of Work Donation had been briefly granted to those who had served their country in the First World War and who had been unable to find work, and there continued to be some minimal 'liability' not only for those unemployed workers who had exhausted their benefits, but also for those able-bodied unemployed in jobs not covered by the unemployment insurance scheme, who therefore had no benefit entitlement.

The first Unemployment Insurance Act had been passed by Asquith's Liberal government in 1911 in response to demands for 'something better than the current system of deterrent poor relief, eked out here and there by spasmodic local relief works and private charities. In those days the majority of the artisan class could and did somehow tide themselves over temporary out-of-work spells, either by saving or by trade union insurances. And as for the unthrifty and the lowest-paid workers, the opinion was that to dispense on easy terms to such people would be the road to ruin.' Much had changed: little had changed.

The Act had 'opened a new chapter in unemployment relief. The government took a leaf out of the trade union book and launched a cautious scheme of contributory insurance . . . the object was to cover short spells of unemployment and help men to eke out their family savings. There were no allowances for the wife and children in those days, and if State benefits, plus savings or trade union benefit, were insufficient or were exhausted, the only other public resource was the Poor Law. And in many areas the rule of the Poor Law Guardians was to offer the workhouse or the labour colony.'

Twenty years after that first Act, there was indeed a safety net in place for the unemployed and their families that had not been there before the First World War. It had been painstakingly knotted together in the growing realisation that unemployment was no longer merely an occasional eventuality that thrifty members of the 'artisan class' would be able to ride out. But the net sagged perilously in places.

Between 1920 and 1934 no fewer than twenty-one Acts concerned with unemployment insurance had been passed as various governments tried to rein in the mounting costs of unemployment benefits, grappling with the problem of those without work in a changed world, informed by the old Poor Law principle of 'less eligibility', meaning that it must not be more financially advantageous not to work than to work.

Until the slump of 1920–21, unemployment had generally been assumed to be cyclical and short-term: economic fluctuations might throw men out of work, but they would soon find another job. This informed the framing of the early Insurance Acts. Indeed, the original Act only covered seven trades, including shipbuilding, iron and steel and the building industry, where it was recognised that seasonal unemployment was frequent. But by 1930 the rate of unemployment averaged not the 4 per cent on which calculations had been made, but around 16 per cent, and in the 'black spots' such as the Welsh Valleys, Teesside, Tyneside and Clydeside it was more than double that. And in such areas more than half of the unemployment was not cyclical and short-term – it was structural and long-term. By 1934, thirteen million workers came under the umbrella of the contributory unemployment scheme, though agricultural workers, public servants (including the armed forces, the police, teachers and civil servants), non-manual workers earning more than £250 a year, domestic servants and the self-employed – which included such categories as shopkeepers – continued to be excluded until 1938, as were workers under sixteen or over sixty-five. But since a rising number of workers – about one in every fifteen of those who registered as unemployed; and again, the figure was higher in the unemployment 'black spots' – had been unemployed for longer than twelve months, they had exhausted their right to statutory benefits, and had to be supported by a series of *ad hoc* measures sequentially known as 'extended', 'uncovenanted' or 'transitional' benefit (the last designation having been adopted in 1927, when a brief upswing in the economy suggested that such relief could be phased out within eighteen months or so).

James Maxton, Independent Labour Party (ILP) MP for a Clydeside seat, attempted to get the centrist Conservative MP Harold Macmillan to agree to the following 'facts' in a BBC debate in December 1932: 'That our present industrial system could not provide regular unbroken employment to the working population: that the earning power of the employed worker was not sufficient to allow of his making provision for extended periods of unemployment: that when the ordinary industrial system was unable to employ him, it was impossible for a man to employ himself remuneratively: that the State had some measure of responsibility for these conditions: that there were not merely breaks in continuity of employment – for some there was no hope of employment at all.'

It was never going to be possible for a series of additional tiding-over benefits to mean that unemployment could be funded by insurance contributions, and it had to be recognised that there were in effect two sorts of unemployed: those generally in regular work who occasionally lost their jobs and would be able to 'cash in' the insurance benefits they had been building up for the relatively short time it took before they found another one; and those who for reasons of their skills (or rather more often lack of skills), the trades in which they worked, the regions where they lived, or perhaps their age, were unlikely ever to find the regular work that would enable them to make unemployment insurance contributions. While the Exchequer contributed roughly a third (along with the employer and the employee) to the unemployed insurance scheme, the heavy financial burden of those out of benefit, for whatever reason, would last as long as there were high rates of long-term unemployment.

When a worker's insurance benefit was exhausted, he or she could apply for transitional benefit, but might be 'disallowed' that benefit for a number of reasons, including refusing the offer of suitable employment. But what was 'suitable employment'? Did it depend on how long they had been out of work? What if a skilled man had been unemployed for two years, but refused to take casual unskilled work, since it was likely to reduce the chances of his ever getting back into his old trade? How long could he be allowed to wait for a job if the industry in which he had previously worked was in decline, and those few jobs that remained were much more likely to go to someone who had recently been working than to one of the long-term unemployed, whose skills may have rusted with disuse? And of course in areas of high unemployment, urging a man to 'take anything' was hardly realistic since there was probably 'very little of "anything" to do'.

If the Labour Exchange decided that a claimant was unreasonably refusing to accept offers of casual work, and that his chances of getting a job in his own trade were negligible, he would be referred to the Court of Referees, which was proclaimed to be independent. If the Court disallowed his claim, he would effectively forfeit his right to be part of the unemployment insurance scheme, and if he could not support himself and his family he would be obliged to apply to what had until recently been called the Poor Law Board of Guardians for relief, assuming he had no other resources. This was also the resort of those unemployed whose work was not covered by the insurance scheme – their numbers were estimated at between 120,000 and 140,000, not counting dependents – as well as those whose benefits or wages were insufficient to keep their family. Not that this was what it was officially called any more: the Poor Law, with its dreaded spectre of the workhouse, had been abolished in 1929, the Boards replaced (in name but often not wholly in personnel) by Public Assistance Committees (PACs), which were locally funded and notorious for the discrepancies of their awards in different areas of the country.

The tenor of most discussion about unemployment dwelt on unemployed men (as indicated by titles of E. Wight Bakke's *The Unemployed Man* and the Pilgrim Trust's *Men Without Work*). Yet a Fabian tract published in 1915, as women flooded into munitions factories, had recognised that 'unemployment in industry affects women as well as men, and often differently from men. How often do we find the state of the labour market treated as if it were solely a matter of the relationship between supply and demand for men?' However, although women tended to outnumber men in such fields as cotton, woollen, worsted and jute manufacture, and in the newer industries producing merchandise for the home market such as light electrical goods, chemicals and drugs, artificial fibres (mainly rayon or 'art' – artificial silk), tinned food and packaging, only 30 per cent of those working in the traditional heavy export industries subject to cyclical unemployment and covered by the 1911 Unemployment Insurance Act were female. Thus, between 1930 and 1932, during the worst of the slump, only 16.8 per cent of the insured unemployed were women, compared to 22.6 per cent men. And since around 50 per cent of working women did jobs that were not covered by unemployment insurance, and thus did not show up in the Ministry of Labour statistics, it is hard to be certain how many women were unemployed at any time, though the figure was undoubtedly higher than 16-odd per cent.

There was considerable prejudice against women workers, and consequently a certain lack of sympathy for those who were unemployed – particularly married women, who were often accused of 'taking men's jobs', and were usually the first to be let go when times were hard. The First World War fear of 'dilution' – that women would be prepared to do the jobs men had left when they went to fight for less money, and would thus depress wages and exclude men from their 'rightful work' when the war was over – persisted long into the peace. The notion that a woman's place was in the home impacted on the attitude to unemployed men – and frequently on their own sense of self-worth – in that a man's wage was intended to support his family, and thus an unemployed man was not the 'provider' society expected him to be, while the 'odd shilling' a woman might contribute to the family budget by odd jobs such as sewing, 'making up', laundry or other domestic work, was seen essentially as pin money, to be dispensed with as soon as the man of the house found work again. In Nelson in Lancashire, for example, the local Weavers' Association agreed to significantly improved rates of pay for male weavers (defined as 'heads of households') who were employed to operate six or eight rather than the customary three or four cotton looms, in return for the dismissal of the married women who comprised 37 per cent of the workforce.

The indignities could be subtle: in her novel *We Have Come to a Country* (1935) Lettice Cooper sketches the scene at the Earnshaw family's tea table. Joe Earnshaw, a skilled joiner, is unemployed, and his daughter Ada has just started work.

> The procedure on these occasions was invariable. Mrs Earnshaw picked out the biggest kipper and laid it on Joe's plate. She gave the next two best to the children, and took the smallest herself. In the days when Joe had been in good work and come home ravenous, there had been two kippers for him. Nowadays there was never more than one each – not always that – but, as the man and the worker, he was still helped first and given the biggest. This evening some idea of celebrating – some feeling that it was Ada's day – made Mrs Earnshaw do a thing she had never done before. She picked out the largest kipper first and slapped it, smoking, onto Ada's plate. 'There you are Ada,' she said, 'eat it up. You'll have to keep well and strong for your work.' None of them realised that a small revolution had taken place in their family life, and that Mrs Earnshaw had paid her first homage to the new head of the house. Henceforth, little fourteen-year-old Ada would be the man of the family.

And in Walter Greenwood's best-selling novel of the Depression, *Love on the Dole*, published in 1933, Sally Hardcastle's fiancé, Larry Meath, breaks off their engagement when he loses his job in a foundry. 'Why can't we be married as we arranged?' Sally demands. 'There's nowt t'stop us. You'd get your dole, and I'm working.' But Larry refuses: 'A humiliating picture of himself living under such conditions flashed through his mind: it smacked of Hanky Park [the working-class area of Salford where the novel is set and where Greenwood had been brought up] at its worst . . . "No . . . " he said, sharply, suddenly animated. "No, no, Sal. No, I can't do it . . . It's no use arguing, Sally. It'd be daft to do it. Yaa! Fifteen bob a week! D'y'think I'm going to sponge on you. What the devil d'y' take me for?"'

As the social investigator and occasional politician Sidney Webb observed, the assumption was that 'a woman always had some kind of family belonging to her, and can in times of hardship slip into a corner somewhere and share a crust of bread already being shared by too many of the family mouths, whereas the truth is that many women workers are without relatives, and a great many more have delicate or worn-out parents, or young brothers or sisters, or children to support'.

For unmarried women, this domestic vision translated into working in other people's homes rather than their own. With female unemployment running at around 600,000 in 1919, various committees and schemes had been set up to investigate the problem. As these committees were composed – predictably – mainly of middle-class women who rather minded the difficulties they were having in finding maids and other staff, their recommendations were invariably that domestic training was the answer. Between 1922 and 1940 the Central Commission on Women Training and Employment trained an average of 4,000 to 5,000 women every year on Home Craft and Home Maker courses. To begin with such training was provided on non-residential courses, but the first residential centre opened at Leamington Spa in January 1930. According to the Ministry of Labour, 'This experiment [was] designed to accustom trainees to live and sleep away from home and to observe the routine which resident domestic service entails.' The experiment was judged a success, and by 1931 seven such centres had been opened, each providing eight-week training courses.

But on the whole women had no desire to do domestic work. A 1931 survey found that while more women in London were still employed in domestic service than in any other industry, their numbers had fallen by over a third since the turn of the century, and they now had a choice of other occupations 'which appear more attractive to most London girls'. Indeed, 'the London girl has always been particularly averse to entering residential domestic service', and most young women, wherever they lived, would prefer to do almost anything rather than opt for life 'below stairs' or, in the case of the prevailing 'cook general' of the inter-war years, accommodated in a poky back bedroom in a middle-class villa. In an unnamed textile town in the North-West a Ministry of Labour survey revealed that of the 380 unemployed women on the employment exchange register who were single and under forty – natural recruits into domestic service, it might be thought – only four were prepared to consider such an option, while in Preston, out of 1,248 women interviewed, a bare eleven were prepared to train for domestic service. It was partly because wages were low – a live-in housemaid in London earned around £2.3s a week and a cook general perhaps a few shillings more (though with board and food included this was not as bad as it might appear); it was partly because domestic service was not covered by the unemployment insurance scheme until 1938, so a domestic servant would not be able to claim benefit if she lost her job; but it was also partly the life: the long hours, the loss of personal liberty – 'No gentleman callers' – entailed in being a servant rather than an employee.

However, an unemployed woman who refused domestic work, or declined to be trained for it, could have her benefit refused or reduced, since she could be said not to be 'genuinely seeking work'. This had been one of the criteria for benefit since 1921, and until it was repealed by the Labour government in 1930 it had put the onus on the claimant to prove that he or she had been assiduously searching for a job, regardless of whether there was any work to be had. It was not until the end of 1932 that the Ministry of Labour finally acceded to pressure and agreed that refusal to accept a training place for domestic service should not automatically lead to loss of benefit: it would only be withdrawn if a young women had accepted training, then taken a post in service, but subsequently left it and refused all further offers of such work.

The abolition of the 'genuinely seeking work' clause caused an outcry that it was a sponger's charter that would encourage opportunists, scroungers, malingerers and loafers. The particular fear was that married women who had no real intention of seeking work, but had accrued insurance entitlements prior to their marriage, would now come forward to claim benefits – and indeed employers wrote in maintaining that they knew of women who had worked for them who were now claiming benefit even though they had left work for reasons of pregnancy or domestic duties.

Sections of the press enjoyed a field day peddling stories of abuse. A Nottingham newspaper attested to the case of a girl of sixteen who had allegedly received £150 unemployment pay in the course of a year, having paid only twenty-four shillings' worth of insurance stamps. Rebutting the charge in the House of Commons, the Minister of Labour, Margaret Bondfield, Britain's first woman Cabinet Minister, claimed that to achieve this remarkable feat the girl 'must have maintained, with dependents' allowances, not only herself but a husband or parent, and at least twenty-three children'.

There were also concerns that by ceasing to require that claimants must be actively seeking work (however ritualistic, and often harsh and excluding, that requirement had been), labour mobility would be impaired. It was argued that there would be no financial incentive for a man or woman to 'get on his or her bike' (or rather go on the tramp) in search of a job in areas away from the depressed regions, though this was hardly a realistic prospect for thousands of men who would either have to maintain a family back home, or move home and family for a job that turned out not to be permanent. Disquiet was not confined to the press: 'Are we to legislate on the lines that these people should think that they need do nothing themselves; that they should wait at home, sit down, smoke their pipes and wait until an offer comes to them?' ridiculed Labour's Attorney General Sir William Jowitt. Even the Prime Minister became prey to alarmist thoughts. Ramsay MacDonald's 'colourful imagination . . . began to picture married women driving up in fur coats to draw benefit: and the retelling of such tales became a staple part of his conversation'.

In November 1930 the Minister of Labour reported that the Act had admitted an extra 200,000 persons to benefit, and nervously cited examples of employers arranging the working hours of part-time workers so that they too would be able to claim. However, the abolition had coincided with a severe recession in the pottery and textile industries, both employers of large numbers of women – indeed, 38 per cent of married women claiming benefit in June 1930 had previously worked in the Lancashire cotton industry, where unemployment had risen from 13.3 per cent in November 1929 to 45.4 per cent in July 1930. That month, with male and female unemployment in the cotton industry at more than twice the national average, 71.3 per cent of claims for transitional benefit came from married women. A year later the figure was still 68.5 per cent.

Pressure continued to grow to stem what were regarded as 'abuses' of unemployment relief – and to take urgent action to reduce the ever-rising borrowing by the Unemployment Fund, which had climbed from £50 million in March 1930 to £70 million in December, plus an additional £60 million from the Treasury to support the unemployed, with the cost of transitional payments alone reaching £30 million. Faced with the conundrum of obviously rising costs and equally obvious rising needs, the traditional prevaricating sticking plaster was applied: a Royal Commission was set up charged with recommending how the National Insurance Scheme could be made 'solvent and self-supporting' and what should be done about those outside the scheme who were 'available and capable of work'.

Reluctant to grasp the political hot potato of actually cutting benefits, as the interim report of the Commission recommended, yet anxious to find a way of reducing costs and staunching 'abuses' (or, as they could more judiciously be called, 'anomalies'), the Labour government rushed through an Anomalies Act which came into effect on 3 October 1931, intended to deal with workers whose attachment to the labour force was considered to be marginal. Such categories included seasonal workers and married women who could claim benefit by virtue of the insurance contributions they had paid when they were single. The immediate effect of the Act was to exclude large numbers of married women from unemployment insurance benefit. Unless a woman had worked for a time *since* marriage and had paid a minimum of fifteen contributions, and could establish that she was normally in 'insurable employment' and was 'actively seeking work' – and likely to find it in her local area – her claim would be disallowed.

By the end of March 1932 over 82 per cent of married women's claims had been disallowed. It had always been difficult to calculate how many women were unemployed. Now it became all but impossible, since there was so little incentive for women to register for unemployment benefit.

While the number of disallowed claims once the 'genuinely seeking work' requirement had been dispensed with confirmed some in their conviction that there had been 'abuse' of the system, it could also be read as revealing a distressingly prevalent aspect of the slump: low wages and widespread underemployment.

Lancashire textile-weaving families needed more than one income to survive even when the main breadwinner was in work. 'We were very poorly paid. The wives couldn't stay at home on a husband's wage. Women have always had to work in Macclesfield,' said one woman interviewed for a study of the Northern silk-industry town. In 1937 a cotton-weaver working full time would make just over £2 a week, while the national average industrial wage for an adult male manual worker the following year was £3.9s. An insured worker with three children who was in receipt of unemployment benefit would receive twelve shillings a week more than an employed cotton-weaver. And in the worst years of the slump Lancashire men's wages were often further depressed by 'playing the warps', or working less than a full complement of looms – and accordingly being paid less.

Moreover, in 1931 when the Lancashire cotton trade was at its lowest, it was hit by another blow when India imposed tariff barriers against imported cotton goods. 'Strong appeals went forth to . . . Gandhi to use his influence towards their abolition,' reported Alice Foley who had started work in a Bolton mill at the age of thirteen and was by 1931, aged forty, a JP and secretary of the Bolton and District Weavers and Winders Association.

> The great Indian leader paid a personal visit to Lancashire. He chose Darwen as his seat of investigation and later came to Bolton . . . He arrived at the Weaver's office, accompanied by his little spinning wheel, but minus the goat which, presumably, he had left in safe keeping with his hostess, Miss Barlow, a member of a wealthy spinning family . . . He was a thin, angular figure, draped in a soft white dhooty [sic] garment, and with kindly eyes peering through round glasses. Gandhi listened gravely to the various appeals from leaders and officials, erstwhile [sic] plying his spinning wheel . . . I think he was gravely moved by what he had heard and seen of the effects of low earning, unemployment and persistent under-employment but could do nothing immediately; his people, he reminded us had always been on the verge of starvation.
>
> In the evening a dinner had been arranged at our local Swan Hotel in his honour, but Gandhi declined to eat anything but bread and water at the repast, somewhat to the embarrassment of his hosts.

After the distinguished, diminutive visitor had left the benighted towns where unemployment for women had reached nearly 60 per cent, some 'hard-headed folks' opined that Gandhi was 'a bit of a fraud', but to Miss Foley he seemed like 'a passing saint in a world of gross materialism' in those hard, grim years.

The 1930s economy is often characterised as one divided between those in work and the unemployed, whereas in fact there were a number of economies operating: full-time work adequate to a family's needs, full-time work inadequate to a family's needs, unemployment and underemployment. When sixteen-year-old Doris Bailey's father, a French polisher in Bethnal Green in East London, was put on short-time work, she was obliged to abandon her matriculation, since the family needed money. She eventually found work in an underwear factory in Holborn, and contributed her wages to the family budget. To qualify for unemployment benefit a worker had to experience three continuous days of unemployment in any one six-day week, which meant that those who worked non-consecutive days, or for part of four separate days, were excluded from benefit. For Kenneth Maher, a miner who was often only in work part-time, it was an iniquitous system. 'Nearly all the pits in Wales were on short time. Even then the coal owners and the government of the day kept bashing the miners. The favourite trick was to work on Monday and Tuesday, off Wednesday, work Thursday, off Friday, work Saturday, or off Monday, work Tuesday, off Wednesday, work Thursday, off Friday, work Saturday. In this way the men could not claim any dole. They were taking home maybe three days' pay – about £1 or 25/-. That was bad enough, but those on the dole were in an awful plight – 18/- for a man 6/- for a wife.'

'The miners were always subject to a day or two days out. If they got four shifts a week they were lucky,' recalled Clifford Steele, whose father was a miner at Grimethorpe colliery in South Yorkshire. 'And then there were the odd occasions, perhaps in wintertime when coal was demanded, that they worked pretty regularly. It was the case of only a few hours' notice. If a man was on day shift starting at six in the morning he had to be hanging about at night to see whether the pit buzzer went. If the pit buzzer went at half past eight it meant that there was no work the following day. So it was a case of don't put me snap [packed lunch] up Mother.'

However, in industries where demand fluctuated but was generally depressed, part-time work *could* act in the interests of both employer and employee. A study of the workings of British industry between the wars has shown that in the harsh market conditions of the 1930s in the iron and steel industry it became imperative for over-capitalised firms to secure orders 'at any price simply to provide sufficient cash flow for their creditors'. Short-time working meant that skilled men were kept on the firm's books in case an order came in, and if this was on a regular basis 'the sequence of idle days almost invariably enables the workers to qualify for Unemployment Benefit'. This suited the employers, since it allowed them flexibility and a team of experienced workers. And the employees knew that if it didn't suit them, there were plenty of unemployed men eager to take their place.

A similar situation affected women workers. As a Macclesfield Silk Trade Association member explained to a Board of Trade inquiry: 'Trade . . . was slack . . . It went up and down – and the married women thought it wasn't fair that they should be put on the dole when work was found for the girls. The boss . . . tried to explain. "My girls will go where there's work," he told them, "and they won't come back when things improve and I'll lose them. They'll find work in another mill. Besides there's only one wage going in with a girl." But he took no notice that many of the men were on short time or the labour [i.e. receiving benefit] too, as well as their wives.'

In the crisis year of 1931, the Ministry of Labour became concerned that payment of benefit for short-time working was 'one of the abuses of the present system'. However, an inquiry into the iron and steel trades revealed that most – though not all – employers believed that 80 per cent of short-time workers needed benefit payments in order to survive. As one employer put it: 'We know all our men and their domestic circumstances, and but for the "dole", they would be physically unable to do their work when there is any for them.' Overall it seemed that only about 15 to 20 per cent of the men normally employed in the industry 'would not be reduced to "needy" circumstances if unemployment pay is not granted' – presumably these men were members of the small aristocracy of affluent skilled labour, for differentials in the industry were very wide.

Far from suggesting that short-time workers were abusing the system by drawing benefit, the employers argued that if benefit was not allowed, there would be no sense in a man being prepared to work three days a week: he would be better off not working at all and drawing a full week's benefit. The government took the point, and the system continued. One effect, however, was to further disadvantage the 'hard kernel' of long-term unemployed, since there was always a reserve pool of short-time labour when an industry began to recover, and it was these men who stood to benefit, since there was little incentive to offer work to those who had been out of the labour market for some time, and whose skills and efficiency might be thought to have diminished. And so the curse was handed down. The sons of men already employed in an industry were much more likely to be offered apprenticeships or training schemes in that industry than other boys. If a boy started work in the same insured industry as his father, both would be eligible for unemployment benefit as of right, regardless of family circumstances. That was not the case for an unemployed youth, nor indeed, more perniciously, for the unemployed father of an employed youth following the introduction of the much-loathed Means Test.

As part of the swingeing austerity package of 1931, which also raised contributions while cutting benefits, unemployment benefit could in future only be drawn as of right for six months: after that, those still out of work and requiring support had to apply for 'transitional payments' paid through the Labour Exchange. Before this was granted, they had to undergo a household means test carried out by the local PAC. The Committee would inform the Labour Exchange of the applicant's circumstances, and the rate of relief he should receive was assessed. In arriving at this figure all forms of household income were taken into consideration. These included any pensions or savings, any money coming into the house from a working son or daughter, even household possessions. The maximum amount which an adult male could receive before losing his entitlement to benefit was 15s.3d a week.

The fact that the total income of a family was assessed led to much bitterness, and sometimes family break-up. 'The Act drove many more young men and women away from home than anything else, because if you had a son working, and the father was out of work, the son was made to keep him,' explained a Welsh miner. 'It was one of the reasons why so many left [the Valleys] for London or the Midlands.'

Various ruses were thought up to get round this deprivation: a working child might leave home and go to live with a relative or in lodgings so that the parent would qualify for benefit. Or he or she might remain at home, but cram into an outhouse or a shed on the allotment when the Public Assistance officer was expected. Stanley Iveson, a mill worker in Nelson in Lancashire, a textile town with high unemployment, recalls the effect of the Means Test there: 'In 1931 when people were being knocked off the dole, there was a big building across [the street] ∴ . . it was a model lodging house. And . . . lads used to go and sleep there, during the week . . . It was a shilling a night. So they were able to draw the dole. But they went home for their meals. And it broke up homes in those days.'

In Dowlais in South Wales Beatrice Wood's father was an unemployed miner, but her brother had a job. The Means Test

meant that everybody working had to keep their parents . . . there was a lot of friction between fathers and sons because the boys resented keeping their parents. We tried to live an honest life, we really tried, but . . . the Government was making honest people dishonest because of their rules. The Means Test man would come often, asking the same question. So we devised a plan with the help of my mother's friend. We would say my brother was living with them. It didn't matter to them because her husband was working. My mother didn't like doing it, but we had to in order to live – if you could call it living. There was a lot of people doing it. The trouble was, my brother couldn't be seen in our house because he wasn't supposed to be living there. The Means Test man came when you least expected him. Sometimes he would call just as my brother had come in from work. He would be eating his food and if there would be a knock on the door there would be one mad rush to get the food off the table (because we only had one room) before we opened the door, and my brother would have to hide in the pantry . . . and stay there until [the Means Test man] had gone. The Means Test man came one day when my brother was bathing in front of the fire in a tub. Well. My brother jumped out of the tub wet and naked and went into the pantry to hide. We didn't have time to take the tub out, so my mother, resilient as ever, caught hold of our dog and plunged him into the tub, pretending she was bathing the dog. My brother was freezing in the pantry. When we opened the door to let the Means Test man in, the dog jumped out of the tub and shook himself all over the Means Test man. It took all my powers not to laugh, because it was like a comic strip if it wasn't so serious . . . Those Means Test men were horrible men, and very arrogant. They would sometimes lift up the latch and just walk in. So my mother went one better – she kept the door locked. They weren't above looking through your window. I was always told that your home was your castle. But not us – we might as well be living in a field: we had no privacy – this was the dreaded nineteen thirties. How people suffered.

If a father was considered to have sufficient means to support an unemployed son or daughter, his or her benefit would be stopped. Donald Kear, an unemployed machine attendant from the Forest of Dean, remembered: 'Any family unlucky enough to have one of their number unemployed were forced to accept a lower standard of living because they had a passenger to carry. In our house I became the passenger. My benefit was immediately cut to 5/- a week. My father [a miner] was paid on production at the coal face. When his earnings rose a little the benefit was correspondingly reduced. The Means Test man went regularly to the office at the mine to find out how much my father was earning so these adjustments could be made.' Occasionally this inquisition meant that a son or daughter without work would find themselves without a home either, as they would be thrown out so as not to be a 'parasite' on the family; this probably happened more when a step-parent was involved.

Any entitlement to benefit passed after six months: after that it was a question of cash handouts at the minimum possible level to keep the unemployed from destitution. The dispensation felt like an act of charity, as the Fabian socialist writer G.D.H. Cole saw it. 'It is therefore – for charity begins at home – to be strictly limited to the smallest sum that will keep the unemployed from dying or becoming unduly troublesome; and their relations as far as possible to be made to bear the cost of maintaining them in order to save the pockets of the tax payers. Behind this system is the notion that unemployment is somehow the fault of the unemployed, from which they are to be deterred if possible; and an attempt is made to persuade their relations to help in deterring them, because they will be made to contribute to their support.'

The ex-Labour MP Fenner Brockway, now an ILP member, attempted to conjure up the effects of the Means Test for those Southerners who could not envisage it, urging them to imagine the Royal Albert Hall 'filled three times over. That would represent the workers on the Means Test in Newcastle. Imagine it filled twelve times over. That would represent their families. It is beyond imagination to realise the anxiety and despair and suffering they would represent.'

In a number of Labour-controlled authorities, PACs were in fundamental opposition to the Means Test, and subverted its operation by always allowing the maximum possible centrally specified benefit, regardless of an applicant's circumstances. County Durham (where an estimated 40,000 people had to face the Means Test), Glamorgan County (where the number was around 27,000), Monmouth, Rotherham and Barnsley were among those warned by the Ministry of Labour against 'illegal payments'. If they persistently refused to conform, as Rotherham and County Durham did, the PACs were suspended and replaced by commissioners from London to 'do the dirty work'. Other authorities felt it was better to submit to the regulations, but to mitigate them wherever possible, as a statement from the London East End borough of West Ham explained: 'We were threatened with supercession, and in face of that threat we prefer to keep our poor under our own care and do what we can for them rather than hand them over to an arbitrary Commissioner from whom they could expect little humanity.'

For workers who had regarded unemployment benefit as a right, earned while they were in work and to be drawn when, through no fault of their own, they were out of it, the Means Test was not only harsh in its effects, it was degrading and humiliating in its association with destitution and the Poor Law, violating the privacy of homes they had worked hard to scrape together, prying into family matters, letting the neighbours witness their shame as their furniture was carted off to be sold.

'If somebody had a decent home, the man from the Means Test came and made a list of what you had. Then you were told to sell a wardrobe this week, some chairs next week, some pictures the week after, until you perhaps you only had your bed, two chairs and a table left. Only then would you be able to claim something off the Public Assistance,' recalled Kenneth Maher. Not all officers were brutal: some clearly felt disquiet at the job they were obliged to perform, and were as respectful and thoughtful as the brutal and inquisitorial system would permit, but nevertheless:

> You were only left with the bare essentials. I bet today, in some upper-class homes there are thousands of pounds' worth of valuable goods stolen by the Means Test men from the poor in the thirties . . . Mother was given thirty bob to feed herself and five kids. We were left with four chairs, a table, a couple of benches and a couple of beds. I remember thinking, 'Good job we've got no rugs on the floor 'cos they'd have took them as well.'
>
> . . . The Means Test bloke arrived with a van to take the best of our

furniture. How I hated him with his smart clothes and the smirk on his face, twirling his stick of chalk in his fingers. I watched as he walked over to two large brass lions standing either side of the hearth, telling my mother they had to go. It didn't matter to him that they had belonged to her grand-mother long since dead. The poor weren't allowed sentiment. We hadn't got much before he got cracking with his chalk. We'd got a damn sight less when he'd finished.

Such confiscations struck at the heart of an unemployed worker's sense of the modest achievements of a hard-working life, as a London sheet-metal worker explained: 'Suppose I would have to sell off that chair over there. There would be more than that chair go out of this room. How many times do you suppose the old woman and I have gone by the store window and looked at chairs like that waiting till we could get one? Then finally, we got it . . . if I had to sell that, I'd be selling more than the wood and the cloth and the stuffing. I'd be selling part of myself.'

The Means Test was not only harsh and often inequitable, it also defied logic. As the *Rhondda Fach Gazette* reported: 'It is in many cases a penalty upon thrift. If a man had been careful and thrifty all of his life and has got a small income he loses exactly that amount from the dole, while a reck-less unthrifty person gets it in full.'

By January 1932 almost a million unemployed were having to register for transitional payments, and were thus coming within the scope of the Means Test. Thousands were cut off from benefit, while others had their relief drastically reduced. It was claimed that in the depressed textile areas of Lancashire only 16 per cent of claimants were awarded the full tran-sitional benefit, while a third were disallowed altogether. Throughout Britain as a whole, half of those applying for transitional payments received less than half the maximum amount, and 180,000 people were judged no longer eligible to receive unemployment benefit under the unemployment insurance scheme as a result of the application of the Means Test. The government saved £24 million in that first year. The cost to society was incalculable.

As James Maxton bitterly lectured Harold Macmillan, 'The Means Test has been useful in disclosing once more how limited were the resources of the working population. But was there any need to set up expensive investigating machinery to discover that the majority of the working class were very poor?'

FOUR

Mapping Britain

You were such an angel to take trouble with my old women and it was really worthwhile. I do not know whether this story of an old castle will affect the Labour vote. People are so odd. They might say, 'He is a humbug: he talks Labour and lives in a castle.' But they might also say, 'How splendid of him when he lives in a castle to come and worry about our little affairs.'

Harold Nicolson writing to his wife Vita Sackville-West, who had entertained fifty ladies from the West Leicester Women's Conservative Association (his constituency) at their home, Sissinghurst Castle in Kent, on 5 June 1937

'Southampton to Newcastle, Newcastle to Norwich: memories rose like milk coming to the boil. I had seen England. I had seen a lot of Englands. How many?', J.B. Priestley asked himself at the conclusion of his *English Journey* in 1933. But although Priestley had roamed (usually by 'motor coach', which he found 'voluptuous, sybaritic . . . This is how the ancient Persian monarchs would have travelled, if they'd known the trick of it . . . they have annihilated the old distinction between rich and poor travellers') from Bristol in the West to Norwich in the East, from Southampton in the South to Yorkshire, Lancashire and Tyneside in the North, by way of Birmingham, Coventry, Leicester, Nottingham and Arnold Bennett's 'five pottery towns' in between, he had not, as most commentators had not, rambled down to England's south-westernmost extremity, Cornwall. If he had, he would have found there unemployment, poverty and despair to equal any found in the reproach that Jarrow, Merthyr Tydfil, Clydeside and the other depressed areas constituted.

The village of St Day, named for a Celtic saint and a stopping place in the Middle Ages for pilgrims on their journey to St Michael's Mount, lies nine miles north of Falmouth and seven miles east of Truro in Cornwall. A prosperous village in the early nineteenth century, its wealth was founded on copper-mining until 1870, when competition from Chile, Bolivia and Peru meant that 2,000 men were thrown out of work when the United

Mines closed down. 'The dismal procession of the Gwennap [the parish in which St Day is located] Mines to the scrap heap had passed, [and] the modern history of St Day had begun. When the Great War came it was trotting down the hill at a leisurely pace. When the war ended the speed of the pace was accelerated and that was the only difference the War made,' explained Richard Blewett, the Medical Officer of Health for the district, in a 'modern historical survey' of St Day he prepared in 1935 for a Board of Education short course for elementary school teachers held at Selwyn College, Cambridge.

The land surrounding the village was 'pocked by mineshafts . . . and scarred by "burrows" or mine tips, over many of which nature is gradually casting a blanket of heather'. In 1935 the rate of unemployment in St Day was nearly 30 per cent, since not only had copper-mining collapsed, but so, in the mid-1920s, had the tin-mining industry around nearby Redruth and Cambourne, from where many of St Day's inhabitants came in search of cheaper housing – even in 1935 the average rent of a workman's house was not much more than two shillings a week. China clay production, which it had been hoped might fill the vacuum left by the decline of mining had done no such thing: by the end of 1932 output had fallen 40 per cent since 1929, and the price had fallen by more than 30 per cent. The Cornish economy was in paralysis, with the population having fallen in the decade up to 1931 by 0.9 per cent (while that of the rest of England and Wales had risen by 5.5 per cent), and the annual average of unemployment between 1930 and 1933 was 21.6 per cent.

Moreover, de-industrialisation at the turn of the century meant that trade unionism amongst the Cornish miners was never the force it was in the Welsh Valleys. Even when a strike was organised by the Transport and General Workers' Union in January 1939 at South Crofty mine, when police and strikers clashed, only 234 men out of a total workforce of 435 stopped work, while the seasonal and scattered nature of the tourist industry meant that unionism did not find a foothold among those toiling in hotels and other holiday amenities. Politically Cornwall, as part of Britain's 'Celtic fringe' and with its strong tradition of religious nonconformism remained a fairly staunch Liberal stronghold during the 1930s (the Conservatives managed to take two seats in the 1931 election and three in 1935), with Isaac Foot, MP for Bodmin until 1935 – the patriarch of a radical dynasty that included the future Labour leader Michael Foot and the campaigning Socialist Workers' Party and *Daily Mirror* journalist Paul Foot – the 'towering presence'. An eloquent preacher and stirring orator, with an 'anti-drink, anti-betting, evangelical stance', Foot was revered throughout the county and the fishermen's luggers at Looe were reputed to be painted in the Liberal colours of blue and yellow in his honour. Indeed, 'Our Isaac' was an important factor in preventing what another Cornishman (though Foot was actually a native of Devon, and began his political career there), the historian A.L. Rowse, who stood unsuccessfully as Labour candidate for Penryn and Falmouth in both elections in the thirties, believed was 'the prime task for Labour in Cornwall . . . to bring home the futility of going on being Liberal [since] Cornish liberalism [was] a fossilised survival' – as, unfortunately, was the inter-war Cornish economy.

Fishing was also in the doldrums in Cornwall by the mid-1930s. 'Outside the Duchy the legend still holds that the fisher is the typical Cornishman,' wrote the former suffragist Cicely Hamilton on her journey round England in 1938, 'but, in sober fact, that race of Cornish fishers is a race that is dwindling fast.' With the Cornish fisheries unable to compete with those of the Artic and the North Sea, there were only two first-class steam trawlers registered in the whole of Devon and Cornwall by 1938, one of which had not put to sea since 1925, and whereas there had been 150 first-class motor vessels in 1919, there were only ninety-one by 1938. The decline in the number of sailing boats was even more dramatic. It was much the same with agriculture: under-investment and out-of-date production methods on family farms that were too small to be economic without a high degree of specialisation meant that there were mutterings by the 1930s of the need to 'collectivise' Cornish farms if they were ever to be economically viable. There were, as Cicely Hamilton found, still some earning a living from the Cornish soil: flower-growers. The trade had started on the Isles of Scilly, taking advantage of the islands' mild winters. At first it had been small, 'a few boxes packed with narcissus and daffodils and shipped on the little mail boat that three times a week makes the voyage to St Mary's, and three times a week makes it back to Penzance'. But by the mid-thirties flower-growing had spread to the mainland, and 'in the spring of the year, the Great Western Railway, night by night, carries the spoil of the daffodil fields to the markets of London and the midlands'.

Apart from its abundance of spring flowers, Cornwall's mild climate appeared to offer its only prospect of economic salvation. Every summer the Cornish Riviera Express conveyed many thousands of tourists, not only 'the privileged minority who might otherwise holiday in the real Mediterranean, but . . . anyone who could afford the price of a third class ticket from Paddington'. The journalist and travel writer S.P.B. Mais helped the romance along with a series of promotional booklets written at the behest of the Great Western Railway hinting at 'a western land of Celtic mysticism'.

Even the trains carried such resonant names as *Trelawney, Tintagel Castle, Tre, Pol and Pen*. When a rival railway company decided to make North Cornwall its own preserve, putting such places as Tintagel and Boscastle on the tourist map, it gave its locomotives such appropriately Arthurian names as *Merlin, Lyonesse, Iseult, Sir Cador of Cornwall, Sir Constantine* – and even the traitorous *Sir Mordred* was briefly considered suitable. Despite their mystic names, the trains were among the fastest in the world. In 1938 the playwright Beverley Nichols was struck by the anachronism of George VI 'flying through a country that even his father would hardly recognise, so quickly are the landscapes passing', to collect 'a grey cloak, a brace of greyhounds, a pair of gilt spurs, a pound of cumin, a salmon spear, a pair of white gloves, a hundred shillings and a pound of pepper', dues owed by the Duchy of Cornwall to its Duke/King.

The South-West's tourism boom had begun before the First World War, and it expanded dramatically between 1920 and 1938, with a rise of 80 per cent in the number of people employed in hotels, boarding houses, laundries and cafés in Devon and Cornwall. Tourists came not only by train but increasingly by coach or car, as roads were improved and car-ownership increased. The tourist traffic was of course seasonal: employment in Cornwall would dip to its lowest point in January, and peak in June.

Cornwall, with its Arthurian romance, its Celtic culture, its periodic 'Cornish revival' movements, now intertwined with the romance of ivy-covered, suggestively gothic, disused mineshafts and engine houses, spectacular coastline and stretches of silver sand, and the charm of 'remote accessibility', also held appeal for those who had no need to fuss with a third-class railway ticket, but could motor down with a wicker picnic hamper (though the journey on A-class roads from London might well require an overnight stop). During the 1930s Cornwall became the summer destination of choice of a number of artistic, literary and generally 'bohemian' types – though with its 'reputable light' Cornwall had been attracting artists challenged to paint its ever-changing seascapes since before the First World War. Vanessa Bell went (as did her sister Virginia Woolf), Augustus John (whose son Edwin had settled at Mousehole), the artist Laura Knight (who also had a cottage in Mousehole), her friend and fellow painter Dod Procter and her artist husband Ernest, as well as the writer who gave Cornwall to popular literature, and whose work is still celebrated in an annual festival that brings literary tourism to Cornwall, Daphne du Maurier.

Although he did move not permanently to Cornwall until 1939, the painter Ben Nicholson was a regular summer visitor to St Ives throughout the thirties. There was already a thriving Society of Artists in the town, which had held an annual exhibition since 1927 and sent work to the Royal Academy Summer Exhibition. It was in St Ives that Nicholson 'discovered' the local fisherman Alfred Wallis, who often painted on cardboard supplied by the local grocer. 'No one likes Wallis' paintings [though of course] no one liked Van Gogh for a time,' reported the artist Christopher Wood, who had been on a walk with Nicholson when they glimpsed Wallis's work for the first time through the open door of his cottage. But they would. Today twelve of his paintings hang in Tate St Ives, and his images of sailing boats circulate on greetings cards.

But St Ives, Newlyn and Mennabilly/Manderley were as far from the concerns of St Day as were the 'professional Cornishmen' of the 1930s, most notable among them the historian A.L. Rowse and the essayist 'Q', Sir Arthur Quiller-Couch. Similarly, the town had little time for a new revivalist organisation, Tyr Ha Tavas (Land and Language), which emerged in 1933, declaring that it stood for 'the unity of persons of Cornish birth or descent who value their Cornish heritage, and who desire to maintain the outlook, individualism, culture, and idealism characteristic of their race', and pronouncing a determination 'to show Cornish people what Cornish men have done and what they still can do to help the World'. There had been a series of earlier Cornish revivalist movements, since 'Every Cornishman knows well enough, proud as he may be of belonging to the British Empire, that he is no more an Englishman than a Caithness man is, that he has as much right to separate local patriotism to his mother-land . . . as has a Scotsman, an Irishman, a Welshman, or even a Colonial, and that he is as much a Celt and as little of an Anglo-Saxon as any Gael, Cymro, Manxman or Breton.' A College of Bards, a Cornish Gorsedd, affiliated to its Welsh and Breton sister organisations, was established in 1927, and held annual ceremonies conducted by blue-robed bards speaking the Cornish language. But by 1937 a newspaper correspondent reluctantly admitted: 'If we are quite truthful we have to admit that the revival of the Gorsedd has scarcely touched the lives of the common people of Cornwall.'

The members of Tyr Ha Tavas, mainly young people, lobbied local MPs to give greater importance to specifically Cornish problems, and produced a magazine, *Kernow* (the Cornish word for 'Cornwall'). However, *Kernow* always sold more copies to those outside Cornwall than to those who lived there, and the marginal political thrust of Tyr Ha Tavas failed entirely to address the social and economic problems of the county, which St Day had in great number.

Those few men still employed in the few mines operating would leave the village just after five in the morning to go down on the early-morning shift, 'up again at 3.30 p.m. then walk home ... there were no baths or showers ... mining was hard, dirty and wet work and the miners did almost everything by hand. The only lighting was candles or carbide lights.' Nevertheless, work was so scarce in the Welsh coalmines that 'A number of families decided to pack up and head for Cornwall, with just a glimmer of hope that their luck might change,' remembers F.R. Clymo, who was a boy at the time.

> I have no idea how many were involved in this trek, but I well remember five or six men coming to St Day ... It took them almost a month to reach us, sleeping rough as they went. They were desperate men who had to make it because their families left behind in the valleys were dependent on them. About a month later when accommodation had been found their families came down in lorries, which were sponsored by the British Legion ... I remember the new intake of Welsh girls and boys who came to our school ... they were like refugees ... [but] at no time did we have any industrial projects since the closing of the mining industry ... very few people were tempted to become residents here.

The only casual work likely to be had, Clymo recalled, was

> when Falmouth Docks would get a shipload of cement in, which would have to be unloaded ... it was a job not done by the dock labourers, so ... the labour exchange would direct a certain number of unemployed men to report to the docks ... There was no such thing as refusal. Refusing meant instant stoppage of unemployment benefits ... I've seen men return after three days of this work with their hands raw and bleeding through continually carrying hundredweights of hot cement from the ship to the warehouse. On another occasion, right here in the village the GPO put the main telephone cables underground from the Exchange ... to the Old Post Office in Market Square. Several villagers who were unemployed were directed to do this work ... they did the work with hammers and gads (steel chisels); first they moved the hard top, then they had to dig down three feet with pick and shovel ... Many of them had not worked for years, so with soft hands and not much muscle they were soon in trouble with blistered and bleeding hands. Some of them got a few bruises as well especially those holding the chisels, because the hammer men, who were out of practice, invariably missed and consequently delivered a blow to the holder's hands. Yet not much sympathy was ever shown because after all it was only a temporary job, as soon as it was finished they would all be laid off and back on the dole again with plenty of time to heal their wounds ... It was quite a common sight to see half a dozen [older] women on a sunny dry afternoon ... heading for Unity Woods and the old Tram Road, their mission to

collect sticks or any broken limbs of trees to keep the fire alight . . . These women wore long hessian aprons (towsers to us), some wore caps and the odd one or two smoked a clay pipe. They would round up as much wood as they could carry in the big aprons. Some would do this two or three times a week to save buying coal. Coal was cheap but they could not afford to buy it . . . times were bad, they were old at forty, no one was ever in a position to help them . . . Life was tough, only the very strongest got through.

There was, reported Richard Blewett in his 1935 survey, 'a noticeable amount of squalor in the village and its surroundings'. Electric street lighting had only arrived at St Day in February that year, no sewerage scheme existed, and water was delivered in barrels by horse and cart. A survey of sixteen households revealed an average of seven children per family, and of six people sleeping in the same bedroom.

'St Day is poverty stricken,' Blewett concluded. Three hundred and twenty of its inhabitants were excused all or part of their rates, and 50 per cent of children on the school register were entitled to free milk, which was provided when the weekly household income did not exceed six shillings per head: in 1937, Merthyr Tydfil's schools were handing out free milk to only 25 per cent of their pupils.

'While 268 St Day men and women were employed in 1935, most finding some sort of work in the village, and others ventured to Truro, Falmouth, Redruth or Cambourne, 82 were unemployed' – 'NEARLY A QUARTER' wrote Blewett in capital letters with heavy underlining. 'The fathers of 53 families are unemployed and their children number 127 at school. I can find no relationship between the unemployment of the fathers and the intelligence of the children.'

The question of the relationship between unemployment and poverty, physical health and psychological well-being (as well as crime) preoccupied politicians, both national and local, committees, commissions and inquiries, social investigators, memoirists, novelists and newspaper pundits in the 1930s. The Pilgrim Trust surveyed a thousand unemployed men drawn from six areas throughout Britain and published its findings as *Men Without Work*; E. Wight Bakke shared the life, insofar as it was possible to do so, of *The Unemployed Man* in the London Borough of Greenwich; Hubert Llewellyn Smith led a team at the London School of Economics assessing what had changed since Booth's turn-of-the-century survey *Life and Labour of the People in London*; Seebohm Rowntree set out to remeasure 'poverty and progress in York' as he had done in a survey published in 1901, and though he found poverty alleviated by 50 per cent, the cause, he noted, was different: in Booth's day it had been low wages, now it was unemployment, which had also struck the London inquiry. Herbert Tout, son of a distinguished Manchester medieval historian, did the same – though much more briefly – for Bristol; Hilda Jennings reported on conditions in the mining community of Brynmawr in South Wales, where unemployment was among the highest in Britain; the Carnegie Trust reported on the young unemployed in the same region; and there were many more specific investigations into the health of the unemployed, the incidence of maternal and infant mortality, and other long-term effects of being without work.

Believing that 'our civilisation was rather like the stock comic figure of the professor who knows all about electrons but does not know how to boil an egg or tie his bootlaces. Our knowledge begins anywhere but at home', J.B. Priestley had set out on his unscientific but evocatively impressionistic journey across England, determined not to be one of those who, because they had 'never poked [their noses] outside Westminster, the City and Fleet Street', were unaware of what was happening in 'outer England'. He was not alone. Throughout the decade Britain (most especially England) would be crisscrossed by those bent on pinning down the true state of the nation – largely by heading north. Honest inquiry, indictment, nostalgic gazetteer, guidebook (although often light on precise information – H.V. Morton's comment on the 'Five Sisters' window in York Minster was, 'No words can describe it; it must be seen,' and he found the pillars of Gloucester Cathedral 'beyond description'), *zeitgeist* entrapper, each book had a different agenda, each traveller was freighted with different baggage. But all had a common purpose: to show Priestley's 'outer England' to those in 'inner England' who would buy their books ('Fact is now the fashion' in publishing), read their articles, take notice, maybe even take action. Towards the end of the decade this documentary impulse would crystallise in the formation of Mass-Observation, which aimed to give voice to the masses it observed, in the documentary films of John Grierson and others, and in the magazine *Picture Post*. But until then the pickings were there to be had for anyone who could get a commission to turn them over.

H.V. Morton had been 'in search of' England (then Scotland, Ireland and Wales) since the end of the 1920s, but he was a self-confessed 'magpie picking up any bright thing that pleased me', and 'deliberately shirked realities. I made wide and inconvenient circles to avoid modern towns and cities . . . I devoted myself to ancient towns and cathedral cities, to green fields and pretty things.' Though Morton found himself drawn more into the inequities of urban industrial poverty as the decade progressed, he never lost his visceral fondness for a pre-industrial, prelapsarian rural world, and scuttled back to its soft embrace as often as he could, defending the country-side against neglect and exploitation.

The journalist J.L. Hodson roamed from the countryside of Norfolk and Suffolk up the north-east coast, taking in Lancashire and Yorkshire, and then back south to the 'English seaside' and 'London town' via the Potteries. He called the resultant book *Our Two Englands* (1936), after Disraeli's concept of two nations, one rich, the other poor. 'We know no more about the un-employed, those of us who live apart from them, than those who stayed at home knew of the Great War,' Hodson concluded of the 'six millions of men, women and children in England [who] have neither enough to eat, nor enough clothes to wear, nothing like enough either on backs or beds'.

An American professor of English, Mary Ellen Chase, found two Englands too, but while her divide was geographic like that of the other roamers, her condemnation was of a different order. Venturing north after a pleasant amble round Southern England, Chase reported in her book *In England Now* (1937) that 'there are few more ugly, more depressing places on this earth than the industrial towns of northern England. Their very names lack the euphony of the south: Manchester, Staylebury, Leeds, Bradford, Sheffield, Crewe and Preston.' Although she noted that the North was known for its radical politics and economics, Chase conjectured that this was partly the result of the 'wilder, freer winds that sweep across wider, higher, more barren moors', she could not wait to leave behind the 'rows upon rows of identical grey houses where strident women with untidy babies stand in doorways . . . the smell of cheap petrol, fish and chips, smoke and wet woollens; tree-less streets; advertisements for Lyons' tea, Capstan and Woodbine cigarettes; miserable shops displaying through their unwashed windows, pink rock candy, drill overalls, tinned sardines, sticky kippers, sucking dummies for babies, garish underwear, impossible hats . . .'

However, Cicely Hamilton, who experienced 'a stirring of the heart' every time she landed at Dover, recognised that the real England was 'essentially urban, living by the office, the factory and the shop'. She made no apolo-gies for devoting two chapters of her survey *Modern England. As Seen by an Englishwoman* to what she called 'hard core unemployment', to 'those Englishmen cast out of industry in the fullness of their skill and experience'.

Beverley Nichols took a 'bird's eye' view of the country in 1938 to 'differ-entiate it from the England of 1928', and although he modestly recognised that the nation's problems 'cannot be settled in a single book . . . at least they can be *indicated*.' Priestley had admitted, 'I have certain quite strong political opinions and I tend more and more to bring them into my writing,' and was clear about what he was looking for before he set out: 'I know there is deep distress in the country. I have seen some of it, just a glimpse of it, already. And I know there is far, far more ahead of me.'

In his indictment *Hungry England* (1932), Fenner Brockway recognised that 'figures and statistics signify little' unless they are translated to a human scale. He described a family of four 'existing on 14*s*.6*d* a week; 5*s* for rent at the lowest 1*s*.6*d* for coal and lighting. Allow nothing at all for clothing and household extras. That leaves 8*s* to provide food for two adults and two children. How can it be done without leaving actual hunger – hunger gnawing at the stomach, hunger making one dizzy and weak, hunger destroying one's body and destroying one's mind.'

The *Daily Worker* journalist and typographer Alan Hutt followed much the same route that Brockway had taken through Lancashire, the Black Country, Tyneside and Teesside, South Wales, Clydeside and Suffolk to investigate the effects of seasonal unemployment on rural poverty, and discovered – or rather confirmed – that 'The stark reality is that in 1933, for the mass of the population, Britain is a hungry Britain, badly fed, clothed and housed.'

The 'lower-upper-middle-class' George Orwell (the pen name of Eric Arthur Blair, another with 'quite strong political opinions' that he tended to bring into his writing) left his part-time job in a Hampstead bookshop and took *The Road to Wigan Pier* for two months, finding no pier (it was a music-hall joke attributed to George Formby's father), but a 'strange country [of] ugliness so frightful and arresting that we are obliged to come to terms with it'. He took the road north partly because he 'wanted to see what mass unemployment is like at its worst, partly in order to see the most typical section of the English working-class at close quarters'. What he found was fury-inducing hard-core unemployment, poverty, deprivation, exploitation, squalor and hopelessness. Some thought his account exaggerated: the right-wing historian Arthur Bryant accused him of being a 'super sensitive' tourist, searching for local colour in the land of the unemployed, producing 'propaganda' in the name of literature.

Others began to publish their autobiographies of the 'hungry thirties' during the decade. John Brown went 'on the tramp' for work before ending up as a student at Ruskin College, Oxford; the young cabinet-maker Max Cohen wrote an account of his life as 'one of the unemployed', mainly in the East End of London; another autobiography was that of George Tomlinson, an uncomplaining coalminer from Nottingham who found that 'After four years of unemployment I get a thrill out of ignoring the pit buzzer,' and set off for a walk in Sherwood Forest, reminding himself that 'If I have lost my job, I have also lost a hard master.' Tomlinson was one of the few unemployed at the time who believed there was 'very little hostility between the "means test" visitor and the family . . . The visitor does his rather unpleasant job in a way that no fair-minded person could object or take exception to. He was probably unemployed himself before he took the job.'

The BBC broadcast a series of talks on unemployment in 1931. The speakers had included John Maynard Keynes, Seebohm Rowntree and Herbert Morrison, with the Conservative leader Stanley Baldwin winding up. These were followed by six lectures by Sir William Beveridge in which he aimed to diagnose the 'disease of unemployment' by tracing its origins back to before the First World War, considering whether the causes were labour or credit, and examining such symptoms as 'social malingering' before trying to calculate the cost of the 'cure'. Beveridge had begun to change his mind on unemployment, moving away from the idea that its main cause was a residual section of the population that would always be unemployable for reasons of physical or moral deficiency, to an under-standing of its structural nature, recognising that 'There is not a special class or kind of people who constitute the unemployed. They come from almost every calling and have as great a variety of interests and capacities as any other member of the community. They are ordinary decent people like ourselves to whom an extraordinary misfortune has happened.' Since this was the case, Beveridge later regretted that he had not made his talks more 'human'. Instead of assailing his listeners with abstract notions and yards of statistics, he reflected, he should have talked more about the social consequences, how actual people were affected.

The human face of unemployment was given more prominence in a series of articles that appeared in *The Listener*, 'the organ of the BBC', and were subsequently published as a book, but never broadcast. *Memoirs of the Unemployed* described the psychological effects of unemployment on people's lives, their politics and their hopes for the future. The idea had come from a similar study carried out in Marienthal, a small industrial village near Vienna, where the closure of the textile mill in 1929 had thrown almost the entire population out of work, and from a competition organised by the Institute of Social Economy in Warsaw which had resulted in the publica-tion of fifty-seven vivid accounts sent in by the Polish unemployed.

In 1932 the ubiquitous journalist S.P.B. Mais had travelled through some of England's lesser-known beauty spots at the behest of the BBC. His seventeen talks, subsequently published as a book, were entitled *This Unknown Island*. The following year the BBC commissioned Mais to give a 'human face' to unemployment on the radio by exploring a different sort of unknown island. This time, rather than idyllic places he visited Labour Exchanges, out-of-work clubs and settlements and other places where species unemployed might be located, talking to organisers and the unemployed themselves, 'black-coated' (now 'white-collar') and former rural workers, women who were either out of work themselves or were bearing the brunt of coping with no regular wage coming in. The intention of the exercise, entitled *Time to Spare*, was largely to give people who had no personal experience of unemployment 'an account from the unemployed themselves of what life is like when one is out of work, what steps they take to cope with the problems of existence . . . since if you have never been out of work you can no more realize the horror of unemployment than you can realize the horror of leprosy . . . If you have never moved outside of Sussex, you can no longer visualize the destitution on the banks of the Tyne than you can visualize a tornado in Japan.'

Mais was eager to learn all he could, but he was a naïve observer. After commenting on the neatness of the women's clothes at a female keep-fit class in Tyneside he was told tartly, 'It's perhaps just as well that you can't see what they've got on underneath.' *Time to Spare* was broadcast in early January 1933, the series introduced by the Prince of Wales. Mais called it 'an S.O.S. message, probably the most urgent you will ever hear and it vitally concerns you. You are called upon to create an entirely new social order. The bottom has apparently fallen out of the old world in which everything was subordinated to a day's work.' He appealed to listeners (who were clearly not envisaged as the unemployed themselves) to rally round and 'make yourself known to the manager of your local Labour Exchange, or if you live in a village, to the Schoolmaster or Parson', to initiate schemes to occupy those without work.

The second series of *Time to Spare*, which started in April 1934, was rather less of an outsider's view of the unemployed: this time the producer Felix Greene toured the country as Mais had, but when he found an un-employed person with a compelling story to tell, he invited him or her to Broadcasting House in London, where he got them talking and their conver-sation was relayed over a loudspeaker to the next room, where secretaries transcribed their words. In his introduction, Mais suggested that things had improved since the first series, but that there was no room for compla-cency. Indeed, the programmes caused a furore in the press, particularly since they started transmission at the same time as the final reading of the Unemployment Bill was going through the Commons. Labour MPs quoted from them (they were reprinted in *The Listener*) to harangue the govern-ment about the Means Test and proposals to further limit the entitlement of the unemployed to benefits.

On 5 June 1934 the *Daily Herald* reported: '*Time to Spare* is shattering too many illusions. Millions are being turned against the Government.'

Sir John Reith, Director General of the BBC, was summoned to 10 Downing Street to be told by Ramsay MacDonald that the series could not continue. Reith recognised that the government had the power to pull the programmes, but told MacDonald that if this were done, there would be a twenty-minute silence at the time they would have been broadcast, and it would be announced that this was because the government had 'refused to allow the unemployed to express their view'. The series continued.

Although the Director of Talks at the BBC, Charles Siepmann, was concerned that the programmes on unemployment merely attempted to ameliorate its effects, rather than probing its possible political causes, Wal Hannington, leader of the National Unemployed Workers' Movement (NUWM), had his request to be allowed to broadcast turned down by the BBC on the grounds that it wished to avoid controversy. Denied a voice on the airwaves, Hannington wrote a number of books castigating government policy and describing the plight of the unemployed, with such unequivocal titles as *Never on Our Knees, Ten Lean Years, Unemployed Struggles*. Several of these were published by Victor Gollancz's Left Book Club, which brought the hardships of those suffering unemployment, as well as suggestions for the problem's solution, to a wider and very engaged audience – Gollancz had also published Orwell's *Road to Wigan Pier* and, in collaboration with his usual publisher, Priestley's *English Journey*.

Others drew on what they had experienced of unemployment or saw all around them, and wrote novels about how it affected men, their families, their communities. Walter Greenwood, who had three spells of unemployment from his work as a clerk and council canvasser, was the author of *Love on the Dole*, which was the probably the best-known novel of the Depression. Nevertheless, in 1936 the British Board of Film Censors twice refused to allow a film version to be shown in cinemas on both moral (too much bad language) and political (a scene of unemployed men fighting the police) grounds. It was, they declared, a 'very sordid story in very sordid surroundings', despite the fact that both the book and a play based on it had enjoyed great success. It finally reached the screen in 1941.

Although *Love on the Dole* was the only 'Depression novel' that was a best-seller, publishers were anxious to find 'authentic' proletarian writers – partly because there were so few of them. As the novelist, reviewer and editor Cyril Connolly pointed out, '90 per cent of all English authors come from the Mandarin class . . . A rigorous class system blankets down all attempts to enlarge these barriers. The English mandarin simply cannot get at pugilists, gangsters, speakeasies, negroes'– or the unemployed, he might have added. In June 1927 the Communist newspaper the *Sunday Worker* had written of having the 'misfortune to be compelled to make do with stories about the working-class who are "sympathetic" but have no first hand knowledge of workers' lives'.

But that changed over the next decade: with time on their hands, men turned to writing about what they knew only too well. Leslie Halward, an unemployed plasterer, had a story accepted by *John o'London's* magazine – and was paid £100 just as the Means Test man was scheduled to call. Another out-of-work plasterer, Jack Hilton, was sent to Strangeways for six months in 1932 for leading an unemployed workers' protest in Rochdale, and wrote his autobiography and a novel – about unemployed workers' protests – while he was in prison. William Holt, a weaver, went to jail for nine months for the same offence, this time committed at Todmorden; when he was released he couldn't find a job and was about to be evicted so he resumed the writing he had always done, but now his subject was invariably the experience of unemployment, selling his books from door to door in the Calder Valley. Walter Brierley recounted the harrowing tale of the depredations wrought by a *Means-Test Man* (1935); the novel sold 6,000 copies in the first year of publication. James Hanley's *Grey Children* was a story of 'humbug and misery' in the lives of unemployed shipyard workers; Roger Dataller's *Steel Saraband* was a tale of unemployment in the steelworks; Lewis Jones's *Cmwardy* and also his later *We Live* told of the hard lives of miners in the Welsh Valleys. Lewis Grassic Gibbon (the stirring pseudonym of Leslie Mitchell) wrote a powerful dialect trilogy of Scotland's ills, *A Scots Quair*, the story of a family moving from rural to urban poverty, of which the third volume, *Grey Granite* (1934), charts their response to unemployment in a fictitious industrial city. Jack Lindsay (writing under the pseudonym Richard Preston) wrote a novel dealing with the collapse of the Cornish economy.

One author had some notepaper printed with the heading 'B.L. Coombes, Miner-Author' after the success of his first book, *These Poor Hands* (1937), another Left Book Club choice, and he continued to work as both. A[rchibald]. J. Cronin, who had been appointed Medical Inspector of Mines in 1924, drew on his experience of the wretched conditions in the coal industry for *The Stars Look Down* (1935), while his sensationally successful next novel, *The Citadel* (1937), was an attack on the system of private medicine, again drawing on his experiences in Tredegar, where he had witnessed the correlation between the inhalation of coal dust and lung disease, and its 'model' treatment with the help of the Tredegar Medical Aid Society.

By the second half of the thirties the prejudice against those who had no intimate experience of working-class life, of poverty and unemployment, seems to have somewhat dissipated: there was an important story to be told, whoever the teller. The one-time editor of the *Strand Magazine* and *John O'London's*, George Blake, wrote a novel set in the shipyards, and in *Ruined City* Nevil Shute (who was an engineer rather than a manual worker) wrote of a rescue package dreamed up by an altruistic businessman for a thinly disguised Jarrow.

Although unemployment seared deepest into the working classes, not all the middle classes escaped: by 1934 an estimated 4,000 black-coated workers were without work, and their plight began to be described in such novels as Simon Blumefeld's *They Won't Let You Live* (1939), in which the graduate protagonist unsuccessfully applies for 187 jobs, eventually deciding to kill himself. Even the thriller writer Eric Ambler used the frustration of a skilled production engineer who could not find work as the basis for the plot of *Cause for Alarm*, published in 1938.

Despite the widespread evocations of unemployment, both real and fictional, which stood as indictments of a system that had failed, political calls to action – let alone revolution – were muted. The BBC dutifully bore vivid witness to the plight of the unemployed, but in its efforts to avoid more controversy than programmes such as *Time to Spare* already whipped up, it largely avoided probing the causes of unemployment and means of relieving it, other than by strenuous voluntary efforts to 'help'. When 'Edward Windsor', as Wal Hannington consistently referred to the Prince of Wales, an active supporter of voluntary movements for the unemployed, came to the microphone in December 1933 to introduce the first series of *Time to Spare*, he set the tone by asserting that 'the causes of unemployment are beyond our control, and we might differ in our estimate of them, but it is largely within our power to control the effects of unemployment. The unemployed are just our fellow men, the same as ourselves, only less [considerably less in his case] fortunate.'

However, novels such as *Love on the Dole* were hailed as a wake-up call, with the left-wing novelist Ethel Mannin hoping that 'It is going to shock smug, fashionable, comfortably-off, middle-class London into a realisation of what the industrial north is really like.' One reader at an Ilkeston public library noticed how many grimy thumbprints such novels bore, evidence, he thought, of their having 'clearly passed through the hands of a variety of curious proletarians'. Thus, in various ways and with varying intensity, by the end of the decade the contours of unemployed Britain in the 1930s had been, if not fully explained, at least comprehensively mapped – even if some declined to listen, or to believe that the topography was quite so bleakly craggy as others portrayed it.

FIVE

Hungry Britain

Oh hush thee, my baby,
Thy cradle's in pawn:
No blankets to cover thee
Cold and forlorn . . .

Thy mother is crying,
Thy dad's on the dole:
Two shillings a week is the price of a soul.

'A Carol', C. Day Lewis (1935)

The death of Annie Weaving, the thirty-seven-year-old wife of an un-employed man in South-East London, mother of seven children, who collapsed and died while bathing her six-month-old twins, offered a stark definition of poverty in 1933. Mrs Weaving had been struggling to keep her family going on the forty-eight shillings a week benefits her husband received. She did so by going without food herself, and though the immediate cause of her death was recorded as pneumonia, the coroner concluded that this would not have proved fatal if Mrs Weaving had had enough to eat, rather than 'sacrificing her life' for the sake of her children. At the inquest, the coroner was blunt: 'I should call it starvation to have to feed nine people on £2.8s a week and pay the rent.'

The press took up the story, and the *Week-End Review* launched a 'Hungry England' inquiry in the spring of 1933, conducted by 'an economist [A.L. Bowley], a physiologist [Professor V.H. Mottram], a housewife, a doctor and a social worker', in the hope that the debate could be settled 'scientific-ally'. It could not. They found that unemployment relief payments were insufficient to provide the minimum diet for a family recommended by the recently established Advisory Committee on Nutrition set up by the Ministry of Health (on which Mottram also sat), and concluded that the 'cheapest practical diet in current English conditions' were about 5s. a week for a man 'not doing muscular work. 4s.2d for a woman; and 2s.9d– 4s.10d for children according to age'.

In November that year the British Medical Association (BMA) established a benchmark for poverty, and this was generally accepted for most subsequent surveys. It specified that an average man required 3,400 calories a day, the cost of providing which was 5s.11d. This figure was later adapted according to whether a man was doing light or heavy work, and proportionately for women and children. Seebohm Rowntree used this standard when assessing the level of poverty in York, but Sir John Boyd Orr, Director of the respected Rowett Research Institute of Nutrition in Aberdeen (who had already been influential in getting free school milk for needy children in Scotland), used more generous figures borrowed from the US Bureau for Economics, which suggested that an active man required 4,500 calories a day and that the population as a whole needed to consume 2,810 calories per head each day.

Until the First World War 'sufficient food' was judged simply by the amount a person consumed: having 'enough to eat' meant just that. But since then there had been extensive research into medical conditions such as rickets, that revealed the importance of the sort of food consumed. There was a growing understanding of the significance of vitamins and minerals, and with it an awareness that large numbers of the low-paid and unemployed could not afford what were known as 'protective foods' – milk, fresh vegetables, meat, fish and fruit – and were subsisting on a largely cheap carbohydrate diet – bread and margarine and potatoes – washed down by copious amounts of tea sweetened with condensed milk. The link between poor nutrition and lack of money was a political question, since, in the view of the think tank Political and Economic Planning (PEP), which had been established as a result of the *Week-End Review*'s campaign, hunger should not be regarded as 'an act of God . . . but a problem which can be analysed and treated by the same methods of common sense that we are trying to apply to other problems'.

'Common sense' suggested it was largely a question of money. A table published in the *Manchester Guardian* in December 1934 showed that to have an acceptable diet a family of a man, his wife and four children (aged five, seven, nine and eleven) needed 35s.2d to live on (excluding rent): what they received in unemployment benefit (also excluding rent) was 29s.6d – a crucial shortfall of 5s.8d.

Using the much more generous calculation that a family of five needed 43s.6d a week to live on at the most basic level, excluding rent, Seebohm Rowntree estimated that 31.1 per cent of the working-class population of

York were living in poverty, as were 18 per cent of the population overall. He concluded that 32.8 per cent of the poverty was due to low wages and 28.6 per cent to unemployment, and that 72.6 per cent of unemployed families lived below the poverty line. In Bristol, Herbert Tout found that over 10 per cent of working-class families were living below the poverty line, an additional 19.3 per cent of working-class families had insufficient income, and more than a quarter of the working class in Bristol as a whole were living in utter destitution; 21.3 per cent of the families suffered as a result of low wages, and 32.1 per cent because of unemployment. But Bristol and York were both relatively prosperous cities, with unemployment rates little more than the national average. Furthermore, these surveys took place in 1936 and 1937 respectively, when the worst of the Depression had passed. What about areas such as the Welsh mining valleys, Tyneside, Teesside and Clydeside, where poverty was much more widespread, and bit far deeper for far longer?

Surveys such as those in York and London, which made comparisons with times when the only recourse for the poor had been charity and the Poor Law, showed that absolute poverty was lower, perhaps half what it had been at the turn of the century. But if poverty was defined as living conditions a little above mere subsistence, then around a third of the working class in Britain – and the manual working class constituted more than 75 per cent of the population, according to the 1931 census – lived on incomes that were insufficient for 'human needs'.

In London in 1929 unemployment and underemployment (short-time working) accounted for 38 per cent of families in poverty, and 55 per cent of the unemployed were living on the poverty line; a survey of Northampton, Warrington, Bolton and Stanley showed that the proportion of poverty due to unemployment had increased more than threefold since 1918; in Sheffield in the winter of 1931–32 it was found that 42.8 per cent of families lived in poverty. All of these calculations presumed the most rigorous housekeeping, that allowed families to exist, but certainly not to live in any meaningful sense.

The Pilgrim Trust calculated the difference between unemployment pay and the average working man's wage. The authors admitted that their sample was small, but concluded that on average, unemployment benefit equalled around 65 per cent of wages; older men, aged between fifty-five and sixty-four, would however receive only 45 per cent of the wages they would have expected had they been in work.

Britain was a world leader in nutritional research, but there was in the thirties no internationally agreed definition of malnutrition, nor a standard measurement for it. Anthropomorphic tests that judged height, weight, hair texture and other outward signs were considered fallible, and blood and urine tests were still in the experimental stage. The seemingly promising evidence of social scientists was proving problematic. Despite the provision to families of measuring jugs, scales and lined exercise books in which to record their income, expenditure and exactly what and how much every member of the household ate (which was regarded as useful training in housewifery as well as yielding survey data) in the course of a month, their findings were 'frustratingly compromised by the human factor', since it was asking a lot to expect poor and often ill-educated families to keep such detailed records over such a period. And for some the natural inclination to resist the spying of outsiders, secrets between husband and wife about money, and even the ever-present spectre of the Means Test man, meant there might be a certain amount of creative accounting in their returns.

However, social investigators on the ground were continually finding correlations between poverty and malnutrition and poverty and infant and maternal mortality, and experiments showed clearly that improved nutrition did bring improved health and life chances. In the Rhondda, the simple expedient of supplementing expectant mothers' diets with a food distribution programme had been tried. The results were startling: 'a sharp fall in the puerperal death rate followed immediately on the introduction of this scheme, the rate dropping from 11.29 in 1934 to 4.77 in 1935'.

Poverty was poverty whatever caused it, and in areas of high unemployment wages tended to be depressed, so the incidence of those with not enough to live on was compounded. Yet the government remained resolute that regardless of what surveys showed, widespread unemployment did not mean an unhealthy nation – or part of a nation – and was quick to blame a lack of education or the fecklessness of the much-maligned working-class housewife, rather than poverty, for inadequate diets. 'There is no available medical evidence of any general increase in physical impairment, sickness or mortality as a result of the economic depression or unemployment,' insisted the Minister of Health, Sir E. Hilton Young, in the House of Commons in July 1933, while the Chief Medical Officer to the Board of Health, Sir George Newman, based his optimism on what he maintained were declining mortality rates and the near eradication of 'malnutrition requiring treatment'.

Those wayward Medical Officers of Health or investigators who declared otherwise were considered guilty of perpetrating socialist 'stunts'. Dr M'Gonigle, the Medical Officer of Health for Stockton-on-Tees, was threatened with removal from the medical register for misconduct if he participated in a broadcast on the problem of malnutrition, while Sir John Boyd Orr was summoned by the Minister of Health, Kingsley Wood, who 'wanted to know why I was making such a fuss about poverty . . . when there was no poverty in this country. This extraordinary illusion was genuinely believed by Mr Wood who held the out-of-date opinion that if people were not actually dying of starvation there could be no food deficiency. He knew nothing about the results of the research on vitamin and protein requirements, and had never visited the slums to see things for himself.' Despite the government's suppression of Boyd Orr's finding in the run-up to the 1935 general election, the Conservative MP and publisher Harold Macmillan, who had seen poverty and hunger up close in his own constituency of Stockton, agreed to publish *Food, Health and Income* in January 1936, thus 'informing the public of what the true position was regarding undernourishment among their fellow citizens' – half of their fellow citizens, Boyd Orr calculated in 1937.

Despite such government complacency – or wilful avoidance – there was a mounting body of evidence from independent investigators that by the 1930s the fall in rates of infant mortality (the number of deaths of children under one year of age), which had been declining impressively since the First World War, with the introduction of maternity and child welfare centres and health visitors, had slowed down considerably, so that England and Wales now ranked ninth in the League of Nations' Table of Infant Mortality, while Scotland was seventeenth. Moreover, there were considerable discrepancies between different parts of the country, and even within small areas. In a comfortable part of Manchester, for example, the rate was forty-four per thousand live births, while in a poorer area it was 143 per thousand. Seventy-six out of every thousand infants died in Glamorgan and Durham, seventy-seven in Scotland, ninety-two in Sunderland and an appalling 114 in Jarrow, whereas in the Home Counties the rate was forty-two per thousand. It was the same with maternal mortality (the number of women's deaths attributed to childbirth): in the North it was 4.36 per thousand, in Wales it was 5.17, whereas in the South-East it was 2.57. Mothers were simply dying in childbirth at a far greater rate in the depressed areas: poor nutrition during pregnancy meant that in the 1930s it was four times as dangerous to bear a child as it was to work down a coalmine. In addition, every five years perhaps a quarter of a million women were likely to suffer disabling and long-lasting 'dull diseases' caused or aggravated by repeated pregnancies and childbirths in adverse conditions. And the wives of unemployed men were not covered by their husbands' health insurance.

Nutrition mattered desperately to the health of the nation – a point that would be taken very seriously at the end of the decade, when after the coming of the Second World War the Minister of Food, Lord Woolton, drew heavily on Boyd Orr's estimates of the standard diet needed to maintain a healthy population – yet, as the leader of the NUWM, Wal Hannington, pointed out, 'The kinds of food . . . necessary to provide the vitamins and calories which have been specified as the minimum requirements [recommended by the BMA] are not being eaten in the homes of the workless since they cannot afford to buy them.' A pint of milk a day would cost 2s.½d a week, while the BMA scale prescribed 2s.8d as the total weekly food allowance for a child of one to two years, and 3s.1d for one aged two to three. Again using the BMA scale, a man eating three meals a day would have exactly 3¼d to spend on each meal, and a woman 2¾d. Furthermore, Hannington quoted the Chief Medical Officer to the Board of Health, Sir George Newman himself, who had estimated in his 1933 report that the milk a pregnant woman needed would cost 4s.1d a week, while the amount allowed for her total food consumption under unemployment benefit regulations was 4s.11d. 'It would, indeed, be interesting,' wrote Hannington, 'to know how the Minister of Health would spend the odd ten pence on buying three meals a day for seven days a week.'

George Orwell quoted – in amazement – a newspaper article that suggested that by eating a diet composed mainly of vegetables and wholemeal bread, with cheese for protein, it was possible for an adult to have a balanced diet for 3s.11d a week. But the 'minimum weekly expenditure on foodstuffs which must be incurred by families of varying size if health and working capacity are to be maintained' recommended by the BMA worked out for a man, his wife and two children aged eleven and nine at 19s.9d a week, out of an unemployment allowance of £1.7s. Since the average weekly rent for three rooms in the East End of London was 12s.6d, and in Stockton-on-Tees the rent for one of the 2,756 new council houses was over nine shillings (which was beyond the reach of most of the unemployed, who continued to live in slum cottages where they paid nearer 4s.8d a week), it was hardly surprising that the Pilgrim Trust found that 44 per cent of the families of the unemployed would not be able to afford the minimum diet once they had paid their rent and allowed for other necessary expenditure. And Rowntree found that in 1933, 72 per cent of the unemployed in York were able to spend less on food than the BMA recommended, 'due to lack of means'. This finding was borne out by Dr M'Gonigle in Stockton-on-Tees, who was convinced that the malnutrition he came across was caused by poverty, and not mismanagement, as was sometimes alleged.

'I learned the meaning of hunger,' wrote Max Cohen of his days as a single, unemployed cabinet-maker. 'I knew what it was to count my pennies carefully and to spend them with hesitation and misgiving. I knew the dull finality of having no money at all.' Cohen

came within the Labour Exchange category of a 'Young Man' (18–21 yrs). Therefore I was receiving fourteen shillings per week . . . apparently it was assumed by the authorities that a 'Young Man' . . . can in some mysterious way support himself on a smaller sum than a 'Man' (21–65 yrs) . . .

Life . . . became divided into more or less rigid periods . . . There was Friday . . . the day, when after feverish waiting at the Labour Exchange, I received the life-giving fourteen shillings. After paying six shillings and sixpence a week rent, I was able, with much care and discrimination, to exist in a more or less normal fashion during the first half of the week. Of course, I could spend nothing on replacing my clothes, or on minor luxuries of any kind, no matter how trifling.

From Tuesday on came bankruptcy . . . I had no money at all, and so, in a sense, nothing more to worry about . . . I lived on whatever may have been left of those things I had bought at the beginning of the week – on dry bread and bits of tasteless cheese. All that was necessary was to pull my belt tighter, ignore the empty ache in my stomach and hang on till Friday and deliverance came round again.

A London housepainter aged forty-seven, married with six children, three of them under six, found himself 'unemployed and unable to fulfil my duties towards my family'. He had a weekly income (including a naval pension and the earnings of three of his children) of £4s.11d, which meant that

after allowing for rent, rates, light, coal and gas with a balance of £2.11s to keep, house, clothe two adults, one adolescent and three children, and provide all other necessaries of life for eight persons, which position a PAC inquisition described as 'not in need of assistance' . . . The chief article of our diet is bread. Margarine comes next, and it is my experience that children prefer this to dripping [from meat] . . . unless the dripping is made use of for frying bread when it often forms a breakfast meal when other food is not available. We invariably take sweetened condensed milk with our tea, a saving thereby being effected in the consumption of sugar; and we often use it for making rice puddings. We usually purchase fresh meat on Friday or Saturday evenings, cash being available on those days, and this being the time when butchers make an effort to sell their odds and ends. Fresh vegetables have been fairly cheap, and these together with cheap sausages, often form our principal meal on two or three days.

A skilled wire-drawer, thirty-two years old, with a wife and one child aged five, who had been unemployed for over three years, had 'little variety in our food since the staple ingredients are bread and butter and tea and cocoa and cheese. Until this year [1933] I had an allotment from which we obtained all our vegetables. A local factory bought the land and I have not yet been able to rent another. We have no garden attached to our house; we share a small back yard with five other houses . . . our rent is 5s6d a week.'

A twenty-five-year-old skilled letterpress printer who had been unable to find work since having a nervous breakdown after the death of his mother five years earlier, was in receipt of 15s.3d benefit. 'How do I exist on my "magnificent bounty"? I pay 8s. for a furnished room which includes laundry. Gas costs 6d weekly; letters for situations 8d; razor blades, soap, shoe blacking, haircuts etc. average 3d; and 6d a week I save to help buy boots, second hand flannels etc. This leaves me 5s6d for food. Can a man keep up health and strength on such a sum? Emphatically no! . . . My breakfast consists of three slices of bread and jam and a cup of tea. Dinner, two slices of bread and about 2ozs cheese. Tea two boiled eggs, or ½lb tomatoes, or a tin of baked beans. If I have 2d left at the week-end (which isn't often) I "mug" [treat] myself and buy some chip potatoes. I have not tasted meat, potatoes (barring the above occasions) or vegetables for over twelve months – and then I am told I get enough money to keep fit and strong.' George Tomlinson, a Nottingham miner, unemployed for four years, explained that 'The real secret of living on the dole [is] potatoes and bread.'

A Scottish hotel-worker, out of work since 1931, had the single man's dole of seventeen shillings a week in 1933, and when he had paid his rent, coal and laundry he was left with 5s.3d, out of which he spent 'about 1 shilling every week on stamps, stationery and typed copies of my references'; 'In the cold wet months of a Glasgow winter . . . my meals, which were few and far between, consisted mostly of tea, bread and margarine,' though he occasionally managed sixpence for some boiling mutton or 4½d for bacon.

Charles Graham, whose father, a merchant seaman, had died when he fell from a ship in dry dock in Australia, and whose stepfather, a miner, was out of work, recalled that his sister 'had just one attic room and two children and with only one gas ring, she couldn't cook an economical dinner. Parents would make soup with a bone, some cabbage, a few turnips and so on. But we usually had a slice of bread in the morning. For dinner a penn'orth of each, that's a penn'orth of fish and a penn'orth of chips; and probably a couple of slices of bread at night . . . now and then with a penn'orth of pease pudding and a saveloy from the local German butcher.' When, during the Second World War, Graham was taken prisoner of war by the Germans for two and a half years, he found his diet much the same as it had been in the 'hungry thirties'.

Graham remembered his mother baking every Sunday (in most North Country families it seems to have been Wednesdays, with washdays on Monday and the Sabbath without work).

> Most of us children would be out collecting orange boxes to stoke the fire. It was a great day, Sunday, because there was plenty of bread, and oven bottom cakes and scones, and so on. We used to buy rusty cans of cheap jam in the market. A housewife would go any distance to save a halfpenny. A halfpenny was a candle and that was four or five hours of light. We were lucky, we had a distant relative of my stepfather who was a butcher and he used to let us have some offcuts of meat at the weekends [a sheep's head was another cheap meat bought for stewing]. Usually sausages was the nearest the average working class got to meat. One of the favourite meals was pan-haggerty. You slice potatoes, put a layer in the frying pan. Put scraps of bacon in the middle then a layer of sliced of potatoes again and fill it with water and just boil away. Or corned beef in the middle. Meat was scarce. I don't ever remember having cheese except for weddings and funerals. And fresh milk was out of the question. It was mainly condensed milk [even though the tin was clearly marked 'unfit for babies'].

John McNamara, an unemployed factory-worker, remembered: 'Lancaster market used to be open till nine Saturday night, and whatever beef and pork sausages they had to sell, they had to get rid of. They couldn't put it away over the weekend because there was no refrigeration, so it would go bad on them . . . especially in the summer months . . . so the stuff went right down to rock bottom prices.' McNamara's mother, 'along with a lot of other married ladies knew this. That was the time they used to go and try and get a bit of meat for Sunday. They'd wait to the last minute. The butcher would practically throw it at them for next to nothing. The fruiterers never threw fruit away. If they'd gone bad, the bad part was cut out. What they called damaged fruit. There was nothing wrong with it but middle class people and the upper crust, they wouldn't think of buying them. But to us it was a godsend. For twopence you could get a handful of damaged apples or oranges . . . The only time you would get to see a chicken was Christmas.

But it had taken twelve months to get that chicken. Mam would find a penny from somewhere to put in the butcher's shop and by the time the year end come she might have five bob.'

Those living on the poverty line or hovering just above it, whether as a result of unemployment, underemployment or simply low wages, lived a dreary life indeed, since 'The minimum standard makes no allowance whatever for sickness, savings, old age or burial expenses, holidays, recreations, furniture, household equipment, drink, newspapers or postage.' There was simply no margin; it was the breadline – and not always that.

With an endless struggle to find enough money to feed a family, it was hardly surprising that there was virtually no money left for anything else. And the longer a man had been out of work, the worse things got. Any small savings were used up, cooking pots, brushes, bedding, towels and clothes wore out. Families got into debt, some had to move to cheaper accommodation if they could find any, or face eviction. Economies on a budget that was already pared to the bone were made on heating and lighting, food got stodgier.

In Sunderland, Mrs Pallas's husband had been 'robust and he had a good job . . . But he fell out of work about four months after I was married, so I've hardly known what a week's wage was.' After thirteen years of unemployment and five children, the oldest boy's trousers had six patches.

I just tell him, he'll be all the warmer, specially in winter. My husband helps me with the darning; I do the patching. I've just put the eighth patch on a shirt of his. I take the sleeves out and put them in another – anything to keep going.

Then when we've finished with the clothes, my husband puts them into making a mat [a peg or rag rug, made by pushing strips of fabric through a sugar sack begged from the grocer or a potato sack]. Everything goes in – vests, stockings, linings.

Many a time my husband has had to make cups for the children out of empty condensed milk tins. He solders the handles on.

Our kettle's got about six patches on it. My husband made the patches from cocoa tins. My husband does all that sort of patching, all the cobbling and hair cutting and spring cleaning . . .

My husband never changes his dole money, but although he doesn't keep a halfpenny pocket money, we still can't manage. And we don't waste nothing. And there's no enjoyment comes out of our money – no pictures, no papers, no sports. Everything's patched and mended in our house.

'It's the women who suffer,' insisted Mrs Pallas. 'The man brings the dole in and he's finished – the woman's got all the rest.' When she married him, Mr Pallas was earning £8 to £10 a week: 'He's a left-handed ship's riveter – a craft which should be earning him a lot. There aren't many left-handed riveters . . . Many a week he's given it [his unemployment benefit] to me and I've just said, "put it in the fire." It's just like an insult to a mother to bring in 33 shillings . . . I'm not blaming my husband. He'd work if he could get it.'

By the time Mrs Pallas had paid ten shillings for coal, gas and rent, and

money for the allotment rent, for burial insurance, to the clubs for the children's clothes, for chapel collection, and cigarettes for my husband, I have about ten shillings left for groceries, two shillings for milk, and about three shillings and sixpence a week for food. It varies a few pence, according to whether we have to make money out of food to buy leather for cobbling or spring cleaning and so on . . . I do the washing every other week because I find I can do a large amount of clothes with the same amount of soap, but it's tiring. I can't manage more than one box of matches a week. Many a time we've sat in the dark – it is gas light, and we haven't a penny for the slot maybe, or we haven't a match.

'A woman had a full time job in the home in those days,' remembered John McNamara in Lancaster. 'It was the blacklead brush to polish the grate. It was the scrubbing brush and a bucket and a floor cloth and a bar of soap [or a donkeystone if they were flagstones] to wash the floors and the tables and the paintwork. And all the paraphernalia to do the weekly washing [often with no running water, washboards to scrub with, blue dollys to make sure the sheets were white, mangling, starching, drying, ironing]. Baking day was Wednesdays. There was a day for everything.'

'It's upon the wives of the unemployed that the real burden falls,' wrote a miner who had been unemployed for eight years by 1934. 'It means they have to scrounge around for the cheapest food and for anything in the shape of clothes, and what our women don't know about jumble sales is not worth knowing. And I cannot imagine a more distressing sight than the average jumble sale in these parts.'

As well as cooking, cleaning and washing, women had to juggle almost non-existent money. Getting things 'on strap' (credit) from the grocer, balancing one tradesman's bill against another, putting a penny or two by in a club for clothing or boots, and putting a brave face on it as she paid her weekly visit to the pawn shop.

Women had to work miracles with the dole, or low wages. 'My father didn't realise how my mother was having to budget. He wasn't aware of a lot of things we had to do, my mother and me, to keep the cart on the wheels. He just tipped his money in and thought it did the job. He just pushed his head in the sand,' recalled Clifford Steele in Barnsley.

Pawn shops were as common as betting shops today. On Monday a woman would pawn her jewellery, often including her gold wedding ring (which she would replace with a sixpenny brass one from Woolworths to stay respectable), or maybe her husband's watch if he had one, or his only suit if he didn't need it that week, and would hope that she would be able to redeem them when the money came in on Friday. Then it would be back to the pawn shop on Monday again, until the family's meagre possessions got too shabby to raise any money against, or even worse, she had to sell the pawn tickets to raise a few pounds, and that would mean the things would be gone for good.

Charles Graham recalled that 'in almost every street [in South Shields] there was the old woman who offered her services as messenger for those people who were too proud to be seen going into the pawn shop. She would be well known to the pawnbroker and could be trusted. She would get a pound loan, the pawn shop would charge twopence a week until the pawn was redeemed. The messenger would get threepence or sixpence from the housewife . . . the parcel would never be opened [by the pawnbroker], it was just a way of getting round the law of money lending. The pawn shop was a bank.' Women would come clattering along the street in clogs and shawls to a pawn shop in Burslem in the Potteries, where unemployment was over 30 per cent in 1931, and stayed high throughout the decade. Its owner 'used to do very well. He used to reckon that it was the only shop in Burslem that had a queue on Monday morning.'

When there was not enough food to go round towards the end of the week, the woman would often go without herself so that her husband and children had a meal on the table – as Annie Weaving must have done count-less times. 'We are told we ought to eat fruit, but it is very seldom that I can afford fruit . . . My husband and I always have to suffer if there is anything to buy. We give it all to the bairns and we have bread and marge,' said Mrs Pallas. 'I was practically living on bread and potatoes,' remembered an Aberdeen women with two small children and an unemployed, unskilled husband. 'But I tried to get something every night for my husband and the girls. Sausages were cheap . . . the men in the fish [shop] would sometimes give us a bit of fish . . . In the winter months I walked over to the New Market. You got a great big rabbit for sixpence and we had that every Sunday, all the months that rabbits were in season . . . But mostly I had potatoes and bread and toast . . . I'd had the two girlies and then I'd had five boys – all dead-born, and I'm certain it was because of the malnutrition.'

John McNamara remembered how 'It was a common thing for a house-wife, for a mother, to do a hell of a lot of sacrificing. Unknownst to hubby. Unknownst to kiddies. It was nothing for them to say, "Oh, I've had mine." And they hadn't had a bite. But you didn't find out till it was too late. A good mother went without many a meal. Kids come first. And husband. She was last though she worked harder than anyone.'

There are few tales of greater poignancy than that of an anonymous mother included in Nigel Gray's superb compilation of voices of the un-employed: 'When our baby was born we had to borrow a mattress from next door and spread newspapers on it. I used to feed the baby on a bottle of warm water. We put her to bed in a drawer. We made nappies out of newspaper. When I went before the public Assistance Committee they asked me if the baby was being breast fed and when I said yes, they reduced the allowance for a child.'

The 'Hatry Crash'

In 1935 the body of a Woking magistrate, Francis Wellesley, was found floating face-down in the river Wey. 'Another Hatry Crash Victim', decided the headline of a national newspaper, though in fact the death turned out to be an accident rather than suicide. Furthermore, Mr Wellesley had never been an investor in any of Clarence Hatry's companies. But the dapper, Chaplinesque Hatry, the son of a silk-top-hat manufacturer who was always so well turned out himself that it was put about that the soles of his shoes were polished as well as the uppers, had become – at least to some – the personification of an attenuated British version of the Wall Street crash, when share prices plummeted and many fortunes were wiped out. And indeed it was on the day after 'Black Thursday', 25 October 1929, that Clarence Hatry had been remanded to Brixton Prison in South London to await trial on charges of fraud and forgery.

Hatry's spectacular business career – and its demise – mirrored the boom-and-bust economy of the 1920s. Given the frenzy of concern about speculation, unstable money and the financial integrity of the City of London in the shaky world economy, it was no surprise that when he and his three fellow defendants faced the formidably 'icy' Mr Justice Avory in the dock of the Old Bailey in January 1930, the prosecution was led by the Attorney-General himself, Sir William Jowitt.

The case was a complicated one, but again Hatry's story embodied another concern – or in this case a suggested panacea – of the times: rationalisation. Almost Edwardian in his spending habits, at various times he had owned race-horses, one of which, Furious, won the Lincolnshire Handicap at wondrously long odds; a yacht which cost £15,000 (almost £700,000 in today's money) a year to keep afloat; and a magnificent house off Park Lane which his wife described as 'a palace in miniature', but which the *Observer* would later sneer at as 'a palazzo in Mayfair with its classical swimming bath above and its sham Tudor cocktail bar below'. Hatry had built and lost his various fortunes largely by consolidating businesses, which was exactly what many economists and industrial pundits were recommending as the way forward for outdated, under-capitalised British industries. While Jute Industries, which he formed in 1920, was a success, there was little 'strategic logic or managerial vigour' in such creations as British Glass Industries or Amalgamated Industrials, 'a hodge-podge of cotton spinning, shipbuilding, and pig farming', according to his biographer.

However, Hatry sold the London department stores (including Swan & Edgar) he had bought and combined into the Drapery and General Investment Trust to Debenhams at a handsome profit, and merged the majority of London's private bus companies, before selling them to London General Omnibus Co., which would eventually become the nucleus of London Transport. He also financed rather less successful ventures, such as the Photomaton Parent Corporation (which operated photographic booths) and the Associated Automatic Machine Corporation (operating vending machines, mainly on railway platforms), both of which perhaps spoke more to his weakness for gizmos than his financial acumen, and leaked funds.

Nevertheless, by 1928 Hatry appeared to be successfully juggling his activities as a proto-asset-stripper under his umbrella company Austin Friars Trust, 'a £300,000 finance house which was to be the linchpin of his later enterprises and the central company in a complicated network of interrelated investment and industrial enterprises', buying companies, amalgamating them, liquidating then reconstructing them under a new name. At his trial, however, the liquidator, Sir Gilbert Garnsey, alleged that the whole group had been insolvent from the very start in May 1927.

Within that cavernous enterprise one particularly successful amalgamation was Allied Ironfounders, a combine of light castings manufacturers, and this gave Hatry the idea of pulling off a similar feat in the ailing steel industry. In April 1929 he acquired control of the United Steel Companies, but the next month the general election returned a Labour government. 'This is ruination,' Hatry lamented to Hubert Meredith of the *Daily Mail*. 'How can I possibly carry through my steel scheme now?' And indeed, in the bear market that followed what might have been anticipated as the beginning of a full-frontal attack on capitalism, Hatry saw the value of his securities take a severe hammering.

To achieve his 'steel scheme' he needed a large amount of money – probably nearly £8 million – but he had a shortfall, and one that he was finding increasingly difficult to bridge, not least because Montagu Norman, the Governor of the Bank of England, was implacably opposed to both Hatry's scheme and its promoter. 'I say he shd stand aside as long as Hatry controls,' Norman advised a director of the merchant bank Morgan Grenfell, which had been approached for a loan.

To raise the £900,000 (more than £40 million in today's currency) necessary to float Steel Industries of Great Britain Inc., Hatry, at the suggestion of one of his directors, an Italian called John Gialdini, tipped from dextrous dealings and sailing close to the wind into illegality. A few years earlier he had audaciously managed to break into the lucrative corporations loans business, and by the end of 1928 he had cornered 90 per cent of the market. Now, in a manoeuvre 'intended to rob Peter to pay for Paul and to reimburse Peter from the profits of selling Paul' he agreed to forge corporation scrip certificates (receipts and contracts) for three of the municipalities with which he had dealings, Gloucester, Swindon and Wakefield, thereby providing security for further loans from the banks until the steel combine was floated, whereupon the forged certificates could be redeemed.

It didn't work. The City's confidence in Hatry, already ebbing, went into free fall, partly as a result of the excessive number of scrip certificates that seemed to be in circulation, and the Stock Exchange suspended dealings in Austin Friars Trust. Gialdini had already done a runner back to Italy when on 19 September 1929 Hatry, who was by now being investigated by Sir Gilbert Garnsey of Price Waterhouse on behalf of worried creditors, and his three other directors confessed to the Chairman of his companies, the 16th Marquess of Winchester, in the Charing Cross Hotel, that there were 'irregularities'. The four then piled into a taxi to tell Garnsey, 'We want to make a complete statement before the investigation is begun.' They subsequently made a formal confession to the Director of Public Prosecutions, Sir Archibald Bodkin, in which the forty-year-old Hatry took full responsibility himself for the misdemeanours. Garnsey revealed that the total liability of Hatry's companies was in the region of £21 million, with Austin Friars Trust responsible for £15 million. The City took the news badly. 'This Hatry affair has besmirched us all, especially in the eyes of foreigners, which we can ill afford,' wrote the Governor of the Bank of England. In his diary he laconically gave his verdict: 'I do not favour bail for Hatry.'

Hatry did not get bail, nor did his young associates. When the case came to trial on 20 January 1930 it took the prosecution a full four days to present the charges, so complicated were the details, so breathtaking the sums of money involved. Hatry was defended by Norman Birkett, KC, but since he and his fellow defendants changed their pleas to guilty of all charges, all Birkett could plead was mitigation. All the lawyer's legendary powers of persuasion (which brought tears to the eyes of the accused) were to no avail. The judge failed to see the difference between Hatry's intention to redeem his fraudulent issue out of the large profits he anticipated making when his ambitious steel combine was floated and 'the threadbare plea of every clerk or servant who robs his master and says that he hoped to repay the money before his crime was discovered by backing a winner. Except that your crime was on a large scale.' Mr Justice Avory sentenced Hatry to a draconian fourteen years of penal servitude, since 'You stand convicted on your own confession of the most appalling frauds that have ever disfigured the commercial reputation of this country.' The 'bird-like' Hatry 'visibly reeled'. His son bitterly concluded that the case had been prejudged in the name of a nation that was itself reeling from the effects of the world slump, but on appeal two months later Hatry's sentence was effectively *increased* by the two months that had elapsed between trial and appeal.

The verdict of some in the City was similar to that of the judge. Hatry's Chairman, the Marquess of Winchester, who had lost money and reputation in the 'Hatry crash', had once thought that Hatry was 'an example of the alert business brain having an unusually quick perception of any proposition, a marvellous gift for shifting the intricacies, a power of putting his case with a clarity of expression rarely found apart from legal training, coupled with an apparent frankness which amounted to a charm of manner'. He now revised his opinion, and decided that in fact what Hatry possessed was 'dangerous optimism coupled with inordinate conceit . . . his brain was honeycombed with crevasses into which unpleasant facts were allowed to slip and there he permitted them to remain in the hope that the glacier would never reveal its secrets'. *The Times* spoke of 'a rogue . . . a signalman who deliberately tampers with the signal'.

But others were less anxious to clamber onto the moral high ground. The left-wing *New Statesman*, which might have been expected to be very harsh about the unacceptable face of capitalism, was kinder. 'Hatry was not a swindler . . . he was rather an unbalanced optimist with a defective moral sense. He set out not to defraud the investors in his companies, but to make money, if he could, for them as well as himself . . . "If only I had been reasonably lucky," a man in a similar position might say, "I would have retrieved everyone's fortunes, and no one would have been a penny the worse for my illegality. How right I should have been!"' For the *New Statesman* it was the City itself that was particularly to blame: 'How in the name of fortune did the banks come to give the Hatry group so much money?' At a time, it probably wanted to add, when it was so unwilling to lend to industry in the depressed areas. Indeed, 'The Hatry case will have done some good if it rivets public attention on the joint-stock banks and reveals what part they are really playing in City speculation and in financing productive industry.'

A model prisoner with influential and eloquent supporters such as Harold Nicolson, eighteen MPs and his lawyer Birkett prepared to petition for him, Hatry was released from prison after serving nine rather than fourteen years. He subsequently borrowed sufficient money to purchase the 'carriage trade' bookshop Hatchard's in Piccadilly. Again he expanded and acquired and amalgamated and diversified, and again his rickety empire crashed. In the late 1950s Hatry was to be found cashing in on the coffee-bar craze, buying up premises in the West End to serve 'froffy coffee' to a newly affluent post-war generation of teenagers. He died of heart failure on 10 June 1965.

PART TWO

The Search for Solutions

R101 Disaster

It would be a *coup de maître*. British prestige confirmed with a stylish gesture. The country's position as an imperial power elegantly underlined. Brigadier-General the Right Honourable Lord Thomson of Cardington, Secretary of State for Air in the Labour government, would stroll coolly into the meeting of the Imperial Conference in London on 20 October 1930 as the delegates were getting down to a discussion of air power. Thomson would have just arrived back from a round trip to India which had taken little more than a fortnight, while the representatives from Australia and New Zealand had taken six or seven weeks to get to the mother country. It would demonstrate that Britain had taken the lead from Germany in the development of 'lighter than air' machines. Furthermore, Thomson was being canvassed as the next Viceroy of India, and the subcontinent had been showing disturbing signs of nationalist unrest for over a decade now. The previous year Jawaharlal Nehru, the President of the Indian National Congress, had pre-empted the Simon Commission's recommendations on India's constitutional future by declaring for *purna swaraj* (complete independence). Perhaps the choice of this destination for the R101, the airship in which Thomson would make his flight, would be read as evidence of how close and how benign the ties of Empire were – at least as far as Britain was concerned.

During the First World War, rigid German airships named after Count Ferdinand von Zeppelin, a German cavalry officer who had been interested in constructing a 'dirigible balloon' ever since he had seen the French using them during the Franco-Prussian war of 1870–71, had become an ominous sight over England. By the outbreak of the war there were a total of twenty-one Zeppelins in service for commercial passenger transport. Recognising their military potential (which Zeppelin had always intended), the German army and navy purchased fourteen airships, most of which were used for reconnaissance. However, on 19 January 1915, in the first ever bombing raid on civilians, two Zeppelins dropped twenty-four fifty-kilogram high-explosive bombs and a number of incendiaries on towns along the Norfolk coast, killing four people, injuring sixteen and causing considerable damage to property. In the course of the war there were fifty-one such raids; 557 British civilians were killed in all, and 1,358 injured. Under the terms of the Treaty of Versailles, all airships were transferred to the Allies as part of the war reparations package.

The British had started to experiment with rigid airships in 1908, but a series of disasters, beginning with the unfortunately appropriately-named *Mayfly* in September 1911, put an end to their development until towards the end of the war. After it resumed, success seemed as elusive as ever: a review in 1923 revealed that out of the 154 rigid airships that had been completed and flown by Germany, Britain the United States and France, 104 (68 per cent) had been lost, along with a total of 584 lives. One life had been lost for every sixty-five airship flying hours. However, one German commercial aircraft company had flown 138,975 miles without a single fatality, and airships had the edge over 'heavier than air' aeroplanes when it came to spaciousness, comfort, load-carrying and quietness.

On leap year's day 1924, Lord Thomson, newly appointed Secretary of State for Air in the first Labour government, announced a three-year Government Research, Experiment and Development airships programme. The gauntlet was picked up by Stanley Baldwin's Conservatives when they came to power in November that year, and in 1926 the Secretary of State for Air, Sir Samuel Hoare, announced that not one but two airships, each capable of long-distance overseas voyages, were to be constructed, in the hope, as Hoare told the Lord Mayor's Banquet, that 'in a few years it will be possible to have a regular airship service between London and Bombay as it now is to have an aeroplane service between London and Paris'. At that time the sea voyage took seventeen days. While an airship could not fly fast as an aeroplane (then averaging around 120 mph) it would be able to sustain a regular 60 mph, and unlike a plane it could remain in the air throughout the day and night. One of the airships (the R101) would be built by the Air Ministry at the Royal Airship Works at Cardington, near Bedford, the other (the R100) by a private company, the Airship Guarantee Company Ltd, owned by the engineering firm of Vickers, at Howden in Yorkshire, where Barnes Wallis, later to develop the famous 'bouncing bomb' used by the 'Dambusters' in the Ruhr in May 1943, was chief designer.

This dual capitalist/state enterprise approach was intended to ensure 'competition in design', and would mean that the failure of one ship would not terminate the whole programme, but what it also did, according to the stress engineer for the R100, N.S. Norway, later to be better known as the writer Nevil Shute, was to ensure that the lessons learned in one experiment were not shared with the other: it was rivalry, not collaboration.

The airships were to be built to the same rough specifications, designed to carry a hundred passengers in comfort, plus ten tons of mail and cargo, and to be capable of flying non-stop for fifty-seven hours at an average speed of 63 mph. But while the R100 was intended as a commercial craft, built along largely conventional lines gleaned from the German Zeppelins, the R101 was to be absolutely cutting-edge, employing the latest technologies.

The plan had been that the R101 would make its first trip to India in the early spring of 1927, but delays, design problems, and costs escalated at Cardington. By the end of 1927 only part of the R101's structure had been delivered, whereas the framework of the R100 was almost finished, despite the fact that at Howden, where Vickers controlled the purse strings, many more calculations were made on the drawing board before work was put in hand. The R100 made its first flight of 150 miles (which took five hours forty-seven minutes) on 16 December 1929, and seven months later, in the early hours of 29 July 1930, took off for Canada. Meanwhile, the R101 had made a couple of flights round Britain, in 'very perfect flying conditions', as its chief designer, Lieutenant-Colonel Richmond, put it, but had not been tested on an overseas route. And the Imperial Conference at which Lord Thomson planned to make his dramatic entrance was due to open on 1 October.

In the early hours of 2 August 1930 the R100 moored at Montreal, having been in the air for seventy-four hours. On 16 August it was back in England, where Thomson congratulated the crew on accomplishing 'this first and successful step in the development of our new generation of British airships'. It never flew again.

Meanwhile, the other great hope of British aviation was being sliced in half in its hangar. The surgical intervention was being performed to lengthen the R101 from 732 feet to 777 feet by adding a further section so that an additional gas bag could be inserted, covered, in the days before plastic, with the stretched intestines of bullocks imported from the great Chicago meatpacking factories. This was being done to give the R101 more lift: as it was, it would only have been able to carry a load of thirty-five tons; the long journey to India required twenty-five tons of fuel, leaving only an impossible ten tons for passengers, crew, luggage and stores. Already everything that could be lightened had been, and what looked like solid oak pillars were in fact balsa wood covered with a paper veneer. But it had been decided that with only weeks to go before the epic flight, drastic action had to be taken.

By 25 September the operation had been completed and the two halves of the airship sewn together again, but bad weather prevented further tests, and it was not until the early hours of 1 October that the R101 was finally 'walked out' of its hangar, some two hundred men (including a number of the unemployed from nearby Bedford) pulling the vast dirigible out of its glove-tight housing with ropes and mooring it to the Eiffel-tower-like structure to which it was attached ready for flight. Already twenty men, the 'gassing and mooring party', had left for Karachi to prepare for the R101's arrival in India. If Thomson was to meet his timetable, it was essential that the airship set off as soon as possible. It has been alleged that Thomson's impatience overrode proper safety concerns for the R101, although the airship's principal biographer strenuously disputes this. Indeed, on the day of its departure for the subcontinent, Thomson insisted to Wing Commander Colmore, Director of Airship Development at Cardington, 'You must not allow your judgment to be swayed by my natural anxiety to get off quickly.'

There were other considerations: six weeks earlier, on August Bank Holiday, the twenty-six-year-old Amy Johnson, daughter of a fish-shop owner from Hull, had arrived at Croydon airport in pouring rain after a nineteen-day solo round trip to Australia, via India. She too had received a warm welcome from the Secretary of State for Air, who nevertheless must have reflected on the contrast between Miss Johnson's pioneering achievement and the fact that although nearly £2.5 million had been spent on the airship development programme since 1924, and questions were being asked in Parliament about such expenditure at a time of intense economic depression, so far there did not seem a great deal to show for it.

Despite the fact that the R101 had never flown in bad weather, and had not flown for even an hour at full speed in any conditions, a Certificate of Airworthiness was issued, and on 4 October 1930, the last day of British Summer Time, the R101 was ready to take off on a 'demonstration flight' of 2,235 nautical miles to Ismalia in Egypt, and then on to Karachi.

At 6.15 that evening the ministerial Daimler drew up on the Cardington airfield and the Secretary of State for Air got out. Earlier that day biscuits had been decanted from tins into paper bags to save weight; Lord Thomson's luggage, which included cabin trunks, suitcases, two cases of champagne, a dress sword weighing three pounds and a Persian carpet weighing 129 pounds to be laid for the state dinners planned for Ismalia and Karachi, amounted to 1,207 pounds. The total weight of the passengers and all their luggage was supposed to be 2,508 pounds.

The mighty silver airship, the largest in the world, with fifty-four people aboard including six passengers, slipped its moorings at 6.36 p.m. in poor weather and steered for London, where it cruised at no more than eight hundred feet above the city, its lights blazing. The practices and uniforms aboard the R101 were, as befitted the name airship, naval, but those not required for watch duty or other chores headed for the spacious dining room, where six tables had been laid with white linen and gleaming silver-ware presented in a gesture of civic pride by the town of Bedford. After a good dinner (for the grandees, or bread and cheese and pickles washed down with cocoa for the crew) most of the passengers retreated to the comfortable wicker chairs in the metal-lined fireproof smoking lounge for a final cigar and a brandy. Given the highly explosive nature of the gas in the airbags, no smoking (or matches) was permitted anywhere else on board. They then trooped out onto the viewing balconies on either side of the lounge, where they caught a glimpse of the mouth of the river Somme, which had such terrible redolence for most of their generation, before retiring to their cabins for the night.

At 2.07 a.m. French time, approaching the Beauvais Ridge, already well known to aviators for its notorious gusting winds, the R101, which had been flying at around 1,200 feet at fifty knots, rolling and pitching through turbulent wind and rain which had not been anticipated, suddenly nose-dived towards the ground. At 2.09 it crashed into dense woods near the hamlet of Allone. The crash ignited leaking hydrogen, and flames imme-diately engulfed the airship, lighting up the countryside around. Forty-six perished, including Lord Thomson and his valet; Sir Sefton Brancker, Director of Civil Aviation; the Director and assistant Directors of Airship Development; the R101's captain, navigator, engineers, petty officers, charge hands and other members of the crew. Eight managed to scramble free, but of those two died of their injuries.

Virginia Woolf watched the funeral procession of the 'heroes' of the R101 on 11 October – but was not impressed.

> The fifty coffins have just trundled by, lorries spread rather skimpily with Union Jacks – an unbecoming pall – & stuck about with red & yellow wreaths . . . the crowd smells; the sun makes it all too like birthday cake & crackers; & the coffins conceal too much. One bone, one charred hand wd. have done what no cere-mony can do . . . why 'heroes'? A shifty & unpleasant man, Lord Thomson by all accounts, goes for a joy ride with other notables, & has the misfortune to be burnt at Beauvais . . . we have every reason to say Good God how very painful – how very unlucky – but why all the shops in Oxford Street and Southampton Row shd. display black dresses only & run up black bars; why people should line

the streets & parade through Westminster Hall, why every paper should be filled with nobility & lamentations & praise, why the Germans should muffle their wireless & the French ordain a day of mourning & the footballers stop for two minutes silence – beats me & Leonard . . .

The inquiry into the disaster, which reported in March 1931, while admiring the 'skill, courage, and devotion' of all those involved in the flight, decided that the immediate cause of the crash was a sudden loss of gas in one of the gasbags at the moment that the nose of the airship was being depressed by a very strong wind. This was probably due to the 'ripping of the fore part of the envelope' (the doped canvas outer covering), which had torn at precisely the place where it had been patched rather than replaced after an earlier mishap, so the wind got in and split open the already punctured front gasbag. In addition the watch had just changed, and the new men on duty had not yet had time to get the 'feel' of the ship. But the conclusion was less contingent:

> It is clear that if those responsible had been entirely free to choose the time and the weather in which the R101 should start for the first flight ever undertaken by any airship to India, and if the only considerations governing their choice were considerations of meteorology and of preparation for the voyage, the R101 would not have started when she did . . . It is impossible to avoid the conclusion that the R101 would not have started for India on the evening of October 4th if it had not been that reasons of public policy were considered as making it highly desirable for her to do so if she could . . . Airship travel is still in its experimental stage. It is for others to determine whether the experiment should be further pursued.

It was not: in December 1931 the R100 was broken up with axes and the pieces crushed by a steamroller so they could be sold for scrap. Workers from a Sheffield firm travelled to France and brought back the remains of the R101, some of which were made into pots and pans, while five tons were sold to the German Zeppelin Company. The sheds that had housed the R100 and the R101 were used to make and store barrage balloons during the Second World War. No more passenger-carrying airships were ever built in Britain. The loss of the German *Hindenburg*, dubbed the '*Titanic* of the sky', which exploded in flames on landing in New Jersey in May 1937, drew what appears to have been a final line under civil airship development worldwide.

SIX

'Can We Conquer Unemployment?'

I reminded myself firmly that I was no economist . . . My childlike literary mind always fastens upon concrete details. Thus, when the newspapers tell me there is yet another financial crisis and that gold is being rushed from one country to another and I see photographs of excited City men jostling and scrambling and of bank porters and sailors carrying boxes of bullion, I always feel that some idiotic game is going on and that it is as preposterous that the welfare of millions of real people should hang on the fortunes of this game as it would be if our happiness hung upon the results of the Stock Exchange golfing tournament . . . I thought . . . how this City, which is always referred to with tremendous respect, which is treated as if it were the very red beating heart of England, must have got its money from somewhere, but it could not have conjured gold out of Threadneedle Street and that a great deal of this money must have poured into it at one time – a good long time too – from that part of England which is much dearer to me than the City, namely, the industrial North. For generations the blackened North toiled and moiled so that England should be rich and the City of London be a great power in the world. But now this North is half derelict, and its people living on in queer and ugly places, are shabby, bewildered, unhappy. I was prejudiced, of course . . . perhaps because I like people who make things better than I like people who only deal in money . . . Perhaps I would not have dragged the City into this meditation at all if I had not always been told, every time the nation made an important move, went on the Gold Standard, or went off it, that the City had so ordered it. The City then, I thought, must accept the responsibility. Either it is bossing us about or it isn't. If it is, then it must take the blame if there is any blame to be taken. And there seems to me to be a great deal of blame to be taken. What has the City done for its old ally, the industrial North? It seemed to have done what the black-moustached glossy gentleman in the old melodramas always did to the innocent village maiden.

J.B. Priestley, English Journey (1934)

It has increasingly been recognized in recent years that Keynes' work cannot properly be appreciated if he is regarded narrowly as an 'economist' . . . the avocation of the economist required a combination of gifts: not only as mathematician and historian, but also as a statesman and philosopher.

Peter Clarke, 'J.M. Keynes 1883–1946:
The Best of Both Worlds' (1994)

Shortly after six o'clock on the morning of Sunday, 5 October 1930, the bedside telephone of Ramsay MacDonald rang in his hotel room. 'The R101 was wrecked and Thomson was not amongst the living!' the Prime Minister wrote in his diary. 'As though by the pressing of a button confusion & gloom & sorrow came upon the world – was the world. So, when I bade him goodbye on Friday & looked down at him descending the stairs at No. 10, that was to be the last glimpse of my friend, gallant, gay & loyal. No one was like him & there will be none . . . Why did I allow him to go? He was so dead certain there could be no mishap . . . This is indeed a great national calamity, & today, I distracted in the midst of it, can but grieve.'

Two days later MacDonald, who was in Llandudno for the Labour Party Conference, addressed the assembled delegates. Looking 'drawn and haggard' he paid tribute to the man who was probably his closest friend in politics before turning to a passionate defence of his government and its attempts to deal with the crushing problems of unemployment:

We are not on trial, it is the system under which we live which is under trial. It has broken down, not only in this little island, it has broken down in Europe, in Asia, in America; it has broken down everywhere. It was bound to break down. And the cure, the new path, the new idea is organisation – organisation that will protect life not property . . . I appeal to you, my friends, today, with all that is going on outside – I appeal to you to go back to your Socialist faith. Do not mix that up with pettifogging patching, either of a Poor Law kind or a Relief Work kind. Construction, ideas, architecture, building line upon line, stone upon stone, storey upon storey . . . I think [it] will be your happiness, as it is mine, to go on convinced that the great foundations are being well laid . . . and that by skilled craftsmen, confident in each other's goodwill and sincerity, the temple will rise and rise until at last it is complete, and the genius of humanity will find within it an appropriate resting place.

With tumultuous applause ringing in his ears, MacDonald hurried back to London, anxious to get to Victoria station in time to greet the flag-draped coffins of the victims of the R101 disaster as they arrived back from France, leaving others at the Welsh seaside resort to puzzle over how these stirring sentiments (or 'MacDonaldite slush and floral phrases. Meaning nothing definite') could be translated to the matter at hand: unemployment, which had stood at 1.1 million when Labour came to power in May 1929, had risen by the time of MacDonald's speech in October 1930 to more than double that. How could the task of realising the 'temple' of socialism accord with alleviating the immediate sufferings of the present crisis of the capitalist one? Or, put more epigrammatically, how could a new Jerusalem be built during the 'economic blizzard', as MacDonald characterised it, that engulfed Britain (and much of the rest of the world) in 1930?

The Labour Party had been founded to give the working classes a voice in Parliament, and it was committed to a parliamentary democratic route to achieving its aims. Now in its second term in office, but still without an outright majority, Labour might – at the outside – have five years in which to effect the transformation from capitalism to socialism, as was outlined in its first detailed programme, *Labour and the New Social Order*, adopted by the party in 1918. As Sidney Webb, the programme's main author, had put it, 'The Labour Party refuses absolutely to believe that the British people will permanently tolerate any reconstruction or perpetuation of the disorganisation, waste and inefficiency involved in the abandonment of British industry to a jostling around of separate private employers . . . What the Labour Party looks to is a genuinely scientific re-organisation of the nation's industry no longer deflected by individual profiteering on the basis of Common Ownership of the Means of Production.' But the radical changes this transformation required would be quite impossible to achieve within a single Parliament: Labour would need at least one further term in office to complete the process. That would mean tailoring policies to win electoral support, while at the same time advancing from a society where explicit government intervention was exercised with a light touch, towards a socialist state with a great deal of public control. It was to be the unfulfilled task of the 1930s for the Labour Party to articulate a practical strategy for accomplishing this goal by democratic means.

Moreover, Ramsay MacDonald, his Ministers and the majority of the Labour Party were committed to this gradualist approach, believing that socialism would be achieved not as a result of the collapse of capitalism, but rather on the back of its success, since it was this that would generate the money needed for wide-ranging community social services and redistributive taxation.

'The election of 1929 seemed to us at the time a wonderful, almost miraculous victory,' wrote the twenty-three-year-old Hugh Gaitskell, at the time a lecturer in political economy at University College, London. 'We had done so much better than I (perhaps because most of my speaking had been in Marylebone!) had thought possible. We paid little, no doubt far too little, attention to the absence of a clear majority. It was enough for us that Labour was in power again, and for the first time held the largest number of seats. Our hopes for peace could be high, we would clear the slums – and, above all, tackle the unemployment.' In fact 1929 was a disastrous time for Labour to come to power, especially with a hung Parliament. As the government struggled to drain the pool of structural unemployment that had been filling up throughout the 1920s, it was knocked sideways by the flood of cyclical unemployment caused by the worldwide Depression. No country was able to cope satisfactorily with the 'economic blizzard' and find an answer to the rising unemployment that resulted. In fact Britain was less hard hit than many other countries, particularly Germany and the United States. Nevertheless, the fate of the Labour government would be in thrall to an unprecedented degree to the performance of the economy. At a time when capitalism, if not in the throes of its final crisis, was certainly being severely tested, socialists were in no doubt that the government should take charge of the management of the economy, and that under a socialist state poverty and unemployment would fade away. But that was a long-term aim (and one without a blueprint for how it would be achieved), and while MacDonald and his colleagues spoke of themselves as socialists they were also members of the labour movement, committed to the defence of working-class living standards, which were under attack as a result of the economic crisis.

The conundrum of whether, in times of crisis, capitalism should be repaired (if made more equitable) or replaced would haunt the left in various degrees throughout the thirties, and contribute to its sense of impotence. 'The capitalist system is ossified, restrictionist and unjust; but it is expanding and stable,' wrote the economist and political theorist Evan Durbin in a book published in 1940 that explored the socialist dilemmas of the 1930s. 'The society based upon the capitalist economy is unequal and restless; but it is democratic, middle class and conservative. What then ought to be done?' However, the immediate problem was that more and more people were being thrown out of work. How could their distress be alleviated without 'propping up' the inefficiencies of the capitalist system any longer than necessary?

Not that there was any lack of ideas about how this should be done. The trouble was that most were contradictory, and several cut across party lines, which is not surprising, since there was no agreed analysis of the causes of the slump among politicians of any of the major parties – although all three had made reducing unemployment the main plank of their election appeal. It was hard to find a solution when what was causing the problem was so perplexing.

The Labour Chancellor of the Exchequer, Philip Snowden, was an exemplar of 'orthodox economics' – 'a High Priest', thought Winston Churchill: 'The Treasury mind and the Snowden mind embraced each other with the fervour of two long-separated lizards,' he wrote. Snowden was adamant that Britain's recovery would only take place as part of a stable international economy based on the Gold Standard. Thus there was an absolute imperative to maintain international confidence by keeping the economy balanced and avoiding a budget deficit at all costs.

This meant that Snowden was implacably opposed to those who saw the solution in expanding the economy through lower interest rates and a programme of public works projects. The Chancellor had made his views clear during the first Labour government in July 1924, and had not budged since: 'It is no part of my job as Chancellor of the Exchequer to put before the House of Commons proposals for the expenditure of public money. The function of the Chancellor of the Exchequer, as I understand it, is to resist all demands for expenditure made by his colleagues and, when he can no longer resist, to limit the concession to the barest point of acceptance.' For Snowden, public works projects had to be strictly evaluated like any other form of investment. Unemployment was a long-term problem that would only be solved if production costs could be brought down – particularly in the export industries. Public works might redistribute unemployment; they would not end it. This was largely the view of the Conservatives too, as well as the City.

As for MacDonald, he had few firm convictions as to what was causing the slump, little confidence in his understanding of the economy (which Labour 'shall have to put under a gyroscope', he once wrote) and few ideas about how Britain was going to get out of it. But, as he made clear in his speech to Conference, he recognised that, along with peace, unemployment was the central issue the Labour government had to tackle – and would be judged by. He started the process as soon as Labour took power. 'Since our return to Whitehall,' wrote Secretary to the Cabinet Thomas Jones (always known as 'TJ'), 'the pace has been furious. The slogan is not "Socialism in our time" but "Socialism before Xmas". Big bills are being drafted on Unemployment, Roads, Factories, Pension, Coal . . .'

The ex-railway union leader J.H. (Jimmy) Thomas had been MacDonald's first choice as Foreign Secretary, but since Arthur Henderson 'would not return to H.O. [Home Office] but put in plea for F.O.', instead agreed to accept the post of Lord Privy Seal with responsibility for coordinating government unemployment policies. In the debate on the King's Speech he reported on his progress less than a month after taking office. Already he had tramped the country talking to industrialists about the supposed panacea of 'rationalisation' to cut costs and improve competitiveness, having discussions with railway managers, business leaders and civil servants, and conducting 'long and delicate negotiations' with the obdurate Governor of the Bank of England, Montagu Norman. He eventually succeeded in interesting the City in 'placing industry on a broad and sound basis and ready to support any plans that in its opinion lead to this end', and by March 1930 what might now be called a Public Private Initiative, the Bankers' Industrial Development Company, had been set up to finance rationalised industry, with £6 million coming from the Bank of England and over forty merchant banks, clearing banks and other financial institutions.

As Thomas was speaking to the Commons, all sorts of other ambitious plans were being drafted. These included a £37.5-million, five-year road-building programme, improvements on the railways, £1 million for colonial development schemes which included building a bridge across the Zambezi – and plans to attract new industries to those areas of Britain where unemployment was highest. Thomas went to Canada for several weeks to try to stimulate the market for British coal and ships. His success was very limited. One of the three assistants who had been appointed to help him in his gargantuan task when they weren't busy with their other responsibilities, Tom Johnston, Under-Secretary of State for Scotland (the other two were the wealthy and arrogant Sir Oswald Mosley, once a Conservative MP but now Labour's Chancellor of the Duchy of Lancaster and fizzing with new schemes, and the veteran politician George Lansbury, whose espousal of 'Poplarism' – named after a rate strike in London's deprived East End in 1921 – had made him a symbol of local defiance of central government in the interest of the poor and needy) pressed for the construction of a road round Loch Lomond (what he got was the reconstruction of the coach road from Aberfoyle to the Trossachs). Lansbury favoured a retirement pension for workers at sixty ('Better pay the old to do nothing than the young,' commented Thomas Jones), a colonising scheme in Western Australia and a land reclamation programme at home.

By November 1930 Thomas was able to report to Parliament that £24 million had already been spent on stimulating public works schemes. But for James Maxton, chairman of the Independent Labour Party (ILP), such initiatives were certainly 'not socialism', and he taunted Thomas with being 'caught in a spider web of capitalism', and prophetically warned that a choice would have to be made between the government and the unemployed – and he knew which side he would be on.

In October 1929 a heavyweight committee was appointed under the chairmanship of a barrister, Lord Macmillan, to examine the workings of the banking and financial systems and to make recommendations 'calculated . . . to promote the development of commerce and the employment of labour'. Macmillan, who later confessed that he 'never learned to move with any ease in the realm of finance', was surrounded by some expert and authoritative minds. There were employers, including the President of the Federation of British Industries, a professor of banking from the London School of Economics, a director of the Bank of England, a merchant banker and a former Permanent Secretary to the Treasury, working alongside a former 'Red Clydesider', J.T. Walton Newbold, while the trade union slot was filled by Ernest Bevin of the Transport and General Workers' Union. The economist John Maynard Keynes, whose hand had been behind the 'remedy for unemployment' set out in the Liberal election manifesto *We Can Conquer Unemployment* (distilled from the famous 'Yellow Book', *Britain's Industrial Future*), was also invited to join.

The Committee, which was criticised in some quarters as being 'packed in favour of finance', took evidence throughout 1930 and into the following year. Keynes presented his – which was in effect a dry run for his two-volume work *A Treatise on Money*, published later in the year – 'like a seminar', seeking to educate the Committee on the fundamental distinction between saving and investment: the world's wealth had not been accumulated by thrift, but rather by enterprise. Savings by themselves achieved nothing: they needed to be put to work. From this followed – though Keynes took several cliffhanging days to expound what followed: 'You are a complete dramatist,' Macmillan said admiringly – his 'favourite remedy': home investment by the government to 'break the vicious circle' of underinvestment and mop up unemployment by increasing domestic demand rather than relying on the vagaries of the export market. Along with this went the further rationalisation of industry, protection of the home market by tariff barriers (a new departure for Keynes), and bringing down interest rates – cheap money.

Reginald McKenna, who had been a respected Liberal Chancellor of the Exchequer during the First World War, and subsequently Chairman of the Midland Bank, agreed, and gave an easy-to-follow explanation of how this could work in practice: with more money in circulation more boots would be bought, more men would be taken on to make the boots, their wages would be spent on cotton goods, which would create employment in the cotton industry, and so it would go on. Ernest Bevin was equally enthusiastic, envisaging the prospect for coalminers, whose purchasing power was almost half what it should have been; if it was raised 'it would lead to a greater demand for boots for children, and clothes and furniture and luxuries and things of that kind'.

But when the ill-prepared and irritable Montagu Norman appeared before the Committee, he rejected Keynes' view that the financial system was 'jammed' and the key to unlock it was obsolete: in Norman's view it was industry that was jammed, and since he saw the Bank of England's relation to the nation as similar to that of a high street bank's to its customers – that is, to ensure that they did not live beyond their means – industry needed rationalisation, not credit, to meet its difficulties. He accepted, however, that rationalisation was hardly a short-term fix, and agreed that unemployment would be 'apt to increase' (the word 'temporarily' was added in the final report to sweeten the pill). In essence the Bank's view – more ably put by others subsequently – rejected the notion that the return to the Gold Standard in 1925, much to the disquiet of Keynes, and indeed McKenna, had resulted in inflated interest rates, or that there were any other monetary shortcomings. The basic problem was that British industry was uncompetitive, and until its house was put in order (largely by wage cuts, 'encouraging' labour mobility by cutting un-employment pay, reducing taxes on profits and – of course – rationalisation) any other remedies would be merely palliative.

By December, after less than six months in office, the verdict of Hugh Dalton, then Under-Secretary at the Foreign Office ('The under secretaries are all aristocrats,' Beatrice Webb had sniffed when the government was formed: Dalton's father had been Canon of St George's Chapel, Windsor, and an intimate friend of George V), was that 'the Labour Government as a whole has been pretty disappointing with bright patches. Thomas and Maggie Bondfield [Margaret Bondfield, Minister of Labour] are two of the most obvious failures. Few have anything good to say about either of them. MacDonald has been messing about again with the idea of the Economic General Staff, and having economists to lunch. But nothing concrete comes of it.' Thomas Jones was not much more optimistic: 'Labour is worried by the growing figures of unemployment. JHT [Jimmy Thomas] for some weeks now seemed to lose his nerve entirely. All criticism from all sides, which used to be spread over several Departments, is concentrated on him. There have been various devices for saving his face, the latest is a luncheon party which I have got to give for the PM.'

This was one of several such soundings-out about setting up 'a new machine which Ramsay could hail as his own creation'. The 'upshot of all this cogitation' was the appointment in January 1930, when employment had risen to just under 1.5 million, of an Economic Advisory Council (EAC) which would be 'the eyes and ears of [the Prime Minister] on economic questions'. MacDonald hoped it would be more than a talking shop: 'If it meets on a Monday, it must be ready for action to be taken on a Tuesday,' he insisted. The Council included bankers, industrialists, two scientists, the socialist intellectuals G.D.H. Cole and R.H. Tawney – and J.M. Keynes, plus Ernest Bevin and Walter Citrine as trade union voices.

There was considerable overlap between the personnel and the remits of the Macmillan Committee and the EAC, and since it had no executive authority and a rather vague brief, Citrine was concerned that EAC was likely to become a dumping ground for 'all the odds and ends that government likes to turn over to us'. Its secretary, the Cambridge economist Hubert Henderson, editor of the *Nation* until it merged with the *New Statesman* in 1930, was equally underwhelmed, since according to one of his colleagues, 'He hated woolly thinking and theorising . . . and scorned Labour's economic theories.' In the event it proved impossible to get a consensus between the businessmen and the economists about the central issue of how to deal with unemployment, and Keynes persuaded MacDonald to set up a smaller group comprising solely economists, with him in the chair as an experiment to test 'the hypothesis, that [economics] can be treated like any other science, and ask for qualified scientists in the subject to have their say'.

By the summer of 1930 the original EAC was meeting less and less, and Bevin and Citrine had become disillusioned. The breakaway group of economists was equally fissiparous, and it proved wearisome to draft a report that was satisfactory to all – when it was published in October, Professor Lionel Robbins from the London School of Economics disassociated himself from the majority view entirely, and wrote a passionate defence of free trade. Nevertheless, no matter how ineffective the EAC was perceived to be, it was the first time a British Prime Minister had received consistent economic advice independent of the Treasury. Moreover, it was a sobering educative experience for those who sat on it, particularly Bevin and Citrine, who saw at first hand just how complex the problems were, and how irretrievably economic and political considerations were enmeshed.

If Dalton thought that the Cabinet was 'full of overworked men growing, older, more tired and more timid with each passing week', the dashing Chancellor of the Duchy of Lancaster was seething with energy and radical solutions. After several frustrating months working with Jimmy Thomas, who was not only 'growing old and tired', but also more lachrymose, and was inclined to drink too much, Sir Oswald Mosley produced what he declared was 'a coherent and comprehensive conception of national policy', which he sent to Ramsay MacDonald on 23 January 1930. The 'Mosley Memorandum' asserted that the government needed to take charge of the economy, with a new department set up under the direct control of the Prime Minister to 'mobilise national resources on a larger scale than has yet been contemplated'. Britain's long-term economic problems would be met by systematic planning to create new industries and revitalise existing ones, while the immediate problem of unemployment would be solved by an ambitious three-year £200-million programme of public works which would cut through all the red tape involved in local authority schemes, and make roadbuilding a national responsibility. In addition, the school leaving age should be raised and retirement pensions paid earlier – shrinking the work-force from both ends. It amounted to a 'British equivalent of the Russian "Gosplan"', thought Fenner Brockway. It didn't really, though it was in favour of pretty heavy – if somewhat ambiguous – state intervention. But for Beatrice Webb its proposals were 'as grandiose as they are vague'.

Nevertheless, the Cabinet debated Mosley's package at length over the next few months. Snowden was obdurate: investment capital was limited, and if it was spent on ambitious public works schemes it would not be available to make Britain's export industries competitive. A loan such as Mosley proposed would push up interest rates and destroy overseas confidence. MacDonald was ambivalent: he was depressed by Snowden's 'hard dogmatism expressed in words & tones as hard as his ideas', yet was unconvinced that massive public spending was the answer. By February 1930 the government had already sanctioned £37 million worth of road improvement programmes but only £27 million worth of schemes had been put in hand, and only 1,620 men had been given jobs.

Mosley was coldly furious. Sneering that a Napoleon could spend £200 million in three years if he wanted to, he quoted Keynes against the Treasury orthodoxy, and resigned on 20 May 1930. His resignation speech to the House on 29 May, during the debate on a Conservative vote of censure on the government's unemployment policy, was a powerful indictment: present government policies were providing jobs for only 80,000 people a year, at a time when unemployment was over 1.75 million and still rising. It was a brilliant performance, and the sharp-tongued diarist and tireless social reformer Beatrice Webb, who recognised that Mosley possessed both 'a young man's zeal' and the ability to 'use other men's brains', wondered, 'Has

MacDonald found his superseder in O.M.?' MacDonald turned in a lamentable performance, seeming completely out of his depth in answering his critics.

The government survived nevertheless, and MacDonald reshuffled. Thomas was shoved off to the Dominions Office (though he was later allowed to retain responsibility for rationalisation), MacDonald put himself at the head of a panel of Ministers set up to develop the government's unemployment policies; that barely noticed rising star Major Clement Attlee, who considered that Mosley 'always speak[s] to us as if he were feudal landlord abusing tenants who are in arrears with their rent', replaced him at the Duchy of Lancaster.

Mosley, showing his arrogance and fatal lack of political judgement, founded his New Party in February 1931, since in his view the 'old men' in the 'old parties' had signally failed to deal with the problems of the postwar world, and thus a new party must be formed 'not to introduce Utopia but to prevent collapse'. His would be a party of neither right nor left, composed of young men with an agenda of parliamentary reform and economic planning, which sought to 'apply scientific method to public affairs to determine precisely what things must be done', untrammelled by party loyalty or political dogma, ready to take ideas from 'anyone so long as they are realist – be they Gladstone, Marx or Joseph Chamberlain'. Its role would be somewhere between a parliamentary 'ginger group', an intellectual think tank and a 'new movement' designed to 'sweep away the mockery and pretence of the old game of party politics'. Nevertheless the party formed to save Britain in its hour of crisis attracted only three Labour MPs, one of whom, John Strachey (a former member of the ILP and future Communist supporter who had resigned with Mosley when his memorandum was rejected – he had been Mosley's best man when he married the daughter of Lord Curzon) soon left. The New Party, which appeared to have 'no vision beyond the immediate emergency', largely disintegrated after failing to win any seats in the 1931 election. In October 1932 Mosley, who felt that the Italian dictator Benito Mussolini had the vision and drive the British government lacked, founded the British Union of Fascists.

'Parliament itself is too big, too clumsy and too inexpert a body even to begin to tackle the complex problems of a modern community,' John Strachey and C.E.M. Joad (a maverick philosopher, writer and self-styled polygamist who became a household name in the 1940s as a member of the BBC's 'Brains Trust') had written in an article on parliamentary reform for the journal *Political Quarterly* in 1931. And in the crisis years of the early 1930s setting up committees to root around trying to find ways out of the blizzard was not indeed the prerogative of Parliament alone. As a young economist, Colin Clark, was to observe, 'The most recent universal remedy is apparently contained in the word "Plan".'

'Everyone has a Plan,' complained the Labour weekly the *Clarion*, though it considered most to be little more than 'undergraduate work', seeking compromises rather than the root-and-branch reconstruction of capitalism it deemed necessary, for which the Soviet Five Year Plan was something of a model. Indeed, there was soon an organisation the rationale of which was planning. On 14 February 1931 a 20,000-word 'National Plan for Great Britain' was published as a supplement to the *Week-End Review*, a magazine started by Gerald Barry and the editorial team who had all resigned from the *Saturday Review* when Beaverbrook converted to his policy of Empire preference. This plan was much needed because, in the view of Barry and its author, Max Nicholson, the country was in the hands of 'elderly men with elderly ideas', working with a 'Heath Robinson contrivance composed of the clutter of past generations and tied together with rotten bits of string'. The 'drift' and 'stagnation' must stop, since 'a great part of the present troubles of this country and the world are due to the failure to adapt erratic and conflicting national policies into a Plan'. The result was wide-ranging and prescient calls for an overhaul of the machinery of government, turning the Post Office and the Ministry of Works into autonomous public utilities – indeed, a measure of devolution from Whitehall and Westminster to industry – the creation of a Bureau of Statistics to inform planners, designating national parks, trying to attract tourists, throwing a green belt around London and redeveloping the South Bank of the Thames. And that June, intending to lobby to turn vision into policy, the Political and Economic Planning (PEP) group held its inaugural meeting, and started to issue regular reports and circulate digests of these reports as 'broadsheets' entitled – what else – *Planning*. With a growing number of research groups – fifteen within a year – beavering away on various topics such as town and country planning, fuel policy, housing, the press, consumer protection and government spin, PEP saw its role as being 'the ginger group of gradualness', in the words of Israel Sieff, vice-chairman of Marks & Spencer, who took over as chairman in December 1932, aiming to influence opinion-formers of any political hue in 'a crusade for continuous change'.

Unemployment hit the trade union movement hard, with falling numbers of members and a greater proportion of the wages of those in work going to support their unemployed brothers and sisters. However, until 1931 the movement had few alternatives to propose, and generally felt that the Labour government was doing its best – certainly no other party would do better – and that in general economic decisions were beyond its remit. But Keynes' attack on the Gold Standard, and the suspicion that Treasury economic orthodoxy was likely to result in a call for wage cuts, led Bevin and Citrine to decide that it was important that the TUC General Council should formulate its position. An Economic Committee was set up, and Bevin and Citrine drew on their experience on government-sponsored committees to call for the nationalisation of the Bank of England (still a private corporation independent of the government, despite its responsibility for the nation's monetary policy), iron and steel, leaving the Gold Standard and increasing government spending to increase purchasing power – very much what Keynes was also saying. If the TUC as a body was slower to develop an alternative economic strategy than its more unorthodox leaders – though by 1932 the Economic Committee had become its most influential policy body, particularly on the public control of industry and trade – defensive in the face of the growing possibility of wage cuts and calling for 'as full a development as possible of the economic relations between the constituent parts of the British Commonwealth', the government was equally unresponsive to trade union pressure.

By August 1930 Bevin was in despair. He considered the situation so serious 'that it warrants a state of emergency. The best brains in the country should be mobilised for the purpose of really tackling the problem instead of "footling about" in the manner we are at the moment.' In early 1931 he joined with some of these 'best brains' as Chairman of the Society for Socialist Inquiry and Propaganda (SSIP – usually referred to as 'zip'), with the former Fabian G.D.H. Cole as Vice Chairman, one of two bodies set up in an attempt to 'ginger up' thinking and activity in the Labour Party and provide it with the nuts and bolts of socialist policy, as Cole was convinced that the government was mired in a 'stagnant swamp' and unable to act.

The other body, the New Fabian Research Bureau (NFRB) (since, according to Cole's wife Margaret, the old one was becoming 'moribund'), was tasked with considering all areas of long-term socialist policy, while the SSIP's role was to diffuse its findings and stimulate discussion in the wider labour movement. G.D.H. Cole's intention was to 'rally the young men, among whom there is some excellent stuff', and indeed both were organisations of all the talents (and not all young or male). Apart from the Coles, participants included Stafford Cripps, a lawyer of great intellectual repute – and earning power – who was wished on a Bristol constituency as its MP in January 1931; George Lansbury; Ellen Wilkinson, the MP for Jarrow; Clement Attlee, who fourteen years later would be Prime Minister in the Labour government that would implement much of what these bodies advocated; the erratically brilliant Harold Laski; the economist Evan Durbin; another economist, the apprentice politician Hugh Gaitskell ('the cleverest and most self-contained of the young men Dalton advanced'); Arthur Pugh, General Secretary of the Iron and Steel Trades Association (who, together with Bevin, represented over half a million workers); and Leonard Woolf, husband of Virginia, who organised the international section.

Never intended as 'parties within a party' (as the ILP was charged with being), these two bodies were rather a collection of 'loyal grousers', several of whom would metamorphose into 'patriotic gadflies' during the Second World War. They were astonishingly industrious, arranging meetings, discussions and 'kite-flying' (today's 'out of the box' or 'blue skies' thinking) sessions, educational meetings for students and trade unionists, and summer schools, in addition to producing a large number of influential books, booklets, pamphlets and memoranda, full of sound analysis and helpful advice. But for some time the government was politely but firmly dismissive of their efforts, and their penetration of the Labour machine proved to be almost as gradual as any old Fabian might have anticipated.

Hugh Dalton, appalled at how woefully ignorant he felt the Labour Party was about the workings of high finance, set out to meet 'as many City blokes as possible' in an attempt to fill in the blanks. One of these was Nicholas Davenport, who had worked with Keynes in the City and wrote the City column in the *New Statesman* under the byline 'Toreador'. Although 'all the claptrap of Clause 4 socialism' was not for him, Davenport considered himself to be a radical, and he was certainly an iconoclast when it came to the workings – or failures to work – of the City. He would look back on the 1930s as a time when 'the City's Establishment was . . . in effect an old boys' racket . . . It was a sort of Mafia in reverse – a gang based on honest dealing instead of blackmail, on good "hard" money (lots of it) instead of easy loot and on simplicity instead of cunning. The only rules were playing safe, resisting change, opposing new ideas, upholding the Establishment and being willing to dress up and go on pompous dinner parade in the City halls . . . the millions spent each year on guzzling [at these] junketings would amaze the underprivileged and enrage the poor.'

Davenport was alarmed that 'Because the Labour Party was so ignorant of the workings of the financial system . . . it was bound to cause havoc if it tried to put it all under government control.' He discussed this possibility 'many times over coffee in City dives' with Vaughan Berry, a City broker who was 'an ardent undercover Labour member', and the two decided to form 'a private dining club where City men could meet the Labour leaders and instruct them in the mysteries of City finance so that they would not make a hash of it when they came into power'. Dalton was encouraging, and Davenport recruited a number of financial journalists, a banker, a stockbroker, an accountant, a statistician, the director of a gold bullion house, and later two economic policy perennials, Evan Durbin and Hugh Gaitskell, plus Douglas Jay, who would be an influential – and profoundly anti-European – advisor to Attlee's post-war Labour government, but was then a staff writer on the *Economist*.

The private dining club, named the XYZ, met fortnightly or monthly in a room above a pub 'over a City alley deserted by night', in the private rooms of quiet Soho restaurants, a Charing Cross hotel, or in members' homes, depending on whose memoirs one reads, but always in great secrecy. Dalton, Herbert Morrison, Stafford Cripps and Attlee, all of whom except Cripps were 'sublimely ignorant of the City and suspicious of its institutions, especially the Stock Exchange which they regarded as a casino where rich men gambled to make money regardless of the state of the economy', were wined and dined so that what Dalton rather grandly called 'my experts' could attempt to 'enlighten them and exorcise the ghosts of Puritan bigotry and prejudice which haunted them'. Dalton's experts wrote papers and produced statistics on such matters as nationalising the Bank of England and the reform of the Stock Exchange, and advocated setting up a National Investment Board and an Industrial Finance Corporation.

'I like to think we did some good,' Davenport reflected forty years later, and quoted one of their number, Francis Williams, who had been City editor of the Labour-supporting *Daily Herald* at the time, and later took over as editor, assuming the role of Attlee's press spokesman after the war, who reckoned that 'Over the years, the XYZ Club drew up a blueprint for Labour's financial policy much of which . . . was adopted by the first post-war Labour government . . . [which it did] in the most private manner without attracting attention to itself.' But useful though that surely was, neither the XYZ Club nor any of the other think tanks, committees and ginger groups managed to find any immediate solution to the problem of conquering (or tackling, as the word had less ambitiously become) unemployment.

'In the chaos of our political life today, there will be many meteors passing through the firmament,' wrote Beatrice Webb in her diary, with little enthusiasm at the prospect. 'Have there ever been so many political personages on the loose?' Mrs Webb was particularly thinking of Sir Oswald Mosley and Winston Churchill, but there were other unaligned souls out there on the loose with notions of how to conquer, tackle, solve the problem of ever-rising unemployment. The Fabian and best-selling novelist H.G. Wells thought there might be some mileage in a scheme to 'grow vines and produce white wine on the slopes of the hills in the South Wales mining area – as they do in Grasse in the South of France', wrote Thomas Jones. 'He also thought we should have large horticultural farms to produce early vegetables. I quickly discovered that he had no sense of the actual position in the derelict areas.'

The modernist poet Ezra Pound was another economic loose cannon. Long concerned about the plight of the under-remunerated artist, after the First World War he was attracted to the economic ideas of Major Clifford Hugh Douglas. Douglas, a Scot, had noticed when he was Assistant Director of the Royal Aircraft Works at Farnborough during the First World War that there was always plenty of money available to pay for what was needed, whereas before the war he was always being told that there was no money to do something useful. He came to the conclusion that there was a simple explanation for the persistence of unemployment and poverty in a modern world that was producing more and more goods. Basically, people couldn't afford to buy the things they produced: it was the persistent problem of under-consumption. So there was widespread poverty 'when physically all could be living in plenty'. If modern technology was leading to increased productivity, then the state would have to step in to increase people's ability to pay for those goods, and this could be done by effectively extending wartime controls, which to Douglas's mind had worked well.

The answer, Douglas argued, was contained in his 'three demands': a 'National Credit Office' to work out how much credit should be circulating in the economy; a 'just price' – a mechanism to absorb profits in times of inflation and return them to the people in the form of subsidised prices when the goods on the market exceeded the money available to buy them; and a 'national dividend' (a bit like a Co-op divi) to give a guaranteed basic income to all, regardless of whether they had a job or not.

This may have been an attractive economic argument, but it was a fallacious one, as G.D.H. Cole and Hugh Gaitskell (and many others) pointed out. Another of Douglas's wackier – though again rather appealing – ideas was reducing the working day of all those who worked in government offices to four hours, but doubling their number, the second shift intended to check the work of the first.

Major Douglas's economics might have been 'heresy' rather than unorthodox, a 'piece of nonsense', even a 'farrago of confusion', and Douglas might indeed be better regarded as 'a religious rather than a social reformer', but he was a hit with 'the political and social crowd that hangs round

Speakers' Corners and joins in any march or demonstration' in the early 1930s. He also managed to snag the imagination of the 'fringes of the left and right', men like Hilaire Belloc, G.K. Chesterton, the poet Edwin Muir, the ex-editor of the *New Age*, a journal of ideas much concerned with modernism in culture, politics, Nietszchean philosophy and spiritualism which had been very influential among the *avant garde* before the First World War, A.R. Orage (who also published Pound on the pound) and of course Pound himself, who not only penned economic treatises, but incorporated his economic thinking into some of his poems: 'and the power to purchase can never/(under the present system) catch up with/prices at large/and the light became so bright and so blindin'/in this layer of paradise/that the mind of man was bewildered'. However, in a time of slavish adherence to the Gold Standard, Pound was prescient in seeing that money was nothing more than a token: 'Money is not a commodity but a measure'. 'Real credit is a measure of the reserve of energy belonging to the community,' he maintained, and he proposed a 'citizen's income' given as of right, much like the vote. And, since 'far from employment bringing riches to a man, employment takes riches away since a person's riches should be calculated according to their store of time and energy, and are diminished by any encroachment on these' (a true creative artist's economics!), working hours should be cut to 'possibly three hours a day for adults between 18 and 40 . . . [which] should supply all men's necessities'.

One of the reasons Ezra Pound found Douglas's economic theory so appealing was that it was an implicit attack on banks and financiers, since inflation and deflation were controlled in 'a dark room back of a bank, hung with deep purple curtains'. So, 'Who my brother controlleth the bank?' For the virulently anti-Semitic Pound, the answer was obvious: a conspiracy of Jewish financiers.

Another maverick thinker frustrated with orthodox economic theories was the British-domiciled Canadian newspaper magnate, owner of the *Daily Express*, Lord Beaverbrook. Like Mosley, Beaverbrook, frustrated with the political party he had tried to influence with his radical ideas, set up a new movement. In Beaverbrook's case it was the Conservative Party that he had lost patience with. And his 'new wine' was Imperial Preference (which had been championed by Joseph Chamberlain in 1903), a tariff-protected internal market between Britain and her dominions intended to bind the Empire together and insulate Britain from the buffetings of the world economy.

In the eighteenth century Adam Smith, the principal theorist of Free Trade, had argued that the removal of trade restrictions between nations would encourage the exploitation of natural advantages, producing an efficient international division of labour and world peace. It was a doctrine perfectly attuned to the industrial hegemony that Britain had enjoyed as 'workshop of the world', buying raw materials in the cheapest markets and selling its manufactured goods in the most costly. But as foreign competition increased in the nineteenth century and the workshop began to look rickety, there were calls for trade barriers to protect British manufacturing industry and the wages of the workers, which free trade imports could undercut.

By 1930 the pressure to protect the home market was beginning to come from some unexpected quarters. It was a highly sensitive political matter, since Labour relied on the support of the Liberals in government, and for the Liberal Party, political and ideological heirs to Cobden and Bright, free trade flowed through their very veins. Snowden, too, was implacably opposed to the erection of any form of tariff barriers. Yet while the Labour government remained firm in its commitment to free trade, a protectionist movement under the leadership of Sir John Simon was stirring deep in the heart of the Liberal Party. And Stanley Baldwin, leader of a Conservative Party that was no more united in its policies to deal with the economic crisis than Labour or the Liberals, felt the breeze too, noting in April 1930 that 'The age of free trade is passing . . . because no new free traders are being born today.' He grew more confident about reviving old Conservative policies of tariff protection, talking cautiously about safeguarding industry and holding a referendum on what had previously been a vote-loser: food taxes. This however was not enough for those in the party who wanted MacDonald to commit to the pursuit of Empire Free Trade.

In early 1930 Beaverbrook jumped the gun and announced the start of an Empire Crusade, since 'The old Parties, slaves of tradition – impervious to new ideas – have let us down too, and . . . out of these old bottles it is no use looking for any new wine.' Beaverbrook's plan was to create a single economic unit from the variety of territories within the British Empire: the Empire would provide Britain with its food, while British industry would provide the Empire with the manufactured goods it needed, all behind a protective tariff barrier.

The Crusade, publicised in Beaverbrook's *Daily Express*, and Lord Rothermere's United Empire Party, supported by his *Daily Mail* (between them these two papers had a circulation of nearly four million), formed an uneasy alliance 'to save the country . . . if necessary at the expense of wrecking every political party' by putting up candidates in every constituency represented by a free trade Conservative (though in fact Rothermere was less concerned about Empire trade than about the loss of British influence in India). In March 1931 the Empire Crusade and the United Empire Party joined together to support an independent, anti-Baldwin Conservative in a by-election in the St George's division of Westminster, the safest (and without doubt the richest) Conservative seat in the country, where the official Conservative candidate was Duff Cooper. Baldwin, who was being attacked from 'under the piecrust' in his own party, was so anxious about the result that he almost considered standing himself. Cooper was a former diplomat and MP, a skilful gentleman-who-lunched, and both the husband of one of the notable beauties of the age, Lady Diana Cooper, and a close friend of the Prince of Wales. In the event, in a campaign in which 'the gloves were off' and there had been 'no baby or butcher-kissing', the socialite Tory 'slayed the dragons', winning a resounding victory despite the 'power without responsibility', as Baldwin accused it, of the popular press.

What Mosley and Beaverbrook advocated *in extremis* – and tainted with their advocacy – also figured in John Maynard Keynes' thinking, found instinctive support from the trade unions, and drew praise from radical young Tories like Robert Boothby and Harold Macmillan, whose Stockton-on-Tees constituency suffered deeply in the Depression, and who was exasperated by 'a shadow Cabinet . . . worn to a shadow by its exertions', a party with too many 'open questions and too many closed minds' – a criticism that could have been levelled at all three parties. Indeed Macmillan, who would in a little more than two more decades preside over Britain's return to affluence, had been tempted to work with Mosley's New Party himself, but had decided that 'Men do better to stick to their own parties and try to influence their policies and their characters from within.' Keynes too recognised much that he advocated in Mosley's proposals. He found the memorandum 'a very able document and illuminating'. And whereas before Mosley's resignation the dispute had been over the efficacy of public works, afterwards the focus of the argument was increasingly about tariffs. Protectionist policies began to find support not just from industrialists, but also from the City of London, economists – including Keynes – and trade unionists. But not from Snowden. The Chancellor remained as intransigent as ever, opposed both to increasing government expenditure to create jobs and also to any form of tariff barriers. Irritated by sniping from his own backbenchers, Snowden decided to give them a cold douche of reality as he saw it. In February 1931, in response to Conservative charges that unemployment costs were too high, the government accepted a Liberal amendment and set up a committee to report on the matter.

Sir George May of the Prudential Assurance Company assumed the role of picky auditor of the government's books, and his committee's report was published on 31 July 1931, the day before the House rose for the summer recess. The deliberations of the men whom Beatrice Webb described as 'five clever hard-faced representatives of capitalism and two dull trade union-ists' were 'sensational' (or 'devilish', as the Bank of England feared). The May Committee forecast a budget deficit of £120 million, and to avoid this it recommended total spending cuts of £96 million, two-thirds to come from unemployment benefit, plus cuts in public works projects and the pay of teachers, the police and the armed forces. 'Luxury hotels and luxury flats, Bond Street shopping, racing and high living in all its forms is to go unchecked; but the babies are not to have milk and the very poor are not to have homes. The private luxury of the rich is apparently not *wasteful expenditure*,' expostulated Beatrice Webb. The Cassandra-like May report, which was considerably exaggerated but not questioned at the time, could not have come at a worse moment. On 11 May the Credit-Ansalt, the most important bank in Austria, had failed, threatening the collapse of the German banking system. France started to withdraw gold in large quantities from London, and by the end of July MacDonald noted 'Run on the Bank of England . . . £5,000,000 exported' as foreign holders of sterling unable to withdraw their money from Germany withdrew it from London instead, in what Treasury officials warned was 'an unprecedented exodus'. What had been a liquidity crisis was turning into one of confidence.

The Labour government was ill-placed to know how to restore it. In line with its election pledges benefit payments had been increased and access to benefits widened in January 1930, but the rapid escalation of unemployment and a shrinking tax base meant that the insurance fund was soon in deficit – by £75 million in 1930, and expected to rise. Unemployment benefits gener-ally had soared as a cost to the Exchequer, from £12 million in 1928 to around £125 million in 1931. To its critics, unemployment insurance had become symbolic of the Labour government's financial 'unsoundness' and 'profligacy'. The Holman Gregory Commission on Unemployment Insurance, set up in December 1930, issued its interim report at the end of June 1931, calling for reductions in unemployment benefits and increases in unemployment insur-ance contributions. And when Lord Macmillan's Committee finally issued its report in early July, 'it was not exactly a document of limpid clarity and gave little practical assistance to a distracted administration' (rather it gave the reverse, exposing the extent of London's short-term foreign indebtedness to the government's putative overseas lenders), while the minority report signed by Keynes and others saw the big picture and the long term, but was equally 'of no immediate help'.

Indeed, even after the publication of the May Committee report (on which his views were not fit for publication), Keynes still thought that MacDonald should consult 'a Commee. consisting of all ex Chancellors of the Exchequer' about the issue. Beatrice Webb, writing her diary at 4 a.m. in the middle of the crisis, considered that 'The only excuse for the Labour Cabinet is that no other group of men, whether politicians, businessmen or academic economists, whether Tory, Liberal or Labour, seem to understand the problem. No one knows either what the situation is . . . or the way out of it to sound finance. Even the fundamental facts of the situation are unknown.'

MacDonald set up a Cabinet Committee consisting of himself, Snowden, Henderson (who despite his position as Foreign Secretary discussing US loans considered that finance was a matter for the Treasury), J.H. Thomas and William Graham, President of the Board of Trade, to consider ways of reassuring foreign investors and easing the strain on sterling. 'Will the country pull through?' the Governor of the Bank of England Montagu Norman was asked on 15 August 1931. 'Yes,' he replied, 'if we can get them [i.e. the government] frightened enough.' Undoubtedly the government was frightened. It was also divided.

On hearing that more than £6 million in gold reserves had leached away during the past month, Snowden wrote to MacDonald on 7 August 1931 stressing the 'terrible gravity of [the whole situation]. Three millions of unemployed is certain in the near future and four millions is not out of the question. We are getting very near exhausting our borrowing powers for unemployment . . . we cannot allow matters to drift into utter chaos, and we are perilously near that.' It was reported in the City that MacDonald was hopeful that a loan to help prop up sterling 'could be placed in New York if satisfactory promises of good behaviour are made here'. But whatever Snowden and MacDonald thought about the imperative of balancing the budget – and by mid-August Snowden was predicting that the deficit would be £170 million, rather than the £120 million the May Committee had forecast – what the City regarded as 'good behaviour' went against the very *raison d'être* of the Labour Party: to represent the interests of working people. Now a Labour government that had proved unable to tackle, let along conquer, unemployment was being expected to penalise those very people who were already suffering most from this failure. 'It certainly is a tragically comic situation that the financiers who have landed the British people in this gigantic muddle should decide who should bear the burden,' again expostulated Beatrice Webb.

The Bank of England's agent in New York, J.P. Morgan & Co., reported that Wall Street needed to have confidence in the financial competence of the British government, and that no further loans would be forthcoming unless an economy package could be put together which satisfied the opposition parties. But this proved impossible. The Conservative Party insisted that taxation must not rise, and Neville Chamberlain, the shadow Chancellor, insisted that the economy package the government was proposing must be increased by around £30 million, while the Liberal leader Herbert Samuel insisted that there had to be 'drastic action' on unemployment insurance.

There was another option to swingeing cuts, one that Keynes had come round to favouring, and even Bevin had ventured was not unthinkable, and that was coming off the Gold Standard, and allowing the pound to settle at a lower value than its parity with gold. But no other member of the government or opposition even contemplated such apostasy: the Gold Standard was a *sine qua non* of the financial stability necessary for a permanent revival of trade, industry and employment, and all other economic decisions had to be taken in light of this given. Anything else would, in the words of the usually cautious economist Hubert Henderson, who was no Treasury man, let loose 'a real *déringolade* [meltdown] which would lead to the complete collapse of the currency which in turn would lead to far harsher cuts than any so far contemplated'. In what is probably an apocryphal story, Sidney Webb is supposed to have gasped, 'I didn't know we could do *that*,' when Britain did abandon the Gold Standard a couple of months later.

Meanwhile, the Cabinet accepted that the budget had to be balanced to restore confidence in sterling, and no one said anything about coming off the Gold Standard (rather Snowden warned the Cabinet on 8 August that the effect of departing from the Gold Standard would be a 50 per cent fall in the standard of living of working men). Hour after hour that humid August the Cabinet wrangled, cutting, trimming. By the twenty-first, agreement had been reached that rather than making economies of £78 million and cutting unemployment benefit payments by £48 million, economies would be reduced to £56 million, unemployment benefits cut by £22 million. But the City dismissed the new targets as inadequate – and warned that gold reserves would probably only last for four more days. Chamberlain for the Conservatives and Sir John Simon for the Liberals said the same; the two opposition parties would 'turn them [the Labour government] out immediately the House met' (being August, Parliament was in recess), insisting that it was MacDonald's duty to avoid the crash. The Conservatives would give him 'any support in our power for that purpose, either with his present, or in a reconstructed government', and Samuel committed the Liberals to that line too – stressing the immense urgency of the situation.

The General Council of the TUC, seeing no 'equality' in the sacrifice they were being asked to make, and convinced that the situation was not quite so desperate as was being alleged, refused to agree to any cuts in benefits or in the pay of teachers or policemen ('Pigs,' spluttered Sidney Webb, meaning the TUC) – though it was prepared to condone those for judges and ministers. 'Practically a declaration of war,' MacDonald noted in his diary; he must have felt he was staring at a brick wall. The bankers insisted on cuts; the trade unions insisted on no cuts. As for support within Cabinet, according to his son Malcolm, MacDonald was 'disgusted with the behaviour of many of his colleagues; they lack grasp of the situation and the guts to face it . . . He will carry on if he can, but it is more likely that the situation will be such that he has no alternative but to resign.' At 10.30 a.m. on Sunday, 23 August 1931, MacDonald set out for the Palace apparently intending to resign 'with the whole Cabinet', but the King made it clear that should the Labour government resign, his view was that MacDonald should attempt to 'carry the country through' with Conservative and Liberal support.

That evening nine of the eleven members of the Labour Cabinet (including the key player, the Foreign Secretary Arthur Henderson) made it clear that they would not agree to a 10 per cent cut in unemployment benefit, by far the most important part of the package. Clearly the government could not continue. MacDonald was confronted with some unpalatable choices: the Labour government could resign, hand over to the Conservatives and Liberals and oppose the cuts in unemployment benefit from the opposition benches, when in fact MacDonald considered them to be necessary; he could resign the Labour leadership and support the cuts; or agree, in his daughter Sheila's words, to be 'P.M. of coalition govt. (this is what King wants) Wld. have to face whole antagonism of Labour movt. Seeming desertion of principle & playing for office. Lose hold of party.' MacDonald havered: on 24 August he returned to the Palace.

The King again tried to persuade him that resignation would be a dereliction of duty: MacDonald must put country before party and head a National Government. The Prime Minister agreed that in the circumstances he would be prepared to remain as head of a government in which the Conservative and Liberal leaders Baldwin and Samuel would also serve 'until an emergency bill or bills had been passed by Parliament, which would restore once more British credit and the confidence of foreigners', after which time Parliament would be dissolved and a general election would be fought along party lines. 'Certain individuals, as individuals, [would be invited] to take on their shoulders the burden of government' in the new configuration. 'MacDonald has been crawling along the hedgerows in search of Labour ministers these last few days,' wrote Hugh Dalton, who was not trawled. In the event, Snowden, Thomas and Lord Sankey, the Lord Chancellor, were the only three Labour Ministers who agreed to serve in the National Government.

'It was a banker's ramp', charged the Minister of Agriculture and Fisheries, Christopher Addison, on the day of his resignation. The TUC also suspected as much, and the *Daily Herald* made the accusation public on 25 August. Bankers, it was claimed, had used the economic crisis to dictate government policy. But no one in government had doubted the bankers' insistence that the budget had to be balanced: it was *how* it was to be balanced that was at issue. The American banks made a loan dependent on a balanced budget, but insisted that the way in which that was achieved was 'quite outside our province'. But in the end, since the other two political parties were insisting on cuts in unemployment benefit payments as a condition of their support, while the TUC and an important and size-able minority of MacDonald's own Cabinet would not agree the 10 per cut, the Cabinet resigned.

'Well – we have what is called a "National Government" – Conservatives, Liberals, and Mr Ramsay MacDonald and a few friends,' wrote the Conservative MP for Barnard Castle, County Durham, Cuthbert Headlam, sceptically. 'I cannot see how such a combination . . . is going to do any good . . . except on paper this is not a coalition. It is a collection of people collected together to save the situation . . . their task, if carried out properly will make them very unpopular – they cannot go on for long without quarrelling among themselves for their policies are widely divergent.'

MacDonald, Snowden and Thomas were expelled from the Labour Party, and Arthur Henderson assumed the leadership. In September Snowden's budget (attacked by Keynes as being 'replete with folly and injustice') raised taxes, proposed a range of cuts in public workers' salaries and cut 10 per cent (though not the 20 per cent recommended by the May Committee) off unemployment pay. On 21 September, with a renewed run on the pound (partly as a result of the Invergordon Mutiny, when naval ratings refused to muster when faced with disproportionate pay cuts), the Bank of England abandoned the Gold Standard, a situation that the National Government had been brought into being to avoid. Within a year this allowed interest rates to fall to as low as 2 per cent and brought about the 'cheap money' that would help build Britain's industrial recovery.

The election that was called for October 1931 was essentially a fight between Labour and the rest: and the rest won. In 1929, 287 Labour MPs had been elected; in 1931 this was cut to fifty-two, and that included Scottish ILP Members (who eventually disaffiliated from the rest of the ILP under their leader James Maxton in July 1932, believing they could answer the need the ILP perceived among the working classes for a more radical socialist party). Labour was all but annihilated everywhere except in coalmining areas. Arthur Henderson lost his seat, as did Hugh Dalton and Herbert Morrison. Only one former Labour Cabinet Minister, George Lansbury, was returned, though two Junior Ministers, the men of tomorrow, Clement Attlee and Stafford Cripps, just managed to hang on. The so-called National Government, which was composed mainly of Conservatives and members of a terminally divided Liberal Party, swept the board with 554 seats.

Thomas Jones felt like 'the Scotch minister who had prayed earnestly for rain, and then had the whole contents of a drainpipe emptied over him' when he heard of the rout. 'The election results are *astounding*,' wrote Samuel Rich, a teacher at the Jews' Free School in London, who considered that 'teachers are the worst hit in the land, except the poor unemployed' when he received his first reduced monthly salary of £29.7*s* instead of the former £32.6*s* on 23 October 1931. 'There will be no opposition . . . "Socialism in our Time" is *off*,' he wrote in his diary, underlining 'off' heavily, twice.

Indeed, it seemed to many that Labour would never again come to power democratically. Hugh Dalton talked darkly about bringing the Durham Light Infantry to London to replace the Brigade of Guards. When Hugh Gaitskell was adopted as Labour candidate for Chatham for the 1935 general election he was rueful: 'The Labour Party . . . tried to get better conditions out of capitalism . . . leaving the economic power in the hands of the same people as before . . . The only way in which Socialism could be got was shortly and fairly sharply . . . [T]hey should get the power, proceed with measures of Socialisation, and smash the economic power of the upper class.' Cripps, for his part, would hint at 'adopting some exceptional means such as the prolongation of the life of Parliament for a further term without an election', and 'overcoming opposition from Buckingham Palace', though when taxed that this sounded a bit like treason, he affected surprise that 'anybody should have thought I was referring to the Crown'.

'The one thing that is not inevitable now is gradualness,' Cripps insisted. The Webbs agreed, and in September 1932 the Fabian-inspired SSIP was merged with the minority wing of the ILP that had stayed in the Labour Party to form what became the Socialist League, another intellectual pressure group, this time with a clear, if broad, Marxist agenda, with Harold Laski and H.N. Brailsford among its members, and soon Sir Stafford Cripps as its chairman. The Socialist League became the main organisation of the left until it too was dissolved by the leadership in 1937, while the NFRB merged with a revived Fabian Society a year later.

MacDonald – and his 'ism' – were, as his daughter had predicted, faced with antagonism from most (but not all) of the Labour Party, though this had as much to do with his disdainful treatment of his parliamentary colleagues and TU supporters as with his initial 'betrayal'. Samuel Rich was amused to receive a '*jeu d'esprit*' about MacDonald that a friend wrote and slipped in a Christmas card:

> If Ramsay MacDonald, you still have brains that work
> Not solely to commands from high finance . . .
> How it must chill your socialistic bones
> Seated upon your unsubstantial throne –
> A transient triumph – then the long alone –
> Sans friends, sans party, salary or loans . . .

History's verdict has been kinder, more prepared to absolve MacDonald from conspiracy and self-aggrandisement, accepting to some extent his reading of the national interest, seeing little culpable substance in his *faiblesse* for eating cucumber sandwiches with and getting sentimental about aristocratic ladies, and finding the explanation for his actions in confusion, being out of touch, having an imperfect understanding (but who did not?) of economic forces, and few mechanisms at his disposal to influence those forces, and thus of clinging to outworn verities, of believing in socialism but having no plan for achieving it. In sum, being blinded by the blizzard that swept the world in which, to strain a metaphor, the windscreen wipers seemed to have frozen.

Could things have been different? Would a 'Keynesian Revolution', an idea which gained favour in the 1960s and '70s, have saved the day? Such an ambitious 'New Deal' public works programme might at least have provided Britain with a creditable infrastructure of roads and bridges. But would it have solved the unemployment problem? Possibly back in 1929 when unemployment was around a million it could have been cut by 600,000, as Lloyd George pledged, the most astute historian of that proposed 'revolution' judges, but by 1931 the Labour government's own two-year public works schemes had become operational, and unemployment remained obdurate in the face of the world slump. The theoretical basis of the 'multiplier effect' (whereby creating primary employment opportunities generates secondary or subsequent ones as a result of increased spending power) of such schemes on employment was imperfectly understood until the mid-1930s. At the time public works projects were advocated as being cheaper and more controllable than the dole, rather than because of 'the beneficial repercussions that will result from the expenditure of the newly-employed men's wages' (though evidence to the Macmillan Committee had suggested something similar, as Bevin and McKenna's enthusiasm showed). And, of course, those in the Labour Party who still imagined they were tramping along the long road to socialism noted that Keynes' solutions were intended to make capitalism work more efficiently and humanely, not bring about its demise.

The month before Labour went down to an electoral ignominy from which it would not recover until 1945, the number of those out of work was the highest ever: 2,811,615.

SEVEN

(Too Much) Time to Spare

If the hours which are designated as leisure time are an important part of
the life of the community, they are an especially important part of the life
of that portion of the community who happens to have no work to do. For
a man who has a job, the day's activities centre round that job. It takes the
greatest share of his time. It eliminates the necessity of constant choices
concerning what shall be done with his day. It provides him with the means
of enjoying his spare time at the various forms of voluntary or commercial
amusement fairly regularly and dressed in clothes of which he need not be
ashamed.

With the man out of a job, it is different . . .

E. Wight Bakke, *The Unemployed Man: A Social Study* (1934)

He could make marvellous things with his hands. He once made a church from
about five thousand matchsticks . . . I think it took him two years . . . He was
always having to invent something . . . an alarm clock, that was a thing of the
past, and he sat for weeks and weeks . . . fiddling with his tools and pieces of
metal and we had a cuckoo clock . . . it occupied his mind for weeks.

Interview by Kate Nicholas with Mrs Bell, the daughter of a long-term
unemployed Teesside man

'What animals cause you the most worry?' the unemployed Nottingham
miner George Tomlinson once asked a gamekeeper: 'I was thinking of stoats,
weasels, foxes and their like. But he answered sourly, "miners". Tomlinson
'knew well enough what he meant, for the collier when he sets his hand to
it is the most skilful of poachers. I loved to watch them go out in the
evening, slipping merrily along a forest path [Tomlinson lived near Robin
Hood's Sherwood Forest], single file like Indian braves but not a bit like
Indians in their appearance. Old slouch hats, short coats with big bulging
pockets, a cosh pulled down the back of the coat and sticking out above
their heads.'

'Rabbits were the thing! And a good dog was half the battle.' George Bestford, an unemployed Durham miner whose father had come north when the Cornish mining industry collapsed, had 'a good whippet! I think we'd have starved if it hadn't been for the dog. Away he'd go and back with a rabbit. They always had the game keepers out and they were there watching to make sure you didn't get any of their game . . . I was lucky because I was well in with a farmer and he used to let me have half what we caught on his land. So on a moonlit night – away with the dogs and catch a few rabbits! Some of the farmers were very good. They would give you some potatoes or a turnip. But some would give you nothing . . . We used to pinch off them.'

A rabbit for the pot would supplement the endless dole diet of bread and margarine, and suet: 'Every miner's house used suet. That was like the basic. Every day you'd have something with suet in for the main meal of the day. To fill you up. You'd buy a big piece of suet from the butcher's for tuppence and every day you grated a bit of suet into the flour. Monday's dinner was always a plain suet pudding with what was left from Sunday's dinner. Another day was "pot pie" we called it. Then "Spotted Dick" with currants in it or you'd roll it out and put blackberries in the middle, tie a cloth around it and put it in the pan.'

It was not just rabbits that nature provided – or rather that the men took. Anything was fair game for scavenging for hungry families. 'We used to live off the land for quite a number of years,' explained a Derbyshire miner. 'You had to . . . it were a matter of getting by. If we were hungry we used to go into the field with a bit of a broken knife and find pignuts and scrape them out and put a bit of salt on . . . we used to go round scrounging what we could get. If we saw a barrow full of peas, we'd come back with a jersey full of peas and that were it . . . we used to eat owt . . . We used to go out and get rabbits and anything, owt what we could catch . . . pigeons, pheasant and ducks off the canal . . . Sometimes we used to pull mangols [sic] and bring them 'ome and stew 'em . . . we had a gaddo [catapult], we got quite expert . . . wood pigeons, we used to wait for dusk for them to settle in the trees to roost and then we'd knock them out of the trees.'

In the mid-nineteenth century the political philosopher John Stuart Mill had claimed that allotments were 'a contrivance to compensate the labourer for the insufficiency of his wages by giving him something else as a supplement to them': a way, in fact, of 'making people grow their own poor rate'. Little had changed nearly a hundred years later. The notion that 'the hungry could grow their own foods and obtain a living from their own methods' was a throwback to Gerrard Winstanley and the Diggers of the Civil War, but it gained a new relevance during the Depression: an allotment could provide potatoes, carrots, cabbages and other vegetables to eke out family meals. The campaign to make Britain more self-sufficient in food production during the First World War, when George V had directed that the geraniums planted around the Queen Victoria memorial opposite Buckingham Palace should be grubbed up and replaced with potatoes and cabbages, had resulted in an astonishing increase in the number of allotments. By 1918 something like 1.5 million allotments dug by a 'new short-sleeved army numbering over 1,300,000 men and women' were producing over two million tons of vegetables. The return to its former owners of land requisitioned by the government during the war and the spread of the suburbs, where most houses had gardens, meant that the number of allotments fell during the 1920s, but by the 1930s the Ministry of Agriculture was recording a revival of interest as both the Ministry and local authorities made land available for allotments, particularly in depressed areas, while the Land Settlement Association, whose main aim was to turn the urban unemployed into small-holders, encouraged not only the cultivation of produce on small plots, but also the keeping of pigs and chickens to provide food and manure.

In a prefiguration of the 'Dig for Victory' campaign during the Second World War, allotments were dug on wasteland and on roadside and railway banks, wherever the soil might yield food for the table. They clung to the steep, scoured hillsides of the Rhondda Valley, perched on riverbanks prone to flooding and huddled under the ugly shadow of gasworks – anywhere the land could not be used more profitably for some other activity. Working his allotment could be a satisfying occupation for a man who felt that was what he no longer had: out of the house, in the fresh air and using his strength to dig. Many took great pride in what they grew on their allot-ment or in their back garden – and many colliery houses had quite large back gardens. Charles Graves, a rather patrician journalist (and the brother of the poet Robert Graves), paid a visit to Ollerton in the Midlands, 'in the heart of the Dukeries' (a large tract of Nottinghamshire in private hands which once contained the estates of no fewer than five dukes), for the society magazine the *Sphere*. He reported: 'All have gardens . . . work in the mines is limited to three days a week . . . All of them like to . . . grow their own vegetables . . . And the Garden Holders Association among the miners is a very powerful organisation with annual cups and prizes to be won. Potatoes, cabbages, carrots all grow well at Ollerton. So do onions and woe betide the man who is caught pilfering his neighbour's celery.'

But pilfer they did: 'There were a hell of lot of allotments. And there used to be a lot of knocking off' in Ashton-under-Lyne. 'They used to be up around three or four in the morning going on the Moss pinching lettuce and celery, anything to make a meal. The Moss was more or less peat. That's why they've never built on it.' Jack Shaw's father, an unemployed miner, 'had an allotment on the Moss. He paid a pound a year. It was just a matter of growing vegetables for our house. Others had big ones and it would be like a full time job.'

But even in those places such as the mining valleys where there was a long tradition of allotment-holding, the Depression, while making such activity all the more necessary, meant it was harder to do. An unemployed man – or one on short-time hours – might well not be able to afford the necessary seeds, tools or fertiliser. The Quaker Society of Friends reported that an unemployed miner in South Wales 'who had been accustomed to grow his own potatoes . . . had become too poor to buy the seed, that for a time he received seed from his companions, and when that was no longer available he went to the rubbish heaps for peelings and took out such "eyes" as he could find in order to plant his allotment'.

The Society of Friends started a scheme 'to supply (at first free of charge) small seeds, seed potatoes, tools, fertilizer and lime'. It was so successful that the government took it up, and in the winter of 1930, 64,000 families were helped in this way. But it was one of the casualties of the 1931 economic crisis, so the Friends stepped in again, persuading the government to give pound-for-pound matching grants to some 62,000 allotment-holders; this rose to over 100,000 grants in subsequent years. In Sheffield over 117,500 unemployed men were provided with 'the requisites for a 300 square yard plot' in 1934, but as the Sheffield Allotments for Unemployed Scheme pointed out, 'This is a scheme to help men who help themselves – how substantial is that self help is shown by the amount the men themselves have contributed towards the cost of supplies – no less than £24,700 collected week by week'. Moreover, such activity was giving a welcome boost to the local steel industry, since in 1933 'over 56,000 spades, forks, etc were supplied nationally, and these were all made in Sheffield'.

Another necessity of life was fuel. It cost at least two shillings a week to heat a modest house, and anyone who could went collecting wood or 'scrat-ting' (scavenging) for coal. Herbert Allen, whose father was a frequently unemployed farm labourer (and as an agricultural worker was not covered by the unemployment insurance scheme) in Leicestershire, always went 'wooding' on a Saturday. 'We never bought any coal . . . My step-brother and myself used to have to go wooding round the spinneys and the hedges and all that. We'd have a pram and a home made truck and we'd . . . walk four or five miles to the woods and pile the old pram right up, put bits of wood round the side so you got a real good height. If ever we was hanging round the house it was always: "If you've got nothing to do you can go and do some wooding."'

Will Paynter, a trade union activist and checkweighman at Cymmer colliery in the Rhondda who was often on short time or out of work during the thirties, spent one day every week with his father and brother on the colliery slag heaps searching for coal. They would only manage to fill one bag each: 'To get three bags could involve turning over twenty to thirty tons of slag which was hard work in any language.' They then had to carry the heavy bags on their shoulders for a mile or more over the uneven and often slippery sheep-tracks on the mountainside.

'Scratting' around for small pieces of coal was particularly humiliating for men who had spent their working lives hewing great lumps underground. 'If there's one thing that makes us bitter here in the Rhondda, it's the question of coal,' said John Evans.

> I have to pay half a crown a week for coal – though there's plenty lying around. When we're in work in the mines we get supplies at a small fixed rate. Why can't we when we are unemployed? We who have worked all our lives in the mines feel we have a kind of a right to it. In these parts there are places where the coal seam comes to the surface on all sides of the hills – they are called outcrops. We could get coal there. But the companies won't allow it – they even use explosives to make it more difficult for us to get at the coal, though it isn't profitable enough for them to use it. Every colliery has its slag tip – where they throw out all the stuff they can't get rid of, and among it are bits of coal. We are sometimes allowed to pick this over at certain times after the contractors have been over it. At these times the place crawls with men trying to find bits of coal – like ants on an ant heap. It's a hell of a job, especially on a cold day, and of course one can never find enough. That's why so many go out at night and try to steal it. But they have policemen, and if one's caught it means fifteen shillings [fine, or worse].

In Ashton-under-Lyne there was a neat scam: coal was brought to the mills in barges, and when it was taken in lorries from the bin, it was shovelled down a chute into the barge below. 'The chaps that was working on the barges would only be on two or three days a week, and they'd be related to the blokes that wasn't working – brothers and cousins . . . well accidentally on purpose [the men shovelling the coal would] throw about six shovelfuls into the canal every time they got the chance. When the barge moved on, there'd probably be three or four hundredweight of coal,' so the men waiting and watching on the bridge 'used to get a bucket full of holes on a clothes line, throw it across the canal and scoop it up. Fill half hundredweight bags. Then they had a pram or pram wheels with boxes on and they used to go round the streets selling it. People used to grumble, "This bloody coal, it's all wet through." But it was only two bob for half a bag,' recalled Jack Shaw.

'Some of them [the unemployed miners] have become coal pirates,' one of their number in South Wales told Fenner Brockway, an ILP MP until he lost his seat in the 1931 election, and a fierce critic of the National Government and the Labour Party's unemployment policies. 'They get caught sometimes and do a turn in prison. But what does it matter? Prison is no hardship these days; food guaranteed and no worry. There are men who raid the coal-trucks . . . Every night a train climbs [the mountain] side. The men jump on it when it's going slow, scramble on top of a truck, throw coal off, and then leap down the other side and gather the coal in sacks to sell. A man was killed doing that the other night: slipped and got cut up by the train . . . it shows to what lengths they're being driven.'

Poverty drove many very close to the wrong side of the law – and then tipped them over. As some scavenged for coal to sell, others poached with the same intention. Charles Graves noted that 'there used to be hundreds of pheasants on Lord Savile's property, Wellow Wood. Two years ago [in 1930] they bagged 900. Last year only 35 and a similar number of rabbits.' An East Midlands miner on short time recalled that 'The best time we 'ad was when we went out pegging one Friday night . . . there were six of us . . . we ran the nets out there three times and we got twenty rabbits apiece . . . Some going that were, three nets for 120 rabbits.'

Dick Beavis, a Durham miner, 'spent a lot of time poaching in the 1930s. I was the "knitter". I used to knit all the nets for the lads. Put them over holes . . . and put the ferret in. I found that more interesting than pit heaps. And that's how I learned my political thoughts. Well whose was the land? You go on all these neglected heaps. I used to think what harm are we doing? We were caught by the police and when we received our summons it was said we were catching "conies". We didn't know what that was. (It wasn't until later in my life that I discovered that "conies" is the old English word for rabbits. Rabbits are classified as vermin – and so you could say you were catching vermin – but "conies" is not.) So the magistrate looked at me and he said, "Where did you get them?" And I said "I found them, Sir." Well, he said he'd never heard such a bloody tale and fined us all.'

A poacher might make as much as eight shillings in a good night, though often he would not make more than three shillings, and sometimes nothing at all. Others might stay on the right side of the law by buying rabbits from a farmer for sixpence, skinning them and selling the skins for ninepence and the meat for fourpence. Selling coal or garden produce could also raise a few pence. Some men set up as cobblers, cutting up old rubber tyres to resole boots, mended clocks, soldered saucepans and kettles, made rag, or peg, rugs, 'did carpentry in their back yards or kitchen, making sideboards out of orange boxes stained brown with permanganate of potash, while their wives cook and tend the children in restricted places round the fireplace, uncomplaining because they realise the necessity of providing some occupation for their husbands in order to keep them even moderately content'. An unemployed man might offer to tend the garden, paint the house or wallpaper a room for a better-off neighbour in exchange for money or goods – a side of bacon, maybe, or a joint of meat. The trouble was that there weren't many – if any – better-off neighbours in most of the depressed areas: perhaps a colliery manager, a works foreman, or a moderately prosperous farmer nearby. But most of the men and women in the towns and villages would be in the same situation: no work, not enough money to live on, certainly not to pay for services.

At harvest time or in the shooting or hunting season it might be possible for those men within walking distance of farms or orchards or country estates to get a few days' work. Often this did not bring in much money, 'but you used to get a drink of beer and that while you were in the fields', and hop-picking drew numbers of East Enders to Kent – as it always had. Some made a bit on the side in less obvious ways, breeding rats, mice or ferrets for scientific research or to sell to London Zoo to feed the snakes – though mice 'had to be alive when they got there or they would not pay for them'. A box of five hundred mice would earn a postal order for around thirty shillings – a tidy sum when the dole for a family with two children was around twenty-eight shillings a week – though collecting five hundred mice and keeping them alive must have been a real team effort.

Women might take in dressmaking, mending or washing, bake bread or cakes, or cook 'potato plates' (scraps of meat sandwiched between two layers of potato) to sell, make toffee or jam, knit or crochet. All these activities assumed not only a few coppers to buy the materials, but also a local market that was better placed financially than the 'petty capitalist'. Some families, already living in cramped accommodation, would double up even more and take in a lodger to help make ends meet – or even 'hot sheet': an Irishwoman in the mining village of Chopwell in County Durham 'had pitmen who slept in the beds during the day and she had men who worked in the coke yard during the night. On different shifts . . . when one would get out of bed, the other would go in.'

Enterprise had its price. The Means Test empowered inspectors to take account of all earnings, no matter how paltry. In March 1934 *The Times* reported that 'In Durham villages one sees that men are genuinely fearful of taking an odd job to earn a shilling or two, doubtful whether their weekly means of livelihood will be cut down if they are found to be keeping a few hens.' Although the newspaper reported that 'The policy . . . is to make no deductions for paid earnings of this sort; on the contrary, they will encourage them,' it admitted that 'Knowledge has not yet filtered through to the men, and because all depends on their Dole they take no risks.' Indeed, the Society of Friends made a point of getting 'a clear statement from the Ministry of Labour that the small amount of produce which a man could sell from his allotment would not affect the amount of his dole. This was a great gain (even although the feeling of suspicion on this point ceased only very slowly).'

A 'worthy woman in Merthyr, who had kept a bakery' told an American sociologist who came to Britain in June 1931 to study the effects of unemployment that 'she had wanted the yard wall of her bakery whitewashed and seeing that there were 6,000 unemployed men walking about Merthyr, she had thought that it would be a good idea to ask one of them to do it in return for a few shillings. She asked one after another, but all refused; they said they "might be seen". Eventually she promised a man that if he would do it, she would undertake to let no one into the yard while he was at work and to keep the gate barred. On that condition she got it done. She then thought she would get one of them to putty the lights on the bakehouse roof. But the roof allowed no hiding place while he did the work; so no one would do it . . . To be "seen" earning a shilling is a terrifying prospect. The regulations may provide for such things, but the unemployed man does not know what the regulations are, and the last thing he wants is to stir up mud.' And there were always neighbours who were quick to make allegations of 'benefit fraud' if they suspected someone in receipt of dole was making a bit on the side. In Greenwich anonymous letters arrived at the benefit office at the rate of two a day, snitching on those the writers thought might be cheating.

In some ways the first weeks after a man lost his job were the easiest: there could be a sense of release, something of a holiday feeling after the tyranny of the pit or factory. The initial days would be filled with the search for work. The Labour Exchange wasn't considered much help. Most jobs were obtained by someone 'speaking for you', a relative or friend already in work who might be able to put in a good word. There was no legal requirement for employers to notify the 'Labour' of any work they might have, and the general view of the unemployed was that employers only used it as a place of last resort, when they were offering worthless jobs no one wanted. And if a man refused such a job when offered it by the Labour Exchange, he lost his entitlement to the dole for six weeks. Across the country, only one vacancy in five was filled through the Labour Exchanges in the 1930s. This is perhaps not surprising at a time when there was such a pool of men seeking work that there was no point in wasting time with the paperwork required by the Labour Exchange.

Believing that finding work was 'down to me', most men would trudge for miles each day from place to place in search of a job, following up leads that led nowhere. 'It became quite customary,' Wal Hannington observed, 'to find men walking miles from their own district, such as from Halifax to Huddersfield, in search of work, whilst men from Huddersfield would walk to Halifax in [the] search for work –often passing each other on the road.' After a few weeks or even months of this dispiriting failure it would become apparent that there just weren't any jobs to be had locally, and this was when some men from the valleys and the smoke-filled towns would go 'on the tramp', moving from place to place in search of work.

'On the main roads leading from the coalfields to the big towns – particularly the Bath road leading from South Wales to London', Hannington saw 'almost any day hundreds of men, footsore and weary . . . trudging towards London having left their families at the mercy of the Boards of Guardians'. But most of the men on the road looking for work in the 1930s were probably young and single. John Brown was one. He had lost his job in the docks and, aged nineteen, left his home in South Shields and took a journey round England that was as extensive as J.B. Priestley's, if less salubrious. From South Shields he and a companion scrambled aboard a lorry bound for Newcastle, from there to York, then hearing about the possibility of a job, Brown managed to get a lift to Salford, then he tried his luck in Liverpool, Grantham, Reading, then Basingstoke, from where he walked to Guildford, where he managed to get a few hours' work painting some railings round a bungalow. Then it was on the road again, with a lift to Winchester, then on to Southampton, where he went round the shopkeepers asking for a 'pennyworth of work'. This netted him enough for a bed at the local workhouse and a shared meal of cocoa and bread and butter.

Over the next months Brown travelled from Dover to Dumfries by way of Bath, Worcester, Shrewsbury and London, where he found work for a bit. Sometimes alone, sometimes with companions – including a young woman, Hilda, who had been sacked from her job as a parlourmaid and had been sleeping out in London parks until Brown took her under his wing, he walked, hitched lifts on lorries, crawled under tarpaulins when the lorry driver was taking a break, and once was offered a lift in a private car. He slept mainly in 'spikes', the casual wards of workhouses, which varied hugely: the one at Winchester was particularly highly spoken of, but others were considered 'not fit to live in', with dirty sheets and blankets, and infestations of lice and nits. He passed nights lying on potato sacks in barns, or under hedges, and when he was temporarily in funds he would stay in cheap 'model' lodging house, or hostels run by such philanthropic organisations as the Salvation Army or the Church Army.

Food was meagre workhouse rations such as skilly (thin oatmeal gruel that must have brought Oliver Twist to mind, though this was officially abolished in 1931, and meat and vegetables added to the diet), usually given in exchange for work such as chopping wood or breaking stones (though stone-breaking was discontinued by the same order in 1931), sometimes bread and a cup of tea, maybe a cold sausage given by someone whose windows or car Brown had cleaned, or fence he'd repaired, or a cheap meal in a café which the grapevine that ran between 'roadsters' recommended, like Nash's in Southampton where a three-course meal could be got for a tanner (sixpence). Brown took whatever work he could get, including bricklaying, washing up and handing out cinema flyers. He discovered that blankets tucked in crosswise, sometimes on a necessarily shared bed, provided the maximum warmth, and learned always to sleep with his trousers under his pillow and the legs of the bed in his boots to prevent them being stolen in the night. But finally, after many months on the road, he grew 'weary of the "spikes" and "models" and barns. The "romance of the road" had turned out to be a sordid tragedy of bread, weak tea, blankets, washing and baked clothes.' John Brown went back home to South Shields – but still no job.

Max Cohen, a frequently unemployed London cabinet-maker, offered a cigarette in a café in the Strand to an unkempt-looking man, his clothes ragged and shabby, his shoes tied up with string, the holes stuffed with newspaper, who told him, 'I tramped the country, lookin' for work . . . But yer can't get any work – nowhere! I tried – honest. I've been out six years . . . never go on the road. You'll be driven from one town to 'nother. A vagrant, that's what they calls you, a vagrant. Y'ave to go to the spike, else you'll get locked up' – 'sleeping out' was an offence under the 1824 Vagrancy Act until it was modified in 1935.

It is not possible to know precisely how many people 'on the tramp' in the 1930s were unemployed men seeking work, and how many were vagrants, but on the night of 21 May 1932, at the depth of the Depression, 16,911 men were sleeping in casual wards; the number had been 3,188 in May 1920 and 10,217 in December 1929.

'It is when a man settles down to being unemployed,' wrote the Reverend Cecil Northcott of his experience in Lancashire, 'that he finds it difficult to know how to fill his time. Beyond the weekly events of signing on and drawing the dole there is not much regulation to his life.' The clergyman spoke of 'helping his missus . . . becoming a permanent occupation. The brass round the kitchen range and anything that shines comes within the duties of the man'; of the fathers who took their children in the pram to the park, 'the same collection of men day after day'; of the 'handicrafts [that] have become so important in many unemployed homes' – an Elizabethan galleon made out of a block of wood, for example.

Joseph Farrington's father, an unemployed iron-moulder, had the skills of a sailor, which was how he started his working life. He would sew two canvas bags together to make a floor covering, or 'cut up different coloured coats and make a pattern. It was as though he'd bought it in a shop when he'd finished it. He could knit . . . he could do anything. He even used to cook the meals because my mother couldn't cook. And he made toys like so many unemployed men, wooden trains, hobby horses, dolls for the girls out of paper and packing and put faces on with indelible pencil. He was clever at making things with newspaper. He'd make a tablecloth with a pattern – just by tearing.' Arnold Deane, an unemployed Oldham man, made a magnificent fifteen-inch model of a hotel, complete with elegant grounds and railings, using cardboard and beads. It had 176 windows, a ballroom, and was lit by electric light. The construction took him two months and was photographed for the local paper.

John Brierley's father Walter, an unemployed Derbyshire miner, was not able to fill his time so productively. He 'felt ill at ease . . . when he was on the dole [from 1931 to 1935]. Hanging about the house and garden when other men were working and the women busy made him feel particularly inadequate. To make matters worse he was clumsy with his hands and could no more build a wall, or put up a fowl house than "fly in the air" my mother said. The tasks he was set required no skill, collecting wood or shovelling coal or muck. If he was set to weed, he would uproot the wrong plants, would knock cups against the taps when washing up, his head probably full of his latest piece of poetry or writing' – one of which, fortunately, found a publisher as a novel, *Means Test Man*, in 1935.

To the observer it might look as it did to the poet T.S. Eliot, in whose poem 'The Rock' the voices of the unemployed intone: 'No man has hired us/With pocketed hands/And lowered faces/We stand about in open places.' But in fact standing about in open places could be a necessary social activity, since there was no longer the camaraderie of work, or the money to go to the pub to meet your mates. Convictions for drunken behaviour fell by more than half between 1927 and 1932, for though the solace of a warm pub and the oblivion of drink might seem an appealing way of blotting out reality, the high price of a pint of beer (a pint of mild cost fivepence and one of strong ale elevenpence) discouraged it, though Jack Shaw reported that men in Ashton-under-Lyne 'used to go round the pubs and off licences and pinch some bottles. There were a penny [deposit] on a bottle. They'd pinch half a dozen and go round and get sixpence and get a gill [half a pint]. You could sit in all night with a gill.'

If they couldn't drink, men might still smoke. 'You could buy five Woodbines for twopence. But that's no bargain if you haven't got twopence. You'd go for maybe a week without a single drag and then when you were given a cigarette, you inhaled so deeply you'd have expected to see the smoke coming out through the laceholes of your boots.' Men would take one drag on a cigarette, pinch it and put it in their pockets for later, or go round the streets picking up butts, which they would mix up together and make their own cigarettes, 'So they were smoking for nothing.' Loose tobacco cost around fourpence an ounce, and this might well be supplemented by dried tea leaves either in a rollup or a pipe.

It seemed that given an extremely limited amount of disposable income (if any at all), an unemployed man would rather spend it on gambling than smoking or drinking: after all, putting a bet on might prove to be the down-payment on a better life. Street gambling was illegal, but that didn't stop it: men would be posted as lookouts while their friends laid bets on pretty much anything. Horseracing was a subject of great interest – though the interest was not in the horses themselves, but in betting on them, which formed a link between the unemployed and the 'sport of kings'. 'It's always been a miner's privilege, a little bit on the horses, the dogs.' 'Blokes used to earn half a crown in the pound as a bookies' runner. There were no licensed bookies. The runners used to stand in the doorways of pubs or else the ginnel [alleyway] of some place. Some of the blokes would go round the mills and pubs and houses. Anything to get a bet.'

Men would not just play billiards, they would gamble on it, a penny or tuppence for the winner. They'd play cards for money, one of their number earning tuppence or threepence a time for 'Keeping Konk' (lookout). Pitch and toss (throwing a coin so it landed as close as possible to a wall) and crown and anchor (a dice game) were almost universal pastimes. 'In most back alleys and lanes young and old men would play their few pennies away on Sunday mornings.' Sometimes bigger events were organised, such as those on a secluded beach at South Shields to which men would come from as far afield as Newcastle or Sunderland, and the bookies came too. While some played for pence, others graduated to 'the bigger school', where the stakes for pitch and toss could be raised to five shillings a time and two lookouts were placed to warn if the police approached. For Joseph Farrington it was 'marbles – flirting. We used to make a ring of tin milk-bottle tops. If you hit one with a marble you took it out. We used to play with money, when we had money.' Jack Shaw and his friends would bet on a 'peggy', a piece of wood that one player would hit and the others had to guess how far away it had landed. Once they had to jump the local canal to get away from the police, and that in itself soon became an activity to bet on.

'They'd gamble on anything. It was the only way they had of getting a few bob. A lot of it was "Why have dry bread when I might have a bit of bread and jam?"' If life seemed an irrational lottery when it came to getting a job, why not take part in a more enjoyable lottery in the hope of turning your luck round, or at least having some control over the choices you made? 'They [the unemployed] have given up all hope of earning anything by work,' Fenner Brockway was told, 'and hundreds of them put all their hopes on horses and dogs and football matches. They put 1s. on. They may lose, they go short on food; but they're so used to going short that they don't trouble much . . . Betting . . . means excitement in the midst of monotony . . . You may deplore the betting mania, but you can't be surprised. What other excitement, what other chance, does existence offer these men?'

Men would keep homing pigeons, as long as they could afford to feed them (and would often bet on races between them), or greyhounds, which 'often received as much attention as any child'. More likely, they would earn a few shillings exercising the greyhounds of an employed friend. Many sports offered reduced rates for the unemployed: bowls or billiards for a penny. Young men would play football on a piece of waste ground – games that would sometimes last all day, with a leather ball they'd pooled their coppers to buy if they were lucky, a blown-up pig's bladder or caps sewn together if they weren't – and men of all ages would go to football matches. In Liverpool in the early 1930s the average gate was 30,000 when Liverpool or Everton were playing, and most professional football clubs would admit the unemployed for half price at half time and free ten minutes before the final whistle. And there was always the opportunity to try to make a few pennies by entertaining the crowds as they queued to get in, singing, juggling, playing a tin whistle, doing handstands.

Boxing was another popular sport. William Saunders would 'go round the boxing booths in the fairgrounds, we used to get £1 for standing up so many rounds'. Some of George Bestford's unemployed friends in Newcastle would volunteer for three-round contests: 'Some of them could box and others couldn't. Those who couldn't just received a good punching-up and the fee which was paid to the boxers was five shillings, out of which they paid two shillings to the seconds. One night there was a man who was so weak and tired it was obvious he should not have been in the ring. The crowd was just beginning to voice their disapproval of his poor show when the referee waved them to be quiet and explained that the man was on the road, had not had anything to eat all day, but had come along to the Hall and volunteered to fight.' But as for the unemployed taking up tennis, badminton, cricket or golf to fill their empty hours, these were, a report on Glasgow's unemployed youth concluded, 'the pursuits of another class'.

The day of one young unemployed man from Lancashire was not untypical. He was 'one of a gang [who] used to stay in bed late in the mornings so as not to need breakfast. I used to have a cup of tea, and then we would all go down to the library and read the papers. Then we went home for a bit of lunch, and then we met again at the billiard hall where you could watch and play for nothing. Then back to tea and to watch billiards again. In the evening we used to go to the pictures. That's how we spent the dole money. In the end, I thought I'd go mad if I went on like this . . . in the end I joined a PT Class. But I found it made me so hungry I couldn't go on with it.'

The public library was somewhere warm to sit, and scouring the 'situations vacant' pages of local newspapers was a daily – if usually frustrating – thing to do, as was checking the racing pages, if the librarian hadn't removed them to discourage such undesirable activities, as quite a number did. The journalist and writer Paul Johnson recalled that the librarian at his local library in Tunstall in the Potteries, the tyrannical Miss Cartlich, was unsympathetic to the unemployed, who 'had no money – literally not a penny – for any form of entertainment and therefore could only walk the streets aimlessly. The reading room of the public library was thus a winter garden of rest.' But woe betide any man who fell asleep, for then Miss Cartlich would 'wake them up and escort them off the premises, if necessary taking a hand to their collar. "Out, out, out!" she would say. "I'll have no men here snoring in my reading room." If they could stay awake, however, and pretend to be reading, the men were safe.'

Many unemployed men found they developed – or now had the time to indulge – a taste for reading books. 'Thousands used the Public Library for the first time,' averred John Brown who read Shaw's plays, Marx, Engels, 'the philosophers of Greece and Rome' and a great deal of fiction in his local South Shields library. 'It was nothing uncommon to come across men in very shabby clothes kneeling in front of the philosophy or economics shelves.' Jack Jones, a Welsh miner, wrote three articles about unemployment for *Time and Tide* in 1931 in which he maintained that 'people were reading for dear life now that they had no work to go to. I tried to show how the depressed mining communities were trying to read themselves through the Depression, and how this was sending borrowing figures in the libraries such as Pontypridd, where there were six and a half thousand unemployed, up and up by scores of thousands.' However, in Deptford in South London the Pilgrim Trust noticed that when unemployment was high, borrowing from the public libraries declined, since all men's energies were focused on getting work, and to them reading was associated with well-earned leisure.

In Greenwich, E. Wight Bakke found that among those unemployed who obligingly filled in diaries of how they spent their days for him, 'an average of 10.7 hours a week was spent in reading'. While more than half that time was devoted to newspapers and magazines, the rest was taken up by books borrowed from the free public libraries. Most of these were fiction: Bakke found little evidence that the men – and presumably the women either – were particularly interested in reading books on 'Socialism or Trade Unionism or other works on economic and political theory'. But some were: an ex-army officer who had been unable to find other work 'joined the public library and read numerous books. I read no fiction at all, but turned my attention to many other subjects, astronomy, physics, economics, history, photography, psychology, and read books on psychic phenomena, the Yogi culture, and other things. I went to lectures by eminent people of all kinds, statesmen and politicians, with the general idea of getting the world and its affairs in perspective and finding out what was wrong with everything.'

One 'brilliantly successful experiment' was the translation of an act of a Shakespeare play into Tyneside dialect in a Workers' Educational Association (WEA) class, while a young unemployed letterpress operator filled his long days by sitting in the parks, swimming or talking with 'other fellows who are out. I am a member of a library and spend most evenings reading until midnight. I find it the only thing that can take my mind off loneliness, poverty and hunger. My choice varies: Fiction –Priestley, Dell, Orczy, Tolstoy etc. (Russian writers are my favourite.) Educational and interest subjects – philosophy, psychology, travel, Socialism, economics etc.' George Tomlinson read *The Canterbury Tales*, Lamb's *Essays*, Darwin's *Origin of Species*, Wilde's *Ballad of Reading Gaol*, 'or anything that I could get hold of' as he sat on his toolbox at the pit head having volunteered for a weekend repair shift. An unemployed miner in the Rhondda was an avid reader of

Balzac, and it was 'during my dole days' that Donald Kear in the Forest of Dean 'became a compulsive reader. I read anything and everything that came my way, from Jack London and Anatole France to medical dictionaries and odd volumes of electrical engineering encyclopaedias.' Kear also listened to 'weekly talks on the radio addressed to the unemployed by a man called John Hilton'. Hilton, a working-class autodidact with a trade union background, was appointed the first Montagu Burton Professor of Industrial Relations at Cambridge in 1931. He was a prolific journalist and broadcaster with an informed and compassionate interest in the plight of the poor. 'I came to have a great respect and liking for him,' recalled Kear. 'His was the only sympathetic voice the unemployed ever heard. He recommended reading as a pastime for us. "Long way ahead in the future," he said, "someone will want to know where you got your know-how, your handiness with words, and you'll tell 'em you were unemployed in the '30s and you did a lot of reading."'

'DON'T BE DEPRESSED IN A DEPRESSED AREA. GO TO THE PICTURES AND ENJOY LIFE AS OTHERS DO' urged a cinema poster outside the Memorial Hall cinema (named in memory of the dead of the First World War, but known locally as 'the Memo') at the Celynen Collieries and Workingmen's Institute at Newbridge in South Wales. The inter-war years were the great decades of cinema-building, with Egyptian, Graeco-Roman, Byzantium, rococo and baroque extravaganzas gradually giving way to 'dream palaces' that were streamlined and modern, sinuously curved, plate-glass-decorated, Art Deco buildings that seemed to pay homage to Manhattan, to ocean liners – or to TB sanatoria. Many were huge: Green's in Glasgow, built in 1927, could seat more than 4,300, while the Bolton Odeon, which opened in 1937, had 2,534 seats and forty-one employees, including usherettes, doormen, chocolate girls and pageboys as well as the expected projectionists and box-office staff.

Cinema-going remained a popular activity for those without work – though the frequency of their visits might be reduced by shortage of money, despite most cinemas selling sixpenny tickets. The reasons were obvious: it was something to do, somewhere warm to go, and a transport out of the dreary reality to romance, humour, drama, thrills. 'For two and a half hours [the viewer] could live in another world where, invariably, the spirit of adventure was given full play, justice triumphed over injustice, and the hero eventually won through.' On Merseyside, where unemployment was high, a 1934 survey found that 40 per cent of the population went to the cinema once a week and of them about two-thirds went twice. In Brynmawr in South Wales there were two cinemas, and both did good business throughout the 1930s, while in Greenwich those unemployed who were encouraged to keep diaries estimated that on average they would spend 2.6 hours a week at the cinema, usually going to an afternoon matinee when the seats were cheaper. The Carnegie Report on unemployed youth in Glasgow concluded that 'attendance at cinemas is the most important single activity' of those they interviewed, with 80 per cent seeing at least one film a week, and a quarter of those going more frequently. This was not, the report considered, altogether for the good: 'It was perhaps inevitable, but none the less unfortunate, that many acquired a habit of attending the cinemas regardless of the standard of the films . . . The harmful effects of indiscriminate cinema attendance are obvious. Young men may come to accept their experiences vicariously. If their only mental sally into adventure comes while they are sitting in a comfortable seat, the enthusiasm and spirit for personal action will soon disappear.' It was hoped that 'increasing endeavour' would be made by the film industry 'to develop a high standard of artistic appreciation'.

Not all cinemas were of such magnificence as the lavish new 'dream palaces': while the patrons of Tooting in South London might watch their films in a building that was a simulacrum of the Doge's Palace in Venice (with a nod to the cathedral at Burgos), the unemployed in the Rhondda Valley were more likely to have their silver screen set up in a Miners' Institute, or a 'fleapit' or 'bug house' unmodernised since its erection possibly before the First World War – the 'Memo' in Newbridge was an exception, seating seven hundred people and decorated with both Art Nouveau and Art Deco flourishes, and murals depicting 'industrial scenes with miners toiling underground'.

Cinemas in Miners' and other Institutes were run by committees that bargained with the film distributors to get the best prices for the films they wanted to show, kept seat prices down – fourpence was not unusual, and at Mardy Workingmen's Institute in the Rhondda, where unemployment was very high, customers were asked to pay what they could afford – and also kept a close watch over what films the patrons watched. Most favoured films with a social message, such as *Broken Blossoms* (1919), a depiction of slum life, though they also responded to customer demand by showing comedies like the nihilistic (and hugely popular) Marx Brothers' *A Day at the Races* (1937) or Shirley Temple's *Bright Eyes*, which was screened 'twice nightly with matinee showings for adults on Thursday afternoons and Saturdays for children' in October 1935. Moreover, in communities where most social activities – the pub, the billiard hall, the Miners' Institute – were organised exclusively for men and either forbade entry to women or made them entirely unwelcome, the cinema was somewhere a woman could go and enjoy herself away from the confines of the home: though while a number of the films shown at Cwmllynfell Miners' Welfare Hall cinema, for instance, such as the swashbuckling *The Prisoner of Zenda* (1937) or American musicals, were unisex in their appeal, an awful lot were clearly 'boy's own' adventures aimed at a male audience.

In the nineteenth century miners' pay had commonly been docked by a penny or two in the pound to pay for their children's education, and when universal free education was introduced this money was redirected to miners' institutes, which were also partly funded by the colliery owners, and in which many fine libraries were collected. Following the recommendations of the 1920 Sankey Commission into coalmining, a Miners' Welfare Fund was established to provide indoor and outdoor entertainment, financed by a levy on colliery owners, and for the first time on the royalty owners (those who owned the land on which the mines were sunk), as well as mineworkers. The fund was administered by a Miners' Welfare Committee on which representatives of all interests sat. This money was used to fund pit-head baths (despite the fact that, according to evidence given to the Coal Industry Commission, wives regarded it as their duty and privilege to wash their husbands' backs and to see that they had their hot bath before the kitchen fire), build or improve institutes, and provide scholarships and libraries. Only about thirty institutes had a cinema (the jewel in the crown was Tredegar's Workmen's Institute, which had an eight-hundred-seat cinema, a film society and hosted a series of celebrity concerts, with the top-price seats costing three shillings). Some were little more than a collection of huts, but all played an important role in the life of the community, offering evening classes and lectures, concerts, theatres and dances, debating societies, gymnastics, photography laboratories and amateur dramatics, and hosting political and trade union meetings, travelling theatrical and opera companies and *eisteddfodau* (Welsh cultural festivals). This strong ethos of education and improvement as well as entertainment led them to be referred to in South Wales as '*Prifysgol y Glowyr*' (the Miners' University), and influenced the choice of films shown in the cinemas, the books on loan in the libraries, and the periodicals lying around in the reading rooms.

By 1934 there were more than a hundred miners' libraries in the Welsh coalfields, with an average stock of around 3,000 books, though some were much smaller, with a local miner acting as a volunteer librarian one evening a week. Despite the strong religious nonconformism of the 'tin bethels' in the Valleys with their crusade for a better life morally, mentally and socially, and the fierce political and union activism of the 'Little Moscows' of South

Wales, even during the 'red decade' of the 1930s few miners seemed interested in reading about politics or economics. The library committees (Aneurin Bevan headed the one at Tredegar) might acquire the complete works of Lenin or Marx, but those volumes remained on the shelves, while the ones that were most borrowed appear to have been Victorian novels (Mrs Henry Wood was much in demand), detective stories or westerns – though, as Jonathan Rose points out, so few borrowing records for the miners' libraries are extant that it is hard to generalise. An Ynyshir library lent books to three hundred out-of-work miners who read on average eighty-six books a year, whereas a survey of 437 unemployed young men from Cardiff, Newport and Pontypridd revealed that while 57 per cent claimed that reading was one of their most significant leisure activities, only 20 per cent ever visited a library, and only 6 per cent borrowed books. To them, reading meant the daily paper, mostly for sport and horoscopes, or cheap paperback novels exchanged with others in the queue at the Employment Exchange.

The institutes had received their funding from miners' wages, the Miners' Welfare Fund and the local authority, so in the harsh economic conditions of the 1930s, when many young men left the Valleys looking for work, and many of those left behind were unemployed, these all but dried up, and the acquisition budgets of most such libraries became non-existent. Miners' libraries were reduced to issuing public appeals for books, approaching sympathetic public library authorities such as those in Manchester, Bethnal Green or Finsbury in London, all of which sent boxloads of books, or reluctantly ceding their hard-fought-for autonomy and becoming essentially distribution centres for their local public library service. By 1937 many had bought no new books for over a decade, so readers were obliged to read whatever was on the shelves over and over again – and presumably most soon became disheartened by a repetition that echoed so many other dreary repetitions in the lives of the long-term unemployed.

The sports pages, the cinema, football, allotment-tending, pigeon-racing, the kazoo band – all these were traditional working-class leisure activities that in substantial areas of Britain were, by the 1930s, no longer something to do at the end of a working day, a working week, but rather had taken the place of work. What if, as seemed increasingly likely, this was not to be a phase, a transition, but a way of life? The 'idle rich' might be an accepted feature of society, but what about the idle poor – even if their idleness was unsought, regretted, enforced, unafforded? Were such men and women to be regarded as the inevitable human cost of industrial decline, to be left to decline themselves, of no further use, supported at a minimal level by the state and allowed to pass their days as if on an unpunctuated weekend, but without the resources to do so? Or were they the vanguard of a new society in which new technologies and a more efficient form of capitalism would mean that there would simply be less work to do and fewer people needed to do it? In 1934 Havelock Ellis, usually described as a sexologist, predicted, rather as Major Douglas and Ezra Pound had done, 'the four-hour working day as the probable maximum for the future. The day of the proletariat is over. Few workers but skilled ones are now needed. Most of the unemployed of today will perhaps never be employed again. They already belong to an age that is past.' However, as a Vice-President of the Eugenics Education Society, Ellis was hard-pressed to see that it would be a bad thing if the 'single proletarian left in England [was] placed in the Zoological gardens and carefully tended', since, after all, 'the glorification of the proletarian has been the work of the middle-class', and the fact was that the 'lowest stratum of a population which possesses nothing beyond its ability to produce off spring' would be phased out as a matter of economic evolution.

When the film-maker Humphrey Jennings came to make a document-ary for the GPO Film Unit at the end of the 1930s, 'a surrealist vision of industrial England . . . the dwellers in Blake's dark satanic mills reborn in the world of greyhound racing and Marks & Spencers', the film's working title was 'British Workers'. But by the time he had filmed, in Sheffield, Bolton, Manchester and Pontypridd, men walking lurchers, releasing pigeons, playing billiards, drinking in a pub, a kazoo band 'razzing away at "If You Knew Susie"' and later carrying a child dressed as Britannia as they play a jazz version of 'Rule Britannia', a fairground, women watching a puppet show, a ballroom slowly filling with dancers, lions and tigers padding round their cages in Bellevue Zoo, Manchester, the title had been changed to *Spare Time*. The voice-over (spoken by the poet Laurie Lee) intoned: 'Spare time is the time when people can be most themselves,' as the miners' cage descended the coalshaft. A re-evaluation of the whole notion of 'leisure' was clearly overdue. If talking about the unemployed as having leisure was to 'mistake the desert created by the absence of work for the oasis of re-creation', how would it be possible to avoid the apathy that various social commentators confidently identified as the final stage the unemployed would pass through, via resolution, resignation and distress. As a 'rough progression from optimism to pessimism, from pessimism to fatalism'? And if the creation of new jobs was not on the cards, how could the unemployed be encouraged to make the 'right' use of the leisure that would be the pattern of their future?

S.P.B. Mais, in his introduction to *Time to Spare* (1935), was convinced that 'Left to themselves the unemployed can do nothing whatever to occupy their spare time profitably . . . This is where you and I come in . . . we have quite simply to *dedicate* our leisure to the unemployed,' and suggested that this meant giving the unemployed man 'a chance to work [since] playing draughts isn't going to fit him for anything except perhaps the asylum'. Mais was full of ideas for 'work': 'I don't care what it is you set up,' he insisted, 'from a forge for men to work on the anvil to a stamp collecting society. It's all grist to the mill. There cannot be too many interests in an unemployed man's life . . . sell him the best leather at the cheapest possible rates and let him learn how to mend his boots for himself and his family . . . make it possible for him to *buy* [Mais stressed: 'you will have noticed my insistence on the word *buy*. The unemployed do not want *charity*. They prefer to pay to the limit of their capacity to pay'] . . . to buy wood, then encourage him to learn how to make chests of drawers, wardrobes, chairs and other necessities of household furniture . . . to buy material and learn to make his own suits.' Give the wife and family of an unemployed man a holiday, or imitate 'the young Cotswold farmer who . . . gave up his summer to entertaining relays of school children from Birmingham . . . This principle of adoption should be extended to towns, and prosperous towns in the South like Brighton should adopt derelict towns in the North like Jarrow.' But Mais recognised that this help should involve neither 'charity (in the wrong sense) nor patronage' (though, however well-meaning he may have been, the latter seemed rather evident). What was needed was either for 'you and I' to 'join a local occupational club', or if there wasn't one, 'get one going . . . all that is required to start with is a disused barn, hut or shop and the goodwill of, say, a dozen unemployed men to pay a penny for the privilege of membership'.

Some initiatives were essentially social clubs, organised locally and spontaneously, usually financed by the members, and intended to be money-making activities. Some, like those in Wales (where drinking in pubs on the Sabbath was not permitted) had licensed bars, and most had a billiards table and a wireless which supplied continuous background music. Such clubs in cities tended to be in the poorer districts. In Liverpool there were reputed to be nearly 150, most housed in empty shops, cellars or basements. Apart from the ubiquitous billiards table, raffles were organised, 'the glittering prize quite often being a box of groceries with a bottle of beer or whisky for the man', card games and other 'petty gambling games – sometimes not so petty – are played from morning to night'. Many clubs organised a football team, and some a 'Wembley Club' into which members would pay a sixpence a week so that every other year when the international football match between England and Scotland was played at Wembley 'a charabanc is hired and club members attend the match and go sight-seeing in London'. At Christmas an outing to the local pantomime would be organised, and 'since some of the clubs are not lacking in the spirit of service to others, an old folk's treat or free film show for the kiddies of the locality is occasionally provided'.

There were, as Mais recognised, already a number of 'occupational clubs' in areas of high unemployment. The Society of Friends had started an educational settlement at Maes-yr-Haf in the Rhondda in 1927, and another in Brynmawr the following year. Mais spoke approvingly of a club in Lincoln where 'unemployed engineers cook the dinners for their own nursery school, mak[e] furniture for the Orphanages, toys for imbecile children, and invalid chairs for the decrepit aged', and still found the energy for 'Greek dancing' in the evening. This was probably the one started in 1927 by the WEA, which had been founded in 1903 to 'link learning with labour', with the motto 'An enquiring mind is sufficient qualification'.

The spread of such centres had been given a boost in January 1932 when the Prince of Wales, the (briefly) future King Edward VIII, who was patron of the National Council of Social Service (NCSS), speaking at a meeting at the Albert Hall called upon the British people to face the challenge of unemployment 'as a national opportunity for voluntary social service', and 'refusing to be paralyzed by the size of the problem, break it into little pieces'. The response was heartening. By that autumn over seven hundred schemes were in operation in various parts of the country, and by mid-1935 the number had grown to over a thousand centres for men and more than three hundred for women, with a total membership of over 150,000. Many provided occupational opportunities as well as the usual facilities for billiards, dancing and reading. In the depressed areas of Lancashire there were 114 centres for men and thirty-five for women. There were nine in Glasgow, the same number in Liverpool and twenty-one in Cardiff. In the Rhondda there were between thirty and forty clubs which offered activities ranging from choral and operatic societies to mining outcrop coal. In Manchester, where there were some thirty centres for the unemployed (seventeen providing facilities for men to repair their own and their families' shoes), an orchestra was formed among unemployed musicians which in May 1933 gave a recital on the BBC North Regional Service, while Gladys Langford, a generally rather discontented North London schoolteacher, went to Queen Mary's Hall, Bloomsbury to hear the British Symphony Orchestra, 'a body of unemployed musicians conducted by Charles Hambourg. He is a stocky little man with a bulging bottom much accentuated by a very short lounge jacket. Enjoyed the music.'

Many clubs used church halls or schoolrooms, which might only be available for a few hours a week, but in some cases disused premises were offered, perhaps a local church, shop, pub or empty factory, or in the case of Salford a fire and police station, and the unemployed spent time painting and equipping them as places in which they would want to spend time.

Some of the clubs received help from their local authority, or Lord Mayor's Fund, others from voluntary social service agencies under the umbrella of the NCSS, the Pilgrim Trust, the Society of Friends, the WEA, which also allowed the unemployed to attend its classes free of charge, or the National Unemployed Workers' Movement (NUWM). Others were 'adopted' by local industrial or other concerns, though they tended to manage them undemocratically, with little input from the members, a situation that 'seems to have been based on the theory that unemployed men were unfitted to take any responsibility for their own Clubs and that the Management Committee, by definition, knew what was good for the men better than the men knew it themselves'.

There were five residential centres, including Hardwick Hall in County Durham, which opened in October 1934, and provided classes in upholstery and bookbinding as well as more usual crafts; The Beeches, Bournville, which was solely for women (courses there only lasted for two weeks rather than the usual six, since it was presumed that women could not afford to be away from home for any longer); and Coleg Harlech, an established adult education college which regarded itself as the Welsh equivalent of Ruskin College, Oxford. In October 1933 the Coleg started running residential courses for the unemployed offering a more academic curriculum rather than crafts and practical skills.

The various organisations received small – if any – grants from the government, usually via the NCSS or the Scottish Council for Community Service. By March 1935 the Ministry of Labour had tipped in £80,000, while voluntary donations totalled more than £125,000. However, while Thomas Jones spoke of 'trying to fob off the unemployed with a miserable grant of a few thousand pounds to Ellis' show [Captain Lionel Ellis was chairman of the NCSS]', the voluntary schemes appeared to value their independence from government funding – and control.

Despite the stringency of its financial support, the government rarely failed to instance the success of such schemes in dealing with the 'residual problem' of the long-term unemployed. And there were many successes: on Clydebank, where one club had 'a membership of seven hundred and twenty three and a waiting list of two hundred', and where men were 'split into fifty groups, occupied in motor mechanics, dress-making, photography, shorthand, music, swimming, boot repairing, metal work, woodwork and wireless'; a Boys' Club in Barnsley where members took 'a nightly run'; Blackburn, which had its own parliament, or Barnard Castle, where traditional quilt-making was being revived.

The Reverend Northcott described a club in Darwen in Lancashire, where only twenty-eight of the sixty cotton mills were still working. It was housed, 'ironically enough, in a building which had been used as a Labour Exchange ... The motto is "Occupation of Hand and Brain".' Facilities were provided for 'cobbling of all descriptions, woodwork classes, discussion circles, lectures and concerts. Twenty men a day pursue the art of rug making. There is first-aid instruction, a physical instruction group, and singing lessons given in a room in the fire station. Men have gone to camp, played cricket regularly, and have learned to swim.'

Since, according to the vicar, the 'Lancashire woman who has gone to the mill has not been a great housewife', a women's centre was 'helping its members in the management of their families' food and clothes', and a number of the occupational centres had women's sections. 'Members bring old clothes and are shown how to remake them ... The men have made wheelbarrows out of old boxes and wheels made out of circular discs. Jig-saw puzzles were made out of magazine pictures and three-ply wood.' In a neighbouring centre an unemployed weaver of fine cloth 'modelled two vases of fine shape' out of old gramophone records he had melted down, 'and felt immediately that he was in the line of genuine potters'. It cost a penny a week to belong to such a club, and this entitled a member to vote for a committee which drew up the programme of activities.

Spennymoor Settlement in County Durham was started in 1931 by Bill Farrell, who had studied at Toynbee Hall, the original example of a settle-ment house founded by Henrietta and Samuel Barnett in Whitechapel in the East End of London in 1884 with support from various Oxford colleges. There the privileged came to live and work among the poor, in the words of Samuel Barnett, 'To learn as much as to teach: to receive as much as to give.' Funded by the Pilgrim Trust, Spennymoor was open to all (though initially there was suspicion that Bill Farrell's title, 'warden', meant 'warder') and offered classes in such things as carpentry, shoe repairing, elementary psychology and the British Constitution. It instigated a debating society, a male voice choir, a children's centre, a needlework class for women taught by Farrell's wife, Betty, and a public lending library, also on her initiative. The Farrells' interest in art and drama stimulated a sketching club and a play-reading group, with scenery made in the carpentry classes. The centre put on its first play in 1934, largely organised by a group of miners' wives, a theatre was built which opened in 1939, and soon Spennymoor was dubbed 'The Pitman's Academy' for its prodigious success in helping its members win scholarships to Oxford and adult colleges. Sid Chaplin, a very successful novelist in the 1950s, honed his writing skills at Spennymoor, as did the miner Norman Cornish his artistic talents at the 'wonderful' Spennymoor sketching club. The Prince of Wales paid a visit in December 1934.

'Ashington, pop. 40,000. Mining town mostly built in the early part of this century. Dreary rows a mile long. Ashpits and mines down the middle of the streets,' was how the 1937 *Shell Guide to Northumberland & Durham* described this Durham town. Not the sort of place to which to take a scenic detour, but some of those – employed and unemployed – who lived in those 'dreary rows' had a yearning for the finer things. There was no public library, but there was a Harmonic Hall, built by the miners so that string bands and brass bands had somewhere to play, as could a children's orchestra with 'violins for about eighty kiddies', and there was a football pitch that doubled as a greyhound track. There was also a thriving branch of the WEA. Harry Wilson, who could have opted to learn music or drama there, instead plumped for 'Experimental Evolution', which took the students out into the surrounding area to poke 'around in ponds and look for flints'. When the course was over, he and some friends felt they were 'at a dead end again so we started on Art'. Robert Lyon ARCA, Master of Painting and Lecturer in Fine Art at Armstrong College, Newcastle, then part of Durham University, was invited by 'a number of men . . . all associated with the pits', to discuss the possibility of forming an art appreciation group in Ashington. After a lecture by Lyon at which he showed them black-and-white slides of Renaissance paintings and classical Greek sculptures, the twenty-four men and two girls (who didn't last long, since 'there's a strict understanding in mining districts where women fit in and where men fit in'), made it clear that that was not what they wanted: they 'wanted a way, if possible, of seeing for themselves'. So Lyon agreed (entirely against the spirit of the WEA, which was 'all theory: nothing which could possibly be interpreted as being of any use for making a living could be taught') to teach the men how to draw and paint, setting them homework each week to produce a picture on a subject like 'The Dawn', 'Deluge' or 'The Hermit', on cardboard or whatever material they could find.

Lyon took his class to look at watercolours in Newcastle Gallery, and in February 1936, thanks to the generosity of the daughter of the chairman of the P&O shipping line, Helen Sutherland, who lived nearby in Alnwick and was a discerning collector of modernist art, to London to see the Chinese exhibition at the Royal Academy, and visit the Tate and other city sights, ending up with a cream tea and madrigals in the Hampstead home of the owner of Kettle's Yard Gallery in Cambridge, 'a celebrated exercise in applied tastefulness'.

In 1936 the Ashington Group held its first exhibition of ninety-seven paintings and several engravings in Newcastle. The 'experiment' received favourable notices; soon the art world (the Surrealist painter Julian Trevelyan and the post-impressionist Clive Bell in particular) began to take notice, and the group was mentioned in a Penguin survey of art in England. Inspired by Ashington's success, other art appreciation groups started to spring up, the British Institute of Adult Education mounted three exploratory 'Art for the People' exhibitions, and in April 1937 the Ashington Group contributed some pictures to what the art historian Anthony Blunt called 'the most important event of the year from the point of view of English Art', organised by the Artists International Association.

'Unprofessional Painting' was the title of an exhibition held at Gateshead in October 1938 to which the Ashington Group sent work. 'They Paint Their Own Lives' was another, held in Mansfield, Nottingham, six months later, and indeed the corpus of work did depict 'ordinary life': a miner reading a newspaper, a Bedlington terrier – 'Miners are keen on Bedlingtons,' explained a critic in *The Listener* – miners with their pigeons, playing dominoes, having Sunday dinner with their families, poaching. But most were of men at work: down the pits hacking coal, in the pit-head baths, eating their 'bait' (packed lunch). In the early days the men sold their pictures for a pound or thirty shillings, 'to get money for painting materials', and found themselves regarded as representatives of the British 'social realist' school. But 'mining pictures would not be welcome to hang on the walls at home; landscapes would be considered more suitable. The women had had enough of mining dominating their lives, and frequently, when there were several workers in the house, reducing them to slaves. Many women were never able to get to bed except at weekends and just dozed in a chair to fit in with the different shifts.'

Such voluntary efforts to help the unemployed (and integrate them into the life of the community, since most clubs and classes were open to all, in work or not) might be rightly admired for what they achieved, but there was a suspicion expressed by the trade union movement that occupational centres would produce semi-trained craftsmen who could be used to undercut existing wage rates, and in some areas pressure was put on unemployed union members not to join them. Others regarded the occupational clubs as little more than opium for the masses, handed down by a government that had no policies to end unemployment. Wal Hannington of the NUWM sneered at 'how craftily the ruling class, by evoking the sentiment of charity, have sought to cover up their sins and omissions in the treatment of the unemployed', and pointed out that the 'honoured gentlemen' of the NCCS had never joined in the demand for the abolition of the Means Test or the restoration of benefit cuts. Frank Forster, an intermittently unemployed casual labourer from Saltney in Cheshire, thought that 'the idea behind . . . the BBC broadcasting of morning talks to Unemployed Clubs . . . seems to be an attempt to keep those who attend the clubs quiet. To dope them . . . They hand out . . . what will keep them out of mischief. They must place their existence on a charitable basis, provide them with voluntarily contributed clubs and games etc . . . All this to prevent them from falling into the hands of Communists.' George Orwell was of much the same mind, arguing in *The Road to Wigan Pier* that the centres were 'simply a device to keep the unemployed quiet and give them an illusion that something is being done for them', though he conceded that what he considered the 'rubbish' the centres offered was probably better for the unemployed man 'than for years upon end he should do absolutely *nothing*'.

The educational and occupational activities at the unemployment centres may have seemed like splendid opportunities to those offering them, but from those on the receiving end, enthusiasm was not always so evident. Since club leaders were poorly paid, suitable people could be hard to find, and a great deal depended on their vitality and organisational skills. Such activities as the centres offered tended to appeal more to the young than to the older long-term unemployed, and class numbers dropped in some districts. 'What we unemployed could do with is a little less of education and a little more of entertainment,' suggested one of their nameless number in a letter to the *Spectator* in March 1933, while the anguish of an out-of-work miner permeates a documentary film made in 1932, when unemployment stood at over two million: 'We can do physical jerks, grow cabbages until we're blue in the face, but it's not paid work. It's just killing time. It's not the real work that we want.'

EIGHT

The Hard Road Travelled

The British working man, employed or unemployed, is very conservative in his allegiance to law, order and tradition. He hates the idea of a Red Revolution, which he knows would make an awful mess ... Communist visitors in the distressed areas get short shrift from men standing unemployed round disused pit-heads.

Sir Philip Gibbs, *Ordeal in England* (1937)

No saviour from on high delivers,
No trust have we in prince or peer.
Our *own* right hand the chains must sever ...

From the third verse of 'The Internationale'

On the first day of 1932 the son and heir of the 7th Earl Fitzwilliam attained his majority. To celebrate, beacons were lit on the hills surrounding the family's magnificent house, Wentworth. Built in the 1720s, the largest privately owned house in Britain, it had a room for every day of the year, and five miles of corridors. In front of the façade, which was the longest in Europe, the Elsecar Colliery Brass Band struck up, and a crowd 40,000 strong joined in singing 'Londonderry Air' and 'We Won't Come Home Till Morning'. And when the birthday boy, Lord Milton, drove with his father in the first car of a fleet of yellow Rolls-Royces on a ceremonial tour of his estates, the eight-mile route was lined with estate workers and the men who worked in the Fitzwilliams' mines (on short time, given the economic climate) and their families, all waving and cheering, delighted that they had each been given a day's paid holiday and a freshly issued ten-shilling note. At various stops en route Lord Milton would open proceedings by cutting a ribbon with a gold pocket knife his father had given him for his birthday, and at the New Stubbin pit the Secretary of the Yorkshire Miners' Association stepped forward to thank the Earl and applaud him as 'the finest idealistic employer in the country today', a mine-owner who had so arranged things that not a single man had been dismissed despite the slump, and shifts had been arranged so the men received 'the fullest benefits of the Unemployment Act'.

The Wentworth miners might have doffed their flat caps and have had reason to feel grateful towards their employers, but in the 1930s most coalminers – the 'sort of grimy caryatid[s] upon whose shoulders nearly everything that is *not* grimy is supported', according to George Orwell, had both particular grievances and a particular militancy. The 1926 General Strike left a bitter legacy for men working in the Welsh Valleys, the Scottish, Durham and East Midlands coalfields, most of whom stayed on strike for months after the nine-day TUC strike collapsed. As a result many were blacklisted by the colliery owners, and never worked again. Wages were cut, hours extended and working conditions deteriorated. Employment in the coal industry fell consistently, from 218,000 in 1926 to 136,000 in 1932, and across Wales as a whole unemployment averaged 39 per cent.

At a time when over 40 per cent of the miners were out of work in the Yorkshire coalfields, a local headmaster would reputedly admonish pupils who answered his question, 'Now then, boy, what are you going to do when you leave school?' 'We're going to pit, sir,' with ''Cos tha' strong in the arm and weak in the head.' Coalmining remained probably the most dangerous occupation in Britain. A West Lothian pit was known locally as 'the Dardanelles pit. It was named that because of the high accident rate – they compared it with the slaughter at the Dardanelles' in the First World War. There was widespread bitterness about the lack of compliance – since compliance invariably cost money – that many mine-owners accorded to health and safety regulations, and in the early hours of 22 September 1934 one of the worst mining disasters in British history occurred at Gresford colliery near Wrexham in North Wales, when an explosion ripped through part of the mine known as the Dennis section during the night shift. Although six miners managed to crawl to safety, three men were killed in the rescue attempt, and on the following night, Sunday, 23 September, it was agreed that the mine should be sealed with the dead miners entombed inside. A further violent explosion a couple of days later killed a surface worker: the disaster had claimed a total of 266 lives.

At the subsequent inquiry, Sir Stafford Cripps agreed to represent the mineworkers' union *pro bono*. Despite the Labour lawyer's relentless, technically informed questioning (Cripps had read chemistry at University College London, since he considered the lab conditions there to be far superior to those at either Oxford or Cambridge, before turning to law) in pursuit of his contention that safety had been sacrificed in the pursuit of profit, it was hard to establish what precisely had caused a build-up of lethal methane gas which had ignited, particularly since the mine-owners refused to allow the sealed section to be opened for inspection. While the report that the Chief Inspector of Mines, Sir Henry Walker, laid before Parliament in January 1937 singled out no one – neither the colliery management, the firemen who worked down the mine, the shot-firers whose job it was to blow up the coal face so the miners could get at the coal to be hewn, nor the inspectors – as having been criminally negligent, he concluded that nor had any of them performed their duties satisfactorily. Yet when charges were brought in the courts by the bereaved against the company and its officials, most of the cases were either dismissed or withdrawn, and no one was convicted of any wrongdoing.

The Gresford pit disaster provoked nationwide sympathy, gifts (over half a million pounds were raised) and unease among many that until the mines were taken out of private hands the catalogue of accidents and disregard for safety would continue, as would the mining industry's generally poor industrial relations and sluggish productivity.

The previous September, unemployed coalminers had marched from South Wales to Bristol to lobby the TUC meeting there, and in September 1932 a contingent from Wales was among the eighteen from all over Britain that marched on London in what the organisers, the NUWM, called the 'Great National Hunger March of the Unemployed Against the Means Test', which culminated in a rally in Hyde Park. The NUWM claimed there were 100,000 unemployed in the park on 27 October, while the Metropolitan Police estimated the number at somewhere between 10,000 and 25,000.

This 'great march' was the largest to date, but by no means the first of the frequent protests by the unemployed since the effects of the Depression had first begun to bite in 1920. As well as numerous local demonstrations, the NUWM organised six national marches between 1922 and 1936, gathering contingents from all over the country to march to London with their demand for 'work or full maintenance at trade union rates'. 'If history is to be truly recorded,' wrote Wal Hannington, 'our future historians must include this feature of the "Hungry Thirties".' To Hannington the marches were a rebuttal of the charge – or, in the case of such proto-sociologists as the Pilgrim Trust survey team or E. Wight Bakke, the sympathetic observation – that the unemployed were apathetic, that they 'quietly suffered their degradation and poverty' despite the evident fact that 'they were hungry; their wives and children were hungry'.

In March 1930, with the number of registered unemployed standing at over 2.5 million, over a thousand men left Scotland, the Durham coalfields, Northumberland, Plymouth, Yorkshire, Lancashire, the Nottingham coalfields, the Potteries, South Wales, the Midlands and Kent to trudge, most of the way on foot, to the capital, where they were joined by the London workless. For the first time women from the depressed textile areas of Lancashire and Yorkshire made up a special – separate – contingent, in the hope that the female Minister of Labour, Margaret Bondfield, might afford their case a sympathetic hearing. This was not to be, and the only success that what Hannington called the 'raiding parties' had was to storm the Ministry of Health, lock themselves in and address the crowds in Whitehall below, until they were forcibly ejected.

In the days after the formation of the National Government in August 1931, protest had escalated, often ending in pitched battles between the unemployed and the police, with the protesters reported as having thrown stones and hammer heads, and attempting to pull the police from their horses, while the police allegedly laid about the protesters with batons. By the end of the year over thirty different towns and cities had seen clashes between the police and unemployed demonstrators. 'This "cuts" business may bring the Empire down,' predicted Samuel Rich, a London teacher who had spent time in September 1931 working out his family's annual budget in anticipation that 'JRM [Ramsay MacDonald] will reduce all *teachers*' salaries by 15% by Order in Council'. Philip Snowden, who had translated his job as Chancellor into the National Government (until the election in October 1931), announced in his budget on 10 September that not only unemployment insurance benefit would be slashed by 10 per cent, but so would the pay of teachers, the police and the armed forces.

Articles had started to appear in the *Manchester Guardian* in the 1930–31 school year highlighting the plight of out-of-work teachers, and it was not long before suggestions were being made that the already very small number of married women teachers might be 'let go'. Although 10,000 teachers marched through the streets of London in protest on 11 September 1931 (members of what Hannington referred to triumphantly as 'the black-coated proletariat . . . embarking on a new experience, marching through the streets carrying banners'), Samuel Rich was appalled at what he regarded as the supine acquiescence of his profession. 'The "L[ondon] T[eacher]" and other teachers' papers all sickening today. The 10% cut is a victory! A victory! What *lice*! I hear that only 218 London schoolmasters voted to be absent yesterday after the meeting. 218! – Bah!'.

As well as demonstrations and clashes with the police over the following months there was one response that was unprecedented – and more disturbing to the government than that of the 'black-coated proletariat' – the incident that Samuel Rich thought 'might bring the Empire down', and which gave an added twist to fears about Britain's stability at the moment of acute economic crisis. 'The Atlantic Fleet has been recalled owing to dissatisfaction among the sailors,' Rich reported. '*They'll* get redress tho' as they are at the right end of the guns.' The largest ships of the North Atlantic Fleet had been gathering in the Cromarty Firth for their annual autumn exercises when the news of the cuts came through – not from official sources such as the Admiralty Board, but piecemeal via newspaper reports and rumours. The cuts were not only swingeing, they were not equitable, and bore most heavily on the lower ranks, as an across-the-board cut of a shilling a day would mean only 3 per cent off the pay of a Lieutenant Commander, while an Able Seamen between the ages of twenty-two and twenty-five would suffer a reduction of 25 per cent. This, a senior officer immediately realised, was 'perfectly absurd'. Six shillings week less money would mean real hardship to the men's families: furniture would be repossessed, clothes and shoes would not be replaced, some families might be evicted, others go short of food. Alan Drage, a Lieutenant Commander on board HMS *Valiant*, was never able to forget 'the queue of dismayed sailors outside my cabin door, each brandishing a sheet of paper covered with elaborate and meticulous calculations, which were explained to me in the utmost detail, each interview concluding, "You see, Sir, I can't possibly manage on this; what am I going to do?"'

In the canteens, which were for the lower orders only, discontent was growing: Len Wincott, an Able Seaman aboard the cruiser HMS *Norfolk*, jumped on a table and called for a strike 'like the miners', but since setting out on a march to London didn't make any sense, it would have to be passive resistance, a sit-down strike. Seamen had long been denied any effective channels of complaint such as a trade union, and were forbidden to communicate directly with their MP to express any grievances about the navy that they might have. But of course any mass resistance by His Majesty's Forces was mutiny – though none of the sailors used that word – in this case 'mutiny not accompanied by violence', but mutiny nevertheless, for which the punishment was death. If the seamen were anxious not to label their actions mutiny, nor was the Admiralty: the Royal Navy was the symbol of Britain's prestige around the world, and rarely had that prestige been more at risk, with an acute financial crisis, a run on gold, and foreign anxieties about the stability and resolve of the British government. The words used were 'disturbance' and 'unrest'. The National Government approached newspaper editors requesting them not to mention Invergordon at this sensitive time for the country. But Ritchie Calder, then a young journalist on the *Daily Herald*, did not feel constrained by such discretion, and the *Herald* ran the story.

On Tuesday, 15 September at 8 a.m. most of the stokers on the battle-ship HMS *Valiant* refused the order to sail from Invergordon on the edge of the Cromarty Firth to take part in exercises in the North Sea, and the crews aboard the battleships *Rodney* and *Nelson* and the battle cruiser *Hood* followed suit, all refusing to move. Over the following thirty-six hours most of the 12,000 men on the twelve ships at Invergordon refused orders.

The Admiralty appeared to be completely out of touch with the situation, taking hours to reply to any communications from the officers, reiterating that in effect every man must do his duty, and it was not until mid-after-noon on Wednesday, 16 September that the order came that ships were to return to their home ports and cases of hardship would be looked into. The strikers' resolve began to crumble, and by that night the ships started to put to sea. The nearest Britain ever came to a Battleship *Potemkin* moment in modern times was over. There were those in the Admiralty, and indeed some naval officers, who portrayed the strike as a mutiny and put it down to 'Bolshevik agitators' – a charge that was perhaps easier to sustain when Able Seaman Wincott, discharged from the navy, joined a front organisation of the Communist Party which capitalised on the 'mutiny' and his claims to have 'led' it. Another leader, Fred Copeman, who was not a member of the Communist Party at the time, became a fellow traveller and active in the unemployed movement and later in Spain. But although twenty-four ratings were discharged – though not until after the 1931 general election – the Admiralty was unable to establish that the events were anything more than the spontaneous actions of a large number of deeply disaffected men, denied any legitimate channels of complaint or redress and faced with a seemingly uncomprehending, unsympathetic and unresponsive Admiralty Board. On 21 September 1931, the same day Britain came off the Gold Standard, the government announced that there would be no pay cuts of more than 10 per cent.

Like the previous national marches and many of the local demonstra-tions that preceded it, the fourth national march which got underway on 26 September 1932, when a contingent of 250 unemployed men left Glasgow, had been organised by the NUWM, which had been set up in 1921 to mobilise unemployed discontent. There was little competition. The Labour Party largely accepted the view, even after 1931, that the government was doing its best in extraordinarily difficult circumstances, while the TUC (whose membership had fallen from 5.5 million in 1925 to under 4.5 million by 1932) was essentially concerned with the interests of the employed, resisting pay cuts and short-time working. The unions' contribution in the early 1930s was confined to mouthing statements 'strongly' condemning cuts in benefit payments and making 'emphatic (verbal) protests' at government in-action. 'Their line was "No illegality, wait, vote for the Labour Party," recalled an unemployed Kirkcaldy man, 'and Pat Devine . . . who was a real agitator . . . says "What is the workers supposed to do? Starve until we get a Labour Government?"'

In 1932, after more than a decade of high unemployment, the TUC began to consider a scheme for 'unemployed associations'. By 1934 such associations numbered 123, with a total membership of around 5,000, but they were essentially local initiatives, with no national TUC guidance or support until 1935, when the TUC offered to pay the expenses of union officials who were prepared to visit associations within their areas 'to stimulate and advise them'.

The NUWM had been established initially as an umbrella group to bring together various district councils for the unemployed which had been active in protests against post-war unemployment, the cessation of the ex-servicemen's 'donation' and what were considered other iniquities. Wal Hannington, the national organiser, was a skilled toolmaker who had been a prominent member of the shop stewards' movement in the engineering trade during the First World War, and Harry McShane, the NUWM leader in Scotland, was also an engineer. Both were founder members of the Communist Party of Great Britain (CPGB), as were many of the activists in the movement. While the NUWM's slogan was 'Work or Full Maintenance at Trade Union Rates of Pay' (which meant in practice thirty-six shillings a week for an unemployed man and his wife; five shillings for each child up to the age of sixteen; a rent allowance of up to fifteen shillings a week plus one hundredweight of coal or its equivalent in gas; thirty shillings for a single person over eighteen, or fifteen shillings if they were aged sixteen to eighteen), all members were required to take an oath 'never to cease from active strife until capitalism is abolished'.

Although a member of the CPGB himself, Wal Hannington was always anxious to distance the movement from the Communist Party and insist on its autonomy. On occasion resolutions would be passed at the NUWM's national conference reaffirming this, and repudiating any notion that the NUWM was in any way an auxiliary of the CP – though there was some substance in the labour movement's charge that any links with the Communists were concealed so as not to alienate Labour and TUC support. Moreover, however much the Communist Party might hope that the unemployed would provide, if not the vanguard for revolution, then its footsoldiers, the vast majority of those who went on the marches did so for tangible, short-term aims: to get a better deal for the unemployed from the existing state.

It is hard to get accurate figures for how many joined the NUWM, since most records come either from the movement itself or from the CPGB: some historians claim that it mobilised 'hundreds of thousands of people', while others dismiss it as remaining 'a minority movement'. One of those who helped organise the Scottish contingent on the march in 1932, and went himself in 1934, Finlay Hart, an unemployed ship-builder, recalled, 'It was as natural as being at work and being a trade unionist, being unemployed and being in the NUWM ... At the time of the '32 march to London the membership of the Clydebank branch of the NUWM would be in hundreds. There were collectors that stood at the Labour Exchange ... There were regular meetings outside the Labour Exchange. Members were recruited there.'

The unemployed signed on on Wednesday and were paid on Friday. So Harry McShane and his comrades 'went always on a Wednesday or a Friday to the Labour Exchange. And we could get a good crowd at the Labour Exchange and hold a meeting on top o' a chair. And from there we organ-ised all our marches and activities.' 'Being a member of the NUWM wasn't a necessary qualification for going on the March,' but Finlay Hart 'couldn't imagine any being on the March that wouldnae had been a member of the NUWM'. Yet in fact nine or ten of the Clydebank contingent of forty-two were not members of the NUWM. Isa Porte, who went on several marches in Scotland, 'wasn't a member myself of the NUWM but I think a lot of the people I marched with would be in it. I wouldnae think there were very many of them in political parties. There would be some in the Communist party, and then there would be Labour Party people. But the majority weren't politically committed in that way. It was just a question of being unemployed and they wanted to do something about it.'

With unemployment at an unprecedented two and a half million, or some 20 per cent of the insured workforce, the 1932 March was the largest so far. It was preceded by months of continuing unrest. Although the NUWM had enjoyed a certain amount of success in opposing the harshest application of the Means Test in some areas of high unemployment and had succeeded in raising the rates of relief benefits by some Public Assistance Committees, a demand for an end to the Means Test in Birkenhead on Merseyside had erupted in a week of protests, bans and counter-protests.

An estimated 8,000 unemployed men marched in a line over a mile long to the PAC offices with their demands. During the ensuing battles between police and demonstrators, stones and bricks were hurled, iron railings torn up, windows smashed and shops looted, batons wielded and police horses charged. Dozens of arrests were made, police reinforcements had to be drafted in from across the Mersey in Liverpool, and thirty-seven demonstrators needed hospital treatment, while seven police were injured, three of them seriously.

In Belfast the next month there was a demonstration by some 2,000 unemployed men demanding better pay for relief work which soon developed into running battles between the police and demonstrators, culminating in the police opening fire on the crowds, killing two men, and having to call on the troops to restore order.

The logistics of the 1932 march were formidable: accommodation had to be found in 188 towns along the route, which was modified in the light of experience of previous marches to try to ensure that the marchers passed through places where they were most likely to be welcomed. Wherever possible reception committees would gather to meet the marchers and march into town with them, provide food, accommodation and entertainment paid for by money raised in advance, and wave them on their way the next morning. St Albans, a prosperous cathedral city twenty miles north of London provided hospitality for thirty-eight women marchers who were met on the road from Luton, escorted into town, accommodated and fed at the Trade Union Club. A concert was laid on to entertain them, and a rally held in the market square to stiffen their resolve. A cobbler took in any shoes that needed repairs, while someone else did the marchers' washing. The women left the next morning with a packet of sandwiches for the road, shouting, 'Unite with us to smash the National Government!' to the citizens of St Albans. Mrs Paisley, a sixty-three-year-old woman from Burnley with sixteen children and twenty-three grandchildren who had suffered much under the Means Test, proclaimed that she 'had had that much good food on the march that I don't want to go home'.

Others were less fortunate: if nothing else could be found, marchers were obliged to seek a bed for the night at the local workhouse (now known as the Institution), where managers had been instructed to accommodate them in casual wards and treat them as tramps or vagrants, which meant searching the men, removing their possessions, insisting on them having a bath while their clothes were disinfected if necessary, locking them in for the night, feeding them a 'spike' diet of two slices of bread and margarine and tea, and refusing to allow them to leave until 9 a.m.

on the second day after their admission, by which time they were supposed to have done whatever work was required to 'earn' their keep. Not all work-house managers insisted on all these conditions: Coventry Council, which had shown 'weakness' in 1930 when it put the marchers up in a school and paid for food provided by the Co-op, was warned that it would be surcharged if that were to happen again.

There were skirmishes along the road, usually over what the marchers were expected to put up with at some workhouses (the Lancashire marchers were seriously batoned by the police at a workhouse in Stratford-upon-Avon, and arrived in Hyde Park heavily bandaged) or restrictions put on their right to hold meetings. Harry McShane, who was in charge of the Scottish contingent, made it a practice that 'if we were banned from marching along a street, we always went up and down it twice'. Some of the Scottish marchers had come from as far away as Dundee, an eighty-mile walk to Glasgow, where they mustered before setting off on the long march south. The men would march on average for twenty-two miles a day, stopping every hour for a ten-minute rest; the cook's lorry would go ahead and 'dish out a good big lunch, usually stew'. Wal Hannington made an effort to march for a stretch with each contingent. 'He loved to lead a big body of men singing. He used to march at the head of the Scots singing "McGregor's Gathering" and get them all waving their caps on top of their sticks – with the Welsh it was "Land of my Fathers".' Most of the contingents had a band which marched all the way to London with flutes and drums, and sometimes cymbals and triangles too. 'Flautists – you cannae stop them . . . they would have played all the way if you'd let them.' The marchers liked to sing as they trudged along too, and the Scots had their own song:

> From Scotland we're marching,
> From shipyard, mill and mine.
> Our banners raised on high
> We toilers are in line.
> We are a determined band,
> Each with his weapon in his hand.
> We are the Hunger Marchers
> Of the Proletariat.

Tom Ferns recalled the unemployed protesters marching through the grounds of Holyrood Palace in Edinburgh, 'with the Maryhill Flute Band . . . leading the contingent and it was playing Connolly's *Rebel Song*, so that was quite an astonishing event going through the Royal territory'. He thought that the songs the marchers sang 'were very simple. Sometimes something simple can explain a situation better than something a bit more complicated,' and instanced songs like:

> Mary had a little lamb,
> Its fleece was white as snow.
> And everywhere that Mary went
> The lamb was sure to go
> Shouting out the battle cry for freedom.
> Hurrah for Mary, hurrah for the lamb,
> Hurrah for the Bolshie boys that don't give a damn.

The Brighton contingent added a further verse:

> Ramsay [MacDonald] had a little lamb
> Whose feet were black as soot,
> Shouting out the battle cry of TREASON.

Some of the women sang (to the tune of 'Oh why are we waiting') 'Oh why are we marching?' and answered in the last line, 'The reason is the Means Test.' Other marchers sang 'The Red Flag' repeatedly. While the Greenock contingent on the Edinburgh March in 1933 sang 'a Russian tune, *Budenny's Cavalry March* . . . the *Red Flag* ["The people's flag is deepest red/It shrouded oft our martyred dead/And ere their limbs grew stiff and cold/Their hearts' blood dyed its every fold"] [it] was a very, very kind o' hymn thing. It was a bit slow and it wasnae much use for marching.'

But 'they [presumably the organisers] were strict about what we sang'. Emily Swankie and the women she was marching with 'were stopped singing one night because it was the wrong type of song – *Land of Hope and Glory*! Someone started to sing it and just because it was a good tune, we all joined in, and the woman came over and said "Just stop that. We don't want that."' It was the same with 'Pack Up Your Troubles in Your Old Kit Bag'. One of the Scottish organisers, Peter Kerrigan, 'blew his top' when that was sung: 'Being the puritanical sort o'Scots Communist that he were, Kerrigan put an end to that song. It was a jingo song – pack up your troubles, nothing to worry about.' Another Scottish marcher recalled that although 'There wis many, many tunes we played . . . we never got to *It's a Long Way to Tipperary*, we never got asked to play that! It wis too capitalistic – it was associated wi' the First World War.' Other marchers 'didn't feel it was a bit militaristic because actually most of our men were ex military men', and sang it a lot.

The marchers carried banners, some with slogans such as 'We Refuse to Starve in Silence', 'No to the Means Test' or 'Wales to London', or simply with the name of their contingent. Those marching from Brighton to London in 1932 carried one that had been embroidered by women NUWM members with 'Solidarity not Charity'. These banners were heavy, and were mostly carried furled until the marchers drew near a town. Hugh Sloan wondered, as the Scottish contingent battled a blizzard through the Lowther Hills in January 1934, 'where the only occupants were sheep . . . why the hell we were carryin' the banner . . . the wind was rackin' the banner around . . . and we couldnae maintain our balance . . . it was the main banner. It just said "The Scottish Contingent". But why we were carryin' the banner in a place like that wi' strong winds blowin', I just don't know.'

Most of the marchers were in their twenties or thirties, though some younger men went too, such as William McVicar, who had only managed to find work for a few days since leaving school at fourteen, and was sixteen and a half when he set off on the march to Edinburgh from his home in Greenock in the summer of 1933. Charles Teasdale of Blantyre, by contrast, was seventy when he set off for London on the 1930 march.

The marchers travelled light, though the Brighton contingent 'borrowed' a wheelbarrow, 'trusting that we would be able to put matters right on our return', to transport their food and a pile of blankets – and to give an occasional ride to their oldest marcher, a seventy-five-year-old woman. Archie McInnes, marching from Glasgow, had 'an old army haversack – surplus equipment. Ye carried your own gear, your knife, fork and plate, and your blankets of course. One tin mug and a plate . . . A change of underwear [though other marchers insisted "We didn' wear underwear in those days," and John Brown, who marched from Glasgow to London in 1932, only took "jist one of everything. I don't think I washed any o' ma underwear or socks during the time I was away" – more than a month!] and shirt, a . . . hand towel, soap, shavin' equipment.' Some wore a waterproof cycling cape – useful in downpours – while John Lochore set off from Glasgow wearing his aunt's old raincoat, 'which buttoned on the wrong side'. Most wore some sort of head covering, a flat cap or what the Scots called 'a bonnet', and carried a stick to help them along. 'The walking stick was a camouflaged sort of weapon . . . a sort of symbol it was in a way and it was very, very helpful,' according to Harry McShane. The police insisted that these potentially offensive weapons must be surrendered on the approaches to London, though some marchers managed to conceal them from the authorities.

On Thursday, 27 October 1932 the marchers arrived at Hyde Park, their ranks of some 1,500 swollen by around 100,000 Londoners, and pressed towards seven carts that had been set up as a platform. They were met by 2,600 police, including 136 on horseback and 758 special constables who lacked the training or discipline of the regular force, and whose presence, in the words of the *Police Review*, was 'calculated to cause trouble rather than avoid it . . . the special is an irritant rather than an antiseptic . . . the less they are seen and used [on hunger marches and demonstrations] the better for everyone'. The 'specials', goaded by the crowd (factory girls in Borough in South London hardly helped, screaming, 'Kiss me, Sergeant!'), attacked the marchers with batons, the mounted police charged, and the marchers retaliated, tearing up railings and breaking branches off the trees. As dusk fell nineteen police and fifty-eight demonstrators were reported to have been injured, while fourteen people had been arrested. There were similar scenes in Trafalgar Square on Sunday, 30 October, when Wal Hannington appealed, 'Let the working class in uniform and out of uniform stand together in defence of their conditions,' and leaflets were stuck on railings urging: 'Policemen! Defeat your own pay cuts by supporting Tuesday's demonstration against the Economies.'

But when Tuesday came, Hannington had been arrested, charged with 'attempting to cause disaffection among members of the Metropolitan Police', and detained in custody. Declining the offer of a Labour MP to sponsor them, since the Labour Party had listed the NUWM as a proscribed organisation in 1930, a fifty-strong deputation of the marchers collected their petition calling for the abolition of the Means Test and of the Anomalies Act, the restoration of benefit cuts and withdrawal of the new economy measures, with, it was claimed, a million signatures ('bigger than the Chartists' petition') from Charing Cross left-luggage office, intending to march from Trafalgar Square down Whitehall to present it at the bar of the House of Commons, as was the ancient right of citizens. However, the police clanged shut the gates, leaving the deputation and their petition inside and a milling crowd of supporters outside.

Those supporters marching towards Parliament – which was illegal, since processions were not allowed within a mile of the Palace of Westminster – were met by 3,174 policemen, including 2,000 on horses – some borrowed from the army for the occasion – detailed to defend Parliament. Fighting broke out which continued until midnight, as far away as the Edgware Road and across Westminster Bridge. Official figures listed twelve police and thirty-two demonstrators injured, and forty-two arrests – though only two of those were marchers. The petition was never presented: it was returned to the left-luggage office, and eventually the marchers set off back to their homes all over Britain in trains, their fares negotiated at greatly reduced rates paid for by the money they had collected en route.

Hannington was sentenced to three months in prison – his fifth term in ten years. Sid Elias, the leader of the deputation to hand the petition in to Parliament, was charged with having stirred the hunger marchers to acts of disorder in a letter written to Hannington (who never received it) while he was in Russia, which allowed the right-wing press to raise again the spectre of a 'Moscow connection', 'Russian dupes' and 'red gold' backing the hunger marches, and received the maximum sentence of two years. Five days after the trial Emrhys Llewellyn, the NUWM's Secretary and Treasurer (who had stashed the petition in the left-luggage office) and the seventy-six-year-old veteran trade unionist, leader of the 1889 Dock Strike, Tom Mann, were also arrested. Both refused to be bound over to keep the peace. Mann addressed the court: 'If I am to be tied, if my mouth is to be closed, if I am not to participate in voicing the grievances of those who are suffering, while the incompetency of those responsible cannot find work for them, and is knocking down their miserable standards still lower, then whatever the consequence may be . . . I will not give an undertaking not to be identified with the further organisation of mass demonstrations and the ventilation of the troubles of the unemployed and of the workers generally.' He went to prison for two months, as did Llewellyn.

The politically engaged writers Storm Jameson, Amabel Williams-Ellis (who was the sister of John Strachey) and Vera Brittain wrote a letter to *Time and Tide* in protest:

> The most important point about the recent demonstrations and hunger marches is this. Other minorities have channels for airing grievances. The unemployed who have the most serious complaint are the least articulate. Their way of saying what they want to say is taken from them if it is made impossible for them to demonstrate or to hold meetings or to state their case directly whether it be to Parliament or to the local Public Assistance Committee. Can it be that the Government are so anxious to silence them because it would rather not hear too much of what it feels like to try to feed a child on two shillings a week? It is with considerable disquiet that we see a National Government attempting to suppress the views of any body of its subjects and especially that section which has the fewest opportunities of making itself heard. The unemployed are muzzled as they have no other means of publicity for their grievances.

Just over a year later, in the bitter cold of January 1934, the unemployed were on the march again. The Labour Party, still hostile to any demands for united action with the Communists, despite the fact that Hitler had come to power in Germany in January 1933 and both the Communist and the Socialist Internationals had called for united working-class action against fascism, continued to class the NUWM as 'a mere instrument of the British Communist Party'. 'One of our troubles was that the Labour Party were opposed to our earlier marches,' recalled Harry McShane. 'The woman organiser of the Labour Party used to go ahead of us and advise people not to have anything to do with us. The Labour Party were opposed to anything, opposed to the Communist Party mainly. It's quite true to say that Hannington and myself were members of the Communist Party. And most of the leading elements were members of the Communist Party, not all of them . . . they did a lot o' that and it did a lot o' harm to us. But later on we managed to get Attlee [Clement Attlee, leader of the Labour Party from 1935] to agree to support a March and speak with us in Hyde Park . . . and we got the assistance of Aneurin Bevan, who was a tremendously fine person . . . He was probably the best speaker I've ever heard. It was on the 1934 March that I first met him.'

Equally, the TUC had refused to involve the NUWM in a rally it had organised in London in February 1933, the sole large demonstration sanctioned by the official labour movement on the issue of unemployment throughout the 1930s. 'The ILP [Independent Labour Party] seemed to do strange things at the time,' mused McShane. 'Sometimes they would support us. They tried to form separate Unemployed Committees, separate entirely from us. They and the . . . TUC were doing the same thing, forming rival bodies.' However, despite the fact that the official Labour Party was 'awfy absent, awfy absent', in the words of Guy Bolton, an unemployed Lanarkshire miner, local Labour Party workers, less concerned with internecine wrangles and more sympathetic to the plight of the individual unemployed, would often turn out to offer support in the form of food, accommodation or entertainment. Hugh Duffy travelled from Scotland 'on the chuck wagon in advance o' the marchers. I chalked the streets and shouted through the loudspeaker, "The Hunger Marchers are comin'! They'll be here at six o'clock! Turn out and support their cause!" And then the lads came marchin' in.'

'Local people were generally sympathetic to the Marchers. They'd come out everywhere in big droves, particularly in England. We had tremendous turn outs to see the Marchers. And we got money from them. The money kept us going.' The local Co-op store might provide food for the marchers as they passed through a town, and even Woolworths sometimes offered meals: 'We made the most of that . . . it saved an awful lot of trouble in cooking.' 'We always got donations,' recalled Archie McInnes. 'A huge box of chocolate wafer biscuits from, I think, the Co-op at Lancaster . . . if you got cigarettes and that . . . ye handed it in to supplies of course. I remember at Macclesfield an elderly lady . . . a bystander . . . pushed cigarettes into my hand . . . They were Capstan. I was a pipe smoker. So I handed them in.' 'We elected people who had the responsibility of taking collections en route and they were very, very good at their job. They made sure they didn't pass anybody. Anybody standing en route invariably found a can under their nose. And the response was very, very good. The people seeing the un-employed marchin', they felt it in their heart. People turned out to see us.' Indeed, so generous were the onlookers that when Finlay Hart acted as treasurer on the Scottish march he was in a position to know that 'we collected on the road down [from Carlisle] to London £991. That was a lot of money. That was just from shaking collection cans and there were public meetings we were passing through . . . The money was used for providing food, leather, sending men home who were ill, expenses like that.'

Since more men had been out of work for longer, more families were having to suffer the indignities of the Means Test. After the government had refused to reverse the benefit cuts that had been introduced as an emergency measure in 1931, a thousand Scots from as far away as Aberdeen and Dundee converged on Edinburgh on 11 June 1933, and finding nowhere to sleep on the second night all bedded down on the hard pavements of Princes Street below the Castle. 'We didnae hae blankets wi' us. We had a haversack for a pillae' and the men slept with their backs to the railings in Princes Street so they couldn't be attacked.' The next morning women protesters had to be cleared from the tramways, the marchers washed themselves in the street fountains, shaved by looking at their reflections in shop windows and set up their field kitchens which had 'a place under-neath where you fuelled them by coal, and they had a chimney for the smoke to go out. So you can imagine what it was like when the fair citi-zens of Edinburgh saw these field kitchens all belching away preparing some food for the Marchers . . . after all Princes Street's the showpiece of Edinburgh . . . you've got all these luxury hotels and big clubs, the Conservative Club and the Liberal Club . . . but the average Edinburgh working-class person was in sympathy with what the demonstrators were in Edinburgh for.'

The newspaper headlines spoke of 'Two Days that Shook Edinburgh', in reference to the Russian Revolution, to the alarm of the authorities, who quickly found the protesters accommodation for the following night; after which 'We were loaded into bloody buses and they just got rid of us.'

Local marches continued throughout autumn 1933. When the Unemployment Bill was published in 1934, it followed the main recommendations of the Royal Commission on Unemployment's report, including no restoration of benefit cuts, the continuation of the Means Test, the transfer of transitional payments away from local PACs which had first-hand knowledge of conditions in their area to a national body, the Unemployment Assistance Board (UAB), and a requirement that could make benefit payments conditional on attending a government training centre.

The government had started a number of training schemes for the unemployed in the mid-1920s, and by the late 1930s there were five funded by the Ministry of Labour. Some million and a half young people had been through junior instructional centres, which were in effect a continuation of schooling, and were compulsory in some areas, while each year about 2,000 young women took courses in 'the various domestic arts, including cooking, needlework and laundry', designed to equip them for domestic service or hotel work. There were grants available for individual vocational training, and in 1928 an Industrial Transference Board had been set up to enable the Ministry of Labour to transfer workers out of their own districts where work was no longer available – miners were natural candidates – and send them to training centres mainly situated in the depressed areas where they, and sometimes their wives, could learn skills which could lead to a new life in Canada, Australia or the more prosperous South of England. Between 1929 and 1938, over 70,000 men passed through such centres, and though in the early days it was hard to place them in work, 63,000 eventually found jobs. Though a number drifted back to their home areas, there were continual complaints that the scheme was draining the life blood from the depressed areas – particularly as the parallel scheme for young unemployed men was transferring them at a rate of over 10,000 a year.

But it was felt that there were some unemployed who were not suitable for these programmes. In December 1929 the Ministry of Labour hatched a plan 'to deal with the class of men to whom our existing training schemes do not apply . . . those, especially among the younger men, who, through prolonged unemployment, have become so "soft" and temporarily demoralised that it would not be practicable to introduce more than a very small number of them into one of our ordinary training centres without danger to morale'. Such men could not be considered for any transfer scheme until they were 'hardened . . . for these people have lost the will to work'.

These Instructional Centres, which catered for around 200,000 unemployed men between 1929 and 1939, did not aim to teach a skill or trade, but rather to toughen the 'fibre of men who have got out of the way of work' by providing a twelve-week course of 'fairly hard work, good feeding and mild discipline' at residential camps, often in remote rural areas, which it was hoped 'would help the [men] to withstand the pull of former ties and associates'.

Although the threats to cut their benefits if men refused to attend the Instructional Centres were never implemented, the NUWM, which was concerned that this was another attempt to generate cheap labour and undercut trade union rates of pay, added them to its list of complaints against the government's attempts to deal with unemployment. It described the centres as 'slave colonies' or even 'concentration camps', though this was a rather excessive description, since men could come and go as they liked, and in any one year up to a quarter left before completing their courses.

Under the toughening-up regime the men were issued on arrival with a 'uniform' of work shirts, corduroy trousers and hobnailed boots, which they could keep if they completed the course. They slept under canvas (in the summer), or in huts, were paid around four shillings a week and issued with a pack of Woodbines and a stamp for a letter home, and were subjected to a strict regime: parading each morning for work, roll calls, lights out, and hard manual labour such as chopping down trees, building roads, digging sewers and stone-breaking. Sometimes men would be 'lent' to work on outside projects, such as the building of Whipsnade Zoo, London University's playing fields, and the Piccadilly Line tube extension, all to accustom them 'once more to regular hours and steady work'.

Len Edmondson's brother was 'sent to a camp in County Durham where the men were employed digging stone and helping to make roads for forestry work. They were accommodated in huts and following breakfast the Union Jack was hoisted [which was a particular irritant to the Welsh and Scottish attendees] whilst they were all lined up and marched to the place of work. In the evening they were lined up again and marched back to the camp when the Union Jack was then lowered.' 'They established one camp in Glen Branter in Argyllshire and a number o' other places. And it is a fact that most of the work they did was afforestation work, mostly for the dukes and the big lords, makin' roads through the forests. And I think it was at Glen Branter they actually had them diggin' holes and filling them up again. The camps were horrible . . . I think they got the idea o' these camps frae Hitler, because Fascism was establishing itself in Germany and they were sending all these young men to these camps,' concluded Tom Ferns, an unemployed Glaswegian who had only ever managed to find short-term jobs and was active in both the NUWM and the Young Communist League. But others enjoyed their camp days, rejoicing in the outdoor life, long walks and sports – particularly football – and rejected any notion of a 'slave camp'.

The camps were clearly authoritarian, with many, it was claimed, overseen by 'civilian sergeant-majors, retired police officers, ex NCOs of the army and officials transferred from the Poor Law Institutions'. But the most numerous complaints seem to have been about the food – stale bread, leathery meat, sandwiches 'with bread an inch thick, with a piece of cheese in between that a mouse wouldn't get up for ... when the men used to be working among the fir trees they'd gnaw the resin off the trunk ... and pick wild mushrooms and eat them raw, they were that hungry,' reported William Heard, a West Ham man with a wife and five children who was sent to Shobdon camp in Herefordshire.

'I still don't know what we learned ... it was a waste of time. The only thing was it took us *away* from something I suppose,' thought Heard (who featured in an NUWM pamphlet, *Slave Camps*). But Alwyn Jones, who was sent to a camp in Suffolk from Oldham, felt 'so much rot is talked about the camps' that he wrote an article for his local paper extolling their virtues. 'A man gets four shillings a week, and of course his wife and children draw if they are unemployed while he is away. He has the best food he ever ate [four meals a day], a bed, and clothes and medical attention if necessary ... in beautiful surroundings.'

Although camps continued to open throughout the 1930s, judged by results they were not particularly effective. Of a total intake of 83,000 'volunteers' between 1935 and 1938, only 12,500 subsequently found employment: 19,500 either gave up or were sacked during the twelve-week course. The last one closed in 1939, and several were converted to house prisoners of war.

The National Government had inherited the notion of transference schemes and training camps, but one initiative of its own was the introduction in 1934 of the Special Areas (Development and Improvement) Act, in recognition of the fact that there was little hope of a sufficient upswing in world trade to bring jobs back to the areas of the old staple industries – coal, iron, steel, shipbuilding. Four special investigators were appointed to examine conditions in the worst-hit areas: Scotland, West Cumberland, Durham and Tyneside and South Wales. Their reports confirmed what the government must have known already: that while trade was beginning to revive in the Midlands and the South-East, massive unemployment persisted in the depressed areas, with no real prospect of improvement. Parts of South Wales were described as 'derelict', with 39,000 men and 5,000 boys 'surplus to requirements', there was a permanent labour 'surplus' in the depressed areas of Scotland, and Durham bore out the claims of a series of influential articles in *The Times* in March 1934 which described the area as 'Places Without a Future: Where Industry is Dead'.

Alongside advertisements for Rolls-Royce, Bentley and Talbot luxury cars, holidays in the Hôtel du Palais in Biarritz, which offered 'Casino-Golf', a broadtail fur coat with a white fox-fur collar on sale at Jays of Regent Street for forty-nine guineas, and a long list of the wedding presents received by Mr Walter Elliot MP and Miss Katharine Tennant, the 'Special Correspondent' (who had reported on the 'stricken areas' of South Wales in 1928) explained that 'There are districts of England, heavily populated, whose plight no amount of trade recovery can ever cure because their sole industry is not depressed but dead.' The articles spoke of places where the 'pits are not only closed but abandoned, the works not only shut but dismantled', of families who had had 'no proper spell of work for eight years . . . people living on the very margin . . . everything superfluous has been pawned or sold . . . and the necessities of life are largely worn out or broken . . . shops are shut and boarded up . . . You may even see the rare sight of a pawnshop closed . . . the men are not starving, but they are permanently hungry.' Alongside stark photographs of mining villages such as Spennymoor and Escombe with their slag heaps, rubble and long, empty, derelict streets making them look truly like war zones, the article declared, 'It would be a failure of humanity to forget them, a failure of statesmanship to ignore them.' An editorial concluded the grim series with a call for the appointment of a director of operations charged with rehabilitating the workforce and reviving the economies of the depressed areas.

Ramsay MacDonald responded by impressing on the Minister of Labour, Henry Betterton, 'the importance of doing something to meet *The Times* leaders, and the growing chorus in the Commons'. Neville Chamberlain, the Chancellor of the Exchequer, agreed, but thought it was essentially 'not a question of spending a great deal of money, but of showing that the matter had not been pigeon-holed'.

Eight months later the Depressed Areas Bill (its name was later changed by the House of Lords to the Special Areas Bill at the behest of the people of Tyneside, who found the title disparaging) was reluctantly introduced into Parliament. It proposed two full-time, unpaid Commissioners for the areas, one for England and Wales, the other for Scotland. Their budget was £2 million, and their remit was strictly limited – there must be no suggestion that 'a sort of financial hosepipe designed to pour assistance into the districts' was being uncoiled, or that this was the thin edge of a public-works wedge.

Grants could be given to local authorities and to voluntary agencies such as the NCSS in the Special Areas to initiate or subsidise amenities such as water supplies, sewerage schemes, drainage and sanitation, hospitals, children's playgrounds, football pitches or open-air swimming pools, and some money was made available for 'back to the land' initiatives such as smallholdings, co-operative farming projects and afforestation schemes – though an imaginative plan for a Welsh national park based on the American model was turned down.

One problem was that the Act was at total variance with the labour transference policies which various governments had been pursuing since the 1920s. As a Ministry of Labour official put it, government initiatives should 'neither waste sympathy nor public funds on any activity which may anchor or attach young or middle-aged people more firmly to the depressed areas'. The 'Get on your bike' attitude which has resonated for the right down the decades as a legacy of the 'hungry thirties' was expressed in the words of the National Government's Chief Industrial Advisor, Horace Wilson: 'The people who wish to work must go where the work is.'

The Act's narrow scope and the limited funds available made it seem little more than a gesture, and it drew criticism from the press and across the political spectrum. The Mayor of Newcastle regarded it as 'a flea bite, a sop'; to Aneurin Bevan it was 'an idle, empty farce', a mere palliative offering 'a bit of colour-washing colliers' cottages' in the hope of attracting new industry (as had already happened at Brynmawr). Lloyd George damned the Act as 'patching' and 'peddling hope', while Harold Macmillan, with patrician languor, ridiculed it as *'Parturiunt montes: nascetur ridiculus mus*. The mountains have been in labour and there has been born a mouse . . . a nice mouse, a profitable and helpful little mouse, but a ridiculous, microscopic, Lilliputian mouse.'

Other depressed areas such as Manchester and Lancashire lobbied to be 'special' too, since they too had moribund industries and high unemployment. By 1936, when the Commissioner for England and Wales, Sir Malcolm Stewart, who had been particularly disappointed at the failure to build a bridge across the Severn, which had first been mooted in the 1840s (but which did not happen until 1965), resigned, ostensibly on health grounds, he admitted that 'No appreciable reduction in the number of unemployed has been effected.' A survey of 5,800 firms that he had undertaken in 1935 showed that only eight would even consider investing in the Special Areas. They gave their reasons as inaccessibility, high local taxes, low consumer purchasing power and high rates of trade union membership. The powers of the Commissioners were increased by an Amendment to the Act in 1937 which meant that rates, rent and taxes could be remitted for industries starting or relocating to the Special Areas, and trading estates were set up with all facilities laid on in which firms could lease premises. It was also agreed that 'steps should be taken to prevent further industrial concentration round London and the South' by diverting industry to areas of heavy unemployment. The Commissioners' budget was increased annually, so that by 1938 they were allowed to spend £17 million. Nevertheless, fewer than 50,000 new jobs were created under the Special Areas legislation.

The 1934 Unemployment Act spurred the NUWM to organise another national march. Given that it was to take place 'in the dead of winter [starting in January], it is essential that proper provision be made for every marcher having stout clothes, good boots and coat, as well as a real Army pack'. Cobblers must accompany every contingent (they would repair boots overnight), and for those coming from Scotland, the North-East, Lancashire and Yorkshire, who would be on the road for more than ten days, hot food would have to be provided. This meant a one- or two-ton truck to transport the field kitchen, which was 'like an old washin' house boiler on the back of a lorry', according to one Scottish marcher. An 'ambulance unit' would also be on hand to cope with the inevitable spate of blisters and other medical emergencies. Every marcher was to be provided with a copy of the Unemployment Bill and the twelve-page *Manifesto of the National Hunger March and Congress* so that he or she would know exactly why they were marching and what for. Generally, money was more forthcoming than it had been on earlier marches. The Tyneside marchers left with generous donations from various Durham mining lodges, and even the impoverished lodges of South Wales managed to scrape together some funds for their representatives. The Scottish contingent collected £45 in the streets of Coventry and £20 in Birmingham, while in Warrington £55 was dropped into the rattled tins of the Lancashire marchers, and they left Oxford £120 better off.

Women were in a very small minority among the membership of the NUWM. 'But there were several capable women who were very active,' recalled Finlay Hart. And when it came to the Hunger Marches, 'We didn't like women with the men in case there was any scandal,' according to Harry McShane, the Scottish NUWM organiser. 'There was a woman's contingent ... and they marched a separate route.' 'We never saw any of the men on the March,' remembered Mary Johnston, who had been unemployed for over a year when she joined the Scottish women en route for London in 1934. 'We never had any contact with them. I don't suppose we ever thought of questioning them. I don't recollect any discussion on the point at all. And of course it would be quite a good thing, really, if the men were using a separate route.'

It was considered that a march from Glasgow to London would be too taxing for the thirty or so Scottish women, so the men 'set off a week or two before us . . . but . . . we would have a send off from Clydebank and we'd get a bus from Glasgow to Derby and join up with the other women, mainly the women from Northern England, Lancashire,' making a contingent of around a hundred. But Emily Swankie, who had decided with her husband John that as the Labour Exchange would have stopped his money if he'd joined the 1934 march (as he would not be available for work if he was on the road – a requirement of drawing benefit) she would march instead, since she was also unemployed. The first day out from Derby

we walked sixteen miles . . . we found that sixteen miles is quite a distance for people not used to marching. And if like me you were in a new pair of shoes, it wasn't funny . . . We never did sixteen miles again. The next day it was twelve miles. And then we cut it down to eight . . . We had black stockings which we were asked to wear all the time . . . they frowned on bare legs. No bare legs on the Hunger March . . . There was a wee bit of puritanism there too, but it was that they wanted to avoid at all costs any bad publicity – women marching with bare legs . . . There were long hours of walking and nothing really happened, passing through villages, people coming out to look at us, curious, interested some of them, not very curious, some of them not very receptive . . . But where we did have receptions, it was great. We had the Co-operative Guild women, some Church Guild women, Labour Party women and Communist Party women. They had made up reception committees for us . . . sometimes they had brought in home baking, and they got us bedded down in halls etc. for the night. In one place they anticipated we wouldn't be very well fed the next day because they knew the area through which we were going. And they made us big bowls of hard-boiled eggs. We had to stuff our pockets with them because it was on the cards that we wouldn't eat next night. And they sent in basins with Lysol – that was the old disinfectant for your feet . . . we were very kindly received.

Like the men, the women always marched in step when they got to a town. 'You march better when you're tuned in with other people,' thought Marion Henery. And it looked more organised and purposeful. As with the men, it was sore feet that were the main problem for the women: 'The Lancashire women wore clogs. You heard the clatter of the clogs but they never had any trouble with their feet . . . but a lot of other women had problems with heel blisters.' The women 'had to sleep in workhouses quite a number of times ... we had always to give our names. The women on the March didnae take kindly to this. So a lot of fictitious names were given – Mary Pickford [the American film star of the silent screen] and names like that.'

Although the Labour Party and the TUC leadership continued to label the NUWM as the Communist party in disguise and to reject attempts to build a 'United Front' against unemployment (though the ILP, which had recently disaffiliated from the Labour Party and would wither henceforth, heeded the call), there was more support among the rank and file this time. The South Wales contingent, for example, had the support of almost all the Labour MPs in the area and many of the local union branches and trades councils for the 1934 march. Reception committees were more likely to turn out as the marchers neared towns, and were more prepared to offer food and accommodation. Many committees included a clergyman who might offer his church hall, or even his church, for the night. However, the reception en route was mixed: as the marchers tramped through Windsor, servants working at the castle threw them money, but at Reading, where there was no reception committee, they had to bed down on used straw in a cattle market.

As the marchers neared Oxford they found 'students were standing on the side o' the road with bundles o' walking sticks and handin' them to us as we passed again after the police [who had confiscated the marchers' sticks] was away. They were sympathetic students, no' Communists or anything like that. But they'd seen what we were goin' through and they decided we needed sticks for walkin',' recalled Frank McCusker. Duff Cooper, who was Financial Secretary at the War Office, was appalled, and said in the House of Commons that he hoped that the university authorities would know how to deal with these undergraduates who fell into step with the Hunger Marchers. When he came to speak at the Oxford Union few weeks later Cooper was challenged about his remarks by Anthony Greenwood, known in Oxford as the 'young Adonis of the Labour Party', the son of Arthur Greenwood, who had been Minister of Health in the 1929 Labour government, but had declined to join the National Government. 'It is a vile thing,' Cooper replied, 'to encourage these poor people, under-fed, ill-clothed, to set out in bad weather, marching the roads to London, knowing perfectly well that they would get nothing when they got there. In a university with traditions, it was a suitable case for the authorities to interfere with the young fools who lost their heads and their sense of proportion.'

The Labour politician George Lansbury was the other speaker, and he disagreed, welcoming the fact that 'Christian charity' still existed among the undergraduates. It was capitalism that had failed to do anything for its victims, 'and that is the greatest condemnation of the system that can be offered'. The President of the Union, the socialist Frank Hardie, questioned the right of Oxford undergraduates to have £2,000 spent on their education while others were pitchforked into the labour market at fourteen. The motion that 'This House believes that in Socialism lies the only solution to the problems of this country' was passed by 316 votes to 247.

The 'young fools' of Oxford were not the only less obvious supporters of the Hunger Marchers. Fifteen-year-old Esmond Romilly, a nephew of Winston Churchill, who was a pupil at Wellington College and who kept a porcelain bust of Lenin on his study shelves under a portrait of his uncle and next to six copies of *The Communist Manifesto*, was a fervent, if unfocused, enthusiast too. With his brother Giles he had started a magazine, *Out of Bounds*, 'against reaction in the public schools', which contained attacks on the Officer Training Corps, fascism (though Michael Wallace of Oundle was allowed space for a defence), traditional public schools which were 'concerned with the production of a class', as well as informative articles on subjects such as masturbation ('some form of auto-eroticism is absolutely inevitable') and progressive schools (including Dartington, which permitted copies of the *Moscow Daily News* as well as the *Times Literary Supplement* in its library) plus some rather memorable poems by the schoolboy Gavin Ewart. The Romillys were delighted to announce in the first issue, published in March 1934, that *Out of Bounds* was 'Banned in Uppingham – Banned in Cheltenham', and they could gleefully add 'Banned in Aldenham, Imperial Service College and Wellington' (from whence it sprang) by the second. Furthermore, the *Daily Mail* had picked up the story under the headlines 'Red Menace in Public Schools', 'Moscow Attempts to Corrupt Boys', 'Officer's Son [the Romillys' father was a colonel in the Scots Guards and had commanded the Egyptian Camel Corps in the First World War] Sponsors Extremist Journal'.

L. Shinnie of Westminster School reviewed the collected *Listener* articles *Memoirs of the Unemployed* for *Out of Bounds*, concluding that 'members of the public schools can only make certain that they will not suffer the conditions depicted in this book if they join with the working classes to achieve a better society'. Esmond Romilly managed to persuade his mother not only to contribute half a crown to the National Hunger March Committee, but also to pen a letter to the *Daily Worker* expressing her 'entire sympathy with the cause of the unemployed who have had their benefits cut and I am glad they are availing themselves of a traditionally British method to voice their grievances'. Nellie Romilly had wished to add

'God Save the Queen' at the bottom, but had been dissuaded. However, young Romilly later realised the political capital that could be made out of a sister of the wife of Winston Churchill writing such a letter, and it never appeared.

One afternoon in February 1934 Henry Crowder, a black American jazz musician and the lover of a wealthy and rebellious socialite with a restless social conscience, Nancy Cunard, went to her flat and found her wearing 'a bizarre collection of garments – a man's overcoat, an aviator's helmet and several scarves – which, she told him, were partly for warmth and partly for disguise. She informed him that she was off to join the hunger marchers and he was to tell no one. Off she went with a small movie camera in her hand.'

Much later, Nancy Cunard wrote to a friend: 'It was at Stamford [that] I met them [the hunger marchers], up that great road . . . One thought the dog of the Inn had been put in the soup, just as we were all sitting down, in pretty great cold, eating stew on the roadside . . . Why the hunger march? In protest against the Means Test.'

'We were on the road when this car drew up,' remembered Tom Clarke, who was on the march from Dundee. 'I think it was a Rolls Royce – I'm not very good on cars. This woman got out . . . [she] was taking newsreels or films. [Peter] Kerrigan said, "That's Nancy Cunard." I didn't at the time know who Nancy Cunard was. To me here we were fighting capitalism and yet ye'd get these people coming along and dropping money, maybe a pound note or more, into a collection bag. I remember quizzing Kerrigan about this. I says, "How the hell does this happen?" He says, "Well, they're so accustomed to giving tips, this doesn't mean a thing." They may have intended well, they may not, but they just gave tips.'

'Eighth day,' wrote Joseph Albaya, who was marching in a Sheffield contingent on 17 February. 'Kettering – one of those towns that didn't know what unemployment was – also where the inhabitants looked at us if were dogs.' The marchers were put up in the workhouse. 'Speech by Mayor to welcome us – (he said he believed in action by constitutional means).' The next day it was 'on to Bedford our longest trek to date – never been so tired as on this day – feet in a terrible condition . . . the trek was about 32 miles on hard roads – admittedly may have done rambles this length but never with the necessity of keeping in step – dark before we reached Bedford – five miles out the leaders had to keep encouraging the marchers – kept telling us we were there – these to my mind were silly tactics as the result was disappointment – had one final rest on the side of the road – utterly fagged out – was stretched out in a ditch – a Good Samaritan came out and dished cigarettes out.'

Aware that the Home Secretary, Sir John Gilmour, and the Attorney General had both warned mothers along the marchers' route to keep their children indoors and shopkeepers to shutter their windows, hinting at the prospect of 'grave disorder, public disturbances', even 'bloodshed', the NUWM was determined to avoid confrontations. 'We're here to demonstrate against the operation of the Means Test and the economy cuts and not to have a diversion or fight with the police which would misrepresent the whole idea of the March,' warned Harry McShane. 'We're here to protest peacefully and with discipline.' Any transgressor would usually be packed off back home – though only after a meeting had been held with all the contingent to decide his fate. Misdeeds might include drunkenness (though according to most marchers this was rare: 'There was no money for drink anyway in the first place.' It took Frank McCusker six weeks to march from Scotland, and 'I could say I had about six pints o' beer frae Glasgow to London'), scrounging, brawling, stealing another man's boots, pilfering the collection boxes or pulling off a scam such as arriving in a town in advance of the main body of marchers, collecting money from sympathetic onlookers and pocketing the proceeds before rejoining the march.

If the marchers were organised, so were the authorities. Instructions were reiterated that any soft-hearted local PAC thinking of offering food or loans of blankets to the marchers would be surcharged for this largesse. Chief Constables along the route were required to file reports about the number, progress and behaviour of each contingent, and whether any marchers had previous convictions for breaches of the peace.

In fact both sides were concerned to avoid any aggressive confrontation as the marchers streamed into Hyde Park on Sunday, 25 February 1934. Unknown to police or marchers, a vigilante committee had assembled in a small flat behind Selfridges, watching the action and hovering by the telephone to report any police brutality among the crowd of over 50,000 marchers. It was a distinguished posse, 'rather like the members of a cultural, intellectual and progressive *Who's Who*': E.M. Forster, Professor Julian Huxley, Vera Brittain, her husband, Professor George Caitlin, and her friend the novelist Winifred Holtby, 'tall, calm and big-boned', and Dr Edith Summerskill were there, as were a couple of barristers, two young solicitors and Kingsley Martin, editor of the *New Statesman*. Claud Cockburn brought H.G. Wells, who had been unwell, and was 'wrapped in mufflers'. The assembled group were either members of, or distinguished left-wingers who had been invited as observers by, the National Council of Civil Liberties (NCCL), since previously reports of acts of harassment by the police had been easy to discredit since they came mainly from the victims themselves.

The NCCL (now Liberty) had been set up by a one-time actor and freelance journalist, Ronald Kidd, who also owned a radical, free-thinking bookshop, the Punch and Judy, in Villiers Street, where unexpurgated copies of D.H. Lawrence's *Lady Chatterley's Lover* or Radclyffe Hall's *Well of Loneliness* could be purchased, as well as books about the Soviet Union which were not 'full of hysterical anti-communism', and the barrister, writer and soon-to-be Independent MP, A.P. Herbert, as a result of Kidd's disquiet at the behaviour of police *agents provocateurs* during the 1932 Hunger March, and Herbert's unease at the police acting as 'bandits', ordering drinks in nightclubs after hours in order to secure convictions. The civil liber-tarians peered down at 'the sea of hats in the Park – caps, trilbies, hard felts and the occasional bowler' marching through the grey, slanting drizzle, and some ventured down to the edge of the crowds to get a closer look. The music of the pipe and flute bands of the Scottish marchers (Glasgow's contingent alone boasted eight flute bands) hung in the air, interspersed with much shouting of slogans and singing of 'The Internationale' as the lines of unemployed marched in step, watched by lines of police, one unit atop Marble Arch with a telephone, ready to direct operations and summon reinforcements in case of trouble.

Joseph Albaya, who had been on the road for sixteen days, recorded:

Got up late for the GREAT DAY . . . put on clean shirt . . . long boring wait at Friends' Meeting House where leaders entertained us in usual fashion by usual speeches – fell in outside, raining on my new outfit . . . put on selling *Hunger March Bulletins* – papers not counted so had plenty of chances of making a dishonest penny – rather alarmed by the reports of the older marchers of not keeping to the ranks consequently rather felt like a hero [sic] lined outside for ration of oranges and cigarettes and the singing of the daily ritual (the 'Internationale') – set off in fine style – rather impressed by the military bearing and dignity of the comrades – the consciousness that it was their Great Day had made the marchers buck themselves up – the contingent headed by Scottish pipers, fifes and drums . . . raining lightly all the time – my papers getting wet and not selling – soon picked up a companion who was trying to convey the usual idea that we were in for a blood bath – crowds increasing – also police contingent headed by three mounted policemen . . . under the command of a military-looking old bastard . . . Noticed that comrades' London banners are much bigger and better than provincial ones and that London comrades are much more militant and less apathetic than provincial comrades [possibly partly because they were less exhausted] . . . the police led us into a better class district off the main traffic roads – blocks of imposing flats – I went berserk

... yelling obscenities at the occupants of the flats – I was sobbing with rage – I never knew what class consciousness was until that moment – I was ready to do anything, charge the police, smash up everything in sight – it was the way the occupants of the flats looked at us ... every flat seemed to have a balcony from which they laughed at us and then contemptuously threw down money – their contempt was so open that even the dullest of the marchers could see it. Christ! ... if they had been on a level on us and not above us on their balconies well ... I should have taken part willingly in my first riot.

Jack Gaster, a young lawyer, was the ILP representative on the London reception committee:

I was based in Marylebone and we were always organising the Hyde Park meetings ... we used to go down to some stables behind Great Ormond Street owned by the Co-op and arrange for eight or ten horse drawn vehicles to come to Hyde Park to form a platform. In those days ... there were no loudspeakers or anything like that ... I had to marshal [the marchers] out of Hyde Park which was a very important job because we were determined to march down Oxford Street. The police were determined that we shouldn't. They wanted to keep the marchers off the main streets. There were hundreds of thousands in the Park. We arranged for part of the march to leave Hyde Park by the Bayswater Road entrance ... and another part to go out via Park Lane ... and both to converge ... There were police lined up, very senior officers because it was a very important thing, 'mounties' too. They said 'Sorry, Mr Gaster, you can't go down Oxford Street.' I said 'We're going down.' I was trembling in my shoes ... but I very carefully put the Scottish marchers behind me. They were the real tough ones. I said, 'These lads haven't walked from all over England to be pushed into the back streets.' 'Sorry, we can't allow it.' I said, 'Very well. We're going down Oxford Street and the responsibility is yours ... There's going to be a fight. Do you want a fight? Does the government want a fight?' They withdrew and we marched down Oxford Street.

In the event the entire occasion went off peacefully: 'not a scuffle, not a baton raised. No report from anywhere of even so much as a pane of glass broken. No bloodshed!' the NCCL observers, who had had no need to pick up their phone, recorded. The same was the case at a rally in Trafalgar Square.

After queuing in the snow some two hundred unemployed marchers were allowed into Parliament, where some struck up 'The Internationale' in the Central Lobby, while those allowed into the Strangers' Gallery interrupted debate by shouting 'Hear the Hunger Marchers!' and 'Down with the Starvation Government!' All were ejected, and they eventually returned home without having been able to present their petition to Parliament, the reduced train fares that had been negotiated with the railway companies covered by money raised on the march.

However, some female textile marchers, led by Maud Brown, the women's organiser of the NUWM, had managed to penetrate 10 Downing Street and confront Ramsay MacDonald's daughter Ishbel, who was 'very friendly [and] offered . . . tea . . . but on a point of honour we refused it', recalled Mary Johnston, one of Miss MacDonald's unexpected visitors. 'We felt it would be weakening our position if we accepted tea.' Before they left the Prime Minister's daughter suggested that maybe the unemployed women might try domestic service, according to one of them.

Ramsay MacDonald refused to grant the marchers an audience. 'Has anyone who cares to come to London, either on foot or in first-class carriages, the constitutional right to demand to see me, to take up my time, whether I like it or not?' he asked rhetorically in the Commons a few days later. 'I say he has not.'

Sir Herbert Samuel, the Liberal leader and former Home Secretary, was despairing:

> No one can say that the grievances of these men, who have walked to this city from many parts of this island, are trivial or imaginary . . . What should they have done other than what they have done, if they want to draw the attention of the nation to their plight, to stir the nation out of what is really a shameful complacency, and to protest against the utterly inadequate measures that have so far been taken? Are we to say to them, 'If you are disorderly, we cannot listen to you; it would be to discourage disorder. If you are orderly, we need not listen to you?' . . .
>
> It is said that they are Communists, and therefore that they ought to be ignored. Let us not attach so much importance to labels, but see the realities behind the name. There is not here, and everyone knows it, any deliberate plan or attempt to overturn society. This march is nothing more than a protest, a bitter cry. They say to us: 'Hear us; see us; help us.' It is that and nothing more . . .
>
> It is said that these men are not representative of the whole body of the unemployed. Perhaps not, but there is no one else to represent them; there is no other organisation that speaks urgently in their name.

That 'bitter cry' was heard again in January 1935, when the 1934 Unemployment Act was implemented, and under what the National Government referred to as a 'Great Social Reform', responsibility for administering Means-Tested relief for those who had exhausted their unemployment insurance entitlement, and the able-bodied uninsured un-employed, were transferred from the 183 local PACs to a new national Unemployment Assistance Board (UAB). A national sliding scale of relief was to replace the various local scales of the PACs, some of which in depressed areas had been lenient in their interpretation of the test. Indeed, as late as 1935 a number of councillors in South Wales boasted that the Means Test had never operated in their area.

When the new rates were announced they turned out to be lower than those previously allowed, and large-scale agitations broke out in South Wales (including the storming of Merthyr Tydfil UAB office, where 90 per cent of claimants had been receiving full rates of benefit), spreading to the North-East (where 10,000 marched on Sheffield Town Hall to demand the repeal of the Act and the immediate restoration of old allowances) and Scotland, with the unemployed besieging local authority offices and PACs with complaints about reduced benefits. Forty-eight per cent of all those in receipt of benefit across the country had seen them cut, while only 34 per cent had seen an increase. An emergency two-day debate in Parliament revealed the divide in the country, as MPs representing seats in the Midlands and the South of England 'listened in often puzzled silence' to the 'virulent attacks' from their colleagues of all parties from the depressed areas. The Chancellor of the Exchequer, Neville Chamberlain, admitted that 'It had been realised for the first time that very large numbers of working men in Great Britain, and particularly in Scotland, were paying rents much lower than had been thought [which meant that their benefit had been cut, since the sliding scale reckoned that rent equalled around a quarter of living costs], and were living under very bad conditions.' A Standstill Act was introduced for two years which allowed the unemployed to choose whichever rate was the higher, that of the UAB or their local PAC.

These protests had been essentially local and spontaneous (though with some NUWM support), and it was not until two years after the previous one that another NUWM-organised march set off. But that 1936 Hunger March was eclipsed, both then and down the years to come, by a much smaller march of only two hundred men, organised with Labour Party and TUC support and led by a Labour MP, Ellen Wilkinson, to protest at the singular situation of one devastated town, Jarrow.

If Jarrow has come to epitomise the 'Hungry Thirties', what, if anything, was the importance of those other seven Hunger Marches from all over Britain? Their success can't be judged in terms of concessions wrung from the government, but though the numbers involved were relatively small, the name – the indictment – 'Hunger March' stuck, giving the decade its epithet. Winston Churchill called them 'Anger Marches', and they were that too. Most of those who took part were realistic about what they achieved. The hated Means Test was still in force when war broke out in 1939, though the government did raise benefit payments after the 1934 march. Rather, marchers spoke in terms of 'showin the authorities that ye are nae prepared to take things lyin' down': 'I felt we had the guts but we had nae policy. I never knew anyone on the March that got a job through it . . . [but] the March meant that you were trying to tae do somethin' about it. They wernae just accepting it'; 'I don't think we achieved any success. We had this approach by Government: you were down and they were trying to keep you down . . . But the Hunger Marches kept alive the spirit to keep fighting'; 'It highlighted the situation that people were in . . . it brought to the notice o' the general public the conditions o' the unemployed at that time'; 'I don't think we achieved that much out o' it. But we let the people in the whole o' the country know the conditions that were going on as far as we were concerned in Scotland, or South Wales, or the North East'; 'Being a Marxist you know you're no' gaun tae get any immediate results. It's a process of development and it takes the form of struggles and the class struggle in a' its aspects. I didn't expect any dramatic victory.'

There was no dramatic victory, but the Hunger Marchers helped to rewrite the concept of 'welfare', reclaiming it as part of the commons, as a social right rather than something given selectively as a matter of discretion to mendicants. This reading would underpin the Beveridge Report of 1942, and subsequent social welfare legislation after the Second Word War.

If the marches achieved few concrete results, did they politicise the unemployed? Did the unemployed come to see themselves as a dispossessed class in revolt against capitalism? Many – politicians of all parties and most of the press – portrayed the unemployed as vulnerable to exploit-ation by the Communist Party for its own nefarious ends. Some charged that the NUWM was controlled by the Communist Party, others saw it as a recruiting ground providing footsoldiers for the Party. The third World Congress in 1921 had directed all Communist Parties to 'partici-pate directly in the struggle of the working masses, establish Communist leadership of the struggle, and, in the course of the struggle create large, mass Communist Parties'.

The CPGB would certainly have liked to gain control of the unemployed movement, build it up as a mass political organisation and direct its activities towards the overthrow of capitalism, but most marchers insist that the overlap of the NUWM and the CPGB was small among the ordinary members, indeed that most members had no particular political affiliation. Very few of the tens of thousands drawn into the agitation went on to join the CPGB – and in fact few actually joined the NUWM. 'The people's flag is deepest pink/It's not as red as people think/And ere their limbs grow stiff and cold/The Dundee workers will be sold'– sang one sceptical marcher. The total number who paid tuppence for an NUWM membership card and a penny a week for a stamp was probably around 15,000 by the end of 1931. When there was government action that was regarded as hostile to the interests of the unemployed, membership would surge: 2,000 a week were recruited in response to the cuts in benefit and the introduction of the Means Test in 1931. Numbers rose throughout 1933 when the NUWM was engaged in active protests and was meeting harsh opposition, but fell again until early 1935, when the announcement of another round of benefit cuts for the unemployed gave a further impetus, and membership rose to above 20,000. But by the time of the final Hunger March in 1936 it had declined to nearer 14,000, and it only rose slightly in late 1938, co-inciding with a campaign for winter relief. Some of the unemployed joined in support of a particular campaign, and then left, most let their membership lapse if they found a job, while a few found even the required penny a week subscription unaffordable. This was not the behaviour of 'a militant army committed to revolutionary change', and throughout the 1930s those who went on hunger marches remained a minority among the unemployed, the un-employed remained a (sometimes, in some places, large) minority within the working class, and moreover a minority without economic power.

The successes that the NUWM achieved among the unemployed were less in politicising them (though a number of Hunger Marchers subsequently did go to fight on the Republican side in the Spanish Civil War) than in drawing attention to the failure of the government to do enough about unemployment, gaining sufficient sympathy for their cause that the government took care not to be seen to be acting provocatively, and particularly in helping unemployed individuals fight for their rights.

The NUWM did have victories in getting local PACs to raise benefit rates, or to impose the Means Test less harshly, and it also evolved a system of local committees trained in legal aspects of unemployment regulations and benefits to advise members, and, supported by advice from the legal department, to represent a member who took his or her appeal to the National Umpire at Kew. So successful was this growing expertise on national insurance questions that the NUWM was sometimes asked for help by a trade union branch, and William Beveridge invited Wal Hannington and Sid Elias to advise official committees on several occasions.

The Maryhill local branch of the NUWM in Glasgow was

> a hive of activity . . . People coming in were getting cut off from benefit as a result of the Means Test and all the other anomalies that were introduced then. And their case was taken up and there was always somebody at the Labour Exchanges representing them . . . the NUWM was organising, fighting appeals against the decision when people's benefits were cut, even turning out when people had been evicted for arrears of rent, advertising the many demonstrations which were taking place in Glasgow – at least one a week, where anything from 5,000 to 20,000 people were turning up . . . we used chalk or whitewash in the streets . . . we had a problem eventually. There were so many demonstrations taking place – unemployed and other – there wisnae enough space left at the street corner to advertise them all.

Michael Clark was 'never a member o' the Communist Party. I was in sympathy quite a lot, but I never did join . . . these fellows read politics and history goin' away back hundreds of years about the Clearances in Scotland . . . the big shot landlords and all that. I'd time for adventure books, but no time for politics!' Nevertheless, Clark took over as rent convenor on behalf of the NUWM in Greenock, taking direct action in disputes. 'We'd go to a house where eviction was threatened [for falling behind with the rent] and sit in the house . . . as many of us as possible, to occupy the house so's they widnae get takin' the furniture. And then we'd negotiate with the Parish Council and councillors . . . to get like a settled fee . . . for them to pay the rent, make up the arrears.'

The NUWM also organised social events for the unemployed: country rambles, football matches, whist drives, socials, study circles, concerts and dances. 'The jiggin', the dancin' was right popular – many of the best dancers in town went. Well, you could say that the unemployed got plenty o' time to practise! They got quite a good band together . . . they could go up to town and at the Palais de Danse they could have held their own wi' the best o' them.' Then there were days out for the children of the unemployed – including an outing to Battery Park near Greenock for 4,700 children who were provided with milk and buns and a bag of toffees to take home.

The charge stuck, however, of a movement controlled from Moscow, financed by 'red gold' and aiming at revolution. Yet if the NUWM attracted only relatively small numbers, the Communist Party certainly did no better. By August 1930 membership, which had peaked at 12,000 immediately after the General Strike in 1926, had fallen to fewer than 2,500, while the Labour Party had around 200,000 individual members. Since 1929 the CPGB had been pursuing the Communist International (Comintern)-dictated 'class against class' policy, identifying the Labour Party as the 'third capitalist party' and 'social fascists', and had severed links with other left-wing organisations including the ILP.

Villages such as Mardy at the head of the Rhondda Valley and Lumphinnans in the West Fife coalfield were demonised as 'Little Moscows' for their industrial militancy, opposition to the coal owners – and to the capitalist system in general – and their supposed unwavering support for communism (though the 'class against class' policy had eroded cooperation in local politics with Labour built up over a decade – as it closed so many doors – and reduced the CP to an opposition party). Miners formed the hard core of the membership, but the party was strongest in London and Scotland. While most CPGB members were relatively young, working-class men, by late 1932, 60 per cent of them were out of work, and that figure was higher in Scotland. There were few female members, since women had been 'completely neglected' in the drive to grow a mass party, and the Young Communist League could only claim two or three hundred members.

Moreover, the avenues of persuasion could be narrow. In Bolton, members of the Communist Party petitioned the central library to subscribe to the *Daily Worker* and periodicals such as *The USSR in Construction* and *Labour Monthly*, as well as to purchase what the local press dubbed 'red' books (such as Lenin's *Complete Works* and Plekanoff's *Fundamental Problems of Marxism*). The chief librarian circulated sample copies for a month, but the Library Committee gave hardly an inch, agreeing only that *Labour Monthly* could be placed in the reading room – and that for a trial period of six months only.

Nevertheless, the decision had been taken not only to try to grow a mass working-class revolutionary movement, but also to engage in electoral politics. However, Communist candidates performed poorly, and seemed unable to capitalise on growing disappointment first with the Labour, and then with the National Government. Even in Seaham, Ramsay MacDonald's own constituency, disgust with the 'great betrayer' did not translate into support for the Communist candidate, who only picked up 677 votes. The Party's most solid support was in London and the depressed mining areas, particularly those in Scotland and South Wales, and at the depth of the Depression in January 1932 membership had risen to 9,000. Yet in the Merthyr Tydfil by-election in 1934, Wal Hannington only managed to pick up 9.4 per cent of the votes, and the Communists were hardly more successful in local elections. In Gateshead even a local 'Douglas Credit' candidate polled more votes than the Communist contender, and no council in England was ever controlled by Communists. Although Communist participation in elections was of considerable 'nuisance value', splitting the left vote and sometimes, as in Whitechapel in London's East End, West Fife and a Sheffield seat, letting in a Conservative or National candidate, it was not until the 1935 election that the Party managed to send an MP to Westminster, when Willie Gallacher won West Fife and Harry Pollitt, the General Secretary, came within a whisker of being returned for East Rhondda.

Attempts to build an industrial base met with little success either: the Minority Movement, the Communist industrial organisation, urged the setting up of alternative unions to rival existing trade unions, but only two ever came into being: the United Mineworkers of Scotland, based in the coal mines of Fife, and the short-lived United Clothing Workers of East London. The Minority Movement never attracted more than seven hundred members, and when it was finally wound up in 1933 it could claim only 550 party members organised in eighty-two factory cells.

The Party's greatest problem in the early 1930s was its retention rate: if the NUWM leached members, so did the CPGB, partly due to 'rotten' organisation, and partly to the rigour and commitment demanded of recruits to the cause. An anonymous member of the Bromley Communist Party in Kent recalled that it had been 'a serious decision' when, after much discussion, eight people 'decided that the time had come to make a commitment to the Communist Party . . . for one thing the police, including the special branch, took a great interest in the activities, however trivial, of even rank and file members of the party. Secondly, a great many employers refused to employ anyone known to be associated with the party, and lastly, it meant virtual segregation and exclusion from the work of the Labour Party and even some Trade Unions.' Cut off from the rest of the 'reformist' left, the CPGB built itself something of a world within a world. 'Like practising Catholics or Orthodox Jews, we lived in a little private world of our own . . . a tight . . . self-referential group,' frequenting cafés such as Meg's in Parton Street in London and the Clarion in Market Street, Manchester ('Communists met in cafés rather than pubs: there was quite a strong inhibition against drink'), the pro-Soviet Scala cinema in Charlotte Street in London, Henderson's 'bomb shop' (which became Collet's bookshop) and others in King Street and the Farringdon Road, as well as meeting at dances and whist drives organised by the Friends of the Soviet Union, the League of Socialist Freethinkers, the Rebel Players and the Federation of Student Societies, and the activities of the Workers' Theatre Movement and the

British Workers' Sports Federation. They rambled collectively at weekends, took holidays at Socialist youth camps or Communist guest houses, or stayed in youth hostels as part of hiking trips (some YHA wardens were rumoured to be 'sympathisers'). If the expenditure of £5 was feasible, they might take a week's holiday with the Workers' Travel Association in the Lake District, or maybe the Trossachs.

Certainly a great deal was asked of a Communist: attending frequent meetings, organising, speaking, selling Party literature, trade union activities, membership of other outside bodies and 'front' organisations. Ernest Trory suggests the level of commitment required: 'I had become engaged to a girl who was not at all interested in the Party. The engagement was later broken off but in the meantime I began to spend more time dancing and taking her to the pictures than was consistent with Party work . . . To make matters worse, I frequented the Empire Club. A real sink of iniquity . . . spending my time gambling and playing cards, when I was needed by the Party at a critical time . . .'

As well as regular attendance at 'advanced political training lectures', the Bromley Communists were expected to sell the weekend edition of the *Daily Worker* (produced in its early days in an unheated office without electricity, the editor typing articles by candlelight) outside Woolworths and Marks & Spencer's in the town centre, although they found they could shift more copies late on Saturday evenings, 'when the bus crews returned to Bromley garage at the end of a day's work'. However, 'sales were not very great, twenty to thirty copies being considered adequate compensation for the long hours worked'. Perhaps that was hardly surprising, since at the time the *Daily Worker*, the first issue of which had appeared on 1 January 1930, echoed the Communist Party's dilemma. It was to contain none of the 'frills . . . dazzle . . . corruption and entertainment' of the popular press, so as not to distract readers from the struggle. But Harry Pollitt, the Party's General Secretary since 1929, was prepared to venture that he thought the paper was 'dull and dismal', and suggested that those who produced it should study the 'techniques of the capitalist press'. 'We constantly talk about being close to the masses,' Pollitt argued in June 1930 when the paper was selling a maximum of 10,000 copies and haemorrhaging some £500 each week from Party funds, 'but no one can say we carry this out in regard to the paper.' What the 'masses' wanted was more general news, sport, humour and topical features, but what they got in the pages of the *Daily Worker* was 'nothing save struggle and death on every page'. Two journalists, one from the *Daily Mail*, the other from the *Daily Express*, were invited to moonlight on the *Daily Worker* to teach the staff how to use capitalism's skills against the capitalists. However, faced with the edict of the CPGB's severe theoretician, R. Palme Dutt, that 'The task is to destroy (not to take over) . . . so-called "general news" and "sport" . . . and replace it by working-class technique,' the pair scuttled back to their day jobs. Despite a gradual dilution of the paper's strict on-message stance with more news – including some investigative 'scoops' – the odd photograph of Gracie Fields, film reviews, excellent cartoons and a women's page with recipes and knitting patterns, it was some time before racing tips, which had disappeared after the first few issues, were allowed back; they remained a distinct selling point for much of the century.

In January 1933, Hitler's assumption of the German chancellorship led to a change in the class-against-class policy, and in the summer of 1935 the Seventh (and last) Congress of the International affirmed the Soviet intention 'to establish a united front on a national as well as an international scale' against fascism – a front that it was argued should include democratic political parties across a wide spectrum. This was not to be a call to which the British Labour Party responded, though the change of policy did bring the CPGB new recruits, among them engin-eers, railwaymen, textile workers, builders and some in the distributive trades. Jack Gaster, who had previously regarded the Party as 'ultra sectarian . . . their concept of a United Front was "We'll unite with anyone who unites with us,"' and had helped expel 'a secret group of Communist Party members within the ILP', had himself lost patience with the ILP by 1935 and joined the CPGB, undertaking frequent legal work for the Party.

Although the CPGB remained an overwhelmingly working-class party, it had always attracted a small number of intellectuals, particularly scien-tists, and in the 1930s it gradually drew in a coterie of undergraduates and recent graduates of Oxford and Cambridge, sometimes referred to sneer-ingly by Rose Macaulay as 'the not-so-very intelligentsia', or, as Beatrice Webb labelled them, 'the mild-mannered desperadoes'.

In 1931 David Guest, son of the Labour peer Lord Haden-Guest, returned to Trinity College, Cambridge, after a year studying in Germany, where he had become convinced that the threat of fascism was dangerously real, and that communism was the only hope, and set about organising the Cambridge branch of the CPGB. This attracted his fellow philosophy student Maurice Cornforth, the poet Charles Madge, John Cornford, James Klugmann and Guy Burgess, all of whom were mentored by Maurice Dobb, an economist and Fellow of Trinity College who had been a member of the Party since 1923, and who had suffered professionally for his affiliation.

The best-known, most-heard (if most tenuously linked) of those Oxbridge students and ex-students who were drawn to communism in the mid 1930s were the 'MacSpaundays' – the poets and would-be poets W.H. Auden, Louis MacNeice, Stephen Spender and Cecil Day Lewis. 'Tell us about the Thirties,' a group of Cambridge undergraduates urged Day Lewis after the Second World War; '. . . it seems to be the last time that anyone believed in anything.' 'We were singularly fortunate compared with the young of today,' acknowledged the poet, 'in believing that something could be done about the social and political evils confronting us . . . no one who did not go through this political experience during the Thirties can quite realise how much hope there was in the air then, how radiant for some of us was the illusion that man could, under Communism put the world to rights.'

What communism offered such young intellectuals was 'substitutes for a faith, heterogeneous ideas which served to plug "the hollow in the breast where God should be"'. Most of Day Lewis's friends who became active in left-wing movements, or sympathetic to them, had similar backgrounds. All had been to public schools, 'with their tradition of both authoritarianism and service to the community'. Three were the sons clergymen – Day Lewis himself, Louis MacNeice and Rex Warner – while W.H. Auden had 'a devout Anglo-Catholic mother . . . we had all lapsed from the Christian faith, and tended to despair of Liberalism as an effective instrument for dealing with the problems of our day, if not despise it as an outworn creed'.

For Day Lewis the attraction to communism had both a religious and a romantic dimension: 'My susceptibility to the heroic, played upon by Russian films in which the worker, mounted upon his magnificent tractor, chugged steadily towards the dawn and the new world, joined up with my natural partisanship of the underdog to create a picture, romantic and apocalyptic, of the British worker at last coming into his own.' Nevertheless, he was, he admitted, 'an extremely odd recruit to the Party' in Cheltenham, where he was teaching at the time (though with a 'gentlemanly refusal to indoctrinate my pupils with Left-Wing ideas'). The CPGB cell there resembled 'more of a combined study-group of a nonconformist chapel than of a revolutionary body', consisting as it did of 'one or two school teachers, a waiter, and several men who worked at the Gloucester aircraft factory . . . as an "intellectual" I was given the job of political education. Never can there have been a more signal instance of the blind leading the shortsighted. I mugged up Das Kapital, The Communist Manifesto, the writings of Lenin, and endeavoured to teach dialectical materialism and economic theories I only half understood to people who lived their lives right up against the fact of economic necessity.'

Although Auden issued a clarion call to his generation to stop 'lecturing on navigation while the ship is going down', he did not join the CPGB. Nor did MacNeice, another 'Marxist of the Heart' for whom 'comrade became a more tender term than lover'. Despite this, MacNeice could see communism's attraction after the 'jogtrot' left of the Labour Party, which was 'notoriously lacking in glamour', and he could appreciate why 'these young poets had turned to the tomb of Lenin . . . The strongest appeal of the Communist Party was that it demanded sacrifice; you had to sink your ego.' Though he was 'repelled by the idolisation of the state', MacNeice was able to console himself with Marx and Engels' dictum that it would soon 'wither away'. Spender did actually sign up, but his membership was short-lived.

Other Cambridge Communist sympathisers who would later gain notoriety for their espionage activities on behalf of the USSR included Donald MacLean, H.A.R. (Kim) Philby and Anthony Blunt, who was always 'thought of as a fellow-traveller, never as a Party member [and who made] extremely cynical remarks about Communism that went beyond the call of duty in suppressing the fact that he was one'.

But there were those who were prepared to make the commitment. In December 1931 the October Club (named after the Bolshevik revolution of 1917) was started in Oxford by an American Rhodes scholar, Frank Meyer, who subsequently translated to the London School of Economics, where he remained active in student politics until he was deported by the government. By January 1933 it could boast three hundred members, though not all of these were card-carrying Communists. However, by 1934 Communists had effectively succeeded in taking over the Oxford Labour Club, hanging a huge portrait of Lenin on the wall of the club's meeting house to signal their entryism. Not everyone advertised their affiliation, but Philip Toynbee, the son of the Oxford historian Arnold Toynbee and grandson of the classicist Gilbert Murray, who had joined the CPGB at the end of his first term at Oxford and 'retired deeper and deeper into this secretive hive . . . was not a clandestine member, but sat on a little iceberg peak above the submarine majority, revealing, as we used to say, "the Face of the Party"'. Toynbee exemplified the song 'we would ruefully sing at our evening socials [the Bromley branch members would, no doubt, have joined in] :

Dan, Dan, Dan!
The Communist Party man
Working underground all day.

> In and out of meetings,
> Bringing fraternal greetings,
> Never sees the light of day.

His undergraduate life consisted largely of sitting through interminable committee meetings, sometimes lasting 'from lunchtime until eight or nine in the evening', leafleting, demonstrating in support of strikes in Oxford factories, taking part in 'slogan-shouting marches through London', attending international Communist Party conferences, going to work alongside the miners in the Rhondda Valley, soaking up 'the whole lively atmosphere of purpose and intrigue'. In 1938 he was elected the first Communist President of the Oxford Union (to be succeeded by Edward Heath two terms later).

While there were probably around two hundred card-carrying Oxford undergraduates, in Cambridge several dons were members of the CPGB, including Dobb, the biochemist 'Doggy' Woolf and the literary scholar Roy Pascal. By 1935 the Cambridge Socialist Society of around five hundred members was dominated by Communists, of whom again some two hundred were Party members. The Cambridge cell, centred on Trinity and King's colleges, was active in the town organising anti-war demonstrations, supporting CP candidates at elections and welcoming the Hunger Marchers in February 1934 (Margot Heinemann owed her conversion to an encounter while at Newnham with the wan and down-at-heel marchers, and remained a Party member all her life), as well as within the colleges agitating for better pay and conditions for college servants, distributing leaflets and selling copies of the *Daily Worker*.

But despite this varied and gifted glitterati, 'traitors to their class' until the Party line changed, the 'entry of the intellectuals' remained something of a trickle, and for every student, scientist or poet who declared for communism there were hundreds of workers. Though the membership of the CPGB rose to a pre-war peak of 18,000 in December 1938, the vast majority of members were working-class. Moreover, distrust of the eggheads did not fade easily: in 1938 one veteran at the fifteenth Party Congress railed against 'these unscrupulous semi-intellectuals who pose as left revolutionaries, who put their "r"s in barricades, instead of putting their arse on the barricades'.

NINE

Primers for the Age

I regard *Nature* as perhaps the most important weekly printed in English, far more important than any political weekly.

Arnold Bennett, November 1930

Mr [H.G.] Wells at one time appeared to think that the scientists might save us. Then more recently it was going to be international financiers. But so many committed suicide. So now it is going to be aviators. Perhaps soon we will be told to pin our hopes on a dictatorship of midwives.

Professor F.S. Blackett, 'The Frustration of Science' (1935)

In October 1933 the writer H.G. Wells gave a dinner party. Since he had invited too many guests to fit round the table in his flat in Chiltern Court, off Baker Street, the party dined first at the Quo Vadis restaurant in Dean Street, Soho – a building in which Karl Marx had once rented rooms – and then repaired to the flat, where it was promised that Moura Budberg (a Russian aristocrat and probably the common-law wife of the writer Maxim Gorky, who had to come to London as Wells' mistress, but continued to maintain distinctly shady links with the Soviet Union) would entertain the assembled company by playing the harp. It was a glamorous evening, with the socialite Lady Emerald Cunard 'in ermine, almost invisible under pearls and diamonds, scenting out the lions', the novelist Enid Bagnold, now married to the head of Reuter's, Sir Roderick Jones, 'brazening out' a nettle rash by covering her face with an orange veil, Harold Nicolson, Max Beerbohm, and 'H.G. at the centre, rosily smiling, all the guests talking at once'.

Unfortunately a number of the guests, including Moura Budberg, were taken ill with food poisoning, so there was no music that night, but there was endless discussion, as there always was at Wells' *soirées*, including one the month before, assembled 'to discuss a magnificent idea he has, to unite science to save the world against all its growing dangers: Fascism, Communism,

Japanism, Americanism and Journalism . . . H.G. "chaired" the meeting in his squeaky voice, which becomes quite a handicap in such circumstances. Nothing was decided, naturally, except the *need for something*, and H.G. will go on giving dinner parties to discuss saving the world.'

'Saving the world' from the list of spectres Wells evoked, as well as those of the economic slump and intractable unemployment at home, was something discussed at a lot of top people's dinner tables in the 1930s. And scientists were at the forefront of such debate, as many were convinced that scientific methods would come up with solutions that inexpert, ill-informed, blundering politicians seemed utterly unable to locate.

Although he was primarily interested at the time in 'the reproductive physiology of monkeys and apes, and the bearing of any evidence on the evolutionary interrelationship of monkeys, apes and man', which he was well placed to research as Prosecutor, or research fellow, at the Zoological Society in Regent's Park (a post he had achieved at the young age of twenty-four), Solly Zuckerman also had a wider range of interests. The atmosphere of the time encouraged him to discuss with some friends, including the young political economist (and great joiner of discussion groups) Hugh Gaitskell and G.P. 'Gip' Wells, the zoologist son of H.G., the idea of forming a small dining club. In the autumn of 1931 'Tots and Quots', an abbreviation and inversion of the phrase in Terence's *Phormio*: '*Quot homines, tot sententiae*' – 'So many men, so many opinions' – convened for the first time at Pagani's restaurant in Great Portland Street.

It was a distinguished (entirely male) table: the robustly confident young scientists who assembled to 'let ideas roam' over the question of 'what role science might play in social development' included the physicist and crystallographer J.D. Bernal (reverentially known as 'the sage' although he confessed that even his encyclopaedic knowledge had lacunae when it came to 'fourth century Roumania'), who believed that science 'held the key to the future', while socialism had the ability to turn it; the geneticist J.B.S. Haldane, perhaps 'the last man to know all there was to be known', with a matchless ability to communicate the complex in public lectures, books and his regular science columns in the *Daily Worker*; the biologist and author of the best-selling *Mathematics for the Million* and *Science for the Citizen*, books he described as 'primers for an age of plenty' intended to equip their readers with sufficient knowledge to become effective citizens in a scientific age, Lancelot Hogben, a conscientious objector in the First World War whose acute mind challenged everything; the prehistorian Gordon Childe (another success with what he referred to as the 'bookstall public'); the sinologist and historian of science Joseph Needham; the

189

zoologist J.Z. Young; the Cambridge economic historian M.M. Postan and the Oxford economist Roy Harrod. Others, such as the literary critic I.A. Richards and the geneticist Lionel Penrose, declined to join but volunteered to 'clock in' as guests when the subject under discussion interested them.

Tots and Quots dinners lapsed for a time in the mid-1930s (not helped by the fact that Hugh Gaitskell probably lost the Minute Book), but the club reconvened in 1939 (with a slightly shuffled membership which now also included Richard Crossman) as a 'platform to proclaim our views . . . about the vast potential [for the] applications of scientific knowledge when dealing with the complicated problems of war'.

But although 'Gip' Wells, who had co-written the best-selling *The Science of Life* with Julian Huxley at his father's bidding, resigned after the first dinner, complaining that 'he had hoped the whole thing would be fun, whereas we were obviously going to become monastic and deadly serious', the small (fourteen was the average number) group of scientists and economists met regularly during the worst years of the Depression, eating well as they pondered the responsibilities of their discipline in a country shot through with social and economic problems.

In 1934 Ritchie Calder, the scientific correspondent of the *Daily Herald*, advocated that the House of Lords should be replaced by what he called a 'Senate of Scientists'. The year before, the Nobel Prize-winning biochemist Sir Frederick Gowland Hopkins, in his Presidential Address to the British Association for the Advancement of Science, had urged the formation of a 'Solomon's House' of the wisest (men) in the land who would assemble to synthesise knowledge, appraise its progress and assess its impact on society. The nutritionist F. LeGros Clark stated that scientists found politics 'a disreputable game', which it was their duty to 'try to transform into a pastime with clean, scientific rules'. Professor Frederick Soddy was explicit: since science was society's 'real master', society should 'insist on being ruled, not by a reflection of a reflection, but directly by those [scientists] who are concerned with the creation of its wealth, not its debts'. J.B.S. Haldane, writing in *Nature* in January 1934, had suggested that refusing to apply scientific method to the conduct of human affairs would bring about the failure of Britain's political and economic system.

When it was suggested to the eminent biologist Julian Huxley that he should stand for Parliament, he dismissed the idea, saying that what guided his life was a passion for truth, not its 'obscuration'. In the book he was invited to write for a series entitled 'If I Were Dictator' (since this was before the full development of Hitler's Third Reich or Stalin's USSR, the word 'dictator' was not freighted with the same terrible associations it later came to carry), Huxley further showed his disregard for democratic politics, proposing instead a corporatist state in which elections would be 'superfluous'. A central planning council would replace Parliament, which was little more than a 'talking-shop', according to Huxley, and lacked the necessary expertise to the run the country (as, presumably by extension, the electorate lacked the necessary expertise to choose a government).

Social issues in the 1930s had a direct bearing on the scientific community: technological advances were charged with having thrown thousands out of work, and creating machines for military savagery; the Hunger Marches were a symbol of the malnutrition of the unemployed, which Sir John Boyd Orr would quantify in 1936 in his book *Food, Health and Income*; Oswald Mosley was using spurious 'scientific' arguments to inflame anti-Semitism; genetic inheritance was the subject of much debate – the sterilisation of 'morons' (defined by the journal *Nature* as making up 'a large proportion of the slum population . . . mental defectives of comparatively high grade . . . people lacking not only in intelligence but also in self-control, which is the basis of morality, and they reproduce recklessly') was seriously discussed in Britain and put into practice in Nazi Germany; while the growing threat of war later in the decade rallied scientific expertise to steel defences and develop weapons of destruction.

Moreover, world events were enlarging Britain's scientific community. British scientists were made acutely aware of the pernicious uses to which scientific theories and inventions could be put when Jewish scientists such as the chemists Gerhard Weiler, E.F. Freundlich and Michael Polanyi, who had been dismissed or resigned from their research or teaching institutes after Hitler came to power, fled to Britain, as did the biochemist Herman Blaschko, the biologist Hans Krebs, the physicists Max Born, Hans Bethe, Heinrich Kuhn, Rudolph Peierls and Kurt Mendelssohn. Boris Chain, a young biochemist, left Germany on 30 January 1933, the day Adolf Hitler was created Chancellor, and came to Britain, where he sought the help of J.B.S. Haldane. Chain eventually moved to Oxford University, and in 1945 he and Sir Howard Florey shared the Nobel Prize for their work on isolating penicillin (though the university denied him even a readership).

After Chain, Haldane sought out more young scientists who needed to flee Hitler's Germany, working alongside Professor F.A. Lindemann (who had himself been born and educated in Germany and later, as Lord Cherwell, would be Churchill's wartime scientific advisor) and an Oxford Professor of Organic Chemistry, Robert Robinson, on the Academic Assistance Council (AAC – renamed the Society for the Protection of Science and Learning in 1936). The Council, chaired by the physicist Sir Ernest Rutherford, director of the prestigious Cambridge Cavendish Laboratory, had come into existence in May 1933 after William Beveridge (then director of the London School of Economics) wrote a letter to *The Times* drawing attention to the plight of Jewish scientists in Germany and Austria. Beveridge had been alerted to the situation by Leo Szilard, a Hungarian scientist who had worked with Einstein (who had declared his intention never to return to Germany and to resign from the Prussian Academy of Sciences in protest at Hitler's racial policies in March 1933), and a young Englishwoman, Tess (Esther) Simpson, who went on to run the organisation.

By 1935 around 25 per cent of all scientists and 20 per cent of all mathematicians had been dismissed from German universities under the Nazis' harsh race laws. The AAC sought to enable such people to continue their research in British universities or industry or, as so many yearned to do, to move to the United States, thus 'salvaging' a number of scientists, in some cases with great difficulty. 'Brains in Germany seem to be going cheap and we have no tariff for them,' wrote W.J. Sollas, the aged Professor of Geology at Oxford. By May 1934, sixty-seven 'wandering scholars', as Rutherford called them, had found positions at London University, thirty-one at Cambridge, seventeen at Oxford and sixteen at Manchester, greatly enriching the British scientific community.

Although the early 1930s were 'by far the richest time there has ever been' for scientific innovation, in the opinion of the chemist and novelist C.P. Snow, with an *annus mirabilis* in 1932, when John Cockcroft and Ernest Walton succeeded in splitting the atom, and James Chadwick did likewise with the neutron, there was disquiet among sections of the scientific community. Many felt that those outside their profession looked down on scientific activities as culturally inferior to the arts, and they themselves were seen as little more than lab rats producing work only 'of great *value in their own departments*', in the dismissive view of T.S. Eliot. The Bishop of Ripon, E.A. Burroughs, in his address to the annual meeting of the British Association for the Advancement of Science in Leeds on 4 September 1927, had invited the scientific community to declare a ten-year moratorium on research, for the general good of mankind, since while science had undoubtedly advanced knowledge, it had done nothing to increase wisdom. (H.G. Wells had recently in effect suggested a similar – though permanent – 'holiday' for the episcopate, also in the cause of human progress.) Society was suffering, in the Bishop's view, from a 'moral lag, a gap between moral and scientific advance, for man's body had in effect gone on growing while his soul had largely stood still or gone back'.

Notwithstanding the Bishop, scientific research carried on, but the

Association strove harder to break down public resistance to the advance of science. Some scientists discussed whether by growing more specialised they might have become 'blinkered' to the wider concerns of humanity, while others addressed the question of whether science had a particular relevance – even a special duty – to society. And a small number of radical scientists at Cambridge (particularly), London and a few other universities, or assembled round the Tots and Quots dining table, despaired that their agenda for the 'social responsibility of science' was not in fact what generally drove scientific endeavour or its public perception. As Zuckerman pointed out, the 'efforts of scientists are generally misunderstood, because they are not interpreted to the world by scientists themselves, and because few of those who are immediately responsible for the conduct of social affairs are scientists. There are, for example, no scientists in the Government.' Moreover, as the Marxist mathematician Hyman Levy argued to Julian Huxley in a BBC broadcast in 1931, 'Since scientists, like other workers, have to earn their living . . . to a large extent the demands of those who provide the money will, very broadly, determine the spread of scientific interest in the field of applied science . . . I know of no scientist who is so free that he can study anything he likes, or who is not limited in some way by limitations such as the cost of equipment.'

J.D. Bernal (whose book *The Social Function of Science* was a manifesto and a blueprint for the unlimited potential of science for progress, especially once it was freed from the shackles of capitalism) took up the theme in response to a criticism from a fellow scientist that 'Bernalism is the doctrine of those who profess that the proper objects of scientific research are to feed people and protect them from the elements, that research workers should be organised in gangs and told what to discover.' It wasn't, he riposted, as if the idea that science had a social function was new. It was 'palpable and admitted fact', and that function was 'largely economic under present conditions and likely to become even more so'. Nevertheless, under capitalism, science was not generally regarded as being capable of 'solv[ing] completely the material conditions of society', Bernal wrote in 1935, 'but rather the best application of science is conceived of as producing such a fatuous and stupefying paradise as . . . *Brave New World* [by Aldous Huxley, Julian's younger brother, published in 1932]; at worst, a super-efficient machine for mutual destruction with men living underground and only coming up in gas masks'.

To Hyman Levy, as to Bernal, Lancelot Hogben, J.B.S. Haldane, Joseph Needham and other radical scientists, only a society transformed along socialist lines into a planned economy producing an abundance of socially useful goods, equitably distributed to all sections of the population who would thus feel 'practically and morally bound to one another in this great collective endeavour' would devote sufficient scientific resources to the solution of economic and social problems. For Levy, what had become clear was 'not only the social conditioning of science and the vital need for planning . . . but the impossibility of carrying this through within the framework of a chaotic capitalism' in which scientists felt unlistened to, undervalued and underfunded (only 0.1 per cent of the Gross National Product was devoted to scientific research and development in the 1930s; by the 1960s it was nearer 3 per cent). For Bernal, 'Science has ceased to be the occupation of curious gentlemen or of ingenious minds supported by wealthy patrons, and has become an industry supported by large industrial monopolies and by the State.' But in a capitalist society this had resulted in 'a structure of appalling inefficiency both as to its internal organization and as the means of the application to problems of production or of welfare'. Bernal's plan, or map, of the future direction of science had analogies with Keynes' economic plan: government would need to take a centralised directional role in the healthy development of science and technology, as in the economy.

But unlike Keynes, Bernal was and continued to be a Marxist all his life (though his membership of the CPGB lapsed in 1933 – or was allowed to lapse, since at the time the Communist Party entertained a certain suspicion of intellectuals). 'During the years of the great Depression I began to study in a more serious way the works of the founders of Marxism, and there I found a philosophy . . . that could be lived and could be a guide to action,' he wrote. *The Social Function of Science* was explicit – and much quoted both by those admiring and those critical of the 'red scientists' of the 1930s of whom Bernal was at the forefront ('that sink of ubiquity', Hyman Levy called him) – in insisting on science's social responsibilities. Bernal also played a key role in the regeneration of the Association of Scientific Workers: 'In its endeavour science is communism . . . In science men have learned consciously to subordinate themselves to a common purpose without losing the individuality of their achievements . . . Only in the wider tasks of humanity will their full use be found.'

Across the river from the laboratories of London University and the Tots and Quots dining tables, an ambitious building designed for a new way of living was taking shape. In January 1935 the young Frances Lonsdale, who would become both a Somerset farmer (as a near neighbour of Evelyn Waugh) and an acute biographer of Edward VIII, was picking her way behind her future husband, Jack Donaldson, through the 'dust and rubble of a new building that had recently arisen in the suburb of Peckham. The building, which had been minutely planned to serve an entirely original purpose, had a front elevation of curved glass windows set in concrete two stories high, and was functional, not in the architectural sense of the word in much use at that time, but in response to the needs of an inspired conception . . . Although built with a flat roof and without decoration, it had an elegant buoyancy which was to remind one, when it was lit up at night, of a great liner at sea . . . It was not quite finished, and it was for me astonishingly material evidence of what seemed an incredible venture.' This modernist wonder had been designed by Sir Owen Williams, a noted structural engineer rather than an architect (a species he dismissed as 'decoration merchants'), who already had to his credit the huge Boots factory in Nottingham and the glittering, black-glass-fronted *Daily Express* office in Fleet Street. Its simple, airy construction was designed expressly for the occupant: the Pioneer Health Centre, a cause to which Jack Donaldson would donate £10,000, nearly half the money he had inherited from his father. Lord Nuffield was also a donor.

This 'form following function' ethos of modernist architecture was particularly salient, since the Pioneer Health Centre was constructed to house a large-scale experiment on the effect of the environment on health, a concentration on preventative rather than curative medicine. The pioneers were a husband and wife team, Dr George Scott Williamson and Dr Innes Pearse, and the new Health Centre was the result of five years' fund-raising activity by the couple to move their work from a small house nearby to this beacon to their conviction that, like illness, health could also be conta-gious. Once a patient presented at a doctor's surgery or hospital ward, Dr Pearce believed that he or she would be in 'the advanced stages of *incapacitating* disorder' – that is, they *felt* ill. She had been appalled when working in a welfare clinic in Stepney in London's East End to realise that she had never seen a healthy baby. The only time mothers came to the clinic was in an emergency, and all she could do was to treat the ailing infant. There was no time to enquire into the circumstances of the exhausted-looking mother, and of course she never saw the father.

What was needed were not just health facilities that acted as a 'sieve for the detection of disease', but conditions in which people could 'keep fit and ward off sickness *before* they were smitten'; these would be provided by a place where the *practice* of health was distinct from the conventional prac-tice of medicine. Only families, which the Peckham pioneers had decided were the 'units for living', were allowed to join, each paying a shilling a week (the Centre was intended to be self-supporting), and every member had to submit to periodic 'health overhauls' designed to check their capacity for individual, family and social life. For an additional few pence they could use a wide range of recreational facilities including a gymnasium, badminton court, roller-skating rink, swimming pool, billiards tables, a theatre space, and rooms for sewing parties or gramophone recitals. There were facilities for children (who had to be restrained from using the glass ashtrays for games of curling along the long corridors) and a nursery club for the under-fives, with specially designed equipment (and much note-taking by the staff) intended to improve family life and enhance personal development. While the Pioneer Health Centre was distinctly modern, experimental and forward-looking in its concept, organisation and habitat, it simultaneously looked back to a pre-industrial community in which a doctor knew his patients in health as in sickness, and the circumstances of their lives, a country village (though without the feudal superstructure) recreated in a busy, fractured inner-city area.

Although Peckham had been chosen because it was a densely populated yet reasonably prosperous working- and lower-middle-class area where such facilities might be expected to add value to the inhabitants' lives, the first survey of five hundred members conducted in 1936 found that 59 per cent suffered from ailments such as diabetes, high blood pressure, tuberculosis or cancer, even though they believed themselves to be healthy. Vindication indeed of the Centre's prophylactic aims, the pioneers thought.

'We are not here to dispense charity, nor to seek out the most help-less and unfortunate in order that we may succour them,' Dr Scott Williamson told the Medical Officer of Health for Camberwell, in whose fiefdom the Pioneer Health Centre was located. Rather the Centre's aims were 'social self maintenance', and the pioneers were 'scientists hoping to find out how people living under modern industrial conditions of life might best cultivate health, and thus to benefit humankind as a whole'. The subscribers to this pioneer 'laboratory' (who described themselves as 'guinea pigs') spent their time there in conditions of 'controlled anarchy': the staff were instructed, 'Don't make rules to make your life easier,' and Williamson encouraged the idea that the somewhat undisciplined chil-dren would eventually evolve their own system of order. Most of the staff lived communally in a large house on Bromley Common, and when not at work in the Centre they 'wrangled all day long'. From 1935 a home farm established on the Common grew organic vegetables and produced fresh milk – 'vital foods' – at cost price for the Centre with the aim of discovering 'how far the early symptoms of trouble [detected in a "C3" population] can be removed by fresh food grown on organic soil' – Williamson and Pearse were both members of the Soil Association council.

The Pioneer Health Centre was high-minded, utopian, convinced ('strong meat', Donaldson thought) – and ultimately not possible to sustain. Partly as a result of the introduction of the National Health Service in July 1948 the Centre was unable to attract sufficient funding, and it closed in 1950.

While it may have been unrealistic to imagine in the economic climate of the 1930s that Pioneer Health Centres could be rolled out all over Britain, health centres practising medicine alongside welfare clinics (which Williamson and Pearce derided as 'polyclinics') were also a rarity (and indeed would be until the 1960s). Although the Dawson Report back in 1920 had advocated a system based on groups of medical practitioners working from publicly funded health centres which integrated preventative and curative medicine, this appeared too much like costly state interference with the autonomy of doctors, and the idea was shelved.

There was, however, a 'polyclinic' in the neighbouring (and much poorer) borough of Bermondsey, which opened in 1936 as part of what the radical borough (which had pulled down the Union Jack from the municipal flag-pole and run up a red flag instead when the ILP won a majority on the Council in 1924) liked to describe as the 'Bermondsey Revolution'. It was the brain-child of Alfred Salter, a doctor and the ILP MP for West Bermondsey, and the husband of Ada Salter, the first woman Labour mayor in Britain. Salter was determined to bring together 'a solarium for tuberculosis, dental clinics, foot clinics, ante-natal and child welfare clinics', formerly scattered in 'ordinary dwelling houses', into one building that would serve as 'the Harley Street of Bermondsey', where the range of services would provide the poor of the borough with 'the best diagnosis and advice that London could provide . . . as good as any the rich could secure'.

Bermondsey did not rest content with a state-of-the-art health centre. It took its message out into the streets, proselytising about healthy living by means of posters, large-print pamphlets (forty-two were produced in 1932 alone), lectures, and electric signs flashing warnings against spitting, messages about the advantages of drinking milk, and pithy slogans such as 'Your son and heir needs sun and air'. Furthermore, a disinfectant van was equipped with a cinema projector and a lantern for outdoor showings of short films made by the Public Health Department (the cameraman's day job was as a radiographer), including such masterpieces as *Where There's Life, There's Soap* (a film for children on personal cleanliness), *Delay is Dangerous* (about the early signs of tuberculosis and the need to seek medical advice) and one with a slightly admonishing ring, *Some Activities of Bermondsey Council,* intended to remind the borough's citizens how much their elected authority was doing for them in the fields of housing and public health (which it undoubtedly was). The open-air screenings took place in the summer months (though not in July and August, as it didn't get dark until 10 p.m., and in any case many Bermondsey residents were away in Kent hop-picking – a film, *'Oppin,* was made about that too). The Council fitted twenty-four lamp-posts in various parts of the borough with special plugs so that the 'cinemas' could be plugged in, and films were shown in the street, in the courtyards of new housing estates, in parks, children's playgrounds and the new Health Centre. By 1932 there were over sixty shows a year, drawing an audience of around 30,000, though both the number of shows and the size of the audiences had begun to tail off by the end of the decade.

An impressive modernist 'drop-in' Health Centre (designed by the Georgian émigré architect Berthold Lubetkin, who had already designed a prototype TB clinic for Dr Philip Ellman, the Medical Officer of Health for East Ham and a member of the Socialist Medical Association, which was never built) opened in Finsbury in North London, another very poor borough, in 1938. Built like a 'megaphone for health', with two wings splayed out from a central axis, it housed a TB clinic, a foot clinic, a dental clinic, a mother and baby clinic, a disinfecting station, a lecture hall and a solarium where the sun-starved children of the borough might benefit from ultraviolet-ray treatment, as well as fumigating facilities and a mortuary in the basement. So representative of a better life for all those who had previously suffered 'C3'-level health – and health care – was Finsbury that it was depicted on one of Abram Games' wartime posters urging 'Your Britain: Fight for it Now'.

But for those not resident in one of those London boroughs and without reasonable means, provision for the unwell in the 1930s remained an example of hotchpotch availability, lack of funding and reluctance to extend state involvement, all resulting in inequality of access to medical services.

Men working in insurable occupations and earning less than £250 a year were covered by a contributory National Health Insurance scheme, introduced in 1913, to (barely) tide them over in times of sickness and provide basic medical treatment and medicines from a 'panel' doctor. However, by 1936 only around twenty million people, about 40 per cent of the total population of 47.5 million, including six million working women, were covered. They did not include dependent wives (except in the case of maternity benefit) and children. Those earning over £250 a year would have to make their own private sickness insurance arrangements – though they could contribute to the NHI scheme through voluntary payments if they could afford to.

The NHI scheme did not cover dental or ophthalmic treatment, though some of the larger 'approved societies' (usually friendly societies or industrial insurance companies, and a few trade unions) which administered the scheme might offer such fringe benefits to attract customers. This meant that for many working-class men and women tooth decay and premature toothlessness were inhibiting and intermittently painful features of life ('Teeth, teeth, teeth, they are half the trouble [with women's health],' wrote a country district nurse in February1938), while Woolworths offered 'do it yourself' eye tests for those unable to afford to consult an ophthalmologist about their need for spectacles.

There were continual complaints that those who received their treatment from the NHI scheme, known as being 'on the panel', got inferior treatment. At least 5,000 doctors remained outside the scheme, and those operating within it in suburban or rural areas often derived most of their income from private patients. A GP employing one assistant could easily have 4,000 panel patients (for each of whom he would receive a capitation fee of about 9s.6d), and it was quite usual for a single doctor to be responsible for as many as 2,500 patients, so those in poor areas with a large percentage of their patients 'on the panel' were likely to give only cursory consultations.

In industrial areas the doctor's surgery would often be housed in a shop where the window would be painted halfway up to ensure some degree of privacy. Patients would queue outside (even when it was raining) until it was their turn to see the doctor. Doctors were not salaried (nor were hospital consultants), so they relied on fees and/or insurance payments, the latter of which were invariably lower, so in general poorer areas, where there were few if any fee-paying patients, were served by either less able or more altruistic doctors. In more prosperous middle-class areas, doctors would usually see their patients in the front room of their own homes. The fee-paying patient would have an appointment and be shown in at the front door by the doctor's wife (or maybe a maid, if finances and status permitted), whereas panel patients would enter by the surgery door, and sit and wait until the doctor was ready to see them. The surgery would smell of phenol, since most GPs were expected to perform operations such as removing appendixes and tonsils, hysterectomies, hernia repairs and suchlike, although increasingly these took place in the local cottage hospitals found in suburbs, smaller towns and rural areas, which by 1935 provided around 10,000 beds.

Or patients might request a home visit (more readily agreed to for private patients), when all the technology available would be the instruments the doctor could carry in his (or very occasionally her) Gladstone bag.

Eileen Whiteing remembered that if influenza or tonsillitis were suspected in her comfortable Surrey home, 'Dr Cressy would be sent for and he usually prescribed the dreaded "slops" which meant that we were only to be given such things as steamed fish, poached eggs, beef tea, milk puddings and so on, until he called again in a day or so.' Doctors' fees varied depending on the area and sometimes on the patient's ability to pay. A doctor attending poorer families would usually require to be paid cash at the time of a consultation or visit (as earlier 'sixpenny doctors' had) rather than sending in a bill. If an operation were needed, the surgeon's and anaesthetist's fees would have to be found, plus nursing home fees.

Having a baby for a middle-class woman often meant a private nursing home, whereas for most working-class women it would be a home confinement, possibly but by no means necessarily with the help of a midwife who delivered babies as the sort of community service that 'wise women' had provided for other women down the ages, often at low cost and sometimes with inadequate standards of medical knowledge or hygiene, as a 'Report on Maternal Mortality in Wales' showed. It was not until 1936 that the Midwives Act obliged local authorities to provide trained midwives, and it was not until 1946 that the number of hospital births exceeded those at home.

So the uninsured, the unemployed who had exhausted their sickness benefit entitlement and whose names were removed from doctors' lists as 'ceased to be insured" (although doctors were no longer paid to treat such people, 'If they were well known to us, we felt morally under an obligation to attend to their wants when asked to'), the dependents of those covered by the NHI and the poor and old, would have to spatchcock together medical care as they did other social services. In the first instance they were likely go to the local chemist for a bottle of patent medicine (almost £30 million a year was spent on patent medicines during the 1930s, and it was not until the 1939 Cancer Act that the advertising of cancer 'cures' bought over the counter was banned), and only if that was ineffective would they seek medical advice. They might be able consult a doctor who participated in the Public Medical Services, or be treated by those employed by enlightened local authorities such as Glasgow, Oxford or Mansfield in Nottinghamshire. Most local authorities, though, provided only those services they were statutorily obliged to, mainly concerned with infant and maternity care, or mental and infectious diseases. People might join a doctor's 'club' and pay a small amount each week, or go to the outpatients' department of a public hospital.

Married women were particularly disadvantaged if they could not afford to pay for their medical care. They were not covered by the NHI scheme, and were considered a poor risk by insurance companies since the mass of burdensome 'dull diseases' contingent on their biology would be likely to prove expensive – a burden the Chief Medical Officer of Health, Sir George Newman, admitted privately he was reluctant to enquire into too deeply, since it was 'a wandering fire to which there are no bounds' that would create demands way beyond the resources of the Ministry of Health. There were few women general practitioners, since most preferred to work directly with women and children in clinics, and many women were reluctant to take their troubles to a male doctor, so they struggled on with varicose veins, anaemia, prolapsed wombs, phlebitis, haemorrhoids, rheumatism, arthritis, chronic backache, undernourishment and exhaustion without ever seeking medical advice. Death in childbirth remained at much the same level – 4.1 per thousand – in 1935 as it had been in 1900, and in the depressed areas of South Wales and Scotland it was 6 per thousand. Better antenatal care as well as improved living conditions might have helped, but the primary cause of death in childbirth was medical, and it was not until the mid-1930s that puerperal fever, which presented the gravest danger, became treatable with sulphonamide drugs.

Hospitalisation was not covered by health insurance, and the choice was between voluntary hospitals, which had originally been endowed by the rich for the care of the poor, and which included some of the most famous London teaching hospitals, and local authority hospitals, many of which had been former Poor Law institutions. The voluntary hospitals were permanently strapped for cash by the 1930s, and were dependent on bequests, fund-raising events such as concerts and fêtes, flag days and patients' fees. Those on low incomes might have been paying a few pence a week which would give them the right to treatment should they need it (or if they were lucky their employer might have made a block provision for employees in this way), or they might be charged whatever the hospital almoner assessed they could afford. But the days of such hospitals were numbered: it was clear that voluntary contributions were no longer sufficient to keep them going, despite the fact that private patients' fees, mostly paid through insurance schemes, covered almost half such hospitals' costs), and by the end of the decade more hospital accommodation was provided by local authorities than by the voluntary sector.

The financial difficulties of the voluntary hospitals and the fact that they were not planned on a national scale according to the needs of the community, gave an opportunity to a group of medical practitioners who had a larger vision for health. The Socialist Medical Association (SMA) had been founded in 1930 with the support of, among others, the first Minister of Health, Christopher Addison, the journalist and propagandist for science Ritchie Calder and medical scientists and practitioners such as Somerville Hastings, a surgeon at the Middlesex Hospital in London and a Labour MP, Charles Brook, a London GP, David Stark Murray, a Scottish pathologist, and Richard Doll, who in the 1950s would prove the link between smoking and lung cancer. The SMA looked to the creation of a socialised medical system which would both streamline the chaotic health provision of the 1930s and ultimately make health care 'free to all rich and poor'. Furthermore, it wanted to end what it regarded as the 'lonely isolation' of the GP by creating salaried posts and locating them in a series of health centres based on municipal hospitals that integrated all aspects of medical care – owing something to the Peckham, Finsbury and Bermondsey models.

Although this blueprint for socialised medicine appears to prefigure the creation of the NHS in 1948, it was at local level – particularly in London – that the SMA came nearest to implementing its ideas in the 1930s. 'Municipal socialism' increasingly seemed to be a plausible strategy for undermining the National Government, and during the 1934 London County Council (LCC) elections the SMA produced a health manifesto claiming that the capital's ill health was due to poverty, bad sanitation and inadequate medical care and treatment (due to lack of resources), for which 'the anarchy of capitalism', reflected in uncoordinated health care provision, was to blame. Seeing health as 'every bit as important as education', SMA members were appointed to a range of LCC committees when Labour won control, and were able to put some of their ideas into practice, such as increasing the allocation of resources to municipal hospitals, improving the conditions and pay of nurses and other medical staff, providing outpatient facilities at most hospitals for the surrounding community and ridding hospitals of any Poor Law connotations, since 'every possible suggestion of charity, subservience, and general second rateness must be banished'. Instead London's citizens should regard 'the municipal hospitals as their own [since they had] every right to use them and expect the best from them'. But although the reform of London's health provision was of considerable interest to other authorities, even Somerville Hastings, chairman of the LCC Hospital and Medical Services Committee, recognised that it was unlikely to be fully possible 'within the limits of existing legislation'.

As well as inadequate hospital provision, the range of remedies doctors could provide was still very limited: during their brief consultation patients would be given a handful of pills, which might come in a range of colours but would in fact probably all be aspirins, though bottles of dilute mixtures of powerful drugs such as kaolin and morphine were also dispensed. A Welsh doctor provided his miner patients with a tincture of chloroform and morphine, effectively an addictive drug, for their chronic chest conditions. Many general practitioners had few aids to diagnosis, a stethoscope, thermometer, ear syringe and maybe a speculum being fairly standard, sterilising instruments was a dispensable luxury, and doctors had to pay for laboratory tests themselves – and therefore tended not to take advantage of new techniques and treatments that were being developed during the 1930s. A Welsh doctor who prescribed little but 'black liquorice' for his miner patients' pneumoconiosis was regarded as a cut above other practitioners in the town, since he had a machine that enabled him to take a patient's blood pressure.

Aware of their limited therapeutic arsenal, doctors essentially bought time by dispensing medicine, hoping that an illness would turn out to be self-limiting and would disappear, while patients appeared to be satisfied if they left the surgery clutching a bottle of medicine (private patients would have their bottle wrapped in white paper and sealed with sealing wax and usually delivered by the doctor's errand boy on a bicycle after evening surgery) or, less frequently, a box of pills, for which they had paid two or three pence. Aspirin powder for pain relief had been available since the turn of the century, and a tablet form had been patented in 1914, insulin injections to control diabetes had been introduced in the 1920s, followed by kidney dialysis, radium treatment for cancers, skin grafts and blood transfusions. Salvarsan was effective as a cure for syphilis and pernicious anaemia could now be treated with iron injections (rather than raw liver sandwiches, as previously), while the significance of vitamins began to be appreciated, leading to new therapies using vitamins C and D in cases of scurvy and rickets.

However, there were few things in the medicine cupboard in Eileen Whiteing's home 'apart from fruit salts, cough mixture, plus iodine for cuts ... and we certainly did not include [the commonplace aspirin] in our home remedies, having to endure headaches and other pains until they went away of their own accord ... cod liver oil and "Virol" were favourite remedies for winter ailments ... and in the case of nerves or depression, a strong iron tonic would be prescribed, with the advice to "pull yourself together".'

Diphtheria in children, an infection resulting in the throat thickening and the danger of suffocation, was one of the spectres hovering over the inter-war years, with some 50,000 cases every year. Two thousand children died each year from diphtheria and whooping cough until effective vaccines began to be used towards the end of the decade. Eileen Whiteing recalled that when she and her sister caught 'the dreaded diphtheria . . . Mother refused to let us go away to hospital, so a trained nurse was engaged at great expense, and, between the two of them, plus the resident maid, we were nursed safely through the long weeks of fever. Disinfected sheets had to be hung over the bedroom doors, all visitors had to wear white coats and face masks, and the whole house had to be fumigated by the local health officers at the end of the isolation period . . . People were endlessly kind . . . since illness was quite a serious event then: I remember hearing the news in hushed tones that straw had been spread over the road outside the house of one of my friends while he lay desperately fighting for his life with double pneumonia in order that the noise of passing traffic should not disturb him until what was known as the "crisis" was past' and the patient's dangerously high temperature either fell, or he or she died of exhaustion or heart failure, since in the absence of any effective medication, all the doctor could do was visit several times a day, wait and watch.

It was not until 1935–36 that real advances in medical treatment were possible with the manufacture of sulphonamides, anti-bacterial drugs effective for the treatment of a range of serious illnesses including streptococcal and meningococcal infections, the 'miracle drug' of those pre-penicillin years.

Tuberculosis was another killer disease that awaited its antidote: in the first decade of the twentieth century it was responsible for one death in every eight, and although that figure was steadily declining by the 1930s, there were still some 30,000 deaths a year from respiratory tuberculosis, and it continued to be seen as a deadly and frightening disease, freighted with social stigma. George Orwell, the most pungent chronicler of the mid-century, who had first contracted TB in 1938, died from its effects in January 1950, aged forty-six. In 1925 the typical tuberculosis dispensary was described by the Chief Medical Officer of the Ministry of Health as 'an out-patient department, stocked with drugs that are mainly placebos', or an annexe of an office for the compilation of statistics', and not much had changed a decade later. Although tuberculosis could be managed to an extent, and a diagnosis was no longer an automatic death sentence, there was no effective treatment until BCG (Bacille Calmette-Guérin) vaccine, after fraught years of trials and considerable resistance from the medical profession, started to be used extensively in Britain in the 1950s. Until then treatment consisted either of radical surgery – usually collapsing a lung, an operation performed on the principle of putting the diseased portion of the body to rest so it could combat disease with its own resources – or exposure to fresh air, on much the same principle of encouraging the recuperative power of nature, since there was not much else on offer.

The notion that sunshine and fresh air helped TB sufferers (and sufferers from other medical conditions) had been popular since the late nineteenth century, and those who could afford it might take the *Train Bleu* to the South of France or head for the bracing air of the Swiss Alps. The first British sanatorium for the open-air treatment of tuberculosis opened in Edinburgh in 1894, and others followed in Glasgow, Renfrewshire and Frimley in Surrey; they soon spread throughout the country, including one funded by the Post Office Workers' Union in Benenden in Kent. Some were for the well-off (though the rich usually chose Menton or Davos), many were funded by philanthropists (although, despite its romantic, artistic connotations, TB was regarded primarily as a disease of the poor, and did not attract the same level of donations or research funding as, say, cancer, despite the fact that even at the end of the Second World War it accounted for more deaths between fifteen and twenty-four years of age in Britain than any other condition). Ireland had one of the worst death rates from TB in the world, and although it had been falling since the turn of the century, it started to rise again in 1937, in stark contrast with the rest of the United Kingdom and Europe, due mainly to poverty and a lack of specialist services such as x-ray machines, which barely existed outside Dublin. Faced with the helplessness of the medical profession, those afflicted turned to folk remedies, desperately trusting in the efficacy of a daily dose of linseed oil mixed with honey, swallowing raw eggs or paraffin oil, goats' milk or dandelion-leaf sandwiches, or positioning themselves in the street outside the Belfast gasworks, since fumes from the vats were reputed to clear the lungs.

Since tuberculosis was 'the principal social disease of our time' in the view of Britain's Chief Medical Officer of Health, with implications for the whole community, the government, in conjunction with local authorities, funded a network of sanatoria (sometimes using old Poor Law infirmaries for the purpose) for free treatment, and aftercare to be provided by tuberculosis dispensaries. If possible the sanatoria were in isolated locations, since statistics showed that tuberculosis was more prevalent in urban areas than rural, and TB was regarded with such suspicion that any proposal to build a sanatorium invariably met with stiff local opposition. (Indeed, local authorities could obtain a court order for a person suffering from pulmonary tuberculosis to be forcibly removed from their home, although they rarely did so.) Ideally they were surrounded by pine trees (which were 'much appreciated for their exhilarating resinous aroma'), recalling Otto Walther's German sanatorium in Nordach in the Black Forest, 'an abode for Spartans' 1,500 feet above sea level and 'exposed to every wind', the model for so many dilute British establishments with names such as Nordach-upon-Mendip and Nordach-on-Dee. They were governed by strict rules – visitors one Saturday afternoon a month was not unusual – with a regime regulated by bells which included rest, a great deal of food (though not always of the highest quality), some outdoor exercise whatever the weather, and indoor crafts such as wood whittling, raffia work, crocheting and painting, and absolutely no sharing of cutlery or crockery. Spitting, a not uncommon habit in the 1930s, was forbidden, since sputum was know to be a carrier of the tubercle bacillus.

Belinda Banham, who had trained as a nurse at St Thomas's Hospital in London, wrote that the treatment provided to tubercular patients in the 1930s by the Royal Sea Bathing Hospital in Margate (founded in 1791 as the Royal Sea Bathing Infirmary for Scrofula)

> consisted, for the main part, in exposure to the elements . . . each ward gave onto two verandahs, one on either side. The verandahs were equipped with shutters which were never to be closed in the day, and at night only with the permission of the night sister. Permission was rarely granted, even when the snow was falling, as it was thought contrary to the patients' interest. Cloaks were allowed to nurses only in moving to and from the wards. Strength and stamina were essential to survival . . . It is difficult today to conceive of the patience and heroism of patients occupying those beds. The length of stay was indeterminate and never less than six months. With tuberculosis of the spine . . . two or three years was common . . . with patients often immobilised for two years or more . . . Efforts were made to protect nurses from contracting tuberculosis, mainly by means of an ample diet . . . nonetheless, several nursing colleagues did acquire the disease and two died in my time there.

When Dr W.A. Murray arrived at Glenafton Sanatorium in Ayrshire in 1934, he found chilblains 'prevalent among staff and patients', which was hardly surprising since the wards had no heating and the icy Scottish wind blew in round the ill-fitting windows, raising the linoleum from the floors in waves 'which made a ward round something like a trip on a roller coaster. Rain also came through the windows to such an extent that a patient with some skill as a cartoonist' depicted the doctor 'doing his rounds in thigh boots while a patient sailed a toy boat round his bed!'

Fresh air was also recommended for supposedly susceptible children who might be 'pre-tubercular' (though some were actually suffering from malnutrition), and could be removed from their infectious homes during the 'delicate years of growth'. By 1937 there were ninety-six open-air day schools in England, catering for 11,409 children; a further 3,985 children boarded at open-air residential schools, while those 2,451 children already affected by pulmonary TB might well attend one of the thirty-six sanatorium schools (or one of the further sixty-five schools catering for children suffering from non-pulmonary tuberculosis). Meanwhile, forty of the 221 schools in Glasgow had been constructed on 'open-air principles', with open verandahs, sliding doors to the classrooms and plate-glass windows, and two 'preventoria' for children who had been exposed to tuberculosis were built. Those children who for whatever reason could not attend such an institution might be shipped out to foster parents in rural areas to get their fresh air that way.

One problem was the reluctance of those who suspected that they had tuberculosis to seek medical advice, since ill-informed prejudice about the disease might well mean that they were shunned 'like lepers' by family and friends, lose their job and find it hard to get another even when they were well again, and have difficulty in getting life assurance cover. 'The world regards the "lunger" as an outcast,' wrote a sufferer in the *Western Mail* in November 1938. 'Filled with an exaggerated dread of any word ending in "osis", unthinking people recoil from anyone who had "had it" . . . Every week scores of "lungers" are released from clinics, hospitals and sanatoria . . . Each patient goes his own way. Yet each one finds himself up against the same problem . . . He is not wanted; he is avoided; he is feared – and then alack! forgotten . . . His own relatives are afraid to have him in the house . . . Jobs are out of reach . . . Two kinds of suffering have attended me through the battle [to get well in the sanatorium]. One was the distressful horror of the disease itself. The other is the mental agony born of my knowledge that when I emerge from the fight . . . I am taboo to my fellow countrymen.' Such considerations sometimes influenced GPs, who were obliged by law to report cases of tuberculosis, which may mean that rates of incidence in the 1930s were actually higher than reported.

Early diagnosis significantly improved the chance of recovery. The information-aware Bermondsey Public Health Department produced a film for their travelling cinemas, *Consumption*, in 1932 which illustrated how 'a consumptive, by placing himself under medical treatment and obeying simple rules of hygiene, can live an ordinary life for many years, without fear or risk to himself or those with whom he comes into contact'. Dr Salter himself played the doctor the patient consults after coughing blood into his handkerchief. He is seen sending the young man to a local authority sanatorium where he gradually gets better and is taught a new trade. On his return home he declines to kiss his wife since he is still contagious, and she makes up a bed for him in a shed in the backyard – provided free of charge by the council.

One way that people might receive treatment was to be admitted to Papworth Village Settlement, near Cambridge, founded by Dr (later Sir) Pendrill Varrier-Jones in 1917 along the lines of Ebenezer Howard's 'garden city' of Letchworth, where, as he explained in an article in 1931, if a tuberculosis patient was found to be 'suffering from extensive and permanent damage he would be able to live and work permanently in a village settlement with his family. The whole tuberculosis problem would be revolutionised. Those who thought they had tuberculosis would present themselves at a very early stage . . . and the success rate in treatment would be revolutionised' – not that Varrier-Jones believed that tuberculosis could be *cured*: treatment was a life sentence.

By 1938 Papworth, which was infused with the same spirit of experimentation ('studying the mechanisms of resistance') and holistic treatment as the Pioneer Health Centre in Peckham – 'We are dealing with persons, not cases,' Varrier-Jones was fond of saying – offered a hospital and a sanatorium consisting of open-air shelters with canvas flaps constructed in Papworth's carpentry workshops for which patients were issued with waterproof blankets to keep off the snow: glasses of water holding false teeth froze solid by the beds. A population of a thousand, including 360 children, lived in the 142 semi-detached cottages to which patients were able to move as they grew stronger, with a verandah and a garden, but no ornaments or wallpaper allowed, as these harboured germs, the windows permanently open. They ate a rich diet that included eggs, milk, porridge and cocoa, and were able to make use of communal facilities such as a swimming pool, join clubs for tennis, cricket, athletics and book reading, and to go to the cinema or pub on site. Since 'not everyone is fitted for a life in Utopia', the emphasis was on self-discipline externally policed. Patients lived under a strict paternalistic regime that censored entertainments they laid on themselves and the films they were allowed to watch, and leave passes were rigorously controlled. There was a psychiatric clinic to counsel the despairing.

As well as families, Papworth admitted single men from 1927 and single women (most of them former domestic servants) from 1929, their hostels sited some distance from each other, with 'a tumulus heaped up' between them to help maintain segregation. However, several inter-patient marriages

Neighbours talk outside a block of flats in London's East End, c.1935.
Photograph by Wolf Suschitzky, who had come to London from Vienna
the previous year. His sister was the photographer Edith Tudor Hart,
who took a series of poweful photographs of the Rhondda Valley,
where she lived, during the Depression.

The funeral cortège carrying the coffins of many of the seventy-one children who were victims of the Glen cinema disaster passes through the streets of Paisley on 4 January 1930.

The Hatry Crash: a newspaper vendor outside Charing
Cross station. Clarence Hatry's trial opened at the Old
Bailey on 20 January 1930.

Brushes for sale in the Caledonian Market north of King's Cross. Originally a cattle market, by 1935 when this photograph was taken by Cyril Arapoff, it sold mostly bric-a-brac and household goods.

A column of men on a hunger march trudge through the rain on their way to London. The contingent towards the back is from Edinburgh.

Hunger marchers climb the railings of Hyde Park
during the culmination of their efforts, a protest rally
against the Means Test on 27 October 1932.

The vicar of St Luke's, Kew Gardens, the Revd H. Maynard, posts a notice on his church on 1 March 1933 inviting his parishioners to vote in favour of cinemas opening on Sundays. The turnout was reported to be impressive.

did take place, and on such occasions Dr Varrier-Jones would present the happy couple with an engraved glass vase.

Varrier-Jones had hoped that the settlement would become financially self-sufficient through farming and market gardening – and in any case he thought it essential that those that could, should work, or they would soon '"throw up the sponge" if they were treated as permanent invalids'. However, the income thus generated turned out to be too little, so he set up a factory turning out travel goods and furniture. Patients were also employed in signwriting, printing, boot repairing and jewellery making, plus some horticulture and poultry farming. By 1930 Papworth's turnover was £85,000, and by 1937 this had increased to over £130,000, with a number of Cambridge colleges purchasing pieces of the well-made furniture.

The incidence and treatment of tuberculosis provides something of a metaphor for a nexus of 1930s attitudes. The clean, sweeping design of tuberculosis hospitals, sanatoria and health centres that rejected Victorian and Edwardian decoration – curtain rails with heavy plush curtains, flocked wallpaper, cornices and curlicues that might harbour dust and therefore bacilli – the fervent belief in the health-giving properties of fresh air, 'aerotherapy' as it was sometimes known, and sunlight, and therefore the use of glass, wipeable venetian blinds, open-air balconies, the curved buildings looking like great ocean liners, such as the expanded Benenden sanatorium, or Harefield hospital, built in Middlesex in 1938 in the shape of an aeroplane floating in the verdant countryside. The Finsbury Health Centre had been explicitly designed to catch the changing angle of the sun, and the interior murals by Gordon Cullen urged 'Fresh Air Night and Day' and 'Live Outside as Much as You Can'.

Flexible interiors were also part of the ethos: Peckham Health Centre had moveable glass partitions which meant that almost whatever they were doing, its members could be observed by the experts like goldfish in a bowl. Such buildings united zealous democratic (and usually socialist) reformist urges with modernist architectural forms that let light into what were formerly dark and hierarchical spaces. Above all there was the debate about what 'caused' tuberculosis. Was it hereditary – the Leicester Schools' Medical Officer was of the opinion that parents with tuberculosis should be prevented from having more children (How? Celibacy? Segregation? Sterilisation?), and the city's Medical Officer of Health made sure that patients were handed a leaflet when they left the sanatorium advising them not to marry or have children. Was it unhealthy living conditions or an inadequate diet that was responsible? Did poverty cause tuberculosis? Or was it that tuberculosis caused poverty (through lack of earnings)? Could an individual take charge of his or her own medical destiny by clean living, or were environmental factors beyond individual agency responsible?

Average life expectancy was increasing: by 1930 it was 58.7 years for men and 62.9 for women, whereas in 1900 it had been 48.5 for men and 52.4 for women, and infant morality was slowly falling. But this was only part of the story. Relief at the decline in the incidence of infectious diseases (such as tuberculosis) overlooked indicators of poor health such as anaemia, debility and undernutrition, and failed to differentiate between different parts of the country. In fact the death rate was rising: between 1930 and 1931 it increased from sixty per thousand to sixty-six, and in the depressed areas of Lancashire, Teesside, South Wales and Scotland the picture was bleak, with the death rate in the early 1930s as high as it had been before the First World War. Infant mortality rates rose, and not just in the depressed areas. There were marked differences between classes: in Lancashire and Cheshire the number of childhood deaths varied from around thirty-one per thousand among the well-off to ninety-three in the poorest class. Deaths in childbirth were 2.6 per thousand in the South of England, but 5.2 in the North and 4.4 in Wales. Surveys indicated that 80 per cent of children in the mining areas of County Durham and the poorest areas of London showed signs of early rickets, which was put down to both poor diet and lack of sunshine under the smoke-laden industrial skies (hence the preoccupation with sunlight of the health centres); modern estimates suggest that between a quarter and a half of all children living in areas of economic depression survived on a diet that was inadequate to maintain normal growth and health.

The charge that there was a connection between ill health and government policies was consistently contested during the Depression. Again tuberculosis provides an exemplary study, with the Chief Medical Officer of Health, Sir George Newman, attributing the rise in deaths from the disease in the industrial areas of South Wales (from 131 per 100,000 in young men aged fifteen to twenty-five in 1921–25 to 197 per 100,000 in 1930–32, and for young women from 185 to 268 in the same period) to 'geographical features of coalmining districts', by which he meant the lack of sunlight in the deep valleys in which the villages were located. He also allowed social factors, such as 'the tendency to crowd into small rooms and halls, some lack of playfields and facilities for open-air recreation, sometimes an unsuitable diet and the tendency to conceal the presence of tuberculosis', while for the mortally afflicted young women it was a question of 'migration to domestic service' and not returning home until the disease was in its terminal stage. Nonsense, a member of the Committee against

Malnutrition riposted: 'There is no evidence that the valleys are deeper and narrower today than formerly, and migration to service does not account for the increase in male mortality.'

Although the Ministry of Health declined to draw a correlation between poverty and the disease, citing 'a complex interaction of a considerable number of factors', those on the ground had no such doubts. A former MoH for Cardiff was unequivocal: 'Poverty has long been recognised as a prime factor in the causation of tuberculosis, principally through its effect on nutrition,' he wrote in 1933. A tuberculosis officer for Lancashire, asked to conduct a survey in Durham, concluded that 'The principal means by which poverty is found to cause tuberculosis are the overcrowding and undernourishment which are the chief distinguishing features between the poor and not poor families [some 3,000] studied,' and considered the link between tuberculosis and undernourishment to be more significant than that between tuberculosis and overcrowding.

In Jarrow, the death rate from tuberculosis was higher in 1930 than it had been before the turn of the century, at a time when rates across the rest of the country were falling by 50 per cent. The fact that there were fewer cases of spinal, bone and joint tuberculosis in Jarrow than might have been expected could be put down to the fact that fewer of the people who lived there were able to afford fresh milk. (In the 1930s almost 30 per cent of non-pulmonary tuberculosis deaths and 2 per cent of the pulmonary strain were caused by tubercular cows' milk or infected meat: in 1931 a thousand children under fifteen died of tuberculosis of bovine origin, and many more were crippled, but by the end of the end of the decade still less than 50 per cent of milk was pasteurised.) 'There is no mystery about the high tuberculosis rate of Jarrow,' flatly asserted 'Red Ellen' Wilkinson, the Labour MP for the town (so named by virtue of both her politics and her flame-coloured hair), scourge of the National Government's policies towards the unemployed. It was not caused by the supposed facts that '"the women do not know how to cook . . . The Irish have a racial susceptibility to tuberculosis . . . The families are too large . . . The geographical formations are unfavourable" . . . all of which reasons have been put forward by various medical authorities'. Rather, it was caused by the vicious cycle of 'bad housing, underfeeding, low wages for any work that is going, household incomes cut to the limit by public assistance, or Means Test or whatever is the cutting machine of the time . . . these mean disease and premature death'.

But still there were those who preferred to see tuberculosis as an individual responsibility, a sickness of advanced civilisation, when the simple life in the fresh air had been abandoned in favour of irregular hours, too little exercise, the stress of modern life, even 'the thoughtless misuse of leisure time'. All of which were ills that could be rectified by a stiff dose of self-help, rather than costly programmes of social welfare.

As the number of unemployed inexorably mounted month on month to over three million by 1931, politicians, economists, scientists, writers and commentators investigated, pronounced, theorised, constituted themselves into committees and wrote reports, and gathered together to lunch and dine, all in an effort to find reasons for and solutions to Britain's economic and social problems. In October, November and December that year the BBC invited a selection of prominent public figures to ruminate in front of a microphone on 'What I would do with the world'. Out of ten speakers, three advocated eugenics.

Lord D'Abernon, a former Ambassador to Berlin and then Chairman of the Medical Research Council, suggested that 'A wise dictator would devote his attention in the first years of his dictatorship to measures calculated to improve the human race,' since 'By excessive latitude given to the weak-minded, by imposing burdens in the shape of taxation on the hard-working to help out the improvidence of the inefficient and less capable, we are doing for the human race exactly what every intelligent breeder avoids in the animal world: we are stimulating breeding from the weak, the inefficient, and the unsound.' Sir Basil Blackett, a director of the Bank of England, agreed that he would ensure that 'we make ourselves and the human race better fitted intellectually and physically to use the scientific knowledge which the twentieth century places so freely at man's disposal'. His programme would make the study of eugenics 'a compulsory item in the training of every man or woman who is destined to take up administrative service in any part of the world', while at home 'we [cannot] afford much longer to follow the aggressively dysgenic course of breeding mainly from the unfit'. Leo Amery, a former (and future) Conservative Minister, decried what he called the 'short-sighted sentimentalism' that he felt had characterised the whole trend of British social and fiscal policy in recent years, discouraging 'thrift and self-reliance' and encouraging 'the actual multiplication of the improvident and the incompetent'.

The term 'eugenics' was first used by Francis Galton, a cousin of Charles Darwin, in 1883. Its etymological roots lie in the Greek words for 'good' or 'well' and 'born'. Eugenics was to be the science (and practice) of improving human stock 'to give the more suitable races or strains of blood a better chance of prevailing speedily over the less suitable'. The Eugenic Education Society (as it was originally called) was formed in 1907 in order to spread the knowledge of hereditary factors and how they could be applied to the improvement of the race – the 'self direction of evolution', as the logo for the Second International Eugenics Conference in 1921 proclaimed. Membership declined after the First World War, but revived again – though never reaching the same level – in the late 1920s and early 1930s, and by 1932 it had reached 768. Obviously this was a select number, but the Eugenics Society never sought a mass membership: rather it aimed to influence the legislative process by permeating the medical profession, the media and universities, and in the 1930s some very distinguished people took an interest in its work, including Julian Huxley, G.K. Chesterton. George Bernard Shaw, J.M. Keynes, J.B.S. Haldane, Richard Titmuss and A.M. Carr-Saunders (Director of the London School of Economics from 1937).

Central to eugenics was the conviction that a large part of those who came to be known as the 'social problem group' of the dependent and destitute were the result of genetic defects. But how could this be relevant to the Depression, when the number of unemployed (those who were necessarily economically and socially dependent, and sometimes all but destitute) had risen to three million, since three million people could hardly be congenitally 'unfit'? How did eugenics shed any light on the fact that unemployment was regional, concentrated in certain industries like shipbuilding, mining and heavy engineering, and not in other occupations?

Eugenicists were sceptical of the notion that poverty and ill health were linked to social and economic factors: rather they blamed the fecklessness and feeble-mindness of the lower orders. Many tended to be persuaded not by the findings of Dr Corry Mann, whose research in the London docklands led him to conclude that poor health was caused by low incomes, and that better pay resulted in better food, with consequent health benefits, but by investigations such as those undertaken by two academics in Glasgow. 'What is not demonstrated,' they wrote, 'is that simple increase in income would be followed by improvement in the condition of children. Bad parents, irrespective of their income tend to select bad houses, as the money is often spent on other things. The saying "what is the matter with the poor is poverty" is not substantiated by these investigations.'

To eugenicists, the ever greater numbers of unemployed served as vindication of what they had 'known' all along: the threat posed by the differential birthrate, whereby those of low intelligence reproduced at a greater rate than those of higher intelligence, and the fear that society was threatened by a small minority of the hereditarily inferior who would 'swamp' it if they were not controlled. If, as eugenicist doctors such as Raymond Cattell 'proved', the unemployed had low IQs, were 'hereditarily defective individuals', 'social inefficients', as the *Eugenics Review* had it, they would just go on breeding more unemployables, a veritable 'standing army of biological misfits'. Unless they were stopped.

The upper and middle classes were clearly producing fewer offspring than those lower down the social scale. For Julian Huxley, the differential birthrate was already dysgenic by 1925: 'The proportion of desirables is decreasing, of undesirables increasing. The situation must be got in hand. But it is impossible to persuade the classes which have adopted contraceptive methods to drop them by appeal to self-control. The way to stop the rot is to diffuse these practices equally through all strata of society.' Although the first birth control clinic had been set up in London by Dr Marie Stopes in 1921, and in 1930 the British Medical Association reluctantly gave qualified approval to doctors providing contraceptive advice to married women, the eugenicists feared that it was upper- and middle-class wives who were making rather too effective use of such knowledge, while those who in their view needed it most were confounded by the mess of pessaries, jellies, douches, 'womb veils', ointments, douches, tablets, condoms and diaphragms on offer, and relied instead on unreliable methods such as *coitus interruptus* or unsuitable domestic substances. What was needed was a foolproof means of contraception – preferably 'the regular consumption by mouth of a substance preventing fertilisation, taken at daily, or better at weekly or monthly intervals' – which 'even the stupidest and therefore the most undesirable members of society' could manage, a Eugenics Society Memorandum concluded.

But 'the pill' was decades away, so would 'diffusion' mean compulsion? 'No public assistance without control of birth rates', the psychologist Raymond Cattell bleakly sloganised. Julian Huxley's solution to the tendency (as he saw it) 'for the stupid to inherit the earth, and the shiftless and the imprudent and the dull', was much the same: to make unemployment relief conditional upon a man's agreement to father no more children. 'Infringement of this order could possibly be met by a short period of segregation in a labour camp. After three or six months' separation from his wife he would be likely to be more careful the next time.' The zoologist Dr E.W. MacBride, who had managed to 'demonstrate' the innate inferiority of working-class children, went further, suggesting in 1930 that 'In the last resort compulsory sterilisation will have to be inflicted as a penalty for the economic sin of producing more children than the parents can support,' though he did suggest that before that last resort was reached, 'Citizens should receive instruction from the State in the means of birth control.'

In 1932 the Minister of Health appointed a committee to make recommendations on the sterilisation of the 'feeble-minded' in England and Wales.

Under the chairmanship of Sir Laurence Brock, the Committee included three enthusiastic eugenicists, one of whom was Brock himself. After untangling the family histories of so-called defectives and assessing whether they produced feeble-minded offspring themselves, the Brock Committee concluded that a quarter of a million people in Britain were suitable candidates for voluntary sterilisation on account of being 'mental defectives'. It was unanimous in believing that it was justified in allowing and even encouraging 'mentally defective and mentally disordered patients to adopt the only certain method of preventing procreation': sterilisation. In reaching this conclusion, the Committee had privileged any studies that suggested that defectiveness was hereditary – 'Broadly speaking stupid people will produce stupid children,' Dr MacBride had asserted – despite dissent from such witnesses as J.B.S. Haldane and Lancelot Hogben, who argued that there could be no scientific certainty on this point, rather that the evidence suggested environmental factors were more likely to be to blame. The Committee did, however, reject compulsory sterilisation.

The Eugenics Society was delighted with the Brock Committee's findings, and confident that if 'the general public could be educated to distinguish between sterilization and castration many members of the Social Problem Group would avail themselves of facilities for voluntary sterilization in order to prevent the birth of unwanted children'.

However, no legislation was forthcoming. It was considered that the public was not behind such a programme, the Roman Catholic Church believed that sterilisation violated the God-given right to reproduce, and by the time the Brock Committee made its recommendations in the summer of 1934, the Nazi Party had embarked on a compulsory sterilisation and euthanasia programme in Germany which increasingly discredited the eugenicists and made repugnant to most people the idea of sterilising – even voluntarily – groups and classes of people.

CODA

Searching for the Gleam

'A party of English doctors and scientists passed through,' wrote the British Consul in Leningrad, Reader Bullard, in his diary on 26 July 1931. 'Mostly much impressed by what they had seen, and as they had been taken to all the showplaces and nothing else this is perhaps not remarkable.' The British footfall through the Soviet Union in the early 1930s was, if not heavy, then at least regular and highly questing. Many on the left regarded the Soviet Union as a successful, planned, egalitarian society, the one place where the problems that beset Britain had, as they saw it, been resolved. Those who went made the journey because they wanted to see the Soviet system for themselves, to have their opinions about what was wrong with Britain – the decay of capitalism, the class system, the searing inequalities of wealth and opportunity – confirmed, and to bring some lessons back home. 'We saw in the Soviet Union the negation of the immoralities of industrial capitalism and the system of private profit,' the political activist and author Margaret Cole recalled. 'We were eager to follow the gleam . . . The hopes for what the makers of the Revolution set out to achieve compared to the dead hopelessness of breadlines and the dole were more than enough to outweigh doubts.'

Sidney and Beatrice Webb went for a two-month tour in the summer of 1932, sailing on the Russian steamer *Smolny*. As befitted two Fabians and rigorous social investigators, in the months before their departure the Webbs had immersed themselves in 'Soviet literature of all types . . . [but] at present we cannot make our way to any settled estimate of success or failure . . . All I know is that I *wish* Russian communism to succeed,' Beatrice wrote.

Lenin had translated the Webbs' *Theory and Practice of Trade Unionism* into Russian ('An example of the quality of boredom being twice blessed,' thought Malcolm Muggeridge), and by virtue of this the Webbs had become 'ikons in the Soviet Union', and were given a superior tour to that allowed to most Intourist visitors, though their itinerary was the usual one: collective farms, schools, clinics, factories. When they came to dine with

Reader Bullard ('At least he came to dinner and she came to two pieces of toast and a glass of red wine. Nine out of ten tourists have their insides upset by bad food, and Mrs Webb is one of the nine') they explained that they were 'mainly interested in the organisation of the State, the way the wheels go round, and they seem to have collected a great deal of information'.

Theirs was a tiring trip, so tiring for a couple whose joint ages totalled 147 years that Beatrice managed to write little more than headings in the black notebook labelled 'Russian Tour. 10 shillings Reward if Lost'. Sidney had viewed the Soviet Union 'with the relish of a scientist whose theoretical proposition has stood the test of practical experiment: "See, see, it works, it works."' Beatrice too felt a sense of satisfaction: 'The problem we have been seeking to solve for the last fifty years – poverty in the midst of plenty – is today being solved, and very much as we should have solved it, if we had had our way.' But her enthusiasm was tempered: she queried, 'How far can you disentangle what is good in Russia from what is bad? . . . Can you take the economic organization of Soviet Russia and reject the "dictatorship" of a creed or caste? . . . These are the sorts of problems which have to be solved by those who wish to supersede, in their own country, capitalist profit-making by the equalitarian production, distribution and exchange of the wealth of the nation.'

George Bernard Shaw paid a visit in July 1931 and was refused permission by his minders to see what he wanted, so Reader Bullard took him to the Kazan Cathedral (which he did 'not find very interesting') and St Isaac's Cathedral ('the anti-religious museum'), then invited the Fabian playwright back for tea at the Consulate, where 'he talked for two hours and told us all a lot about Russia . . . just waving away anything that did not fit in with his preconceptions'. Hugh Dalton (former Labour Under-Secretary for Foreign Affairs and future Chancellor of the Exchequer) and Frederick Pethwick-Lawrence (from the Treasury, and a keen suffragette-supporter) tipped up in that busy summer of 1932. 'They have come to look at Soviet finance,' noted Bullard. The feminist author and journalist Cicely Hamilton, one of the few visitors to speak any Russian, arrived in June, intending to write an article about the country (which she found drab, though she approved of the way young Soviet children in nursery schools were dressed alike and had their hair cropped so that you could not tell their sex) for *Time and Tide*. A vinegar merchant, one Mr Cook, arrived with a letter from the Mayor of Leeds addressed to the President of the Soviet Union, 'whom he had been unable to see', so the Consul invited him to dinner, at which 'the innocent' praised a factory canteen he had just seen as 'better than anything in Leeds'.

Naomi Mitchison, a tireless traveller and writer, the sister of J.B.S. Haldane and the wife of a future Labour MP, was one of the Fabian Dalton/Pethwick Lawrence group that also included the formidable bookshop-owner Christina Foyle. Mitchison arrived in Leningrad wearing a garment of her own invention, a white jacket with 'pockets all around it like purses in a belt', and professing that her interest was mainly archaeological – though she made a particular point of finding out about birth control, and also about abortion practices, since Russia was the only country in which abortion was legal. 'She'll be pretty closely watched,' commented Bullard darkly. On her return Mitchison was overheard 'advocating a revolution for England'.

J.D. Bernal had been among a party of English doctors and scientists the previous summer. His enthusiasm for the USSR had been aroused by the unexpected visit to London a few weeks previously of Nikolai Bukharin, a close associate of Lenin and head of the Academy of Science's section on the history of science and the Director of Research for the Supreme Economic Council, who led a delegation of Soviet scientists to the second International Congress of the History of Science and Technology. Bukharin (who would perish in Stalin's 'great purge' in March 1938) had somewhat dominated proceedings, speaking of how 'a new science' to parallel the new economic system had been born in the Soviet Union. Bernal, who considered the Congress 'the most important meeting of ideas that has occurred since the Revolution', could not wait to see this 'new science' for himself.

Two tours – in July and August 1931– were organised by the *Manchester Guardian*'s science correspondent, J.G. Crowther, under the auspices of the Society for Cultural Relations. The doctors – some of whom were shocked to see women undergoing abortions in state clinics in Moscow without benefit of anaesthetics, which was normal practice – were in the majority, but Julian Huxley, who was very impressed that the Soviet authorities were 'preparing to increase expenditure on pure scientific research far beyond that attempted in any capitalist country', was one of the handful of scientists. In July Bukharin had hosted a lavish banquet (paid for by the Soviet government) at the Dynamo sports stadium in Moscow; the August party was rather less sumptuously entertained, and Bernal 'saw very much of the difficulties as well as of [the] achievements. I saw the construction camps for the Dnieper dam, and at the same time saw something of the hard times that were produced in the period of early collectivisation . . . and yet there was no mistaking the sense of purpose and achievement in the Soviet Union . . . It was grim but great. Our hardships in England were less: theirs were deliberate and undergone in an assurance of building a better future. Their hardships were compensated for by a reasonable hope.'

Bernal was to return to the USSR several times, once in 1934 with his then lover Margaret Gardiner, who soon got bored with the November celebrations in Moscow, watching 'column after marching column, gun carriages, tanks, all the grisly paraphernalia of power and war, with that row of grey men sitting there hour after hour to take the salute and acknowledge the applause'. Although Gardiner found Russia 'drab', she detected a feeling of hope, and was distressed and disturbed when, during her and Bernal's visit, Sergey Kirov, the Communist Party leader in Leningrad and a member of the Politburo, was assassinated – possibly on the orders of Stalin.

The art critic and travel writer Robert Byron set off for Russia in January 1932, determined to concentrate on the paintings and buildings he wanted to see, and to ignore politics: 'I almost went out of my way to avoid the state manifestation of communism – factories, clubs etc . . . as for Bolshevism and the Five Year Plan and all that – it seems too uninteresting to bother with . . . though I daresay I shall become interested.' Ten days later he had indeed become very interested:

> No more shall I be deceived by English intellectuals who all come on conducted tours – by our standards it is all *evil* . . . If the five-year plan works, it will be the industrial barbarism come true – apes in possession of machines, violently, madly nationalistic, hating and hated by the opposing human beings. But will the five-year plan work? It may seem stupid to write like this after a fortnight here – but there is the other side. They have cast so much off, all the futilities and extravagances that hamper us – somehow in spite of the devil worship one breathes a fresher air, and however much their experiment may menace our civilisation, one can't wish it different or fail to wish them success up to a point. In fact one's mind is filled with a flat contradiction – apparently insoluble, and the only concrete impression is simply one of intense interest.

Robert Haslam, a comfortably-off businessman, joined the rush to check out a (relatively) new social experiment, leaving his home in Bolton 'in the Rolls' in August 1932, bound for Hay's Wharf in London and thence to the Soviet Union. He spent a month travelling around on a trip arranged by Intourist, but found little to commend post-Revolutionary Russia, with its generally poor food, lukewarm baths, unflushable lavatories, uncomfortable trains and what he decided were hopelessly inefficient factories – though he was impressed by a pioneer camp near Yalta. Haslam found it 'increasingly difficult to come to an opinion on much of it, but I do feel there is no stability'. Defiantly he wrote in the visitors' book of the Russian ship that bore his party back to Britain: 'St George for Merrie England/No Soviets for me/I quite enjoyed the Sibier/But then, thank God, I'm free!'

Malcolm Muggeridge had shared the intellectual left's enthusiasm for the Soviet Union. Disillusioned with his work on the *Manchester Guardian* and with Britain under the new National Government, he resolved in 1931 'to go where I thought a new age was coming to pass; to Moscow and the future of mankind', as the newspaper's Russian correspondent. Muggeridge and his wife Kitty (a niece of Beatrice Webb, who considered that she and Malcolm were 'the most gifted and certainly the most "proletarian" of my nieces and nephews') 'sold off pretty well everything we had, making, as it were, a bonfire of our bourgeois trappings: my dinner jacket, for instance, Kitty's only long dress . . . as well as most of our books, which we considered to be bourgeois literature of no relevance in a Workers' State . . . We even wound up our bank account. What possible use would a bank account be in a country where bankers along with industrialists, landlords and priests had all been eliminated? . . . Kitty was pregnant again, so that our next child would be born a Soviet citizen [the Muggeridges had left their three-year-old son Leonard behind at school in the Lake District]. It all seemed wonderful.'

But it wasn't. Soon Muggeridge grew impatient with life in the Soviet Union: 'We might as well have been back in Didsbury. Revolutions, like wars, upset things far less than might be superficially supposed. As the very word "revolution" implies, they have a way of ending up where they began.' He grew wearily amused too, as did Bullard, by the endless procession of distinguished visitors and their pronouncements:

Shaw, accompanied by Lady Astor (who was photographed cutting his hair), declaring that he was delighted to find that there was no food shortage in the USSR [the Ukraine in particular was enduring a famine at the time]. Or [Harold] Laski singing the praises of Stalin's new Soviet constitution [though Laski, who visited in 1934, tempered his enthusiasm for Russia as 'a land of hope' with concern about the repressive nature of the regime, declaring that he was sure that 'if I lived in Russia I should court difficulty from my sense of the need to form a Council of Civil Liberties']. Or Julian Huxley describing how a 'German town-planning expert was travelling over the huge Siberian spaces in a special train with a staff of assistants, stopping every now and again to lay down the broad outlines of a future city, and then pushing on, leaving the details to be filled in by architects and engineers who remained behind . . . I shall treasure until I die as a blessed memory the spectacle of them travelling with radiant optimism through a famished countryside, wandering in happy bands about squalid, over-crowded towns. Listening with unshakeable faith to the fatuous patter of carefully trained and indoctrinated guides, repeating like schoolchildren a multiplication table, the bogus statistics and mindless slogans endlessly intoned to them.

Within months of his arrival Muggeridge left the country of which he had entertained such high expectations and travelled to Montreux in Switzerland, where he and Kitty had decided to run a guest house for the Workers' Travel Association (a Labour Party tourist agency). Before he left, Muggeridge had written a series of articles for the *Manchester Guardian* which were published in March 1933. '"We must collectivize agriculture", or "We must root out the Kulaks" (the rich peasants). How simple it sounds! How logical! But what is going on in the remote villages? In the small households of the peasants? What does the collectivization of agriculture mean in practice in the lives of the peasants? What results has the "new drive" produced? . . . That is what I wanted to find out.' What he found was that 'the civilian population was obviously starving in its absolute sense: Not undernourished as, for instance . . . some unemployed workers in Europe . . . There had been no bread for three months . . . The only edible thing [in the markets] in the lowest European standards was chicken . . . the rest of the food offered for sale was revolting and would be thought unfit, in the ordinary way to be offered to animals.' It was 'the same story in the Ukraine – cattle and horses dead; fields neglected; meagre harvests despite moderately good climate conditions; all the grain produced was taken by the Government; now no bread at all, no bread anywhere, nothing much else either; despair and bewilderment'.

Muggeridge's reports, which were confirmed by Gareth Jones, a former Political Secretary of Lloyd George who had gone on a walking tour of Russia that same year, were the first accounts of the famine by a Western journalist, the first indication that collectivisation, far from being a socialist dream, was turning into a nightmare. But not everyone wanted to hear them: the editor of the *Manchester Guardian* was lukewarm, wishing that Muggeridge had restricted himself to 'plain, matter-of-fact statements of what you saw . . . If we denounce we are apt to be in unpleasant company.' George Bernard Shaw (who, Jones reported, was 'after Stalin the most hated man in Russia') had written to the *Guardian* after an earlier report from Muggeridge, describing his comments as 'a particularly offensive and ridiculous attempt to portray the lot of the workers as one of slavery and starvation. We the undersigned are recent visitors to the USSR . . . We desire to record that we saw nowhere evidence of such economic slavery, privation, unemployment

... Everywhere we saw a hopeful and enthusiastic working class, self-respecting, free up to the limits imposed on them by nature and the terrible inheritance from the tyranny and incompetence of their former rulers ... setting an example of industry and conduct which would greatly enrich us if our system supplied our workers with any incentive to follow it.'

Muggeridge, despairing, 'discarded the *Manchester Guardian*' and wrote a further series of articles, 'as bitter and satirical as I knew how to make them', about what he had seen, which he sent off to the *Morning Post*, a 'reputable Tory newspaper of the extreme Right' (which was taken over by the *Daily Telegraph* in 1937).

Some who kept the faith in the Soviet model had a disquieting time as news of Stalin's purges and show trials became known, while others were able to accept these as the inevitable 'infantile disease' of a revolutionary society; the few who lost their faith found the disillusion hard, and felt rudderless as they drifted through the crises of capitalism, their lodestar tarnished.

PART THREE

Planning England
(and Scotland and Wales)

PROLOGUE

Follies

When the journalist Henry Vollam Morton (known as Harry), encouraged by the warm reception and almost bi-monthly reprints of his book *In Search of England* set off *In Search of Wales* in 1932, his route wound round the mountains of Snowdonia and along the craggy coast of what he called the 'Land's End of Wales'; he met the ex-Liberal Prime Minister David Lloyd George, 'a strong wind in the war years', walking down a lane in his home village of Criccieth. Morton then struck inland through the Llanberis Pass, bound 'through the thin rain' for the small town of Betws-y-Coed. Had he instead stuck to the coastal route, he would have come across a strange private fantasy demesne, a sliver of Italianate Surrealism that clung to the Merioneth Peninsula.

Aber Iâ ('estuary of glass') had been bought in the mid-1920s by the 'intuitive' (that is, virtually untrained) architect Clough Williams-Ellis, the son of a local Welsh squarson, whose professional training amounted to three months' study at the Architectural Association in London. He intended to make an imaginative gesture by building a 'holiday retreat for the more discerning' among the 'cliffs and woodland rides and paths that crisscross the whole headland between high crags', replete with 'an exuberant jungle of exotic and subtropical flowering shrubs (mainly rhododendrons)'. Portmeirion, as Williams-Ellis christened his fiefdom, owed nothing to prevailing notions of functional architecture; rather it was a Mediterranean extravaganza of campaniles, piazzas, an observatory tower which incorporated a camera obscura, Regency-type colonnades, colour-washed baroque houses, a vaguely Jacobean-style town hall, *trompe l'oeils*, pillars, obelisks, orbs, ponds, terraces, grilles and a range of architectural jokes and whimsies.

A hotel opened for visitors in 1926, and throughout the 1930s Williams-Ellis extended Portmeirion with fifteen more buildings, many incorporating architectural salvage that he had acquired over the years. In that decade (and indeed during the Second World War too) the resort served as a retreat for celebrities such as Noël Coward (who would write *Blithe Spirit* during a week's stay in 1941), George Bernard Shaw, Augustus John (who liked to speak Romany with a gypsy who lived in a tent in the woods until he was killed by a motorcyclist leaving the car park), Bertrand Russell (who wrote *Freedom and Organisation, 1814–1914* at Portmeirion in 1934) and the Prince of Wales (the future Edward VIII), who also spent time there in 1934, and required that a bath and lavatory be installed in his bedroom, since it was not appropriate for a royal to share such facilities. Williams-Ellis even acquired a hotel, renaming it the Mytton and Mermaid, near Shrewsbury, so that those travelling from London and the South-East could break their journey for a night. Visitors could come for the day, too, and paid on a sliding scale: the more people there were, the higher the entrance fee. Usually the entrance fee was around one shilling, but it rose to a dizzying ten shillings (around £25 in today's money) when the Prince of Wales was in residence.

Williams-Ellis admitted that while he had 'an acute inborn instinct for architecture', he remained 'in some respects half-baked as a technician', and many saw him less as an architect and more as a stage designer. Few if any of his exuberant excesses would have been possible had he followed his own precepts, as set out in a letter to the *Manchester Guardian* while he was on leave from France during the First World War: 'Anyone who cares for England must be interested in national planning, the provision of a comprehensive co-ordinated and compulsory development and conservation scheme for the country as a whole, urban and rural, public and private.' In fact the building of Portmeirion was only possible because there were then 'no Building Regulations, no Town & Country Planning Act, no regulations about Historic Buildings'. Although Williams-Ellis thought there ought to be all these things (and said so repeatedly), 'privately, secretly, he relished their absence', wrote his wife. So effective was Williams-Ellis at 'calling my own tune' that when Snowdonia was declared a national park just after the Second World War, something he had long agitated for, its boundaries were drawn to exclude Portmeirion.

No planning permission was needed, or sought, for another 'world-class folly' that opened to the public for the first time in the summer of 1929. Roland Callingham, a London accountant, owned a large house and garden in the leafy commuter suburb of Beaconsfield in Buckinghamshire. Callingham was a model-railway enthusiast, and commissioned the largest outdoor Gauge 1 railway layout in England for his garden, dragooning his gardener and other household servants, family and friends into making scale models of houses, shops, a castle, pubs, a cinema, a station and a church to set alongside his railway line, constructing roads and streets to connect them, and fashioning Lilliputian-sized people to inhabit his construction. Named 'Beckonscot' (an amalgam of Beaconsfield and Ascot, where Callingham's railway collaborator lived), the first model village in the world covered a site of around two acres. It was visited by Princess Elizabeth on the eve of her eighth birthday in April 1934 with her grandmother Queen Mary, wife of the by then ailing King George V. The serious-looking, cloche-hatted, white-gloved child, third in line to the throne, peered through shop windows at the miniature goods for sale, watched 1:12-scale trains leaving from Maryloo (an amalgam of Marylebone and Waterloo) station, listened to the 'choir' singing in one of the several churches (they would later include a model of one built in Beaconsfield as a memorial to G.K. Chesterton, who died in 1936), and took it upon herself to rearrange the sheep in the fields.

By May 1937, when the American magazine *National Geographic* featured Beckonscot, the miniature country town was attracting over 57,000 visitors a year, and boasted a racecourse (Epwood – combining Epsom and Goodwood) a fairground, docks and an Art Deco aerodrome which looked remarkably similar to a miniaturised Croydon airfield.

The intention was that Beckonscot should grow and develop just like any other town, so as the decades passed, modern concrete slabs were erected in place of some of the pargeted buildings, elaborate ironwork at the railway station was replaced by concrete and glass, and the original steam trains gave way to diesel. But in 1992 it was decided that the 'progress' of the past sixty years should be reversed, and Beckonscot returned to how it had been when Princess Elizabeth (who by then had been on the throne for nearly forty years) had visited. 1960s-style blocks of flats were torn down, concrete offices destroyed, glass and metal bus shelters uprooted, all to be replaced by work-shops and mock-Tudor cottages, while individual shops, many modelled on actual Beaconsfield establishments of the 1930s, replaced a supermarket and all the buildings were repainted in 'the drab colours relevant to the time'. The children's author Enid Blyton, creator of Noddy and Big Ears, had moved to Beaconsfield in 1938, and a replica of her house, Green Hedges, was re-created as part of a village that now stands in a perfect 1930s time-warp, viewed through binoculars the wrong way round, with its tea-drinking matrons sitting under shady umbrellas, its edge-of-town roadhouse next to the tiled swimming pool with its two-foot diving tower with five spring-boards, its eternally grazing cows, sheep and horses and more exotic animals in the zoo, its pink-coated huntsmen permanently in full Tally ho!, its polo field, its miller perpetually carrying sacks of grain into the windmill, watched by two archetypal figures from the 1930s countryside, hikers in shorts with rucksacks on their backs and carrying stout sticks.

TEN

Accommodating the Octopus

In 1930 . . . enemies could be particularized: advertising hoardings, concrete kerbs, conifers, filling stations, power lines, ribbon development, alien building materials, flat roofs: the only thing to do was to go for them one by one, first a letter to *The Times*, and then, if possible by legislation.

> Lionel Esher, *A Broken Wave: The Rebuilding of England, 1940–1980* (1981)

The attitude of this generation to Nature is perversely contradictory. We have developed a quickened sense of the beauty of the countryside and, assisted by the petrol engine and the electric train, inaugurated a new return to Nature; yet no race of human beings has done so much to destroy the countryside which they profess to enjoy.

> C.E.M. Joad, *A Charter for Ramblers, or The Future of the Countryside* (1934)

In the country, recreation is recreation. You make up your spiritual losses whenever you have time to 'stand and stare'. Half of the tragedy of unemployment is due to the urbanised minds of the unemployed. The establishment of the 'recreational centre' – which is recognised as an outstanding need – is far more elaborate and costly than it need be because the happy countryman's means of recreation are not understood and can with difficulty be brought home to the urban dweller.

> Sir William Beach Thomas, 'Why I Live in the Country', *Countryman*, April 1935

Just as 'day was slipping into an unpleasant evening, cold and wet' on 13 January 1933, a black London taxi pulled up outside 7 Buckingham Palace Gardens near Victoria station. 'A lady, heavily masked, got out and announced herself to the commissionaire as "Red Biddy" of "Ferguson's Gang".' But this 'bandit' was not intent on plunder, 'her mission was one of benefice'. The premises were the headquarters of the National Trust, and the masked woman, 'bent with the weight of a heavy bag . . . desired to see the secretary, with whom, without lifting her mask, she deposited £100 [worth almost £5,000 today] in silver' before getting back into her taxi, and, 'recognised by no one', disappearing into the gloaming.

'Red Biddy' was the *nom de guerre* chosen by one member of a strange gang of well-connected, well-educated young benefactors dedicated to 'preserving England and frustrating the Octopus'. The octopus was what Lord Curzon had called London – 'a great octopus stretching its tentacles in order to lay hold of the rich pastures and leafy lanes of the countryside' – when he had opened a National Trust property, Colley Hill in Surrey, in 1913. Clough Williams-Ellis had taken the image as the title for *England and the Octopus*, 'an angry book written by an angry man', in 1928, which was described in the preface to a new edition nearly fifty years later by the town planner and architectural critic Lewis Mumford as the 'flying banner of the ecological movement that is now sweeping the planet'. It was to this cause of 'preserving England and frustrating the octopus' that the 'Ferguson Gang' decided to donate money in various enigmatic and flamboyant ways to the National Trust.

The gang was all female, its members taking aliases such as 'Sister Agatha', 'Kate O'Brien the Nark', 'Erb the Snark', 'Silent O'Moyle', 'See Mee Run', 'Black Maria', 'Bloody Bishop', and the ringleader, 'Bill Stickers' (as in 'Bill stickers will be prosecuted'), who it later turned out was Peggy (Margaret) Pollard, a great-niece of the zealous Victorian Prime Minister William Gladstone, and herself a fine Sanskrit scholar, the first woman to gain first-class honours in the Oriental Languages tripos at Cambridge. Stickers/Pollard was also a gifted writer of comic verse, a fervent Cornish conservationist and reviver of the ancient Cornish language, a bard, a harpist and a committed Roman Catholic convert who penned hymns in both Latin and Cornish. In addition she was to earn an entry in *The Guinness Book of Records* for having embroidered a tapestry with scenes from C.S. Lewis's Narnia books, which was 'nearly as long as the Bayeux Tapestry'. 'Red Biddy's' father was a major general, her epithet bespoke her politics, and she later became a paediatrician, achieving notoriety by absconding with a child whom she considered to be at risk from its parents. 'Bloody Bishop' was an art student at the Slade, while 'Sister Agatha' was a talented musician, and in her middle years a stalwart of the Red Cross. As for 'Ferguson', s/he probably never existed – Ferguson's signature was always a rubber stamp – though a man purporting to be him broadcast an appeal for the National Trust on the BBC in 1935 which brought forth donations of £900 plus six hundred new members.

The gang raised money by levying a 'tax' on their own private incomes and collecting any Victorian coins that came into their possession, and they made their donations with dramatic whimsy: stuffed into the carcass of a goose, wrapped round a cigar, £500 accompanying a bottle of Ferguson-gang-bottled sloe gin as a 'ransom' for the entire supply of the Dorchester Hotel's toothpicks at a banquet held there to celebrate the anniversary of the National Trust in 1935. In 1932 they took charge of the near-derelict medieval Shalford Mill in Surrey, endowed the National Trust with £500 for its repair and upkeep, and persuaded the Trust's architect, John McGregor (whom they named 'The Artichoke') to create a 'cell' for the gang's secret meetings in the basement, which took place round the millstone, accompanied by much Latin chanting. By the time the Ferguson Gang disbanded for marriage and other forms of respectability they had raised £4,500 (more than £200,000 in purchasing power today), enabling the National Trust to acquire disparate bits of England, including Newtown Old Town Hall on the Isle of Wight, cottages in Oxfordshire and stretches of the Cornish coastline.

The National Trust had been founded by Octavia Hill, Canon Rawnsley and Robert Hunter in 1894 'to act as a Corporation for the holding of lands of natural beauty and sites and houses of historic interest to be preserved intact for the nation's use and enjoyment'. In the 1930s 'the nation's use and enjoyment' of the countryside was a contested issue, charged with political, economic, social, ideological and aesthetic resonances – and the remit and aspirations of the National Trust, run by what might be described as cultivated amateurs, several with a military background, mirrored many of these. Originally more concerned with its role as protector of 'unspoilt' rural landscapes – the majority of them in the more affluent South of England, though the Lake District, large tracts of which were acquired as a result of the generosity of the author of *Peter Rabbit* and other anthropomorphic tales, Beatrix Potter, in 1929, was an exception. By the end of the 1930s the National Trust held as much as 50,000 acres in England and Wales, many of which (especially those along the coast) would otherwise no doubt have been developed.

'One hears and one reads a good deal of sentimental gush about the heart-break of old established landowners forced to see their ancestral acres through the hardness of the times,' wrote Clough Williams-Ellis, claiming that this was often due to the owners' 'folly or mismanagement, or . . . expensive tastes incompatible with the low returns from land owning'. However, although he had scant sympathy with their owners, he nevertheless regarded it as 'unthinkable that the great houses of England should be allowed to perish away – the really great houses that is – those that are great in their architecture, their associations and the beauty of their settings, not merely great in size'. But since there were 'more great country houses in England than there are great men to inhabit them', some new solution had to be found.

Williams-Ellis's notion was to get the editor of *Country Life* to draw up a list of 'every house of real distinction in the land' (though in his view the standard of distinctiveness might have to be lowered for Wales, where he himself was still building his own whimsical fable village, 'or they might find themselves with no house at all that was dignified by State protection and assured to them as an ornament in perpetuity'). Once identified, the owners of these 'truly great houses' would 'enjoy substantial remissions from rates and taxes', and in return would have the obligation to maintain their properties, to make no alterations without permission, and to grant members of the public access 'under carefully framed conditions' so that they might enjoy these time capsules of an unchanging world, for an entrance fee.

When Philip Kerr succeeded to his title as 11th Marquess of Lothian in 1930, he was obliged to pay almost 40 per cent of the value of his properties in death duties (a measure he had himself helped to guide through Parliament as Lloyd George's Private Secretary). Four years later, by which time the rate had risen to 50 per cent, Lothian revived a version of Williams-Ellis's notion, suggesting that the sixty large (over twenty bedrooms and a suite of state rooms) and six hundred smaller houses that *Country Life* had identified as being dwellings of 'real historic interest and artistic merit' should be exempt from death duties, and the cost of maintaining them could be set against tax provided that the owners kept the house, garden and historic contents intact and allowed the public in 'from time to time' – a scheme he recommended as 'planned private enterprise'.

A provision in the 1931 Budget allowed owners to offer their house or land in lieu of death duties. However, the Inland Revenue had no desire to collect country houses, while the National Trust could not afford to accept many (either as a direct gift or via the government), since it could not pay for their upkeep. However, the 1937 National Trust Act made it possible for the Trust to become the life support of country houses fallen on hard times, guarding them from 'untrammelled market forces' (as it sought to protect rural landscapes from the same predator) and itself from undue state interference by making any endowments the owners made for the upkeep of the property they had donated to the Trust tax-free. This could hardly be an uncontentious matter, since by 'saving' the houses from being sold and estates broken up and parcelled off to developers, the National Trust would also be preserving the existing social arrangements, since the terms of the Act allowed the owner to continue to live in his or her house rent-free after gifting it to the National Trust with tax-free maintenance arrangements – thus protecting this way of life from the buffeting forces of modernity and economic hardship that were racking so much of the nation. Lord Lothian immediately donated his own home, Blickling Hall, a Jacobean manor house in Norfolk with grounds of 4,600 acres, to the Trust.

Harold Nicolson, the author and ex-diplomat, who liked his friends to be 'well-read and well bred', recommended an unemployed young Old Etonian, James Lees-Milne, to his wife, Vita Sackville-West, as 'an aristocrat in mind and culture', and in turn Sackville-West recommended Lees-Milne for the job of Secretary to the Country Houses (later Historic Buildings) Committee, with a salary of £400 a year. This enabled Lees-Milne to follow the vocation he had discovered when, as a student at Oxford, he had been outraged to witness potshots being taken at a statue of Apollo at Rousham, a William Kent architectural gem near Oxford, after a dinner party there. He had then and there 'made a vow . . . that I would devote my energies and abilities such as they are to preserving the country houses of England'. In his new role he set off round the country by car and bicycle to attempt to persuade grandees in magnificent houses (preferably eighteenth-century establishments, in Lees-Milne's taxonomy of architectural desirables) that it was greatly in their interest to become tenants in their own homes.

The first house to be acquired under the scheme, however, hardly fitted Williams-Ellis's (or most others') view of a historic house. Wightwick Manor, a mock-half-timbered Arts and Crafts-influenced brick building on the outskirts of Wolverhampton, built less than fifty years previously by the architect who was responsible for many of the buildings in Lord Leverhulme's model village for the workers of Port Sunlight on Merseyside, Edward Ould, was offered to the Trust by its owners, the paint and varnish manufacturer Sir Geoffrey Mander and his wife. The house came with a very substantial endowment and fine Pre-Raphaelite interiors and artefacts: the Trust accepted.

The Countess of Warwick, mistress of the late King Edward VII and a recent convert to socialism, was unsentimental in her prognosis: 'Times change, and we must learn to change with them . . . The stately homes of England have had their selfish day. Nothing could be better than they should make atonement, in emptiness and disrepair, in the hope that a nobler future awaits them.' In some cases it certainly did: Sir Charles Trevelyan, a Liberal turned Labour politician who had been Labour's Minister for

Education, had inherited the 13,000-acre estate of Wallington in Northumberland in 1928. However, he regarded himself not as the owner 'but as a trustee of property which under wise and humane laws would belong to the community', opened the hall and gardens free of charge at weekends and public holidays, and allowed it be used for adult education and workers' theatre activities (he gifted it to the National Trust in 1941). Some trade unions converted manor houses into convalescent homes for their members. The Workers' Travel Association acquired or rented 'many of the great houses that were built by workers of other generations who were never fortunate enough to find even a night's shelter within their walls': 'Thus does Time (with the help of the WTA) bring in his generous revenges.' Other country houses functioned as schools: the Countess of Warwick offered her own seat, Easton Lodge, as a Labour college in the aftermath of the General Strike, but given its reduced circumstances at the time, the TUC reluctantly turned down the opportunity of running the substantial country house.

The original intention of the National Trust had been primarily to conserve Britain's natural heritage, rather than its houses. In studiedly simple prose, Clough Williams-Ellis put the case: 'Today unspoiled country is one of the things that people value most of all.' Unspoiled it might be, but untouched it was not, except for places such as 'the Scottish Highlands, or Dartmoor, or Snowdonia . . . thrilling because of their wildness and loneliness'. England's scenery was primarily 'man-made'. Hundreds of years of farming, planting and building, and innumerable tiny alterations, additions and subtractions have gone to make up the English countryside with which we are so familiar.

And what would the country be without its buildings? asked Williams-Ellis. 'The English countryside is landscape in harness, and the most substantial part of that harness is architecture.' But that harness, which had once consisted of 'simple, vernacular villages . . . which grew bit by bit, round the church and along the main street', taking in 'the squire's house, the vicarage and one or two other buildings [with] a decorative formality which marks them out – much as the parson's black coat and the squire's well-fitting tweeds mark out their wearers from the other villagers', maybe a manor house too, and certainly an inn, was changing. Although 'England had enjoyed almost perfect health until the beginning of the last century, when the first sporadic signs of a disfiguring malady began to show themselves here and there in the busier and more populous parts of the land,' by the 1930s the 'infantile rashes' raised by a *laissez-faire* attitude to the needs of industry and the requirements (and activities) of 'a monstrously swollen population . . . had affected the general complexion of the land' – Britain was a mess, 'and the end is not yet'.

These disfiguring rashes were various: from urban sprawl, 'ribbon development . . . straggling strips of building which fly out in all directions from the plan of the town', factories, 'crude and unsightly things in a landscape', 'weekend cottages . . . usually in the form of a bungalow . . . almost always ugly', hotels and roadhouses (often built in a 'sham antique' style) and petrol stations, all of which the architectural aesthetes thought could be 'perfectly presentable . . . if placed in a neat row', but not if it they attempted to imitate 'a Cotswold cottage or a Chinese pagoda'.

Frank Forster, during his frequent spells of unemployment, often went cycling around his home in Cheshire, and decried the despoliation of the countryside just as much as Williams-Ellis did. 'Houses built haphazardly, no traces of a plan. Why should private individuals with money be allowed to make such a hideous mess of the country? They extract their profit and leave the mess they have made no matter what it looks like. As a man facing connection with a woman. After his enjoyment has been fulfilled, away he goes and cares nothing of what happens to the other . . . It seems a great pity so much of our countryside should be in the hands of private people . . . The whole country should be in the administerial [sic] hands of the State.'

Whereas in the nineteenth century the movement of population had largely been from the country to the towns, that was now reversing. New light industries and commercial enterprises, mainly clustering away from the traditional industrial conurbations in the South-East and the Midlands, were employing an increasing number of people. These people needed housing, hence the strangling tentacles of suburban growth around London and Manchester and many other industrial cities, leafy habitats for commuters. But while these suburbs extended the girth of the towns and gestured to some of the delights of the countryside, they were hardly rural. There was also what Patrick Abercrombie, a town planner, called the 'urban attaque' on the countryside, 'congeries of shacks, bungalows and caravans-grown-stationary'.

This 'attaque' had been made possible by a combination of what Williams-Ellis called 'improved locomotion' – road and rail links – cheap land, since British agriculture was in a parlous state in some regions and many landowners were eager to sell their land for development, enthusiasm for the open air and the charms of the countryside – all this with negligible planning restraints and 'no official guardianship of our country's beauty'. The result, as far as the conservation lobby was concerned, was 'mean building all over the country that is shrivelling up old England – mean and perky little buildings that surely mean and perky little souls should inhabit with satisfaction'. Although Williams-Ellis, whose words those were, applauded people visiting historic houses (a maximum of thirty open-to-the-public days each year was the usual with National Trust properties), he was decidedly less appreciative when they sought to pitch their 'pink asbestos bungalows' on 'Salisbury Plain or Dartmoor or the South Downs, or some commanding hill in the Cotswolds or Chilterns where they can be seen for miles around'. However, while deploring the realisation of the rural dream of the pink asbestos home, Williams-Ellis had a country weekend bolt-hole of his own, shielded from public view, rented on the Bray estate at Shere, near Guildford in Surrey, where his neighbours included a number of Labour Cabinet Ministers and the historian G.M. Trevelyan.

'The hut dwellers both get a view and spoil it,' complained the prolific writer S.P.B. Mais of the 'bald bungalows' strewn almost everywhere he travelled in Southern England, the railway carriages converted to tearooms atop every hill with a view (or 'a flimsy bungalow with pink asbestos roof and gimcrack verandah enclosed with coloured glass announcing that it was the Lucky Dip Café'), the ubiquitous advertising hoardings – by 1938 an eighty-mile stretch of road from Manchester to the Lake District was lined with 755 advertisements, some proclaiming the virtues of household names such as Oxo or Vimto or Bovril, others, locally scrawled, offering 'Eggs for sale'. Legislation to restrict roadside advertising did exist, but it only applied to hoardings that were more than twelve feet square, and local authorities were often reluctant to embark on costly court cases with uncertain outcomes. 'Letting the great syndicates with the long purses do just what they like . . . results in confusion, increases the discomfort of all, and the ruin of much that is life-giving . . . modern highwaymen seizing on the roadside and the landscape, obliterating and defiling it,' complained the Arts and Crafts architect C.R. Ashbee in a BBC broadcast in April 1930 of a tendency tenaciously fought by the Society for Checking the Abuses of Public Advertising (SCAPA), founded in 1893 and served by a journal with the hopeful title A Beautiful World.

'Leave all your troubles in those drab old towns/And fly, fly, fly/There's still a plot or two upon the Downs/Left for you to buy' was a lyric intended to be sung to the tune of 'Pack Up Your Troubles In Your Old Kit Bag' which appeared in the Peacehaven Post (later changed to Downland) just four years after the end of the First World War, but by the1930s Peacehaven on the Sussex Downs had come to exemplify all that the self-appointed custodians of the rural idyll found most malign, most desecrating. The 'poison began at Peacehaven' on what was once 'a piece of unspoilt downland' but was now 'a colony of shacks'. Standing proudly atop the rolling downs overlooking the sea, Peacehaven offered a choice of seventy-five different styles of bungalows, whose owners gave them names such as 'Dunroamin' and 'Kia Ora' (a Maori phrase for 'Good Health' – also used for a fruit squash). There were many gaps between the houses, since often plot-holders found they could not actually afford to build on the land they had purchased for as little as £25, there was scant provision for drainage, and roads were often little more than a line on a map. Previously known as 'New Anzac-on-Sea' as the result of a somewhat fraudulent competition to name the new estate during the First World War, and originally with road names such as Louvain, Mons, Marne and Ypres (later changed to the innocuous Sunview, Piddinghoe, Gladys and Dorothy), Peacehaven, which had grown hungrily during the 1920s and early 1930s, did not only infuriate the conservationists – particularly since it was advertised as a 'a garden city by the sea', while they thought it violated all the tenets of Ebenezer Howard's vision. It also riled Brighton and Hove Planning Committee, more on economic than aesthetic grounds, since it required costly piped water services, made-up roads, refuse collection and other local authority services, while all the council could do was insist that the asbestos houses be demolished and the common cesspool enlarged.

The same division of the land into small plots, the same mismatch of bungalows, chalets, converted railway carriages (as little as £15 would buy a Victorian railway carriage, obsolete stock bought from a railway company and delivered to your own site), redundant trams, ex-army huts and caravans could be found at Shoreham and Pagham not far from Peacehaven; Waterlooville near Portsmouth; Jaywick Sands in Essex, advertised as 'a motorist's mecca by the sea', its main highway named Brooklands and other thoroughfares designated as Chrysler Crescent, Austin Avenue, Singer Street and Renault Road; the Isle of Sheppey; Canvey Island; on a swathe across the north Kentish Downs from Box Hill via Biggin Hill; Camber Sands on Romney Marsh and Dungeness peninsula. 'Jerry-built wooden erections' disfigured miles of the Lincolnshire and Norfolk coasts, 'tawdry flippancies' straggled the banks of the Thames in Surrey and Berkshire, west around Exmoor, south from Liverpool into the Welsh hills and along the Yorkshire coast, the Humber estuary, the Ayrshire coast, even the banks of Loch Lomond.

Some were associated with poverty and desperation: huts built on allotments rented from the council for 2s.6d a year by unemployed miners evicted from their colliery-owned homes. But many plotland developments were bids for freedom, made possible by ineffective planning legislation, often built on marginal land that no one had previously had any use for, and advertised for sale in local papers, on pub noticeboards, even on the backs of tram tickets issued by the London County Council as 'a home of one's own', at a time when acquiring conventional property was out of the question. Numbers of the Essex plotlanders were the children of rural workers who had left the land for work in the East End of London during the agricultural depression of the late nineteenth century. They paid £5 at open-air auctions for a plot on which they might first erect a second-hand army tent, before graduating to a wooden or corrugated-iron 'built' dwelling. Clusters of discordant shanties, their 'cheap incongruity', in the words of the historian John Lowerson, 'masking the hundreds of individual hopes and patiently saved-up for ambitions' that these retirement homes and weekend retreats represented. 'Whose haven was it? Whose haven is it?' Sir Nikolaus Pevsner would ask decades later of Peacehaven. But he would have been unlikely to have got the answer he was expecting – at least from its 1930s residents – considering 'every man his own house, even if only a few feet from the neighbours!'

It was one thing to explode apoplectically at the growing 'uglification' of Britain. What was much harder was to work out (or 'plan', in the favoured terminology of the1930s) how to reconcile the desire to preserve the beauty of the landscape with the needs of the multitudes of people for whom the 'development of the motor car has made it possible to "live in the country"', as J.C. Squire, who had been active in the campaigns to preserve Stonehenge from neglect and encroaching development, challenged in an article in the *Observer*. The Council for the Preservation of Rural England (CPRE), an umbrella organisation bringing together some forty organisations including the Country Gentlemen's Association, the Royal Institute of British Architects, the National Trust, the RAC (Royal Automobile Club), the AA (Automobile Association), the Society for the Preservation of Ancient Buildings and the National Federation of Women's Institutes, all in some way concerned with the countryside, was formed in 1926, largely as the result of a crusading pamphlet written by Patrick Abercrombie. The CPRE recognised that protecting the countryside could not mean preserving it as it was in an earlier era, but wished to 'promote suitable and harmonious development and to encourage the rational enjoyment of rural areas by urban dwellers'.

Many thoughtful conservationists – Clough Williams-Ellis among them, and on occasions C.E.M. Joad – wrestled with this problem, even if it didn't always show in some of their more flamboyant and snobbish writing.

If the chiaroscuro of modernity was bound to upset the natural order – no longer was the rich man in his castle, since death duties had caused it to be sold, its lands dispersed – then who was going to be the new guardian of the countryside? Were the mistakes of the Industrial Revolution, every-where manifest in Britain's towns and cities, simply going to be exported into the countryside by a growing population? Would it be a question of 'What Manchester looks like today, the English countryside will look like tomorrow?', wondered Patrick Abercrombie. Development was unplanned, 'Towns spilled over their boundaries in all directions, their inhabitants rifling the deepest recesses of the country.' It was the 'higgledy-piggledy' nature of such plotland developments that distressed the conservationists (and the ardent socialist Frank Forster), built by speculative builders who seemed to have acted like 'tidy-minded wizards playing unauthorised blind man's buff in no-man's land, and had been punished for their skittishness by being petrified on the instant just wherever they happened to stand'.

Yet thoughtful conservationists recognised the impulse that drove men to want their own 'three acres and a cow', and rejoiced in the urge for open country, fresh air, a morality founded in nature, not in a capitalist, consumer economy. The drive could not, indeed should not, be resisted: but it must be tidy, organised, ordered – planned. Just as others threw their energies into campaigning for a planned economy (Joad was Director of Propaganda for Oswald Mosley's New Party until the summer of 1931), Abercrombie and Williams-Ellis were among those seeking to have an overall professional plan for the countryside before it was too late. Along with his predictable *bêtes noires* – roadside advertisements, the AA, bungalows – Williams-Ellis included Borough Surveyors in his 'Devil's Dictionary', since they failed to insist that new buildings were designed by professionals with proper architectural training, instead ordering what they considered to be 'tasty' ornamentation from catalogues. 'It is thus that the worst band-stands, tram-shelters, park-gates, pavilions and public lavatories come into being' – though Williams-Ellis too had a soft spot for 'tasty' ornamentation, as Portmeirion showed, though his was not acquired from a catalogue, but gathered over the years, and had acquired a patina of age.

What Williams-Ellis believed was needed sounded distinctly Mosleyite: 'a new direction and leadership as never before, because now, in this gener-ation a new England is made, its form is being hastily cast in a mould that no one has considered as a whole . . . If there is no master founder, and no co-related plan, we may well live aghast at what we have made – a hash of our civilisation and a desert of our country.' Reluctant to blame working men and women for their rural aspirations, the conservationists railed against the developers who left 'the immemorial resort of peaceful [urban] wanderers . . . a forlorn and struggling camp of slatternly shacks and gimcrack bungalows, unfinished roads and weather beaten advertisements', and instanced the 'Cottabunga' – a 'charming bungalow cottage delivered carriage paid to any goods station in England or Wales, ready to erect for £245.10s nett' as an atrocity that could be found dotted all over the country-side. It was far removed from the ancient practice of Feng Shui, Williams-Ellis lamented, which guided the Chinese to 'harmonise human additions with natural features that a new complex landscape might result'. But then, 'China for a thousand years or more has been devoting its unrivalled artistic genius to this very question (. . . of the inevitable artificialisation of the natural landscape)', whereas Britain had only seemed to begin to notice the problem in the 1930s.

Voluntary bodies such as the National Trust managed to mount periodic campaigns to save areas of natural beauty under threat of development: an appeal had been launched to ensure that rows of villas or 'Druid's bunga-lows' Cottages' were not built on the perimeter of Stonehenge ('England is Stonehenge, not Whitehall,' the Ferguson Gang had resolved at the height of the furore). But these were essentially *ad hoc*, seat-of the-pants initiatives, as the Labour Minister of Health Arthur Greenwood (who was responsible for such matters) recognised in 1931. It was, he said, essential to consider 'the whole question of how to deal with our national amenities . . . we cannot go on dealing with this part and with that separately, raising funds for purchase and so on'. What was required was a national policy regarding 'our most precious historical monuments and our finest bits of national scenery'. It was not just ancient monuments, historic houses and prehistoric burial grounds that needed protection. As Patrick Abercrombie recognised, 'The greatest historical monument that we possess, the most essential thing which *is* England, is the Countryside, the Market Town, the Village, the Hedgerow Trees, the Lanes, the Copses, the Streams and the Farmstead,' a remit that was of course far beyond the resources of the CPRE or any other body.

A start was made with the 1932 Town and Country Planning Act (which became law in April 1933). The highly complex Act was criticised by some who saw it as 'the shepherding of a grandmotherly government' (today's 'nanny state'), but a decade later it was condemned by the Scott Report into the countryside as having been a tale of 'high hopes and subsequent disappointments'. Although the Act was 'called a Town and Country Planning Act, practical experience quickly proved that it was entirely inadequate for the formulation of country planning schemes'. It was not until 1947 that a more prescriptive Act was passed, with greater powers for local authorities. The Restriction of Ribbon Development Act of 1935 suffered from many of the same inhibitions as the earlier Act: essentially it was permissive legislation for local initiatives with no Exchequer funding for compensation payments and no central overview.

The 1932 Act did have some successes: by the outbreak of war in 1939, 85 per cent of the Sussex Downs were protected from building developments, while the 1938 Green Belt Act restricted urban sprawl to an extent by proposing the throwing of a rural girdle round London, and gradually thirteen other urban areas, to preserve rings of open space that halted tentacles of urban encroachment and towns from simply merging into one another. However, the emasculation of the Town and Country Planning Act during its lengthy passage through Parliament, with endless objections from vested interests protesting against state interference in what they regarded as their inalienable property rights, and objections to the likely cost of compensation, raised a question that would be heard throughout the 1930s from a number of different perspectives: what was the countryside actually *for*?

Although it represented by far the largest part of the land surface of Britain – around thirty-three million acres, whereas towns and cities took up little more than four million – the countryside was underpopulated: by the 1930s only about six million people out of a population of forty-one million lived there. Moreover, only 6.7 per cent of the nation's workforce worked on the land. The number of farm workers (both men and women) had fallen by around 10 per cent between 1921 and 1931. In some places the change was more dramatic: in Oxfordshire, for example, the number working on the land had fallen by 32 per cent, with some 3,000 ex-farm labourers working at the Morris car factory near Cowley in Oxford, out of a total workforce of around 5,000. Miners, who throughout the nineteenth century had been the third largest group of rural workers (after agricultural workers and domestic servants) were also in decline during the 1930s, unemployed in the country, if they had not already left for factories or building sites in towns.

'Derelict', 'unkempt' and 'neglected' were among the words used to describe the inter-war countryside, and novels of the period such as Adrian Bell's (father of the BBC war correspondent and white-suited short-time independent MP Martin Bell) early 1930s rural trilogy, *Corduroy*, *Silver Ley* and *The Cherry Tree* and Stella Gibbons' parodic *Cold Comfort Farm* (1932) sustained a picture of rural gloom caused by government lassitude and urban indifference. A 1934 Labour pamphlet mourned that 'No keen observer can travel far through the once pleasant and prosperous country-side of Britain without realising that there is something badly wrong with agriculture and the conditions of modern life today . . . Fields that were cultivated are going back to poor grass. Farms that were bustling and prosperous are silent. Sadly lacking over vast stretches of land is any sign of active, energetic cultivation . . . Empty, untilled fields: miserable cottages: farmhouses in bad repair.'

In many ways rural Britain could be compared to a one-industry town that had fallen on hard times. But since the effects were dispersed, they were less easy to grasp, and in fact there were some areas of the country which dairy farming and livestock-rearing, including poultry farming, made reasonably prosperous. It was cereal farming – particularly in East Anglia – that was in decline, and those farmers who had bought their own small farms on mortgages after the First World War were hit particularly hard. During the Depression the already falling price of wheat dropped by 50 per cent. Consequently arable land fell by four million acres between 1918 and 1939, making livestock heavily dependent on imported foodstuffs and meaning that as much as 70 per cent of food for the British people was imported rather than home-grown or raised.

In any case, agriculture was no longer a question of producing food merely for the local market. Production had to be for a national, or even a world, market, with prices beyond the control of the farmer. Tariffs to protect British agriculture were one solution always aired by the Conservative Party, and from 1931 a series of quotas and import taxes were imposed on a range of agricultural goods from Europe, while those from the Empire were allowed free entry. More radical Tory thinkers such as Harold Macmillan, working with the Next Five Years Group, recognised that this was no long-term solution. Britain was primarily an industrial country, and needed a flourishing export industry; tariff barriers would bring retali-ations and lead to higher food prices, which would hit the already suffering industrial population for the sake of – possibly – protecting the interests of the 10 per cent employed on the land. The only answer was increased productivity through land drainage and soil improvement schemes, greater mechanisation (in 1938 there were only around 4,000 tractors in the whole of England, and most of these were on large farms of over three hundred acres), improved credit facilities and marketing boards – by 1939 there were seventeen such boards, the most famous of which was the Milk Marketing Board. The Labour Party regularly and dutifully brought up the idea of land nationalisation, but the prospect of the compensation payments this would incur made it seem a utopian chimera.

Rural wages were low – £1.10*s* was the average for an agricultural worker, around a third of the pay of an urban labourer – and conditions poor. It was not until 1936 that agricultural workers were included in the National Insurance scheme. Scattered around the countryside, few belonged to a trade union (though the National Union of Agricultural Workers claimed 50,000 members by 1939), and many had the continual insecurity of living in a tied cottage that went with the job, and from which a worker and his family could be evicted. Mary Emerson and her husband worked under an arcane bondager system, known as the 'hinds', which persisted in Northumberland into the 1930s. 'Under the system a man and his wife were hired for one year. My husband got 30 shillings a week and I got 5 shillings for milking five cows night and morning and other jobs as well: I spread muck, I cut thistles, pulled potatoes, pulled turnips. If the farmer wanted you, you could stay on another year, or you could leave. When we left the tied cottage, all our furniture was piled up on to a wagon and taken to the next farm we were moving to. We had no idea what kind of cottage we were going into. You'd go and see it and you had to live there, however awful it was. You just tried to make it habitable. Work started the same day.'

Marian Atkinson, who lived with her husband and fifteen children on an isolated sheep farm in Cumbria, had to use sacks for her family's outdoor clothing. 'We had miles and miles of binder twine and we tied the sacks around our waists. We made a three-cornered hood out of them, too, to keep our heads dry. Sometimes we had one round our waist, one round our bottoms, one round each knee . . . they kept us as warm as a top coat or shawl.' From May to October or November the family went barefooted. 'It was a sense of freedom in one way and a sense of saving up in another, because while you weren't wearing your shoes, you weren't wearing them out.' Mrs Atkinson would serve lambs' tails, 'cut off when they were five or six weeks old, skinned and cooked with a handful of barley, a handful of peas and a handful of rice . . . they made a jolly good stew . . . Nothing went to waste on the farm, absolutely nothing . . . I never had no wages, I worked for rent and home.'

Almost half the parishes in England and Wales lacked a sewerage system, a third had no piped water, and fewer than one in twelve farms had electricity as late as 1938. Inside picturesque, whitewashed, rambling-rose-covered, thatched-roof cottages could lurk dank earth floors, a wooden board over a hole in the ground in an outhouse the only lavatory, rooms lit by candles or oil lamps, and miserable poverty. Unsurprisingly, almost any land that could be was sold off for housing: between 1919 and 1939 more than 860,000 houses were built in rural areas, of which 700,000 were the work of private builders. But these were rarely for country people, who could not possibly afford the rents. Instead they brought town-dwellers to live in the country, many of whom commuted to the towns and cities to work.

Traditional rural industries such as hurdle-making, weaving, potting, dry-stone walling, thatching, quilting and basket-making were threatened by new technologies, new forms of production. In Berkshire, for example, the number of blacksmiths had fallen from twenty-two to six in forty years, and all the water mills were derelict. Yet while the many books and magazines devoted to rural life liked to depict age-old craftsmen doing age-old crafts in age-old ways – bending willow, whittling wood, making lace, weaving yarn, polishing with beeswax – there was a realistic appreciation that 'If the village blacksmith will not adopt modern methods, will not make the best use of modern machinery, will not meet a changing market, he will disappear, and no amount of sitting under chestnut trees and singing in the choir will save him. And we should not want to save him . . . The decrepit must not be bolstered up, it must be changed or abandoned,' wrote the Secretary of the Cambridge Rural Communities Council, E.R. Vincent, briskly.

Although the employment opportunities offered would invariably be small-scale, there were considerable attempts (helped by such organisations as the Rural Industries Bureau) by many local craftsmen and women to diversify, to mechanise and to market their products. Most village garages started in blacksmiths' shops, while others turned to fashioning wrought-iron gates or such suburban hearthside must-haves as firedogs or coal scuttles. And the influx of town-dwellers into the countryside sometimes brought a new aesthetic, an appreciation for the 'arts and crafts' aspect of rural life, even a willingness to pay more for the handmade, the cottage-spun.

'The English have the ugliest towns and the most beautiful countryside in the world, and it was inevitable that sooner or later they would discover the fact. The credit for that discovery must go to our generation,' wrote the popularising philosopher C.E.M. Joad. By train, charabanc, motor car, motorbike, bicycle or on foot this discovery was made (or more likely re-affirmed) as town-dwellers set out into the countryside, encouraged by the outpourings of inter-war paeans to rurality and clutching a map and possibly a compass.

The first journey ever made in Britain by a 'petroleum motor carriage' was claimed to have been taken in July 1895 between Micheldever in Hampshire and Datchet near Windsor, a distance of fifty-six miles, which took five hours and thirty-two minutes, 'exclusive of stoppages'. By 1930 some cars were advertised as being capable of 70 mph, and the speed restriction of 20 mph had been abolished in 1930, since it was almost universally flouted (a limit of 30 mph in towns was reimposed in 1934). Whereas there had been around 100,000 cars on British roads in 1918, there were over two million by 1939. And with this mass production – and consumption – prices were falling: in 1936 an average car cost almost half what it had done in 1924. Although a Rolls-Royce cost £2,500 (when the average cost of a London house was around £500), a small family car such as an Austin 7, a 'Bullnose' Morris 8 or a Ford would set a motorist back about £165.

By the 1930s Britain's countryside was criss-crossed with tarmacked roads, some following the line of earlier, much wider highways, others constructed (often as part of an unemployed labour scheme) as new trunk roads or bypasses. But Britain was not a land of autobahns or autostradas. The total road network had only increased by 4 per cent between 1899 and 1936, the year an Act was passed to 'provide a national system of routes for through traffic', and this had to be put on hold when war broke out three years later. While the railways had opened up Britain for leisure (as for other purposes) in the previous century, transforming small coastal villages such as Bournemouth into major towns, the car brought a rather different form of exploration and exploitation. As Patrick Abercrombie judiciously put it, 'The immediate physical assault upon the landscape by motoring can indeed in no wise be compared with the scars inflicted by the railways: but the complete permeation is more thorough.'

This 'permeation' was partly made possible by the facts that cars were rather more mechanically reliable than they had been in the early years of the century, there were more and better-equipped garages outside the towns, and the frequency of petrol stations along country roads had increased, as had the ubiquity of AA and RAC telephone boxes, patrolling motorcyclists and 'get you home' services. Membership of the AA cost £2.2s a year, which covered all legal costs in the event of prosecution. The AA had been founded in 1905 to frustrate police road traps, using cyclists and motorcyclists to warn motorists of upcoming speed traps. By 1937 it claimed to have 600,000 members.

In addition to a map in the car's glove compartment there might be an itinerary produced by one of the motoring organisations – in the summer of 1934, 700,000 were provided. These ranged from direct routes (though as scenic a direct route as possible) to *Day Drive Booklets* from towns recommended as touring centres, or 'Tourlet' guides, useful for the Sunday-afternoon spin or half-day excursion. There might also be the popular

Hotel and Boarding House guide, or a list of AA- or RAC-recommended places to stay – though the habit of touring was not popular with hoteliers and guest-house keepers, since a one-night stay involved the same necessity for clean sheets as the traditional week- or fortnight-long holiday. Then there was the booklet the AA brought out annually from 1933, *Caravan and Camp Sites in England, Scotland and Wales*, although at £50 to £100 for the smallest model, caravans were beyond the purse of most motorists (and below the social acceptability sightline of others), so there were only 3,500 privately owned caravans by 1933, though they could be rented from five guineas a week.

Motorists could nose their cars down minor roads, stumbling on 'undiscovered' byways. The covers of Ordnance Survey maps depicted first walkers, then cyclists; by 1935 the quarter-inch series showed a motorist. It was an individualistic, particularly middle-class, form of penetration (with the help of hire purchase, a new 10–15 horsepower car was within the reach of most white-collar workers), one which G.K. Chesterton likened to the tanks of an invading army. The motorcar completely 'shuts in' the motorist, who sits looking 'inward at his speedometer or his road book' as he drives along roads that do not go 'to places; but through places'.

The motorist was further encouraged to meander 'through places' by the avalanche of countryside books that were being published to acquaint him or her with the delights of rural England ('England' seeming the natural companion of 'rural' to such pastoralists, even if what they referred to might include Wales or Scotland), many with numerous brightly coloured photographs, since colour printing was now relatively cheap.

Such books proved very profitable to publishers, and every year dozens of new titles like *English Byways, Green Fields of England, The English Inn* or *The English Country Town* appeared in the Longman's 'English Heritage' series (started in 1929). Batsford's 'British Heritage' series (begun in 1930) included remarkably similar titles such as *The Old Towns of England* and *The Old Inns of England*. Dent's 'Open Air Library' included the poet Edward Thomas on *The Heart of England* and *Out of Doors with Richard Jeffries*, and between 1930 and 1940 the ever-prolific S.P.B. Mais wrote more than twenty guidebooks with such titles as *England's Character, England's Pleasance, Glorious Devon* and *England of the Windmills*. The urban pootler might subscribe to the green-jacketed quarterly the *Countryman*, published from rural Oxfordshire, and read about 'Disappearing Crafts' or, surely the embodiment of the new way in which town-dwellers approached the country, 'Bird Watching by Car and Telescope'. This involved rather a lot of fiddling around with bits of wood and wingnuts, but it did enable the motorist to 'drive within twenty yards of a buzzard'. Or he might have settled down with H.V. Morton's *In Search of England*, which was in its twenty-sixth impression by 1939, although 'a glance at the route followed will prove that this is not a guide-book'.

These outpourings of rural advice and enticement were invariably illustrated with photographs or sketches of the beautiful places the car-owner was in fact being invited to despoil, if not directly by dropping orange peel or leaving sandwich wrappers at the rustic spot at which he and his family had elected to picnic, then indirectly as far as rural purists were concerned by requiring petrol stations to fill up his car and tearooms to nourish its occupants.

Most of these books and magazine echoed the conservationists' plea that the countryside was perfect as it was (though ripe for discovery). Taking a journey back into the past as well as out into the country, they tended to gloss over those modernist elements that might be less than picturesque, but they rarely had a campaigning edge against change, since their readers would most likely be more than happy to consume scones and jam in fake half-timbered thatched ye olde tea shoppes, might well put up for a night at a Trust House (formed in 1920 to convert old country pubs into tasteful roadhouses) or a farm which did thriving business with B&B guests – during the Depression some Devonshire farmers probably derived as much as three-quarters of their income from offering accommodation, serving teas or letting campers pitch tents on their land. And they would almost certainly stop at a garage or filling station, which might be a blot on the landscape with its corrugated-tin roof and scabby forecourt (despite the advice of the CPRE to opt for timber-framed walls and thatched roofs while eschewing exaggerated rusticity), but without which no long out-of-town journey would be possible.

The commercial investment in this duality – presenting the countryside as a tranquil, unchanging place while bringing increasing numbers of people and their essential accoutrements to assault this quality – was most explicit in those publications sponsored by companies that would benefit most from people buying and using cars. Every major motor-vehicle manufacturer produced its own magazine. The *Morris Owner* (which claimed a readership of 43,000; the *Austin Magazine, Vauxhall Motorist, Standard Car Review* and the Rootes-group-owned *Modern Motoring* were not far behind) was the glossiest and longest-running, presenting an idealised vision of the countryside, backed up with free film shows extolling 'Our Beautiful England' – accessible in your very own Morris 8.

Jack Beddington had been Shell oil's man in Shanghai before returning to head office in London, where he criticised Shell's poster designs. Told to do the job himself, he decided that rather than concentrating on the petrol's technical properties, since there was no detectable difference between one brand of petrol coming out of the pumps and another, he would seek to identify Shell with Britain's most beautiful countryside, made accessible by the car. Shell had already stacked up some credit in this area, since it had started to remove its advertising signs from rural areas in 1923, and since 1927 it had encouraged garage-owners to take down their enamel Shell signs and to concentrate their advertising instead on 'lorry bills', hoardings on the sides of delivery tankers. Advertisements appeared in magazines featuring letters of praise from environmental organisations for this initiative, and photographs of English beauty spots were reproduced, promising: 'The proprietors of Shell do not advertise their petrol in places like this.'

The artists Beddington commissioned to produce these 'lorry bills' included most of the finest British artists and graphic designers at work in the 1930s, including John and Paul Nash, Vanessa Bell, Duncan Grant, John Piper, Edward Bawden, Rex Whistler, Eric Ravilious, Graham Sutherland, Ben Nicholson, Barnett Freedman, Edward Ardizzone, Mary Kessell and later the American expatriate E. McKnight Kauffer. Some of the posters were knowing and witty, while others portrayed the English countryside, unsullied by telegraph poles, billboards or, somewhat disingenuously, garages, but dotted with unusual and intriguing features – follies, ruins, monuments, geographical phenomena – accompanied by slogans such as 'To Visit British Landmarks You Can be Sure of Shell'. Throughout the 1930s exhibitions of these posters were mounted (two of which were opened by Kenneth Clark, the young Director of the National Gallery), and the normally rather acerbic critic Cyril Connolly was soon hailing the oil company as 'the Medici of our time'.

In 1933 the poet and architectural conservationist John Betjeman was working at the *Architectural Review* (or the *Archie Rev* as he called it) when he suggested to Beddington a series of guides to the British counties, for which he would act as general editor. The guides were to be published by the Architectural Press (which owned the *Archie Rev*), though later, mainly as a result of Betjeman's manoeuvrings, they and their general editor moved into Shell Mex's 1931-built Art Deco offices on the Thames Embankment near the Savoy Hotel, designed by Ernest Joseph, a leading architect of synagogues.

Betjeman had a clear vision for the guides, 'which interest me more than anything else because I hate urban life and am really cut out for archaeology, make up [in the book design sense] and photography and know England pretty well'. They were not for 'the uncritical tripper', but 'everything an intelligent tourist could want to know is touched upon . . . No writer of a Shell Guide is allowed to use those worn out words "picturesque", "fine", "beautiful", "quaint". The writers are selected for their powers of observation and their ability with prose. There is no guide-bookese in a Shell Guide.'

Since he had lived in Cornwall for much of his life, Betjeman chose that county for the first of the series. The slim, spiral-bound book came out in 1934, selling for 2s.6d. Apart from the usual 'guide-bookese' gazetteer there was an article on fishing written by Betjeman's father Ernest, and a handful of recipes for Cornish fare, including one for pasties, though not for 'Stargazy pie', since this was made only in St Ives. *Cornwall* was considered sufficiently successful for the series to continue, and much as Beddington had corralled talent to advertise Shell's petrol, Betjeman did the same for the guidebooks, commissioning authors who were 'generally poets with a bump of topography' – invariably his friends. Peter Quennell wrote the guide to Somerset with his father, the architect and social historian C.H.B. Quennell; Paul Nash was the editor for Dorset and John Nash for Bucks; Anthony West, the illegitimate son of Rebecca West and H.G. Wells, wrote on Gloucestershire, Robert Byron on Wiltshire (Betjeman contributed a slogan to the Shell poster campaign on that county: 'Stonehenge Wilts but SHELL goes on for ever' – the megalithic stones pictured drooping limply), while Betjeman himself wrote the guide to Devon. The guides included articles by other hands: the Dean of Rochester contributed one on his cathedral for the Kent guide, and Miles Sargent (a master at Marlborough College) a rather patronising one on hop-picking for the same volume, while its editor Lord Clonmore pronounced that 'To travel in Kent without visiting Canterbury is rather like eating Christmas pudding without brandy butter.'

John Piper had been recommended for his work on the abstract art magazine *AXIS*. 'Dear Artist,' Betjeman wrote, 'Would you like to do Oxfordshire?' Piper, who was a keen photographer, drove around in a second-hand Lancia, which he had bought for £15, with his soon-to-be second wife Myfanwy Evans and a ridge tent, photographing Anglo-Saxon and Romanesque carvings, which he thought were 'the forebears of pure abstractionists today . . . Many a Picasso-like profile is to be found on twelfth-century fonts and capitals.' *Oxon*, a guide to 'one of the most ordinary of English counties', was published in 1938 with text, photographs and sketches by Piper. Since it was a Shell Guide to the *countryside*, it expressly did not include the city of Oxford, which Betjeman had labelled 'motopolis' anyway.

The guides 'were not expected to pay. They were prestige advertising, subsidised by Shell. There were no publisher's contracts and the whole thing was done on a personal basis.' As useful guidebooks, the Shell Guides were sadly deficient. What they represented was the work of a coterie of clever and talented young men, each with an interest in words and design (in Betjeman's case particularly typography), producing books that stunningly embodied the selective nostalgia of progressive connoisseurs (particularly for the 'fast disappearing Georgian landscape of England'), replete with stark modernist and generally very un-nostalgic black and white photographs, used large, since Betjeman had learned that 'large blocks should be of small objects – details of carving, trunks of trees, facades of buildings – and that small blocks should be of what are termed "general views"' – more geological slabs of granite than winding lanes and thatched cottages. The guides provided a view of England that had formerly usually been left to the middle-brow ('poets with a bump of topography' generally neglected to write about their homeland in favour of more distant explorations), celebrating England and an Englishness that the commercial intentions of their sponsors was set to dilute if not despoil.

If there was a persistent tension between wanting to leave the country-side in an unsullied time warp, yet eroding its tranquillity by making it easier and faster to get deep into, between conserving and observing (one magazine even proposed that all roadside hedges should be scrubbed up and replaced with clear plastic screens so motorists could see round corners), it was hardly a straight path for the less environmentally disruptive cyclist or walker.

C.E.M. Joad was one of the most explosive proselytisers against the 'irruptions' of the car and the motorcycle in the 1930s. One particular irri-tation was the *Observer*'s 'menacing' motoring correspondent, 'a man who obviously loves the English countryside . . . [yet drives] his car up and down and round the counties of England until no lane is safe from his molesta-tion, no village unvisited by his peripatetic mechanisms. And week by week he divulges in the *Observer*, carefully, charmingly, the results of his depre-dations, devoting all his considerable powers of persuasion to the task of inducing others to follow in his train.' What especially irked the fluent philosopher was the detailed instructions given in each column to enable motorists to 'shatter the peace. They are to leave the Hog's Back or the Kingston Bypass, and are then to follow the carefully given directions to find their way through the deep-cut lanes of Surrey . . . The better to find these lanes, you are advised to take a *large-scale walker's map*,' he exploded.

Walking or rambling (or the rather more purposeful hiking) were the way in which the carless and the motorbikeless could reclaim *their* rural idyll. 'People in shorts were everywhere,' shaking off the workday city, breathing that highly-prized thirties commodity 'fresh air', feeling the warmth (sometimes) of the sun on pale urban skins, swinging limbs, clasping sturdy sticks, even possibly singing 'I'm Happy When I'm Hiking', a communal song popularised by the *Daily Herald* in the early 1930s.

Manchester's Central Station early on a Sunday morning was 'an unforgettable sight' for Joad, 'with its crowds of ramblers, complete with rucksacks, shorts and hob nailed boots, waiting for the early trains to Edale, Chinley, Hope and the Derbyshire moors, it might lead one to suppose that the whole of Manchester was in exodus. And it is, indeed, true that this generation has replaced beer by "hiking" as the shortest cut out of Manchester.'

As far as Joad was concerned, those in the South had little conception of 'the hold which the rambling movement has in the North'. This did not mean that Southerners did not ramble over the South Downs and the Chilterns, the Mendips and the moors of Devon and Cornwall, sometimes with single determination, or in small groups of friends or on outings arranged by youth clubs, churches, chapels, scout troops or Boys' Brigade battalions or political organisations such as the Fabians or the Young Socialists. The Ramblers' Association, founded in 1935, organised country rambles, lobbied for cheap railway fares for walkers, particularly on Sundays, and negotiated 'Walking Tour Tickets' that enabled ramblers to alight from their train at one station, and depart from another after a day's walk. For those who preferred to cycle – sometimes on a tandem, which was a popular courting (and after, until the babies arrived) mode of transport – the Cyclists' Touring Club (CTC) arranged tours for its members, campaigned to persuade local authorities to improve roads so cyclists would not somersault over their handlebars when their bike hit a pothole, and tried to negotiate special 'cyclists' rates' for meals and accommodation at hotels and B&Bs.

Such wholesale invasion did not find unquestioning favour. J.B. Priestley found when he returned to his home city in 1935 that Bradford folk were still, as they always had been, 'streaming out to the moors . . . I have known men who thought nothing of tramping between thirty and forty miles every Sunday.' But whereas when Priestley was young they had set out 'in twos or threes, in ordinary working clothes . . . Now they were in gangs of either hikers or bikers, twenty or thirty of them together and all dressed for their respective parts . . . I doubt whether this organised, semi-military, semi-athletic style of exploring the countryside is an improvement on our old casual rambling method. The youngsters looked too much as if they were consciously taking exercise; they suggested the spirit of a lesser and priggish Wordsworth.'

Joad too was less than thrilled at the masses he found walking on the Derbyshire moors: on 'a gorgeous day commanding wide views over miles of moorland country . . . so close were we packed that we looked for all the world like a girls' school taking the air in "crocodile" on a Sunday afternoon'. The apogee of the mass ramble must surely have been in July 1932, when 16,000 people joined S.P.B. Mais (who revelled in the title 'Ambassador of the British countryside') in a midnight excursion to watch the sun rise over Chanctonbury Ring on the Sussex Downs. Four special trains had to be laid on, though unfortunately the dawn was cloudy and the rising sun obscured.

Tension between cyclists and motorists, both of whom claimed the rolling English road for their pleasure, grew intense in the inter-war years, with invective about cyclists' 'poor roadmanship' in motorists' magazines such as the *Autocar* matched by ripostes in the *CTC Gazette* claiming that motorists seemed to think that because they paid road tax they owned the road. While cyclists had little option but to share the roads and lanes with cars, ramblers could choose to strike off along footpaths over grassland and through woods. The Commons, Open Spaces and Footpaths Preservation Society, founded in the 1860s, found itself endlessly fighting to safeguard public rights of way threatened by landowners, and although the Rights of Way Act which became law in 1934 did not create new footpaths, it allowed that a right of way could be established if it could be proved that a particular footpath had been in use consistently over several decades.

The right to roam collided with the same prejudices as did other incursions into the countryside such as ribbon development and caravan parks, and raised again the question: what was the countryside *for*? In the South there were areas such as the South Downs which were intersected by a reasonable number of footpaths across grassy land where walkers would not interfere with any farming interest, but it was markedly different in the North. In an area of 230 square miles of uncultivated moorland between Manchester and Sheffield there were only twelve footpaths that were over twelve miles in length. Those who worked in the grimy, smoky industrial towns had virtually no access to the heather-clad moors almost on their doorstep – much of it owned by the Duke of Devonshire – because it was shooting country: breeding grouse had to be protected so they could be shot. Moreover, Sheffield Corporation, which owned land around Bleaklow Head, refused access to its own ratepayers to walk on it, with the excuse that the reservoirs into which the bogs drained might get contaminated – and in any case it was making a tidy sum from letting the moor for grouse-rearing.

People had trespassed on the land for centuries, and every summer brought a crop of skirmishes with gamekeepers, but by the 1930s it had become a matter of the right of access for thousands of people intent on spending their limited leisure time in the fresh air. 'I'm a rambler, I'm a rambler from Manchester way, I get all me pleasure the hard moorland way,' sang the Young Communist League folk singer Ewan MacColl when still a teenager. 'I walk where I will, o'er mountain and hill . . . I may be a wage slave on Monday, but I'm a free man on Sunday.'

In 1931 members of the Communist-inspired British Workers' Sports Federation (BWSF) had been camping close to Bleaklow, and when they were turned back from an attempt to walk on the moor they resolved on a mass trespass. 'Wild Scenes on Kinder' reported the *Manchester Evening News* of the climb of somewhere between 150 and six hundred ramblers (estimates vary wildly), led by Benny Rothman, the Secretary of the Lancashire BWSF, up the bleak, slate-dotted Kinder Scout from the village of Hayfield, where wardens and reinforcements were waiting. Fights broke out, and the ramblers marched back down the hill, singing revolutionary songs. When they reached Hayfield the police as well as the press (alerted by Rothman) were waiting. Five of the so-called ringleaders were arrested, charged with violent affray and grievous bodily harm to one of the keepers, and subsequently sentenced to between two and six months in prison.

Other mass, and less mass, trespasses followed; a poignant booklet of photographs, *Views of the Forbidden Moorlands of the Peak District*, surreptitiously taken by a Sheffield man, showed what barren beauty was being kept from the view of the Northern common man. An Access to Mountains Bill, first introduced in 1886 and 'so often but so unfruitfully' reintroduced, was thrown out by Ramsay MacDonald's National Government when Ellen Wilkinson had a go in 1932. MacDonald had deeply ambivalent feelings about access to the countryside. He himself often took to the hills and moors around his home in the fishing village of Lossiemouth on the east coast of Scotland to get a perspective on things political, believing that it was 'as necessary . . . to initiate young folks into the love of the hills and the physical endurance which is the homage exacted by the hills [as it is] to initiate them into Marxian economics'. But when it came to endorsing a 'Welcome to Scotland' initiative to bring tourists – and their money – to his native land, he declined, squirming unpleasantly that 'I am always for opening up the country to the crowd, but to help to open the flood gates for a turgid crowd is quite another matter.' He was likewise unhelpful when Princes Risborough Labour Party complained about lack of public access to the grounds of the Prime Minister's official country residence, Chequers, in the Buckinghamshire Chiltern hills.

The Labour MP Arthur Creech Jones who introduced the Access to Mountains Bill yet again in 1938 was himself a keen hill-walker and his Private Member's Bill sought to ensure that 'No owner or occupier of uncultivated mountain, heath or moorland or uncultivated downland shall be entitled to exclude any person from walking or being on such land for the purpose of recreation or scientific or artistic study, or to molest him in so walking or doing.' The Bill was passed, but it was not the measure the Ramblers' Association, Joad or any other right-of-way campaigner had hoped for. Access was not automatically granted to the hills, moors and bogs of Britain: it had to be applied for by local authorities or bodies likely to benefit, such as the Ramblers' Association, with all the bureaucracy and cost that would entail, since the landowner was almost bound to object. Even if an order were to be granted, the owner of the land would be allowed to specify conditions, such as no access allowed in the nesting or shooting seasons in the case of a grouse moor, for example – and since these were during the summer months, this was a cruel privation.

It was predictable that the Bill would disappoint those who had campaigned so tirelessly for it, including both the Ramblers' Association and the London-based Progressive Ramblers' Association, and men who had written books with such robust titles as *The British Highlands with Rope and Rucksack*, *Striding Through Yorkshire*, and Joad's own *A Charter for Ramblers*. It was equally to be expected that most landowners would object not only on the principle of the violation of property rights, but also to the damage 'trespassers' might cause to the countryside, with crops trampled down, hedgerows pushed through, gates left open, livestock startled, fires lit, litter ('that grimy visiting-card which democracy, now on calling terms with the country insists on leaving after each visit').

In fact Joad was not really all that happy with the idea of *people* in the landscape at all, certainly not noisy and vulgar town-dwellers. The countryside should echo to the sound of the skylark or the curlew, not be polluted by 'the hordes of hikers cackling insanely in the woods, or singing raucous songs as they walk arm in arm at midnight down the quiet village street . . . There are tents in meadows and girls in pyjamas dancing beside them to the strains of the gramophone . . . there are fat girls in shorts, youths in gaudy ties and plus fours, and a roadhouse round every corner and a café on top of every hill for their accommodation.' But his answer was not to deny access: it was to 'educate the public', to 'have every child required to pass an examination in country lore and country manners before he left school', while any town-dweller who had not passed such an examination would be obliged to 'wear an "L" upon his back when he walked abroad in the country, for until he has learnt the elementary manners of the country-side, he is no better qualified to be at large in a wood than a learning motorist is to be at large on a road'.

Educating an uprooted urban population to reinhabit its own backyard was a task undertaken in various ways by a number of organisations. The Youth Hostel Association (YHA) had been started in Germany before the First World War as part of the *Wandervögel* (Wanderbirds) movement, with *Jugendherbergen* (youth hostels) dotted around the country, each one a day's walk from the next. The idea spread to Britain with the support of various groups of ramblers, hikers and cyclists who wanted somewhere cheap to stay, and the national YHA (covering England and Wales) came into being, soon followed by parallel associations for Scotland and Ireland. The first President was the historian G.M. Trevelyan, who was also a member of the governing body of the National Trust, with Patrick Abercrombie of the CPRE as Vice Chairman. By Easter 1931 the first four hostels had opened, one of which was a wooden hut in Flintshire specially designed for the YHA by Clough Williams-Ellis, and by the end of the year there were seven, serving between them almost 10,000 outdoor types. The accommodation was simple – iron bunks in dormitories – and cheap at a shilling a night. The rules were firm: no smoking, gambling or intoxicants, lights out (and strict silence) from 10.30 p.m. Dormitories were segregated, but elsewhere the sexes mixed, and guests were required to carry out duties such as bed-making, food preparation and washing up cheerfully.

A quarterly journal, *YHA Rucksack*, was sent to members, containing exchanges between 'self cookers' and those who ate the food provided (at extra cost), between ramblers and cyclists, and between those who liked large hostels (such as the 130-bed Derwent Hall in the Peak District, opened by the Prince of Wales in July 1932, when he commended the idea of 'tramping holidays away from the atmosphere of our big cities') and those who thought a rustic hut more in keeping. By 1939 there were 280 hostels and 83,417 members. Yet being free to roam and to rest your head when the sun went down was no longer that easy, particularly on bank holidays, when far-sighted booking ahead was required.

The YHA, which had given cautious support to the Access to Mountains Bill lobby, was committed not only to accommodating countryside users (a number of hostels were so isolated in the Welsh mountains or the Lake District that they were hardly suited to the purpose of the working-class rambler who had neither the money nor the time to take such an expedition) but to educating them. In an article in *Rucksack* in 1935 the rural writer and passionate advocate of traditional agricultural husbandry H.J. Massingham congratulated the YHA on the 'noble work' it was doing in 'purging the countryside of its more barbarous elements', and argued that 'There is no innate disharmony between those who make their living from the land and those who explore it for their pleasure or find pleasure in the spiritual contemplation of its beauties.' An early Country Code was pinned up in each hostel, instructing members how to respect the countryside and what equipment they needed while doing so.

Those who became members of two other organisations, the Kibbo Kift or the Woodcraft Folk, were expected to do much more than contemplate the beauties of the countryside: they were encouraged to 'return to the early conditions of the wilderness'. Kibbo Kift had developed out of, but also in reaction to, the Boy Scouts, founded by Robert Baden-Powell in 1908, which could claim close to half a million members in Britain by 1938. John Hargrave, an artist and writer who had served as a stretcher-bearer in the First World War, had been the Scout Headquarters Commissioner for Woodcraft. But on his return from the war, Hargrave (who used the name 'White Fox') had become increasingly critical of the patriotic, imperial jingoism of the Scouting movement. In 1920, strongly influenced by the ideas of Ernest Seton, who had been born in South Shields but had spent most of his life in the Canadian backwoods, learning Native American lore, he set up a breakaway group, the Kibbo Kift Kindred – '*kibbo kift*' being Old English for 'proof of great strength' (or, some argued, 'skilled left-handed') – which many similarly disenchanted scoutmasters joined. The movement, which had mystic, indeed occult aspects, was devoted to strenuous hiking, camping and various other woodcraft activities. Its members wore a green and brown uniform modelled on a Saxon cowl and jerkin. While it never commanded a large following and attracted not inconsiderable ridicule as being made up of cranks and faddists, it formed links with the Co-operative movement – several 'Wheatsheaf' (the symbol of the Co-operative Society) branches were established – and was increasingly involved with Major Douglas's Social Credit schemes.

However, under the autocratic Hargrave, Kibbo Kift soon had its apostates, one of whom, twenty-year-old Leslie Paul, started the Woodcraft Folk for children and young people in 1925 with himself as its Headman, or National President. Still profoundly influenced by Kibbo Kift, the Woodcraft Folk had a German *Volk*-like identity with the landscape, decried capitalism, industrialism and all things urban, and pledged to 'develop in themselves, for the service of the people, mental and physical health and communal responsibility, by camping out and living in close contact with nature'.

The Woodcraft Folk originated as a pantheistic organisation that acknowledged 'the longing to live a kind of poetry'. It was communalistic, strongly socialistic – 'training young people . . . for service to the working-class movement', and demonstrating in favour of a National Health Service in 1932 – but also had supremacist undertones. Woodcraft Folk would be a new breed of 'the physically fit with . . . quick sure brains and boundless vitality. We are the revolution.' Somehow, by camping, hiking, learning to follow animal tracks and light fires, they would 'pav[e] the way for the reorganisation of the economic system which will mark the rebirth of the human race'.

Members were given 'woodcraft names' on joining (Leslie Paul's was 'Little Otter'): their birth name would be inscribed on a piece of birch bark and ceremoniously burned. Rituals even included a reported Woodcraft wedding near Sheffield in July 1932. In front of two hundred onlookers, a tom tom was beaten and a blazing torch held over the bridal pair as 'Brown Eagle' (Basil Rawson, who succeeded Paul as Headman in 1934) intoned, 'Your trails have run together, your trail is one.' Membership rose from 116 in 1926 to 4,521 in 1938. The Woodcraft Folk acquired a nine-roomed house in distinctly unrural Tooting in South London as their headquarters (the Folkhouse), and their journal, the *Pioneer*, had a circulation of around 2,000.

'We were socialists . . . of the Edward Carpenter stamp, in love with a mystical vision of England,' John Hargrave declared of Kibbo Kift. The 'New Nomads', as Hargrave called those who hiked out from the city to rekindle a communion with nature, were embedded in a long tradition of socialist ruralists that included William Morris, Richard Jeffries and Eric Gill, seeking escape from the ugly sores of industrialisation, the stifling conventions and enervating routines of town life. The England they sought was a simple one of 'the hedgerow and the village spire', the retrieved folk song (Cecil Sharp had done a thorough job by then, but there were those who found its revival 'artificial in the age of jazz') and the reactivated morris dance, the maypole on the green and the hay cart along the (unmade-up) lane. But what the 'back to the land' movement increasingly found by the 1930s was a rural population more likely to be excited by the prospect of a visit to the cinema than by gathering round the piano to sing 'One Man Went to Mow'.

'They don't know how lucky they are in towns,' an unemployed East Anglian carpenter and wheelwright complained. 'When I read or hear over the wireless about their clubs and occupational centres and all the rest of it, I wish I was one of them . . . That is what we want here. They at least have got lamp posts and street corners to loll up against.'

ELEVEN

Accommodating the People

I lunched with [George Lansbury, Labour MP for Poplar and leader of the party from 1931 to 1935] on one occasion at his office in Whitehall, and because he had a guest, he added roast mutton to his usual menu, which consists of bread and cheese . . . for Mr Arthur Greenwood [the Minister of Health] was with us . . . When [lunch] was over we looked out of the windows over St James's Park.

'I shall not count my work complete,' said George Lansbury, 'until I have cleared away every railing from London parks and squares. I can't bear to look at railings – they stand for everything I dislike.'

Arthur Greenwood looked at him pensively. 'You have an easier job than I have,' he commented. 'I shall find no rest until every slum is removed from the face of London and the big cities all over England. A slum is harder to shift than railings.'

Frances, Countess of Warwick, *Afterthoughts* (1931)

'The problem of Leeds is the problem of back-to-backs,' wrote H.V. Morton in a series of articles for the *Daily Herald* which the Labour Party gathered together as an indictment in book form in 1933. Back-to-back houses had been built around the beginning of the nineteenth century as cheap accommodation for those flooding to work in the new factories, 'with the object of packing in the population on a principle since adopted by sardine salesmen'. Consisting of one room downstairs which served as a combined kitchen, scullery, parlour, wash house and larder, and one room upstairs (often divided into two bedrooms), or occasionally two on each floor, such houses were surrounded on three sides by their neighbours, so that the three walls of one house were also the walls of three others. The oldest ones were airless, lightless, and inevitably lice-, bug- and rat-infested, the walls often so damp that wallpaper peeled off as soon as it was pasted up, and patches of mould gave the house a musty air to mingle with the rest of the foul odours.

The rents were low, so there was no incentive for all but the most altruistic landlords to carry out repairs. As a result doors hung off hinges, lath and plaster ceilings were in danger of collapse, chimneys were cracked, windows broken and old newspapers served for curtains in many of the houses. Nearly all were without modern sanitary facilities – residents in the courtyard developments did their washing in what in Birmingham was called a 'brew'us' (wash house), or even a large barrel in a communal yard, using a cold-water tap affixed to a standpipe (which also supplied drinking water), with washing strung across the courtyard in fine weather or festooned around the small house in wet. 'Drip, drip, drip on the family heads, the kitchen floor, day after day . . . perennially hanging washing' added to the unhealthy squalor. Tenants had to wash themselves at the kitchen sink and walk down the street to a communal, stinking, often out-of-order lavatory (some mere pail closets) shared by as many as six households, crammed in a side passage or between the blocks of houses, and surrounded by dustbins. Those for whom there was no electricity laid on, and who could not afford gas for heat and lighting, had to cook in small, dark foetid rooms over an open grate, summer and winter alike. 'It used to take a scuttleful [of coal] to cook an egg,' recalled a housewife living on the Dunstan estate in Hackney who rejoiced at having 'gone all electric' at a halfpenny a unit.

Rats were endemic: Ada Chesterton, a writer and lecturer who had reported on her experiences living 'down and out' for the *Sunday Express* in 1926, and who took a keen interest in housing the poor, visited a slum dwelling in Southwark in 1935 where the tenant, Mr Hibbert, told her he had 'killed sixteen of 'em [rats] last weekend . . . I sent mother out with the girls and a neighbour took in the baby. I let fly then – and worked steadily for hours – rows of corpses laid out good and proper . . . But it doesn't make any difference in the long run. They're back again. I trapped four last night and they'll be another four tomorrow morning . . . The landlord breeds them . . . We've sixteen families in this block, and none of us has got a dustbin. All the refuse – potato peelings, vegetables, muck, and bits and scraps of fat – are thrown into a cellar just outside the door . . . the rats grow sleek on it.'

The Reverend Charles Jenkinson, Anglican vicar of one of the poorest parishes in Leeds, Holbeck, wrote in 1934 of a house where a doctor attending a woman in childbirth 'had to erect props on either side of the bed with a large sheet covering the bed to catch the falling bugs'. A Sanitary Inspector told of bugs dropping into his cup of tea should he be so unwise as to accept one when visiting a slum property, and repeated the wry comment of his colleagues that if they entered such a dwelling wearing a blue suit, it would be brown by the time they left. Most families would do what they could to eliminate such vermin, scrubbing their homes with carbolic soap, dragging mattresses into the backyard where they would sleep on warm nights, and smearing their bodies with turpentine or paraffin.

By the middle of the nineteenth century back-to-back houses were already recognised as disease pits, with above-average death rates from tuberculosis, bronchitis, pneumonia, phthisis, measles and diarrhoea. Strenuous efforts were made by social reformers and clergymen to have them banned, and some local authorities did prohibit their erection. But Leeds continued in the old unwholesome ways, building seventy to eighty such houses to an acre, until the 1909 Town Planning Act made them illegal. However, Leeds continued to build back-to-back houses (albeit improved models in terraces of four, all with access to the street and most with cellars) until the mid-1930s. By 1930 the 74,805 back-to-back houses in the city represented more than half its total housing stock; 33,632 were at least sixty years old, and some had been built before 1844. Most were owned by small private landlords (whose family probably lived in one, while he let others he owned), charging rent of around six shillings a week. While an ambitious road-building scheme was put in hand, speculative-built private estates were springing up on the outskirts of the city, complete with the odd swimming pool and recreation ground, and Leeds' civic and commercial façade continued to increase its prosperous and august appearance, the slums at the heart of the city remained a nasty threatening scabrous relic of the early Victorian age.

There had been an acute housing shortage in Britain at the end of the First World War – perhaps a shortfall of 600,000, which rose to 805,000 by 1921. This was partly caused by the fact that although there had been a housing deficit before 1914 only around 50,000 houses were built during the four years of the war, and partly because social unrest had necessitated a Rent and Mortgage Interest (Restriction) Act passed in 1915 that had pegged rents to their pre-war level. While this had been seen as a wartime emergency, given rapid inflation coupled with the housing shortage, it had proved politically inexpedient to repeal the Act after the war, with the result that there was no incentive for private builders to build low-cost housing for uneconomic rents, particularly since building materials and labour costs were spiralling upwards.

The effect of this was that during the inter-war years the private landlord's role in housing the poor was gradually ceded to local authorities – though this was a role that almost all were reluctant to take on other than as a short-term emergency measure. In Leeds, England's fifth largest city, there had been thirty-six council houses before the First World War: by 1939 14 per cent of Leeds' housing stock was council-built. Throughout the country, the picture was much the same: before 1914 probably about 1 per cent of the population lived in local authority housing and 10 per cent were owner-occupiers. At least 85 per cent of the total housing stock was private rented accommodation, with the remainder provided by employers or philanthropic housing societies such as the Peabody Trust or Sydney Waterlow's Improved Industrial Dwellings Company. However, in the two decades between the First and Second World Wars 31.5 per cent of all houses built were council houses, 49.1 were built by or for owner-occupiers and only 19.4 by private landlords, while a large number of houses built before 1914 had been bought by owner-occupiers.

Coupled with the obvious need for more low-cost housing was an enthusiasm for improving such accommodation. A committee chaired by the Liberal MP Sir Tudor Walters, which reported in 1918, was strongly influenced by the turn-of-the-century garden city movement, and recommended building spacious, light-filled, cottage-like houses that would last for sixty years, with gardens and proper privacy, clustered in cul de sacs and small terraces rather than in the grim, squalid, monotonous rows that disfigured most industrial cities. But who would build these dwellings? The notion that the state should provide housing other than as a short-term expedient was anathema for most local authorities. Indeed, for Conservative councils owner-occupation was, as the *Yorkshire Post* put it approvingly, 'possibly the best and surest safeguard against the follies of Socialism'. Even the influential chairman of Birmingham's Housing Committee, J.S. Nettlefold, believed that the role of local authorities should be to provide the necessary infrastructure, such as roads and services, to enable private builders to fill in the grid with houses for sale or rent.

The 1919 Housing Act made it mandatory for local authorities to survey their housing needs and submit schemes for Treasury approval and funding. Despite the fact that the houses built would be far superior to almost all existing working-class housing, rents were to be kept in line with the controlled rents of those houses. The houses that were built, to the designs of architects employed by the Ministry of Health or, more often, the engineering department of the local authority, were generally of a high standard – 'immensely in advance' of existing working-class housing, admitted Seebohm Rowntree in 1936 of the houses built in York, though he didn't much like 'the little sheds with flat cemented roofs' intended for tools and bicycles but which 'look like privies'.

Unfortunately, however, there were not many of them. Of the 500,000 houses it had been estimated were needed, only 170,000 had actually been built by 1923, when all approval was stopped. Another Housing Act introduced by the Conservative Minister Neville Chamberlain that year cut off the subsidy entirely, but then reintroduced it with a much reduced amount, on the assumption that somehow the private sector would be able to do without financial assistance what local authorities had been unable to do with it. Between 1923 and 1929 only 75,000 local authority houses were built throughout the whole country, though houses for owner-occupiers were positively proliferating, which made rather hollow the bold speech King George V had made to representatives of local authorities ten years previously, when he had declared that 'The housing of the working classes has never been so important as it is now. It is not too much to say that an adequate solution to the housing question is the foundation of all social progress.' It was hard to see where the solution was to come from, though, since private builders were only building for those who could afford to buy or pay economic rents, and local authorities were not stepping in to provide housing for those who couldn't.

The so-called Wheatley Housing Act (John Wheatley was the new Labour Minister for Health), passed in 1924, had changed tack again, giving local authorities subsidies to build houses for let at fixed rents, and between then and 1933, when the Act was repealed, 508,000 houses had been built, all but 15,000 by local authorities. But of the two and a quarter million houses built between 1919 and 1934, only 31 per cent were local authority, 'council' housing. Again, most of these houses were of a much higher standard than most tenants in inner cities had been used to, with fitted kitchens, gas cookers and indoor bathrooms – but often without a front parlour, which was disquieting to working-class sensibilities, which required a 'best room' for occasional family celebrations, formal entertaining, and laying out the dead. Although the renowned architect, exponent of the garden city movement and member of the Tudor Walters Committee (and later Chief Advisor to the Greater London Regional Town Planning Committee and President of the RIBA), Raymond Unwin, regarded it as 'worse than folly to take space from [the] living room, where it will be used every day and every hour, to form a parlour, where it will be used only once or twice a week', a Mass-Observation survey concluded that since people had 'a strong aversion to eating in what they regarded as their "best" room . . . in this respect at any rate, the new houses built between the wars have proved themselves much less in accordance with the needs of the people who live in them than the old houses of the nineteenth century'.

Despite the Wheatley subsidy, rents for these desirable new properties were well beyond the reach of low-paid workers, and certainly of the un-employed, whose numbers had reached three million in 1931. In Manchester, for example, average council house rents, at thirteen to fifteen shillings a week, were almost double those of inner-city slum properties, and in Sheffield over 7 per cent of council tenants were paying a third of the house-hold's income in rent, which meant they were not left with enough to live on. The writer Alan Sillitoe was born in 1928 in 'the front bedroom of a red-bricked council house on the outskirts of Nottingham', but when his father was laid off from his job as a painter and decorator, the family got into arrears with the rent and had to move to 'a cheap bug-ridden back-to-back in the middle of the city', the start of a childhood of helping pile possessions onto a handcart, moving from one inner-city slum to another after a brief taste of respectable living.

How were working (and unemployed) families to be housed in decent accommodation at rents they *could* afford? Salvation was supposed to come via what was known as a 'filtering up process', by which those who moved into new houses would vacate old but acceptable properties which could then be occupied by slum-dwellers. But this was never going to work: there were more new families needing houses than there were houses, despite the spate of building, and during the Depression upward mobility was an impossible aspiration for the unemployed, underemployed and low-paid, who were not able to afford higher rents, particularly if they were living in controlled-rent accommodation (and were probably in arrears anyway). If they moved the rent would not be controlled, and they would need to pay it in advance.

Overcrowding blighted inter-war lives. In November 1934 Ramsay MacDonald called solving it 'the second chapter' of the National Government's housing programme (the first being slum clearance). Under the terms of the 1930 Housing Act, rent books had to specify the maximum number of people who could occupy a dwelling, but landlords who broke these rules were rarely prosecuted, since the onus could then fall on the local authority to rehouse the surplus tenants. The 1935 Housing Act set the bar low, defining overcrowding as when two or more persons occupied each 'habitable room' in a dwelling. This excluded bathrooms and sculleries, but included kitchens and living rooms – though in England, unlike Scotland, such rooms were rarely used for sleeping. 'Persons' were defined as being over the age of ten: under that you counted as a half person, and babies did not count at all. Whole people of the opposite sex who were not married were not expected to share a room. The Act gave statutory powers to local authorities to deal with overcrowding, and modest subsidies to do so.

In order to implement the Act it was obviously necessary to find out how extensive overcrowding actually was, and in April 1936 local authorities all over Britain were sent detailed forms, and instructed to fill them in and return them to the Ministry of Health, together with proposals of how they were going to deal with the overcrowding they discovered. In Islington, in North London, fifty-two unemployed men and women were signed on to carry out the survey, but instructed not to call on 'premises known to be occupied by persons of the professional classes'. 44,400 of the borough's stock of around 46,000 dwellings were visited (though probably around 13 per cent of these would not have qualified as working-class housing). If overcrowding was suspected, a survey assistant would return with a tape measure, instructed not to include chimney breasts and fitted cupboards when calculating the size of rooms: calculations based on the resulting findings showed that 6,757 families – around 7.5 per cent of Islington's population – were living in overcrowded accommodation. Throughout the country an average of 3.8 per cent of families were judged to be overcrowded, although in Newcastle-upon-Tyne the percentage was 11, in Manchester it was 14, and in Birmingham (where there were 26,046 people on the waiting list for a municipal house in 1933) it was 13.5.

Thus thousands might technically have a roof over their heads, but what lay beneath that roof might be unacceptable for human habitation, and often grossly overcrowded even by a very conservative definition of over-crowding. 'No other civilized country has such vast tracts of slumdom. For size and density, for foul air and wretchedness, the slums of Britain are a class apart,' the Chief Sanitary Officer of Whitstable in Kent claimed in 1935. In 1928 the National Housing and Town Council had reported that the slum problem had not improved since 1918: there were still at least a million houses unfit for human habitation, and two million that were over-crowded. In October 1930 Birmingham Anglican Nonconformist clergy organised a 'House Improvement Sunday', when preachers across the city denounced these 'time capsules of neglect' from the pulpit. 'The slums remain a festering sore at the heart of the city's life, breeding disease and degeneracy and depriving the children born into them of their birthright of a home,' one charged. 'We must look on slum clearance as a social duty, like the cleaning of a sewer,' declared H.V. Morton.

In Bolton a reporter found a seventeen-year-old girl having to share a bed with her parents, as their condemned slum house was so damp, with water pouring in every time it rained, that the family could only use one room; the girl slept wearing gum boots. In the St Clements district of Oxford ten people in one family 'all slept top to tail; they had to cook in the cellar';

in Burslem in the Potteries investigators found conditions 'so bad that we were amazed . . . in a square flanked at one side with a pot bank, on another a public house, side by side with a slaughter yard, and on the other two by rows of five and three houses. It can well be imagined how effective this is in keeping out sunlight and fresh air . . . the only way for tenants to get rid of dirty water is to throw it into the gutter, from where it will run past other people's houses into a grid. [The square] contains one tap for the use of six houses and four W.C.s which are very often stopped up . . . to accommodate eight families comprising thirty eight people including children. None of the houses have sinks or wash boilers and in consequence all the washing has to be done over the fire in the kitchen, which is the only room downstairs. The food stores have no doors, and are therefore a hunting ground for flies and insects . . . none of the houses have gas, but use an oil lamp.'

In one of the houses they found a family consisting of 'husband and wife, wife's sister aged 21, three boys aged 7, 5 and 1½ and two girls aged 5 and three. The two eldest boys sleep in the same bed as the father, the baby sleeps with his mother and her sister, one girl sleeps on a board across the foot of the bed, and the other in a small cot.' In another house 'of the two up two down sort . . . troubled very much with bugs, beetles and mice', they found 'the tenant family consist[ing] of the mother and five daughters, aged 22, 16, 14, 10 and 8, and one son aged 19 who all use one bedroom and the lodger's family is a man and wife and three sons aged 22, 20 and 17, who use the other room'. In addition, 'the windows will not open and plaster is falling off the walls'. 'We could,' the investigators wrote after four pages, 'go on quoting instances of this kind, but these will serve to enlighten our readers as to the awful conditions existing in our midst.'

In Manchester, H.V. Morton came across a man and wife, two teenaged sons and two adult daughters living in a one up one down terraced house in the Ancoats Street area who all slept in one small upstairs bedroom, the parents in a double bed with the fifteen-year-old son lying 'with his feet towards his parents' head'. The eighteen-year-old boy slept in a single bed, and the two women 'in a kind of shake-down in another corner'. A survey on Merseyside in 1938 found an eight-room house consisting of two parlours, one kitchen and five bedrooms. Six households of fourteen people lived there, while a ten-roomed was home to eight households of twenty-five people. In both houses the occupants shared a single tap, and there was one lavatory in the first house (for six households) and two in the second (used by twenty-five people). Those living on the upper floors had to haul everything – shopping, coal, water, slops, babies' prams – up and down the narrow, dark stairs.

Frank Forster was invited home for dinner by a man with whom he had been doing some casual work.

> The house (well it has to be called that for the sake of distinction though it has little claim to it) is in Volunteer Street near the Drill Hall [in Saltney]. When I got there I found that he was married with one little kiddie. The place where they lived was not fit for human habitation. There was no trace of exceptional filth or dirt but the awfully cramped quarters denied the inhabitants any freedom. They could hardly move in the house. What an environment for young children! They had a few bits of old furniture in the kitchen. Two or three chairs that had seen far better times. A table which was crippled in one leg ... the back kitchen of the house was in a cellar down some steps. The child was about 15 months old. A pretty little thing, very sharp indeed. Her name was Ellen. The wife seemed dulled by the place in which she had to live. Moving about as though accepting that there is no respite for her against the terrible condition of their 'home' ... I thought as I sat with them at their table, how cruel living conditions were for many workers. And how hypocritical the utterances of those who govern.

In Glasgow, where dark, dank and foul-smelling Victorian tenements with their shared 'close' or passage and single staircases were notorious, more than half had families living in only one ('single end') or two rooms until well after the Second World War. At night a 'hole in the wall' bed in a recess opposite the sink in the kitchen would be pulled down, the area beneath used for storage. Its occupants would sleep, 'heel to head', on a feather or straw ('donkey's breakfast') mattress, with maybe a curtain pulled across the recess for some modicum of privacy at night and to cover the bedding by day. A baby's crib was invariably a drawer on the floor. Several families in the same tenement would have to share a lavatory, either in the yard or a 'cludgie' on the half landing.

A Sanitary Inspector reported on one Glasgow house where sixteen of the twenty-three children were still living at home in a four-roomed slum cottage. Eight children – six boys aged from four to fifteen and two girls aged eight and twelve – slept on straw mattresses in one room, the walls of which were stained with urine, one mattress with recent menstrual blood; in another bedroom slept four older girls and two toddlers, while the father and two grown-up sons slept in a made-up bed in the living room. A little more space was available than usual, since at the time of the inspector's visit the mother was what was known as 'in' – detained at His Majesty's Pleasure for shoplifting some tins of condensed milk.

The 1931 Census showed that fifty-four families in the City of London were living more than seven to a room, and throughout the metropolis a third of the population lived more than three people to a room, while only 37 per cent of families had a house or flat of their own. An 'ex nursing sister' (Joan Conquest) wrote about the London slums she visited: a married couple with eleven children occupying two small upstairs rooms; four adults (including a pregnant woman) and five children housed in one basement room, with the coal cellar next door let out to a lodger to help with the twelve shillings a week rent; an old woman and her mangy cat occupying a room eight feet by five, the 'walls black with grime, the plaster has dropped off most of the ceiling'; a couple with ten children living in two basement rooms and a kitchenette of 'a huge Early Victorian mansion [with] stone lions guarding the fine flight of steps up to a colossal portico', but, with rent of twenty-five shillings a week, compelled to sub-let the smaller room to a lodger with whom the eldest girl 'sometimes sleeps . . . and what she gets for the defilement of her young body helps to mend the boots'; a family living in one room, the father and mother in a single bed and six children in a double – in which the distraught mother had caught a son and daughter committing incest; a single room for a couple and their five children and another one on the way, costing ten shillings a week and let as furnished because a table and one chair were nailed to the floor; another couple with six children living almost underground and paying fifteen shillings a week rent for two rooms, though one was uninhabitable, dripping with water, sprouting fungi and overrun with rats, yet with 'the fatuous text "God Bless Our Home" hung above the one-time kitchen grate'.

Part of the slum problem in London was the low standard of building at the end of the nineteenth century (this of course was not unique to the capital), with scrappy foundations, no damp courses, and poor-quality bricks and mortar so that walls soon bulged. There was also the increasing 'peppering' of formerly residential areas with industrial and commercial enterprises. The update of Booth's London survey between 1931 and 1935 found that in North Lambeth, 'There are candle and toilet-soap works, beer and vinegar breweries, printing works, laundries, a flour mill, a lead smelting works, potteries and factories for the production of boot polishes, sauces and meat essences, hydraulic packing and emery paper and polishes,' with their contingent noxious smells, and tall industrial buildings dwarfing substandard cottages, cutting out their light and polluting their air.

In 1936 Mrs Chesterton reported similar trends in Shoreditch: 'The spread of commerce has steadily decreased living accommodation; more and more dwellings have been converted into workshops, with the consequence that site values have so increased in price that housing work has been almost at a standstill . . . The people are domiciled in ancient cottages, small houses, pre-war flats and modern LCC and council dwellings. There are still a few Georgian houses in the old squares, but these, like the rest are mostly let in tenements. There are 2,000 basement homes in Shoreditch. I sometimes feel that London's subterranean housing is undermining the whole city – but, as far as darkness is concerned, some of the ground floors of the cottages are as dim as any cellar . . . with the living room so dark that electric light had to be used all day.'

The middle classes were fast moving out of such areas as Islington, the streets around Paddington station, Brixton, Hammersmith, Fulham, Lambeth, Poplar, Southwark and Camberwell, attracted by homes and gardens in the new suburbs. Working-class families were moving in, filling what had been family houses with multiple occupants: the number of tenement houses in St Pancras was reported to be steadily increasing in 1930, as middle-class family houses were let out in rooms to working-class households, while boroughs like Shoreditch and Bermondsey were found to be housing entirely the working classes by the early 1930s. The 'worst property in the Metropolis' was to be found on 'the great plain south of the river, between Wandsworth and Deptford, originally flat marshy land . . . In Southwark and Bermondsey the riverside is flanked by great warehouses and factories, behind, a chaotic jumble of narrow streets, alleys and courts.' Notorious slums were also found in the East End, and from Poplar to Kentish Town. Indeed, in 1933 the Medical Officer of Health for Stepney declared that the borough contained so many unfit houses and slums that the only answer was to pull everything down and start again. In Southwark it was much the same, with 'hopelessly defective and all together deplorable' properties that were damp, dilapidated and of 'Obsolete design and construction, vermin . . . abound throughout the whole borough, and impart to much of it a character of unrelieved defectiveness.'

However, some districts of London, such as the area around Buckingham Palace and parts of Hampstead, were becoming 'gentrified', as were recalcitrant areas of Kensington and some streets in Paddington and Battersea. The middle-class population had doubled since the end of the nineteenth century in St Marylebone, Holborn and Westminster, while Bloomsbury was the beneficiary of 'fashion flowing backwards' from west to east, so that by 1935 it was as bohemian as Chelsea had been in the 1890s, whereas in Chelsea H.G. Wells watched in amazement as 'perverted coachmen's houses' became the smart mews homes of those who could pay 'quite an aristocratic rent'.

Mrs Chesterton thought this was not a tendency to be welcomed:

the attraction of pseudo-Bohemianism to the picturesque also complicates
the housing problem; just as in Knightsbridge, cottage and mews properties
have been made over for the well-to-do, so unthinking people have staked
out claims in or about Shepherd's Market [in Mayfair], thus dehousing the
working-class inhabitants and sending up rents. It is undoubtedly good fun
to camp out in a mews, but what is amusement for the thoughtless results in
actual hardship for the dispossessed. All over Westminster you find this craze
for the possession of antiquated spots and historic association. Houses which
otherwise would have been pulled down through sheer age, thus making room
for working-class flats, are perpetually being reconditioned and decorated on
a lavish scale for tenants who are not indigenous to the locality, but are part
of a fashionable incursion from other districts.

Manchester had 70,000 unfit dwellings, and there were 68,000 back-to-back
houses still occupied in Sheffield, more than 38,000 in Birmingham and
30,000 in Bradford. As Ernest Simon, a wealthy industrialist, former Lord
Mayor of Manchester and author of the influential book *The Anti-Slum
Campaign* (1933) wrote in 1935: 'Manchester has hitherto been housing
the middle-classes and the aristocracy of labour, and has done almost
nothing for the lower paid workers.' Even Leeds, which had built more than
20,000 council houses between 1919 and 1939, and ranked as one of the
'big five' provincial housing authorities which together accounted for 20
per cent of total local authority building in the inter-war years (the others
were Birmingham, Liverpool, Manchester and Sheffield), still only managed
to demolish fewer than 4,000 slum dwellings in the same period. As the
city's Medical Officer of Health, Dr Jervis, reported in 1933: 'For all the
thousands of new houses erected the slum population has not diminished
by so much as one family, nor have the conditions of the poorest wage
earners been meliorated in the slightest degree.'

The Greenwood Act, passed by the second Labour government in 1930,
allocated government funding specifically for slum clearance. To make sure
that this was a comprehensive rehousing programme rather than just an
encouragement to demolish, people rather than houses were subsidised at
the rate of £2.5s per person per annum for forty years, or more if the cost
of land was particularly high. The local authority could cook up what subsidy
or rebate scheme it liked, providing that the rents charged were what tenants
could reasonably be expected to be able to afford. Moreover, the building
schemes submitted were supposed to solve the problem within five years.

However, given that 1931 was the trough of the Depression, the Act did not take effect until 1933, when the major barrier to its effectiveness turned out to be its failure to specify exactly what constituted a slum property, which meant that local authorities that were so inclined could save money by designating only their most squalid and collapsing properties as slums. The London County Council, for example, condemned only 33,000 out of 749,000 houses; in the Potteries, Arnold Bennett's 'five towns', 'a formless chaos of red brick that fill the little valleys and climb the hills' 'with a blanket of smog sagging over the whole area, so foul that at times it is impossible to see from one end of the road to the other', 8,585 out of 51,000 working-class homes were condemned as unfit for human habitation (Stoke-on-Trent was known locally as 'Smoke upon Stench'); in Manchester it was 15,000 out of 180,000, and in Newcastle only 1,000 out of 61,000. Overall the Ministry of Health approved schemes covering only a quarter of a million of the 9.4 million houses in England and Wales.

Leeds, however, with the largest slum problem in the country, was galvanised to replace almost a quarter of its entire housing stock in six years, demolishing 30,000 back-to-back dwellings. This had not been the city's initial response. In 1931 the council announced that 2,000 houses would be demolished over five years, while a further 9,000 would be 'reconditioned' or patched up, even though ten years earlier the Committee on Unhealthy Areas had reported that Leeds had 33,000 back-to-back houses in such a poor state of repair that it was 'difficult to suggest any method of dealing with them short of complete clearance'. This cautious approach was not acceptable in the view of the tireless social reforming Reverend Charles Jenkinson, who, taking as his battle cry 'Clear Up the Slums!' had been elected to the city council for one of the worst slum areas in Leeds, North Holbeck, in November 1930.

On the platform of a fifteen-year programme to demolish 45,000 back-to-back houses, Labour gained an overall majority in the November 1933 municipal elections. This ambitious programme – the most extensive in the country – was not realised: after the Conservatives returned to power nationally in 1935 the pace of demolition slowed, houses so scheduled might wait two or three years between the order and the act so deteriorated further, and building costs soared. Despite these delays and setbacks, 30,000 slum properties were demolished. Although an exception was made for a very few well-looked-after houses, no compensation was paid for most properties that the Medical Officer of Health had decided were unfit for human habitation, on the logic that they were probably at least sixty years old, and sixty years' worth of rent was compensation enough. The deeply inappropriately-named Sweet Street, Humane Place and Paradise Row were no more – but then nor was Gasholder Place – and more than 20,000 dwellings were built in Leeds between 1933 and 1939.

But being able to pay the rents for such new homes continued to be a huge inhibition. There was evidence that when poor families were moved to the new Mount Pleasant estate in Stockton-on-Tees, they went without sufficient food in order to pay their rent, which was nine shillings per family per week, compared to the 4s.8d they had been paying for their old, unhealthy accommodation. The result was malnutrition, illness, premature death: from an expected 8.12 deaths per thousand, the rate rose to 33.5 per thousand – a fourfold increase.

Local authorities faced a genuine dilemma: there was no point in moving people out of slums if they could not afford to pay the rent for their new homes. On the other hand, paying hefty subsidies would reduce the councils' income, so they would be able to clear fewer slums and build fewer houses.

By 1938 more than a hundred local authorities in England and Wales were operating some sort of differential rent scheme. Barking in East London drew up a table by which rents were worked out according to a family's income and the number of children. Other authorities set a standard rate and then worked out rebates according to the tenants' circumstances. Stoke-on-Trent, for example, charged the standard rate if a household's income was £3 a week or above; below that a rebate was allowed of one shilling per child when there were more than two, and so on until a household with a total income of £2 would only pay the minimum rent. In Carlisle, rebates were calculated on rent as a fixed proportion of income. Twenty per cent of a family's income was spent on rent, less sixpence a week for each child of school age, and there were various variations on these schemes. But in the main they applied only to those families rehoused as a result of slum clearance, since there continued to be the residual (and unrealistic) feeling that most council house tenants were, as they had largely been in the 1920s, moderately comfortably-off artisans, able to pay reasonable rents.

This was not, however, the system that Leeds adopted. For the Reverend Jenkinson, rents should be fixed solely according to the ability of the tenant to pay. To implement this radical approach, Leeds Council introduced a complicated housing means test. A tenant's rebate would be worked out by calculating the number of his dependents and their ages in relation to the required subsistence allowance laid down by the BMA Committee on Nutrition, and this amount would be deducted from the family's income. What was left over was considered available to pay the rent, though in fact the tenant was not expected to pay all his or her residual income in rent – that depended on the family size and the type of house they were occupying. These rebates were granted on a week-to-week basis, so tenants had to turn up at the rent office every week clutching their 'grey book' in which all their family's financial circumstances – income, outgoings such as school meals, travel expenses and insurance – were recorded. The result of these complicated calculations was that some families were paying as little as two shillings a week rent, and around 11 per cent of council tenants were paying no rent at all (though they still had to pay rates).

Despite its noble intent, the Leeds scheme was deeply resented both by those who had to submit to what they regarded as another humiliating means test (some were even prepared to forgo a rebate rather than undergo the little-grey-book inquisition) and those who felt they were subsidising their neighbours' rebates by paying higher rents themselves. The fact that Leeds, with its diverse industries including a fairly healthy clothing manufacturing sector, escaped the worst of the Depression meant that there were sufficient numbers of tenants paying an economic rent for the differential rents scheme actually to accrue a surplus; but the symbolic effect of the scheme was enough to scupper the Labour majority at the next election.

The return of the Conservatives signalled the end of rent-free houses in Leeds, with every tenant obliged to pay a minimum of about 20 per cent of the standard rate. Tenants designated as 'compulsory' (inhabiting council houses as a result of slum clearance) were eligible for higher rebates than 'voluntary' ones (who had opted to move), who paid rather less than they had under Labour's scheme. 'Public money being paid to those who do *not* need it,' complained the Reverend Jenkinson. The scheme soon ran into deficit, and discontent over how to set rents equitably was still rumbling on when war broke out in September 1939, rather overshadowing the considerable achievements that Leeds had made in slum clearance and rehousing in the 1930s.

By 1939 the official estimate of slum houses in Britain requiring demolition was 472,000 – almost twice the 1935 estimate: 245,000 had been demolished or boarded up and 255,000 replacement homes had been built. In addition, 24,000 properties had been built specifically to house those in overcrowded accommodation. It could be said that the problem of the slums was half solved by the time war broke out, and over the next five years German bombs and V weapons would contribute dramatically to the demolition process.

What, though, was to replace the slums? It was a question that vexed Ernest Simon when he came to consider 'The Future of Our Great Cities'

in 1935. 'On what lines should the slum areas be rebuilt and redeveloped?'
he wrote. 'The slums are the older part of the city, and so they tend to be
near its central areas. Should these areas be used for rehousing, and if they
are so used, at what density should rebuilding be carried out? Or should
all the new houses be built in the suburbs, or outside the city altogether?'
'Town planning of a non-existent town is a delightful occupation in which
many people, architects and others have entertained themselves, but planning
for a densely-populated and built-up borough . . . is less easy,' pointed out
a commentator on the problem in Stepney.

It was largely a question of density: slum houses tended to be crowded
together at the rate of fifty or seventy to the acre, whereas the 'modern
Tudor Walters municipal house with its own garden is built at twelve to
the acre'. It was these Arts and Crafts-influenced cottage-type estates, built
on what would now be called greenfield sites, that appealed to most local
authorities – at least initially. The Ministry of Reconstruction had laid
down the idea at the end of the First World War: 'street frontages should
be considered as a whole, and an endeavour made by recessing certain of
the groups . . . to avoid the monotony of a long straight building line . . .
The disposition of the houses should obscure, so far as possible, the view
of back gardens and drying greens. Attention should be given to the possibility of grouping a number of houses round three sides of a quadrangle
or other open space.' Gone were the serried terraces of industrial cities, to
be replaced with small crescents, cul de sacs and open spaces, a homage
to the village green: fresh air and green spaces would rejuvenate former
pasty slum-dwellers, and disease and even crime would be eradicated in
these inter-war utopias. The 'cottage estates' absorbed the thinking of
Ebenezer Howard and Raymond Unwin and the garden city movement
(indeed, Unwin travelled from Howard's garden city at Letchworth to
advise the First Scottish National Housing Company on housing for workers
at the new dockyards at Rosyth). It was also cheaper for councils to purchase
undeveloped agricultural land unencumbered by existing services, drains,
foundations and disputed land ownership, that could be levelled and
developed with relative speed. The sheer scale of the housing required
compelled a 'suburban solution of mass production', in the words of a
historian of Glasgow's housing policy.

Indeed, it was a social revolution: between 1919 and 1937 twelve million
people – almost 30 per cent of the British population – were rehoused. 'Removals
on so large a scale involving so high a proportion of the population have never
taken place before in the whole course of our history,' as Sir Kingsley Wood,
the Minister of Health remarked in 1937.

Moreover, more than 90 per cent of the 1.1 million council houses built between the wars were on suburban estates. There were some spectacular examples of the 'mass suburb'. The slum tenement population of Glasgow was decanted into various large estates built on purchased land that would 'swaddle the great city in swathes of development', much to the disgust of a Scottish landowner speaking to the Royal Institute of British Architects' conference in 1935, who complained that 'trees and hedges, cottages and farm buildings have all been swept away and replaced by the stock plan, and the stock house exactly like all the others. The country is blotted out.'

Between the wars something like one-fifth of Birmingham's population was rehoused, many on estates on the outskirts of the city named after the rural land they had erased – Glebe Farm, Gospel Farm, Billesley Farm and Pineapple Farm. In Wythenshawe, twelve miles from Manchester, a model 'satellite town' built between 1927 and 1941 by Manchester Corporation covered over 2,500 acres of farmland on land bought by Ernest Simon and his wife Sheena and sold to the Corporation for the relief of the city's over-crowding. This so-called 'garden town' (a term that was frequently misbestowed on any new development away from the inner cities and with a bit of grass and a few flowers) housed 35,000 people by 1935 in gabled and mansarded 'cottages' served by a four-lane 'parkway', the first in Britain. For the Women's Co-operative Guild Wythenshawe revealed 'the world of the future': every working mother would have 'a clean, well-planned home, which will be her palace – so well and wisely planned that her labour will be lightened and her strength and intelligence reserved for wider interests'. For Sheena Simon, the estate represented 'a century's progress'.

The building of Becontree, at the time the largest planned residential development in the world, on reclaimed marshland near Dagenham in Essex, an area with 'very few natural advantages', had been started in 1921. When it was completed in 1934 it covered 2,770 acres (around four square miles), with over 25,000 dwellings providing housing for some 112,000 people. This was larger than Norwich, Bath or Preston, and almost as large as Wolverhampton. But since the housing density was so low (about twelve houses per acre), Islington in North London had a population of nearly 322,000 in an area only marginally larger than that covered by Becontree.

Most of the houses, which were allocated on the basis of family size, had either two or three rooms plus a kitchen/scullery, while a few had five rooms, and a very few had six. The residents were overwhelmingly working-class, which was defined in the Pilgrim Trust report as applying to 'a group of people ... engaged in work who are employed at a wage or salary either not liable to be assessed for income tax or else only just liable'. Indeed, it would have been 'extremely difficult, if not impossible, to have found another area in England containing such an overwhelming proportion of working-class people'. More than eight out of every ten men were manual workers, and fewer than two could be described as 'black-coated workers'. A high percentage of women workers – nearly 6,000 of them, mainly unmarried daughters – worked in offices or shops, while others were employed in factories or as hairdressers, waitresses or barmaids.

Mr Brown, whom Ada Chesterton had quizzed in his Shoreditch slum, had replied 'Nothing doing, mate,' to her suggestion that he might consider removing to Becontree. 'My wages are £2.10 shillings a week. If we moved, the fares [to his work] would cost between five and six bob. I can't afford that, with the children to keep.' Although there was no shortage of applicants for houses on the Becontree estate (a peak of 225,000 in 1933 either wrote in or called into the office), it was only the elite among the working class who were able to live there or in Watling, Roehampton, St Helier and similar estates. Cottage estates were not going to be the solution for slum-dwellers. A prospective tenant had to establish need, but also that he could pay the rent – and usually that the family had lived within the LCC boundaries for at least two years. As Terence Young's report on Becontree for the Pilgrim Trust noted tartly: 'Most slum dwellers could not afford the rents and travelling expenses and their problems are being dealt with quite separately by slum clearance and rehousing schemes. The enquiries which casual visitors to the Estate sometimes make about whether the tenants store their coals in the bath, and whether slum habits are changed by the new surroundings, or is the place going to turn into another slum area, are therefore rather pointless.'

The median wage of Becontree residents was £3.15s a week, and 40 per cent earned over £4. As Terence Young explained, 'It would be impossible [for a family] to continue to live at Dagenham with an income of much under £2, and with an income of over £5, sooner or later the attraction of house ownership becomes effective unless the family is very large.' Unemployment on the estate was relatively low – around 8 per cent in April 1931 and 11 per cent in the same month in 1932, when the national average was over 20 per cent and 21 per cent respectively. This was partly because the majority of men were between thirty and forty – ages when unemployment tended to be lowest. It was also because the unemployed were soon removed, since they would no longer be able to afford rents which were between ten and twenty-two shillings a week in 1933, according to the size of the house. (This was well below the economic rent, and in fact rents had been reduced in 1929 and in January 1933, making Becontree's the lowest rents on all LCC cottage estates.) Almost all the housing was for families. Single women were excluded from municipal housing, and often had to pay well over the market rate for private rooms – out of wages that were invariably lower than those of men. Out of a total of 68,629 LCC dwellings in 1935, only 277 were one-room tenements, though 130 out of every thousand London families were 'one-person families' – and it was predicted that this number would rise.

There were rent rebate schemes, but the LCC was unenthusiastic, partly because of loss of revenue, added bureaucracy and an attitude summed up by Lewis Silkin, Chairman of the LCC Housing Committee in 1937. 'It is possible,' he said, 'to go too far and create a special favoured class out of those who happen to be council tenants. The large majority of working-class people are not, and never can be, council tenants, and after all, they have to help foot the bill.' Then, as Mr Brown had pointed out to Ada Chesterton, men – and women – had to find the money to travel to work in inner London, since there was little industry in Becontree until the Ford motor plant arrived in 1931, with plans to employ a workforce of 10,000 people producing five hundred cars a day. It was rumoured that though Ford's managing director was unimpressed by Dagenham and would have much preferred Southampton, Henry Ford himself felt moved to do something about unemployment in the East End, so opted for the clay wastes of Essex.

Initially there were not many jobs for local men, since a lot of existing Ford workers moved south from Manchester. The huge plant, 'the size of nine or ten football pitches with long oblong bays split up into sections, each of which dealt with a different part of the car', and with a jetty on the Thames for loading and unloading, offered 'the best paid jobs available but it was very difficult and competitive getting in. An unskilled man working at Fords on a forty-hour week got paid £3.10s, while a qualified tradesman who didn't work for the company, was at least £1.10s under that rate and he probably had to do more hours.' But, as Mrs Chesterton sagely remarked, 'One plant hardly makes a forest,' and in 1938 between 60 and 70 per cent of Becontree residents were not employed locally: Ford employed 12,650 workers; Becontree had a population of well over 100,000.

Bill Waghorn, who had been working on the docks, got a job at Ford as soon as he could, since it meant he would earn ninepence a week more, and also an end to the journey he had had to make ever since his family had moved to Becontree in 1929. 'At the time I was working on the Isle of Dogs and had to start at eight in the morning. The train wasn't properly in service so I also had to take a bus, which was often delayed and unreliable . . . you couldn't be late for work, what with three million unemployed and no work anywhere, so I ended up cycling the fourteen-mile round trip to and from work. I had to get up at five o'clock every day, and I didn't finish work until 9 o'clock. So it was quite an ordeal. Lots of people travelled to work along the A13 and in the winter it was bitter cold . . . when a lorry came along all the cyclists would crowd behind it, jockeying for position, because it gave us protection from the wind.'

During a debate in Parliament, the case of a young Becontree worker who was obliged to spend 7s.6d on railway fares out of a weekly wage of £1.14s.8d was cited, and in 1934, 75 per cent of Becontree's 75,000 workers were not able to find jobs locally; most travelled into London to work. It was hardly surprising that many people decided they could not afford to move out to the cottage estates, particularly if their work was irregular and they needed to be on the spot to get it, as dockers or piece workers did. When the District Line was extended to Becontree in September 1932 there was a huge queue at one of the stations, and over 2,000 workmen's tickets were sold on the Sunday evening for the following day.

Then there was the question of furnishing: the few sticks that might have sufficed in a pokey inner-city tenement would hardly fill a new house. Many of the moves were organised by women, who hired the services of a removal van or a friend with a lorry, since their husbands 'daren't have the day off for moving because there might not have been a job for you when you went back into work the next day'. In Leeds, families were offered the facilities of the council's 'bug van' for their move, which was popular because this on-the-move fumigation service was free of charge. Some families ditched their old furniture when they moved, some supplemented it with a few new things invariably bought on the 'never never' which was a regular part of a working-class budget – probably with repayments of about three shillings a week for furniture, and maybe a wireless or gramophone. When Rosina Evans' family moved to the Downham LCC estate near Bromley in Kent, which had been opened in 1925 and had 32,549 inhabitants, her mother went to Holdron's in Peckham, which 'used to be famous for selling things on the never never'. Since she had 'aspirations which my dad didn't agree with . . . she bought a walnut veneer bedroom suite which was like something out of a novel. She also bought at the same time a rexine suite [a sofa and two armchairs] with brown velour cushions, a sideboard with twist legs, a square table with four chairs. I thought we were posh, but Dad was dead against it . . . He yelled and raved and screamed but it made no difference, we still got the furniture.' Some local authorities, including Leeds,

Glasgow, Birmingham, Bolton, Rotherham and some of the London boroughs, set up schemes to buy furniture in bulk and sell it to tenants at cost – though this was hardly popular among local retailers, whose profits were undercut.

Although every house on the Becontree estate had gas, not all had electric lighting, and one of the main complaints of tenants was that they could not afford to use electric irons or fires because the charge per unit was so high. By contrast St Helier, near Carshalton in Surrey (named after Lady St Helier, a former LCC alderman; its population of 39,845 made it the second largest estate after Becontree), had no gas when it was built, and residents used electricity for lighting and cooking. In 1930 the utility companies, battling for the right to provide energy to the new estates, offered to lay the necessary pipes and cables free of charge, and were given a list of names and addresses so they could solicit custom. 'The Gas Company was touting for business when we moved in,' recalled Alfred and Hetty Gates. 'You could get a cooker for almost nothing, and if you decided to have gas instead of electricity your cooker came almost free.'

Roehampton, built on land in South-West London formerly owned by an American financier and completed in 1921, when building standards were high, was generally considered to be the most desirable of the LCC 'cottage estates'. Set in a 146-acre parkland landscape of mature trees with a large shopping parade, wooded play area and allotments, it captured to near perfection Raymond Unwin's model of an estate for 'superior artisans'.

An indoor bathroom with a lavatory that was solely for the use of their own family was the greatest thrill to most residents, and children had to be restrained from running upstairs to flush it all day. On the St Helier estate some houses had the bath in the kitchen:

> when not in use it was covered with a wooden flap which then could be used as a table. Under the kitchen window was a deep square sink, fitted with a cold tap. As this was the only running water in the house, everybody used the tap all the time, from early in the morning when Dad got up to wash and shave, till last thing at night when we [children] washed or bathed. In between all this coming and going, Mum had to do all the washing up, laundry and anything else that needed doing. We had to be very well organised otherwise there would have been chaos . . . the kitchen window sill was neatly arranged with household cleaning things on the left and Dad's shaving mug and bristle brush on the right together with soap in a dish and a nail brush.

A roller towel hung behind the kitchen door for drying hands. We each had our own towel for washing and bathing, and these were hung over the ends of our beds.

Other houses had the bathroom upstairs, and hot water had to be pumped up from the coal-fired copper in the kitchen for the weekly Friday-night bath. On the Downham estate, 'The water used to spurt into the bath through a hole between the two taps. Each pump would send up about two cup-fulls of hot water so by the time it was full, the water was cold.' As a result John Edwin Smith's parents 'finished up carting water upstairs in a bucket'.

The houses were decorated about every five years by the 'council's own painting gang of about 20 to 25 painters who used to go from estate to estate. Practically all the external paintwork was white except the front and back doors which were done in Brunswick green. The decorators used to put a coat of varnish over the paint which gave it a beautiful finish.' Tenants had a choice of colours for inside the house: yellow ochre (which some generously referred to as 'buttercup yellow') or pale green for the walls, while the woodwork was 'always a sort of beige, pastry colour'. The bedrooms would be distempered, a mixture of whitewash and size. 'The ceilings were painted white, and the decorator used to put a bit of blue in with the ordinary white because it made it look nice and bright.' Later tenants could choose wallpaper for downstairs rooms – the association of wallpaper with lurking bugs had made the authorities wary at first. The decorators 'had a book with half a dozen patterns . . . and you could choose whichever pattern they had. But if you didn't like any of the patterns and you wanted to go out and buy your own paper you could, the council still put it up for you. Most people waited for the council decorators though because they really couldn't afford to pay for paper and paint.'

Tenants did get into financial difficulties; a doctor who had arrived at Becontree in December 1925 knew that 'any fees not collected in cash at the time of treatment could be labelled "bad money"'. Some tenants ran up arrears and were evicted. Eric Phillips, who worked in the Estate Office in Becontree, recalled: 'If people were a week in arrears with their rent, we would send a "First Arrears Letter", which would be a gentle reminder. If it continued for another two or three weeks, you would send a second letter of rather sterner stuff, "Look here, you've got to pull yourself together and get paid up, or else." If there was no effort being made, you would serve a notice to quit . . . As I recall there were very few actual evictions during my couple of years before the war. Usually the family would skedaddle, leave without giving their notice.' But May Millbank remembered, 'If you didn't pay the rent [on the Watling estate], you were given a month to move out irrespective of whether you had one or ten children, you was out! I think if a family had to leave, they'd be put in a halfway house. There used to be one up at Edgware General Hospital.' Florence Essam of Becontree recollected 'coming home from school and sometimes seeing people being put out of their house by the council . . . with their furniture on the pavement. If it was raining a kind neighbour might come out with a bit of tarpaulin to cover their belongings . . . [My mother] would say "Those people couldn't pay the rent, so the council have put them out."' In fact 12 per cent of tenants were 'removed' from Becontree in 1931–32, though most of these were not evicted but left because they were dissatisfied in some way with life on the estate – amenities, travel, neighbours –missed their old surroundings, could no longer afford to live there, were now too well-off to live there, or their family circumstances had changed.

Some tenants found ways of supplementing their incomes. One Becontree resident, Grace Foulkes, made jam when plums were ripe, and took in washing from men working at Fords. 'Front parlour' shops opened repairing shoes, selling confectionery or haberdashery, or acting as stockrooms for tally men. These were illegal, and although they were welcome since there were few neighbourhood shops on the estate, they were closed down. And a regular feature of Becontree life was the 'pawnshop bus' which left for Barking every Monday morning at 9.30 – though of course goods bought on hire purchase could not be pawned. In 1931, presumably in response to demand, a pawnshop opened in Dagenham village, which saved the bus fares.

Despite the cost of travel, of using electric irons, of restrictive clauses in tenancy agreements that forbade 'driving nails or allowing or permitting nails to be driven into the walls of the premises', 'erecting or permitting to be erected any structure in the garden of the premises', changing the colour of your front door, keeping 'on the premises or any part thereof any pigs, rabbits, fowl or pigeons', being obliged to clean the windows 'at least once a week', to 'have all chimneys in use swept once a year', to 'have a fireguard for the children' and to keep the front garden 'in a neat and cultivated condition' (though privet-hedge clipping was usually a council responsibility) and your children under control 'on any part of the estate', the majority of the 258,126 tenants on the LCC cottage estates appeared to be content there. A Mass-Observation enquiry found that 80 per cent of tenants 'liked their homes'; 50 per cent 'liked their kitchens'; 43 per cent liked the neighbourhood, and only 6 per cent would like to live in a town instead, and 14 per cent in the country.

On 'Oak Estate', which for some mystifying reason was what M-O called Becontree, 85 per cent 'liked their houses'. On 'Elm Estate' (Roehampton), 'quite the most pleasantly situated of all the LCC estates', which the 'general bearing of the people . . . good working-class C types' marked out as a 'high-class estate' (it was known locally as 'uniform town', owing to the number of bus drivers, tram drivers, policemen and postmen living there), the percentage was 86, and the main complaints were about poor transport links and shopping facilities. And on 'Ash Estate' (Watling), with 'its natural charm . . . its hills, its trees [and with] many of the new streets bearing the names of the old fields on which they have been built', the score was 70 per cent.

It was much the same on the Wythenshawe estate. Although early residents described themselves as 'pioneers' as they trudged through slush and cinders, having to push their prams across the fields to the shops, since there were no roads on the estate at first – nor schools, cinemas, libraries or medical services, all of which had been promised but which had hardly materialised by the outbreak of war in 1939 – 90 per cent of those interviewed were very enthusiastic about living there. They liked it for the same reasons that other cottage-estate-dwellers liked their estates: having a bathroom, a better kitchen (Raymond Unwin's cousin Barry Parker, also a town planner, had recommended that sculleries should always be built on the south side of the house so they caught the sun, since 'the housewife spends nine hours in the scullery for every one she spends in the living room' – though this didn't happen), a garden, privacy, fresh air – in sum, they were proud to live in a 'showplace for the world'.

Where there was dissatisfaction it tended to focus on domestic details such as badly planned kitchens, draughty rooms, shared entrance porches. Almost all the residents liked having a garden, 'the care of which formed their principal leisure-time occupation' for many, which was used for growing flowers and vegetables, as somewhere for the children to play (most estates would not allow children to play in the open spaces, many of which were fenced in), for keeping rabbits or chickens (not officially allowed, but usually tolerated), drying clothes and relaxing. Becontree Council recommended that tenants should 'strive to obtain a natural look [for their gardens] rather than an artificial effect. Bordered edging and concrete paths do not give the restful effect of turf with neatly trimmed edges.' Most gardens were a blaze of colour in the summer, with 'every inch used for growing flowers of every kind', and vegetable patches in the back garden for potatoes, cabbages and Brussels sprouts; some gardeners 'even gave celery and cucumbers a try'. A garden club was started at Watling where residents, who were 'all new to gardening and . . . learnt everything from scratch . . . could buy plants and anything you wanted at cost price', as well as bartering surplus produce.

What was repeatedly mentioned in residents' replies to M-O's enquiries was the appreciation of privacy, of being able to keep oneself to oneself, to be self-contained. 'I like it very much indeed,' said a fifty-year-old woman on the Watling estate. 'It's got a front door and a back. You can go inside and it's nobody's business.' People wanted higher fences between gardens, their own porch rather than a shared one, no possibility of being over-looked. 'Less than one person in a hundred [M-O was so shocked by this figure that it was reported in italics] mentioned any form of activity that involved co-operation with their fellow citizens.' There must have been a good deal of weary headshaking back in the office when it was realised that 'To an extent unbelievable to those who have not investigated it, many people are passive minded, letting things be done to them, hardly thinking of what they could get done, if they would co-operate with their neigh-bours and fellow citizens.' Women seemed most to blame (presumably this was largely because men spent so much time working and travelling to and from work that they had little time for leisure, and certainly not leisure that involved 'community activity' rather than digging the garden, listening to the wireless or going to the pub): 'the average housewife's view of the neighbourhood in which she lives is bounded by its physical character-istics, its shops, its mass entertainment – notably the cinema – and the neighbours', rather than 'political . . . social, cultural or religious activity'.

The one generally admired feature of the slums was the camaraderie, the community spirit that living hugger-mugger in appalling surroundings was supposed to engender. Remove people from those surroundings (not that the cottage-estate incomers were former slum-dwellers, but most were certainly from crowded inner-city environments) and the bonds of commu-nity seemed to dissolve overnight. In Manchester, 68 per cent of those living in Ancoats and 59 per cent in Hulme very much wanted better housing, but not at the cost of having to leave their neighbourhood. A survey of Bermondsey noted that while people preferred cottage homes to flats, they nevertheless preferred flats in Bermondsey to cottages elsewhere: 'One reason for the happy atmosphere of the Borough is the fact that 95 per cent of its population is working class.' It was 'mixed boroughs' such as Kensington and Wandsworth that lacked 'civic pride and consciousness and sense of unity'. In the eyes of the socialist G.D.H. Cole, 'the comradeship of the street in a poor working-class quarter', which he contrasted unfavourably with the reserve on a model housing estate, had been lost by relocation.

Although Ruth Durant, writing about the Watling estate, which with its 19,012 residents by 1936 almost qualified as a self-contained town, had defined community as 'a territorial group of people with a common mode of living, striving for common objectives', it would seem that in reality community in fact meant proximate family. This was disquieting to those thirties progressives who viscerally believed that rural life had the moral edge over a crowded existence in the cities. As well as being healthier, it was felt that going 'back to the land' would prove redemptive to those who had been made feckless, even criminal, by their dreadful industrialised urban environment. The point of the garden cities had been to provide 'a self-contained entity offering inhabitants home, work and community amenities . . . based on the traditional symbol of community: the common entitlement to land'. And even in the watered-down version the LCC and other authorities were offering, it wasn't just about cherry-blossom trees and patches of green. It was a model for a new life.

Raymond Unwin and his cousin Barry Parker both considered town planning to be 'a civic art': the architect was merely a 'disinterested mentor' to the citizens of England's 'emerging democracy', there to give shape to the aspirations of a community – though it was hard to see in the 1930s how such aspirations might be made known to the architect, since there were no conduits of consultation, and informal exchanges between would-be council-house tenants and blueprint-producers seemed unlikely. Since such communities were based on replicating the structure of rural villages, where the squire lived in close(ish) proximity to the farm labourer, a balanced social mix of the classes 'became for many planners and social commentators the defining characteristic of good town planning'.

But what had happened in the case of cottage estates was the reverse: they were almost entirely working-class in composition. An urban problem had been shunted into a series of very large suburban extensions. How, commentators and planners wondered – covertly sometimes – could this new 'mass society' (i.e. the working classes) be accommodated? They were, of course, being accommodated in the bricks-and-mortar sense, in as near rural village conditions as councils could manage (increasingly, it had to be said, on the cheap), with their own patch of green front and back, but they were proving intransigent to a wider accommodation within the political, social and cultural values they might have been hoped to embrace. Instead they seemed to prefer their old individual pursuits – including the cinema.

Although H.G. Wells had confessed in his *Autobiography* that in the early days of socialism, 'We did not say what we meant by the "community" because none of us knew or had even thought that it might need knowing,' F.R. Leavis believed that by 1933 'the organic community has gone'. It seemed important, given these 'mono-class estates', the mass-suburbanisation of the working classes, to work out not only what community did mean, but also how a new version could be encouraged.

There was not much to encourage a community spirit on the estates. Planners had been ambivalent about whether they were supposed to be dormitory towns (which by default most largely were, since industry was slow in coming – this was as true of Wythenshawe near Manchester as it was of Becontree) or self-contained towns, which, given their limited amenities, they were not. As well as having a paucity of shops (in Becontree there was on average one shop for every 241 people, while in older towns the average was one to forty or fifty), there were no street markets (the presence of which was 'much missed'). In Watling in the early days 'there was nothing but bricks and mortar and acres of mud . . . no shops, no schools, the children running wild'.

There was also a shortfall of most other facilities, including pubs, which George Orwell complained were 'banished from housing estates almost completely, and the few that remain are dismal sham-Tudor places fitted out by big brewery companies and very expensive . . . for a working-class population, which uses the pub as a kind of club, it is a serious blow at communal life'. On the Downham estate, with 35,000 residents, there was but a single pub, albeit the largest one in Britain. And even this tried to break the cultural mode, providing a new way of drinking for a new way of living, aiming to encourage a more respectable family 'refreshment' rather than the drunkenness that the small, smoky, traditional pubs were thought to engender among the working classes. One LCC member had expressed his distaste for 'perpendicular drinking', and customers in the new-style establishments could not buy their drinks at the bar, but had to sit at tables where they were served by waiters in 'monkey suits, bow-tie and so forth' who expected a tip.

Becontree, a community of more than 110,000 people, could claim only five public houses (whereas in the communities from which most of the new inhabitants came they would have passed one at least every sixty seconds) and two off-licences. Other amenities were also thin on the ground, with fourteen doctors' houses (which meant roughly one medical practitioner to every 8,000 people), three clinics, twenty-seven churches, thirty schools (including only one nursery school, a voluntary one), two cinemas (one, the Princess, which opened in the autumn of 1932, was huge, with 2,750 seats, and was described as 'probably the most palatial place in the country'), six public buildings, and only eleven garages for rent, since councils felt it would be 'inconvenient . . . if the majority of the tenants became rich enough to need garages'. The Kingstanding housing estate in Birmingham, which was home to around 30,000 people in 1932, had one church, one church hall, one cinema, one pub, and no parks, sports ground or hospital. By comparison, the slightly smaller nearby town of Shrewsbury boasted thirty churches, fifteen church halls, two public libraries, four cinemas and 159 pubs.

Community centres might have been thought to encourage a sense of community by providing 'a building designed to provide facilities for the social, educational and recreational welfare of the members of the community living in the neighbourhood it is intended to serve'. In the introduction he wrote to the Pilgrim Trust survey of Becontree, the Conservative Prime Minister Stanley Baldwin had argued that 'to provide no halls, or other buildings in which people can meet seems a serious mistake', and generally such places were considered to be a good idea – particularly for the educative work in citizenship that might be expected to take place within their walls. But community centres were expensive to build, and the LCC considered that it was in the business of building houses, and that ratepayers could hardly be expected to subsidise facilities for estate-dwellers that they themselves could not use.

It was not just the cost: there was confusion of purpose here too. If a community was to be welded together, should not the people who would form that community work together to provide their own facilities? Would not the provision of a ready-made social centre sap initiative and lead to a lack of respect for the amenities provided? But if the community had to raise money to build a centre, this would take several years, and would leave little time for the very educational and cultural events that were supposed to bond the community together. That is, if busy, cash-strapped people were prepared to give up their meagre 'leisure time' for such activity anyway.

By 1937 only two LCC cottage estates, St Helier and Downham, had community centres, and when one was built on the Watling estate as a result of an interest-free loan from the Pilgrim Trust only 6 per cent of the adult population joined the Community Association, and only 2 per cent stuck with it for a year or more. The Loan Club, by contrast, could boast 1,320 members, and the District Nursing Association 3,000. As Ruth Durant concluded in her survey, all residents wished Watling to be furnished with amenities, yet the majority wanted merely those they had known before: 'working, shopping, cinema-going, "listening-in", and perhaps whist-playing, they reverted to "keeping themselves to themselves"'. There were various societies and organisations, but they 'do not correct, but merely reflect social atomisation. In the long run, Watling is not much more than a huge hotel without a roof.'

On the Roehampton estate a mansion was rented and provided medical and dental services, music rooms, hard tennis courts, billiards rooms, and bars for men, but by 1937 paid-up membership had fallen to 205, and the Estate Superintendent reported sadly that very little was being done in the interests of the estate tenants 'beyond catering for those who would make the house just a place where drink could be obtained at club prices, and billiards played'.

Perhaps such reluctance was partly because, as a survey of Bristol council housing estates conducted in 1938 found, 'People dislike to think that some paternal outside authority is trying to teach them how to be pally when mutual help is a virtue which they were practising for generations before the new estates were planned.'

Churches did not do much better as a focus for community life: on the Becontree estate only about 3 per cent of men over twenty-five and 11 per cent of women went to church, though 12,000 children under fourteen, about a third of Becontree's children, were sent to Sunday school. But sending your children to Sunday school was a traditional way of couples getting time to themselves on a Sunday, and most children stopped going as soon as they could, though some 10 per cent belonged to organisations such as the Boy Scouts or the Girl Guides, which often met on church premises.

It seemed as if Orwell was right when he wrote that 'All the culture that is most truly native centres round things which even when they are communal are not official – the pub, the football match, the back garden, the fireside, and the "nice cup of tea".' Estate-dwellers went to the cinema – particularly those who were courting – and children went to the Saturday-morning screenings; they went to the dogs: a greyhound track was opened on the outskirts of Becontree in 1931 with space for 5,000 spectators; they bet on horses; played football; went for walks; tended their gardens, and although, as Grace Foulkes, who moved to Becontree from Wapping in 1932, wrote, 'We knew nothing about gardening and nor did our neighbours', most soon learned. Mass-Observation found that only 17 per cent of cottage-estate gardens were neglected, and that 'Most of the people owning a garden treasure it and look after it well.' The LCC awarded silver cups and cash prizes for the best-kept gardens, which they chose by walking round the streets and peering over hedges. The women knitted and sewed, both sexes listened to the wireless, and the men might well nod off, exhausted by their hard day's work and the often long and tiring journey home. As the report on Watling put it, after travelling miles to and from work, 'a few yards to a meeting place can seem an insuperable distance', and 'everywhere in Watling it can be observed that daytime hurry is followed by apathy in the evening'. Yet its author defended what she had seen: the estate-dwellers were not 'apathetic or anti-social'; rather they were 'preoccupied with the necessity of existence'.

Nevertheless, this reluctance to reconstitute a new sort of community was a sad disappointment to those observers who had had such high hopes of the attenuated form of garden city that local authorities were building in the 1920s and '30s (though those who lived on them were rarely asked what *they* wanted). Colonising the countryside, decanting the urban poor and ill-used into new and healthy surroundings was not working out as they had felt confident that it would.

As Terence Young pointed out in his report for the Pilgrim Trust, 'If Becontree had happened in Vienna, the Labour and left Liberal Press would have boosted it as an example of what municipal socialism could accomplish.' But this was Britain, and here commentators talked about 'architectural monstrosities', 'annoying monotony' (in fact there were some ninety different types of houses in Becontree), 'huge and dreary building schemes', the 'isolated wastes of Dagenham'. Even Mrs Chesterton, who had asked a Shoreditch slum-dweller why he did not apply to move his family to a new LCC estate, described Becontree as 'that black and mournful spot known as Dagenham'.

The estates were overwhelmingly working-class, and the working class seemed to lack the aspirations that the middle classes thought they should have. Given half a chance, it was thought that they would use their baths not for the proper purpose but to keep coal in (if not dirty clothes, rabbits and litters of puppies), pull doors off the jambs and use their stairs for firewood, foment communism, root up trees, and resolutely decline to be educated for citizenship. It was as if, detractors thought, you could take the family out of the slums (although that was not usually where it had come from) but you couldn't take the slums out of the family.

As well as largely eschewing community facilities, most cottage-estate residents seldom issued out into the roads or the cul de sacs (known as 'banjos' because of their shape, with a circle of green at the end) or the 'circuses' to replicate the street life they had known in the teeming cities. Besides this, the depopulation of the inner cities concerned some planners. Elizabeth Denby, who had been given a grant by Lord Leverhulme's foundation for the purpose, toured Continental cities in the summer of 1933.

In her report, *Europe Re-Housed*, she was acerbic about Britain's current housing policy, maintaining that there was ample room to build within existing city boundaries. 'Vienna with 1,800,000 citizens has 14 miles of built up area and 93 miles of woodland, while Manchester with only 759,000 inhabitants covers 43 miles only 4 square miles of which is open space... How absurd for questions of existing city density to be disregarded. How lazy to advocate decentralization and the creation of new satellite towns! Is there not a good case for examining the structure of each town and relating the new areas to the best traditions of the past instead of indulging in the extremes of beehive building in the centre and chicken-coop building on the outskirts of town; of new estates spread over agricultural land, and of densely developed tenements for working men and their families in central city areas?'

In Liverpool, where the slum problem was acute, Charles Reilly, the tirelessly energetic occupant of the Chair of Town Planning at Liverpool University – the first in the country – proposed a way of rejuvenating the inner-city areas that showed an appreciation for the vitality of their life. Reckoning that it would take more like ten to fifteen years than the estimated five to demolish all the 'dark and dismal streets and courts' of Merseyside, he proposed that some patching work should be done with regard to drainage, water supply and leaking roofs, and then the whole area should be sprayed with a 'colour wash – light cream, light pink, or light blue, as one sees in France [or at least the Professor did], or even plain white-wash over whole streets and courts, roofs and all'. He would then 'paint the windows and doors really bright colours like they use in Holland – vermillion, cobalt blue or emerald green'. The resourceful Professor proposed to 'close most of the streets to ordinary traffic with posts and chains. In this way they would become safe playgrounds for the children... and in summer safe sitting out places for the older folk', and to 'borrow from the Parks and Gardens Committee shrubs of privet and myrtle in tubs (brightly painted ones of course)'.

In its inquiry into housing, Mass-Observation gave its readers a simple history lesson: 'The origin of flats on the Continent was the need for a large number of people to crowd together for safety within the walls of a city. As there was no serious warfare in England after the seventeenth century, English towns were able to spread themselves during the great period of population increase between 1760 and 1900, and flats were only built in a few of the largest cities.' It reported that 'there can be no doubt... that flats are unpopular with the great majority of English people'. Indeed, 'For every one person who said that she would like to live in a flat, ten said that they would like to live in a small house or bungalow.' Birmingham's Medical Officer of Health would have been sympathetic to this view, believing that in no time at all, flats would become even more unwholesome than the back-to-back houses they might replace.

Birmingham was just not 'flat-minded' (in 1930 a local paper put this down to the 'independence of character which has done so much for Birmingham'). It was not until 1935 that the principle of building flats was accepted by the city council, and prevarication continued until the outbreak of war four years later. There had been one mildly ambitious scheme, begun in 1927 with the construction of three-storey blocks on a former claypit at Garrison Lane, near Birmingham City football ground. The three hundred dwellings were built in a distinctive Dutch style, with baths installed, but with rents set at between 8s.1d and 8s.11d they were let to better-off workers, and soon earned the nickname 'The Mansions'. This was changed to 'The Barracks' when they were occupied and tenants realised how small they were, how few amenities they had and how rapidly the area around them was deteriorating.

Throughout the country there were approximately only five flats erected for every hundred houses built. Yet in Liverpool it was two out of ten, and of every ten dwellings that the LCC built in the 1930s four were flats: in 1936, for the first time, flat-building in London exceeded cottage-building. In M-O's opinion, this represented a clear case of 'public policy flying directly in the face of public opinion'.

Although the 1933 Wheatley Act had offered a subsidy for building flats, economy does not seem to have been the reason for this departure from the 'Tudor Walters' tradition of two-storey single-family cottage homes, since five-storey blocks of flats proved to be between one- and two-thirds more expensive to build than non-parlour houses, and to cost almost double for the equivalent floor space. While London and Liverpool, with high land values and shortages of housing and space, had a long tradition of flat-building, it required a considerable conceptual about-turn for many local authorities – and prospective tenants – to stop regarding flats as suitable only for special cases such as the single or the elderly, to erase the image of Victorian tenements for the poor, and to envisage them as desirable urban dwellings rather than as 'vertical slums' which were 'opposed to the habits and traditions of the people'.

The impetus came partly from the recognition that inner cities would become wastelands if housing was demolished and the population exported, and that many people needed or wanted to live near their place of work; partly from the arithmetic that the high price of inner-city land made it uneconomic to build anything other than high-density dwellings on it once it had been cleared of slums; partly from a fear that Britain would become seamlessly covered in endless suburbs; partly from the growing reluctance of landowners to sell their land for estate development – Lord Jersey had given short shrift to the LCC's offer to buy Osterley Park for this purpose; and partly from a recognition of the value of communities and a reluctance to scatter them. Additionally, there was also a modernist architectural urge, influenced particularly by the achievements in housing the working classes in Europe, where the developments were considered by the more *avant garde* British architects as perfect high-rise, ferro-concrete examples of 'machines for living' (in Le Corbusier's phrase) that combined aesthetics and function, and were sufficiently imaginative to include a whole range of social amenities (just as the cottage-garden estates had been intended to do).

Since no ambitious architect could consider his (or occasionally her) training complete until he had studied 'workmen's dwellings in Vienna on the spot', delegations set off to Austria, Germany, Czechoslovakia, Holland, France and Scandinavia to see how it was done. Perhaps fortunately, few copied the politicians and economists in venturing as far afield as the USSR to check out the Soviet model. Rather than British planners picking up tips from the United States, American architects were, in advance of President Roosevelt's introduction of a Federal Housing Programme, being sent to Britain and other European countries to study housing solutions for low-income families.

A deputation from the West Yorkshire Society of Architects, fresh from a visit to Vienna, put the case for flats to Leeds Corporation Housing Committee, which though it had sanctioned the building of two-storey 'cottage flats' in the late 1920s, had by 1933 decided to build no more since they were proving, largely for reasons of noise, unsuitable for the 'normal family'. 'We have nothing to learn from the Continent when it comes to our two-storey council houses,' reported the architects, 'but to those who associate barrack-like monotony and drabness with tenements or flats, what has been done in Vienna comes as a revelation. By pure artistry in simple inexpensive architectural design, together with very large scale layout of courtyards and amenities, some of the Vienna working-class flats make the old Viennese Baroque palaces look trivial and tawdry.' They went on to praise 'the best scheme, the Karl Marx House . . . to see this under a summer sky in Vienna is to see a very fine example of humanized architecture largely due to the problem having been tackled in a sympathetic and imaginative manner', and assured the committee that among their ranks there was 'the ability and spare' to do the same in Leeds.

But could what had been achieved in Austria, where some 60,000 flats had been built between 1920 and 1933 to solve the acute post-war housing crisis, work in Leeds? Mrs Chesterton had also been impressed by 'what an impoverished city like Vienna can accomplish', with the 'dignity of outline implicit in the splendid structures . . . their feeling of sweetness and light', and asked, 'Why should we not reach out to similar achievement? Why should working-class housing be branded with ignoble design, mean perspective, and lack of dignity? Why should our housing be bounded by cheap standards when the whole world beautiful lies before us where to choose?'

It appeared that it was Leeds rather than London, 'the wealthiest capital in the world', that was indeed 'reaching out to similar achievement'. A new estate 'on continental lines' was announced in March 1934. It was to be built using a cutting-edge prefabricated system of building designed and patented by a Frenchman, Eugène Mopin, who was invited to tender for the development in the notorious Quarry Hill area of Leeds, less than a mile from the Town Hall: street after street, court after court of atrocious back-to-back slums, described by the Archbishop of Canterbury, Dr Cosmo Lang, when a curate at a nearby parish church, as 'the most squalid part of Leeds . . . I never saw anything worse, or indeed as bad, in East London.' The plan was for flats for eight hundred people. Not more than a quarter of the site should be taken up by buildings; a community hall with seats for 520, with a stage and dressing rooms, was to be provided, as were twenty shops, basement storage for prams, a central laundry, indoor and outdoor swimming pools, wading pools, gardens and other delights, including a private balcony for each flat and a profusion of windowboxes and troughs, since the riot of flowers on the Karl Marx Hof had so impressed the visiting Leeds architects.

The plans evolved: the swimming pools were dropped in favour of tennis courts and a bowling green; household rubbish was to be disposed of by the Garchey system, copied from the Drancy estate just outside Paris, by which it was thrown down chutes to be burned in an incinerator, which, inexplicably, was the first thing residents or visitors would see when they passed under the monumental concrete Oastler Arch – named after Richard Oastler (the nineteenth-century Leeds social reformer known as the 'Factory King' for his campaigns for a ten-hour day and against the Poor Law) – at the entrance to the estate, next to the estate mortuary. Most innovatively, it was decided to include eighty-two passenger lifts, which meant that the blocks could soar to eight storeys, twice the height of the usual council flats built in Britain (though some swanky blocks in London's West End and in seaside resorts topped twelve storeys), increasing the number of flats to 938. There was even talk of roof playgrounds, but these were dropped in favour of the usual water tanks and chimneys.

When it was built, the Quarry Hill estate paid homage to modernist cinema building, with sinuous curving structures faced with alternating strips of brown-pea gravel and white spar that compared, some thought, to 'the grandeur of Beachy Head at sunset'. There were five different sizes of flats, intended to be able to cater for different social needs and thus to produce a balanced community. They were all of a high standard, and thought had been given to making sure that all living rooms were 'facing sunwards' (though bedrooms faced the noisy perimeter roads). There was a back-to-back range that provided an oven for the scullery (which had been included because it was thought that Northern housewives would still want to make their own bread), and an open coke fire with a gas poker, to make fanning newspaper and blowing bellows a thing of the past, in the living room (which was fitted with trivets so the kettle-on-the-hob tradition could still be observed). The scullery ('the housewife's workshop', the architect called it) was small, but then it did not have to be used for washing, since there was a central laundry and it was forbidden to hang washing on the balconies, and under the sink was a refuse container: when sufficient waste had accumulated, a lever could be pulled and the contents would be flushed down the waste stack – this in flats that would not have had fitted cupboards, a refrigerator, washing machine or even a vacuum cleaner. The living room, which was painted 'buff' as were all the rooms, had 'vermin proof' concrete skirtings, iron window frames and metal picture rails – no timber was used except for cupboards, which were the ubiquitous 'internal green' or brown. There was no separate lavatory (an undreamed-of luxury at the time, though a few London estates managed it before the Second World War), the master bedroom opened directly off the living room, and the balconies were a bit of a disaster, being 'dark and unfit for any constructive purpose'.

Building work was endlessly delayed, and in the summer of 1940 those parts of the estate that were not finished were given up as a bad job and abandoned to the imperatives of wartime. One of the two planned shopping parades was finally finished in 1952, the other was never built; nor were the sports grounds or the communal gardens. Although the much-heralded playgrounds were completed, with swings, seesaws, slides and toilets, three of the five were surrounded by high fences and were locked at night. They soon became dumping grounds for rubbish, and by the 1960s they were nothing more than asphalt wastes, one used for car parking.

Moreover, the windowboxes consistently failed to cascade with a riot of colour, since few residents troubled to plant them.

By 1938, the average cost of building each flat, including decorating, wiring and a proportion of the costs of the land, roads, waste-disposal system, laundry, roads and lifts, was around £600, which was not far out of line with the national average for council properties. However, the rents (which included utilities and a small charge for using the laundry) meant that a skilled working man earning between £3.2s.6d and £3.7s.6d (which would have been his weekly wage in Leeds at the time) would have been paying a fifth of his income in rent. They would have represented at least half of an unskilled worker's wages, making Quarry Hill flats beyond his reach, though those who were compulsorily rehoused in the flats as a result of slum-clearance programmes (two hundred in the first intake) could apply for rent relief. But generally, this particular utopia was not for the poor.

The promised community centre was never built (its site was used for water storage tanks during the Second World War), though a suite of rooms in one of the blocks was designated for community activities in 1942, and tenants who had been brought together by fire-watching duties during air raids and organising concert parties for the troops and VE-Day parties for the children, banded together to form a Tenants' Association in 1946. Tenants' Associations, though, were usually of a rather different stripe to Community Associations, and were concerned less with leisure activities than with rights, protection and grievances.

The Tenants' Association in Quinn Square, dilapidated blocks of flats in Bethnal Green in East London, organised a rent strike against their private landlord in the summer of 1938 over the issue of decontrolled rents, which meant a landlord could charge whatever rent he could get. Given the shortage of houses for rent, this could mean an increase of 25 per cent or higher, with no security of tenure. The strike spread to neighbouring Stepney, with its appalling housing conditions, where the huge Tenants' Defence League, led by the well-known radical Anglo-Catholic priest Father Grosser, could rally thousands of members.

With the support of the Communist Party, street after street organised rent strikes, most of which were successful, and most landlords signed 'collective agreements'. But one, C&G Estates Ltd, refused, and the tenants of two large blocks it owned went on strike for twenty-one weeks, ignoring notices to quit and clashing with police when the bailiffs tried to evict them on 27 June 1939. It was, C&G Estates declared, 'no longer a private matter between a particular landlord and his individual tenants. It is a struggle between mob law versus the law and order of the country.' If the 'mob' prevailed, then 'none of us in this country is safe with our posses-sions and rights'. To an extent, despite the rhetoric, the 'mob' did prevail. The Bishop of Stepney invited both sides to his house to negotiate, and C&G Estates agreed to reduce the rents of all decontrolled tenants, and to spend £2,500 on repairs at once and a further £1,500 every succeeding year. As the weekly magazine *Picture Post* pointed out, 'In the short space of six months, the [tenants'] league has reduced rents by a total of nearly £18,000 a year, has induced landlords to refund £20,000 of excess rent, and has helped thousands of tenants to obtain repairs.'

The league set up a number of evening legal advice centres, issued a handbook called *The Tenant's Guide*, and 'so enthusiastic are the members that a good many have become experts on this subject themselves, and are fully competent to advise their neighbours. They have also instituted a series of lectures by professors of hygiene, and run concerts and dances for the young and parties for older folk.' Community action indeed, though the shortage of decent housing at affordable rents in London's East End remained unresolved.

Quarry Hill flats in Leeds did not remind everyone of Beachy Head at sunset, and not all marvelled at the 'dignity and even majesty in the bold sweep of the blocks'. Some regarded them as communistic and brutal, symbol-ising 'the descent of the mass-man . . . to his last home, the termitary'. Nevertheless, it was generally reckoned that the flats were the most advanced built for the working classes in Britain at the time. They represented a dramatic break with the tradition of cheap, undistinguished blocks of flats for low-income families. Their self-conscious modernity was a deliberate rupture with the 'blind faith that the only decency is Georgian', which had resulted in most local authorities building traditional blank-walled, high, small-paned-windowed blocks, their rears dominated by access balconies and staircase turrets.

The Quarry Hill flats proved very popular – for a time. In the 1950s there were always seven or eight hundred people on the waiting list, although the Reverend Jenkinson (who was never convinced that flats were the answer to working-class housing needs, but had come to see Quarry Hill as the best worst solution, and had thrown his considerable energies into its realisation) had always regarded them as a halfway house between the slums and a little cottage on a suburban estate with a garden fore and aft. By 1958 nearly half of the tenants had been living there for over ten years, and while the reputation of the estate declined after that, many new tenants moved there voluntarily, and many old ones remained.

In November 1973 the end of the Quarry Hill experiment in living was announced by Leeds Council's Labour-controlled Housing Committee. The reason given was that the structure was obsolete – particularly the Garchey waste disposal system – and anyway, a planned six-lane motorway would have a devastating effect on several of the blocks of flats. By 1978 the entire 1930s utopian estate had been demolished.

TWELVE

Accommodating Other People

Do you know the world I live in? Ellesmere Road, West Bletchley? Even if you don't you know fifty others exactly like it. You know how these streets fester all over the inner outer suburbs. Always the same long, long rows of semi-detached houses . . . as much alike as council houses and generally uglier . . . The stucco front, the creosoted gate, the privet hedge, the green front door. The Laurels, the Myrtles, the Hawthorn, Mon Abri, Mon Repos, Belle Vue. At perhaps one house in fifty some anti-social type who'll probably end in the workhouse has painted his front door blue instead of green.

George Orwell, *Coming Up for Air* (1939)

So there it is, our own contemporary vernacular, spread thinly but ubiquitously over English hill and dale – or what was hill and dale before the speculative builder or the municipal councillor so aptly interpreted people's instincts and carpeted them with this intricate jungle of red peaked gables and evergreen hedges, multi-coloured chimneys and winding, tree-shaded avenues. From Becontree to Wythenshawe, from Port Sunlight to Angmering-on-Sea, the startling consistency of suburban character – despite its notorious vagaries in detail – indicates its origins in the living present. It could be the product of no other age but ours.

On account of its ubiquity alone we cannot afford to ignore it. During the twenty years between the two wars, four million new houses were built in England – enough to accommodate nearly a third of the population – and a very large percentage of these can be classified as suburban houses. So the suburban environment determines the style in which – for good or ill – England Lives.

J.M. Richards, *The Castles on the Ground: The Anatomy of Suburbia* (1946)

Frank Forster, who was mostly unemployed during the 1930s, picking up the odd bit of gardening or labouring here and there, was invariably at odds with his father, who worked in the sanitation department of Hawarden Rural District Council. In August 1936 he wrote in his diary: 'Even during an ordinary conversation [Father] will find some way of bringing in a mention of my being out of work . . . of late I have been drawing up plans for the alteration of the garden . . . Once or twice I have attempted to explain my plans to him. But my attempts have been met by the reminder that when I get a job then he will listen to whatever plans I may have.'

Forster Jnr's was a complex philosophy. On the one hand he had 'strong communist ideas'. A subscriber to the Left Book Club whenever he could afford to be, he was anti-royalist, anti-capitalist, pro-intervention in the Spanish Civil War. Yet Forster, who was in his mid-twenties, was neverthe-less drawn to the notion of *embourgeoisement*, and went 'out of my way to cultivate the friendship of the middle class and the lower middle class' rather than 'getting on intimate terms with my own', which he felt would mean that he 'would have to lower all the standards (intellectual, moral, ethical) that I keep at the height that I am able'. For that reason he had decided to sever his membership of the Chester Unemployed Association. He justified this by assuring himself that 'should a revolution occur then I am a Communist. But for the advancement of myself socially, I must "do in Rome as the Romans do"!'

During dinner one day in May 1935, Frank Forster had another idea about what the Romans might do. 'I suggested to father that we should have a name put on the front gate. He immediately showed strong oppos-ition to such an idea. He thought that it was too stuck up. Accused me of wanting to appear big, to be one in a hundred. For myself, I think that a beautiful sounding name on a front gate is very becoming' (though he conceded that a number was necessary too, for the postman's sake). 'Perhaps the presence of the name on a gate has associations with the upper class . . . the working class, generally, does not inhabit places worthy of a name.'

Housing by the 1930s had become an increasingly salient indicator of the distinction between the working classes and the middle classes (particu-larly the lower-middle class). Where you lived, the sort of house you lived in, and how you lived, depended of course on your income, but also on your sense of your social status, and on your aspirations and achievements.

Of the nearly four million houses built in England between 1919 and 1939, nearly three million were built by private builders, and just over one million by local authorities – despite the initial post-war intention to make building homes fit for working-class 'heroes' the priority. In 1935, 287,500 new private houses were built and 275,200 in 1937, the peak years of the inter-war housing boom. The vast majority of these were for sale rather than rent. The number of owner-occupied houses in Britain had been around three-quarters of a million in the early1920s; by 1938 it had soared to more than three and a quarter million. And the vast majority of this vast majority of new homes were the result of 'spec' (speculative) building, houses built in large numbers to be sold rather than individually commissioned architect-designed houses, which were still 'homes for the few'. The vast majority of these spec houses went up where the market was – in the Home Counties, the flourishing towns in the Midlands, and pockets around large industrial cities such as Manchester, Liverpool and Sheffield.

Owner-occupation mapped British society. It was an obvious pattern: in places of economic boom, houses were being built and people were buying them; in economically stagnant areas, people were either migrating, or were unable to contemplate taking on a new financial commitment. A striking example of this was the Welsh mining town of Merthyr Tydfil, where 47.5 per cent of workers were unemployed in 1935, and 25 per cent of residents left the area between 1929 and 1938. In Merthyr, which had had a strong tradition of owner-occupation (albeit on short leases) before the First World War, only 596 houses were built between the wars, and only twenty of the twenty-eight built by private builders were owner-occupied.

In more prosperous areas with a more middle-class population, the percentage of owner-occupiers was much higher. Hastings and Great Yarmouth, for example, both seaside resorts with a large number of retired people, had over 50 and 35 per cent respectively, and the percentage was similarly high in administrative centres where there were jobs for large numbers of white-collar workers, such as Exeter (46 per cent) and Bristol (51 per cent). In Plymouth, 68.5 per cent of houses were owner-occupied, and in Portsmouth 48.8 per cent – both were naval towns with a tradition of home purchase. It was the same in county towns with a large middle-class population such as Norwich (36.8 per cent) and Chester (32.3 per cent). Edinburgh (40 per cent), with its range of employment opportunities, had not suffered from the Depression as much as the rest of Scotland. In areas where new industries had mushroomed in the inter-war years, such as Oxford and Coventry – both dependent on the rapidly growing car industry – the ratio of owner-occupation to rented accommodation was similarly high. But the most striking discrepancy of all was between the North and South: in the North the percentage of people buying their own homes was less than half that in the South.

In 1935 the population of Greater London was around 8.5 million; it had been growing at the rate of three quarters of a million every year – the equivalent of the entire population of a provincial city being absorbed within a twenty-five-mile radius of the centre. But it was the population of the suburbs that was expanding; by almost a million and a half between

1921 and 1937, while that of inner London had declined by half a million. With its wide variety of jobs, the capital had not, in general, suffered as much from the Depression as other parts of the country. It acted as a magnet for those seeking work in the new consumer durable industries or in the service and administrative industries that were expanding as the old manufacturing ones withered and declined. With wages in such sectors stable, prices falling and credit easier to obtain, home ownership became something that more and more couples were able to contemplate. The *Evening News* had been able to sustain a weekly 'Homeseeker's Guide' since the mid-1920s, a page of illustrated advertisements for new suburban developments. In 1931 nearly 45,000 houses had been built in the London area; by 1934 that had increased to just under 73,000.

Medium- to large-sized building companies, household names like Laing, Wates, Wimpey, Taylor Woodrow, Nash, New Ideal Homesteads, most founded only in the 1920s, were buying up land all around London. Smaller developers were cashing in on the boom too, sometimes needing to sell a few houses at one end of a road in order to be able to finance the building of those at the other end.

Some of the new housing hugged the arterial roads radiating outward from London and other major cities. These created the notorious unregulated ribbon developments, rows of low-cost houses that J.B. Priestley described as 'miles of semi-detached bungalows, all with their little garages' and, he presumed, for he could hardly know for certain, containers for their owners' 'wireless sets, their periodicals about film stars, their swimming costumes and tennis rackets and dancing shoes'. They jostled alongside small parades of shops, mock-Tudor roadhouses, petrol stations and factories, sprawling along the Great West Road, the Kingston Bypass, the North Circular Road, the North Orbital Road, the Watford Bypass, Eastern Avenue, Great Cambridge Road and more. The jam of their attendant cars and buses, trams and motorbikes clogged up these arteries, confounding their purpose, which was to slide traffic effortlessly out of the cities and away. Such housing was popular with builders, since it meant they did not have to pay frontage charges; but living on an arterial road could be treacherous, particularly on summer weekends: four times more children were killed by traffic along ribbon developments than elsewhere in the country. In 1935 the Restriction of Ribbon Development Act forbade building within two hundred yards of such roads (or any other road the local authority decided needed the same protection). The urban sprawl was halted; or rather it was redirected.

New estates were springing up in increasing numbers outside the city boundaries – how far depended largely on the size of the town or city. In Oxford it was around two miles, in London, six to ten miles from Charing Cross. The rows of houses infilled the space until they abutted the green belt, land that in 1935 local authorities had been encouraged with a £2 million government grant to purchase as a buffer to further encroachment, and 'to provide a reserve supply of public open spaces and of recreational areas, and to establish a green belt or girdle of open space lands, not necessarily continuous, but as readily accessible from the completely urbanised areas of London as practicable'. It had been intended that a continuous belt up to five miles wide would encircle the capital: that never happened. Less a belt, the 72,000 acres formed more of a series of scattered green handkerchiefs (a few of them substantial) by the time the money ran out during the war.

In Middlesex, to the west of London, where land was no longer required to grow forage for the capital's horses, new estates provided private housing for some half a million people between 1931 and 1938. The houses were cheaper around Harrow, Potters Bar, Uxbridge, Feltham and Friern Barnet, while superior estates – bigger, better-built houses, and fewer of them – mushroomed in Edgware, Mill Hill, Southgate, Norwood and parts of Wembley. In Surrey, Merton and Morden grew prodigiously, as, to a lesser extent, did Malden, Epsom, Ewell, Sutton, Cheam, Croydon, Banstead and Kingston, while Weybridge and Esher became the Mill Hills of the South. Kent, which had been relatively undeveloped until the early 1930s, soon succumbed to the suburban embrace around Bexley, Chislehurst, Sidcup, Orpington and, further afield, Sevenoaks, the county's higher-priced houses clustering around Petts Wood, Bromley and the southern edge of Sevenoaks. To the East, home to the vast Becontree estate, owner-occupiers pushed out to Chingford, Hornchurch, Romford, Ilford and Barking, most buying modestly-priced houses, although there were pockets of more luxuriously sited and appointed residences around Wanstead and Loughton, both within easy reach of Epping Forest.

The parents of the future arts broadcaster Paul Vaughan had been living in rented accommodation in Acre Lane, Brixton, and while his father, who was 'something in linoleum', was content to stay near his close-knit family, his mother yearned for a 'nicer life', which, to her meant their own home in the suburbs. In 1934 she achieved her wish when the family moved to a pebbledash-rendered £1,000 'Swiss-chalet'-style house on a Wates-built estate in New Malden. 'This was where the postal district numbers came to an end. We weren't in London, we were in Surrey and it mattered.' Their house, which fronted the Kingston Bypass, was 'the last in a row of about twenty in the same style, but it was a little bigger than the others and £250 dearer. This conferred on us a small but lasting social advantage, as did the fact that we were on the corner, and had a garage at the end of the garden.

Inside the bedrooms were larger. There was an extra room downstairs, too, for which, as it happened my parents found it difficult to hit on any specific use. It was variously designated the Breakfast Room, the Morning Room, and the Study, even though none of the functions indicated by those names was important enough to deserve a special room in our household.'

Although a Ford Popular might sit in the garage of such a new suburban house, such a modest family car would still be beyond the means of most new home-owners, who were likely to be having to do a spot of belt-tightening in order to afford their £500-odd house, and would be much more likely to rely on public transport to get them to and from work. Even those who did own a car would probably have used it primarily for weekend outings, or perhaps for driving to the station so they could take the train to work.

'Live on the Live Line, Southern Electric – The Quickest Way Home', and 'Live in Surrey Free from Worry', urged Southern Railway, promoting its network of electrified commuter lines that criss-crossed the county. Each year the company published a series of free promotional handbooks that gave all the necessary information about train timetables, fares and the length of journeys, and also provided details – copiously illustrated – of the new housing developments that particular line served. 'The Country at London's Door' promised the cover of one, showing a train winding purpose-fully into a generic rural scene. Reciprocally, builders' advertisements for houses would invariably include information that the estate was 'on the Southern Electric'.

Those wishing to sell land for housing could sometimes be persuaded to subsidise the building of a station or the extension of a line, which would maximise the development potential of their land. At Stoneleigh, near Epsom, a farmer who had sold two large farms to a property developer in 1930 agreed to contribute both the land and half the cost of the building for a railway station. By 1935 the concrete station, built in the middle of a field, was entirely surrounded by small semi-detached houses, and more than 300,000 commuters a year were catching trains from its platforms – a three-fold increase from two years before. A large public house was built close to the station, and a 1,462-seat cinema, the Rembrandt, opened nearby in 1938.

When it was first built in the mid-nineteenth century, the London Underground had been intended to circle the centre of the city, connecting with mainline stations bringing in workers and visitors from the provinces and outlying areas, or with trams (forbidden in the West End) carrying passengers from places such as Peckham or Archway. From 1900 the steam system had been electrified, and gradually the inner circle was broken into, while lines also extended outwards. In 1923 the Hampstead Line had been extended north to Hendon, and the following year it reached Edgware (which involved building a viaduct over the North Circular Road); it could hardly continue to be called the Hampstead Line, and since to the south the line had stretched to Morden in 1926 (in the teeth of fierce resistance from the recently amalgamated Southern Railway, and an eventual standoff which would leave South London permanently bereft of tube lines compared to the other three points of the compass), various names were canvassed – Medgeway, Mordernware, Edgmorden – until, thankfully, in 1937 the simple 'Northern Line' was settled on. The line not only linked the densely populated districts of Balham and Tooting to central London, but by connecting with buses provided a commuter transport hub that included the St Helier estate – whose high proportion of postal workers needed late and early trains to get them to the main sorting office near Blackfriars. Until the formation of the Passenger Transport Board in 1933 regulated bus routes, most passengers had a choice of either a bus running on a scheduled route by a large company like the General, or one of the four hundred or so independent or 'pirate' buses that stopped wherever there were enough passengers waiting to make it worth their while, and often varied their routes for the same reason.

'Now pioneer, now camp follower . . . vigorous but uncertain,' was how Patrick Abercrombie described the London Passenger Transport Board, since it enabled the building of some suburbs by providing transport links, and obliged others, diverting or extending existing routes to developments that speculative builders were already erecting. But underground lines were notoriously expensive to build – over £1 million a mile (over £45 million in today's money). In 1929 the Underground Group – a precursor of the London Passenger Board – set up by Albert Stanley (later Lord Ashfield), which controlled most buses, tube lines and trams in London, had taken advantage of the Labour government's scheme for unemployed men to be given work on public utility schemes to extend the underground network so that increasingly commuters could travel directly from the outer suburbs to the centre without having to use buses or trams first.

By 1934 the underground was carrying 410 million passengers a year, and such labour was used to extend its reach further, extending the line past the massively over-used Finsbury Park station in North London to Wood Green, and deeper into Middlesex. Charles Holden (the architect responsible for 55 Broadway, the headquarters of London Transport, as well as London University's starkly beautiful Senate House in Bloomsbury, completed in 1937) was commissioned by Frank Pick, chief executive of London Transport, to design 'inviting doorways . . . that cannot be missed by the casual passerby' for the new extension. Outstanding modernist buildings resulted along the Piccadilly Line, including the circular glass and brick a-spaceship-has-landed type construction at Arnos Grove (1932), and stations at Southgate (1935), Cockfosters (1935) and Enfield West (now Oakwood, 1933).

Nevertheless, the underground could be confusing to navigate. In 1931 Harry Beck, an employee on the underground, was paid five guineas by Pick to devise a diagrammatic map of the tube. Beck's topological map, with a close affinity to an electrical circuit board, first issued free to the public in 1933, is still in use today, with new lines breaking through the circuit as they are constructed.

This push out of the capital further promoted the delights of 'Metroland', 'a country with elastic borders each visitor can draw for himself', as the publicity brochure put it, housing built on land that had been surplus to requirements for London's first steam underground railway, the Metropolitan Line. 'Metro-land' had been promoted in brochures and advertisements since 1915 (when the annual guide was renamed *Metro-land* rather than *Guide to the Extension Line*, as it had been since 1904). As a popular song had it, 'Hearts are light, eyes are brighter/In Metroland, Metroland.' It has become the archetypal vision of 1930s suburbia (in its most rural and grandest manifestation), memorialised by John Betjeman in what one of his biographers called a 'telly-poem' paean to the line that runs from Marylebone station by way of Pinner, Wembley, Harrow, Rickmansworth, Chorleywood, Chalfont and Latimer to the immaculately ordered and leafy outer limits of Buckingham suburbia at Amersham and Chesham.

A regular annual wage or salary of around £200 was considered just about adequate security for a mortgage. Someone earning £3.8s.9d a week could comfortably afford mortgage repayments which put a house costing £500 to £600 within reach, with weekly payments of £1.0s.5d plus rates of 4s.3½d. Building societies calculated that outgoings on housing, including rates, should not exceed a quarter of a man's income – a much higher proportion than that usually paid for rented accommodation. Given the substantial rise in real incomes (for those in work), the cost of houses was dropping, due to falling construction costs and new labour practices which led to fierce competition between building firms, and price-cutting – a house built to Tudor Walters' specifications in 1920 cost more than £1,000 to build: by 1932 the same house could be built for £350. Interest rates were also lower after Britain came off the Gold Standard in 1931 and the government adopted a cheap money policy in the hope of kick-starting the economy, while the willingness of building societies to lend meant that lower middle-class people such as elementary schoolteachers, senior technicians and draughtsmen, better-paid shop assistants or buyers were able to buy their own homes in the 1930s, an option that had been denied to them in the 1920s.

Mortgages were increasingly easy to obtain. After the financial crash of 1929 and subsequent unease about overseas investment, those with capital to invest increasingly favoured building societies as a secure home for their savings. Assets in the Woolwich Building Society, founded in 1847 and attracting funds in its early days from men working at Woolwich Arsenal, had only risen from £1.6 million to £2 million between 1920 and 1925. By 1934 they had shot up to £27.1 million. The Abbey Road Building Society (named after its first address in St John's Wood), formed in 1874 by members of the Free Church, had assets of three quarters of a million pounds by the outbreak of the First World War. By 1938 this had multiplied by seventy, and the Abbey Road was one of the largest building societies in the country, others being the Halifax (which had a tradition of being prepared to lend to owner-occupiers and rentiers on modest incomes), the Leeds Permanent and Woolwich Equitable, which between them held around a third of the total assets of all building societies. In 1938, £137 million was lent to house-buyers by these and other building societies that had opened branches all over London and in other towns and cities, as well as in the areas where they did most business: the suburbs.

Awash with money, the societies, which up until 1930 had required 25 per cent of the purchase price of a house for a deposit, relaxed their require-ments and were prepared to accept 10 or even 5 per cent of the valuation – which was much nearer the sort of sum people were used to paying as 'key money', demanded by landlords of rental properties before the keys were handed over.

Repayment periods were extended from fifteen to twenty years, then to twenty-five or even thirty, mortgage interest rates dropped to 4½ to 5 per cent, and the building societies contrived various ways to reduce legal and survey charges, offering 'all-in packages' that included absorbing legal and other fees into the price of the house and thus transferring them to the mortgage. To make it even easier for those on a low income to scramble onto the housing ladder, since with the rapid pace of building more people wanting to buy a home of their own had to be persuaded to do so, a 'Builders' Pool' was established. In theory this helped those who found it difficult to raise the necessary deposit, since the builder would advance cash to a building society to make up the difference between the mortgage and the valuation, so that the purchaser might have to come up with even less than 5 per cent of the purchase price. This proved to be a successful tactic for extending the owner-occupier market to the lower-paid: the builders Laing estimated that the pool system tripled the rate of house sales in the early to mid-1930s.

While all this made home ownership a realistic possibility for *some* higher-paid and thrifty manual workers, it remained a largely middle-class pattern. By 1939 something under 35 per cent of housing in Britain was owner-occupied. Yet almost 60 per cent of the middle class either owned or were buying their houses, whereas less than 20 per cent of the working class were owner-occupiers, fewer than in 1915, and of that number quite a few probably took in lodgers to help with the mortgage.

Ever anxious to extend the market, builders and developers took out advertisements in the national, regional and local press and on roadside hoardings, urging, 'Why Pay Rent When You Can Own Your Own Home?', and promising easy terms for house purchase. Jane Walsh, wife of an Oldham cotton-piecer, saw 'a big signpost' while out for a walk one Saturday evening. 'It said "Own Your Own House. Price £449. Deposit £20. Repayments, rates, taxes, 18s weekly. Exhibition house now open." We went and had a look at the exhibition house . . . How we admired and exclaimed! We discussed ways of raising the £20 deposit – which seemed an impossible sum. And if we could raise it, what about the 18 shillings? . . . In comparison with our present rent of 6s.9d a week, it was tremendous. But then so was the difference between the exhibition house and the slum we were living in.'

Grace Foulkes and her husband Reuben, who worked as a stoker on a tug moored near Woolwich, had run the gamut of housing possibilities during the early years of their married life, moving first from a slum in Wapping to rented rooms in Whitechapel, from there to the LCC Becontree estate at Dagenham. Various problems meant that the family was obliged to return to private rented accommodation in Forest Gate, East London. However, Mrs Foulkes missed life in Dagenham, and when she heard of a new housing estate that was being built at Hornchurch, 'a small country village with beautiful country' not far from there, with houses for sale for £495 freehold, the couple and their two small daughters set off to investigate.

> You could go and inspect a show house, fully furnished, but before this was shown to you, you were invited to a specially built house which was a representation of Snow White's House; the inside was furnished according to the pictures in the story, together with seven dwarfs and Snow White. Where the dwarfs came from, I shall never know but there they were, shaking hands and escorting you around. This was a very good sales gimmick, for after you

had seen the house you were given a wonderful tea. When this was finished you were driven around the estate and invited to choose your plot of land or your house. They were very good, well-built houses, with three bedrooms, a large lounge and a kitchen. There was also a very large rear garden and a smaller front one. Each house had garage space. You could secure your house for a down payment of £1. You were then allowed one month to make this up to five pounds. By the end of three months this must be made up to £25. You could then move in. The mortgage was arranged by the builders and the loan was spread over 25 years. The repayments were 12s9d a week, plus rates, which at the time were 4s6d a week. So for under a pound a week you were buying your own house. The interest on the loan was 2½%.

The couple decided to buy one of the houses, raising the required £25 by pawning a gold watch and chain that had belonged to Grace Foulkes' mother – which they were never able to redeem. With Reuben earning £3.10s a week, the family could just about afford the mortgage repayments on their new house, although 'we could not buy luxuries . . . we could not save either and we had no pleasures outside our home, for we could not afford them. But we worked in the garden, growing what vegetables we could and we went for country walks, through Hornchurch on to Upminster Common, where on fine days we could picnic.'

Life on the new estate was delightful, with various milkmen plying the family with gifts of free milk, eggs, cream, even a tea service, in an effort to get their custom, and a baker left a free loaf every day for a week for the same purpose. 'It seemed a good beginning to another kind of life, for now we were owner occupiers . . . We were all so very proud of our new houses, and each occupier named his house. Of course we had a number, but a name we must have just to be the same as all the rest. Ours was called "Arcadia" which means "simple happiness". This is what we had; this is all we wanted.'

Nevertheless, the struggle to keep up the payments on a home of their own could be daunting for the estimated 5 per cent of owner-occupiers earning £3.10s a week or less. After Reuben Foulkes had an accident at work, several of his toes had to be amputated. 'Now he had lost his balance and we both knew that he could no longer work on ships or tugs; for men who work on the river must be sure-footed as ships are never still.' Unable to keep up the mortgage payments and with no response to an appeal for help from the building society, Grace Foulkes 'registered the keys and returned them to the Building Society', and the family went to live in a tied cottage that went with a job in Hampshire.

The danger of low-paid workers taking on commitments that they could barely afford – encouraged by the offer of small deposits particularly enabled by the 'builders' pool' system – was recognised by some of the building societies. Walter Harvey of the Burnley Building Society cautioned his industry colleagues, 'We are taking on increasing numbers of the type of buyer-borrower who is entering into obligations beyond his means . . . it is no real service to the house buyer to lend him more than he can afford to borrow.' Although, for obvious reasons, building societies were loath to publicise the level of mortgage defaulters for fear of discouraging others, it is probable that the annual rate of default was around 2 per cent. Building societies dealt harshly with those in arrears, seeking repossession regardless of circumstances, and often despite the earnest intention of the defaulter, who most likely had fallen on hard times due to illness or unemployment, to pay when possible. Even after they had vacated their house and sent the keys to the building society, Grace and Reuben Foulkes were sued for the outstanding loan. The judge threw the case out of court.

Elsy Borders was also a victim – albeit a remarkably resourceful one – of the corner-cutting practices of some of the builders of the cheaper houses and the sharp practices of some building societies. In October 1934, with her husband Jim, a London taxi-driver (and part-time law student) acting as guarantor, she had taken out a 95 per cent mortgage with the Bradford Third Equitable Building Society on a £690 semi-detached house that, owing to the state of the unmade-up road, the Borders had not actually seen, on the 1,200-house Coney Hall estate at West Wickham in Kent built by Messrs Morrell (Builders Ltd).

It became apparent at once that the house was highly unsatisfactory. The roof leaked, tiles fell off if there was a high wind, damp patches appeared on the bedroom walls, ceilings cracked, wooden frames were warped so that doors and windows could not be closed, the woodwork and eaves were infected with vermin, the foundations were inadequate and the electrical wiring was dangerously faulty, which meant that the Borders and their small daughter received an electric shock if they touched the walls. It was, in fact, a perfect example of a 'Jerry-built' house (Jerry from Jericho, the walls of which came tumbling down), though the house still stands today, and Mrs Borders withheld the mortgage payments. When the Bradford sued for repossession, Mrs Borders, advised by a Communist solicitor, Bill Sedley (father of the current senior appeal judge Lord Justice Sedley), counterclaimed, alleging that the society's statement that the house was well built was misleading, and that she had been persuaded to buy by the builders (who had gone into liquidation the previous year).

The case was heard at the High Court in January 1938. Known variously as the 'Tenant's KC' and, less appealingly, as 'Portia in a Jumper' (though describing herself as a 'mere housewife'), Elsy Borders proved an eloquent advocate for home-owners' rights, and soon four hundred other Coney Hall estate householders also started to withhold their mortgage repayments. Some older residents complained that it wasn't only the building work that was shoddy, but that the 'tone' of the estate – and hence its house prices – was going down, since a number of members of the working class had moved in, and were letting the side down by going to and from work in their uniforms rather than a suit, collar and tie.

The complicated case, during the course of which Mrs Borders scored points off Norman Birkett KC in a libel case brought by her husband against the builders, who had labelled him a 'bad egg', dragged on until 1940, when the House of Lords finally threw out the Borders' claim and the family lost their house. But what Elsy Borders' lengthy battle had done was expose the iniquities inherent in the 'builders' pool' system, whereby many who could not really afford to buy their own homes were encouraged to do so by collusion between spec builders and building societies which was to the financial advantage of both. Since the system gave builders the assurance that their houses would be sold, there was little incentive, in a competitive market, to maintain high construction standards rather than produce 'Jerry-built' houses. Following the Borders' case, the Building Societies Act of 1939 put an end to such practices by attaching such stringent conditions to the 'builders' pool' system, that it was effectively unusable. Hundreds of other Coney Hall withholders found that, unlike Mrs Borders, their houses could not be repossessed.

Perhaps unsurprisingly, not everyone who theoretically might be able to buy their own house wanted to do so. Mass-Observation's housing report showed that those on low incomes who lived in relative comfort on estates where it was not possible to buy a house were not particularly interested in becoming owner-occupiers. Only 14 per cent of the people living on the Becontree estate, for example, wanted a home of their own, though on the Watling estate 29 per cent did.

The main disincentive was money: some respondents had no desire 'to be in debt for the rest of my life', though others totted up the rent they had paid over the years and wished that they had been able to buy. Those who preferred to rent also cited the costs of repairs, 'always having your hand in your pocket if you owned your own home' (and presumably the chore of having to actually arrange for the repairs to be done, whereas in rented accommodation that would be the landlord's or local authority's responsibility), and many felt they were more mobile if they were renting, and could move for a job, or retire to the seaside, without the aggravation of selling their home.

For those who did decide to embark on the suburban lifestyle, it was a different world of glimpsed rurality, long commutes, neat, sapling-lined streets punctuated by shopping parades, often with a branch library and a sub-post office, teashops and pubs, invariably a cinema or two, and possibly a nearby paddling pool, swimming pool or lido such as the enticingly named 'Surbiton Lagoon'.

There was much less concern about the loss of community in the owner-occupier suburbs than there was on the new LCC suburban estates. Or at least there were fewer surveys. Perhaps it was because the move had been voluntary, usually involving considerable sacrifices to achieve it; perhaps it was because the middle classes were considered not to have had much of a community to lose; perhaps they were considered capable of arranging their own entertainments, and so would not suffer from the aimlessness that social observers were so anxious to identify and to channel among the working classes. Perhaps it was that 'citizenship' was not at issue when it came to the middle classes: their stake in the social order was presumed and evidenced by their eager acquisition of property and the amount of time and money that went into its upkeep and adornment.

Yet there were concerns – rather patronising concerns – about what suburbia would do to women, for whom 'the question was ... how to lay out time ... She did not have to go out, for shopping was delivered' – though for many such women 'going to the shops' constituted a daily ritual: even if the weekly groceries were delivered, there was always the butcher, the fishmonger, the greengrocer to visit, dry cleaning to be picked up, knitting wool bought, some necessary errand to the post office, library books to be exchanged. She daydreamed afternoons away in the cinema, or turned to cigarettes or aspirin, while reading 'best sellers' was 'a means of easing a desolating sense of isolation and compensates for the poverty of their emotional lives'.

In March 1938 the doctors' weekly the *Lancet* had identified (or rather imported) an angst that would unfurl down the decades, 'suburban neurosis'. Dr Stephen Taylor of the Royal Free Hospital sketched a typical (if composite) case, 'Mrs Everyman', a twenty-eight- or thirty-year-old housewife who came to his outpatient department complaining of pains, weight loss, sleeplessness. She and Mr Everyman had saved for two years in order to buy a 'small semi-detached hire-purchase villa on the wonderful new Everysuburb estate adjacent to one of our great by-passes and only twenty minutes from the station ... All their savings went on the first instalment of the house and furniture. Mr Everyman was an inexperienced lover, and the physical side of marriage shocked and disappointed his wife. After a year of rather unsatisfactory birth control, during which time the thrill of a "home of her own" had worn off, they decided to risk a baby.' This kept Mrs Everyman's 'hands pretty full' for eighteen months,

> then things began to slacken up. She had developed a routine for doing the housework quickly. She had to think a little about the shopping, but the cooking she did almost blindly. The [Daily] Peepshow didn't take long to read, and the wireless was always the same old stuff. They hadn't been able to get away for a holiday as they had hoped; baby had cost more than they had bargained for. Hubby had started to grumble at her [complaining that her loss of weight meant that 'she wasn't so nice to cuddle any more'] ... Mrs Everyman had begun to worry – all the time. Was she ill, who would look after baby if she was? Might hubby get ill and lose his job? Then what? They'd fall behind with the instalments. They'd take away the furniture. And they'd have to live in rooms – or take a lodger. Perhaps they couldn't get one. You never saw notices up in Acacia Row with 'Bed and Breakfast. Gent preferred' on them, like you did in London. What would the neighbours say?

Not that poor Mrs Everyman knew many neighbours, and though the curate had called, 'hubby had said no' to her going to the church social. So with no one to talk to about her worries, Mrs Everyman went to her doctor, but he just said it was 'nerves'. 'Nerves! What had she to be nervous about?' Mrs Everyman contemplated 'taking something. Or putting her head in the gas oven,' but decided instead to try the hospital outpatients, where she was seen by Dr Taylor, who 'put her miserable little story . . . into medical jargon' and wrote it up for his colleagues. He identified the main problem as boredom 'occasioned by lack of friends', not enough to do and not enough to think about, anxiety, money worries, the fear of unwanted pregnancy, and 'a false set of values' largely engendered by 'making a fetish of the home' and aspiring to a life portrayed by the Daily Peepshow and the cinema. 'One cannot blame her for expecting at least a little of other people's thrills. But there *is* no thrill in Everysuburb.'

What did the doctor propose for this unhappy suburbanite? A team of psychoanalysts on each new estate would be one solution, but Taylor found that 'an inverted and costly' one, and concluded that 'one must try to reawaken interest in life'. The pub might have been a possibility, but 'by an unwritten law that is for men only. A carefully graded reading list is perhaps more use than a bottle of medicine. Another baby rather than a new wireless if it can be afforded, may effect a permanent cure.' But Dr Taylor was not optimistic: 'As long as life offers the suburban woman so little to live for', she will 'continue to add to the numbers in our out-patient waiting rooms ... We have, I fear, let matters go too far in the jerry-building, ribbon-development line to institute an entirely satisfactory scheme of prophylaxis.' All he could hope for was that these 'rotten little houses will in due course collapse. Perhaps when the children grow up they will break down the barriers which separate family from family ... they may see through the values of their family and come to despise it.'

In the meantime Dr Taylor saw a salvation in 'establishing on these new estates social non-religious clubs catering for all possible interests ... with a swimming bath and gymnasium, a cafeteria, a day nursery, the public library and reading, smoking and games rooms – something not unlike the Pioneer Health Centre in Peckham, without perhaps such a positive emphasis on health'. 'The prevention of the suburban neurosis, then, is in the hands of the social workers and politicians,' he concluded. But the politicians and the handful of social workers most local authorities employed were in general too occupied with the welfare of the working classes to worry about cases of 'neurosis' in privately owned Everysuburb.

It was, indeed, a very different world to be grasped: suburban roads, closes, crescents, drives, ways and avenues – 'street' was considered all together too urban – had names that gestured to their rural or some other leisured recent past: Meadow Rise, Fir Tree Close, Barnfield, Deepdene, The Clumps, Meadowside, Chestnut Close, Hawthorn Way, or Linksway, Greenaway, Crossways. Or they followed a theme that was to the developer's fancy. In Raynes Park, where Paul Vaughan went to school, there was a 'painters' estate' where 'you wandered along Gainsborough Road, Romney Road and Millais, Landseer, Turner and Kneller Roads'.

When it came to the naming of houses, individual choices could be puzzling. Sometimes the name would suggest a rather grander residence than a small semi, 'The Hollies', 'The Laurels', 'Grey Gables'; sometimes the name might recall the owners' honeymoon joys, 'Charmouth', 'Coniston', 'Lynton'; sometimes it would entwine their names, 'Gladbert', 'Ethelroy', Lesrene'; and sometimes it would speak a whimsical, if rather heavy-handed, truth or hope, 'Dunroamin', 'Mon Repos', 'Bakome'. This was not an exclusively lower-middle-class suburban practice: the Russian sculptor Dora Gordine and her husband, the Hon. Richard Hare, son of the 4th Earl of Listowel and the first Professor of Slavonic Studies at the University of London, merged their names to form 'Dorich' for their very grand house built in 1937 on Kingston Hill, with fine views of Richmond Park.

Paul Vaughan's father, like most suburban dwellers (and Frank Forster), considered it essential for his house to have a name as well as a number. 'My father settled on one he thought appropriate to its situation next to the bypass: "Wayside". Through a crony in the City, he had some writing paper printed with the address set diagonally across one corner in old-fashioned gothic script, giving, of course, both the name and the number [14]. Unfortunately the Post Office which had as much trouble as everyone else keeping up with the rush to the suburban countryside, had decided Malden Way ought to begin a few miles further east towards Wimbledon. We were given a new number [248] and my father's fancy headed notepaper became obsolete at a stroke,' as did the 'villagey scale of our new address'.

As a house's name – spelled out in metal letters screwed on the gate of the more modest houses, painted on a ceramic plaque of the mid-range, engraved on a brass plate at the top of the range – bore witness to the desire for choice, so, as much as possible, did its design. The basic shape of most suburban houses was very similar: a rectangle containing a sitting room and dining room plus a hall and kitchen downstairs, with two bedrooms and a small box room, bathroom and separate WC upstairs. But to give the impression of individual choice there were usually a number of different styles of house on a new estate, all variations on a basic design that owed much to the early-twentieth-century vernacular of architects such as Sir Edwin Lutyens, Norman Shaw and C.A. Voysey. 'No two houses the same,' estate builders would boast, though thankfully that meant no *pair* of semi-detached houses: the two conjoined semis that made up a whole were identical, like a Rorschach blot opened out.

The Farm Estate in Catford offered 'Queen Anne, Jacobean, Georgian or Tudor'-style houses (in that order). Fascias might be hung with red tiles, usually above pebbledash render (cheap to do, easy to maintain, and avoided the need to regularly repoint the brickwork), and either the upper storey or part of the roof gable would gesture to 'Merrie England' with strips of half-inch boarding nailed up to resemble oak beams, often with startlingly tall (and sometimes quite elaborate) chimneys teetering above. The front of the house might be interrupted with barge boarding, scalloped leading, or panels of bricks laid in a herringbone pattern. The woodwork was invariably painted green, either darker Brunswick or the paler apple.

Almost every suburban house had a bay window which enabled the inhabitants to 'peep up and down as well as across' the road. It also provided more light, the illusion of a little more space, and room to display an ornament – galleons were very popular, as were coy plaster Dutch girls and boys – or a vase of flowers. And, according to one modern authority, such

311

a window represented a swelling maternal bosom, an infallible sign of security. Furthermore, a bay window was a mark of owner-occupation, since it was a feature never found on council houses. Windows were frequently made more 'historic' by the inclusion of small leaded panes, or even bottle glass. Porches might be a gracious swoosh of brick down from the roof, elliptical, keyhole-shaped, or, occasionally, absent. Stained glass was much favoured, though it sometimes cost extra: leaded motifs dotted along the upper panes of windows, panels inset in the front door, round windows on the stairs. Again, galleons were a popular motif, as were lighthouses, seagulls, heraldic shields, crinolined ladies and the ubiquitous sunburst, its rays radiating into the corners, an image sometimes repeated on the wooden front gate. Paths curved wherever there was room, and by the 1930s gravel had invariably ceded to crazy paving. Front doors might be heavily studded to suggest a medieval stronghold, with a sonorous iron ring knocker, or wood grained to resemble oak with a small round porthole window to let in light and enable the person within to check out callers.

Front gardens, which were all that could usually be seen by the passer-by, were small and not intended to be sat in, played in or for cultivating vegetables. Such activities were for the fenced-in back garden. Front gardens were only for looking at. Gardening had become an increasingly popular leisure activity in the 1930s: newspapers and magazines published regular gardening columns, part works and gardening encyclopaedias filled bookshops, and Mr (C.H.) Middleton's gardening talks were among the BBC's most popular programmes, a number of them being published in book form. But perhaps the greatest recognition came when W.D. & H.O. Wills issued a set of fifty cigarette cards, each one a handy hint for the gardener. It was probably no exaggeration to claim, as a gardening writer did, that 'Countless new homes and gardens have brought into being thousands of additional gardening enthusiasts, gardening is [today] man's chief hobby.'

Flowerbeds might flank the path or be cut in a half-moon shape under the window, full of indiscriminately coloured bedding plants, or a more austere flare of feathery pampas grass. There might be a rockery, the 'rocks' a useful final resting place for builders' rubble, sheltering a range of small alpine plants. Gnomes might nestle there too, or on the lawn, relaxing, fishing, smoking a pipe, out of proportion, but no matter, with perhaps a cast stone birdbath. A low front wall marked the boundary, in brick and probably castellated, or using waste material from a blast furnace to give a rough, 'rustic' appearance, the whole topped with a clipped privet hedge and/or heavy iron link chains, again channelling the notion of home as secure fortress.

Inside the house, the hall would be dark and narrow, space perhaps for a hat stand, a small table for letters to post, the telephone if the family had one (in the hall to discourage overlong calls) and a drawer for gloves, and maybe a stand for umbrellas and walking sticks. It could become awkwardly cramped if it was also required to accommodate a pram or bicycle. More expensive houses might have wood-panelled halls (the panelling might extend to the dining room). More modest ones would make do with lincrusta, or, increasingly anaglypta paper, brush-grained and varnished to match the interior woodwork, which was fairly likely to be brown 'oak' – certainly in the hall – up to a wooden dado rail atop which might be displayed pewter plates or sporting trophies.

Floors would be parquet downstairs if possible; if not, then parquet-printed linoleum. Turkish rugs were popular in the dining room, and in the sitting room there was likely to be a wool rug between sofa and fireplace, rectangular or half-moon-shaped, perhaps with a floral pattern or something rather Cubist, swirling or 'jazz', owing a debt to the contemporary designs of Marion Dorn or Marion Pepler. Upstairs the floors might be carpeted – not usually fitted, but with a dark-stained and varnished surround – and if not, then linoleum again. Or 'linolsquares', *faux* 'slip mats' bought perhaps from Catesby's in Tottenham Court Road, which was reputed to stock the most comprehensive range in the world. The linoleum that Paul Vaughan's father's firm manufactured included a range of patterns, but in his own home Mr Vaughan preferred imitation parquet, or *jaspé*, which was meant to look like marble, for the bathroom and perhaps the kitchen.

The suburban kitchen, painted in cream, *eau de nil* or duck-egg blue matt oil, might have a fitted cupboard or two, and as space was at a premium, what could be built in would be, as in a caravan. There would be a deep white ceramic sink with one or two wooden draining boards attached (stainless steel was not unknown in the 1930s, but was unusual in a domestic setting) and a gas cooker – electric cookers were not usual either, indeed a number of newly built houses had no electrical sockets, and were only wired for electric lights, so that the increasingly popular electric irons, and even kettles and toasters, had to be run from a lighting socket.

Without central heating a coke boiler would supply hot water – and keep the kitchen warm; and without a washing machine, the housewife might send sheets and shirt collars to the laundry, but would do most, if not all, her washing at the kitchen sink with perhaps a mangle in the shed and a rope washing line stretching across the back garden. A kitchen cabinet would hold crockery and have shelves for dry goods such as flour and sugar, a drawer for cutlery and a drop-down enamel flap for food preparation. As fridges were still a rare luxury (and most were gas), food would be kept in a small pantry on the north side of the house, with a small wire-meshed window to keep it cool. Since the kitchen was small, the family might eat there on a table that doubled as an ironing board with a blanket over it, while a hatch in the wall would allow food to be passed through to the dining room when company came.

There would be fireplaces in the dining and sitting rooms, no longer ones that needed weekly black leading, but built of brick or faced with glazed tiles in a mottled grey, brown, cream or dark green lustre, some with a geometric motive and a ziggurat top that served instead of a Victorian marble mantelpiece. A coal scuttle in metal-lined polished wood or brass would stand by the fireplace, and there would be a set of fire dogs on the tiled hearth. Some homes would have a socket for a gas poker. Small fireplaces might be provided in the bedrooms, but would most likely be fitted with a two-bar electric wall-mounted fire.

Although show houses might be furnished wall to wall from Waring & Gillow or some local furniture emporium, most suburban houses were a more eclectic mix. A few pieces might have been inherited or brought from previous rented accommodation, but most families were anxious to start afresh in their new surroundings, even if that meant waiting or buying a few things on the 'never never' from Whiteleys, Maples, Hamptons or Drages, partly because the size of the houses meant that Victorian and Edwardian furniture was too large, and partly because it just 'didn't suit'.

The future sociologist Phyllis Willmott's mother was delighted by the possibility of hire purchase, since it enabled her to throw out her 'solid Edwardian oak dressing table bought secondhand in her early married years . . . in favour of the new veneered walnut suite she could never get – with matching wardrobe and chest of drawers – on the "never never of hire purchase"'.

But a social worker cautioned against such reckless behaviour: 'A few bits of sticks that meant home to many of them would not do on the new estate – they must have a rexine suite, a Jacobean sideboard and a gate-legged table . . . soon they found they had surrounded themselves with debt and first one thing then another had to go. They found attractive advertisements were just a myth, and instead of the shopwalker who showed them round and said "Won't you stay for lunch and let us send you home in a car?" they found on their doorstep one morning a very different type of man, and when he went, their furniture went with him.'

The interior style was most likely to match the exterior: cottage vernacular with chintz curtains and loose covers on an uncut moquette three-piece suite, though more boxy, rexine-covered sofas and armchairs were becoming very à la mode by the 1930s. A bookcase – maybe made by Minty, perhaps with sliding glass doors to keep the dust off books which may or may not have been rarely consulted – and a nest of occasional tables (which were unlikely to see many occasions) would complete the sitting room furnishings. Except for the wireless. While television was hardly even in its infancy as far as most British households were concerned until well after the Second World War, nine million British households owned a wireless (so called because it transmitted through the airwaves rather than wires like a telephone, and was powered by an accumulator battery which required periodic charging at a local garage). It was a sturdy piece of equipment, housed in either a wooden cabinet, often with a fretwork panel over the loudspeaker, or in bakelite, a new plastic, usually made in brown, black, dark green or maroon and also used for door handles, clocks, ashtrays, dressing-table sets and telephones (should such a modern wonder be possessed: a telephone was not of the highest priority in the suburbs. There were an abundance of public phone boxes in built-up areas, mail was collected and delivered several times a day seven days a week, and the telegram was a frequent means of urgent communication. Having a phone was clearly an index of being comfortably off. There were over a million telephone subscribers in Britain in the 1930s, but while one in every 3.5 households in Epsom was on the phone, in Merthyr Tydfil the ratio was one telephone per forty seven households). 'Listening in' was an evening's entertainment – or commitment – not something one did while preparing a meal, say, and meals on a tray were for invalids, not families. But some concession to relaxation while listening to a programme could be detected from the selection of bottles and glasses in the sideboard (the very chic might have a glass-fronted cocktail cabinet), the pipe rack on the mantelpiece and the metal ashtrays on weighted leather straps hanging over the arm of the sofa or the armchairs

Pictures hung from a high, narrow wooden rail that circled the room. Paul Vaughan's father, who smoked Ardath cigarettes, collected the cards in each packet and pieced them together until he could make Franz Hals' portrait of *The Laughing Cavalier*, which he then posted to the manufacturers and in return received a small framed reproduction of the same picture. Other popular prints included Constables and Turners – occasionally a vivid Van Gogh – hunting scenes, jolly cardinals or monks at table, country views, seascapes, coaching inns, bar scenes and exotic moonlit views – usually over the sea or some indeterminate desert. Some people screwed plaster scalloped vases or plaster heads – Spanish dancers perhaps, or three ducks in upward flight – to the walls, while a glass-fronted cabinet might display a collection of Goss china, some cut crystal glass, an inverted test tube containing layers of coloured sand, the silver horseshoe from a wedding cake and other souvenirs of events and holidays.

In the dining room there would usually – eventually – be another matching set. This time a gate-legged dining table or one that could be extended to seat guests, with matching upright chairs (including a carver with arms to denote the head of the table) and a sideboard on which would likely rest a wooden biscuit barrel, a blue Chinese ginger jar, and maybe an arrangement of flowers or dried leaves, perhaps in a vivid orange-and-green Clarice Cliff vase, if that was not standing in the centre of the table. The wood might be mahogany or oak, or, with the shortage of timber since the 1920s, plywood with a fruitwood veneer. The style, almost invariably, 'Jacobean', with heavy turned and bulbous legs, the default position for British furniture design at the time – and for long after.

Downstairs, lighting might be a modern striplight in the kitchen; elsewhere most likely a central hanging light, perhaps an upturned glass bowl, opaque, painted, engraved or milky and mottled (the wattage of electric lights was much stronger by the 1930s, and a naked bulb could be irritating). Or it might be a stubby wooden 'candelabra', with *faux* wax dripping down the 'candles'. Wall uplighters were popular too, and most suburban homes would have a standard lamp in the corner, its wooden stem turned like a stick of barley sugar or fashioned in wrought metal, topped with a parchment shade fringed or bobbled, plain or decorated.

Walls were papered (except in the kitchen and bathroom), invariably in porridge-coloured and rather porridge-textured papers enlivened with contrasting borders or framing corners, usually in the thirties' ubiquitous 'autumn tints' of cream, orange, brown, green and red – used on everything: carpets, linoleum, fabrics, pottery and above all wallpaper – either discreetly in a frieze of trailing leaves, vines and flowers or geometric shapes, or more boldly in swirling, jarring 'jazz' patterns (Sandersons offered a huge range of all of these, some expensive). Pasting up corners or contrasting panels as recommended by magazines such as *Ideal Home* and wallpaper manufacturers could be tricky, and usually required the services of a professional decorator – a disincentive for cash-strapped new semi-owners.

Upstairs, as sitting and dining rooms had their matching suites, so did bedrooms. Walnut or maple were favoured for the main bedroom if it could be afforded, the furniture consisting of a bed headboard, wardrobe, chest of drawers and a dressing table with drawers and a mirror, invariably placed in the front window so that what was seen by passers-by was the unattractive back of the mirror. The dressing table might also have a glass top to protect against cosmetic spills, and would be furnished with a matching set of hairbrush, clothes brush, comb, hand mirror, powder bowl and maybe scent spray made in glass and metal or bakelite. This set the tone of the bedroom, which was distinctly 'feminine' (though invariably shared in an average suburban home), with a heavy pelmet, rayon 'damask curtains' and a satin-covered eiderdown (or eiderdowns for the twin beds that were increasingly popular), probably in a shade of pink or peach, stitched in a vaguely Art Deco pattern above a frilled valance-encased bed.

No matter how retrospective the rest of the house, the bathroom would be a temple of modernity, representing most decisively a break with tin baths in front of the kitchen range and outside, shared privies. Almost universally it would have an iron or ceramic low-level, boxed-in bath along one wall, a free-standing pedestal handbasin, both with gleaming chrome taps, a signature repeated in accessories like a toothbrush stand, bath tray and towel rail (which was perhaps even heated). The walls would be tiled in ivory, pale green, pale blue, pink or primrose glazed tiles probably edged with a chequerboard pattern incorporating black and stretching as high up the wall as the owner could afford, with wipeable paper above if that was not all the way. In one corner would be an airing cupboard for towels and sheets, and in another might well stand a cork-topped stool and a glass-topped Lloyd Loom linen basket (made of tightly twisted paper, though you would never have guessed). The lavatory would literally be the 'smallest room', adjacent, containing nothing but the pan, cistern, toilet-paper holder and a cleaning brush – but *separate*.

Not all suburban semis were exactly like this, of course, but almost all would have had a number, if not most, of these elements present. And not all suburban semis fell into the 'Tudorbethan' design mould either – within or without – though most did. Simple, rectilinear, Georgian-style architecture held little appeal for an aesthetic raised in Victorian taste and, despite protestations, reluctant to entirely forgo the excesses that signified status and possession in the nineteenth century, and that could so easily mingle with a generic 'historic' style that elided with elements of ye olde English. In addition, Georgian austerity was irredeemably associated with slum tenements, and to an extent with the plainer, bay-windowless council houses of the 1920s and '30s.

Furthermore, few developers experimented with '*moderne*' houses, those influenced by the Continental Modern Movement buildings to be found in Germany and Holland, and most associated with Walter Gropius and Le Corbusier, which insisted that earlier architectural forms were obsolete, and a new, post-war age required new buildings based on industrial materials and techniques, though in fact using traditional methods and materials, but with some modern-looking flourishes. A few flat-roofed, plain white-walled houses complete with distinctive metal Crittall windows were being put up by spec builders from around 1932. Most were angular boxes, others sinuous and streamlined like small, beached ocean liners or miniaturised sanatoria, their 'sun trap' metal windows curving round the corners of the house.

In 1934 the *Daily Mail* Ideal Home Exhibition at London's Olympia showed a 'Village of Tomorrow', grouping a selection of such houses by a number of builders including Wates, Laing, Berg, Morrells, Davis and Crouch. But it was Haymills, a long-established firm, that had picked up the gauntlet in January that year when it announced that it was about to 'capture the modern spirit' with 'great advances in design, flat roof, soft grey facing brick', in a selection of houses to be built at Wembley Park. Similar *moderne* houses were erected in Hendon and Surbiton (where the developers confidently claimed that they were 'building the house of 1950'). Howard Houses tried to bring such homes within the reach of the less well-off in West Molesey, where in March 1934 a two-to-three-bedroom semi was advertised for £395. It had 'a flat roof [which] offers you a whole floor of extra space, and delightful means to revel out-of-doors . . . easy access to the roof can be arranged. There your children can play in safety and unrestricted sunshine. There you can take your meals in the open, entertain your friends, enjoy the peace of the moonlight, and sleep *al fresco* if you wish.'

It would appear that few wished to sleep *al fresco* in suburban Surrey – maybe mistrusting the promise of 'unrestricted sunshine' – for within twelve months the builders had covered over the delights a flat roof offered with a traditional pitched, tile one, finding the public reluctant to buy and building societies to lend on properties they suspected might have a low resale value. 'Modern' might be all right for factories and cinemas, but a cottage-style semi was what most house-buyers sought in suburbia.

Such a dwelling was not Arcadia, not an aspiration, not a source of contentment to some, however. Rather it was an aesthetic insult, an inexcusable regression, an assault on the very concept of architecture and design. 'A man who builds a bogus Tudoresque villa or castellates his suburban home is committing a crime against truth and tradition: he is denying the history of progress. Denying his own age and insulting the very thing that he pretends to imitate by misusing it,' wrote an architectural critic in 1935.

Two years earlier the International Congress of Modern Architecture (ICAM) held its fourth meeting on the steamship *Partris II* as it sailed from Marseilles to Athens. The British contingent were all members of MARS (Modern Architectural Research): Ernö Goldfinger, F.R.S. Yorke, J. Morton

Shand and Wells Coates, a Canadian living in Britain and a pioneer modernist, and Geoffrey Boumphrey, an engineer. The latter two had, the previous year, debated 'Design in Modern Life' in a series of programmes broadcast by the BBC, and puzzled over why 'people cling to the same old forms in their houses – or what seems still more curious, go even further back . . . to Tudor, or some other "period" – while at the same time they are very careful indeed not to be behind the times in the matter of clothes'. Other luminaries aboard included the French painter Fernand Léger, the Hungarian artist and photographer László Moholy-Nagy, and the Finnish architect and furniture designer Alvar Aalto. As the *Partris II* cleaved through the cerulean blue Mediterranean, those on board attacked suburbia. It was 'the symbol of waste . . . a kind of scum churning against the walls of the city . . . a reproach to the city it surrounds . . . an example of black ugliness'. Garden cities, on which so many suburban estates were modelled, were 'an illusory paradise, an irrational solution . . . urbanistic folly . . . one of the greatest evils of the century' (a century that had seen one world war in which more than eight and three quarter million had been killed, and would in six years bear witness to another).

Back in England, the same thread ran from Anthony Bertram, whose Pelican book *Design* was published in 1938, through to the urbane cartoonist and writer Osbert Lancaster, who mocked 'bypass variegated', writing: 'If an architect of enormous energy, painstaking ingenuity and great structural knowledge, has devoted years of his life to the study of the problem of how best to achieve the maximum of inconvenience, in the shape and arrangement under one roof of a stated number of rooms, and had the assistance of a corps of research workers ransacking architectural history for the least attractive materials and building devices known to man in the past, it is possible, just possible, although highly unlikely, that he might have evolved a style as crazy as that with which the speculative builder, at no expense of mental energy at all, has enriched the landscape on either side of our great arterial roads.' And in the year that the Munich crisis had brought Britain to the brink of war with Germany, Lancaster considered that the destruction of these 'slums of the future' was 'an eventuality that does much to reconcile one to the prospect of aerial bombardment'. Which was what Lancaster's friend John Betjeman, the poet and assistant editor of *Architectural Review*, thought too, gleefully encouraging, 'Come friendly bombs, and fall on Slough,/It isn't fit for humans now' (even if Slough was not, strictly speaking, suburbia).

It is perhaps understandable that architects should decry the thousands and thousands of houses that had been built with little guidance from their profession. 'This was a period in which quantity took absolute precedence over quality,' wrote the architect and planner who in the 1960s was elected President of the Royal Institute of British Architects (RIBA), the architects' professional body, Lionel Brett (later 4th Viscount Esher). 'Practically none of the interminable square-miles of speculative building was planned by architects or with any pretence of consumer consultation, and most of the council housing was little better.'

Most spec building was innocent of architectural plans; the houses were builders' 'potboilers', turned out in a mass pressing from a single (or some-times several) blueprints from the drawing board of a jobbing architect (or builder's draughtsman) with a now unremembered name. Ironically, a criticism often levelled at suburban estates was that they were 'monotonous', whereas in fact they were generally a great deal more varied and haphazard than any austere Georgian terrace, buildings that are still the gold standard for most architects and architectural connoisseurs. Indeed for a trained eye it was the 'accumulation of happy accidents', the sheer asymmetrical variety of styles, the excess of decoration, the functionless inauthenticity of materials – beams not used as part of the structure, but tacked on as pure decoration – the wilful ahistoricism of so many designs that proved such an affront.

But was it only the bay window, the leaded glass, the oversized chimneys, the crazy-paved path, the red pitched roof – even the obviously fake 'Tudor' beams – that were so offensive, so repellent and reprehensible? Or was it also the people that lived in such houses, and what the semi-detached suburban villa represented about their lives, their culture, their aspirations? Was it aesthetic refinement, architectural discernment that was assaulted, or simple social snobbery that made the suburbs seem so contemptible, so undermining?

It might appear so: Hilaire Belloc described

> The miserable sheds of painted tin:
> Gaunt Villas, planted round with stunted trees
> And, God! The dreadful things that dwell within.

For Graham Greene, the red-bricked, Tudor-gabled, half-timbered 'Cozyholmes' 'represented something worse than the meanness of poverty, the meanness of spirit', while John Betjeman's ode to Middlesex mocked:

> Gaily into Ruislip Gardens
> Runs the red electric train
> With a thousand Ta's and Pardon's
> Daintily alights Elaine.

J.M. Richards, reflecting on the suburbs of his homeland, 'part of the background of the England in which we have all grown up', as he saw out the Second World War in Egypt, recognised what was at stake in the contradiction between 'the alleged deficiencies of suburban taste' and

the appeal it holds for ninety out of a hundred Englishmen, an appeal which cannot be explained away as some strange instance of mass aberration . . . We well know the epithets used to revile the modern suburb – "Jerrybethan" and the rest – and the scornful finger that gets pointed at the spec-builder's Tudor [it was not just spec builders who favoured Tudor: many expensive, bespoke houses, blocks of flats, refurbished pubs and hotels, shopping parades, Liberty's department store in Regent Street, golf clubhouses and even a cinema in New Oxted embraced the style too] . . . though perhaps we should not criticize so fiercely the architectural idiom the suburb has adopted as its own if we understand the instincts and ideals it aims to satisfy and how well, judged by its own standards, it often succeeds in doing so . . . If democracy means anything, it means deciding – for a change – to pay some attention to the expressed preference of the majority, to what people themselves want, not what we think they ought to want.

For Richards the suburbs had 'the one quality of all true vernaculars, that of being rooted in people's instincts'. It would seem that one of the compelling instincts, certainly when it came to housing, was the desire to better oneself, and to mark that upward mobility as definitively as possible. As the eminent planning barrister Sir Leslie Scott, a member of the Council for the Preservation of Rural England, lamented in 1936, 'there has been a revolt against the artistically good simplicity of the well-designed Council house . . . This re-action had manifested itself in a demand for the kind of house which is an abomination; a house which is bought just because its exterior is so different from the decent exterior of the Council house that the casual observer must see at a glance that its owner is *not* living in a Council house.' 'Since [council houses] were plain, the [spec] builders made their houses as fancy as they could afford so that there could be no possibility of confusion,' concurred Lionel Brett.

The suburban owner-occupier was not content to be set apart only by architectural features. What was wanted was a more concrete expression: a brick wall, in fact, like the one topped with jagged glass that had been erected by the residents of a private estate at Bromley in Kent in 1926 to keep out those who lived on the neighbouring LCC Downham estate. In 1925 Oxford City Corporation had bought Summertown, some largely agricultural land in North Oxford roughly two and a quarter miles from the city centre. North Oxford was (and is) the posh end of the city: to the east were William Morris's (Lord Nuffield's) Cowley car factories, which had made Oxford prosperous and which by the end of the 1930s employed over 10,000 people, some 30 per cent of Oxford's workforce, many of whom lived near their work. To the north was the city's previous largest single employer, Oxford University Press (labour force around three hundred), and roads of upper-, upper-middle- and middle-class housing, many occupied by dons and their families (once they had been permitted to marry), and a high proportion owned by the university.

In 1931 Oxford City Corporation started to build the Cutteslowe estate, comprising 298 terraced and semi-detached houses, on the land it had purchased in Summertown. A year or so earlier the Corporation had sold the adjacent land to the Urban Housing Company (UHC), and in June 1934 the UHC started to build an estate of 208 semi-detached private houses costing £650 each. Clive Saxon, managing director of UHC, soon complained that building materials were being filched from his site by trespassers from the Cutteslowe estate which was also in the process of construction at the time, and a wooden security fence was erected to keep the intruders out. In December 1934, just as the Corporation's estate was finished and occupied, this temporary fence was replaced by two permanent brick walls, each 'seven feet tall ... supported at intervals by buttresses, and ... topped by a set of revolving iron spikes which ran its entire length'. Thus the residents of the 'highly desirable' private estate, 20 per cent of whom were professional men (and a few women) and only 3 per cent were partly skilled or unskilled workers, were totally segregated from (and could not even see) *hoi polloi* on the council estate a few yards away, none of whom were professionals and 36 per cent of whom were in partly skilled or unskilled occupations. Moreover, the blanking off of the two roads that connected the estates meant that the Cutteslowe residents were obliged to walk an additional 633 yards in order to reach the Banbury Road, where some of them had jobs, there was a frequent bus service, and shops and schools for their children were located. UHC justified its action by citing complaints from residents that the proximity of the council estate was adversely affecting the quality of their lives and the value of their properties, and particularly objecting to the fact that twenty-eight slum-dwelling families (out of a total of 298) had been rehoused on the Cutteslowe estate, reneging, UHC claimed, on a promise made during the negotiations to purchase the land for private development; though, as the Council pointed out, these tenants were perfectly respectable and indistinguishable from the other tenants on the estate.

Led by Abe Lazarus, a young local Communist, trade unionist and political activist who was nicknamed 'Bill Firestone' after he had successfully led a strike at the Firestone Tyre and Rubber Factory at Brentford in July 1933, a committee of Cutteslowe residents was formed, and on 11 May 1935, 2,000 people including Cutteslowe residents and undergraduates wearing red shirts or fancy dress gathered to watch a pantomime recounting a history of the walls, and then, armed with picks, set off to demolish the offending structures. Advised by the police that anyone who tried to do so would be arrested not for attacking the walls but for assaulting the officers who were there to defend them, the demolition party reluctantly retreated.

A Councillor Gill visited the walls and reported to his fellow members: 'There was this high wall with barbed-wire entanglements and behind it, cut off like wild animals or savage creatures, there was a collection of citizens of this city . . . These are the methods of the Stone Age, and this is a country fit for heroes to live in. The people are herded behind walls and barbed wire like Germans in a concentration camp . . . Cost what it may, either in money or effort, we will have to have these walls down.' But that was not going to be easy: legal opinion advised in effect that UHC could do pretty much what it liked with the roads it had built. The only solution seemed to be a Compulsory Purchase Order, partly argued on the grounds that the demolition would provide work for the unemployed of Oxford – of whom there were very few, while the job would hardly have kept those set to do the work off the dole for more than a couple of days.

Nevertheless, the Chief Constable of Oxford strongly supported the application, as did the City Engineer, who reckoned that the walls increased the cost of refuse collection by £16.6s a year, and an additional labour force of one had to be employed to sweep the streets since so much time was wasted – 156 hours a year – walking the long way round from one estate to the other. UHC proved impervious to such compelling practicalities: its intention was primarily to protect the social status of its residents from not very dissimilar people living in rather similar (if plainer and somewhat cheaper) houses a few yards away. If the Cutteslowe residents found the walls 'a perfect insult' to the working classes, the middle-class private estate dwellers avowed that they would find their removal an equal insult. An Oxford undergraduate, called by UHC for its defence, spoke in censorious tones of 'children and dogs everywhere' on the council side of the walls, with 'trees damaged . . . and drawings in chalk executed on the walls'. Since he had purchased his house on the UHC estate with the intention of having somewhere quiet to study, were the walls to be knocked down he would 'without a doubt, have to move'. After some months of deliberation, the

Minister of Transport, Leslie Hore-Belisha, rejected the plea for a Compulsory Purchase Order.

And so the impasse remained: suggestions were made by Hore-Belisha that the Corporation should build its own walls, which might be used as a bargaining ploy to demolish UHC's; Sir Stafford Cripps, who lived in a nearby village, was consulted – though the committee was nonplussed to find that the King's Counsellor's usual minimum fee for a case lasting longer than a day was a thousand guineas, which would almost have enabled him to purchase two houses on the private side of the walls for perhaps two days' labour (before tax, of course), had he the inclination. Cripps advised that, having been built over sewers without permission, the walls contravened a local bylaw. UHC took no notice of the Council's resulting order to demolish.

Finally, it was decided that the Corporation would demolish the walls itself, and if UHC wished to take it to court, the matter could be hammered out there. On 7 June 1938 a municipal steamroller charged the first wall, and the job was completed by Corporation workmen with sledgehammers and chains, and the two halves of the roads joined to form continuous thoroughfares. The next day UHC workmen started to rebuild the walls; the Corporation was alerted and its men arrived with sledgehammers and shovels to knock them down again. The case went to the High Court on 20 July 1939: after a hearing lasting four days, Mr Justice Bennett gave his ruling: Oxford City Corporation had acted illegally. UHC was awarded £180 damages and told it could rebuild the walls, which it did, an expensive appeal against the judgement having failed. During the Second World War a possibly mischievous member of the local Home Guard drove a tank into one of the walls, claiming he thought it was a roadblock, and demolished it. The War Office issued an immediate apology and agreed to pay for the rebuilding.

It was not until 1959, twenty-five years after they had been built, that the Cutteslowe walls were finally demolished. What had formerly been secure cul de sacs for the middle classes and formidable barriers for the working classes were now two ordinary suburban roads. However, one owner-occupier refused permission for the small portion of wall erected in *his* garden to be demolished until the 1980s. All that remains today is a blue plaque marking the site.

THIRTEEN

Grand Designs

Civilisations are rightly judged by their architecture, not because buildings are more permanent than other artistic achievements, but because they represent a greater collective effort. They concern equally the drawing-room and the servants' hall.

W.H. Auden, *Architectural Review*, August 1933

We have got into not one but a thousand battles, left and right, black, red (and white too, for the fools who won't take part and so constitute a battle line all on their own), Hampstead, Bloomsbury, surrealist, abstract, social realist, Spain, Germany, Heaven, Hell, Paradise, Chaos, light, dark, round, square. 'Let me alone – you must be a member – have you got a ticket – have you given a picture – have you seen the *Worker* – do you realize – can you imagine – don't you see you're bound to be implicated – it's a matter of principle. Have you signed the petition – haven't you got a picture more in keeping with our aims – *intellectual freedom*, Freedom, FREEDOM – we must be allowed, we can't be bound – you can't, you must fight – you *must*. That's not abstract, sir – that's not surrealist, sir – that's *not*. Anything will do – send it along . . .

Myfanwy Piper, *The Painter's Object* (1937)

Far better that painters and poets should think of themselves as grocers than that they should think of themselves as seers!

Eric Gill, *Architectural Review*, March 1930

> Art is not life and cannot be
> A midwife to society.
> For art is a fait accompli,
> An abstract model of events
> Derived from dead experiments.

W.H. Auden, 'New Year Letter, 1940'

On the night of 2–3 October 1932 a bastion of tradition, and the authoritative voice of the governing classes, underwent a revolution. *The Times* changed its typeface. Not only did the text look different, the masthead changed too. Out went the heavy old script which the typographer Stanley Morison, who had been appointed to oversee this redesign in 1930 (and who took over the editorship of the *Times Literary Supplement* in 1936), considered had become 'a stale mixed grill of underdone gothick, underdone chinoiserie ... only too consistent with a degenerate background of paste-board pinnacles and bogus [Strawberry Hill] battlements'. In came a type designed expressly for the newspaper – an 'aristocratic type' suitable for a dignified newspaper intended to be read by people with leisure. It was a modernised version of the sixteenth-century Dutch typeface Plantin, Times New Roman, a font still to be found on every computer in the Western world today.

The decision had not been taken lightly: Morison, rightly concerned with what he called 'fundamental ocular laws', had pored over the Medical Research Council's 1926 *Report on the Legibility of Print* and had checked proofs set in the new type with Sir William Lister, the country's leading eye specialist. The debate had raged over months, with Morison on occasion banging his fist on the table in frustration at the conservatism of many on *The Times* who seemed to want a masthead that would resemble (according to him) the label on a bottle of Châteauneuf du Pape. Readers had been given more than a week's notice of the impending change, with two lengthy articles in justification. 'The print of newspapers must change with social habits; and in no period have social habits been more transformed than in our own. In the eighteenth century, *The Times* [or the *Daily Universal Register* as it had been called from its inception until 1787] was largely read in coffee houses; in the nineteenth it came to be read in trains; and in the twentieth it is read in cars and airliners.' Although there were some dissenting voices – including one from a member of the Athenaeum who had been a reader since 1857 – faced with a *fait accompli* most readers proved robust, sending congratulations on the readability of the new design and embracing change cheerfully.

The response must have been a relief to the young and energetic assistant editor (later editor) Robert Barrington-Ward, who had anticipated that such a change would shock the public, 'but the shock would be good ... and however shocked they were, it was highly improbable that readers would cancel their orders on an issue like this ... Altogether it would give the paper a valuable reputation for modernity, taste and efficiency.'

'Modernity, taste and efficiency': these were resolutions that were making waves far beyond the redesign of *The Times* in the 1930s. Modernism found expression in all the visual arts – architecture, design, painting, sculpture, photography, fashion – and spilled into literature, poetry, music, drama, film and psychoanalysis. And modernists equated design with morality, taking a stance, believing that the world could be made a better place. It was the role – more than the role, the duty – of creative people to harness modern knowledge and modern technologies to build that better world, a more 'honest', pared-down, unfussy world free from hypocrisy and illusion in which mankind could function better, live more equitably. The word 'modernism' took on a proselytising hue for those committed to its project, colonising education, religion, politics, sex. On the ruins of a world ravaged by war, tarnished by an uneasy peace, sullied by a clearly malfunctioning society – 'The old forms are in ruins, the benumbed world is shaken up, the old human spirit is invalidated and in flux towards a new form. We float in space and cannot perceive the new order,' as the architect Walter Gropius put it – the new, the functional, the efficient, the rethought were proving compelling. To paraphrase Stanley Morison, there were to be no more Chippendale chairs dominating the living room of modernity. But while for the majority who had neither modern living rooms nor any Chippendale chairs to put in them, modernism might hardly colour their world, better lives for these 'masses' were theoretically always in the forefront of the minds of the progressive 'grand designers' of modernism, even if most of their designs seemed to circulate only amongst themselves.

There was to be one thing in *The Times* that would not change: 'The "Perpetua" capitals cut from a design by Mr Eric Gill and adopted from December 28 1929 for the main heading of the picture page, could not be surpassed.' It was Morison who had persuaded his friend, the free-thinking engraver and sculptor Eric Gill (with whom he shared the favours of the so-called 'Queen of Typography', Beatrice Warde), that the typefaces he designed and cut laboriously by hand – particularly Perpetua and the continuingly popular Gill Sans – could be adapted for Monotype machines, an invention at the end of the nineteenth century as decisive to letter design as Gutenberg's press had been in the fifteenth century.

In 1930 the BBC had relocated to Portland Place near London's Oxford Circus from its original home, Savoy Hill, off The Strand. Writing in the London *Evening Standard*, Harold Nicolson enthused about the new building, the architect Val Myer's solution to the difficult task of fitting a pod representing the latest in technological communication in with John Nash's surrounding Georgian buildings:

In a few weeks this mass of Portland stone will terminate in three iron masts recalling such modern conceptions as Meccano, a battleship of the US navy or even the Funkturm of Berlin . . . The new headquarters of the BBC are sparing in their use of decoration . . . above the entrance, immediately below the centralised window of the Director General will stand a statue of Prospero and Ariel, fresh from the chisel of Mr Eric Gill. ['Who are Prospero and Ariel?' Gill had queried, 'and why are they appropriate to the BBC?' He wondered if maybe it was some sort of pun on 'Ariel' and 'aerial'.] For the BBC worship beauty only if it be in harmony with purpose, even as they philosophise without a touch of the effeminate. The new palace is expressive of these ideals. Stark it may be, but oh! how strong! how true!

However modern the new communications hub was, Gill sat out the months working on the front of the BBC like a medieval stonemason, perched on scaffolding and chipping away at the massive stone figures (Ariel was largely modelled on the actor Leslie French, who was playing the part in Shakespeare's *The Tempest* at the Old Vic at the time). Wearing knee-high socks and a belted smock, Gill was dubbed the 'Married Monk' by the popular press. It was observed from below that he wore no underpants as he worked. When the sculpture was finished, the BBC governors, invited behind a tarpaulin to view the figures, were shocked at the size of Ariel's genitals and requested that they should be reduced before the figures were exposed to the public gaze.

Since Gill's sculpture was public art viewed by all who passed by, rather than seen by appreciative art lovers in a gallery, it was likely to arouse strong feelings – as had the work of his fellow sculptor Jacob Epstein, culminating in his massive *Night and Day*, commissioned by Frank Pick for the new London Underground headquarters, 55 Broadway by St James's Park station, designed by Charles Holden and built in 1928–29 (this also required genital modification). Writing in the London *Evening News*, the President of the RIBA, Sir Reginald Blomfield, was particularly vitriolic about Epstein's figure: 'bestiality still lurks below the surface of our civilization, but . . . why parade it in the open, why not leave it to wallow in its own primeval slime?' Subsequent statues met with similar abuse. The robust G.K. Chesterton found himself 'outraged' by Epstein's *Ecce Homo* (1934–35), while, with the popular press's usual sensitive appreciation of non-traditional arts, the *Daily Express* jibbed at the heavily pregnant *Genesis* (1930–31) as 'Epstein's Bad Joke in Stone', the *Daily Telegraph* called it 'Unfit to Show', and the *Daily Mail* 'a simian-like creature whose face suggests, if anything, the missing link', while the Mothers' Union regarded it as 'an open insult to motherhood'.

While Epstein and Gill's graphic, flamboyant, large-scale portrayals of nudity and sexuality might well have been offensive to some (and there was often also an unpleasant undercurrent of anti-Semitism in attacks on Epstein), they were emblematic of a deep and jagged fissure that had opened up in the arts between the 'modernists' and those whose tastes and beliefs were more traditional. Indeed, RIBA's Sir Reginald Blomfield was the author of a book, *Modernismus*, published in 1934, a pugnacious, if sometimes witty, attack on Continental modernism (though Blomfield's position on the matter was somewhat compromised by his acceptance of a post advising the Central Electricity Board on the design of their pylons – the perfect modernist icon).

For the modernists such attacks were hardly surprising. In their view British art since the Post-Impressionist exhibition in 1910, organised by the Bloomsbury art critic Roger Fry, which had been its 'shock of the new' moment, had become anodyne, 'lukewarm', lacking in 'criticism of life', according to Kenneth Clark, Director of the National Gallery. Watered-down English versions of the French Post-Impressionists by painters such as Vanessa Bell, her husband Clive and her lover Duncan Grant, dominated the London Group with their soft, pleasing landscapes, still lifes and portraits of each other, and were popular with the general public – though the most enduring 'Bloomsbury portrait' is possibly that of J.M. Keynes and his wife the ballerina Lydia Lopokova by something of an outsider, the working-class artist William Roberts, Britain's 'only cubist', whose work was much in the style of Léger. Likewise, the annual Royal Academy Summer Exhibition, 'the art event of the year' for public and critics alike, still tended to select works of 'pedestrian naturalism' such as the horse paintings of the RA's President, Sir Alfred Munnings, the circus pictures of Dame Laura Knight or the work of the Cornish artist Dod Procter (whose painting of a Newlyn fisherman's daughter, Cissie Barnes, dreaming on her bed at dawn, had caused such a stir that the *Daily Mail* had responded by buying it for the nation).

When in June 1931 the *Architectural Review*, the mouthpiece of architectural modernism in the thirties, provocatively quizzed a number of painters and sculptors about whether they had or ever would submit their work to be hung in the Summer Exhibition, the replies were unequivocal, from Rex Whistler (whose evocative eighteenth-century-style murals graced the Tate Gallery's tea room) to Mark Gertler (a vivid Expressionist painter whose patron was Lady Ottoline Morrell): no. The Vorticist artist and writer Wyndham Lewis, who had parodied the London literary and artistic scene with cruel portraits of Vanessa and Clive Bell and other Bloomsberries as well as the three Sitwells, Osbert, Sacheverell and Edith, in his savage satire *The Apes of God*, published in 1930, was affronted even to be asked, since he regarded himself as 'a one-man show'. The sculptor Frank Dobson thought 'The Institution should be allowed to die,' while Henry Moore opined that 'The sculpture at the RA is of an even lower standard than the painting.' Paul Nash, who had made his reputation as a war artist in the First World War (and would be one again in the Second), and had recently been working on the design of a sumptuous ultra-modern bath-room for the Viennese dancer Tilly Losch in Wimpole Street, in which a motif of Losch's wet feet had been woven into the carpet, thought it would just be too confusing to include 'one, or even a few "modern" paintings among "Academy" paintings'. A *salon des refusés* was clearly on the cards.

In June 1933, Nash took action. In a letter to *The Times* he announced the formation of Unit One, a group of artists in whose work could be found 'the expression of a truly contemporary spirit, for that thing which is recognized as peculiarly *of today* in painting, sculpture and architecture'. The art critic, poet and writer Herbert Read, who edited the *Burlington Magazine* from 1933, was one of the group, which included Ben Nicholson (who had been a member of the *avant garde* Seven and Five Society, which at his insistence in 1931 expelled all artists considered too staid, and introduced an abstract art-only rule), Edward Burra, Nash, the sculptors Henry Moore and Barbara Hepworth, Wells Coates, an engineer who had designed buildings but had never trained as an architect, and the architect Colin Lucas. Read explained that Unit One, the name of which fused the individual and the social, 'did not stand for any new principle in art'. Nash agreed: 'It was to be a small group of painters and sculptors [and architects] each of whom was making an individual contribution to contemporary art and yet all of whom shared certain qualities which seem to unite them. Exactly what these qualities are was not easy to define' – though one of the things that united the members might have been proximity, since most of them lived in Hampstead in North London, the 'Nest of Gentle Artists', Read dubbed it, paraphrasing Turgenev. The 'nest' accommodated Moore, Nicholson and Hepworth (they married in 1938) and Read himself, all of whom had homes and studios in the same road, while Stanley Spencer, Adrian Stokes, Roland Penrose (who, to the chagrin of his neighbours, had one of Moore's abstract statues in his front garden) and by the mid-1930s émigré artists fleeing persecution in Nazi Germany, all settled in the same postal district.

For Herbert Read, art wasn't just about production: the artist 'must also be a propagandist of his painting . . . he must devise subtle and . . .

suggestive means of arousing an interest in the always apathetic public'. One way of doing this was 'to join together in a band: a band of instrumentalists not only makes more noise than a solo player – it can do interesting things which cannot be done by the players separately . . . though the essential bond in such a unit is spiritual'.

The band or bond was not to last long: to coincide with the publication of its manifesto, Unit One held its first and only exhibition in April 1934 at the Mayor Gallery in Cork Street, which had been opened the previous year as a venue for contemporary art. An abridged version of the exhibition then toured the country, bringing the experience of contemporary art to the (not always fully appreciative) citizens of Liverpool, Manchester, Hanley, Derby, Swansea and Belfast. However, 'Whether we like it or not, there is a great change taking place in our ideas of design, and not a town or village in the country is escaping it . . . we are in the midst of a new movement,' the *Derbyshire Advertiser* recognised, insisting portentously that 'Least of all can those in business, manufacture or trade afford to ignore modern art.'

Unit One dissolved in 1935, but its members went on to be significant forces in British art, and to take it in new directions. The two major directions (which Unit One had straddled) were abstraction and Surrealism. Abstract art was defined by Herbert Read in *Art Now* (1933), the first comprehensive defence in English of modern European art, as work that possesses 'an aesthetic unity in no sense relying on an objective equivalence'.

Ben Nicholson, the son of the distinguished painter and woodcut printer Sir William Nicholson, exhibited several of his 'White Reliefs' at the second abstract art exhibition to be held in London, in April 1936, displayed alongside sculptures by Barbara Hepworth and Henry Moore, paintings by John Piper and Eileen Holding and the work of famous European artists such as Piet Mondrian, Fernand Léger, Joan Miró, László Moholy-Nagy, Naum Gabo and the American Alexander Calder. Nicholson's geometric monotone carved works divided those who saw them as 'preparing the death rites of painting', devoid of feeling, a 'lavatory art form, clean antiseptic bathroom art', and those who thought they 'explored the potentialities of light' and represented 'a world of absolute and permanent values placed above the shifting world of appearances and free from all the arbitrariness of life'.

In June 1936, two months after the abstract show, the International Surrealist Exhibition opened in London, representing what seemed to be the polar opposite of abstract art. An import from Paris (André Breton's first *Surrealist Manifesto* had been published there in 1924), Surrealism exhibited a fascination with the bizarre, the incongruous and the irrational, its plot being 'to reveal the images we all censor within ourselves'. 'How many Surrealists does it take to change a lightbulb?' 'A fish.'

'Do not judge this movement kindly,' Herbert Read wrote in the catalogue to the 1936 exhibition. 'It is defiant – the desperate act of men too profoundly convinced of the rottenness of our civilization to want to save a shred of its respectability.' It was not simply a question of a new aesthetic (though as Read pointed out, 'a nation which has produced two such surrealists as William Blake and Lewis Carroll is to the manner born'), but a series of strategies the anarchistic purpose of which was to jar, to jog, to shock the observer out of easy complacencies, to upend society: many of the French Surrealists were members of the Communist Party, which was then Trotskyist. The Surrealist artist had a moral and political duty to 'precipitate revelation by any method, no matter how violent, in order to start a vertiginous descent into the hidden territories of the subconscious' – to 'extend the possible', in Breton's words.

In Britain the 'spectral voices' of Surrealism brought together a diverse group of people. Paul Nash, John Armstrong and Tristram Hillier from Unit One (Henry Moore had a brief engagement too), Roland Penrose, who had studied in Paris and found the 'glittering treasure' of Surrealism there, as had Julian Trevelyan, the artist scion of a distinguished family of historians, John Banting (a 'wild creature at this time [sometimes dyeing his hair green and cutting off the toes of his shoes so his painted toenails peeped through], dancing in night clubs all night and creeping home to his mother's house in Roehampton by the first Underground') and Eileen Agar, whose *Quadriga*, which challenged the way Westerners read from left to right, was one of the four paintings chosen by Read and Penrose for the Surrealists Exhibition in London. The poet David Gascoyne, who wrote the *First Manifesto of English Surrealism* – in French – in 1935, and whose *A Short Survey of Surrealism* was published six months later (Cyril Connolly considered it to be 'one of the prettiest books of the year'), followed by a collection of poems with the Surrealistic title *Man's Life is This Meat* in 1936; Hugh Sykes Davies, a Cambridge don with interests in Freudian theory and dialectical materialism whose 'strange indefinable text' *Petron* resonates with Surrealistic images of sacks of butterflies and a man who has string passed through his head and out through his nostrils and sculpts his own face with a mallet and chisel; the documentary film-makers Len Lye and Humphrey Jennings, who also painted and used photomontage techniques in constructions such as *Mountain Inn and Swiss Roll* (1936). And there was the immensely rich patron of the arts Edward James (by 1936 the ex-husband of Tilly Losch after a sensational, contested divorce case), who liked to hint that his father *might* have been Edward VII, and who had published John Betjeman's poems *Mount Zion* with a dramatically experimental typographical dust jacket in 1931. Although it is the back of James' head that features (twice) in René Magritte's painting *La Réproduction interdite* ('Not to be Reproduced'), commissioned in 1937, his connection was particularly with Salvador Dalí, who referred to him as a 'humming-bird poet', and many of whose finest paintings James bought. It was with James that Dalí constructed two of the most enduring Surrealist assemblages, the aphrodisiac *Lobster Telephone* and a luscious shiny pink satin sofa made in the shape of Mae West's lips. James once sealed a contract with Dalí by sending him a stuffed polar bear.

James commissioned Ben Nicholson's younger brother, the architect Christopher (Kit) and his young colleague Hugh Casson to 'cope with the architectural execution' of a Surrealistic patina as envisaged by Dalí for the Lutyens-designed holiday home Monkton House on the South Downs in Sussex that he had inherited. Dalí suggested that the exterior walls should be painted puce (which they were), and that one room should be painted red and made to pulsate to suggest a panting (or retching) dog. James, seeking authenticity, wanted the walls to be coated in dogs' hair, but as Casson, who gamely experimented with 'walls made of rubber sheets which contracted and expanded irregularly by means of compressed air jets', later explained, 'It would be easy today, but we didn't have suitable materials then.' However, if there was to be no dog's stomach simulacrum, James did get two carved wooden palm trees to flank the front door that were so tall that the roofline had to be raised to accommodate them, carved wooden panels representing laundry hung out to dry beneath the upper windows, bamboo drainpipes, one chimney converted into a clock that told the days of the week, concealed speakers that wafted music across the lawns, and, inside, a huge sweeping staircase with a porthole aquarium set in the wall, which might also afford 'a glimpse of people bathing as you ascended the staircase'. Rather more Brighton Pavilion than Surrealism, remarked James's biographer sniffily.

But the project did not stop there: in April 1937 the Georgian Group had been established (as part of the Society for the Protection of Ancient Buildings) in a small office in Cork Street lent by the architect Basil Ionides, in an attempt to halt 'the tide of careless destruction that is daily menacing the architectural beauties of our country', as a concerned young peer put it in the House of Lords. Nash's Regent Street Quadrant had already been rebuilt in 1928 (to the designs of Reginald Blomfield, who wanted to demolish

Carlton House Terrace but was thwarted by a campaign orchestrated by the *Architectural Review*), Lewis Vulliamy's 1840 *palazzo* in Park Lane had been replaced by the reinforced-concrete luxury Dorchester Hotel which opened in April 1931, and in 1936 the Adelphi, the magnificent terrace of houses fronting the Thames, had been demolished in order to build an office block. Waterloo Bridge, completed in 1817 to the designs of John Rennie, which the Italian sculptor Antonio Canova had considered 'the noblest bridge in the world . . . alone worth coming to London to see', was now a mountain of debris on the Embankment, and the British Museum had put in a planning application to redevelop the entire east side of Bedford Square, considered the finest example of Georgian town planning. Predictably, the Group's supporters included James Lees-Milne and John Betjeman (and an early Betjeman love, 'Billa' Harrod), but then Cresswell – formerly of the Council for the Protection of Rural England – was appointed its secretary. One of its first projects was to save the façade of the Pantheon in Oxford Street, designed in 1772 by James Wyatt. In the onwards march of commerce, the building had been sold in 1937 for a new branch of Marks & Spencer, which had agreed to remove the façade and contribute £200 towards its relocation. Edward James excitedly claimed it for one of his homes, West Dean in Sussex, and Nicholson and Casson drew up plans for its incorporation into a new bailiff's house on the estate with androgynous caryatids designed by John Piper without, and effects that included the hanging of an entire bearskin within. It was not to be: war, money, and the difficulty of finding anyone who wished to live in such a 'freak house' put paid to the grand design.

Opening the International Surrealist Exhibition at the New Burlington Galleries on 11 June 1936, André Breton, dressed entirely in green, declared that a revolution in the relationship between perception and representation was taking place 'around the visitors'. Twenty-seven of the artists represented were British (out of a total of sixty-nine: 'The English contribution is comparatively tentative,' admitted Herbert Read, but he was sure that British artists 'may recover . . . the courage of their instincts').

Since there was no Surrealist group in existence in England prior to the exhibition, the organisers, Read and Roland Penrose, had to make the decision as to who was a Surrealist and who was not. The pair selected three paintings of Julian Trevelyan's, 'and so, overnight, so to speak I became a surrealist', while rejecting the work of Francis Bacon, who they decided was 'not sufficiently *surreal* for inclusion'. The catalogue cover was designed by the German artist Max Ernst, who had settled in France, finding that Surrealism had rather failed to take root in his native soil. The 'surrealist phantom' Sheila Legge, 'an attractive girl . . . who became for a while a sort of mascot of the Surrealist group', and who had been photographed feeding the pigeons in Trafalgar Square to publicise the exhibition, came to the opening wearing the same long white satin dress, her face entirely obscured by roses and dotted with ladybirds – an idea David Gascoyne had adapted from Dalí. It had been intended that she should wander round carrying a pork chop, but the weather was so hot that that was disposed of, and instead she carried an artificial leg wearing a silk stocking. The poet Dylan Thomas went from guest to guest offering teacups full of boiled string, enquiring, 'Do you like it weak or strong?' In a Surrealistic gesture of his own, the composer William Walton pinned a kipper onto one of Miró's paintings, but Paul Nash removed it because the smell threatened to overpower the occasion. Herbert Read stood on a sofa to lecture on 'Art and the Unconscious', while Hugh Sykes Davies remained on the floor to discourse on 'Surrealism and Biology'.

Salvador Dalí, who had been staying in the country with the designer and photographer Cecil Beaton, and had already had several Surrealistic moments, playing a piano in a swimming pool, the black keys replaced by chocolate éclairs, arrived later wearing a deep-sea diving suit lent to him by the composer, writer and aesthete Lord Berners (since he intended to make a dive into the unconscious, 'plunging down deeply into the human mind'), accompanied by two white wolfhounds or borzoi (depending on the observer) and clutching a billiard cue, with a jewelled sword in his belt, to give a lecture entitled 'Authentic Paranoiac Pleasures' about a philosophy student who had taken six months to eat a mirror wardrobe. Unfortunately it was almost impossible to hear what he was saying, so Edward James, sitting in the front row, had to translate. And for some time no one realised that Dalí was suffocating and was unable to unscrew his helmet. A spanner was fetched, but proved useless; in the nick of time a workman hammered off the catch, and James prised off the helmet using Dalí's billiard cue. Dalí continued his presentation by showing slides, some sideways, a few the right way up, but most upside down.

The exhibition was a great success, and turned in a profit, since 23,000 visitors came in the heat to gaze at the 360 paintings, including Man Ray's pair of red lips floating above a landscape, sculptures, drawings, collages, photographs, children's drawings (including one by 'Freddy' entitled *The Water Mug Gets Lost in the Playground*), 'the powerful biomorphic sculptures of Henry Moore', 'the sinister creations of Edward Burra', several African and Oceanic artefacts, two walking sticks, Meret Oppenheimer's fetishistic *Fur-Covered Cup, Saucer and Spoon*, Dalí's *Aphrodisiac's Waistcoat*, an old tailcoat with 'lots of little glasses of *crème de menthe* sewn all over it', and Eileen Agar's collection of *objets trouvés*, rusted metal, shells, bits of driftwood and netting, most of which she had found while out walking on the beach with Paul Nash, with whom she was conducting a passionate extra-marital affair (adulterous on his part too) in Swanage in Dorset, which Nash found had 'a strange fascination, like all things which combine beauty, ugliness and the power to disquiet', a location that transformed them both into 'seaside surrealists'.

The newspapers were entirely nonplussed and mostly hostile, writing of madness and 'meaninglessness for the sake of meaninglessness', 'a travesty of everything that's decent'. Clergyman called for a ban, J.B. Priestley spoke of 'moral perversions', while the *Daily Worker* sternly admonished, 'The general impression one gets is that here is a group of young people who haven't the guts to tackle anything seriously.'

The Surrealists continued to meet in Roland Penrose's house and in various studios, planning further exhibitions and other activities: 'for we never tired of pointing out that Surrealism was not a way of painting, but a way of living'. But though the word 'surreal' entered the language, it was usually used to mean bizarre and inexplicable, rather than a subversively and erotically revolutionary means of liberating the subconscious. And the Surrealist movement was seen as socially irresponsible and a bit silly, rather than at the cutting edge of radical politics, self-advertisement rather than transforming profundity. But several of the Surrealists, including Julian Trevelyan, had strong left-wing political engagement and a commitment to change, and the European irrationality that had its dress rehearsal in the same year as the Surrealist Exhibition could make the anxious disorienta-tion the Surrealists produced by their metaphors seem tragically apposite, even if it 'lost much of its impetus during the [Second World] War. It became absurd to compose Surrealist confections when high explosives could do it so much better, and when German soldiers with Tommy-guns descended from the clouds on parachutes dressed as nuns,' thought Trevelyan.

But, as Kenneth Clark pointed out, however publicity-attracting and skirmish-involving they were, Surrealists, abstractionists, all were a 'small clique', while for the young art historian Anthony Blunt such work was 'the affair of a small minority [who have] cut themselves off from the wide public among the bourgeoisie. They have, of course, lost all contact with the proletariat.' Some other artists were very anxious to reconnect. The slump had made William Coldstream 'aware of social problems, and I became convinced that art ought to be directed to a wider public . . . it seemed to me important that the broken communication between the artists and the public should be built up again and this most probably implied a movement towards realism'.

Coldstream had trained as a painter at the Slade under Henry Tonks, but by 1930 he had decided that film was a medium better able to communicate his social concerns, so he joined the GPO Film Unit, where he worked under John Grierson, as did Len Lye, an experimental film-maker who had been one of the exhibitors at the International Surrealist Exhibition. In 1935 Coldstream edited *Coal Face*, a short, stark documentary about the bleak conditions in the Welsh mining valleys with music by Benjamin Britten and words written and spoken by W.H. Auden – 'O lurcher-loving collier, black as night'. Britten and Auden also collaborated on the GPO Unit's most famous production, *Night Mail*, made in 1936, and planned a film about the slave trade using African artefacts from the British Museum, but it was never made.

Auden had advised a schoolboy would-be film-maker, Lawrence Gowing, 'You only want to become a film director because you think it is the art of the future. It isn't. Art is the art of the future,' and he also discouraged Coldstream from the same perception. With his friend and impecunious fellow artist the South African-born Graham Bell, Coldstream devised 'A Plan for Artists', which proposed a movement to combat 'the influence of Paris [in abstract and Surrealistic art] which had become almost a tyranny', and which Coldstream regarded as a 'dead end', with a return to rendering on canvas exactly what the painter saw in the real world, in street and café scenes, in still lifes and portraits. This plan was submitted to Kenneth Clark whose response was to create a fund offering modest financial support to struggling artists, to enable them to escape the economic pressures that might otherwise oblige them to produce formulaic work that would sell.

Out of this grew a school which opened on 4 October 1937 in London's Fitzrovia, and moved to a vacant car showroom in the Euston Road in February 1938. The 'Euston Road School' was named partly in homage to – and was down the road from – the Camden Town School of Walter Sickert, an artist much admired by Coldstream. The director was Claude Rogers (who was teaching at the new Raynes Park School for Boys, where Paul Vaughan was one of his suburban pupils), and the other artists, all of whom had been forced by economic hardship to earn their livings by taking part-time work, included Coldstream and Victor Pasmore (who had been working as a clerk in the LCC, and only painting at weekends until he received a stipend from Clark). Graham Bell, whose patron and landlord Clark became, was a close supporter and an inspiration, as was Clive Bell, while Vanessa

Bell and Duncan Grant both taught occasionally. Lawrence Gowing, taking Auden's advice, proved an outstandingly talented pupil. All were committed to 'training the observation', and all (Graham Bell to the greatest extent) to making their art accessible to the ubiquitous 'man in the street'.

While working at the GPO Film Unit, Coldstream had met Humphrey Jennings, and in April 1938 he and Bell spent three weeks in Bolton with Jennings closely observing that (largely working-class) 'man in the street' under the direction of the ornithologist turned anthropologist Tom Harrisson, who with Jennings and Charles Madge had founded an innovative people-watching (and listening-to) organisation, Mass-Observation, in 1937. Their intention had been for volunteer 'researchers' to 'collect a mass of data based on practical observation, on the everyday life of all types of people'. The data-collecting must have mostly been fun: it included observing such things as 'Behaviour of people at war memorials, Shouts and gestures of motorists, Female taboos about eating, The aspidistra cult, Anthropology of football pools, Beards, armpits, eyebrows, Distribution, diffusion and the significance of the dirty joke', though other subjects such as anti-Semitism, sadly a widespread and cross-class phenomenon at the time, and later people's attitudes to the threat of war, would have been less fun. This data was supposed to provide the raw material for 'the scientific study of Twentieth-century man in all his environments', which it didn't, but it did produce a series of vivid insights into the lives of ordinary people (largely working-class people, since these were in the main the subjects of the largely middle-class observers) that added up to an informal and historically invaluable 'anthropology of ourselves' from the late 1930s through the war years.

The Old Harrovian Harrisson had already 'gone native' and, like so many other thirties observers, gone north, his anthropological fieldwork involving working an eleven-hour day in a cotton mill in Bolton for twenty-seven shillings a week, selling ice creams in the street and other casual jobs, and spending his evenings in the pub or at political meetings. It was decided that 'Worktown', the generic name Bolton was given in M-O reports, should become the Northern outpost for the first M-O survey. Harrisson was joined by a variety of usually unpaid 'participant observers' to watch, eavesdrop and compile statistics on such subjects of moment as how long it took to drink a pint of beer.

These observers included, on occasions, Humphrey Spender, the photographer brother of the poet Stephen, who worked for the *Daily Mirror* until he joined the new illustrated, socially aware magazine *Picture Post* in 1938.

Spender 'saw in the cotton workers of Bolton the descendents of Stephenson and Watt, the dwellers in Blake's dark satanic mills reborn into a world of greyhound racing and Marks & Spencer . . . His interest was intense but not long-lived.' Another was Julian Trevelyan, who made collages of what he saw out of 'newspapers, copies of *Picture Post*, seed catalogues, old bills, coloured paper', which tended to blow about in the wind as he gummed them onto the paper while sitting in the open air between the cotton mills and a reservoir, watched by the occasional 'suspicious and reserved' Boltonian. Trevelyan also kept a day diary for M-O, as did William Coldstream, noting such matters as smoking, drinking, bus journeys and superstition. The poet and literary critic William Empson, whose influential book *Seven Types of Ambiguity* had been published in 1930 when he was only twenty-four, was dispatched to report on the displays in sweetshop windows, and the future politician and journalist, then an Oxford undergraduate, Woodrow Wyatt, as well as two other future politicians, Richard Crossman and Tom Driberg (who was also a gossip columnist on the *Daily Express* under the name 'William Hickey'), came and went.

In April 1938 Coldstream and Bell had been invited to take part in one of Harrisson's Mass-Observation experiments to test the public's reaction to art by painting the 'honest, unvarnished scenery of soot and factory, cobbled street and washing hung out at the back' in Bolton with the unswerving veracity for which they were known. The artists set up their easels on the roof of the municipal art gallery – Coldstream closing one eye to help him represent three dimensions as a flat image – and produced two panoramic views of the town. Harrisson's intention was to bridge the gap between the artist and 'the wider public', and to test whether that public would really rather have paintings of 'Highland Cattle in the Scottish dawn' on its sitting room walls than anything more contemporary.

The two paintings (Bell referred to his as a 'squalorscape') were photographed and passed round the pubs, working-men's clubs, dance halls and barber shops to find out what Boltonians thought of the realist view of their empty streets and belching chimneys. They were not 'particularly smitten'. 'It certainly looks like a distressed area,' said one man. 'We're dead, we are! Our people are dead! It must be the two minutes' silence,' was an elderly woman's response. Bell concluded: '(1) The Boltonians are not interested in art (2) but they are interested in Bolton.' However, Trevelyan's vivid collages appealed more (even if some thought them 'plain daft'), though he suspected that this might be because people liked the idea of newspapers with stories about royalty being torn up and used to represent Bolton's cobblestone streets.

Anthony Blunt, writing his art critic's column in the *Spectator*, recognised that 'In art, as in morals, honesty is often unexciting at first sight. But the test comes not at the first, but the fiftieth hour; and it is not obvious which will look duller then – a Picasso or a Coldstream.' The Euston Road School did not survive long enough to see. It was closed on the outbreak of war, though at Kenneth Clark's instigation a small 'Members of the Euston Road Group' exhibition was mounted in Oxford in 1942. The artists dispersed: Pasmore was imprisoned for a time as a Conscientious Objector, Bell was killed in 1943 when his Wellington bomber crashed on landing, and Coldstream became an official war artist, as, briefly, did Claude Rogers.

While Trevelyan had never really left Surrealism (and in a sense he took it to war in his work in camouflage, in which he disguised one thing – a gun emplacement, say – as another – a public lavatory, a seaside café or a chicken coop), Jennings left M-O because he felt that Harrisson had moved it too far away from the Surrealist undertow, which had been implicit from its inception in its exploration of England's collective unconscious, towards the 'scientific'. But both the Surrealists and what might be seen to be their antithesis, the Euston Road School, were in dialogue with a social realist organisation, Artists' International. There was a joint meeting between the Marxist AI (renamed the Artists' International Association by then) and the Surrealists during the International Surrealist Exhibition in June 1936 at which Anthony Blunt had replied to a paper given by Herbert Read stressing the materialist and revolutionary tendencies in Surrealism.

The AI was a collection of social realists who extolled art as a weapon in the class struggle. It had been started in 1933 by a group including the advertising illustrator Clifford Rowe, who had been a member of a similar group in Moscow, the stained-glass artist and ceramicist Pearl Binder, who had a lifelong fascination with pearly kings and queens and settled in London's East End the better to study them (and who in 1937 married Elwyn Jones, who in 1974 would become Lord Chancellor in Harold Wilson's second Labour government), and the art critic Francis Klingender. As well as publishing a collection of essays, *Revolutionary Art*, to which Eric Gill and Herbert Read contributed, and providing savage cartoons for *Left Review*, the definitive magazine of the British left in the 1930s, the group produced leaflets, pamphlets and placards, and put on street puppet shows during May Day celebrations, all to give them 'the experience we need of direct contact with the masses'.

In 1935, the year Mussolini invaded Abyssinia, the AI softened its hard line somewhat, added 'Association' to its name, and appointed an advisory board – that probably never met – of such art luminaries as Vanessa Bell,

Duncan Grant, Eric Gill, Jacob Epstein, Herbert Read, Augustus John, Dame Laura Knight, Henry Moore and Paul Nash in the cause of unity against a greater threat, and organised a broad-based exhibition, 'Artists Against Fascism and War', in Soho Square in November. The art was realist, the 350 exhibitors a mixture of professional artists and amateurs, photographers and illustrators, cartoonists and designers, including miner-painters from the Ashington Group. One emblematic exhibit was the wealthy, Marxist, Slade-trained painter Clive Branson's *faux* primitive work *Selling the Daily Worker Outside the Projectile Engineering Works*. Six thousand visitors came.

When the 'Euston Roaders' had contributed to an exhibition of paintings of London held in Nottingham in 1938, which included Lawrence Gowing's painting of a red London bus going past the draper's shop in Mare Street, Hackney, above which he had been born, they were so anxious to ensure that the general public saw their work as well as the 'connoisseurs' that they sent out invitations to the private view to everyone whose name was Brown (or it might have been Green) in the Post Office directory.

Art was also seen outside a tight London circle in the form of murals, which became so prevalent in the 1930s that the Tate Gallery (its name had been changed from the National Gallery of British Art in honour of its founder, the sugar magnate Henry Tate, in 1932, after it had acquired a significant collection of modern art) mounted an exhibition, Mural Painting in Great Britain, 1919–39, in the early summer of 1939. Chelmsford Town Hall had a series depicting 'John Ball Leading the Peasant Rising' painted by Bernard Fleetwood-Walker in 1938. In 1933 Stanley Spencer executed a number of paintings for the Burghclere Memorial Chapel near Newbury, in memory of those who had been killed in the First World War. Frank Brangwyn, a prolific muralist, had been commissioned to produce a series of panels for the House of Lords commemorating those peers who had lost their lives in the war, but his initial attempts were considered too grimly realistic, and his second, including tropical fruit and vegetation, suggesting the colonies and the losses they had suffered, as merely flamboyantly decorative. The Corporation of Swansea (Brangwyn was of Welsh origin) finally bought them to display in the Guildhall.

Holiday-makers could take tea and scones beneath murals of seaside panoramas by day and night painted in 1932 by Eric Ravilious and his wife Tirzah on the curved walls of the new Midland Railway Hotel at Morecambe Bay. The hotel, for which the architect Oliver Hill had also designed much of the furniture and Marion Dorn the carpets, also boasted carvings of seahorses and *Odysseus and Nausicaa* a by Eric Gill, with an inscription from

Wordsworth, who had lived nearby. Unfortunately the white modernist building soon proved unequal to the rainswept Lancashire coast: the flat roof leaked, the walls subsided and cracks appeared in Ravilious' murals, which he had to repaint.

Ravilious, Edward Bawden and Cyril Mahoney painted murals depicting scenes from Elizabethan and Jacobean drama on the canteen walls of Morley College for Working Men and Women in Lambeth in South London. Between 1933 and 1936 Mahoney supervised Evelyn Dunbar, a recent graduate from the Royal College of Art, painting a series of murals at Brockley County School for Boys in Lewisham, South-East London. These depicted Aesop's fables, located in the Kentish countryside, as well as a panorama of the school, the largest of which was nearly forty feet wide and took a whole year to complete. Though hardly for the general public, Rex Whistler added Plas Newydd, the country seat of the 6th Marquess of Anglesey, to his list of mural sites that included the Tate tea room, painting a massive work depicting an Arcadian coastline incorporating coded references to Whistler's passion for the Marquess's eldest daughter, Lady Caroline. Doris Zinkeisen, a Scottish artist, painted a thousand-foot square mural on the subject of *Entertainment* for the Verandah Grill which served as a nightclub, cocktail bar and restaurant aboard the *Queen Mary*, while her sister Anna produced a mural of *The Four Seasons* for the cabin-class ballroom. Vanessa Bell and Duncan Grant were commissioned too, though Grant's three large panels were rejected, and though not invited to paint a mural, the Surrealist Edward Wadsworth managed to have two of his (quasi-Surrealistic) nautical paintings hung in the cabin-class smoking room, both of which 'received more than their fair share of criticism', according to one of the *Queen Mary*'s biographers.

The provinces did not just receive artists' work on tour: they generated it. L(aurence) S(tephen) Lowry, who worked as a rent collector during the day (though he had had some art-school training, and fearful of being considered a 'Sunday painter', did not admit to his dual life) painted mist-infused grey industrial scenes of his native Manchester and Salford in the evenings after supper which had some sombre affinity with the Camden Town School. Although Manchester City Art Gallery bought some of his work and Lowry was elected to the Royal Society of British Artists in 1934, his matchstick-men figures did not have their first major London airing until 1939, in a one-man show at the Lefevre Gallery. Frank Rutter, who had been a great supporter of the Post-Impressionists (and critic of the stuffiness of the Royal Academy) as curator of Leeds City Gallery, was an important mentor of Herbert Read, and was regarded as the 'elder statesman of [British] art', author of some twenty important and influential books of art criticism, numerous articles in the *Sunday Times* and other periodicals, and apparently an entire room of catalogues to which he had contributed the introduction or preface. Susie Cooper was born in the Potteries the year Arnold Bennett's *Anna of the Five Towns* was published (1902). When she was twenty-seven Cooper left the pottery where she had been making vivid Cubist-style decorated work, rather similar to that of Clarice Cliff (another Burslem potter), and with a family loan started her own workshop in Burslem. Despite the inauspicious economic climate and high unemployment in the Potteries, Cooper managed to succeed. Her 'art ware' designs, including a quintessential Art Deco motif, 'Leaping Deer', proved very saleable: she was invited to exhibit at the British Art Industries Fair in 1931, Queen Mary bought one of her breakfast-in-bed sets, and Greta Garbo one of her masks. Nikolaus Pevsner was much taken with her work, and by the end of the decade she was providing hand-decorated earthenware pottery for enterprises as diverse as the restaurant in the modernist new Peter Jones department store in Sloane Street designed by Slater and Moberly, the new Peckham Health Centre and Imperial Airways' London to Paris flights, as well as being a regular supplier of such useful everyday objects as cups and saucers, plates and bowls, teapots, honey pots and vases to John Lewis in Oxford Street, Heals, Harrods, Grants of Croydon, Dunns of Bromley, and other 'fashionable shops from Bath to Scarborough'.

Cooper was an active member of the Society of Industrial Artists, founded in 1930. 'The professional artist of the future would be a professional designer,' prophesied Paul Nash. Such an integration proved to be 'a talisman invoked against economic decline, social polarisation and political chaos', and was further encouraged by the Council of Art and Industry (CAI), established by the Board of Trade in 1934 under the chairmanship of Frank Pick, the man who had revolutionised the running of London's transport system – and its design. Both organisations were concerned with raising standards of design, but while the Society of Artists was naturally concerned with its members' employment opportunities, the CAI's main aim was to improve the design of British products, which were perceived to be lagging behind those of other European countries, meaning the country was losing out on much-needed export opportunities. This situation was highlighted by the report of the Gorell Committee on Art and Industry, published in 1932, which queried how 'an artistic nation . . . now finds itself handicapped in the world market by lack of artistic quality in so many of its manu-facturers'. Nikolaus Pevsner considered that more than 90 per cent of English industrial products were artistically objectionable.

The idea was that as well as producing 'an oblong of canvas to be hung on the drawing-room wall . . . modern artists of the stature of Henry Moore,

Vanessa Bell and John Nash [would] turn quite naturally from painting a picture or carving a statue to designing a lampshade or wall paper or a book cover', thought *The Listener*, commenting on the Gorell report (though Roger Fry, Clive and Vanessa Bell and Duncan Grant had been doing just that for some years on a small scale at their Omega Workshop), and that manufacturers would welcome this turn.

The Prince of Wales, perhaps recalling his great-grandfather Prince Albert's encouragement of art and industry, was enthusiastic too. Speaking at the Albert Hall in 1934 he advised artists 'to go abroad and study the demand which this machine age has evolved in foreign countries as regards taste, fashion, design, convenience, practicability, etc. Having studied these characteristics, they should then settle down and produce ideas combining the best details which they have discovered abroad with what, for want of a better term, I will call "a new British art in industry".'

In ways that fulfilled the Arts and Crafts movement's belief in the fusion of art with the everyday, businesses such as Imperial Airlines, the Cunard and Orient shipping lines, Cresta Silks and other manufacturers of fabric and china joined Shell in hiring artists. Barbara Hepworth and Ben Nicholson were commissioned by Edinburgh Weavers to produce designs for a 'Constructivist Fabric'. In order to help educate the consumer's eye, Zwemmer's Gallery in Cork Street included furniture, textiles and pottery in an exhibition of paintings and sculpture mounted to coincide with the publication of Paul Nash's *Room and Book* in 1932. Tooth's Gallery introduced a hire-purchase scheme enabling works of art to be bought for a deposit and monthly payments, 'just as for wireless sets and washing machines'. An exhibition of Midland Industrial Art attracted over 28,000 people in 1934. Art exhibitions were dispatched around the country, so those who lived in places that did not have a museum or gallery could appraise modern art and design for themselves. Lectures were given, and observers (called 'animated catalogues') stationed in exhibitions 'to keep an eye on people who were puzzled or seemed at a loss about how to look at pictures'. A defining moment came in 1935 when the Royal Academy, the last bastion of the fine arts, amended its constitution 'for the sake of the country' and mounted an Art and Industry exhibition.

Frank Pick campaigned unsuccessfully to create a series of regional 'monotechnics' – a National College for Pottery in Stoke-on-Trent, for example, one for the wool industry in Bradford, for the cotton industry in Manchester, and so on. The BBC broadcast a series of talks in 1933 on 'Design in Daily Life' which were later published as a book, and another series in 1938 which resulted in a Pelican paperback in which its author,

Anthony Bertram, chastised those whose view of art was 'too "arty" . . . to recognise those great works of art that man has recently produced in aeroplanes, cars, locomotives, buses and coaches'. A series of art exhibitions were staged at Charing Cross Underground station, and department stores were encouraged to hold exhibitions of the best designs they stocked, which could not only be admired, but also purchased, since, as the Gorell Report had recognised, 'It is probably true to say that for one person who visits a museum or gallery, a thousand enter a shop to buy a cup and saucer' – and, a review of the report added, 'five thousand look into a shop window'.

In the summer of 1927, J.M. Richards, who would become editor of the influential, *avant garde Architectural Review* in 1935, but was at the time a student at the Architectural Association (AA) in London, went on holiday to Germany with 'an itinerary that would take in several prominent examples of the new architecture that, although ten years old on the Continent, was only now beginning to interest young architects in England . . . We saw Ernest May's housing at Romerstadt . . . [Eric] Mendelsohn's department store [in Stuttgart] and spent a long time at the Weissenhof *siedlung* [settlement – an estate of working-class housing also in Stuttgart] where, in 1927, a group of the most modern architects in Europe – [Walter] Gropius, Mies van der Rohe, [J.J.P.] Oud [a Dutch architect], Le Corbusier and others – had been brought together to expound the functional and stylistic potentialities of modern architecture . . . nearly the whole of the visual vocabulary with which modern buildings were to be identified for many years afterwards – white walls, flat roofs and horizontal windows – Weissenhof was a place of pilgrimage for every young enthusiast.' Richards and his companions then 'decided on impulse and in spite of the expense, to fly – something none of us had done before. We flew from Tempelhof [Berlin airport] to Croydon, then the airport for London' – itself an arresting example of Art Deco architecture and interior design.

The same year that Richards took his modernist odyssey, Le Corbusier's *Vers une architecture* had been translated into English by Frederick Etchells, a painter turned architect who designed the first modernist office building in England, Crawfords advertising agency in High Holborn, but would end his days restoring churches in Berkshire. Could Le Corbusier's concept of the house as a 'machine for living' find acceptance on English soil, where the President of the RIBA, Sir Reginald Blomfield, was 'prejudiced enough to detest cosmopolitanism'? Was 'going Modern and being British', as Paul Nash put it, possible? Could modernism as a functionalist rebellion against 'style', unnecessary ornamentation or decoration, 'the inevitable logical product of the intellectual, social and technological conditions of our age', in the words of Walter Gropius, who had established the legendary *Bauhaus* (School of Building) in Germany, be translated into an English idiom?

The architectural historian Nikolaus Pevsner, whose Jewish ancestry had made it expedient for him to leave his native Germany in 1933 and settle in London, saw this as no problem. There was nothing 'un-English' about 'simplicity, uniformity, rectangularity, abrogation of ornamentation' – as austere Georgian and Regency terraces showed. Nevertheless, when the influential 1932 International Style Exhibition opened in New York, there were only two examples of English architecture in halls dominated by buildings from Germany, France, Scandinavia and the United States: Joseph Emberton's Royal Corinthian Yacht Club at Burnham on Crouch in Essex (though not his façade for the great Empire Exhibition Hall at Olympia in 1930) and Amyas Connell's 1929–30 house for the archaeologist Bernard Ashmole, High and Over at Amersham in Buckinghamshire (though in fact Connell was a New Zealander).

The claims for modernist architecture were ambitious. In paring down buildings to their functionalist form, ridding of them of unnecessary and 'hypocritical' decoration, a new way of life was opened up. As science in the minds of politically-minded scientists such as J.B.S. Haldane and J.D. Bernal needed to move beyond mere technological possibilities to address the discontents of the age, so it was with architecture. In 1935, the architect and writer Serge Chermayeff contended, 'architects can no longer concern themselves with construction in a separated professional compartment. They must concern themselves with the reconstruction of society.' Sir Giles Gilbert Scott, President of RIBA and the architect of Liverpool Cathedral, described an architect as 'a PLANNER, and as one of the most important servants of the community, with a valuable contribution to make towards an improvement in the art of living'. Wells Coates, an engineer by training, who had been working in shop design for Cresta Silks and had been commissioned to design the sound studios for the new BBC building in Portland Place, was convinced that 'the properties of steel-concrete and glass' had unleashed 'new forces'. He too believed in 'an architectural solution to the social and economic problems of today . . . a Future that must be planned rather than a Past that must be patched up'. The old ways of living had to change: 'We don't want to spend as much time as we used to on our homes. So the first thing is that our dwellings have got to be much smaller . . . We cannot burden ourselves with permanent, tangible possessions, as well as with our real possessions of freedom, travel, new experience – in short, what we call "life".'

In 1929 Coates happened upon the opportunity to design for 'life' when he met Jack Pritchard, who worked for the Estonian-based Venestra Plywood Company and had admired how Coates used wood in his shop designs, and his wife Molly, a bacteriologist and psychologist. The Pritchards were great enthusiasts for Le Corbusier, had been to Germany to see Weissenhof and the *Bauhaus*, and had managed to meet most of the stars of the modernist movement. They set up a company called 'Isokon' (Isometric Unit Construction) in December 1931 so that Coates could design houses, flats and all that went in them, and also commissioned him to design a house for them, a project that soon evolved into a block of 'minimal housing' flats. Coates, though Canadian, had been born and brought up in Japan, and had absorbed an appreciation of minimalism from there. But he was not a trained architect, and the flats were his first building commission.

Completed in 1934, the stark, four-storey concrete block, painted pale cream with a shell-pink tinge, in Lawn Road in Hampstead, housed twenty-nine service flats, of which twenty-two were very compact and minimal (the Pritchards had a penthouse for themselves furnished with exquisite chrome tubular and bent plywood modernist furniture by the Finnish designer Alvar Aalto and Marcel Breuer, which they had ordered from Zürich), with sliding doors and furniture that folded away, the 'equipment for the living of a free life'. 'All you have to bring with you is your rug, armchair and favourite picture,' promised a prospectus. The flats were intended for busy, baggage-free professionals who could avail themselves of the flat-cleaning, window-cleaning, laundry and shoe-cleaning facilities provided, plus 'meals from the central kitchen at moderate prices', since the flats' own 'kitchenettes' were tiny and minimally equipped for these busy, busy tenants. Rents were around £110 for a single or £160 for a double a year, or slightly more if furnished, so the Isokon (or Lawn Road) flats were not for the poor, no matter how refreshingly possession-free they might of necessity be, but for 'middle-class people of moderate means'.

The 'Peabody atmosphere' (of philanthropically-funded social housing) was to be avoided, according to Pritchard. In the basement a dining club, the 'Isobar', was opened in November 1937, so called because 'Molly [Pritchard] was interested in the weather', and Marcel Breuer designed an installation showing the workings of a barograph with a photograph of clouds behind it. The club restaurant, which soon attracted local artists such as Ben Nicholson and Barbara Hepworth, was entirely furnished with Isokon furniture, most designed by Wells Coates. Philip Harben (who would later make his name as one of the first British television chefs) was employed to do the cooking.

Harben, who had briefly worked as a documentary film-maker on John Grierson's *Drifters*, was also a founder member of the Half Hundred Dining Club with the Pritchards and the journalist Raymond Postgate (a left-winger, son-in-law of the Labour leader George Lansbury, who would later start the *Good Food Guide*), part of 'the movement for improving food in England', but entirely different from the wine merchant and gourmet André Simon's Wine and Food Society, which the Half Hundreders considered to be 'too large, too expensive and too pompous'. Members (who included the zoologist Julian Huxley and most of Pritchard's architect and designer friends and colleagues) cooked or supervised dinners on a rota basis. No meal could cost more than ten shillings a head (including 4s.6d for wine and sixpence for service): if it did, the person in charge would have to make up the difference. The Isobar kitchen provided some meals; on other occasions members were taken to a restaurant in the East End of London for 'an authentic Chinese meal', and by Huxley to the club at London Zoo in Regent's Park, where the menu consisted of bison's hearts and silverside of nylghau (an antelope), but not snake soup, as had been eagerly anticipated, as 'not enough middle-sized snakes needed culling'. On another occasion the typographer and founder of the Nonesuch Press, Francis Meynell, provided camembert ice cream, which was found to be a bit cloying. When it came to the turn of Postgate, who was the brother-in-law of G.D.H. Cole and considered himself something of a wit, he devised a menu such as might be offered by an English boarding-house landlady – though an extraordinarily imaginative, one might almost say Surrealistic, one – with mashed potatoes coloured with edible pigment to resemble the flag of Jamaica, and a soup turned blue by the use of methylene, which caused great anxiety to Marcel Breuer when his urine turned bright blue later that evening.

Breuer was one of the first residents of the Isokon flats. The *Bauhaus* where he had worked as a furniture designer had been closed down by the Nazis in 1933, and he continued the work he had been doing in Berlin for Isokon, designing distinctive furniture in tubular metal or pressed and bent plywood, which he used for one of his most famous pieces, the long chair, advertised as 'giving scientific relaxation to every part of the body . . . it is an even better aid to digestion than any medicine under the sun'. Other émigré residents included the Hungarian graphic designer and photographer László Moholy-Nagy and the architect and furniture designer Walter Gropius, founder of the *Bauhaus*, who arrived in London with his wife in October 1934. Gropius became design director of Isokon before he took off again for a professorship at Harvard. While living in Lawn Road he worked on plans for a block of Isokon flats to be built in Didsbury, Manchester, though it never materialised; nor did a similarly ambitious scheme for flats abutting Windsor Great Park with a view of the Castle in the distance (presumably, had they been built, the royal family would equally have had a view of the Isokon flats on *their* horizon).

With a number of projects aborted through lack of money, few commissions for architects (who had become by the mid-1930s part of a much more tightly controlled and regulated profession) and none from central or local government (unlike Germany and the Netherlands), there was a regrettable lack of welcome for the fleeing newcomers. In order to work, all had to go into partnership with practising British architects. These forced (if often brief) collaborations resulted in some of the finest examples of British modernist buildings, including a house at Angmering on Sea by F.R.S. Yorke and Marcel Breuer, a house by Gropius and Maxwell Fry in Old Church Street, Chelsea, and the one next door by Erich Mendelsohn and Serge Chermayeff (who was not a refugee, but though born in the Caucasus had been educated at Harrow), and perhaps Britain's modernist masterpiece, the De la Warr Pavilion in Bexhill on Sea (opened in December 1935), an entertainments venue, a superb liner-like, welded steel, curved glass 'socialist palace by the sea', also by Mendelsohn and Chermayeff, who won a competition (which, given the parlous state of the architectural profession, attracted an astonishing 230 entries) organised by the Parliamentary Secretary for Education in the National Government, who was also the energetic Mayor of Bexhill on Sea, 'Buck', the 9th Earl de la Warr.

When the Russian-born architect Berthold Lubetkin had come to Britain in 1931, he found it 'about 50 years behind, as though locked in a deep provincial sleep'. The following year he and five other young students training at the Architectural Association School (a relatively new departure in Britain, where previously most architects had learned their skills as apprentices) formed the Tecton group (*tecton* being Greek for 'carpenter' and so, by extension, 'builder').

Tecton's first commission was for a TB clinic for Dr Philip Ellman, but when that failed to get off the drawing board, the group was in danger of collapse. Lubetkin was thinking of returning to the Soviet Union when the first of its 'zoo jobs' materialised. In 1932 the London Zoological Society had acquired two gorillas from a zoo in Bordeaux, which it had had to put in with the lemurs. Solly Zuckerman approached Tecton to design more appropriate accommodation. The resulting Gorilla House, an uncompromisingly modern, drum-shaped, swivel-doored, building, proved so popular with man and beast that Tecton was commissioned in 1934 to provide a pool for the zoo's penguins. This elegant modern design was as far removed as could be imagined from the traditional constricting cages, and with its concrete ribbon ramps (constructed using the expertise of the engineer Ove Aarup) and splash pools, it provided endless delight to animals and visitors alike. Some even wondered sadly 'why human beings cannot be provided, like penguins, with an environment so well adapted to their needs'.

Further commissions followed: for Whipsnade, London Zoo's out-of-town branch near Dunstable in Bedfordshire, for which Lubetkin designed the elephant house, the giraffe house – and a *dacha* for himself and his family; and in 1936 for a zoo in the grounds of Dudley Castle near Birmingham, which included ravines for bears and tigers and a terrace where chimpanzees could stage 'tea parties'. On the opening day on 16 November 1937 of what was described as 'at once a scientific centre, an example of an ultra-modern town plan in miniature, and a source of entertainment for a huge industrial population', there was a near riot as a quarter of a million people flocked to see the wondrous menagerie.

Ernö Goldfinger, who came to London from his homeland, Hungary, via Paris in 1934, had designed a beauty parlour for the cosmetics manufacturer Helena Rubinstein in 1926, and both functional wooden toys (most of them small versions of modern transport) and, in 1936, their Wimpole Street shop, for Paul and Marjorie Abbatt, the design of which 'encouraged children to interact with the toys and furniture on show – a radical idea at the time', according to Goldfinger's biographer. But it is his own modernist family house, 2 Willow Road in Hampstead, for which he remains best known.

Despite their decisive influence, not all modernist houses in Britain were the work of architects from the Continent. Patrick Gwynne designed The Homewood in Esher, Surrey, for his wealthy parents in 1937; Maxwell Fry designed the Sun House in Hampstead for himself; and Oliver Hill's 'Joldwynds', at Holmbury St Mary in Surrey, was voted 'House of the Year' by *Country Life* in 1933. Unfortunately it proved so unsatisfactory, with leaks and cracks and buckled doors, that its owners, the Master of the Rolls Sir Wilfred Greene and his wife, acidly pointed out to Hill that 'Your job does not come to an end as you seem to think when you have got something that looks nice in a photograph.' In 1939 the Greenes despairingly commissioned the Tecton group to build a small, pitched-roof house in the grounds for them to actually live in.

Women architects also made an impact, with increasing numbers entering the profession in the 1930s. Charlotte Bunney designed a modernist house with her husband that blended with its Georgian neighbours in Downshire

Hill, Hampstead; Elisabeth Benjamin was the joint architect of a sanatorium, and in the mid-1930s designed three modernist houses including one for the left-wing politician Dr Edith Summerskill in Highgate; Mary Crowley designed a number of schools. And in 1928 Elisabeth Scott, a twenty-nine-year-old architect with a distinguished architectural heritage (her great-uncle was the designer of St Pancras station and the Albert Memorial, Sir George Gilbert Scott, and her cousin was Sir Giles Gilbert Scott of Liverpool Anglican Cathedral and Battersea Power Station fame), won a competition to design a replacement for the Shakespeare Memorial Theatre at Stratford-upon-Avon, which had been destroyed by fire. The new theatre, which was opened on St George's Day (also Shakespeare's birthday), 23 April 1932, was a severe, functionalist brick construction on the banks of the Avon. It did not win many plaudits: seeing it just before it was finished, the composer Edward Elgar, who lived in nearby Malvern and had been appointed the new theatre's Musical Director, vowed never to set foot in it, and complained that he was so distressed he would be unable to eat for a month. 'Beachcomber' in the *Daily Express* referred to the 'new Soviet barracks at Stratford', while the actors were unhappy with the stage. 'On a clear day you can just see the boiled shirts in the front row. It's like acting to Calais from the White Cliffs of Dover,' complained one. Others were kinder, praising the capacious and 'icily elegant' foyer and the uncluttered auditorium, while the *Architectural Review*, pursuing its modernist mission, was thrilled at a building that was 'uncompromisingly a theatre with no attempt at disguise', and even hymned the architect-designed knives and forks in the restaurant, and fixtures and fittings that were 'worthy of Stockholm Town Hall' – high praise indeed.

Among the most distinctive features of houses of the 'Modern Movement' were the windows: usually long horizontal, sometimes curved, panes of glass in metal frames. Most of them were made by the Crittall metal window company of Braintree, Essex, which had been producing them since the mid-nineteenth century. Buildings for which the family firm had supplied windows included the House of Commons and the Manchester Corn Exchange, as well as the Lots Road Power Station in Chelsea, which at the time could boast the largest windows in the world. Located away from a ready source of labour, Crittalls had decided to build a village to house its employees, on the lines of Bournville or Port Sunlight (or more recent 1920s examples: the London Brick Company village in Bedfordshire, Bowater Paper's settlement in Kent, Pilkington Glass in South Yorkshire, or the Kent colliery villages), and purchased two hundred acres of farmland in the village of Silver End, four miles from Braintree, for the purpose.

Anxious that the development should avoid 'suburban monotony', the firm's artistic and technical director, Walter Crittall (who was always known as 'Pink'), 'zoned' the site and commissioned several architects to design houses for each zone. C.H.B. Quennell (who as well as being an architect was co-author with his wife Margery of the best-selling series of books 'A History of Everyday Things in England' and father of the louche *belle-lettrist* Peter Quennell) came up with fairly traditional designs, but Thomas S. Tait, architect of the Kodak building in Kingsway and other prestigious corporate buildings, who was also making a name for himself with hospitals and sanatoria (and was later one of the judges for the De la Warr Pavilion competition), was 'given a free hand within the limitations of cost'.

According to Pink Crittall 'the result is a pleasing and successful experiment in what can be done with the limited problem of artisan's dwellings'. The houses cost £500 each to build (rather less than the £3,000 Le Château, the luxurious house Tait designed for a member of the Crittall family at Silver End), and had a lavatory in the scullery. The streets of small, uncompromisingly modernist, rectangular, flat-roofed, white-painted brick houses attracted respectful acclaim from the architectural press, as did the social facilities on the estate, including 'the best village hall in Britain' with its four-hundred-seat cinema/theatre, dance hall, restaurant, lecture hall, billiard room, library and infant welfare clinic. However, when the residents were allowed the right to buy the houses they occupied from Braintree Council, which took over the estate in 1969, many compromised Tait's severe designs with the addition of 'inappropriate' porches, extensions and PVC windows in place of Crittall's metal windows.

Not far from Silver End was another modernist construction, this time a replica of an Eastern European 'workers' settlement' set amidst the flatlands of Essex. Starting in 1933, the shoe manufacturer Tomás Bata built at East Tilbury a replica of his factory and housing for his employees at Zlín in Czechoslovakia. 'Bataville', a fusion of the English Garden City movement with standardised concrete construction systems, provided much-needed employment not only for local people thrown out of work by the construction of the docks at Tilbury, but for the unemployed from Wales and the North of England. Accommodation consisted of houses rather than flats, with a few hostels for single employees, since in Bata's view a man with a garden was able to 'potter about there so he doesn't go to the pub or political meetings'. Canteens, shops, a school, a technical college, a library, a cinema and a swimming pool were provided to enable Bata's employees, in his words, to 'work collectively and live individually' – though of necessity socialising pretty collectively too.

The onward (if very limited) march of modernist architecture did not go unchallenged. For a start, no matter how much modernist architects genuinely espoused social concerns and saw architecture as transforming lives, virtually none worked for local authorities rather than in private practice, and few of their commissions were for working-class housing – though Sassoon House, built on land adjacent to the Peckham Health Centre, was an exception, as were Kent House in Chalk Farm, North London, and Kensal House in Ladbroke Grove. These were social housing projects, funded by wealthy individuals or foundations, a modernist response to the anxiety that slum-dwellers were being rehoused by local authorities in 'barracks' rather than the light, airy homes that social reformers and socially-minded architects thought they needed.

Sassoon House was designed by Maxwell Fry in collaboration with the self-styled housing consultant Elizabeth Denby, organiser of the campaigning 'New Homes for Old' exhibitions held between 1931 and 1934. It was funded by a wealthy Mayfair philanthropist in memory of her deceased merchant banker husband and steeplechasing son, and was intended as a model dwelling for workers, with flats for rent for as little as nine shillings a week. The first families moved into the modernist block of twenty three- and four-roomed flats, each with its glazed 'family balcony', in November 1934.

Kent House, designed by Amyas Connell (the New Zealander who had designed the modernist landmark 'High and Over') and Basil Ward, was commissioned by the Anglican priest Father Basil Jellicoe's St Pancras House Improvement Society (SPHIS). The reinforced-concrete block rehoused families from the vermin-infested slum blocks of Somers Town in sleek modern flats with hot and cold running water, a 'surrogate garden' in the form of a cantilevered balcony with a windowbox for each flat, and a playground on the roof. 'Your Society is not only opening flats. You are opening avenues, windows, doors to new lives for men, women, and most important of all, the rising generation,' Sir Wyndham Deedes, a high-ranking-army-officer-turned-Bethnal-Green-social-worker and chair of the National Council of Social Service's London council, told the fortunate residents at the opening ceremony on 2 December 1935.

Denby and Fry again collaborated on the design of Kensal House, an 'urban village' in North Kensington for the Gas, Light and Coke Company intended to demonstrate the cheapness and efficiency of gas. It was 'the last word in working-class flats', said the design critic Anthony Bertram in a BBC programme on the subject of 'Housing the Workers' in November 1937. The reinforced-concrete block provided the tenants of its sixty-eight flats with not one but two balconies, one large enough to accommodate a dining table or allow space for children to play, the other screened for drying clothes, since it was recognised that 'very poor people are sensitive about displaying their underclothes to the neighbours'. The rents were 9s.6d a week for a two-bedroomed flat, and 11s.6d for three bedrooms, including gas heating. Residents also enjoyed the benefit of two social clubs. One, the first of the Prince of Wales initiatives for community facilities for slum dwellers (and the unemployed), was the Feathers Club Association, where during the day women could socialise or attend dressmaking or cookery classes, and carpentry tools and sewing machines were provided for residents to mend furniture or shoes, or to make clothes and curtains. The other was intended as a city equivalent of the village hall, a place to meet at the end of the day with neighbours, play darts, listen to music, put on a dance. Allotments were dug between the blocks, and children's needs were catered for with a playground and a nursery school on the premises. Here children could stay from 8 a.m. until 5 p.m. in a tastefully designed environment with structured play and nutritious meals. Close attention was paid to their manners, their cleanliness and their health, in the hope that each child would 'learn to cooperate with others and to reconcile the needs of self with the equally legitimate claims of society'.

Nevertheless, most architects designed homes for wealthy private clients – the house in Chelsea designed by Fry and Gropius had accommodation for two or three housemaids and a butler. Moreover, most of their work was largely confined to the more prosperous South of England. When Jeremy Gould compiled a gazetteer of 'modern' ('a flat roof is in general taken as the criterion') houses built between 1919 and 1939, he listed nine hundred, of which only one hundred are north of Cambridge. W.H. Auden had noticed this too: 'A world of . . . Huge plate-glass windows, walls absorbing noise/Where the smoke nuisance is utterly abated/And all the furniture is chromium-plated/Well you might think so if you went to Surrey/And stayed for weekends with the well to do . . . But in the north it simply isn't true/To those who live in Warrington or Wigan? It's not a white lie, it's a whacking big 'un.'

And few people seemed to welcome huge plate-glass windows set in white boxes on their patch (in fact many modernist buildings were not white, but the stark architectural photographic style honed by such as Dell and Wainwright, staff photographers on the *Architectural Journal* in the 1930s with the use of coloured filters, gave the impression that they were). The simple, undecorated designs submitted for an RIBA building competition in 1932 were described by one judge as 'very undressed indeed, and many of them it would have been a real kindness to cover up'. The 1932 Town and Country Planning Act had given local authorities the right to regulate the size, height, design and external appearance of buildings, and they could turn down plans for any building that they judged would be 'likely seriously to injure the amenity of the locality'. For conservative-minded authorities this could mean open season on modernist architecture. Appeals could only be made to the Minister of Health (whose brief included housing), who could then request that the President of the RIBA send in an arbitrator – and if the President happened to be Sir Reginald Blomfield, the case was as good as lost.

Chermayeff's 1936 design for a timber-clad house for himself, Bentley Wood, to be built on wooded downland at Halland in Sussex, described by Professor Reilly of Liverpool School of Architecture as 'a regular Rolls Royce of a house', was opposed by Uckfield Rural District Council, which compared it to a garden shed. On appeal to the Minister, the building was allowed to proceed – and Henry Moore's modernist sculpture *Recumbent Figure* was positioned in the front garden. 'A house which had the bad manners of refusing to parody past building styles with greater or lesser ghastliness is therefore to appear in Sussex,' rejoiced the *Architect's Journal*.

In 1933 Basil Ward and Amyas Connell (who had previously met opposition over his design of 'High and Over') submitted plans for a pair of semi-detached houses to be built at Ruislip in Middlesex. The proposals were turned down by the council, which considered them to be 'deliberately odd. We see nothing in the planning which would render it necessary that it should be treated in this fashion which is not new but of Continental origin . . . Architects might be interested to see these designs carried out, but we conceive it to be the duty of elected representatives to have some regard to the feelings and wishes of the community . . . and in our opinion, nine out of ten of the Ruislip population would view these houses . . . with active disfavour.'

The RIBA arbitrator upheld the decision, agreeing that the design would be 'injurious to the neighbourhood', and although the houses were eventually built with only minor modifications, the *Architect's Journal* was disquieted by the behaviour of the RIBA, and warned that if it 'allows its more reactionary members to obstruct the enterprise of its more progressive members . . . the younger men, the future backbone of the profession, will be forced to join themselves into a defensive *bloc*'.

Lubetkin and Tecton's Highpoint Two (1936–38) in Highgate, a more decorative scheme than Highpoint One (1935), with museum casts of classical caryatids flanking the entrance, also ran into opposition from the local council, which 'expressly forbade a replica of Highpoint One'. The battle delayed building for over a year. Ernö Goldfinger's plans for a terrace of three houses in Willow Road, of which the largest was to be his own family's home, were opposed by the Hampstead Heath and Old Hampstead Protection Society, led by Henry Brooke (later a draconian Conservative Home Secretary), which considered that the borough had quite enough angular modern buildings, such as Maxwell Fry's Sun House, which they felt were not in the 'English tradition', and out of character with the proposed new build's Georgian and Victorian neighbours (though Hampstead was – and is – a total mélange of architectural periods and styles). Moreover, the windows would be too big, and the building material would be *concrete*. Goldfinger wearily riposted that the houses were to be built mainly of brick, not concrete, that they were in fact an adaptation of eighteenth-century style, and thus in keeping with the finest local houses, and that 'Only the Eskimos and the Zulus would build anything but rectangular houses.' The habitués of the Isobar and other aesthetes rallied to Goldfinger's defence, and the houses were finally built. In 1995 number 2, Goldfinger's own residence, was one of the first modernist buildings to be acquired by the National Trust.

Even those who lived in modernist buildings seemed a little equivocal sometimes. When Jack and Frances Donaldson, who were so involved in the building and running of the Peckham Health Centre, commissioned a house for themselves from Gropius to be built at Shipbourne in Kent, they 'decided in a most crusading spirit that the only intelligent thing was to build in the architectural style of our own day. This crusading spirit almost completely prevented me from asking myself whether I actually liked it,' mused Frances Donaldson. In 1931 Hugh Dalton and his wife Ruth had commissioned a weekend home in Wiltshire from Frederick McManus of Thomas Tait's practice, the Daltons having admired photographs of the Silver End houses. Costing £2,500, the house was regarded by their friends as 'impracticable and ugly . . . it bore the mark of its creators: inelegant yet at the same time, bold and original', according to Dalton's biographer. And when Dalton's 'Uncle' Arthur Henderson, the Labour Foreign Secretary, came to visit, he asked 'which is the front', recorded Dalton in his diary.

A 'defensive bloc' of progressive young architects could serve as a description of MARS (Modern Architectural Research), the English chapter of the Congrès International d'Architecture Moderne (CIAM) founded in 1933. It was never large – seven members in 1933, rising to around seventy in 1938 – and was possibly influential only in a small, networking circle. But the aims of its members (of whom several were also members of Unit One) were certainly ambitious. 'Research' had a satisfyingly scientific ring to it, but members were less concerned with researching techniques and materials than with making 'an analysis of the growth of a new conception of architecture' which would include 'rather deep probings into the whole structure of society'. Yet when it came to collaborating on a 'New Homes for Old' display at the Building Trades Exhibition at Olympia in September 1934, MARS declined to offer solutions to slum clearance in Bethnal Green, preferring to analyse the problems. The next year, a new group, the Architects and Technicians Organisation (ATO), was formed by Lubetkin and several members of MARS, which offered to work with any organisation that was working to improve housing conditions. It regarded the contemporary architectural scene as the product of 'reactionary forces of privilege and reaction', and was overtly critical of the National Government's housing policies.

An exhibition of 'New Architecture', mounted in the belief that modern architecture's best hope of success lay in appealing to the public's visual sense, opened at the New Burlington Galleries in January 1938. The catalogue, the foreword to which was – startlingly – written by George Bernard Shaw, explained that architecture seemed to have 'attained one of those periodic plateaux which occur in the historical ascent of every intellectual movement', and 7,000 visitors trooped in to see the tricksy and confusing exhibition designed by Mischa Black, in which the 'modern period' was represented by a 'typical block of workers' flats'. Nevertheless, the exhibition was a financial disaster, and though Le Corbusier (who flew in) praised the 'lyrical appeal of those poems in glass and steel', it was attacked by John Summerson for its 'captions and exhortations of the most vacuous pomposity', and by some AA students for its lack of overt opposition to the 'anachronistic social system'. Subsequently MARS splintered, with some members continuing, under the aegis of the Marxist émigré architect Arthur Korn, to work on a plan for London so immensely radical it was as if they had a *tabula rasa*. The capital was to be 'drained of its parasitic elements' (that is, industry and excess population) so the centre could 'breathe'; huge areas were to be demolished and replaced with a series of 'hubs' combining housing with workplaces and leisure facilities, while a series of continuous green 'parkways' would traverse the city.

Other members quit, including the left-leaning Lubetkin, who castigated MARS as being 'a flat roofs club ... based on a gentleman's agreement', while younger architects considered it too conservative. Gropius was already at Harvard, Breuer followed, Moholy-Nagy went to Chicago, Mendelsohn increasingly did most of his work in Palestine, and the partnership of

Connell, Ward and Lucas, which had produced so many buildings that had become domestic ideograms of the Modern Movement, including the contested Ruislip houses and various 'Sun Houses', was dissolved through lack of work in 1939.

While for many years all but the most ambitious and expensive work of the 'flat roofers' was allowed to crumble and peel (and it did seem to do so rather easily) some public and corporate buildings built in the 1930s became icons, and were preserved in the face of the urge to demolish when their original function had been long displaced by new technologies and changing work practices. Perhaps the greatest, certainly the most imposing, was 'the temple of power', Battersea Power Station, built on the south bank of the Thames, for which Sir Giles Scott was the consulting architect, though he had nothing to do with what went on inside to produce electricity, and was not happy with its 'upturned table' appearance. Completed in 1933, but not operational until 1935, with its solid brick exterior, Art Deco detailing and massive, towering flue chimneys, fluted like classical columns, Battersea Power Station was soon being compared to a 'brick cathedral' and hymned as 'Modern Architecture for Modern Industry'.

When a number of celebrities, including the film star Charles Laughton (whose *The Private Life of Henry VIII* was the box-office smash of 1933, and for whom Wells Coates had designed a flat in Bloomsbury which Laughton's wife, the actress Elsa Lanchester, described as 'open, liveable . . . free from the oppressive weight of the past'), the writer Rebecca West and Kenneth Clark were asked to nominate the five best modern buildings in Britain in 1939, Battersea Power Station came second, trailing Peter Jones department store in Sloane Square. No one nominated any of the remarkable buildings designed by Owen Williams, which included the Dorchester Hotel (1930), the Boots Wet Goods (1931–32) and Dry Goods (1935–38) factories, Peckham Health Centre (1933–35), the black-glass *Daily Express* building in Fleet Street (1929–31) and offices and plant for the newspaper in Manchester and Glasgow. Nor did the starry lay critics much applaud the spread of Art Deco factory buildings strung out along the Great West Road, providing work for thousands in the suburbs: the Guinness brewery at Park Royal (1933–36), for which Sir Gilbert Scott was the consulting architect; the Hoover Building at Perivale with its colourful Art Deco/Egyptianalia façade, housing some six hundred workers, designed by Wallis, Gilbert and Partners (1932–38); and the Firestone tyre factory at Brentford, built by the same architects in 1928, with a similarly elaborate façade, possibly gesturing towards the discovery of Tutankhamun's tomb six years earlier.

As well as factories, the 1930s gave some architects the opportunity to design schools that were in keeping with new thinking about the young, how they should be taught, and in what surroundings. The Hadow Committee, set up by the 1924 Labour government, had recommended in its 1926 report the abolition of the elementary school system and its replacement by primary schools which children would attend until the age of eleven, followed by secondary education, either of the more academic sort at grammar schools (which would include the existing, renamed higher or secondary schools) or at 'modern' schools (the senior departments of old elementary schools), and an increase in the school leaving age to fifteen. The Depression delayed the implementation of these changes, though by the outbreak of war in 1939 almost two thirds of children over eleven were receiving some sort of secondary education. It was not until 1947 that the leaving age was finally raised to fifteen.

The slump had meant that there was no funding for new schools, but by the mid-1930s the buildings required to implement the Hadow Report's recommendations were being planned, and in 1937 Liverpool's enterprising Professor Reilly persuaded Gerald Barry, by then editor of the *News Chronicle*, to run a competition to design the 'ideal school'. Wells Coates, Tecton, Breuer and Yorke, Oliver Hill, Raymond McGrath and Denys Lasdun all entered, but the winner was twenty-six-year-old Dennis Clarke Hall, a newly qualified architect who designed a girls' high school at Richmond in Yorkshire (despite initial objections from the local authorities), a modern glass, concrete and wood building from which pupils could gaze across the Yorkshire dales to the moors thirty miles away, unlike Victorian Board Schools where windows were placed so high that pupils would not be distracted by being able to see out.

Oliver Hill designed several schools in Yorkshire. Ernö Goldfinger's ingenious plan for an expanding nursery school never got off the drawing board, but one idea that did come to fruition realised the vision of the Director of Education for Cambridgeshire, Henry Morris. This was for a series of 'Village Colleges' which would be used as schools during the day, but in the evening would serve as leisure and educational centres, 'bringing together . . . various vital but isolated activities in village life' such as evening classes, the Women's Institute, the British Legion, Boy Scouts and Girl Guides, library facilities, etc., thus 'creating a new institution for the English countryside . . . it would provide for the whole man, and abolish the duality of education and ordinary life. It would not only be the training ground for the art of living, but the place in which life is lived.' Since Morris also believed that 'The design, decoration and equipment of our places of education cannot be regarded as anything less than of first class importance – as equally important indeed, as the teacher,' it was not surprising that the partnership of Walter Gropius and Maxwell Fry was awarded the contract for Impington, the fourth of seven such colleges, which opened just after war broke out in 1939, and was later described by Pevsner as one of the best, 'if not the best buildings of its date in England'.

Education was a contested subject in the 1930s, both for those who were anxious for their children to get a better start in life than they had themselves, and for those whose families' economic circumstances meant they needed another income as soon as possible, and who regarded secondary education as an unaffordable luxury in harsh economic times. Then there were 'progressives' such as Henry Morris, who recognised that if society was going to change, the way its children were educated had to change too. This impetus took several forms.

For those who intended to build a better world on the ashes of the old, it was necessary to start with the young. Frank Pick had envisaged a new curriculum for schools that included art education at both primary and secondary levels, to produce 'little warriors' who could take part in the battle for 'a New England. A beautiful England again.' Others were more radical, wanting not just a new subject mix, but an entirely new way of educating children. Some twenty 'progressive' schools were established between the end of the nineteenth century and the outbreak of the Second World War, and they were particularly popular in the 1930s, when breaking the mould was on many minds. Some were small and had only a brief flowering; a few persist to the present day. All shared the same broad intentions: to emancipate the child from the harsh routines and philistine attitudes of the traditional public schools, to break out of narrow academic formalism and create a 'free' school in which the child was not repressed or moulded but was liberated to discover the world for him or herself, in his or her own way, learn at his or her own pace, explore his or her own passions and interests.

Gordonstoun was founded in 1934 by Kurt Hahn, a Jewish education-alist who had been forced out of his school in Germany by the Nazis and fled to Scotland, where with the support of such British establishment figures such as the novelist John Buchan (Lord Tweedsmuir), the future Archbishop of Canterbury William Temple and the historian G.M. Trevelyan he established a school on the lines of the Salem school he'd been forced to abandon. Located in rugged countryside on the Moray coast, Gordonstoun aimed to provide the 'moral equivalent to war', in which 'the craving of a man to test his powers in earnest' was privileged by 'increasing the range of active pursuits that should be regarded as educationally relevant from team games to such things as sailing, climbing, canoeing etc', providing a 'healthy pasture' for all in pursuit of the Platonic ideal of the 'whole man' who is 'spirited, swift and strong' as well as 'gentle and alert to the arts'. The school motto 'More is in You' hardly hints at the way that might be realised by the spartan regime to which pupils were subjected: cold showers, early-morning hill runs and hazardous physical adventures. This was perhaps not far removed from the average public-school regime, but Gordonstoun was 'comprehensive' in its acceptance of children with a wide range of abilities and financial circumstances, and its insistence on self-discovery rather than imposed rules, and the secondary place of examination attainments. One of Gordonstoun's first pupils (there were 135 by 1939) was Prince Philip of Greece, who some years later would marry the granddaughter of King George V and take the title of Duke of Edinburgh.

After Wellington, the rebel public schoolboy Esmond Romilly had been sent briefly to a moderately progressive school, Bedales, which put less emphasis on sport and more on the creative aspects of education, but he was no more attuned to Bedales than he had been to Wellington. Had he instead been dispatched to a school about which his subversive magazine *Out of Bounds* published an article written by one of its pupils, he might have fared better. Dartington, which took its first six pupils in 1926, was the 'experiment' of an immensely wealthy American, Dorothy Whitney, and her second husband, Leonard Elmhirst, an agricultural economist who had spent four years in India working with Rabindranath Tagore, the Nobel Prize-winning poet and social reformer.

Dartington Hall was a large, almost derelict estate near Totnes in Devon with many buildings dating back to the fourteenth century when the Elmhirsts bought and restored it. The school they established there appealed to what one of its earliest pupils, the sociologist Michael Young, called 'high-minded middle-class parents who would not send their sons to a State school because it made religion compulsory or to a public school because it made military training compulsory . . . [the Elmhirsts] were to be a magnet for devotees of naked bodies and cabbage juice'.

The sons and daughters of Bertrand and Dora Russell, Aldous and Juliette Huxley, Clough Williams-Ellis and his wife Amabel Strachey, were pupils at Dartington in the thirties, as was Ernest Freud, the son of Sigmund (who would grow up to be a modernist architect), and the children of the novelist Ernest Raymond, the actor Miles Malleson and the publisher Victor Gollancz. Dartington's prospectus insisted that 'Education be conceived as life, and not merely a preparation for life.' The children were to 'learn by doing', whether that meant building shelters, cutting down trees, growing vegetables, making cider, keeping bees, caring for livestock, raising chickens and collecting their eggs – then wringing their necks for the pot – keeping accounts, or any of the multifarious other tasks that were needed to sustain the community, preferably undertaken in the open air.

There were no compulsory games, no compulsory religion, no OTC, no uniforms, no corporal punishment (initially no punishments at all, but this was modified in operation), no segregation of the sexes ('Boys' and girls' rooms are arranged as in a hotel, without distinction of sex,' explained a pupil. Teenage pregnancies were feared, but rarely happened), no Latin, no Greek, no anything that would remind Leonard Elmhirst of the bruising educational experience he had endured at Repton. 'On the Library table are to be found on a basis of equality, *The Times*, and the *Moscow Daily News*, *The Times Educational Supplement* and *Out of Bounds*,' explained a satisfied pupil. Furthermore, Dartington Hall was to be a democratic, self-governing commonwealth, with teachers known as seniors and children as juniors. Rules were at a minimum, punishments clearly explained, and decisions were made at a General Meeting at which all had an equal voice. Dorothy Elmhirst also held a regular Questions Club where 'any issue could be raised': most seemed to be about sex (though sometimes concerns about the League of Nations surfaced). However, a 'kissing club' founded by one of the pupils was discouraged and disbanded.

The original plan had been not to have a headmaster, since 'no one was good enough to be allowed uncontrolled authority over a child', and instead there were to be rotating chairmen, but this principle too was breached in the light of experience. Bill Curry, who had been running a progressive school in Philadelphia, was appointed 'Director of Education to the Social and Educational Experiment now being carried out at Dartington Hall' on a salary of £1,000 a year, and took up his post in 1931, living in a splendid modernist house in the grounds, 'High Tor', and aiming to turn Dartington into 'a miniature copy of the world as we would love to have it'.

After his bitter and protracted divorce from their mother Dora, with whom he had started a progressive school, Beacon Hill in West Sussex, the philosopher Bertrand Russell had removed two of his children, John and Kate, and sent them to Dartington Hall. Beacon Hill had opened in 1927, a year after Dartington, and the two schools were run on similar lines, since 'Bertie rather feared the imposition of orthodoxy and the stifling of unusual talent' for children.

Although both Russells had written weighty books on theories of education, they 'were not very clear at the start as to how we should organise things. But there were certain definite principles. There was to be no corporal punishment; the children were free to come into the classroom and work and learn, or not to do so. If they came in intending to disturb others, they would be asked to leave and occupy themselves outside . . . Other principles were that there should be no suggestion that naked bodies, or any part of the body, were obscene or "dirty". This meant not scolding for masturbation; it also meant freedom to run around without clothes when the children found it warm enough . . . there was complete freedom of speech, no topic of discussion being ruled out [which] also meant that the grown-ups were not treated with exaggerated respect . . . they were addressed by their first names and not with "Yes, Sir" or "Yes, Miss So and So". The pupils were divided into three groups 'who got called the Bigs, the Middles and the Smalls'.

Jack and Molly Pritchard's two boys were pupils, as was Sylvia Pankhurst's son Richard (while she rented a cottage in the grounds to write her book on the suffragette movement), and the offspring of the writer David Garnett and other 'well-known English intellectuals'. Although 'the parents who were most inclined to try new methods were those who had difficulties with their children', and Beacon Hill 'got an undue proportion of problem children', the school only ever rejected one child. Although 'visitors who saw our small tribe, sometimes nude, sometimes, by their own choice, dressed in odd garb, and also rather grubby' might not have realised it, the Russells were rigorous about twice-daily showers, regular bowel movements (Bertie was particularly keen on those), no religion or anything military, fresh food, the open air and open discussion, practical learning and democratic decision-making. Dora taught those who wanted to learn French or German, while Bertie 'soon found it impossible to undertake much teaching' since he was writing books on education, and frequently going abroad to lecture on education, in order to finance the school, as some progressive parents seemed to regard it as 'a charitable institution' and omitted to pay the fees.

Beacon Hill's parlous financial state (particularly after Bertie left in 1932) meant endless appeals, a peripatetic hand-to-mouth existence and renting the school buildings and grounds out in the holidays to such organisations as the Progressive League, the foundling of C.E.M. Joad which 'advocated sex reforms': some of its members 'liked to put certain of these, such as free love and nudism, into practice'.

The Russells could have considered sending their children to an existing progressive school rather than going to the enormous trouble and expense of starting their own, but they considered that academic standards at A.S. Neill's Summerhill in Suffolk, founded in 1921, were too low, because for Neill the 'social side' was more important than the 'learning side'. Education, Neill believed, was about 'the instinctive side of the child . . . the child must be free to express itself in the manner that its dynamic driving force demands'. If it was suppressed, that energy would 'find a way out in destruction' rather than 'expressing itself in love and creation'. Thus a child *should* be 'active, noisy, indifferent to adult values of manners, cleanliness, language, property &c . . . We began by abolishing adult authority' and creating a democracy which was 'more complete than any other democracy with the possible exception of a village Soviet in Russia'. All 'laws' were made at a weekly Saturday-evening meeting at which each child and each teacher had a vote. There were 'innumerable laws' made by the children, including a no swearing outside the school grounds edict, since, as an eleven-year-old explained, 'The townspeople don't yet know that swearing doesn't matter'. Miscreants were tried by a jury of their peers, and punishments included forgoing the regular Monday cinema visit (whatever film happened to be showing – no censorship), helping level the hockey pitch or building a new tennis court.

As at Dartington and Beacon Hill and the other small (often very small – Beacon Hill had twenty-five pupils by 1934) boarding schools for the progressive middle classes who could afford to experiment with their children's education, the emphasis at Summerhill was put on children finding out things for themselves, coming to learning because they wanted to, not because they were timetabled to. In the morning lessons were arranged, but they could be about 'plating pennies in order to make them into florins' or making ink or soap ('but they have no intention of using the latter'). There were no set lessons in the afternoon, but they resumed at five 'for those who want them'.

Interrogated, as he frequently was, about how 'children brought up in this free manner [would] fit into a stern life afterwards', Neill responded with chilling prescience in 1934: 'We have had disciplined schools for a long time in Europe . . . Today Europe is an armed camp ready for war . . . at a rough estimate I should say that a school of today that was fitting youth for after life would be teaching pupils the exact dose of castor oil for an enemy, the easiest way to make poison gas, the best way to keep the wage slaves down . . . In a world that is obviously going to be in the near future a battle-ground between Fascism and Communism it isn't easy to say exactly how a system should prepare children for after life.'

CODA

The Edge of the World

In June 1936 the film-maker Michael Powell came by sea to what the Romans had called 'Ultima Thule', the edge of the world, the outer isles of Scotland. Powell (who would later combine with Emeric Pressburger to make some of Britain's most original and acclaimed films, including *The Life and Death of Colonel Blimp*, *A Matter of Life and Death*, *The Red Shoes* and *Black Narcissus*) landed with his crew on the lonely Shetland isle of Foula to make a film about the evacuation of St Kilda that had taken place six years earlier.

The St Kildan archipelago, which had been owned by the Macleod of Macleod for six centuries, had been sold in 1934 to the Earl of Dumfries, and despite Powell's pleadings the laird had refused permission for the film to be made there. Hirta, the main island, and the only one that had been inhabited, had been deserted since its small community had been ferried forty miles across the Atlantic to start a new life in the Highlands of mainland Scotland in 1930, and Dumfries, a keen ornithologist, had no desire for its rich birdlife to be disturbed by the activities of a film crew. So the almost equally lonely Foula, which had the same craggy hills, treacherous cliffs and rocky inlets was chosen to stand in as the location for a way of life that had been deemed unsustainable in the modern world.

Powell, dismissive of documentaries as films made by 'disappointed feature film-makers or out-or-work poets' (he seems to have been thinking of the Humphrey Jennings/W.H. Auden *Night Mail*, also made in 1936, with music by Benjamin Britten) resolved that *his* film was going to be a '*Drama!* an *Epic!* About people!!' His script personified the conflict, and used well-known actors such as Finlay Currie and John Laurie to convey the question that lay at the heart of the St Kilda depopulation: whether it was possible to live as the community had for over a thousand years, or whether increasing incursions by the outside world had disrupted and changed that life in ways that meant it was no longer viable.

Even without the love affair and the atavistic feuds that Powell wove into the film, employing the native population of Hirta as well as his

365

imported stars, the story was dramatic. By 1929 the population of St Kilda, almost all of them crofters living in small stone houses, had dwindled to less than forty. Theirs was a hard life. The islands could barely sustain the necessities of existence: potatoes, meagre quantities of barley and corn were about all that could be grown; houses were heated and food cooked by burning peat cut from the hillsides; illness was rife in the harsh winters, and infant mortality tragically high. Although sheep grazed on Hirta and its two neighbouring islands, Boreray and Soay, which were little more than outcrops of rock, the community rarely fed on mutton. The sheep – those that did not stray over the highest cliffs in Britain or were not dashed into the sea by the fierce gales – were kept not for meat but for their fleeces. In the winter the soft brown wool was spun and woven into fine-quality tweed which was sold to the tourists who had first started to arrive in the 1830s, coming to marvel at the islanders' simple life, wander down the one main street and buy blown speckled guillemot eggs from the local boys.

Birds – gannets, fulmars and puffins – were crucial to the economy of St Kilda. 'Bird people', Julian Huxley called the St Kildans, and from an early age boys were taught to clamber down the precipitous cliffs to take the birds from their nests. Indeed, so staple a fare were the birds that when the Preservation of Sea Birds Act was passed by Parliament in 1869, a clause was inserted specifically excluding St Kilda from its provisions because of 'the necessities of its inhabitants'. From the arrival of the birds in March till their departure at the end of November every year, 'all the energies of mind and body' of the islanders were centred on 'one continued scene of activity and destruction', wrote George Atkinson, who had taken 'a few weeks' ramble among the Hebrides in the summer of 1831'. A hundred years later, little had changed. In March the puffins arrived in their hundreds and thousands on the rocks of Stac Lee and Stac an Armin, and boats would be launched and islanders scale the cliffs to kill the birds, and the adult gannets that had returned from months at sea in January, and take any eggs they could. In August it was the turn of the fulmars, thousands of which would be killed: in 1929, the year before the evacuation from the island, it was estimated that the harvest of fulmars totalled around 4,000, about 125 for every inhabitant. It was an exhausting and hazardous cull: gannets have a five-foot wing span and are fierce in defence of their young, and a footing lost on the cliff face, a rope frayed, could mean a plunge to almost certain death in the raging sea below.

It was the flesh of these seabirds – boiled or stewed, or wind-dried in stone *cleits* built for the purpose, to be stored for sustenance during the winter months – that the St Kildans ate, mixed with oats or a few potatoes.

Some of the birds' feathers were plucked and bundled up, along with the woven tweed, to pay the islanders' rent to their landlord, while the rest were exported to the mainland, where the government bought large quantities for use in army pillows and mattresses. The oil of the fulmar, found in its feathers and its stomach – and spat viciously at predators – found ready takers too, since it was considered to have medicinal properties similar to cod liver oil; any that was not sold was used to light the lamps of the St Kilda crofters.

By the end of the 1920s, the islanders' connection with the mainland economy was much closer than it had been a century earlier. A mail boat called as regularly as weather permitted – which in the winter months was not at all – and a post office had been opened on the island in 1899. When an influenza epidemic struck the island in 1913 the outside world in the shape of, among others, the *Daily Mirror* newspaper and Gordon Selfridge, owner of the department store, sent relief supplies to ward off starvation, and during the First World War St Kilda had become a War Signal Station, keeping an alert eye on enemy shipping in the North Atlantic. The occasional leavening of imported jam and cocoa, butter and tea had become a welcome change from an unremitting diet of seabirds, and paraffin a pleasing alternative to fulmar oil for light and heat. Inexorably, what had traditionally been a barter economy had been infiltrated by money. The bird oil, feathers and cloth that the Kildans could export were losing their currency in an increasingly mechanised and synthetic world, where the cost of artisanal extraction and production plus lengthy transportation were making their goods uneconomic.

Increasingly, St Kildans began to glimpse what seemed to be an easier way of life than their ceaseless round-the-clock battle with nature to scratch a bare livelihood. It seemed to some outsiders that the 'nibbling at socialism' as one of them characterised the islanders' communal life, sapped enterprise, making St Kilda uncompetitive in the modern world. Young men, and then whole families, started to drift away, to Australia, Canada, England, Scotland. On 10 May 1930, having endured a long and bitter winter, with acute shortages of food and shelter, the islanders petitioned the Scottish Office 'to assist us all to leave the island this year and find homes and occupations for us on the mainland . . . since for many years St Kilda has not been self-supporting and with no facilities to better our position, we are therefore without the means to pay for the cost of removing ourselves and our furniture elsewhere'.

On 30 August 1930 the remaining thirty-seven islanders left St Kilda aboard HMS *Harebell*. A few days earlier, 667 of their sheep had been trussed

and loaded onto a boat, to be sold to cover the cost of the evacuation –
until outraged public opinion demanded that the proceeds should go to
their island owners. The able men, none of whom had ever seen a tree,
since none grew on Hirta, were employed by the Forestry Commission in
Argyllshire, where there were murmurings about 'special treatment' at a
time of high unemployment in Scotland; the old and the widows, none of
whom of course had been part of the National Insurance scheme, had to
submit to a means test in order to obtain relief to buy rather than to catch
and grow their food.

It was the story of this community out of joint with the times, a remote,
near-subsistence economy that no one was any longer prepared to support,
that Michael Powell and his crew arrived to recreate on a simulacrum of
St Kilda for the cinema-going public in 1936, and by October that year he
had *The Edge of the World* 'in the can'.

Passengers wait patiently at Victoria Coach Station in 1939. Photograph by Wolf Suschitzky.

British Union of Fascists nuptials. T. Naylor and Edith Taylor seen leaving the Free Catholic Church, Edmonton, through a fascist guard of honour after their wedding on 5 February 1934. The happy couple were both keen Blackshirt hikers, having done the walk from Lands End to John o' Groats.

Children playing at a nursery school on the site of the
old Foundling Hospital in Bloomsbury on 24 March
1936. The hospital, founded in 1739 by the sea captain
Thomas Coram for 'the education and maintenance of
exposed and deserted young children', was demolished
in 1928, and the children were eventually relocated to a
purpose-built Foundling Hospital at Berkhamsted,
Hertfordshire, in 1935. But in 1937 the hospital bought
back some of the land and built a new children's
centre on the site.

Ramblers and hikers demonstrate on 1 January 1932 in support of the Open Air Charter for the preservation of public rights on roads and footpaths.

Twenty-nine-year-old Richard Crossman calls on the Robbins family during his unsuccessful by-election campaign to become Labour MP for West Birmingham in April 1937, the same year that the brilliant Oxford don's *Plato Today* was published. Crossman was finally elected as MP for Coventry East in 1945.

'I gotta horse.' Ras Prince Monolulu
(real name Peter Carl Mackay),
the successful tipster, at Epsom
racecourse on 28 May 1933.

PART FOUR

1936

FOURTEEN

The King is Dead

If out of such an appalling, tense decade it is possible to select one particular year as the most disturbing and turbulent, that year would have to be
1936. To read through the newspapers of 1936 . . . is to realise what a frenet-
ically hectic, helter-skelter of a year that was.

Valentine Cunningham, Introduction to
The Penguin Book of Spanish Civil War Verse (1980)

> Spirits of well-shot woodcock, partridge, snipe
> Flutter and bear him up the Norfolk sky:
> In that red house in a red mahogany book-case
> The stamp collection waits with mounts long dry.
>
> The big blue eyes are shut which saw wrong clothing
> And favourite fields and coverts from a horse;
> Old men in country houses hear clocks ticking
> Over thick carpets with a deadened force;
>
> Old men who never cheated, never doubted,
> Communicated monthly, sit and stare
> At the new suburb stretched beyond the run-way
> Where a young man lands hatless from the air.

John Betjeman, 'Death of King George V' (1937)

George V died on 20 January 1936. He was seventy, and had been king for
more than a quarter of a century. It was not a role he had expected or
wanted, but when his older brother, the indolent and dissolute Duke of
Clarence, died of pneumonia in 1892, George became heir to his father,
who in 1901 acceded the throne as Edward VII. He dutifully married his
late brother's fiancée, Mary of Teck, and succeeded his father in 1910. It
was a fairly harmonious marriage: 'the sailor King' (George had been in

the navy) fathered six children and was a dauntingly strict disciplinarian, continuing to espouse the 'Victorian values' of morality and probity that seemed to have leapfrogged over his father, and rather bypassed his elder son, Edward, Prince of Wales. Reserved, shy, of limited intellect and rather dull in the manner of a conservative English country gentleman with hobbies, George nevertheless proved a dutiful and ultimately popular monarch. His stature was enhanced by his morale-boosting activities during the First World War, and perhaps also by his moderating role in the con-stitutional crisis of 1931, when he urged Ramsay MacDonald to form a 'National Government' and the Liberal and Conservative leaders to serve in it. Although the 1926 General Strike had unnerved him, and he had advocated the use of military force before being dispatched to Sandringham so the politicians could resolve things, it was a well-judged gesture to announce in September 1931 that the King had surrendered £50,000 of his Civil List entitlement at a time of severe economic recession. The *Daily Worker* was predictably scornful about 'George Windsor' giving up a portion of his 'kingly emoluments . . . the straits to which the King will be reduced should bring a lump to the throat of the most callous. Now the royal housekeeper will have to make do on a mere £488,000 a year or £9,384 a week, [a sum] equal to a worker's dole for 225 years or about 90 years' pay for a miner.'

On a hot May day in 1935, George V and his family had driven to St Paul's Cathedral in an open carriage for a thanksgiving service to mark his twenty-five years on the throne. The Silver Jubilee was celebrated by 'by far the greatest number of people in the streets that I have ever seen in my life. The enthusiasm was indeed most touching,' noted its object. Bunting was hung between buildings, flags run up flagpoles and lamp-posts decor-ated; there were street parties and free cinema shows for the children (Mickey Mouse cartoons were particularly popular); a chimpanzee at London Zoo was named 'Jubilee'; Buckingham Palace was floodlit as were St Paul's and the Houses of Parliament; embroidery kits were produced that bore the lines 'Prince of Sportsmen, brilliant shot/But happiest aboard his yacht'; special Jubilee postage stamps were issued, and the keeper of the King's stamp collection (a first-rate one) was knighted; the unemployed and old-age pensioners were given vouchers which they could exchange for half a crown; and banners were waved in the East End of London proclaiming 'Lousy but Loyal'. But not every knee was bowed: H.G. Wells had been 'puzzled at the readiness of liberal-minded English people to acquiesce in and conform to the monarchy. The king is necessarily the head and centre of the old army system, of the diplomatic tradition, of hieratic privileges, a sort of false England that veils English life.' And in the coalmining area of Lumphinnans in Fife, where a fifth of the miners were unemployed, local Communist councillors opposed any notion of celebrating the Silver Jubilee of the 'royal parasites', since in their view there was nothing to celebrate, and children needed food, not bunting.

Frank Forster was similarly unimpressed: 'There appears in the newspapers much about the coming "Jubilee Celebrations". They make much of the bonuses which some people will receive on the day. Charity cannot support a nation so that people can live decently . . . There is a surfeit of tradition, of patriotism, of the need to keep this country as it is. O how deeply are people taken in.' He found the flags decorating the streets 'a mockery': 'There were decorations down the whole length of Salisbury Avenue. People living there seem to have gone mad. Nearly every door had a Union Jack stuck on it . . . The lampposts were festooned, some of them having coloured paper shades placed over the electric bulbs . . . there was a crowd in the middle of the avenue dancing to the strains of the gramophone . . . When people who live in abject poverty make such a show over royalty, one is brought to realise the superhuman task of communist educators. And when the Labour party makes much show over the Jubilee Celebrations and cares little for the state in which people live one is driven to cry out against hypocrisy. To stroke the soft expensive fur of those who live in abundant wealth is only to keep oneself down in the depth of filth and poverty.' Forster, who was mostly unemployed throughout the 1930s, had managed to find a temporary job, so opted to go in to work on Jubilee Day, rather than take part in the shenanigans of the 'fur strokers'.

And now the King, who most people had last heard giving a Christmas broadcast just over a month before, a practice he had initiated in 1932, was dead. Stanley Baldwin had thought at the time of the Jubilee that the King had 'seemed to be packing up his luggage and ready to depart'. But for Madge Martin, the wife of the vicar of St Michael's, Oxford, it was 'a great shock when the wireless announced that "the King's life was drawing peacefully to its close" . . . Everyone loved him and everyone must feel much as I do, sad at heart, and lost without such a wonderful and wise ruler.' 'It is odd how a man's trade seizes him,' thought the editor of the *Sunday Dispatch*, Collin Brooks, when he heard 'the unexpected bulletin that the King is ill' on 17 January. 'My first and dominant emotion was one of readiness for a congested and complicated week-end with the paper.'

The bulletin about the King's life drawing to a close had been scribbled by Lord Dawson of Penn, the royal physician, just before he put his words into effect by administering a hefty dose of morphine and cocaine into the dying King's jugular vein, in order to relieve his suffering but also to ensure that his death would be announced in the dignified *Times* rather than the evening tabloids. 'Obvious that Sister B was disturbed by this procedure,' Dawson jotted down in his private notebook, though the Queen had left the matter in his hands. Perhaps strangely, Dawson would vote against the Voluntary Euthanasia Bill when it came to the Lords on 1 December 1936, arguing that this was 'something which belongs to the conscience of the medical profession, not to the realm of law'. The Bill was defeated, though of course, then as now, such acts did take place.

Vanessa Bell had come out of the cinema to 'bulletins about "closing hours"' on 20 January, 'so having the car, we [she and Duncan Grant] thought we'd drive by Buck House. It was rather an amazing sight, crowds so thick we couldn't get near the railings to read the bulletin and cars parked all the way along the Mall . . . As we could hear nothing new, we decide to drive home.' They sat up listening to the quarter-hourly bulletins until it was announced that the King had died, 'news given in extremely pompous manner and voice by Sir John Reith [Director General of the BBC] himself . . . Public life has been intolerable ever since. The wireless has practically stopped, as it won't give anything of a cheerful nature and unfortunately doesn't give all the superb melancholy music it might. I don't think the general public feels anything but mildly amused curiosity, but they have to dress in black and newspapers have practically no news.'

The black-bordered press spoke of 'our sad loss', 'a well-loved King', 'service in war and peace', 'the King we mourn' and 'the King we salute', and claimed that 'The death of no sovereign of these realms throughout their history has created more profound or widespread grief than that of George V.' The *New Statesman* endorsed the epithet 'the crowned bourgeois', while congratulating the late King for not being particularly clever, 'an advantage in a country which distrusts cleverness in high places'. The people of America were reported to be mourning 'as if for their own King; & the Japanese are in tears'. Edmund Blunden contributed a noble elegy for *The Times*: 'An honest King's the noblest work of God/Now passes one whom all the world termed so . . .' The Poet Laureate, John Masefield, who always included a stamped, addressed envelope with every poem he sent to *The Times* so it could be returned if not considered suitable, cabled in his ode on this momentous occasion from Los Angeles, 'This man was King in England's direst need/In the black battle years, after hope was gone . . . /His courage was a flag men rallied on . . . /The best, the gentlest and the most beloved . . .'

Virginia Woolf noticed that 'most of the men in Southampton Row wear black ties wh. are brand new, or dark blue ties, which are the nearest they can get. In the stationers the woman spoke with a subdued kindness as if we were both mourning a great uncle we had never seen . . . The shops are all black. "We always carry a large stock" the woman at Lewis's said. But there'll be nothing doing after this rush at all. There'll be no work for us . . . Mourning is to outlast the London season. A black Ascot.'

The public seemed swept up in such a gigantic wave of lachrymose emotion that the journalist Philip Gibbs declared, 'I am beginning to think that the death of the King is the greatest event in human history since the crucifixion,' and the psychoanalyst Ernest Jones somewhat laboriously tried to unravel why the British demonstrated such craven feelings towards their rulers. But one Birmingham man, though 'not a republican', was nevertheless 'bored and irritated by the endless, exaggerated eulogies of the late king', and like H.G. Wells before him, marvelled at 'the ease with which the inhabitants of this country can be swept back into the middle ages of belief despite the education of our schools'.

When the Prime Minister, Stanley Baldwin, had announced the news of the King's death in the House of Commons, he had just returned from the funeral at Westminster Abbey of another stalwart of a passing age, the poet and writer Rudyard Kipling, who also happened to be Baldwin's cousin. Kipling, who in the words of Secretary to the Cabinet Thomas Jones 'had the fecundity which is the mark of genius', had died on 18 January at the age of seventy, his passing overshadowed by that of his King. 'The death of poor Mr Kipling has passed almost unnoticed,' wrote Vanessa Bell, but her sister Virginia Woolf observed that Kipling's death 'has set all the old war horses of the press padding round their stalls'. One 'war horse' writing in *The Times* lauded the breadth of Kipling's compass, for he had 'watched so many customs from Cathay right round to Sussex'. 'The whole world was his writing desk,' providing the 'avowedly banjo strains' of much of his writing and making him 'a household word among thousands of men of action not otherwise greatly devoted to literature'. 'A nation already in mourning found it in its heart to pay tribute to one of its greatest writers,' the paper concluded sonorously.

On 23 January the royal coffin was brought from Norfolk to London. Virginia and Leonard Woolf watched the stately progress of the gun carriage draped with the royal standard and surmounted by the Imperial Crown from King's Cross to Westminster Hall, as did Duncan Grant and Vanessa Bell, who noted that 'Indians in turbans were climbing the trees' in Tavistock Square to get a better view.

Despite her cool detachment, Vanessa Bell found the procession 'unexpectedly lovely', that is until the new King Edward VIII hove into view, 'looking utterly miserable, very small, disreputable, patchy and debauched, and his hardly handsomer brothers [the Dukes of York, Gloucester and Kent]. What a pity they aren't like you and Quentin,' she wrote to her younger son Julian, away teaching in China.

En route to Westminster Hall the Maltese cross on top of the Imperial Crown had fallen to the pavement: one of the Grenadier Guard escorts bent down and picked it up. 'Christ! What will happen *next*?' exclaimed Edward VIII as he plodded along behind the cortège, weighed down 'in a thick long overcoat looking utterly done'. The cross was refixed once the procession reached the Hall, but Harold Nicolson thought it 'a most terrible omen' for the new reign.

The royal corpse lay in state for four days while not far short of a million mourners filed past, 'silent on the thick felt that had been laid on the pavement of history'. Many of them had come on a tube train, since for the first time the Underground ran all through the night. Lady Diana Cooper, wife of the Secretary of State for War, Duff Cooper, had privileged access and did not have to queue for hours. 'I went almost nightly. Through a secret door one could slide into the centre of the moving masses, and there I would lead, in patriotic and monarchic pride, any foreign friends visiting London.'

Edward VIII (who had wept hysterically at his father's deathbed, clutching his mother, while the Queen had remained controlled in her grief) and his three brothers mounted guard at each corner of the catafalque on the final night. The coffin was then taken by train to St George's Chapel, Windsor, for the funeral on 28 January. Behind the bier, under a leaden sky, slowly, solemnly, heads bowed, walked five kings, including Britain's, and representatives from all over the world, including one from Nazi Germany, where Adolf Hitler had assumed the Chancellorship in January 1933. In Portsmouth people were so glued to their wireless sets that 'Everyone ceased to use water for cooking, washing etc., while the broadcast of the King's Funeral was on.'

The King is dead: long live the King. But what sort of monarch would Edward be? The Prince of Wales had 'always been a hero' of Madge Martin's, and 'I hope he will make a fine king.' *The Times* was hopeful too. Edward VIII 'comes to the throne as no stranger to the people', and referred to his 'travels to almost every part of his Empire'. It added that though the Prince of Wales had received a somewhat sketchy education – 'Men not books are his library,' as the newspaper kindly put it – 'he is gifted with a genuine interest in . . . all sorts and conditions of people . . . [and] takes the fullest part in bettering the condition of his people'. This had led him to contribute to the miners' relief fund during the General Strike while at the same time lending his car to help distribute Winston Churchill's *British Gazette*.

Such contradictions coursed through the new King. On the one hand, with his 'vitality . . . which is the key to other men's hearts', Edward Albert Christian George Andrew Patrick David (so called to emphasise the unity of his four kingdoms in the person of the King) had a lively, if transitory, sympathy for the unemployed, and was particularly popular in ex-servicemen's associations and working men's clubs. Clarence Huff had been very taken with him when he came to an Unemployed Club in Bradford: 'No plush carpet down. The Prince sat on an ordinary plain chair; with him was a very elegant lady and they had tea and cakes just the same as the rest of us . . . After staying about an hour the Prince left accompanied by detectives and a police escort. Unbelievable that a possible future King of England would come to a place like [that] but he did.' The Secretary to the National Council of Social Services (NCSS) had been impressed too by the Prince of Wales's concern for the unemployed: 'The Prince knew more than some of his Ministers about the problems of the derelict valleys and the silent mills.' 'I am thinking . . . of each member of the unemployed population as a single, separate personality, beset by depression, labouring under a sense of frustration and futility,' Edward had told a meeting of the NCSS at the Albert Hall in January 1932, in a triumphantly successful appeal for volunteers to help the unemployed and their families. He gave practical effect to his concern with the Feather Clubs, the first of which opened in Ladbroke Grove in 1934. These were originally intended to provide amenities for the unemployed, though they increasingly embraced those on low pay too. The clubs were largely run by a woman who had in effect been the Prince of Wales's *maîtresse en titre* for sixteen years, Mrs Dudley (Freda) Ward, but Edward took an interest in their activities and visited them on occasion.

On the other hand, the new bachelor King, who was good-looking in a slight, pale, sandy, baby-faced English way, with a predilection for loud checked suits, spent as little time as he could on the tedious official duties of a constitutional monarch, preferring the high life. He exuded a warm charm to most people he met, though he could get bored and fidgety, and enjoyed a glitzy, hedonistic lifestyle of travelling, partying, West End night-clubs, weekending, yachting, swimming, hunting and playing golf, spending money extravagantly, being at forty-one a middle-aged 'bright young thing' in the mould of the previous decade. Again, *The Times* was tactful, main-taining that Edward's 'versatility . . . was not necessarily fickleness', and of course it did not mention a series of affairs with (usually married) women.

'The passing of an epoch,' Harold Nicolson had noted on the death of George V, and Edward did indeed seem very modern. His arrival at his father's deathbed in his own plane – 'hatless from the air', as John Betjeman put it – the first royal to fly, seemed to exemplify this. And the new King aspired to be seen as 'Edward the Innovator' (which he would prove to be in a way he had not anticipated), letting 'fresh air' into the 'venerable institution of kingship'.

But despite Thomas Jones's optimism that Edward would 'rise to his responsibilities though he may discharge them in his own way', and *The Times*'s upbeat talk of a 'good augury and high hopes' for the new reign, Nicolson felt 'uneasy . . . that the Prince of Wales is in a mess'. This mess was largely caused by his intimate friendship with a divorced and remarried American, Mrs Wallis Simpson, whom he had first met in 1931. J.H. Thomas, the Lord Privy Seal and former railwaymen's leader, who had been very close to the old King, was even more uneasy, as he told Nicolson (who had a go at reproducing Thomas's eclectic working-class accent), ''ere we 'ave this obstinate man with 'is Mrs Simpson. Hit won't do 'arold, I tell you straight. I know the people of this country. I *know* them. They 'ate 'aving no family life at Court.' Baldwin felt the same: 'It's a tragedy he's not married,' he said, and wondered to the Labour leader Clement Attlee if the new King would 'stay the course'.

The *New Statesman*, which regarded Edward VIII as a throwback to his grandfather, Edward VII, rather than to his father, a 'country gentleman [whose] industry and devotion to duty were beyond praise', spoke with vatic seriousness: 'An immeasurable fund of loyalty and affection is always at the disposal of the King of England. It is not a blind devotion and it has often been forfeited in the past. How far it is evoked or retained depends on the actions and character of the Sovereign himself.'

In the same month that the old King died and was buried, three high-profile left-wing intellectuals met for lunch. The highly successful barrister and politician Stafford Cripps, the Marxist theorist and writer John Strachey and the pacifist schoolmaster turned publisher Victor Gollancz were all concerned with how best to counter-attack the growing menace of fascism in Europe, and to persuade those on the left that what united them in this opposition was more important than what divided them on other matters. This unity should include Communists, since the CPGB, in common with other European Communist Parties, had dropped its 'class against class' strategy under which any Social Democratic or Labourite parties were regarded as 'social fascists', as much the enemy as openly fascist parties. In December 1934 the Comintern had decreed that Communist Parties should form anti-fascist alliances of workers across the political spectrum. This meant taking the masses 'as they are. And not as we should like to have them,' as Georgi Dimitrov, the head of the Comintern explained. In Britain this would mean working to form an alliance with the Labour Party. However, the Labour Party consistently rejected Communist overtures, and in October 1936 the party conference decided by 1,728,000 votes to 592,000 to reject affiliation with the CPGB.

Cripps thought a weekly newspaper would serve the anti-fascist cause best; Gollancz suggested a book club based on the American 'Book of the Month' club, that would provide its members with a steady diet of radical books at cheap prices. The publisher's view prevailed, and the next month an advertisement appeared in the press maintaining that understanding politics was a matter of 'terrible urgency at the present time, when the world is drifting into war, and fascism is triumphing in country after country'. The Left Book Club intended to publish books that would 'provide an armoury from which a weapon could be selected for argument on any conceivable subject'.

Members had to agree to take a 'Left Book of the Month' for 2s.6d for a minimum of six months – and enthusiasm or inertia usually kept them as members beyond that. The books, most of which had been specially commissioned for the Club, would arrive on publication day, having been dispatched from bookshops rather than by direct mail, so as not to jeopardise the booksellers' goodwill that Gollancz relied on for the sale of the other books he published, among them an extremely successful crime series which included the adventures of Dorothy L. Sayers's Lord Peter Wimsey. Subscribers would also receive a free monthly leaflet, *Left Book News* (later *Left News*, which soon expanded into a journal of sometimes sixty pages) containing reviews of the books, a summary of the Club's activities, an editorial by Gollancz and a monthly report on the USSR. Persuading people to '*undertake* to buy books' by subscription was, Gollancz believed, the way to bypass the 'ninety-nine booksellers out of a hundred [who] quietly boycott socialism'.

The response was immediate: within a year 40,000 members had joined, guaranteeing that a serious political book would achieve a circulation of at least this number every single month, when few books sold in conventional ways got anywhere near that figure, and four hundred local groups had been formed to discuss that particular month's choice. By the outbreak of war in 1939 there were 57,000 members, and more than two million books had been distributed by the Club. 'It is,' wrote Gollancz excitedly, 'not too much to say that the Club has already begun to take on the characteristics of a genuine *movement of the masses.*' By 1939 the number of discussion groups, including ones for scientists, musicians, taxi drivers, architects, accountants, busmen, teachers, journalists, actors and sixth formers, had swollen to 1,200. There were LBC author tours at home and abroad, summer schools, annual national rallies – the first, in 1937, packed the Albert Hall 'from floor to ceiling with the vast auditorium filled with eager and earnest youth', and thousands more unable to get a ticket. This spawned local rallies, a total of forty in 1937, and twice as many the following year. Other attempts to gather the previously politically unawakened into the fold included such things as photography, music, travel, swimming, cycling and other sports, since 'walks, tennis, golf and swimming are quite different when your companions are "comrades of the left"', as well as classes to teach Russian and show Russian films.

A later commentator sketched a hypothetical typical day for an LBC member, 'waking to find his Left Book Club monthly selection on his doorstep; attending a Left Book Club Russian language class; going to the local Left Book Club travel agency to arrange for a Left Book Club tour to the Soviet Union; spending the remainder of the morning selling Left Book Club publications in the town market place; attending a Left Book Club luncheon, organized by some local businessmen; then going to the Left Book Club Centre to play ping-pong and then to relax reading left periodicals; selling Left Book Club pamphlets and leaflets for the remainder of the afternoon; in the evening attending a Left Book Club discussion meeting, followed by a Left Book Club film-showing on Spain and a one-act play performed by the local Left Book Club Theatre Guild Group; chalking a few slogans on his way home; reading his *Left News* and then dozing off to sleep, secure in the knowledge that the Left Book Club was Not So Much a Book Club, More a Way of Life', and all the time wearing his bright orange LBC badge bearing the words 'KNOWLEDGE, UNITY, RESPONSIBILITY'.

However much this way of life might have appealed to Frank Forster, it was out of his reach as long as he was unemployed. But as soon as he found a job he 'intended to become a full member once I am in the money. Have coupon already filled up to send to Gollancz. I intend concentrating on obtaining books this time, instead of clothes like last time.' As soon as he started work he set aside 7s.6d from his first week's wages to cover three months' subscription to the LBC, and he planned to keep thirty shillings aside for his subscription in case he was thrown on the dole again. By 1938 LBC meetings around Chester took up a lot of Forster's time, though he noted that 'of late the attendance of the meeting of the discussion group has not been too promising. It is really a pity for the LBC presents a glorious opportunity of meeting people of advanced views.' It was sometimes hard to keep the faith: in March that year 'there was supposed to have been a film show organised by the LBC held in the Temperance Hall, George Street, Chester, but the affair turned out to be a failure. The show was due to start at 7.30 but the chap with the films didn't turn up until 9.15. By that time most people had gone home . . . As Press Secretary to the LBC, I am supposed to send a report of the meeting to the local papers. But it would not do to send a report of a would-be film show. Best to let that go,' he concluded wisely.

Although the full-time, paid organiser of the network of discussion groups, Dr John Lewis, estimated that 75 per cent of the members were 'white collar workers, black-coated professionals and left-wing intellectuals', there were members who fell into none of these categories, including thirty Aberdeen tram workers who formed their own group to discuss the monthly choice, while a Communist shop steward in Manchester recalled that 'The Left Book Clubs did have an impact . . . I went into the factory at ten o'clock to address the night shift and as I walked up the aisle a man opened the door to one of these great big cupboards and showed me row after row of these books. They were reading them on nights, so they did have an influence.'

The first titles published in the LBC's distinctive limp orange covers were *France Today and the People's Front* by Maurice Thorez, leader of the French Communist Party (most months subscribers could acquire a book on either the popular front or the Soviet Union) and *Out of the Night*, which was the biologist Hermann Muller's attempt to rescue eugenics from the perverted form it had taken under Hitler. These were followed by a stream of books that 'dealt with every aspect of the world about which it was possible to hold a Left opinion'. One was an indictment of the prison service, *Walls Have Mouths*, by the Communist Wilfred Macartney, who had spent eight years behind bars for spying, which was something of a hit with members. Others included A.L. Morton's *A People's History of England*; Wal Hannington's *The Problem of the Distressed Areas* and *Ten Lean Years*; the autobiography of a miner, *These Poor Hands*, by B.L. Coombes; a book on the Paris Commune; another on the *People's History of Germany*; works on India and China, colonialism, democracy, the English Civil War and many more. John Strachey's *The Theory and Practice of Socialism* was the choice for November 1936, and became the Club's 'bible', with four-week courses arranged for 'disciplined study' of a book that was 'rooted in fact and illuminated by theory', according to one of the organisers. The 'Red Dean', Hewlett Johnson, contributed a volume on *The Socialist Sixth of the World*; Simon

Haxby wrote *Tory MP*, an analysis of the family and business connections of Conservatives. In June 1936 members received *World Politics* by the CPGB's leading ideologue, Rajani Palme Dutt, while the Labour leader Clement Attlee was persuaded to describe *The Labour Party in Perspective*, which was almost as dull as it sounded.

The books were selected by three men: Gollancz (generally progressive, a Labour Party member, though 'For about 15 months I was as close to communists as one hair to another.' However, the hairs would separate somewhat after the Munich crisis in 1938); Strachey, who was 'in broad sympathy with the aims of the Communist Party', and claimed to have 'a stock answer to dear old ladies who ask me, "and why Mr Strachey, did you become a Communist?" "From chagrin, madam," I reply, "from chagrin at not getting into the Eton Cricket XI,"' though in fact the CP would never issue him a party card; and Harold Laski, a theoretician who mixed his inborn liberal sympathies with Marxist ideas. He served on the Labour Party's National Executive Committee, and was a prodigiously fast reader with an almost photographic memory, which was to prove useful, even if his comments scrawled on manuscripts tended to be cryptic.

This rather impressive triad, three of Beaverbrook's 'four horsemen of the socialist apocalypse' (Kingsley Martin, editor of the *New Statesman and Nation*, was the fourth) represented a microcosm of 'popular frontism' – uniting anti-fascists in a political alliance – and they confronted the same problems that bedevilled the national effort. In July 1937 Gollancz noted that since the Club had been started only three of the fifteen monthly choices so far were not by Communists: 'I think we ought to remedy this . . . our whole aim must be to win the maximum number of members and frighten the minimum.' The Club was to be a 'reading Popular Front by representing every point of view'. However, the Labour Party regarded the LBC as pretty much a front for the Communist Party, and an inhibition to the development of a Popular Front movement in Britain through the fear of Communist domination. Indeed, at one point it threatened to declare membership of the Left Book Club incompatible with membership of the Labour Party.

George Orwell's depiction of a Left Book Club meeting in his 1939 novel *Coming Up for Air* was profoundly unsympathetic, describing 'a little wooden hut with a corrugated tin roof . . . the usual crowd of fifteen or sixteen people had rolled up. On the . . . platform there was a yellow placard reading "The Menace of Fascism". This didn't altogether surprise me . . . There's always a moment during the evening when I find myself thinking the same thought: Why the hell are we doing this? Why is it that people will turn out on a winter night for this kind of thing? . . . the seats of all the chairs were dusty . . . You know the line of talk. These chaps can churn it out by the hour like a gramophone . . . stirring up hatred . . . We're the West Bletchley revolutionaries . . . It struck me as I looked round the audience that only about half a dozen of them had understood what the lecturer had been talking about, though by this time he'd been pitching into Hitler and the Nazis for over half an hour. It's always like that with meetings of this kind.'

Another of Orwell's books was to be the most successful and enduring of all the LBC's choices. In December 1936 he delivered the book Victor Gollancz had commissioned on poverty and unemployment in the North-East, *The Road to Wigan Pier*. This turned out to be, in effect, two separate books in one: the first half was a grim, detailed and deeply affecting picture of the effect of mass unemployment. The second was a barbed satire on the ineffectiveness of the left, mocking 'astute young social literary climbers who are Communists now, as they will be Fascists five years hence'. It sneered at the 'streak of soggy and half-baked insincerity that runs through all "advanced" opinion', and 'all that dreary tribe of high-minded women and sandal-wearers and bearded fruit-juice drinkers who come flocking towards the smell of "progress" like bluebottles to a dead cat'. Despite his distaste for this argument, Gollancz's publisher's instinct recognised the appeal *The Road to Wigan Pier* would undoubtedly have for Left Book Club members. But would they be so incensed by the second half of the book that it should be lopped off, since Orwell refused to change it? Instead, Gollancz wrote a long introduction suggesting (incorrectly) that Orwell was playing devil's advocate for socialism, that it was important to 'rouse the apathetic by showing the utter vileness' that Orwell had exposed, and that somehow the second half was less an attack, more a timely call for the left not to dissipate the goodwill it had mobilised in sectarianism and ineffectuality.

Gollancz's instincts proved to be right. *The Road to Wigan Pier* infuriated the left. It was lacerated by Harold Laski in the LBC's own *Left News*, while Harry Pollitt thought the second half was little more than the whingeing of a 'disillusioned little middle-class boy', and a regrettable distraction from the real issues of poverty and unemployment. However, discussion groups devoured it. Readers 'profoundly shocked' by Orwell's revelations of life in the North wrote in by the hundreds, asking, 'Tell us, please, what can we *do*?' Forty-four thousand copies of *The Road to Wigan Pier* were sold through the LBC and 2,000 in bookshops, and it is still in print today – though Gollancz's convoluted introduction did not survive beyond the Left Book Club edition.

Given its concern that the 'Left' in Left Book Club meant a persuasive flow of Communist propaganda, the Labour Party started its own club under the auspices of the TUC. It was not a success, any more than the so-called Socialist Book Club founded in 1938 by Ronald Batty. Gollancz dubbed it the 'Batty Book Club' before it folded within a few months, having recruited no more than three hundred members. Batty had been a senior employee of Foyles bookshop in the Charing Cross Road when he married the boss's daughter, Christina, who would later take over the shop. Alarmed that the right-wing case was being lost by default and the nation submerged in 'a flood of communist and semi-communist literature . . . pouring forth from the printing presses and threatening to engulf the saner members of the reading public', Christina's father W.A. Foyle had started the Right Book Club in February 1937, which she effectively ran under the slogan 'Might is Right'. Its aim was to prove, in Christina's words, 'that truth neither began nor ended with an aged Victorian called Marx, and to show . . . that you need not be unprogressive because you happen to be a Conservative'.

Although the Right Book Club was run on the same subscription model as the LBC and the books cost the same, they were not specially commissioned works, but cheaper editions of recently published books chosen by Foyle and her selectors, who included a couple of keen sympathisers with National Socialism who were associated with pro-Nazi British organisations. It was an eclectic list that included *Ordeal in England*, the riposte by the right-wing journalist Philip Gibbs to Orwell and J.B. Priestley's journeys into social conditions; *Famine in England* by Viscount Lymington, a pro-Nazi environmentalist; and books by other right-wingers such as Douglas Jerrold, Arnold Lunn and Hugh Kingsmill, as well as Edith Sitwell's biography of Queen Victoria. By the end of 1937 the Right Book Club claimed to have 25,000 members (about half as many as the LBC), and although Christina Foyle admitted that there was considerable difficulty in finding 'good Right books', the RBC had managed to provide its members with more than thirty titles by September 1939.

On 5 February 1936 *Modern Times*, written by, directed by, produced by and starring Charlie Chaplin (and with music by him) opened at the Tivoli cinema in The Strand. Alistair Cooke, who would later broadcast *Letter from America* but was at the time the BBC's film critic, described Chaplin as 'the most famous man on earth in the early 1930s', quoting the aphorism of Will Rogers, Hollywood's top-paid star, that 'The Zulus know Chaplin better than Arkansas knows Garbo.' Cooke had been offered a job as assistant director on *Modern Times*, but to his later regret had turned it down.

Chaplin had what could be described as a 'Dickensian' childhood, raised partly in Lambeth workhouse, son of a periodically insane mother and an alcoholic father, an orphan by fourteen. He had worked in the music halls since the age of nine, and had evolved a hugely popular film persona as an outsider, an outcast, a tramp in urban society. *Modern Times*, which was to be the tramp's last appearance, showed the alienation of modern man in the machine age, and opened with a scene in which a flock of sheep morphed into a hurrying crowd of workers. The huge factory in which Chaplin's character laboured seemed to produce nothing, while turning its workers into mere appendages of the machines. In the film's most famous image, Chaplin is stretched round a giant cog wheel, part of the machinery he is servicing; when he walks away from the production line he moves like a jerky automaton, depersonalised, another piece of machinery.

The first film with sound was *The Jazz Singer*, starring Al Jolson. Made in 1927, it opened in London the following September, and within a few years the 'talkies' had effectively killed the silent screen. But Chaplin was reluctant to use speech in his films, since he thought silence made his art universal. *Modern Times* was his late farewell to that genre. It was also a comment on the unintelligible (yet universal) sounds of 'modern times': the characters don't speak – the only sound apart from the music and the noise of inanimate objects (and a 'big brother'-like, all-seeing factory boss) is Chaplin's gibberish, incomprehensible song near the end. For the Russian film-maker Sergei Eisenstein, who in 1925 had made *Battleship Potemkin*, *Modern Times* was a contemporary tragedy, a depiction of man's displacement by machine. The *New Statesman*, however, was just disappointed that it wasn't as funny as Chaplin's earlier films.

At dawn on Saturday, 7 March 1936 a token force of 22,000 German troops marched into the fifty-kilometre-wide strip of territory bordering the Rhine, goose-stepping smartly through Essen, Düsseldorf, Frankfurt and Cologne in direct contravention of the terms of the Treaty of Versailles signed at the Peace Conference in 1919. It was not the first breach: Hitler had reintroduced conscription in March 1935, and two years earlier had withdrawn from the League of Nations and the disarmament conference. Now, having seen the impotence of the League of Nations when Mussolini had invaded Abyssinia (Ethiopia) in 1935 and the League had failed to implement effective sanctions against Italy, the Führer was unconcerned that it would act decisively to enforce the terms of Versailles.

The 'Rhineland Pact' had been the principal treaty of the post-Versailles renegotiation that took place in Locarno in Switzerland in 1925 in an attempt to 'normalise' relations with the defeated Germany by binding Britain, France, Germany, Belgium and Italy in guaranteeing each other's frontiers against aggression by any of the signatories. However, France, riven by internal political difficulties, and ever fearful of German intentions on her border, signed an additional pact with the Soviet Union in 1935. Hitler was thus able to represent his remilitarisation of the Rhineland as an act taken 'more in sorrow than in anger', as a result of France's 'contravention of the Locarno provisions'. For France the reoccupation was a provocative act, and her loss of an eastern buffer against Germany was threatening, but she was unable and unwilling to act alone. Britain made it clear that she 'could not and would not take part in any actions conducive to war', since the country was poorly armed, unsure of the strength of German forces, and anxious to see a peaceful and satisfied Germany brought back into the 'European family'. Hence the country's diplomatic energies were expended as much in restraining France as in confronting Germany.

There had been another example of the British policy of 'appeasing' European aggression the previous year when news of a secret pact between the Foreign Secretary, Samuel Hoare, and the French Prime Minister, Pierre Laval, to partition Abyssinia, allowing only a port and a 'corridor for camels' to the sea for the Abyssinians between areas of Italian occupation, was leaked to the press on 13 December 1935. The ensuing uproar against the craven acceptance of Italian aggression meant that Hoare was obliged to resign. The plan was dropped, and Mussolini turned to Hitler for support. Hitler concluded, rightly, that neither France nor Britain would prove much of an obstacle to his intentions.

'Great excitement at Hitler's coup. House crowded,' recorded Harold Nicolson. '[Anthony] Eden [Hoare's successor as Foreign Secretary] makes his statement . . . very calm. Promises to help if France attacked, otherwise, negotiation. General mood in the House is one of fear. Anything to keep out of war.'

That was the general mood in the country, too. Anything to keep out of war. Uneasy about the punitive terms of the Versailles settlement on Germany, aghast that Britain appeared too pusillanimous to check Mussolini's violent invasion in Africa, where bombs and chemical warfare had been deployed, it was easy for people to shrug that after all, Hitler was only moving into his own backyard. The German ambassador to Britain reported back to Berlin on 10 March: 'The so-called "man in the street" generally takes the view that he does not care a damn if the Germans occupy their own territory with military force . . . He has not the slightest intention of getting himself involved and possibly allowing himself to be drawn into war.' It would seem that the ambassador was largely correct. A Captain W.A. Harrison undertook his own survey 'in hotels, public-houses, country inns, "buses" and Railway trains 3rd. class', and came up with the intelligence that 'the average man' was forgiving of Hitler's 'symbolic act': 'Can't say I blame Gerry for sticking his head up when he can. He took his licking all right, but them Frenchies can't keep their boots off him . . . I can't think how you can keep a nation of 65 million down for ever unless you exterminate them . . .'

Speaking for the left, Hugh Dalton, chairman of Labour's National Executive Committee, declared 'bluntly and frankly' that public opinion, especially in the Labour Party, would tolerate neither military nor economic sanctions to drive German troops out of the Rhineland, since a clear line could be drawn between Mussolini's war in Abyssinia and 'the actions . . . of Herr Hitler, which, much as we regard them as reprehensible, have taken place within the frontiers of the German Reich'. The Cabinet's policy was 'peace with as little dishonour as possible', decided the Conservative president of the Board of Education Oliver Stanley, while Edward VIII put it about that he had been influential in restraining Britain from taking any action against Germany – which he hadn't.

In May, the date for Edward's coronation was fixed for a year hence, 12 May 1937, and the ship named after his mother, Queen Mary, that had languished so long in John Brown's shipyard on Clydeside as Job No. 534 (unfinished), a symbol of Britain's industrial decline, finally set sail on her maiden voyage from Southampton to New York via Cherbourg on the twenty-seventh. A radio message was received just prior to sailing from the new King. The 80,733-ton luxury Cunard liner (weighing more than the total weight of the entire Spanish Armada), completed with a government loan of some £3 million, was carrying 1,840 passengers who had paid £53.15s Cabin Class one-way, £28.10s Tourist and £18.10s Third Class. They would be 'protected by luxury [as] you sail the ancient path between continents . . . before arriving on landfall, refreshed and richer in company, with the light of the sea on your salt-tanned cheeks and a look of distance in your eyes'. Facilities included a promenade deck specifically for dogs, equipped with a lamp-post, three cinemas, a beauty parlour, a swimming pool, Turkish baths, a daily newspaper, the *Ocean Times*, a chapel and a synagogue. Larry Adler was on board with his mouth organ, as were Henry Hall and the BBC Dance Orchestra.

The poet Laurie Lee was offered a free trip in return for an article in a Cunard magazine. He described the *Queen Mary* as 'elegant, romantic, almost medieval', with decks 'as long as a village street', and eulogised about 'deck chairs in the sun . . . a book or siesta in the afternoon, tea and cakes at four o'clock; dinner at the Captain's table . . . you meet your fellow passengers. There are actors, writers, steel magnates and wives, professors, Italian princesses [he did not, presumably, encounter any Third Class passengers].' The captain, 'lean as a Scottish loch, orders his guests like a flagged flotilla . . . bringing them trimly alongside each other'. In the bar, 'the martini . . . in one's hand trembles faintly. One feels the throb of the liner's thrust. Black ties and tuxedos, bare arms and pearls . . . hot canapés of bacon and liver . . . 40 choices of the best brand whiskies.' At dinner 'lobster, pâtés and fruits . . . Pressed Boar's Head . . . Braised Haunch of Venison . . . Entrecote Steak Henri IV . . . One settles perhaps for Caviar de Beluga, Boston Sole and a split Bordeaux pigeon, with a bottle of Chablis and a light Bordeaux wine, and brandy and figs to follow . . . As the night settles down, gala dancing and cabaret . . . the honeymoon ocean unfolds to the sultry throbbing of the saxophone . . . with champagne in buckets.'

On 3 June His Imperial Majesty Haile Selassie I, Conquering Lion of the Tribe of Judah, King of Kings and Elect of God, arrived in London. He had led a guerrilla war against the invading Italian army in Abyssinia since October 1935, urging his countrymen to 'fight a nomad war' against Mussolini's forces whose intention was to create a bridge between the Italian possessions of Eritrea and Somalia. Under attack from a large European power armed with 'unlimited quantities of the most death-dealing weapons', including bombs and poison gas, and with no sign that the collective security the League of Nations promised was about to be activated, his impoverished nation of twelve million inhabitants was defeated. Marshal Badoglio entered the capital Addis Ababa on 5 May, and Mussolini declared Ethiopia an Italian province and King Victor Emmanuel III its new Emperor. *The Times* wrung its metaphorical hands over Abyssinia, asking, 'Is there another in history who had deserved more fortune and received less?', but no effective help was forthcoming from the League of Nations, several members of which were prepared to recognise the Italian conquest.

Selassie set off to Geneva to plead his case to the League on 30 June. His powerful, dignified speech about the slaughter of his people, delivered in his native Amharic, made him an anti-fascist icon around the world, and *Time* magazine named him 'Man of the Year'. Anthony Eden, the Foreign Secretary, suggested to the King that it might be a popular gesture if he were to receive him. 'Popular with whom? Certainly not the Italians,' retorted Edward VIII, who was opposed to the policy of, as he saw it, 'coercing' Mussolini, and sent his younger brother, the Duke of Gloucester, to do the courtesies.

In early October Selassie moved from the London flat in Princes Gate where he had been staying into a £3,500 house he had bought and refurbished for himself and his large family in Bath. He was soon able to fill it with imperial regalia, furniture, rugs and other possessions, wheedled out of the occupying Italians and brought to Britain free of charge by the P&O Steamship Co. The Emperor lived out his exile in a style that was both lavish and litigious until late June 1940, when, after Italy had entered the war in support of Germany, he was allowed to return to Abyssinia in great secrecy and, with the help of British, Commonwealth and other Allied forces, was eventually able to reclaim his country from the invaders.

On 12 June Harold Nicolson, who had been narrowly elected as National Labour MP for West Leicester in the November 1935 general election, went to the Commons to hear 'poor Jim Thomas [do] his stuff. He read it standing just behind me. I felt that the tears would drop on to my head . . . When he had finished he walked out, turned and bowed to the Speaker. Then his PPS [Parliamentary Private Secretary] took him by the arm and he left the House for ever. Poor man. Poor man. The House murmured a sort of low sound of sympathy for him.'

'Poor Jim' was the Secretary of State for the Colonies, J.H. Thomas, who had been appointed by Ramsay MacDonald in 1930 to 'deal' with un-employment. In 1935 he had been given a Cabinet post largely to lend credence to the notion that the government was National rather than Conservative, when in fact Stanley Baldwin, who had replaced MacDonald as Prime Minister in June 1935, had won 425 seats to the opposition's 180. But within months of the election Thomas had been accused of leaking budget secrets to a Conservative MP, Sir Alfred Butt, and an old business associate, Alfred Cosher Bates, who had taken out insurance against taxation increases that were announced in the budget soon afterwards. The evidence was circumstantial, and may well not have stood up in court, but though the ex-railwaymen's union leader with a penchant for the high life had not bene-fited personally from the leak, he had acquired a total of £1,600 from some rather dubious previous transactions with the pair (including placing a bet on the outcome of the general election). A week before the tribunal set up to investigate the matter delivered its verdict Thomas resigned as a minister, and three weeks later, in the emotional scene Nicolson witnessed, as an MP.

MacDonald was sad to lose his oldest and most loyal friend in politics; Baldwin was sad because he was very fond of Thomas, who in his view had 'fallen victim to the two weaknesses of his class', namely the turf and drink;

and George V, had he still been alive, would have been sad too, because Thomas used to make him laugh uproariously.

It had been a confusing election: when Harold Nicolson presented himself for selection at Leicester in October 1935 he was 'perfectly willing to stand as a National Candidate under any of the minor labels, Tory, Liberal or Labour . . . I had offered myself as a National Liberal two years ago. I had offered myself to the Tories at the time of the Sevenoaks bye-election.' He had also, briefly, been a member of Mosley's New Party. Nicolson, who was 'at sea about these labels', was informed that though he should not call himself 'National Labour candidate', if pressed, 'I must say that I was a follower of Ramsay MacDonald.' Still 'muddled', he was sharply told 'not to fuss about MY HONOUR', and stood as the 'National Government Candidate' (meaning he supported Baldwin but with no other commitments). Unfortunately, the local printers made an understandable mistake and printed placards describing him as the 'National Conservative Candidate'. The word 'chameleon' could be heard on the streets, but he got in anyway – though by only eighty-seven votes – in a fight against Labour and Liberal candidates. Nicolson actually thought of himself as 'an Asquithian Liberal', and indeed the divided Liberal Party effectively disintegrated in 1935; from then forward the contest that would dominate the British electoral system was a two-party Conservative–Labour one.

The opposition was, if possible, even more muddled: its policy was to represent some vague concept of 'Tory socialism', while taking a quasi-independent line on foreign affairs (which would attract a growing number of government dissidents in the coming years of growing international tension). Moreover, the health of the sixty-nine-year-old Ramsay MacDonald, who had lost his seat in the general election, but had been retained in government and was returned to Parliament in a by-election in January 1936, was failing, as was his grip on events. He was, according to his biographer 'a forlorn, and, as time went on, an almost forgotten figure'. Labour's first and second Prime Minister finally resigned as Lord President of the [Privy] Council in May 1937, and on 9 November that year, while on a voyage to South America with his youngest daughter, he died of heart failure.

FIFTEEN

'I am Spain . . .'

O understand before too late
Freedom was never held without a fight.
John Cornford, 'Full Moon at Tierz: Before the Storming of Huesca' (1936)

What's your proposal? To build a just city? I will.
I agree. Or is it the suicide pact, the romantic death? Very well, I accept, for
I am your choice, your decision. Yes, I am Spain.

W.H. Auden, 'Spain' (1937)

They [the poets of the Spanish Civil War] talked in an almost empty theatre
as if it were a packed Wembley stadium. They argued, proved, disproved and
judged as if the whole nation were listening. They had, in fact, discovered a
drama and invented an audience.

Robin Skelton, Introduction to *Poetry of the Thirties* (1964)

There is no longer any point in trying to untangle the web of lies and confu-
sions which lay behind that dreadful Civil War. It arose out of total confusion
and chaos. There were individuals on both sides who committed every possible
form of cruelty and beastliness. And nobody, from either side, came out of it
with clean hands. We, of the International Brigades, had wilfully deluded
ourselves into the belief that we were fighting a noble Crusade because we
needed a crusade – the opportunity to fight against the manifest evils of Fascism
which seemed then as if it would overwhelm every value of Western civilization. We were wrong . . . but . . . the whole thing was not in vain . . . I have
never regretted that I took part in it. The situation is not to be judged by what
we now know of it, but only as it appeared in the context of the period.

Jason Gurney, *Crusade in Spain* (1974)

'The Spanish Tragedy', read *The Times* leader headline on 29 July 1936. It
described the military rebellion that had broken out in Spain on 17 July,

speaking magisterially of an anachronistic struggle irrelevant to modern Europe, an age-old battle rooted deep in Spanish history that had more to do with Goths and Vandals and the excesses of the Spanish Inquisition than modern ideologies. This was a struggle in which 'communist' and 'fascist' were inappropriate labels, and in which Britain should most definitely not take sides, nor get involved in any way. That was how the British government would have liked to see it too, but the war was to be a cruel and protracted conflict that aroused British public opinion and would take British lives – at least five hundred of the 2,500-odd who volunteered to fight – and involve thousands more in political and humanitarian campaigns.

In February 1936 a Popular Front coalition of various Spanish socialist, Communist, liberal and nationalist parties and groupings had won a hair's-breadth election victory. A period of instability followed: the socialists refused to join the new government, there were assassinations, failed assassinations, woundings and strikes, and 160 religious buildings were destroyed – usually torched. On 13 July Joseph José Calvo Sotelo, a monarchist and leader of the opposition in the Spanish parliament, the Cortes, was gunned down in a revenge killing. Five days later General Francisco Franco, who was regarded by the Spanish middle classes as the man who would save the country from political and social revolution, was flown from the Balearic Islands, where he had been sent into exile to serve as military commander, to Spanish Morocco, from where he launched what was intended to be a swift *coup d'état* to overthrow the democratically elected Republican government: the subsequent conflict took on the coloration of a world war in embryo, becoming 'the screen on to which foreigners projected their own concerns with such luminous clarity'.

From the outset Britain's official aim was, in the words of the acting Foreign Secretary Lord Halifax (since Anthony Eden was on holiday), to 'localise the disturbance . . . and to prevent outside assistance from prolonging the war'. The National Government appeared less interested in which side won – the Republicans (who spanned the spectrum from liberal centrists concerned to uphold constitutional government through to revolutionary Communists and anarchists) or the Nationalist insurgents (a disparate mix of fascists, falangists, monarchists and Catholics united only in opposition to communism) – as long as the resulting government was stable and Britain's strategic interests were not threatened.

When the representatives of twenty-seven nations met in London on 9 September 1936 to decide their policy towards the war, Britain took the lead in advocating non-intervention – a stance that was severely compromised when Germany helped airlift Franco's army from Morocco to Spain at the end of July; over the course of the war Germany and Italy supplied aircraft, tanks, guns and 'volunteer' troops to the rebels. In late September the USSR started to provide the Republicans with tanks and planes (though never in such large quantities as those supplied to the Nationalists by Germany and Italy). The British government was clearly aware of these breaches, and of the fact that the policy of non-intervention benefited the Nationalists far more than the Republicans, but in Eden's words, 'Better a leaky dam than no dam at all.' 'An elaborate policy of humbug', Winston Churchill, then a Conservative backbencher, called it, though he had supported non-intervention at first. The Spanish Civil War would cut across party alignments, and made many political dilemmas explicit and uncomfortable: Was Britain going to take a stand against fascism? Or was Bolshevism the greater threat? How realistic was an Anglo-Italian rapprochement in the face of Germany? What were Hitler's intentions in Europe, and how could these be contained? Could pacifism be an absolute, or were there circumstances when to fight was the lesser evil?

Most Conservatives supported non-intervention, seeing the Civil War as a matter of 'Rabble against Rebel', an irrelevant distraction from the problem of Germany, though some were fiercely pro-Franco as a bulwark against communism, and would have echoed the *Daily Mail*'s line that the Generalissimo's forces were 'Crusaders of Righteousness', or Stanley Baldwin's sentiment: 'We English hate fascism, but we loathe bolshevism as much. So, if there is somewhere where fascists and bolshevists can kill each other off, so much the better.' Others came to fear Franco as a threat to the British Empire – as Churchill did.

The most notable Tory dissident was Katherine Murray, the Duchess of Atholl, MP for Kinross and West Perth, an unlikely Republican supporter with her strong anti-communism and her fervour for Empire (she had opposed the government's India Act, which offered a degree of self-government to the subcontinent in May 1935). Moved by the suffering of the Spanish people, she chaired the National Joint Committee for Spanish Relief, and in April 1937 went to Spain with the Committee's vice-chair, Eleanor Rathbone, an independent MP, and the left-wing Labour Member Ellen Wilkinson. The women travelled around Spain ('flitted', according to a critical George Orwell), meeting leaders on both sides and victims of war, although they were refused permission to visit the front. The Penguin Special the Duchess wrote on her return, *Searchlight on Spain*, sold 300,000 copies in Britain and was translated into Spanish, French and German. However, many of her constituents were 'dancing with fury' at her support for the Republican cause, feeling that the interests of the Spanish sierra were far removed from those of the Scottish Highlands, and picking up the taunt 'the 'Red Duchess', though as a Labour MP wrote, it was 'a complete misnomer. She is a quiet, unobtrusive, rather pale and tired-looking old lady. She possesses absolute courage of conviction.' In December 1938, with almost no support from her former Conservative colleagues, the Duchess lost her seat in a by-election she herself instigated (admittedly with a wider agenda including that of anti-appeasement), and in which she stood as an independent.

While the Communist Party celebrated the war in Spain as a vindication of its recent Popular Front policy, with working-class parties uniting to fight a common enemy in fascism, that was not what actually happened in Spain, nor in Britain, where the left continued to fragment.

The Spanish conflict pointed up the powerlessness of the Liberal Party, which continued to put its faith in the League of Nations, though the former party leader Lloyd George loudly proclaimed that he had almost gone to Spain, since he saw his own political battles as analogous to those of the Republicans: 'I have been in the same fight all my life. The landed aristocracy, conservative churchmen, and vested industrial and financial interests have always fought me. And I them.' But he didn't go, and this vainglorious attempt to revive a spent career was recognised for what it was. However, one Liberal MP, Wilfred Roberts, who visited Spain in 1936 with an all-party delegation, worked tirelessly for the National Joint Committee for Spanish Relief, attracting charges of being a fellow traveller for his willingness to work with anyone, including Communists, to get things done.

The Labour Party had declared its support for the Republic, and the TUC organised a fund for humanitarian relief for their Spanish brothers at the outset, but the party decided to support the policy of non-intervention in the hope of averting a wider pan-European war, as well as having no wish to alienate its Catholic supporters – though even if Labour *had* opposed non-intervention, the small number of seats (154) it had won in the previous year's election would not have changed government policy. It was not until the Labour Party Conference of October 1937 that support for non-intervention was jettisoned, as increasing numbers of stories of insurgent atrocities appeared in the press. Even then Labour leaders were reluctant to divert resources to a campaign they felt might further fracture an already fissiparous party, and rather than bringing pressure to bear on the government to intervene in Spain they largely confined their initiatives to humanitarian ones, organised by individuals or small local groups. Various Labour MPs visited Spain, including the party leader Clement Attlee, who went in December 1937 with a group that included Ellen Wilkinson. They stayed in a hotel in Barcelona where most of the rooms were used as hospital wards for the wounded, since the fighting was only four miles away, and visited the Communist British Battalion of the International Brigade (which named a company the 'Major Attlee Company' in honour of Labour's cautious leader). Attlee returned much impressed by the Spanish 'People's Army' – though this had no effect on Labour policy.

The Independent Labour Party (ILP) had disaffiliated from the Labour Party in 1932, presenting itself as a revolutionary socialist party, but by 1935 its membership had plunged from over 16,000 members to little more than a quarter of that – though it remained a powerful force in Glasgow, where four ILP MPs were returned in 1935, including James Maxton, its widely respected leader. When war broke out in Spain, at just the moment when the Comintern had eschewed revolution, it seemed that here was an opportunity for Britain's only revolutionary party, and the ILP immediately threw its support wholly behind one Spanish party, POUM (Partido Obrero de Unificacíon Marxista), created in 1935 with an aim of 'permanent revolution'. The ILP channelled funds to POUM to be 'used by our comrades in the way they think best', including, presumably, buying arms. It also provided medical supplies, an ambulance and a military contingent which arrived in December 1937, campaigned, and cared for Basque refugee children.

By the 1930s Spain had begun to be a holiday destination for those for whom 'Blackpool and Brighton . . . ceased to suffice'. Comfortably-off middle-class British travellers ventured in small numbers to the 'Spanish Riviera' from Málaga to Almería, to Granada and Seville, or took a coach trip with Thomas Cook, Pickfords or Lunns; a thirty-two-day tour organised by a London-based coach company, Motorways Ltd, cost ninety-eight guineas – about £5,000 in today's prices – though the Workers' Travel Association offered trips to Spain for £10 to £12. But most preferred the Basque coast, and San Sebastián was a favourite resort. Small colonies of Brits, attracted by the climate, though rarely by the 'oily' food, settled in Spain or on the islands such as Mallorca, where there were reckoned to be some 4,000 British expats by 1935 – including the poet Robert Graves – providing there was a golf course nearby and a circulating library. But though holiday-makers might have a good time in 'the poster world . . . of gamboge and cerulean blue, of singing and lounging and carnations in the mouth', and expatriates enjoyed their new life in Spain, few sloughed off their preconceptions about the country, seeing it as a backward, superstitious place with a '*mañana*' mentality, in the sway of a religion that was tainted by the Inquisition, and after 1931 politically turbulent, regrettably 'socialistic' and strike-riddled. To a large extent this would be the attitude of most of the British to that 'far away country' throughout the Civil War – until stories of atrocities and suffering stirred a compassionate response in many.

However, there were some for whom Spain's tragedy dominated the horizon from the start of the war, as an indictment, a clarification, a compulsion, a call to take sides, to take action. A few went to fight for Franco's forces, including four Catholic seminarians from the English College at Valladolid and a contingent raised in the Irish Free State by Eoin O'Duffy, leader of the fascist Blueshirts. So did Peter Kemp, who as a 'traditionalist Tory . . . viewed communism and fascism with equal loathing. But of the two I believed communism presented the greatest danger to Europe.' Kemp abandoned his legal career to join a Carlist cavalry regiment, and was soon transferred to the Spanish Foreign Legion, where he served as an officer before being almost killed by a mortar bomb in the summer of 1938.

But it was the Republican cause that inspired almost all those from Britain who went to fight in Spain. 'I suppose it's a fever in the blood of the younger generation that we can't possibly understand,' wrote Virginia Woolf to her sister Vanessa Bell, whose son Julian had the 'fever'. For the writer John Lehmann, 'The Spanish war . . . turned the scale and thereafter I knew where I stood . . . everything, all our fears, our confused hopes and beliefs, our half-formulated theories and imaginings, veered and converged towards its testing and its opportunity, like steel filings that slide towards a magnet suddenly put near them.' As Lord Byron had fought for liberty in Greece in 1824, so numbers of young Britons felt drawn to take that fight to Spain. Just outside Chester, Frank Forster, once again signing on the dole, and worrying about not being able to afford a new pair of shoes, read of the rout of Nationalist forces in a battle outside Madrid one Sunday in *Reynolds' News*:

> The struggle appears to have been quite a grim one. Pictures which I have seen in the newspaper depicting scenes in Spain during the present fighting, show workers in shirt sleeves using rifles and machine guns just as though they had come straight from the factory or home and hastily flung up barricades behind which they have crouched to repel the raiders. Such a life as this is one that I would like so much to live. Events must happen so quickly that the ordinary petty squabbles and bickering of everyday family life are swamped out and everybody of the working class loyal to the proletarian cause is welded together in such a solid body of comradeship. There must be a great thrill in living through times such as the ones now in Spain.

In place of the humdrum everyday existence here is excitable thrilling adventure for the sake of high aims. Would I were now in Spain!

Many other idealists felt that same urge and left for Spain, finding their own way in the early months, attaching themselves to some militia or other that they found congenial, sometimes staying a few weeks or months, then peeling off and coming back home. No structure, no question of desertion. It was what one historian of the Spanish Civil War, Hugh Thomas, called the 'heroic period' before bitter infighting between the different factions of the left vitiated this unity.

The first British casualty in Spain was an unlikely one. Felicia Browne was a young, middle-class artist who had spent time at the Slade and had exhibited at the 'Artists Against Fascism and War' exhibition in November 1935. A member of the Communist Party, she was in Barcelona when the war broke out, possibly to sketch the People's Olympiad (a left-wing alternative to the Olympic Games currently in progress in Berlin). She managed to enlist, and volunteered to join a commando raid on a rebel munitions train. Taking first aid to an injured colleague, Browne was shot and killed around 25 August 1936. Her notebook was retrieved, and her sketches of Spanish militia were auctioned to raise money for the cause.

The rebellious ex-public schoolboy Esmond Romilly was eighteen when he went to Spain in October 1936. Crossing France by bicycle, carrying a copy of Aldous Huxley's *Eyeless in Gaza* and wearing boots and underwear he had bought at the Army & Navy Stores on his father's charge account, Romilly attached himself first to the Tom Mann Centuria (named after the veteran British trade union leader), commanded by a Jewish East London clothing worker, Nat Cohen, who had been on a cycling holiday in Spain when war broke out. Soon, bored with inaction, the volunteers attached themselves to the XII (German) Thaelmann International Brigade, and, with rudimentary training and equipment, were sent to fight on the Madrid front, the British contingent standing out, according to the *Daily Express* journalist Sefton Delmer, who visited them, 'like a schoolboy team from the Blues'. At the battle of Boadilla there was chaos, desertion – 'we only *thought* we were an army' – and death. Romilly was one of only two English men to survive.

He left Spain with severe dysentery, arriving back in England in January 1937, and wrote an account of his war, *Boadilla*, which was published that autumn. Since there was already a flood of books about Spain on the market, it sold few copies (though when Diana Mitford, who married Oswald Mosley in 1936, read it, 'It made me be on the Government side in Spain for about three days . . . he can tell a story well'), and the nineteen-year-old Romilly had to make a living by writing advertising copy. While convalescing he met his second cousin, the sparky Jessica ('Decca') Mitford, sister of the fascists Diana and Unity. For some time Jessica had 'cut pictures of woman guerrillas out of the papers, determined, steady-looking women, wiry, bright-eyed, gaunt-faced, some middle aged, and some little girls', and had wondered 'How to take my place at their side?' Meeting Romilly, who had been commissioned by the *News Chronicle* to report from Spain, gave her the opportunity. Now she 'pored over pictures of Spanish guerrilla women fighters in the weekly illustrated papers', and decided what to wear to war: 'a brown corduroy ski suit with a military-looking jacket and plenty of pockets . . . a good-looking running away outfit' on which she planned to sew Cash's name tapes 'bearing the legend DECCA MITFORD, INGLESA', which, Romilly assured her, 'would protect my things from getting appropriated'.

The young couple managed to get to Bilbao. They were pursued by the 'Grown-Ups' – Jessica's 'Muv and Farve', Lord and Lady Redesdale – and the British press, and finally packed off back to France by the consul; they married in Bayonne on 18 May 1937, with both mothers' reluctant blessing, lots of presents, and a promise from Hitler, extracted by Jessica's sister Unity, that the story of Jessica 'running away with the reds to Spain' would not appear in the German press. The newlyweds sadly decided not to return to Spain: 'We felt that all the recent publicity about us had already harmed the cause of the Spanish Republic. The endless stories about our adventures had driven the war news off the front pages, as well as making a farce of our own convictions.'

Esmond's brother Giles had a similarly high-profile war in Spain. He joined the International Brigade, and when his uncle Winston Churchill tried to use his influence to keep him out of the fighting, Romilly went awol in order to be punished by being sent to the front line, as he was during the battle of Brunete near Madrid in early July 1937, in which he distinguished himself.

'Famous Poet to Drive Ambulance in Spain', announced the *Daily Worker* on 12 January 1937. The poet was Wystan Hugh Auden, who had been in Iceland with his fellow-poet Louis MacNeice when war broke out in Spain. 'Europe is absent,' he had written there. 'This is an island and/Unreal.' He went to Spain knowing that 'I shall probably be a bloody bad soldier but how can I speak to/for them without becoming one?' Auden was 'profoundly shocked and disturbed' by the fact that 'all the churches were shut, I realized I didn't like it. I wanted them to be open. I didn't at that point want particularly to pray myself, but I wanted people to be able to,' and by the massacre of priests by the Republicans. He spent little more than a month in Spain, from where he filed his impressions for the *New Statesman* and perhaps did some propaganda broadcasting.

The pro-Franco South African poet Roy Campbell, who was also in Spain at the time, accredited by the Catholic magazine the *Tablet* and always critical of the left – 'first clenching fists and then throwing up their hands' – spoke viciously of Auden's contribution as 'playing table-tennis on behalf of the Republicans'. Auden himself complained that he 'waited around and could find nothing to do'. A poem he wrote on his return was simply called 'Spain': 'I am whatever you do . . . I am your choice, your decision: yes, I am Spain'. It was published as a sixpenny pamphlet, with the proceeds going to the work of Medical Aid in Spain. George Orwell thought it was 'one of the few decent things that have been published about Spain', though he had his criticisms: 'Mr Auden's brand of amoralism is only possible if you are the kind of person who is always somewhere else when the trigger is pulled.'

Other poets were drawn to Spain too. 'We had a greater need of going to Spain than the Spanish Republic had need of us,' said one. Julian Bell, the son of the Bloomsbury artists Vanessa and Clive Bell, a Cambridge-educated, rather minor poet, went not to fight, since his family had strong pacifist inclinations, but as an ambulance driver. Bell was wounded in the battle of Brunete on 18 July 1937, and died later that day. His aunt, Virginia Woolf, wondered if his mother would ever get over the 'perpetual wound' his death had caused.

Laurie Lee had been in Spain when war broke out – 'no announcements, no newspapers, just a whispering in the street and the sound of a woman weeping' – but left almost at once, and though he later liked to pretend he was drawn straight back, it was over a year before he slipped across the border from France, leaving a mess of emotional entanglements behind him, and with an exceptionally cold winter in Spain ahead. He presented himself to the 15th International Brigade, who, desperately short of men, reported of the poet-volunteer carrying a violin: 'He seems a perfectly sincere comrade, who is very sympathetic to the Spanish government [but as he is] generally speaking, physically weak, he will not be any use at the front. He agrees that the added excitement will be too much for him.' (Lee suffered from epileptic fits.) Within less than two months, as the brutal battle of Teruel raged, in which the International Brigade took desperately heavy losses, Lee had returned to England.

Stephen Spender had been reviewing poetry for the *Daily Worker* since October 1936, and when his book *Forward from Liberalism* was published by the Left Book Club in early January 1937, Harry Pollitt, the Secretary of the CPGB, suggested that the poet might join the newly formed International Brigade. Spender demurred, saying that he had 'no qualification as a soldier', and that since he couldn't drive, he could hardly join the ambulance brigade. The avuncular Pollitt allegedly joked that at least Spender could 'get himself killed, to give the party its Byron', but since that didn't appeal much either, Spender was sent to Spain by the Communist Party (of which he was not yet a member) to find out what had happened to the crew of a Russian ship sunk by the Italians. Mission accomplished, he returned to England, but was back in Spain for six weeks later in the year to broadcast anti-fascist propaganda. He hitched a lift south in an ambulance emblazoned with the slogan 'Fuck Franco' driven by Wogan Philipps, the Communist artist and later active peer, and husband of the writer Rosamond Lehmann. Philipps was wounded at the battle of Jarama, but later returned to Spain and organised the evacuation of nearly 2,000 refugees to Mexico after Franco's victory. Meanwhile, Spender spent most of his time trying to get a former lover, Tony Hyndman, who had joined the International Brigade when Spender married, and had been traumatised by fighting on the Jarama front, about which he had written his disillusioned poem, 'no slogan/no clenched fist/except in pain', released from serving with the Brigade.

Spender called the Spanish Civil War a 'poet's war', and it generated almost as much poetry as had the First World War, inspired by violent death among the olive groves: 'The flower of freedom needs blood at its roots,' wrote George Barker. It was not only the blood of soldiers on the parched ground or on city pavements, but women and children killed and mutilated too, by snipers or from the air. Most of the poems were written in support of the Republican side, though some were penned for Franco too.

Many British writers who didn't go to Spain nevertheless had strong partisan views. The socialite Nancy Cunard, rich from shipping-line money, and with a passionate and effective, if erratic, social conscience, fought for causes in 'a state of fury in which, in order to defend, she attacked every windmill in a landscape of windmills'. Deeply committed to the straightforward notion that the Republicans were fighting for freedom, she visited Spain several times, travelling to the front with a typewriter and her possessions slung over her shoulder in a spotted handkerchief, distributing food, cigarettes and what money she could, and sending reports back to the British press. In January 1939, as the Nationalist victory became inevitable, she would turn in powerful, searing accounts of refugees teeming across the border into France for the *Manchester Guardian*, concluding that 'Franco stands condemned and judged for eternity.' At Cunard's prompting, the *Guardian* set up a fund to help the refugees in that terrible early spring of 'human wretchedness' when many of those who did escape were effectively penned up in camps in France with no facilities.

But before that, in 1937, Nancy Cunard had decided to survey the views of British writers on the conflict, since they were, she thought (or flattered them) 'amongst the most sensitive instruments of a nation . . . [and] it is impossible any longer to take no side'. It was a profoundly unscientific poll, and several of those she solicited refused the invitation. 'Will you please stop sending me this bloody rubbish,' wrote George Orwell. 'I am not one of your fashionable pansies like Auden and Spender. I was six months in Spain, most of the time fighting. I have a bullet-hole in me at present, and I am not going to write blah about defending democracy or gallant little anyone.' Nevertheless, the results were as Cunard had believed they must be – and possibly to a degree had engineered, since there is no certain way of knowing whom she approached, and the refuseniks are not listed. When 3,000 copies of *Authors Take Sides on the Spanish War* were published as a pamphlet by *Left Review* in the autumn of 1937, with the proceeds going to the Republicans, they sold out immediately.

One hundred and twenty-seven of the 148 who contributed were 'For the Government'. These included the ILP General Secretary Fenner Brockway; the poet George Barker, who took the opportunity to inveigh against the US car manufacturer Walter Chrysler and the Archbishop of Canterbury, as well as Hitler, Mussolini and Franco; the playwright Samuel Beckett – whose response, '!UPTHEREPUBLIC!', was the shortest, and he would not be induced to write more; Margaret Cole; Cyril Connolly; the Satanist Aleister Crowley, who wanted to see Franco 'swing in chains at Execution Dock' as a 'common murderer and a pirate'; Havelock Ellis; William Gallacher; William Forrest (a 'labourer's son. I am a trade unionist. I am a writer . . . And you ask me where I stand . . . ? In the name of God!'); David Gascoyne; Victor Gollancz; Aldous Huxley; C.E.M. Joad; Rose Macaulay (who was as succinct as Beckett, answering 'AGAINST FRANCO'); Sylvia Pankhurst; and against type perhaps, the editor of the *Countryman*; Stephen Spender (whose reply was the longest) and the other 'MacSpaundays', Auden, MacNeice and C. Day Lewis; Rebecca West; the Williams-Ellises, Amabel and Clough; and Leonard (but not Virginia – 'All I can do is write') Woolf.

Sixteen were 'Neutral'. They included T.S. Eliot, who felt 'convinced that at least a few men of letters should remain isolated, and take no part in these collective activities'; Seán Ó'Faoláin, who barked, 'Don't be a lot of saps. If X and Y want to cut each other's throats over Z, why on earth do people who do not believe in the ideas propounded by either X,Y or Z have to "choose between them"?'; Ezra Pound, who found the whole idea of such a questionnaire 'an escape mechanism for young fools who are too cowardly to think'; Vita Sackville-West and Vera Brittain, who as 'an uncompromising pacifist . . . [held] war to be a crime against humanity whoever fights it and against whomever it is fought'.

Only five were 'Against the Government'. These included Roy Campbell, Wyndham Lewis, Geoffrey Moss ('Major, late Grenadier Guards') and Evelyn Waugh, who knew Spain 'only as a tourist and a reader of newspapers', but felt that if he were a Spaniard 'I should be fighting for General Franco', though he found it 'mischievous' to suggest that the choice between 'fascism and Marxism . . . is imminent'. George Bernard Shaw's opinion that 'In Spain both the Right and Left so thoroughly disgraced themselves in the turns they took in trying to govern their country before the Right revolted, that it is impossible to say which is the more incompetent' arrived so late that it was printed inside the front cover under the heading 'unclassifiable'. Graham Greene did not commit himself, since he was anti-Franco but was disturbed by Republican brutalities. Many others were measured in their support for the Republicans, 'questioning the certainties on which that commitment was built' and sobered by what happened when their idealism came up against the grim realities of Spanish politics.

Those realities had to be confronted early by some. John Cornford was born into an upper-middle-class academic family, the great-grandson of Charles Darwin, and joined the Communist Party while he was a brilliant undergraduate at Trinity College, Cambridge. As soon as he heard news of the outbreak of war in Spain and rumours of the dual nature of the fight in Catalonia, to defeat fascism and to establish a workers' state, he arranged accreditation from the *News Chronicle* – though he spoke no Spanish – and set off for Port Bou. He was in Barcelona by 8 August 1936, one of the first Britons to arrive, and found there what he thought was 'a genuine dictatorship of the majority supported by the majority', as he wrote to his love, the equally stellar, equally politically committed Communist Margot Heinemann. Within three days Cornford had thrown in his observer status and joined one of the POUM militias.

Barcelona in the early days wove a heady spell for most who arrived there en route to war. Philip Toynbee wrote: 'The place had a sort of carnival atmosphere, "en pleine revolution". It is a workers' city at war . . . it was intoxicating.' George Orwell was similarly impressed when he arrived in late December 1936. He had first gone to see Harry Pollitt about going to

Spain, but refused to join the International Brigade, insisting that he wanted to go and see for himself before making a commitment. Pollitt 'decided I was politically unreliable' and refused CP assistance, so Orwell contacted the ILP, and they agreed to help. Arriving in Barcelona with his size-twelve boots strung round his neck, he found 'much in it that I did not understand, in some ways I did not even like it, but I recognised it immediately as a state of affairs worth fighting for.' Orwell joined the POUM militia, fighting under his real name, Eric Blair. He was sent to the Aragon front as a *cabo* (corporal) in charge of twelve men, where he stayed for 115 days, mainly in trenches, experiencing the 'mingled boredom and discomfort of stationary warfare', since his was a quiet part of the line. 'This is not a war,' his commander Georges Kopp, a Belgian ex-engineer, used to say, 'it is a comic opera with occasional death.'

Despite the hardships, the lack of weapons, uniforms and equipment, the poor food, the stench, the rats and the often bitter cold, Orwell felt he was 'breathing the air of equality', and imagined that all those fighting for freedom all over Spain were too. He would argue with his comrades in the trenches that there was a difference between Stalin's tyranny in Russia (news of the Moscow show trials was beginning to circulate) and Communist tactics in Spain, and in fact intended to transfer to an International Brigade himself, seeing the point of their slogan 'The war first, the revolution after' rather than of the POUM's insistence that the Civil War be a revolutionary war, since 'We must go forward or we shall go back!' But while Orwell was recuperating in Barcelona in May 1937 after having been shot by a sniper, the POUM (who had been declared covert fascists) was suppressed and its units were absorbed into the Republican army. Orwell, along with ILP and other foreign supporters, was obliged to flee for his life.

Back in England, Orwell sought a publisher for his account of his experiences in Spain: 'Gollancz, is of *course*, part of the Communism-racket, and as soon as he heard that I had been associated with the POUM and Anarchists . . . he said he did not think he would be able to publish my book.' *Homage to Catalonia*, Orwell's personal, vivid and moving account of his time in Spain and what he saw as the loss and suppression of the revolutionary spirit there was published in April 1938.

'O understand before too late/Freedom was never held without a fight,' John Cornford wrote in September 1936, though for him 'Our fight's not won till the workers of the world . . . Raise the Red Flag triumphantly/For Communism and for liberty.' Cornford, though, had grown increasingly concerned about a militia hamstrung by 'incompetence . . . by lack of technicians, of discipline, of training, of intermediate officers'. And in December

1936 'bad luck' in the shape of machine gunfire during the battle of Boadilla laid Cornford's 'strength into a shallow grave'. He was just twenty-one. Ralph Fox, a founder member of the CPGB and one of its leading intellectuals, was killed on the same day.

Tom Wintringham, the military correspondent of the *Daily Worker* who had arrived in Spain from Abyssinia, urged that what was needed was a trained, disciplined international force, rather than 'amateur anarchist' militias. At a meeting of the Comintern (the Communist International) on 18 September 1936 it was decided that despite the fact that the USSR was still adhering to the policy of non-intervention – which it abandoned a month later – each country should be given a quota of men and women to be recruited to fight in Spain.

The British Communist Party was small, though growing – from 6,500 in February 1935 to over 11,000 in 1936 (and 17,750 by July 1939). Charlotte Haldane, the journalist second wife of the scientist J.B.S. Haldane, who was herself to become enmeshed in the war, suggested that 'In spite of the fact that Marx and Engels had spent most of their lives in England, their doctrines had made comparatively little headway in a country where social-democracy had produced a powerful Labour Party and legal trade unions that satisfied and absorbed the socialist-minded workers.'

Harry Pollitt, leader of the CPGB, and his Politburo colleagues in London had the hard task of raising sufficient volunteers for Spain to meet the Comintern's quota. Their first target was the Young Communist League, and Pollitt's weekly column in the *Daily Worker* called for volunteers. 'If every working-class organisation would only . . . see that all its members with the necessary experience were asked to go to Spain, the British unit would number thousands,' he urged on 21 December 1936. Help from any quarter was welcome, in line with the Party's current (if rebuffed) popular-front policy. Eventually the so-called 'Comintern Army' (though this spoke of a homogeneity and discipline that was never fully the case) would number around 32,000 volunteers drawn from fifty countries, with most coming from France, while the CPGB sent around 2,000 volunteers.

Volunteers would present themselves at the Communist Party's headquarters in King Street, Covent Garden, to be quizzed about their family background – those aged between twenty-five and thirty-five without family commitments were preferred – and whether they had any military experience, or skills that might be useful. Party membership wasn't necessary, but all were interrogated about why they wanted to fight in Spain. Although the majority who joined the International Brigades from Britain were Communists, others were members of the Labour Party or small left-wing groupings, while 224 declared they had no political affiliation. However, nearly all needed CP help, since it was all but impossible for those without money, a passport and connections to get to Spain under their own steam – though some stowed away on Barcelona-bound ships leaving Marseilles. The CP provided a way for those who wanted to activate their commitment to help the Republican cause, and gained much credit, a number of recruits, and some opprobrium, particularly from right-wing newspapers which maintained that there was virtual press-ganging of innocent (or drunken) recruits to the cause. 'Misguided stiffs', a British Foreign Office official in Madrid called them.

Jason Gurney was a young sculptor living near Manresa Road in Chelsea, which in the 1930s was 'largely a slum area, in which most of the rooms were let off as squalid bed sitters for ten bob a week', but which attracted 'a community of artists and students'. For Gurney, who regarded himself as a radical in politics, the Spanish Civil War seemed to provide the chance for an individual to take a positive and effective stand on an issue that appeared to be absolutely clear: 'Either you were opposed to the growth of Fascism and went out to fight against it, or you acquiesced in its crimes and were guilty of permitting its growth. There were many people who claimed that it was a foreign quarrel and that nobody other than Spaniards should involve themselves in it, but for myself and many others like me, it was a war of principle, and principles do not have national boundaries.'

In December 1936 Gurney made his way to King Street and explained that he had come to join the International Brigade. One of the women in the office 'looked at me as if I was likely to be more of a liability than an asset', but led him into the office of 'Comrade Robson':

> Within about ten minutes the room had filled up . . . Nobody seemed to know anyone else and we all sat round and fidgeted until Robson finally turned round and delivered himself of a short and rather threatening lecture. He was completely fair and frank in what he had to say. It was a bastard of a war, we would be short of food, medical services and even arms and ammunition. If any of us believed we were going into a fine adventure we might as well pack up and go home right away. He could promise us nothing but the opportunity to fight Fascism, on the evils of which he enlarged at great length . . . One individual became very insistent about the conditions of service, whereupon Robson snapped at him 'If you are looking for conditions of service, you're not the kind of bloke we want in Spain. So get out.' That seemed to be the right attitude and I was impressed. I was going to regret it later, but at the time it seemed almost indecent to ask conditions for the privilege of serving in a crusade. We were not submitted to

any kind of medical examination. Robson asked if we were fit and healthy and took our word for it. We were given twenty-four hours to make our personal arrangements and told to report back at the same time on the following day.

For John Londragan, a Scottish railwaymen, it was straightforward too: 'Being a member of the Communist party and an anti-fascist I thought it was my duty to go and help the people in Spain. And the fight, whether it be here in Aberdeen against the British Union of Fascists or against Hitler and Mussolini in Spain, was exactly the same fight to me, no difference at all.' Londragan was told firmly, 'We don't want adventurers. We want people who really are anti-Fascist, who really want to play a part against Fascism in Spain.'

Although those applying at the Passport Office for visas or new passports would be refused if it was suspected that they intended to go to fight in Spain, there was a way around this that the Communist Party exploited. Volunteers were given tickets for a weekend excursion to Paris: 'They used to call them "dirty week-end tickets". You didn't need a passport, or anything.' Even despite the announcement on 20 February 1937 that the 1870 Foreign Enlistment Act (designed to prevent the sale of arms during the Franco-Prussian war) made it an offence to recruit or volunteer to fight in Spain, and carried a penalty of two years in prison, a fine, or both, no prosecutions were brought, and the authorities could do little about groups of men setting off from Victoria station who swore that they were going to visit the Paris Exhibition, or just taking a short holiday across the Channel. Three quarters of those who went to fight with the British Battalion did so *after* the ban.

When Jason Gurney returned to King Street on the morning after Comrade Robson's lecture, 'the original eight men I had met on the previous day had now increased to fifteen. They were all working-class fellows, about my own age, poorly but respectably dressed; most of them in their Sunday suits, raincoats and cloth-caps. Everybody was subdued [but] once aboard the Channel steamer, however, the whole atmosphere changed completely. We had left England and there was no going back on our decision . . . on arrival at the Gare du Nord the taxi-drivers, who were all Red enthusiasts, recognised us at once for what we were and gave us a free ride to the *Bureaux des Syndicats* which was the assembly place for foreign volunteers coming from all over Europe.'

Charlotte Haldane, whose son Ronnie was, at sixteen, the youngest member of the International Brigade, was employed (under the code name Rita) to meet the volunteers at an office in the aptly-named place du Combat in Paris. A few, 'not more than half a dozen', were found unsuitable for fighting and were returned to London. She found that of the others – 'by no means all Communists' – many were 'unemployed lads, miners often from the valleys of South Wales, or the mining villages of Scotland. Years of depression and the dole had forced them into enlistment. Spain's gain was Britain's loss here.'

The volunteers were put up in 'little, shabby, unobtrusive hotels . . . whose owners' discretion could be counted on'. To ensure that no one got drunk or visited a brothel, all their money was confiscated. (Haldane sent what was invariably a few coins or a 'grubby ten shilling or pound note' back to London 'with the request it be refunded to their families through the Dependents Aid Committee'.) Each man was issued with ten francs a day, so all he could buy was some Gauloises and a couple of drinks. The men were put in charge of a *'responsable'* (Gurney was chosen to be one of these, since he was the only one of his group with any military experience, though this was 'limited to the OTC which I had so bitterly detested at school', and he spoke French). They were issued with blue French berets to make them look less obtrusive and, forbidden to carry any luggage, told to stuff a clean shirt and socks, soap, toothpaste and shaving materials into their pockets before they set off for the frontier accompanied by a guide provided by the French Communist Party.

'The departure of the "Red Train" from the Gare Austerlitz had become one of the sights of Paris,' recalled Gurney. 'There was no secrecy about the whole affair and crowds with banners came to wave us off . . . It was rather embarrassing to be treated like heroes before we had done anything and we were delighted when the train finally pulled out.' The volunteers arrived in Perpignan near the French–Spanish border, from where buses took them across the Pyrenees by night to Figueras on the Spanish side. Despite France's adherence to non-intervention, officials usually turned a blind eye to the traffic, and even after the border was closed, guides managed to find a number of routes across the Pyrenees and into Spain by which men crossed on foot, often wearing plimsolls or rope-soled espadrilles they had bought for a few francs.

The volunteers came mainly from urban and industrial areas all over Britain, with the largest numbers from Scotland (five hundred), London, the North-West and the North-East, where there were strong links between shipbuilding and communism. There were 250 volunteers from the Irish Free State, and another sixty from Northern Ireland. Most were in their twenties or early thirties, though one, Joseph May, later admitted to being sixty-three, while others exaggerated their age since volunteers under eighteen were discouraged, and after February 1937 were not accepted at all, sent home if they were already in Spain, or transferred away from the front line if they refused to return. Most were not poets nor artists (Valentine Cunningham, who edited a volume of the poetry of the Civil War forty years later, reckoned that a 'graduates' war was nearer the mark than an intellectuals' one') but working-class. A high percentage were trade union members or, as Haldane had noted, unemployed: those without work probably accounted for between a quarter and an eighth of the British Battalion, thought Tom Wintringham (and these might well be members of the NUWM). Some may have become 'mercenaries' for the money, but that was doubtful, since the pay was erratic and was only the equivalent of £1 a week when it was paid. Some had been in the army or the Territorial Army, or like Gurney, the Officers' Training Corps if they had been to a public school, and considered Spain to be a just cause in which they could use their training.

For some, fighting in Spain had a glamour that hanging around the dank streets of Britain without a job lacked: Spain seemed to offer 'an aliveness that could not be crushed out by the Labour Exchange and hopeless monotony of odd jobs'. Some wanted to escape from intolerable family situations: a few crept away in the night, while Harry Stratton told his pregnant wife that he was taking a new job in Southampton, when in fact he had decided to volunteer for Spain. Some were driven by unswerving Party loyalty, but nearly all went because they believed that fascism had to be defeated and they wanted to help those they perceived as the underdog.

Among the volunteers who listed their occupation were clerks, salesmen, electricians, miners, labourers, drivers, seamen, painters, bricklayers, carpenters and steelworkers. The docker and later Transport and General Workers' Union leader Jack Jones, believing that since the British and French governments were 'standing on the side-lines' it was right for individuals to give the Republicans 'what ever help we could in supporting them', went, and was badly wounded at the battle of Ebro. Fred Copeman, a Communist who had started life in the workhouse and had been involved in the Invergordon mutiny, had been active in the NUWM as had another volunteer Peter Kerrigan, a Hunger Marcher activist. Copeman took over as the British Battalion's commander after the battle of Jarama, alongside Jock Cunningham, who had been a soldier in the Argyll and Sutherland Highlanders. Clem Becket, Joseph Norman and George Brown were among those who taken part in the Kinder Pass trespass, as had Wilf Winnick, a hero of the Manchester YMCA boxing ring (a large number of those who went from Britain were keen boxers).

George Green, a cellist who got work when he could playing in Lyons Corner Houses or cinemas (until the 'talkies' all but did for that) and was active in the Musicians' Union, went to drive an ambulance and act as a medical orderly. He was soon pleading with his wife Nan, who was secretary of the local London branch of the Communist Party, to join him as a nurse, which she did, sending their two young children to board at A.S. Neill's Summerhill (courtesy of Wogan Philipps, who paid the fees for a while). George Green was killed on the banks of the Ebro on 23 September 1938 in a battle that claimed fifty-six lives out of the 116 members of the British Battalion fighting there. J.R. Jump, a newspaper reporter, joined up, as did George Jackson, a coalminer from Cowdenbeath in Scotland, and a clerk who worked for Edmonton Council in North London. A West Country farm labourer, a founder member of the Bromley (Kent) branch of the Communist Party, went to Spain in early 1938 and died during the Ebro offensive that July.

Will Paynter, a check weighman at Cymmer colliery, a trade unionist and Communist Party organiser for Wales, was one of the more than two hundred miners from the Valleys who formed what almost amounted to a cadre within the British Battalion. Paynter didn't volunteer, since he was newly married and his wife was expecting twins (she was to die in childbirth while he was in Spain), but was sent to take up the post of political commissar at the International Brigade's HQ at Albacete to deal with questions of disaffection, desertion and the repatriation of the wounded. Christopher St John Sprigg (who wrote under the pseudonym Christopher Caudwell, but whose friends called him 'Spriggy'), a member of the Poplar Communist Party in East London, was learning Russian with the intention of visiting the USSR one day when the Spanish Civil War broke out. In December 1936 he drove a van that the citizens of Poplar had bought to serve as an ambulance to Spain, where he joined the International Brigade and became a machine-gun instructor. Caudwell died on the bloody killing field of Jarama on 12 February 1937. He left behind a collection of Marxist analyses of culture, published after his death as *Illusion and Reality* (1937), *Studies in a Dying Culture* (1938) and *The Crisis in Physics* (1939), work so intellectually powerful that when Harry Pollitt read *Illusion and Reality* in manuscript he decided the Party could ill afford to lose such a fine, theoretically-attuned mind, and sent off a telegram recalling Caudwell. It arrived too late.

However deep their commitment, the realities of war came as a terrible shock to most of the volunteers. Some of them had earned their political credentials in street fights with members of the British Union of Fascists or on hunger marches, but they were totally unprepared for what they found in a conflict where, in the words of one volunteer, John Lepper, 'Death stalked the olive trees/Picking his men/His leaden finger beckoned/Again and again.' Many were unable to stave off disillusion with the increasingly strict regime imposed by the Battalion commanders to weld their disparate and sometimes unsuitable volunteers into a competent fighting force. Plummeting morale and high rates of desertion – some 298 during the course of the war, while others ended up in Spanish jails or prison camps – were among the many problems that beset the Battalion: the informal way in which volunteers enlisted meant that some found it hard to accept that they couldn't simply go home when they had had enough of war. Despite sensational stories to the contrary, deserters from the Battalion who were caught were not shot, but were set to work digging trenches, fortifications or latrines, or had their pay docked. This last was hardly punitive considering how paltry and irregular it was, and how little there was to spend it on.

Most volunteers had little or no military experience, but training at the International Brigade base at Albacete was minimal in the early days, consisting of 'a couple of days of marching, and one or two mock attacks'. There was also an acute shortage of weapons, uniforms and equipment. The battle of Jarama in February 1937, in which the Nationalists launched a surprise attack in an attempt to encircle Madrid, was the British Battalion's first real experience of battle. Many of them were 'city-bred young men with no experience of war, no idea how to find cover on an open hillside, and no competence as marksmen . . . the propaganda machine had so reduced the reality of the situation that we were convinced that we only had to advance for the enemy to retreat,' wrote Jason Gurney. Two hundred and seventy-five of the four hundred men of the British Battalion were killed on the first day at Jarama defending a position that became known as 'Suicide Hill' (before the war was over there would be 'Suicide Hills' all over Spain'), a fatality rate of 68 per cent: on the first day of the Battle of the Somme in July 1916, British units took around 50 per cent losses. Tom Wintringham was wounded and had to cede his command, though he remained in the battle. Left in line for months, the British volunteers would sing to the tune of 'Red River' a poem by Alec (or Alex) McDade that would become, in slightly more heroic form, the official song of the International Brigade:

> There's a valley in Spain called Jarama
> That's a place that we all know so well,

For 'tis there that we wasted our manhood,
And most of our old age as well.

In July 1937 the first major Republican offensive at Brunete, north-west of Madrid, proved another massacre. Despite acts of great heroism, 268 Britons were lost. This led to a reassessment of command structures and tactics, with the leaders recalled home and several refused permission to return. Thereafter the Battalion became more like a conventional army, though still with a strong political impulse, and along with the rest of the International Brigade was incorporated into the Spanish 'People's Army' by September 1937.

The British Battalion fought on the Aragon front, in the battle of Tereul in December 1937, and on 31 March 1938 it suffered devastating losses on the river Ebro when an encounter with an Italian tank division killed or wounded 150 out of 650, with 140 being taken prisoner. Yet although any hint of romance must have gone out of the crusade by that time – almost all volunteers were wounded at least once, and the mortality rate exceeded 20 per cent – sufficient volunteers continued to arrive to reconstitute the Battalion after the terrible losses of March 1938.

'You are history. You are legend,' declared 'La Pasionaria' (Dolores Ibárruri), the Spanish communist leader, when on instructions from the Spanish Prime Minister Juan Negrín the International Brigades withdrew from Spain in October 1938, in the forlorn hope that this would encourage Italy and Germany to withdraw their forces too. Many of those who fought in Spain looked back on those years as the central experience of their lives, a moral crusade, a time of comradeship and satisfaction at fighting for the 'last great cause'.

Yet there were others for whom the legacy was bitter. They had discovered that 'sheer idealism never stopped a tank', that the war in Spain was not simply a matter of good versus evil, but was also embedded within the conflicts of Spanish history and international politics. That political credentials could take precedence over military ability despite the fact that all wrote simply '*anti-fascista*' under the heading 'Political Affiliation' in their Republican Army pay book. That the 'at all costs' mentality, as Tom Wintringham called it, a 'boastful, romantic view of war . . . that makes courage more important than brains', pertained among some commanders who were fatally convinced that 'Marx + courage = success'. That the Communist Party, while quick to recruit, could be slow to care for its fighting recruits: complaints were likely to be met by political lectures, or visits from prominent political figures, rather than respite from the fighting, and initially little provision was made for the volunteers' dependents, and news of their fate was frequently tied up by red tape for weeks.

Many Brigadiers found that their passion for the cause was not as widely shared as they had hoped. Hubert Humphries, a Birmingham Labour councillor who went to Spain on a fact-finding mission in early 1938, was 'at a loss what to do next' on his return. 'I keep talking to meetings and groups but it was not exactly inspiring to find only fifty people in Birmingham sufficiently interested to turn up at my meeting for first hand information.'

Some 2,400 British volunteers – men and women – went to fight in Spain: 526 died there, and around 1,200 were wounded. The overall loses in the war were nearly a quarter of a million in total – one in every ten Spaniards who fought was estimated to have been killed in combat, while others were summarily executed, mainly by the Nationalists. Most of the British who did make it home received a rousing public welcome on their return, 'a frenzied welcome' that disrupted traffic from Victoria station to Buckingham Palace was how the *Daily Herald* (which had always supported them) described the return of the International Brigade, while Bill Cranston, who had been in Spain for eighteen months and had fought at the battle of Ebro, 'got a reception in Glasgow and we got a big reception in Edinburgh. Right down Leith Street to the Picardy Place Hall . . . it was a good reception, a good reception.' The first memorial to the slain of the International Brigade – there would be fifty more – was erected in Swindon in April 1939, in memory of twenty-three-year-old Percy Williams, a railway engineering apprentice who was killed at the battle of Caspe in March 1938, just two months after he had joined the Brigade.

The communist *Daily Worker*, fervent in its support of the Republican cause, devoted most of its space to Spain from July 1936, its pages often black-bordered with lists of casualties, others carrying photographs of militia bearing arms with captions such as 'On Guard of Freedom', 'Ready for the Rebels' and 'To Defend Democracy'. Reports from Claud Cockburn (under the pseudonym 'Frank Pitcairn') frequently appealed for supplies and medically trained volunteers, though stopping short of calling on readers to come and fight. During the early months of the war the *Worker* managed to raise a staggering £3,000–£4,000 each month for Spain. But the paper's circulation, at around 60,000 in 1937, accounted for only 1 per cent of all newspapers sales, so most people never read it. While the *News Chronicle*, the *Daily Mirror* (which saw its readership as being young working-class men and women, and 'the politics had to be made to match') and the *Daily Herald*, with a readership of around two million a day, were sympathetic to the Republicans and to those who went to join them 'although their own country was not at war' and 'their own homes not at risk', they broadly supported non-intervention.

Though the Cardiff *Western Mail* was initially for Franco's side, a number of influential regional papers, including the *Manchester Guardian*, were more inclined to support the Republicans, but nevertheless aimed at balance, scrupulously reporting atrocities on both sides: 'The summary execution of prisoners, the murder of innocent civilians, and wanton acts of violence . . . reported from all parts of Spain give a shocking picture of the horrors of civil war.' *The Times* and the *Daily Telegraph* were reasonably impartial in the early days, and strongly supported the government's non-intervention position. However, the *Observer*, the *Morning Post* (which was acquired by the *Daily Telegraph* in 1937), the *Daily Mail* (with a circulation of over one and a half million) and the *Daily Sketch* were avid for Franco's victory against the 'Bolsheviks' or 'Reds', and portrayed British volunteers as stupid, deluded, avaricious, venal and 'idle', although probably more than three quarters of those who went to Spain left jobs. Cinema newsreels were generally pro-Nationalist when they did show news from Spain, though they made little attempt to explain the causes of the war, with voice-overs distancing the conflict by talking of the country as the 'lazy garden of Europe [in which] brother raises his rifle against brother'.

It was the provincial papers that brought news of Spain to most people, albeit less the 'big picture' and more human-interest stories of locals who were in some way involved. Each week the letters column of local papers would become a forum for strong opinions about the war, while returning volunteers were interviewed for eye-witness accounts. A Sheffield man and Labour Party member, Joseph Albaya, who managed his father's sweetshop, went to Spain to fight with the International Brigade, sending his fiancée a ring from London on the way 'in case I didn't come back'. But Albaya's linguistic ability took him out of the fighting to act as a translator, and he was allowed to return home when his father died.

'I hope by the following impressions and anecdotes, to convey to the people of Oldham, a true picture of Government in Spain as I have seen it during my service with the International Brigade,' wrote Kenneth Bradbury, a twenty-one-year-old compositor and member of the Young Communist League, from a Spanish hospital after he had been wounded in an air raid. The 'Oldhamer', who had been sustained in the trenches by copies of the 'Green Final' with news of Oldham Athletic Football Club sent by his father, toed the line, telling of Spain 'awakening to a great future . . . that we were privileged to witness . . . the people being solidly behind the government', and his pleasure at seeing that 'the only big building, as always in Spain, is the church, now used as a cinema and "cultural centre" for the village'. Bradbury was killed at Tereul on 20 January 1938.

A partisan but very powerful conduit of news and images from Spain was *Picture Post*, bankrolled by Edward Hulton and edited by the Hungarian émigré Stefan Lorent, the first issue of which came out on 1 October 1938. It printed Robert Capa's now iconic photographs of the war, and was at pains to remind its readers at the time of the Munich crisis that month that Spain was no 'faraway country', but was very much part of Europe and of concern to Britain.

That might be; but in the opinion of Eleanor Rathbone 'the attitude of His Majesty's Government to the Spanish Civil War was like that of a fastidious gentleman walking with an averted nose past a butcher's shop. Or, in view of their responsibility, a better analogy might be a housewife anxious to be rid of a litter of unwanted kittens, who, as she hands them over to the executioner remarks perfunctorily, "Poor little things."' The policy of non-intervention affected humanitarian aid: the government refused to provide financial assistance 'except as part of an agreed international scheme previously accepted [by] both parties in the Civil War', which obviously was most unlikely. However, it did stump up £73,000 for the naval evacuation of refugees in 1936 and 1937, and eventually allowed £25,000 to be sent to the International Commission for Assistance of Child Refugees in Spain, while at the end of the war the Red Cross (which until then had been singularly reticent) gave £5,000 to help Spanish refugees in France. In general, however, the government saw its role as primarily being to try to stop individuals and organisations from sending funds to Spain, on the grounds that they might be used to purchase arms. But just as in practice there wasn't much it could do to stop volunteers going to fight, there wasn't a lot that could be done to stop voluntary collections.

The Society of Friends, or Quakers, were determinedly impartial in their relief efforts, maintaining that their role was to give succour to whoever needed it in time of war. They sent blankets and clothing to refugees, set up mobile canteens in areas conquered by Nationalist forces and a refugee children's colony in the then tiny fishing village of Benidorm, and raised nearly £90,000 for post-war relief aid. But the majority of organisations involved in relief work did take sides.

Within two weeks of the outbreak of the war, the Spanish Medical Aid Committee had been formed, largely at the instigation of the Communist Party activist Isabel Brown, who had received a telegram from Madrid on the second day of the war asking for 'medical supplies, ambulances, doctors, nurses, all the help you can get. Please send us what you can, quickly.'

Brown already had considerable experience of helping the victims of fascist regimes in Italy and Germany, and was legendary for her ability to persuade people to part with their money for a good cause. In three days £1,500 had been collected, and by 23 August 1936 the first medically equipped ambulance group was ready to leave Victoria station for the Aragon front with a team of doctors, nurses, medical students and six drivers. The leader, Kenneth Sinclair-Loutit, a twenty-three-year-old medical student, was threatened by his father that he would be disinherited if he went to Spain (he proved inefficient and was soon replaced). Julian Bell was one of the unit's stretcher-bearers. By the summer of 1938 the Committee was supporting six forward field hospitals, a base hospital and a blood transfusion centre, and British nurses were treating the Republican wounded and training Spanish women and girls in nursing skills, while the trade union movement had either bought or given donations for forty vehicles.

The Scottish Ambulance Unit Committee was founded in September 1936 by a Glasgow businessman and Chancellor of the university, Sir Daniel Stevenson, with the support of wealthy friends and the Scottish TUC. It was not very successful, with indiscipline among some who went to Spain, rivalry with the Spanish Medical Aid Committee, and accusations that it was getting too involved in politics. Despite the support of the Labour movement (which was disenchanted with the political complexion of the Spanish Medical Aid Committee by then), the Scottish Unit was withdrawn, though its commander, Fernanda Jacobsen, worked on helping get food to Spain, for which she received an OBE in 1937.

While most support from Britain flowed through the better-organised pro-Republican organisations, the Catholic press took the lead in raising money for the Nationalist side. The weekly publication the *Universe*, which printed regular pro-Franco reports from such enthusiasts as Arnold Lunn, the religious controversialist and founder of the Alpine Ski Club, and Douglas Jerrold, a cantankerous publisher and would-be Conservative MP who had chartered a private plane to carry Franco from the Canaries to Morocco, started a fund which had reached £8,084, largely from small donations, by the end of 1936, while warning readers that those who contributed to the Spanish Medical Aid Committee were funding 'the Reds'. The *Catholic Herald* also launched an appeal, but both initiatives were soon subsumed into the Bishops' Committee for the Relief of Spanish Distress, headed by Cardinal Hinsley, the blunt-speaking Yorkshire-born Archbishop of Westminster, and with Gabriel Herbert, Evelyn Waugh's sister-in-law, in charge of funds and administration, and Waugh himself as a member. The Committee's intention was not only to relieve distress, but also to support those fighting 'atheistic communism', and to show that not all Britons were for the Republic. It raised some £12,500 during the course of the war, most coming from large donations from wealthy individuals, but never came anywhere near the amount collected for the Republican side.

By late 1936 it had become obvious that the various funds and services needed to be coordinated. In response to an all-party visit of MPs to Spain in November 1936, a National Joint Committee under the chairmanship of the Duchess of Atholl was set up, which by 1938 was overseeing at least 150 pressure and fund-raising groups across the political spectrum devoted to aiding the Republic. This grassroots Popular Front in action brought joy to some, although the Labour movement was determined not to cooperate with what it perceived as a Communist-dominated organisation, opting instead to participate in socialist- and trade-union-organised efforts with fellow Spanish workers – though this was not conspicuously successful: in the first two months of the war the TUC and the National Council of Labour managed to collect less than one penny per member for Spain. Equally, although they were prepared to come under the umbrella, the Quakers were so anxious about compromising their impartiality that they insisted (as did the non-partisan Save the Children organisation) that a statement of impartiality must be read out at the start of each meeting.

A similar umbrella organisation, the General Relief Fund for Distressed Women and Children of Spain, was allegedly impartial, although in fact it was monarchist, since it was unfurled by the Infanta Beatrice, cousin of the Spanish King Alfonso XIII, who had fled Spain on the election of the republic in 1931. Despite being supported by such notable non-right-wingers as the classicist Professor Gilbert Murray and the historian Lord David Cecil, its committee was largely peopled by right-wing pro-Francoists, and those who sheltered refugees including the Bishops' Committee. This organisation was never very successful, and by 1938 it had been wound down, its efforts assumed by the Society of Friends.

Substantial amounts of money were raised in Britain from those moved by the suffering in Spain, but the organisations responsible for distributing this largesse, while humanitarian, were almost invariably partisan, channelling resources specifically to either the Republicans or the Nationalists, rarely to both. However, most individuals who gave so generously were probably largely unaware of these distinctions, and were simply prepared to make a sacrifice 'for Spain'.

Such sacrifices (which included £54,000 donated to Spanish Medical Aid by the middle of 1938) came largely from individuals and local collections. A scheme for buying threepenny milk tokens in Co-op stores raised £32,000 in sixteen months – well below the £200,000 anticipated. Most towns and villages in Britain had some form of 'Aid Spain' campaign, and in large towns there would be more than one. Isabel Brown had 'a card index of every Trade Union, of every co-operative guild, of every individual that had ever sent anything for the victims of Fascism. And we were able to get circulars out to them. We then began to organise public meetings. Put me up to ask for money for wounded men, and my God, we got it. The biggest collection I ever took was on the return of the International Brigade . . . £3,800 in less than ten minutes was handed up to the platform. That is the scale on which we worked . . . The first meeting in the Albert Hall, Paul Robeson came and spoke and sang "Joe Hill".' 'Robeson was the great man of the evening,' wrote the artist William Townsend. 'He bestrode this meeting so that the negroes and the Spaniards seemed to be the same thing; then he sang and so easily filled the air and it seemed everything at that moment that he was singing not only for two oppressed peoples but for the oppressed everywhere and all the generous aspirations of the unoppressed as well.'

Stafford Cripps spoke, continued Brown. 'Lord Addison [Christopher Addison, the much-respected Liberal-turned-Labour politician] was in the Chair . . . It was the first time I'd spoken in the Albert Hall. And we got over £2,000 at that first meeting. I spoke with Jack [J.B.] Priestley in Bradford, his home town. The biggest hall in Bradford was packed . . . At these meetings £5 notes would come up . . . women would take the rings off their fingers and put their brooches in the collecting plate and they'd send them up to the platform . . . they'd be weeping because of the story I was telling . . . that was my big role during that period.' Even Virginia Woolf was – grudgingly – impressed. 'Oh what a bore those meetings are,' she wrote in June 1937. 'We sat for three hours behind the Duchess [of Atholl] and talked about Spain – I mean we listened and they talked into megaphones, or microphones . . . However, by hook or by crook, really by means of a fat emotional woman in black velvet called Isabel Brown, they raised £1500 for the Basque children.'

Noreen Branson, who was branch secretary of the Battersea Communist Party and whose husband Clive was fighting with the International Brigade, recalled going round with a collecting tin for Spain. 'If you went round knocking on doors, arguing for this or that, they would usually pretend they didn't know you, particularly if you were canvassing for candidates, Labour or not, they would always say, "I must consult my husband" – that was very much the habit. Spain was an exception . . . they always rushed back to get a tin of milk or something, immediately . . . very few people had refrigerators . . . and although people had milk delivered, it had to be drunk very quickly before it went off, so everyone had lots of tins of milk as a back up.'

It was the same in Hackney in East London, where 'they gave tins, soup, whatever they could, everyone wanted to do something'. 'There was always something going on,' recalled the wife of a Rhondda miner who had joined the International Brigade. 'Collections up the Valley, although God knows, they didn't have much to give because they were half starved.'

In South Wales miners took collections and held flag days. The wife of a miner imprisoned during an industrial dispute sent £1.10s to the *Daily Worker* 'Aid Spain' campaign 'with best wishes for the conquest of the Spanish Government'. Concerts were held in chapels and miners' halls, pithead collections were held and clothing was collected (some, given the poverty of the districts from which it was donated, was not suitable to be transported). Left Book Club circles gathered to discuss the numerous books the LBC published on Spain, including Arthur Koestler's *Spanish Testament*, published in December 1937, or to watch a screening of the film *Defence of Madrid*. In Sheffield, one such group met every Friday evening in a vegetarian restaurant called the 'Sunshine Café' to discuss the book of the month. The members were urged to form a support group for the Spanish Relief campaign: 'We used to meet in the evenings and on Sunday mornings and do door-to-door collections for non perishable food – tinned foods, packet foods and so on – and also money.' Beryl Barker's mother agreed that their house could be used as a depot for food collected on their council estate. 'A man came up from London . . . and he had a loudspeaker on his van . . . He always played a record of Paul Robeson, singing, "Sometimes I feel like a motherless child". We also had a campaign for knitting four-inch squares to be made up into blankets and people would give us odd balls of wool and so on for this . . . Isabel Brown came, because she was the champion money collector for Spanish Relief . . . and she went round the working men's clubs . . . and I'd go round with a tin after she'd spoken.' Collectors learned that they did best if they went round with their tins on a Friday, since that was pay day. The Young Communist League helped, as did members of the Woodcraft Folk.

At a village near Bethesda in North Wales, a Spanish militia man's hat and a militia girl's scarf were auctioned, both reputed to have been bought with the unopened wage packets of slate quarrymen, while the South Wales Miners' Federation ('The Fed') levied half a crown on its members' wages, an unheard-of amount and ten times that usually raised during an industrial dispute. When Harry Pollitt thought of 'the appalling poverty that is rampant in these mining valleys and the extent of the sacrifices that this money means, it seems to me the outstanding thing that has happened in the whole Spanish campaign'. In 1938 the Durham miner Will Lawther (later to be leader of the NUM) told the TUC conference that £16,000 – over three-quarters of a million pounds in today's money – had been received from the distressed areas of England, Scotland and Wales.

Students at Girton College, Cambridge, organised collections and 'knitted innumerable garments both for the government forces and the civil population', while the Cambridge Spanish Society regretted that 'the unhappy situation in Spain . . . had diverted the interests of its members from literary to more practical matters'.

In Dorchester, the novelist Sylvia Townsend Warner, who with her lover Valentine Ackland had joined the Communist Party in 1935, appeared on a platform with the writer John Cowper Powys in early autumn 1937 talking about her experiences in Spain, where she and Ackland had been twice. Initially Ackland's offer to take her own 'small, fast two-seater' car in a convoy of self-funded volunteers who had first-aid knowledge was turned down by Communist Party HQ, but at the invitation of Tom Wintringham, Ackland and Townsend Warner went to work with a Red Cross unit in Barcelona in September 1936. Although this foray lasted only three weeks, Warner found it exhilarating, 'the nearest thing I shall ever see to the early days of the USSR', and compared Spain favourably to 'this mealy-mouthed country' (Britain). She had taken particular pleasure in seeing an office with a large sign reading 'Organisation for the Persecution of Fascism'. However, the pair were not at all thrilled by the attitude of some of the English they encountered in Barcelona, with their refusal to learn Spanish and tendency to treat the 'natives' as inferior beings.

The couple's second visit was in June 1937, when they were invited to attend the Second International Congress of Writers in Defence of Spain. Organised before the war broke out, it was to be held in three cities, Barcelona, Valencia and Madrid. Despite considering the rest of the delegation (which included the poet Edgell Rickword, Ralph Bates, Frank Pitcairn – the *nom de plume* of Claud Cockburn – John Strachey, and a new comrade whose party membership would be short-lived, Stephen Spender) to be 'depressingly puny and undistinguished', they went, and were deeply moved to be greeted with shouts of '*Viva la republica! Viva los intellectuals!*' Spender, however, thought, probably rightly, that all the 'speeches, champagne, food, receptions, hotel rooms were a thick hedge dividing us from reality', and that the notion that the writers could make a real difference had 'something of the grotesque about it'. But now one of '*los intellectuals*' was back in Dorset talking about Spanish life and literature, and appealing for contributions for a fund she and Ackland had set up to alleviate the soap shortage, since it had been pointed out to her that it was very demoralising for the militia not to be able to wash properly. Contributions positively flowed in, with the Dorchester meeting raising £4.10s; four train dining-car attendants had a whip-round and produced five shillings, four London shopgirls gave ten shillings, Ackland's sister gave nothing, but the sister's maid donated five shillings. Although Vita Sackville-West did send a pound note, she confessed that she thought the appeal 'the funniest I have ever had', and made a rather inappropriate joke about the Spanish needing soap all the time, and not just because of the war, which seemed to Warner to show just how far removed from the real world the Sissinghurst-closeted writer was.

In Battersea, a solidly working-class area in South London, a thousand people turned up to hear Aneurin Bevan speak in the Town Hall, and £35 was raised; an 'Aid to Spain' week was held in December 1936, with members of the Young Communist League (of which the future playwright and screenwriter – creator of *Dixon of Dock Green* and *The Blue Lamp* – Ted Willis was the secretary) pushing wheelbarrows to receive donations of sugar, tinned milk and other tinned food: a tonne was forthcoming (they estimated that it would take 5,000 tins of milk to make a tonne) and was sent to Spain as part of a ninety-three-tonne shipment. The science correspondent of the *News Chronicle*, John Langdon, who had been in Spain, told a meeting that 'if we didn't defeat fascism in Spain, France and Britain would be next . . . so "Save London Save Madrid" became the slogan'.

People went carol-singing for Spain, and in the window of the People's Bookshop (an enterprise started by a Communist mathematician and writer, David Haden Guest, who was killed fighting with the International Brigade in 1938) in Lavender Hill in South-West London, a group of women sat all day, furiously knitting a total of sixty garments to be sent to the front. The Battersea Aid to Spain movement set themselves a target of £750 to send an ambulance to Spain: it seemed over-ambitious, but endless whist drives, swimming galas, children's parties and concerts were arranged. A fête opened by the Spanish ambassador, with the stallholders dressed in Spanish costumes and with boxing matches, egg and spoon races, a 'strong man' who could break out of an iron cage, a performance by some Basque refugee children, and a peculiarly joyless-sounding event billed as 'dancing to the South West Area Young Communist League Bugle Band', as well as substantial trade union donations, swelled the total. Clive Branson 'drew a huge map of the road from London to Madrid and stuck it up on a great placard in the window of the People's Bookshop, and we got a toy ambulance and moved it along another section every time we raised £50'. The amount was achieved by August 1938, and the ambulance left with 'Battersea' proudly painted on the side.

As well as sending ambulances, food and supplies, a number of men and women with medical training decided to volunteer. 'I didn't go . . . for any political reason,' explained Penny Phelps, a State Registered Nurse who had been working in Hertfordshire at the time, and had got into trouble for taking time out to minister to some Hunger Marchers. 'There was a need somewhere . . . you see a gap and you think "Oh, dear that's dangerous," or "they need help," and so I thought I could perhaps help in some small way.' Most women who went to Spain went to nurse, though Patience Darton's matron at the British Hospital for Mothers and Babies strongly disapproved, calling it 'an emotional extravagance'. It turned out to be extremely hard work. The British nurses' 'silly little blue frocks with white collars and turned up cuffs' were deeply inappropriate in war conditions, where they had to care for their patients in huts, train carriages, disused railway tunnels, even a cave near the Ebro river, the premises often infested with rats, and lit only by candlelight, the nurses sometimes giving blood transfusions by the flickering flame of a cigarette lighter.

Annie Murray, who had gone from Aberdeen to Spain, where her two brothers were fighting with the International Brigade, worked first at a small hospital in Huerte, nursing 'about 80 per cent Spaniards, and the rest were Internationals from all the countries . . . Americans, Germans, Italians, Russians . . . every country you could think of that sent volunteers, French, Yugoslavs . . . all for the anti-Fascist side . . . We got in a wounded Fascist officer, a high ranking sort . . . the young Spaniards, the casualties, were shouting at us, "Leave him to die, leave him to die." But of course we were there to treat all the people. We weren't sorry, though, when that man died.' Later Murray, who was transferred to a large hospital in Barcelona but went out to the front lines in a hospital train, recalled assisting at an operation that took place under a railway bridge as bombs fell all around. Language difficulties did not help. Instead of ordering 'aguja' (needles), Gabriel Herbert, who worked as a link between Franco's forces and the Bishops' Committee, found she had put in a request for 10,000 'anguilas' (baby eels) in assorted sizes.

Priscilla Scott-Ellis, the daughter of Lord Howard de Walden and his Spanish wife, who after brief training went to nurse in front-line Nationalist hospitals, found that while nuns carried out some nursing duties, the general care of the wounded was usually considered to be the family's responsibility. She was appalled at the level of hygiene she found, with medical staff 'picking up sterilised compresses with their fingers. I am not surprised that so many of the wounds get infected.'

Nurses broadcast from Spain calling for volunteers. 'I know of a hospital where there are 500 wounded and only two trained British nurses. Can you come and give us a hand?' entreated Penny Phelps from Madrid just before Christmas 1937. Several nurses sent accounts of their life in Spain to their local papers, and few passed up an opportunity to ask for supplies or money for their wards. Madge Addy sent news to the Manchester Spanish Medical Aid Committee, and when it responded with a gross of Izal toilet rolls, she reported that such was 'the shortage of everything' these could not be used 'for the purpose they were intended for', but the office clerks were having to use the paper to type on. When they were on leave, or invalided back home, some nurses toured the country appealing for help for Spain. At Hornsey Town Hall, Penny Phelps's talk was so heart-wrenching that an old lady pressed a cheque for £100 (nearly £5,000 today) into her hand for Spanish Medical Aid. 'Most of the nurses who came out that I met were politically conscious and knew why they were coming out,' thought Annie Murray. 'But there were a few who just went out to be a nurse for a humanitarian reason and had no idea which side they were on even when they went out . . . But most of them came back and have been very active anti-fascist workers since.'

On the afternoon of Monday, 26 April 1937, when the war was in its tenth month, the small Basque market town of Guernica, which lay in the hills of Northern Spain between Bilbao and San Sebastian, was almost completely destroyed by bombs dropped by German and Italian planes. Perhaps as many as a thousand people were killed – the *Daily Express* correspondent, who arrived that night, claimed to have counted six hundred corpses, with more being pulled out from the rubble, though recent estimates put the dead at more like two hundred, but no one can know for sure – and hundreds more were injured.

The news of Guernica was conveyed to Britain almost immediately by George Steer, who was reporting the war for *The Times*, as he had the war in Abyssinia, and who drove there as soon as news of the raid reached him in Bilbao, arriving there at 11 p.m. that same evening, while the conflagration was still blazing. Newsreels were shown at Gaumont cinemas on 6 May showing 'the Holy City of Guernica, scene of the most terrible air raid our modern history can yet boast . . . Four thousand bombs were dropped out of a clear blue sky into a hell that raged unchecked for five [it was actually nearer three and a half] murderous hours. This was a city, and these were homes, like yours.' Although the Japanese had bombed

Shanghai in March 1932, the Italians had bombed Abyssinia (and used poison gas) in 1935, and in Spain nearby Durango had been all but destroyed a few weeks earlier, it was Guernica that seized the imagination as a symbol of the impact of war on innocent, defenceless civilians – and fuelled fears about Germany's future intentions towards Britain. 'Euskadi's mines supply the ore/To feed the Nazi dogs of war:/Guernika's thermite rain transpires/In doom on Oxford's dreaming spires:/In Hitler's frantic mental haze/Already Hull and Cardiff blaze,/And Paul's grey dome rocks to the blast/Of air-torpedoes screaming past,' wrote the poet Edgell Rickword with terrible prescience.

Franco denied responsibility for the carpet-bombing attack, claiming it was the work of 'Red incendiaries', Basque Republicans desecrating their own stronghold, an independent republic that had been granted wartime self-rule. Guernica was a place that Basques held in almost mystic regard, with its famous oak tree beneath which every King of Spain was obliged to stand to swear to uphold the traditional laws and rights of the Basques, making the town an internationally known symbol of democracy, one that Wordsworth had hymned in a sonnet written during the Peninsular War. However, T.S. Eliot, who considered the Spanish Civil War to be 'the perfect opportunity for extremists of both extremes', was prepared to believe the Catholic publication the *Tablet*, which reported that 'the most likely culprits . . . were the Basques' own allies, their shady friends in Catalonia'. *The Times* telegraphed George Steer requesting 'a judicious statement', since the 'other side' was dismissing his account of the raids. Steer's response was published on 29 April: 'I have spoken with hundreds of homeless and distressed people, who all gave precisely the same description of the events. I have seen and measured the enormous bomb-holes at Gernika, which, since I passed through the town the day before, I can testify were not there then. Unexploded German aluminium incendiary bombs were found in Gernika marked "Rheindorf factory, 1936".'

In Paris, the Spanish artist Pablo Picasso read Steer's original account of the bombing when it appeared in *L'Humanité*, the French Communist Party newspaper, on 29 April. Within days he started work on what would become his most famous painting. Mural-sized at 7.8 metres (twenty-five feet) long, the black-and-white oil painting is an anguished representation of the tragedy, expressing Picasso's outrage at the violence and suffering. *Guernica*'s first showing was in the Spanish Pavilion at the Paris International Exhibition in July 1937. Julian Trevelyan found it 'incandescent', and the next year the Surrealist painter Roland Penrose, a friend of Picasso, arranged for the painting to come to Britain.

It was displayed for three weeks in October at the New Burlington Gallery in the West End, along with a number of Picasso's preparatory sketches, to raise funds for Spanish relief. However, reviews were mixed, and only about 3,000 paying customers came to see it. The painting then went on the road to Leeds and Oxford, returning to hang in the Whitechapel Art Gallery in London's East End for two weeks in January 1939. Clement Attlee, the leader of the Labour Party, opened the exhibition. This time, the reception was overwhelmingly enthusiastic. Twelve thousand people queued to see the work, vindicating Penrose's conviction that Anthony Blunt and other critics were wrong in their belief that Picasso's art was irrelevant to the concerns of the working classes and that *Guernica* would appeal only to 'the limited coterie of aesthetes who have given their lives so wholly to the cult of art that they have forgotten anything else. The rest of the world may see it, shudder and pass by.' £100 was raised on the first day alone – sufficient to send a food ship to Spain.

Four days after the assault on Guernica, a letter was published in *The Times* calling for Basque children to be brought to safety in Britain. Among the signatories were Ellen Wilkinson and the Duchess of Atholl. Since the beginning of April, Franco had been blockading Spanish ports to prevent British ships carrying food from getting through. Although this contravened international law, an emergency meeting of the British Cabinet on 11 April acquiesced, and British vessels were advised not to proceed to Bilbao, despite the fact that George Steer had wired assurances that the blockade was a bluff, that minesweepers had cleared the approaches to Bilbao, and the Francoists were being held at bay by Basque guns. One British ship, the *Marie Llewellyn*, captained by 'Potato' Jones (so named for the cargo he was carrying), failed to reach port. However, on the night of 19 April the *Seven Seas Spray*, captained by the Welsh Captain William ('Earthquake') Roberts, with his daughter Florence (Fifi), the 'brave lass' of Edgell Rickword's poem, aboard, 'turned the historical blind eye' to the Morse signal instructing it to return to St Jean de Luz, ran the gauntlet of 'Franco's sham blockade' and landed food at Bilbao, receiving an ecstatic welcome from the starving Spaniards. She was soon followed by other British ships.

The siege of Bilbao and the threat of air attacks gave added urgency to the mission of Leah Manning, an official of the British National Union of Teachers who had briefly been Labour MP for East Islington, and who was in Bilbao at the invitation of the Spanish government, trying to arrange the evacuation of children on behalf of the National Joint Committee for Spanish Relief. Large numbers of children had already gone to France

(70,000 by October 1937, and 440,000 by the end of the war), and others to Belgium, the USSR and later Mexico, but the British government remained deaf to Manning's petitions until the bombing of Guernica – though the Foreign Office would maintain its opposition – and other aid organisations advised strongly against removing young children from their homes and families.

Finally the British government agreed to accept 4,000 children, aged from five to fifteen, with the strict proviso that they were not to be a charge on the British taxpayer, but were to be the sole financial responsibility of those who brought them. The Duchess of Atholl suggested that the government should match each pound privately subscribed, but this was turned down. 'They demanded that the London Committee should guarantee ten shillings per head for each child – this at a time when they expected the children of their own unemployed to survive on five bob a week,' recorded an outraged Manning. Furthermore, the children were to be sent back to Spain 'as soon as conditions permitted'. The Basque Children's Committee, which had representatives from organisations including Spanish Medical Aid, Save the Children, the TUC, the Catholic Church, the Society of Friends and the Salvation Army, took responsibility for the refugees' care, and two British doctors were flown out to give the children a thorough medical check before they left.

On 23 May 1937 an ageing, slightly rusted liner, SS *Habana*, designed to carry eight hundred passengers, docked at Southampton after a rough three-day crossing during which the 3,681 *evacuados* had been 'laid head to tail on the bulkheads, in the swimming pool, in the state rooms and along the alley ways, for all the world like the little *sardinas* about which they were always singing'. They were accompanied by ninety-five women teachers, 120 young female helpers (the *señoritas*) and fifteen priests. It was the largest single influx of refugees ever to come to Britain. Nine Southampton medical officers clambered aboard to inspect the refugees again. Each child was tagged with a tape tied around his or her wrist: a white tape indicated 'clean' and allowed children to proceed straight to their destination; a red tape meant the child was verminous, and was sent to the Corporation baths for delousing (this usually involved shaving the head, which distressed the children); while blue indicated that they were suffering from a contagious disease – those so identified were conveyed to an isolation hospital.

At first *los niños* were taken to a camp at North Stoneham, near Southampton, where Boy Scouts and other local volunteers had been drafted in to erect five hundred bell tents on a thirty-acre site provided by a local farmer, lay on gas and water pipes, dig latrines, erect marquees for use as kitchens and stuff cotton sacks with straw to serve as mattresses. It was a traumatic time for the *niños*, some of the older of whom considered themselves to be adept guerrilla fighters. They had been torn from a war zone, and had left their families there. Few spoke any language other than Basque, while most of the helpers had no Spanish. Fights broke out between different political groups, the younger children were scared and homesick, the older ones confused and unsure, and could be resentful of camp discipline.

On 19 June news of the fall of Bilbao was relayed through the loudspeakers that played 'Land of Hope and Glory' every morning, causing the children great distress. 'A pandemonium of weeping and wailing broke out ... a very few boys tried to smash the radio, calling it a fascist liar, and then rushed out of the camp in their furious anger,' determined to find a boat to take them back to fight the rebels themselves, 'but soon came back remembering that they had responsibilities to younger brothers and sisters'. A commandant was brought in to keep order and to calm the local population, ex-servicemen were hired to patrol the perimeter fence at night, and twenty of the older boys who were considered to be 'troublemakers' were dispatched to France.

North Stoneham was only supposed to be a transit camp, and work began at once to try to place the children in other accommodation – a task made no easier by the right-wing press running scare stories of out-of-control youths and calling for their repatriation, while the Birmingham branch of the British Union of Fascists demanded 'Britons Before Basques'.

In total ninety-two private homes and hostels throughout Britain, in cities such as London (which had five) and Manchester (four) or in small villages, from Scotland to Wales, financed by organisations or by the generosity of individuals, took in refugees. Catholic schools took some, as did the London Teachers' Association, while the Salvation Army provided a hostel in Hackney for four hundred. A 'colony' of Basque refugees moved into an empty hotel by the Thames at Maidenhead, and others were accommodated in country houses in Oxfordshire, Hertfordshire and Somerset (this one, at Street, provided by the Quaker shoe manufacturer Roger Clark, was reserved for the sons and daughters of anarchists, since it was funded with the help of the ILP MP Fenner Brockway); a redundant rectory at Pampisford, a village outside Cambridge, where John Cornford's mother was among those helping to care for the children; at Watermillock in Cumbria; a disused sanatorium at Keighley in Yorkshire; Aldridge Lodge, near Walsall; an empty workhouse at Wickham Market in Suffolk; rows of bleak wooden huts at Brechfa near

Carmarthen; similar ones on the Berkshire downs and on the Essex coast; in the medieval castle at Herstmonceux in Sussex; in a field of canvas tents at Diss in Norfolk; and a dreadful encampment at Margate.

Virginia Woolf saw 'a long trail of fugitives – like a caravan from the desert' as she walked home to Bloomsbury after buying whitebait at Selfridges in June 1937. 'Spaniards flying from Bilbao which has fallen, I suppose. Somehow brought tears to my eyes, tho' no one seemed surprised. Children trudging along: women in London cheap jackets with gay hand-kerchiefs on their heads, young men, & all carrying cheap cases & bright blue enamel kettles, very large, & saucepans, filled I suppose with gifts from some Charity – a shuffling trudging procession, flying – impelled by machine guns in Spanish fields to trudge through Tavistock Square.'

After the fall of Bilbao, sending the children home became even more problematic, since families had dispersed in the face of the Nationalist advance, some parents had been killed and homes destroyed. Moreover, the unfortunate children became political pawns, with the British government always mutedly anxious to be rid of them, Nationalists in Spain demanding that they belonged in their own communities, and most of the aid agencies reluctant to repatriate them until they were sure that conditions were safe for them to return.

Under pressure from Father Gabana, former chaplain to the English-speaking Catholic community in Barcelona, 152 children were sent back to Spain in November 1937 (Gabana had wanted eight hundred), and a further five hundred in January 1938, once the British agencies were persuaded that they had homes to go to and parents who wanted them to return. But it was soon clear that there were almost 2,000 children whose parents were either unable or unwilling to have them back. The aid agencies were finding that caring for the refugees was absorbing all their funds, leaving little for them to send to Spain, but their responsibilities to the children could not easily be discharged. The older ones received official dispensation to work to support themselves ('My God,' exclaimed one British employer, 'we can't call this boy Jesus. We'll have to call him – Jim'), while younger ones were offered for adoption wherever possible. Various fundraising events were arranged by local aid groups with the children singing and dancing, dressed in Basque costumes, to raise money for their keep. The enterprising concert organiser Frida Stewart, who had founded the Aid Spain committees in Hull and York, even took a party of refugees to several fashionable Swiss ski resorts to entertain holiday-makers. They raised £300, and a booklet, *Songs of the Basque Children*, with an introduction by the Duchess of Atholl, added more to the coffers.

It had been hoped that the evacuation of the Basque children was merely a crisis measure, and that as soon as the battle for northern Spain was over they would be able to return: they were coming to Britain for 'three months only'. In fact, after the victory of Franco and the end of the Civil War, over a thousand children remained in Britain, and there were 450 who never left.

'May God bless your work for reconstruction and reconciliation,' wrote Archbishop Hinsley from Westminster Cathedral, sending congratulations to Franco, 'the great defender of the true Spain', on 28 March 1939. His hope was not realised. After the war at least 500,000 people were killed in Spain, and the subsequent 'white terror' probably claimed the lives of a further 200,000 of those who had opposed Franco's forces. For many Spaniards who survived the grossly destructive civil war there would be years of recrimination, suspicion, repression and isolation – until the return of democracy in 1977, two years after the Caudillo's death.

For the British, the ominous awareness that in Spain they had witnessed a war by proxy for the World War that would engulf the globe a few months after its end was coupled with ever-present anxiety about whether Franco would throw in his lot with the Axis powers. (He did not, remaining officially neutral throughout the Second World War.)

Those on the left in Britain who had been involved in the struggle of Republican Spain, and of course particularly those who had joined in the fight, would have profound memories of 'the last great cause', a fight for liberation that would be evoked in subsequent conflicts from Vietnam to post-Soviet Europe.

> And the next day took the boat
> For home, forgetting Spain, not realizing that
> Spain would soon denote
> Our grief, our aspirations;
> Not knowing that our blunt
> Ideals would find their whetstone, that our spirit
> Would find its frontier on the Spanish front,
> Its body in a rag-tag army,

wrote Louis MacNeice.

Yet George Orwell's concerns would also increasingly be reprised, and would colour debates about the true nature of the conflict, particularly about the role and effect of the *Partido Comunista de España* (PCE) on its course and resolution, and the implications of that for understanding future world conflicts.

SIXTEEN

Wanting the Palm not the Dust

I soon found I was humming a tune called 'Here's to Romance' – remember it? Nice tune. It used to be on a record, about 1936. On the other side of 'These Foolish Things'.

A woman watching the Duke and Duchess of Windsor driving in a
coupé in the Bahamas during the Second World War

On 1 August 1936, Siegfried Eifrig, a tall, blue-eyed German, holding a flaming torch aloft, sprinted down the Unter den Linden, Berlin's main thoroughfare, to the massive Olympic Stadium, built to hold 100,000 spectators. Berlin, with a population of over four million, was the third largest city in the world at the time, trailing London and New York, and Germany had won the bid to host the Olympics back in 1931, two years before the Nazis came to power: the games now offered the Führer a perfect opportunity to show the power of his Third Reich, its efficiency and sporting prowess, to the rest of the world.

There had been efforts among the Jewish populations of Britain and America to organise a boycott of the games. Walter Citrine, TUC leader, railed against the Nazi success in bringing all German sports 'under the heel of Hitler', but while the British Olympic Association was debating a possible boycott in December 1935, the Football Association was hosting the German national team for a game against England at White Hart Lane, Tottenham Hotspur's ground, which was located in a neighbourhood with a fair-sized Jewish population. Despite anxieties about demonstrations and potential violence, the match was uneventful. Germany lost 3–0, and at a gala dinner afterwards, the Reich Minister for Sport, Hans von Tschammer und Osten, spoke about 'the blue sky of friendship between the two Nordic countries'. The next evening, at the inaugural dinner of the Anglo-German Fellowship, its spokesman, Lord Temple, warned those who had tried to cancel the game to 'mind their own damn business . . . The Germans have always been our good friends. They have always fought fair in war . . . If another war comes . . . well, I hope the partners will be changed.'

The proposal for a boycott was withdrawn on the usual fallacious grounds that 'sport should be above politics', and forty-nine nations took part in the magnificently orchestrated spectacle, the largest and most lavish Olympics ever mounted, filmed as a striking modernist propaganda exercise by Leni Riefenstahl. Hitler opened the games, barking a welcome to the assembled masses beneath a sea of banners bearing both swastikas and the linked rings of the Olympic movement. The athletes then marched past the dais: some, like the French contingent, giving what was either a smart Nazi salute or the 'Olympic salute' – though no one quite seemed to know what that was. The British simply inclined their heads giving a military 'eyes right' acknowledgement to Hitler, though the *Daily Express* thought 'It would not have done the British any harm if they had made a gesture to the country housing the games by following the unexpected example of France.'

For the first time the Olympics, the tenth since the Games had been revived in 1896 when they were held – naturally – in Athens, were relayed over the airwaves in twenty-eight languages, by a fleet of radio-transmitting vans positioned around the stadium. It had been rumoured that Oswald Mosley would be picked for the British fencing team. He was not, but his wife-to-be Diana Guinness (*née* Mitford) was there with her sister Unity, at the invitation of Hitler. Diana found the Games a great bore (she preferred a trip to the opera to hear Wagner's *Parsifal*), but used the opportunity while staying with Goebbels and his wife Magda, of whom Hitler was also a guest, both to solicit money for Mosley's British Union of Fascists (the request was 'wearily' turned down 'for the moment') and to check with the British Consul in Munich about getting married to Mosley in Germany.

Chips Channon, an immensely rich, gossipy, socialite US-born Conservative MP, was at the Games too, with his wife Honor, daughter of the Earl of Iveagh, at the invitation of the German Ambassador to London, Joachim von Ribbentrop. They too found the Games boring, but the impressionable Channon, who thought the 'Horst Wessel Lied' had 'rather a good lilt', mused during a state banquet at the Royal Opera House that evening that he was 'more excited to see Hitler [even though he thought the Führer 'looked exactly like his caricature – brown uniform, Charlie Chaplin moustache'] than I was when I met Mussolini in 1926 in Perugia, and was more stimulated, I am sorry to say, than when I was blessed by the Pope in 1920 . . . One was conscious of the effort the Germans were making to show the world the grandeur, the permanency and respectability of the new regime.' The future Labour politician Richard Crossman, then a young Oxford don, went to the Games too, but what he felt was distinct unease.

'Germany to-day is openly and defiantly a nation at arms,' he wrote. 'Hitler, largely thanks to British foreign policy, has won the masses.'

The Games lasted until 16 August. German athletes won a total of eighty-nine medals, including thirty-three gold. Britain, which sent forty-two athletes, after a shortfall in funding that required contributions from such private benefactors as Lord Nuffield, Imperial Tobacco, the Greyhound Racing Association, the *News of the World* and Horlicks Malted Milk, won four gold, seven silver and three bronze medals, not a brilliant haul, and one that disgusted a clergyman who wrote to the *Daily Telegraph*: 'It is not pleasant to think of the Union Jack waving over a company of "also rans" . . . a maritime people, we are beaten at rowing by the inland Swiss. In boxing (pre-eminently a British sport) we occupy a back seat . . . What are the reasons for this decline . . . ?' He went on to answer his own question: too much 'democracy' had sapped Britain's virility and competitive edge, with the result that the country had 'gone soft'.

The medal count left 'no doubt of the supremacy of the United States, the rise of Germany and Japan as athletic as well as political powers, and the eclipse of Great Britain', in the equally harsh view of the *Spectator*. And indeed it was an American who was the hero of the games, the black athlete Jesse Owens, who broke eleven Olympic records, won four gold medals, and was acclaimed by his German long-jump rival, Luz Long, and the banks of spectators who cheered wildly every time his name was announced, despite his being 'racially inferior' according to Nazi categorisation – and subject to segregation laws back home in the US.

Tennis had not been an Olympic sport since 1924 (and it would not become one again until 1988), but the previous month, on 3 July 1936, the twenty-six-year-old Fred Perry, a former ping pong champion and the son of a Labour and Co-operative MP, gave the British a *frisson* of sporting achievement when he pulled off a hat trick by winning the Men's Singles at Wimbledon, as he had done the two previous summers. Perry, who had turned down a lucrative offer to endorse Daks ready-to-wear trousers and be paid a shilling for every pair sold, in order to maintain his amateur status, turned professional after his achievement – to this day he remains the last male British player to win the event.

On 26 August nearly 7,000 people queued at the Radiolympia Exhibition in Earl's Court, to see the first talking pictures on television, transmitted from Alexandra Palace ten miles away. The actor Leslie Mitchell appeared as Britain's first television announcer. It was not a particularly auspicious debut, since he appeared to have a black eye (though make-up had done its best), was perspiring heavily and visibly, staring into space, and generally seemed rather ill at ease. The transmission showed clips of Paul Robeson singing 'Ole Man River' from the film *Showboat*, a moving scene from *Rembrandt* starring Charles Laughton and Gertrude Lawrence, and a made-for-television documentary in which Julian Huxley and A.P. Herbert traced the history of writing from scrawls on cave walls to modern newspapers.

The first television sets to be commercially available cost between £50 and £125, and had screens that measured only twelve or fourteen inches. However, even if you could afford a set at a time when the average working man's wage was around £3 a week, only people within a twenty-mile radius of the studio at Alexandra Palace could pick up the flickering image without a 'booster'. Television was still 'a mere toy or hobby for the well to do, and will make little change to social life', decided the *Spectator*, though it doubted it would be long – ten years maybe – before 'we may find as many people enjoying television as radio'. While *The Times* delighted at the prospect of being able to watch 'Hammond bat and Larwood bowl, Perry play tennis and Padgham play golf', the *Spectator* sounded a note of caution, pointing out that into your sitting room would come nightly images of 'rebellions in Spain, misery in the depressed areas, concentration camps in Germany . . . not forgetting the speeches of Mussolini, Hitler, Goering, Goebbels'. The magazine gloomily evoked Charlie Chaplin's *Modern Times*, wondering who would decide what was to be shown. 'Is it only the King, the athlete, the dictator, the boss, or other figures well known to us now on the news reel – the wife of the Cabinet Minister breaking a bottle of champagne on a battleship, the inspector of guards of honour, the politicians making an election address, the Dionne quintuplets – whom we shall be allowed to see?'

On 30 August the *Queen Mary* set a record for the fastest transatlantic crossing. On her sixth voyage, the *Queen* had taken three days, twenty-three hours and fifty-seven minutes, at an average speed of 30.63 knots, to sail from the Ambrose Light, New York, to the Bishop Rock, off the Scilly Isles, taking the record from the French liner the *Normandie*, whose time she had bettered by three hours and five minutes. 'Heartiest congratulations on completing the record,' wired the King, who was also at sea, cruising in the Mediterranean aboard a hired yacht with a party of friends including a married American woman, Mrs Wallis Simpson.

On its previous voyage the *Queen Mary* had won the coveted Blue Riband for the fastest westbound Atlantic crossing. The blue pennant was proudly flown by the ship that had had such a painful gestation period, eloquent evidence of acute economic problems of North-East England, but Cunard was not to enjoy the honour for long. The next year, the *Normandie* snatched the prize back, only to lose it again in 1938 to the *Queen Mary*, which then hung onto it until 1952. Moreover, the ship's future depended almost entirely on sales of passenger tickets, since it carried 'practically no cargo except bullion and mail'. Would the 75 per cent capacity of 2,139 passengers her owners predicted be achieved? 'The Blue Riband always brings passenger trade,' conceded a correspondent. But 'whether this will give her 1,100 passengers a trip, in all seasons, remains to be seen'.

On Sunday, 4 October, violence flared on the streets of London. It came as no surprise. Oswald Mosley had decided to celebrate the fourth anniversary of the founding of his British Union of Fascists with a march through the East End. The BUF had been launched on 1 October 1932, four months before Hitler came to power in Germany. The thirty-two founding members regarded themselves as embarking on 'a great and hazardous adventure . . . to sacrifice all . . . to dedicate their lives to building in this country a movement of the modern age'. On the back of the membership card was printed the movement's aim: 'To win power for Fascism and thereby establish in Great Britain the Corporate State'. Recruits wore black shirts that fastened at the side, modelled on Mosley's fencing shirt – though his was in silk – and a badge with a *fasces* (a bundle of sticks, the symbol of the fascist movement). It was undoubtedly a more mesmerising – if more sinister – uniform than the one Harold Nicolson had suggested in the early days, of 'grey flannel trousers and shirts'.

Mosley hoped to attract to his new party all those disillusioned with the 'spineless . . . old gang' of politicians – the 'old muttons', he dubbed them – who, 'when faced with problems . . . squat impotent in front of them like a hypnotised rabbit in front of a snake'. Unemployment would never be solved without planning: planning of resources, labour, financial power. But planning was ineffective without a strong centralised executive government. The BUF's corporate state would be a totalitarian regime 'with no room . . . for those who do not accept the principle "all for the State. And the State for all."' 'A pinchbeck candidate for dictatorship', the *Manchester Guardian* called Mosley.

Mosley believed that fascism would come to power in Britain as it had in Germany: when the economy collapsed and people sought extreme solutions, either fascism or communism would triumph. For Mosley, it would be fascism that would bring order out of economic chaos, and he insisted that in Britain it would succeed by constitutional means and not by violence, which would only be used when it was necessary to save the country from the 'red terror' of communism. But the situation in Britain was different from that in Germany, as an article in the *New Statesman* pointed out: 'Conditions do not exist in Britain for the growth of fascism. We have no ruined middle class . . . we have no economic suffering extreme enough to drive men to desperate measures . . . and we are not suffering under the psychology of defeat' – though some ex-servicemen, many of them the 'temporary gentlemen', wartime officers of 1914–18, disappointed with the deal they had got in the peacetime world, were among Mosley's supporters. There *was* unemployment and unrest in Britain, but it was not to the BUF that the vast majority of people turned for the solution.

In the early days of the BUF Mosley was still a respectable figure, invited to debate at a Foyles Literary Lunch, and to tangle with Attlee at the Cambridge Union. A Fascist Union of British Workers (FUBW) was established in 1933 by a Covent Garden porter who had been an NUWM leader, to 'protect the interests of workers whether employed or unemployed' by fighting the Means Test and cuts in wages and benefits – it also hectored the Labour and Communist Parties for putting the interests of foreign governments before those of British workers. Mosley's first wife Cynthia ('Cimmie' the daughter of Lord Curzon) set up a Women's Section, since women made up 20 per cent of the membership. Mary Richardson, a former suffragette who had endured forcible feeding in her struggle for the vote, became its second head, after the first, Lady Makgill, was obliged to resign for embezzling funds. Female Blackshirts were trained in ju-jitsu and encouraged to become members of the St John Ambulance Brigade – both useful skills for fascist meetings – but those who held power and decided policy were men, and machismo was an intrinsic part of the appeal of fascism which the swaggering, debonair, virile Mosley personified.

In January 1934 the *Daily Mail* came out for fascism. 'Hurrah for the Blackshirts!' it trumpeted, asserting that Britain's survival depended on 'the existence of a Great Party of the Right with the same directness of purpose and energy of method as Hitler and Mussolini have displayed'. By the spring of 1934 the BUF's membership was around 34,000: there were forty-two branches in London and 122 in the provinces, most along the South Coast from Kent to Devon, in the Midlands, where the movement enjoyed the support of small traders and middle-class businessmen, in a few Northern non-industrial towns such as Blackpool and Hartlepool, and among the Lancashire cotton towns, where Mosley promised to protect their industry from foreign competition. There were a few rural members, mainly landowners, and while fascism was predominantly an urban working-class phenomenon, by 1934 the movement was attracting what the Home Office called 'a better class of recruits', including 'Generals, Admirals, big business men, and the Debs of the period with Union Jacks round their lily white shoulders'. A number of Tory MPs were also sympathetic – as many as 230, it was rumoured – believing that there was 'no fundamental difference between the Blackshirts and their parents, the Conservatives'.

Members paid a shilling a month if they were employed and fourpence if they were not; these fees raised about £12,000 a year. The BUF's two propaganda sheets, the *Blackshirt* and the more upmarket *Fascist Weekly*, had a circulation of 25,000 and 30,000 respectively, and were self-supporting. The newspaper magnate Lord Rothermere, owner of the *Daily Mail*, gave money for a time, as possibly did the car manufacturer and philanthropist Lord Nuffield. Other wealthy donors – landowners and businessmen – also gave generously, sometimes anonymously, and it was rumoured that the then Prince of Wales, the future Edward VIII, had sent a cheque. And substantial amounts of money came from the Italian dictator Mussolini – an annual subsidy of £86,000, totalling £234,730 by 1937: almost £11.5 million in today's money – and later from Goebbels, who in 1936 alone managed to extract £91,000 from a Nazi regime that was generally unwilling to subsidise foreign fascist enterprises, but coughed up for the BUF, in the view of MI5 'for purposes likely to be favourable to German policy'.

On 7 June 1934 Mosley held his biggest ever rally in London's Olympia. The *Daily Mail* offered free tickets to readers who sent in letters explaining 'Why I like the Blackshirts'. Union flags were waved, trumpets played, and the leader bounded onto the podium in a halo of spotlights; but unfortunately his speech could hardly be heard in most parts of the hall, as the loudspeakers had not been plugged in. Mosley started by talking about the need for action, but soon launched into a virulent anti-Semitic diatribe, evoking 'European ghettoes pouring their dregs into this country'. Not all those present were supporters of Mosley, and pandemonium erupted, with coshes, knives, knuckledusters, socks stuffed with broken glass, hoses filled with lead and chair legs wrapped in barbed wire being wielded by both sides (though Mosley had banned the use of offensive weapons). Hecklers were summarily thrown down flights of stone stairs by Mosley's 'Biff Boys' – once comprising public-school hearties, but soon working-class toughs formed the nucleus – and then kicked while they lay on the ground. Since it was, theoretically, a private meeting, the police, who tried to intervene, were asked to leave. Five people were so badly injured that they were detained in hospital, and fifty more needed hospital treatment. A report to the Home

Office expressed surprise that no one had been killed 'since there was so much bloodshed'. Mosley refused to apologise for the violence, maintaining that Communists had made an orchestrated attempt to disrupt the meeting. Thomas Jones, the Deputy Cabinet Secretary, thought that 'Organised Communists had not only got what they asked for, but a great deal more, with excessive brutality.'

The fall-out from the Olympia rally was profound. The event sounded the death knell for the BUF's support among respectable political opinion, which had been intrigued by Mosley's economic solutions, perhaps attracted by his vitality and eloquence – and in some cases probably covertly agreeing with his anti-Semitism – but who now saw the BUF as the 'thugs' party', to be given a wide berth. Others, however, found the violent spectacle thrilling, and the Home Office reported that 'for the next few days people from different classes queued from morning until night at the National Headquarters' to enlist. 'One must recognise,' admitted one Conservative MP, who was a critic of the BUF, 'that a movement of this kind which is capable of filling first the Albert Hall . . . and subsequently Olympia with 15,000 people has its roots in something in this country, and is not to be ignored.'

Lord Rothermere withdrew the *Daily Mail*'s support from the movement, which was a body blow. Mosley claimed this was because Jewish advertisers such as Joe Lyons of Lyons Corner Houses were threatening to boycott the *Mail* and the rest of his press empire, but in fact the unfavourable publicity following the Olympia meeting was decisive, and Rothermere claimed that he could 'never support any movement with an anti-Semitic bias'.

By 1936 the active membership of the movement had dropped to about 4,000, funding from Mussolini had been cut back by 70 per cent, and any hope of winning power through the ballot box had long evaporated. Mosley never attracted a leading politician to the ranks of what Churchill dubbed 'the suicide club'. The BUF never won a parliamentary seat, and never had a local councillor elected. In the 1935 general election they did not contest any seats, but made their presence felt with the 'dismal slogan' 'Fascism Next Time', while in 1939 the fascist candidate in a by-election at Hythe in Kent, the spy Kim Philby's father, Harry St John Philby, only polled 578 votes.

Moreover, Mosley was not attracting recruits from those places that might have been expected to turn to extremist solutions, the depressed areas of Wales and the North-East of England. Most of his support came from the South-East, London in particular, and the growth in the number of supporters in 1934, when the movement swelled from 12,000 to 40–50,000, was largely due to the disillusion which many Conservative voters felt with Baldwin, and the general ineptitude of Ramsay MacDonald's National Government – the main reason why Rothermere was in Mosley's camp for a time.

That spring Mosley dropped 'fascist' from the name of his organisation: in future it would be called the British Union, and on Empire Day, 24 May, he showed off the BU's new officers' paramilitary uniform. It consisted of a military greatcoat, peaked cap and jackboots, the similarity to Nazi dress emphasised by an armband with a lightning-flash emblem in red, white and black. With his 'metallic charm and Douglas Fairbanks smile', his lithe fencing-master's physique and aristocratic bearing, the uniformed Mosley looked compelling – if chilling. The year before, he had bought the lease of the Whitelands Teachers' Training College in the Kings Road, Chelsea, next to the Duke of York Barracks. This became the Black House, the HQ of the movement, with offices and accommodation, and room for balls, cabarets, concert recitals and community singing and others of the 'manifold activities' that Blackshirts enjoyed, until the need to retrench made Mosley abandon it for cheaper premises in 1935.

After the Olympia débâcle, anti-Semitism became the predominant political force of the BU. It was, of course, implicit in the movement's insistence on 'Britain for the British' and its opposition to 'high finance', which was supposedly dominated by 'big Jews', while 'little Jews' allegedly took jobs from British workers and proved more successful in commerce. With the economy stabilising in 1936, the BU increasingly turned to blaming Jews for Britain's ills – or imagined ills.

The East End of London proved fertile soil for the BU's anti-Semitic message: there had been strong anti-Semitic tendencies in its teeming impoverished streets since the turn of the century. One third of all Jews in Britain had settled there, most escaping persecution from Eastern Europe before the First World War. Some had proved spectacularly successful, which led to envy, while Jews were blamed for various unsavoury business practices such as sweated labour, rent extortion by slum landlords and an increase in crime. An area of small businesses, mainly tailoring and furniture-making conducted in back yards and front bedrooms, where one bankruptcy would trigger a chain of similar collapses, the East End was never a mono-industry depressed area like Merthyr Tydfil, Jarrow or Govan. But much of it was grindingly poor, and it was largely un-unionised, overcrowded and unsanitary, and honeycombed with explosive prejudices, suspicions and political passions. While fascism never made much headway in areas of Irish settlement such as Wapping, it found its most ready response in Shoreditch, Bethnal Green and Stepney, which were among the most overcrowded boroughs of London. 'The narrow streets of Bethnal Green straggle across London, hidden like a shameful secret behind the City's façade of wealth . . . to accommodate the unhappy population which manufactures the City's goods,' wrote Anne Brock Griggs, the wife of an architect and the BU's Women's Organiser for Southern England, who stood as candidate for Limehouse in elections for the LCC in March 1937. And these were the boroughs with the highest number of Jewish families. Half the BU's membership came from there and from Hackney, and the movement's only grassroots leader, Mick Clarke, was based in Bethnal Green.

Anti-Semitism was, regrettably, not the prerogative solely of the BU. There were other fascists who were virulently anti-Semitic. These included the burly bachelor vet Arnold Leese, an expert on the diseases of the one-hump camel, and leader of the Imperial Fascist League (which the Special Branch estimated never had more than 150 members), whose 'solution' to the three million Jews he claimed lived in Britain by the early 1930s (in fact there were fewer than half a million) predated the atrocities of the Third Reich. Leese suggested 'extermination by some humane method such as the lethal chamber', or failing that, deportation to Madagascar, from where the existing inhabitants would be relocated and compensated with 'Jewish money'; the island would become a massive Jewish Alcatraz, patrolled day and night by the world's navies to stop a single Jew ever escaping.

The Britons, formed by Henry Hamilton Beamish, the son of an admiral who had been aide-de-camp to Queen Victoria, and brother of the Conservative MP for Lewes, was another organisation that uncritically accepted the 'revelations' of the odious forgery *The Protocols of the Elders of Zion* of a 'Judaeo-Masonic plot' to achieve world domination. However, after he had had been successfully sued for libel by the Jewish industrialist and former Cabinet member Sir Alfred Mond, Beamish fled abroad in 1919, and the main impact of his organisation was in publishing endless versions of the *Protocols* and other provoking books with titles like *The Jews' Who's Who* (edited by Beamish), *Britain Under the Heel of the Jew* and *Why are Jews Hated?*.

The Nordic League provided an umbrella for a number of racial nationalist groupings. Its guiding spirit was the vehement anti-Semite Archibald Maule Ramsay, Conservative MP for Peebles since 1931, who was also leader of the Right Club, a marginally more respectable dining club that aimed to infiltrate the Establishment, lessen the alleged Jewish influence in the Conservative Party, and influence the armed forces. A great deal of secrecy surrounded the activity of both organisations, though the Nordic League went public in 1938, pro-Nazi appeasers to a man, on the grounds that the war that threatened was yet another example of the worldwide Jewish conspiracy. The League premiered anti-Semitic Nazi propaganda films, including one showing the ritual slaughter of animals, drank a toast at each meetings to 'PJ' (Perish Judah), and was linked to the White Knights of Britain, a version of the Ku Klux Klan which had spurts of activity between 1936 and 1937. It advocated shooting Jews, or stringing them up from lamp-posts.

Entrenched anti-Semitism was not confined to the far-right lunatic fringe. Although the number of people who feared a 'Judaeo-Masonic plot' or saw Jews as 'the tsetse fly carrying the poison germ of Bolshevism from the breeding ground of Germany' was small, 'parlour anti-Semitism', which led to business and social ostracism and a distaste for things Jewish, seems to have permeated every level of society. There were casual references to 'Jew boys', the belief that certain residential areas were hostile to the notion of Jewish 'incursions', that Jews were money-grubbing, vulgar and ostentatious – 'money in furs', in T.S. Eliot's formulation – unclean, in general 'alien' to Britain. The *Jewish Chronicle* complained of an advertisement that appeared in the *Daily Telegraph* stipulating that 'no Jewesses' need apply for a job in a typing pool, the *Hackney Gazette* carried one offering unfurnished accommodation but insisting 'No children or Jews,' while after a lengthy discussion the majority of town councillors decided that an advertisement for a boarding house in Shanklin on the Isle of Wight that proclaimed 'No Jews catered for' should be permitted in the official guide. Anti-Semitism was evident in the Civil Service recruitment policy, in the 'quota system' in some public schools, in the membership policies of too many golf clubs, in anti-Jewish jokes and in the 'fat Jewesses' and 'sheenies' characters of much inter-war detective fiction, and in a jingle that the Mayor of Wigan, a 'quack herbalist doctor, ultra-socialist', produced for the amusement of the Earl of Crawford and Balcarres:

> Onward Christian soldiers
> You have nought to fear
> Israel Hore Belisha
> Will lead you from the rear
> Clothed by Montague Burton
> Fed on Lyons pies
> Die for Jewish freedom
> As a Briton always dies

– though at least the War Office did forbid this to be used as a marching song for the army.

Indeed, Leslie Hore-Belisha suffered grievously from anti-Jewish prejudice, and when he was appointed Minister of War in 1937, the military top brass ran an effective campaign against him, partly fuelled by racism, with the Chief of the Imperial General Staff, Sir Edmund Ironside, referring to him as 'Horeb Elisha'.

During a debate on the BUF in the Commons in July 1934, William Greene, Conservative MP for Worcester, enquired disingenuously, 'Is it not a fact that 90 per cent of those accused of attacking Fascists rejoice in such fine old British names as Ziff, Kerstein and Minsky?' while another Conservative, F.A. Macquisten, chipped in, 'Were some of them called Feignbaum, Goldstein and Rigotsky and other good old Highland names?'

Sir Arnold Wilson, a Conservative MP who was no anti-Semite himself and who wanted a more generous attitude towards Jewish victims of Nazi persecution, had 'watched with alarm and anxiety the growth of anti-Semitism . . . certainly the basis of anti-Jewish feeling is primarily economic; the sooner we realise it the better. Fascism in some aspects is really an indictment of this house,' he charged in 1936.

While Mosley refused to associate the BU with the wilder shores of the 'Jew-baiting' groupuscules that existed in the 1930s, he was tactically adroit at exploiting grievances such as those Wilson identified, turning 'a mere dislike into active hostility'. As the National Liberal MP Robert Bernays wrote:

> Today he is the most formidable mob orator in Great Britain. He is the only politician with the exception of the Prime Minister who can attract large audiences . . . 'Mosley is coming' announce the posters. That is all, but it is enough in a great many towns to fill the largest halls. He is, moreover, in a good tactical position. Having been out of parliament for five years [Mosley] has escaped any responsibility for what has been done or left undone. He can canalise the popular discontents, and very effectively he does it. Whether it is the grievances of the tithe payers in the southern counties or the anti-Semitic feeling in the East End or indignation at the worsening position of the distressed areas, Mosley is there to aggravate and inflame the general disgruntlement. What is more, he is able to personalise these discontents. He sets out to prove to his audiences that their troubles are all due to some concrete evil – the 'sweating' Jewish employer, or the international banker or the crafty politician on the make. He gives his audience something to hate, and next to fear, hatred is unhappily the most powerful recruiting-agent in politics.

The announcement that 'Mosley is coming' to the East End on 4 October 1936 drew a swift response. There had been violent clashes between fascists and anti-fascists all that summer in Manchester, Hull and Bristol, culminating at the end of September with forty fascists being injured when anti-fascist protesters threw rocks at them on Holbeck Moor, Leeds. Riots between fascists and their opponents broke out in Victoria Park in Hackney in July 1936 when Mosley addressed a crowd of 5,000, and there had been constant attacks on East End Jews, Jewish shops and market stalls. William J. Fishman, then a sixteen-year-old Stepney Labour League of Youth activist, recalled that the BU 'deliberately played on the irrational fears and hatreds of slum dwellers. Fascist incursions were mounted against the Jews. Attacks were stepped up as Blackshirt gangs made daily, more often nocturnal, forays into the ghetto . . . East End Jews, in the front line of attack, had no alternative but to resist.' And 'night after night squads of their comrades used to receive the riot call. And from Chelsea old vans would rush to extricate the venturesome speaker from a hostile crowd,' recalled John Beckett, former Labour MP for Peckham, but by 1934 a leading Mosleyite who ran the party's propaganda machine and edited its two weekly magazines.

It was entirely predictable that there would be worse violence if Mosley were allowed to lead his Blackshirts on a march through the East End, as he planned. The Commissioner of the Metropolitan Police, Sir Philip Game, wanted to have the fascist movement outlawed, as had his predecessor, Lord Trenchard, but the only person who could ban the march was the Home Secretary, Sir John Simon, and he refused to do so, considering it would have been an infringement of freedom of speech, despite deputations from the mayors of the five East London boroughs affected, the Labour leader Clem Attlee (who had been Mayor of Stepney and whose parliamentary constituency was Limehouse) and the Labour leader of the LCC, Herbert Morrison (one-time Mayor of Hackney and MP for a seat in the borough). So strongly did some East Enders feel that the police should not be used to protect the Blackshirts that Bethnal Green Borough Council proposed that the portion of the rates devoted to the Metropolitan Police should be withheld in protest.

On 4 October 1936 police leave was cancelled, and special constables took over the beat of regular officers in East London as 6,000 foot police – a third of the Metropolitan force – plus the entire mounted division were drafted in, with an autogiro flying overhead to facilitate communication, all to ensure that the march could take place. But the East End had different ideas. By the middle of the afternoon 100,000 anti-fascists – the largest such demonstration yet seen in London – had made for Whitechapel and were milling round Gardiner's Corner in Cable Street, just off the Commercial

Road. They had been alerted by announcements chalked or whitewashed on pavements and walls 'Everybody to Aldgate on 4th October 1.00 p.m. THEY SHALL NOT PASS' (a reference to the *No Pasaran!* of the Spanish Civil War Republicans).

However, the Jewish Board of Deputies was ambivalent about what action Jews should take in the face of fascism, and were unwilling to associate themselves too closely with radical activist East End Jews. Their President, Neville Laski, issued a letter to Jewish youth clubs telling their members they must not get involved in anything that broke the law, and to 'stay away from disorder, close your windows and curtains and stay indoors'. This message was also published in the *Jewish Chronicle*.

Near Aldgate, in Royal Mint Street, Stepney, 2,000 Blackshirts (including four hundred women) were assembled. Mosley swept up in a bulletproof car to inspect his storm troops. The Blackshirts' route would take them through Cable Street, which had been barred by an overturned lorry full of bricks that the protesters had hijacked from a builder's yard, with more bricks used as makeshift barricades and a missile store. The Stepney Jewish People's Council against Fascism and Anti-Semitism (which had gathered 100,000 signatures in forty-eight hours for a petition to stop the march) was out in force, as were the International Labour Defence League, the ILP, the Labour Party and the Communist Party. Like the Jewish Board of Deputies, the CP had also been ambivalent about the action it should take. The official attitude was that the Party should work to affiliate/infiltrate trade unionism and the Labour Party rather than use its energies agitating on the streets, as too much emphasis on Mosley would give him gratuitous publicity and would dilute the CP's broader opposition to the National Government. Although this line was to change, and anti-Mosley activities were to prove a recruiting ground for the Communist Party, the initial advice on the eve of Cable Street had been to 'avoid clashes . . . no excuse for Government to say we, like BUF, are hooligans'. Rather than fight Mosley and his Blackshirts, the *Daily Worker* instructed its readers to march to Trafalgar Square, 'where London's youth will show solidarity with the Spanish people' at the very moment the fascists were starting *their* march through the East End. Joe Jacobs, secretary of the Stepney branch of the CPGB, was in no doubt that this was the wrong strategy. 'Whether we liked it or not, other people were taking to the streets in opposition. We could not do anything but try to head this opposition in the direction we thought it should go. That's the job of a vanguard.' Not that the Stepney branch was united: Jacobs was all out to 'bash the fascists wherever you see them', according to Phil Piratin, who was elected Communist MP for Mile End in 1945; his own attitude was less confrontational.

With days to go, the official CP line had changed. Leaflets calling for solidarity with Spain were overprinted with instructions to 'Rally at Aldgate at 2 p.m.' to oppose Mosley. 'It was an impressive demonstration of working-class solidarity. It was also quite bloody,' recalled Louis Heren, later Deputy and Foreign Editor of *The Times*, but at the time 'growing up poor' in the East End. 'In those days the police . . . dealt firmly with the lower orders . . . .Whatever Mosley stood for, and no matter the rabble at his heels, he was an obvious gentleman and a patriot, which is more than you could say for the mob at Gardiner's Corner. We were Cockneys, unemployed, Jews, a few Irish, and I suppose some agitators. We shouted, *They Shall Not Pass.'*

The confrontation that ensued became known as the 'Battle of Cable Street'. Bricks and stones flew, horses reared, the police moved in, wielding truncheons, Sir Philip Game, himself on horseback, ordered the mounted police to charge, protesters threw marbles under the horses' hooves, lemonade bottles thrown from roofs and windows exploded. The plate-glass window of Gardiner's store was smashed and protesters fell in; some started looting the woollen goods. Taxi drivers – most of them Jewish – organised themselves into a mobile column, ferrying reinforcements from one street to the next and retrieving the wounded, an exercise Heren likened to 'the Paris cab drivers who rushed French troops to the Marne in 1914'. The anti-fascists included a sizeable contingent of Wapping dockers: 'It was the dockers who stopped them,' Bernard Kops's father told his ten-year-old son proudly as they walked home.

The Metropolitan Police Commissioner telephoned the Home Secretary in the country, but was advised that since it was a legal march he could not ban it; the only solution was to reroute it through the West End. Mosley reluctantly acquiesced, since though 'the government surrenders to Red violence and Jewish corruption', '*We* never surrender . . . the British Union obeys the law and does not fight the police.' He and his Blackshirts set off towards the Embankment, a pipe band at their head. Later that night fascist youths went on the rampage, smashing the shop windows of Jewish premises along Roman Road.

The next day Mosley left for Germany, where he was to marry Diana Guinness, *née* Mitford, at Goebbels' house with Diana's sister Unity and Magda Goebbels as her witnesses, two BU officers as his. Hitler, who gave the couple a photograph of himself in a silver frame with an eagle on top as a wedding present, was a guest. The marriage was kept secret for two years, ostensibly to protect Lady Mosley from harassment, 'since I was living alone [in the country] and politics were rough', but maybe also to preserve Mosley's magnetism as the 'Rudolph Valentino of Fascism' for women – or some women.

The 'Battle of Cable Street' had resulted in relatively minor injuries, and eighty-five arrests, of which around eighty were anti-fascists, and of those eight were women. When Ubby Cowan, who had been pushed through a draper's shop window, presented himself at the London Hospital at the end of the day, he told the doctor his injuries were caused by 'a vase falling off a wardrobe'. 'Of course,' the doctor replied sceptically. 'And that's why I have had over 400 policemen in here today.'

The Special Branch reported that far from the 'Battle' dampening enthusiasm for the BU, it had excited enthusiasm. As Harold Nicolson had recognised back in the old days of Mosley's New Party (when it had been proposed that the youth wing should be named 'Volts' – Vigour-Order-Loyalty-Triumph), action, novelty (by contrast to the 'dun ranks of British politicians') and macho power were essential ingredients of Mosley's appeal; if that should tip over into violence, as frequently happened later, there were those who found that *very* invigorating. Some 2,000 new recruits signed up in the aftermath of the 'Battle', and BU meetings in Stepney, Shoreditch, Bethnal Green and Stoke Newington later that autumn drew large crowds, though Special Branch concluded by the following spring that the BU's support was falling off, and would do so further if only the press would ignore them.

'The best thing that has happened for some time was the refusal of the populace in the East End to allow Sir Oswald Mosley's march,' congratulated the *New Statesman*. 'For it was not Sir Philip Game who banned the parade; the common people banned it . . . Jews and Gentiles alike would not have it.' And, as Joe Jacobs was quick to point out, 'It should not be forgotten that in East London, some of the local churchmen played a big part in the fight against Mosley. Father Grosser and the Rev. Jack Boggis were outstanding examples.'

On 1 January 1937 the Public Order Act became law: it banned the wearing of political uniforms, outlawed paramilitary organisations, and strengthened the law on marches, assemblies and the use of insulting language to provoke a breach of the peace. This 'silly business of playing at Mussolini . . . with the folly of coloured uniforms and tin trumpets' was checked, in outward show at least. The Act also allowed the police to audit the accounts and require disclosure of the sources of funding of any party deemed to be violating the law, which proved a further blow to the BU's finances. Increasingly, local authorities refused to permit the BU to use their halls and open spaces to hold meetings. The party was effectively banned from the BBC, and coverage of its activities disappeared from newsreels, while fewer and fewer newsagents were prepared to sell *Action* or the *Blackshirt* – in other words, the BU's marginal, fringe status as little more than a rowdy party of the streets became increasingly obvious.

Nevertheless, Mosley was able to march through Bermondsey in South London in October 1937, fascist activity continued in the East End, where there were four active BU branches – in Bow, Shoreditch, Bethnal Green and Limehouse – and the Act probably inhibited protest against fascism as much as, if not more than, fascist activities. The poisonously anti-Semitic William Joyce (later to become Lord Haw-Haw, the notorious propaganda broadcaster from Nazi Germany during the Second World War) stood as a candidate in the 1937 LCC election, the first time the BU had contested LCC seats, and achieved 14 per cent of the vote, though he split from – or was forced out of – the party in March 1937, and with John Beckett founded a rival party, the National Socialist League. Even though many of Mosley's supporters were young men, too young to vote, other fascist candidates did even better, polling 19 per cent in Limehouse (where, according to the Women's District Leader 'they would follow Mosley through fire and water ... and they were a pretty rough crowd') and 23 per cent in Bethnal Green, but none won a seat, whereas a Communist, Phil Piratin, was elected for Stepney.

For the remainder of the decade, strapped for cash, denied opportunities to broadcast or hold meetings, and inhibited by the Public Order Act from wearing uniforms or holding political marches without police consent, the BU continued to decline, with a brief revival for the 'Peace Campaign' Mosley organised to try to appease Germany in 1939, since 'the jackals of Jewish finance are once again in full cry for war'. In May 1940 Oswald and Diana Mosley were interned, and they remained in prison, then under house arrest, for the rest of the war.

The morning after the Battle of Cable Street, on Monday, 5 October, two hundred men left Jarrow, a Tyneside shipbuilding town where 70 per cent of the citizens were unemployed, to march the three hundred miles to London.

The Jarrow March has come to epitomise the despair of the unemployed, of men driven to trudge the length of the country to put their case to a Prime Minister who refused to listen. But in fact the march from Jarrow – a town probably best-known to most people until 1936 as the home for sixty years of an eighth-century Benedictine monk, the Venerable Bede

– was among the last, and certainly one of the smallest, of the hunger marches of the 1930s. Indeed, as the men from Jarrow plodded south, so did three other marches: the 1,400-strong sixth National Hunger March, the Scottish Veterans' march, and a particularly poignant expedition by the National League of the Blind, 'tapping their way to London to ask for justice' on behalf of 67,534 registered blind persons in England and Wales who wanted the age at which a blind person could draw a pension reduced from fifty to forty years.

All these marches took much the same route, occasionally passing each other on the road, but the complexion of the Jarrow March was different – indeed the words 'Jarrow Crusade' were appliquéd on the banners the men carried to distance it from earlier marches and to show how serious an enterprise it was. The Hunger Marches had been organised by the communist-dominated NUWM, but the Jarrow crusade was intended to be non-political, and the Conservative Party in Jarrow, conscious that un-employment impacted on its members too, particularly among small shops and businesses, supported it. And, as Ellen Wilkinson noted, all along the crusade's route the marchers found 'Conservative mayors, hesitatingly taking the chair, nervously afraid of "politics", and then themselves at the end of the meeting banging the table heartily and moving resolutions themselves to be sent to the Premier demanding that "something be done to bring work to Jarrow"'.

The shipworks Palmers Yard had brought industrial prosperity to Jarrow in the nineteenth century, and had so dominated the town that it was unof-ficially known as 'Palmersville'. But the yard, which had built a thousand ships between 1852 when it opened and 1932, was hit hard by the slump, and had closed down in 1933. Most devastatingly, the prospect of a modern steel-works, which had looked like the town's salvation, offering work to some 2,000 men and spawning ancillary industries, had been snatched away at the last minute that summer by what seemed to be the machinations of the powerful British Iron and Steel Federation acting as a cartel to refuse Jarrow a quota for the production of steel. 'It appears that the Jarrow scheme was not rejected [by the Board of Trade] because of the inherent defects but that it was wrecked by the jealousies and rivalries of the Federation in the North Eastern area,' proclaimed a leader in *The Times*. As a result the town was 'utterly stagnant. There was no work. No one had a job except a few rail-waymen, officials, the workers in the co-operative stores, a few workmen who went out of the town,' wrote its MP, Ellen Wilkinson. And poverty took its toll. Average infant mortality in England and Wales was thirty-eight per thousand births: in Jarrow it was ninety-seven. The tuberculosis death rate for England and Wales was 702 per million: in Jarrow it was 1,273. Two and a half times more schoolchildren suffered from malnutrition in Tyneside and Durham than in the South-East in 1936. And while obviously Jarrow had much greater need for social services such as school meals, a penny on the rates there would yield £436, whereas in nearby Whitley Bay and Monkseaton, both of which had smaller but better-off populations, the same penny increase would produce £1,091. In Newcastle the council was able to spend £1.5s.10d on each child for school meals, medical services etc.: Jarrow could only spend seventeen shillings.

The cancellation of the proposed steel plant on top of the closure of Palmer's, and the feeling that no notice was being taken by the rest of the country in the plight of the North-East in general and Jarrow in particular, gave rise to the crusade. Alternative ideas had been floated, such as that the people of Jarrow should refuse to pay income tax, or the unemployed ship-builders should march to Palmer's Yard, seize what materials and tools they could, and build – and maybe even launch – a vessel of some kind to draw attention to their plight. The Mayor of Jarrow put it movingly: 'In every town and city and village on our way to London we are going to put to the people of this country the plight of our depressed town, so that public opinion, which is the greatest factor in this country . . . may make itself felt. We don't want people to be fed always by charity . . . We feel that after fifteen years of hardship, while the rest of the country may be progressing, we in the north eastern corner are left entirely on our own . . . Jarrow has been termed the most depressed town in the country, but we are here on behalf of all towns in a similar position to our own. All we are asking is that our unemployed men shall be allowed to work and earn sufficient money to keep their wives and children.'

This feeling that Jarrow was a forgotten place was real. Nationally, un-employment was falling by 1936: down from near on three million in 1932 to one and three quarter million by the summer of 1936 – 13 per cent of insured workers rather than over 22 per cent. The 'march of pylons' across the countryside, bringing electricity through the National Grid under the auspices of a Central Electricity Board set up in 1926, was all but complete by 1933, and enabled industry to be dispersed to new areas, since proxim-ity to coalfields was no longer necessary. Despite the slump, electricity output grew fourfold between 1925 and 1939, and by then there were almost nine million consumers of electricity, as compared to less than three quarters of a million in 1920. By the end of the 1930s two houses out of every three were wired for electricity – it had been only one in seventeen in 1920. And this stimulated a growth in all sectors that used electricity: the cinema, broadcasting, underground trains, plus manufacturers of domestic appliances such as cookers, vacuum cleaners, heaters, radios, irons and, still in relatively small numbers, refrigerators.

The British car industry was another success story. By 1937, 507,000 cars a year were rolling off the production lines of factories clustered around Birmingham, Coventry, Luton, Oxford and Dagenham, and a small family car was half the price it had been ten years earlier. Although the industry was successful overseas, exporting some 65,000 cars by 1938 (considerably more than their nearest European rivals Germany, France and Italy), most were sold in the home market. The motor industry hardly qualified as 'new', since it had grown out of the heavy engineering and transport industry, but other 'new sector' industries such as light engineering and chemicals were never able to equal the export markets of the pre-slump 'old' industries such as iron, coal and textiles, and relied for their success on an expanding number of domestic consumers with higher disposable incomes.

The growing success of the chemical industry, which by 1939 employed 100,000 people, was based on new products – fertilisers, dyes, artificial silk (rayon) and plastics such as bakelite, which was used for a mass of household and industry products. And the mid-1930s housing boom, and the construction of factories, shops, schools and other public buildings meant that there were almost a million jobs in the construction and related industries by the late 1930s.

There was even evidence by 1936 of a glimmer of hope in the depressed 'old' industries. Coalmining was still in the doldrums, since the growth in electricity generation meant declining demand for coal, but new, mechanised production techniques meant that output was growing, and while the cotton industry remained flattened, the woollen industry, which was never so dependent on overseas sales, was doing better on the home market. Steel output, which had reached an all-time low of 5.2 million tons in 1932, had climbed to thirteen million tons by 1937, and new plants had been opened in Corby, Ebbw Vale and Shotton – but not Jarrow.

The slow national recovery had failed to reach the severely depressed areas of Scotland, South Wales, West Cumberland and Tyneside, and it was here, in what were by 1936 called 'Special Areas' (a renaming of depressed or distressed areas that held out the promise of intervention), that the problem of the long-term unemployed persisted, with paltry resources devoted to revitalising industry. Resentment at the Means Test and the low rates of benefit, while the rest of the country seemed to be prospering, made such areas feel bitterly neglected. When Sir David Runciman, President of the Board of Trade, replied to a delegation from the North-East in

July that 'Jarrow must work out its own salvation,' his 'icily polite indifference to the woes of others' as Ellen Wilkinson was to describe it in the book she wrote about the Jarrow crusade, *The Town that was Murdered*, for the Left Book Club, proved a powerful spur to a month-long crusade intended to draw attention to the problem that had not gone away, and that could not be solved by the town on its own, as the steelworks débâcle had shown only too starkly.

The two hundred marchers were blessed by the Bishop of Jarrow and inspected by the Mayor, who had 'personally written to his fellow-Mayors on the route long beforehand, impressed them, and secured their willing co-operation', with the town council all present, before they set off, led by 'wee' (four feet eight inches tall) red-haired Ellen Wilkinson MP (a mixed blessing: good for publicity, less good for speed), who would march most of the way, taking days out occasionally to attend the Labour Party Conference and fulfil other engagements. They were accompanied by Palmer's band. 'We would like to have had a thousand . . . but we couldn't have accommodated them . . . the question of food [and] sleeping had to be considered,' explained an organiser. Many men felt frustrated that they were not chosen, but as Ritchie Calder, one of the journalists who accompanied the march, explained: 'In one family there were four volunteers from whom only one could go. And the brothers gave the trousers and the jacket and the father gave the boots and the uncle gave the raincoat. And the family marched with one man.'

'The detailed arrangements to the last blanket planned out by Councillor Riley and his staff at the Town Hall worked like clock-work. All the men had to do was to walk and that they did magnificently,' wrote Ellen Wilkinson proudly. However, the reception the marchers (or 'crusaders', or 'pilgrims') received in the various places they went through, or stopped for the night, varied: in Northallerton there was no official reception, but the Methodist church laid on plates of ham and tinned salmon sandwiches; in Ripon they were warmly welcomed by the Bishop and the Mayor, the Conservative Party donated two guineas to their funds and entertainment was provided at the Palladium cinema; in prosperous Harrogate, a Conservative area, welcoming crowds caused a traffic jam, the Rotary Club provided supper and the *Harrogate Herald* grew dewy-eyed about Ellen Wilkinson, who reminded its gossip columnist 'somehow of Joan of Arc'; in Leeds Sir William Nicholson, a local industrialist and former Lord Mayor, provided a lavish silver-service meal for the men, with a choice of beer or wine, the crusade's mascot, a black dog, was given a silver tureen to eat from, and £7.15s was collected to help the marchers on their way; in Barnsley they fed on meat and potato pie, had another free cinema visit, but just missed George Formby, who had come to the town to raise money for the families of the fifty-seven miners killed in the Wharncliffe pit disaster nearby on 6 August; in Chesterfield, £19.13s had been raised among local business people, but Labour councillors boycotted the marchers, concerned that there might be communists among their ranks, though the Mayor came to talk to them, as did another Labour councillor who informed them that in general he 'deprecated marches on London, but theirs was an exception'.

The crusade had got lost on the way to Nottingham, but when the men arrived they were showered with 'cascading coins', given a good meal and provided with two hundred new sets of underwear and medical supplies from local industries, while the Co-op stores donated thirty-two pairs of boots and twelve pairs of trousers; both at Loughborough and at Leicester the marchers occupied sleeping quarters that the blind marchers had only just vacated on their journey south. They had a particularly warm welcome in Bedford, where they arrived on 26 October, being plied with cigarettes and tobacco, and presented with pounds of sausages by local master butchers. Bedford was among the places participating in one of sixty adoption schemes whereby a prosperous area would 'adopt' a distressed town or village and raise money for it, provide holidays for the children and try to find work for the unemployed. Jarrow had been adopted by Surrey, while Bedford's adoptee was Eden Pit in Durham, where almost all the men were out of work.

News coverage of the Jarrow Crusade was extensive, and it received publicity usually denied to the NUWM Hunger Marches: the BBC broadcast nightly reports, journalists from two Tyneside papers marched all the way, the local press would pick up the story wherever the procession stopped for the night, and the national press and provincial press ran frequent stories – most of them sympathetic, though not all. Some thought the march was 'ill advised', it 'would serve no purpose', the unemployed were 'being exploited for political ends' and the whole thing was just 'cheap showmanship'. The controversy was kept alive by the upper echelons of the Church. First the Bishop of Durham wrote to *The Times* to complain that the crusade was 'revolutionary', a 'stigmatisation' Ellen Wilkinson regretted, when for her it was 'the quiet exercise of our constitutional right to offer a petition to parliament'. She quoted the remark the Bishop of Sheffield made when the marchers had stopped in his city: 'All governments are like wheelbarrows, useful instruments, but they need to be pushed.' Meanwhile the Bishop of Jarrow (who Wilkinson suspected of having been leant on by Durham) wrote to explain that though he might have blessed the crusaders, he certainly did not support them, and concluded that 'Such marches can do no good . . . and are liable to cause unnecessary hardship to those taking part [though the crusaders were much better fed – many put on weight – clothed and medically cared for during their month on the road than they ever were in their ordinary lives in Jarrow] and are altogether undesirable.' Mr Dodds, who had been Mayor of Jarrow the previous year, rather closed the matter by pointing out soberly that the crusade 'may not be the best way of dealing with these terrible problems, but it is the only way the men know'.

From the top of a number 19 bus Gladys Langford, a somewhat acid-spirited London elementary schoolteacher, complained that the Jarrow Crusade 'held up our bus for a very long time' as it marched into the capital. At the Royal Academy Summer Show the following year, the Academician Thomas Cantrell Dugdale exhibited an oil painting that showed the same scene. But his watchers were not on a bus (though the artist had been when he had the idea for the painting), they were in a smart London flat in evening dress: as an elegant woman leans out of the window to get a better view of the men of Jarrow marching through Piccadilly, a man, with studied indifference as to what is happening in the street below, slouches in a chair, blowing smoke rings. The painting both suggests that the plight of the unemployment was little more than a passing spectacle to the wealthy, and indicates to a considerable extent a microcosm of what happened when the crusade arrived in the capital.

The men marched to Hyde Park, where Ritchie Calder estimated there was a crowd of 50,000: the police put it at only 3,000. It was an emotional occasion. Many young people had left Jarrow and moved south to look for work, the girls as waitresses and in domestic service, the boys in whatever jobs they could find. 'There was a great reunion in Hyde Park, families coming together again . . . and it was a very tearful occasion, I can tell you,' wrote Calder, 'because they weren't going back with the marchers. They just weren't going back.'

The Communist Party was holding an 'Aid for Spain' meeting in the park when the Jarrow men arrived, but according to Ellen Wilkinson they ceded the platform for an hour, and listened to the speeches. There were several, including, of course, one from Wilkinson, who spoke of 'a town that has been murdered . . . What has the Government done? . . . It does not want anyone to tell the truth about these black areas in the North, in Scotland, and in South Wales that have been left to rot. These are the by products of a system where men are thrown on slag heaps . . . They will not be treated like slag, like things that can be thrown away.'

The government had already made it clear that neither the Prime Minister nor any other minister was prepared to meet the marchers, so all that was left was for Ellen Wilkinson to present the leather-bound petition in a specially-made wooden box with gold-leaf lettering, which had been lodged at a police station for safekeeping at every town they passed through, to the Commons. The crusaders were not present: they were off on a steamboat on the Thames to Tower Bridge, a trip paid for by Sir John Jarvis, the former High Sheriff of Surrey, who saw himself as Jarrow's saviour – 'Santa Claus' the press called him, when at a public meeting the previous day he somewhat diminished the crusade's purpose by announcing that he had a plan for a new steel tube works on Palmer's old site. It was a move that attempted to leverage the crusade for Jarvis's own agenda, and it let the government off the hook, though as Matt Perry, a historian of the crusade, points out, when the works finally opened – with a substantial government grant – in December 1937, it only employed two hundred skilled and semi-skilled workers, hardly an answer to Jarrow's problems.

In the House of Commons Ellen Wilkinson read out the petition from Jarrow, 'where formerly 8,000 people, many of them skilled workers, were employed, only 100 are left now . . .' She broke down in tears. The petition was not discussed: along with a companion petition from Tyneside it was referred to a committee, which found all sorts of procedural reasons, such as its being typewritten rather than handwritten, to disqualify it: only twenty of 68,502 signatures collected from across Tyneside were allowed. The marchers 'had imagined an imposing ceremony and a long discussion'; what they got was a cup of tea and a sympathetic meeting with a group of about a hundred cross-party MPs at which the leader of the Labour Party, Clement Attlee, was present but did not speak to endorse their petition.

On Guy Fawkes Day, 5 November, the crusaders went back to Jarrow, by train this time. Among the hundreds at King's Cross station to see them off was Sir Malcolm Stewart, who resigned later that month as Commissioner of the Special Areas, frustratedly admitting that 'No appreciable reduction in the number of the unemployed has been effected.' 'I have not been invited to meet you,' he told the men, 'but was determined that you should not go back without a word of encouragement. Your march has done good . . . I am not making promises or raising hopes – but don't lose courage, I have hope for Jarrow.' Ellen Wilkinson professed to share this hope. Although she had not expected 'that we should come back with a shipyard under one arm and a steelworks under the other', as she told the local paper, 'The march has put Jarrow on the map and has made Parliament realise, even if the Government did not, that something has to be done for Jarrow.'

The crusaders were less sanguine. 'We got nowt,' said one. 'Our march didn't do us a bit of good – we were out of work at the end,' said another later. And more than fifty years after the Jarrow Crusade, the oldest survivor gave his verdict: 'It was a waste of time. It had no effect on unemployment. The only thing that saved Jarrow was the war when the shipyards were needed again.'

There was a rumour that the King would be visiting Jarrow and other distressed areas in the North-East in the near future, and on 18 November, ten months after his accession to the throne, though as yet uncrowned, Edward VIII embarked on a two-day tour of South Wales. He took a detour to the abandoned steelworks at Dowlais, where more than 2,000 people were waiting in the cold drizzle to see their sovereign. Three quarters of the men were unemployed, but there were cheers as the King's car hove into view on the road from Merthyr Tydfil. Lines of children, many dressed in hand-me-down clothes provided from the Mayor of Merthyr Tydfil's Distressed School Children's Fund, waved the flags they were clutching, and the Dowlais Aged Comrades' Club struck up 'God Save the King'.

Whereas when he had come to Wales a quarter of a century before to be invested as Prince of Wales at Caernarvon Castle Edward had been welcomed with 'brilliant flags and princely paraphernalia', this time he was met by 'humble arches made of leeks from Government-sponsored co-operative farms, and of unlighted Davy lamps strung together by jobless miners'. The King gazed sympathetically around at the gaunt, ill-dressed, badly-shod men, the excited, malnourished children, the roofless build-ings and redundant, twisted girders. 'Even a King, who would be among the last to feel the pinch of a depression, could see that something was manifestly wrong.' Turning to an official who was accompanying him he said solemnly, 'Something must be done.'

This empathetic and well-meaning, but essentially ordinary, remark had a rather astonishing effect. 'Certain Government circles were not pleased. It was intimated that by saying that "something must be done" I had suggested in effect that the Government had neglected to do all that might have been done.' It was a reminder for some of how the deceased King George V had continually had to sternly warn his son that he must 'keep out of politics', whether over unemployment or Nazi Germany, to which he extended the hand of friendship on his own initiative.

When a constitutional crisis of unprecedented magnitude engulfed Edward within days of his return from Wales, there were those who hinted that the Prime Minister, Stanley Baldwin, and other senior politicians would not be all that sorry to see such a potential stirrer-up and troublemaker dispatched from the throne in favour of his younger, but more solid and reliable, brother Albert, who was always known as Bertie until he became King, when he started to be called George (in public) in an effort to repair the continuity of the ruptured royal line.

However, the expression of a sentiment which many felt, but few, including the King himself, knew how to take much further, consolidated Edward's reputation as the 'people's King'. He had undertaken a similar expedition to the Durham coalfields in 1929 – which had not greatly pleased Baldwin either – and was well known for his 'field work' in working-men's clubs and below decks, and for his sporadic efforts to help the unemployed and the poorly paid. He had considerable empathy for and an easy, relaxed way with the poorer portion of his kingdom, and was a frequent champion of their needs. It had been anticipated that as King he would flout convention, stare down the Establishment and bring the wind of change whistling through the corridors not only of Buckingham Palace (where his economies – or penny-pinching – caused much distress) and other royal residences, but of the seat of government too. In sum, he appeared to be a thoroughly modern, maybe even democratic monarch, oddly representative of the decade, as it would transpire, with his chromium-plated social life, his sympathy with, but inability to resolve, the nation's social problems, and his predilection to drift, confident that events would somehow resolve themselves for the best.

However, while Edward's sentiments were no doubt sincerely held, they were paternalistic rather than socialistic, and of the moment, for as Geoffrey Dawson, editor of *The Times*, judged, the new King had 'never shown the slightest interest in social distress when away from his popular tours'. He 'made his historical statement "something will be done,"' charged the Liberal MP Robert Bernays, 'knowing that he himself could not do it, would not bother to do it, and in any case had no ideas on how it could be done . . . He never really did any hard work. He responded instinctively to human misery but he had no idea as to how it could be remedied. He never met politicians. What an opportunity he could have had as a bachelor to give male parties of six or eight and really get down to the problems at issue.'

Furthermore, what the unemployed of Dowlais, those queuing hopelessly for work or benefit payments at Merthyr Tydfil Labour Exchange who had received encouraging words from the King, the residents of a run-down Pontypool housing estate he had promised, 'You may be sure that all I can do for you I will,' did not know was that their solicitous ruler had decided to abdicate the throne, and had already informed Baldwin, his mother and his brothers of his decision.

Edward VIII had met Mrs Wallis Simpson in 1930, but he had not really got to know her until his mistress Thelma Furness, the twin sister of Gloria Vanderbilt (mother of the future fashion designer), who had introduced them, had playfully left him in Mrs Simpson's charge when she went on holiday to America in January 1934. Wallis (*née* Warfield) Simpson was the daughter of a well-born Baltimore couple, in somewhat straitened circumstances. Christened Bessiewallis (an amalgam of two relatives' names, as was the Southern custom), she soon dropped Bessie, and in 1928, having divorced her abusive and alcoholic first husband, had married Ernest Simpson, a British citizen with an American mother who had been born and educated in the US. The couple moved to London, eventually establishing themselves in a flat in Bryanston Court which, according to Edward VIII, was 'in exquisite taste and the food, in my judgment, unrivalled in London'.

The then Prince of Wales was profoundly attracted by 'the grace of [Mrs Simpson's] carriage and the natural dignity of her movements . . . her deft and amusing conversation' and the fact that, in his view, she was 'extraordinarily well-informed about politics and current affairs', since she read 'the four leading London newspapers every day, from cover to cover. She kept up with the latest books and knew a good deal about the theatre.' But what the then Prince most admired was her forthrightness. 'If she disagreed with some point under discussion, she never failed to advance her own views with vigour and spirit. That side of her enchanted me. A man in my position seldom encountered that trait in other people . . . I always welcomed an opportunity to argue . . . perhaps because I had so few opportunities to do so.'

Others found her 'not beautiful: in fact she was not even pretty. But she had a distinct charm and a sharp sense of humour . . . Her eyes, eloquent and alert, were her best feature,' said Lady Furness, whom Wallis had usurped in the King's affections. 'Chips' Channon thought her 'Jolly plain, intelligent . . . she has already the air of a personage who walks into a room as though she expects to be curtsied to. At least she wouldn't be too surprised. She has complete control over the Prince of Wales.' On another occasion he described her as 'glittering, and dripped in new jewels and clothes . . . literally smothered in rubies, and looking very well as she has been on a fish diet for four days . . . [the King] must give her new jewels every day . . . her collection of jewels is the talk of London . . . quick and American, but not profound, but whose influence upon the King, until now, has been highly salutary – in that it was supposed to have calmed him, encouraged him to cut down on his alcohol consumption, and obey certain social conventions'. Channon, though American, had English roots and education, and disliked America while loving the England of 'London Society and large country houses, of rank, privilege and wealth' – which of course included Edward. The society beauty Lady Diana Cooper, wife of Duff, by 1936 Secretary of State for War, who spent quite lot of time in Mrs Simpson's company, thought 'She is wearing badly; her commonness and her Becky Sharpishness [the amoral, social climbing anti-heroine of Thackeray's *Vanity Fair*] irritate.' Harold Nicolson, though he was prepared to 'stick up for' Mrs Simpson on occasions, privately considered that, 'After all, every American is more or less as vulgar as any other American.'

The smitten monarch fell into the habit of calling at Bryanston Court for cocktails around 6 o'clock most evenings, whether Ernest Simpson was in town or not, and of inviting the pair to stay with him at Fort Belvedere near Windsor Great Park, 'a child's idea of a fort. Built in the eighteenth century and enlarged by Jeffry Wyatville for George IV, it had battlements and a cannon and cannon-balls and little furnishings of war. It stood high on a hill, and the sentries, one thought, must be made of tin,' according to Lady Diana Cooper, who was often a visitor too. Edward had asked his father for the use of the grace-and-favour residence in 1929. 'What could you possibly want that queer old place for?' asked George V. 'Those damned weekends, I suppose.' (George had disapproved not only of his son's weekend habit, but also of Soviet Russia – a prejudice his son shared – and of 'painted fingernails, women who smoked in public, cocktails, frivolous hats, American jazz', modernities Edward embraced with enthusiasm.) In fact the 'pseudo Gothic hodge podge' became more Edward's home, where he entertained frequently, gardened strenuously and did *petit point* embroidery. Fort Belvedere was to be the stage upon which most acts in the abdication crisis would be played out.

Mrs Simpson's name had been published in the Court Circular as attending one of the King's dinner parties in late May 1936, but it was not until later that summer that the relationship between the two began to cause acute anxiety in official circles. In August Edward chartered a yacht, the *Nahlin*, and took a party sailing off the Dalmatian coast – he had actually wanted to join the boat in Venice, but had to be persuaded that this was out of the question since it would look as if he was condoning Mussolini's regime. Among the party were Duff and Lady Diana Cooper, and of course Mrs Simpson, but not Ernest, since by now she had decided that the time had come for a divorce.

According to Robert Bernays, who was not a guest, 'life aboard was simply a dreary round of cocktails and gramophone music' – and doing erotic jigsaw puzzles, judging by photographs of the trip. The lovers spent their entire time together, and were photographed by the press in attitudes of some intimacy wherever they went, Edward often wearing what Lady Diana Cooper described as 'spick-and-span little shorts, straw sandals and two crucifixes on a chain round his neck . . . If he walks to see the sights (the churches and old streets) they [the "jostling crowd"] follow shouting "Cheerio" and surround him so that he can see nothing.'

'[The King] has been brazen, almost foolish,' Chips Channon thought. 'The Mediterranean cruise was a Press disaster,' and Edward's slight when he declined to open some new hospital buildings in Aberdeen on the grounds that he was still in mourning for his father, yet was seen collecting Mrs Simpson in an open-topped car when she arrived from London for a visit to Balmoral, was 'a calamity. Aberdeen will never forgive him.'

Most of the British public still knew nothing of the relationship, although the US press showed no reticence about publishing photographs of the couple together and speculating about the romance, 'King Will Wed Wally', the *New York Journal* predicted on the eve of the Simpson divorce in October 1936. When American publications arrived in Britain the offending pages were scissored out, which roused the suspicions of some, and prompted Ellen Wilkinson to ask the President of the Board of Trade in the Commons on 17 November, 'What is this thing the British public are not allowed to know?' She was told, 'My department has nothing to do with that.'

'It is maddening to think of our King as the central figure of unsavoury gossip on both sides of the Atlantic,' complained the Reverend Alan C. Don, secretary to Cosmo Lang, Archbishop of Canterbury, towards the end of October. 'So far our English press has been effectively muzzled' by a 'gentleman's agreement' secured by Lord Beaverbrook, something of a royal sycophant, and a long-time foe of Baldwin, who had accused the newspaper magnate and sometime politician of exercising 'power without responsibility', in the resonant phrase of Baldwin's cousin Rudyard Kipling. Thus, when the Simpson decree nisi was granted (in Ipswich, since it would not have been possible for the case to have been heard in the London courts for a year or more) on 27 October 1936 on the grounds of Ernest Simpson's adultery at the Café de Paris in Bray with a woman named Buttercup Kennedy, it was noted in the British press only by a formal paragraph, whereas 'the American newspapers have had a Roman Holiday. The headline of one . . . read "King's Moll Reno'd in Wolsey's Home town",' reported Channon.

Lord Balneil, a Lancashire Conservative MP who would succeed as Earl of Crawford in 1940, described Edward as being guilty of 'all-absorbing egocentricity' and agreed with a fellow peer that he would be 'blackballed by any respectable London club', considered the fact that the British papers 'never breathe a word on the subject . . . most unfortunate, for it has given the King a false sense of security'.

A week before the Simpsons' divorce, which obviously raised the stakes considerably, Baldwin had been to see the King at Fort Belvedere, carrying with him a large folder of 'American newspapers . . . and even Chinese vernacular newspapers . . . carrying stories about your behaviour'. The Prime Minister had wanted the King to 'have this coming divorce business put off', to which Edward replied disingenuously that he could not, since it was 'the lady's private business'. Baldwin urged that Mrs Simpson should go abroad for six months, with the unspoken hope – which was a general sentiment among the Establishment – that in her absence Edward's puppy-like passion would cool somewhat.

However, on 16 November the King summoned the Prime Minister to Buckingham Palace to inform him of his determination to marry Mrs Simpson. Under the terms of the Royal Marriages Act of 1772 there was no legal impediment to this, but if he elected to do so against the advice of his ministers, he would be acting unconstitutionally. Baldwin pointed out that 'the position of the King's wife was different from the position of any other citizen in the country; it was part of the price which a King has to pay. His wife becomes the Queen; the Queen becomes the Queen of the country, and therefore, in the choice of a Queen, the voice of the people must be heard.' Edward's riposte was that if the government and the people found the marriage unacceptable, he would abdicate. Baldwin was 'deeply grieved' by the King's decision.

Edward's mother, Queen Mary, whom he called on later that evening, was likewise 'grieved beyond words' at the news, though it was hardly a total surprise. 'It seemed inconceivable to those who had made such sacrifices during the war that you, as their King, refused lesser sacrifice,' she wrote later. And she declined to receive the 'adventuress' who had snared her son. The Queen, an intimidating and distant parent, as had been her husband, had not had much luck with her sons. Prince Henry, Duke of Gloucester, was a man in the mould of one of Victoria's many renegade Hanoverian uncles, while Prince George, Duke of Kent, before he married the meltingly beautiful Princess Marina of Greece in 1935 had been a predatory bisexual with a cocaine habit acquired by mixing with the Kenya 'Happy Valley' set.

The next day, Edward told his brothers. Bertie, who would become King if Edward did abdicate, 'minds terribly . . . but it's awfully difficult for [him] to say what he thinks, you know how shy he is', according to his wife.

The King then departed for his highly successful progress through the slag heaps and deserted factories of South Wales.

On his return, a *Daily Mail* leader invoked the 'King Edward touch', which it claimed had 'started a fresh chapter of endeavour for the distressed areas', and contrasted his practice of going to see national problems for himself with the way in which they were usually approached: 'There is consultation, committees are appointed and conferences take place in the solemn apartments of Whitehall, but how often does a Minister . . . go boldly forth to see for himself and measure the problem by independent judgment, following this with action.' The unspoken premise was that the loss of such a monarch would clearly be a disaster – not that the *Mail's* readers had the slightest idea that it was on the cards. Esmond Harmsworth, the son of the *Mail's* owner, Lord Rothermere, invited Mrs Simpson to lunch at Claridge's to float a compromise solution to the bubbling constitutional crisis: a morganatic marriage, meaning that she would not take the title of Queen, and any children of the union would be without right of succession. She suggested the idea to Edward, who raised it with Baldwin. Baldwin agreed to ascertain what Parliament and the dominions thought of the plan. The answer was equivocal. A morganatic marriage would require an Act of Parliament, and would in effect be an admission that the King was marrying someone who was unfit to be Queen. New Zealand was prepared to accept what Edward chose to do, but Canada, Australia and South Africa were adamant that this was not an acceptable solution: indeed, while abdication would be 'a great shock', a morganatic marriage would be 'a permanent wound'.

Clement Attlee, as leader of the Labour Party, reported that while its members felt 'sympathy for the King and the affection which his visits to the depressed areas had created, the Party – with the exception of a few of the intelligentsia who could be trusted to take the wrong view on any subject', they were opposed to any notion of Queen Wallis, and would equally object to a morganatic marriage. This was a view Aneurin Bevan thought they shared with a 'typical middle-class woman in Surbiton'.

Of the Cabinet, only Duff Cooper was prepared to consider the morganatic solution, suggesting that the matter should be shelved until after the coronation – though that would have put the Archbishop of Canterbury in an invidious position. The other members were unanimous: a morganatic marriage was both impractical and undesirable. On 4 December Baldwin went to tell the King that if he persisted in his intention of marrying Mrs Simpson, the only course open to him would be abdication, though he assured him that he fervently hoped this would not be the option he chose.

It was at this time, when in effect the matter had already been decided, that the King's subjects, whose unexpressed interests had been a shuttle-cock in the affair, learned what was going on. 'The country is in a turmoil because the King had stated that he wants to marry Mrs Simpson with whom he has been friendly for some years,' reported vicar's wife Madge Martin on 5 December. 'His ministers have advised him not to do so, as they consider her an unsuitable person as she has already been married twice. Everyone is anxiously waiting to see what the new King will decide to do – marry her and resign the Throne, or give her up, or marry her and dismiss the Cabinet. There doesn't seem to be any happy way out, only I do hope above all that we do not lose our wonderful King.'

The dam burst, the storm broke, the cat was out of the bag on 3 December, following an address by the Bishop of Bradford ('aptly named Blunt') to a Diocesan Conference two days earlier in which he had upbraided the King for not being a regular churchgoer, and called on him to 'do his duty'. The Bishop denied that his remarks had anything to do with the Wallis Simpson crisis, but they were the catalyst that encouraged the press to lift its self-imposed silence. A 'confused muddled jumble' written by its editor, Geoffrey Dawson, appeared in *The Times*, a fine leading article in the *Daily Telegraph*, while the other papers wrote 'in sorrow rather than anger' and billboards on the street 'flamed' with the words 'King and Mrs Simpson'. 'The Country and the Empire now know that their Monarch, their young King-Emperor, their adored Apollo, is in love with an American twice-divorced, whom they believe to be an adventuress. The whole world recoils from the shock,' wrote Chips Channon that morning.

'Everybody in England must be thinking about the King,' thought Madge Martin, who certainly was. 'A long reading afternoon seeing what the papers have to say on the matter. Most of the cheaper ones seem in favour of him marrying Mrs Simpson, but at all costs not to abdicate when he is so much loved.' *The Times*, the *Daily Telegraph*, the *Sunday Times*, the *Observer*, the *Daily Herald* (after some equivocation) and the *Manchester Guardian* all proclaimed for the 'constitutional solution': that the King had to either renounce Mrs Simpson (who by this time had fled to the South of France, accompanied by the loyal but dim Lord Brownlow) or abdicate, as did the entire provincial press, with the exception of the *Western Mail*, and the *Spectator*. The *Daily Mail*, (whose lead story was headlined 'The People Want Their King'), the *Daily Express*, the *Daily Mirror* and, rather surprisingly, the non-conformist *News Chronicle* plumped for a morganatic marriage, as did the *New Statesman*; with a difficult-to-follow argument about Mrs Simpson not being Mrs Simpson at all, since her first husband was still alive, so did the *Tablet* and the *Catholic Herald*.

When it came to the political parties, the majority of Conservatives accepted Baldwin's rather drifting position, though the Chief Whip reported that probably some forty-odd Tory MPs were for the King. The most notable among them was Winston Churchill, whose private nickname for Mrs Simpson was 'cutie'. But Churchill finally lost the sympathy of the House, was shouted down, and his political ambitions were put back several paces as a result of his support for the King and his demand for more time. 'What is Winston's game?' wondered the Reverend Alan Don. 'Does he see himself as future leader of the "King's Party" should a constitutional crisis lead to the resignation of the government?' Most Labour and Liberal MPs also accepted Baldwin's stance, though there were some in the Labour Party who supported the proposal for a morganatic marriage, hoping it would force Baldwin to resign. If Labour refused to join an alternative government a general election would have to be held, during which they would campaign on the King's concern for the unemployed and attack the government on its policies towards Abyssinia and Spain – though whether this would have been a winning ticket seems highly doubtful. Harry Pollitt, secretary of the Communist Party of Great Britain, was able to stir things up by declaring that 'the spectacle of the National Government laying down a code of morals and behaviour for the King, is indeed a sight . . . there is no crisis in all this business for the working class. Let the King marry whom he likes.'

On the other political extremity, Oswald Mosley was a pro-King man ('Stand by the King' was his slogan), lined up 'with Churchill, Beaverbrook and the communists [and his erstwhile supporter Rothermere] in lonely agreement against the Establishment'. Edward VIII was 'fascism's ideal King', according to Mosley's biographer, 'young [ish – he was forty-two at the time of the crisis], unconventional, anti-Establishment [and standing] for friendship with Germany and action on unemployment'. Mosley seemed to imagine for a time that the crisis could be his opportunity for power. *Action* published a photograph of the King getting out of an aeroplane with the caption 'A Symbol for the Modern Age which the old men hate', and the BU brought out a four-page *Crisis* special, the front page of which showed the King standing in front of some derelict pits on his recent tour of South Wales, while the text of a speech Mosley had delivered in the East End on 4 December was printed inside. He had urged that the King should be allowed to choose for himself whom to marry, and insisted that that was what young people thought, while the 'old gang' took the same constitutional line as Baldwin, a 'gang' member himself. It sold 37,000 copies, but a 'King's Party' which would benefit Mosley was never a serious possibility. After a 'night of soul-searching' Edward, recognising that a move towards such a party would leave 'the scars of civil war', rejected the idea, and on 6 December he wrote to Mosley with 'polite thanks for his offer of support', of which he 'felt unable to take advantage', having no wish to associate himself with the BU.

But what about the people? Was the country divided into cavaliers and roundheads again, as Chips Channon ventured? Were the British romantics to a man and woman, buying into 'the greatest love story ever told', and the notion that constitution or no constitution, middle-aged love should be allowed to triumph? Were they all hearts in mouth like Madge Martin about losing their 'wonderful King'? Harold Nicolson thought not: addressing a chapel audience in Islington on the subject of biography on the evening the news broke, he found that only ten out of an audience of four hundred joined in the singing of the National Anthem. 'The upper class mind her being American more than they mind her being divorced. The lower class do not mind her being an American but loathe the idea that she has had two husbands already.' However, Nicolson did 'not find the people angry with Mrs Simpson. But I do find a deep and enraged fury against the King himself.'

Gladys Langford, herself perhaps of 'the lower class' to whom Nicolson referred, since there seemed to be no middle ground, would not have agreed with his analysis. Deserted by her husband within twenty-four hours of the wedding, her marriage annulled, she 'env[ied] Mrs Simpson who is loved by a man who is prepared to let a Kingdom totter for her sake', and thought that 'the King is to be congratulated on having the courage to break free from hypocrisy and precedent . . . My views are not common though. Women are furious. They keep exclaiming, "she's already had two husbands". Men seem to think he might have continued "an affaire" and not imperilled "Big Business".'

Letters flooded into newspaper offices: 90 per cent of those who troubled to write were alleged to be in favour of the King marrying Mrs Simpson, while crowds packed Downing Street chanting 'We want our King' and singing the National Anthem. At Marble Arch banners were waved bearing the legend 'After South Wales You Can't Let Him Down'. Women paraded up and down outside Buckingham Palace carrying placards that read 'God save the King from Baldwin', while five hundred fascists among the crowd of 5,000 intoned rather more brutally, 'One two three four five/We want Baldwin, dead or alive!' A gang of small boys was encountered in the Kings

Road 'marching along, singing to the music of a well-known hymn-tune, a paraphrase they had concocted, beginning: Hark, the herald angels sing/Mrs Simpson's pinched our King!', and Woolworths reported that Edward VIII coronation mugs, which up to then had been slow to move, had now sold out completely, though other retailers reported that Christmas trade was well down on the previous year.

Anthony Heap, a twenty-six-year-old London civil servant who in 1933 had 'developed a fervent enthusiasm for Fascism', nevertheless disagreed with Mosley. He considered that the Cabinet '*rightly* opposes this scandalous match [which] would not only make the King appear cheap and contemptible in the eyes of the whole country but depress our trade and lower the country's prestige enormously as far as the rest of the world is concerned. In fact, he's made a complete and utter fool of himself.'

Collin Brooks, editor of the *Sunday Dispatch*, reported in his diary on 3 December that 'the city and the lobbies feel that [Edward] must abdicate. If it is a choice between the King and the Empire, Britain will be almost solidly against him, even to the point of dethronement and banishing. But he may do anything ... he may dismiss Baldwin and send for Mosley, and attempt a fascist coup d'etat. All is very much on the hazard. The situation has had the effect of swamping all other news – the Spanish war, the German menace, the distressed areas have all fallen into the obscure background of the national mind. In preparing the paper for the weekend I have even had to allow for a Royal suicide, for the King is obviously out of the realm of rationality, and in the realm of nerve storms. Wally herself is ill, and little wonder. The pity is that such fools as Baldwin should have allowed the situation to develop in this way. The pistol should have been used earlier,' he concluded dramatically.

'We can't have a woman Simpson for Queen, that was the sense of it. She's no more royal than you or me, was what the grocer's young woman said' to Virginia Woolf, though Woolf noticed on 7 December that 'We have developed a strong sense of human sympathy; we are saying Hang it all – the age of Victoria is over. Let him marry whom he likes.' But while 'all London was gay and garrulous – not exactly gay, but excited ... In the Beefsteak Club, however, only Lord Onslow and Clive [Bell] take the democratic view. Harold [Nicolson] is as glum as an undertaker, & so are the other nobs. They say Royalty is in Peril. The Empire is divided. In fact there has never been such a crisis. That I think is true. Spain, Germany, Russia – all are elbowed out. The marriage stretches from one end of the paper to another ... Mrs Simpson is snapped at midnight as she gets out of her car. Her luggage is also photographed ... We are all talking 19 to the dozen;

& it looks as if this one insignificant little man had moved a pebble wh. dislodges an avalanche. Things – empires – hierarchies – moralities – will never be the same again . . . And the King may keep us all waiting, while he sits, like a naughty boy, in the nursery, trying to make up his mind.'

'It is now a clear fight to a finish between King and Parliament with no possibility of compromise on either side,' wrote Anthony Heap on 5 December. 'Unfortunately the popular press in order to appeal to the loose-thinking, sentimental mob is veering round in support of the King.'

'"End of the Crisis" blithely announces the *Express* today,' Heap was able to report on 8 December. 'This on the strength of Mrs S's offer to withdraw from the match. ["She is willing, if such action would solve the problem to withdraw from a situation that has been rendered both unhappy and untenable," is what her statement from Cannes said.] Offer is the operative word which is anything but a solution to the difficulty. It merely amounts to challenging the King "Desert me now if you dare." And he, no doubt, will be duped into falling for the sham heroism and become more obstinate still. End of crisis be damned. It's hardly begun yet.'

But in fact just two days later, on 10 December, 'History was made today,' reported Heap. 'The crisis at last reached the most dramatic end it possibly could – the King abdicated in favour of the Duke of York. This was I think the most thrilling and exciting news I've ever experienced. It had no other reaction on me whatever. No sorrow or regret and certainly no sympathy for the King for how can anyone other than a muddle-headed sentimentalist sympathise with a man who can so lightly abandon his great heritage and fail so dismally in his duty to his people for the sake of a commonplace cow like Mrs Simpson. Especially after having gone out of his way to gain immense popularity in behaving like an impetuous schoolboy. He's let the country down badly and cost it many millions in lost trade. Still the worst disgrace of all, Mrs S becoming queen has thank heavens been avoided thanks to Mr Baldwin who alone emerges from this sorry business with honour and esteem. His speech in the Commons after the abdication was first announced there this afternoon was magnificent. He'll go down in history as the saviour of his country on more than one occasion. A truly great man.'

'Baldwin's speech was an amazing performance,' agreed Robert Bernays. 'I shall always remember the crush in the press gallery and the banging of doors and the wild stampede at the first sentence of the King's statement that he had renounced the throne irrevocably. I had never seen the House in grander form [than] when they heard Baldwin's unstudied almost chatty account of all that had happened. There was a tremendous sense in everyone that we were on a great stage and the world was taking account of how we were comporting ourselves . . . I gather that never for a single moment would the King waver in his determination to go and that his last words to Baldwin were, "If the Angel Gabriel came through that window and told me not to do this thing I would still do it."'

The craggy, principled James Maxton, ILP Member for Glasgow, a man rather loved throughout the House, had seen the crisis as the perfect opportunity to get rid of the monarchy altogether, but only four other MPs supported his demand for a 'stable and dignified government of a republican kind'. Aneurin Bevan, who sat in the Labour interest for the Welsh mining constituency of Ebbw Vale, could not agree that the issue was, as Baldwin presented it, between King and Parliament, since Parliament had not been consulted. 'The Prime Minister, who has a natural gift for the counterfeit, surpassed himself,' Bevan sneered after the speech. 'He spoke as a pilot who had guided the ship of State safely to harbour through stormy seas, past jagged rocks, and in the strength of buffeting winds. The winds, indeed, were boudoir hysteria, the rocks threatened to wreck only his own career, and the official Opposition has not blown even a zephyr across his path.'

But later, when Robert Bernays 'ran up against Baldwin . . . and congratulated him on his speech . . . He said a crisis was bound to come and that it might have come on a far more difficult issue.' Was he referring to Edward's wish for greater rapprochement with Hitler, perhaps?

Although Madge Martin was impressed by Baldwin's performance, she saw 10 December as 'A black day for England. All else seems to fade away except the fact that in the afternoon our beloved King VIII abdicated and gave up the throne. All because he cannot marry his Mrs Simpson. I feel almost broken hearted as I have always adored him. It is strange, but I always said too that he would never become King. Mr Baldwin's excellent and thoughtful speech was read out over the wireless and he almost convinced us that this is the only way, but it is all terrible, and I can't bear the thought of losing such a wonderful personality for ever this way. It is more tragic than the late King's death.'

Later that evening the former King broadcast to the nation. He had wanted to 'put his case to his people' before, but this had been refused. Now, it was suddenly urgent to decide on a title for him, since the BBC Director General Sir John Reith was proposing to introduce the ex-sovereign as 'Mr Edward Windsor'. This would never do, explained the new King George VI testily. Since he had been born the son of a duke, that made him

Lord Edward Windsor. But if that was to be his title, he could be elected 'to the H. of C. Would you like that?' pressed the King. The Lord Chancellor's representative 'replied no. As D of W he can sit & vote in the H of L, Would you like that?' Again the representative demurred. 'Well if he becomes a Royal Duke he cannot speak or vote in the H of L and he is not being deprived of his rank in the Navy, Army or Air Force.' So that was how it was, and at 9 p.m. His Royal Highness Prince Edward broadcast to the nation from Windsor Castle.

> A few hours ago, I discharged my last duty as King and Emperor, and now that I have been succeeded by my brother, the Duke of York, my first words must be to declare my allegiance to him with all my heart.
>
> You all know the reasons which have impelled me to renounce the throne. But I want you to understand that in making up my mind I did not forget the country or the Empire which as Prince of Wales, and lately as King, I have for twenty-five years tried to serve. But you must believe me when I tell you that I have found it impossible to carry the heavy burden of responsibility and to discharge my duties as King as I would wish to do without the help and support of the woman I love . . .

'The King's abdication is an unhappy solution to an unhappy situation. In the circumstances it is nevertheless the best solution,' pronounced the *New Statesman* two days later.

The former King having managed to secure highly advantageous financial arrangements for his future – at huge cost to relations with his brother and with Winston Churchill – he bade his family farewell before being driven through the cold winter's night to Portsmouth, where at 1.30 in the morning he boarded the ship the *Fury* and sailed the Channel into exile after a reign of 325 days. 'Thus it has come about that a King with an Empire at his feet nine months ago, has gone into the wilderness as an exile from his native land for the sake of a woman who has already made a failure of two marriages,' regretted the Archbishop of Canterbury's chaplain. Although he later paid occasional fleeting visits to Britain, the Duke of Windsor, as he became, made his permanent return conditional on his wife being received by his family and accorded the same rank as the wives of his younger brothers. This was refused. So it was only in death – his on 28 May 1972 in Paris, hers in the same city fourteen years later – that the ex-King and his consort (whom he had married at Tours on 4 June 1937) came home, their corporeal remains to lie next to each other in the royal vault at Frogmore.

On 11 December Chips Channon, who recognised that he had 'backed the wrong royal horse', went to the Commons to hear the Abdication Bill read. 'We woke in the reign of Edward VIII and went to bed in that of George VI . . . and Edward, the beautiful boy King with his gaiety and honesty, his American accent and nervous twitching, his flair and glamour was part of history.'

That day Madge Martin tried to be resolute. 'The papers full of the new King George VI whom we shall just have to learn to love, though I have always considered him dull, and his wife too "charming".' But she had been 'terribly upset' when, on the evening of the abdication, she had gone to a whist drive in Oxford, and found that 'most of the people were reviling our beloved King'. The reviling seems to have been rather general. Osbert Sitwell called it 'Rat Week' when the Duke's erstwhile friends and supporters scuttled off the already sunk ship. 'Where are the friends of yesterday/That fawned on Him,/That flattered Her . . . Oh, do they never shed a tear/Remembering the King, their martyr/What do they say, that jolly crew,/ So new and brave, and free and easy,/What do they say that jolly crew,/Who must make even Judas queasy?' While others weighed in with moral strictures.

'We loved him. We would have drawn swords for him. And then, by God, *didn't he let us down*!!' expostulated an officer in the Royal Fusiliers, of which Edward had been Colonel-in-Chief. 'Feeling has hardened against poor King Edward very noticeably,' reported Alan Don on the day of the proclamation of George VI (or Albert I, as Virginia Woolf referred to him). 'The more one hears what really took place behind the scenes, the more thankful one is that he decided to go – he could never have made much good. He was a dual personality, a mixture of much that was good and charming with much that was rotten and unstable. His infatuation for "the woman I love" . . . amounts to madness.'

A dinner of those 'bidden to discuss future relations of the [Unemployment Assistance Board] and the National Council of Social Services', found themselves talking of 'nothing but the recent Palace crisis . . . [Lionel] Ellis was still full of grief for the fall of the Prince, with whom he had worked closely from the inception of the Albert Hall meeting on unemployment onwards'. Anthony Heap was having 'second thoughts on the King's abdication [which] convince me that it is the best thing that could possibly have happened. [Noël Coward would have agreed: he suggested that statues of Mrs Simpson should be erected throughout the land in gratitude for having saved Britain from the reign of Edward VIII] . . . He has never been really suited to the position either in temperament or outlook or seemed over keen on having it despite immense popularity – or perhaps because of it. He rather seems to have made himself too popular by half. After all a dignified and gracious bearing and demeanour are the first essentials of Kingship and in this aspect he was totally lacking, though it mattered little when he was Prince of Wales. On the other hand, his brother, the Duke of York, who succeeds him as George VI fulfils these qualities admirably and will therefore I think make a better King. If he errs it is only on the right side of quietness and reserve. The only possible snag is his wife who (now Queen Elizabeth) has shown an unfortunate tendency in the past to play to the gallery on similar lines to Edward. Still, the new responsibility will perhaps arrest that tendency somewhat.'

Walking down Whitehall just before the abdication, Virginia Woolf had felt 'slightly yet perceptibly humiliated . . . I thought what a Kingdom! England! And to put it down the sink . . . Not a very rational feeling. Still it is what the Nation feels.'

'I suppose [Edward] will go down in history as the typical product of the war generation,' mused Robert Bernays. 'For four years he saw the world crashing to ruins and he thought, like so many of his own age that all that mattered was pleasure.' Bernays had been a harsh critic of the ex-King, believing that Edward had been 'intent on abdication . . . but that the King's death was so sudden that he could not escape . . . he was suddenly caught-up in the tragedy and hypnotized by the bright lights of the throne [and] was powerless to escape . . . He has never really tried to make Kingship work. Apart from public appearances he really has been astonishingly idle . . . He never read his papers and was only prepared to play the King at intervals, never realising that for a public man there is no private life and that he is always on duty . . . He never kept his appointments. Ministers used to be kept waiting for nearly thirty or forty minutes and he has used Buckingham Palace merely as an office. Vital cabinet papers have been scattered about. He was so selfish that he refused to have a secretary at the Fort with the result that when the cabinet wanted to retrieve important papers they had to ask the butler to send them back.' This caused great unease: there was a fear that the official red boxes were left lying around, and it was suggested that Mrs Simpson may have read highly confidential documents, and even passed their contents on to her German contacts – the ambassador Ribbentrop, in particular – though there is little evidence for this. However, 'To combat this, for the first and last time in history papers were screened by the Foreign Office before the red boxes went off to the King,' according to Edward's biographer.

'He never read a book,' continued Bernays, 'he never accepted anything and never took his pleasures in moderation. When he took up something he would do it so feverishly that he soon grew tired of it . . . he was passionate about golf and at one time would play three times a day. Then he became so bored that he would never play at all. He always wanted the palm without the dust, failing to understand that it is the dust that makes the palm worthwhile.' Nevertheless, Bernays conceded that Edward 'had some great qualities. I was terribly moved at the broadcast address, not because I had any sympathy for him but at the stark tragedy of his failure. It was like seeing a man of great promise committing suicide before one's eyes.' A cartoon appeared in the press of a workman laying down his tools and turning to his mate to ask, 'How can I do my work without the help and support of the woman I love?'

'And so ends a year as eventful as I am likely to see,' concluded Alan Don on 31 December 1936. The chaplain had been shaken by the 'Arch's' maladroit criticism of Edward and his circle in a broadcast on 13 December, though the Primate had offered scant spiritual or practical guidance during the crisis. 'Certain years seem to have been desperately charged with fate,' a leader in the *Daily Telegraph* read on that same last day. 'Of their number is the year whose last hours are now passing. It is not that 1936 will be memorable by the magnitude of its actual catastrophes. But it has abounded with events which have seemed to bring catastrophe near. Serious alarms at home, graver alarms abroad, a deepening sense of gathering storm. Feverish military, naval and aerial preparations, revolution and civil war have kept Europe continually on tenterhooks . . . Yet the British people have not escaped affliction. Within a single twelvemonth three Kings have reigned over us.'

PART FIVE

Feeling the Texture

An Iceberg on Fire

On the night of 30 November 1936, as the abdication crisis neared its climax
– not that most people in Britain knew that – the sky above London was
such a vivid blood-red that an orange glow could be seen as far away as
Brighton, fifty miles away. It was a sight that would become ominously
familiar during the Blitz in 1940, but on this night it was that symbol of
high Victorian achievement, the Crystal Palace, that was on fire.

The alarm had first been given at 7.30 p.m., and within an hour the
flames, fanned by a strong westerly wind, were so fierce that the hoses of
438 firemen, summoned from all over the capital, were ineffectual as molten
glass and iron crashed to the ground and sparks and shards of glass whirled
in the plumes of acrid smoke. It might seem surprising that glass should
prove so combustible, but heating pipes below the floorboards had dried
the floors to tinder, layers of dust had settled in the cracks, and 20,000
wooden chairs were stored under the enormous orchestra pit (which was
itself made of wood).

All night the fire raged, with flames leaping as high five hundred feet,
it was said. Richard Dimbleby phoned in the story to the BBC from a public
phonebox. Cracking flames, excited crowds and fire engines could be heard
in the background of this, the first major on-the-spot live report of a major
news event, and it scooped the newspapers. A reporter on the *Daily Mail*
hired a plane, and from the air the Palace looked like 'the blazing crater of
a volcano', while next morning the *Daily Express* compared it to 'an iceberg
on fire'. At about 8 p.m., the whole 384-foot-long transept collapsed, 'sinking
slowly and with a continuous rumble' that could be heard five miles away,
revealing an incandescent pillar of fire as a great spiral staircase burned,
hundreds of rats swarmed out of the burning building, and most of the
goldfish swimming in the pools and fountains would later be discovered
to be 'missing believed boiled'.

Crowds flocked to see the inferno, their cars gridlocking the roads of
South London. Private planes were chartered from nearby Croydon airport

for an aerial view, and a mass of sightseers had to be held back by the police from hampering the work of the firemen. Primrose Hill and Hampstead Heath to the north and Blackheath to the east were crowded with spectators, and MPs hurried out onto the terrace of the House of Commons, or peered from the windows of committee rooms and offices at the blaze. Chips Channon, on his way to the Commons, 'found the dark sky ablaze with light. It looked like a Venetian sunset . . . It was one of the largest fires ever known in London . . . now there is only one tower left, a reminder of Victorian London.' Sir Henry Buckland, the manager who had done so much to restore the fabric and the fortunes of the Sydenham 'white elephant' in the past twenty-five years, wept as he watched the Crystal Palace's involuntary 'last and biggest firework show of all'.

Anthony Heap found the fire very affecting too. 'It really horrified me when I read it in the paper this morning. For that grand old gigantic glass edifice always had a very warm spot in my heart. It had a most impressive grandeur and majesty and somehow stood for all that was great and glorious in the Victorian age . . . Strangely enough it was so beautifully clear and moonlit last night that I had the strong inclination to go for a walk across Hampstead or Parliament Hill, which I have never done at night. Would to God that I had obeyed that uncanny intuition. I should then have seen the tragic but awe-inspiring sight of that tremendous blaze away in South London. Even had I learned of it on the radio in the 9 o'clock news, I would have gone up there like a shot. But no, I was destined to miss it as well as lament its passing evermore. We shall never see its like again.'

In North London, schoolteacher Samuel Rich had just picked up a letter from his doormat at around 8 p.m. – 'the last post of the day' – when he saw 'a bright glare in the sky! People hurrying. The Crystal Palace on fire . . . with Amy [his wife] in spite of her cold to the top of the Avenue . . . what a sight! A long sheet of flame . . . We got back to hear the news summary. The announcer began: "There is no Crystal Palace" . . . to [his grandchildren] the palace will be just a name, something in history, and when the present generation goes none will remember the various "courts", the organ, the Handel festivals, the big clock, the grounds . . .'

It was not until dawn the next day that the conflagration was finally brought under control. The Duke of Kent, dressed in a hastily borrowed fireman's tunic and brass helmet, inspected the damage and spoke to the smoke-blackened, exhausted firemen. All that was left of the magnificent glass structure that had been designed by Joseph Paxton for the Great Exhibition of 1851, Britain's industrial and artistic showcase masterminded by Queen Victoria's consort Albert, were the two 282-foot-high water towers designed by Isambard Kingdom Brunel. A molten lava of thousands of tons of fused glass and iron covered the Sydenham hillside to which the painstakingly dismantled structure had been transported from its original site in Hyde Park and re-erected in 1854. The rebuilt and enlarged Crystal Palace had been a magnificent local landmark, compared by some to a giant crinoline, a glass edifice rising to six storeys high, a quarter of a mile long and over five hundred feet wide in places, visible for miles around, and used for exhibitions, concerts, public meetings and offices. Its soaring transept contained a gigantic organ and a concert platform for 4,000 performers. It had housed circuses, and the celebrated Blondin, who had breathtakingly crossed the Niagara Falls on a tightrope, had strung his rope between the glass towers and edged across, pausing to consume an omelette on the way. It had been home to the world's first aeronautical exhibition in 1868, and the first national motor show, as well as the usual pet shows, baby shows and flower shows, and the translucent glass palace provided a dramatic reflective backdrop to the spectacular Brock's firework displays held every summer since 1865 in the surrounding 349-acre park. During the First World War the glass structure had been used as a naval depot, and when it was reopened in 1920 it was the first home of the Imperial War Museum.

The Crystal Palace was, according to the 'London Diary' in the *New Statesman*, 'just on the point of regaining the admiration of the public'. The diarist regarded it as 'architecturally the best building in London erected in the last hundred years', and quoted an appreciation in the *Athenaeum* written on its opening in 1854: 'The Sydenham Palace is what it pretends to be. It asserts loudly that it is glass and iron – and *it is* glass and iron, and everyone can see through it . . . It reports the state of nature and the weather. It shows the dull sky when the sky is dull, just as it shows the blood red flushings of its summer sunsets . . . Thus . . . it has a poetry of its own – the poetry of fact and of nature, rather than of fantasy. It is the poetical product of a materialistic age – it is a realised idealism worked out in a century of reality . . . There is in this structure, fragile as it might seem – mere petrified air and crystallised ice as it is – self-supporting and unbuttressed as it appears – a durability that may deride the Pyramid.' And now, less than a hundred years later, that durable monument to an age was no more.

The fire, an inquiry later concluded, was an accident, probably started when a gas leak ignited, though it might have been an electric short circuit in the office staff lavatory, or even a carelessly tossed cigarette butt. And the thirty-four minutes it had taken for the local Penge fire brigade to get to the scene hadn't helped.

The fire had happened at a particularly unfortunate time: not only had a major £300,000 renovation just been completed, but there had been ambitious plans for a celebration of the coronation of Edward VIII at the Palace: 30,000 children were to have come there to hear Gracie Fields sing, but now, no palace: just a fortnight later, no Edward VIII either.

David Gascoyne was on a train home to Richmond after a visit to the Blackheath home of his fellow poets Charles Madge and his then wife Kathleen Raine, and the documentary film-maker Humphrey Jennings. They had spent the evening discussing the formation of a Mass-Observation movement. From the train Gascoyne saw 'a great glow in the sky', which he found out the next morning had been 'the great fire of the old Crystal Palace'. For Gascoyne, with his interest in the surreal, the fire had an added significance: it 'represented in a sort of symbolic way an image of the world-conflagration which we were already beginning to think of as about to break out'.

The fire gripped the imagination of the British public too – photographs and stories filled the newspapers for days afterwards. The would-be Mass-Observers interpreted this fascination with an event that had 'torn up the remaining roots of the nineteenth-century' as evidence that 'the people' had the same unconscious understanding of the significance of the event as they themselves did, seeing in the Crystal Palace fire much the same sort of augury as the sinking of the *Titanic* in 1912, which had become in retrospect a portent of the end of an era, of approaching Armageddon.

Should the Crystal Palace be rebuilt? The Victorian symbol re-erected? A letter in *The Times* pointed out that it would cost less to reconstruct the Palace than it would to build a battleship, but building battleships was a key part of the rearmament programme that had been announced in a white paper in March that year. The army was to be modernised, with four new battalions added and the Territorial Army overhauled; the number of aircraft for home defence would rise to 1,750; and two new battleships (to add to the existing fifteen), an aircraft carrier and nineteen cruisers would be laid down, while all existing battleships would be modernised. Defence expenditure had been £140.8 million in 1935–36; £158 million had been estimated for the following year: the actual figure spent was £183 million, and in February 1937 the government asked for a £400 million defence loan, and estimated that the total cost of rearmament over the next five years was likely to be around £1,500 million. Germany at the time was believed to be spending £1,000 million a year on arms. Set beside this, the cost of rebuilding the Crystal Palace did indeed seem a drop in the ocean. It might also seem a rather wistful project.

However, since the fire had left the nation in possession of 'an extensive site in a commanding position in South London', *The Listener* invited a 'number of distinguished persons, interested in the fields of entertainment, sport, music, art, town-planning, etc., to express briefly their opinion as to the best use to which this site may be put in the national interest'. Lord Sempill advocated its use as an aerodrome, with a great tower topped by an illuminated globe 'which would symbolise the Empire on which the sun never sets'; the Bishop of Southwark (in whose diocese the site lay) opted for a hospital which would be 'a sort of halfway house between the General Hospitals and the Convalescent Homes'; the film director Alexander Korda suggested that this was an opportunity to recreate a 'Regency pleasure garden' similar to the famous Vauxhall Gardens; Frank Pick, Vice Chairman of the London Passenger Board, proposed a 'Social Health Centre' on the lines of the one in Peckham. Other worthies put forward ideas for sports fields, concert halls, exhibition spaces, play and educational facilities for children – the mixture much as before.

What in fact happened was that two hundred of the Palace's seven hundred employees were given notice, Baird studios decided that their premises in the South Tower were sufficiently undamaged for television transmissions to continue, and when war broke out less than three years later, military equipment was stored in the remaining buildings, anti-aircraft guns were installed, and Brunel's magnificent twin water towers, survivors of the inferno, were demolished lest they became landmarks for German bombers. 'The same reason could have been given for the dynamiting of St Paul's Cathedral,' one of the historians of the Crystal Palace commented tartly.

SEVENTEEN

Choosing Between Gas Masks
and God's Tasks

I believe that Christ was neither meek nor mild, nor frail, but a man magnificently built, tall and strong and that His mind was even stronger than His body . . . By the keenness of His brain all those who argued with Him were outwitted and subdued.

H.W. ('Bunny') Austin, champion tennis player and convert to the 'Oxford Group',

writing in the *Daily Express*, 1932

'What a bloody shit! Now we are going to get a republic,' exclaimed Baroness Rothschild when she heard of Edward VIII's abdication. She was proved wrong, of course, but nevertheless the unshakeable determination of the King Emperor to marry an American woman who had 'a couple of living husbands still scattered around' was a major constitutional issue, and there were worries as to whether the monarchy would survive, or would 'crumble under the shock and strain'. No King of England had abdicated since Richard II in 1399 (and he had hardly departed of his own volition), but although the matter of Edward and Mrs Simpson soon faded for most people, and its importance to the life of the nation proved to be transitory, it sometimes illuminated currents already coursing through the law, the Church, society, fashion, and of course the monarchy itself.

For a start, there was the small matter of the coronation mug. The artist Eric Ravilious, who had established a considerable reputation as a watercolourist, engraver, lithographer and decorator of ceramics, was commissioned by Josiah Wedgwood to produce some designs that could be transfer-printed onto pottery, a traditional eighteenth- and early-nineteenth-century English technique. In July 1936 Ravilious travelled to Stoke-on-Trent to finalise designs for a special mug to celebrate the coronation of Edward VIII, planned for the following May. Wedgwood, which had also commissioned a commemorative mug from Dame Laura Knight – Ravilious thought it was 'bloody beyond belief' – was delighted with Ravilious's exuberant, colourful design with its 'submerged royal arms with the heads of the beasts sticking out into the [exploding] fireworks above'. The large mug, like 'a mantelpiece ornament', exclaimed Ravilious when he first saw the finished product, went into production straight away, and the first shop in London to stock it was Dunbar Hay in Albemarle Street, run by a friend of Ravilious. The first customer through the door to buy one was Wallis Simpson. However, when Edward VIII abdicated on 10 December 1936, the mug had to be hastily withdrawn, and reissued with the 'ER' changed to 'GR' and the background colours changed from turquoise and yellow to green and pink.

A royal visit, planned for Edward and announced by him in his one and only speech to Parliament as King, during which the British monarch would be crowned King-Emperor of India at the Delhi Durbar, was postponed. This was partly because George VI declared he wanted time to 'settle in' to his role, partly because he was regarded as quite physically frail, but also because of the tensions following the passing of the Government of India Act the previous year, which had established a federation without conceding self-government. As a result the Indian National Congress had declared its intention of boycotting the event. It was decided, however, that the coronation itself could not be postponed, and that George Rex would be crowned, as it had been planned that Edward Rex would be, on 12 May 1937. And it was to be a glorious occasion to expunge the humiliation of the abdication, a royal pageant that would cost £524,000 – more than two and half times the amount spent on the crowning of George V.

George VI was, as one of his early biographers says, a supreme example of a *roi malgré lui*. Indeed, on the first night of his reign he had blurted out to his cousin Lord Louis Mountbatten, 'Dickie, this is absolutely terrible. I never wanted this to happen; I'm quite unprepared for it . . . I've never even seen a State Paper in my life. I'm only a Naval Officer, it's the only thing I know about.' Mountbatten tried to reassure the quailing monarch that 'There is no more fitting preparation for a King than having been trained in the Navy,' but even in that he had not been a conspicuous success. In his first year, George (or 'Bertie', as he was at home) came sixty-eighth in a class of sixty-eight candidates, and had only managed to scrape up to sixty-first place by the time he passed out. Shy, nervous, a chain smoker with a duodenal ulcer, an unpredictable temper and a sometimes incapacitating stammer, Bertie was probably best known before his rapid ascension to the throne as a good sort in shorts and open-necked shirts who promoted scouting for boys as a way of bringing together public-school types and junior proles at Duke of York Camps for Boys. He joined in the activities himself, self-consciously tapping his head at the appropriate moment as the company sat in a circle around the camp-fire singing 'Under the Spreading Chestnut Tree'. While Edward winged (or more usually sailed) round the world, ambassador to Britain's far-flung dominions, George was usually left at home to mop up the factory visits, and was soon referred to as the 'Industrial Prince'. If Edward was the 'cock pheasant', George was the 'ugly ducking' who seemed unlikely ever to turn into a swan. All his life he had been in awe of his blue-eyed, golden-haired older brother, so he was dismayed and distraught when it became apparent that he would in effect have to turn into him.

During the brief reign of Edward VIII, the Archbishop of Canterbury Cosmo Gordon Lang had had the idea that the coronation could be an opportunity for a 'Call to Religion addressed to the Nation', but given the circumstances, the idea had to be dropped as 'inopportune', though some religious issues persisted. First there had been Ramsay MacDonald's ecumenical request that Nonconformist Churches should participate in the ceremony, but the Archbishop firmly scotched that, informing the Coronation Committee that 'he had after full consideration decided that it was not possible to find any place in the religious part of the ceremony for any Free Church Minister'. 'They do not grasp that it [the coronation service] is a totally different matter to the Jubilee service in 1935, being, in fact, a celebration of the Holy Communion according to the Anglican rite into which the actual coronation is incorporated,' Lang's chaplain, the Reverend Alan Don, explained. Then there was the question of the Oath, for since 1911, when the last coronation had taken place, the status of British possessions had changed: the countries of the Empire now enjoyed Dominion status, and were not prepared to be lumped together as 'this realm' of Britain. Moreover, the Prime Minister of Canada Mackenzie King on behalf of French Canadians, the Roman Catholic Australian Prime Minister Joseph Lyons and Éamon de Valera, President of the Irish Free State, objected to the solemn promise that the sovereign would 'uphold the Protestant faith' in *their* countries. After weeks of the 'air being thick with messages' a formula was agreed, but a month after the coronation, a new constitution was promulgated by the Dail by which Ireland became a republic and the King was eliminated from all its internal affairs.

As the day approached, the employees of the London General Omnibus Co. went on strike: 'not a bus running. This is a serious business coming so near the coronation when London is crowded with people,' wrote Alan Don anxiously. There had been a successful bus strike in 1932, when the company had made similar demands to those of the coalmine and railway companies – longer hours, lower pay and redundancies – and there had also been an unofficial strike of busmen in 1933. The men's contracts came to an end on 30 April 1937, and mindful of improving economic conditions, and perhaps not unmindful of the publicity such action would attract at the time of the coronation, against the advice of their Union Secretary Ernest Bevin, 26,000 London busmen walked out on 30 April. Their demands were for a seven-and-a-half-hour working week, and an inquiry into conditions of work, which they maintained had worsened over recent years with more traffic regulations, larger, heavier (seating sixty instead of thirty-four) and faster (capable of going at 30 rather than 12 mph) buses. Moreover, expert medical opinion showed that busmen suffered from more gastric illnesses than other workers, probably due to nervous strain and snatched, irregular meals.

On 1 May thousands of busmen wearing their white summer uniforms marched through the streets of London carrying banners declaring 'Twenty-Five Thousand Busmen Can't be Wrong', and leaflets entitled *London Busmen Demand the Right to Live a Little Longer* were handed out to the crowds.

The result of the industrial action was chaos, with 'trams and tramcars packed almost to suffocation, large crowds accumulating at railway stations', streams of cars flooding into the capital and parking anywhere, since the police were excessively lenient. The situation was made much worse by the barriers erected in the area of the coronation processional to control the crowds. 'The streets look odd,' thought Virginia Woolf, 'all aflutter with banners . . . & no omnibuses; a lower level in the streets; all taxis & innumerable private cars; & droves and herds trudging the pavement.' The strike lasted for four weeks, but when the men went back to work on 28 May they had not achieved their objectives.

The week before the coronation, the *Lady* was getting in the swing. 'Quite a lot of people who have been talking of superior plans to "escape" the twelfth of May in London, are beginning to think that it's going to be – in the Londoner's language of understatement – "rather fun". A height-of-the-season air already prevails in Mayfair . . . and those who have been causing amusement by their cautious ability to remember the last Coronation may do so without betraying that they are really over thirty.'

Bunting went up, shops put on loyal displays, lamp-posts were festooned. There might not have been any red buses on the streets, but the garlands and streamers made a splash of red, white and blue, 'clearly the right colours for our London sky and architecture . . . Bond Street looks very elegant with long Chinese banners in white,' thought the *New Statesman*, although it regarded 'the ubiquitous use of what is called "gold" but is in fact a dirty yellow' as a grave mistake. It was the department store Selfridges that in the magazine's view reached the 'absolute bedrock . . . of pretentious bad taste. The thing must have cost thousands to do; and it is spectacularly ugly and deforming. The building . . . is smothered with huge half-reliefs of gilt and silvered plaster, enormous gilt lions, swollen tassels, fussy and over-decorated hangings of every kind.' Not everyone shared this aesthetic shudder. Crowds trekked nightly to gaze on these *faux* splendours, and an Indian rajah was reputedly so impressed that he bought the whole façade, which was dismantled when the festivities were over and shipped back to adorn his palace in Rajasthan.

Windowboxes sprouted red, white and blue flowers, large photographs of Their Majesties were stuck on pieces of cardboard and displayed in front windows with streamers of crêpe paper, anyone who had a flag dug it out, unfurled it and stuck it out of the window, on the gatepost or garage roof. In the East End some residents, who might have been thought to have had little reason to rally to the monarchy, showed an admirable generosity of spirit, hanging out banners that proclaimed 'God Bless Our King and Queen *AND* the Duke of Windsor'. In Oxford, Madge Martin's 'spirits drooped in sympathy with the wilting decorations' (it was a very wet May), but then 'John came in [to the vicarage] and successfully got our electric light to go which illuminated our letters G &E . . . Mr Butler came in . . . and we all drank their majesties' health in Bristol Cream sherry. We went out to look at the illuminations being tried out in St Giles and chatted till nearly eleven. A nice evening.'

Fuelled by the number of recent issues of stamps to commemorate royal events such as the Jubilee in 1935 (George V had spent many hours engrossed in his stamp collection) and the ascension of Edward VIII, philately had become very popular: Edward VIII stamps sold out on the day of the abdication, and the price of a set of Jubilee stamps had soared to £20, while those for George VI were 'the best stamps we have had since early Victorian days. They are designed by Mr Eric Gill: the lettering is excellent, the spacing just, and the head itself, designed by Mr Dulac, quite dignified.'

Newspapers printed pull-out supplements of the processional route, and a child's guide to the complicated ceremony. Crowds flocked to London by coach and train – a thousand special trains were laid on for 12 May – hotel rooms overlooking the procession had been booked out long ago, most at vastly inflated prices, and some people slept on the pavements and in the parks to ensure a good view. 'Camps & latrines in all the parks, like the Crimea,' noted Virginia Woolf.

'The Coronation! Nothing but the Coronation. Clothes, uniforms, robes, ermines, miniver, rabbit, velvet, velveteen. Where were the coronets? In the bank, at Carrington's, or in the attic? There were fears for bad places behind stone pillars, absurd fretting over starvation and retiring rooms, alternative routes to the Abbey via Ealing or Purley' (most of the eight hundred peers elected to take a 'special underground train which carried them from Kensington High Street to Westminster . . . the fare was threepence a head'), wrote the legendarily beautiful Lady Diana Cooper, who wore a gold dress embroidered by Molyneux with a crown of golden flowers in her hair, and looked, she thought, 'faded but not, thank God, overblown'.

'12 May, The great day of the Coronation,' wrote Madge Martin, who wasn't there. 'No rain – but dull. I went to a short thanksgiving service and then back, to sit solidly listening to the wireless, which thrillingly described the procession and the service in the Cathedral [*sic*]. We sat spellbound from 11.0 till 5.0 and gloried in all the pageantry as described and the music and the cheering. It was the most wonderful broadcast we've ever heard.' It was the first time a coronation had been transmitted on the wireless. There had been discussion about televising the event, but that had been dropped 'inasmuch as the results of this Television could only be seen by a limited number of people within twenty-five miles of London who happened to have the necessary apparatus in the house' (when George VI's daughter Elizabeth was crowned less than twenty years later, more than twenty million people watched the event on television). Another reason was that, as the Archbishop of Canterbury admitted, there was 'no possibility of censoring' a live broadcast, whereas he was able to approve the newsreel film before it was shown in cinemas.

Harold Nicolson looked in on Ramsay MacDonald as he was dressing for the occasion, but when Nicolson complimented him on how distinguished he looked in his Trinity House uniform, the Labour statesman mordantly replied that when he had been 'a visitor to a lunatic asylum I always noted how well the worst lunatics looked'. Chips Channon got much more into the spirit of things, dressed in 'my velvet Court suit. Honor [his wife] looked splendid in grey, all sapphires and diamond tiara.' The Channons had seats in the South Transept:

> We had an excellent view . . . on all sides were MPs I knew and their be-plumed, be-veiled, be-jewelled wives . . . My mother-in-law on the Countesses bench looked magnificent . . . the North Transept was a vitrine of bosoms and jewels and bobbing tiaras . . . soon the procession began: the foreign royalties and their suites; our own tupenny royalties, i.e. . . . . the Mountbattens etc . . . After a little the real Royalties arrived . . . the gaunt Queen of Norway appeared,

followed by Queen Mary, ablaze, regal and over powering [a break with tradition, but there to show her support for her second son]. Then the Queen's procession, and she appeared, dignified but smiling and much more bosomy. Then, so surrounded by dignitaries carrying wands, sceptres, orbs and staffs, as to overshadow him, George VI himself. He carried himself well . . . And soon the long ceremony began: it seemed endless, [Later the King was to tell Ramsay MacDonald 'that for long periods of the Coronation ceremony he was unaware of what was happening'] and the old Archbishop intoned in his impressive clear voice that was heard so well over the amplifiers . . . Opposite me, near the throne, sat the 8 representatives of the Free Churches, like crows at a Feast, in their drab 'Elders of the Kirk' black cloth. They looked so glum and disapproving that they reminded me of the present Government as it sat decreeing the Abdication, relentless, perhaps right, but forbidding . . . The sun shone through the windows and the King looked boyish suddenly. Then it was the Queen's turn . . . and my thoughts travelled back to the old days when I called her 'Elizabeth' and was a little in love with her . . . The heat and airlessness were . . . overpowering. Then at last the procession formed up, and we watched, spellbound, as it uncurled and slowly progressed down the nave . . . There was a long wait after the Royalties and processions left and impatience broke out. Chocolates were munched and flasks slyly produced . . . The few Socialists and their wives seemed subdued and impressed by the ancient Service and the grandeur of the feudal capitalistic show. One of them remarked to me, 'Why should we sit behind these Peer Johnnies?' 'It's their show, after all. You are lucky to be here at all,' I answered, and he stopped smiling.

There was a rumour that Queen Elizabeth's 'bosominess' was due to her being pregnant. The Duchess of Hamilton, who had started the Scottish Society for the Prevention of Vivisection in 1912, refused to wear the traditional ermine. Everyone had worried about the King's stammer, but he had been having coaching on his breathing and stretching his diaphragm from Lionel Logue, an Australian-born engineer with no medical training whose dictum was 'There is only one person who can cure you and that is yourself . . . I can tell you what to do but only you can do it.' With lots of practice, and help from a microphone expert at the BBC, the King's responses in the Abbey and his broadcast later that evening in what Harold Nicolson described as 'a fine perfect English voice' (George pronounced his 'r's; as 'w's, whereas Edward had been criticised for an American twang even before the advent of Mrs Simpson) were all but faultless. At the Château de Candé in the Loire Valley, the until-very-recently Edward VIII sat knitting a dark-blue jumper for Wallis Simpson, listening to what should have been *his* coronation on the wireless.

Then it was all over. The rackety months of yore were past: a family was on the throne again. The Queen's public warmth started to win hearts, and 'As Used in the Royal Nursery' became the must-have endorsement for baby soap, prams and teething rings, even though the 'little princesses' Elizabeth and Margaret Rose were long past such needs. The official decorations were sold off: the crowns that had been placed on top of the masts in the Mall went for £1 each; the stools used in the Abbey fetched twenty-five shillings. 'The crowds . . . are returning to their homes in the remotest parts of the Commonwealth and to Killiecrankie, Cardiff, Puddleton, Brixton and Bow. The Dominion Premiers have stayed on to tackle the grim task of deciding to what extent and under what conditions they will tax their people to arm the Empire. In the countryside bonfires have blazed and the village sports have been run. In the great thoroughfares and mean streets alike the flags and the bunting, now a little draggled in the rain, still remind us that England for a week at least has touched the carnival spirit.'

But there were those who would not have thought that 'carnival' hit quite the right note. Frank Forster 'saw and heard the Coronation ceremony in Westminster Abbey in a newsreel. When the Archbishop (how medieval that sounds) has crowned the King he turns to the peers and assembled wealthy people (this is important) and asks them if they accept George VI as their King. Of course as the schedule says, they accept him. But this is the point. When the Church big figure addresses the peers, he refers to them as "the people". Now was ever there more misrepresentation. Only people of certain social standing were allowed at the ceremony. Which meant that poor people were banned. And those people present who were of a definite social status and had very easy access to money were addressed as "the people". What of the millions who were outside? It cannot be taken that the peers inside the Abbey were representative of the rest of the population for the mere existence of their social conditions sweeps that contention away. It is such as this which bears evidence of the ridiculous relationship which exists between the governing class and the workers. The social structure of the ruling class was built under conditions which have long disappeared. And for attempts to [be] made to keep that structure intact in conditions radically changed, is nothing less than madness.'

The travel writer Robert Byron was predictably not particularly concerned about the people being bypassed: what incensed him was what he saw as the ongoing ruination of London, and since so many visitors from home and abroad had come to the capital for the coronation, he used the occasion as a peg on which to hang a polemic about its despoliation. The 1900 Ancient Monuments Act authorised the listing of buildings that were considered to be of national importance, which could then be protected. However, churches were excluded, as were structures erected after 1714, and although the 1932 Town and Country Planning Act gave local authorities the power to protect buildings of architectural or historical merit, they had to compensate the owners, so the Act was virtually a dead letter, and no building had been saved as a result of it. Furthermore, if the façade of a building was saved, none of the usual government grants would be available for its rebuilding. Addressing the 'gentle visitor from overseas', Byron admitted that London was 'ugly – muddled, smoky and lacking in those grand vistas and symmetrical spaces which are the proper adornment of a great capital'. But, he insisted, 'We like London's ugliness, just as one likes the ugliness of an old woman because it tells of a long life and strong character.' Yet, 'slowly and furtively, but only too surely, England and the Empire are being defrauded of their ancient capital, against their wish and without their consent . . . It means that when May is over, and the flags are down, and the crown is back in the Tower, the capital of the greatest political association ever devised by man will revert to her usual status of a local bucket-shop.'

Byron was appalled by the proposed destruction of Bedford Square, Waterloo Bridge, Sir Joshua Reynolds's house in Leicester Square, the Adelphi. He named the 'barbarian' villains as 'the long-nosed vampires of high finance and the desperate avarice of hereditary landlords', and 'if possible . . . more odious still . . . the spiders of the church', under whose care such wonders as Sir Christopher Wren's church of All Hallows, Lombard Street, were supposed to be safe, but were in fact threatened with demolition in order that their sites could be sold off. So bitter did he feel that when his polemic was republished as a pamphlet, Byron included 'for the convenience of inquirers' the telephone numbers of some of the despoilers, including the Trustees of the British Museum, the Ecclesiastical Commissioners, the Bishop of London and the Archbishop of Canterbury.

Part of the reason why the Church was able to contemplate such vandalism, Byron believed, was that attendance at church services was generally low. Hence the Archbishop of Canterbury's thwarted hopes of a 'Return to Religion' campaign at the time of the coronation, the supreme moment of the established Church's role in the state. The 1930s were a testing time for the Church, which since before the First World War had seen its political influence waning. At the 1938 Empire Exhibition held in Glasgow, one of the exhibits, alongside new homes, machinery, domestic appliances and the artefacts of Empire, was an Anglican church. Few people entered it. Churchmen complained that new municipal housing estates prioritised the building of community halls over that of churches, resulting 'not [in] congregations of worshippers, but congregations of whist players, dancers and people seeking social recreation', though some of the more progressive clergy saw such developments as a God-sent opportunity for 'outreach' programmes.

During this decade the Church's authority was tested by social and legal changes, its doctrines were challenged, its importance in many people's lives diminished, and its role of giving a clear spiritual and moral lead to the nation was reduced not only by its own divisions in the face of shifting social and moral attitudes, but also by the confusion and volatility of domestic and international politics. The Church had become an 'effete establishment . . . moving like a rudderless vessel over a rock-haunted ocean', accused Bishop Henson of Durham, who regretted the realignments it had to make in the modern age.

Mass-Observation found occasional hostility to the Church among those it interviewed on the streets of London: 'There's a lot of good people in the world, but people that call themselves Christians are the sort that go to church and put "No Hawkers, No Circulars. Keep Out" on their gate and wouldn't do a kindness to anybody under the sun.' However, most Britons in the 1930s would have said that they were Christians, though many might well have added, 'But of course, I'm not religious.' While something like 60 per cent of the population professed to be Church of England, about 15 per cent Free Church and 5 per cent Roman Catholic, 'being Christian' frequently meant that a person was baptised, married and buried by the Church, and generally adhered to a sort of morality which was considered to be how a 'good Christian' should live. Far smaller numbers than that were churchgoers – in 1930 it was estimated that there were 5,529,000 active members of the Protestant (Anglican and Nonconformist) Churches and 2,781,000 Roman Catholics out of a population of almost thirty-five million adults – and the numbers were declining.

A Mass-Observation survey had shown that in 'Metrop', as it called Fulham, in West London, 'about one person in ten goes to church fairly regularly and another two go at intervals ranging upwards to once a year'. As with the rest of the country, 'the congregation on an ordinary Sunday consist[s] of about three quarters women'. Even those who rarely if ever went to church themselves thought it a good idea for children to receive religious instruction at school. 'They look on it as the best way of imparting ethical principles – or, rather, they know of no alternative way of doing so.'

Church attendance varied across the country: it was lower in the North of England than in the South, except in parts of Lancashire and the North-West, where there was a substantial Catholic population. A survey of Liverpool reckoned that between 15 and 20 per cent of the population of Liverpool ever went to church.

The higher your social class, the more likely you were to attend church, and those living in the country were more likely to be regular churchgoers than urban dwellers (although places with a high Catholic population like Liverpool and Glasgow bucked this trend, with over 80 per cent of the congregation in Merseyside churches being manual workers). Young and older people were more likely to fill up the pews and benches, and women were, on the whole, more likely to go to church (particularly the Anglican Church, where on average – at least on Merseyside – the ratio was 163 females to a hundred males) and to belong to groups attached to churches such as the Mothers' Union, to teach in Sunday School and organise the flower rota.

When J.B. Priestley passed though Birmingham on his 'English Journey' in the autumn of 1933, he felt that since the city 'has long been one of the strongholds of Nonconformity' he should visit one of its chapels. He found the service 'exactly like the ones I remembered from thirty years ago, and the people taking part had not changed a great deal. The chief difference in the congregation was that there were fewer young people in it, and especially young men. I doubt if there were half-a-dozen men under thirty-five in the chapel. If there were any boys present, they escaped my eye. There were a few little girls, a sprinkling of older girls and young women, and all the rest of the congregation and the choir were middle-aged ... I suppose that in my chapel-going days, there would actually have been twice the number of people at the service.'

The decline of churchgoing did not necessarily mean the diminution of the Churches' influence, as Mass-Observation reported in their survey of 'Worktown' (Bolton). 'It is necessary to understand the tremendous power of "Nonconformity" in Worktown, for it influences the social life and success of the pub. This influence is not at all "obvious". It would be easy to spend a year in Worktown and, if you didn't go to church, think that the Church was less important than the tram or the political party. But its leaders are also leaders of politics, police, magistrates' benches, local press and business men.'

Though only a child at the time, Eileen Whiteing picked up on a similar Church of England dominance. She lived a comfortable middle-class life in Surrey, in a house called 'The Myrtles' which had a 'conservatory, aviary ... and outside lavatory for the gardener and visiting workmen', a live-in maid (who was summoned by a set of bells that rang in the kitchen) plus an older woman who came every Monday to help out with the washing. She had been 'sent to Sunday School at an early age, followed in due time by confirmation into the adult church . . . [which was] Holy Trinity . . . what one would call a "middle-of-the-road" church, being neither too "high" nor too "low" in its approach. Great store was set on this, particularly as the trend in the parish church at Carshalton was to be Roman Catholic in all but name . . . There was, of course, a great deal of religious intolerance at the time and Ecumenism had not been thought of.'

The regular congregation included two sisters 'who came to church in winter swathed in grey squirrel fur coats and smelled deliciously of "Attar of Roses" scent on their lace handkerchiefs . . . a really eccentric lady . . . who was always dressed completely in black from head to toe . . . [and who] occasionally had an Indian missionary to stay in the house (well chaperoned by two resident maids, of course) and this was a point of great interest locally since it was almost unheard-of to see an Indian or an African in our neighbourhood . . . Major Pothecary with his family . . . also attended the church.'

Eileen Whiteing was a member of the 'Crusaders' movement, which was 'very popular among young people and much sought after . . . although I realise it had great snob value. The prevailing strict rule of membership that only admitted children from grammar or public schools did not then strike me as at all unsuitable or unchristian. Indeed, I was very proud to be admitted to the select band of girls who gathered for bible reading and the singing of "choruses" every Sunday afternoon in a private house. I suspect that the occasional meetings at what we called "squashes" with the boy crusaders in their own hall . . . had something to do with the attraction also!'

Whereas Conservatives had traditionally been staunch Church of England, and this largely persisted in the inter-war years, Liberalism and Nonconformity had been as recto and verso, particularly in Wales, Cornwall and parts of the Midlands until the First World War. This was breaking down by the 1930s, partly because the Depression meant that many men moved away from their communities and often lost their churchgoing habits, while some who remained in places like the Rhondda Valley were shy of attending chapel, since the tradition of Sabbath smartness was so strong, and these men could no longer afford smart clothes, In addition, the 'great causes' of Nonconformity – temperance and non-denominational education – had lost much of their currency. In any case, the Liberal Party was in freefall. Its replacement, Labour, was more secular, though several of its leaders, including George Lansbury, Stafford Cripps and Clem Attlee, were

Anglicans, and Philip Snowden and Arthur Henderson were active Methodists. Moreover, dissenters and other minorities such as Catholics and Jews were more likely to find a home with Labour, as were the full gamut of humanitarians, rationalists, agnostics and atheists.

Only the Roman Catholic Church's numbers were sustained in the 1930s, partly because of a rapid expansion of the clergy, a forward church-building programme, particularly in the new out-of-London estates – suburban Kent was positively deluged, with twenty-two new Catholic churches built between 1930 and 1939 – and showcase edifices including Buckfast Abbey in Devon, and Prinknash Abbey, planned to exceed the nearby Gloucester Cathedral in magnificence. There was also an aggressive missionary campaign, an expansion of Catholic public schools such as Ampleforth and Downside, and an increase in the number of Catholic dons at Oxford and Cambridge. Furthermore, an unyielding attitude towards mixed marriages brought in a large proportion of the 12,000-odd converts each year. And although the influx of Irish Catholic working-class immigrants with a high birthrate did not peak until the 1950s, there was a steady stream of them, particularly to Liverpool and Glasgow, throughout the decade.

The demographics of this growth led to what almost amounted to a schism between Northern and Southern Catholics. In Liverpool, with its large, working-class Irish Catholic population, the Archbishop behaved rather like a medieval palatine, telling the Archbishop of Westminster, 'Do not forget, your eminence, that I rule the north.' Given the conditions in which many of his flock lived, that rule included a degree of political radicalism alien to the Westminster 'wing', where Archbishop Bourne had condemned the General Strike of 1926 as a 'sin', whereas the Anglican Archbishop of Canterbury had pleaded for conciliation, a plea the BBC refused to broadcast and the official *British Gazette* to publish.

'Westminster Catholicism' took a rather more conservative coloration, close to government and to Rome, with a fashionable aspect of old-money recusants and 'snob Catholic' converts associated with the Brompton Oratory or the Jesuit church in Farm Street, Mayfair, such as Maurice Baring, Hilaire Belloc, G.K. Chesterton, Eric Gill, Graham Greene, Ronald Knox and Frank Pakenham (later the Earl of Longford). Many of these were brought into the fold by the worldly, subtle 'aristocratic-featured' Father Martin D'Arcy, who had studied and ministered at Farm Street before returning to Oxford to teach moral philosophy, becoming Master of the Jesuit foundation Campion Hall in 1933, where he commissioned Sir Edwin Lutyens to design a magnificent new building for the college.

D'Arcy worked on the principle that 'The bigger the stone, the bigger the ripple,' and among the glittering converts of this 'drawing room apostle' with the *noli me tangere* aura were the writers Muriel Spark and Evelyn Waugh. He shared with Waugh (who wrote a biography of Edmund Campion, the founder of Campion Hall) a 'specialised enthusiasm for domestic architecture' – ideally gracious country houses (and of course churches) – and a nostalgia for the English rural past, particularly as represented by the Catholic gentry. Indeed, Father D'Arcy had compiled his own genealogical table, which stretched to eleven feet and traced his family back to the Norman Conquest. He was supposed to be the model for Father Rothschild in Waugh's *Vile Bodies*, published in 1930 (and dedicated to Bryan and Diana Guinness – later Mosley), and it would be D'Arcy who Waugh would ask to check the proofs of *Brideshead Revisited* 'for verification of details of Catholic practice and morality'.

Although ecumenism might have been frowned on in suburban Surrey, it was something the Archbishops of Canterbury and York both worked hard to promote. Cosmo Gordon Lang had himself been Archbishop of York until his translation to Canterbury in 1928, when he was almost sixty-four. The previous year, the established Church's lack of political clout or spiritual independence had been painfully demonstrated by the refusal of the House of Commons to allow the revision of the Book of Common Prayer to gesture towards more 'Romanish' practices (a veto that Lang attributed to those who could not forget 'the bishops who had dabbled in the Coal Strike'). He was a rather austere, increasingly pompous prelate. According to Alan Don he sat through Noël Coward's affecting *Cavalcade* with his emotions unaroused: 'He neither wept nor laughed, while all around him, those in the stalls were dabbing their eyes throughout the performance.' He would 'rather go in his motor to Bognor and potter about there under a leaden sky' than seek the sun on the Continent as his doctors advised. Lang was a lifelong bachelor, clever, snobbish, dazzled by high office and high society, 'more Wolsey than St Francis of Assisi', as a friend cruelly assessed him. He was a great admirer of Margot Asquith, whose barbed lunchtime conversation he found 'brilliant', and was the first Archbishop since the Reformation always to dress in a mitre and cope. This made him feel like a 'popinjay' as he 'strutted round' the streets of Somers Town after opening a block of flats built by the St Pancras Housing Association as part of his work to promote better housing for the urban poor.

Cardinal Arthur Hinsley was almost seventy when he succeeded Francis Bourne as Archbishop of Westminster in 1935. Known by Pope Pius XI as 'Africanus' after his many years working in that continent, he and the nearly equally elderly Lang had warm and close relations – Lang even managing to introduce his Catholic counterpart to the Athenaeum club, traditionally a stronghold of Anglicanism. Lang understood and sympathised with the workings of Rome, though he found Nonconformism less to his liking, and was active in promoting cross-Church cooperation, seeing the ecumenical movement as having a role to play in the promotion of world peace, and a spiritual analogy to the League of Nations, which he also supported.

There was to be a constant tension in the 1930s caused by the view of some well-placed clergy that, faced with the misery of the Depression, the Church should restrict itself to generalised moral guidance, rather than pronounce on matters best left to others. Archbishop Temple, for example, considered that 'The Gospel contains no illumination concerning the rights and wrongs of bi-metallism, or social credit, or "technocracy" [and] between such theories the Christian is no more competent to judge than anybody else.' The true concern of Christianity was 'human welfare [and] . . . it has a great deal to say about it'.

However, a number of prominent churchmen did consider that they had a more direct role to play in improving the lot of the poor. Hensley Henson, Bishop of Durham, who had been very pleased to be called a 'Jacobin lacquered over to look like a Tory', could be ambiguous in his approach to social problems, chastising both the coal owners and the miners during the General Strike. However, he was deeply critical of the modern tendency, as he saw it, of considering Christianity to be 'in the category of private opinion which man may cherish but by which he must not seriously guide his civil behaviour'. In 1931 Henson circularised his clergy prior to a visitation, wanting to know what they knew about unemployment in their parishes and what they had done to help.

The Convocation of Canterbury, held in February 1930, had unanimously passed a motion condemning 'the overcrowded and insanitary conditions under which so many are now compelled to live as a menace to the moral and physical welfare of the nation', and urged the government 'to do their utmost to remedy those evils in their own parishes as elsewhere'. Cyril Garbett, who had had an apprenticeship in poverty and poor housing as Bishop of Southwark before being appointed to the See of Winchester in 1932, and who was the Church's spokesman on housing, published an influential pamphlet, *The Challenge of the Slums*, in 1933. Basil Jellicoe, who regarded the slums round where he worked at the Magdalen College Mission in Somers Town as 'the devil's work', was instrumental in founding the St Pancras House Improvement Society to rehouse slum dwellers in 1924. By 1930 hundreds of families had been moved into low-rent flats built by the Society. Charles Jenkinson, who was the vicar of a slum parish, a Labour

Councillor, and Chairman of the Leeds Housing Committee, led the crusade to demolish acres of Leeds' notorious back-to back-terraces and build new homes. The Archbishop of York (late of Manchester), William Temple, a member of the Labour Party, who had chaired the interdenominational Conference on Christian Politics, Economics and Citizenship (COPEC) in the 1920s, instigated a Committee on Unemployment (other members included George Bell, Bishop of Chichester, and A.D. Lindsay, Master of Balliol), and it was this committee that, funded by the Pilgrim Trust, produced 'the best social study of unemployment made in the thirties', *Men Without Work*.

Several bishops spoke out in the House of Lords in opposition to cuts in unemployment benefit, chastised the government for the severity of the Means Test and the slowness of slum-clearance programmes, railed against the exploitation of labour and called for a better deal for the low-paid, while men like Bishop Bell were eloquent in their opposition to rearmament. But though their speeches might be heard, reported and appreciated, the actual political influence of the Church was hard to measure. As well as some heroic efforts at slum-clearance initiatives, a number of churches and chapels were tireless in providing premises and activities for the unemployed, and sometimes clothing and food too – the Society of Friends was particularly active in such initiatives. But although the Bishop of Jarrow had initially blessed his town's Crusade, he tempered his support after the swingeing attack by his fellow Bishop of Durham, and with a few exceptions it was rarely priests, vicars or non-conformist ministers who trudged alongside the hunger marchers.

Being 'above politics' in the years of the Depression could seem like being 'above the people' too, unwilling to abandon the individualist route to salvation, and press for the collectivist solutions that were so obviously required. As a Canon of Westminster wrote in 1931, 'Christian teachers are apt to observe that if everyone would accept Christianity our economic problems would solve themselves but unless the Churches show themselves capable of constructive and realistic thinking to vindicate these enormous generalisations they are bound to appear futile and almost meaningless.' The price could be high, argued Joseph Needham, the Cambridge scientist and scholar of China, in his contribution to a series of essays published by Victor Gollancz in 1935 which were intended to explore the points at which Christianity and communism might meet: 'The phoenix of the Kingdom [by which he meant Marxism] is rising from the ashes of the Church's failure.'

International affairs increasingly challenged the Churches, and could make them cautious: 'We have suffered so many disillusions,' wrote Archbishop Lang at the time of the Italian invasion of Abyssinia. The Spanish Civil War was deeply divisive. There was the official Catholic 'Bishops' Fund for Aid to the Spanish Nationalists', a prominent Catholic, Douglas Jerrold, played a key role in General Franco's return to Spain from Morocco, Douglas Woodruffe, editor of the *Tablet*, committed the weekly to the wholesale support of the Nationalists, and Cardinal Hinsley displayed a framed photograph of Franco on his desk. Other Church organisations and groups, meanwhile, worked equally hard for the Republicans, while the Society of Friends gave aid to both sides. The Catholic and both Anglican Archbishops were disquieted by the rise of Nazism, but tended not to raise their voices to say so, taking the line that it was better to 'abstain from the pleasing task of continuously scolding other nations and attempt to understand them', as the Bishop of Gloucester, A.C. Headlam, wrote to *The Times* in July 1938. Archbishop Lang's own profound hatred of war, and his unease at the terms of the Treaty of Versailles, led him to condone the government's recognition of Mussolini's conquest of Abyssinia in May 1938, which he did 'with a reluctance almost amounting to pain', and to support Chamberlain's policy of appeasement until March 1939. He was, however, active in denouncing Nazi policies towards the Jews – including to the German Ambassador to London, Joachim von Ribbentrop, with whom he had frequent conversations.

Bishop Headlam chaired the Church of England Council on Foreign Affairs from its inception in 1933 until the end of the Second World War, and his pro-Nazi pronouncements – he praised them for their self-discipline and self-sacrifice, and sided with the pro-Nazi faction when the German Protestant Church split – incensed many of his fellow Bishops. Hensley Henson, Bishop of Durham, dubbed Headlam 'the pertinacious apologist for of the Nazi government', and George Bell, Bishop of Chichester, who worked tirelessly to aid Jewish victims of Nazi persecution, called for his resignation. But Headlam dug in his heels and stayed put; the matter was played out in the letters column of *The Times*, with Bell urging Lang to disassociate the Church from such views, which the Archbishop did.

If Headlam was pro-Nazi, the Dean of Canterbury, Hewlett Johnson, stood at the other end of the political spectrum. Johnson's pro-Soviet sympathies earned him the epithet 'the Red Dean' – though he was never a card-carrying member of the Communist Party. He had wanted to be a missionary, but had been rejected by the Church Missionary Society on account of his liberal views. As vicar of Altrincham in Cheshire he campaigned doggedly for better housing conditions for his parishioners, and he and his wife ran holiday camps for young people. It was the extremes of wealth and poverty that he saw around him in his parish, fused with the example of the Russian Revolution in 1917, that sowed the seeds of his conviction that communism and Christianity were based on entirely compatible moralities. Ramsay MacDonald appointed him Dean of Manchester Cathedral, and in 1931 Cosmo Lang made him Dean of Canterbury. There he continued the activities that had brought him his nickname, helping to organise the 'Cathedral Pilgrimage for the Unemployed', which sought 'radical remedies for the modern problem of want amidst plenty' by recruiting pilgrims to visit a cathedral of their choice for the cost of half a crown, proceeds going to the unemployed. Fifty-five cathedrals took part, and hundreds of thousands participated in this modern-day 'Pilgrimage of Grace': the King and Queen agreed to be 'pilgrims' to Westminster Abbey. The Pilgrimage was advertised on railway stations throughout the country by posters drawn by the young woman Johnson would marry four years later. He was able to convince himself that 'The Pilgrimage has helped to bring home to one half of England the tragedy suffered by the other half', though that was surely wishful thinking.

'If a system inevitably brings disastrous results, it is surely up to us to frame another,' Dean Johnson argued, and not content with action at home, he roamed abroad in search of answers. Intrigued by Major Douglas's Social Credit movement, he went to Canada to see it in action ('Social reformers will always owe a debt to Douglas,' he wrote credulously later). He also travelled to China to investigate the devastation caused by the floods of 1931, and to Spain in 1937, where he witnessed the bombing of Durango. In 1937, already chairman of the editorial board of the *Daily Worker*, and since 1935 Vice President of the Society for Cultural Relations with the USSR, Hewlett was finally granted a visa to visit the Soviet Union for the first time at the age of sixty-three, from whence he returned after three months, convinced despite Stalin's purges and show trials, which were going on at the time, that, to echo the Webbs, he had seen the future and it worked.

On his return, the 'Red Dean' gave many talks on the Soviet Union, and published *The Socialist Sixth of the World* (1939), which was a massive best-seller, reprinted twenty-two times and translated into twenty-four languages. He expounded his belief that communism was not in any way antipathetical to Christianity, but rather was its logical continuation. Although the Archbishop of Canterbury was frequently exasperated by his radical, dome-headed Dean, he was personally very fond of him, and was always grateful for Johnson's support when, during the First World War,

Lang had written to *The Times* reminding its readers that the Germans were God's children too, and had received much opprobrium for his sentiments. Despite many attempts to unseat the somewhat 'baffling' Johnson, he remained in post for over thirty years.

At the opposite end of the ecclesiastical spectrum from the Red Dean in terms of political sympathies and pronouncements stood the somewhat isolated 'Gloomy Dean'. Son of a country curate whose maternal grandfather had been Archdeacon of Cleveland, William Ralph Inge was upper-class, Eton-educated, a professor of divinity at Cambridge, a brilliant scholar of mysticism, a romantic, backward-looking Conservative who was not at all keen on 'the court-chaplains of King Demos', as he called the more progressive clergy. He was well-known through his many books and as a regular columnist for the *Evening Standard*. He confessed: 'I have made some thousands by my pen,' and was canny when it came to commercial decisions, agreeing with his publisher to change the title of his book *Cosmology and Theism* to *God and the Astronomers*.

For Inge the proper concern of Christians should be matters spiritual. He regarded Church institutions as relatively unimportant, and cared more about the 'cirrhosis of the moral sense' in individuals than crumblings in the Church. Yet he dismissed the idea that being a Christian necessarily implied social responsibility, and opposed any notion of the state looking after the welfare of its citizens, on the grounds that such provision – even in the years of desperate unemployment – would lead to feckless, work-shy behaviour.

Appointed Dean of St Paul's in 1911 by his friend Asquith, who saw him as squarely in the literary tradition of other great deans of that cathedral such as John Donne and John Colet, Inge was a questing, fluent intellectual who numbered George Bernard Shaw among his close friends. He was also something of a snob, with a distinctly non-ascetic taste for comfortable living, who was much concerned with the 'servant question', considering it to be a matter of national importance that young girls were increasingly less prepared to enter domestic service in the inter-war years. His robust defence of middle-class interests extended to a strong belief in eugenics: not only did he consider that the working classes were over-procreating (producing what he called 'sub men'), but he advocated state licences for those couples allowed to breed, the sort of intervention he roundly condemned when it came to welfare provision. In Inge's view of an ideal future, 'social prestige is attached to the family who can show A1 ancestors on both sides for three generations'. But if Inge sounds anachronistic, something of a caricature (though on his death aged ninety-three *The Times* cautioned that the Gloomy Dean should not be dismissed as a 'Blimp in a dog collar'), regrettable even, the middle-class man-or-woman-in-the-pew was probably more likely to find Inge's brand of Christianity to his or her liking than those 'progressive clergy' he so castigated in his writing and preaching.

When Hitler succeeded as Chancellor of Germany in January 1933, the possibility that Britain would need to respond to German aggression some-time in the future gradually coloured attitudes and debate not only among politicians, military strategists, intellectuals and churchmen, but a much wider public. There were international events that heightened tension – Germany's withdrawal from the League of Nations and disarmament talks, the reoccupation of the Rhineland, the Italian invasion of Abyssinia, the Spanish Civil War – and then a rapid escalation in 1938 with the occupation of the Sudetenland and the crisis over Czechoslovakia, by which time the dreadful inevitability of war had permeated most people's thinking, no matter how fervently they continued to hope for, and in some cases search for, an escape. As unemployment had seemed the intractable problem in the first half of the 1930s, so international tensions and their impact on Britain moved gradually centre stage after 1933. Not that unemployment was in any sense 'cured' – it still stood at nearly two and a half million in 1933, and it was not until 1937 that it fell below one and a half million – to a considerable extent as a result of the threat of war and the need to rearm.

One of the conundrums of these years is how widespread the fear of war actually was. When did it start to dominate people's thoughts and influence their actions? Was opposition to rearmament primarily an aspect of a general distrust of the National Government? To what extent was Britain a strongly committed 'pacific' nation, and how much did this underpin the government's policy of appeasement? Or, as seems likely, did most people simply not want to go to war, and looked to the government to see that it did not happen for as long as possible, rather than holding deep-seated pacifist convictions, or informed views on foreign-policy options? On the whole, diarists and letter-writers only articulated their views (if they did so at all) at times of crisis – the Rhineland, the Sudetenland, Munich – while memoirists and biographers naturally write with the knowledge of what came next.

Moreover, sophisticated polling techniques were still in their infancy. The British Institute of Public Opinion was set up in 1938 on the model of Dr George Gallup's US organisation; its first findings appeared in

Cavalcade magazine. In 1937 a regular column based on Gallup's findings was published in the *News Chronicle*, and the same year Mass-Observation, a surveying rather than a polling organisation, with no claims to be scientific or representative, started its investigations. Nevertheless, there are moments when it is possible to net at least some indications of the mood of the country, though these can be fleeting, tentative and partial, and may have assumed more importance in retrospect than they had at the time.

One example was the so-called 'Oxford Pledge' or 'Oxford Oath'. In the Hilary Term of 1933, the Oxford Union organised a debate to which, unusually, two outside speakers were invited. On 9 February, Professor C.E.M. Joad (actually he wasn't a professor, but a reader in philosophy at Birkbeck College, described by Leonard Woolf as a 'quick-witted, amusing, intellectual scallywag') proposed the motion 'That this House will in no circumstances fight for its King and Country.' Joad was opposed by the Hon. Quintin Hogg, the twenty-five-year-old son of Lord Hailsham, Secretary of State for War, who was a Fellow of All Souls, and had just been called to the Bar. The undergraduates spoke first, and then Hogg took the floor, arguing that pacifism was more likely to lead to war, and that by failing to arm itself Britain would have no influence on Europe. In his response, Joad, who, by common consent made the better speech, drew on his experiences in the First World War, when his best friend from student days at Oxford had died in agony in the trenches, impaled for twenty-four hours on barbed wire, his entrails hanging out. The motion, Joad pronounced, really meant 'That this House will never commit murder on a huge scale whenever the Government decided it should do so.' It was carried by 275 votes to 153.

The debate probably caused little stir among most people, who are likely to have agreed with the headline 'Children's Hour' over *The Times* leader on the subject, which spoke of 'a little clique of cranks', or the *Daily Mail*'s condemnation of 'posturers and gesturers'. There were suggestions, though, that it brought bad publicity abroad, by suggesting to the rest of Europe that the British were 'soft', 'decadent', 'won't fight', thus 'sowing dragon's teeth' for the future. And the result certainly roused 'old Oxford', one of whose (brief-stay) members, Randolph Churchill, organised a risible 'expunging debate' in the forlorn hope of 'correcting' the record. Such men saw the outcome as evidence not so much that their Alma Mater had gone soft, but that it had gone 'red' – though in fact few 'reds' were at the debate. And since Oxford (and to a lesser extent Cambridge) was still regarded as a nursery for future politicians and leaders of men, such white-feather radicalism was a threat to the nation's future security as well as to its standing abroad.

A by-election in October 1933 in East Fulham, then a largely working- and lower-middle-class area, which the Conservatives lost by a large margin to Labour, has been seen as evidence of 'pacific democracy'. The result was used by Stanley Baldwin to argue that he had no mandate at that time to embark on a major rearmament programme, and that to have done so would have been political suicide – or at least would have lost the overwhelmingly Conservative National Government the 1935 election. On 14 October 1933 Germany walked out of the Disarmament Conference in Geneva, and gave notice of its intention to withdraw from the League of Nations, a situation blamed to some degree on a speech by the British Foreign Secretary Sir John Simon in which he appeared to shift away from multilateral disarmament to a position that in effect put Germany 'on probation' for five years. So the threat of war was probably on voters' minds, but although peace was mentioned by the Labour candidate, John Wilmot, and particularly by his wife in her appeal to women voters, the main issues of the campaign were housing, high rents and unemployment in the building trade, and it was probably these that swung the vote, though general criticism of the government's foreign policy may have played a part too – there is no definitive way of knowing.

In the wake of the collapse of the Disarmament Conference a so-called 'peace ballot' was held in which over 11.5 million British adults – an esti- mated 38.2 per cent of the population over eighteen – took part in an unprecedented test of public opinion. Organised by the League of Nations Union and conducted by half a million volunteers, mainly Communists or from the left, who had to get used to 'calling several times and finding everyone out, then finding everyone in but the form lost and another one needed. It meant calling at houses where the house-holders shouted at you or at houses where people were totally indifferent and apathetic.' The results came in from late November 1934 until the end of June 1935, and although the exercise has come to be viewed as a contest between militarism and pacifism, in fact people were being asked to make a choice about how peace could be secured, between isolationism and the sort of collective security that the League of Nations and the Disarmament Conference were supposed to ensure. The peace ballot sought approval not for unilateral disarmament, but rather for disarmament by international agreement, and raised the possibility of nations combining to 'compel an aggressor to stop by . . . if necessary, military measures'. The result, announced at a triumphant rally at the Albert Hall addressed by the Archbishop of Canterbury, was an over- whelming yes to all five questions – though there was more overwhelming support for Britain remaining a member of the League of Nations and for multilateral disarmament than for the possible use of military as well as economic force against an aggressor.

The *Daily Express* was opposed to what it called a 'Ballot of Blood', seeing it as a way of trying to coerce the government, and advised people to tear up their ballot papers, while the Foreign Secretary initially – and rather ill-advisedly – suggested that such matters were beyond the competence of the general public. Less a scientific survey than a very successful propaganda exercise, the 'peace ballot' demonstrated clearly that the British people (or at least those who responded) were anxious about the threat to peace, and sought security in international cooperation – or collective security, as it was increasingly called. However, a series of events starting with the Italian invasion of Abyssinia and the Spanish Civil War and ending with Hitler's invasion of Poland, showed that this would be no guarantee of peace – and it was peace that the people of Britain wanted, some would later say at almost any price.

Until the end of the First World War pacifism had been largely restricted to Quakers and Nonconformists, but after 1918 a number of peace societies, including the Fellowship of Reconciliation, the Union of Democratic Control, the International Committee of Women for Permanent Peace (British section) and the No War Movement were started. The man who took the lead in the 1930s was the son of a minor canon at the Royal Chapel, Windsor, secretary to Cosmo Lang when he was Bishop of Stepney, vicar of St Martin-in-the-Fields, where he turned the crypt into a sanctuary for the homeless and destitute, and Hewlett Johnson's predecessor as Dean of Canterbury. On 16 October 1934, as newly appointed canon at St Paul's Cathedral, the Reverend Dick Sheppard wrote to the press declaring himself to be 'now convinced that war of every kind or for any cause, is not only a denial of Christianity, but a crime against humanity' and calling on those (men, that is) who agreed with him to send him a postcard announcing that they denounced war. Despite the fact that only three national newspapers published his letter, he received 100,000 postcards within a year, and new pledges continued to arrive with every post – on average, four hundred a day.

The first mass meeting of the Peace Pledge Union (PPU), formed by Sheppard in the hope that these laudable but vague sentiments could somehow be channelled into effective action, was held in the Albert Hall on 14 July 1935. It was addressed by Sheppard himself, the First World War poets Siegfried Sassoon and Edmund Blunden, and Maude Royden, a writer and preacher (women had recently been admitted to the PPU, but remained in the minority). Other active members included Vera Brittain (whose 1933 memoir *Testament of Youth* was a powerful anti-war indictment, but who only came out for all-out pacifism in 1934 after hearing Sheppard speak), the Methodist ministers Leslie Weatherhead and Donald Soper, the novelist Rose Macaulay, Eric Gill, Bertrand Russell and the Labour Party leader George Lansbury.

The PPU rented offices in Regent Street prior to buying its own HQ in Bloomsbury, employed staff, and published a weekly paper, *Peace News*. It sent letters to the press, stuck up posters, raised funds, organised meetings, huge rallies and demonstrations at militaristic occasions such as the annual RAF air display. It also campaigned against the 'whited sepulchre' of the League of Nations, not because the League sought international cooperation, but because the PPU thought collective security was either impractical in an age of aerial warfare and given the conflicting interests of nation states, or was simply a diplomatic cloak for aggression. Believing that the Versailles settlement had been provocatively harsh, the PPU bent over backwards to understand German foreign-policy aims, and while its members were certainly not pro-Nazi (even if they might be pro-German), there was sometimes a tendency for *Peace News* to show callous disregard for the victims of Nazism both within Germany itself and later in Czechoslovakia – though from 1938 the paper did appeal for its readers to sponsor Jewish refugees during the time they were in London.

Sending a postcard was the only action required for membership of the PPU: the pledge to peace was what mattered, since Sheppard's intention was to demonstrate the strength of commitment in the country, and so influence the government to make the pursuit of peace its overriding foreign-policy objective. Therefore the PPU would have to be a broad church, finding a space for all those opposed to war. But this would make it a church that was unlikely to survive the vicissitudes of events, since under its arches sheltered those who shared the Quaker tradition of an absolute refusal to condone war or take part in it whatever the circumstances and whatever the consequences, as well as those for whom pacifism (or pacificism, as the historian A.J.P. Taylor called this strand, resurrecting the original term that had become largely arcane by the 1930s) was political, forged in the circumstances of the day. Their number included those whose guilt about the Versailles settlement led them to believe that Germany had some legitimate grievances, who opposed rearmament, putting their trust in collective security and the League of Nations to sort out conflict without resorting to military action. In short, those who sought 'the conference table not the battlefield'.

On 31 October 1937 Dick Sheppard, who had just beaten J.B.S. Haldane and Winston Churchill in the election for the Rectorship of Glasgow

University, died unexpectedly aged fifty-seven of a heart attack. Vera Brittain was in the United States, and heard the news in a letter from her husband, George Caitlin. 'The Devil seems to be reaping this year,' he had written, and Brittain had the 'feeling that the sun had gone down . . . To all of us who cared for spiritual values, the shock of Dick Sheppard's death to his own country was comparable to the blow dealt to India a decade later by Gandhi's,' she wrote later. 'For two and a half days G[eorge] told me, the people of London had passed by Dick's coffin in St Martin's. He had attended the farewell service, in church – "all those clerics non-committal, using generalisations like blankets . . . " From Trafalgar Square he had followed the funeral procession along the Thames Embankment to St Paul's Cathedral – "with police holding up the traffic . . . people standing hatless, the police on point duty saluting; most touching of all, Thames barges and tugs, and the men coming up on board and taking off their hats. Up Ludgate Hill to the thousands, four deep, standing round the churchyard – into the Cathedral crowded to the doors, all that immense area; never since the King's funeral, and this without pomp or commerce, have I seen anything like it."'

When Sheppard died, leaving his followers 'literally as sheep not having a Sheppard', the PPU had a membership in excess of 118,000, and *Peace News* was selling around 15,000 copies a month. Although this may have seemed encouraging, in effect it meant that only just over 100,000 Britons were prepared to denounce war by writing a postcard, a number that fell far short of the million Sheppard had reckoned was necessary to block any government attempt to declare war. Moreover the PPU was a predomin-antly white-collar – and male – organisation, while the Labour Party, which might have provided the footsoldiers for pacifism, remained firmly committed to a belief in collective security. Indeed, the party's saintly leader, George Lansbury, an absolute Christian pacifist, was subjected to a cruel taunt from Ernest Bevin at the 1935 party conference in Brighton at the height of the Abyssinian crisis, and since no member of the Labour National Executive came to Lansbury's rescue, he resigned the following week and was succeeded as leader by Clement Attlee.

Virginia Woolf, herself a pacifist, had been in the hall. 'It was very dramatic. Tears came to my eyes as L[ansbury] spoke. And yet he was posing I felt – acting unconsciously, the battered Christian man. Then Bevin too acted I suppose. He sank his head in his vast shoulders till he looked like a tortoise. Told L. not to go hawking his conscience around ["from body to body asking to be told what to do with it"] And what is my duty as a human being? . . . Do I trust Bevin to produce a good world, when he has his equal rights? . . . My sympathies were with [Dr Alfred] Salter [MP] who preached non resistance. He's quite right. That should be our view. But then if society is in its present state? Happily, uneducated and voteless, I am not responsible for the state of society. These are some of the minnows that go round my head & distract me.'

Woolf's 'minnows' would continue to swim in others' ponds. With the Church seemingly no more adept at finding answers to the problems of the age than the politicians, any new initiative seemed welcome. 'The enthusiasm of these young converts attracts CC [Cosmo Canterbury],' wrote the Reverend Don in July 1935 of his Archbishop. 'It is an interesting and remarkable movement which attracts and repels me by turn and its effects on different people are so conflicting.' The 'movement' was the Oxford Group (not be confused with the Oxford Movement, a mid-nineteenth-century attempt to revive the Catholic outlook of the Church of England). The journalist and future politician Tom Driberg had come across 'the revivalist cult led by Dr Frank Buchman from Pennsylvania' when he attended a meeting at the Randolph Hotel in Oxford in February 1928, and reported it in the *Daily Express* under the headline 'Revival Scenes at Oxford. Undergraduates' Strange New Sect. Prayer Meetings in a Lounge' – a 'scoop' that would later lead to a job as the paper's gossip columnist 'William Hickey'. From that moment Driberg took 'a desultory but increasing interest in the Buchman movement', and he later wrote a polemical book about it.

Buchman was a Lutheran pastor with the 'scrupulous shampooed and almost medical cleanliness of the hygienic American', who grew to look a bit like a country stationmaster or small-town bank manager and, as one of his admirers suggested, could almost have been the love child of Mr Pickwick. He was not particularly charismatic, yet he managed to found a worldwide movement very much based on his own personality. He had had a conversion experience in a chapel at Keswick in the Lake District as a young man, and set out on a 'peripatetic fellowship' to convince other young people – particularly well-off university students – that they were in need of a spiritual reawakening which was most likely to happen during the 'quiet time' observed by the Group, a 'drawing room conversion' at a house party. Many of these so-called 'house parties' would hardly have fitted even into a many-roomed mansion. In the summer of 1933, 5,000 people (including almost a thousand clergy and twelve bishops) turned up to an event that filled six Oxford colleges, and two years later 6,000 somehow crammed onto the lawns of Lady Margaret Hall. The Group had no formal connection with Oxford, and some people were uneasy with the apparent association, but Buchman was particularly successful among Oxford students, and his followers had supposedly taken the name the 'Oxford Group' after a railway porter wrote the words on the window of their carriage as their train passed through Switzerland.

Buchman denied that the Group was a religion: it was an 'organism rather than an organisation', he insisted. It had 'no hierarchy, no temples, no endowments, its workers no salaries and no plans but God's plan'. Its followers saw themselves as simply 'Holy Crusaders in modern dress' whose chief aim was 'a new world order for Christ the King', cleaners-up of the moral order and fighters against communism.

The Oxford Group attracted followers of all denominations, mixing social groups through an ever-expanding network of house parties, with personal evangelical entreaties intended to lead those present towards 'God Control', guidance from God, which was received when a convert had 'surrendered his or her own ego and . . . fully surrendered to God's will'. Based on 'four absolutes' (absolute honesty, absolute purity, absolute unselfishness and absolute love), the Group's gatherings had a strong confessional tone of sin-and-tell. 'Bunny' Austin, the tennis champion, who seemed to believe that Christ was a bit like him in build, was a typical convert, as was Eric Liddell, the Olympic gold medallist athlete who refused to run on the Sabbath, and the sentimental columnist Godfrey Winn. But the playwright Beverley Nichols, who had been an early convert, soon shuddered at 'all that business about telling one's sins in public . . . it's spiritual nudism', the actress Margaret Rawlings was reported (by Driberg) to consider that exposing one's soul through public confession was 'as shocking as undressing in Piccadilly', and Queen Marie of Romania, granddaughter of Queen Victoria, shared their distaste: 'He [Buchman] wanted . . . me to get up . . . before my children and confess everything I had ever done!' She particularly objected to Buchman's snobbishness: 'He spoke of God as if He were the oldest title in the *Almanach de Gotha*.'

The Church was somewhat confounded by the Oxford Group, not a little envious of its vitality and appeal, but also somewhat wary. The Lambeth Conference had discussed it for two days in October 1933, without coming to any agreement. Archbishop Lang recognised that 'There is a gift here of which the church is manifestly in need,' and a prominent member of the Church Army 'admired their pluck. Let us help them all we can.' But Bishop Henson had strong misgivings about the 'sect', since Buchman concerned himself with the 'up and outs', rather than, as did most evangelical movements, the 'down and outs', while Dick Sheppard regarded the 'Buchmanites' as 'the old-fashioned [late-nineteenth-century American evangelists] Moody and Sankey business in modern dress'. Hewlett Johnson thought 'The "house-parties" idea smacks of snobbishness [and] the doctrine of guidance gets dangerously near to magic,' though he was pleased to see 'a new orientation Godward'. And Canon Arnold Mayhew asked the rather salient question, 'How are we to make use of it? To direct all this energy and enthusiasm into revitalising the Church, which needs it so much. Can any of the new wine be put into old bottles without a general bust up?' or would the Group 'become one more sect – the Salvation Army of the Middle Classes?'

The mid-1930s were, in Driberg's description, 'years of exultant advance' for the Oxford Group. Kingsley Martin, the editor of the *New Statesman*, went along to a meeting at the Albert Hall in July 1936 – the same hall that Mosley had filled two years previously. The audience was

> predominantly well-dressed, upper-class people with rather high proportion of women. The keynote of the meeting . . . is to be 'national safety' only to be obtained by God-control (Does God need a big air force or not?) God must govern England through God-controlled homes, God-controlled schools, God-controlled business, God-controlled professional life and God-controlled international policy. A Brigadier-General who controls race horses . . . tells us how he enlisted in the Oxford Movement and was changed. He used to swear at his men as they swore at the horses. Now the men too are changed. No more war. To change society is a God-guided basis is a bigger task than an army command. We have to choose between 'gas masks and God's tasks' . . . A chartered accountant, a DSO and an International rugby player, tells us how God controls his business and home life, and a journalist, who used to drink too much, looks forward to the time when newspapers will be different because people who make the news will be changed ['But what,' wondered Martin, 'happens to changed journalists if proprietors and advertising managers do not change too?' – but questions were not allowed at Buchman meetings] . . . The Labour Lord Mayor of Newcastle spoke long and eloquently . . . he had been in 'seventh heaven' since his conventional Methodism had been turned into a reality by the Groups. God would save Newcastle from unemployment. Five workers from the woollen mills of Yorkshire, who had been changed, had travelled down that afternoon to tell us about it and would be at work again at seven o'clock in the morning . . . Each of the five told us how they had not always worked honestly and well. One of them used to drink; they slacked off on flat rates and scamped through on piece work. They had confessed to God and the foreman and now they worked for God and made everyone happy in the workshop.

Martin was sceptical, noting that 'God does much of his work through people with titles and decorations' as baronesses and princesses took the platform, and he 'badly wanted to know whether God approved of the colour bar and pass system for Natives' when a former champion of Boer rights 'told us how he had been changed, formed a coalition with his adversaries, now loved England and the British Empire and saw God's solution for all the racial problems of Africa'. He was also troubled, wondering whether this 'new Salvationism was really so very different. The shape has changed; doctrine is unfashionable; Heaven and Hell are gone. This is religion without tears. To-day with the world tumbling around us, members of the Oxford Group want, as we all want, war and class conflict to cease. To face the causes of war or the causes of class conflict is too great a strain for many of us. How much easier if God's message is that these problems can be solved by national unity, if we can throw our burden upon the shoulders of God-controlled experts under a God-controlled leader. I think I know the social and political movement of which the Buchmanite movement is unconsciously a part.'

The very next month, Buchman, whose crusade for 'God Control' had taken him to the portals of national leaders and trade unionists, went to the Berlin Olympics, where he met Heinrich Himmler (he had encountered him previously at Nuremberg rallies) and tried unsuccessfully to meet Hitler. This did not go down well in Britain, where there were others besides Kingsley Martin who entertained suspicions that Buchman was pro-fascist, a view hardly mollified when he declared in an interview, 'I thank heaven for a man like Adolf Hitler, who built a frontline of defence between anti-Christ and Communism.'

In May 1938 Buchman adopted the call for Moral Re-Armament (MRA) at a meeting at East Ham Town Hall in London, arguing that it was not military rearmament that was needed, but spiritual rearmament – 'guidance not guns'. (After Buchman's death in 1961, MRA would be lead by the charismatic ex-rugby player Peter Howard, who had been leader of Oswald Mosley's 'Biff Boys' in the 1930s.)

'What is Moral Re-Armament?' demanded a poster pasted up outside Canning Town public hall a few days after the East End meeting:

> It's not an institution.
> It's not a point of view,
> It starts a revolution
> By starting it in you!

The revivalist energy of MRA, its promise of a fresh start, of a better life, of peace in a world where war was again beginning to threaten, of a higher authority that would take charge, was particularly attractive to young men disillusioned with the 'old gang' of secular and religious leaders. But for many, the slow but inexorable decline of the Church's authority was less noticeable. Most people still professed a belief in God and considered themselves to be Christians, even if they rarely went near a church other than for life's rites of passage. Around 70 per cent of babies were baptised, most people chose to marry in church (and since neither the Anglican nor the Catholic Church permitted the remarriage of divorced persons in church, there were probably quite a few more who would have done so if they had been allowed), and almost everyone had some sort of religious funeral. Moreover, a third of English people claimed to say their prayers every day, and even more claimed to do so 'regularly'. About half the population said they believed in an afterlife, though fears of hell and damnation no longer held the same sway as in former times.

Many of those who did not have any contact with the Church as an institution, yet claimed in a general way to be Christian, could be described as being influenced by what an Edwardian clergyman had called 'diffuse religion' – accepting and trying to live by Christian values and morality, perhaps getting involved in charitable activities, and if not the Mothers' Union, then the Women's Institute, which had a religious ethos too. The Church's hold on children remained strong: Sunday Schools and Bible Classes kept up their numbers as those of adult churchgoers declined, as did Brownie and Girl Guide packs and their male equivalents, meeting in church halls and with special services held in church. In the economically depressed areas of high unemployment in particular, the Boys' Brigade with its strong commitment to God and its gritty opposition to the temptations of the modern world such as cinemas, gambling and smoking flourished (though less so in Wales, with its anti-militarist tradition). The Brigades would join church parades in full uniform, beating drums, blowing bugles, twirling sticks, and sometimes carrying dummy rifles. In September 1933 its Jubilee 'Conventicle' (named after the seventeenth-century Scottish Covenanters' services 'under the canopy sky') held in Hampden Park football stadium, Glasgow, packed in 130,000 with another 100,000 eager lads locked out, supposedly the largest open-air service ever held in Scotland.

The belief in some sort of unexplained entity was strong. *Psychic News* claimed in 1932 that there were five hundred societies affiliated to the Spiritualists' National Union (SNU), and it was rumoured that there were at least forty spiritualist meetings in and around London every Sunday night in the mid-1930s, at which attempts were made to put the dead in touch with the living. The 1930s saw the high-water mark of spiritualism. As well as the activities of the SNU, there were frequent meetings in London and the provinces, the medium Helen Hughes could draw crowds of 3,000 or more, while 9,000 packed into the Albert Hall to witness Estelle Roberts 'speaking to the dead', books about spiritualism sold in large numbers, and *Psychic News* claimed that there were around 100,000 round-the-dining-room-table séances in British homes. Even allowing for the exaggeration of the spiritualist press, the slaughter of the First World War had made bereavement a common experience, and the desire to make contact with the deceased was tragically pervasive, while the spread of wireless and telegraphic communications reinforced the notion that 'out there' in the ether were those who wished to communicate and could be heard.

The Catholic Church was fiercely hostile to the notion of a hotline to the dead, and had been so concerned that 'superstition' might seize its members that a society called the Catholic Crusade Against Spiritualism had been formed in 1926 to staunch the 'considerable leakage among Catholics', with lectures organised to expose the dangers of such cults. The Church of England was more equivocal: the Archbishop of Canterbury set up a committee chaired by the Bishop of Bath to investigate the phenomenon. Many clergymen reported that members of their congregations were attracted to spiritualism, which they found a comfort, and while a minority report dismissed the idea that spiritualism had any scientific basis, most members recognised that the fact that the Church of England was 'too cautious' when it came to praying for the departed made the unsatisfied 'drift' towards spiritualism.

Almost every national and regional newspaper (not including *The Times*, the *Manchester Guardian* and indeed the *Daily Worker*) and most mass-circulation magazines published a horoscope, some had more than one, others had an astrology column, and most working-class women would 'look at their stars' every day. Articles in women's magazines wrote of lucky numbers, colours, days of the month. Children avoided the cracks in pavements lest something dreadful would befall them, people worried that breaking a mirror would bring seven years' bad luck, and an article in the *Daily Mail* observed that modern glass versions of 'old-fashioned witch balls' were being incorporated into the décor of modern houses, since they were supposed to bring good luck to the occupants. Wood or metal car mascots, including dogs, cats and tigers, often came with a new car, advertised as being a way of ensuring the reliability of the vehicle, and a St Christopher medallion might be affixed to the dashboard for a similar reason. Green stone or jade, mostly imported from New Zealand and fashioned into charms and pendants, was popular in the 1930s and regarded as efficacious in warding off bad luck.

When it came to filling the pews on Sunday, the family car proved as seductive an alternative to church as the bicycle had to an earlier generation. Eileen Whiteing noticed that whereas as a child her Sundays had consisted of 'going to church morning and evening, and to Sunday-school in the afternoons . . . as we grew older our parents liked to take us out for a drive in the afternoon, and it became very fashionable to try out the various new road-houses or country cottages where cream teas would be served, catering for the growing number of motorists visiting the countryside at weekends; which I suppose was the beginning of the great decline in Sunday observance and church attendance'. The *Church Times* was realistic: 'The natural reaction against the Puritan gloomy Sunday has had the inevitable result of going too far. The day of rest has become a day of rush and hustle . . . Sunday was the family day. Now on the Lord's Day the family is distributed all over golf courses and tennis courts, and is dashing about the country in Baby Austins . . . What can be done about it? We are entirely opposed to the banning of games in the park on a Sunday afternoon . . . We do not believe that to shut the cinemas would mean filling the churches.'

In July 1932 the National Government had passed the Sunday Entertainments Bill. This allowed cinemas, though not theatres, to open on Sundays in places where it was already common practice (mainly in big cities and seaside resorts, many of which were circumventing the 1780 Sunday Observance Act), while elsewhere it was left up to the local authority. By 1934 nearly all London cinemas had performances on Sundays, and so did about a quarter of those in the rest of England – but not in Scotland or Wales, where sabbatarianism was stronger. Only around 7 per cent of cinemas there opened on Sundays, and this did not change until after the Second World War.

If people were reluctant go to church, at least the church could now go to them. As the Rector of Whitechapel marvelled in the first religious radio broadcast, made in 1922, he was speaking to more people at that moment than St Paul had in his whole lifetime.

Sir John Reith, the first Director General of the BBC, wrote that he was 'more anxious about the general religious policy of the BBC in matters great and small than in anything else', and there would indeed be a number of anxieties on the subject throughout the 1930s. Religious policy was determined by a committee under the chairmanship of Dr Cyril Garbett, Bishop of Southwark. It dealt with such issues as how many hours of religious broadcasting there should be, at what times and of what sort. In the early days of the Corporation, religious programmes had been confined to Sundays, the seventh day that Reith insisted should be entirely different from the other six. However, as a result of the persistence of sixty-four-year-old Miss Kathleen Cordeux of Watford, who wrote to the *Radio Times* and organised numerous petitions urging that 'a large number of those who listen-in [particularly the sick and housebound] long to hear something daily of God and his love', a fifteen-minute service was broadcast every weekday morning at 10.15 from January 1928 (it still persists today). Seven thousand listeners wrote in to welcome the innovation, though Miss Cordeux was not granted her subsequent request, daily evensong to follow *Children's Hour*.

Religious broadcasting was supposed to fall 'within the mainstream of the Christian tradition', but that could be contentious. Both Reith and Garbett (and later the Reverend Iremonger, who had provided the religious commentary during the coronation, and was appointed as the BBC's first Religious Director in July 1933) aimed to be even-handed and ecumenical. Their Committee was made up of Anglicans, Roman Catholics and Nonconformist clergymen (no laymen), and the scheduling aimed to reflect this balance, with an emphasis on the established Church, which was allocated roughly 45 per cent of the broadcasts, with most of the other 55 per cent shared between the Free Churches (24 per cent) and the Roman Catholics (12 per cent), with the rest divvied up between the Church of Scotland and others such as the Salvation Army and the Quakers. Christian Scientists, Mormons, Theosophists and spiritualists were among those denied airtime, and no service from a Jewish synagogue was broadcast for many years, though the Chief Rabbi was permitted to give a talk around Passover time.

Then there was the quality of the broadcasts. A religious studio had been incorporated into the new BBC building in Great Portland Street in 1933, designed by Edward Maufe, the architect of Guildford Cathedral, but increasingly outside broadcasts became more popular – listeners liked to think they were part of a church congregation while sitting in their armchairs. Some clergy proved to be natural broadcasters. Dick Sheppard was one (he was also a member of the advisory committee), and his services from St Martin-in-the Fields were broadcast regularly on the second Sunday of the month. The Reverend W.H. Elliott's broadcasts from St Michael's Chester Square proved so popular that when he went on holiday in the summer of 1932, over 11,000 people wrote to the BBC pressing for them to continue. Others were less attuned to what was required, some using a 'holy voice' entirely suitable perhaps for reaching the far pews in an echoing church, but the 'parsonical drone' was ill-suited to radio, and likely to make listeners switch off. In an effort to raise standards the BBC had issued a handbook, *Hints to Sunday Speakers*, in 1928, which advised speakers to remember that their 'vast audience is not a crowd or congregation, but various individuals to whom you are speaking in the intimacy of their homes'. Talks had to be submitted ten days in advance, and 'must avoid sectarian propaganda or provocative argument' – though later series were commissioned in which controversy was permitted providing it was not 'offensive' or 'injurious'.

Some churchmen thought the whole notion of broadcasting church services trivialised religion. The Bishop of Southampton complained in 1935 that 'wireless services give inoculation of the mildest form of Christianity yet discovered'. Some worried that it would prevent people coming to church if they could get all the religion they wanted in their living rooms, while others hoped that religious broadcasts would serve as a sort of trailer for the real thing. And most thought there were not enough of them, and a lot that they were never quite right. A complaint from an Aberystwyth Free Church Council about a regular gardening talk at 2 p.m. every Sunday was given short shrift by the *Church Times*, which commented that good men could be very silly men, and that criticism of 'the engagement of an expert to explain on Sunday afternoons how best the amateur can prune his mulberry bushes [was] ridiculous'.

Audience measurement was an inexact science in the 1930s. 'There is at present no simple and direct method of measuring the response which listeners make to the varied supply of information they receive through the broadcast programme,' the editor of *The Listener* told an audience of librarians in October 1935. By 1938 religious programmes took up nearly 5 per cent of the ninety-six hours of broadcasting on the national network and 3.75 per cent on the regional ones, where the hours were marginally fewer. A survey of 4,000 people who were required to keep a logbook of their listening habits (they were already probably unrepresentatively keen listeners) showed that those living in the West Country were most likely to tune in to religious broadcasts; that the highest number listened to the Sunday service (more working-class than middle-class listeners, who might have been in church anyway), about 13 per cent listened regularly to the Daily Service, and only about 10 per cent listened to religious talks.

For Reith, the ideal Sunday was a silent one, but pressure was mounting from within and without the BBC to increase the number of broadcasting hours, particularly to fill the slots between 10.45 a.m. and 12 noon and 6.30 p.m. and 8 p.m. on a Sunday, when nothing was broadcast in case it tempted people to say at home rather than go to church. Continental stations such as Radio Luxembourg and Radio Normandie, whose broadcasts could be heard by British listeners with good sets, had no such inhibitions, and were putting out light-music programmes from 8 a.m. until late at night every Sunday, and a *Littlewood's* [Football] *Pools Programme* was broadcast on Radio Luxembourg at 2 p.m. every Sunday, so it wasn't necessarily that people weren't listening to the wireless on Sundays, but that most just weren't listening to the BBC.

Although the BBC gathered in the public's money in the form of a ten-shilling per person licence fee (though not all of the revenue went to the BBC), it was still in hock to the Church when it came to what people could listen to on what was for most their only day off. Throughout the 1930s the BBC strongly resisted the notion that listeners constituted a market: in its patrician view they remained an audience. It was not until the Second World War, by which time 98 per cent of the population could listen on a cheap wireless set to one BBC service, and 85 per cent could choose between two, that an unremitting Sunday diet of religious services, serious talks or dramas, interspersed with classical pieces played on the BBC organ (rather than the Wurlitzer, which was regarded as the rock bottom of vulgarity by Reith and Iremonger), or the occasional venture into opera, and rounded off with an epilogue, gave way to Reith's 'lowest common denominator' of light music, comedy and quizzes, and Sunday became, in yet another way, a day much like any other.

If dance and light music were considered unsuitable Sunday fare, when it came to classical music the BBC had no competition in the 1930s. It was a 'musical juggernaut', the largest single employer of musicians in the country, and a powerful patron. As well as filling the slots in the Sunday schedule that were not taken up by religious broadcasts or serious talks, classical music pervaded the rest of the week's output too. In 1931 Adrian Boult was invited by Reith to take the post of conductor of the BBC Symphony Orchestra, the formation of which hugely raised the low bar of orchestral music in Britain, and it was soon recognised as one of the finest orchestras in the world. Boult also oversaw the BBC's Music Department, the largest programme department in the Corporation, with a staff of fifty-four by 1937.

Despite the misgivings of Sir Thomas Beecham, who thought that 'the performance of music through [the wireless] cannot be other than a ludicrous caricature', and who went on to form the London Philharmonic Orchestra the following year, the BBC's remit was to broadcast opera, symphonies, chamber and 'modern' music so 'the shepherd on the downs, or the lonely crofter in the farthest Hebrides and, what is equally important the labourer in his squalid tenement in our all too familiar slums, or the lonely invalid on her monotonous couch, may all, in spirit, sit side by side with the patron of the stalls and hear some of the best performances in the world'.

As well as performances, the BBC broadcast regular talks of varied ambition to ensure that the delights of Bach, Beethoven, Mozart, Bartok, Schönberg, Stravinsky or the English composers Elgar, Delius (who both died in 1934), Ralph Vaughan Williams, William Walton, Frank Bridge, Gerald Finzi and Constant Lambert (though he was better-known as a conductor by the 1930s) – would pass none of its audience by. However, it was the Proms (Promenade Concerts) acquired by the BBC in 1927 under the direction of their founder, Sir Henry Wood, and broadcast from the Queen's Hall (until it was destroyed in the Blitz), that truly succeeded – and continue to succeed – in bringing a wide range of music to a wide range of people.

EIGHTEEN

A1 Men and Consuming Women

Semi-naked races have no knowledge of science nor hygiene. They live in the midst of smells. They drink foul water. They know nothing of germs. But they live fairly long and are amazingly strong and healthy. Why? Because they have a plus which we lack. They have the Ultra-Violet rays on the skin of the whole body . . . The fact is that the bleached clothes-wrapped races are physically weaker than the natural-colour races. The dockers of London cannot compare, for strength and endurance, with the coolies of China and the natives of Africa. The law of compensation has made us pay dearly for our comfort and our inventions.

Herbert N. Casson, *The Story of Artificial Silk* (1928)

Only in the Thirties could the 'Keep Fit' movement have come into being without exciting mocking laughter from the 'intelligentsia' or suburban Left. But none went up. Keeping fit was as serious a problem as any other: one might not practise it, but at least one did not joke about it.

Robert Graves and Alan Hodge, *The Long Weekend* (1940)

Streamlinism is a modern movement reflected equally in clothes and loco-motives and in an indefinite way connected with the cult of fitness.

Patrick Abercrombie (ed.), *The Book of the Modern House:*
A Panoramic Survey of Contemporary Domestic Design (1939)

'We have no desire to exchange our form of government for that of a total-itarian state,' Neville Chamberlain, then Chancellor of the Exchequer, assured the Conservative Party's annual conference at Margate on 2 October 1936. 'But in the matter of attention to physical development we may surely learn something from others. Nothing made a stronger impression on visitors to the Olympic games in Germany this year than the splendid condition of German youth, and though our methods are different from theirs, in accordance with our national character and traditions, I see no reason why we should not be equally successful with our results.' Indeed, so disappointing had Britain's performance in Berlin been three months earlier that a delegation from the Board of Education had gone to Germany to investigate the way physical education was being taught there. The delegates had been particularly impressed by the 'excellent work' of the 'Strength through Joy' initiative, which was 'certainly the most agreeable and possibly the most instructive phenom-enon of the Third Reich', though there was concern that the policy had gone too far, with the body being regarded as a 'mere machine to be kept constantly tuned up to the highest possible pitch of efficiency', while 'the whole population [was] under the legal and moral obligation to train'.

The health of the nation had been a concern for some time. During the Boer War, alarm at the fact that only 14,000 out of 20,000 volunteers were fit enough to join the army had led to the fear that the British race was degenerating physically. Now, in 1936, evidence that Britain's athletic prowess left a lot to be desired revived the spectre of the First World War, when only 36 per cent of those examined for recruitment to the army were graded A1 (fully fit for combat), while 31 per cent were C3 (unfit for combat). The fitness of its citizens seemed an allegory for the fitness of the nation to compete, if necessary to fight. The desire to produce A1 men (and women) began to guide government policy in this area, which until then had been restricted to the physical education of school children.

A report in 1935 estimated that 91 per cent of boys between fourteen and eighteen years of age never engaged in any form of physical activity at all (Newcastle presented a particularly inert picture). While boys at public schools were drilling in Officer Training Corps, playing strenuous games of rugby and springing effortlessly over vaulting horses in the gymnasium, it was rather different for other chaps. Yet, to the disquiet of the Board of Education, officer recruits to the elite military academies of Woolwich and Sandhurst were found to be pretty weedy too, and it was claimed that the War Office was having to review the amount of baggage a soldier could be expected to carry. It seemed pointless to contemplate undertaking a compre-hensive and cripplingly expensive military rearmament programme if the bodies required to operate the arms or drop the bombs would not be up to the task.

The government was reluctant to emphasise something that was likely to alarm the public, so keep-fit campaigns tended not to stress the military dimension. In January 1937 a White Paper outlining a £2 million scheme for physical fitness training was published. It firmly rejected any notion of this being compulsory, partly on the grounds of the problems of enforce-ment, but also because it would be 'wholly alien to the national temper and tradition'. The Physical Training and Recreation Act, which was passed in June, gave grants to local authorities and voluntary organisations to provide facilities for such activities, and a year later the Board of Education launched the National Fitness Council, which within the space of a year had provided grants of nearly £1.5 million for swimming pools, sports clubs, playing fields, youth hostels and a number of other ways in which the young could get exercise and fresh air.

However, any whiff of training for war was to be resisted: Walter Citrine, General Secretary of the TUC, spoke for his members (and many more) when he insisted that 'anything approaching the militaristic bias of German physical training activities must be firmly resisted'. Hence Chamberlain's insistence that though the nation must keep (or more likely get) fit, it must do so in the British way, a point he again emphasised when on 30 September 1937, now Prime Minister, he inaugurated the 'National Fitness Campaign'. *The Times* endorsed this with a special issue on 'The Nation's Health' (reprinted as a 2s.6d book), which was given a possibly rather alarming urgency by the announcement that many of the contributors had 'interrupted their holidays' to write their articles, 'evidence of the importance to which they attach to it and the faith they cherish in its ultimate usefulness'.

'The improvement of the National Health is among the first aims of a progressive government,' *The Times* declared: 'If cleanliness and good food and exercise are concerns of the individual man and woman, the means for the attainment of all of them must be provided and protected by public authority.' Articles on health and education, health and broadcasting, dental care, mental health (which noted that the 1930 Mental Health Service Act had 'abolished the meaningless term "lunatic"' and replaced 'asylum' with 'mental hospital', which 'emphasises the need for remedial rather than merely custodial methods') were all very upbeat, insisting that the 'doctor today takes pride in the idea that he is an ambassador of health as well as a healer of sickness and disease and devotes, as a rule, both time and care to the inculcation in the minds of his patients of that "will to fitness" which is the necessary foundation of national strength.' However, in the end, fitness was a personal responsibility: 'The success of the campaign depends . . . upon the co-operation of those whom it is being sought to benefit.'

Although undoubtedly such urgings were needed, there had been a considerable 'will to fitness' abroad in the land for some years. This had little – at least in the minds of those doing the exercising – to do with war, though an undertow of the need for national superiority could usually be detected from its proselytisers. By 1930 there were 100,000 members (including some women) of the Health and Strength League, which had been relaunched at the end of the First World War; by 1936 the figure had risen to 133,670, and by 1939 to 162,987.

In 1930, 374 physical culture clubs were listed by the League throughout Britain. They usually charged one or two shillings to join, and sixpence per evening. When Chamberlain had first spoken of the need for a 'really healthy nation' in 1936, the National Fitness Campaign's magazine *Health and Strength* crowed: 'At last our objective is achieved! We want a physical culture club in every town, village and hamlet . . . but our greatest wish is to see that every man develops that essential quality which makes for national fitness – Pride in Body – an opinion we have held for 35 years!'

The notion of a fit and healthy body had been the aim of reformers since towards the end of the nineteenth century, but such advocates tended to be gentle souls who felt more at ease in a rural environment and sought their route through vegetarianism, herbalism and other relatively minority 'fads' of the simple life. By the 1930s a more robust approach to health was taking a grip. Eugenicists saw selective breeding as the way to achieve a race of citizens healthy in mind and body, rather than the poor specimens that seemed to be what Britain increasingly had to offer. But the new health reformers looked to dietary reform and hygienic living as the answer – though this laid responsibility for health squarely on the shoulders of the individual – and called for discipline and resolve, rather than better housing, increased wages or welfare initiatives.

Sir William Arbuthnot Lane, a consultant surgeon who was particularly keen on the regular evacuation of the bowels, since he saw constipation as the root cause of 'all the troubles in civilised life', had founded the New Health Society in 1925 to promote exercise, a healthy diet, sunbathing and personal cleanliness, and to combat the degenerative elements of an urban, industrial life where everyone had the 'habit of keeping the trunk erect from morning to night' rather than squatting as 'savage races' did. Lane advocated much that Edward Carpenter and his ilk had in the 1890s: a diet of wholemeal bread and flour, milk, fresh fruit and vegetables and 'strict moderation' in 'flesh foods'. This high-fibre diet would help inner cleanliness; exercise, sunlight and loose clothes were also part of the prescription. The Depression put a brake on ambitious plans for New Health exhibitions extolling this way of life, but books, pamphlets and newspaper articles continued to appear advising on diet and urging people to take up outdoor pursuits such as hiking and camping to promote good health.

The Sunlight League was started in the mid-1920s by Dr Caleb Williams Saleeby, an advocate of heliotherapy, or helio-hygiene (treatment by expo-sure to direct sunlight). Saleeby, who also had a long interest in what he called 'positive' – later known as 'reform' – eugenics, contributed a regular column to the *New Statesman* under the pseudonym 'Lens'. Sunbathing clubs opened in a number of places including Finchley, Sidcup (the site of the Arcadians Club). The Yew Tree Club, 'devoted to physical culture and nudity', and which gradually allowed nudity all day rather than just in the afternoon, opened in Croydon in 1931, and a 'naturist' holiday resort on the Isle of Wight took its first guests in 1933. Several of these ventures were the initiative of Captain Harold Hubert Vincent, who started the Sun Ray Club and the Sunbathing Society, organised lectures and meetings (which in 1931 drew 'over 150 members from the professional and business classes') at his home, Sun Lodge in West Norwood, and suggested a parade of two hundred naked men and women through Hyde Park to promote the cause.

It was not an entirely popular one. In 1930, two hundred angry residents living near land in Hendon, North London, which the owner allowed to be used for nude sunbathing, invaded the area. The police were called, but they turned out to be rather more sympathetic to the sunbathers than to the objectors. Various progressives including George Bernard Shaw, Vera Brittain, Winifred Holtby, Laurence Housman, Naomi Mitchison, Dora Russell and Julian Huxley were shocked at this prudish attitude towards naturism, and wrote a letter to *The Times* in March 1932 in protest. Wisely recognising that with Britain's climate sunbathing was better described as 'active air bathing', they extolled the benefits of its 'decentness and wholesomeness' to 'the health and happiness of the indoor worker', and regretted that while 'many groups . . . have been formed to practise air bathing . . . they have found it necessary to secrete themselves in the woods round London in order to avoid the attention of the public, the Press . . . and their neighbours. This need for secrecy is iniquitous! Semi-nudity can be viewed on stage by paying for it, but it cannot, it seems, be indulged in for health and well being in the open air, until for lack of it, one is ill enough to go to hospital or a home for crippled children!' The enthusiasts thought there 'should be the same liberty in clothing for air bathing (away from public highways) as is now allowed on the stage; public authorities could well set aside grounds for air bathing exercises, private people could well make similar use of their own grounds; light and air clubs could be founded, and so on'.

This reverence for open air and sun was nowhere more pronounced than in lidos, those 'urban beaches' whose name derives from the Latin *litus*, meaning shore, that teemed with swimmers and sunbathers. Many of them looked like ocean-going liners, with their decks and handrails. Lidos were (usually literally) the concrete expression of the health and fitness ideology that swept Britain in the 1930s. They were also the nearest thing to a seaside holiday a lot of city and town dwellers ever had. Although Morecambe in Lancashire was by the seaside, it also had an open-air pool, and when Sir Josiah Stamp, Governor of the Bank of England and Chairman of the LMS railway company, opened it, he declared that 'bathing reduces rich and poor, high and low to a common standard of enjoyment and health. When we get down to swimming, we get down to health.'

The first lido, so-called, in Britain was the Serpentine in Hyde Park, opened by the Labour leader George Lansbury in 1930. Somehow the word 'lido', with its connotations of a pool with lawns for sunbathing, a café and a terrace for spectators, sounded more enticing than 'swimming pool'. This was partly, the LCC recognised, because of its Italian overtones (after all, the original lido is an island in the Venice lagoon), shared with other words that 'enriched the English language' such as 'concertina, ditto, broccoli, soda, motto, umbrella, salvo and influenza'.

There had, of course, been open-air swimming pools in Britain before the 1930s – some fifty perhaps: the first purpose-built one was probably in Finsbury in the mid-eighteenth century. But lidos represented something of a new era. A combination of health and hygiene regulations introduced in 1934 forced the closure of some older pools, while paid holidays, marginally shorter working hours and a celebration of the outdoors and the efficacy of the sun provided additional impetus. So did the fact that the government was prepared to give grants to local authorities for public works, providing that they benefited the community and used unemployed labour and British materials.

Between 1930 and 1939 at least 180 lidos were built in Britain, sixty-four within the London area alone: Herbert Morrison, leader of the LCC, promised in 1937 to turn the capital into 'a city of lidos'. The first of the decade was Kennington lido, opened in 1931. London Fields, Hackney, opened in 1932, followed just two years later by another, larger, grander lido less than a mile away at Victoria Park (Morrison had a particular understanding of the area's needs, since he had been Labour MP for Hackney South). Soon lidos were scattered all over the metropolis, from Brockwell, Bexley and Bromley to the south, Surbiton, Chiswick and Twickenham to the west, Willesden, Gospel Oak on the edge of Hampstead Heath, Hornsey, Highbury and Edmonton in the north, Dagenham, Poplar, Silvertown and West Ham to the east. Charlton lido, opened in 1939, was almost the last to be built in London, since after the outbreak of war there were other priorities. Most were demolished in the later years of the twentieth century, a dazzling decade of facilities that lay halfway along an axis from 'suburbia to the Côte d'Azur' proving to be but transitory.

Lidos were usually, but not always, rectangular. Enfield's in North London was a perfect oval; the massive pool at New Brighton near Liverpool, said to be the largest in Europe with space for 2,000 bathers and 10,000 spectators, opened by Lord Leverhulme in 1934, was D-shaped, and so was the pool at St Leonards, the posh end of Hastings. Chingford in Essex boasted a cruciform design, while the 1935 Jubilee Pool at Penzance, was triangular. Several built on the coast incorporated sea-water pools too. In most lidos bathing was mixed, so bodies were clad, unlike early days when young men joyously splashed around swimming pools naked; but some, such as Southampton, were segregated.

Filtration plants brought pools up to health and safety standards, which were much less stringent in the 1930s than they have subsequently become – sometimes with tragic results. Turnstiles allowed visitors to be charged an entrance fee. Most made provision for children and non-swimmers (and in the 1930s that meant a lot of people, though the spread of outdoor pools was a great encouragement to learn) and had purpose-built changing rooms and diving boards – diving was a cult that reached its apotheosis in the 1930s, as can be seen in the swallow-like images in the film Leni Riefenstahl made of the 1936 Berlin Olympics. The platforms would be made of wood or metal, or in the case of Weston-super-Mare, West Ham, Black Rock at Brighton, Scarborough and others, were magnificent reinforced concrete structures, with springboards made of Douglas fir covered in coconut matting. All needed a minimum depth of fifteen feet of water. So fine was Weston's huge ziggurat construction that it became as iconic as Blackpool's tower for the West Country resort that boasted of having 'air like wine'.

The pools were almost always painted Mediterranean blue, and had wide, white-painted brick or flagstone surrounds, many with benches or deckchairs, and usually flowerbeds and some grass. Scarborough – always a cut above neighbouring resorts – had Italianate gardens and colonnades, and the lido at Southport – a town referred to as 'the Paris of the North', though admittedly only on railway posters– resembled nothing so much as a Roman amphitheatre. Some had ornamental fountains which filtered the pool water. Margate had a total of six licensed cafés, with seating for 3,000, and pitches for six orchestras to serenade the swimmers. Britain's 1936 Olympic swimming team trained at the Hilsea lido, Portsmouth, and most of the larger lidos had spectator stands. Health and beauty classes were held on the terraces, and some pools installed underwater lighting to encourage night-time bathing – Margate lido at Cliftonville sometimes stayed open until midnight at the height of the season.

Morecambe's pool was so large and magnificent that even the name 'lido' would not do. It was named the 'Super Swimming Stadium', and as Sir Josiah Stamp said when he opened it in July 1936, 'it put the more into Morecambe'. It was the perfect complement to Oliver Hill's modernist Midland Hotel, described by *Country Life* as 'the most beautiful building in this country' when it opened in 1932. Portobello pool in Edinburgh, opened in May the same year, had a wave machine (as did Wembley), and given the inclement Scottish climate, it was heated by hot water, a byproduct of the adjacent power station. Others lidos staged 'attractions' to pull in the punters when no one wanted to venture into the water – such as log-rolling, parades of bathing beauties (or aqua lovelies), 'ornamental floating formations' and diving displays – for the sun didn't always beat down in the 1930s: 1938 was a notably wet and cold summer, though there were several heat waves in the first half of the decade, which was just as well, since most open-air pools were unheated.

A fit body is a trim body. By the 1930s the link between obesity and heart disease was accepted, and the *Lancet* had started to publish research about the necessity of roughage in diets. Frederick Horniman had 'lost ten thousand pounds of fat and deflated innumerable waistcoats' with his abdominal exercises based on native dances that toned the body of saggy, baggy, middle-aged industrial man. Vitamins had been identified, lettered from A to E and sold in health shops. Advertisements no longer suggested that people might like to 'gain two and a half pounds of healthy fat in six weeks', but that they might rather prefer to shed it within the same time frame. Such weight loss would be achieved through special diets (calories were rarely mentioned), strenuous exercise and running special rubber rollers over your fat bits, or by taking metabolism-enhancing drugs (though by the end of the 1930s these were regarded by the medical profession as hazardous), rather than by simply eating less, at a time when unemployment pay would not buy a healthy diet, or even a sufficient one: in some depressed areas as much as half the population was reckoned to be suffering from malnutrition.

Mary (Mollie) Bagot Stack, a young war widow with a small daughter, believed that a rigorous routine was required to 'build the body beautiful'. She would 'spring out of bed (much against my will)' at 6.45 in the morning and plunge her face in cold water before exercising for half an hour, 'stripped, with all the windows open (but sufficiently curtained) to gramophone music' before embarking on a day punctuated with a great many glasses of water, lunch of vegetables, dinner of lean meat or fish, teeth-cleaning after every meal, and several lapses in the form of cups of coffee '*with cream* (because I like it)'.

Bagot Stack had started the Women's League of Health and Beauty in 1930: 'People were enthusiastic about joining associations at that time, and the word League was in vogue.' By the end of 1932 it was holding classes on the beach in the summer, new centres opened in Glasgow and Birmingham, and it had 4,500 members; by 1935 there were centres in Éire, Australia, Canada and Hong Kong; by 1939 the number of members had risen to 170,000 in Britain and the Dominions. The League's motto was 'Movement is Life' (a lift from Isadora Duncan), and its aim was 'Racial Health', changed to 'Racial Health Leading to Peace' in 1936. The League was not concerned with racial superiority but with the harmony, as Bagot Stack saw it, between beauty and peace. Members, who could be any age, 'cultured or uncultured', had to sign a pledge committing themselves to regular exercise based on 'some practical knowledge of the mechanism of the body', as well as promising to buy at least one copy of each issue of the League's magazine, *Health and Beauty*. They were also advised to shave under their arms, use a deodorant, and make sure they always had a clean handkerchief stuffed up their left knicker leg.

Membership fees were reasonable in comparison with the rates for most private exercise classes: the League's annual subscription was 2*s*.6*d*, plus two shillings for an entrance badge to be worn at every class. Each class cost sixpence, and in the depressed areas they were sometimes held free of charge. So the League was, as Mrs Bagot Stack intended, mostly within the reach of 'business girls and women, slum children, factory workers, mothers' who 'worked long hours, earned low salaries and had little opportunity during their scanty leisure time to indulge in dance or sport'. Its aims were realistic, too: 'In these days of rush, fifteen minutes a day is the utmost time most of us can spare. It's a pity, but it is a fact. The following exercises are designed to give the maximum results in the minimum time.'

The 'classlessness' of the League was stressed continuously, and all members wore the same uniform: black satin knickers (daring at a time when movement was usually associated with figures clad in Roman-like drapes) and a sleeveless white blouse, which meant that distinctions of class or money were left in the cloakroom, where 'fragile crêpe de chine will dangle on the next peg to "art silk", and Bond-street suits jostle bargains from the basement', while inside the hall, 'the girl who drives her own car will link hands with one who has snatched an evening from selling stockings in a street market'.

From the outset Bagot Stack sought publicity for her League, organising displays in the Albert Hall and Hyde Park (where 2,500 members performed together in 1935), at Wembley Stadium for the Coronation Pageant in 1937, and again in June 1939, when 6,000 members participated in an Empire Pageant of Health and Beauty. The synchronicity of hundreds of waving legs could seem rather fascistic, but in fact it was more Busby Berkeley than Nazi. Women, 'the youngest and the oldest, fattest and thinnest, most elementary and most veteran', joined the League to do a combination of dance, callisthenics and rhythmic exercises to music both because they wanted to get fit ('training the body to be its own instrument in the great orchestra of Life') and to enjoy the companionship of other women. Men had their own League classes from 1937, but they were segregated from the women and cost more.

In 1935 Mollie Bagot Stack died of cancer aged fifty-one, and the mantle passed to her daughter, Prunella (hailed by the *Daily Mail* as 'the most physically perfect girl in the world'; another paper described her as 'strapping' and 'Nordic'). Two years later, when she was still only twenty-two, Prunella Stack was invited to join the board of the National Fitness Council to help in the work of overseeing the government's Physical Training and Recreation Act, set up 'to make Britain an A1 nation'. On 15 October 1938 she married a Scottish laird, Lord David Douglas-Hamilton; 10,000 League members turned up to see the wedding in Glasgow Cathedral, including some who had come from London in a specially hired train.

Dean Inge was fairly fitness-disposed (and certainly eugenics-minded), and in 1929 he had joined Caleb Williams Saleeby and others in developing the clothing subcommittee of the New Health Society, on which they both sat, into a fully-fledged Men's Dress Reform Party (MDRP). There was a degree of catching up to do. The women's Rational Dress Society, founded in 1881, protested against 'any fashion in dress that either deforms the figure, impedes the movements of the body, or in any way tends to injure [women's] health', and set its guns on tightly fitting corsets, high heels and bulky, heavy underwear. The organisation sold whaleboneless stays, insisted that seven pounds was the maximum weight of underwear any woman should be expected to wear, and pressed for the adoption of 'bi-furcated garments' (a fashion instigated by Amelia Bloomer in the US). Now it was men's turn to do away with stiff collars, starched shirt fronts and 'leather coffins' on their feet. Hats should only be worn as protection against rain or sun, coats were only needed when it was cold, loose blouses should replace starched shirts, and sandals hard leather shoes. Underwear should be non-constricting, and trousers had to go, replaced by either shorts or a kilt. Moreover, men should be allowed to dress with as much individuality as women: more than a decade had passed since the end of the war, yet men might as well still have been in khaki for all the difference that could be seen between one grey suit and trilby hat and the next.

Men's clothes should let air and sun get to the body, and as much skin as possible should be exposed to ultra-violet rays. While a tanned body had previously indicated outdoor labour, it now came to suggest outdoor leisure. A brown baby was seen as a bonny baby, and a sunlight-measuring device was distributed to 'health resorts and other towns', with *The Times* publishing the results every day.

The exercise necessary to produce A1 men required loose, functional clothes, and in one of his fruitless attempts to reform male dress, Dr Caleb Williams Saleeby had written to the Lawn Tennis Association encouraging it 'to persuade men to give up the handicap of heavy trousers and play in shorts'. He instanced the then Duke of York's appearance in an open-necked shirt and well-cut shorts at a Scouts' summer camp – and after all Lord Baden-Powell, founder of the Scouts, had 'lived all [his] life in shorts without collar-studs whenever possible'. But though 'no one feels like jeering when eleven hefty footballers run onto the field in "shorts"', they were not regarded as suitable for the more middle-class location of the tennis court, and certainly not the cricket pitch (as remains the case), where it was thought the players would look like 'funny little boys'. On public tennis courts some women were running around in long shorts or divided skirts – though if stockingless, this caused comment: British men, with exception of the upper-class pin-up tennis star 'Bunny' Austin, who daringly wore shorts on the Centre Court at Wimbledon in 1932, wore trousers. His opponent Fred Perry was not at all grand (though he proved to be the superior player), and was thus unwilling to defy convention in the way the more insouciant Austin had.

In May 1931 Dean Inge gave a lecture to the Royal Institution about 'The Future of the Human Race' in which one of his predictions was that 'everyone would simply wear a tunic over which a cloak may be thrown in cold weather'. However, despite such suggestions and compelling arguments, the MDRP made little headway, and in 1937 the New Health Society, which had supported it, was declared bankrupt. British men proved resistant to showing a leg, or a portly stomach, partly on aesthetic grounds and partly because there was a feeling that sartorial drift could lead to moral plunge. A 'sturdy and virile *man*' was perfectly 'capable of withstanding the rigours of a stiff shirt', and as a contributor to a debate on 'Shall Man be Redressed?'

on 24 June 1932 suggested, 'The man who, alone in the jungle, changes into his dinner jacket does so to convince himself that he is not a savage – soft, sloppy clothes are symbolic of a soft and sloppy race.' The movement had some successes, however – in the underwear department, on hiking trails and some sports fields, in the increasing ubiquity of sports jackets and open-necked shirts, blazers and white flannels, and in men's bathing suits, which grew rather scantier even in areas of mixed bathing.

In men's clothes, form followed function – and class. Wealthy and professional men would have their suits tailored in Savile Row if they could afford it, or at small bespoke establishments elsewhere, where inside legs were carefully measured, and much thought given to a nip here, a slight turn there, but nothing that would distinguish one City (or business, or civil service) type from another. The less well-off lower middle classes and those working-class men who wanted a 'Sunday best' suit bought them at shops like Burton or Horne Brothers, paying fifty to sixty shillings for a 'tailor-made' garment for which they would choose the style from a catalogue and the fabric from a swatch, and have their measurements taken by a shop assistant who was encouraged to cultivate the dignified style of a 'Quaker tea blender' rather than the 'severe style of the income-tax collector' or the 'smooth tongue of the fortune teller'. The customer would pay a deposit (often to the only woman working in this male world) and collect the finished suit a week or so later; adjustments would be made if necessary. In 1919 Burton had had forty shops, half of which were in London; by 1939 their reach was national, with 565 shops, over 90 per cent of them outside the South-East – twelve in Birmingham alone. During the thirties, ready-to-wear, off-the-peg suits took over from tailor-made, and shops were adapted to deal with this more cost- and labour-effective fashion.

The subtle calibrations of class, measured less by income than by occupation and status, were signalled in numerous ways including accent, domestic situation, and dress. A menswear style guide from 1935 makes this very clear, depicting a 'black-jacket ensemble . . . which can be seen at a glance to belong to the large room with the pile carpet, often distinguished by a neat card on the door, marked "In Conference". It blends just as well with a Harley St. address, as with Throgmorton Street, or, for that matter, the Inns of Court and there is no fear of confusing it . . . with a kind of junior clerk version.' An early market research exercise conducted by Austin Reed, which along with Simpson of Piccadilly provided a bridge between the bespoke and the mass market, was also revealing. It showed that in Preston collarless coloured shirts outnumbered formal white ones by eight to one, whereas in Liverpool and Manchester the ratio was 50:50. Austin Reed took the decision to close their Preston branch forthwith, since the town clearly did not have the middle-class population necessary to sustain such a shop.

Teachers, shop assistants and a vast army of clerks all wore suits to work in the 1930s, some shabbier and shinier than others, if their owner did not have the money to purchase several to wear in rotation. Although John Osborne's grandfather was 'always dressed . . . as if ready to go out' at week-ends – or rather on Saturday afternoons and Sundays, since most firms still worked on Saturday mornings, and older men would still be seen in the football stands, at the greyhound track or in the pub in a suit, younger middle- and lower-middle-class men would be more inclined to shed their suits and replace them with a sports jacket or knitted cardigan or hand-knitted v-necked sleeveless pullover (maybe in the Fairisle design favoured by the Duke of York) to hide their braces, since it was considered most 'common' for those to be evident, a short-sleeved, tieless shirt, flannel trousers or shorts, or even plus fours and argyle-patterned socks, though these were considered rather risible by the 1930s.

Evening wear was something of a minefield, since rules were very unbending: a black tie, never a white one, and never, ever, a pre-tied one, the giveaway buckle visible from the back, with a black evening jacket and black patent shoes that could not be worn on any other occasion. Evening clothes would be worn to dances and dinners, receptions and the opera and to the stalls in the theatre, though by the 1930s the 'immaculates' were in danger of rubbing elegant shoulders with 'tweedy patrons' – especially at a Shakespearean play that attracted the 'youthful intelligentsia'. No wonder Moss Bros, which since the turn of the twentieth century had been hiring out ceremonial dress and campaign uniforms, was much in demand for evening dress among 'those who have all the impulses towards gentility, but lack the necessary money to equip themselves in accordance with their real or imaginary status in life'.

Whereas in the 1920s the fashionable female had been a 'short-haired, boyish girl with no breasts and no waist but exposed legs' (since she was wearing a short, tunic-like 'flapper dress'), by the 1930s the emphasis had changed. The 'torso was of paramount importance, but the legs of little account', pronounced Madge Garland, a journalist working for *Vogue* who advised Virginia Woolf on her wardrobe as well as commissioning articles from her. And 'with the indecision characteristic of the decade an occasional asymmetrical décolletage covered one shoulder with a slight drapery but left the other bare, while even more drastic was the halter neckline which left back, neck and shoulders totally exposed'. Unfortunately, the new fashion required 'nothing less than a perfectly proportioned body with a naturally indented waist, small rounded breasts which needed no support, perfect shoulders, an absolutely flat back and exceptionally slender thighs ending in extra long legs'. Which was not how most women were built

Fashionable clothes, for those who minded about or could afford such things, were sophisticated, clinging, since bias-cut dresses were all the rage, décolleté. Satin slithered over those perfect rounded breasts and taut torsos, white was 'dominant for evening', indeed Patou's white satins 'were to be found in the wardrobe of every well-dressed woman'. Gladys Cooper wore 'a white chiffon and carried a white ostrich feather fan when she played opposite Sir Gerald du Maurier in *Cynara*', and another actress, Gertrude Lawrence, 'scored the maximum marks when she appeared in Molyneux's white bias-cut satin, plus gardenias, diamond ribbon bracelets, and a black velvet wrap edged with white fox'.

Women were advised to 'dress husky' for the country in tweeds and tartan (the young Duchess of York was a model here), but in town 'special cocktail dresses became part of every woman's ["every" in fact being a limited circle] wardrobe', since it was 'necessary to find something which fitted the hours between day and evening dress'. Coats were often made of fur, and 'in the latter part of the decade there were foxes everywhere except, perhaps in the Arctic region where many cannot have been left . . . Every smart woman's wardrobe included one or more fox wraps, there were short silver fox jackets and capes, white fox stoles for evening.' Hats were *de rigueur* for all daytime occasions, and these varied from plate-sized models to toques, which Queen Mary had popularised, hats inspired by Portuguese fisherwomen, berets, turbans, fezzes, boaters, pillboxes, snoods, 'tall pointed cones trimmed with spiky feathers', and for afternoon and early evening, tiny wisps of chiffon, 'bits of nonsense, tit bits of feathers, oddments of flowers and ribbons which made up in cost what they lacked in size', though 'no woman with anything on her head was allowed into restaurants or night clubs where evening dress was obligatory'). When unhatted, heads were as 'polished and shiny as brushing and brilliantine could make them', though permanent waves were a problem, 'more often frizz than curl'.

Gloves were essential too, and bags too small to carry anything much. Cellophane bags were all the rage in 1935, but were fragile, and had to be handled with almost as much care as Schiaparelli's 'glass dresses' for evening. Orchids were an accessory of choice, pinned on bosoms, bracelets, belts, even on fur coats. Costume jewellery was popular, with pigeon-egg-sized glass baubles, while sparkling diamond bracelets were worn over black, elbow-high evening gloves, and Princess Marina of Greece, who married the Duke of Kent in 1934, revived the fashion of pearls. Pierced ears were considered very last-decade by the young, but fortunately the French jeweller Cartier had a brainwave while watching a maid hang out clothes, and adapted the mechanism of the clothes peg for earrings. Platinum, which apparently had previously only been used by Siberian peasants to make buttons, now entered the fashion world, but not on the whole for wedding rings, 'which some thought hardly binding unless they were of the traditional gold'.

Make-up was still regarded by the older generation as 'fast', the badge of the actress – or worse. A little *papier poudré* dabbed on a shiny nose was acceptable, with eyebrows and lashes brushed with brilliantine or Vaseline, but not lipstick or nail varnish, even though *Vogue* was always talking about coral, carmine or pomegranate lips (or, as war approached, Helena Rubinstein's 'Regimental Red' or Cyclax's 'Auxiliary Red'), cyclamen rouge, deep-blue eyelashes and polished nails. Eileen Lawrence (later Whiteing), who was 'a slave to whatever current trend was in vogue', recalled that 'make-up was quite limited: being mostly a vanishing cream and a dusting of loose powder, with a discreet touch of lipstick – but certainly nothing like eye shadow, mascara, bright nail varnish, hair-spray or deodorant.'

However, in 1935 the average reader of *Good Housekeeping* – hardly a magazine in the vanguard of fashion – reported that a typical 'town dweller' would spend £15.1s.3d a year on cleansing cream, powder, lipsticks, rouge, a twice-yearly permanent wave and a fortnightly shampoo and set, plus manicures three times a year. For a typist in a provincial town it was more like £3.2s.2d, but then she had a 'roseleaf complexion', due apparently to not eating between meals and munching four apples a day, and she *had* used the same threepenny lipstick for the past two years. A 'well-preserved' forty-two-year-old actress, however, was high-maintenance, spending £743.14s on permanent waves, bleachings and 'touching up's, twelve boxes of face powder a year, not to mention wax baths, electric belt treatments, and the budget buster, an annual 'cure' at Carlsbad or Vichy 'for slimming, skin rejuvenation and general toning up of the system'.

Advertisements (often for 'inner cleanliness') showed husbands delicately shuddering, 'I wish you wouldn't use so much make-up, Mary!' Unpleasant, if not downright vicious, articles continued to be published occasionally in women's magazines written by men who were deeply critical of women using cosmetics, and talked of their red nails 'like bloody talons', their lips so red that 'they looked like a butcher's shop', faces rendered 'grotesque and disfigured' by having their eyebrows plucked, and short skirts revealing 'roly-poly legs'.

The length of skirts was indeed a question of great importance, and nowhere was 'this perennial dispute more acrimonious than over the length of the Ascot dress – the problem split families, broke friendships' – floor-length, calf-length, mid-calf-length? Unfortunately, one way out of this dilemma seemed closed off. Madge Garland reported that it was 'eccentric' for women to wear trousers, though she conceded that they looked better than 'rumpled pullovers and shapeless skirts' on the golf course, and were acceptable on the grouse moor, the beach or in the boudoir.

'Modern' notions were beginning to come in, with man-made fibres like Lanielle, Nicolaine and Tricolene that no one can remember any more, since they were replaced by better ones, and by 1936 the zip, which until then 'had not always been a dependable piece of modern mechanism', had 'finally ousted the hook and eye'.

In the 1930s Paris ruled when it came to fashion, but there were seven leading couturiers in London, including Norman Hartnell, Charles Creed, Digby Morton, Victor Stiebel and Molyneux (who was British, though he had made his name in Paris). Most women did not of course patronise *hauts couturiers* but bought their clothes in shops, had a dressmaker 'run something up', or used a paper pattern to make their own clothes. The film stars Gloria Swanson and Norma Shearer, perhaps feeling the effects of what *Vogue* called the 'new economy' in 1931, were among the women who sent off for the paper patterns advertised on the cover of the magazine, and probably most children – certainly most girls – wore home-made clothes in the 1930s, their jumpers, cardigans and hats hand-knitted. A shop-bought dress was a rite of passage to adulthood.

If women were poor, they wore clothes passed on from friends or relations, and bought second-hand from markets and jumble sales, or if they were poor but middle-class and wanting to keep up appearances, responded to advertisements in the *Lady*. Most of these were placed by private individuals who were as (or more) circumspect in proffering their wares than those who use lonely hearts columns today, describing themselves as a 'widow in reduced circumstances', a 'titled lady', a 'London lady', maybe a 'barrister's wife', though their customers were probably not so socially elevated. Another source of cheaper, but good-quality clothes were the dress agencies that also advertised in the *Lady* and other periodicals, and usually had discreet premises in places like Sloane Square or Buckingham Palace Road, invariably on the first floor so that customers could not be spied buying second-hand clothes. E.M. Delafield's *Provincial Lady* had a trying experience with a dress agency when once more in the bad books of her bank manager: 'March 12th Collect major portion of my wardrobe and dispatch to address mentioned in advertisement pages of *Time and Tide* [to which Delafield was a regular contributor] as prepared to pay Highest Prices for Outworn Garments, cheque by return ... March 14th Rather inadequate postal order arrives, together with white tennis coat trimmed with rabbit, which – says accompanying letter – is returned as unsaleable. Should like to know *why*.'

In May 1939 Mass-Observation talked to women when they were shopping for clothes, and found that most spent time window-shopping first, used magazines for inspiration (*Vogue* was mentioned most frequently) or looked at photographs of film stars or royalty (the Queen and the Duchess of Kent were cited as role models). When it came to buying, clothes were expected to last: 'quality not quantity' was a frequent mantra, with seams being closely examined when a purchase was contemplated.

A 1932 review of British retailing pointed out that 'no other industry so widely affects the public as does [the] work of retailing, in none other is there such a wide range of scale'. Its author, the managing director of the Kensington children's clothing store Daniel Neal, best known for Chilprufe vests, sensible Startrite shoes (after the child's foot had been thoroughly x-rayed) and school uniforms, divided Britain's shops into six categories: department stores; multiple shops such as Freeman Hardy & Willis (shoes); speciality shops such as Austin Reed; small independent shops, often of a 'family type'; the Co-operative Movement shops; and 'fixed price' chain stores such as Woolworths, Marks & Spencer and British Home Stores. By the 1920s all major cities and most reasonable-sized towns had at least one department store; these sold the nation about 10 per cent of all its clothing and footwear. By 1939 it was 15 per cent, and smaller independent shops were losing out.

Shopping in the 1930s was a different experience from what it had been before the First World War: in the chain and department stores no imperious shopwalkers or assistants interposed themselves between the customer and goods kept out of reach on shelves and in drawers. She (or less often he) was free to wander around open-plan departments, looking, touching, comparing the price and quality of merchandise. The size of such shops was revolutionary, made possible partly by the growth of suburbia and improvements in public transport which gave them a far greater catchment area, while falling prices and rising wages for those in work gave customers greater spending power, and the easing of credit was a further incentive for shops to expand their stocks. Stores worked hard to dispel any suggestion that hire purchase was either a nice little earner for the shopkeeper at the expense of the customer, or in any way analogous to the pawn shop. Drages, a large Oxford Street furniture emporium, enlisted the endorsement of

Margot Asquith, Countess of Oxford, who proclaimed that as 'a woman of taste [who] could never live in ugly surroundings or with ugly things' she was enchanted by the wares she saw on offer, as well as with the 'kindly and wise provision' Drages made for hire-purchase defaulters.

The volume of HP trading increased twentyfold between 1918 and 1938, and according to the Board of Trade its annual value in the late 1930s was about £100–£120 million, roughly 3.5 per cent of retail sales and 2.5 per cent of total personal expenditure. Furniture and carpets accounted for 30 per cent of HP transactions: the Board of Trade estimated that more than 70 per cent of sales of working-class furniture was on the 'never never'. Drages perhaps notwithstanding, not all hire-purchase defaulters were treated with 'kindly and wise provision'. Until the 1938 Hire Purchase Act, introduced by Ellen Wilkinson, tightened up regulations, unlike other credit providers, who had to use the courts to sue defaulters, HP traders could simply re-possess the goods, which remained their property until the end of the contract.

Moreover, defaulters not only lost the goods, but also all the payments they had made, regardless of how near they were to having fulfilled their contract. And they had probably been either paying at a very high rate of interest, or had paid a much higher price for the goods than cash purchasers – often a mark-up of 100–110 per cent. Customers were frequently not provided with a copy of their HP agreement, so it was difficult for them to check their obligations, or if they did have a copy the jargon was so obfuscatory that they would have been most unlikely to fully understand what they were signing. Contracts might include a clause that allowed the trader to forcibly enter a purchaser's home and seize the purchases in case of default, while other clauses exempted the trader from being required to ensure that the goods were 'fit for the purpose intended and of merchantable quality'. As a Liverpool county court judge noted in the case of a shore foreman who was forced to continue payments on a twelve-guinea radio although it had only worked for a few hours and could not be mended, 'We will sell you rubbish and you will have no remedy.'

Married women were not legally allowed to enter into hire-purchase agreements without their husbands' consent, but they were often respon-sible within the family for making the weekly payments, and if they fell into arrears they might be 'terrorised with threats of their husbands being told . . . and possession of the goods is often retaken without any compen-sation when large instalments have been paid' – a process known as 'snatch back'. By 1937 there were an estimated six hundred repossessions a day, some of which were made within hours of the purchaser missing a single payment.

The abuses were perceived to have become so iniquitous by 1937, with judgement summons having risen from 267,000 in 1931 to 327,000 in 1936, and HP being denounced as a 'major social evil' for the poor, that judges were increasingly sympathetic to defaulters, setting monthly repayments at such a negligible level that the trader might have to wait a hundred years for the final payment. In a BBC broadcast John Hilton, 'the people's friend', advised those who felt that HP salesmen had misrepresented their position to refuse to pay, since the courts were likely to treat them leniently. When the Hire Purchase Act, which gave greater rights to purchasers, including protection from repossession (unless the trader had obtained a court order) once a third of the payments had been made, came to Parliament in April 1938, it passed both the Commons and the Lords with almost no opposition.

'On almost every main street you will find the same shops in similar proportions,' wrote Jan and Cora Gordon in their book *The London Roundabout* (1933), in which they described the capital as 'an overgrown country town'; but the range of shops was much the same in any undergrown country town: 'a Woolworth's, a Boots, an A.B.C. and Lyons', an Express and a United Dairy, a Greggs and a Home and Colonial, a Partners's and a Maynard's, two dyers, two bookshops, two family chemists, half a dozen fruit shops and tobacconists'.

The first British Woolworths store, with its red fascia with gold lettering proclaiming 'F.W. Woolworth & Co. Ltd 3d and 6d Stores', had opened in Liverpool in 1909, masterminded by a Birmingham man, William L. Stephenson, who had formerly been an English buyer for a New York store, and reckoned that he knew how to translate an American retail concept into a British success. When the slump hit Britain in 1931, the year Woolworths was floated as a British public company with Stephenson as the chairman, there was gloom about the operation on the other side of the Atlantic, where 'approximately three million men were living below a standard "below which" the social experts said, "no worker should be forced to live". One and three-quarter million women were on the same level. They were not likely to be renewing their lipsticks very often, or buying many pairs of new rayon stockings. For them to burn out a saucepan or break a jug was a small disaster not to be automatically remedied by popping round to Woolworths . . . Even among those who were relatively well-placed there was a spiritual pulling in of horns. Nobody was in a mood to try anything new,' diagnosed Claud Cockburn, a journalist who had worked in New York and Washington for *The Times*, but had returned to London in the early

1930s, joined the Communist Party, started his own news-sheet, the *Week*, and in 1935 also joined the *Daily Worker* as its diplomatic correspondent (and later covered the Spanish Civil War for the *Worker*). But 'Stephenson was looking for people who did earn a little money . . . The slump had . . . jolted British attitudes, knocked some old bits of thinking about a bit, sharpened people's economic eyesight. Millions who had any money left at all, were not going to let habits or traditions impede them when it came to getting value for money. If a new Woolworths in an old town could prove better value, then the available money would come to Woolworths.' Woolworths' potential customers included 'everyone between a shadowy line drawn somewhere through the middle of the middle class and another drawn somewhere near the top of the working class'.

The reason for Stephenson's success with Woolworths, Cockburn concluded, was that he had 'recognized the emergence of a new type of consumer demand in the Britain of the thirties'. This was based on the fact that consumer demand in Britain was regional – in the 'old industries' there was unemployment and no money, while in the newer service industries of the Midlands and the South-East there was some, if not a lot of, disposable income; and by the late thirties almost a third of those employed worked not in producing goods but in the servicing of people or things, in selling or in the bureaucracy needed to administer government and industry. So far, so obvious; but what Stephenson also understood was the psychology of flux – that new jobs, new places to live, changed mindsets, unfroze petrified social relations and created expectations. This stimulated consumer demand. And Woolworths was able to satisfy that demand among those who did not have much money. 'Mr Woolworth's success,' wrote Thomas Burke in his book *London in My Time* (1934), 'is due to the fact that millions of people can spend six pence [the maximum price charged] at five different times, or three pence at ten different times, who never at any time have half a crown to spend.' If someone decided they wanted the latest colour lipstick, or a new screwdriver, and it was on sale at Woolworths at a cheap price, they would buy it, rather than thinking that they shouldn't because further down the line they were going to have to buy a new carpet. Moreover, in times of uncertainty, goods as much as money, became a 'hedge' against hard times maybe to come. Buy it now when you've got the money to do so – just as the rich always had when it came to diamonds or pictures or fine antiques. Thus Woolworths became a hugely popular high-street store where people bought necessities and small luxuries, where children spent their pocket money, where you could linger over the goods laid out in trays rather than having to ask a snooty assistant to fetch something for you.

'By a clever act of legerdemain Woolworth has contrived to insinuate himself into a peculiar position. He has identified his shops with the hunting instinct, he has become the covers of continual quest,' according to the Gordons. 'Woolworth "news" is bandied about at suburban tea-parties almost as eagerly as the League matches are discussed in the pubs, or the hunting prospects in the country smoking-rooms, "Do you know, my dear, the Woolworth's in Walham Green is selling the most marvellous coffee grinders. Only sixpence and you'd pay one and fourpence for the same thing in Soho. But there are only a few left . . . " Woolworth's slyness consists in this, that nobody gives him credit for the bargains found in his bazaars. Each takes the credit for himself. Mr Woolworth no longer counts. He is there . . . just as rocks are to the geologist, jungles are to the zoologist . . . there's little doubt that in sum Woolworth has done a noble duty; he has brought more happiness to the mere modern woman than all the husbands ever found. "For", as Lorelei might have said, "marriage is a toss up. But a Woolworth bargain is a joy for at least a month."'

In 1931 Rachel Ferguson called her novel *The Brontës Went to Woolworths*; in her novel about the thirties, *Our Spoons Came from Woolworths* (1950), Barbara Comyns mentions buying 'a lot of blue plates from Woolworths', and when the jeweller from whom the couple bought their wedding ring declines to give them a set of real silver teaspoons, 'our spoons came from Woolworths too', an indication of Bohemian penury. In 1937 thirty-four new Woolworths stores were opened, forty older ones were refurbished and extended, and by the end of the year there were 711 in Britain, each turning over a very satisfactory profit. (Now, almost overnight in early 2009, there are none.)

Boots was another ubiquitous high street store. Founded by Jesse Boot, the son of a Wesleyan herbalist, it started trading primarily as a chemists in 1883 in Nottingham, Boot's home town and the beneficiary of much of his largesse. The company was bought by an American pharmaceutical firm which suffered catastrophic losses in the Wall Street crash, and when Jesse Boot died in 1931, his son John took the opportunity to lead a banking consortium to buy it back for £6 million. Determined to prove his commercial acumen –his father had sold the firm because he had such a low opinion of him – John Boot commissioned an architecturally distinguished and technologically advanced 'wonder factory' at Beeston near Nottingham, designed by Owen Williams, which his mother Florence opened by smashing a bottle of eau de cologne at the foot of the main staircase in July 1933. It was a modern and efficient place to work, and productivity rose so satisfactorily that Boots gave its workers every Saturday morning off – making it reputedly the first large company in Britain to introduce a five-day working week.

Throughout the 1920s Boots shops had opened at the rate of one a week. On 19 October 1933, the thousandth store was opened (two hundred more would be added by 1939). The shop was in Galashiels in Scotland, but the opening ceremony was performed at a lunch at the Savoy Hotel in London, at which Jesse's widow, Florence, pushed a lever, and simultaneously the latch was released on the door of the Galashiels shop, admitting the first customer, a Miss Cochrane, whose shopping list, which included Ovaltine, Bovril, aspirin, cod liver oil and Lifebuoy toilet soap, was broadcast live to the possibly enraptured party at the Savoy.

Simon Marks, impressed but also alarmed by the success of Woolworths, 'this commercial giant whose red signs were beginning to dominate the main shopping streets of Great Britain', had set off to America to see how it was done. Marks & Spencer's shops, with their green and gold fascia, were usually to be found at the 'top end' of the high street or shopping parade, away from such places as the fish and chip shop. By 1939 there were 234 stores, providing nearly forty miles of counter space, with a turnover of £23,448,000 and employing a total staff of over 17,000, selling goods – 94 per cent of which were manufactured in Britain – at a maximum price of five shillings (the company had started as a 'penny bazaar' – 'Don't ask the price – it's a penny' – in Kirkgate market, Leeds, in 1884). Goods were sold under the brand name 'St Michael', registered in 1928, which was the name of Simon Marks' father, the founder of the firm, as well as being the patron saint of Jewish people.

Marks & Spencer's had sold a wide range of goods including hardware, cutlery, china, fancy goods, toys, confectionery and particularly haber-dashery, but during the 1930s it increasingly came to concentrate on textiles – mainly clothes: 'a forest of apparel' was how the flagship Pantheon store in Oxford Street advertised its wares. A combination of mass-production manufacturing techniques, cheaper fabrics such as rayon, and greater spending power for those in work – by 1939 the cost of living was 11 per cent lower than in 1924, while average wages were 3.5 per cent higher – made the decision to pioneer the provision of fashionable clothes (or fairly fashionable – at least M&S introduced 'French knickers' to sell alongside 'passion-killer' *Directoire* ones gathered with elastic just above the knee) a feasible one, since women comprised the majority of Marks & Spencer's customers in the inter-war years, and of its staff too. A notional 'Mrs Goodwife', featured in the *M&S Magazine* in the summer of 1932, managed to buy a 'tennis frock, hat, blazer, stockings, shoes, a slip and knickers' for £1.0s.1d.

The dropping of so many haberdashery lines suggests that fewer women were now making their own clothes, preferring to buy ready-made.

Marks & Spencer's target customers, who in its early market-stall days had been solidly working class, came to include lower-middle-class women too, but it still saw itself as very much in competition with Woolworths, with the same stained wood floors, wooden counters, opaque glass pendant lights (one electric, one gas, in case the electricity failed), with prices well below stores such as C&A (a 1920s arrival from the Netherlands), but with the emphasis on 'quality'. But Marks & Spencer's main competitor was the Co-op, which in 1938 was selling a third of all women's and children's clothes (the Co-op was particularly strong in underwear and overalls, less so in fashion, which is where M&S scored). Marks & Spencer's solid middle-class customer base was not established until after the Second World War, though in the thirties there was a 'flattening out' of distinctions between the dress codes of different classes, and M&S undoubtedly contributed to that. Some wealthy customers reputedly also took to that level playing field, with the excuse that they were buying not for themselves but 'for their maid'.

Many branches of Marks & Spencer had been rebuilt and extended in the 1920s; more were built or rebuilt in the South and the Midlands during the early years of the slump. In 1930 a new store was built in the mining town of Bishop Auckland in County Durham, one in Glasgow, and another in Sunderland; in 1931 stores in Middlesbrough, Paisley and Wigan were enlarged; and in 1933, the worst year of the slump, new shops opened in Halifax, Rotherham and Rochdale. A large London store had opened at Marble Arch in 1930, and in October 1938 another flagship 'superstore' opened in Oxford Street, the 20,000-square-foot 'Pantheon', on the site of James Wyatt's 'Palace of Pleasures', built in 1772 (the original façade having been shipped to the Surrealist patron Edward James in Sussex).

Other stores that flourished in the 1930s included food chains such as Home & Colonial, Sainsbury's, Liptons, Dewhursts the Butchers and, rather surprisingly, Mac Fisheries, a chain of fishmongers set up by Lord Leverhulme after the First World War to sell the catch of the fishermen of Lewis and Harris; the Southern chemist and hardware chain Timothy Whites; clothes shops like Dorothy Perkins (named after the popular climbing rose, its shops were cottagey, its logo a crinolined lady), Evans Outsize, Cresta Silks (for which Wells Coates had designed several shops), C&A, which soon had stores in Liverpool, Birmingham and Manchester as well as London; W.H. Smiths, Littlewoods, the Times Furnishing Company, and the shoe-shop chains Freeman, Hardy & Willis, Dolcis and Lilley & Skinner.

Lewis's of Liverpool was a department store that behaved like a chain store: it had branches in Manchester, Birmingham and Glasgow, all industrial cities that had 'an industrial population of more or less the same character'. The shops were of as standard a design as practicable, and one buyer controlled the purchasing of merchandise for all four stores, which allowed 'all the economies of bulk purchasing to be enjoyed and also materially reduces the actual buying expense itself'. This was a form of rationalisation 'unique not only [in Britain] but so far as is known, in the world', and in 1932 there were plans afoot to 'control the whole process of production and distribution . . . from the raw material upwards' – a route Marks & Spencer's and other chain stores were also developing.

The chains carried a uniformity of lines, and their identifiable brand was carried through in their logos and also often repeated in the standard-isation of the architecture (or refurbishment) of the buildings which signalled their presence in whichever high street or shopping parade they were located. Boots, for example, which had favoured mock-medieval timbering before the First World War (and occasionally afterwards, in Farnham in Surrey in 1930, for example), switched to neo-Georgian designs, followed by the sort of classicism that gave its shops the gravitas of a 'vener-able financial institution', though sometimes they were designed to fit in with other buildings, particularly if they were in a historic town such as Colchester, Norwich or Cambridge, or given a 'frankly modern' treatment in newer industrial cities such as Coventry (1932), Liverpool (c.1935) and Leeds (c.1935) for example.

Montague Burton, the 'Tailor of Taste' (who negotiated the purchase of sites for new shops through a third party so the firm would not be iden-tified and, Burton feared, overcharged), set up its own architects' department in 1932, which produced classical façades, often decorated with Art Deco motifs such as chevrons and sunbursts, and in Wolverhampton and Halifax magnificent, angular elephants' heads. Burton was a teetotaller and a supporter of the Temperance Movement, and his larger shops might have a billiard or snooker hall on the top floor, so men could relax in an alcohol-free environment, having also perhaps been lured into the shop itself *en passant* to make a purchase.

Marks & Spencer appointed Robert Lutyens, the son of the eminent architect of New Delhi and the Cenotaph, Sir Edwin Lutyens, as its consultant architect in 1934, and to ensure the uniformity of M&S stores wherever they were, Lutyens designed a grid system with flat-fronted stone-clad façades. However, the Pantheon in Oxford Street was superior in every way, faced in 'ebony' granite (a material much favoured by Burton's too), with walnut counters and wall panelling. Cafés, teashops and fish bars had become popular in Marks & Spencer's stores as in Woolworths, and the Pantheon was equipped with the ultimate word in chic, a Manhattan-style 'luncheonette', its walls clad in primrose and black vitroline, with red leather-covered stools providing seating for 150.

Woolworths stores were mostly built of solid red brick during the 1930s, with Crittall metal windows, and often with a weighing machine in the lobby that could be used even when the shop was shut. Their architecture tended to be less uniform than that of Marks & Spencer, and was, like Boots, sometimes sympathetic to the local vernacular, with a neo-Georgian branch in Bath and mock-timbered shops in Kingston upon Thames and Lincoln. Woolworths' most dramatic shops were the 'superstores', which Montague Burton admired as 'American sky-scraper architecture', built in Blackpool, Brixton, Dudley, Morecambe, Preston, Southend, Sunderland and the Edgware Road in London. The most thrilling of all was in Lewisham in South-East London, which looked much more like a cinema, a veritable 'palace of dreams', than a mundane chain store selling nothing over sixpence.

Several architecturally distinguished department stores became part of the London cityscape in the 1930s – and one didn't: Daniel Neal's children's clothes shop in Kensington High Street, planned with baroque towers, arches and a pergola'd roof garden, was never built. D.H. Evans (which was then owned by Harrods, as were Dickins & Jones and Kendal Milne in Manchester) was designed with elegant soaring mullioned windows which looked rather skyscraper-like, by the architect of Harrods, J.S. Beaumont, who also designed Kendal Milne's new store in Manchester (which unfortunately was requisitioned by the civil service as soon as it was finished in 1940; it was not until after the war that it opened as a shop). Sir Edwin Lutyens had a hand in the design of Gamages in Holborn, while some stores such as Welwyn department store in the Garden City and John Barnes in Swiss Cottage, North London, were planned with flats on the upper storeys, because by the mid-1930s it had become smart to live in a flat.

The architect for Simpson's in Piccadilly (1935–36) was Joseph Emberton, who had designed the Olympia exhibition hall and several shops for Austin Reed, and who greatly admired Erich Mendelsohn's De la Warr Pavilion at Bexhill. Simpson's, which had seven floors devoted to men's wear (women's came later), had 'glascrete' canopies at ground and top-floor level, and neon strips on the fascia that pierced the dark. Peter Jones in Sloane Square (1936–39), which was owned by John Lewis, had broad horizontal bands of glass curving round the corner into the King's Road. A survey in the *Architectural Review* voted it the best modern building of the year by a wide margin.

Innovatory shops were being built all over Britain: Whitaker's in Bolton, Kingstone's in Leicester, the Urmston Gas Showrooms in Manchester, St Cuthbert's Co-operative Association furnishing store in Edinburgh, Randall's furniture store in Uxbridge, an extension to Fenwick's in Newcastle, Bradford Co-op, 'His Master's Voice' gramophone store, rebuilt after a fire in 1936 with an amazing pictorial neon façade setting Oxford Street ablaze with colour.

But it wasn't architecturally distinguished buildings that drew in the shoppers, it was what was on offer inside. The escalators in the modern stores whisked customers up, but were designed to make their descent slow, since they had to walk through each floor on their way down, impulse-buying on the way, it was hoped. Special features included the neon-lit circular basement barber's shop in Austin Reed's flagship Regent Street store, and the elegant 'Rainbow Room' restaurant at Derry & Toms in Kensington, built between 1929 and 1933. Customers taking tea at Kennards of Croydon were entertained by 'the strains of light music from the inevitable trio or quartette [sic], often of ladies only, hidden behind a bank of palms and plants'. 'Why go to the West End – there's Bentall's of Kingston' advertised another suburban department store which hosted baby shows, bought the floral decorations from the Royal Box at Ascot every year, imported a Lancashire 'Cotton Queen', Marjorie Knowles, chosen from among mill operatives, and serenaded its customers with a gipsy band one week and a czardas band the next as they travelled up and down the escalators. Bentall's rivalled the attraction of aviatrix Amy Johnson at Selfridges by displaying Malcolm Campbell's *Bluebird*, which had just broken the world land speed record, in its windows, put on a circus with the lion kept overnight in the lift shaft, and even brought over a Swedish gymnast to dive sixty-three feet down the escalator hall into a tank of water twice a week. Not to be outdone, Selfridges signed up Suzanne Lenglen, six times Wimbledon ladies singles champion, to give demonstrations on a temporarily erected court in September 1933. In 1930 Kennards hired three baby elephants to promote their 'Jumbo Sale', while Simpson's arranged for three light aircraft to land on their roof. When the Prince of Wales launched a massive 'Buy British' campaign in March 1932, Selfridges invited the Mayor and Master Cutler of Sheffield to fill 6,000 square feet with their city's steel products; at the same time, the store's windows were filled with a million pounds worth of diamonds, displayed in special burglar-proof glass octagonal cases. This was a particularly odd juxtaposition, since a year before, in June 1931, Selfridges staff, apprised of the fact that in the slump money was flowing out of the business faster than it was flowing in, offered to work until 7 p.m. with no overtime. Contests to find 'Miss England' were held in the same store, and 27,000 people crowded in to watch the US and British bridge champions play in a special soundproof room. There was a stylish mannequin theatre in the magnificent new Derry & Toms store in Kensington High Street, finished in 1933, and since department stores found their cosmetic and perfumery departments particularly profitable, most had hairdressing salons, beauty parlours and manicure lounges: warts could be removed free at Selfridges, and corns winkled out at Kennards.

But above all it was the roof gardens that were the biggest draw in the thirties: the one on the East Ham branch of the London Co-operative Society, which opened in May 1935, boasted 'a cafeteria, flowerbeds, crazy golf, rookery nooks, lily pond, fountain, kiddies playground, giant telescope, and many other attractions'. One day Marjory Allen, a landscape architect, had followed a group of maintenance men onto 'a vast grey empty expanse [of roof] stretching from one end of [Selfridges Oxford Street] store to the other.' It had not always been unused: there had been a golf training school, and later an ice rink up there, plus occasional costume balls in the 1920s. 'The sun was brilliant, the air fresh, and I thought with regret of all those salesgirls, secretaries and office workers . . . eating their lunch sandwiches in the dim recesses of the underworld. Why not put a few seats up here for them? Why not make a garden where they could enjoy some peaceful relaxation? Why not have an outdoor exhibition of sculpture?' Anxious to help establish her new profession (the Institute of Landscape Architects had only been founded in 1929), Allen persuaded Gordon Selfridge to allow her to design such a garden at minimal cost. '"Anything that attracts people into my store is good for business," he said. "None of them will be able to resist spending a few shillings."' He got Marjory Allen to inscribe her name on his window with his diamond – 'This was our contract.'

It was a considerable challenge: soil could be laid no more than eighteen inches deep because of the weight, and hundreds of tons of earth, rocks, stones and a thousand tons of 'rich country loam and farmyard manure' had to be transported by lift in the early hours of the morning before the store opened, but in six months it was complete, and it opened in the spring of 1930. There was an English garden filled with 'old fashioned flowers – stocks, pinks, snapdragons, wallflowers, lupins, lavender, roses', hollyhocks six feet tall, a cherry-tree walk, vine walks, a clematis-covered gazebo, fantail pigeons that bathed in a pool and nested in dovecots designed by the Surrealist painter Julian Trevelyan's son. There was a rose garden, a winter garden, a scent garden, and a view north to Hampstead Heath. In all 60,000 plants a year were planted, including 30,000 spring bulbs. Thirty-five thousand people a week came 'to bask in the sun, surrounded by lovely flowers and cool pools . . . [finding] real peace and grace, away above the noise and fumes of the street'. Shoppers came for lunch, coffee, tea, to see mannequin shows and the sculpture displays – including the work of Jacob Epstein and Henry Moore. The gardens bloomed for three years, but then the management 'decided to use them for the display of garden equipment, including gnomes, toadstools and other God-wottery'. They fell into disuse, and were closed during the Blitz, but in 1941 Selfridges' roof was again turned into a garden, this time a victory one growing vegetables to supplement wartime rations.

Ambitious though Selfridges' horticulture-in-the-sky may have been, by far the grandest roof garden was the one and a half acres that covered the roof of Derry & Toms, laid out between 1936 and 1938 and comprising a Spanish garden based on the Alhambra in Granada, a Tudor-style garden, and an English woodland garden with over thirty species of trees, all surmounted by the perfect exotic touch, pink flamingos picking their way delicately through the plants.

With 'destination stores' such as these, it was hardly surprising that small, independent 'speciality' shops were being squeezed out. The department stores and chain stores snapped up prime locations – Gordon Selfridge bought up every shop that came up for sale in the vicinity of Selfridges so he could expand – forcing smaller establishments to relocate to side streets, depending increasingly on the loyalty of existing customers. The success of the 'speciality shop', Lawrence Neal wrote, depended on 'the first-hand knowledge and personality of its proprietor, and other characteristics of enthusiasm and initiative which will always enable it to out-distance less intelligent competition'.

Every town would have several such small shops, often called 'Madam Someone's' if, as they often did, they sold women's wear, where personal service would be paramount, customers' tastes remembered and their foibles pandered to. Eileen Lawrence's mother patronised 'a large drapers known as Aldis and Hutchings [in Wallington, Surrey] . . . We were always treated as VIPs when we shopped there . . . The head buyer, Miss Atkinson, [came] forward when Mother entered the "Baby Linen", for instance, and [we were] given chairs to sit in while we made a leisurely selection of some tiny garment or other . . . The same treatment was given to us when we shopped in Croydon at the large drapers known as Rowbotham's, where our family was also known to the owners. Shop-walkers, or buyers, as they were called, were very important people in their sphere and could command instant attention from their staff to look after a customer's needs.'

'Looking after a customer's needs' could, unfortunately, be something of a euphemism. The Mass-Observation survey found that one reason women liked shopping for clothes in department stores was that staff in many small clothes shops in city centres were paid on commission, and tended to be Jewish. Hence the commonplace anti-Semitic remarks about 'falling into the clutches of the Jewish type of saleswoman, who will over-persuade you with glib patter', whereas it was the commission system that made it imperative for the sales person to secure a sale from anyone who walked through the door if at all possible, otherwise their wage packet would suffer, and possibly their job might be on the line.

NINETEEN

Holy Deadlock

Have you any views of loving your own sex? All the young men are so inclined, and I can't help finding it foolish; though I have no particular reason, at the moment.

Virginia Woolf to Jacques Raverat, 24 January 1925

Who are the girls who have voted for the marriage bar? Nine out of ten swing daily to their offices in suburban trains and trams and buses, carrying in their suitcases a powder puff and a love story or *Home Chat* . . . they think on foggy mornings when the alarm clock goes, that they loathe above every-thing the scramble to the office. They think if only they could marry and have a little home of their own all will be well.

Winifred Holtby, 31 January 1930

I would like to have married Robert . . . but he was a total pederast . . . This wretched pederasty falsifies all feelings & yet one is supposed to revere it.

Nancy Mitford writing to her sister Jessica about Robert Byron

When Edward VIII abdicated, he had given as his reason, his wish to marry 'the woman he loved'. But in December 1936 Wallis Simpson was not free to marry the King or anyone else. She was still married to Edward Simpson, whom she had sued for divorce on grounds of his adultery, which he had not denied, and had been granted a decree nisi on 27 October 1936. Neither Wallis nor Ernest, however, would be free to remarry until a decree absolute was granted, and that usually took six months. So it would not be until at least May 1937 (the month of his planned coronation) that the ex-King would be able to take the American 'adventuress' as his bride.

The reason for this two-stage process was so that enquiries could be made to ensure that the grounds on which a divorce was granted were genuine, and there had been no collusion between the two parties. Divorce by consent, which might have seemed the simplest way to end a marriage, was not an option. Moreover, adultery was the only grounds on which a marriage could be dissolved. In order to obtain a divorce, there had to be an 'innocent' and a 'guilty' party, and Mrs Simpson's innocence seemed suspect. She was probably the King's mistress, and it was rumoured that she had (or had had) other lovers too. It was just such undefended divorces that the King's Proctor (a government lawyer) would investigate to make sure that the 'innocent' party really was innocent, that no one had been lying. If he found evidence that all was not as it should be, he could intervene in the process, put the facts before the court and have the decree rescinded, which would stop the husband and wife from remarrying. It did not have to be the King's Proctor who took this step: any private individual could pay five shillings in order to fulfil the same function, providing evidence as to why the decree nisi should not be made absolute.

In the case of Edward and Mrs Simpson, there were those who thought that the King must be 'saved from himself': if Mrs Simpson's divorce could not go through, and the King could therefore not marry her, why would he need to abdicate? But in fact Edward was in a privileged position: given the principle that 'the King can do no wrong', the Simpson divorce case could not be investigated while he was on the throne, since such an investigation might involve him. But once he abdicated, the King's Proctor could get on the case straight away. So Edward's best course would have been to stay on the throne until May 1937, when the decree would be made absolute, since it had not been possible to investigate it. By then, who knows, government and people might (just possibly) have become reconciled to the prospect of Queen Wallis. But this option was anathema to the government, as it was to the impatient, lovesick King. And in any case, there was nothing to stop a patriotic citizen from suggesting that there were dirty deeds afoot (the couple's 'comings and goings' as the Home Secretary, Sir John Simon, put it) that called for an enquiry.

Somehow, the decree absolute had to be expedited, either by bringing pressure on the divorce court (the waiting period was occasionally shortened if there was a pressing reason, such as the imminent birth of a child who would otherwise be illegitimate) or by special Act of Parliament. But the government refused to do either of these things. Everyone waited anxiously for the 'citizen's intervention' which they felt sure would come. Mrs Simpson, who had declined the advice of her own solicitor to withdraw her petition for divorce, urged Edward to 'get the legal side fitted up' – that is, to appeal to the new King, George VI, to instruct the Attorney General to 'suppress the suit'.

Indeed, a solicitor's clerk did exercise his right of intervention, claiming that Mrs Simpson had not disclosed that she had 'habitually committed adultery' with the King. He then tried to retract, apparently satisfied that Edward's abdication put an end to the matter, but this was not legally possible, and the papers were referred to the King's Proctor, Sir Thomas Barnes. By this time the King's Proctor had received shoals of letters complaining that there seemed to be one law for the rich and another for the poor, and that there was a conspiracy to protect the King. He decided that the time had come when he must investigate the circumstances of the Simpsons' divorce.

Government legal officers were dispatched all over the country, from Newcastle to Cornwall, to collect evidence – if evidence there was. The staff of the *Rosaura*, the yacht on which the King and Mrs Simpson been guests in 1934, were interviewed, and admitted having examined the sheets on Mrs Simpson's bed, but found no telltale marks of sexual activity on them. The captain of the *Nahlin* (the yacht on which they had cruised the Mediterranean in the summer of 1936) also denied any evidence of intimacy. Amazingly, Wallis Simpson's maid was not interviewed, on the grounds that her first loyalty would be to her employer, nor were members of the Royal Household, though the King's Proctor interviewed Mr Simpson himself.

A formal hearing before the President of the Probate Divorce and Admiralty Division of the High Court was held on 19 March 1937. It concluded that the Simpson divorce case had been treated no differently from any other, that gossip in the Garrick Club and the foreign press did not add up to 'evidence', and that there was indeed 'no evidence whatever' of anything that would be a bar to Mrs Simpson obtaining her divorce. She and the Duke of Windsor were married on 3 June 1937 in France.

But as Stephen Cretney, who has made an exhaustive study of the case, points out, the servants, surely the people most likely to be able to provide firm evidence of 'intimacy', were not questioned. Moreover, Special Branch reports which spoke of Mr Simpson as being 'of the bounder type', and of Mrs Simpson as being 'very partial to coloured men', and of having 'another secret lover' – a well-bred car dealer – and which were in the hands of the Metropolitan Police Commissioner, Sir Philip Game, were, amazingly, not considered at all. It is hard to shake off the suspicion of, if not a cover-up, then some sort of wilful refusal to look too closely into the case, since with the abdication firmly behind and the coronation ahead, there must have been a strong desire to see the ex-King dispatched, rather than a reopening and mauling over of what might turn out to be a rather unworthy and sordid episode.

At the very time that the Simpson divorce was under the spotlight, legislation was going through Parliament that would change Britain's divorce laws for the first time in eighty years. A[lan]. P[atrick]. Herbert was a brilliant barrister who did not practise law but instead wrote light operas, comic musicals and books, including a best-selling novel about living on canal barges, *The Water Gipsies* (1930). He was also a regular contributor to *Punch*, writing articles, verse and a regular column, 'Misleading Cases', which satirised the anomalies of the law. In 1935 Herbert was elected as an Independent MP for Oxford University (after a campaign orchestrated by Frank Pakenham, later Lord Longford). The previous year he had published *Holy Deadlock*, a fictionalised indictment of the nonsenses – and cruelties – of the current law on divorce: 'If two young persons made a mistake and married: and did their best to make the partnership work: and after seven years agreed that it could not be done: and decided that the false partnership ought to be brought to an end: and made some friendly honourable plans to do so – that was some kind of criminal offence. There was no decent way in which that mistake could be wiped out.' That was why the novel's protagonist, a publisher of school books, was 'behaving like a gentleman' and 'travelling down to Brighton with a strange young woman in a first-class carriage' in order to provide evidence of adultery which would enable his wife to petition for the divorce they both wanted.

Herbert set out to right the wrongs his novel had described: he introduced a Private Member's Bill in November 1936, not, as he explained, 'because I am a lifelong Bohemian who is anxious for sexual licence ... but because I believe it will bring new strength to the institution of the family'. Quoting the Archdeacon of Coventry, he continued: 'as the law stands at present those who wish to bring an end to the marriage were forced to take one of two alternatives – either one must commit adultery or one must commit perjury. The law as it stands is a distinct incitement to immorality ... An extension of the grounds of divorce does not necessarily mean making divorce easier.' As well as being an 'incitement to immorality' the law meant, in effect, that the rich could divorce by mutual consent, an option not open to others. In fact Herbert's Bill was cautious, being largely based on the recommendations of a 1912 Royal Commission, and he was always careful to carry the Church (or rather the non-Roman Catholic Church) with him (albeit guardedly and rather confusedly). The 500,000-strong Mothers' Union, however, was vociferous in its opposition, as it was to birth control and abortion: no divorced woman could become a member, nor could any woman guilty of 'infidelity', though that was harder to track. Herbert was subjected to an avalanche of 'fiery' postcards and resolutions from MU branches concerned about the spectre of a 'woman in her forties, no longer young or particularly attractive', whose better-preserved and better-looking husband 'might easily fall for someone younger and more entertaining' and cast her off without an income or a home of her own. The MU might have consoled itself with the fact that between 1931 and 1935 (that is, prior to Herbert's Bill) over half of divorce petitions had been filed by women.

After a somewhat cliffhanging passage through the Commons and the Lords, the Matrimonial Causes Act became law on 1 January 1938. Henceforth people could petition for divorce after three years of marriage (less in very exceptional circumstances), and the grounds could be adultery, desertion, cruelty, habitual drunkenness, or if one of the parties was of 'incurably unsound mind'. A wife could also petition if her husband was guilty of rape (of another woman), sodomy or bestiality. This was far from no-fault divorce, nor did it make it any easier for those – particularly women with children – without independent means to contemplate divorce: that would take another thirty years. But it was an improvement on the hypocrisy of earlier legislation that forced parties into the farce of being 'surprised' by a chambermaid in bed with a paid colluder (having probably spent the night sitting up playing cards, drinking or sleeping in separate beds), with the hotel bill being cited in evidence. Since 90 per cent of petitions after the passing of the Act were undefended, obviously collusion continued. And despite the fears of the MU, the stability of marriage was probably not much affected.

The cost of divorce remained a deterrent for most (though since 1920 'Poor Person's' undefended divorces could be heard in various assize towns, which reduced the cost, rather than at the High Court in London; hence Ipswich for the Simpsons, though for rather different reasons). Those with incomes under £2 a week, or in special circumstances up to £4, might be able to obtain some legal aid at the discretion of the Law Society, since divorce cases, though heard in the civil courts, could not be settled out of court and had to be bought to trial. After the Act the number of Poor Persons seeking divorces rose slowly, but it remained a small percentage of those seeking divorce, which rose by almost 60 per cent to 7,935 in 1938. Nearly 70 per cent had been married for ten years or more, and perhaps surprisingly, the number of divorces on the grounds of adultery did not rise significantly. The increase was mainly due to those seeking a divorce on grounds of desertion, or much less often, cruelty or insanity. This suggests that the 1937 Act allowed people who had long wished to end their marriage to at last be able to do so, rather than, as critics of the Bill had charged, destabilising the institution of marriage.

However, until the after the Second World War the less well off were more likely to separate than to divorce, since the cost of a divorce was around £50, or more than £100 if the case was defended, and though legislation in the 1920s had allowed that a wife could be awarded a small sum for her own maintenance and up to £1 a week for each child, this could stretch the resources of a working man to breaking point. By the early 1930s men who had defaulted on maintenance payments to their families constituted 7 per cent of the prison population. Moreover, for the middle classes – as opposed to the upper classes – divorce, though accepted, still carried a considerable social stigma, and many solicitors were reluctant to accept matrimonial work, since it was felt to be unpopular with their predominantly middle-class clientèle.

Gladys Langford had been in a 'less than angelic temper' for some time, finding that the children she taught at an elementary school in Islington 'smell and are lazy, have vermin and sores on them'. However, on Boxing Day 1937 she felt '*much* improved in spirits after a violent bout of love-making, more befitting Cleopatra than me. Stanley [her intermittent, younger lover] came this afternoon and we made the very most of our hour and a half together. *He* was quite exhausted when he left, but I was merely gleeful. I am forty-seven and two thirds [and Langford considered herself to be "of enormous bulk" – she weighed ten stone seven pounds] and am still able to rouse him to a frenzy . . . couldn't settle down to reading after this afternoon's excitement.'

Langford might have found such snatched sex temporarily satisfying, but what she desperately longed for was marriage: she had been married once, twenty-three years previously, but her husband, George, had left her almost immediately, and the marriage had been annulled. An intelligent, educated (for her time), cultured woman in a job she found unfulfilling and badly paid, her fate was to move from small flatlet to small flatlet, sharing a bathroom and kitchen or cooking on a gas ring on the landing, feeding pennies into a meter, continually petitioning her landlady for 'something to be done about the dirty beige patterned wallpaper' and chipped paint. She later moved into a small residential hotel in Highbury, North London, where she was scornful of the other residents who shared the breakfast table day after day, irritated by their conversation and repulsed by their appearance and physical habits. Langford was socially – and sexually – frustrated. 'I didn't realise how sex hungry I was,' she confided to her diary, 'until I realised that no strange man touched me in the Tatler' (a local cinema). She was highly critical, and becoming more so as her hopes of a relationship that would develop into a proposal of marriage rather than occasional snatched, illicit sex, were constantly confounded. 'I *wish* "Darling Charles" [or Stanley or Roger] would marry me' was a frequent diary entry.

Gladys Langford was typical of no one but herself – and she was hardly a young woman by the 1930s – but her predicament flags up what could be the lot of the unmarried, unmoneyed woman in the 1930s, with limited career opportunities and a perceived shortage of eligible men. Marriage was seen as the normal state, the only ambition for all young girls except the exceptionally well-educated, ambitious and independent, and a high premium was put on the security of family life and home ownership.

There was an abundance of advice for the so called 'bachelor girl', that semi-glamorous figure who later in the century would evolve into the well-paid 'singleton' with her (short-term) elected independence and sociable community of like-minded others. 'Agony aunts' in women's magazines tended to be bracing. In 1934 'Alex', who had grown bored with the domesticity of marriage was firmly reproved : 'Just think how many women would gladly give up their so-called independence to have a home and a husband of their own, to have the chance of making a success of married life and a home. Women who will never have that chance because the war took their lovers and their husbands and made them the real tragedy and pathos of our times – the surplus women.' In the years of Depression the advice of such 'aunts' took a more overtly economic turn. They were particularly keen that a young woman should 'better herself' by marriage: in December 1929 *Peg's Paper* advised a woman to drop her fiancé of two years, 'as there seems no prospect of him ever going to be in a position to marry you', since he was unemployed.

Although a number of magazines for women started in the 1930s – *Woman's Own* in 1932, *Woman's Illustrated* in 1936 and *Woman* in 1937 (which was selling three quarters of a million copies a week by 1939) – they all concentrated on the concerns of married women, particularly those women 'worth their salt' who wanted to be 'the best housewife ever . . . and then some'. This tendency reached its apogee in *Housewife*, launched in 1939 with the proclamation, 'Happy and lucky is the man whose wife is houseproud . . . who likes to do things well, to make him proud of her and her children.' Such mass-sale magazines, with their apparent conviction that happiness was only obtainable via 'a husband, a cosy home and kiddies', must have seemed designed to make a spinster feel an incomplete woman staring into a world of pullover patterns, late-flowering herbaceous borders and milk teeth that she could never fully enter.

There was, however, ostensibly, help at hand. Significantly perhaps, along with the label 'bachelor girl' itself, most advice manuals for her species originated in America, such as the bracing *Live Alone and Like It: A Guide for the Extra Woman* by Marjorie Hillis, published in Britain in 1936, which was full of rousing exhortations on such subjects as 'A Lady and Her Liquor', 'Etiquette for the Lone Female' and 'The Pleasure of the Single Bed', though most such manuals still carried the underlying assumption that the single life was a transient state before this fun-loving 'extra woman' attracted (or snared) a husband. As Hillis wrote: 'This book is no brief in favour of living alone. Five out of ten of the people who do so can't help themselves, and at least three of the others are irritatingly selfish. But the chances are that some time in your life, possibly now and then between husbands, you will find yourself settling down to a solitary existence.' Hillis recognised that the 'problem of the solitary woman is . . . intrinsically more intricate than that of the solitary male. The lonely male, no matter how unprepossessing, really has no problem. He just looks for an unattached female – usually unprepossessing – and goes on looking until he finds one. One might think that the female would simply reverse the process and search assiduously for the unattached male. But it isn't as easy as that. In the first place, she mustn't appear to be looking . . . the lonely male is an elusive creature, once he realises he is being fished for. He is too shy or too cunning to be caught, or else, once hooked, he proves so unbelievably dreary that he has to be thrown back again.' There were ways of 'hooking' a man, Hillis believed, but they did not include domestic 'hobbies': 'modern men don't like to be sewn and knitted at'. She advised taking up new interests such as 'astrology, numerology, palmistry, graphology and tarot', and using them 'to intrigue and waylay men'.

For working-class girls there was always the 'monkey parade' of a summer evening or a Sunday afternoon, strutting youth on the lookout for a date, while for their middle-class sisters advice tended to be more discreet. They were advised to 'go where men are' by joining a tennis club, taking ball-room-dancing lessons or attending dances, which were reckoned to be the most likely places for 'picking up' and 'getting off with' the opposite sex, or even learning to fly. Hillis thought one answer might be to merge 'University Clubs [male] and all the fashionable women's hostelries: fifty per cent of the clubmen to move into the hostelries, and fifty per cent of the vestals to flutter into the clubs'.

There were advertisements: *Matrimonial Times* proclaimed itself to be a 'bona fide medium for introductions', and carried pleas from advertisers such as 'Spinster, 31, looks 25', '50, but pass as 40', 'Spinster, 31, not painfully plain COLINDALE'. In April 1939 Britain's first marriage bureau opened in New Bond Street, Mayfair, after having been refused a licence by the

LCC the previous year. Its proprietors were two ultra-respectable single women, both of whom had been debutantes: Heather Jenner (daughter of a Brigadier-General) and Mary Oliver (whose father was a country vicar). On the first day 250 applicants wrote in, telephoned or turned up at the door. In the first months Jenner and Oliver took on as clients wealthy widows, retired generals, tea planters on leave, farmers, an artificial-limb maker, an MP, teachers, nannies, shorthand typists, shop assistants, insurance clerks, a plumber, a woman surgeon and a female dentist, actresses, a master from Eton and the widow and daughter of an earl (different earls). Half those seeking a life partner were men: they were charged five guineas to register and dunned for twenty guineas on their wedding day (if there was one), while women were charged according to their means, which might mean only ten shillings.

The desire for love, companionship, a home, children, is of course not specific to any one decade. There had been a perceived 'problem' of 'surplus women' since the 1890s, and the carnage of the First World War, when over three quarters of a million British and Dominion men were killed on active service, had added to the problem, creating a 'lost generation' of potential husbands. This was coupled with the fact that the mortality rate was higher among baby boys than girls. According to the 1921 census there were 1,720,802 more women than men in Britain: that meant 1,096 women to every thousand men. This was against a background of a long-term falling birthrate and a trend for smaller families – women married in 1880s had an average of 4.6 children; by 1930 it was around 2.19. At least the attractions of Empire were no longer draining off eligible young men in the way they had before the First World War – 750,000 of them between 1901 and 1910 – so that so-called 'fishing fleets' of not-quite-so-young-any-more women had been obliged to travel to India and other far-flung lands to find someone to marry.

By the 1930s women were out in the world, visible in society, employment, politics and the economy in numbers and ways that they had not been before the First World War. Since 1923 Oxford had caught up with London and provincial universities in awarding degrees to women (Cambridge held out until 1948), though the number of women undergraduates was tiny compared to men. In 1936 only around 500,000 girls were receiving secondary education in state or local-authority schools, while those who could afford to would send their daughters to boarding school or one of the girls' public day schools, most of which had high academic standards and ambitions for their pupils, or would have them educated at home.

Women over twenty-one had been allowed to stand for Parliament since 1918, and were granted the vote on equal terms with men ten years later. The first woman MP to take her seat (Nancy Astor) did so in 1919, and Margaret Bondfield, who admitted that she 'just lived for the Trade Union Movement', with 'a concentration undisturbed by love affairs', was appointed Minister of Labour, Britain's first woman Cabinet minister, in 1929. Although the first female Justice of the Peace had not been appointed until 1920, by 1931 there were around 4,000 woman JPs and magistrates: these were largely middle- and upper-middle-class women, unpaid and untrained (unless they sought training out for themselves, which many did), since 'common sense' was regarded as the only necessary qualification.

The 1919 Sex Disqualification (Removal) Act had given women the theoretical right to 'assume or carry on any civil profession or vocation', though that is hardly what happened. The Synod of the Church of England would not admit women, nor would the Stock Exchange, and while women could enter the Civil Service, they could not take overseas postings. Women had made great strides in medicine during the First World War, but after-wards their contribution to the health of the nation was not encouraged, except as nurses – most London hospitals would no longer accept women as medical students (University College and the Royal Free were excep-tions), usually on the grounds that they would only get married and waste their training. Those who had already qualified in medicine were invari-ably general practitioners (often in partnership with their husbands) or worked in clinics: female consultants were extremely rare in the 1930s, even in gynaecology and obstetrics. Women did not manage to penetrate many other professions very successfully either: in 1928 there were twenty-one women members of the RIBA in a sea of nearly 6,000 male architects; there were two female structural and two female civil engineers, and one solitary female mechanical engineer.

Helena Normanton had applied to the Middle Temple in 1918 and was refused entry, but when she applied again within forty-eight hours of the passing of the Sex Disqualification (Removal) Bill (which she had helped bring about), her application was accepted, and she was called to the Bar in November 1922, only the second woman barrister in Britain.

Normanton, unusually, was married (though childless, and she refused to take her husband's name), as was Nancy Astor – indeed she took over her husband Waldorf's Plymouth seat when he went to the Lords. While the modern notion of combining a career with a family was not unknown, it was extremely rare (juggling the demands of low-paid work with the care of children was, of necessity, a different matter for working-class women). In 1931, out of a total of five and a half to six million women in the workforce, around one and a half million worked in public administration, commerce and the professions, and another one and a half million found jobs in the new, expanding light industries of South-East England and the Midlands. The vast majority of these were single. Essentially – of course there were exceptions – middle-class married women did not work outside the home, even before they had children, and the assumption (if not the practice) held true for working-class women too, as the 1931 Anomalies Act showed. In 1931, 84 per cent of the female workforce was single, widowed or divorced.

It wasn't only the responsibilities of caring for a family that fuelled objections to married women in the workplace. There were reservations about a woman's 'proper' role, a carry-over from the fear of 'dilution' from the First World War, sharpened in the years of unemployment, that women would undercut men's wages and take their jobs, and women found themselves refused 'men's jobs'. Sir Herbert Austin, who employed a large workforce of women in his car factories, nevertheless wrote vehemently to *The Times* in September 1933: 'I don't think a woman's place is in industry. If we were to take women out of industry, I believe we could absorb all the unemployment. I think that men ought to be doing the work instead of women.'

The principle was enshrined that a man should be paid a 'family wage' (though thousands weren't), and that if a married woman worked, she was merely doing so for 'pin money'. Ellen Wilkinson put the argument succinctly: 'Men say that they ought not to be expected to keep a wife and family on the same wage a single woman gets for keeping herself. To which women reply that single men get the same wage as married men, and that many have family responsibilities.' But most married women were denied the opportunity to continue in employment. The so-called 'marriage bar' operated in the Civil Service (except in the Treasury, which had the discretionary power to retain married women, but had only exercised it eight times by 1937), in medicine – including nursing – in teaching, and in numerous private firms.

The BBC, at first committed to welcoming women on equal terms with men, had a *volte face* in 1934, deciding to dismiss women when they married on the grounds that they would be taking jobs from single women who had no other means of support. But it seems the true motivation was more than concern for the single sisterhood. In 1939 a BBC executive sketched a scenario: 'Take a regular management meeting – every Monday morning say. It's a closely knit little circle of men meeting. It knows its own mores, language – and then suddenly a species with entirely different reactions is introduced into it . . . They don't like it.' And it was significant that the marriage bar at the BBC did not apply to lavatory attendants, cleaners – or wardrobe mistresses, since it was 'normal custom [for] women of this class' to work outside the home.

In 1931 the average age at marriage was twenty-seven for men and twenty-five for women – though working-class couples tended to marry younger than middle-classes ones. While only 34 per cent of women between the ages of fifteen and thirty-nine were married in 1901, this had increased to 41 per cent by 1931. That still left a not inconsiderable part of the female population single (including those who were widowed or divorced): in 1931 a third of women who had not married by the age of twenty-nine would not do so – at least while they were still able to conceive. Most single women would have to support themselves while either living in the parental home, if that was practicable, in a hostel connected to their workplace, in 'digs' with a landlady, or in a small flat, usually with a shared bathroom and kitchen. They would invariably be less well paid than a man in whatever job they did, and they enjoyed no job security and rarely any pension scheme. And as a woman got older, and her colleagues married and became housewives and mothers, the overweening contemporary perception that this was what a woman was made for would add to her sense of isolation.

Before the First World War, the most usual occupation for a single working-class woman was domestic service. After 1918, many women having had a taste of independence (and better pay) in some sort of war work, this was the last thing most of them wanted to do, and they held out as long as they could until the slump and lack of jobs forced them back into service. But to be a servant in the inter-war years – and in 1931, 35 per cent of the women in the workforce were – was in many ways an even harder and more dreary existence than it had been before 1918, when there was a wider range of domestic positions to be had. They were, wrote the sociologist Joan Beauchamp in 1937, 'the Cinderellas of the labour market . . . obliged to slave from dawn to dusk for a miserable pittance'. Unlike the life of a woman who worked 'below stairs' in a grand house, with the camaraderie that involved, and where a live-in cook or housekeeper could earn £65 a year, that of a 'cook general' in a suburban villa could be harder and more lonely than one would like to contemplate. Pay could be as low as 12s.6d or fifteen shillings a week (food and board was 'found', though both could be minimal and of poor quality), and hours as long as the day, with half a day off midweek and every other Sunday, no visitors, no independent life. Hardly surprisingly, there was little rush for women to avail themselves of the schemes the government set up in the depressed areas during the worst of the slump to train them for such work.

Whereas traditionally there had been numbers of married women employed in the 'old industries', particularly textiles, and women were valued in the new electrical consumer industries for their small, nimble fingers that could twist wires and stitch car seats, in the 1930s most were very young – and single. In 1931, out of 50,000 or so women working in car manufacture and the electrical and clothing industries, 35,000 were under twenty-four, and of these 11,500 were under seventeen (many would be sacked when they reached eighteen, after which they would have had to be paid more). Their wages were less than those of men working in the same factories, and they were employed on unskilled, deadeningly repetitive tasks such as filling tubes with toothpaste, stuffing studs through shirt collars, fixing widgets or wiring radios. Increasingly, as in *Modern Times*, such labour was on a production line instead of piecework as it had been, and women had to work at an exhausting breakneck speed to keep up with the conveyor belt, with a rare five-minute toilet break.

Leonora Eyles, a journalist who had been deserted by her first husband and left to bring up their three children, and who subsequently married the editor of the *Times Literary Supplement*, David Murray, had made an immensely successful career as a novelist as well as writing for newspapers and magazines: she was the agony aunt for *Woman's Own* from its beginning in 1932, billed as 'the woman who understands'. Having been a single parent and poor herself, she wrote not only *Commonsense About Sex* (1933) but also *Careers for Women*, published in 1930, in which she stressed that 'the young woman of today' should have 'a trade or profession that enables her to support herself', though she was 'saddened' to note that 'Very rarely is the payment for women's work in the professions like teaching and medicine and science, which entail a big outlay of time and money, at all representative of the expenditure. Many women with high qualifications, after years of training, are getting something like £3 a week – in London.'

Taking a Keynesian approach, Eyles argued against the idea that women entering the workplace were 'taking the bread out of the mouths' of anyone at all: 'Work means wages and creates spending power which in turn creates demand for further service or commodities.' She instanced herself. The fact that she was a journalist, who kept poultry and had a garden, meant that she could pay the wages of others to look after her chickens and tend her herbaceous borders out of what she earned from writing. In this spirit she explored the jobs a woman could do, from entering the medical profession, massage and medical gymnastics, dairy farming, librarianship, being a mannequin or a kennel maid or even a veterinary surgeon, garment-making, the stage – and of course teaching, nursing, catering, office and shop work, all of which were considered suitable jobs for women.

By 1931 there were some 200,000 women teachers, more than 50 per cent of the profession. Gladys Langford's monthly pay packet for teaching in a London elementary school was around £24 (tax deducted), and she was 'always in debt'. This was only about four-fifths of the salary of a male teacher who had received the same training and was doing the same job, but it was not a bad wage for a single woman, and 85 per cent of women teachers were unmarried in the 1930s – three-quarters of local authorities discriminated against married teachers, and the words 'teacher' and 'spinster' seemed all but conjoined. Furthermore, popular sexology manuals linked psychological well-being with sexual fulfilment, and women without male partners were portrayed as 'prey to complexes and neuroses', being forced to sublimate their frustrations in sheer hard work. Though as Winifred Holtby, the writer and close friend of Vera Brittain, pointed out, a spinster doctor, teacher or political organiser was likely to find life much more fulfilling than an under-occupied middle-class housewife. 'I have not yet seen the newspaper which refers to those eminent bachelors, Noël Coward, Colonel T.E. Lawrence, Herr Hitler and the Prince of Wales as "this distressing type"' – which was how *Fascist Week* had referred to unmarried women.

'Today there is a far worse crime than promiscuity: it is chastity. On all sides the unmarried woman today is surrounded by doubts cast not only on her attractiveness or her common sense, but upon her decency, her normality, even her sanity,' wrote Holtby with some bitterness in a survey of women's sexuality over the previous sixty years on the occasion of George V's Jubilee in 1935 for *Time and Tide* (known as the 'Sapphic Graphic', reflecting the male perception that many of that persuasion wrote for the very successful magazine). The magazine was owned and edited by the divorced Lady Rhondda, who lived for many years with one of her contributors, Theodora Benson, and was very close to another, Cicely Hamilton, who as a turn-of-the-century 'new woman' had written a stinging indictment of *Marriage as a Trade*.

The prescription of hard work wasn't easy for female teachers to follow, though. There was growing unease that boys taught only by women might turn into 'spinster sons', while women who taught girls might transmit feminist – or worse, lesbian – tendencies to their pupils. In arguing against the marriage bar, it was easy to slip into a discourse that suggested that the celibate induced the cloistered, that to grow up well-adjusted, children needed the example of 'normal' – i.e. married – teachers.

'That decision of twenty, thirty years ago, was it the wrong one? Ought I to have been doing something else all these years?' wondered Dorothea Hiley, a headmistress, in her book of advice about the teaching profession, *Pedagogue Pie*, published in 1936. Gladys Langford endlessly wondered the same thing: was it being a schoolteacher that was the bar to her marrying? But she never quite took Hiley's wise advice that 'it is a good plan . . . at about the age of forty to do something strange such as beginning golf, or buying a car, or writing a detective story. There is nothing very wild-oaty that a respectable, professional female can do, but do let a free part of your personality flap in the wind. Madness is so vitalising.'

In 1931 there were fewer than 3,000 female medical practitioners; there were nearly 120,000 nurses. Nursing, which before the First World War had been akin to domestic service in terms of hard drudgery, had subsequently instituted a registration scheme which raised the status of the job, but it was still an all-female one, convent-like and bound tight with regulations and intrusions into private as well as working lives, its practitioners dressed in starchy uniforms, snowy caps and highly polished leather shoes and surveyed by 'dragon' matrons (Mary Milne of St Mary's Paddington was held up as an exemplary, humane exception, believing that a high standard of patient care was only possible with contented and comfortable nursing staff). A nurse worked up to sixty hours a week for £25 a year 'all found' in 1937 as a probationer, rising to a maximum of £65 as a qualified nurse, £80 as a staff nurse and £125 as a sister. Nursing duties were regarded as totally incompatible with marriage – indeed most nurses lived in hospital accommodation – and so it was a profession of single women.

In George Orwell's *Keep the Aspidistra Flying*, published in 1936, Julia Comstock, sister of the main character, Gordon, is 'a natural spinster soul. Even at sixteen she had "old maid" written all over her.' Having had 'as nearly as possible no education at all [having attended] one or two poor, dingy boarding schools', Julia worked a seventy-two-hour week as a waitress in 'a nasty ladylike little teashop' near Earl's Court, for which she received her lunch and tea and twenty-five shillings. At J. Lyons' teashop chain waitresses had replaced waiters (though not in Lyons' 'grand hotels', where male waiters reigned supreme), and earned an average of £1.16s.4d a week – rather more than poor Julia Comstock. Lyons' waitresses were known as 'Nippies', a name chosen as the result of a staff competition. Fortunately other suggestions such as 'Sybil-at your-Service', 'Miss Nimble', 'Miss Natty', 'Dextrous Doris' and 'Busy Betty' had lost out.

The young actress Anna Neagle (then known as Marjorie Robertson) dressed as a Nippy in an advertisement for Lyons' tea shops, wearing the uniform of a black dress with rows of pearl buttons and a white collar (easily removable for washing, which the waitress had to do herself), cuffs and small apron, with a pad and pencil for orders tied round her waist. By the end of the 1930s there were 7,600 Nippies working in Lyons' London teashops. Most were from the capital, but others came from remote parts of the British Isles, particularly the depressed areas of the North, Scotland, Wales and Northern Ireland. Nippies had a day off a week, and according to *Picture Post* 'being a Nippy is good training for a housewife': eight or nine hundred Nippies got married every year to customers 'met while on duty' (though possibly not to those who frequented the Coventry Street branch, a favourite venue for homosexual men in the 1930s). The image of the Nippy became a powerful inter-war brand for smart but not expensive meals. In a series of photographs the Austrian refugee film-maker and photographer Wolfgang Suschitzky, used a Lyons Corner House as one of the archetypal images of thirties London, and the actress Binnie Hale starred in a successful musical comedy, *Nippy*, in 1930. But for the Nippies themselves – and even more for the women working behind the scenes in the kitchens – it was hard, poorly paid life, with a kitchen hand reportedly working a ten-hour day for 17s.6d a week plus dinner and a cup of tea.

Shops were another spinster-dominated workplace. During the First World War women had taken over from male assistants, and by 1931 there were close to 400,000 women employees in the retail industry, 91 per cent of whom were single. Many of those who worked in big-city shops lived in dormitories, hostels or appalling 'digs'. Stores varied, of course, from 'small and dirty shops in slums, often doing a negligible trade in "gob stoppers", liquorice, boot laces etc.' to family-run corner shops, 'madam shops', chains (or 'multiples') and grand department stores. Again, the hours were long: shops often stayed open until 9 p.m., the assistant would have been on her feet since 8.30 a.m., and certainly in the larger department stores discipline and an impeccable dress code were strictly enforced – for dragon matron substitute eagle-eyed martinet shopwalker. Wages were low, and women were paid less than men: in 1937 Lewis's stores were paying male assistants 52s.6d a week and women 37s.6d. The 1934 Shop Act, which did not come into effect until 1937, made it illegal for those under eighteen to work more than forty-eight hours a week exclusive of meal breaks, but it also permitted fifty hours of overtime per year, which was usually unpaid. Women working in 'madam shops' suffered particularly. They would be un-unionised (as many shopworkers were), often working on commission and at the whim of the owner. Marjorie Gardiner, who worked for a smart Brighton milliner, was typical. Refused tea and coffee breaks, she was frequently obliged to work more than the contracted ten- or twelve-hour day, and suffered colds and chilblains since the shop door was flung wide open all winter to attract (coat-wearing) customers to try on a range of feather-, mink- or ermine-trimmed confections the assistants could never contemplate buying for themselves.

Florence White ran a small confectioner's shop in Bradford. She was a spinster herself, and in her view 'the young and wise get into the protected industry of marriage'. However, in 1936 there were 175,000 women between fifty-five and sixty-five who had been sufficiently unwise to remain single, and it was for them that Miss White founded the National Spinsters' Pension Association. Although the Association was 'not planning anything militant as the Suffragettes did', White was determined to draw public attention to the plight of unmarried women with low incomes, often no home of their own, and the constant fear of redundancy: 'There are many cases of this kind, especially among women industrial workers, who with advancing age, have been unable to keep up with the pace of the modern factory and have lost their jobs to young girls.' Under the slogan 'Equity with the Widow' (who received a pension of ten shillings a week providing her husband had been insured under the government scheme), the Association campaigned for pensions for spinsters who had been contributing to the National Insurance Scheme to be paid at the age of fifty-five, rather than sixty-five, and a contributory pension scheme for those thousands of women, including domestic workers, and those 'leading quiet, heroic lives' caring for relatives, who had no pension entitlement, and would have to rely on Public Assistance. Only 80,000 spinsters between fifty-five and sixty-five were entitled to a state pension: the other 95,000 were 'lapsed spinsters' who through ill health or family responsibilities had ceased paying their pension contributions for a time.

In the 1935 general election Florence White issued a questionnaire to all prospective MPs; the next year she stood as a candidate herself at the Preston by-election; in 1937 she organised a petition, collected a million signatures in less than a month, and took it personally on a decorated lorry to the House of Commons. Meetings and rallies were held all over the country, and on 5 June a train, its windows carrying posters reading 'Reserved. Special Train for Spinsters', left Keighley station in Yorkshire bound for London, stopping en route to pick up members carrying banners and wearing sashes and badges that read 'Pensions for Spinsters at 55' and

'Support Our Cause'. The women gathered at Kingsway Hall to hear Florence White harangue the Conservative Minister of Health, Sir Kingsley Wood (who wasn't present) and point up the unfair comparison between war widows and 'war spinsters'. Widows might well be comfortably off for the rest of their lives, even if they had only been married for a matter of days before their husband was killed, whereas spinsters who had lost their loved one, or whom the war had deprived of the opportunity of finding a husband, were condemned to a future that was likely to be penurious and uncertain. Rousing cheers greeted the speech, and then the spinsters marched off in a four-deep crocodile, accompanied by a brass band, to Hyde Park, where they heard Norah Blaney sing a verse specially composed for the occasion by her partner, Gwen Farrar:

> We spinsters are a happy lot
> And do the things we should,
> We should be far happier
> If only Kingsley would . . .

Kingsley wouldn't: it would be ruinously expensive, he protested. But in 1938 a Bradford MP introduced a Private Member's Motion about the spinsters' cause, and a committee of inquiry was set up. The committee rejected the idea of pensions for spinsters at fifty-five, a decision that was, perhaps surprisingly, welcomed by some feminists, who thought that such differentiation would mean that spinsters would have the status of a 'permanent semi-servile class', and that it would be an open invitation to employers to dismiss single women when they reached pensionable age. However, the 1940 Old Age and Widows' Pension Act reduced the age at which insured women (this would have included most working spinsters), and the wives of men in receipt of a pension, were entitled to draw a pension from sixty-five to sixty. Florence White hailed this halfway measure as a victory, but in fact the pension was given only on retirement, so women would be deprived of their health insurance benefits at precisely the age when they might need them most.

'Children by Choice not Chance' was the slogan chosen by the Family Planning Association, which brought together various similar organisations in 1939. It had been a long trudge from the first such venture, the Mothers' Clinic for Constructive Birth Control, opened by Marie Stopes in the Holloway Road in North London in 1921, which had been prosecuted for obscenity over a birth-control leaflet with a diagram showing a finger indicating the mouth of the womb on the grounds that it might not be the woman's own finger. A health visitor in Edmonton in North London was sacked by the Public Health Department for telling mothers where to go for birth-control advice, and there was opposition from local authorities, the Roman Catholic Church, individuals who associated contraception with promiscuity, and women who were afraid to tell their husbands that they had been seeking contraceptive advice.

Gradually birth-control clinics spread throughout Britain: the first one outside London opened in Wolverhampton in 1926, and two horse-drawn caravans, converted into mobile clinics, toured the country bringing advice and instruction to women in remote areas in Wales and the North of England for over a year. In some places there was fierce opposition. The caravan was vandalised and ransacked in Tredegar in 1930 (probably by a gang of unemployed youths), and in Bradford it was torched, allegedly by a Catholic mother. The Bishop of Salford raged against 'these strange filthy things' in his diocese, and the Catholic Church spoke of birth-control clinics as 'infinitely worse than the unnatural vices that were practised in the wicked cities of Sodom and Gomorrah'. The Archbishop of Cardiff urged Catholics to 'fight tooth and nail' to prevent local authorities sanctioning clinics, and even suggested 'refusing to pay our rates [to show] that we are in deadly earnest'.

Many doctors were opposed to birth control, and were reluctant to work with the clinics, or to send patients to them. In any case, most working-class women, who were not insured under the National Health Insurance Scheme since it excluded the dependents of insured workers and the unemployed, rarely saw a doctor, calling on his or her services only in an emergency. In 1927 the Labour Party conference had voted by an overwhelming majority against local authorities being able to fund birth-control clinics from the rates, though by 1930 dozens of local authorities, including Brighton, Shoreditch, Bootle, St Helens and Warwickshire were urging that they should be able to do so; that year the government conceded that existing Maternity and Child and Welfare clinics could instruct those women for whom another pregnancy would seriously affect their health about birth control.

Advocates of birth control thenceforth largely switched from national campaigns to urging local authorities to open clinics. By 1939 some sixty clinics (or sixty-five, or eighty-four, or ninety-seven; there is little consensus among historians) had been established – including, after much wrangling and denouncing, one in Belfast in November 1936, the first and only one in Ireland for almost another twenty years – a result of co-operation between local authorities and the Stopes-founded National Birth Control Association, which by this time had become the Family Planning Association. Progress was much slower in Scotland, where by 1939 only five out of fifty-five local authorities were providing advice on contraception, though there were also a handful of voluntary clinics doing so.

In 1930 the Lambeth Conference voted by 193 to sixty-seven to give cautious permission for the use of artificial methods of birth control by married members of the Church of England in special circumstances. Though the Archbishop of Canterbury spoke piously of his wish for sex to take 'its rightful place among the great creative and formative things', it was clear that the licence was reluctantly given. Several leading clerics, including Bishop Henson of Durham, objected, maintaining that 'contraceptive intercourse is always, in all circumstances and prompted by whatever motive, unchaste', and the bishops urged that contraceptives should not be on sale openly, and that advertising should be restricted. However, the decision meant that Anglicans now had only their own consciences to guide them – that is, if such pronouncements from on high had much influence on their sex lives. The Roman Catholic Church remained intransigently opposed to anything other than the use of the so-called 'safe period'. In December 1930 Pope Pius XI's encyclical *Casti Conubii* expressly prohibited Catholics from doing anything that would hinder the 'natural power of procreating life', and declared the use of artificial contraception to be a 'grave sin'.

Birthrates were falling dramatically from the large families of the Victorian and Edwardian eras. By 1940 only 9 per cent of women had families of more than five children, and only 30 per cent had three or more: the post-First World War middle-class norm of the two-child family was beginning to permeate to the working classes. A large family makes less economic sense in an urban than a rural society, particularly in times of high unemployment such as the 1930s, when in addition the Means Test allowed only two shillings extra benefit per child and penalised the family for any contribution adult children might make to the household budget, and the raising of the school leaving age meant that children were a financial drain on their parents for longer. A reduction in infant mortality rates, which had fallen by 70 per cent between 1901 and 1935 (though they remained disturbingly high in some areas of economic depression such as South Wales) contributed to the decline of the birthrate since children were more likely to survive, as did the clear correlation, commented upon since the end of the nineteenth century, between large families and poverty. And despite all the obstacles put in their way, more married women were working outside the home – 6,250,000 by 1931, a rise of 750,000 from 1911 – particularly in clerical jobs and the new light industries, which was another inhibition to large families. There was also the incentive of an easier life than couples' parents had had, the opportunity to have more fun, a nicer home, a car, to buy more things, to 'do better by the kiddies'. Although there were still very large families of ten, twelve, fourteen or even more in the 1930s – particularly in poor areas such as Liverpool, Glasgow and the East End of London, where there were a large number of Catholics and life could be chaotic – it would appear that despite religious and other objections, many couples were making use of one or other of the artificial, or so-called mechanical, contraceptive devices on the market.

Marie Stopes (who was not a doctor but a fossil-plant specialist) recommended what she called a 'racial cap', a small rubber dome that fitted over the cervix and was held in place by suction. Vulcanised rubber, developed in the nineteenth century, had been used for early diaphragms (usually known as Dutch caps). These were 'thick heavy things made from something like car tyres', or from metal and cellulose, until latex came from America in the 1920s and began to be used for both diaphragms and for men's sheaths, or condoms – which had been issued to the troops during the First World War in an attempt to curb an epidemic of venereal disease. The English Rubber Company, which started to manufacture latex condoms in 1932, was soon producing two million a year, and more were imported from abroad. The more expensive latex ones were disposable. Others were more durable; the careful husband would need to wash them after use, inspect them for tears or holes, and store them, covered in talcum powder, in a box. By the late 1930s a unisex sheath was on the market, adaptable for use by either partner, and guaranteed 'to last for years'. However, it was recommended that a belt-and-braces approach be taken, using some sort of spermicidal jelly or paste such as Volpar (Voluntary Parenthood paste) as well. Other methods included a sponge (an artificial one rather than a sea sponge was recommended) soaked in spermicidal jelly or olive oil and inserted into the vagina (Marie Stopes was keen on olive oil, since it was cheap and easily obtainable without embarrassment from the grocer – at least where she lived – but its reliability as a contraceptive was pretty suspect); spermicidal tampons that dissolved; pessaries (the most widely sold were made of quinine and cocoa butter) inserted by syringe, douches, or even home-made ones. In 1930, 40 per cent of middle-class couples were reckoned to be using some form of artificial birth control, as were around 28 per cent of working-class couples.

But despite the wave of manuals about sexual fulfilment in marriage, starting with Marie Stopes' *Married Love* (1918), and the birth-control advice found in such works as her sequel, *Planned Parenthood: The Treatise on Birth Control for Married People: A Practical Sequel to 'Married Love'* (also 1918), Dr Helena Wright's *The Sex Factor in Marriage* (1930) and Leonora Eyles' *Commonsense About Sex* (1933), which were to be found largely on middle-class bedside tables (or in drawers, according to the memoirs of several children of the thirties), and the relative proliferation of clinics offering advice and devices, fewer people were using 'modern' methods than the age-old traditional strategies of abstinence, withdrawal (*coitus interruptus*) or abortion to limit the size of their family.

Sheaths weren't cheap: reusable ones cost around a shilling, but disposable ones were much more expensive; and pessaries, at two shillings a dozen, were considered too expensive for the poor. Many men disliked wearing sheaths, describing the effect as like 'washing your feet with socks on' or 'having a toffee with the paper on', while others associated their use with sex with prostitutes, not their wives, or found purchasing them from chemists, barbers, 'hygienic stores' or market stalls (they were invariably kept 'under the counter', and had to be asked for) embarrassing, though presumably less so via mail-order companies or from vending machines in pub toilets. Women might have to pay to register with a birth-control clinic, and then pay for any appliance provided, though this might be waived at the discretion of the nurse. Many found it difficult to insert a diaphragm correctly, they had to be checked regularly, and some were afraid that they might somehow 'get lost' in their insides, never to be retrieved. They were regarded as messy, and taking the spontaneity out of love-making, and it was felt that a woman looked 'calculating' if she fitted herself up in anticipation of sex. Moreover, the use of caps, pessaries and douches passed responsibility for birth control to the woman rather than the man, which was against most working-class cultural norms, in which a man initiated sex and took responsibility for the consequences. A woman's supposed unawareness of birth-control methods was believed to be an indication of her innocence and virtue, the historian Kate Fisher suggests. It was not seemly for women to know, or talk, about such matters: that was men's talk, pub talk. So while some couples decided on abstinence – 'We were very strong-willed and slept in single beds' – most opted for what they recognised could be an unreliable method, withdrawal, variously referred to euphemistically as 'being careful', 'taking the kettle off before it boils' or 'getting off at Edge Hill [Birmingham]'.

'Family planning' was what most health officials had come to advocate by the 1930s, rather than the population-limiting-sounding birth control, but whatever it was called it wasn't what most married couples practised. A 1949 report on 'An Enquiry into Family Limitation' found that 84 per cent of those who married between 1910 and 1924 did not 'plan' their families, and even by the 1940s less than 50 per cent did, and the matter was often not discussed. Rather, couples tried to limit their families, not to space them systematically; most were aware that there might be 'accidents' – a wife 'falling' for a baby, rather than 'going in' for one – and many half-expected this eventuality with a certain degree of fatalism. Indeed, for some women, not overburdened with a brood of infants, the risk of conception could almost be part of sexual arousal. The writer Naomi Mitchison, who had borne seven children, wasn't very keen on this lackadaisical approach, arguing that although many people were 'thrilled' by 'happy or surprising accidents', it was 'braver and nobler and more civilized to have only intentional children'. And in *her* book on birth control Mitchison insisted, 'There is a particular thrill in saying "Now is the time, to-day or to-night, in such a city or forest, we will beget our child."' But, romantic though that sounds, it does not seem quite how it was in most marital beds in the 1930s.

Birth control was seen within the context of planned families: sex was connubial, love (in the physical sense) married. Pre- and extra-marital sex appeared to be largely the prerogative of the wealthy or the *avant garde*, though that was clearly not the case, as the unfortunate Gladys Langford's diary shows. However, although no unmarried women would be advised at a birth-control clinic, illegitimacy rates were relatively low – about 5 per cent of all births in the 1930s – though the Registrar-General, commenting on the birthrate for 1938–39, suggested that nearly 30 per cent of mothers conceived their firstborn out of wedlock. However, since though they may have been conceived out of wedlock, most children were born within marriage, this suggests that many courting couples did have sex, and fixed (or advanced) the wedding date when pregnancy occurred, which rather contradicted the standard view (and exhortation) that all 'nice girls' were virgins on their wedding night.

'Our sex-life was expected to be (and generally was) non-existent before marriage,' recalled Eileen Whiteing. 'Certainly abortions or illegitimate babies were never heard of in our circle. We certainly had numerous boy friends and there was plenty of scope after dances or tennis parties, so perhaps our very innocence and lack of knowledge protected us from disasters! Girls and boys alike seemed to know by instinct the limits to be imposed on any love-making, even during the longish engagements which were normal.' Eileen Lawrence, as she then was, met her future husband soon after her twenty-first birthday at a meeting of the local debating society. After a year, she and Dennis Whiteing, who worked in Wallington council's rates office, got engaged, and for eighteen months both saved 'very hard in order to fill the traditional "bottom drawer" and to buy the necessary furniture and furnishings for our future home. It was out of the question to start married life on second-hand bits and pieces.'

The couple married in April 1939, Eileen wearing a 'lace wedding-dress complete with three-foot train . . . made by the dressmaker Ann Beaufort of the Arcade Sutton for around three pounds, with hand-finished satin bindings and minute satin buttons', the four bridesmaids 'delightful in their pale green organdie full-skirted dresses with lilies-of-the valley in their hair'. The guests, 'dressed to the hilt, dripping with picture hats, wraps and jewels', enjoyed a sit-down meal that had cost the bride's parents £1 a head and that included 'sandwiches (various fillings), sausage rolls, lobster patties, fruit jellies or fruit salad, meringues and cream', washed down with coffee, lemonade or orangeade, before the 'radiant young couple left by train from East Croydon for their honeymoon in Eastbourne – a favourite resort at that time – amid clouds of confetti and cries of good luck'.

If that was the reward of those who 'knew the rules' and stuck to them, it was different for girls who 'got into trouble' and did not marry, but continued with their pregnancy rather than seeking an abortion. They had a bleak time unless their family was supportive, sometimes bringing the child up believing that its mother was its sister. A middle-class girl would be most likely to be sent away to a mother and baby home, or to a relative in the country, the baby adopted, her grief at the loss never acknowledged or spoken of again. A working-class girl whose family refused to help, or which couldn't afford to feed another mouth, might have nowhere to go but the workhouse – known after 1929 as 'public assistance institutions', although very little but their name changed until the coming of the welfare state after 1945.

'It makes me wild,' wrote a nurse to Marie Stopes in 1939, 'mothers with a pram full of children *always* complaining – yet they say – Oh I don't want to come [to the birth-control clinic]. Oh I wouldn't like to use this or that. Oh I couldn't touch myself, *No* – but they will touch themselves plenty if to produce aborsion [*sic*] and spend money and take all sorts of things.' Abortion was indeed for numbers of women almost an alternative form of contraception, routinely used, sometimes even before there was any evidence of pregnancy. Such women were sometimes perplexed when clinics informed them that they dealt with birth control, fussed around with caps and jellies and leaflets, but refused to help with a termination. 'The unlawful side of it had not struck them at all . . . [One woman] said "surely you are going to do something for me".' The nurse 'had to explain to her that we did not teach how to destroy life'.

To some women, if 'quickening' (the moment a woman could detect her foetus move, generally around three months after conception) had not occurred, abortion did not seem a moral issue of 'destroying life', but rather 'bringing on' a delayed period. This was decades before the 'blue stripe' test could be purchased over the counter to confirm – or not – pregnancy. As a government Committee on Abortion, chaired by Norman Birkett, reported in 1936, 'many mothers seemed not to understand that self-induced abortion was illegal. They assumed it was legal before the third month, and only outside the law when procured by another person.' Dr Dunstan Brewer, who practised in Swindon, gave evidence that in his view 'The average British matron respects the law only where its provisions tally with her conceptions.' Having questioned his married women patients who had two or more children, he found general agreement that 'a woman was quite justified in attempting to get rid of an unwanted pregnancy by simple means prior to the child quickening'. Dr Helena Wright concluded as a result of her work at her birth control clinic in North Kensington that middle-class women with four or more children did everything they could to terminate subsequent pregnancies, in the best interests of their existing families, as they saw it.

Working-class women 'had a sort of secret service to help anyone with an unwanted pregnancy', sharing tried and tested remedies and the names of sympathetic pharmacists and abortionists who would 'help'. It was alleged that once a marriage or birth announcement appeared in the newspaper, the couple would receive through the post pamphlets on birth control which were 'frequently a blind for the sale of abortifacients and the addresses of abortionists'. There were believed to be several ways that an early abortion could be self-induced. 'Bumping down stairs' was one, drinking copious quantities of gin, preferably while sitting in a scalding bath, was another. Women would get pills from the chemist, advertised as 'Curing *All* Ladies' Ailments' or 'Getting Rid of Blockages', or even, with some truth, 'National Insurance for Women', but they were not cheap at 2s.9d to 4s.6d a box, or even more – sometimes they carried a warning that they were *not* to be taken if a woman was pregnant, a subtle way of advertising their abortifacient properties. A woman might swallow quinine – sometimes laced with tobacco – or pennyroyal, bile beans, quantities of Beecham's powders, washing soda, lead scraped from lead plaster, gold leaf, a potion made by soaking nails and pennies in water, even rat poison. Slippery elm bark might be inserted into the vagina using a syringe and soapy water, so it would swell when wet, dilate the cervix and cause a miscarriage; even more dangerous was prodding around with a knitting needle that had been heated to 'sterilise' it. The father of Ted Willis was unemployed during much of the 1930s apart from the odd casual labouring job. His mother, who worked as a charwoman and took in other people's washing, already had two children and 'a depressing catalogue of unpaid debts and a thickening wad of pawn tickets in the left hand drawer of the kitchen dresser' in the family's home in Tottenham, North London, when she found that she was pregnant again – with him.

> It is no wonder that the thought of another child drove my mother to desperation. She tried everything possible to get rid of me. She bought gin she could ill afford and drank it neat. She carried the tin bath in from the back yard, filled it with near-boiling water and then lowered herself into it, scalding her flesh so painfully that she was in agony for days. She ran up and down stairs until she was exhausted. And when all this failed to check my progress, she procured some gunpowder – enough to cover a sixpence – mixed it with a pat of margarine and swallowed it. That was reckoned in those days to be almost infallible, but it succeeded only in making her violently sick.
>
> In the end she reconciled herself to the inevitable, and I emerged, none the worse for these adventures . . . She bore me no ill-will for my perverse behaviour: once I was there, to be accepted and fed and loved along with the others. Years later she told me about my narrow escape, and added with a wicked twinkle in her eye: 'Think yourself bloody lucky I didn't buy enough gunpowder to cover a half-crown.'

What Mrs Willis could presumably have done as a last resort was to go to an abortionist – usually an older women, a neighbour or a relative, most with no medical training, though some were ex-midwives or nurses. They operated in less than sanitary conditions in their own back kitchen or that of the client, keeping a 'jar of slippery elm and pennyroyal in the oven for the benefit of harassed younger neighbours' and using heavy 'massage' or instruments – usually a metal knitting needle heated up. This was where working-class women with little money and great desperation were most likely to fetch up, most knowing such an act to be illegal but having to rely on the female solidarity (and sometimes the avarice) of friends or strangers.

Meanwhile, their better-off counterparts might visit a Harley Street specialist or someone euphemistically called an 'osteopath' or similar, or book into one of the many private nursing homes (largely unregulated, but which offered an estimated total of 3–4,000 beds in London) that were prepared to perform such an operation for a hefty fee. 'It is perfectly possible,' the National Conservative MP Mavis Tate told the House of Commons, 'for a woman in the West End of London, with sufficient money, to have a miscarriage brought about any moment she wants, through doctors of the recognised medical profession.' 'It costs about £50,' Vita Sackville-West claimed authoritatively in one of her novels (though a backstreet abortionist was more likely to settle for two guineas). A.J. Cronin, in his novel about the medical profession *The Citadel*, published in 1937, described such a surgeon, Ivory, as 'nothing but a damned abortionist' specialising in 'love's labour lost . . . There's a couple of nursing homes where they do nothing else – all very pretty and above board of course – and Ivory's the head scraper.'

How many abortions occurred is impossible to know: in 1936 the British Medical Association reckoned that 20 per cent were illegal (that is, neither spontaneous nor performed by a doctor to save the life of the mother), while one historian has calculated that there were a total of 68,000 criminal abortions in 1935 alone. The Birkett Committee, reporting in 1939, estimated that of around 110,000 abortions each year, 66,000 were probably spontaneous and 44,000 procured. However, it was often very hard to tell the difference between a spontaneous and an induced abortion, particularly if it was carried out by a skilled medical practitioner, and doctors often suspected that early miscarriages were in fact abortions. A midwife working in a Welsh mining village in the 1930s believed that of the 227 miscarriages the 122 women of the village had over a period of seven years, few were accidental. A survey of 3,000 Birmingham women in 1936 showed that 35 per cent of them had had an abortion. Meanwhile, although maternal deaths were falling, still on average 3.27 women out of every thousand died in childbirth – or, put more starkly, one woman lost her life every 330 births. This attrition did begin to improve around this time with the introduction of sulphonamides, which dramatically reduced incidents of sepsis and made natural childbirth, caesarean sections and induced abortions safer.

In 1926 the Infant Life Preservation Act had confirmed that abortion was illegal once the foetus was viable (at twenty-eight weeks), except when it was performed to save the life of the mother: it was not clear whether it was illegal if performed for the same reason *before* twenty-eight weeks. The British Medical Association (BMA) set up a committee in 1935 which recommended that abortion should be legal to remedy the effects of a failed criminal abortion, in case of rape and of incest for young girls, as well as on eugenic and other exceptional grounds. In Scotland the Aberdeen Medical Officer of Health performed abortions on social grounds, which was against the law in England. Clearly clarification was needed.

On 14 June 1938 Dr Aleck Bourne, obstetric surgeon to St Mary's Hospital Paddington, was arrested by a Chief Inspector Bridger as he came out of the operating theatre having performed an abortion on a fourteen-year-old girl who had been gang-raped by some soldiers. Her case had been brought to Bourne's attention by Dr Joan Malleson, a member of the Abortion Law Reform Association which had been founded in 1936 by seven women, including Stella Browne, Frida Laski and Dora Russell, and which sought a change in the law since they argued that too many women were dying from botched abortions. Dr Bourne did not claim that the girl was likely to die if her pregnancy continued to term, but said he had decided to operate because of the threat of 'mental and nervous' injury if she gave birth, and he had informed the Attorney-General what he intended to do. Hence the presence of Chief Inspector Bridger.

The trial opened at the Central Criminal Court on 18 July. Bourne pleaded not guilty to having performed an illegal act, denying that there was a clear distinction between the danger to life and to health, and stating that many cases showed that if a person's health was seriously depressed, their life might be curtailed. In his summing up, the judge accepted Bourne's argument that 'Life depends on health, and it may be that health is so gravely impaired that death results.' He directed the jury that if 'the probable consequence of the continuation of the pregnancy will be to make the woman a physical or an emotional wreck', they were entitled to take the view that 'the doctor who, under those circumstances and in that honest belief, operates, is operating for the purpose of saving the mother'. In the case before the court a 'normal, decent girl' was likely to become 'a mental wreck' if the pregnancy was allowed to continue, he concluded. Dr Bourne was acquitted.

Treated as something of a legal landmark, the case was more a reaffirmation, or clarification, of the law as it stood. That had been what Bourne had intended, rather than a reform of the law. Though obstetricians might now have felt more confident about the circumstances in which an abortion would be within the law, the judgement left ambiguities. Human life was still to be considered sacred, and 'the unborn child in the womb must not be destroyed unless the destruction of the child is for the purpose of preserving the yet more precious life of the mother'. This defence was only available to members of the medical profession, who it was assumed would not 'venture to operate without consulting some other doctor of high-standing'. But if the grounds for carrying out an abortion were to be 'mental anguish', might not a psychiatrist be needed to pronounce? And only the educated or relatively well-off had recourse to psychiatrists.

Backstreet abortions would continue to be illegal. The grounds for legal abortion were purely medical: no economic, social or eugenic (the strong possibility that the baby might have a serious hereditary disease) circumstances could be allowed, and any doctor who performed an abortion 'merely because a woman does not want a child' did so at his or her peril. But it was on the first two grounds that most working-class women sought abortions – too many children already, the family living in poverty and in poor housing. The family of one London woman who was in hospital as a result of a failed abortion in 1937 was living in two rooms for which they paid seven shillings rent out of a weekly income of £2.10s. Her husband refused to use a sheath 'because of the fear of cancer', but as far as she was concerned, 'We cannot let the children go without shoes. We must look after those we have got and I can't manage to clothe them any more.' A woman in Glasgow, hospitalised for the same reason, already had nine children, and her family too was living in two rooms.

The judgement in Dr Bourne's case was a long way from the spirit of a paper given to the BMA in 1926 by the consulting obstetric physician at the Charing Cross Hospital, Dr Thomas Watts Eden, who had suggested that it is 'an ethical question of great interest to what extent we as doctors have the right to insist that a woman shall pass through an ordeal which she is unwilling to face, even if we do not think that she will sustain any permanent injury from doing so'. It was the rigidity of the medical profession, Dr Eden claimed, that drove women to 'abortion-mongers'.

'It is impossible,' claimed one London doctor in 1937, 'to practise gynaecology without being overrun with abortions.' The number of legal abortions in London had risen to 3,892 – it had been 2,667 in 1931 – and probably as many as 95 per cent of them were picking up the pieces of 'incomplete' self- or illegally performed operations. London was seen as the abortion capital, accounting for 35.1 per cent of all deaths of women due to abortion, whereas rural areas only contributed 19 per cent. It was claimed that abortionists set up near the main railway termini such as St Pancras and Paddington to serve women arriving from the depressed areas.

During the worst years of the Depression, 1931–32, the incidence of abortion rose in cities like Birmingham, Bradford, Glasgow, Manchester, Derby and Sheffield, which in 1934 had 6.11 maternal deaths per thousand, nearly 40 per cent of which were as a result of abortions. Sheffield was, the chair of its Health Committee feared, in danger of being 'regarded as an abortionist City', and Bolton was not far behind. The unemployment rate in Sheffield was between 50,000 and 65,000 between 1930 and 1939 and a 1932 study showed that the unemployed had 49,333 dependants, including 29,370 children, meaning that 'The huge total of about 100,000 persons [are] directly affected by the unemployment problem.' The city's industries employed few women: in textile towns such as Rochdale, where traditionally a high percentage of married women worked in the mills, female workplace networks enabled them to gain access to birth control rather than having to resort to abortion. Consequently deaths due to abortions were lower there than in Sheffield and similarly male-dominated places.

In 1937 a committee of inquiry under the chairmanship of Norman Birkett KC was set up to 'consider what steps can be taken by more effective enforcement of the law or otherwise to secure the reduction of maternal mortality from this cause'. The members of the committee were the usual great and the good – only one of the five women members did not have a title. Although the rest were doctors and other professionals, no doubt with long experience of legal and medical matters relating to abortion, most were hardly in touch with the lives of the women who most frequently sought abortions, or with the poverty, unemployment, poor accommodation and too-frequent pregnancies that drove them to do so. Dr M'Gonigle, Medical Officer of Health for Stockton-on-Tees, the author of a damning report on malnutrition among the unemployed, and Dorothy Thurtle, a social worker and daughter of the Labour politician George Lansbury, were the exceptions.

The usual arguments were paraded, some muddled, some contradictory, all eventually inconclusive. Abortion would encourage promiscuity. It was most prevalent among the 'smart set' who did not want to be distracted from their pleasures and indiscretions, according to the Chief Constable of Cardiff. Prosecutions for prostitution were falling because there was more 'amateur competition', and easier abortion would only exacerbate that. The Union of Catholic Mothers went so far as to say that the increased avail-ability of birth control had encouraged 'excessive coitus', and this had led to 'imperfectly developed spermatozoa', which meant more spontaneous abortions. Abortion was strictly a medical matter, and decisions on whether to carry out the procedure must be made purely on clinical grounds: social factors were of no account, and to insist on them encroached on doctors' professional standing. Yet on the whole women were 'rather afraid of doctors', and birth-control clinics were not well advertised: in some cities only a handful of women attended them – 19,000 per year across the whole country, a paltry figure in comparison to the number of women who had an induced abortion each year. Furthermore, since most local authorities dismissed women employees on marriage, there were few married women doctors staffing the clinics, which meant that those who were dishing out advice were either young and single, or old and single, and did not on the whole 'inspire confidence'. The plight of the professional woman was movingly sketched by one of the witnesses, Beryl Henderson. She was caught in 'an impossible position': she could not marry, could not have a baby, and could not have an abortion.

Abortion was, *de facto*, a response to inadequate birth-control methods, many witnesses argued. Others worried about falling birthrates. The Chancellor of the Exchequer, Neville Chamberlain, had raised child allowances slightly in 1934, since he viewed the fall in the birthrate 'with considerable apprehension'. The Abortion Law Reform Association stated that botched abortions could make women sterile, and pointed out that if the government was serious about encouraging women to have more babies, it needed to improve their social and economic situation, rather than conscripting them unwillingly into maternity.

Although the Abortion Law Reform Association sought a liberalisation of the law – the USSR had been held up as a shining example of how it should be done, until in the interest of greater productivity it reversed its early abortion on demand policy in the late 1930s. It advocated that abortion should be readily available for single as well as married women. Only one member of the committee, Stella Browne, took the more radical stance of a 'woman's right to choose', which would be the cry of feminist reformers in the 1960s, echoing the 'ethical question' that Dr Thomas Watts Eden (who was also a member of the Committee) had raised more than a decade earlier. Browne, by then nearly sixty and a lifelong spinster, startled the Committee by announcing to them conclusively, 'If abortion was necessarily fatal or injurious, I should not be here before you.'

The Birkett Committee's recommendations essentially clarified the status quo and upheld the firm implementation of the existing law. Dorothy Thurtle, concerned to 'work for a real improvement in the lives of working women', dissented and issued a minority report arguing that it was 'reasonable and legitimate for women to want freedom from perpetual childbearing', and that abortion should be available as a right for any woman who, having had four pregnancies, wished to terminate any subsequent ones.

Marie Stopes was not at all sympathetic towards abortion; neither did she look favourably on sex out of wedlock, and certainly not on same-sex sex. 'The correct name . . . for what is now so euphemistically called Lesbian love is homosexual vice,' she wrote in her book *Enduring Passion*. 'Keep your mind off the physical side of that aspect as much as possible and lead as healthy and as busy a life as you can,' she advised a Miss Redcliffe who had written to her concerned that she had 'a very strong tendency to be attracted by my own sex'. 'Hard brain work' would probably do the trick, thought Stopes, and assured her correspondent that 'You will find the normal sex attraction will assert itself and the phase pass entirely away.' But if the 'phase' didn't pass, if it wasn't a 'crush' or a 'pash' or a 'rave', then unless the 1930s lesbian moved in forward social or artistic circles, she might have to put up with considerable misunderstanding, being thought ill, unnatural, an 'invert'. Even the sexologist Havelock Ellis, who was tolerant of some rather odd heterosexual practices, described women who preferred women as 'abnormal', 'perverts', the result of 'defective breeding', while Sigmund Freud – whose work was almost unknown in Britain until after the Second World War – thought the causes of lesbianism could be traced to a difficult childhood.

In 1921 there had been an attempt to make sexual acts between women illegal, but the Bill was rejected by the House of Lords, with Lord Desart saying incredulously: 'You are going to tell the whole world that there is such an offence, to bring it to the notice of women who have never heard of it, never thought of it, never dreamed of it. I think that is a very great mischief.' The Lord Chancellor, Lord Birkenhead agreed: 'I would be bold enough to say that out of every 1,000 women . . . 999 have never even heard a whisper of those practices.' But in July 1928 the whisper had become a roar with the publication of Radclyffe Hall's *The Well of Loneliness*, which brought lesbian practices out into the open. The novel, written as a plea for 'merciful toleration' according to Radclyffe Hall (whose first name was Margaret, but who was always known as 'John', and wrote under her surname alone), is a desolate story, portraying the handsome, slim, athletic Stephen Gordon (her parents had wanted a son), a member of the 'third sex', a male soul and mind trapped from birth in a female body and thus doomed to misery. 'I am,' she declares, 'one of those whom God marked like Cain.' Stephen falls in love with a 'femme', Mary Llewellyn, and the two set up home together until Stephen, stricken with remorse about Mary's future happiness, engineers it so that she falls in love with a good man, leaving Stephen to face a bleak future alone – yet not alone, for behind her stand a 'legion' of the unborn, who look to her to champion their cause.

Copies of *The Well of Loneliness* filled the windows of W.H. Smith, and the print run of 1,500 sold out in a week, though lesbians such as Romaine Brooks and Vita Sackville-West criticised the novel, calling it 'ridiculous', 'trite', 'superficial' and 'loathsome'. But though it was hardly a torrid book – one 'sex scene' consisted of the words '. . . and that night they were not divided' – the editor of the *Sunday Express* famously asserted that he would rather 'give a healthy girl a phial of Prussic Acid than this novel'. The publishers panicked, and sent a copy to the notoriously zealous Home Secretary, Sir William Joynson-Hicks, resulting in a prosecution being brought under the 1857 Obscenity Act. Same-sex-friendly intellectuals such as E.M. Forster and Virginia Woolf offered to appear for the defence (though as Woolf, who found the book 'meritorious and dull' – and 'so pure, so sweet, so sentimental that none of us can read it' – wrote, 'Many of our friends are trying to evade the witness box, for reasons you may guess. But they generally put it down to the weak heart of a father or a cousin which is about to have twins'). Vita Sackville-West felt 'very violently about *The Well of Loneliness*. Not on account of what you call my proclivities; not because I think it is a good book; but really on principle. (I think of writing to Jix [i.e. Joynson-Hicks] suggesting that he should suppress Shakespeare's Sonnets.)'

But neither they nor Evelyn Waugh, who also volunteered to testify on the book's behalf, need have bothered: the chief magistrate declared that literary merit was inadmissible as a defence – the question was a straight one of obscenity. The bench decided that *The Well of Loneliness* 'is a book which, if it does not commend unnatural practices, certainly condones them, and suggests that those guilty of them should not receive the consequences they deserve to suffer'. The 'disgusting . . . dangerous and corrupting' book was banned in Britain until 1949, though it could be ordered from the US, and was prominently displayed on bookstalls at the Gare du Nord in Paris, where English visitors could hardly miss it.

Even during those relative underground years the book at least gave lesbians some affirmation of their existence and the certainty that there were others who shared their feelings. Equally, it no doubt caused others to look askance. 'Oh! The vicarages and country homes who felt their peace of mind forever poisoned as they contemplated Daphne, Pamela, Joan and Margery all living together with unthinkable consequences,' wrote Beatrice Gordon Holmes, who considered *The Well of Loneliness* a 'dreary book', but equally thought that 'Real homosexuality is an extremely rare thing . . . it's completely suitable and natural for all human beings to form deep and tender attachments, permanent or passing, irrespective of age or sex – and rather unnatural if they don't.'

During the trial, Radclyffe Hall had received 5,000 letters, mostly from women. Only five were abusive, the rest thanking her fervently for writing the book. When Barbara Bell, a lesbian living in Blackburn who joined the police force in 1939, found a copy in the 1930s she was ecstatic. 'It was a revelation, I thought well I must join the club, I'm all for this,' though she would put the book in a paper bag before lending it to friends, 'it was so secret'.

The author Sylvia Townsend Warner lived with her lover Valentine Ackland from 1930 when they met until Ackland's death, a 'glorious span of thirty-eight years of love and trust and happiness . . . My love, my Love,' Townsend Warner wrote to Ackland. The night after Jessie Monroe appeared in the novelist Elizabeth Goudge's garden as a result of an advertisement seeking someone to keep her company in Devon after her mother died, Goudge was 'flooded with happiness', and after twenty-one years together she described the younger woman's arrival as 'the most wonderful event that has ever happened to me'. The writer Elizabeth Bowen had an affair with the then very young May Sarton at the end of the thirties, which Sarton intimated was not the first such liaison Bowen had had, and was unlikely to have been the last. The reformer Eleanor Rathbone set up home with Elizabeth Macadam, a Scottish social worker who was 'part and parcel of the whole pattern of Eleanor's life and cannot be unentangled from it', as Rathbone's biographer Mary Stocks wrote. Hannah Gluckstein, daughter of the hugely wealthy owner of the Lyons chain of corner houses and teashops, was a painter who went under the name of Gluck. After a fling with the thirties version of the domestic goddess, the flower arranger Constance Spry, Gluck fell deeply in love with Nesta Obermer. Her feelings were reciprocated, but Obermer continued to live with her wealthy older husband and to participate in the round of social and charity events befitting a married woman in her position.

Vita Sackville-West, who was in most ways devotedly married to the bisexual Harold Nicolson – the couple gave a talk for the BBC about their connubial bliss – had many lesbian affairs, including with Violet Trefusis, Evelyn Irons, Ethel Sands and the Head of Talks at the BBC, Hilda Matheson (indeed it was Matheson who arranged for Sackville-West and Nicolson to talk about their marriage – without mentioning its openness – on the wireless). Virginia Woolf and Sackville-West had a long *tendresse* which gave rise to Woolf's androgynous parody *Orlando*, published the same year as *The Well of Loneliness*. Though Woolf's preference for her own sex led her to intimacies, she declined to define herself as a Sapphist, or to place herself in any other category. Her remorseless pursuit by the septuagenarian composer Dame Ethel Smyth throughout much of the thirties came increasingly to irritate her, and even more so her husband Leonard. Some lesbians

During his brief occupancy of the throne, Edward VIII visited the Welsh mining village of Abertillery while on a tour of the 'black hillsides, slag heaps and dingy houses' of unemployed miners and their families in November 1936. 'Something must be done,' he pronounced.

A family taking a midday break during an 'opping 'oliday, picking hops in the Kent countryside. Photograph by Cyril Arapoff, who had left Russia after the Revolution and opened a studio in Headington, Oxford.

In July 1937 the inauguration of Weston-Super-Mare's
magnificent concrete cantilevered diving tower – the
highest platform was ten metres – was watched by a
crowd of 4,000 Despite protests from conservationists,
the structure was demolished in February 1982.

Dolls being distributed in June 1937 to the fifty Basque children, refugees from the Spanish Civil War, being cared for at Watermillock, Bolton.

Eric Gill stands next to his monumental *Creation* in 1937. Nearing completion, the sculpture was destined for the League of Nations Building in Geneva. The centre panel was 'practically entirely filled with the naked figure of a man...a vast and grand figure of Man with hand outstretched and the tip of his finger touching the tip of the finger of God'.

A family enjoying a day on the beach at Blackpool on 1 July 1939.

such as Evelyn Irons and Radclyffe Hall dressed in trousers (rather less exceptional for women by the 1930s), shirts and ties, fitted tweed jackets and in Hall's case men's socks and spats in winter and a brocade smoking jacket in the evenings. Hall, Ethel Sands and Valentine Ackland had their hair cut in a severe Eton crop, while some women wore signet rings on their little fingers to signal their sexual preferences. No doubt other female teachers, shop assistants, typists, civil servants and daughters of the vicarage, eschewing the dramas, scandals and *ménages à trois* of others, spent the thirties dressed indistinguishably from other women in quiet, unflamboyant, same-sex domesticity and fidelity.

Virginia Woolf recorded a Bloomsbury dinner party at which the company had fallen to discussing *The Well of Loneliness*. 'Morgan [E.M. Forster] said that Dr Head [the Woolfs' doctor] can convert the sodomites. "Would you like to be converted?" Leonard asked. "No", said Morgan, quite definitely.' Nor would a host of other thirties figures for whom sodomy, mutual masturbation, fellatio, bisexuality, cross dressing and 'rough trade' had become either a persistent way of life or an interregnum between youth and maturity. Young men at Oxford and Cambridge, Cyril Connolly's 'homintern', were as radical in their sexual practices as in their politics. 'There was [a sodomy club] at Oxford between the wars and I am informed there was another at Cambridge,' fumed the Bishop of Rochester during a debate on homosexual law reform in the 1960s. Younger members of the fraternity included W.H. Auden ('Wystan – whose preference was for fellatio – could always on the brief journey to London make a contact,' wrote his Oxford contemporary A.L. Rowse, who was pretty adept at that too), Christopher Isherwood, John Lehmann, Stephen Spender, Tom Driberg (who favoured 'bright green Oxford bags' and who was nearly thrown out of the historian A.J.P. Taylor's twenty-first birthday party for pestering a married waiter), Guy Burgess and Anthony Blunt. Among the older 'queers' (as the nomenclature was in pre-gay days, since the term 'homosexual' sounded rather clinical and diagnostic) were Forster, J.M. Keynes, Cecil Beaton (a bird of paradise in dress when young, and 'really a terrible, terrible homosexualist and [I] try so hard not to be'), Noël Coward (whose song 'Mad About the Boy', written for a 1932 review, *Words and Music*, had to be sung by a woman, Joyce Barbour) and Lytton Strachey.

These were all privileged men moving in artistic or intellectual circles where difference and eccentricity were appreciated and esteemed. 'I propose to call them Lilies of the Valley,' decided Virginia Woolf, as 'William Plomer, with his policeman then Stephen [Spender], then Auden and Joe Ackerley [the saturninely handsome literary editor of *The Listener* from 1935] all lodged in Maida Vale, and wearing different coloured Lilies. Their great sorrow at the moment is Siegfried Sassoon's defection; he's gone and married a woman.'

Young working-class men would stand at the back of Collins Music Hall in Islington being masturbated by an unknown hand, pick up and be picked up in the criss-cross warren of arches and alleyways under the Adelphi between Charing Cross and the Embankment, in the Rotherhithe Tunnel, have encounters in St James's Park, Hyde Park (where the police detected thirty queer incidents in 1932), Hampstead Heath, Shadwell Park, Victoria Park, Kennington Common, Hackney Marshes, and their equivalent provincial open spaces – where there were plenty of bushes. In the pubs along Waterloo Road, where servicemen stayed at the nearby Union Jack Club, a honeypot for female prostitutes too. Pansies, nancy boys, 'Dilly boys, soliciting in the West End, spending their 'pink shilling' in bars or cafés where one was bound to find a like-minded soul. 'Day after uneventful day, night after loveless night, we sat in this café [the Black Cat in Old Compton Street, Soho] buying each other cups of tea, combing each other's hair and trying each other's lipstick,' recalled a one-time 'Dilly boy, Dennis Pratt, who changed his name to Quentin Crisp in 1931. Lyons Corner House in Coventry Street, on the corner of Leicester Square, was the 'absolute mecca' for queers, who had to queue to get in on a Sunday afternoon. 'The first floor was known as the Lilly Pond. You went in, ordered your tea and toast and table-hopped.' They encountered each other in the Turkish baths of Jermyn Street or Bayswater, the Savoy or the Imperial Hotel, Russell Square – sixteen were still open by the mid-1930s, including one in Bermondsey – murmuring through the steam, 'Is she so?', 'Is she musical?', 'Is she TBH [to be had]?' to be sure.

'Painted boys' might find some dive – perhaps the Adelphi in the Edgware Road, or the Caravan, a basement club in Endell Street tricked out in Oriental style which boasted nearly five hundred members within six weeks of opening in July 1934 – where they could dance cheek to cheek. But not in Soho clubs like the Festival in Dean Street, the Careless Stork in Denman Street, the Sphinx in Gerrard Street, owned by Muriel Belcher and Dolly Mayers who also owned the Music Box in Leicester Place, which opened in 1937. They might be 'men only', but they were respectable and exclusive: the entrance fee was steep, the dress code strict (ties had to be worn) and the doormen vigilant in screening out any exhibitionist 'queans' or working-class trade.

They had sex in lodgings – a 1928 survey had estimated that there were nearly 17,000 single, unskilled working-class men living in London lodging houses – in cheap hotels, leaving an ochre-coloured stain, a 'map of Ireland', for the chambermaid to find on the sheets; up against the wall in dark alleyways, an overcoat strategically draped over an arm; swiftly on the top deck of night buses; on the back seat of a parked car; in the dark of the cinema (less than satisfactory, since the LCC insisted on shaded lights to pierce the gloom, and usherettes were instructed to shine their torches along the rows of seats at intervals). Approaches were made and coupling achieved in public urinals such as the one on the corner of Tooley Street in Bermondsey, near London Bridge, which was 'of such a nature and in such a position as to lend itself to acts of indecency, being an old round iron structure with small holes from which any approach from outside can be observed'. More prosperous men on the lookout would frequent the magnificent men-only Long Bar of the Trocadero in Shaftesbury Avenue (owned by J.J. Lyons, but which in 1937 started to admit women and was renamed the 'Salted Almond Cocktail Bar'), or the Criterion bar or the Regent's Palace Hotel on Piccadilly Circus, Gennaro's in New Compton Street, or maybe the Running Horse pub in Shepherd Market, well placed for that other sort of gentleman's club in Pall Mall and St James's.

All illegal. All criminal offences under Section 11 (Labouchère's amendment) to the 1885 Criminal Law Amendment Act ('the blackmailer's charter'), which defined any act of 'gross indecency' between men, even those between consenting adults in private, as against the law. It was not an offence to be homosexual, but it was to indulge in any practice that could be defined as homosexual. There were additional local by-laws against 'indecency', and another Criminal Law Amendment Act in 1912 had made it an offence to 'persistently importune for an immoral purpose'. In fact, private premises could only be searched with a warrant, so those men who were able to take their lovers or pick-ups home (as well as those who lived discreet, regulated, though often anxious, lives with a male partner), or who kept away from notorious West End 'black spots', were safer from police surveillance and arrest than those driven to public or semi-public places to satisfy their urges. But even they were not entirely safe, because the police could apply for a warrant if there were public complaints or private information that homosexual acts were being committed on any premises. 'The police thought of homosexuals as North American Indians thought of bison. They cast about for a way of exterminating them in herds. With the aid of informers they discovered where the great drag balls were being held, and turned their attention thither. These balls were organised by private individuals and held in any of the large banquet rooms that can be hired for parties. They couldn't, of course, be advertised, but no publicity was needed.

The network always managed to reach anyone who might want to go and had half-a-crown to spare for a ticket. About three-quarters of the men who attended these dances went in drag. In one raid a hundred or more screaming, shrieking, fighting, kicking boys in feathered head-dresses and diamanté trains could be scooped, pushed or flung into vans by a relatively small squad of policemen.' But away from the febrile West End of rent boys and drag events, frippery and cottaging, the scene was a great deal calmer. Many queer men managed to live lives, have relationships and friendships, that never came into contact with the law.

'I got pretty shrewd at finding books – Edward Carpenter . . . had the most influence on me . . . Walt Whitman . . . J.A. Symonds . . . *A Problem of Greek Ethics*. There was very limited availability of information [about homosexuality] in the thirties. I was very much a person who found out by books,' recalled Trevor Thomas from South Wales who worked in art galleries after finishing university. Others read 'Havelock Ellis . . . And of course Plato . . . authors like Walter Pater and Winckelmann and people like that, and they all sorted of pointed in that direction.' But books were not how most 'found out'. Homosexuality in the East End of London had always been accepted to an extent. A working-class Tynesider who had come to London to work as a dancer used to go to East End pubs 'where the mums and dads used to go. And they referred to the boys by their camp name. "Hello Lola, love. How are you, dear? You going to give us a song?" The East End of London, which had very tightly-knit families living in their streets of terraced houses, in and out one another's, they know about their sons and it was accepted.'

The historian Matt Houlbrook suggests that homosexual relations between young working-class men might not have been at all unusual in the inter-war years. Such men would not necessarily have regarded themselves as homosexuals, in the way that effeminate exhibitionists were in their book – cissies, poofs, nancy boys – but rather as simply seeking sexual relief in a predominantly male culture of work and pub, a practice that would cease when they 'grew up', married and became the 'man of the house' and the breadwinner. Houlbrook instances (among others) the writer John Lehmann's lover, Fred Turner, a Coldstream Guard who ended their longish-term relationship when he married his pregnant girlfriend in 1934.

Money and class: the decade's sexuality acted like a distorting mirror. 'The difference of class . . . between [us] . . . .provide[d] some element of mystery, which corresponded to a difference of sex. I was in love . . . with his background, his soldiering, his working-class home,' wrote the poet Stephen Spender of his ex-Guardsman love, Tony Hyndman. What was acceptable in one stratum of society could bring social disgrace, ostracism, the loss of a job and family, blackmail, even suicide in another. Men who would never have met in the usual course of professional or social life might do so in the pursuit of an alternative sexual freemasonry. A middle-class, boarding-school-educated professional male prostitute 'never saw myself as anything like the street boys. The first man I was with taught me everything. We used to go along Piccadilly and he'd say, now don't you ever do that. You see them being picked up. He said, you're better class than that, you're educated. That's for silly little queens . . . I never had any brushes with the law . . . mainly because being educated, I was sensible enough not to do things in parks and things like that.'

There had been established homosexual networks since at least the 1920s in places like Liverpool, Manchester, Glasgow, Blackpool, Brighton, but unemployment brought young men from the distressed areas of Wales and the North to the capital in search of work. A few, unable to find it, might have been exploited for, or themselves exploited, their sex. The Church Army mapped what it called 'the curse of the Embankment' along the Thames, where young men were able to 'earn bed, board and pocket money easily' by 'tapping' wealthier men there, or by hanging around Trafalgar Square and Piccadilly, The Strand or Soho, preening in the plate-glass windows of shops, asking the time or for a cigarette from anyone who might be a middle-class 'steamer' (punter/client), or a gentleman who fancied 'a bit of the rough' and knew where to go for it.

Urinals were particularly favoured locations. In 1937 the respectable publisher Routledge brought out a guidebook by one 'Paul Pry', *For Your Convenience: A Learned Dialogue Instructive to All Londoners and London Visitors*. The slim, pocket-sized volume offered 'some of the things a man often wants to know . . . [such as] what to do if one were walking through Wigmore Street after three cups of tea'. It indicated with a green dot 'the precise location of every refuge . . . one of those zinc or iron enclosures painted a grateful green'. Places of that kind 'which have no attendants, afford excellent rendezvous to people who wish to meet out of doors and yet escape the eye of the Busy . . . to exchange information out of earshot of their friends, or the observation of the Dicks'. Yet it was urinals that the 'Dicks' (plain-clothed policemen) particularly had in their sights, clamping down on any examples of 'cottaging', acting as *agents provocateurs* to entrap the eager and unwary.

In 1927 a schoolmaster, Frank Champain, who was an Oxford Blue and a war hero, was arrested for importuning in the Adelphi arches urinal and sentenced to three months' hard labour. However, on appeal – he cited a weak bladder as the reason for his frequent visits to the stalls – his conviction was overturned, and a committee was set up to investigate police practices. Following its cautious recommendations, fewer such 'stings' were mounted, partly because they were considered too demeaning (or distracting) for the police involved: they were 'a sacrifice a police officer should not be required to make . . . to invite and endure an insult to his manhood of a gross character' that not only affected the individual officer's self-esteem, but also the 'dignity of the force'.

In 1932 there were 162 cases of homosexual behaviour in London resulting in prosecution – by far the majority occurring in the West End and being tried before Bow Street or Marlborough Street magistrates. In 1937 the number had risen to 251, but the map remained the same. One of the humiliating rituals of arrest was when the police ('Brendas' in queer speak, short for Brenda Bracelets) would rub a suspect's cheeks with blotting paper to establish if he was wearing make-up on his 'ecaf' (back-slang for 'face', part of a rich queer language of inclusion and wariness).

In 1929 there had been ten arrests for importuning; increased police surveillance meant that the following year this number had risen to 113. This was evidence of a gradual change that Matt Houlbrook traces throughout the 1930s which would inform legislation more than thirty years later. A distinction increasingly began to be drawn by law enforcers, the progressive medical establishment and the wider public between the flamboyant, effeminate, painted, usually working-class or 'bohemian' 'screaming quean', and the discreet, unremarkable homosexual who was 'normal' in every way other than his sexuality, and was seen as posing no threat to society.

In 1932, thirty officers of the Metropolitan Police Force burst into the ballroom on the ground floor of a house in Holland Park. The partygoers were all male, mostly working in domestic service or in nearby hotels. Half were in lounge suits, half in evening dresses and wearing make-up. The organiser of the ball was 'Lady Austin' (in fact a twenty-four-year-old barman from Baron's Court). Her ladyship was arrested along with fifty-nine others. However, he confounded the Inspector who was arresting him on being told that one of the plain-clothes constables was a policeman too. 'Fancy that, he is too nice. I could love him and rub his Jimmy for him for hours,' he trilled. When cautioned, he insisted, 'There is nothing wrong with that. You may think so, but it is what we call real love for a man. You call us Nancies and bum boys, but . . . before long our cult will be allowed in this country.'

TWENTY

Regimenting Mass Happiness

My holiday snapshots disclosed
A thing that I hadn't supposed
That I'd lain on the shore
For a fortnight or more
Underdeveloped and over exposed.

C.H. Lewis, Liverpool, one of the winners in the *Evening Standard*
'Holiday Limerick' competition in August 1932, prize half a guinea

August for the people and their favourite islands . . .
Lulled by the light they live their dreams of freedom,
May climb the old road, twisting to the moors,
Play leapfrog, enter cafés, wear
The tigerish blazer and the dove-like shoes.

W.H. Auden, 'To a Writer on His Birthday' (1935)

One day, 'out of the blue' while sitting on the front at Bognor watching 'an endless drift of faces stream by', an idea for a novel came to R.C. Sherriff, the son of an insurance clerk who was born in Kingston upon Thames, never married, and would die a few miles away in Esher. He felt rather diffident about it when it was finished, and submitting it to the publisher Victor Gollancz 'seemed like offering a fruit drop to a lion.' Gollancz had published the play that had made Sherriff a household name, *Journey's End*, based on his own experiences in the First World War (he had been badly wounded in the battle of Ypres) and first staged at London's Savoy Theatre in 1929.

Sherriff's novel, *The Fortnight in September*, was published in 1931 and was acclaimed as 'lovely', 'enchanting' and 'a little masterpiece'. It sold 'like hot cakes: 10,000 copies as quick as they were printed; 20,000 in a month. An American publisher had it out in record time. It got enthusiastic notices there and sold as well as it did at home. It was taken for Germany, France and Scandinavia, Italy and Spain.' Sherriff's career revived, and he was whisked off to Hollywood to script the film of H.G. Wells' *The Invisible Man* in 1933, and *Goodbye, Mr Chips*, James Hilton's sentimental story of a schoolmaster in 1939. Later, back in Britain, he was employed as a screenwriter on several of Alexander Korda's hits.

The Fortnight in September is a perfect, relentlessly detailed evocation of a lower-middle-class family's fortnight by the sea in the 1930s. The Stevens' holiday has been eagerly anticipated all year. The budgie has been left with the neighbours, the milk cancelled – except for half a pint a day for the cat – all newspapers and magazines stopped, but the newsagent keeping that month's *Family Gardening* for their return, the silver (consisting of an inkstand that had been a wedding present and some cups the oldest son had won for running at school) locked up. 'Dad' exchanges his usual suit and stiff collar for 'flannel trousers and his cricket shirt . . . and a tie of course for the train journey, but at the sea he would leave the neck open'. Their destination is 'Seaview', the same Bognor boarding house they have stayed at every year since Mr and Mrs Stevens spent their honeymoon there. The rates are £3.10s a week including service and cooking, food bought by the family – or rather Mrs Stevens – to be cooked by Seaview's proprietor, Mrs Huggett, and served by the maid, Molly, with an extra charge of a shilling a week for the cruet. There is 'the first walk along the front, the first ice cream of the holiday' – and so it goes on: nothing really happens for more than three hundred pages. It is the annual repetition that gives the holiday meaning, the retreading of family dynamics and hopes, not novelty or discovery. The sun shines, the family watch the end-of-the-pier show, doze in deckchairs, hire a beach hut where tea can be brewed, bathe in the sea, listen to the band, send postcards home. Finally they pack their suitcases, take a 'short stroll down to the front for a blow of sea air', and return by train via Clapham Junction to their house in Dulwich, its 'garden cut short by the railway line', for another year.

The TUC had passed a resolution in favour of holidays with pay way back in 1911, but war and then the Depression had put an end to hopes of any such government legislation, even though the Commissioner for the Special [that is distressed] Areas, Sir Malcolm Stewart, argued in 1935 that compulsory paid holidays were one way, along with shorter working hours, raising the school leaving age and lowering the retirement age, to alleviate unemployment. On average, male manual workers put in just under forty-eight hours a week and women 43.5, including overtime, and though it might seem unlikely that there was much on offer during the Depression, the Ministry of Labour estimated in 1933 that on average eight hours' overtime a week was being worked in a number of trades, including the woollen industry and brick manufacture.

In April 1937 only about four million manual workers earning £250 a year or less, out of a total workforce of 18.5 million, were entitled to paid holidays, and perhaps another million had also wangled the right – both the Soviet Union and Nazi Germany were rather more progressive than Britain when it came to paid holidays for the workers. Following the introduction of a Private Member's Bill in November 1936 the government set up a committee to look into the whole question of holidays with pay, taking evidence from employers, the trade unions, representatives from holiday resorts, the transport industry and a host of other interested parties. All sides agreed that workers needed holidays; the matter for debate was whether industry could afford to pay for them. The TUC, which was seeking twelve paid working days a year, ideally between April and October, maintained that every worker had a right to 'regular periods of freedom from daily toil, commonly described as periods of leisure', and that industry could afford such a modest concession, which would represent less than 4 per cent of the total wage bill. The unions had heard the argument too often that such measures of social advancement would be 'the straw that broke the camel's back', would kill 'the goose that laid the golden eggs of prosperity'. But 'The camel goes on and the goose still lays eggs,' a Midland's miners' representative acidly pointed out.

On the other side, the employers argued that paid holidays would cost industry far more than the 4 per cent the TUC estimated, would make British industry uncompetitive abroad, and far from helping unemployment, would be likely to increase it, would be nothing but a covert pay increase, and that employers had no right to 'take a portion of the [workers'] wages and spend it for them', which is what they would effectively be doing. Austin Hopkinson, an industrialist National Government MP, asked a fundamental question: If the social services were abolished, would workers receive increased wages as a result? He seemed unconvinced when he was told that they would.

The Committee's recommendations, a cautious compromise between the arguments advanced by the two sides, were enshrined in the 1938 Holidays with Pay Act, which set up a special 'Holiday' branch in the Ministry of Labour to oversee voluntary schemes before legislation was planned to be introduced in 1940–41. By June 1939 over eleven million white- and blue-collar workers were entitled to holidays with pay – one working week plus bank holidays was usual. As the MP for Blackpool, Roland Robinson, said during the debate on the Bill, 'The summer holiday, so recently a privilege of a minority, has become the prerogative of the million.'

But, of course, having time off work is not necessarily the same as being able to take a holiday – the rent or mortgage still had to be paid, and there was the cost of transport and accommodation and 'incidentals' like new clothes, buckets and spades and more. Some people had managed to take a holiday before the Act either because their particular industry or employer had agreed a deal, or through putting money aside all year in thrift clubs and other forms of saving. As the TUC chairman Sir Walter Citrine rightly predicted, the advent of holidays with pay would not lead to 'a sudden rush to the seaside'. The cost of a week's holiday away for the family was beyond the reach of those thirteen million workers who earned less than £4 a week. And of course for the unemployed there were no holidays with pay. 'We are a town mostly existing on the dole, and a great many of us have had too many holidays,' noted a Dumbarton newspaper on the edge of Glasgow in 1932.

However, paradoxically the 1931 financial crisis had benefited a number of Britain's seaside resorts at a time when it was seen as unpatriotic to go abroad: money should be spent on Britain's failing economy, and in any case when the pound was devalued after Britain left the Gold Standard, foreign travel became more expensive. The 1921 Health and Pleasure Resorts Act had permitted local authorities to spend modest amounts of the revenue raised from the hire of deckchairs and beach huts, and from other tourist attractions, on promotional advertising. By the mid-1930s resorts such as Torquay were spending substantial sums on advertisements in newspapers and large-circulation periodicals such as the *Radio Times* (which sold three million copies weekly in 1935), brochures, guides, even films shown in cinemas. Railway and coach companies gained too, with the increasing popularity of camping and rambling holidays. 'Hiker Special' and 'Mystery Excursion' trains were run for those who wanted to take that sort of holiday, and reduced coach fares were offered to campers. A film, *Dawdling in Devon*, was released in 1933 and shown in the US as well as the UK.

The combination of an increasing number of people having paid holidays, falling prices and rising standards of living in some regions meant that while large parts of the country were in decline, or certainly static in terms of development throughout the 1930s, a number of seaside resorts were booming. An estimated £3 to £4 million was spent on improvements to the seafront every year of the decade, with promenades being extended and entertainment facilities built. Rhyl in North Wales acquired a new theatre, three cinemas, an open-air swimming pool and a bowls pavilion, while Blackpool spent £3 million in the 1930s on its parks, promenade and Winter Gardens. At Barry Island in South Wales and Ilfracombe in North Devon, projects to attract holidaymakers were started in order to provide work for the local unemployed.

Seaside holidays were as socially calibrated as any other activity. Some resorts attracted the middle classes whose idea of a holiday was to have a rest, stay in a 'nice hotel' if they could afford it, or a boarding house if not, sit in a deckchair and read, knit or doze, stroll along the esplanade, have a knickerbocker glory in a café, listen to a band playing on the promenade bandstand, admire the municipal floral clock, maybe play a game of bowls, tennis or mini-golf while the children paddled, built sandcastles, shrimped in rock pools or watched Punch and Judy on the beach. Bognor Regis was one such (until its post-war redevelopment), Torquay another, as were Lytham St Annes, Bournemouth, Eastbourne and Poole. Westgate in Essex aimed to distinguish itself from the more 'common' Margate, and Frinton on Sea, where nannies were often sent with the children while parents holidayed abroad, fought hard to keep its exclusivity from nearby Clacton and Southend (though there was a fast young crowd that also favoured Frinton in the inter-war years, their 'pranks' disturbing its sedate pleasures). Southsea, near Portsmouth, promoted itself as the resort for those 'who prefer their seaside stay to be spent among surroundings that are peaceful, quiet and refined without being dull' (subtext: unlike Margate or Blackpool). The 1932 official guide for Torquay made it clear that the resort held little attraction for those 'whose idea of a holiday is compounded of Big Wheels, paper caps, donkeys . . . tin whistles, and generally a remorseless harlequinade'. Its natural clientèle were 'the thoroughly normal, healthy and educated people who are the backbone of the nation'. Sidmouth in Devon was equally exclusive, and worked to keep it that way, vetoing plans for a holiday camp to be built nearby, making a supreme effort to limit day-trippers, declining to lay on any entertainment or publicise itself. Bexhill, with its De la Warr Pavilion and active Philosophical Society, while not being in the Devon resorts league, considered itself a cut above nearby Hastings. In general, resorts that were beyond the reach of railway lines, such as those in parts of North Devon, Cornwall and Norfolk, remained smaller and more exclusive, since a car was required to reach them.

As well as being pestered by photographers taking their picture – albeit without a film, until they found someone who agreed they would like a holiday souvenir – a family's stroll along the promenade might be enlivened by an encounter with 'Lobby Lud' (so called after the telegraphic address of the *Westminster Gazette*, which had introduced the character in 1927, and carried on from 1930 by the *News Chronicle*) or one of his imitators, who was to be challenged by a holidaymaker carrying a copy of the appropriate newspaper and uttering the approved words, 'You are Lobby Lud [or whoever] and I claim my £5.'

Mr Lud was but one trilby-hatted, belted-raincoated, pipe-smoking mani-festation of the 'circulation wars' of the 1930s, when the popular press, battling for readers, offered ever more fantastic inducements to people to buy their paper. A legal judgement in 1928 put an end to competition lotteries, leading to an avalanche of free gifts as troops of canvassers rapped on doors throughout the land offering sets of encyclopaedias, or Dickens novels, cameras, wristwatches, kettles or silk stockings – free fire insurance was the come-on the *News Chronicle* offered, while the *Daily Mail* prom-ised to pay £100 school fees for children whose 'bread winning parent' had met with a fatal accident, and £10 for Boy Scouts and Girl Guides who had suffered 'accidents involving a broken bone' – in the hope of getting the householder to take out a subscription. In 1933 this strategy cost the *Daily Express* more than £55,000 over a ten-week period. Indeed, between 1930 and 1932 each new reader of the *Daily Herald*, which at one point offered cash for the birth of twins to its subscribers, providing they survived for forty-eight hours (the *Daily Mail* did the same), was costing the paper £1, while the price of the paper was a penny. By 1937 the typical news-paper employed more canvassers than editorial staff. Since this was such an expensive and ultimately self-defeating war, the inducements gradually dried up.

Eileen Whiteing recalled childhood summers spent at Bognor, Eastbourne or Worthing (though towards the end of the thirties the family was venturing further afield to Dorset, Devon, Somerset and Cornwall). Their prepara-tions were similar to those of R.C. Sherriff's fictional Stevens family: two large trunks packed with summer dresses, sunhats, 'bathing costumes, sandals, mackintoshes and umbrellas, and so on, to cover all types of weather possible in the normal English summer', were sent on in advance; dust covers were fitted over the furniture; the household silver and pets were taken to grandparents for safekeeping. Accommodation was at a boarding house or in private apartments, with catering laid on – 'my mother had no intention of cooking on holiday' – and they usually took the maid with them, 'to give my parents plenty of freedom to go off to concert parties or listen to the band'.

Before the advent of paid holidays, workers would save up all year, paying a small amount each week – sixpence was usual – into a 'going off' club organised by their factory or by a local pub, club or corner shop: 90 per cent of the 4,500 employed at Lever Brothers' Port Sunlight works in 1938 contributed to such a club. The money would be paid back, with interest, on the eve of the holiday, with the 'divi' from the Co-op used to buy some new clothes or a pair of shoes. This meant that 'the miners and mill-hands and other thousands who come to Blackpool in their thousands for their annual holiday have each saved up about £20. This they deliberately spend,' wrote the journalist Charles Graves, who made a tour of holiday spots in 1930. 'They go back home having spent their last penny, take a cab home, give the driver 1s.6d which they left behind the clock for this very purpose, and start saving for the next year again the next day.'

The notion of blowing a year's savings in a week drew opprobrium from some London journalists, who regarded this as 'thrift of a sort, but hardly of the right sort'. In Oldham in 1931 at the depth of the Depression, the 148 'going off' clubs paid out considerably less than in any year since 1924, but nevertheless disbursed £185,000 to their members. The local paper congratulated the 'Oldhamers', recognising that this sum had only been achieved 'by strong determination and the most careful management of household budgets'.

Even after paid holidays were introduced, a holiday away was beyond the reach of many. Full board in places such as Brighton, Southend, Clacton or Ramsgate would cost 35 shillings a week, rising to 42 shillings at the height of the season. This meant that a family with two children would have to spend £6.6s in July or August. When the cost of travel and spending money was added, the total would come to over £10 – more than three weeks' wages for most working men.

In 1937, the year before the Act, it was estimated that fifteen million Britons took an annual holiday – that is roughly a third of the population. A survey of London's leisure habits suggested that that included around half of all working-class families. Brighton and Hove and other resorts along the south coast grew rapidly, providing more accommodation for holiday-makers as well as becoming increasingly popular to retire to. It was the same along the Essex coast and for seaside towns in Kent, such as Whitstable and Ramsgate, that were easily accessible from London, as well as for the resorts along the coast of North Wales, and Douglas on the Isle of Man, that were in easy reach of the Midlands and North-West. Some villages in Devon and Cornwall grew in popularity – Brixham, for example, saw its fishing industry decline as the number of its boarding houses doubled, and it was much the same in Hastings in Sussex, where beaches and quays were cleared of nets and capstans, and mooring for fishing boats was replaced by car and coach parks and a boating lake. Resorts on the east coast, not too far from the Yorkshire industrial towns, such as Whitby, Redcar, Filey and Scarborough (considered rather posher than its neighbours) that offered sand (or shingle) and bracing sea breezes flourished.

And then there was Blackpool, and its marine conurbation sprawling from Crosby up to Fleetwood by way of Southport and Lytham St Annes. Blackpool had meant fun by the sea for many years before workers had paid holidays. Though 'some, eccentrically went to Morecambe or even Rhyl ... Blackpool was full at any one time with neighbours from the same town ... groups of relatives and friends would share lodgings, or take them in the same street and young and old, children and courting couples and married folk alike, would spend a year's savings in a glorious spree'. The holidaymakers were on a 'Wakes Week', when the mills, shops, post office and schools would all pull down the shutters. Wakes Weeks had started in the Lancashire cotton industry towards the end of the nineteenth century, often around an established local festival. The custom had spread to the Yorkshire woollen mills and then to the pottery towns of Staffordshire and some other industries in the Midlands, so from mid-July to mid-September one town after another would shut up shop for a week – and by the mid-thirties often a fortnight – and the place would be deserted as people took their annual holiday *en masse*: so many of them in Blackpool that the resort was known as Oldham or Rochdale or Halifax or Bradford or wherever 'by the Sea'.

Night and Day, a short-lived attempt to provide a British equivalent to the *New Yorker* magazine, for which such literary luminaries as Evelyn Waugh, Graham Greene, Rebecca West, Peter Fleming, Aldous Huxley and Christopher Isherwood wrote, and which made a specialty of getting down and dirty with reports of bottle parties and rather dubious nightclubs, gave its readers a taste of 'Blackpool Belle' in September 1937. 'Whatever way you come to Blackpool the first you see of it is the Tower, Eiffel's not so much smaller sister ... You can dance here for a shilling and choose any of Lancashire and Yorkshire's neat-fingered little mill girls you see for a partner ... and for an extra sixpence go up the Tower and look down on Blackpool's swarming sands and the Prom.' The author of this Blackpool experience was Ralph Parker, one of the team of some eighty Mass-Observers who descended on Blackpool in August 1937, since the resort was where so many of the people of Bolton ('Worktown') decamped to spend their magical 'fifty-second' week of the working year. The largely middle-class Mass-Observers wanted to see the industrial North, that 'race apart' they found so gratifying to study in great detail, at play. Bolton was characterised as a 'town that offers few prospects of a better life for the individual and where looking forward to a good afterlife has nearly disappeared'. The 'possibility of a win on the football pools and the certainty of a week's leisure ... are the only two releases from the routine of life'.

In the case of this particular exercise, M-O's primary motivation seemed to be a somewhat prurient interest in sex-by-the sea. Its observers acted more like ornithologists than anthropologists, creeping around in the dark, crouching in bushes, crawling under the pier, pretending to be drunk so they could observe couples in the sand and check out exactly what they were doing, sidling along the beach timing embracing couples with a stop-watch. However, this energetic surveillance ended in disappointment: out of 234 cases of 'lovemaking' observed it had only been possible to confirm three incidents of actual copulation, and that included one of their own number who had sex up against a wall with a married woman from Leeds.

Blackpool was reckoned to be a good-value holiday. The journalist Charles Graves decided that the secret of its success was the fact that '2d in Blackpool goes as far as 1s. in London . . . 4s. in Paris, 5s. at Le Touquet, Deauville, Cairo, Biarritz, and Monte Carlo . . . what you can do with 1s. is incred-ible. At the Tower, the almost fabulous red-brick building on the front, you can see for 1s. an aquarium full of Japanese salamanders and other odd fish; you can inspect the menagerie with its lions, monkeys and other animals; you can dance in a ball-room about twice the size of any London palais de dance; you can watch a child's ballet with 150 performers; you can go up to the roof gardens and see the midgets' entertainment . . . Yes, Blackpool is flabbergasting. You are like a cheerful straw in an organised whirlpool of ridiculously inexpensive gaiety. Blackpool takes off its jacket to give you a good time, and give it does. It has been described as a pleasure factory. That is apt. What a factory!'

But the town was changing. Blackpool's annual publicity budget had been ratcheted up, and the 'Blackpool habit' was drawing visitors from further afield than the traditional 'Wakes Week' towns – Glasgow, the Midlands, South Wales, London, the Bristol area. Housing developments were being built round its outer edges in the hope of attracting permanent residents to an area whose economy was over-dependent on holidaymakers and day-trippers – unemployment was as high in Blackpool as in factory towns in the 1930s, and between 1930 and 1933 poor relief soared by £16,000 a year. As well as modernist redesigns along the seashore and new department stores, the number of pawn shops, salerooms and second-hand shops in the borough increased.

The Big Wheel, which had creaked round at such a snail's pace that the only people for whom it held any thrills were courting couples, had been demolished in 1928, its carriages sold off for garden sheds. Rejuvenation of the town centre started as Blackpool emerged from the slump years. This 'Mecca of Health and Pleasure', as its guidebook proclaimed, took as its motto the single word 'Progress'. The Olympia Amusement Arcade was erected on its site, and a new, six-storey Woolworths, reputedly the world's largest, opened on the Promenade in 1936, drawing some visitors straight from the Central Station, with never a thought of seeing the sea. The Promenade was extended, the ballroom at the Tower refurbished, a covered swimming pool and sun lounge built on the North Promenade, and what the architect Hugh Casson called 'a tangle of kiosks' was replaced, thus 'creating an air of order and unity on the beach'. Joseph Emberton, the architect tasked with smartening up the Pleasure Beach area, designed a miniature railway that included a replica Forth Bridge in 1933, an Ice Drome (a venue for skating, ice hockey and extravaganzas on ice) which opened in 1936, and a new casino to replace the wedding-cake-style one built in 1913. Owing something to the De la Warr Pavilion at Bexhill, it opened in May 1939. The last word in thirties modernist chic, it boasted a tower in the shape of a giant concrete corkscrew echoing the spiral staircase inside, air conditioning and 'magic eye' doors that opened when someone approached them. The building was, Hugh Casson pronounced, 'one more step towards developing an amusement area on rational lines'.

Blackpool's attraction can perhaps best be understood by looking at the Automobile Association Member's Handbook for 1939. The handbook listed only two four-star hotels (the Metropole and the Imperial, which had its own orchestra, ballroom and Turkish and sea-water baths, hard tennis court and a Louis XVI restaurant), six with three stars and only one with two, far behind the totals of Bournemouth or even Southend, or much smaller places such as Torquay, Llandudno or Sidmouth. Most visitors to Blackpool stayed year after year in one of the boarding houses presided over by Mrs Porter, Mrs Peel, the Misses Lawton or one of the other 4,000 Blackpool landladies, many of them widows or spinsters.

The Blackpool landlady, a stock figure of fun in comedy shows, on the radio, screen and picture postcards in the 1930s, could be a motherly, welcoming soul, but equally she might be a fearsome figure. Most insisted that they were offering their guests a regular 'home from home', but the notion of allowing visitors their own key was unthought of, and the Boarding House Keepers' Association opposed any extension of local licensing or entertainment hours, on the grounds that this would keep visitors out late having fun, and thus their landlady sitting up waiting for them to come in. But at least by the 1930s guests might possibly expect a family table at meal-times, rather than a long communal one, and might find a washbasin with running hot water in their bedroom rather than a bowl and pitcher.

If the North Pier, the nearby beach and the streets around Stanley Park (a huge area of grass, flowerbeds and sporting facilities named after the

Derby family and opened by the Earl in 1926) considered itself the smart end of Blackpool, the Golden Mile, the stretch of promenade facing the sea between Central Station and Central Pier which culminated in the 550-foot-high Blackpool Tower was where most trippers took their pleasures.

While Bournemouth, Southport and Redcar attracted around two million visitors a year, Rhyl and Hastings between two and a half and three million, and Southend five and half million, Blackpool claimed that seven million visitors a year flocked there annually. On August Bank Holiday weekend in 1937, 425 special trains were laid on, and as many as 31,000 cars, 5,300 motor coaches and 6,360 motorcycles joined the throng. Not all of the visitors were the traditional families: young people – usually in all-female or all-male groups – were drawn by the amusements, the dancing, the singing booths, the opportunity to hook up with someone of the opposite sex: a 'passion express' late train ran from Blackpool to Bolton, so that day-trippers could get home at the end of the evening.

The problem for all British seaside resorts was the shortness of the season. Despite valiant attempts to portray Blackpool as an all-year-round resort, its main trade was from June to September. The famous illuminations – '27 miles of festoons', reckoned Mass-Observation – comprising 300,000 lightbulbs outlining the piers, the Tower and other important buildings, a row of plywood, illuminated laburnum trees stretching from Central Station to the Pleasure Beach, and a series of ever more complex tableaux from life, literature, stage and screen and nursery rhymes, many of which appeared to move, were an attempt to extend the season. The lights were switched on in mid-September (often by the town's benefactor, the Earl of Derby, or another local dignitary; in 1937 it was the Duke of Kent, who happened to be in Blackpool for other purposes), drawing thousands of trippers to take a slow tram ride (most of the carriages were disguised as something else – a fairy coach, a galleon), or increasingly to drive their cars, along the front, marvelling at the ingenuity and topicality of the garish displays. The 'flowerless town is suddenly festooned with vegetation, in which electric parrots flap their wings'. The illuminations were an outstanding success, bringing an unprecedented two million visitors to Blackpool in the six weeks that the lights blazed during September and October.

The sheer crush of people seems to have been an attraction to many. On August Bank Holiday Monday, 1934, the journalist William Holt noted 'three thousand dancing in the tower ballroom, six hundred dancing in Winter Gardens, and "pictures" packed . . . Day-trippers swarming very near sea. A black fringe all along the water's edge . . . boarding-house steps crowded, guests sitting or standing out. Melodeon and banjos playing.

Footpaths crowded. Greatest congregation of pedestrians between Central Station and Central Pier. Sluggish, gregarious, happiness packed like sardines . . . Promenade and sands an intensely moving sea of humanity, but without any definite currents . . . trams move through it like crowded ships.'

Blackpool's greatest attraction was the Tower, 'the best-known symbol in Britain . . . in Worktown [and the other industrial towns from which so many visitors came], every outlook is stamped with the indelible finger of a factory chimney. In Blackpool there are none, except the Tower, a chimney which will never smoke.' 'From the seahorse tank in its bowels to the brilliant lights on its tip, it guarantees good fun,' with Reginald Dixon playing his 'Wonder Wurlitzer organ to the four corners of the world by radio . . . a grotto aquarium, the vast dance hall . . . a zoo, a roof garden, aviary, criminal slot machines, palmistry, clairvoyants, tea bar, restaurants, lifts, circus, children's ballet, and palm grove'. It provided an unequalled view across Blackpool, which in 1937 boasted four theatres, five pierrot halls, a circus, the ice drome, an Indian theatre and nineteen cinemas which together could seat 70,000 patrons at two shows every evening. Stars of stage and screen came to perform at Blackpool, of whom two were particularly popular. The first was 'Our Gracie' – Gracie Fields, who was born above a fish and chip shop in Rochdale and who exemplified the mill-girl 'rags to riches dream' in such films as *Sally in Our Alley* (1931) and *Shipyard Sally* (1939). The second was another Lancashire entertainer, George Formby from Wigan, married to a champion clog dancer who managed his career. Formby's *double entendre*-packed comic songs held the same appeal as Donald McGill's saucy seaside postcards – which were also very popular in Blackpool.

Most visitors headed straight for the Golden Mile, intent on claiming an inch somewhere along the 'seven miles of golden sand' that the town's brochures claimed. There they could snooze in a deckchair, build sandcastles, watch Punch and Judy, bathe – or more likely paddle – in the sea, buy ice creams, oysters, fish and chips, candy floss and sticks of pink Blackpool rock (or sweets suggestively labelled 'Mae West's Vest' and 'Sally's What Nots'). They could have their weight guessed, their photograph taken by a 'smudge artist', record their voice in a song booth, buy risqué postcards of the fat man peering over his stomach complaining 'I've lost my little Willie' variety to send home. Or take a turn on one of the 'thrilling big dippers' or the 'Social Mixer', a large bowl that 'rotated at increasing speed . . . Everyone is churned up . . . As it stops . . . three [people] are violently sick.' Or the Ghost Train, Noah's Ark or the Fun House with its cakewalk and currents of air suddenly blowing up giggling women's skirts, slot machines or palmists' booths.

They could then wander among the endless titillating exhibitions that had been there since Victorian times, but that reached a new plateau of freak-ishness in the mid-1930s thanks to the entrepreneurial energies of 'Blackpool's Barnum', Luke Gannon, a Burnley man who had started his career in patent medicines, but after marrying a clairvoyant had begun exhibiting compelling examples of human oddity. There was the 'headless girl', with a 'professor' showing how she was fed and how she breathed (a mirror illusion), and an 'Educational Museum of Human Anatomy' with 'excellent replicas of the ravages of syphilis'. Another Blackpool attraction, Madame Tussaud's waxwork museum, added to the spectacle with a Chamber of Horrors displaying figures on the rack, a Chinese execution, the Torture of the Hook at Algiers, Dr Buck Ruxton's library (something of scoop: Ruxton, a Parsi surgeon who had settled in Lancashire and had killed his wife and maid and chopped their bodies up into such small pieces that the crime came to be labelled the 'jigsaw murder', was hanged at Strangeways Prison, Manchester, in May 1936). There was also a very topical – and partisan – exhibit, the 'Spanish Revolution Scene', depicting the massacre of the priests at Huelva during the Civil War, with replicas of their heads impaled on spikes and a promise that 'The Management, at very great cost, and much forethought, are endeavouring to place before our . . . patrons some idea of the every day atrocities, which are now taking place in Spain.'

On show too were a tableau of the Last Supper (in wax, threepence to view), various *tableaux vivants* (also known as *poses plastiques*) purporting to be representations of classic works of art, in fact providing an opportunity to stare at artfully posed 'nude' women (actually covered by body stockings). There were tattooed women, the 'ugliest woman on earth' – Mary Anne Bevan, a thirty-three-stone Irishwoman with jagged teeth – 'La Belle Eve', hailed as the 'most beautiful', a bearded lady from Russia, a woman from Accrington with no arms but who could knit with her feet, a dog-faced man, a bird-faced man (sometimes such exhibits were in fact animals), a three-legged boy, a boy with a lion's mane, a five-legged cow, a woman with 'lobster claws' instead of hands, a forty-two-year-old 'Hop o' my thumb' who weighed just twenty-four pounds and stood less than two feet tall, and a man crucified on a cross, reputedly to earn the money to return to his missionary work in the South Seas.

If possible even more bizarre than these stunts, aberrations, deceits and cruelties were the ashen-pale 'Starving Brides', of which there were several at different Blackpool locations, each wearing a wedding dress and going without food for an indeterminate reason. Gannon went one further, immuring a 'bride' and two 'bridegrooms' in separate coffins and offering them £250 if they fasted for thirty days, their only sustenance a quart bottle of water a day. When police swooped and ordered the exhibit to be closed, Gannon refused, pausing only to change the message on the blackboard outside to read, 'The bride too ill to be moved. Still on view after 23 days starvation'; and still the eager crowds pressed forward.

'Hermaphrodites' seemed to exercise a particularly prurient appeal: there were several 'half man/half woman' exhibits. 'It is always a man who is turned into a man-woman.' One side was left a 'wiry, strong, muscled and crop-headed man', while the other would be a womanly 'pink and white, plump and powdered with waved hair and jewelled hand', the effect achieved by 'long months of massage, shaving, injections of paraffin under the skin to make it rise gracefully where it is meant to rise; make-up on one half of the face; one jewelled earring, one high-heeled shoe – and behold the man-woman'. This spectacle was given renewed popularity by the Colonel Barker exhibit, mounted by Gannon in 1937. Barker was in fact a woman, Lilias Irma Valerie Barker, who had been married and borne two children before masquerading as a virile male boxing champion, 'marrying' a woman in 1923, and then living with another. The 6'2" tall, eighteen-stone Barker, who had adopted a military persona and dress, was unmasked as a woman when she was arrested for perjury and imprisoned. She became an exhibit in Gannon's dreadful galaxy under the banner 'Strange Honeymoon', accepting a fee of £200 not to consummate the marriage she had allegedly contracted (with another woman) until the season was over. The couple lay in twin beds, a Belisha beacon and a pedestrian crossing between them (it would be intriguing to deconstruct why), with the public paying to file past and 'guess whether Barker was a man or a woman'. Mass-Observation reported the confusion of the onlookers: 'I think she's one of those women who like women . . . he's a man and a woman . . . I can't tell what he is . . . I call him a Gene, Jack [the speaker's husband] calls him a Moxphrodite.' The exhibit was Blackpool's hottest attraction that summer.

But neither 'intersexuals', 'hermaphrodites' nor other unfortunate or constructed aberrations of nature could equal Gannon's greatest coup: the vicar of Stiffkey in a barrel. Harold Davidson was a Church of England clergyman who had fallen from grace. The incumbent of Stiffkey-with-Morston in Norfolk, he had, with his bishop's permission, embarked on a mission to minister to those in London's West End. He soon found himself returning to his parish only at weekends as he tried to save the souls of young girls, particularly shop assistants and Nippies in Lyons Corner Houses, who he decided, with no family around them and low wages, were vulnerable to the lures of casual prostitution in the big city. Davidson approached 'an average of 150 to 200' young girls a year (sometimes having removed his dog collar beforehand), offering cups of tea, sympathy, advice (he even paid for the treatment of syphilis for one) and help in finding jobs and accommodation. He brought some of them back to Stiffkey for some sea air, a break from the temptations of London life, if possible, a job in service – and a slightly more than avuncular caress, but probably not a great deal more. In 1931 the Bishop of Norwich decided to investigate Davidson's 'slackness', and the self-styled 'prostitutes' padre' was charged with offences against public morality under the 1892 Clergy Discipline Act. The case opened at Church House, Westminster, on 29 March 1932, and attracted widespread press coverage. One of the main witnesses testified that she and Davidson had slept in the same room for several nights, and that he had tried to have 'connection' with her. He was shown to have keys to several girls' rooms, and to have called on them late at night, but it was a (possibly faked) photograph of the clergyman with a fifteen-year-old girl, her back to the camera, clutching a shawl but clearly with nothing on underneath, that did for him. On 8 July he was found guilty on all five counts of immoral conduct and stripped of holy orders.

Davidson never ceased to protest his innocence, appealing twice to the Privy Council, and in 1936 he gatecrashed a meeting of the Church Assembly, showering leaflets on the heads of the delegates protesting at the injustice he had suffered. Cosmo Gordon Lang, the Archbishop of Canterbury, remained impervious to his pleas, refusing him the right to speak.

Deprived of his living and needing money, Davidson announced that he would shortly embark on a lecture tour of the US, but in fact headed north, where he had been offered £500 by Luke Gannon to fast, like Diogenes, in a barrel for fourteen days on the Golden Mile. Between 2,000 and 10,000 people (accounts vary) queued up to pay tuppence to see the vicar sitting in a barrel, preparing papers for his next appeal or addressing the crowd. Traffic ground to a halt and Blackpool Corporation summonsed Davidson and Gannon for obstruction, but any fine was chickenfeed compared to the nearly £1,500 the public paid that summer to see the (briefly) Oxford-educated vicar, who sometimes varied his act by locking himself into a refrigerated chamber, vowing to freeze himself to death; at another time he sat in a 'roasting pit', being prodded in the buttocks by a mechanical 'devil' with a pitchfork.

Confounding Blackpool Corporation's attempt to dignify its image, the vicar of Stiffkey was back on the Golden Mile for the 1935 season, planning to fast in a glass coffin and then spend twenty-four hours encased in ice. The Corporation tried again, this time charging Davidson with attempted suicide, but it lost the case when a doctor testified that he was in better health when he emerged from the coffin than when he had entered it. But, his popularity with the public fading, Davidson was driven to more desperate measures. In 1937 he moved to Skegness, which was in the process of changing from a small coastal town to one of Britain's busiest resorts, where he appeared locked in a cage with two lions, Toto and Freddie. On 28 July 1937, Freddie suddenly savaged the ex-rector, carting him around the cage 'as a cat does a mouse', either because he had inadvertently stepped on Toto's tail, or because the carnivorous animals had deliberately been kept hungry. The mauled Davidson died in hospital two days later, probably from an injection of insulin administered by a doctor who mistakenly believed that the vicar was diabetic. A verdict of misadventure was returned at the inquest – as in life, so in death.

Gannon, who had given Davidson his entrée into 'show-business', was ever eager to find a crowd-puller. In 1935 he had cabled the Queen of Abyssinia on hearing that she had just achieved a sixteen-day religious fast as a protest against the war that was raging in her country. Declaring himself to be a fellow pacifist who was planning a 'Pageant of World Peace' in Blackpool, he offered the Queen the opportunity to repeat her fast, this time in one of his barrels. There was no reply.

'Include Your Wife in This Year's Holiday', urged the *Manchester Evening News* in May 1935, concerned that for many married women a holiday was 'just a continuation in other surroundings of the work and worry which is usually her lot' – which was undoubtedly the case in a rented self-catering apartment or caravan, or on a camping holiday. But a holiday camp represented just the sort of 'regulated fun' that was likely to be attractive to a weary mother, offering board 'all in', meals provided, 'something to keep the kiddies happy', plenty of company and non-stop activities and entertainment for both sexes and all ages.

Holiday camps, communal tented or hutted ventures of a 'pioneer' stripe, had been popular since the turn of the century among Fabians, trade unionists, some religious groups, Clarion Club cyclists, Young Socialists, naturists and other progressives – those who espoused what the socialist campaigner Edward Carpenter had revered as 'plain food, the open air, the hardiness of the sun'. Unsurprisingly most were pretty Spartan and, in their way, middle-class and exclusive.

Thomas Cunningham, a Liverpool flour merchant, had set up a holiday camp for young men on the Isle of Man in 1908. At first visitors slept in bell tents lit by candles (later, chalets and bungalows were provided), but all the elements of later 'Hi de hi' camps were there – shops, a swimming pool, a vast dining room for communal meals, organised team games and sing-songs. The camp mainly attracted shop assistants, clerks, teachers and other 'black-coated' male workers – on average 60,000 a year by 1936.

There were small, family-run camps like Fletcher Dodd's and Potters, both on the Norfolk coast, others in Suffolk, the Robinson Crusoe Club and Holiday Camp in wooded Berkshire countryside, the Golden Sands camp 'Right on the Beach' at Rhyl. Squires Gate holiday camp sprang up on the edge of Blackpool, offering unwelcome competition to boarding-house landladies with cheap accommodation in huts, chalets or tents, allowing holidaymakers to cook their own food, bathe, dance, sing and take part in treasure hunts. Some camps were constructed as extensions to 'plotland' developments, such as at Withernsea on Humberside, where unemployed joiners built thirty-five wooden chalets for holidaymakers, though the 1936 Public Health Act was invoked to insist that they could only be occupied between 1 March and 31 October.

Socially-minded companies provided camps to give their workers a break – swapping one form of enlightened regulation for another. Lever Brothers had one, as did Needler's chocolate manufacturer of Hull. In 1924 the Civil Service Clerical Association started a camp for its members at Corton in Suffolk, and this proved so popular that another was opened on Hayling Island. NALGO (National and Local Government Officers Association) found an 'ideal spot' at Croyde in North Devon and bought an existing camp with 'ninety five asbestos huts, a recreation room and dining hall, a tennis court and putting green'. They were so pleased with their acquisition that they built another one near Scarborough for 252 guests which opened in July 1933. Derbyshire miners could holiday in their own camp at Skegness from 1939, paid for by contributions from the Miners' Welfare Fund and by the colliery owners: it cost a miner and his wife 33 shillings for a week's holiday and 8s.6d for each child, and they could even travel there cheaply thanks to a discount negotiated with the railway company. Various Co-operative Societies ran holiday camps for their employees and customers: people queued for hours in the February cold to secure a place for the summer. In 1938 the Co-operative Society linked with the Workers Travel Association to set up Travco Ltd, a non-profit organisation intended to make a 'practical contribution towards the holiday problem of the family as well as individual workers of limited means'. Its first camp, Rogerson Hall near Lowestoft in Suffolk, opened in August 1938, with accommodation for two hundred holidaymakers in rows of barrack-like huts.

Children were catered for by the Holiday Fellowship, which had three seaside camps in 1932, with room for up to five hundred children a week in 'well built army huts', while some local authorities had started to provide holiday camp places for their most 'necessitous children' after the First World War. By the outbreak of the Second in 1939 there were twenty such camps, some for children who were sick or in need, others simply providing an opportunity for children to take their lessons in a healthier place than they were used to. The unemployed were catered for too, but in the humiliating, segregated manner of old Poor Law institutions. Women and children could holiday at the Yorkshire Unemployment Advisory Camps at Cloughton and Filey, while men could stay at Redcar School Camp in August – provided no women were booked in. The National Fitness League had plans for several camps where its creed could be lived out, but war put paid to that. However, by the mid-1930s an estimated half a million people a year took their holidays in some sort of holiday camp or tented accommodation. A magazine, *Holiday Camp Review*, the first issue of which came out in April 1938, was confident that 'the Holiday Camp movement has come to stay ... and is destined to spread'.

Two years earlier Billy Butlin had opened his first holiday camp at Skegness. Butlin was a showman: he had started his working life running a hoopla stall, but had realised that his plan to make a living travelling around country fairs was becoming less and less viable now that charabancs were beginning to take more and more people further afield. In 1927 he persuaded the Earl of Scarbrough to lease him a hundred-yard-long strip of sand dunes at Skegness on the Lincolnshire coast, at the time a small, windswept place, 'little more than two streets and a short promenade called the Grand Parade'. There he established an amusement park, followed by a chain of similar parks stretching from Mablethorpe to Hayling Island, Bognor, Felixstowe, Portsmouth, Bexhill and the Isle of Man, filled with all manner of fairground attractions including thrilling rides on the big dipper, the figure of eight and dodgem cars (which he was the first to import into Britain). Butlin's ambitions grew. Recognising that however much they might look forward to them, most people's holidays weren't that much fun – turfed out of their boarding houses after breakfast, they had to mooch around in often inclement weather for most of the day, in and out of amusement arcades, and many resorts banned all entertainments on Sundays – he decided to build a camp that would keep holidaymakers entertained whatever the weather. Butlin's Skegness opened on Easter Saturday 1936, a quotation from *A Midsummer Night's Dream*, 'Our True Intent is all for Your Delight', emblazoned across its entrance. 'Holidays with three meals a day and free entertainment from thirty-five shillings a week to £3 depending on the season' proclaimed a half-page advertisement in the *Daily Express* that cost Butlin £500 to announce the opening of the 'Butlin luxury holiday camp' (the ceremony to be performed by the aviatrix Amy Johnson). Within days all the 1,000 places were booked for the season, and there were plans to extend the camp to accommodate 2,000 in 1937.

'Happy Campers' days were fully organised from the minute they were woken in their chalets at 7.45 a.m. by cheerful Redcoats (camp workers wearing red blazers and white flannels) bellowing greetings through loud-hailers: 'Roll out of bed in the morning/With a great big smile and a good good morning/Get up with a grin/ There's a good day tumbling in!' Included in the cost of the holiday were regular meals eaten *en masse*, trips, 'ambles', swimming lessons culminating in a gala, a variety of sports, health and fitness classes, dances – by 1938 there were two resident bands at Skegness, Mantovani's and Lew Stone's – concerts, talent shows, fancy-dress competitions, 'kiddies entertained by Uncle Mac', snooker, beauty contests, quizzes, church services on Sunday, non-stop synchronised activity (the programme broadcast by 'Radio Butlin') until 'Good night, campers' at 11.45 p.m. That is, if you could face it, though you didn't have to. 'Please don't get the idea that you've GOT TO BE GAY,' reassured a brochure. 'No chivvying you to do this or that . . . it's *your* holiday.' Redcoats were on duty at all times to make sure everything went swimmingly. Instead of somebody bossily shouting 'Time!' in the bars, holidaymakers were encouraged to conga out as if it was all part of the fun, rather than a legal requirement.

So successful was Skegness that in 1939 Billy Butlin opened a similar camp at Clacton in Essex. He decided on the slogan 'Holidays with pay – Holidays with play. A week's holiday for a week's wages', and hired a special train to bring every MP who had supported the Paid Holiday Bill to the opening. By 1938 Skegness and Clacton together were catering for 50,000 visitors a year, and the number rose to nearly 100,000 in 1939. Thomas Cook put a foot into the holiday-camp business in 1938, building a 'Chalet Village by the Sea' at Prestatyn in Wales in partnership with the LMS railway company. It could house 2,000 and had a more sophisticated appeal than Butlin's – no Redcoats or megaphone exhortations, and the brochure showed couples dancing in full evening dress. Another Butlin's camp was built at Filey on the Yorkshire coast, where previously the Princess Royal had taken her children shrimping, but when war broke out this was requisitioned by the army (and Butlin's Skegness camp by the navy); so barracks-like were the facilities holidaymakers had enjoyed in peacetime that the transition was relatively seamless.

*   *   *

Not everyone wanted to spend their precious week's holiday in a camp, or was drawn to the seaside by such alliterative appeals as 'Sunny Southend' or 'Ramsgate for Rest, Ramsgate for Residence, Ramsgate for Recreation, Ramsgate for Rejuvenation', and some were sceptical about Weymouth's claim to be 'the English Naples'. Alternative destinations, though sharply declining in popularity by the 1930s, were the spas: Bath, Buxton, Matlock, Cheltenham, Harrogate (probably the most successful spa in Britain before the First World War, partly because it was 'a particularly useful place to stay between the end of the London season and the grouse shooting in Scotland'), Malvern, Leamington (which had gained a Winter Hall Bath in the 1920s, the largest covered pool in the Midlands, as well as a Pump Room restaurant on the same lines as that at Bath), Tunbridge Wells (where a new spring was discovered in 1935 'with qualities unique in this country', but plans to bottle the water and market it came to nought), Woodhall in Lincolnshire (famous for its mud and its iodine baths), and Droitwich where one hotel organised aqua cocktail parties, with guests serving themselves from floating tables. In Scotland hydros such as those at Gleneagles, Dunblane, Melrose, Callander, Clunyhill, Taymouth Castle, Crieff, Bridge of Allan and Peebles revived somewhat after the First World War, aided by the development of golf courses and opportunities to ride and shoot, but on the whole they attracted only the elderly, and, as the manager of one noted in 1932, visitors from the US and the Dominions had dwindled 'owing to the Depressed times in which we live'. The appeal of spa towns in the 1930s was to those who, no longer able to afford a week at Continental spas such as Baden Baden, yet remained convinced of the curative properties of hydrology, 'taking the waters'.

Then there was the appeal of the countryside, an Arcadia opened up by the growth of cars – over two million on the roads by 1939 – and motor coaches, which carried 82 million passengers in 1936–37, advertising 'Make your journey part of your holiday'. Farmers' wives and cottage-owners in picturesque spots found it profitable to offer bed and breakfast or cream teas (particularly since agriculture had suffered in the slump as well as industry), and those with plenty of land laid on 'facilities' (a standpipe at least) for campers and caravaners. The annual Motor Show had had a caravan section since 1934, and by then there were some ninety-two models in production, including very sophisticated ones that would have made a holiday a compact home from home, with large windows, walnut panelling, sinks with running hot and cold water, stowaway beds, tables and benches, full-sized baths, fitted wirelesses, even lockers for golf clubs and fishing rods. One model, retailing for £320 in 1937, even boasted central heating, a dressing table with triple mirrors and a cocktail cabinet.

The most-visited destinations were Scotland, North Wales and the Lake District, where smart hotels such as the White Cross Bay at Windermere prospered, while at the other end of the scale day-trippers poured into the area by car or coach, or parked their caravans or pitched their ridge tents in the sites that dotted the fells. The four YHA hostels there had been in the Lakes in 1930 had trebled to twelve by 1935, and by 1938 were offering accommodation for more than 72,000 walkers and cyclists a year who didn't object to sleeping in bunks in dormitories and helping with the chores.

The appeal of the Lakes was quite different to that of nearby resorts. 'Although from the sea front of Morecambe the hills which look down upon Windermere can be seen in the distance, from the shores of Lake Windermere one cannot even *imagine* Morecambe,' commented a local newspaper. Visitors came for the scenery, the great outdoors and the solitude, which was under increasing threat in the 1930s as inevitable tensions mounted between the desire to maintain the essential character of the lakes, while at the same time making provision for the tourists their economy badly needed. The area's romantic literary associations were reinforced when the 'Lake Poets' Wordsworth, Coleridge and Southey were joined in hymning the delights of Coniston and Derwent Water, Grasmere and Windermere, by Beatrix Potter in the early years of the century, and then by Arthur Ransome, a journalist who had met and married Trotsky's secretary in Russia, and returned with her to settle on the fells near Windermere and started to write books about children messing about in boats. The first, *Swallows and Amazons*, was published in 1930, to a muted reception, but in 1932 the series took off with the third book, *Peter Duck*, for which Ransome drew the illustrations himself), further enhancing the call of the lakes – as his next books such as *Coot Club* (1934) and *Pigeon Post* (1936 – chosen as the best children's book of the year) did for the Norfolk Broads and the Essex estuary.

Other visitors headed to the New Forest, the West Country or the Forest of Dean (a designated National Park since 1938: Snowdonia and Argyll were the other two – all belonged to the Forestry Commission). Those who lived near to it were drawn to the Derbyshire Peak District, an awesome escape for the industrial workers of Sheffield and Manchester in particular, though it was never popular with those from the South of England. According to a 1934 guidebook its rugged, untamed crags and peaks were 'forbidden country, a little terrifying, the never-never land from which the southerner turns away'. For those with rather different holiday requirements there was Stratford-upon-Avon, where the Shakespeare Festival, first held in 1879, drew 200,000 visitors in 1938 during its twenty-four-week season – many to visit or possibly just to gaze on the new theatre which had opened on a bitterly cold day in April 1932.

Not everyone could afford to go away even after the introduction of holidays with pay; or if they did, it was to stay with friends or relations. Colin Ferguson, who worked in the pattern shop of Babcock & Wilcox, an engineering firm in Renfrewshire, went to visit his cousin William and his family in Letchworth in Hertfordshire in July 1933. He travelled from Glasgow in a convoy of four coaches, paying 50 shillings return to London, which he considered something of a rip-off since the coach was 'very cramped . . . no room to stretch my legs' and there was no deduction for being dropped off at Baldock, 'which is 38 miles by road from London'. Ferguson's 'large brown composition case' was hauled onto the roof of the bus and covered with a tarpaulin.

He was impressed by Letchworth – 'it is very well laid out – as one wd. naturally expect a garden city shd. be' – but rather less so by the capital, finding King's Cross 'a dirty, dismal, mean spirited station for a city like London, larger perhaps, but even more miserable than that disgrace to the Glasgow stations – Queen Street'. At Selfridges in Oxford Street he took a lift to the roof garden, but it was too hazy to see much so he spent some time watching the seismograph, though there had been no signs of an earthquake shock since the machine had been installed three years earlier. He wrote home on Selfridges stationery: 'Here I am in Selfridges's in London . . . looking for Reid Dick's work.' (Reid Dick, a Scot appointed sculptor-in-ordinary for Scotland by George VI in 1938, had produced bas reliefs for Selfridges: 'Two bronze figures at pavement level and 22 plaques representing industry and sport around the centre section and two figures at third floor level.')

Then it was down in the lift again, off for a quick peek into Westminster Abbey (which to Ferguson's mind looked better on the postcards), an iced drink at Lyons', and to the House of Commons where James Maxton, Ferguson's MP, had got them seats in the public gallery. This too didn't quite come up to scratch, since the speaker wasn't wearing his wig and the Labour MP (soon to be leader) 'Major Attlee' was 'loafing' on the front bench, 'hands deep in his trouser pockets and both feet – legs crossed – on the table which runs halfway down the floor and divided one side of the House from the Govt. side'. Ferguson could just make out '"porky" [Stanley] Baldwin', Labour leader George Lansbury, who 'seemed as if he was asleep', and another

Glasgow MP, David Kirkwood, who was working hard to revive John Brown's shipyard at the time. 'MPs who wish constituents to retain respect for Parliament should refrain from sending on free tickets to see the show,' noted Ferguson caustically. At 2.15 p.m. the search for Reid Dick's sculpture resumed. Ferguson found two on Unilever House on the Embankment, and his 'fine piece in the Kitchener Memorial' in St Paul's Cathedral.

It was 10.35 that night before Ferguson got back to Letchworth, and he reflected that 'what I saw [of London] by no means thrilled me. A great deal of it was very mean and dirty.' He left for Glasgow the next day, having pressed £1 on his hostess ('she would take no more') and spent half a crown each on toys for his cousin's children. He reflected that the total cost of his ten-day holiday had been 'about £8.4s8d . . . including sweets and spools [film for his camera]'.

London had begun to cater more for tourists by the 1930s, and though it would never compete with Paris, Rome or Florence, over £31 million was spent by tourists to Britain in 1937, which was not much less than the country earned from the export of coal or the products of the woollen industry. Large modern hotels were being built in Park Lane to accommodate wealthy visitors: the Grosvenor, on the estate of the Duke of Westminster, opened in 1929, and the Dorchester, built on the site of the demolished Dorchester House, once one of the finest houses in London, opened in April 1931. Sir Stephen Tallents, secretary to the Empire Marketing Board, which had been set up by the Colonial Secretary in 1926 to promote trade around the Empire and to persuade consumers to 'Buy Empire', ruminated in 1932 on what might appeal about Britain to tourists. He put the monarchy first ('with its growing scarcity value'), followed by 'parliamentary institutions (with all the values of a first edition)' and British virtues of 'coolness . . . fair dealing . . . fair play . . . and quality (in manufacture)'. When it came to what events there were to see, Tallents opted for 'the Derby and the Grand National, the Trooping of the Colour, the Boat Race, Henley, Wimbledon, the Test Matches, and the Cup Final'. His list of 'excellencies' included 'Oxford and St Andrews . . . English villages, the London omnibuses and Underground Railways, Piccadilly, Bond Street, Big Ben, and Princes Street, Edinburgh . . .'

But most English visitors came to London just for the day. They might take a trip down the Thames, either west to Richmond and Kew or east to Greenwich, passing under Tower Bridge, a 'pretentious piece of bad medievalism' yet an essential sight on most tourist itineraries, which was thrillingly opened an average of fourteen times a day in the 1930s to allow boats to pass beneath, a bell being rung to alert pedestrians and vehicles.

Ward Lock's 1938 *Guide to London* recommended that London be seen from the top of a bus. It offered an exhausting schedule for 'London in a Day' that included the National Gallery, the National Portrait Gallery, Whitehall, the Houses of Parliament, Westminster Abbey, Westminster Cathedral, Buckingham Palace, St James's Park, London Museum (Lancaster House) and St James's Palace, all before lunch. In the afternoon it was off at a canter again, taking in pretty well everything of interest between Piccadilly and St Paul's Cathedral, including the Royal Academy, a drive through Hyde Park, the Wallace Collection, the British Museum, Lincoln's Inn and Fleet Street.

What was not mentioned, even if the tourist had a week to spare, was Madame Tussaud's waxworks in Marylebone Road. The building had been devastated by fire in March 1925 – only 171 of the 467 models had been saved – and it was not until April 1928 that it was able to reopen. By October that year there had been a million visitors to the main exhibition and 700,000 to the Chamber of Horrors, from which an opium den showing British sailors with a Chinese host had been removed at the request of the Chinese government. In 1930 an original model of a guillotine used in the French Revolution was discovered not to have been destroyed in the fire as had been thought, so it was restored and put back on show in the company of other 'horrors' such as models of Dr 'Buck' Ruxton, Alfred Rouse, the 'blazing car murderer – wearing suit worn on night of the crime', the 'Margate Murderer', Reginald Hinks, and a chilling tableau of medieval instruments of torture, including a figure hung by its stomach from a hook. Despite the prurient interest in such displays, Tussaud's suffered in the Depression: apart from financial constraints, newspaper photographs were now of such high quality that visitors complained if models – such as the one of George V – failed to meet the required standard of lifelikeness. Visitor numbers dwindled, staff were made redundant and opening hours shortened. An attempt was made to go upmarket with a new cinema and a restaurant and dance floor where a Duke Ellington-style band played jazz and 'hot foxtrot' numbers. But these weren't very successful either. The relentless conveyor belt of public figures and events meant that 'The Men Who Won the War' of 1914–18 were dumped in 1934, while a year earlier the US President, Herbert Hoover had been melted down, replaced by Franklin Delano Roosevelt at Madame Tussaud's as he was at the White House. Joseph Stalin arrived a year later, though Gandhi had been on display since 1931.

Among the endless rows of politicians were wax models of sports stars such as the Everton footballer Dixie Dean, the Wimbledon tennis champion Fred Perry, the boxer Jack 'Kid' Farr and the Australian cricketer

Don Bradman. The aviatrix Amy Johnson appeared with her fellow pilot and husband (for a while) Jim Mollison. Hollywood stars such as Greta Garbo, Mae West (in the dress she had worn in the film *I'm No Angel*), Marlene Dietrich, Charles Laughton, Shirley Temple and Mickey Mouse (playing a piano) were there alongside home-grown entertainers including George Robey, Gracie Fields, Anna Neagle and the cartoonist Strube. J.M. Barrie, the author of *Peter Pan*, was on display (annoyingly, more than a hundred of his pens were stolen by visitors between 1930 and 1937), and Adolf Hitler arrived in 1933, the year he took over as Chancellor of Germany, though the model was soon defaced with the words 'mass murderer' in red paint. However, it was the British monarchy that gave the greatest boost to visitor numbers. Tussaud's exterior was floodlit for George V's Silver Jubilee in 1935, but it was the Abdication that proved a real winner. Edward VIII's speech was relayed throughout the galleries and a model of Mrs Simpson was quickly made, dressed in red satin and wearing her trademark rubies, with a guard standing nearby in case the 'American adventuress' was savaged. The number of visitors soared by 10,000 in a fortnight.

In an attempt to attract families, Tussaud's had introduced tableaux from fairy stories such as 'Little Red Riding Hood' and 'Jack and the Beanstalk', and near the entrance stood Sam and Barbara, two stuffed polar bears who prior to their demise had been among the attractions around the corner at London Zoo. Once it had been possible to see wild animals at the Tower of London – lions since the thirteenth century, later an elephant and a polar bear – or in the upper rooms of a house off The Strand, the site of 'Pidcock's Exhibition of Wild Beasts', or to throw pennies at bears dancing in the street. Since 1828 exotic, dangerous or just interesting specimens had been housed by the London Zoological Society in Regent's Park. The zoo had been established as a place for scientific study, and it was not until 1848 that it was opened to the public. Nearly a century later it was undergoing a rather necessary modernisation that would, it was hoped, attract more visitors and make the animals' totally unnatural lives a little more bearable. In 1924 George V and Queen Mary opened what was at the time the largest aquarium in the world, built beneath the Mappin Terraces (named after the silversmiths Mappin & Webb, which had made a generous donation), that had been built just before the First World War on land donated on condition that animals housed there could be seen from Regent's Park. In 1932 the Tecton architectural practice, which included the émigré architect Berthold Lubetkin, worked with the famed Danish engineer Ove Arup to design a home for two huge young Congolese gorillas the zoo had recently acquired. The building was circular: one half formed the animals' living quarters; the other, a caged play area, had a concrete wall that could be swung back in summer to give the primates some watery London sun, and visitors a chance to watch them at play.

This was considered to have 'solved the problem in a brilliant fashion', so Tecton and Arup were commissioned to design a penguin pool that would 'preserve the birds from the boredom which generally overtakes all zoo inhabitants'. This was achieved in 1934 with 'a sensational and dramatic design' involving two cantilevered ramps that spiralled round each other, giving the enclosure 'a theatrical quality and provid[ing] a suitable stage for the waddling gait of the penguins'. 'A glass-fronted diving tank at the level of spectators . . . showed the contrast between their great agility under water and extreme awkwardness on land.' The new enclosure was a great success, with spectators queuing up to watch the penguins shuffle around and leap for the fish the keepers threw them at pre-announced times.

In 1935 Edward and Robert Kennedy, sons of the US Ambassador, performed the opening ceremony of a small 'Pets' Corner' with animals that were sufficiently tame for children to handle, including a young chimpanzee, a lion cub, a Shetland pony, a small python, an infant yak, a giant tortoise and a selection of rabbits, piglets and kid goats. The entrance fee was a shilling, and children could watch the chimpanzees' tea party that took place at 5.15 every afternoon in a nearby cage. Pets' Corner (later renamed the Children's Zoo) drew almost 7,000 visitors the first summer it was open.

A report had recognised in 1909 that Regent's Park, 'in the smoky atmosphere of a great city, can never be an ideal place for animals'. There was no point in moving to another site in London: 'transporting the beasts to Richmond Park, the Crystal Palace, or somewhere near Hampstead or Highgate would be a dangerous experiment financially and no great gain from the point of view of soil or climate'. There was, however, another option. In 1927 the Society bought the derelict six-hundred-acre Hall Farm at Whipsnade near Dunstable in the Chiltern hills. Using the labour of 150 unemployed men from the distressed areas of the North and Wales, it was transformed into an open-air rural outpost of London Zoo. Whipsnade Park Zoo (as it was then called) was an immediate success with the public, drawing 38,000 visitors on its opening day, Whit Sunday 1931, with queues so long that many never actually got in. Whipsnade's success was predictable: it was an accessible distance from London, in good picnicking country and offering the chance to see birds, cheetahs, llamas, deer, bears, a herd of white rhinos and lions (in whose enclosure a foolhardy employee died in 1932 after accepting a bet to retrieve his bowler hat) 'in the wild'. A year later the Society added to this cohort by buying the stock of a defunct travelling menagerie.

Midlanders soon had their own zoo, too. Dudley Zoo, set in five hundred acres of parkland, the grounds of Dudley Castle, opened in 1938, a number of its buildings designed by Lubetkin's Tecton practice, which was consolidating a reputation for the modernist housing of animals. Belle Vue in Manchester celebrated its centenary in 1936 with the refurbishment of the elephant house, which sheltered the famous Indian elephant 'Lil', who had come with her keeper, the Orientally-clad Fernandez, from Malaya in 1921. The aquarium in the reptile house was enlarged, and was opened by Gracie Fields; a large gibbon cage was constructed (this was not a success, as the animals had a habit of attacking the keepers); a Monkey Mountain for 'a seething mass of Indian monkeys' didn't work either, as the monkeys kept escaping, particularly when the moat surrounding their 'mountain' froze, and a racoon pit were also constructed. A jaguar, 'the first Belle Vue will have had for twenty years', was reported to be on its way, as was a rhinoceros from Kenya, and two pandas ('extremely delicate creatures, which are said to resemble a cross between a cat and a small bear') from the Himalayas. The miniature railway was extended so that visitors could take in all these new sightings in comfort.

Some Londoners had had their own summer holiday tradition for generations, leaving the city for a working holiday in the Kent hop fields. For those from the East End or the poor areas of South London or Notting Hill, hop picking meant three or four weeks in the open air with the chance to earn some money. Mostly it was the women who went, with their children – the older ones taken out of school, lying about where they had been, but their sunburned faces giving them away – with husbands coming down at weekends. If the menfolk were out of work, casual workers on the docks or in the building trade, or fancied a bit of a break, they would come for the whole time, working alongside the women as pole pullers, cutting down the bines so the women could strip off the hops.

'There is a fairly close correlation between the poverty of a district and the proportion of the inhabitants who go hop-picking,' noted the *New Survey of London Life and Labour*, 'and within the poor areas it is, generally speaking, the poorest and roughest households which provide the largest contingents.' Thousands of people would make their way to London Bridge station in the early hours of the morning, the children lifted over the wall so a ticket would not have to be bought for them, to catch the 'Hoppers' Special' to Paddock Wood or Marden or other nearby stations in Kent. Some travelled in the guard's van, the possessions they were bringing with them tied up in bundles, children hiding under the seats when the ticket inspector came along. At their destination it would be a question of pushing a pram or a box on wheels with everything piled on it a mile or so to the hoppers' camp, though the brewers Whitbread would send a horse and cart to collect hoppers bound for their farm. More fortunate were those who clubbed together to hire a greengrocer's van, or a lorry or a furniture van, to drive down the A21 to Kent laden with bits of furniture, lino, rugs, tins of whitewash, mattress covers (or a feather mattress if there was room), blankets, pots and pans, candles, hurricane lamps, plus the family cat or budgie, since as grandma came too, there would be no one left at home to look after it.

In the 1920s Whitbread had acquired a large hop farm at Beltring, near Paddock Wood. There they built 750 huts (tin at first, later wooden ones with platform beds) with cookhouses, washing facilities, hot and cold water (including primitive showers, a real advance), proper sanitation and even shops and recreation facilities. But for most the accommodation was more basic. The pickers usually stayed in windowless corrugated-iron-roofed huts (sometimes used for animals in winter) about eight by ten feet in size. Sheds 'like sentry boxes with their backs to the camp' were put up for lavatories. These 'were supposed to be out of noseshot, but on a warm day with a breeze our way we could smell them.'

Families didn't just turn up: 'If you wanted to go hop picking for the first time, you'd write to the farmer beforehand . . . If there was a vacancy, depending on how many pickers he needed, you'd get a reply. If someone had died since the last hop-picking time, there would be space for a new picker . . . We used to get this card saying we could go hopping . . . we were all running up and down, all lots of excitement, waving this card.' Some families, considered good workers, would be invited back every year and claimed the same hut each time, so they may have left a few bits and pieces from their last visit – a scrap of lace curtain maybe, a few sacks – to establish residency.

Some huts had brick floors, but most had earth or chalk, which hoppers preferred because it was warmer. The first tasks on arrival were to cover the floor with bundles of sticks and twigs, make mattresses with the straw provided, bang some nails into the walls to hang things from, set up apple boxes for chairs and a table, dig a pit for cooking (some people would bring the inside of their oven from home) and another one for a larder, build a fire outside the doorway and get the water boiling for tea.

The working day started early, with a wash in a bucket, breakfast, and off to the fields with sandwiches ready to start picking at 7 or 8 a.m. and finish at 5.30, with a break for lunch at noon. Families would work together. The hops were 'like little acorns only much softer', but the bines were rough and would tear hands and arms, so some pickers wore gloves, or an old sock; others wore a sacking apron. It was hard work. George Orwell did a stint in September 1931 on a farm near Maidstone, and soon his hands were 'stained as black as a Negro's with the hop juice, which only mud will remove [or in fact soda] and after a day or two they crack and are cut to bits by the stems of the vines'. Pickers had a bin to tip the hops into, attached to a light wooden frame which they would pull along with them as they moved down the rows; children would collect those hops that had fallen on the ground. 'The laws about child labour are utterly disregarded,' noted Orwell as he watched exhausted small children sleeping on the ground, though he concluded, 'They liked the work and I don't suppose it did them more harm than school.' Some parents would let their children collect hops in an umbrella, and give them pocket money in return.

A whistle would signal the arrival of the measurer, who would tip the hops into a wicker bushel basket. The bin number noted, the hops would be thrown into an enormous ten-bushel sack known as a poke, then dried in an oasthouse before being loaded onto goods trains to be sold at the Hop Exchange, near Borough Market in Southwark. The picker would be paid according to the number of bushels he or she picked: the going rate in 1931 was six bushels to the shilling: 'that is we were paid two pence for each bushel we picked . . . a good vine yields about half a bushel of hops, and a good picker can strip a vine in ten or twenty minutes'. But in practice it didn't work out like that: some vines were much harder to strip than others; some hops were much bigger than others; pickers had to wait to move onto a new row, 'with no compensation for lost time'; it might pour with rain; the measurer might short-change the pickers, since the hops were measured in bushel baskets of standard size, and 'Hops are not like apples or potatoes . . . they are soft things as compressible as sponges, and it is quite easy for the measurer to crush a bushel into a quart if he chooses.' Orwell and the friend he had gone with earned about nine shillings a week: 'We were new to the job, but the experienced pickers did little better. The best pickers in our gang, and among the best in the whole camp, were a family of gypsies, five adults and a child; these people spending ten hours a day in the hop field, earned just ten pounds between them in three weeks.' There were farms nearby where 'the tally was eight or nine bushels to the shilling, and where even twelve shillings a week would have been hard to earn'. 'You never got paid weekly,' recalled one of the regular 'hoppers', Ellen

Russell. 'You used to have a sub, Tuesday, Thursdays and Saturdays. If they paid you weekly, you might spend it all, or you might just go home! . . . We never had much money to take home at the end, but we had a cheap holiday. A fine holiday.'

In the evening the hoppers would cook a meal outside, or in a smoky cookhouse if it was raining – mostly stews with vegetables – over an open fire, and then sit round the fire singing songs such as 'My Old Man Said Follow the Van', 'It's a Long Way to Tipperary' and 'The Quartermaster's Store', or telling ghost stories.

At the weekends, when many husbands came down, it was off to the pub for beer at fourpence a pint and a shilling deposit on the glass. On Sundays there was plenty of religion on offer – with so many souls to save, so many problems of poverty and deprivation to sort out, the Churches were much in evidence in the hop-picking areas. The Salvation Army, Anglo-Catholic missions, a mission from Oxford University, sent out barrows with tea and slabs of cake for sale at a ha'penny in the hop fields, ministered to the sick, gave advice and held Mass daily in the village churches and open-air services on Sundays. The Salvation Army ran crèches where infants could be left for a penny a day while their mothers picked, and children could have a good wash in one of their tin tubs at the end of the day – soap and use of a towel one penny. With a white sheet hung up as a screen, 'magic lantern' shows were put on –biblical stories for the children, and films for the adults.

'On the last morning, when we had picked the last field, there was a queer game of catching the women and putting them in the bins. Very likely there is something about this in *The Golden Bough*. It is evidently an old custom, and all harvests have some custom like this attached to them,' reported George Orwell, who thought that hop picking was 'in the category of things that are great fun when they are over'. The fields picked bare, the bines rolled up and the tall poles and wires naked to the sky, the hoppers would queue up with their tally books to be paid anything they were still owed, then it was back home to the smoke with a pillowcase full of scrumped apples, a couple of chickens still with their feathers on, a bag of hops as a souvenir, probably stopping at The Bull at Swanley for a comradely drink 'till next year'. Since it was well known that 'Go down hopping, come back jumping,' the children's first port of call would be 'Nitty Norah' to get rid of the vermin before going back to their classrooms, after a long and usually enjoyable open-air truancy.

Hopping was a way of life that would disappear not long after the Second World War with the widespread use of 'wonder machines' which 'could do in one hour what it would take two people thirty-five hours to do'. 'The machine is not intended to oust human pickers,' explained one of the joint inventors, 'but is intended to . . . work in co-operation with the hand pickers.' But oust them it did.

The sun, so fleeting and elusive in Britain, was a motif of the thirties. It burst from the top quadrant of suburban windows, from garden gates, the panels of front doors, tiled fireplaces, fretworked wirelesses, dressing-table sets, enamelled cigarette cases, powder compacts and gold cufflinks. Cacti – emblem of desert heat and aridity – became fashionable houseplants. Sunlamps were believed to be healing and energising, and with a tan no longer regarded as evidence of a hard outdoor life, but as the badge of a leisured existence, the cult of sunbathing was popularised by the *chic* French designer Coco Chanel. International cosmetic houses such as Cyclax and Helena Rubinstein started to market 'sunburn oil' to aid the browning process. 'I've got masses of lovely oil to rub all over myself,' says Amanda Prynne in Noël Coward's *Private Lives* (1930). 'When I'm done to a nice crisp brown you'll fall in love with me all over again.'

Flat sunbathing roofs were a modernist architectural idiom, and 'Vita' glass was used to allow as much sun as possible into the solariums of hotels and other public buildings since ultraviolet rays were seen as health-giving, rather than health-threatening. Swimming costumes shrank to expose more skin to the sun, with two-pieces for women ('bikini' was a post-Second World War term) or sleek Jantzen costumes, while bathers wore tight-fitting rubber swimming caps to protect their hair from salt water or chlorine. The costumes that covered manly chests were also growing skimpier. Occasionally a woman might be spotted wearing a pair of plastic-framed sunglasses, usually white, but they were more likely to be seen on the Continent, where the fashion had spread – along with beach pyjamas – from America. In 1936 sunglasses started to be manufactured with 'Polaroid' filter lenses, and the craze really took off, though their appeal was more as a glamorous sea and poolside accessory than as protection from the sun.

In Britain, local authorities were perturbed by the growing habit of holidaymakers changing into their swimsuits under a towel or wrap on the beach rather than hiring a beach hut. This deprived seaside resorts of valuable income, and in 1930 Eastbourne introduced a 'no hut no bathe' rule which the police enforced by taking the names and addresses of hundreds of 'mackintosh bathers', as they were known. Day-trippers, never great contributors to the seaside economy, particularly if they brought their own sandwiches with them, had even less need of council facilities, as most did not don a costume, instead rolling up their trouser legs and taking off their socks or stockings to paddle.

Railway advertisements offered to take passengers to the 'Sunny South': Bournemouth was advertised as a 'Mediterranean Watering Place'. Along with Cornwall, Torquay, with its mild climate, villas and palm trees, was claimed to be the 'English Riviera'. But whatever the posters promised, the sun could not be guaranteed, and so those privileged few who could afford the time and money went in pursuit of it on the French (or, less often, the Italian) Riviera, boarding the luxuriously appointed *Train Bleu* at Victoria station. 'Sleep your way from the City's fogs to the Riviera sunshine' was how the train was advertised. However, whereas before the First World War it was the moneyed who had fled abroad in the winter months, by the 1930s it was mainly the elderly who sought the winter sun's warming rays abroad: the young wanted full-on sun in the hottest months, and sought it in Antibes, Menton, Juan-les-Pins, Nice and Cannes.

Travel to Europe had declined during the slump, and after Britain came off the Gold Standard in the '*annus terribilis*' of 1931 holidays abroad were 'practically 50% dearer for English people', the travel firm Thomas Cook calculated. The company cut its workforce, shut offices and discontinued its contributions to its employees' pension funds, while still calling on their 'unremitting work . . . and unswerving loyalty'. However, by 1935–36 trade had begun to revive, and in 1937 nearly a million and half Britons travelled to the Continent, not all of them holidaymakers of course, though a large number were. Most went to France – besides the Riviera, Paris, and Deauville with its golf courses, elegant promenade and casinos were popular too. Some took day trips to Boulogne or spent a week at Saint-Malo or Le Touquet – 'like a piece of Sussex dotted with pine trees . . . spiced by the possibility that the Prince of Wales will be playing on the golf course ahead of you . . . and that Lord Birkenhead will be playing *chemin de fer* at the same table as you . . . and Sir Philip Sassoon may be playing *boule* in the next room'.

Thomas Cook arranged pilgrimages to Lourdes and Rome, and was permitted to print the Papal emblem on its brochures. Monte Carlo was another popular destination, with its casinos where nuns waited silently in the foyer to collect alms from those who had won at the tables. Then there was Switzerland, particularly in winter for the skiing, since 'The Prince of Wales did for winter sports much what the Prince Regent had done for the seaside,' though while 5,066 clients of Thomas Cook went on sports holidays in the winter of 1930–31, the number fell to 661 the following year after the abandonment of the Gold Standard. The fashionable flocked to

St-Moritz with its thrilling bobsleigh run, Gstaad and Davos. For most tourists Italy meant a rather truncated 'grand tour', taking in Rome, Florence and Venice (where motorboat racing on the Lido was an added excitement). A trip down the Rhine was a popular German holiday – Poly Tours advertised these with a swastika blazoned on the cover of their brochure under the slogan 'The Land of Dreams Come True' – as was a visit to Bayreuth for the music festival. In Austria, the Tyrol and Salzburg, again for music, were the main draws – Vienna had become less of a favoured destination than it had been in the nineteenth century. Jugoslavia (as the former Yugoslavia was known) was increasingly attracting British tourists – 7,000 a year were going by 1935 – as was Scandinavia. Apart from the Moorish appeal of Granada, Spain had never been a particularly popular destination for British visitors, and the Civil War made it all but impossible, and certainly unlikely.

There were even more ambitious choices for the well-off. Thomas Cook organised big-game shoots in Africa, and Intourist (formed in 1930) took people to shoot bears in the Russian forests. The Caribbean islands added such exotica as flying fish, tropical fruit and flowers and endless silver beaches to the sun-and-sea mix the Mediterranean offered, while those in search of culture as well as sun travelled to Egypt, Greece and North Africa. One could go on an all-in tour of the Soviet Union for £17, and it could cost less than £37 to cross the Atlantic on the *Queen Mary* and stay for four nights in New York. When the ancient city of Sodom was 'rediscovered' near the Dead Sea, Cook's took a party, and in 1930 it offered a trip to watch the coronation of Haile Selassie as Emperor of Ethiopia for £325, with a game-hunting safari included in the price. The Booth Line took people on a seven-week tour of the Brazilian jungle, sailing from Liverpool and ending up in Manaus, nearly 6,000 miles away, where the travellers could find 'alligators, jaguars, parrots, giant water lilies and armadillos'. The Indian State Railways offered trips that could 'furnish sport such as few countries can give; the tiger in the forest, the great mahseer in many rivers, the wily snipe on the jheels, the strong winged duck, the jinking pig'. If these weren't thrills enough, there was always the Taj Mahal: 'By moonlight its seduction is irresistible.'

'Cruising was a word that until four years ago meant practically nothing to the British public,' maintained the *Daily Telegraph* in a special supplement in 1935. That was a considerable exaggeration: since the First World War the surplus of ships had supplied the means, and cruising around Europe and beyond had grown increasingly popular. In 1931, 70,000 passengers took a cruise and this number had risen to 550,000 by 1937. It cost

£6.6*s* for a six-day cruise to Norway, while a weekend cruise to Northern France, Belgium and Holland was £3.5*s*.6*d*.

Cruises with a purpose were increasingly popular. Swan Hellenic led the field, employing first-class lecturers so that passengers learned as they glided towards the ruins of the ancient world. The Wayfarer's Travel Agency started a programme of activity cruises just before the war, with chamber music, madrigal singing, gramophone recitals and lectures, reading groups and play readings, as well as the usual offerings of deck quoits, dances, fancy-dress parties and trips ashore. 'Every hour of the cruise full of interest . . . a round of social interest and enjoyment' designed to 'banish taciturnity', proclaimed the *Daily Telegraph* in its supplement, which listed nearly four hundred cruises. It sounded suspiciously like a very upmarket Butlin's on the open seas.

The National Union of Students offered the young the opportunity to canoe along the Danube, or ride horses in the Carpathians, or go mountaineering in the Alps, the Pyrenees or the Dolomites. But some young men saw travel less as a holiday and more than as a means to self-discovery and self-definition. Until 1932, in order to be accepted as a member of the select Travellers Club in Pall Mall, a man had to be able to prove that he had travelled at least a thousand miles from London: now some who had never been further than Paris were admitted. But travellers' tales, a genre that became a 1930s art form, redolent with sensibility, erudition and manifestos, ranged further. Patrick Leigh Fermor set off in 1933 to walk across Europe to the threshold of Asia, starting at the Hook of Holland and ending up in Constantinople (present-day Istanbul), sleeping in barns, police stations, *Schlossen* and *châteaux*; but it was not until more than thirty years later that the first part of his account of a well-connected young man's odyssey (his father was a distinguished geologist) was published as *A Time of Gifts*.

The aesthete and art connoisseur Harold Acton felt that if he did not travel far from England's shores he would remain 'an unbaked mould'. With the assistance of a generous American uncle he left Florence for China in January 1932, finding that in Peking, 'I belonged to myself again'. He bought a Chinese house, wore Chinese clothes, learned Mandarin partly in order to translate Chinese poetry, appreciated Chinese art and *objets*, adopted Chinese customs and tried to cultivate Chinese thoughts, writing about his experiences in *Escape with Me* (1939) and in a rather brilliantly malicious novel about the expat community in Peking, *Peonies and Ponies*, published two years later. But when the Japanese invasion of China, which had started with an attack on Shanghai in the summer of 1937, escalated in early 1939, Acton fled back to Europe, never to return.

Peter Fleming, older brother of the later to be more famous Ian, joined a hare-brained expedition in 1932 to look for a lost explorer, and wrote a best-selling book about his hilarious escapades, *Brazilian Adventure* (1933). He then trekked 3,500 miles on foot and horseback from China to India, filing copy on the way in his role as Special Correspondent for *The Times*: his account of this thrilling and hazardous journey was published in 1936 under the title *Tales from Tartary*.

Patrick Balfour, 3rd Baron Kinross, who was working as a gossip columnist on the *Daily Sketch* and obliging his ex-Oxford friends by dropping their names in such a way that they sounded *au courant*, found 'the atlas a notorious seducer', and visited so many countries in a mere six months that he was 'almost ashamed to tot [them] up'. Travel, Balfour thought, was no longer the educational experience it had once been: 'Now it is primarily an avenue of escape, both actual and spiritual, from the complex liabilities of modern life.' His modern-day *Grand Tour: Diary of an Eastward Journey*, published in 1934, took him to France, Italy, Cyprus, Syria, Iraq, Persia, Afghanistan, India, Nepal, the Andaman Islands, Malaya, Siam, Indo-China and Sumatra, all in twenty-four weeks.

Travel was an escape for Evelyn Waugh too. His book *Labels: A Mediterranean Journal* described a voyage he had taken with his first wife, also named Evelyn (their friends called her She-Evelyn to distinguish her from him). By the time he came to write it the marriage had broken down after She-Evelyn had run off with one of He-Evelyn's best friends, so Waugh represented himself as a bachelor and the erring She-Evelyn as Juliet, the wife of a fellow passenger. It had been a wretched journey. She-Evelyn had been frighteningly ill, coughing up blood and looking 'distressingly like a corpse', but as the trip had been wangled by Waugh's agent in return for his writing articles, he had to sit in their cabin composing amusing pieces every evening and conscientiously checking out the sights every time the *Stella Polaris* put into port.

The voyage began in Monte Carlo and ended in Lisbon, via Haifa, Cairo, Athens, Corfu, Barcelona, Algiers, Gibraltar and places in between. Published in 1930, *Labels* prefigures Waugh's later novels, comparing the Serai, the Palace of the Sultans in Istanbul, unfavourably with the Exhibition Hall at Earl's Court. And while he greatly admired Gaudí's unfinished cathedral of the Sagrada Família in Barcelona, Waugh wrote of Mount Etna at sunset: 'the mountain almost invisible in a blur of pastel grey, glowing on the top and then repeating its shape, with the whole horizon behind radiant with pink light, fading gently into a grey pastel sky. Nothing I have ever seen in Art or Nature was quite so revolting.'

Waugh wrote four travel books, including one exercise in contempt rather than humour, the punningly named *Waugh in Abyssinia* (for which he disclaimed responsibility, having preferred the unselling title *A Disappointing War*), published in 1936. He had gone to Abyssinia (he had been there before for the coronation of Haile Selassie in 1930) to cover the war there for the pro-fascist *Daily Mail* (as Patrick Balfour had for the *Evening Standard*), and came back with an admiration for the way Mussolini's forces were attempting to impose European 'civilisation' on the Abyssinians. The book did not sell well: none of Waugh's travel books really did, but they were to prove excellent source material for his successful novels *Black Mischief* (1932), *A Handful of Dust* (1934) and *Scoop* (1938), in which Abyssinia morphs into Ishmaelia, and Waugh (or more likely his journalistic colleague William Deedes, or another hapless journalist, William Beach Thomas) into the novel's main character, William Boot.

Like Harold Acton, Robert Byron was another scholar-traveller who was somewhat disenchanted by Western civilisation. In this he was much influenced by Oswald Spengler (as was Waugh, who had slipped *The Decline of the West* into his suitcase as he set off of on his *Labels* cruise) and by what he saw as the wilful destruction of the finest of Britain's architectural heritage. His itch could only be satisfied by going east – in his case to Central Asia. His fare to India was paid by Lord Beaverbrook, who commissioned an article on the new England–India airmail service for the *Daily Express*, but it was his account of his journey to Oxiana, the plains of the river Oxus, that more than any other book defined the travel literature of the thirties: 'what *Ulysses* is to the novel between the wars and what *The Waste Land* is to poetry'. *The Road to Oxiana* is crafted like a series of traveller's notebooks (in fact with book-learning added in later), describing a journey starting in Venice, then going via Jerusalem, part of the way in an unreliable charcoal-burning Rolls-Royce, to Mesopotamia, the land between the Tigris and the Euphrates, known as the 'cradle of civilisation', but to Byron the 'mud plain', and thence to Persia – Tehran, Shiraz, Persepolis. At the end of April 1934 Byron and his travelling companion Christopher Sykes reached their Holy Grail, the monumental, formidably austere Gumbad-i-Kabus or Tower of Qabas, a tomb that Western travellers had been forbidden to visit until 1932 and that in Byron's eyes ranked with the great buildings of the world. From there they crossed the border into Afghanistan and Turkestan, but for political reasons they were never able to get to the Oxus itself, the site of Matthew Arnold's epic poem *Sohrab and Rustum*, which 1930s schoolboys committed to memory: 'And the first grey of morning fill'd the east/And the fog rose out of the

Oxus stream'. They then returned through India, sailing to England from Marseilles.

The Road to Oxiana was published in April 1937. It achieved disappointingly average sales, but gratifying critical acclaim. Reviewing it in the *Sunday Times*, the historian G.M. Young located Robert Byron on a continuum with the poet Lord Byron, to whom he was distantly related, representing 'the last and finest fruit of the insolent humanism of the eighteenth century'. In just over two years the world would no longer be open for 'insolent humanists' to take such meandering odysseys and write books about them.

TWENTY-ONE

Spittoons in Arcadia

Those entering the Saloon Bar of 'The Midnight Bell' from the street came
through a large door with a fancifully frosted glass pane, a handle like a dumb-
bell, a brass inscription 'Saloon Bar and Lounge', and a brass adjuration to Push
... Given proper treatment ... it swung back in the most accomplished way, and
announced you to the Saloon Bar with a welcoming creak. The Saloon Bar was
narrow and about thirty feet in length ... At the far end the Saloon Bar opened
into the Saloon Lounge. This was a large, square room, filled with a dozen or
so small, round, copper-covered tables. Around each table were three or four
white wicker armchairs, and on each table there lay a large stone ash-tray supplied
by a Whiskey firm ... This was no scene for the brawler, but rather for the
principled and restrained drinker, with his wife. In here and in the Saloon Bar
'The Midnight Bell' did most of its business – the two other bars (the Public
and the Private) being dreary, seatless, bareboarded structures wherein drunkenness was dispersed in coarser tumblers and at a cheaper rate to a mostly
collarless and frankly downtrodden stratum of society. The Public Bar could
nevertheless be glimpsed by a customer in the Saloon Bar.

Patrick Hamilton, *Twenty Thousand Streets Under the Sky* (1935)

Approximately one in every nine of the working population of Bolton was
still unemployed in 1938. Yet, employed or unemployed, 'more people spend
more time in public houses than they do in any other buildings except
private houses and work-places. Why?' asked Tom Harrisson in *The Pub
and the People*, a survey of the minutiae of the drinking life of 'Worktown'
undertaken by Mass-Observation in the last two years of the decade.

One answer must have been the sheer number of pubs: three hundred
in a town with a population of around 180,000, as compared to thirty cinemas
and two hundred churches and chapels. And in a town where mill-workers
– still wearing clogs for the main part – worked forty-eight regimented hours
a week, and holidays amounted to one week a year if that, there was a strong
yearning for time that was unregimented, for men to be with their mates

in what was largely a 'masculine republic', to talk, play darts, cribbage or shove ha'penny, read the racing pages of the paper, or just stare into a pint glass with no compulsion to do anything. But most men confined their drinking to Friday and Saturday evenings, and those strapped for cash would 'wait for the last hour; never mind what time you open or what time you close. It's all they've got the money for,' a barmaid observed.

Traditionally men 'tipped up' their wages to their wives and received back a small allowance for 'beer and baccy'. Most pubs ran a slate, whereby a man would owe for his drinks and pay when he was in funds. Such a system was 'vital in the pub economy', as it was in other low-wage or no-wage places. There were rarely defaulters among the regulars, and Mass-Observers found some pubs where the landlord did not need to note what his patrons owed him: they kept a small notebook and jotted it down themselves.

Unemployment kept some men out of pubs, a study of Greenwich found in 1931 – they hadn't the money to stand a round: 'Yes, I miss the Green Man but you can't drink alone, and it costs money when there is a crowd.' And this denied them more than just the beer: many pubs organised charabanc outings in the summer, and maybe fielded a darts, football or cricket team.

Cyril Dunn, a journalist working in Hull, was as aware as the novelist Patrick Hamilton of the nuanced social geography of the public house. The Black Boy was where he and a colleague whom he referred to as the 'Little Welshman' used to repair for a beer. 'We always go into the Front Room, lacking the courage to go down the whitewashed passage to the Smoke Room entrance. We sit and listen to the fights and the coarse swearing of the women, instead of watching them as we would wish. The bar connects the Front and Smoke Rooms and from the former you can see just a little of the latter – a woman leaning on the bar counter with a cigarette in the corner of her mouth and a glass of beer in front of her. She calls the barmaid by her Christian name, as one woman to another.'

Fewer women than men spent time in the pub: Mass-Observation observed 712 people in a range of pubs in Bolton in 1937–38, and reckoned that only 16 per cent were women, though in York at around the same time over a quarter of the drinkers in working-class pubs were women, while in London it was about the same. Not only would a woman find herself outnumbered, she would be segregated, either formally or informally, barred from the 'vault' or 'tap room' where men drank, and relegated to a separate 'best' room, even if she had come with her husband, which she usually had – though he was likely to pay for her drink.

However, while relatively few women were to be found in traditional working-class pubs, and some men strongly disapproved of their wives drinking, it was increasingly more acceptable for middle-class women to drink in hotel bars – Seebohm Rowntree estimated that over 40 per cent of drinkers in such establishments in York were women – in country pubs and in the new roadhouses on the arterial roads out of cities. Basil Nicholson, reading proofs of *The Pub and the People* in 1941– the only copy in existence, he was told, since 'owing to blitzes' all others had been lost – marvelled at the 'magic casement' the book provided on 'a foaming fairyland of ale and cakes'. 'In 1938 we never knew,' he wrote wistfully, 'that those spittoons were in Arcadia.'

But that Arcadia had already begun to change. New suburban developments attempted to reconfigure the concept of the pub, often calling new examples 'hotels', whether they had accommodation or not, and emphasising that they catered for families. The Stoneleigh Hotel, a Tudorbethan half-timbered 'superpub', opened on the Surrey edge of London in November 1935. Designed to look as much as possible like a huge country pub, with beams and mullioned windows, it had, in addition to the usual bars and an off-licence (known in older pubs as the 'bottle and jug' room, since customers would come with a jug to have it filled with beer to take home), a restaurant, a billiard room and a large hall that could hold 150 people and was let out for receptions, dances and meetings. The Downham Tavern in Kent was a similarly massive edifice, the only pub on an estate of 35,000 people. On the Becontree estate near Dagenham in Essex the LCC built what it called 'licensed refreshment houses' to replace old-style beer houses; by 1938 there were nine such establishments serving a population of more than 120,000. As at Downham, these had a series of 'refreshment rooms' where once there would have been bars. This sanitisation of drinking, a large airy room replacing a fuggy, nicotine-stained snug, with propping up the bar discouraged and the 'civilising' influence of families encouraged, was an attempt to rewrite a traditional space and culture, to restructure working-class habits. George Orwell regretted the advent of these 'dismal sham-Tudor places fitted out by the big brewery companies . . . for a working-class population, which uses the pub as a kind of a club', and regarded it as 'a serious blow at communal life'.

On his journey round England in 1933, J.B. Priestley, another professional observer of Northern life (and in his case a Northerner himself) had found not one England, but three. The first was the 'Old England, the country of the cathedrals and minsters and manor houses and inns'; the second was 'nineteenth-century England, the industrial England of coal, iron, steel, cotton, wool, railways; of thousands of little houses all alike'; the third was the England of 'arterial and by-pass roads, of filling stations and factories that look like exhibition buildings, of giant cinemas and dance-halls and cafés, bungalows with tiny garages, cocktail bars, Woolworths, motor-coaches, wireless, hiking, factory girls looking like actresses. Greyhound racing and dirt tracks, swimming pools and everything given away for ciga-rette coupons.' And he didn't like it, though he recognised that this England might be 'democratic': 'You need money in this England, but you do not need much money . . . The young people in this England do not play chorus in an opera in which their social superiors are the principals: they do not live vicariously, enjoy life at second hand, by telling one another what a wonderful time the young earl is having, or how beautiful Lady Mary looked in her court dress; they get on with their own lives. If they have heroes and hero-ines, they choose them themselves from the ranks of film stars and sportsmen and the like.'

Nevertheless, for Priestley this democratic modernism was leading to the loss of something that was valuable, something that was quintessen-tially English. Men no longer gathered in 'Glee Unions' to sing part-songs into their beer, as they had when he was a lad, but instead (some) young things headed off to cocktail bars, evidence of the regrettable 'cheap' Americanisation of British life, along with films, music, dance – and, of course, Woolworths. *The Savoy Cocktail Book* was a plangent exemplar. Published in 1930 with a vivid 'jazz' cover designed by Gilbert Rumbold, its 750 recipes were compiled by Harry Craddock, who presided over the American Bar at the Savoy Hotel – he had come to London in the 1920s from his native America since Prohibition had deprived him of his trade. Craddock was credited with inventing the White Lady cocktail (two parts gin, one part Cointreau, one part lemon juice, and a twist of lemon peel) and with popularising the dry Martini; he was pretty keen on absinthe, too, and many of his cocktails, such as the Monkey Gland and the Rattlesnake, were based on a combination of absinthe and gin or whisky, maybe some grenadine or an egg white, cognac or triple sec, perhaps the glass served with a rime of salt or sugar. Such concoctions would be drunk in the Savoy, obviously ('gay and very smart particularly during the ballet season. Cabaret twice nightly'), the Ritz ('crowded and fearfully smart'), Claridge's, the Dorchester, the Mayfair ('attracts a transatlantic crowd') and other smart hotels, bars – and nightclubs.

Lady Marguerite Strickland, the daughter of the Earl of Darnley, was a stunning thirties beauty who advertised everything from kirby grips to Gordon's gin, and whose photograph could be seen on a hoarding high up among the neon lights of Piccadilly Circus advising people to 'Drink Horlicks' to ward off 'night starvation'. Presented at Court in 1931, she 'went to a lot of nightclubs every night. The Florida . . . was popular with the debs, and that was great fun. The men wore black coats and there were telephones on all the tables, so that you could be rung up by the man across the room, it was very romantic . . . the most popular club was the Four Hundred, everyone loved it because it was completely dark. Then there were the Monsignor, The Embassy, The Nest, The Kit Kat, there were lots and lots of them, and often you didn't know where you were, you'd go from one to another when a party dragged on and it was all the dark . . . the idea of the darkness was that you'd be dancing with someone else's husband and your husband was across the room with the man's wife. The dancing was so important, the new band music was so marvellous, I used to know all the tunes and the band leaders who used to play in the clubs were all friends of ours. It was all so exciting.'

The American-born musician Roy Fox, known as the 'Whispering Cornetist' since he played the quietest trumpet in the West End, was the star name playing at the newly reopened Monseigneur Club in a basement on the corner of Piccadilly and Lower Regent Street. The head waiter and the cloakroom attendant were both dressed as a 'Monseigneur [in] a white wig and a blue velvet coat with lace ruffles', and the bar served a special pale-blue Monseigneur cocktail with a gin base. 'White tie and tails was the order of the day [though] if you weren't dressed you could eat in the gallery running round two sides of the restaurant . . . a lot of undergraduates used to go there late at night and eat bacon and eggs and coffee' for the not inconsiderable sum of 10s.6d. 'In those days the bandleaders were comparable to film stars. They were *the* attraction of any club: and you could see the way the eyes of the girls as they were dancing past would be automatically drawn to the bandleader,' recalled Fox.

In 1931 Gerald Cock, who was in charge of outside broadcasts and dance music at the BBC, gave Roy Fox a contract for a live broadcast which was transmitted every Wednesday at 10.30 p.m. Fox and his band 'made no concessions except to blow a little louder . . . a card was displayed saying "BAND NOW BROADCASTING"'. This was still a novelty, and 'the effects of the broadcasts was staggering. A mass of fan mail followed the first transmissions, taking the band completely by surprise. They had no conception of the size of the radio audience.' Fan mail was also addressed to the band's resident crooner, Al Bowlly, and crooners (from a Dutch word meaning to groan or whisper, in effect singing at an intimate half-volume which the Deputy Director General of the BBC, Cecil Graves, considered 'a particularly odious form of singing') would soon become as much in the spotlight as band leaders, Bowlly in particular with songs like 'Just Let Me Look at You', 'With My Eyes Wide Open I'm Dreaming' and 'Easy Come, Easy Go'.

All over the country people were tuning in to the vicarious enjoyment of a night out in the West End, and becoming hooked on the elegant, sophisticated music of the dance bands. 'Tiny' Winters, a 'jazz-minded young string bass player', tuned in and thought it was 'just great'. He was from 'a nice home in Hackney, but a poor one: but when you listened in to the radio and heard these sounds coming from the Savoy [where Carroll Gibbons played] or the Dorchester [the venue for Jack Jackson], or the Monseigneur, it was like tuning in to a dream world'.

The top-notch bands played in West End clubs, including at the *thés dansants* held regularly at the Savoy or the Café de Paris (entrance fee four or five shillings), and hotels, and many had lucrative BBC and gramophone recording contracts too – Jack Payne and his Dance Orchestra earned most of their income from the BBC. Those on the next rungs down the ladder performed in less prestigious London and provincial nightclubs and hotels (the Regent Palace Hotel also held regular afternoon tea dances, for which it charged only two shillings), brasseries, cafés, dance halls and *palais-de-dance* (Hammersmith had the first custom-built dance hall in Britain), or at 'gigs', temporary engagements such as society balls, college or political dances or social events at factories and offices, or toured the country playing one-night stands in village halls.

In 1930, *Melody Maker* (established in 1926 as a trade magazine for musicians) reckoned that there were approximately 12,500 to 20,000 dance bands in Britain, consisting of five to eight musicians playing saxophones, trumpets, trombones, drums, guitars, clarinets, bass, sousas and pianos. The largest concentration was in London, though Manchester was also a major centre for dance music, with regular bands engaged at the Ritz Ballroom, the Plaza Ballroom, the Midland Hotel and the new Lido at Sale, while Mameloks musical instrument store on the Manchester Road had a ballroom, café and lounge and teaching rooms attached. Birmingham could also 'be fairly regarded as one of the most advanced cities syncopationally speaking outside London', with dances at the Tower Ballroom, Tony's Ballroom, the Palais de Danse and the Masque Ballroom. Glasgow boasted 127 professional musicians and many more semi-pros playing at such venues as St Andrew's Halls (where Charlie Harkinn and his Kit Kat Band were the main attraction, along with the Philco Dance Band), the Locarno, the Gordon Ballrooms and the unpromisingly named London, Midland and Scottish Railway's Central Hotel, with regular tea dances at the St Vincent Tea Rooms. Nottingham was well provided with dance halls.

In Leeds the Gaumont cinema chain engaged dance bands – fifteen-piece orchestras at the Majestic and the Coliseum – and the practice soon spread to other chains. Musicians found summer employment at seaside resorts such as Torquay (which was advertised as being 'exceptionally well served in the way of dance bands'), Newquay ('the dance musician's Mecca during the summer season ... all the large hotels employ resident bands who play for a continual round of dances from one week to another', according to *Melody Maker*), Cleethorpes (which had a Café Dansant on the Promenade), Skegness and Chapel St Leonards (where, according to *Melody Maker*, 'Find a café and you will find a dance band! In fact, it would be quite difficult to take a meal without music'), as well as the new holiday camps: at Caister, north of Great Yarmouth, for example, Percy Cohen's Band was playing to 1,500 dancers a night by 1935.

Unemployment hit music just as it did other areas of work, and the number of professional musicians dipped in the early thirties, with semi-professionals who still had to keep their day jobs outnumbering the pros by something like twenty to one. Such bands, whose members usually had no musical training, learned their skills from the number of 'self tutor' books that flooded onto the market, from courses run by *Melody Maker*, from gramophone records and from listening to the wireless. It was much the same for those wanted to learn to dance to their music: newspapers carried features showing complicated diagrams of the new dance steps; the Mecca ballroom chain gave lessons; middle-class children who had learned ballet graduated to 'ballroom dancing' in their teens with the waltz, the veleta, the foxtrot and maybe even the tango being particularly popular. The would-be dainty-footed rolled up the carpet and cavorted around their sitting rooms trying out the latest steps as they listened to records – a portable gramophone was advertised for sale in the *News of the World* in 1931 for £3.15s, with the suggestion that it was 'the very thing' as a Christmas present or for parties, and could be enhanced for a further £1 by filling the album in the lid with 'eight acceptable records'.

The BBC broadcast big bands at 10.30 until midnight every night except Sunday (naturally, given the DG Sir John Reith's insistence on a sombre Sabbath), featuring a different band for the full hour and a half each night: Lew Stone on Tuesday, Harry Roy on Friday, and so on. Henry Hall, who had been Musical Director for the chain of London, Midland and Scottish Railway hotels and so was well attuned to provincial and suburban tastes (unaffected by 'the virus of West-Endism' as the *Radio Magazine* described him), was appointed leader of the BBC's own Dance Orchestra in succession to Jack Payne in March 1932, and his signature tune 'Here's to the Next Time' (composed by the BBC's Director of Entertainment, Roger Eckersley) was the first music transmitted from the new BBC building in

Portland Place when it opened in May that year. Hall's name was soon synonymous with dance music, and he proved something of a heart-throb with the public, though his easy-listening, 'four-beats-in-a-bar' music was generally despised by musical highbrows.

In the West End the Prince of Wales had a corner table permanently reserved for him at the Embassy Club in Old Bond Street in the 1920s, as did Lord Louis Mountbatten and his wife Edwina, granddaughter of the immensely wealthy Sir Ernest Cassel, financier and friend of Edward VII, and 'Bendor' the also fabulously rich – and extravagant – 'Golden Duke of Westminster', former lover of Coco Chanel, but at this time married to his third wife, Loelia Ponsonby. Lady Diana Cooper had been a habituée too, as were intimates of the Prince of Wales, Lady Furness and Mrs Dudley Ward and Lady Alexandra 'Baba' (Black Sheep – because of her fascist leanings) Metcalf and her husband Major 'Fruity' Metcalf, ADC to the Prince. Thursdays had been the most fashionable night to be seen there, and no society hostess would have been so clueless as to hold a party on that night. The Prince of Wales was no more competent on the dance floor than he was in many other areas of his life, but he was a Royal, so when he had caught the eye of Bert Ambrose, the Embassy bandleader (until he was lured away to the Mayfair Hotel) as he steered some unfortunate partner around the small dance floor in a two-left-footed waltz, the band was obliged to continue to play 'his' tune until he sat down.

However, by the mid-1930s the fashionable crowd were beginning to drift away from the Embassy, and the romantic novelist Barbara Cartland was employed to woo them back. She did so by softening the lighting, getting rid of 'a ghastly cubist carpet', recovering the banquettes to look like her own bed at home, and generally making the place look 'romantic' (as might have been expected). 'What designers forget,' she said, 'is that smart restaurants and night clubs are full of unhappily married people – the happily married ones stay at home, the young unmarried ones are not good payers.' It was important to make these malcontents and misers 'feel glamorous, to imagine themselves in love if only for the evening'. The actress Anna May Wong performed the cabaret on the opening night, and 'though it was her first effort and she wasn't very good', she gave the newspapers something to write about. Cartland persuaded the management to lure back Bert Ambrose, and soon the club was doing so well that her services were dispensed with.

A former head waiter at the Embassy had opened the Café de Paris in Coventry Street, and the Prince of Wales, who had known him at the Embassy, patronised the new establishment. By the mid-1930s it had become a great success, hosting cabaret acts by such stars as Marlene Dietrich,

Maurice Chevalier, Josephine Baker and the risqué female impersonator and pantomime dame Douglas Byng (dowagers and mermaids were his speciality), attracting European royalty as well as such glitterati as Noël Coward, Gertrude Lawrence and Gloria Swanson. The Kit-Cat in Haymarket, the Silver Slipper in Regent Street (which boasted a glass floor), Ciro's in Orange Street, Monseigneur in St James's, the Five Hundred in Albemarle Street and the Bag o'Nails in Soho were other popular venues for drinking, eating, dancing and cabaret. They were, however, hardly establishments for *hoi polloi*. Their exclusivity was guarded by their membership lists, their dress codes and their cost: a bottle of champagne cost around thirty shillings – almost half the average working man's weekly wage. As the nightclub owner Kate Meyrick, who admitted that she added something like a 100–150 per cent mark-up to a bottle of champagne, explained loftily, 'The prices charged in West-End night-clubs are not prices at which food and drink is supplied in an A.B.C. tea-shop.'

There were a host of other establishments in the 'bottle party belt' that ran 'from midnight to milkman's round'. They included the Four Hundred ('favourite haunt of the rich, very subdued lighting after 2 a.m.'), the Coconut Grove ('South Sea Island setting – dress optional'), the Havana ('Cuban band, rhumbas, cabaret, air cooled, breakfast'), Uncle's and The Bat. These clubs, or *boîtes*, as the smaller ones liked to be known, got away (most of the time) with being cavalier about the 2 a.m. closing time usual for most licensed clubs by insisting that they were holding private 'bottle parties', with patrons required to order their drinks twenty-four hours in advance. The law was, in the view of the gossip columnist Patrick Balfour, 'simply a variation of the principle "one law for the rich, another for the poor", but with the bias on the side of the poor for once. It is only the rich, because of the late hour at which they dine, who wish to drink after ten o'clock at night.'

The best-known nightclub was probably the 43 at 43 Gerrard Street in Soho (depicted by Evelyn Waugh as the Old Hundredth in *A Handful of Dust*), owned by Mrs Kate Meyrick, the stepdaughter of a clergyman and the estranged wife of a Dublin physician. After the break-up of her marriage, with three sons at Harrow and three daughters at Roedean to educate, she had started in the hospitality business by organising tea dances in Leicester Square, and was soon the undisputed 'Queen of Nightclubs', owning several besides the 43, including the Silver Slipper in Regent Street (which had been the Bobbin before it was raided and, as was the way, opened under a new name, but was henceforth known by its aficionados – who included Charlie Chaplin – as the 'Slippin') and the Manhattan in Denman Street, and she had a part interest in the Folies Bergères in Newman Street.

In the mid-1920s the notoriously illiberal Home Secretary Sir William Joynson-Hicks decided to clean up London, and declared war on nightclubs in particular, since they tended to be run by Italians, with clientèle so mixed that titled persons might well find themselves sipping a cocktail next to a dancer, a provincial businessman on a spree in London, a boxer – '"Kid Lewis" after spending £100 or so entertaining a big party of friends to dinner at the Savoy, would bring them to the "43" and get rid of another £30 or £40' – or even a criminal. Clubs would be raided, names taken, they would be shut down, and would reopen a week later under another name. Mrs Meyrick found herself in court frequently, usually for selling drinks out of hours or to non-members, and was periodically jailed for six months. This did not seem to affect her businesses overly: every time the police mounted a raid they returned to the station 'with notebooks like the Almanac de Gotha', and two of her daughters married very well indeed, one to an earl, the other to a baron.

In 1928, just after her release from Holloway after serving another six-month sentence, Meyrick was rearrested and charged under the Prevention of Corruption Act. It was alleged that she (and others) had been bribing a certain Station-Sergeant Goddard, who on wages of £6 a week managed to own a large freehold house in Streatham, two cars and two bulging safe-deposit boxes. When the case came to trial in January 1930, Meyrick was found guilty of bribing Goddard by slipping him £100 a week not to raid her clubs, and was sentenced to fifteen months' hard labour. After her release she continued to hold the law in contempt, and was jailed twice more for licensing offences. After a final raid of the 43 in February 1932, she was bound over for three years, and forbidden to run any premises at which alcohol was sold. Meyrick made the unlikely statement to the press that all she wanted was to 'retire . . . to some country village and have my three grandchildren stay with me at holiday time', but her spells in Holloway proved deleterious to her health, and she died of broncho-pneumonia in 1933, aged fifty-seven. She died a poor woman, some £500,000 having 'melted away' in the course of her years as a nightclub owner, on such incidentals as bounced cheques, hefty lawyers' fees and paying off blackmailers.

Night and Day published the report of 'a fairly extensive tour of contemporary Night-Town' by Maurice Richardson, 'collecting fierce hangovers and an overdraft' in July 1937. He found that 'in ten years nothing seems to have changed except women's clothes and the names of tunes [the] dance-music is lukewarm and would give Bojangles [Bill "Bojangles" Robinson, a black American tap dancer] of Harlem pneumonia . . . Snooty boredom is the correct facial expression . . . and plenty [of nightclubs] are still indistinguishable from their glorious ancestors of the Goddard-Meyrick regime:

same chlorotic rickety dance "hostesses" reeking of scent as pungent as "Flit"; same exasperated drunk banging the fruit machine against the wall. Purveyor of night life is still a popular profession among ex-army officers of the chronically unsuccessful type. You know the sort. "Poor old Jacko never has any luck. First there was the tobacco plantation in Rhodesia, then the riding school, then the garage and the flooded chicken farm. And now there's a nasty little spot of bother over his bottle-party place.""

Mass-Observation found several 'spots of bother' when its observers spent a 'Night in Soho' in spring 1939. There were prostitutes, and fights broke out with 'razors, chairs, bottles . . . they break off the tops of tumblers and dash them under your chin . . . at one affair . . . two negroes had been having a gun fight and one was shot in the mouth and the other in the head'. In several clubs 'dope' and cocaine were openly on sale, and couples danced suggestively to the music of a band, or more likely a radiogram in the corner.

Maurice Richardson picked out two nightclubs in particular. The Nest was presided over by 'Mrs Cohen, the finest specimen of a night club queen in London', who 'with her brilliant hair, and . . . aquamarine dresses . . . would certainly rate four stars in the language of the guide books . . . The band blows the roof off in a little pen at one end, and at the other handsome suave grey-haired Mr Cohen, distinguished-looking as a Pall Mall antique-dealer, stands behind a little bar that is stuck all over with photographs of coloured stars . . . All colours, sexes and professions. Plenty of negroes – bandsmen, music hall performers, students, West Indians, Americans, Africans. But very few coloured girls, and those few are nearly all London-born or from Cardiff . . . you will find the atmosphere . . . very friendly, quite democratic, very international. Left-wing poets can be guaranteed a dusty puff of afflatus here.' And there was the Frisco, 'shaped like a railway carriage . . . matting and palm grass on the walls try to introduce a jungle motif . . . All sorts of people go there – smarties, tired business[men], films, press, higher bohemians . . . Frisco is a large, astonishingly well-preserved West Indian negro . . . There are two schools of thought about the cabaret: the naïves say it's marvellous; the sophisticates sigh deeply for Harlem. The band is good, better than anywhere else. There used to be a clever little creature from Trinidad in it. He was called Cyril Blake and played the trumpet and sang. Even the most Harlem-blasé sophisticate would admit that his version of the "St James Infirmary Blues" was nearly if not quite classic. The number of "clubs" in the Belt must run into hundreds. There are six or seven in Kingly Street [behind Regent Street] alone. They range from the high-class Four Hundred where you have to be dressed [i.e. in evening clothes] to little cellars where poor old tarts with sore feet stamp about to the noise of one accordion . . . Many of these clubs may be shut down at any moment, but each will figure in somebody's individual history as a landmark of the thirties.'

Evelyn Waugh too had noticed the interest in black entertainers and entrepreneurs that rode a wave of increasing fascination in the mid-thirties with 'everything Black'. Lady Astor, who only ever served lemonade at her Cliveden parties (being a teetotaller herself, and considering that everyone else should be too), laid on 'negro folk songs and spirituals with banjo accompaniment' to follow the dancing at one of her evenings, reported Thomas Jones. Stars of the Harlem renaissance, a movement in literature, poetry, art and music influenced by the African-American folk memory and the experience of slavery, became part of a European diaspora – and Britain, as the centre of the Empire, became a 'junction box' for wide areas of the black world.

The Jamaican poet Claude McKay, one of the leading lights of the Harlem renaissance, 'a new black modernity in which, for the first time, black men and women could hope to enter the modern world on their own terms', had come to London in 1919, but left two years later, deeply disillusioned by the 'mother Empire' and convinced that prejudice against black people had become 'almost congenital' among English people. They could not think of a black man, he believed, as anything but an entertainer, a boxer, a Baptist preacher or a menial.

Among the black entertainers who enchanted white Europe were Josephine Baker, the toast of Paris, and the 'Blackbirds'. The Prince of Wales had been much taken with one of their stars, the delightful Florence Mills, whose song 'I'm a Little Blackbird Looking for a Bluebird' gave their revue its name, and he had kept returning to watch her when the show was playing at the Pavilion Theatre in London. Lena Horne starred in the last Blackbirds revue in 1939, which was a flop, but kick-started her career. Ken 'Snakehips' Johnson, born in British Guiana but educated in Britain, declined to follow his family's medical tradition, and instead went into show business, going to Harlem in 1935, where he learned African vernacular dances. A 'fluid and flexible dancer' (which is how he got his nickname), Johnson returned to Britain intent on forming an all-black hot jazz ensemble. His West Indian Dance Orchestra became Britain's most popular swing band, touring the country, featuring on the infant BBC television service in March 1939 and appearing at high-end nightclubs such as the Old Florida in Bruton Street and the Café de Paris, where in March 1941 Johnson, together with members of his band and the audience, was killed in an air raid.

Despite Johnson's popularity, his frequent radio broadcasts bringing his music to thousands who would never hear him in person, the most successful of all black inter-war entertainers was the American actor and bass singer Paul Robeson. His first appearance in Britain had been in the play *Voodoo* at the Blackpool Opera House in 1922, and in 1928 he thrilled audiences with his rendition of the slave song 'Ol' Man River' in Jerome Kern's *Show Boat*, which opened in Hammersmith. Robeson made his home in London, playing in *Othello* with Peggy Ashcroft in 1930, the first black actor to take the role since the 1860s. One critic was moved to write: 'That Mr Robeson should be stripped to the waist is my first demand of any play in which he appears.'

This uneasy (homo) eroticism and exoticism of black entertainers was something that had first been picked up in several books in the previous decade with titles that would be unacceptable today, monuments to the fascination of white writers with raw, proud 'primitivism' and an aesthetic that attracted the Surrealists too. Ronald Firbank (a Wildean aesthete, son of an MP for Hull) wrote *Prancing Nigger* (1924: this novel about a Caribbean republic – a compound of Cuba and Haiti – and the failure of a black rural family to gain social acceptance was a great success in the US under Firbank's preferred title, *Sorrow in Sunlight*, but was less noticed in Britain). Then there was Carl van Vechten's *Nigger Heaven* (1926, a love story set in Harlem: the title refers to the balconies of cinemas where black people were obliged to sit in the decades of segregation). *Africa Dances* (1935) was written by Geoffrey Gorer, a Cambridge-educated writer who had received a crash course in anthropology from Margaret Mead, whose controversial study *Coming of Age in Samoa* had been published in 1929. Gorer's book follows an African dancer the author had met at the Folies Bergères in Paris back to Senegal, and he journeys through West Africa observing tribal cultures with the stern intention of deconstructing ill-informed colonial myths – particularly about black sexuality.

The prejudice against black men consorting with white women, and the fear of miscegenation compromising the 'purity of the race' had been inflamed in 1919 when E.D. Morel, a trenchant left-wing critic of anti-colonialism, had written an article for the *Daily Herald* about France's use of black troops in occupied Germany. The piece, 'Black Scourge in Europe', described the 'bestial threat' that 'syphilitic barbarians' supposedly posed to white women. It was reprinted as a pamphlet, 'The Horror on the Rhine', and proved an instant best-seller, handed out to all delegates to the TUC Congress, and inspired similar pieces in other journals. The supposed attraction black men held for white *avant-garde* women was satirised by Winifred Holtby in her novel *Mandoa, Mandoa!* (1933).

In 1931 Nancy Cunard, the daughter of Emerald Cunard (*née* Maud

Burke), a pillar of London society (which Nancy dubbed the 'corrupt coterie'), and possibly of Emerald's husband Bache, a Leicestershire landowner and grandson of the shipping magnate, or possibly of the Irish writer and poet G.M. Moore, published an article in W.E.B. Du Bois' African-American journal *Crisis* entitled 'Black Man and White Ladyship'. The first half was a vicious attack on Cunard's mother Emerald, 'the most conscientious of ostriches', as a snob, a hypocrite, a profligate materialist ('I have not the faintest idea how much I spend on clothes every year. It may run into thousands. I have never bothered to think about it,' she had told the *Daily Express*), a control freak and a racist ('As yet only the shadow of the Negro falls across the white assembly of High Society and spreads itself, it would seem, quite particularly and agonisingly over you'). The second half was an impassioned exposition of the slave trade, lynching and all the cruelties and indignities inflicted on black people by a society that believed that 'the damn niggers had to be kept in their place' while relying on them to look after their children and fight their wars. But, Cunard concluded, 'The days of Rastus and Sambo are long gone and will not return . . . the pore [sic] old down-trodden canticle-singing nigger daddy who used to be let out to clown for the whites has turned into the very much up-to-date, well educated, keen, determined man of action.' Cunard had her article printed as a pamphlet, and sent it as a sort of Christmas card to about a hundred people, many of them her mother's friends, including her lover, the conductor Sir Thomas Beecham, and possibly the Prince of Wales, a former beau.

Presumably Emerald was deeply wounded, though her reaction was dignified, but even Nancy's friends thought her actions were regrettable, and sprang more from a hatred of her mother than from any real wish to help race relations. Although the situation between mother and daughter had been strained for some time, the tinder seemed to have been Lady Emerald's disgust at the fact that not only was her daughter importing an allegedly blasphemous and obscene Surrealist film, *L'Age d'Or* (made by Luis Buñuel and Salvador Dalí), banned in France, to have it privately screened in London, but that she had a black lover, Henry Crowder, a mild-mannered jazz pianist who worked with her at the very successful Hours Press which she had set up in France. Lady Cunard had allegedly threatened to have Crowder apprehended at his port of arrival and refused entry to Britain, but her daughter was told that there were no legal grounds for doing so.

Nancy Cunard resolved to produce a book demonstrating the injustices meted out to black people, as well as the power and magnificence of black achievement. 'It was,' she wrote, 'a question of erecting a monument [to black culture] – denouncing the fallacious arguments about the benefits of civilization so generously brought to the blacks.' There were contributions from the poets Langston Hughes and Sterling Brown, and rather tossed-off pieces from Norman Douglas and Ezra Pound. Harold Acton wrote on Pushkin, and there was a short extract from William Plomer's *African Notebook*. The struggling playwright Samuel Beckett, who the Hours Press had published, undertook many of the translations from French. Abraham Lincoln's Proclamation of Emancipation was included, Zora Neale Hurston wrote on black folklore and speech patterns, 'shouting the sermon' and spirituals, William Carlos Williams contributed an uncomfortable piece about how he'd fancied his family's black maids as a youth, there were profiles of great black men such as Frederick Douglass and women such as Harriet Tubman, and pieces on such stars of the 'Negro firmament' as Duke Ellington and his orchestra, jazz, and the influence of black music on European, with pages of spirituals, songs and blues. The black East End former prize-fighter Bob Scanlon (another 'suspiciously close' friend of Nancy's, who she claimed gave her boxing lessons) wrote on 'The Record of the Negro Boxer', and Henry Crowder wrote on 'hitting back' at racial injustice. Nancy contributed several articles herself, including one on the 'Colour Bar' (which included a dig at her mother, 'an American-born frantically prejudiced society woman' who was perfectly content to be photographed – photograph reproduced – with 'an Indian rajah', presumably, Nancy concluded, because '*Rajahs have money* and are "important people", chiefs etc.').

A long section on Africa included history, ethnography, personal experiences, and a large number of striking photographs of African art and artefacts – several of the pieces were owned by Nancy herself, including the ivory bracelets she customarily wore from wrist to elbow. The final section on the wrongs of colonialism included an article by George Padmore on 'White Man's Justice in Africa', along with contributions from two African nationalists who would later lead their respective countries, Jomo Kenyatta of Kenya and Ben Azikiwe of Liberia, but who were living in London at the time.

The book was a vastly ambitious, profoundly passionate undertaking. It was at times incoherent, deeply moving, and of course highly political – and although Nancy Cunard was prepared to subsidise its production (in the end it was largely paid for by the settlement of libel cases against several British newspapers that had covered her visit to London with Crowder in 1931), it was hard to find a publisher. It was, she despaired, 'like selling oriental rugs to manure merchants'. Jonathan Cape declined, as did Victor Gollancz. Eventually, through the good offices of the left-wing English poet Edgell Rickword, whom Nancy had met when both were involved in the Scottsboro case,* the radical publisher Wishart, for whom Rickword was working, agreed to take it on, though Nancy insisted on eagle-eyed surveillance of her masterwork at every stage.

With a print run of a thousand, the eight-hundred-page, hessian-bound, heavily illustrated, two-inch-thick *Negro* (the title had originally been *Colour*), 'Dedicated to Henry Crowder, my first Negro friend' and with a frontispiece of a striking painting of the 'rail thin' Nancy by her friend the Surrealist artist John Banting, was finally published on 15 February 1934. It sold for two guineas (£2.2s), and copies were sent by Nancy to various libraries in Britain and America, which, given the weight of the tome, was a costly exercise. The *New Statesman* liked it, and the *Daily Worker* gave it a good review, which was not surprising since Nancy declared in her introduction that 'It is Communism alone which throws down the barriers of race as finally as it wipes out class distinctions.' But *Negro* did not receive either the wide press coverage or the public acclaim that Nancy had hoped for, though several contributors wrote to say what a 'damn fine and serious' book it was. And it did not sell well. When the Blitz came to London in 1940 there were still several hundred copies in Wishart's warehouse: all were destroyed in an air raid.

Apart from entertainers, there was a relatively small black community in Britain in the 1930s, mostly centred round the ports: the East End of London, Liverpool, Glasgow, and particularly Cardiff. Many of them suffered overt discrimination and occasional violence, usually triggered by fear that in a depressed economy, black labour costs would undercut white, and white men would lose their jobs to black. Accumulated bitterness against discriminatory employment practices led to race riots in Cardiff in 1935 (there had been similar riots there and in other seaports in 1919). The police had systematically and wilfully misapplied the Aliens Act by classifying black seamen of undisputed British nationality as 'aliens' between 1931 and 1933, at a time when unemployment among seamen ran at one in three. The situation was, a report concluded, 'a new monument to economic ignorance and racial animosity in Britain'.

*Nine black youths had been arrested in Scottsboro, Alabama, in March 1931, charged with raping two white girls on a goods train. All were found guilty in a travesty of a trial in front of an all-white jury with a lynch mob baying outside the courthouse, and all but the youngest (aged thirteen) were sentenced to the electric chair. Nancy Cunard campaigned tirelessly for justice, and raised money for the numerous appeals that dragged on until 1938.

In the 1930s there were also a number of black intellectuals in Britain, many studying law before returning home to play their part in the anti-imperialist struggle. The first Pan-African Congress had met in London in 1900, as had sections of the second and third in the 1920s, and the Webbs, the Woolfs, H.G. Wells and R.H. Tawney had been among those left-wing establishment figures who took an interest in their deliberations, demands for Home Rule for British West Africa and the West Indies, and the call that 'in all the world . . . black folk be treated as men. We can see no other road to Peace and Progress.'

Many of these black intellectuals from the colonies stayed in dismal bedsitters in North London, and trafficked in ideas and hopes, linking London to the rest of the black world by mounting soapboxes at Speaker's Corner, organising meetings in the Conway Hall or the Friends Meeting House on the Euston Road, and distributing smudged Gestetnered leaflets.

Harold Moody, who had come to London from Jamaica to study medicine, and had encountered the usual prejudice and professional setbacks, married an English nurse, and in March 1931 at a meeting in the YMCA in Tottenham Court Road inaugurated the League of Coloured Peoples to look after 'the welfare of his people in an alien land'. Though Moody was dismissed by younger black radicals as an 'Uncle Tom' figure, his coat-tails tied to the Colonial Office, the League succeeded in providing 'Humanitarianism, Pan-African Style', sorting out housing and employment issues, taking black British-born children on a summer outing to Epsom each year and arranging a Christmas party for them. Moody became an advocate for black interests in public affairs. He upbraided the BBC for its use of the word 'nigger', which he described as 'an unfortunate relic of the days of slavery, vexatious to present day Africans and West Indians'. He was involved in helping the black community at the time of the Cardiff seamen's riots, and also raised sufficient awareness of the Trinidadian oilfield riots in June 1937 for the British government to set up a royal commission to inquire into economic and social conditions in the West Indies. However, the League's membership was small – it was largest in Cardiff – and always included more whites than blacks; Moody refused to admit Asians.

Also in 1931, the Quakers set up another voluntary organisation, the Joint Council to Promote Understanding between White and Coloured Peoples in Great Britain (modelled on the South African Joint Councils). More radical black activists in London increasingly made connections between the treatment of black people in Britain and colonial oppression, and saw the way forward as a pan-African one, uniting black people throughout the world in solidarity and self-help – without the help of white liberals, to whom 'you are not a person you are a problem, and every crusading crank imagines he knows how to solve your problem'.

C.L.R. James arrived from Trinidad steeped in Victorian culture in 1932, and stayed in England for fifteen years, going first to Nelson in Lancashire to lodge with his fellow Trinidadian the cricketer Learie Constantine before settling in Bloomsbury. James was a more radical figure in black politics in the 1930s than Harold Moody, as were George Padmore, Ras Makonnen, Jomo Kenyatta and I.T.A. Wallace-Johnson. He made his living by writing about cricket for the *Manchester Guardian* and the Glasgow *Herald*, joined the ILP but left it to form the Trotskyist Revolutionary Socialist League. A most eloquent, inspiring and intellectually curious man, James published a Trotskyist 'bible', *World Revolution 1917–1936* in 1937, as well as his classic *The Black Jacobins* (1936), a history of Toussaint L'Ouverture and the Haitian Revolution.

George Padmore (a pseudonym), another Trinidadian, came to Britain via New York, where he had joined the Communist Party, and Moscow, where despite being unable to speak Russian he had been appointed Head of the Negro Bureau of the Red International, helped organise the first International Conference of Negro Workers in 1930, and edited the *Negro Worker*. When the Communist International suddenly dissolved the International Trade Union Committee of Negro Workers, Padmore resigned his various roles and came to Britain in 1935, where he worked as a tutor and journalist, writing for *Tribune* and other left-wing publications. He collaborated with the Labour MP Fenner Brockway on colonial matters and also as a member of the No More War Movement.

Padmore shared a flat in London with British Guianan-born George Thomas Nathaniel Griffith, who took the name Ras Terafi Makonnen as he was drawn deeper into the Ethiopian cause after the Italian invasion in 1935. He had come to London in 1937 via Denmark, from which he had been deported for publicising the fact that the Danes were manufacturing mustard gas, in contravention of the terms of the Geneva Convention. He soon left London for Manchester, where he lectured to Co-operative Unions, read Anglo-Saxon history at the university, and started a chain of teashops, first the Ethiopian teashop on the Oxford Road, and later the grander Cosmopolitan (where Jomo Kenyatta helped out), which became a social centre for black people living in Britain, particularly during the Second World War. So successful was Makonnen's expanding chain that he was able to help Britain's growing black community in numerous ways, including financing a bookshop, a publishing house, a monthly journal – and eventually the fifth and by far the largest and most significant Pan-African Congress, which was held in Manchester in 1945.

Isaac Theophilus Akuna Wallace-Johnson, the son of a farmer and a fishmonger, was born in Sierra Leone, and as a young man was involved in trade union activities, representing Sierra Leonean railway workers at the first International Conference of Negro Workers in Hamburg in 1930. He came to Britain in 1936 to appeal to the Privy Council to set aside charges for seditious libel for an article he had written for the *African Morning Post* on the Italian invasion of Abyssinia, and while in London before returning to carry on his fight against colonial oppression in Sierra Leone he worked with Padmore, James, Makonnen and Jomo Kenyatta to found the International African Service and edit its bulletin, *Africa and the World* (later the *African Sentinel*).

Jomo Kenyatta, later President of Kenya, was another Pan-African activist living in London in the 1930s. Educated at a mission school, Kenyatta had come to Britain in March 1929, seeking redress for Kikuyu grievances, and returned in 1931 to study under the famous anthropologist Bronisław Malinowski. In 1938 he published an anthropological account of his own society and culture, *Facing Mount Kenya*. Kenyatta was hounded by the Special Branch, which believed he was spreading 'poison by word of mouth' every time he spoke to WEA classes about colonial oppression in his country. He was so poor at that time that when letters arrived from Kenya he would sell the stamps to buy a penny bun; another way he supplemented his almost non-existent income was working as one of the 250 extras in Alexander Korda's film *Sanders of the River*, starring Paul Robeson.

Korda's brother Zoltán had gone to Africa in 1933 to film tribal ceremonies and dances as well as the flora and fauna. He had no script, but had the feeling that this footage would come in useful for the film the Hungarian brothers intended to make based on Edgar Wallace's very popular stories. It did. Back in England a Congolese village was built at Denham studios, black dockers (and Jomo Kenyatta) were brought from London, Cardiff, Liverpool and Glasgow for the crowd scenes, and filming starting in autumn 1934, with Leslie Banks playing Sanders, the sort of chap 'we could not run the show without'– 'the show' being the British Empire. Paul Robeson took the part of Bosambo, one of the 'keepers of the [British] King's peace' and thus a 'good African'. Another black American singer, Nina Mae McKinney, played his wife Lilongo. Although the film was set in the River Territories of West Africa, none of the cast ever made it out of England during production. Released in April 1935, *Sanders of the River* opened with a map of Africa and the legend 'Africa – tens of millions of natives, each tribe under its own chieftain, guarded and protected by a handful of white men, whose work is an unsung saga of courage and efficiency.'

The film was a huge box-office success, and Robeson's recording of 'Canoe Song' was a hit too. Most critics welcomed the film's insights into 'our special English difficulties in the governing of savage races', as the *Sunday Times* critic put it. But not all. The documentary-film-maker Paul Rotha was scornful: 'So this is Africa, ladies and gentlemen, where the White Man rules by kindness and the Union Jack means peace! . . . You may, like me, feel embarrassed for Robeson.' Robeson felt embarrassed for himself. He also felt deceived, agreeing with a black American journalist who told him that the film was 'a slanderous attack on African natives who were pictured as being satisfied with the "benevolent" oppression of English imperialism . . . You became a tool of British imperialism.'

Robeson refused to work for Korda ever again, since he had, in his own words, 'discovered Africa' in London – though not the Africa that Korda had portrayed. He enrolled to study African languages at London University, and became a patron of the West African Students Union. Increasingly interested in communism, he visited the Soviet Union for the first time in 1934, and committed himself to the anti-colonial struggle along with his London-based friends James, Kenyatta and Kwame Nkrumah, who would later lead Ghana and its predecessor, the Gold Coast. 'The artist must take sides. He must elect to fight for freedom or for slavery. I have made my choice. I had no alternative,' Robeson declared in a speech at the Albert Hall on 24 June 1937 (though his commitment here was to Republican Spain, rather than to the struggle for black freedom).

'I am tired of playing Stepin Fetchit comics and savages with leopard skin and spear,' Robeson decided, and in future he tried to balance his performing career (which included going to Hollywood in 1936 to film *Show Boat*, which had been a Broadway as well as a Shaftesbury Avenue smash hit) with his growing political commitment. He gave concerts in huge cinemas in largely working-class areas to 'reach the people', and appeared in films such as *Song of Freedom* (1936), which he felt was the first film to 'give a true picture of many aspects of the life of the coloured man in the west', with its tale of a British-born black docker who discovers he has an exceptional singing voice.

Filming of *The Proud Valley*, the last feature film Robeson made in Britain, started in August 1939, mainly in the Rhondda Valley. Robeson played a miner, David Goliath, who dies in a pit accident at the end of the film, a reference perhaps to the terrible Gresford colliery disaster in September 1934 that claimed 226 lives. Robeson had a particular affinity with the South Wales miners, meeting the Hunger Marchers, visiting miners' social clubs, donating the entire takings of a concert he gave at Caernarfon to the 160 widows and two hundred fatherless children of the Gresford miners. In 1938 he sang in front of a crowd of 7,000 at the Welsh International Brigade's memorial at Mountain Ash in 1938 to commemorate the thirty-three men from Wales killed fighting in Spain. He was introduced by Arthur Horner, President of the South Wales Miners' Federation, as 'a great champion of the rights of the oppressed people to whom he belongs'.

As long ago as 1920, when the cinema was still young, the Labour Party had recognised that 'the eyes are more exact witnesses than the ears' in a circular on 'Labour Cinema Propaganda', but it then seemed to forget its own wisdom. Despite the best intentions of committed film-makers such as Paul Rotha, and generous offers of help from the *Daily Herald*, it was not until 1938 that Labour, prodded by the success of the Co-operative Movement in this area, established a Workers' Film Association to make use of the medium.

Perhaps surprisingly, the Conservative Party had been much more prescient in its use of film. During the 1931 LCC elections Neville Chamberlain noted that the party might book a hall and engage an excellent speaker, but still only fifty people would turn up, whereas speakers going round with a 'cinema van' were reckoned to draw as many as 3,000 people in a night. Cinema vans were seven-ton pantechnicons with a hooded viewing screen at the back. They would stop in the street and offer a free film show to passers-by, holding their attention so the politician who accompanied the van could then make a speech. The vans were rather like – though probably not modelled on – the Russian Bolshevik cinema vans or trains.

In 1926 Conservative Central Office had started to commission the party's own films. Many were 'Felix the Cat'-type cartoons which ridiculed their Labour opponents, showing Prime Minister Ramsay MacDonald and Chancellor of the Exchequer Philip Snowden as incompetent plumbers, for example. These would be part of a programme that included a speech from the party leader lasting ten minutes or so, vaudeville sketches by well-known artistes but with a political message, documentary 'shorts' on the beneficial effects that Conservative policies were having on agriculture, steel, shipbuilding or fishing, and were rounded off by a dialogue in which one 'working-class type' explained to another why the Conservative Party was best.

In those innocent, pre-television days, such infotainment clearly appealed to what Central Office called the 'untrained mind', particularly in rural areas, and prior to the 1935 general election, 1.5 million people watched such films. Whether or not they were persuaded to vote Conservative is of course impossible to know.

Even if the Labour Party lagged behind when it came to harnessing the power of film, a number on the left worked very hard to use the medium to point up the 'deadly parallels' in Britain between 'sumptuous wealth on the one hand; abject poverty on the other'. Based on Continental models such as the German *Volksfilmverband*, whose chairman was Heinrich Mann, the Workers' Film Society's primary aim was to allow British workers to see Soviet films such as Eisenstein's masterpiece *Battleship Potemkin*.

The 1909 Cinematograph Act was concerned merely with safety regulations, and had no powers to censor films exhibited by cinema-owners. The British Board of Film Censors (BBFC), a self-appointed body set up by the trade in 1912, took it upon itself to fulfil this function, though it had no actual legal authority to so. The only ways round its *diktats* were to appeal to the local authority (such appeals were unlikely to be successful, since most accepted the BBFC's rulings without demur) or to show nonflammable film, since the 1909 Act only covered flammable film, though such films would have to be shown on premises not licensed under the terms of the Act. Thus throughout the 1930s a ludicrous cat-and-mouse game was played between socialist film societies renting halls to show 16mm (or even 9.5mm, essentially home-movie format) films, and local authorities trying to stop audiences seeing the cinematographic products of the world's first 'workers' state'.

Soon there were such film societies dotted all over the country – Salford had a particularly active one – showing mainly Soviet films such as Eisenstein's *Battleship Potemkin* (about the 1905 Kronstadt rising), Pudovkin's *Storm Over Asia* (an indictment of imperialism) and *Mother* (based on Maxim Gorki's novel), or *Bed and Sofa*, a rather scandalous film showing the effects of the housing shortage which obliged a woman and two men to share an apartment in contemporary Moscow. The films were intended to be politically educative, and attracted the dedicated to sit on a hard bench in a cold, probably dingy, room, watching a silent film, 'halting four times in one picture while reels are changed', when they could have been sitting in a comfortable seat in a warm cinema, losing themselves in romance, adventure or humour – admittedly at a slightly higher cost, since if (and it was a big if) 120 viewers could be mustered, a film society need only charge sixpence a head. In November 1930 a thousand membership cards had been ordered for the Salford Workers' Film Society; by the end of the season only 350 had been needed.

However, there were successes: Charlie Mann (son of the veteran trade union leader Tom Mann), who had set up Kino (*kino* being the Russian word for cinema), a distribution and production company for left-wing films, 'in the backyard of an old garage in Bloomsbury', was ferrying reels of the one copy of *Battleship Potemkin* Kino owned between three crowded London halls in his old Morris two-seater, so that as one reel finished the next (it was hoped) arrived. Mann reckoned that by mid-February 1934 the LCC ban on screenings of *Potemkin* had been broken nearly twenty times in the London area.

The government reacted by announcing that the ban would be extended to non-flammable film. An outcry ensued, since schools and numerous political and religious organisations used such film stock too, for educational and instructive purposes. Following a failed prosecution after a showing of *Potemkin* to an audience of four hundred at a miners' hall at a Durham colliery in October 1934, and pressure from the NCCL and the *Manchester Guardian*, the idea was dropped, though the ban on *Potemkin* was not lifted until 1954.

Educating the people was not just about showing them the Soviet model. The Socialist League had come together as a ginger group in the dreary days of the Labour Party travails of 1931, uniting ex-members of the ILP with other socialists including Stafford Cripps and Harold Laski. Another member was Raymond Postgate, an expert on trade unions, later better known as the founder of the *Good Food Guide*, who criticised the BBC in a splenetic broadcast from Moscow, where, with the 'help of Hugo's paperback grammar for tourists' he was on a fact-finding trip, in the summer of 1932: 'You are expected to assume that the whole of your audience consists of backward clergymen and prudish old ladies. Don't mention wine! Don't mention sex! Don't mention Marxism! Don't mention the world revolution! . . . Never wear a smoking jacket when you ought to have tails and a boiled shirt. Never say anything new or unexpected. Let your mind be as narrow as [BBC Director General] Sir John Reith's . . .'

Postgate may have been unable to influence one medium, but there were others. Rudolph Messel, the young film critic of the *New Clarion*, had also been on the USSR trip, and with Postgate and his wife Daisy, and with the sponsorship of the Socialist League, the Socialist League Film Committee (soon renamed the Socialist Film Council) was formed 'to make propaganda films which would be shown at meetings of the Labour Party, Co-operatives, Trade Unions and so on'. Stafford Cripps lent ('permanently it transpired') a 16mm ciné-camera, and the collective made their first film, *What the Newsreel*

Doesn't Show, in 1933. Essentially it was a collection of stills juxtaposing construction work in the Soviet Union with slums in London and Glasgow, and May Day celebrations in London showing the Labour leader George Lansbury (Mrs Postgate's father) addressing crowds in Hyde Park.

Their second venture was more ambitions. Written by Messel and starring the polytalented Naomi Mitchison as a be-overalled 'Mrs Smith', *The Road to Hell* (which only cost £66 to make, so presumably the performers gave their time for the cause) told the story of a drunken playboy (played by Messel) who runs over a working-class father without even noticing. The injured man, Mr Smith (played by Postgate), is unable to work and loses his job, but is ineligible for benefit because his sons are working. When they too lose their jobs, one commits suicide; the other loses his girlfriend (Daisy Postgate took this part) because he has no money, takes up with a criminal gang, and after a smash-and-grab raid is apprehended in a citizen's arrest by the very man who injured his father and started the whole dreadful cycle. The film, which ends on a moment of uplift with a distraught Mrs Smith leading her family in a resolution to 'Unite and Fight the Means Test!', was shot largely in the kitchen and back yard of Lansbury's home, 39 Bow Road in London's East End. *The Road to Hell* was occasionally shown to Labour and Co-operative Movement members, who generally applauded, but it was not terribly well received by other film-makers, even left-wing ones. The documentary-maker John Grierson was disquieted by its sensational title, lack of professional polish and rather confusing political message: it seemed to suggest that if top-hatted capitalists driving cars could be got rid of, the problem of unemployment would be solved. Paul Rotha was so incensed that he criticised the patronising 'cultured accents' of the cast, which was a bit excessive, since *The Road to Hell* was in fact a silent film.

The SFC's next film, *Blow, Bugles, Blow*, released in 1936, did have a sound-track, though it consisted largely of music (including both the National Anthem and 'The Red Flag') and sound effects, with the dialogue conveyed in subtitles. Raymond Postgate wrote the screenplay and a had a bit part as a 'bloated Tory' in a story about how workers could avert war by calling simultaneous general strikes in their own countries (Britain and France in this case) and persuading soldiers to give up their arms. Unfortunately, this was even less well received than *The Road to Hell* had been: Messel lost the £1,500-odd he had invested in the film, and that was the end of the SFC.

Kino made films as well as distributing them. There was a strong feeling on the left that the two main newsreel companies, British Movietone and Gaumont, were unduly sympathetic to Conservative aims – showing hunger marchers as unruly and the police as provoked, for example. The first

Workers' Newsreel was released in August 1934: it opened with the explicit statement that 'This is an attempt to present NEWS from the working-class point of view,' and the subjects covered included the *Daily Worker* Gala at Plumstead, the opening of a new Co-op, the Hendon Air Display, the Youth Anti-War demonstration in Sheffield, an anti-war demonstration in Hyde Park, and demonstrators against Mosley's Blackshirts at Olympia, all accompanied by a pungent commentary and filmic juxtapositions that made political points. The Gresford colliery disaster was covered in a subsequent newsreel, with footage of grieving wives and children. Kino also made feature films. *Hunger March* portrayed the 1930 march – and gained certain currency since the Metropolitan Police had 'requested' the newsreel companies not to film it or the 1932 or 1934 marches; all but Paramount complied. *March Against Starvation* was a more ambitious film about the 1936 'National Protest' that included information in graphic form about how much food the dole would buy, and had a cliffhanging narrative thread: would Baldwin agree to meet the marchers?

The Workers' Film and Photo League (WFPL) was set up in November 1934 to 'coordinate the activities of . . . all those who appreciate the possibilities of the camera as a weapon in the class struggle'. Its secretary, 'Peter Porcupine' (aka Jean Ross, the *Daily Worker*'s film critic), encouraged readers to film 'their local demo' against the introduction of new scales of unemployment benefit on 24 February 1935; a prize of 'a copy of Marx-Engels-Leninism' would be awarded to the person who came up with a title for the resulting film. Another WFPL film, *Jubilee*, was an against-the-grain polemic that suggested that the Silver Jubilee of George V on 6 May 1935 was merely 'a publicity stunt [by the National Government] masking sinister preparations for war'.

The WFPL encouraged workers (at least, those workers who owned a camera or a ciné-camera) that 'The time has come to produce films and photos . . . showing their own lives, their own problems, their own solutions to solve these problems.' One result was *Construction*, filmed by building workers on a site in Putney where there had been a nine-day strike in October 1934 over the sacking of a shop steward. It had to be an undercover job, so a carpenter and amateur film-maker employed on the site concealed a camera beneath a sacking apron. Unfortunately this resulted in a large number of shots of nothing but strands of hessian, but the workers re-enacted the strike, and a watchable film was assembled which, it was hoped, would encourage other trade unions. *Defence of Madrid*, made by the Progressive Film Institute and distributed by Kino, proved to be the greatest success: shot in Spain on 16mm film, it raised an estimated

£6,000 for the Republican cause, much of it in small donations from areas of high unemployment, and played to a much wider audience than most other socialist film-makers' efforts.

John Grierson, who had regarded the efforts of the Socialist Film Council as misguided and amateurish, can be considered the architect of a documentary film-making movement that remains perhaps the most resonant legacy of the 1930s' visual production. A Scot who had become committed to the idea that for democracy to function properly people needed to be educated, and that the best way of doing that was through film, Grierson had gone to work for the government Empire Marketing Board (EMB), which had been founded to promote trade within the Empire as a riposte to calls for protectionism. Grierson's first project for the EMB was possibly his greatest film. *Drifters* (1929) is a lyrical, detailed documentary about the North Sea herring fleet which was heavily influenced by Soviet cinema, its stunningly beautiful silent images of the sea and the work of the people who harvest it montaged in such a way that the message is clear: there is a high price paid by fishermen to bring food to the nation's table. Other films made by the EMB included Basil Wright's *Song of Ceylon*, originally intended as four short films on the tea industry, but which grew into a celebration of the communal life of traditional labour in contrast to the commodification of the market; and John Grierson's *Industrial Britain* (1933), which lingered longer on craft skills, such as glass-blowing and pottery-throwing, than industrial processes.

When the EMB became redundant with the introduction of tariff reform legislation in 1933, Grierson moved to the GPO Film Unit, taking the talented film-makers he had assembled with him. Soon Basil Wright, Arthur Elton, Harry Watt, Edgar Anstey, Paul Rotha, Marion Grierson (John's younger sister) and Stuart Legg were joined by others including Alberto Cavalcanti, a Brazilian *avant garde* film-maker who had worked in France with Jean Renoir, René Clair and Jean Vigo.

At the GPO Unit, the team continued to make documentaries celebrating workers' skills. These 'creative treatments of actuality', detailed expositions of working lives, included a number of films about the various forms of communication the GPO was involved in, the most famous of which was Harry Watt's *Night Mail*. Made in 1936, it shows the progress of a letter posted in London to its arrival in Glasgow the next day. The twenty-three-year-old Benjamin Britten wrote the score, and onomatopoeic verses by W.H. Auden were read over images of the steam-driven Night Mail speeding north ('This is the Night Mail crossing the border/Bringing the cheque and the postal order/Letters for the rich, letters for the poor/The shop at the corner and the girl next door'). *Coal Face*, made by Cavalcanti and others in 1935, showing how coal was mined, but also how miners and their families lived, while Humphrey Jennings' *Spare Time*, with a commentary by the poet Laurie Lee, showed the ways that industrial workers spent their leisure time. As far as Grierson was concerned, such documentaries (he was the first person to apply the word 'documentary' to film – he thought the word clumsy, but could never think of a better one) were not 'this or that type of film, but simply *a method of approach to public information*', though some clearly had higher aesthetic and political agendas than that.

From 1935 on a number of independent film companies started to make documentaries for various sponsors. Shell had such a unit, and there was also the Strand Film Unit, but the most significant was Realist Films, which made films about such subjects as schooling, pollution, unemployment and housing, the best-known of which was probably Arthur Elton and Edgar Anstey's *Housing Problems* (1935), sponsored by the gas companies and the LCC, which brought to the screen the problems of slum housing through the testimony of those who were forced to live in it – although, given who the sponsors were, the film insisted that this was a problem that was being solved.

What the documentary film-makers did so effectively was to represent working-class experience, and validate it, in itself a revolutionary act and part of a progressive agenda, their fans claimed. Such 1930s documentaries undoubtedly influenced future film-makers, and they remain a compelling source for historians. And possibly since, as Basil Wright said, 'It is the task of the documentary worker to be in the forefront of policy,' they awakened some understanding and compulsion to action among those who were in a position to take it. But until the Second World War, when documentaries made under the auspices of the Ministry of Information were shown as part of feature-film programmes in commercial cinemas, the output of the various documentary-making outfits was mainly distributed on an educational circuit of schools, libraries, film societies or WEA classes, and few documentary-makers – Cavalcanti was one of the exceptions – would find success in the commercial film world.

Many Left Book Club members felt that simply buying a book a month did not exhaust their political and social energies, and wanted to exchange and promote ideas by grafting discussion groups and other activities onto their subscription. This made them natural partners for left-wing film-makers. The first meeting of the LBC Film Group was held in London on 15 December 1938, with J.B.S. Haldane speaking on how film studios should deal with

ARP (Air Raid Precautions) regulations if war came. The WFPL and the LBC co-operated in making a film, *Red Right and Blue*, which showed Victor Gollancz and John Strachey speaking at the LBC's conference. Although Frank Forster found that the group in Chester was a bit of a wash-out – on 4 March 1938 'the chap with the film didn't turn up', and the next evening 'attendance was not very great. Say perhaps 40–50 people which goes to point to the LBC films not being too great a draw, though those there were decidedly interested.' Nevertheless, LBC Film Groups were established throughout the country, showing films distributed by Kino. An LBC Theatre Guild was also spawned, organised from the Unity Theatre in London, to which groups could affiliate for 2s.6d year, which entitled them to advice on plays suitable for performance in small halls requiring little or no scenery and few costumes, but which nevertheless dealt with pressing political and moral problems. By 1938 there were some 250 such groups.

The Workers' Theatre Movement (WTM), which came to fruition at the time of the General Strike in 1926 and withered nine years later with the coming of a 'Popular Front' movement and the abandonment of the 'class against class' Party line, marking the end of the 'revolutionary epoch', presented 'agitprop' theatre. It was a child of the Communist left, involved (as was the CPGB at the time) in a war of class against class. Its task was not a reformist one, its intention neither to represent the working classes as the documentary film-makers did, nor to bring workers into contact with 'great dramatic art', but rather to convey a political message, to 'edit present-class-struggling experiences . . . the form should be episodic, not epic; short stories with punch, rapid and exciting actions, satirical revues; not big canvases'. The WTM was made up of a number of local initiatives – Bowhill in Fife presented dramas of working life in the coalfields; there was a workers' theatre at Plumstead Radical Club in South London; at the Memorial Hall, Farringdon Road, Upton Sinclair's *Singing Jailbirds*, about the US 'Wobblies" (IWW – Industrial Workers of the World) strike was a great success and toured the country. Charlie Mann (later of Kino) convened the Lewisham Red Players, while Ewan MacColl, later a renowned folk singer and author of 'Dirty Old Town' ('I met my girl by the gasworks wall/Dreamed a dream by the old canal') and 'The Manchester Rambler', commemorating the Kinder Scout trespass ('I may be a wage slave on Monday/But I'm a free man on Sunday') helped set up the Salford 'Red Megaphones': 'I knew bugger-all about theatre. But I knew a great deal, or rather I thought I knew a great deal, about politics . . . I wasn't impressed with the theatre I'd seen. I thought there must be something better, and I thought that the theatre should become a weapon, it should be something that spoke for all the people like me, the people who'd gone through their childhood with a red haze in front of their eyes: the people who wanted to tear it all down, and make something better.'

The WTM saw the street as its stage, performing in parks, on street corners, outside factory gates, from the backs of lorries, entertaining the hunger marchers. Performances were linked wherever possible to political events – the 'Becontree Reds' for example wrote and performed a sketch about eviction, and performed it outside a house on the Dagenham estate where an eviction was taking place. *Murder in the Coalfields* was performed in the Rhondda, and WTM members raised money for the families of miners killed in a pit accident during the run of the play, and for strikers seeking union recognition at Rego's tailoring factory in North London. During the 'more looms' agitation in Lancashire in 1931–32, when workers were reqired to operate twelve rather than the usual eight looms, thus increasing productivity and profit but at the cost of lost jobs among their fellow weavers – particularly women – the 'Red Megaphones' (most of whom were unemployed themselves), coached by the millworkers on the intricacies of the industry, wrote sketches about the threat which, the weavers argued, would cut 50 per cent of jobs, putting on as many as twelve performances a day in mill towns all over Lancashire and Yorkshire, performing as the workers came off a shift, urging them to take action and raising funds for those out of work or on strike.

WTM troupes were used as warm-up acts at Communist street meetings before the speaker arrived, or made a stage out of a couple of trestles and a plank before they were moved on by the police. Their simple imagery – bosses always wore a top hat, workers a cloth cap – and their 'magazine' repertoire of sketches, mimes and songs, made the snatched performances ideal for the crowds that gathered. The audiences tended to be working-class, and while many of the players were of working- or lower-middle-class origin, others were 'bohemian rebels', unemployed most likely, but not the manual labourers, miners and factory hands they sang about.

The Hackney People's Players, which had started with the modest aim of livening up Labour Party branch meetings, became a branch of the WTM in 1928. Finding few plays that contained the message they wanted, one of their members, Tom Thomas, started to write his own plays for a 'propertyless theatre for the propertyless class – no costumes, no props, no special stage'. He adapted Robert Tressell's novel *The Ragged Trousered Philanthropists* – omitting the final scene in which the central character, Frank Owen, coughs up blood from his tubercular lungs as he resolves to kill his wife and child to save them from destitution and starvation after his death, so the play can end on the uplifting note that 'socialism is the only remedy for poverty and unemployment'. 'Aye!'

roared the audience night after night as it played in halls and working men's clubs round London. Thomas's plays were 'flexible': if someone in the audience interrupted, the cast would 'argue it out with them then and there . . . it didn't matter. It added to the theatre.'

By 1931 the Hackney WTM – now calling themselves the 'Red Radio' – had taken over existing groups all over the country, their names proclaiming their political allegiance: 'Dundee Red Front Troupe', 'Sunderland Red Magnets' (the Woolwich group took the name 'Red Magnets' too), 'Greenwich Red Blouses', 'Southampton Red Dawn'. It put on a monthly all-London show, brought out a paper, *Red Stage* (produced by the indefatigable Charlie Mann), toured Scotland, holding a 'monster rally' on the Mound attended by more than 25,000 people, and sent a number of groups to Moscow in 1933 to take part in the International Workers' Theatre Olympiad. Then the line changed. A 'theatre of attack' whose targets were as likely to be Ramsay MacDonald and James Maxton as Stanley Baldwin was no longer what was needed. 'Class against class' conflict was dead; what had to replace it was 'an alliance of everybody threatened by fascism'. By 1937 the WTM had 'come inside' to curtains and proscenium arches, proper seats and technical equipment.

In that year the Unity Theatre, which grew out of the Rebel Players and had been performing in a church hall, acquired new premises, a former Presbyterian chapel being used as a mission to the unemployed and down-and-outs run by an ex-naval officer at 1 Goldrington Street, Somers Town, in the railway triangle between Euston, St Pancras and King's Cross stations – the area that figures so vividly in Patrick Hamilton's novel about pub life in the 1930s, *Twenty Thousand Streets Under the Sky*. Advertisements appeared in the left-wing press offering free beer and sandwiches to 'anyone willing to help build THE WORKERS' THEATRE'. Four hundred people came forward, including five architects, 115 carpenters, thirty-four artists and signwriters, seven dress designers and nine plumbers, while 'a bevy of helpers (women)' provided refreshments. A socialist (but clearly not a feminist) theatre was completed in two months at cost of around £800. With seating for more than 320 people, it had a large, well-equipped stage, rehearsal, dressing and club rooms, a bar and storage space. On the opening night, 25 November, the London Labour Choral Union sang, the Workers' Propaganda Dance group performed an anti-fascist ballet, *A Comrade has Died*, Paul Robeson sang ('like he's got a whole orchestra in his throat'), and there was a performance of *Waiting for Lefty* by the American dramatist Clifford Odets, a play about a New York taxi-drivers' strike which had been performed many times by left-wing British theatres. It gained a new currency with the busmen's strike at the time of the coronation in 1937, with performances held in some sixteen bus garages raising money for the strikers and attracting a new audience for the theatre.

Alfie Bass started his acting career at the Unity, as did John Slater, and in 1938 Paul Robeson, who had begun to feel that he was 'drying up . . . acting in plays that cut against the very people and ideas that I wanted to help', turned down several offers to appear in the West End and films to act, unpaid, with a cast of amateurs at the Unity Theatre. The play, *Plant in the Sun*, by a young American, Ben Bengal, was about black and white trade unionists uniting in a sit-down strike at a chocolate factory. Robeson played a part originally written for an Irishman alongside a cast that included real-life carpenters and clerks. The play won an award in the annual national amateur drama competition in 1939.

The Unity was the first theatre in Britain to stage a full-length play by Bertolt Brecht (*Señor Carrar's Rifles*, in 1938), Sybil Thorndike pronounced it 'the most exciting movement in the theatre of our day', and Elizabeth Bowen, writing as drama critic for *Night and Day*, felt that it had a 'real purpose, so a real energy', and urged those who disapproved of 'propagandist art' to 'visit the Unity to see whether Art suffers'. By September 1938 the Unity Theatre had more than 7,000 individual members and over 250,000 affiliate members belonging to various labour movement organisations. There were a number of Unity Theatres on a smaller scale in other cities. Predictably, Frank Forster was an enthusiastic member of the Chester branch, which met in the Nag's Head Tea Rooms. He recorded one meeting 'with 18 people present, a good proportion of them women. The main business of the evening was the casting of two short plays which we intend to give at a Left Book Club dinner . . . I made a date with a chap called Harrap . . . we intend to get some facts together for the writing of a play about the Gresford colliery disaster. Harrap seems very keen on the idea. I am to meet him at 2.0 on Friday at the YMCA.'

While in Manchester Ewan MacColl had transformed the Red Megaphones into the Theatre of Action, and though he was accused of wanting to 'dance our way through the revolution', the enterprise was transformed by the arrival of a young RADA-trained actress from London, Joan Littlewood, who became MacColl's co-producer and then (for a time) his wife. The Theatre of Action had no permanent home, but performed wherever a space could be found, the crew lugging around essential props and lights made from biscuit tins – on one occasion looping the wires out of a window and connecting them to the cable of a tram car when there was no other source of power. The venture lasted little more than a year, torn apart by vicious Communist Party infighting, but its short florescence had more than equalled the reach and scope of the London Unity.

Many of the Unity Theatre performances were 'didactic, fashioned too obviously for propaganda purposes, but they never pretended to be anything else', thought Ted Willis. And 'They had a verve and a feeling of excitement . . . and the producers were not afraid to experiment boldly . . . It ignited a fuse.' *Babes in the Wood*, 'a pantomime with a political point' performed in the aftermath of the Munich crisis in September 1938, by which time the Unity was deeply in debt, deliberately employed the 'rapier of wit' rather than the 'battle axe of realistic drama'. The 'babes' were Austria and Czechoslovakia, Hitler and Mussolini were the 'robbers', accomplices of the 'wicked uncle', who resembled Neville Chamberlain. Robin Hood saved the babes to the melody of 'Affiliate with Me'. The Cliveden Set* were portrayed as 'four motionless and *soignée* aristocrats with metallically indifferent expression and an enervated assurance of voice' singing a parody of the hymn 'We Plough the Fields and Scatter': 'We own the press and scatter/Confusion in the land./Reaction's fed and watered/By our exclusive band,' and expressing their support for appeasement to the tune of 'Land of Hope and Glory' 'with an assurance that is merciless and magnificent' while the Fairy Wishfulfilment waved her tinsel wand, 'hoping with the sob sisters of the press that all might yet turn out for the best'. Sometimes the satire was pretty limp, but it was good knockabout stuff, sentimental and funny. Lawrence Gowing painted most of the scenery, and the music was 'unashamedly derivative of Cole Porter and the big dance bands'. 'It slides from broad farce to pathos without slipping up anywhere, and it doesn't lose its punch anywhere either through being so funny,' thought the artist William Townsend. 'I had no idea such a stage had been reached in the development of theatrical propaganda – popular, truly dramatic, economical and inescapable. We enjoyed it with a tremendous sense of freedom and relief; something here that is alive, real and for us all.' The press was lukewarm, but audiences loved it. The six-month run attracted almost 48,000 people, and the haunting song 'Love on the Dole' was the hit of the show and remained popular for many months.

---

* A term coined by the left-wing journalist Claud Cockburn to describe the upper-class social circle that included Geoffrey Dawson, the editor of *The Times*, and Lord Lothian, centred around Cliveden in Buckinghamshire, the country house of the Conservative MP Nancy Astor and her husband Waldorf, and pilloried by Cockburn as pro-appeasement and pro-Nazi.

TWENTY-TWO

Dreamland

The cinema gives the poor their Jacob's ladder
For Cinderellas to climb.

Louis MacNeice, 'Autumn Journal' (1939)

The exploitation and individual destruction of the divine gift of the public
entertainer by prostituting it to the purposes of financial gain is one of the
worser crimes of present-day capitalism.

John Maynard Keynes, 'Art and the State', The Listener, 26 August 1936

My generation learned how to be human beings from films. You learned how
to smoke ... from films. You learned how to hold a cigarette ... in a sense
everything you learned about being a unit in modern society came from films.

Denis Norden, recalling his childhood visits to the Trocadero
at the Elephant and Castle in the 1930s

What was the 'capitalist dope', the narcotic for the masses, that left-wing
dramaturgs and film-makers were so anxious to wean audiences away from?
In the theatre it was likely to have been a 'well-made play' depicting upper-
middle-class sexual intrigue, often in a country house, its most notable
providers Noël Coward or Terence Rattigan, or a musical imported from
America.

Coward was already an established and very high-earning playwright in
both Britain and America with a string of light – and not so light – successes
to his credit: *The Vortex* (1923) dealt with drug abuse. *Private Lives* opened
at the Phoenix Theatre in 1930 after a provincial tour, starring Laurence
Olivier, Gertrude Lawrence and Coward himself. It was 'light and required
light handing ... Gertie was brilliant. .. the witty quick-silver delivery of
lines; the romantic quality, tender and alluring, the swift, brittle rages;
even the white Molyneux dress.' Though the critics were divided – one
comparing the slight play to a paper boat in a bathtub, liable to be

submerged at any moment – *Private Lives* provided a 'delicious frisson' for its middle-class audience, particularly in its sexual ambiguity, which could apply to Coward's own persona as much as to the adulterers on stage. 'I think very few people are completely normal really, deep down in their private lives,' says Gertrude Lawrence's character, Amanda. Like many of Coward's plays, *Private Lives* teetered perilously near to what was permissible on the public stage, and Coward was frequently at odds with the Lord Chamberlain.

Coward's next venture was entirely different. He had discussed with the theatrical impresario C.B. Cochran the idea of 'a big spectacular production at the Coliseum . . . Even the idea of Decline and Fall of the Roman Empire flirted with me for a bit.' After chancing on a bound collection of the *Illustrated London News* in a second-hand bookshop in the Charing Cross Road, he trimmed his ideas to a history of Britain since the Boer War.

Coward's extravaganza *Cavalcade* recounted the decades from New Year's Eve 1899 (the year of his own birth) to New Year's Eve 1929, the vapid and directionless eve of the thirties:

> In the strange illusion,
> Chaos and confusion,
> People seem to lose their way
> What is there to strive for,
> Love or keep alive for? . . .

sings nightclub performer Fanny in the opening scene.

Cavalcade opened at the Drury Lane Theatre on 13 October 1931. The story is told through the lives of an upper-class family, the Marryotts, and their servants, but stringing together popular songs of the decades – 'Goodbye, Dolly Gray', 'It's a Long Way to Tipperary' – its 'emotional basis . . . was undoubtedly music'. It had a huge cast, but once the stars – including the young John Mills – had been selected, Coward found the process of choosing the rest 'a depressing business. We needed about four hundred and over a thousand applied. Hour after hour we sat on stage at a long table set against the lowered safety-curtain whilst an endless stream of "out-of-works" passed by us – all of them professional actors or actresses, every one of them so in need of a job that the chance of being engaged as a super for thirty shillings a week was worth queuing up for . . . times were hard, almost too hard to be borne.' He was particularly riled when he found out that Cochran had employed 'three stage-struck society girls' who did not need a job for walk-on parts. The dispute was only resolved when 'Cockie' agreed to Coward's demand that he would take on an additional two unemployed actors for each society miss.

After the curtain fell on the opening night – 'the most agonising three hours [Coward] had ever spent', with it looking as if the complicated hydraulic machinery that raised the orchestra and lowered the stage as the vast pageant of British history unfolded was jammed – Coward walked onto the stage and 'managed to make a rather incoherent little speech which finished with the phrase: "I hope that this play has made you feel that, in spite of the troublesome times we are living it, it is still pretty exciting to be English."' This was received with 'a violent outburst of cheering, and the orchestra, frantic with indecision as to whether to play my waltz or "God Save the King", effected an unhappy compromise by playing them both at once. The curtain fell, missing my head by a fraction, and that was that.'

While *Cavalcade* delighted audiences, and stirred the more right-wing press and most of the critics, with its patriotic appeal, it appalled others. Sean O'Casey found it 'tawdry . . . Coward codology . . . the march past of the hinder parts of England, her backside draped in a Union Jack', while Beverley Nichols declared that it was 'the finest essay in betrayal since Judas Iscariot'. Reluctant to stay in England and 'cash in on my tin pot glory', Coward left for America in October 1931.

The theatre had entered the blood of Terence Rattigan, the son of a diplomat whose career came to a premature end when he made Princess Elizabeth of Romania pregnant, at prep school, and as a member of Oxford University Dramatic Society (OUDS) he had a one-line part in *Romeo and Juliet* with Peggy Ashcroft and John Gielgud. Rattigan and Gielgud collaborated on a never-produced stage version of Charles Dickens' *A Tale of Two Cities* in 1934, and Rattigan's play *French Without Tears* opened at the Criterion Theatre in November 1936, starring the youthful Trevor Howard and the not much older Rex Harrison. The critics were divided as to whether it was enviably witty or without plot or point. But again, the audiences were the arbiters, and the play ran for over a thousand performances, and continues to do the rounds in rep today.

Brilliant, entertaining and 'bittersweet' though Coward and Rattigan could be, their work was pretty solidly middle-class (and above) entertainment. Other forms of dramatic endeavour in the thirties straddled the divide between commercially successful light theatre and the resolutely heavily political, largely amateur, alternative. The Group Theatre was founded in 1932 by Rupert Doone, who had worked with Diaghilev, been a lover of Jean Cocteau and a schoolfriend of W.H. Auden. Others involved included Tyrone Guthrie, the ballerina Lydia Lopokova (who was married to John Maynard Keynes) Benjamin Britten (who composed music for several productions), John Piper (who designed sets) and Auden, who was a schoolteacher at the time. It was to be a permanent company, albeit without a permanent home, and aimed to rekindle what T.S. Eliot believed Elizabethan drama had achieved, 'aimed at a public which wanted *entertainment* of a crude sort, but would *stand* a good deal of poetry'.

Auden wrote three plays for the Group, all designed to 'sweep away the cobwebs that hung around English drama at the time' and declare the 'decline of a class' (the middle one). All – predictably – received mixed reviews. The first, *The Dance of Death*, first performed in February 1934, was a fusion of dance, mime and words spoken and sung – all the devices of 'low theatre' – combining 'German cabaret and English pantomime [and] Marxist analysis in rhymed verse and offering an active and decisive role to its audience'. It was very short, so it played in a double bill with Auden's adaptation of one of the Chester medieval mystery plays, and later with T.S. Eliot's macabre fragmentary melodrama *Sweeney Agonistes*: 'I knew a man once did a girl in/Any man might do a girl in/Any man has to, needs to, wants to/Once in a lifetime, do a girl in . . .' The *Times Literary Supplement* spoke of Auden 'desiring revolution . . . like a gamin jeering at the tumbril', while the *Spectator*'s critic complained that 'in place of acting the evening offers a great deal of acrobatic posturing, some peculiarly tedious dancing . . . and some Swedish drill', and saw the 'two charades' as another example of thirties intellectuals' 'flight from reason'. 'We should like less prancing and bad dancing . . . and more stiff thinking,' instructed the critic and poet Geoffrey Grigson, the combative editor of *New Verse*.

The next two plays Auden (or 'Uncle Wiz', as he was called by his colleagues) wrote for the Group Theatre were collaborative efforts with his great friend Christopher Isherwood. *The Dog Beneath the Skin* ('Dogskin', as the cast christened it) opened at the Westminster Theatre in January 1936, the Lord Chamberlain having insisted on some cuts, but not as many as he might had his pompous eminence understood cockney rhyming slang. Acclaim was muted when the play was published – 'a shoddy little affair', thought the *Spectator*'s drama critic, and F.R. Leavis considered that 'very little of the play stands up to cold perusal' – but it was better received in performance. Although Julian Symons compared it to 'the work of a church hall dramatic society', the *Daily Worker* thought it 'one of the best plays of the season', the *Observer* found it comparable to Noël Coward, and the *Sunday Times* predicted that it would run for five years, though it fact it ran for six weeks. In 1936 Auden again collaborated with Isherwood (Auden

writing the 'woozy bits' – the verse, Isherwood the 'straight bits' – the prose)
to produce *The Ascent of F6*, a play about mountaineering, salvation and
the deadly stranglehold of maternal love, dedicated to Auden's geologist
brother John, who had climbed the Himalayan mountain K2, and with
music by Britten. Like all the Group Theatre's plays this was produced in
a small theatre that was easily filled with an audience of the favourably
inclined, and though again critics had reservations, the play transferred to
the West End, and still has periodic outings at drama festivals.

Since 1880 the Victoria Theatre in Waterloo Road, Lambeth, known
affectionately as the 'Old Vic', had aimed to raise the cultural sights of the
working classes (and to keep them off the booze). It tended to patronise
its potential audiences with 'high class drama especially the plays of
Shakespeare' done on the cheap in a melodramatic Victorian style that irritated the young and kept them away in droves. After the First World War
the iron-willed Lilian Baylis (niece of Emma Cons, who had acquired the
Old Vic in 1880 and set it on its redemptive path) had introduced
Shakespeare in rep to meet 'the crying needs of working men and women
who want to see beyond the four walls of their offices, workshops and
homes into a world of awe and wonder', and by 1923 all thirty-seven
Shakespeare plays had been performed there. Though many of the performances were of the highest quality (John Gielgud, Edith Evans and Sybil
Thorndike all appeared at the Vic), money was always a problem – Gielgud
was offered £10 a week for starring roles and £5 for all others, and the
maximum total budget for a production was £20. Smart theatregoers were
not often prepared to trek south of the river, the working class ('our people',
Baylis called them) could never afford enough to make the theatre viable,
while teachers, who provided a regular audience, were less able to do so
after their pay was cut as a result of the 1931 financial crisis. Even so, in
1930 there were three versions of *Hamlet* running concurrently in London,
including one at the Old Vic with the twenty-six-year-old Gielgud in the
title role. The often fierce critic James Agate had 'no hesitation whatsoever
in saying that this is the high-water mark of English Shakespearean acting
in our time', and Sybil Thorndike thought it was 'the Hamlet of my dreams,
and I never hope to see it played better', while from the stalls Harold Nicolson
compared Gielgud to Sir Henry Irving. His reputation established, Gielgud
subsequently tackled Romeo, Richard II, Oberon, Hotspur, Prospero,
Macbeth, Antony and Lear (at age twenty-seven) at the Old Vic, all directed
by Harcourt Williams, who invited him to direct *The Merchant of Venice*
in 1932.

In 1934 Tyrone Guthrie, who had impressed Baylis with his direction of

Love's Labour's Lost the previous year, was invited by her to take over the direction of the Old Vic. Under his direction it flourished, and high-profile actors such as Laurence Olivier, Charles Laughton (the Pilgrim Trust agreed to subsidise any play in which Laughton appeared), Robert Donat, Emlyn Williams, Flora Robson and Elsa Lanchester, who could command five times as much money in the West End theatre and more from Hollywood, were prepared to slum it for the opportunity to work with Guthrie.

Shakespeare's plays could of course always be seen in his home town after the brutalist Memorial Theatre reopened in Stratford-upon-Avon on St George's Day 1932 (having been destroyed by fire in 1926). And in 1933 the 3,000-seat Regent's Park Open Air (i.e. summer-only) Theatre put on its first play, *Twelfth Night*, subsequently staging some of the less-often performed Shakespeare plays, as well as the perennial *Midsummer Night's Dream*, and Ben Jonson, Milton and Goethe on occasions too. Some critics were decidedly sniffy about 'lolling around in deckchairs' to watch a play, but most audiences enjoyed the 'back to nature' experience.

By 1938 Shakespeare had somewhat seized the hour: Tyrone Guthrie directed Alec Guinness in a modern-day *Hamlet*, *Troilus and Cressida* was performed as an anti-war play in modern dress (Dorothy L. Sayers hailed the production as 'restoring the emphasis to the places where Shakespeare put it'), and *Julius Caesar* was the first full-length Shakespearean play to be televised by the BBC.

As well as running the money-haemorrhaging Old Vic, Lilian Baylis, with the help of a committee that included Winston Churchill, Stanley Baldwin, Dame Ethel Smyth and Sir Thomas Beecham, had bought another theatre in a then poor part of London, Islington. Sadler's Wells had a long and distinguished history but had fallen into disrepair, being used as a roller-skating rink among other indignities. The new theatre reopened on 6 January 1931 with an appropriate production of *Twelfth Night* and a cast headed by John Gielgud as Malvolio and Ralph Richardson as Sir Toby Belch.

The idea had been that the Old Vic and Sadler's Wells should each offer alternating programmes of drama and opera, but it soon became clear that this was confusing for audiences and made dubious commercial sense, since drama flourished at the Old Vic but was never as popular at the Wells as opera and dance. In 1931 Baylis invited Ninette de Valois (an Anglo-Irish woman, born Edris Stannus), who had danced with Diaghilev's Ballets Russes and had her own ballet school, and whom Baylis had employed for £40 a season to teach her actors 'how to move', to form a ballet company at Sadler's Wells Theatre and move her school there too. The ballets were choreographed by de Valois, designed by such as John Piper and Oliver Messel – sometimes waiving their fees – and danced by Frederick Ashton, Anton Dolin, Alicia Markova, and even occasionally the rather ageing Lydia Lopokova (which meant that J.M. Keynes made generous personal contributions – he once booked seats for eight hundred economists in London for an international conference), and soon the young Robert Helpmann and Margot Fontes (later Fonteyn). All the dancers were paid a pittance, and often wore cast-off evening dresses or even peers' robes that Baylis had been given, with head-dresses made from 'a pennorth of pipe-cleaner and ping pong balls'. Nevertheless the performances proved such audience-pullers that Baylis gave up her confusing idea of running drama and ballet in repertory, and established drama at the Old Vic, and opera and ballet at Sadler's Wells. Starting with the 1935–36 season, the first truly British ballet company performed a mixture of classical ballet and contemporary work with music by Constant Lambert (who became the musical director), Vaughan Williams, Edward Elgar and Geoffrey Toye. The audience was part Bloomsbury of course, but also part locals who queued up for cheap seats, and threw pennies onto the stage to help costs if they enjoyed the performance. When Lilian Baylis died in November 1937 the Vic-Wells resident company consisted of twenty female and ten male dancers, two resident choreographers and a resident conductor, plus a ballet school (which would become the Royal Ballet School) with some forty students.

Music was heard in the West End too. Intimate revues showcasing stars such as Hermione Gingold, Hermione Baddeley (who in Gladys Langford's opinion 'seems to have assumed the mantle of Marie Lloyd') and Bea Lillie (supposedly 'the funniest woman in the world') were staged with knowing and sophisticated sketches and songs. The Palais de Luxe cinema, one of the earliest exhibitors of silent films, just off Shaftesbury Avenue, was bought in 1931 by Laura Henderson, who had it remodelled as a theatre, renamed it the Windmill, and hired Vivian van Damm to produce 'Revudeville', a non-stop programme of variety that ran from after lunch until 11 p.m. The first one opened on 3 February 1932, but lost money until van Damm, inspired by the Folies Bergères and the Moulin Rouge in Paris, added glamorous nude models to the song-and-dance routines. These would initially stand stock still on stage (binoculars were strictly forbidden), and could thus credibly be described as *tableaux vivants*, with themes such as Annie Oakley, Mermaids – even Britannia – so avoiding the Lord Chamberlain's censorship. They proved a great draw, particularly when fan dances were introduced, and several other West End venues introduced similar 'non-stop' drop-in entertainments.

The Broadway production of *Show Boat*, starring Paul Robeson with songs by Jerome Kern, had been a major success in London in 1928, and adaptations of German operettas – *White Horse Inn* and *Waltzes from Vienna* (both 1931) and *Casanova* (1932) – were followed by the lavish *Glamorous Night*, written specially for the huge but rarely filled Theatre Royal Drury Lane in 1935. It was to be one of Ivor Novello's earliest stage triumphs (he had written 'Keep the Home Fires Burning' during the First World War and had been a lizard-smooth matinee idol in silent films). Its appeal was its sheer spectacle, with a gypsy wedding, lines of royal guards and the simulated on-stage sinking of an ocean liner. The plot laced together an old-meets-new story of a Ruritanian princess and a television inventor with dollops of operetta, musical comedy and ballet. The romantic extravaganza established Novello's reputation for lavish sets, impossibly heady romance (with none of Coward's sophisticated angst), lush melodies. *Glamorous Night* was followed by *Careless Rapture* (1936), *Crest of the Wave* (1937) and *The Dancing Years* (1939), the story of a German-Jewish operetta composer (played by Novello – he invariably took the lead role in his productions) who is finally saved from a concentration camp, which ran until the Blitz started.

But the real musical success of the inter-war years was *Me and My Girl*, with music by Noel Gay and starring the comedian Lupino Lane as a working-class Cockney barrow-boy who inherits an earl's title and fortune – but nearly loses his girl. It opened at the Victoria Palace in 1937 and ran for 1,646 performances. One of its numbers, 'The Lambeth Walk', a knee-and-elbow-slapping cakewalk that ended with a cocked thumb and the cockney cry 'Oi!', became a hit song and a hugely popular dance: when George VI and Queen Elizabeth attended a performance, they gamely raised their thumbs and shouted 'Oi!' along with the rest of the audience.

Madge Martin, the wife of an Oxford vicar, was a reasonably cultured woman with a certain amount of time on her hands. At the end of 1936 she noted in her diary that she had read fifty-five books, and seen twenty-nine plays – one of them, 'the high brow play we saw at the Duchess in the afternoon of 17 [December], "Murder in the Cathedral" all about Thomas à Beckett was the most dreary thing in the world' – and sixty-six films (*Top Hat* starring Fred Astaire headed her 'super excellent' category, and she saw it four times). This was fewer than her usual annual total of cinema visits, but like almost everyone else in Britain, Mrs Martin was a regular cinema-goer. By the 1930s the cinema had taken over from the theatre and the music hall as the most popular form of entertainment for most people.

Nine hundred and three million cinema tickets were sold in 1934; by

1939 this had risen to 990 million, an average of nearly twenty million every week. The number of cinemas multiplied to cater for these ever-expanding audiences The first purpose-built cinema, as opposed to the 'penny gaffs' housed in converted shops, probably opened in Stourport in 1904, and by the First World War nearly every town had at least one 'picture palace' or 'fleapit'. The larger ones had many more: in 1939 Liverpool had ninety-six cinemas, Birmingham 110 and Leeds seventy. In 1926 there were around 3,000 cinemas; by 1938 there were 4,967. While many of these were large modern replacements for old cinemas, between 1932 and 1934 alone 302 new cinemas were built.

The term 'picture palace' was hardly hyperbole: cinemas were constructed as dream worlds, escapist fantasies, maharajahs' palaces or Italianate villas, Egyptian temples, *faux* Alhambras. Many of them were huge constructions, dwarfing the drab, mean streets of the poor working-class areas in which they were located. The Trocadero at the Elephant and Castle in South London, which opened in December 1930, was one such. Named after the fashionable Shaftesbury Avenue restaurant, yet set among a complex mesh of tram routes and busy roads, the Troc with its 'Renaissance' interior provided 'three hours of Piccadilly luxury and comfort for the price of a big sandwich'. 'It was a very poor area with all the tensions of an inner city – tremendous conflict with the police, no mercy shown on either side. When you came into the cinema you really were getting the only touch of luxury you could possibly acquire in those days,' remembers the comedy writer and television presenter Denis Norden, who as a child was a regular at the Troc in the thirties, and then got a job working at the cinema. 'The seats were more comfortable . . . than anything at home . . . People had the same seats every week and sometimes it would pass from father to son . . . You were expected to know them by name and greet them. A big thing in this kind of depressed area, to be greeted by your name, you were somebody – you might have a very menial job in a factory or something like that, but when you came into the cinema, it was "Hello Mr Brown, you'll enjoy it tonight."'

The Troxy on the Commercial Road in Stepney, East London (Troxy being an amalgam of Trocadero and the Roxy, New York), which opened in August 1933, was an equal fable in magnificence which presented a stark contrast to its surroundings, though in this case the interior was a stunning Art Deco design by the Troc's architect George Coles. The Astoria in Brixton was (and still is) a stage set, an indoor fantasy of trailing vines, 'antique' statuary and Lombardy poplars, with the ceiling changing like the sky, from dawn to dusk to starry night, 'And they used to put up on the screen "This cinema is perfumed with Yardley's Lavender". And you used to sniff – "Doesn't this smell lovely!'" recalls Vi Turner. The Finsbury Park Astoria was tricked out like a Moorish walled city, complete with fountains; the Palace, in Southall in West London, resembled a Chinese pagoda decorated with dragons with writhing tails; the New Victoria (opposite Victoria station) opened in 1930, the interior resembling what the architect Ernest Wamsley Lewis imagined a 'mermaid's palace' would look like, with a translucent underwater effect achieved with concealed lighting, glazed stalactites, glass fountains, the seats upholstered in deep blue-grey with a wave pattern.

The Pyramid in Sale (a Manchester suburb), which opened in 1933, had a double python façade, with bell-leaf capitals and Pharaohs' heads staring down at the audience from the organ housing. The Egyptian theme (much influenced by the excitement caused by the discovery of Tutankhamun's tomb by the Englishman Howard Carter in 1922) also featured at the equally appropriately named Luxor in Twickenham, an example of what John Betjeman called 'Egypto-Commercial-Renaissance-cum-Georgian' architecture (add other adjectives of choice). The Beaufort cinema in suburban Birmingham was an exercise in olde Tudor, with 'a riot of fake beams', panelling and armorial stained glass, a suitable setting for Alexander Korda's *The Private Life of Henry VIII* (1933), which could also have been said of the positively baronial Gaumont Palace in Salisbury, Wiltshire. Perhaps the most magnificent of all was the Granada at Tooting in South London. Completed in 1931, it was pure gothic extravaganza, Strawberry Hill in the foyer and a pastiche of Rheims Cathedral crossed with Notre Dame for the main auditorium, with wimpled maidens and troubadours painted along the balcony walls, and furniture that 'would not have disgraced Pugin' dotted around.

As far removed as it is possible to imagine from these baroque excesses was the 'Odeon style', the defining modernist symbol of the thirties, with its stark lines and sleek, minimalist exteriors, strongly influenced by German cinemas. Many took the same curved idiom as TB sanatoria, the De la Warr Pavilion, ocean liners and Charles Holden's London Underground stations, but often with tall flat towers and slab-end angular fins slicing through the faience, tile or brick exteriors, sometimes housing a staircase, but often merely to signal the presence of a cinema. The effect was starkly industrial, making the cinemas look like power houses. The Odeon chain was owned by Oscar Deutsch, the son of a Birmingham scrap-metal dealer, who had begun to indulge his schoolboy passion for film by acquiring cinemas in the West Midlands. (The chain's name derived from the Greek name for ancient amphitheatres, but also served to provide the slogan 'Oscar Deutsch Entertains Our Nation'.)

By 1933 Deutsch had acquired twenty-six cinemas and launched his Odeon circuit, no longer building mainly in working-class areas but targeting upmarket South Coast resorts and smart London suburbs, where he realised a vast new potential audience lay. By 1939 there were 142 Odeons, with as many as six new ones opening a month. Deutsch's architects took inspiration from Margate's 'Dreamland', a cinema built on the site of an amusement park that had been destroyed by fire in 1931. Designed by Julian Leathary and W.F. Granger, it opened in 1935 with a striking fin tower carrying its name. The Odeon Worthing, built in 1934, had a five-storey tower to draw holidaymakers' attention. The largest Odeon ever built, with seating for 3,000, was in Blackpool; the Odeon Muswell Hill, opened in 1936, was architecturally restrained on the outside since it was sited opposite a church, but inside it boasted a superb double-height auditorium. Bury St Edmunds, Bournemouth Kingstanding, Birmingham, Colwyn Bay in North Wales, Chingford in Essex, Well Hall, Eltham, Balham and Camberwell in South London, Acton in West London, Sutton Coldfield, all had magnificent Odeon cinemas. But the flagship was the Odeon Leicester Square, on the site of the demolished Alhambra Theatre, designed by a team of architects led by Harry Weedon, who had designed many other cinemas for Deutsch's chain (as had George Coles). Its huge black polished granite façade, outlined with neon lighting in tribute to the 'night architecture' so beloved in Berlin and other German cities, dominated the square, while the interior had elaborate cove lighting, a display of flying female figures and seats upholstered in imitation leopardskin.

Besides his prodigious construction programme, Deutsch also acquired some 150 cinemas from smaller circuits. But the Odeons were far outnumbered by the Gaumont British Picture Company, owned by a merchant banking family, the Ostrers, who with Isidore Ostrer at their head became effectively 'the first family of the British entertainment industry', owning cinemas, a newspaper (the *Sunday Referee*), Baird Television, Bush Radio and Radio Luxembourg. Gaumont merged production companies, distribution circuits and cinemas to show the films it made and distributed. By 1930 it controlled three hundred cinemas, and embarked on a building programme that constructed new ones all over Britain. Most were striking modernist buildings, the first of these being Wamsley Lewis's New Victoria. Though by the mid-thirties Gaumont was building cinemas with a seating capacity of around 1,500 in places with a largely middle-class catchment such as Stroud in Gloucestershire, Worcester, the Wirral, Chippenham and

Carshalton, its earlier projects had been mega-cinemas in more working-class areas. The Gaumont at Hammersmith could seat 3,560, while the largest cinema in England was the Gaumont State in Kilburn, North London, with seats for 4,004 and a tower that looked like a miniature version of the Empire State Building in New York, a striking contrast to the elaborate pillared interior, with a chandelier copied from one in Buckingham Palace. Green's vast Playhouses in Scotland, one in Dundee, the other in Glasgow with 'It's Good – It's Green's' woven into the carpet, were even larger, with seats for more than 4,300 in Glasgow, with a ballroom and a miniature golf course attached.

The third mighty cinema chain, Associated British Cinema (ABC), was built up by a Scottish solicitor, John Maxwell, who by 1937 owned 431 cinemas, having failed to take over Odeon, but acquiring a smaller chain, the Union, with 136 cinemas, to add to the eighty-odd he had had built, which included large cinemas in Brighton, Birmingham and Belfast, others scattered across North London and suburban Kent and Surrey, and the 1931 Liverpool Forum, with its interior modelled on the Chrysler Building in New York, itself only completed in May 1930.

Who went to these cinemas? Who lost themselves in the warm, comfortable interiors, the 'smoking permitted' plush seats? Who found the screen 'an oblong opening into the world of fantasy' and escapism? More of them were female than male, except in adolescence, when the genders were evenly balanced. A survey of the East End found in late 1936 that 'middle-aged and elderly men continue to find their main relaxation in pigeon clubs, in darts matches and championships, in their workingmen's clubs, their trade unions and political organizations and more recently in radio construction and listening. But women and young people depend nowadays almost entirely for their entertainment on the cinema.' Cinemas were a permissible public space for unaccompanied women, for whom going to the pub was frowned on, they were somewhere couples could go together, and they fitted in with women's lives – a mother could take in a matinee before the children came home from school, before she had to prepare the family meal. A middle-class woman like Madge Martin might do her shopping, change her library books, have a light lunch (maybe in the cinema café) and then see a film in the afternoon, with a friend or alone.

Younger woman, a survey of London noted, 'worship the various "Stars" ... and form clubs which take the name of their favourite star of the moment, such as the [Greta] Garbo club, or the [Rámon] Navarro club. Members of these clubs write to Hollywood or Elstree for signed photographs of their favourites.' Moreover, 'the influence of the films can be traced in the appearance of the women and the furnishings of their houses. Girls copy the fashions of their favourite film star. At the time of writing [1935], girls in all classes of society wear "Garbo" coats and wave their hair *à la* Norma Shearer or Lillian Harvey. It is impossible to measure the effects the films must have on the outlook and habits of people.'

Rose Mullett worked in the West End of London, and after work she would go to 'the cinemas where the "big" films were shown before reaching the suburbs. The Empire Leicester Square was *the* place to go for sheer luxury of seating and where glamorous film stars of the 1930s had their films shown.' Denis Norden recalled that at the Empire, 'Before they opened, the ushers used to line up in the foyer and smoke Havana cigars and puff out the smoke, so as to give you that smell which is what you pay for.'
Mullett remembers:

We queued outside the cinema for an hour or so ... no matter how cold the weather, or heavy the rain, we stood there patiently, just longing to be inside the cinema in the warmth and comfort, lost in the illusion of the film world ... the film programme consisted of a second feature film, usually very poorly acted and with a boring story, sometimes a crude thriller or a maudlin love story. Then there was a travelogue, a news film called Movietone News or Pathé Gazette, and of course the big film. The travelogues were very good as a rule ... they were educational and interesting. The news films, too, were eagerly watched ... At the big West End cinemas, and some of the suburban ones too, a highlight of the programme was an organ recital, probably about 10 minutes duration. I didn't care for this item myself but I believe most people really enjoyed it and it was certainly billed as an 'attraction'.

About half way through the programme of films, the curtains would come across the screen, and the organist seated at the instrument would rise up from the well of the cinema, on a sort of platform ... He usually gave us a medley of popular songs of the day but you could be sure that 'In a Monastery Garden' would be included, and also 'In a Persian Market'. The body of the instrument was made of a kind of transparent material with translucent panels [Denis Norden compared such organs to 'a big jelly mould that changed colours all the time'], and as the organist played, pastel coloured lights would gleam and flash from the panels ... the player wore a white suit and the whole effect was very theatrical. These organists were usually household names in their own right ...

One irritating habit the management of the cinema had was allowing the sale of ice-cream, chocolates, cigarettes etc. during the showing of films and this could be very distracting if you were seated at the end of a row.

The salesgirls would come up and down the aisles with their tray of things for sale and murmur, 'Chocolates, Cigarettes, Ices', at the same time flashing a torch to attract your attention. As these trays were also lit, you could miss whole minutes of the film, especially when, as often happened, people sitting several seats in would ask those at the end to buy something for them, and money etc. would be passed along . . . The 'big' film was usually very dramatic and moving, or it could be a great Hollywood musical (deafening if you were seated in the cheap front seats).

Not all cinema experiences were had in the new *luxe* chain cinemas, the Odeons, the Gaumonts, the ABC: more than two-thirds of cinemas in the 1930s were either individually owned or the property of a small local chain, and some of these could indeed be 'fleapits' or 'bug hutches', many converted from music halls, devoid of comfort or even cleanliness. The cinema, like almost every other thirties experience, was class-calibrated. In Greenwich E.Wight Bakke reported that 'One interesting feature of the cinema audience is its sense of class distinction.' Skilled workers spoke of two cinemas in the borough which were 'not attended by a very good class of people'. The patrons did not dress up but wore their working clothes, the men invariably leaving their caps on. 'We always go to the Prince of Wales where the class of people is better,' said an engineer. Leslie Halliwell, who grew up to be a great authority on film, recalled the smell of Bolton's fleapits as a potent mixture of 'sweat, oranges and cheap Devon Violet scent', while for others the abiding memory is of Jeyes Fluid. In his novel *A Frost on my Frolic* (1953), Gwyn Thomas claimed that the common name for such places in Wales in the 1930s was 'The Laugh and Scratch', or simply 'The Dog', because of 'the way people have of itching after a few minutes'.

Mass-Observation found that in Bolton, which was 'a mecca for the film fanatic', there were 'forty-seven cinemas of varying size, quality and character' in 1937. None was more than five miles from the town hall, and the average seat price was sixpence. The Bolton Odeon, an Art Deco showplace built on a slum site, with seats for 2,534, a car park and a balcony café, opened in 1937. The staff numbered forty and included projectionists and under projectionists, usherettes wearing natty pillbox hats ('There was no career path there,' noted Denis Norden. 'There wasn't ever a woman cinema manager'), pageboys, doormen and a 'chocolate girl' who paraded up and down the aisles with a tray. There was an organ with resident organist, and a café which unfortunately had the reputation of serving 'the toughest buttered crumpets for miles around'. The Crompton cinema, which opened the same year, was less grand: it only seated 1,200, had no café but had a change of programme midweek, daily matinees and a children's cinema club on a Saturday morning. Its seats were slightly cheaper than those at the Odeon, starting at threepence, with 1s.6d for the best seats in the house.

The Palladium, like the Crompton part of a small chain, was more of a fleapit: it had opened in 1919 and hadn't had a facelift since, so it was dingy, 'oddly dark and sinister'. Its audience was largely working-class, drawn from the surrounding area. It offered the same continuous programme, matinees and children's programmes as the more upmarket picture houses, and could seat around the same number as the Crompton, while entrance tickets ranged from fourpence to a shilling for the best seats.

What Boltonians liked to see was probably not very different from the rest of the country – Northerners went to the cinema on average more than twice as often as Southerners, though Londoners were an exception. The first choice of both sexes was musical romances, and the second was 'drama and tragedy'. Then women preferred 'history', whereas men opted for crime – particularly if they were Palladium habitués, for whom it topped the list. Cowboy films were also popular with the fleapits' male patrons, whereas no women seemed to like them, and only a few men who were quizzed at the Odeon. Neither sex seemed very keen on war films, while slapstick comedies and cartoons unsurprisingly appealed more to children and young people – 'More Popeyes, Mickey Mouse, Laurel and Hardy,' urged a fourteen-year-old who went to the cinema twice a week.

What is clear from this survey, as from most other reports, is that the films most people went to 'dream palaces' to see were not British. Gladys Langford said of Stanley Lupino's *Sleepless Nights* (1933): 'I never saw such piffle. No wonder no one wants English films.' Denis McDermott, a four-teen-year-old youth who went to the cinema in Bolton at least six times a month put it equally brutally. 'American films are . . . 100% better than British ones. Not a matter of money but of brains.' They were 'far superior to British on every point: action, direction, humour, yes, everything!' American films were considered slick, fast-paced, with plenty of action, whereas British films had 'no tension about them, no life, when anyone sees an English film, it's nearly always got a mist in it same as a foggy day. Why don't they spend a bit of money and get some proper scenery?'

Part of the reason was the 1927 Cinematograph Films Act, which was misguidedly introduced to protect the British cinema industry, which had been all but destroyed during the First World War, from being swamped by Hollywood films – by 1925 only 5 per cent of films shown were British. The Act had been introduced partly because the film industry was potentially lucrative (though the maverick MP Josiah Wedgwood, who opposed the Bill, thought that Britain had no more need of a film industry than it did of a banana industry), and partly because 'It is not only that films are a medium of entertainment . . . but are also a powerful medium for propaganda,' and the President of the Board of Trade, Sir Oliver Stanley, wanted to see 'British films true to British life, accepting British standards and spreading British ideals'. During the 1920s Hollywood studios had insisted on a system by which cinema owners who wanted to book a particular film had to book a block of other films unseen, and in some cases even unmade. In an effort to create a more level playing field for British films, the Act obliged renters to offer, and exhibitors to show, a proportion of British footage (films made anywhere in the Empire were eligible) which rose by annual steps to 20 per cent in 1938. The result was that distributors who wanted to screen foreign films – of which American films were by far the greatest number – needed a large number of British films to balance those imports. Hence 'quota quickies', made as cheaply and as quickly as possible, with scant regard for quality, either by companies set up solely to do this, or by American companies such as MGM, Paramount or Warner Brothers in British studios. This had a disastrous effect on the British film industry, with cinema owners complaining that they were being forced to rent films which they would never be able to show (a number of interminably long Indian films fell into this category), while there were not enough good-quality British films being made to draw audiences that would make them financially viable.

The film that most 'Worktowners' picked out as their favourite in 1937 was *Mutiny on the Bounty* (1935), and it was highly popular in the East End of London too. Much of it filmed in Tahiti, it was the most expensive film MGM had made since *Ben Hur* in 1926, telling the true story (though with much licence) of the rebellion led by Fletcher Christian against Captain Bligh. It starred Charles Laughton and Clark Gable, with James Cagney and the young David Niven in bit parts. Other 1930s Hollywood blockbusters included *Mr Deeds Goes to Town* (1936), starring Gary Cooper as a tuba player tried for lunacy after deciding to give his $20 million fortune away to help dispossessed farmers in the Depression.

Portsmouth was a relatively poor town, but the cinema culture thrived there as it did in Bolton. In 1932 there were twenty-two cinemas for a population of roughly 250,000, and by 1939 another seven had opened. The Regent, the most luxurious of them, had been bought by the Gaumont chain in 1931. It had seats for 1,992, a tea room, an organ (the only cinema for miles around to have one) and in the early 1930s its own small orchestra, plus plush fittings and stars that twinkled in its blue ceiling as the lights went down. Its cheapest seats cost sixpence, the most expensive two shillings. It was an 'exclusive first run' cinema, showing major films before they had been seen elsewhere for a whole week, rather than changing the programme on a Wednesday as smaller cinemas did.

Just like the patrons of Bolton's cinemas, those of the Regent preferred American films to British. In the years between 1931 and 1939, 311 Hollywood films were shown there as first features, as compared to 142 British, and when it came to the supporting films (or B movies, as they came to be called) the US predominance was even more marked: 270 US films, forty-nine British. Only four British films drew audiences of over 25,000 to the Regent in the decade, while nine American films topped that number. The film version of Noël Coward's *Cavalcade*, which led the charts at the Regent in September 1933 and won an Academy Award for Best Picture, was in fact made by Fox studies in Hollywood, as were two other high-grossing films which were filmed in England but with Hollywood stars and a Hollywood budget. *A Yank at Oxford* (1938) was naturally filmed in Oxford, and introduced the unknown British actress Vivien Leigh (a year later she would become a major star as Scarlett O'Hara in *Gone With the Wind*), but was made by MGM. *The Lives of a Bengal Lancer* (1935), which starred Gary Cooper and mapped a fictional British triumph (and a lot of in-fighting too) during the supposedly glorious British Imperial adventure in India, was made by Paramount. It too was very popular: 'superbly acted, full of action, colour and drama', thought a twenty-year-old Bolton cinema regular, while Leslie Halliwell noted that 'The whole town turned out to see this oddly-titled Indian adventure.' The film was nominated for seven Academy Awards, and a phrase used by the villain, 'We have ways of making men talk,' has resonated in bad films down the decades.

'Talking pictures were in their infancy, and screen writers were hard to come by. The old-time writers employed to supply captions for silent films were rarely any good at dialogue. The way was wide open for a generation of young writers, with golden opportunities for those who could master the new technique for talking film,' recalled R.C. Sherriff, who was invited by James Whale, who had directed the 1930 film version of Sherriff's *Journey's End*, to go to Hollywood to script a film version of H.G. Wells's *The Invisible Man* for Universal Pictures in 1932. Despite the dire warnings of friends that it was 'the place where writers go to lose their souls', Sherriff remembered 'the magic lure of Hollywood, the memory of evenings when I used to pay 4*d* for a wooden seat in a local cinema', and accepted the offer. Sherriff's script was a success; *The Invisible Man*, which starred Claude

Rains (Boris Karloff had refused the role) was named by the *New York Times* as one of the best ten films of 1933, and Sherriff was offered more lucrative work by Universal, including an adaptation of A.E.W. Mason's novel *Four Feathers*, directed by Alexander Korda. In 1938 MGM studios asked him to write the screenplay for the adaptation of another novel by an Englishman, James Hilton's *Goodbye, Mr Chips*, a celebration of the traditions and values of an English public school, starring the British heart-throb Robert Donat, whose performance won an Oscar.

MGM made two extremely successful films based on novels by A.J. Cronin. *The Citadel*, published by Victor Gollancz's Left Book Club in 1937, had sold 40,083 copies in nine days – a bookselling record. Until his success as a novelist enable him to write full time, Cronin had been a doctor, and his novels are deeply autobiographical, drawing particularly on his experience as a medical inspector of mines. *The Citadel* tells the story of an idealistic young Scottish doctor who works in the South Wales mining valleys before coming to London, where he is saved from the temptations of a high-society practice by a good woman. A critique of poverty and private medicine ('There must be a better way'), though not yet an advocate of a National Health Service ('hopeless – bureaucracy chokes individual effort – it would suffocate me'), the film version, directed at Denham Studios by one of Hollywood's most powerful directors, King Vidor, and starring Rosalind Russell and Robert Donat, with Ralph Richardson and Rex Harrison, opened in 1938 to critical and popular acclaim – it was the top British box-office film that year, and received four Oscar nominations, including Best Picture. MGM were encouraged to film an earlier Cronin novel, *The Stars Look Down* (1935). The film, starring Michael Redgrave and Margaret Lockwood, and set in a fictional mining community, 'Sleescale', on the coast of Northumberland, and 'Tynecastle' (Newcastle upon Tyne), in effect lobbied for the nationalisation of the mines. It opened in 1939.

A number of British writers were lured to Hollywood in the 1930s. Anthony Powell stayed for a few months, but not finding a niche in the studio system, came home. P.G. Wodehouse, who quipped that it was 'an era when only a man of exceptional ability and determination could keep from getting signed up by a studio in some capacity or other', went early, since several of his novels had already been made into silent films when he arrived in 1930. He stayed a year, tried his hands at several scripts, none of which really worked, and his contract with MGM was not renewed, although he managed to mine his experience there for a number of short stories parodying the star system he had briefly become part of. J.B. Priestley went in 1935, driving from Arizona where he was staying with his family to pick up bits of freelance scriptwriting and editing, though his name never appeared in any credits, an omission for which he professed to be grateful. Aldous Huxley, believing that 'old Europe' was finished, took the long way: in 1937 he and his wife Maria bought a Ford in New York and with their son drove for weeks across America, stopping for some time to stay with Frieda, D.H. Lawrence's widow, on her hacienda in Taos, New Mexico, before hitting dreamland USA, where Huxley intended to write a book about 'remedying the wrong functioning of society'. He was not an instant success in Hollywood despite the reputation that had preceded him from his books *Crome Yellow* (1921), *Brave New World* (1932) – which was reportedly being used as a classroom text in one school in Michigan, to the alarm of the FBI – and *Eyeless in Gaza* (1936). He passed up the chance to turn John Galsworthy's *Forsyte Saga* into a film, a screenplay about Marie Curie was quietly shelved, and his contract with MGM was not renewed. But with the encouragement of Anita Loos, the author of *Gentlemen Prefer Blondes*, Huxley started to make it, crafting a script for *Pride and Prejudice* (known throughout the studio as 'Pee and Pee'), a task he did not find easy, as war broke out in Europe.

However, just about the most popular film of the decade in Britain was a distinctly Hollywood production. *Snow White and the Seven Dwarfs* (1938) was Walt Disney's first animated full-length film (the adventures of Mickey Mouse and his team, Minnie, Pluto and Goofy, were shorts). Despite Disney's wife having warned him that 'No one's ever gonna pay a dime to see a dwarf picture,' the Technicolor story of Bashful, Doc, Dopey, Grumpy, Happy, Sleepy and Sneezy – and Snow White – was a box-office hit on both sides of the Atlantic, drawing an audience of 35,671 in Portsmouth and more than twenty-eight million in Britain overall.

Feature films were not specially made for children until the 1940s. While Leslie Halliwell's mother had been taking him to the cinema regularly since he was four years old, even she drew the line at *Werewolf of London* (1935), an advertisement for which in the *Bolton Evening News* warned: 'THIS FILM HAS TERRIFYING SCENES AND PARENTS ARE ADVISED *NOT* TO BRING THEIR CHILDREN TO SEE IT.' At first the British Board of Censors had insisted on an 'A' certificate for *Snow White*, meaning that a child could only see it if accompanied by an adult (presumed to be a parent or guardian), which led to under-fourteens hanging around and pleading with cinema-goers, 'Take me in with you, Mister?' But most local watch committees were prepared to grant it a 'U' (Universal) certificate provided a mildly scary scene involving a witch and a skeleton was cut, so 'for the next month the entire town [of Bolton and no doubt many others] seemed to be singing "Whistle While You Work"'.

In 1932 the LCC surveyed 21,000 children from a sample of twenty-nine schools about their cinema-going habits. Nearly 40 per cent went to the cinema at least once a week, and a further 17 per cent went at least once a month, which meant that more than half London's schoolchildren were regular cinema-goers. Over half of all London children aged under five also went to the cinema, 30 per cent of them at least once a week. Other cities, including Edinburgh, Birmingham and Sheffield, conducted similar surveys, and came up with similar results: 'Seven children out of every ten go to the pictures at least once a week. Most children spend longer at the cinema than they do at school subjects.' Poorer children went to the cinema more often than those from better-off families, and in contrast to adolescents and adults, more boys went than girls. (Why? Preference? Or were girls expected to stay at home more to help around the house?) The younger the child, the more he or she was likely to enjoy cartoons most. Slightly older children of either sex liked cowboy films (though boys rather more than girls), but by eleven their tastes divided, with boys opting for war and adventure, while girls preferred the romances that boys found 'soppy'. An Edinburgh survey found a class difference: among working-class children, love stories were very popular, whereas girls from middle-class homes 'will have none of them'.

The same inconclusive debate that continues today about the effect of television on children resonated around the cinema in the 1930s. There were those who unequivocally blamed films for high rates of juvenile crime, certainly for the Americanisation of language – 'Yep', 'Nope', 'Sez you', 'OK chief' (in place of 'Yes, sir') and 'Attaboy' being particularly disliked. Educationalists tended to think cinemas were unhealthy places – they were airless, the screenings ended late so children were tired at school the next day, and tellingly children found lessons boring after the excitement of films. Naturally, cinema owners saw things differently. Sidney Bernstein, managing director of the Granada cinema chain, was understandably anxious to instil a cinema-going habit early, and pointed out that the cinema was often used as a way of disciplining a child: be a good boy or girl all week, and the reward would be a ticket for the Saturday matinee, or 'tuppenny rush'. Bernstein advocated such special performances, since adult movie-goers did not want to be disturbed by children: 'they fidget, they talk, they express their enthusiasm with a vehemence which is not soothing to an adult audience, and they are equally clamorous in displaying their boredom at what they do not understand, appreciate or approve. All this can be very trying and distracting to adults.'

Many cinemas did put on special shows for children, usually on a Saturday afternoon, but most were far from satisfactory. An observer at the Coliseum cinema in Spital Hill, Sheffield, on Saturday, 29 November 1930, estimated that there was a crowd of around three hundred children, ranging in age from three to fourteen, who had each paid a penny admission. The show started with 'lusty' community singing, music supplied by the organist, and a news short, mainly about football, which was 'applauded with enthusiasm' (other cinemas also included a cartoon – usually Mickey Mouse or one of his paler, poorer imitations, whose creators 'copied only the techniques but not the artistic taste of Disney'). The feature films that followed, however, seem deeply inappropriate. The first, *Love Comes Along*, starring Bebe Daniels, lasted an hour and a half, and while it probably did little harm as 'most of the film consisted of love scenes which passed over the children's heads'; the second, a twenty-minute comedy, was 'very unsuitable. A scene of two men drinking in a café with too much rough play and silly coarse talk. The children were very amused at the drinking and fighting parts.'

The observer concluded that though 'for thousands of Sheffield children these performances are the great event of the week . . . unfortunately the children's matinee is of very little concern for the average cinema proprietor. It occurs once a week; it yields very little in box office receipts . . . Some cinema proprietors have given up the Saturday matinee as an uneconomic proposition; many others would not be sorry to do so, but are held back by such considerations as the desirability of pleasing parents, who are their regular patrons and who wish to get their children out of the way on a Saturday afternoon, and the need to "educate" the next generation of cinema patrons . . . The easy thing to do, and from a purely business point of view, the only thing to do when booking films is to consider the standard evening audience and choose according to an estimate of its taste. The entertainment needs of a once-a-week audience of children can hardly enter into it. Thus it is that in most cinemas children's matinee performances are identical with the performances given in the evening to adult audiences.'

The result was that while the children were generally well-behaved, there was clearly boredom and restlessness during long, sentimental films with often incomprehensible dialogue, with catcalls and boos. One observer noticed games going on in the back row during the film, yet the Sheffield children came back Saturday after Saturday – some 10,000 each week. The explanation for this 'huge patronage', the report concluded, was 'overcrowded homes, drabness of life, lack of open spaces and playing fields, and the absence of healthy alternative forms of entertainment . . . With all its faults the cinema still provides a way of escape from dullness to glamour and excitement.'

Even so, it was felt that there must be a better way. In 1937 Oscar Deutsch commissioned Richard Ford of the Odeon chain's publicity department to look into the question of children's screenings. Ford decided that Saturday mornings were a better time than afternoons, since not only were cinemas not used at that time, but the children might still be in possession of their weekly pocket money. The shows must be cheap, and certainly not educational, for no child wanted an extension of school. 'What the school builds up during the week *may* be entirely nullified on Saturday morning,' mourned the sociologist J.P. Mayer. The Saturday cinema clubs had an important place in a child's life, with toffees to be eaten, peanuts shelled, comics swapped and general friendly rowdiness; above all they provided an effectively grown-up-free zone – most working-class parents (whose children constituted most of the clubs' membership) had no idea what their children were watching. While the Gaumont clubs refused entry to the under-sevens, Odeon admitted children almost regardless of age, and 'in the more proletarian areas, the elder children take their baby brothers and sisters with them which is certainly a great relief to their mothers'. Nevertheless, Ford envisaged the Odeon clubs as having a higher purpose than merely serving as nurseries with entertainment. There were to be badges, rules about being kind to animals and obeying your parents, and working to 'make the country a better place to live in', with slogans such as 'Odeon Billy wishes you not to push while you are waiting in queue'. There would be a children's committee to help choose the films and organise things like charity collections. The club had its own song ('To the Odeon we have come/Now we can have some fun'), and each Odeon Saturday morning ended with the children standing while the National Anthem was played. By 1939 Ford reckoned that there were seven hundred such cinema clubs – 160 of them were Odeon clubs, while the Granada circuit had Grenadier Clubs, the Union cinemas their Chums Club, and Gaumont could claim Shirley Temple, whose singing of 'On the Good Ship Lollipop' in *Bright Eyes* (1934) made the six-year-old a star, as president of their clubs.

Whatever Bolton audiences thought of most British films, there were some that won their unstinting praise: those starring Grace Fields, the 'Lancashire lass' from nearby Rochdale who starred in a number of gutsy Northern working-class films. Fields was 'sturdily built', not particularly young or beautiful when she hit the silver screen, and the roles she played called for sensible blouses and skirts, rather than vamp attire. It was not only her personality that 'bounced off the screen', or her powerful and adaptable singing voice, her vitality and sense of comic timing that made the music-hall performer a film star: it was her 'ordinariness', her 'naturalness', her 'one of us-ness' that made her so appealing. 'Listen to her for a quarter of an hour,' recommended the Yorkshire-born J.B. Priestley, 'and you will learn more about Lancashire women and Lancashire than you would from a dozen books on the subject.' Field's first two films, *Sally in Our Alley* (1931) and the more schmaltzy, showbiz *Looking on the Bright Side* (1932), were set in London East End tenements (recreated in the studio); both showed a working-class Northern lass confronting metropolitan snobbery and winning through. By 1934 'Our Gracie's' films had come to preach a more direct message of hope during the Depression.

Sing as We Go, scripted by J.B. Priestley ('the Gracie Fields of Literature'), was filmed in Bolton. When Greybeck Mill closes down, Fields vows, 'If we can't spin, we can sing,' gets on her bike and finds work in Blackpool, which gives plenty of opportunity for familiar seaside locations – the Tower ballroom, the Pleasure Beach – and for homely, humorous stereotypes, most notably the seaside landlady. She then saves the day – and the town – by getting a plutocrat to invest in t'mill, so that a Union Jack-carrying Gracie is able to lead the workers back to the looms to the accompaniment of a brass band. *Shipyard Sally* (1939) 'set the seal on Gracie as Britannia'. It is not rearmament that gets a Clydebank shipyard, closed during the Depression, reopened, but Gracie's warm-hearted faith that Britain will pay the debt it owes its workers, exemplified in her lusty rendition of 'Land of Hope and Glory' as the men gratefully stream back to work. Not everyone was uplifted by the film's simple, conservative message. C[aroline].A[lice]. Lejeune, film critic of the *Observer*, acidly pointed out that 'We have an industrial north that is bigger than Gracie Fields running round a Blackpool funfair.' Graham Greene, writing in the *Spectator*, mocked the fact that in Fields' films 'unemployment can always be wiped out by a sentimental song, industrial unrest is calmed by a Victorian ballad and dividends are made safe for democracy'. But in Bolton 'packed houses were the order of the day', as they were throughout the country, and Fields was an international star – one of Britain's very few.

Among British stars who, while not hitting the international circuit were nevertheless very popular domestically, was another Lancashire comedian, George Formby, an ex-jockey, the son of the 'Wigan Nightingale', the music-hall entertainer who invented Wigan Pier, to which George Orwell would take the road in his search for the depressed post-industrial North. Formby's cheeky, irrepressible 'little man' persona had something in common with Charlie Chaplin. But his humour was verbal (often accompanying himself on a ukulele), a winning mixture of innocence and smutty *double entendre* in songs like 'My Little Stick of Blackpool Rock' and 'When I'm Cleaning

Windows' (banned by the BBC). After two low-budget, made-above-a-garage films, Formby was signed up for Ealing Studios by Basil Dean, who recognised in him the same larger-than-life screen presence as Gracie Fields had, and the same potential for feisty working-class-hero-makes-good roles.

Walter Greenwood, author of the defining British novel of the Depression, *Love on the Dole* (1933), was commissioned to write the script for *No Limit* (1935), in which Formby plays a chimney sweep's assistant who dreams of becoming a TT motorbike-racing champion on the Isle of Man (the second most popular working-class holiday location after Blackpool) riding his home-made bike. It was an immediate and enduring success, as were subsequent films such as *Keep Your Seats Please* (1937), in which Alastair Sim played a crooked solicitor, *Feather Your Nest* (1937), in which the plot centres round the song Formby would make his signature, 'Leaning on a Lamppost', *Keep Fit* (1938), a send-up of the movement of the same name, and *It's in the Air* (1938), which presaged the war which had by then come to seem inevitable, with Formby initially rejected by both the RAF (since he can't tell his left from his right) and as an ARP warden. This film meant that Formby would exemplify the democratic, all-in-this-together spirit that was called upon when war did break out a year later. Gracie Fields played a similar role until, to considerable criticism, she temporarily left Britain for Canada in 1940 to avoid her husband, Monty Banks, an Italian who had directed some of her and Formby's films, being interned.

Binkie Stuart never caught on as Britain's answer to Shirley Temple, but the considerable charms of Jessie Matthews, the seventh of the sixteen children (only eleven survived) of a Soho market greengrocer, did cross the Atlantic – indeed, her films did rather better box-office in the US than in Britain, though among middle-class British audiences, for whom presumably her elocution-trained voice did not jar, she rated third, behind Gracie Fields and Cicely Courtneidge. The recipe that Matthews, a very pretty, talented dancer, actress and singer, offered for difficult times was less feisty achievement than glamorous and romantic escapism, a British version of the twirling, twinkling, spangled glitz of Fred Astaire and Ginger Rogers. One of C.B. Cochran's high-kicking 'young ladies' in the 1920s, Matthews starred in fourteen films during the 1930s, the second of which, *There Goes the Bride* (1933), was a spectacular success, as was her role opposite John Gielgud in a film musical version of J.B. Priestley's play *The Good Companions* in 1933, which was followed by a string of musicals, the most successful of which was *Evergreen* (1934).

But somehow Matthews never quite drew the masses that Gracie Fields did: she was never able to find her Fred Astaire, and she always seemed at one remove from her audiences, too hidebound perhaps by her acquired cut-glass accent and 'the *mores* of the county drawing room' that so bedevilled British film-making in the thirties. She was never quite able to achieve the effortlessly classless glamour of Hollywood, though her real-life rags-to-riches story might have been thought to make her a natural contender.

In 1924 the film producer Michael Balcon set up Gainsborough Pictures with the help of Maurice Ostrer of the Gaumont chain, who, very aware of the need to create stars – and if possible to stop them from decamping to Hollywood when they were successful – had spotted and nurtured Jessie Matthews's talents. Balcon also restarted the career of a talented British director, Alfred Hitchcock, who had been making films since the early 1920s and had a notable success with his first sound movie, *Blackmail* (1929), but had then had a string of flops until his adaptation of John Buchan's novel *The Thirty-Nine Steps* (1935), starring – again – Robert Donat. Perhaps his best-known early film, the comedy thriller *The Lady Vanishes* (1938), starring the upcoming stars Michael Redgrave and Margaret Lockwood, proved to be the most successful British film of the decade. But in 1937 the Essex-born Hitchcock, regarding his native land as irredeemably class-bound and priggish, left for Hollywood, where he would make more notable films with the producer David O. Selznick.

The film that had first revitalised the British film industry and cracked the Hollywood hegemony was neither a thriller nor a piece of musical uplift, but a historical extravaganza. *The Private Life of Henry VIII*, made in 1933, infuriated those who thought that what the British cinema needed was a realistic portrayal of everyday life that 'ordinary' people could relate to. It was made by a Hungarian director working in Britain, Alexander Korda, whose most successful picture to date had been a romp through ancient history, *The Private Life of Helen of Troy* (1927). Korda applied the same formula to the English monarch, played by Charles Laughton, with Korda's wife-to-be Merle Oberon as Anne Boleyn and Laughton's wife Elsa Lanchester memorable as Anne of Cleves. It was deeply dubious history, but a rollicking film, with 'Bluff King Hal' going in for a great deal of eating and drinking, belching and wenching, and was a smash hit in Britain and America, spawning imitations including *Nell Gwyn* (1934), a remake of a silent film that made a star of Anna Neagle, and Korda's much less successful follow-up, *The Rise of Catherine the Great* (1934), with Douglas Fairbanks Jr and Flora Robson.

In 1937, the year after the abdication of Edward VIII, an event that had shaken belief in the monarchy, came a steadying film about a British queen, *Victoria the Great*. Produced and directed by Herbert Wilcox, it starred his future wife, Anna Neagle, regal after her saucy diversion as Nell Gwyn, and Anton Walbrook as the indefatigably upright Albert. So delighted were British audiences with this reassuring history – though James Agate criticised Neagle's accent as 'overlaid by layer after layer of suburban refinement' – and it did well in America too, that Wilcox made a sequel, all in Technicolor, a 'vast canvas of Victoria's life' called *Sixty Glorious Years*, for which access to the royal palaces was granted (exterior shots only). Queen Mary attended the film's premiere on 14 October 1938, just two weeks after the nation had tried hard to believe the assertion of Prime Minister Neville Chamberlain that he had secured 'peace for our time' in his meeting with Hitler at Munich.

TWENTY-THREE

Not Cricket

Most of us would prefer to have inscribed on our tombstones 'He was a good sportsman' to anything else. A lad going up to university would rather have the prospect of a Blue than becoming a Cabinet Minister.

John Foster Fraser writing in the Sunday Graphic, 6 July 1933

No amount of legislation has ever yet been able to stop the growth of traffic . . . the phrases 'the increase of traffic' and 'the increase of travelling' have recurred all too often. People travel more now than they have ever travelled, and in the future they will travel still more. If they want more roads to travel by, you may be sure that they will get them, for in the last analysis nothing can stop the development of the road.

R.M.C. Anderson, The Roads of England (1932)

On 10 July 1934, the newly appointed Minister of Transport Leslie Hore-Belisha nearly became a traffic statistic while crossing Camden High Street in North London. 'You cannot say that I don't take risks,' he joked, to 'general laughter'. It is hard to see why there was even the hint of a titter. At the time Hore-Belisha was involved in a public-relations exercise to demonstrate the supposed efficacy of what were known as 'uncontrolled crossings', introduced as one way of trying to halt the slaughter of pedestrians on British roads, when a sports car shot along the street without stopping, and it was only by 'standing stock still' that the minister was saved from serious injury or worse.

By the 1930s the motor was king on Britain's roads. Horse-drawn vehicles had all but disappeared from urban streets: there were only 12,000 horse-drawn carriages licensed in 1937 (compared to 207,000 in 1923), and electric trams, once seen as the transport of the future, were in sharp decline, with a third of tracks abandoned by 1933 and tram operators investing in buses instead – particularly since trams were regarded as 'workman's transport', and thus resisted by those whose social mobility had brought them to the new suburbs. There were 2,405,392 motor vehicles on Britain's roads in 1934, and of that number just over half were private cars.

It was a hazardous situation. Motorists caused 80 per cent of all road accidents. In 1934 the highest ever number of road casualties was recorded. Half the deaths were of pedestrians, and of these three-quarters had occurred in built-up areas. Hore-Belisha spoke of 'mass murder'. As that year saw 7,343 deaths and 231,603 injuries, and the trend appeared to be rising inexorably, it would seem that the new Minister did not grossly mis-speak. In 1932 a correspondent to *The Listener* claimed to have worked out that more people had been killed on the roads in the previous three years than on any battlefield during the entire revolutionary and Napoleonic wars with France.

The 20 mph speed limit had been abolished (with the exception of a few notoriously dangerous stretches of road) by the 1930 Road Transport Act, steered through Parliament by Herbert Morrison, then Labour Minister of Transport. The limit had been almost universally flouted, leading to an unmanageable backlog of court cases, and it was hard to secure a conviction anyway, since primitive speed traps permitted endless claims and counter-claims, with both the motoring organisations, the Automobile Association (AA) and the Royal Automobile Club (RAC), bristling in defence of their members. In 1935 the AA (larger and more pugilistic than the RAC) claimed that half the cases brought by the police against motorists allegedly exceeding the speed limit were either dismissed or 'leniently dealt with', and the following year 7,400 speeding cases were dismissed.

The 1930 Act did however make some contribution to road safety by insisting that only one pillion passenger could be carried on a motorbike (and that person 'astride a proper seat securely fixed') and making third-party insurance for motorists compulsory. It limited the maximum number of hours that bus and lorry drivers could work, introduced the Highway Code, gave local authorities the power to regulate traffic by such devices as one-way streets, roundabouts, road signs and traffic lights, an American invention, originally known as 'traffic control robots'. The first in Britain had been erected as an experiment in Wolverhampton and Leeds in 1927, and proved so efficacious that they soon spread throughout the country, reaching London in 1931, where unfortunately lights controlling traffic from side streets were situated on the pavement and did not overhang the road, so a policeman had to be stationed by each set to convey its message to motorists.

These advances were somewhat negated by the continuing primacy given to the interests of the motorist over that of the pedestrian, who was being felled in increasing numbers by latterday Mr Toads on Britain's roads. Mr Toad had his defenders: Colonel Moore-Brabazon (later Baron Brabazon of Tara), a Conservative MP who had been Parliamentary Secretary to the Minister of Transport (and who would take charge of transport in Winston Churchill's wartime coalition), was a wealthy maverick with a pioneer's love of speed, a robust sense of humour (he once piloted an aircraft with a pig as his passenger) and a careless disregard for the lives of pedestrians. 'What is the point of such concern over 7,000 road deaths a year?' he demanded. 'Over 6,000 people commit suicide every year, and nobody makes a fuss about that.' The *Motor* was, unsurprisingly, on the side of the motorist, observing tartly, 'Nobody who drives a motor vehicle in the streets of London can fail to be astounded at the folly of which pedestrians are capable. Considering what traffic is today, the risks taken appal the man at the wheel of the motorcar who – it is no exaggeration to say – is constantly saving the life of walkers.'

By way of contradiction, A.P. Herbert, in 'Misleading Cases', a regular column he wrote for *Punch* on the Byzantine idiocies of the legal system, described the imaginary case of Mr Albert Haddock (the unfortunate victim of many accidents and miscarriages of justice in Herbert's articles) who, while crossing the road, had been knocked over by a car driven by a Mr Frank Thwale, against whom he had brought an action for damages. Rebutting the contention that he himself was to blame as a 'jay walker', Haddock contended that 'Mr Thwale's motor car should in law be regarded as a wild beast; and the boast of its makers that it contains the concentrated power of forty-five horses makes the comparison just. If a man were to bring upon the public street forty-five horses tethered together, and were to gallop them at their full speed past a frequented cross roads, no lack of agility, judgement or presence of mind in the pedestrian would be counted such negligence as to excuse his injury. And the fact that the forty-five horses of Mr Thwale are enclosed in a steel case and can approach without sound or warning, does not diminish, but augment, their power to do injury.' One of the appeal judges saw the principle as analogous to 'the movements of ships at sea . . . [where] it is the rule . . . that a steam vessel shall, at her peril, keep out of the way of weaker vessels . . . the greater the power, the greater the duty; not, as the respondent seems to say, the greater the power the greater the right . . . The sailing-vessel, like the walker, may be almost obsolete, but she retains her rights.' Haddock won his case.

The motor car remained the focus of a number of fascinating questions throughout the decade (and beyond) about rights and responsibilities, about power and money and class. The use of the phrase 'motor accident' – or even 'incident' – was one, suggesting an act of God or technology, rather than human agency or lack of care. The use of cars at elections was another. In 1930 a Bill introduced by a Liberal MP to ban the use of cars during election campaigns, since this could only be to the benefit of Conservatives, was defeated, but in 1938 another Liberal MP, Richard Acland, who claimed that during the 1935 election campaign he had had thirty-five cars at his disposal while his Tory opponent had had over two hundred, tried again. This Bill failed too.

Insurance was another issue ripe for ideological position-taking. How far was it the inalienable right of an Englishman to drive his car on the public highway regardless of the consequences? And if a motorist was obliged to have insurance cover, that would give insurance companies the right to withdraw that cover, and with it his rights on the highway. On the other hand, if a motorist drove without insurance and injured or killed someone, the victim would have no way of enforcing payment for medical treatment or compensation. The insurance companies declined to pronounce on the desirability of compulsory insurance, while hospitals, witnesses to the results of road accidents, urged that it was essential. The RAC considered it would be unfair to expect all motorists to take out insurance just because some might be unable to pay the costs of an acci-dent, and the Scottish Motor Club ridiculed the idea: no one had expected a butcher's boy in a horse-drawn van to be insured against injuring a road user, so why should a car driver?

However, the principle was admitted and enshrined in the terms of the 1930 Act, as was an obligation (as a result of a Lords' amendment) that insurance companies should be required to pay £25 to hospitals treating accident victims, to be reclaimed later from the driver's policy (though in practice this rarely worked). Herbert Morrison, the then Minister of Transport, muttered darkly that this wouldn't be necessary if all hospitals were a public service run by local authorities, but this was deemed an irrelevance.

Bicycles were still a relatively cheap form of transport – a new model Raleigh, for example, could be bought for £5.10s, or five shillings a week on 'deferred terms' – and there were more than ten million cyclists on Britain's roads in 1934, double the number there had been in 1929. Like the pedestrian, the vulnerable cyclist was frequently demonised as a major cause of accidents. But by the mid-1930s increasing numbers were becoming motorised. Car-ownership was no longer solely the preserve of the wealthy, since car prices had fallen dramatically, to less than half what they had cost in the 1920s, and they were cheaper to run too. An Austin 7 tourer (officially designated the 'Mighty Miniature', but more often referred to as a 'bath on wheels' or a 'bed-pan') cost £125, and a saloon (a 'tin gin palace') £135; a Morris Minor Tourer with triplex safety glass throughout and a chrome finish cost much the same; and the first £100 car, the Morris Minor SV, first rolled off the production line in 1931.

Even if there were few working-class motorists among the 350,000 people who by 1935 had purchased such vehicles, they might be able to scrape together sufficient funds, either individually or as part of a small syndicate of family, friends or workmates, to buy a second-hand model. Hire purchase was not an option for buying a car, since the 1938 Hire Purchase Bill (introduced by Ellen Wilkinson) set an upper limit of £50 on articles covered against unscrupulous repossession.

The statistics on the ownership of motorcycles, or motorcycles with a side carriage attached, which had been a very popular working-class form of transport in the 1920s, are open to interpretation. By the early 1930s sales were falling, but were they losing out to the small 10 hp cars which constituted 60 per cent of all cars on the road? Or to no private motorised transport at all, since their putative owners might be unemployed or on short time?

The fact that motoring was no longer the prerogative of the wealthy (though car-ownership prior to the Second World War was overwhelmingly middle-class) rather changed the terms of the debate. In 1934 the ever-escalating casualties, combined with a widening car-driving constituency, encouraged Oliver Stanley, the then Minister of Transport (the ninth since 1918, which hardly indicates a high regard for the brief), to introduce a further Road Traffic Bill in 1934. However, by the time it reached the Lords, Stanley had been promoted to Minister of Labour, and his place taken by the man with whose name the safety of the pedestrian is most associated, Leslie Hore-Belisha.

The 1934 Road Traffic Act reintroduced a speed limit, this time of 30 mph in built-up areas, gave local authorities the power to introduce pedestrian crossings for the first time, and required new drivers to take a test before they could obtain a licence, whereas previously anyone over seventeen could drive a car, whether they had ever sat behind a steering wheel or not. Again, the supporters of the combustion engine objected fiercely. Speed-limit signs were torn down or defaced, and the *Motor* spoke of the Act as being 'designed to apply still more shackles to the motorist', though in general the press had come round to the idea that some restraint was required. There were arguments that the definition of a 'built-up area' (where the speed restriction would apply) would cause confusion – the Member for Clitheroe wanted the words 'a populous place' substituted, as if motorists could be expected to do a headcount as they drove along – but Hore-Belisha stuck to his guns: a built-up area, he declared, was one with street lighting, though he was opposed to 'cluttering up the roads' with signs informing motorists that they were entering a speed-restricted zone.

Others were concerned that requiring a person to take a driving test would not prevent the 'reckless driver [from] subduing his restlessness for long enough to pass, and then presumably going back to his old ways as soon as he had the required licence'. The object of the test, a government spokesman explained wearily, was 'not to put people off the roads but to put people on the roads with some sense of responsibility'. It was Moore-Brabazon whose opposition was the most extreme. During the debate in the Commons he thundered that this 'anti-motorist bill' was 'absolutely reactionary legislation . . . It is true that 7,000 people are getting killed in motor accidents, but it is not always going to be like that. People are getting used to new conditions . . . No doubt many of the older Members of the House will recollect the number of chickens we killed in the early days. [Moore-Brabazon had been driving since the turn of the century, and had spent his vacations from Cambridge acting as an unpaid mechanic to Charles S. Rolls, of Rolls-Royce.] We used to come back with the radiator stuffed with feathers. It was the same with dogs. Dogs get out of the way of motorcars nowadays and you never kill one. There is education even in the lower animals. These things will right themselves.'

'Crude irrelevancies,' sighed *The Times*'s leader, 'which nevertheless served the purpose of showing the House of Commons that the exclusive or preponderating regard for one class of road users leads nowhere.' It welcomed this 'wisely experimental' measure, which 'was only part of a campaign to making the roads safer' – though the other part, building better roads, was endlessly delayed for reasons of cost. Although on the same visit north in 1934 George V had opened the Mersey Tunnel, 'the greatest under-waterway in the world', linking Liverpool with the Wirral commuter belt, and a new road connecting Liverpool with Manchester, and three bridges had been built over the Thames, a substantial road-building programme was urgently needed in order to cope with the huge increase in motor traffic. There were no autobahns or autostradas or parkways in Britain at the outbreak of the Second World War. The Great North Road that ran the 276 miles from London to Newcastle had not a single mile of dual carriageway its entire length. It had already become obvious that 'roads to by-pass the by-pass' were needed, since busy main routes had become, in the words of the secretary of the pressure group the Pedestrians' Association (which was consistently denied airtime by the BBC when motoring matters were discussed) roads of 'blood and tears'. The new arterial roads built so optimistically in the 1920s had become among the most dangerous stretches of road in the whole country.

Once the 1934 Act became law, Hore-Belisha flung himself into a frenzy of publicising its provisions, taking a 'secret all-night tour among the "tootless" cars of London' – one of the experiments of the Act had been a prohibition of the sounding of motor horns between 11.30 p.m. and 7 a.m. within a five-mile radius of Charing Cross. This meant that a 'silence zone' stretched from Highgate in the north to Streatham in the south. So impressed was Hore-Belisha by what he failed to hear that he expressed his desire that 'the boon of sleep and rest shall be conferred as quickly as possible on as many people as possible', and immediately made every built-up area in Great Britain a silence zone.

Since 1,894 pedestrians had been killed in 1933 while attempting to cross roads, an experimental scheme of 'crossings for foot passengers' at which pedestrians had the right of way was introduced at junctions in London. After Hore-Belisha's near-accident in Camden Town, it was clear that white lines painted on the road and a signpost marked 'C' (for crossing) were inadequate, and metal studs were punched into the tarmac to slow down motorists and 19,000 'Belisha beacons' – the name was probably coined by a journalist – amber globes mounted on seven-foot-high black-and-white posts, were installed in London. These were provided, according to a 'motorist' writing in *The Listener*, for the 'pampered pedestrians . . . without the motorist's consent but out of the motorist's pocket'. At first the beacons were unilluminated, since electrification was deemed too expensive; the *Spectator* thought they made London look as if it was 'preparing for a fifth rate carnival'. But W.D. & H.O. Wills brought out a set of 'Safety First' cigarette cards, of which no. 45 showed a pedestrian crossing with a Belisha beacon, and a board game called 'Belisha' was marketed, involving a road journey from London to Oban. The beacons became a ubiquitous and evolving feature of Britain's urban landscape.

However, politics still being considered a profession for gentlemen, Hore-Belisha's use of self-promotion to draw the public's attention to his safety initiatives was regarded as vulgar by many of his colleagues. He 'looks like being *le Disraeli de nos jours*,' thought the journalist Collin Brooks, who had described Hore-Belisha as 'able and energetic, but greatly disliked in the City as a pushing Jew' when he was Financial Secretary to the Treasury. 'Chips' Channon, who considered Hore-Belisha had a 'Hollywood mentality', also gave his anti-Semitism an outing. 'I went for a walk with Hore-Belisha, the much advertised Minister of Transport,' he wrote in January 1935. 'He is an oily man, half a Jew, an opportunist, with the Semitic flare for publicity. Belisha beacons, unheard of a few weeks ago, are now world famous.'

Neither Belisha beacons nor the reintroduction of the speed limit had such a dramatic effect as had been hoped: in the following year road deaths fell by 841 to 6,502, and injuries by 10,877 to 221,776. Pedestrian road deaths remained high too, falling by nearly five hundred to 3,079, though deaths and injuries in built-up (where the speed limit was in effect) were reduced.

An attempt to effect some reconciliation between motorist and pedestrian was the trial use of 'courtesy cops' who rode around on bicycles with megaphones 'advising' motorists rather than arresting them for misdemeanours. Government-funded pilot schemes were rolled out in Lancashire, Cheshire, Liverpool, Manchester and Salford in spring 1937, with police officers given special training for their educative role at Hendon police college.

If the sunburst was one pervasive symbol and summation of the thirties, 'streamlined' was another. The 'Silver Lady' mascot on Rolls-Royce cars, the 'Spirit of Ecstasy' leaning forward, cleaving into the wind, based on one Lord Montagu of Beaulieu had commissioned for his Silver Shadow from the sculptor Charles Robinson Sykes in 1911, was at first an optional extra but was subsequently affixed to the radiator grilles of all Rolls-Royces. Its image seemed to appear, reworked and replayed, in everything from fabrics to pottery whose pointed shapes seemed to urge forward (Poole Pottery even named a two-tone mushroom range of crockery 'Streamline'); in chrome, marble or alabaster ornaments; in clocks supported or leant against by languorous women, perhaps with the leash of a windswept Borzoi, greyhound or other similarly 'streamlined' animal wound round their wrist; in the aerodynamic forms of cars, trains, planes and ships, all suggesting sleek modernity, effortless speed, finely honed technological advance.

Luxury cars such Bugattis, Lagondas, Rolls-Royce Phantoms, Jaguars, Daimlers, Bentleys and Sunbeams had long been essays in sinuous, powerful curves, but by the later years of the decade the 'boxy' and 'bull nose' shapes of the average family saloon were beginning to look 'as archaic as your grandmother's hat'. The pseudonym of the *New Statesman*'s motoring correspondent was 'Streamline'.

The height of the streamlined aesthetic form might have been expected to be aircraft, but development of the bullet- (or cigar-) shaped airships had been abandoned after the disastrous loss of the R101, and long-haul air travel remained largely the prerogative of wealthy business travellers, government officials – and the intrepid. The pioneer aviatrix Amy Johnson despaired of the British government's 'complete lack of airmindedness' and reluctance to engage with the potentials of aviation, which not only hampered Britain's commercial competitiveness, but retarded its military preparedness. Apart from the mail-carrying services (in 1938 nearly 3,000 tons of mail went by air), airlines were not viable without government subsidies.

Imperial Airways had been formed in 1924, as had Britain's other public corporation, the BBC. It was intended to link Britain (or more specifically London) with her Empire and dominions, but very much on imperial terms: attempts to 'sectionalise' routes by allowing national proposals to establish air services within the Empire were firmly resisted. At first Imperial Airways flew between London (using Croydon airport) and Continental Europe; by 1934 it was operating commercial services to Cairo, Calcutta, Rangoon, Singapore, Cape Town, Hong Kong, Khartoum, Nigeria and, in conjunction with the Australian airline Qantas, Australia. But it was not until 1936 that political air rights were sorted out and passengers were able to fly directly from London to far-flung points in the Empire rather than needing to go by train from Paris to Brindisi to board their plane.

It was believed that passenger services would never make airlines self-supporting. The answer was thought to be that Imperial Airlines should carry the Empire's first-class mail at the cost of a 1½d an ounce regardless of its destination. Large seaplanes were used: the main purpose of this was to save money by landing on the sea rather than needing to redevelop inland airports with longer runways, though this disastrously discounted the cost of the infrastructure needed to land in such places as the crocodile-infested shores of parts of Australia. The seaplanes could carry both passengers in *wagon lit* comfort and a large tonnage of mail, but they cost Britain the competitive advantage of speed – US planes were achieving 200 mph, while British seaplanes chugged along at around 115 mph. 'It is wrong,' opined Amy Johnson to the Oxford Women's Debating Society. 'It is speed which counts; and that is why business is going to foreigners.'

Imperial Airways was of necessity heavily subsidised (though not as heavily as the French airline). It offered passengers 'Africa in Days Instead of Weeks', although the 8,539-mile journey to Cape Town took eleven days, only marginally less time than going by sea. Nevertheless, passenger traffic had only risen from 10,321 at the airline's inception in 1924 to 66,324 by 1935.

Imperial's Empire Flying Boats (designed and made by Short Brothers) were elegant and comfortable – an important requirement, since passengers spent so long aboard – with Lloyd Loom chairs bolted to the floor, spacious promenade decks and smoking cabins, and since they flew low, at around

3,000 feet, they afforded excellent views of the land below. But they had to make frequent touchdowns to refuel, with passengers taking in foreign sights much as they would have done on a ship's cruise, and they were easily damaged – 'iron turkeys with paper bottoms', concluded one engineering historian.

Airline publicity and travel writers described the glamour of air travel while providing reassurances of its safety. One conjured up the image of a magic carpet, claiming that as an air passenger he had a better sense of Constantinople than did Jason and his Argonauts, Mohammed or Suleiman: 'They did not know, as I knew, how truly magical it was, how fabulously beautiful. They had not soared into space above their palaces.' But the Suez Canal looked 'ridiculous, little more than a ditch'. The reality of air travel could be less glamorous than promised: passengers were nonplussed to find 'a special basin beneath each seat' for air sickness, planes vibrated and juddered, the noise of the engines was sufficient to make conversation all but impossible, and the small amount of luggage travellers were permitted to take (usually two hundred pounds including the passenger's own body weight) did not please those women who customarily had several heavy trunks carried aboard when they travelled by sea. Moreover, Imperial Airways found that carrying passengers proved incompatible with running an efficient airmail service, since one required speed, the other comfort. When the bargain price for conveying Christmas cards led to the service being completely swamped in 1938, the sea planes had to be stripped back to cram in ever more mail sacks, and the RAF had to be called in to help.

Continental flights did not fare much better than long-haul ones. It cost around £12 to fly from London to Paris, which compared unfavourably with a first-class train and boat ticket at £5.15s. Although the number of flights between Britain and the Continent rose from 42,000 in 1930 to 161,000 in 1938 (the year a nervous Neville Chamberlain took his first flight, tightly rolled umbrella in hand, to attempt to broker a peace with Hitler), over 60 per cent of passengers chose to fly with the more heavily subsidised Continental airlines rather than with British Airways, formed as an expeditious government-subsidised merger of a number of failing private airlines in 1935. Nor did the multiplicity of compact airlines flying domestic routes make much impact in a small island where trains were fast and largely reliable: internal passenger traffic increased from 72,000 in 1932 to 121,000 in 1935, services to the Channel Islands proving the most popular, and apart from mail, freight on the whole went by land, not air.

Despite their concerns, the railways did not lose a significant number of passengers to air travel, and even during the Depression the number of people making train journeys did not decrease significantly, and had risen to over 1,800 million a year by 1938. Whatever the reality, though, there was a sense of decline, a feeling that the terms of transportation had changed, that roads could meander wherever demand lay, and planes had the freedom of the skies, while trains were confined to Victorian-built tracks, laid out on a grid that no longer accorded with newer, flexible demands of work and leisure, and the railways were restrained by costs and regulations that made them uncompetitive. While the number of passengers taking trains rose, the railways were losing their overall share of the market – the growing mobile population was more inclined to go by car if they could, or by coach if they couldn't, for their holidays and days out.

The 'big four' railway companies (an amalgamation of 121 small companies had taken place in 1923) – or five counting the nationalised London Passenger Board, which had taken over the London Underground group in 1933 – could have fought back by rationalising their services, doing something of a pre- Beeching cull of uneconomic branch lines and over-frequent services. But on the whole they didn't. They went for modernity, speed, streamlining. Southern Railway had invested some £21 million in electrifying 60 per cent of its lines by 1938, the great majority in the London commuting area, others around Glasgow, Manchester and the North-East of England were also upgraded in this way. However, this modernisation was limited, partly because of expense, but also, as the historian Harold Perkins explains, because coal-owners who sat on railway boards objected to it since steam trains used a great quantity of coal (although the production of electricity involves burning large amounts of coal too).

Until 1932 there had been an agreement not to compete on speed between the two railway companies that ran trains to Scotland, the London Midland & Scottish (LMS), which steamed up the west coast to Glasgow, and the London & North Eastern Railway (LNER), which, as its name suggests, took the east coast route to Edinburgh. In 1932, given competition from aircraft, that agreement was scrapped: advertising films were made showing a plane, a train and a boat all speeding north, with the train pulling ahead, and both companies sought to attract passengers – particularly business passengers – by finding ways to cut the leisurely eight and a quarter hours it took to cover the four hundred miles from London to Scotland.

Nigel Gresley had been appointed Chief Mechanical Engineer of the LNER in 1923, responsible for the maintenance and repair of over 7,000 locomotives and a staff of 30,000. He started work straight away on upgrading the comfort, the look and the speed of the company's trains, improving the sleeping cars and installing all-electric cooking facilities in new restaurant cars. Gresley had exhibited a cutting-edge *Flying Scotsman* locomotive at the 1924 British Empire exhibition at Wembley, and in the following years the train's coal capacity was increased and various adjustments made, enabling it to achieve its first 392-mile non-stop run to Edinburgh in 1928. By 1934 the *Flying Scotsman* had achieved 100 mph, and the appearance of the formerly solid, rounded 'Thomas the Tank Engine'-type steam train had been transformed. The *Silver Jubilee*, so called to celebrate George V's twenty-five years on the throne in 1935, pulled by a 'Silver Link' engine, clad in silver-painted metal to make it look like a streamlined, aerodynamic bullet, shot past excited crowds lining the platforms and track, whistle screeching, steam billowing. As it sped from London to Newcastle on 27 September 1935, the 110th anniversary of the first railway line, crammed with press and photographers drinking champagne and port in the bar, the *Silver Jubilee* achieved an average speed of 100 mph over long stretches, and twice touched 112 mph. Gresley (who was knighted the year after the *Silver Jubilee*'s triumph) considered that the cladding was little but a marketing device; the train's performance was minimally enhanced, if at all, by the new design, but it gave the desired impression of speed, modernity, technological progress.

Gresley's counterpart at the LMS, William Stanier, had been poached from the Great Western Railway (GWR), which for many years had run Britain's fastest train, the *Cheltenham Flyer*, which by 1932 was averaging 81 mph over the seventy-seven miles from London to Swindon. On 29 June 1936 the LMS *Coronation Scot*, another arrow-like, beaver-tailed train, its livery a striking metallic blue with white stripes, named in tribute to the crowning of George VI, seized the steam-train record, briefly clocking up a speed of 114 mph on the London Euston to Glasgow run. So thrilling was this that the engine was shipped off for a celebrity US tour, debuting at the New York World's Fair in 1939.

But, as every schoolboy used to know, the inter-war laurels went to an LNER locomotive called the *Mallard*, designed by Sir Nigel Gresley and built at Doncaster, which 'ate up the miles' along the east coast route during a special trial run on 3 July 1938. With driver Joseph Duddington at the controls it streaked along the track at 120 mph – two miles a minute – touching 126 mph for a brief moment on the downhill run from Grantham, setting a world record for steam locomotion that would never be beaten, since the days of steam were numbered: diesel would power the trains of the future. When war broke out just after a year after the *Mallard*'s triumph, the cosmetic cladding was stripped from high-speed trains and, painted battleship grey, they went to war.

The records that made up the 'triple crown' – for the fastest speed by land, air and water – were tossed around quite a bit during the thirties, with Britain at various points holding all three. In August 1936 and again in August 1938 the *Queen Mary* wrested the record for the fastest Atlantic crossing from the French liner the *Normandie* – despite the fact that the *Normandie* had cost twice as much to build as the more conventional British ship. The *Normandie* with its huge public rooms – the dining room could seat seven hundred at a sitting and was longer than the Hall of Mirrors at Versailles, its children's nursery decorated with scenes from Jean de Brunhoff's *Babar* books – was a glittering Art Deco sea palace, even more fabulous than the *Queen Mary*. When the *Normandie* first won the Blue Riband she flew a blue pennant that was thirty feet long to signify the crossing's 30-knot average speed. In fact neither the French nor the British admitted they were in competition – the tragic sinking of the *Titanic* in 1912 had made the notion of sacrificing everything to speed an unacceptable one – and the liners' respective captains sent polite 'bravos' to each other when the other won the palm.

There were no such inhibitions about another water-speed record. Malcolm Campbell and Henry O'Neal de Hane Segrave (known as 'de Hane') had a lot in common, though while Segrave, the son of an Anglo-Irish landowner, was comfortably off, Campbell, who was the son of a diamond merchant, was considerably richer. Both had flown during the First World War, both – Campbell in particular – had matinee-idol good looks. Both had been glamorous crowdpullers at the racing track at Brooklands in Surrey, but they had grown bored with the limited rewards of circuit racing, and set out to be the fastest man on both land and water, seeking out opportunities to push themselves and their cars to the limit, edging year by year to formerly unimaginable speeds.

On 15 February 1931 at Daytona Beach, Florida, Campbell in his custom-built car *Bluebird* (named after Maurice Maeterlinck's play about searching for the bluebird of happiness), reached 231.4 mph, beating both the previous record-holder, the American driver Ray Keech, and Segrave, the first person ever to reach 200 mph on land, whose monster chain-driven *Sunbeam* had managed only a fraction of a mile less. On his return to Britain Campbell was knighted for his achievement (George V asked him what good was achieved by these repeated record attempts, which added only a few miles per hour to the existing mark), as Segrave had been earlier.

Campbell was to go even faster, achieving the magical 301.13 mph at Bonneville salt flats, Utah, on 7 March 1935, but Segrave had moved from land to water. On 13 June 1930 he broke the world record when his Rolls-Royce aero-engine speedboat *Miss England II* reached 98.76 mph on Lake Windermere. However, on his third run, Segrave hit an object floating in the lake, the boat capsized, his engineer drowned and Segrave was mortally injured. The Prince of Wales and the Prime Minister were represented at his funeral, and Segrave's ashes were scattered over the playing fields of Eton (where he had been a pupil) from a plane that had been his.

Campbell also took to the water, achieving the world record in August 1939 when another *Bluebird* reached 141.44 mph on Coniston Water. Unlike Segrave, Campbell was to survive his various dangerous exploits – but his son, Donald, would be killed on Coniston Water on 4 January 1967 during an attempt in his own *Bluebird* to exceed 300 mph on water.

A rather pale air imitation of the Blue Riband was the King's Cup race, instigated in 1922 by George V in the hope of encouraging the design of light aircraft and developing engines ahead of Britain's rivals. Competitors were required to make a round trip from Croydon airport to Glasgow, with an overnight stop. In 1933 the Cup was won by Geoffrey De Havilland, who went on to start the De Havilland aircraft company, and in 1938 by Alex Henshaw with a never-bettered record of 236.25 mph.

Despite its worthy intentions, the King's Cup never captured the public's imagination in the way that the Schneider Trophy for sea planes did. The £1,000 prize, originally sponsored by Jacques Schneider, a wealthy French balloonist and aircraft enthusiast, had the same objective as the King's Cup – to encourage technical advances in aviation – but it soon became a simple speed race, attracting huge crowds. Britain won the trophy in 1914 and 1922, and in 1927 and 1929 RAF pilots flying a Supermarine triumphed. But in 1931 the beleaguered British government withdrew its financial support, whereupon the wildly eccentric, hugely wealthy Dame Lucy Houston, who had a pathological hatred of the National Government in general and of Ramsay MacDonald in particular (she used to display an eight-foot illuminated sign on her yacht *Liberty* declaring, 'To hell with the traitor MacDonald'), gleefully picked up the tab to keep Britain supreme in the air with a donation of £100,000. Watched by an estimated half a million spectators lining the seafront at Cowes on the Isle of Wight on 13 September, the British teams flying the triangular course above the Solent beat the world record; on 29 September the Supermarine S.6b crashed through the 400 mph barrier

– the first plane ever to do so. The sleek, aerodynamic appearance of Supermarine was to exert a considerable influence on the iconic design of Spitfire fighter planes in the Second World War.

Dame Lucy Houston also funded an expedition in 1933 during which aircraft flew over the summit of Mount Everest for the first time, not only to show that Britain was Best, but as an indication of her own displeasure at any move to grant independence to India. Independent, courageous women – though most were neither as rich nor as unbalanced as Houston – played highly visible roles in the forward march of aviation in the 1930s.

The first woman to fly the Channel had been an American journalist, Harriet Quimby, who did so in 1910, remarking that 'Flying seems easier than voting.' A year later, Hilda Hewlett became Britain's first certified woman pilot. She ran a successful flying school at Brooklands, and worked in aircraft manufacture throughout the First World War. In August 1928 the American Amelia Earhart was the first woman to fly solo across the American continent, and in May 1932 she became the first woman to emulate Charles Lindbergh and fly the Atlantic solo, taking fourteen hours and fifty-six minutes to cross from Newfoundland to Co. Derry, Northern Ireland.

The daughter of a vicar, Mary du Caurroy Tribe married the man who would succeed as Duke of Bedford, and led a busy life as sportswoman, nurse and radiographer for over thirty years before taking up flying at the age of sixty-one in an effort to relieve her deafness, probably contracted as the result of a bout of typhoid fever in India as a girl. With a co-pilot she flew to India and the Cape in what turned out to be record-breaking flights. The 'Flying Duchess' gained her pilot's licence in 1933, and in March 1937, aged seventy-two, she took off to complete her 200 hours of solo flying. She was never seen again, though parts of her plane were washed up on the beaches of East Anglia.

Jean Batten was a New Zealand dentist's daughter with an unusually imaginative mother who pinned pictures of the French pioneer aviator Louis Blériot, the first man to fly across the English Channel in 1909, above her baby daughter's cot. In 1930 Jean and her mother moved to London, where, inspired by Lindbergh's non-stop flight from New York to Paris in 1927, Batten gained both a private and a commercial pilot's licence at the London Aeroplane Club. In April 1933, in a Gipsy Moth plane that had once belonged to the Prince of Wales, given to her by the latest in a string of smitten young men, she took off for Karachi, aiming to better Amy Johnson's record time from England to Australia. She failed, as she did on her next attempt, but in May 1934 Batten flew to Australia in fourteen days twenty-two and a half hours, knocking four days off Johnson's time.

When, after yet another romantic interlude, she flew back to Britain, she became the first woman to fly to Australia and back. Record-breaking flights to Argentina and Brazil (crossing the South Atlantic with only the aid of a watch and a compass) followed, and in October 1937 the glamorous aviatrix piloted a Percival Gull monoplane from New Zealand to London in five days and eighteen hours – a record which was not bettered for forty-four years.

Beryl Markham was yet another magnificent woman in a flying machine. She spent a wild childhood and a promiscuous young adulthood in the Rift Valley in British East Africa. When Henry, Duke of Gloucester accompanied his brother, Edward the Prince of Wales, to Kenya's 'Happy Valley' in 1928, he fell in love with Markham and brought her back to London, setting her up in a suite of rooms in the Grosvenor Hotel. At the insistence of his mother, Queen Mary, Gloucester settled a capital sum of £15,000 on Markham to avoid a scandal, since she was claiming that her son, born in February 1929, was his, though the timing made this highly unlikely. In England Markham learned to fly, and having obtained her pilot's licence in 1933, accepted a dare to cross the Atlantic, which she did without a radio, crashing into a bog in Nova Scotia, having run out of fuel. The twenty-one-hour-thirty-five-minute flight made her the first woman to fly the Atlantic from east to west, and the first person to make it in a solo non-stop flight. It was her last adventure in the air: she then wrote a best-selling account of her Kenyan childhood and spent the rest of her days training horses in the Rift Valley.

The energetic romantic novelist Barbara Cartland was another unlikely pioneer. At the request of the nightclub queen Kate Meyrick's son-in-law Lord Clifford she had organised a bevy of former debutantes to drive supercharged MGs around the track at Brooklands. 'The race was ostensibly to show the public that women could drive as well as men [as indeed the "Speed Queen", Kay Petre, frequently showed] – actually to publicize the cars.' Cartland, who personally disliked driving, completed three laps with Lord Clifford in the passenger seat, and the leather-helmeted, goggle-wearing women she had managed to collect –'quite a difficult feat in 1931 – few young society beauties drove well enough' – were endlessly photographed and filmed and their exploits shown on newsreels to cinema audiences.

But at that time 'flying was the main interest of the young and dashing . . . people who could afford it had their own private Puss Moth [a three-seater De Havilland monoplane with an impressive speed record], poorer folk contented themselves with gliding' (and most people, of course, never left the ground). Gliding was a craze that had come from Germany, where it was a way to get round the constraints of the Versailles Treaty, which forbade the use of single-seater powered aircraft. While a number of British gliding clubs had been forced to close during the Depression, some survived, including the London Gliding Club, which flew from Ivinghoe Beacon and then the Dunstable downs in the Chilterns. Cartland and two RAF pilots commissioned a glider (or more likely Cartland acted as a glamorous front person for the enterprise) which they intended to fly across the Channel. However, when the *Daily Mail* offered a prize of £1,000 for the first glider to cross the Channel, Cartland and co. decided this was too much like a 'stunt', and on the same day set off in the opposite direction in the red and white *Barbara Cartland*, flying overland: 'a cricket match stopped and waved at us, golfers stared at us from famous courses, the world was very beautiful and we were excited at what we were achieving', which was to fly a distance of about a hundred miles from Manston airport in Kent to Reading airport, 'where the Mayor was waiting to greet us'. That summer of 1931 the *Barbara Cartland* took part in several air rallies (sometimes with Cartland in the passenger seat), easily beat an express train in a race from London to Blackpool and set a British record for gliding over four and three-quarter hours before being blown over three times on landing after another record-breaking attempt. Although the pilot escaped injury, 'what remained of the "Barbara Cartland" was taken to the scrap heap'.

Of all these beautiful, daring and sometimes reckless women, it was Amy Johnson who was the iconic British aviatrix in the 1930s, who in 1932 came second after Edith Cavell, and above Joan of Arc, among schoolgirl visitors to Madam Tussaud's asked who they most wanted to be like when they grew up. An economics graduate of Sheffield University and the daughter of a wealthy herring importer ('fishmonger's daughter' was the usual description), Johnson was the first woman recipient of the Air Ministry's licensed engineer certificate, and was allowed to fly the planes manufactured by the De Havilland aircraft company, where she worked, since if a 'slip of a girl' could fly them, then anyone could.

On 5 May 1930, twenty-four-year-old Johnson, who had only a hundred hours experience of flying solo and was one of only sixty women among the 2,000 British amateur pilots, set out from Croydon airport in her biplane *Jason* (named after the voyager of Greek legend, and also the telegraphic address of her father's fish business) to attempt to break the England-to-Australia record of fifteen and a half days set by an Australian squadron leader two years earlier. The *Manchester Guardian* was impressed, commenting that 'she ran very great risks in passing over savage counties and risks to a woman are greater than risks run by a man'. Certainly she was flying over a great deal of terrain marked only 'unsurveyed desert', including an area near Baghdad where another pioneer aviator, Sir Alan Cobham, had been shot at from the ground by a Bedouin as he flew from England to Australia four years earlier, his engineer being killed. Although Johnson (or Johnnie, as she liked to be called) made it to Karachi in five days, wearing 'khaki shorts, puttees and a green sun helmet', bad weather and fuel shortages delayed her, and it took her nineteen and a half days to get to Brisbane.

She was nevertheless garlanded by enthusiastic crowds, hailed as 'Queen of the Air', or 'Lady Lindbergh', received a congratulatory telegram from George V and was later made a CBE. On her return to Croydon (having been refused a place on the ill-fated R101, for which an all-male contingent was wanted) the short journey to London took two and a half hours as crowds stood four or five deep along the route. The *Daily Herald* hailed Johnson's achievement as 'the vindication of womanhood', while the aviation-mad *Daily Mail*, which had bought her story, threw a grand lunch at the Savoy in her honour at which Louis Blériot, Malcolm Campbell, J.B. Priestley and Noël Coward were among the guests, and she was presented with a gold cup and £10,000 (nearly £500,000 today).

Over the next few years Amy Johnson notched up more record-breaking achievements in the air: London to Moscow in less than a day, and then on to Tokyo, the whole trip taking ten days in July 1931; Lympne in Kent to Cape Town, 6,200 miles in a Puss Moth in four days, six hours and fifty-four minutes (ten hours less than her then husband and fellow star aviator, Jim Mollison, had taken). In July 1933 Johnson and Mollison left Pendine (Pent-tywyn) sands in Carmarthen for New York. After thirty-nine hours in the air their heavily loaded ten-seater De Havilland Dragon Rapide 'Seafarer' ran out of fuel, and they ended up in a swamp in Connecticut. Nevertheless the 'flying sweethearts', as the press had it, were the first husband and wife to cross the Atlantic westwards, and they received a tickertape welcome parade along Wall Street. The marriage broke up, but Amy Johnson continued to pursue records, even though she had never learned technical navigational skills, and found her way mainly by following coastlines, rivers and tracks. Although Jean Batten took the women's London to Australia record, Johnson's round trip to Cape Town in May 1937 broke both the outbound record (she took three days six hours eleven minutes) and the round-trip record.

There were other, rather less daring, records broken in the 1930s. In 1934, 1935 and 1936 Fred Perry won the Men's Singles title at Wimbledon, and a prescient crowd queued all night for tickets for a triumph that would never be repeated by a British man. In 1937 Oxford won the Boat Race by three lengths, ending Cambridge's unbroken sequence of victories since 1923. For a race with direct tribal relevance to very few, this battle between the dark and light blues generated an amazing amount of interest. 'Everybody who lived on the river gave a boat race party,' asserted J.M. Richards, the editor of *Architectural Review*. 'Eric and Tirzah [Ravilious, who had a house at Chiswick] did so too, crowding their sitting room with their friends, who, after the race was over, made their way up or down the riverside to join other parties at other friends' houses, parties which went on for the rest of the day. The parties mattered more than the race, the latter providing the necessary sense of occasion and anticipation, a sense enhanced by the riverside spectacle, crowded with incident: droves of people displaying dark or light blue rosettes or little ribboned celluloid dolls backed by crossed oars; flags on all the buildings; programme hawkers; the craft on the river. The most remarkable of these were the crafts that followed the race just behind the Oxford and Cambridge boats – steamers and launches piled high with people and appearing enormous in contrast to the fragility of the racing shells, bearing down in a cloud of spray like a water-borne cavalry charge. This was a moment to which Eric specially looked forward. He celebrated his enjoyment of it some years later when he depicted the scene on a boat-race vase for Wedgwood.' Those who were not invited to party-hop along the Thames got their pleasures from the fun-fair atmosphere, which included the opportunity to get drunk and to have a flutter on the result. The fact that Cambridge nearly always won shortened the odds and meant there was more to play for.

The BBC had been broadcasting a live commentary on the Boat Race since 1927, with John Snagge providing it from 1931. In 1939 a survey reported that 70 per cent of a BBC listeners' panel's members had listened to a broadcast of the Boat Race, whereas boxing drew only 51 per cent, football and cricket 50 per cent, and Wimbledon 34 per cent. Nevertheless, a somewhat perplexed German observer noted that 'both banks of the river are crowded for miles with thousands of spectators among whom the lower classes predominate. Little can be seen of the race, and before you can get a glimpse of it, it's all over.'

Although there had been initial resistance from newspaper editors who feared a drop in sales, the first sports broadcast, of a rugby international between England and Wales at Twickenham, had been transmitted on 15 January 1927, the Grand National was broadcast for the first time in March, with listeners able to follow a map of the course printed in the

Radio Times, and the FA Cup final followed on 23 April. Naturally, there were fears that if people could listen to sporting events from the comfort of their own armchairs, the number of live spectators was bound to decline. The Football League was particularly uncooperative, frequently banning the broadcasting of League matches, and the BBC was also in intermittent dispute with the Football Association about broadcasting Cup finals.

Sports broadcasting was not an unmitigated success in the early days: the equipment required for outside broadcasts was heavy, bulky, slow to position and unreliable. It was difficult to describe a fast-paced football match so that 'the listener gets a mental photograph of what is taking place', so the *Radio Times* printed a diagram of a football pitch divided into eight numbered squares and two commentators were employed, one to describe the action – 'Richard has got the ball . . . Come on Mercer . . .' – while the other interjected the section number. Nor was it easy to find commentators with 'the power to make a listener feel that he was present at the event'; one newspaper noticed that 'It is easier to make a commentator into a temporary expert than the true expert into a commentator.' But the BBC's Director of Outside Broadcasting, Gerald Cock (promoted to be the first Director of Television in 1935), insisted that it was worth persevering, since wireless was giving 'the blind, the invalid and the poor' the opportunity to join in a national obsession.

Soon the service had improved and expanded, and by 1934 the BBC was offering whole afternoons of continuous commentary covering sports including football, rugby, cricket, tennis, horse- and pigeon- (but only occasionally greyhound-) racing, and less mass-participation activities such as speedboat racing, TT trials from the Isle of Man (speedway racing, introduced from Australia in 1928, proved immensely popular: by 1933 there were five tracks in the London area, and nationwide attendance figures were almost one and a quarter million), fencing, boxing, gliding, clay-pigeon shooting, darts, baseball and table tennis.

A golf demonstration was the first sporting event to be televised, in October 1936, and the next year Wimbledon and the FA Cup final were shown as an experiment. By 1938 the Derby and the Boat Race (technically one of the most challenging events to cover) could also be watched by the handful of households that owned sets and lived near enough to the studio at Alexandra Palace to pick up a signal.

The year was soon punctuated by regular broadcasts of sporting events – football, rugby, steeplechasing – with highlights including the Grand National, the Boat Race, the FA Cup final, Wimbledon, the Derby and

Royal Ascot, creating a national 'calendar' for members of the nine million households that by 1939 had a wireless set, who would probably never have actually been a spectator at any of these events.

Betting on sport consumed the time and interest of far more people than played or even watched it. The laws on gambling were not watertight, having been built on various judges' edicts and decisions of local authorities, and they were occasionally challenged, but under the terms of the 1906 (Street Betting) Act credit betting off course with licensed bookies was legal. Many of the larger bookmaking firms had a regular upper-middle-class, professional and business clientele. Cash betting on course was also allowed. Cash betting off course, however, was not, although this was how most working-class bets were placed, with an army of unlicensed bookies operating on street corners, in pubs, clubs and workplaces – usually with a 'watcher' to keep an eye out for the police. Numerous small shopkeepers would take cash bets, while milkmen and window cleaners were also well placed to collect bets as they did their rounds.

The office of one bookie in the back room of a Salford terrace house was 'complete with a telephone and "blower" [the London and Provincial Sporting Agency's telephone service, established in 1929] . . . A simple cover over a back yard led to a door with a "window" cut in, this window was just a hole with a removable shutter/cover and it had a small shelf on the inside. Bets were placed by knocking on the shelter if not open and handing the bets through the opening . . . look-outs ("dogger out") were placed at strategic points to warn of police activities, these were usually assisted by enthusiastic local youngsters. The bookie usually had a "mug" [in London a "mug" was known as a "percher"] whose main job was to be caught by the police with nominal evidence only,' to deflect attention from the real quarry. Street bets would be placed by wrapping the stake in a scrap of paper with the race and the name of the horse scrawled on it, along with a pseudonym so that the punter could not be traced by the police. Although bookmakers were often portrayed as wily or flash characters, out to make a quick buck out of the innocent (Sam Grundy in Walter Greenwood's *Love on the Dole* is archetypal), many were respected in working-class communities for their ability to outwit the law, and some could be relied on to defer payment, or even lend money, in times of hardship.

The police were ambivalent about their role in stamping out illegal betting: some profited from bribes or protection money, many no doubt placed bets themselves, and almost all recognised how deeply the habit was embedded in working-class communities, how many of those who had an illegal flutter were otherwise law-abiding citizens, and how blatantly the legislation was weighted against poorer people who dealt in cash in hand. Moreover, the fear, oft voiced by politicians and the Churches, that betting was bringing financial ruin and the collapse of the family, seemed ill-founded in the main. Although probably around four million people placed regular bets on the horses and around half a million on the dogs, the Chief Constable of Manchester, giving evidence to a Royal Commission on Betting in 1923, maintained that 'the majority of [workmen] act very modestly indeed in betting transaction', wagering only from sixpence to 2 shillings a week. This figure probably stood throughout the thirties, though in areas of high unemployment, sixpence or less would have been a more likely stake.

People bet for all the obvious reasons: in a world with few choices, this is one; it might be the opportunity to make the sort of money a working man could never hope to save, or an unemployed man could only dream of. 'The cheapest of all luxuries', Orwell called betting. 'Even people on the verge of starvation can buy a few days' hope ("Something to live for" as they call it) by having a penny on a sweepstake.' One man told a social investigation in York that he would 'rather have six penn'orth hope than six penn'orth of electricity'. If some bounty was to descend, dreams were not of yachts and fast cars, but of being able to 'buy a gramophone, or to buy a new wireless set or to go on holiday', or if it was a real windfall, 'a new house, which would be built to our own idea, so we could getter a better scullery'. Betting was also simply something to do – studying the racing pages in a shared newspaper, a common topic of conversation in the pub and on the streets. Studying form, becoming a bit of an expert on the horses or the dogs or football teams, was a cerebral exercise that kept men's wits active, and the man who had a win 'acquires thereby a definite social standing, and his views on very different matters are heard with respect'.

Until commercialised greyhound-racing was introduced in 1926, horse-racing had been the only sport on which it was legal to bet. Between the wars horse-racing was big business: horses, trainers and jockeys came from all over the world to compete in British races, and in London alone 500,000 copies of the racing editions of evening papers were bought daily. *Sporting Life*, the only specialist sports newspaper, had a circulation of around 100,000, and almost all newspapers employed tipsters, including, with some reluctance, the *Daily Worker*, though the Liberal *Manchester Guardian*, which was strongly anti-betting, held aloof. The facts that *The Times* devoted almost as much space to racing as the *Daily Mail* by 1937, that cinema newsreel companies regularly covered major races, that the royal family attended major race meetings, and that the BBC broadcast such 'national' races as the Derby, the Grand National and the St Leger, plus the fact that *Sporting Life* carried advertisements for Austin and Morris cars, Burberry coats and Schweppes tonic, all suggest that interest in horse-racing – and thus undoubtedly betting on it – embraced all classes.

The industry gave employment to thousands of bookmakers, since around £221 million a year was spent on legal betting by 1938, and informal employment to many more. In 1937–38 the turnstiles at racecourses took a total of £3.1 million, whereas football took £2.7 million. Race meetings were very varied: Ascot was a society fixture; Newmarket was an occasion for Jockey Club members and other serious racegoers – George V, who was good on bloodstock and form, was a frequent attender, and also liked to watch the Grand National from the box owned by Lord Derby, who with the Aga Khan was one of the great stud owners and breeders of the inter-war years. The Derby run at Epsom, the St Leger at Doncaster, the Grand National at Aintree and, increasingly, the Gold Cup at Cheltenham attracted huge crowds (an estimated 300,000 at Epsom and Aintree), many from Ireland, others coming by special trains laid on for the occasion: forty-three such trains ran to Aintree on Grand National day in 1930, including nine from London. On the whole, working men could not afford to be regular racegoers, but the Derby or the Grand National might well be the occasion for a 'grand day out' for the family with fish and chips, jellied eels, ice cream and fortune-tellers, and swings for the children, while women, who might not usually bet, were inclined to have a flutter on such occasions.

A 'Tote' (Horserace Totaliser Board) system had been introduced in 1929, intended to provide a safe, state-controlled alternative to illegal off-course betting and to make a financial contribution to racing by deducting a percentage of the pool of 'totalised' bets. But the Tote attracted only a rela-tively small number of punters – mainly those placing small bets, including women – though it grew in scale, so that by 1934 all racecourses offered a Tote service. Its takings reached £4 million in 1936 and it made a modest surplus, though it never approached the amount bookmakers netted. Most punters preferred the more haphazard, traditional way of placing bets with on-course bookmakers who employed 'tic tac men' to signal information about odds, and used back-slang to further mystify punters. One of the most colourful on-course tipsters was 'Ras Prince Monolulu', who claimed to be chief of an Abyssinian tribe but in fact was born on St Croix in the Caribbean (his real name was Peter Mackay or McKay). The 'Prince', dressed in brightly coloured clothes, feathers and beads, with his cry 'I Gotta Horse!', was a fixture at thirties race meetings such as Epsom, Ascot and Doncaster.

He had made his fortune, and also his reputation as a tipster, in 1920 when he backed Spion Kop to win the Derby at odds of 100–6, making him richer by £8,000 (nearly £400,000 today).

Greyhound-racing was a thirties phenomenon: the third largest commercial leisure activity in Britain (after cinema and football), attracting some nineteen million spectators a year – including women, who according to a female breeder who wrote the first standard history in 1934 were 'the keenest supporters of track racing since its commencement: they form a large proportion of the huge crowds seen at the various tracks'. Whippet- and greyhound-racing and hare-coursing had been popular sports for generations, mainly in London and the North. The first circular course on which the dogs chased an electric hare, an import from the US, opened at Bellevue, Manchester, in 1926, advertising 'All the thrills and skills of coursing without the cruelty'.

The craze spread like wildfire. By 1930 the abandoned White City, built for the 1908 Olympics, had been developed as a high-class stadium with covered terraces, a restaurant and club room, as was some waste ground in Harringay, north London, where the detritus thrown up by building the Tube line had been dumped. Wembley stadium, empty since the 1925 Empire exhibition, was purchased for a bargain price and let out for Cup finals, but its main activity was greyhound-racing. Other stadia had opened in Edinburgh, Glasgow, Birmingham, Belfast, Cardiff, Manchester, Hull and elsewhere, and by 1932 there were fifty tracks and many more in the pipeline (though a proposal to bring greyhound-racing to the Crystal Palace was rejected after concerted local opposition), as well as numerous small un-licensed or 'flapping' tracks, where dogs were released to run across a field towards men flapping towels, a sport popular mainly in Wales and the North-East, and mainly patronised by working men.

'All classes patronise the races,' the New Survey of London found. 'Favourite dogs are followed from track to track [the most favourite being Mick the Miller which won fifty-one races in two years, his retirement covered by newsreel cameras, he starred in a film about himself, *Wild Boy*, in 1934] . . . A certain element of the picturesque enters into the race meetings . . . before each race the electric hare whirrs round the track: as it passes the kennels the betting ceases, the kennel doors fly open, the dogs rush out, the crowd roars; a few seconds and the dogs are round, the white-coated attendants lead the dogs away, the lucky spectators collect their winnings and the betting begins again.'

In the early days many tracks operated five or six nights a week, including

Sundays, and in 1931 over one and three-quarter million people attended greyhound races in Manchester, and over two million in Glasgow, where there were five tracks. The fact that each race lasted only a matter of seconds provided 'practically unlimited facilities for continuous gambling', in the words of the 1932–33 Royal Commission on Lotteries and Betting. Indeed, greyhound-racing was to the forefront of the Commission's concerns. As the Home Secretary, Sir John Gilmour, informed the House during the passage of the subsequent Bill in June 1934, 'There are only seven race-courses within 15 miles of Charing Cross, with 187 days of racing, whereas in the same area there are 23 greyhound tracks with over 4,000 days racing a year. Greyhound-racing has brought on-the-course facilities, often as an almost nightly event, into most of the large urban centres in the country.' The tracks were unlicensed, and the profits could be enormous: 'King Solomon's mines cannot compare with the money that has been raked out of greyhound racing,' claimed an MP during the debate.

There had been discussions about banning Tote betting at greyhound tracks, but this was a problem since on-course betting (including the Tote) was allowed at horse-racing courses, so it could have been seen as blatantly classist to ban it at greyhound tracks. But to the official mind what was excessive betting had to be curbed, particularly as it was feared that women were becoming inveterate track gamblers. One Glasgow track even provided a crèche where mothers could leave their children while they bet on the dogs, and 'two see-saws, and a round sandpit complete with spades and buckets are some of the amusements provided for kiddies' at Harringay. Greyhound-racing must cease to be 'an animated roulette board', in the words of Winston Churchill, and become a sport like any other, with betting in no way essential to its enjoyment, and spectators presumably expected to go for the sheer pleasure of watching a clutch of sinewy dogs flash by in pursuit of an electric gizmo.

Under the terms of the 1934 Betting and Lotteries Act, greyhound-racing was legitimised but controlled: tracks had to be licensed by local authorities, betting was limited to 104 days a year and no more than eight races in four hours were allowed. The Home Secretary assured the House that it 'cannot be over emphasised that the Bill does not place any limit on the number of days on which greyhound racing can take place. Greyhound racing can take place on every day of the week if they so choose. What the Bill seeks to do is to prevent commercial organisations from providing organised facilities for gambling to a degree which experience has shown to result in serious consequences to the social life of the country.'

However, in places where there was more than one track, owners would usually come to an arrangement whereby they would open on different evenings, so punters could gamble more frequently than the legislators had intended. In 1938 twenty-five million people attended meetings at tracks owned by the National Greyhound Racing Club, and perhaps as many as ten or fifteen million at others.

The thrill of greyhound-racing was the immediacy of watching a race, heart in mouth, on which you had a bet on one of the runners, but the 1930s saw two other immensely popular forms of gambling which required simply posting a stamped addressed envelope. One was the Irish sweepstake, which was first run in 1930. Started by a wealthy Dublin bookmaker with the support of the Irish Free State government, the lottery aimed to provide funds for Ireland's hospitals and medical services to supplement the impoverished state's contributions. The first draw took place at the Mansion House in Dublin under the eagle eye of General O'Duffy, the Commissioner of Police, with Irish nurses turning the barrel and a blind child drawing the winning ticket. The sweepstake was so popular that it was soon run three times a year, based on such classic English races as the Grand National and the Derby. Tickets cost ten shillings each, the prize was £100,000, and by March 1932 it had raised £4 million from ticket sales, with twenty-three hospitals each having benefited by £2.8 million from the first five lotteries. Over the water British punters were quick to organise themselves into syndicates of families, workmates or customers from the local pub or working men's club to buy tickets, and probably more than £3 million in postal orders was mailed from Britain to Dublin for each draw. Lotteries and sweepstakes were illegal in Britain, and it was also illegal to purchase tickets for foreign lotteries, but it would have been a Herculean task to stop the outflow of postal orders to Ireland: even though the GPO did open some 9,000 envelopes and return the stake money, there was no chance that the government of the Irish Free State would cooperate in renouncing an income stream that was such a support to its medical services.

It might have been thought that rather than banning participation in the Irish sweepstake, Britain might have imported the model, and indeed a Conservative MP, Sir William Davidson, did introduce a Private Member's Bill in March 1932 with the aim of raising money 'by means of lotteries for charitable, scientific and artistic purposes or other public projects'. He asked, 'How much sickness and suffering in this country might have been saved had this money been available to us?', since out of seven million tickets sold an estimated five million had been purchased by British citizens, a total of about £6 million in 1931 and nearly £11 million in 1932 flowing over the sea to 'rebel Ireland', while *The Times* listed 'the names of 1,000 criminals who had won prizes in the Irish sweepstake'. The Bill was lost for lack of time – Clement Attlee, George Lansbury and Nye Bevan were among those anti-betting Labour MPs who voted against it. However, while the 1934 Act did not legalise a national lottery, and made it an offence to purchase lottery tickets from abroad, though prosecutions were rare, it did allow private lotteries (such as whist drives) to continue, and legalised lotteries held for charity – but only if they were not the main purpose of the bazaar or garden party or whatever.

John Hilton, a statistician with a human face (or voice), had become something of an avuncular figure to the poor and unemployed. Working at the Ministry of Labour, he was not content simply to compute unemployment figures; he wanted to find out about the lives of those the lists represented, believing that too many economists neglected the social side of statistics (an impression of which he was not disabused when he was appointed to the first Montague Burton Chair in Industrial Relations at Cambridge University in 1931). In 1933 Hilton started to give regular talks on the BBC, and between 1936 and 1939 he contributed a weekly column to the *News Chronicle*. His sympathetic manner and interest in ordinary people – 'I believe . . . in Tom, Dick and Harry (and of course in Peggy, Joan and Kate) . . . I know how important in the scheme of things are Sir Thomas, Professor Richard and the Right Honourable Henry . . . but if they start throwing their weight about too much and I have to take a side, I side with Tom, Dick and Harry' – won him a large audience and sackloads of post, including so many letters about why people did the football pools that he collected them into a book on the subject, published in 1936.

Hilton's view was clear. Writing about what he defined as 'wealthlessness' (lack of capital), he explained, 'fifty million pounds a season have been spent on the Pools. You will never suppress the Pools. They have flourished and they will flourish . . . because they are supplying a need. They are satisfying a craving; the craving for the redistribution of wealth by irrational windfalls.' He went on to advocate that the privately owned wealth of the country should be confiscated, pooled and redistributed 'so that everybody had his £1,500', which would fructify in some pockets and trickle rapidly out of others. But until that unlikely reform happened, the pools would flourish.

Ever since football matches became regular fixtures in the mid-nineteenth century, various forms of pre-match betting had proliferated in newspapers and through coupons sold on the streets and outside football stadia on match days, all sailing close to contravening betting and gambling laws. There were spasmodic prosecutions, but by 1913, by which time book-makers had got in on the lucrative business, around two million coupons were issued nationally each week. John Moores, a Liverpool telegraphist, started his pools business, Littlewoods, in a modest way in 1923 with capital of £150, employing his family to send out coupons and check them against the match results. Punters predicted the result of a number of football matches – the home or the away team to win, or a draw – by filling in a column of twelve squares: each column cost a penny, and there was room on the coupon for thirty guesses, which would have cost half a crown. By the end of the 1926–27 football season turnover had risen to £2,000, meaning that when the money was pooled substantial prizes could be won for small stakes – most as low as a few shillings but others soaring to £22,000 – even after Littlewoods (or Vernons or Zetters or Shermans and other smaller rivals) had taken their 5 per cent commission and a further percentage for expenses – a system much like the Tote.

Littlewoods, the largest of the pools companies, was based in Liverpool, as was Vernons, with armies of women working as checkers (though known as 'clerks') or stamp-lickers in huge converted warehouses, super-vised by women and, in the case of Littlewoods, with generous social and welfare provision, including a ballroom and a sports ground, to counter-act the mind-numbing boredom of checking endless rows of crosses, the coupons delivered by Littlewoods 'postmen' working two days a week. The pools promoters managed to circumvent the 1920 Ready Money Pools Act by getting punters to send in their postal orders ('the working-man's cheque') in arrears to pay off the previous week's debt. The formula is still in operation, largely unchanged, today. Moreover, in 1932 Littlewoods entered the lucrative world of mail-order shopping, exploiting lists of customers who were already sending in a football pools coupon each week, many of whom had organised themselves into clubs for this very purpose. Vernons, Littlewoods' Merseyside pools rival, started its own mail-order retail business in 1936.

By the 1930s it was reckoned that around a quarter of the adult popula-tion of Britain – some five to seven million people – did the pools regularly. Seebohm Rowntree thought that roughly half the households in York did so. John Hilton suggested that 'The postal order business of the Post Office gives some clue to the rate of growth . . . the sale . . . of sixpenny postal orders alone have gone up in the last nine years from 4 million to 22 million, and shilling postal orders from 8 million to 24 million.' While not all these postal orders were accounted for by the pools, Hilton reckoned that they represented 'the vast bulk of the increase. The Post Office now sells these low-amount postal orders in books, like the books of stamps, for the greater convenience of Pool clients in sending in their investments and Pool Promoters in paying out small winnings.'

For many people the pools were a central feature of their lives. A York workman explained that he spent 'three days in considering next week's football, a day filling in his coupon, and three days in keen anticipation of the following Saturday's result'. Hilton

> drew a fancy picture of the scene as I saw it in thousands of the five million or so happy homes of England, Scotland, and Wales whose members like to have their shilling or two in the Pool . . . I pictured on the Thursday or Friday night the family seated round the table. Father with the master coupons, mother with the spare coupons to keep a record of the bets placed; grown-up sons and daughters seated councillor-wise around the table; the younger ones on the sofa; grandma in the rocking chair. The discussions have been going on all week, of course. Each has taken council [sic] of friends in the know: some have studied form in form books and newspapers. It is Friday night; wages or dole have been drawn; the spare pennies are burning holes in the pockets; and now the discussion begins: will Hull City win, draw or lose against Blackpool next Saturday? Father presides. Sons and daughters state their views; from the sofa comes a childish treble: grandma tries to make her voice heard; mother rules. Down go the figure 1,2, or X in the first of the 300 tiny squares on this one coupon. Now the next. Will Aston Villa, win, draw or lose against Leeds? Another discussion, another decision, another square filled in. And so on for twelve matches. Twelve little squares filled; a pennyworth of the family's collective bets for that weekend is made . . . then again and again column by column, penny by penny . . . Then the postal order, or the money paid over to the agent, and that week's family Pool-investment is done . . . late on Saturday afternoon there is a rush for the early and late evening papers . . . it is the football results in the stop press column. I say well that is very nice; all this burning interest in a manly sport. I am told no, they have little interest in the game as a game or the teams as teams, they are only interested in the results . . . The odds are, of course, the very heavy odds are, that they won't have won anything at all; but you never know, and a day may come . . .

There were various attempts to ban football pools: a Liberal MP introduced a Bill in 1936 arguing that they were a lottery, and should therefore be banned. His attempt failed since opponents argued that doing the pools required some skill rather than being pure chance (a definition of a lottery).

In 1938 A.P. Herbert, by then Independent Member for Oxford University, tried again: he too was unsuccessful.

'I see in the attempt to stop Football Pools the desire of the "ruling class", i.e. the "monied" , to defend all and every one of their present privileges. One of these is certainly that the rich alone should be permitted to gamble, speculate, or whatever name they give to it,' wrote an East End man to John Hilton, while a Scottish correspondent complained that 'many members of the House of Commons and the House of Lords own racehorses and bet in large sums and still there is no comment on this. The Government have a Tote for betting. What about this? And again there is the Stock Exchange. Seems funny allowing betting in one way and not another . . . even at a Church bazaar one pays for guessing how many peas there are in a bottle.'

The attempts to outlaw football pools were fully supported by the football authorities: those who organised sports did not on the whole see those who organised betting on those sports as complementary, and did what they could to frustrate what they regarded as their parasitical and demeaning and possibly corrupting activities. That was as true of the Jockey Club as it was of the Football Association (FA). In October 1935 the recently appointed new president of the Football League (formed in 1885 to administer professional fixtures and players' terms and conditions), who was a Methodist, tried to stymie the pools operators by forbidding League members to carry advertisements for the pools in their programmes or at their grounds, and even persuaded the FA, which remained the custodian of the game itself, not to publish the list of fixtures until two days before kick-off. This caused outrage; George Orwell happened to be in Yorkshire on his way to Wigan Pier: 'Hitler, Locarno, Fascism and the threat of war aroused hardly a flicker of interest locally, but the decision of the Football Association to stop publishing their fixtures in advance (this was an attempt to quell the Football Pools) flung all Yorkshire into a storm of fury.' In response the pools companies simply picked up the phone, rang round the football clubs and managed to produce coupons that way, and business carried on, though disputes about who legally owned the copyright of the fixture list would rumble on for another two decades.

Not everyone who sat by the wireless of a Saturday teatime ticking off their pools coupons ever went to a football match, or played the game. But an awful lot did. Football, long a game of the *demos*, needed little equipment apart from the ball, no special clothing or even full teams. Kicking a ball around on a piece of waste ground, or in the street in the days before the press of traffic made that impossible, by whoever could be mustered, the goal 'chalked on the wall, or a pullover artfully laid on the ground, that was football'. Boys played football (though public- and grammar-school boys were more likely to play rugby), men played football – many factories had teams – and some women had played football; but in 1921, when there were some 150 women's teams, including one from Lyons' Tea, the FA banned women's football matches from its grounds. This 'appeared to be just another attempt to subjugate a sport that was competing strongly with male football in terms of skill, crowds and gate receipts' – a match between a Preston team and the St Helen's AFC at Goodison Park that year had attracted a crowd of 53,000. Women, however, had to find other sports: by 1938, 160,000 played netball for clubs affiliated to the All England Women's Association for Netball, there were over a thousand women's hockey clubs, and probably over 6,000 women played for women's cricket clubs.

Watching football was a mass activity too, with unsurpassed crowds flocking to Wembley Cup finals and other major fixtures. When Scotland played England at Wembley in 1932, fifty-two special trains brought 23,000 supporters south; 93,000 watched Manchester City win the Cup final 2–1 against Portsmouth at Wembley in April 1934; and on New Year's Day 1939, 118,577 packed into a Rangers–Celtic game at Hampden Park in Glasgow. 74,088 went through the turnstiles at Tottenham's ground when they held the Cup holders, Sunderland, to a draw in 1938, and even League games from outside the top flight packed in the fans: 49,335 attended a Second Division game between Fulham and Millwall in 1938. Most spectators would have paid a shilling to get in, more if they wanted to sit under cover.

The star inter-war player who could pull in the crowds like none other was Stanley Matthews. Son of a barber who was also a professional boxer, Matthews first played for the team of the pottery town of Stoke in 1932 when he was seventeen; when, in 1938, it looked as he might transfer to another club, a packed public meeting, convened by local industrialists, met to dissuade him. The local newspaper, the *Evening Sentinel*, appealed, 'He is a star of the first magnitude. He cannot be replaced . . . Stanley Matthews must not be allowed to go,' and declared that this was the biggest story since the Abdication.

In the thirties Matthews, a right-winger with legendary dribbling skills, was paid the maximum wage for a footballer of £8 (which was more than double what the average working man earned). Many players earned less, though transfer fees were high – the first £10,000 fee had been paid in 1928, and in 1939 transfer fees totalling £272,000 were paid for players in the four Football League divisions. Wages were ostensibly pegged to ensure that the richer clubs did not corral all the best players, but also, covertly, to keep the game as far from being 'professional' as possible – though this hardly made the players amateurs, but rather 'emphasised their status as working-class hirelings'.

If Matthews was the star player, Arsenal was the star team. Though football's heartland had been in the industrial North in the earlier part of the century, Arsenal helped widen the focus. The team had been formed by a group of workers at the Woolwich armaments factory in South London in 1886, and moved to Highbury in North London in 1913. Under the chairmanship of the ex-Huddersfield Town manager Herbert Chapman, appointed in 1925, Arsenal dropped the 'Woolwich' from its name and changed its kit, pioneering the use of numbers on football shirts. Chapman also tried to introduce playing matches under flood-lights, which was common on the Continent, but the FA was having none of that, so he compromised, using a white ball when the light was poor. He brought in top-notch players, and rebuilt Arsenal's stadium in 1936 in a striking Art Deco style designed by the Scottish architects Claude Ferrier and William Binnie. The previous year he had persuaded the London Transport Board to change the name of the nearest Tube station from Gillespie Road to Arsenal. In the thirties Arsenal won five First Division titles and two FA Cups, one in 1930, the other in 1936. In 1939, managed after Chapman's untimely death by George Allison, who had been the BBC's first football commentator, known as 'By Jove', the team's members morphed into film stars in a thriller directed by Thorold Dickinson called *The Arsenal Stadium Mystery* – though only Allison, with his BBC accent, was given a speaking part.

Since football is closely tied to national and local identities, it was always likely to arouse strong, sometimes violent, emotions. In the inter-war years crowds would throw bottles and other missiles, swarm onto the pitch, swear, chant provocative songs and taunts, and fights and scuffles would break out on occasion. However, according to a historian of sport, Richard Holt, '"hooliganism" in the collective and contemporary sense did not take place at football matches' in the 1930s. Sectarian violence was an altogether different matter. Matches in Glasgow between the city's 'Old Firm' of Rangers (Protestant) and Celtic (Catholic) mobilised tens of thousands of spectators, adding a further incendiary spark to religious antagonisms that were tribal rather than doctrinal. The Protestant community, which comprised about three-quarters of the population of the city, a number of whom worked in the shipyard of the Belfast-based Harland & Wolff which had opened in Govan in 1912, was vociferously anti-Catholic and anti-Irish Republic, and had close links with Ulster loyalists, holding an annual 'Orange walk' that drew as many as 50,000 people. They tended to live in mainly working-class areas such as Govan and Partick. The Catholic community, living on the fringes of the city centre in areas such as the Gorbals, were of Irish descent (though most were Scottish-born) and identified strongly with Irish nationalism. Like their fellow Catholics in Northern Ireland, they were discriminated against in the labour market.

Violence frequently flared up outside the Ibrox and Celtic Park stadia, and fans on their way to matches were often viciously attacked with sticks, stones and bottles by rival gangs. There were two dominant street gangs: the fearsome Protestant 'Billy Boys', named after both King Billy and the gang's leader Billy Fullerton – 'Hello, hello, we are the Billy Boys!', their most well-known chant had it, 'Hello, hello! You'll know us by our noise!/We're up to our knees in Fenian blood,/Surrender or you'll die,/For we are the Bridgeton Billy Boys'; and the notorious Gorbals gang the South Side Stickers (not all its members were Catholic: there were a fair number of Jews and even Protestants). The sectarian battles were largely, but by no means exclusively, fought by young men. But older fans were keen to pitch in too, as in the case of thirty-eight-year-old Rangers supporter John Tranquair, who was accused of seriously injuring a Celtic fan when he and five to six hundred Rangers fans ambushed a train on its way to Ibrox for a match in March 1934. If it was hazardous to cross 'enemy' territory by foot or bicycle to get to a match, or to travel by train or coach to an away match, there were frequent altercations between Celtic and Rangers supporters in the city even when there was no match, some of which ended in serious injury, and on one occasion death. At the trial of a man accused of attacking a Rangers fan for making a derogatory remark about Celtic, the bemused judge remarked to the jury that 'For some mysterious reason that [he] could not understand, football and religious prejudice seemed to be very much mixed up in the minds of the particular class of people with whom they were dealing.'

Since the British considered their footballers – at the time – to be the finest in the world, the 'people's game' was inevitably enmeshed in the nation's international prestige. Sporting prowess was increasingly also regarded as evidence of a nation's virility, particularly among totalitarian regimes, as was brutally obvious during the 'Battle of Highbury' on 14 November 1934. Italy, the victors of the second World Cup (in which the British had declined to take part), came to play England at Arsenal's stadium, a match presumptuously billed as the 'real' World Cup final. It was rumoured that Mussolini had offered the Italian players the equivalent of £150, an Alfa Romeo car and exemption from military service if they beat the English. The game got off to a bad start: within two minutes the Italian centre-half broke his foot, and since no substitutes were allowed, the visiting team had to play the rest of the match a man down. It was the most violent game the young Stanley Matthews had ever seen: soon three British players were walking wounded, one with a broken nose, another with an injured ankle, the third punched and with a fractured arm – but they played on to victory, beating the ten-man Italian team 3–2.

In the years immediately after the First World War, the Allies refused to engage with Germany either politically or at sporting events. Germany was not invited to either the 1920 or the 1924 Olympic Games, and the FA vetoed football matches against Germany (as did its Scottish, Irish and Welsh counterparts). This isolationist (or insular) attitude, which kept the focus of British football narrowly domestic, spread to an on-off relationship with the international football governing body FIFA, and a refusal to take part in the first three World Cups, held in 1930, 1934 and 1938. However, since by the mid-1930s totalitarian regimes had come to equate sporting prowess with national power, the British Foreign Office started to make it clear that sport constituted an important flag-waving exercise and that it was essential that British teams acquit themselves well when they played countries such as fascist Italy and Nazi Germany, though the FO chose to deny this when it suited them, bluffly maintaining that such sporting exchanges were all about European unity and friendly cooperation. In December 1935 the German team was due to come to London for a friendly match against England at Tottenham Hotspur's White Hart Lane. The newly knighted TUC leader Sir Walter Citrine demanded that the match should be cancelled, both because sport was Nazi-controlled in Germany, with Catholics and Jews excluded from national teams, and in case fascist thugs infiltrated the crowd and made political capital of the occasion. The Home Secretary, Sir John Simon, declined. 'I do not think that interference on behalf of the government is called for . . . Wednesday's game has no political significance whatever . . . it is a game of football, which nobody needs attend unless he wishes, and I hope all those that take an interest in it from any side will do their best to discourage the idea that a sporting fixture in this country has any political considerations.' But it did: the German team gave the Nazi salute as they paraded onto the field, and the Nazi flag fluttered alongside the Union Jack. In front of a crowd of 60,000 (including some 10,000 Germans) Germany won 3–0.

A return match was played in Berlin in May 1938. Sir Robert Vansittart, the Chief Diplomatic Advisor at the Foreign Office, contacted Sir Stanley Rous of the FA to impress on him that 'it really is important for our prestige that the British team should put up a really first-class performance. I hope that every possible effort will be made to ensure this.' After much soul-searching, the English team gave the Nazi salute before the game, and went on to win a 6–3 victory, one of the goals scored by Stanley Matthews. So delighted was the FA with this demonstration of British supremacy on the football field that each player was presented with a canteen of cutlery on top of his £8 match fee (plus ten shillings travelling expenses). A further England v. Germany match was unavoidably delayed by war, and was not played until 1954.

'You do well to love it, for it is more free from anything sordid, anything dishonourable, than any game in the world,' Lord Harris, a dominant force in the MCC (Marylebone Cricket Club, founded in 1787), the sport's governing body, told young players in 1931. That was hardly true: though children played cricket in the streets with a plank of wood for a bat and a dustbin standing in for a wicket, cricket at national, international and county level was a sport embedded in a political, social and cultural morass in the thirties. Although the game was widely played throughout the country – except in areas where there was a large Irish population – it was a simulacrum of the British class structure, though one deeply imbued with a sentimental ruralism of whites on the village green, the squire bowling, the blacksmith scoring an impressive number of runs, the vicar's wife serving tea and cucumber sandwiches, the village coming together to the soft thwack of leather on willow.

'The football public is a cloth-capped fried fish lot . . . the cricket public is on an altogether higher plane,' wrote one cricketing journalist, though there was a rigid hierarchy within cricket too. The game was compulsory at most public schools and grammar schools, while elementary schools rarely had a playing field, and local authorities were reluctant to allow cricket to be played in their parks, so 'sport' for their pupils meant touching toes and stretching arms in the asphalt playground, unless they were fortunate enough to have a teacher who would arrange Saturday-morning games. Nor was it always easy for adults wanting to play recreational cricket either: between 1924 and 1934 seventeen Bolton cricket clubs had been disbanded because their pitches had been sold for house-building, and the National Playing Fields Association claimed that 1,700 out of a total of 13,000 acres available for sport within ten miles of Bermondsey was lost to housing by 1933; this was true wherever speculative building encroached. Those who were able to join a works team did better, since employers might be expected to provide a pitch.

Cricket mattered deeply in Yorkshire, which with Lancashire had more cricket clubs than any other part of the country. When the Yorkshire player Len Hutton broke the record for the highest score in a Test innings with 364 against Australia at The Oval in 1938, the Mayor of his home town of Pudsey sent him a telegram each time he scored another fifty runs, the church bells were rung 364 times, and a civic dinner was laid on for his return. Yet even in Yorkshire cricket was a class-attenuated activity,

The MCC was a self-perpetuating all-male elite. English county cricketers were divided into two separate camps: amateurs, or 'gentlemen', who were sufficiently wealthy to be able to play for the love of the game without needing to be paid; and professionals, or 'players', who were paid on a game-by-game (or tour-by-tour) basis. Professionals and amateurs playing for the same team would have separate changing rooms, go out onto the pitch through separate gates, and eat their meals separately. Amateurs had 'Mr' before their names on the scoreboard, while professionals just had their initials. Moreover, the England captain was always an amateur, in parallel with the distinction between officers and 'other ranks' in the army. It would have been no more thinkable for a professional to captain a cricket team than it would have been for a private to have been put in charge of a military unit. Even Jack Hobbs, possibly the greatest English batsman of all time, was never considered for the captaincy: 'He certainly should have captained England,' thought another professional batsman, Patsy Hendren, '. . . but he was a "pro" and I take it that on this account he was never even considered as a possible.' Hobbs, the son of a Cambridge college scout, seems to have accepted this discrimination without complaint. A dignified, church-going sports-shop owner, he 'knew his place' despite opening the batting for England in sixty-one Test matches, and scoring 61,760 first-class runs including 199 centuries between 1905 and 1934.

Some international Test matches attracted capacity crowds, especially when the Australians came as they did in 1930, 1934 and 1938. Huge crowds also packed into County Championship matches when old rivals were playing – Lancashire against Yorkshire, Northamptonshire against Leicestershire – games traditionally played over the Whitsun or August Bank Holiday weekends. However, the smaller crowds who flocked to most County Championship matches, which were played over three days, were predomin-antly middle-class, since the working classes found it harder to take that much time off, and particularly in the industrial North and Midlands tended instead to support their local league teams: 'The workers settled for league cricket. It was played on Saturday afternoons when they were free, and, what was more, little was demanded from the travelling point of view. As one old-time cotton worker put it: "Tha's got to be a man o'means to watch first class cricket . . . and besides, tha's expected to wear a collar and tie when tha goes to Old Trafford."'

League matches could attract huge crowds. Most teams employed paid professionals both to advise them on their play and to attract spectators. The star West Indian all-rounder Learie Constantine, who was paid more than £1,000 a season in the Lancashire League, could draw gates of 10,000; and another West Indian, the opening batsman George Headley, was also offered £1,000 to play for a Lancashire League team in 1934. League clubs were usually loyally supported in their locality, with members – or rather their wives – organising fêtes, bazaars and galas to raise money to pay the professionals' fees, and the numbers through the turnstiles were large enough to keep ticket prices low.

'Everybody seems to be a member of their respective Lancashire League club,' wrote a former England bowler who joined the Todmorden club as a professional in 1933. 'They would rather miss joining the Co-op than the cricket club, and when bad times make money scarce their sacrifices to enable them to pay their annual subscriptions are almost pitiful. In addition to paying their subscriptions, they do anything in their power to assist the club . . . [including] "ironing out" pitches – and I have seen men do as much voluntary work on Lancashire League grounds in a week as a paid groundsman in county cricket does in a fortnight.'

In the summer of 1930 the England cricket team was trounced by the visiting Australians, with the 'young Australian wonder batsman' Don Bradman breaking the then record for a Test innings at Headingley with 334 runs. During the return tour to Australia in 1932–33, England regained the Ashes using a tactic that caused great upset, called into question the notion of 'fair play', and threw an unsettling light on the British class system and the notion of Empire.

The English team was captained – naturally – by an amateur, a 'dour Scot', Douglas Jardine. Born in India and educated at Winchester and Oxford, Jardine was not, strictly speaking, a gentleman, since he earned his living as a barrister. Determined to counter the brilliant Bradman and regain the Ashes, Jardine devised a devastating tactic which the English referred to as 'fast leg theory' but which became known as 'bodyline', bowling fast, short deliveries directly at the unprotected upper body of the batsman, who was surrounded by a 'semi-circle of menacing fielders placed within yards of the wicket'.

No Australian batsman escaped the menace of the furious, phenomenally fast bowling of the Nottinghamshire ex-miner Harold Larwood and two of his almost equally fast colleagues – indeed the Australian wicketkeeper, Bert Oldfield, sustained a fractured skull – though injury was not the intention; rather the aim was to force the batsman to defend his body with his bat, thus providing an easy catch for the encircling fielders. The Australians complained that this was 'preventable brutality', and their captain, Bill Woodfull, who was himself hit over the heart by Larwood's onslaught, declared, 'There are two teams out there. One is playing cricket. The other is making no attempt to do so.' For their part the English maintained, in the words of *The Times*, that 'there was nothing unfair or unsportsmanlike or contrary to the spirit of the game in the tactics of the English captain and his men', and accused the Australians of being 'squealers', poor losers.

Possibly more than cricket was at stake. Australia was constitutionally sovereign, and not committed to imperial defence, and economically increasingly remote from British interests; 'the chief sentimental link that bound the two countries together, after the Crown, was a common devotion to cricket'. But it was still an imperial relationship: Australia had been the first nation that the MCC considered of sufficient standard to play Test cricket against England, and was still regarded as the only serious cricketing rival of the 'mother country', but the recent losses of the Ashes, first in 1920–21 and again in 1930, had come at an unfortunate time for British prestige, while the country was still suffering from the shock of the First World War and seemed to have lost its way, plunged into economic depression and political instability. An upstart 'young country' with a disdain for class differences and a strong commitment to democracy (at least for white, non-Aboriginal Australians) and 'barracking' vulgar crowds had seized the trophy, and then accused the Mother Country of unsportsmanlike behaviour when Jardine employed what the *Manchester Guardian*'s cricket writer Neville Cardus called 'tit for tat' tactics to get it back. Australia too had its grievances: a heavy war debt owed to Britain was eating up its export revenue, and it too had suffered in the Great War, losing thousands of men at Gallipoli in what many felt was an unnecessary sacrifice occasioned by the leadership of the British officer class, that same class whose representative was now trying to outwit Australia's legendary sportsman, Donald Bradman.

The sporting controversy further soured relations between the two countries: English immigrants were cold-shouldered by previously friendly Aussies, businesses in both Britain and Australia boycotted each other's goods, and a few years later a statue of Prince Albert in Sydney was vandalised and daubed with the legend 'Bodyline'. It was not until the Second World War that the strained relations between Britain and her former colony improved.

England duly regained the Ashes by winning the bodyline series, but the following summer, after the English team had played the West Indians, who used the same tactics against them in the second Test at Old Trafford that they themselves had so controversially used down under, the MCC, which had demanded that Australia withdraw the accusation of 'unsportsmanlike behaviour', decided that 'direct attack bowling' was 'unfair . . . and must be eliminated from the game'. Jardine never captained an Ashes team again, and Larwood was never again selected to play for England. In 1934, deprived of their lethal bowling tactics, England again lost the Ashes to Australia, which retained them for almost twenty years. As far as the West Indian Marxist intellectual and cricket writer C.L.R. James was concerned the bodyline controversy signalled the 'decline of the West . . . it was not an incident, it was not an accident, it was not a temporary aberration. It was the violence and ferocity of our age expressing itself in cricket.'

CODA

'The Only Thing We Have to Fear is Fear Itself...'

'Your readers may be interested to learn that Mr D.W. Brogan, MA, fellow and tutor of Corpus Christi College, Oxford, and author of *The American Political System*, has kindly agreed to lead a Study Tour to the United States to examine on the spot some of the more constructive aspects of the New Deal,' wrote Frank Darvall of the English Speaking Union to *Time and Tide* in January 1937. The intention was that the hoped-for party of 'university teachers, students, journalists and others especially interested in contemporary America' would leave England on the *Queen Mary* on 17 March and spend just over three weeks in the USA studying 'such aspects of the Roosevelt Experiment as the Tennessee Valley Authority, the Civilian Conservation Corps, the Subsistence Homestead Projects etc.' They would have the opportunity to meet 'a number of high officials responsible for the administration of the Experiment' as well as some of its critics.

Unfortunately, it would be an expensive trip: 'It is impossible to take the group over and back across 3,000 miles of ocean and over an itinerary of nearly 3,000 miles in the United States for less than £84.10.0 [nearly £4,000 today].' But the ESU hoped that 'the novelty and value of such a first hand experiment of such significance to a capitalist democracy like Britain will induce interested people to consider even such an expense'.

In July 1932, a year Beatrice Webb described as 'lurid with the sights and sounds of disintegrating capitalism', the US stock market had reached its lowest point, having fallen 89 per cent from its peak in 1929. Unemployment, which had been around 1.5 million in 1929, rose to 12.8 million, or 24.75 per cent of the workforce, and some 5,000 banks had failed. In November the citizens of America went to the polls. 'The whole world is directly concerned in the decision of the American electors,' wrote the *News Chronicle*, which while recognising that it was 'no part of a foreigner's business to interfere or take sides in the domestic politics of the United States', nevertheless welcomed the signs that victory looked likely for the Democratic candidate, Franklin D. Roosevelt, since, in the newspaper's view, if Herbert Hoover were to be returned for a second term, that would almost certainly mean higher tariffs, which would be disastrous for the British economy. J.M. Keynes referred to the 'magic spell of immobility' which hovered over Hoover's White House, with interest rates kept high to encourage saving rather than the investment that was necessary to kick-start the American economy. And there could be no worldwide recovery without a US recovery.

The Conservative MP Robert Boothby, who was in America on election night, considered that while the Americans were still committed capitalists they were aware of the system's 'grave defects' which had become apparent since 1929, and were 'ready and anxious to try something new and throw all their vitality and enthusiasm into it'. He was right. On 8 November 1932 Roosevelt won a landslide victory by over seven million votes, and the Democrats secured a substantial majority in Congress too. It was a new dawn, the *News Chronicle* decided: 'Twilight is fast descending upon America's gods of the last decade.'

The socialist Harold Laski, a frequent visitor to the US and probably better informed about the country than anyone else on the British left, caught a whiff of what he thought might be 'an American renaissance', and welcomed Roosevelt as 'the most hopeful figure who has entered the White House since Woodrow Wilson left it'. But he was doubtful about whether Roosevelt had the strength 'to take the right road' to cure America's economic and social crisis, and feared that his election would turn out to be 'in fact a pill to cure an earthquake'. The 'earthquake' being, in the words of the *Economist*, 'such trifles as the relief of twelve million unemployed, a new banking crisis . . . the vast agricultural population of America clamouring for relief . . . a huge budget deficit'.

Roosevelt's inaugural address was broadcast to Britain, the first time this had happened. *The Times* was delighted with a speech that in its view promised action, while the *New Statesman* was nothing short of incredulous: 'What is all this? The clap-trap of an international Socialist orating in Hyde Park? No, the solemn inaugural address of the President of the United Sates . . . Nothing about "economy" or "tightening our belts" . . . but the plain recognition of the need for a different basis of society.'

Recent manifestations of 'old' American society had not been much admired by the British public. There was the ever-looming issue of Britain's war debts, with 'Uncle Sam as an international Shylock'. New York had clearly taken over from London as the citadel of international capitalism, and as far as the left was concerned the main reason the

Labour government had collapsed in 1931 was the demands for heavy spending cuts by American bankers before any more loans were forthcoming. Apart from the question of domestic US pork-barrel politics, the lawlessness of American society, from Al Capone and the Chicago ganglands of the 1920s to the kidnapping and murder of the aviator Charles Lindbergh's toddler son in March 1932, sent shivers down British spines. 'Kidnapper headlines, gangster movies, their own inability to come over and see for themselves, and our peculiar conduct when we are on their shores have given the English unflattering ideas about us,' wrote the American journalist Kathleen Norris in *Reader's Digest*. And Denis Brogan's mother was amazed that her historian son should wish to study the 'murderous country' that had executed the Italian-born anarchists Sacco and Vanzetti for supposed murder in 1927, a case that became an international *cause célèbre*.

Roosevelt acted decisively: he excoriated the bankers, and dealt with the banking crisis by closing all banks for ten days. This stemmed the panic, although it hardly reformed the system, but the British press was delighted. The right was prepared to see it not as an assault on capitalism, but rather as an attempt to curb irresponsibility and selfish money-making. In a remark that seems remarkably up-to-date, Philip Guedalla, writing in *The Times*, defined an American banker as one who 'makes a dubious fortune by lending other people's money on insufficient security in the interval that he can spare from selling worthless bonds'. The Glass-Steagal Act in June 1933 separated investment banks (engaged in the capital market) from commercial banks (handling loans and deposits), since the blurring of this line was thought to have contributed to the Crash. Without warning Roosevelt took America off the Gold Standard, which devalued the dollar and pushed up the cost of US exports on the world market, and in effect he cancelled the outstanding debt Britain owed America from the First World War.

During his election campaign Roosevelt had declared, 'The country needs and, unless, I mistake its temper, the country demands bold, persistent experimentation. It is common sense to take a method and try it. If it fails, admit it frankly and try another, but above all try something.' In 1933 he embarked on a series of experiments which from the outside appeared like a cohesive programme, a New Deal for the American people.

The contrast with Britain seemed striking: optimism rather than defeatism, action rather than inaction, a plan rather than a flounder. 'I think,' Clement Attlee told the Commons, 'President Roosevelt is setting us a great example of energy in the way of dealing with things.' This was in stark contrast to the pronouncement of the President of the Board of Trade, Walter Runciman: 'We have terminated our schemes for dealing with unemployment by way of capital expenditure works and we shall not reopen these works no matter what may be done elsewhere.' In the US the initiatives were coming thick and fast: a massive programme of work relief, in the vanguard of which were the National Recovery Act (NRA) and the Works Progress Administration (WPA), which though derided by some as 'We Piddle Around' employed five million people by 1938, most on construction projects such as building roads and bridges, hospitals and airports, though professionals were also set to work overhauling public libraries, teaching in schools and running theatre projects. Denis Brogan was particularly impressed that under this scheme 'out-of-work actors were not offered jobs as navvies on the roads but as actors', and 'painters were encouraged to paint in post offices, which now have tolerable frescoes where we have air mail posters of a devastating competence'. He also applauded the 'most bold experiment of all, authors . . . enrolled by the "Federal Writers' Project"' to produce an impressive series of guide books to America'.

America's Social Security Act of 1935 established what Britain had had since 1909, old age pensions and unemployment compensation paid for out of taxes, though large numbers of the unskilled poor, particularly women and blacks, were excluded. That same year the National Labor Relations Act permitted US workers to organise unions and participate in collective bargaining. The Rural Electrification Administration (REA) set out to provide electricity to the countryside, where only one in ten farms had it, meaning that the other nine had no reason to buy the consumer durables that electricity made possible: fridges, vacuum cleaners, irons. The Tennessee Valley Authority (TVA), established in 1933, was an ambitious scheme to break the stranglehold of private power companies and establish a regional planning agency in one of the poorest parts of America, providing decent housing, improving crop yields, and putting thousands to work building dams and irrigation systems. But it was a one-off: entrenched interests vetoed the extension of the TVA to other states.

It was as if, Harold Laski wrote, Roosevelt was seeking 'with a passionate suddenness, to do, as it were overnight, something akin to what the Liberal Government in England had done after 1906'. Indeed the New Deal did pull off the shelf numerous ideas that had been tried in other countries, as well as those circulated at home. Joseph Chamberlain's programme of municipal socialism was one model, Lloyd Gorge's welfare reforms another, as were the British Industrial Disputes Acts from 1907 to the end of the First World War.

It was the comprehensiveness, the energy of the package, that exhilarated the British. A New World with a New Deal. A New Deal for a New World. For the first time in a generation America could be seen as a laboratory of social change, in which the economic ideas of John Maynard Keynes could be tried out in ways that they had not been in Britain, confounded as they repeatedly were by the 'Treasury View'. Even the staunchly Conservative *Morning Post* found it 'impossible not to contrast the energy and initiative of President Roosevelt's Government with the comparative inactivity of our own . . . no one would suggest that the same plan which meets America's needs would be suitable for the needs of this country . . . but that is not to excuse the British government from doing next to nothing . . . what message of help or leadership to spur on our nation as President Roosevelt is spurring his, as Signor Mussolini and Herr Hitler [who had come to power two months after Roosevelt] have spurred on theirs?' 'It is an immense experiment,' marvelled Lloyd George, who felt it dwarfed those in Italy or Russia. And Keynes himself, who was to have a rather unfortunate meeting with Roosevelt at which it was clear that the American President didn't have much of a clue what the British economist was talking about, nevertheless saw the New Deal as the most promising liberal experiment of the age. As he wrote in an open letter to Roosevelt in December 1933: 'You have made yourself the trustee for those in every country who seek to end the evil of our condition by reasoned experiment within the framework of the existing social system . . . If you succeed, new and bolder methods will be tried everywhere.' Roosevelt's programme offered a chance, Laski hoped, 'of showing that there is a genuine alternative to fascism and Communism' in those troubled times.

The New Deal would answer the pressing conundrum of the age: whether capitalism could be reformed to provide a decent standard of living for all the people, and whether that would be possible within a democratic system. 'Not only the citizens of the United States, but businessmen, politicians and economists all over the world are waiting for experience to furnish the answers to a hundred unanswered questions,' suggested the *Economist*. 'It will,' wrote J.A. Hobson, a Keynesian before Keynes, 'bring us the answer of history to the question whether a planned and ordered economy can be built on the foundation of private enterprise and ownership.' Several interested persons on the left hurried across the Atlantic to check it out. Margaret Bondfield, the former Minister of Labour, went in 1933: there was a 'real revolution of ideas ... sweeping through America', she reported to her Labour colleagues, and 'only wished that there could be the same enthusiasm, the same vitality, the same energy here'.

H.G. Wells went twice, paid generously by *Collier's* magazine to comment on the New Deal. He then flew to Moscow to try to convince Stalin that the American and Soviet experiments had much in common. Stalin was not persuaded: 'The United States is pursuing a different aim from that which we are pursuing ... the Americans want to rid themselves of the crisis on the basis of private capitalist activity without changing the economic basis ... The banks, the industries, the large enterprises, the large farms are not in Roosevelt's hands ... the army of skilled workers, the engineers, the technicians, these too are not at Roosevelt's command, they are at the command of the private owners.'

While most British people probably rarely gave the New Deal a passing thought, it continued to absorb the interest of those holding the centre ground in British politics, and anxious to investigate the practicality of a mixed economy in solving the problems of unemployment and economic decline. The New Deal had a significant impact on the thinking of the Next Five Years group, founded in 1935 by the marginalised Labour supporter Clifford Allen and the dissident Conservative Harold Macmillan among others. But for committed Conservatives who had no doubt that capitalism was the best possible economic system, and state planning was an anathema, the New Deal had proved, if had proved anything, that governments ought to refrain from 'interfering in matters in which they have no concern and confine themselves to their sole responsibility ... [namely] such things as balancing the Budget and reducing taxation'.

The TUC, however, was enthusiastic at its annual conference in September 1933, with one delegate praising the New Deal as the 'greatest adventure in systematic planning and control of industrial operation ... ever undertaken by a democratic nation'. Walter Citrine more circumspectly recognised that while the model was not an exact fit for Britain, 'the direction was essentially right. In the United States there was the first glimmer of real industrial recovery which had taken place in the post war world.' But there were dissenters who warned against forging 'a united front with capitalism'. The youthful Aneurin Bevan was scornful of the way, as he thought, delegates had been taken in, and Stafford Cripps expressed the view that it was futile, or worse, to attempt to modify capitalism, and was concerned that when the New Deal failed, as he was sure it would, disillusioned American voters might turn to the 'distinctly American type of fascism' represented by 'stunt politicians' such as Huey Long and Father

Coughlin.* Fenner Brockway (who journeyed to Washington too) decided that 'President Roosevelt will be regarded as the undaunted adventurer who challenged Destiny by attempting to rebuild a system that was crashing about him,' but was of the view that the task of 'sustaining an economic system which has outlived its day . . . is beyond the achievement of any human being', and he too feared that America might slide into fascism.

G.D.H. Cole, in a long and thoughtful article in the *New Statesman* in September 1933, insisted that while what was happening across the Atlantic was not the advent of socialism, Roosevelt was 'doing his best to boost Capitalism back to prosperity by an extensive policy of state control'. Cole understood why the TUC 'have naturally a keen desire to get their members back to work', which was why they were prepared to 'push any immediate Socialist policy into the background lest it should interfere with the prospects of a "Rooseveltian" capitalist revival', though he thought the model was worth trying. In fact, despite their critics, this was essentially what most union leaders thought too. Socialism was the goal, but it was a long-term project, and in the meantime their members needed work and security.

Even those who were perfectly prepared to put capitalism on the bench and tinker with the model until it was working again were somewhat uneasy about the legerdemain that the New Deal could be seen to be performing at great speed. William Beveridge had long recognised an 'unresolved conflict of opinion between the planned economy (such as the Russians are trying to work out though with many unnecessary mistakes of their own) and an automatic system using the mechanism of prices and the motive of profit to adjust the wishes of the consumers through their issue of purchasing power', and was 'not sure that there is any practicable half-way house' between the market and a command economy. He went to the US in November 1933 to report to the Rockefeller Foundation, and though he was impressed by what he saw in a country that had formerly 'derided dole . . . lectured the world on the wickedness of unbalanced budgets' and seen unfettered business enterprise as the precondition for economic growth, he was deeply pessimistic about the outcome, and still concerned – correctly – that Roosevelt was trying to pursue what were bound to be contradictory objectives in the conditions of the Depression, those of social reform and of economic stability.

---

* Long, a demagogic Senator from Louisiana, ran a campaign to 'Share Our Wealth' through progressive taxation, making 'Ev'ry man a king', able to buy his own home, car and radio, which is credited with moving Roosevelt to the left. Coughlin drew millions to listen to his radio talks blaming international financiers and Wall Street bankers for starving the nation of money. By 1934 he had withdrawn his support for Roosevelt and the New Deal, and was advocating monetary reform and blaming 'Jewish conspirators' for America's plight.

The ESU apparently did manage to attract sufficient interest to take a party to America in March 1937. They had a full programme, ranging from a talk by the labour organisation leader John L. Lewis to a special concert arranged by the Fisk University Glee Club in Nashville, Tennessee, during their tour of the TVA project. 'America seems a little undecided as to how far private enterprise should be assisted, controlled or perhaps entirely eliminated,' the group uncontroversially decided on their return.

By the following autumn, British interest in America had become more acute: the debate would no longer be about how capitalist or socialist the New Deal might be, how successful or disappointing it was, but rather about what the United States's attitude towards Europe would be in the event of war. Would America be prepared to be the 'arsenal of democracy' that Britain would so desperately need?

PART SIX

1938 to 1939

TWENTY-FOUR

A Scenic Ride to Catastrophe

Thank God our Prime Minister is a true angler! He possesses the patience, he strikes quickly at the right moment, he is willing to travel far for the fish he is after – whether the fish is salmon or Peace. His methods are always sporting and for the benefit of his brother anglers. He does not admit defeat.

Fishing Gazette, 8 October 1938, on the return of Neville Chamberlain from his meeting with Hitler at Munich

And still we finish where we started. What a pity the world's round! The most depressing discovery ever made.

Henry Trebell, speaking in Act IV of Harley Granville Barker's *Waste* (first performed in public at the Westminster Theatre, London, 1 December 1936)

I can see the war that's coming . . . There are millions of others like me. Ordinary chaps that I meet everywhere, chaps I run across in pubs, bus drivers, and travelling salesmen for hardware firms, have got a feeling that the world's gone wrong. They can feel things cracked and collapsing under their feet.

George Orwell, *Coming Up for Air* (1939)

'Well this was the day we were to have gone to war,' wrote Cyril Dunn, a twenty-eight-year-old journalist working on the *Hull Daily Mail* on 1 October 1938. 'Instead the Munich Agreement has been signed and Hitler has marched his army into Czechoslovakia without having to fight for it. Ivy, Peter and Mary [Dunn's wife, small son and live-in servant] have got their gas masks. (I didn't bother about mine – Peter was so pleased with his he was reluctant about even taking it off). They've stopped digging shelter trenches. Today the janitor has been trying to wash the black paint off the office windows without noticeable success . . . I'm dam' relieved war has at least been postponed . . . But I'm definitely unhappy about the Czechs and a bit uneasy about the loss of democratic prestige. I'm not alone in this. Moscow's paper [presumably a reference to the *Daily Worker*] called the Munich conference "The Committee for the Co ordination of Fascist Aggression". Hannen Swaffer [the *Daily Herald* journalist] said he had heard of crossed cheques; Chamberlain had shown him that Czechs could be double-crossed.'

Despite Dunn's unease at the price at which peace had been purchased, he had desperately wanted to avoid war in the tense weeks of September. 'We're learning the reality of a bad dream,' he had written. The situation really came home to him when 'I went to hear Professor Haldane lecture on the inefficiency of the government's ARP and learnt that no protection whatever against gas attack was proposed for children under four. That did it. John is 2½, Peter is 4 and likely to be made a gibbering idiot by a high explosive bomb . . . From the train [going to Liverpool] I saw people and soldiers digging trenches . . . Every night Ivy and I discussed plans for evacuating Hull which Haldane said was more dangerous than London. My idea was that they [his wife and children] should go to Bridlington leaving me here to carry on at the "Mail" office until I was "fetched" – when I should go in the Navy . . . As I came to bed last night, Peter whimpered in his sleep and I lay on my bed for ages in an agony. The kids have hopelessly complicated the idea of war for me. I haven't felt any personal fear – except of being a failure as a fighting man – but thinking upon the possible death, mutilation or crazing of the youngsters has made me a nervous wreck. We've listened to every possible word on the wireless. Ivy has even started to read the political news in the papers, to ask bewildered questions and to wonder why someone doesn't bump Hitler off.'

With the Munich Agreement, it appeared that the threat of war had lifted – 'Peace for our time', Chamberlain had promised when he landed at Heston airport on 30 September, after weeks of shuttle diplomacy between London and various German towns and spas. But as many suspected, 'our time' would have a short shelf life, and October 1938 would turn out to be the start of a countdown to war, what George Orwell called 'a scenic ride to catastrophe'.

By 1935 it had become apparent that Adolf Hitler's aim was no longer simply for German post-war recovery, but that his imperial ambitions would threaten the stability of Europe as Japan's had that of the Far East with the invasion of Manchuria in September 1931. On 12 March 1938, in yet another contravention of the 1919 Versailles Treaty following Germany's rearmament and reoccupation of the Rhineland, Austria was annexed in an *Anschluss* (link-up, or incorporation); in September that year Hitler took the next predictable step along the route of creating an empire that included German-speaking lands and the territories Germany or Austria had lost after the First World War. He demanded that the pro-Nazi Sudeten German minority in Czechoslovakia, 'this new-old country, this land of pleasing diversity', as holiday advertisements in the British press described it, should be reunited with their homeland.

This Sudeten fringe was of great strategic and defensive value to Czechoslovakia. However, the British Foreign Office had argued strongly against giving a guarantee of British protection to Czechoslovakia. 'I shall be called "cowardly"', Sir Alexander Cadogan, the Permanent Under-Secretary, had conceded in March 1938, but 'we *must* not precipitate a conflict now – we shall be smashed.' Ramsay MacDonald's son Malcolm, the Secretary for the Dominions, spoke of 'the massacre of women and children in the streets of London. No government could possibly risk a war when our anti-aircraft defences are in so farcical a condition. No Cabinet, knowing as they do how pitiable our defences are, could take any risk. All we can do is by wise retreat and good diplomacy diminish the dangers being arrayed before us. The Cabinet knows full well that we are shirking a great responsibility. But they cannot undertake such a responsibility.'

Although Czechoslovakia had an alliance with France and a treaty with the Soviet Union, and Britain was committed to aid France if Germany attacked her, the Western European powers had no desire for war; they were alarmed by what they believed to be Germany's overwhelming military might, and the British were conscious of the need to speed up their rearmament programme. Nor, in fact, did Italy's dictator Benito Mussolini, who was wary of German intentions, or indeed the Germany military, only too aware of the real state of its preparation. The stage was set for conciliation, which in effect meant persuading Czechoslovakia to 'make the best terms she can with Hitler'.

On 12 September 1938, at a speech at a Nuremberg rally, Hitler was unyielding in his refusal to accede to the more conciliatory Czech proposals and settle the dispute along the lines Britain was suggesting, and urged the Sudeten Germans to insist on their maximum demands, promising the armed support of German forces if necessary. The following day the Sudeten leader's ultimatum was rejected by the government in Prague, and a Sudeten uprising supported by German forces seemed likely. 'Europe seemed on the very brink of conflagration,' reported the *Annual Register*. 'At this critical moment the Prime Minister took a step as dramatic as it was unexpected with the object of staving off the impending evil.'

The dapper Neville Chamberlain, scion of the great Birmingham political dynasty, had none of his father Joseph or his half-brother Austen's flamboyance, but looked rather more like an Edwardian haberdashery counter assistant with his frock coat and stiff wing collar ('the Old Coroner', Conrad Russell, farmer nephew of Bertrand, called him in a letter to Lady Diana Cooper). Chamberlain had taken over from Stanley Baldwin as Prime Minister in May 1937, though he liked to think of himself as having been a 'sort of acting PM' for a couple of years before that, and had dominated Cabinet discussions throughout the 1930s. On 15 September 1938 the sixty-nine-year-old Prime Minister took to the air for the first time in his life. Believing that diplomacy and persuasion were Britain's most potent weapons in keeping the peace in Europe and limiting Hitler's aggrandisement, and that he himself possessed remarkable skills in those departments, Chamberlain had decided to confront the Führer in person, hoping that the initiative might 'appeal to the Hitlerian mentality . . . it might be agreeable to his vanity that the British Prime Minister should take so unprecedented a step'. It might have, but Chamberlain had misread Hitler's determination to seize the Sudetenland if it wasn't ceded by the Czechs. The British press was largely supportive of the 'dramatic stroke', and Mass-Observation reported that 70 per cent of those it polled believed Chamberlain's excursion was 'a good thing for peace'. But the First Lord of the Admiralty, Duff Cooper, was more pessimistic, believing there were three alternatives, or 'horses left in the race': '1. Peace with honour; 2. Peace with dishonour; 3. Bloody war. I don't think that no. 1 has an earthly. The other two are neck and neck.'

The trip to Hitler's mountain lair at Berchtesgaden in the Bavarian Alps was the first of three the Prime Minister would make that early autumn. It was brief and inconclusive, with Chamberlain saying that he could not agree to self-determination for the Sudetens without his Cabinet's approval, but feeling satisfied that he had 'established a certain confidence' with Hitler, and forming the impression that 'here was a man who could be relied upon when he had given his word'. Others disagreed. Trusting Hitler did not appear a sound option to Duff Cooper: 'He has got everything he wants at present and he has given no promises for the future.' For Harold Nicolson, Chamberlain and Sir Horace Wilson, the civil servant who was the Prime Minister's closest adviser and who had accompanied him, had had 'the bright faithfulness of two curates entering a pub for the first time; they did not observe the difference between a social gathering and a rough house; nor did they realise that the tough guys assembled did not speak or understand their language'. Hugh Dalton for the Labour Party was appalled at how Chamberlain had been flattered by the Führer, as if he had been 'a British working man with an inferiority complex' and Hitler 'a British nobleman', and warned the Prime Minister that this was unlikely to be the last of Hitler's demands: 'I believe he intends to go on and on until he dominates first all Central and South Eastern Europe, then all Europe, then the world.'

On 22 September Chamberlain travelled to the Rhine spa resort of Bad Godesberg near Bonn in a confident mood. The Czech President Eduard Beneš had effectively had to accept the partition of his country, since an Anglo-French visitation had made it clear that Britain would not support Czechoslovakia if she resisted German demands, and that the French were not prepared to honour their treaty obligations. The once and future Conservative MP Cuthbert Headlam was uneasy: 'Even if we are not actually pledged to go to the assistance of the Czechs, we were a party to the calling into existence of their unhappy country and are supposed to stand up for the smaller nations.' Indeed, Chamberlain's concession did not earn him much acclaim at home: only 18 per cent polled were supportive of his policy, while 44 per cent were 'indignant' at the concessions. Headlam reckoned 'we had been caught with our trousers down . . . This time we shall be lucky if we get out of this mess without war . . . clearly we must preserve the peace if we can – and this is obviously what Neville is out for – even if it means being called a "traitor" etc.' Winston Churchill went further, issuing a statement denouncing the partition of Czechoslovakia as 'a complete surrender by the Western democracies to the Nazi threat of force'. Crowds gathered in Whitehall chanting 'Stand by the Czechs!' and 'Chamberlain must go!', and as Chamberlain told an unsympathetic Hitler, he had been booed as he left Heston airport.

'Chamberlain is at this moment wrestling with Hitler for the second time,' wrote the Reverend Alan Don, chaplain to the Archbishop of Canterbury. 'The country has been very divided by what the PM's critics call the "betrayal of Czechoslovakia". Personally I cannot see what other choice was possible if war was to be avoided last week. If Chamberlain fails this week, he will at least have demonstrated to the world that he has gone to the last limit of concession and that only Hitler's brutal intransigence makes war inevitable. Meanwhile we wait in suspense, watching helplessly while the nations of Europe slither down into the abyss. Is it possible that in a week's time there may be bombs raining down from the sky on half the cities of Europe? Here in London we are hopelessly unprepared and the prospect is too horrible to contemplate.'

Although the Prime Minister received an ecstatic welcome from the German people, who shouted 'Heil Chamberlain!' and waved Union Jacks and swastika flags, he found when he crossed the Rhine from his hotel to Hitler's that the Führer had ratcheted up his demands, and was no longer prepared to accept peaceful progress towards redrawn Czech frontiers on the basis of self-determination for the German inhabitants. A 'solution must be found . . . either by agreement or by force . . . the problem must be settled definitely and completely by 1st October', he insisted. Chamberlain declined the ultimatum and returned to London 'with all the marks of failure', thought Cyril Dunn: 'war looks like certainty'.

The Cabinet rejected the Bad Godesberg proposals, as did the French, who promised to stand by the Czechs. Czechoslovakia had already mobilised. Now preparations were put in hand in France and Britain. Despite the fact that Chamberlain did not think that 'great issues' were at stake, and was well aware of the sketchiness of British military preparations, he seemed prepared to fight if German troops occupied Czechoslovakia by force.

As Queen Elizabeth broke a ceremonial bottle of champagne over the 'noblest vessel ever built in Britain' at the launch of the ship that bore her name at Clydebank on 27 September, the 'ARP are going ahead – trenches are being dug in the Archbishop's parks, – plans for the evacuation of practically all London schoolchildren are ready to be put into operation', reported Alan Don. 'The dislocation of normal life will be staggering at first, if the worst comes. The crypt, reinforced with sandbags . . . will be our "funk hole" it can accommodate 200 easily and will be available for outsiders.'

Thousands more sandbags (many of the sacks ordered from Forfar, giving a welcome shot in the arm to Scotland's ailing jute industry) were stacked round 'vital buildings'; anti-aircraft batteries were erected on Horse Guards Parade and along the Embankment, with the muzzles of the guns pointing to the sky; trenches were dug in London parks – including Hyde Park, Regent's Park, Green Park, St James's Park, Hampstead Heath, Hackney Downs and London Fields – by men working through the night under the glare of flares or the headlights of lorries. It was the same throughout the country. In Manchester, trenches were dug in parks and gardens, and a contractor friend of the businessman Raymond Streat was 'ordered to get 800 men to work day and night'. The ARP Committee in Hull produced a 'last minute scheme, mobilising all the building contractors in the city to dig a shelter trench for every family. It's going to cost "about a million" but nobody says a word', reported Cyril Dunn, though 'some householders are refusing to have shelter-trenches dug on the grounds that it will spoil their gardens!'

Through every letterbox in the land a leaflet plopped advising on the 'choice and preparation of refuge rooms in houses', precautions against fire and the operation of the Air Raid warden system, as well as giving instructions for how to construct 'a quick refuge for six in the back garden', using 'a corrugated iron roof, sandbags or boxes filled with earth and old boards'.

Tree trunks were whitewashed in anticipation of the blackout that would have to be imposed; loudspeakers were installed at all main railway stations to instruct civilians and soldiers. Gas masks were issued – though there were none for children under four; the best that could be done was to wrap them tightly in a blanket and carry them to the nearest gas-proof shelter – and people were taught how to put on and care for the monstrous rubber contraptions. Announcements were made at football matches urging people to go to have their masks fitted, and the same instruction was flashed on cinema screens, broadcast on the wireless, urged from the pulpit.

Lady Diana Cooper, whose husband Duff was deeply critical of any attempt to trade with Hitler, arguing presciently throughout Chamberlain's to-ing and fro-ing that the choice was 'not between war and a plebiscite but between war now or war later', was busy at her local ARP station with the 'grisly job [of] clamping snouts and schnozzles onto rubber masks, parcelling them and distributing them to queues of men and women', and having to explain that there were none yet for infants.

Cyril Dunn, who as a journalist had received 'a "Private and Confidential" from the F.O. asking us not to mention that coastal defence units had been mobilised', discovered that there were not enough people to distribute the gas masks in Hull. At one depot, 'The masks were all the same size! East Hull was . . . being attended to by *one woman* volunteer who couldn't even lift the boxes containing the masks.' In Oxford, Madge Martin and her husband Robert 'went to the Old Playhouse where we have seen such jolly, light-hearted plays, and were fitted for gas masks. It really depressed me more than anything to see the ordinary, patient crowd of men, women and children waiting to be fitted with these hideous monstrosities, just in the day's work . . . The waiting for news is *awful.*' In Wilmslow, 'the Legion Hall (where otherwise the Green Room Society would have been rehearsing a play) was used by the police as a warehouse to unpack the component parts, assemble them and distribute them by the hands of volunteers. In Manchester the schools were closed to children and used for the distribution of gas masks, and Raymond Streat 'saw long queues on my way home each evening'.

Streat toyed with the idea of whether he ought to join the army again, and wondered 'who was to determine where duty would lead a man of my age [forty-one] in my position'. He discussed with his wife what they should do about taking in evacuees in the event of war, since 'every householder in places other than cities was asked to state how many refugees they could and would shelter'. Doris Streat volunteered to take two, but the couple decided that 'if the refugees were dirty and unreliable, we thought we would let them live and sleep in the morning room, to which they could gain access by a separate entrance'. Fortunately it didn't come to that – yet.

On 28 September William Townsend, who had trained at the Slade under the intimidating artist Henry Tonks, called on various friends in London who were hastily packing up their studios as hired vans drew up to take their paintings to the country in case of war. That afternoon he went with another friend to the National Gallery in Trafalgar Square. 'The central galleries were already closed and while we were there some others were being shut up, but there were still Goyas and Grecos to see and the Venetians and the French and the English and we managed to enjoy them, and to be interested in the strange manoeuvres by which the glass was removed from the huge Van Dyck equestrian portrait. It was pleasant to see quite a lot of people in the gallery and to be able to believe that art was some use in a crisis: that there were some people who thought that pictures were the best thing for to-day, – the blackest day of all so far. It seemed to us then the last afternoon before war.'

As Chamberlain was reporting the dismal outcome of his latest visit to Germany to the Commons, news came through that Hitler had climbed down and agreed to an international conference to work out a solution to the Czech crisis. The Prime Minister hurried once again to the airport. This time a posse of politicians and diplomats flew with him to Munich. The Czech President was not present as the future of his country was decided. Nor was Stalin consulted. After twelve hours' heated argument it was agreed that the Sudeten Germans would be allowed self-determination within the boundaries of the Third Reich. The 'Munich Agreement' was signed, and Chamberlain asked to see Hitler alone. In the Führer's private flat, with only an interpreter present, Chamberlain asked and Hitler agreed to jointly sign a pact ruling out war between Britain and Germany and agreeing to accept negotiation and consultation as the basis for solving problems in the future. This was the piece of paper that Chamberlain was to wave so dramatically on his return to England. 'Peace for our time'.

The relief in Britain was palpable. As he went into chapel, Alan Don heard 'the thrice blessed news that the "Big Four" [Chamberlain, French Prime Minister Daladier, Mussolini and Hitler] had reached an Agreement in the early hours of the morning. Neville Chamberlain has brought it off. *Laud Deo*. It seems like a miracle . . . the universal relief is indescribable.'

'What a shave!' wrote Virginia Woolf. 'It would have meant our last 15 years of life spent in battling for a thread of liberty; keeping the [Hogarth] Press going among the deaths of the young. And now suddenly we can travel & move and use our normal faculties . . . I wonder if we could have faced it even here [in Sussex] – entertaining East end children in the hall; writing; getting all the dismal fag ends of things thrown at us; & reading casualty lists.' Chamberlain had himself lived through the horrors of the First World War and vowed that there must be 'no more Passchendaeles', and Raymond Streat mused, 'all this has forced anyone over the age of forty to recall 1914. A generation that has known war must be frightened of the prospect of having to endure it again.' Chamberlain was – briefly – a hero, 'Man of Munich' not yet the indictment it would soon become. As many as 40,000 letters and telegrams, nearly all of thanks and congratulations, flooded into Downing Street, and gifts came in embarrassing profusion. It was suggested that Chamberlain's umbrella should be broken up, the fragments sold like holy relics.

The Archbishop of Canterbury, Cosmo Lang, decreed that as Sunday, 18 September had been observed as a day of prayer, Sunday, 2 October should be a day of national thanksgiving. The publishers Eyre & Spottiswoode sent the Archbishop copies of the orders of service from 1919 and the end of the Boer War for reference. Cardinal Hinsley directed that *Te Deums* should be sung in all Roman Catholic churches, General Evangeline Booth ordered special services at all Salvation Army citadels, and in Westminster Abbey the ecclesiastical procession paused at the tomb of the Unknown Warrior as the congregation sang 'Now, Thank We All Our God'. Prayers were said for the 'stricken people of Czechoslovakia' and collections taken for their relief. In Liverpool, where intercessions had been held every quarter of an hour from midday to 2 p.m. during the height of the crisis, one of the clergy toured the streets in a car using a megaphone to urge shoppers to come to church to give thanks. The Archbishop of York divined the hand of God in the outcome of Munich. Britain's prayers had clearly been answered. What about those of the Czechs, one wonders.

Speaking in the House of Lords on 3 October, Archbishop Lang, who had roundly condemned the Italian invasion of Abyssinia in 1935, and the failure of Britain to do anything about it, was now 'sure that everyone would agree that almost any price was worth paying to avert the calamity', and spoke of 'three million people in a small district in the centre of Europe' towards whom 'Britain was under no obligation.' Dean Inge, late of St Paul's Cathedral, agreed: the nation should not be dragged into war for 'a ramshackle republic, not twenty years old that does not concern us in the least'.

Raymond Streat noticed that 'everybody is glad to escape the horrors we have been fearing but I do not find people jubilant. Thoughtful people are asking what are to be the consequences of peace secured by the terms agreed last Friday [i.e. 30 September]. Will it be real peace and will it last? Or have we yielded to a bully who will very soon press further demands until at length he presses on something that matters to us in a way that Czechoslovakia never mattered? Nobody has an answer.'

Virginia Woolf wrote when the procured peace was but two days old: 'Other emotions rapidly chase each other . . . peace seems dull. Solid . . . the opposition is already marshalling . . . some obliquity: after all we admired Ch.[amberlain] in the crisis. Is it fair to abuse him now?' Her husband Leonard was already predicting that 'we have peace without honour for six months'.

Rayon headscarves available in a London department store that October showed battleships, marching troops, gas masks and bombs. 'Peace in Our Time, 1938', read the ironic legend printed round the edge. And there were two high-ranking ecclesiastical dissidents: Bishop Henson of Durham and the Dean of Chichester, A.S. Duncan-Jones, believing that Munich was not peace but 'an international coup d'état', wrote letters to *The Times*, that stout organ of appeasement, but they were never published.

The debate on the Munich Agreement in the House of Commons had been scheduled to last for two days, but so many Members wanted to speak that it was extended to three and a half. For Labour, Clement Attlee was sonorous. It was a victory not for reason and humanity, he claimed, but for brute force. The Liberal leader Sir Archibald Sinclair spoke of the country 'wobbling to war', and from Chamberlain's own party Antony Eden was critical, Duff Copper had already resigned over the matter, and Winston Churchill was a tornado of fury and reproach, talking of total and un-mitigated defeat and humiliation. But Chamberlain received support from an unexpected quarter: James Maxton, the ILP leader and Glasgow MP, thanked him for doing 'something that the mass of British people want done'. When the vote came the government had a majority of 366 to 144 – 'so the PM can go and fish on the Tweed knowing that his policy has the support of [most] of his party'. But in fact, though pacifists within the Labour Party and the ILP voted in favour of the Munich Agreement, thirty Conservatives had abstained, including Churchill, Eden, Macmillan and Leo Amery.

'After the crisis – the cost.' *Picture Post* made the calculation after 'wide enquiry and exhaustive cross-checking' that 'Gone with the wind which blew out of Nuremberg last month is over £50,000,000 sterling . . . there is scarcely a householder in Britain who hasn't paid out some of his own money to convince Hitler that this country means business.' There had been the loss to industry and business, but almost half of the money had gone on the protection of the British civilian population: 'gas masks – £6,000,000

The roof gardens of Selfridges in Oxford Street, decorated to celebrate the Silver Jubilee of George V in May 1935. The theme was 'Empire', the statue of Britannia, flanked by two golden lions, stood eighty feet above the roof and trumpeters blew.

Princess Margaret Rose and Princess Elizabeth with their mother the Duchess of York and their aunt the Duchess of Kent at the celebrations to mark their grandfather's twenty-five years on the throne with a service of thanksgiving at St Paul's Cathedral on 6 May 1935. The Duke of York (within eighteen months to be King George VI) and the Duke of Kent can be glimpsed in the background.

Local residents crowd round the gates of Sandringham, Norfolk, to read the bulletin about the illness of George V being put up by the lodge-keeper's wife on 19 January 1936. The King died the next day.

On 21 January 1936 the swastika flew at half-mast on the German Embassy at 9 Carlton House Terrace as a mark of respect for the death of George V. In October that year Hitler's protégé Joachim von Ribbentrop was appointed German Ambassador to Britain.

The erstwhile Edward VIII, now Duke of Windsor, walks with his mother, Queen Mary, in the grounds of Marlborough House on 6 October 1945. It was the first time they had met since Edward's abdication nine years before.

In an effort to relax court formality during his brief reign, Edward VIII replaced what he regarded as tedious presentation ceremonies with garden parties. At one such event in Buckingham Palace gardens that summer of 1936, guests, caught in a sudden downpour, scurry for shelter.

'All my long struggle to win peace has failed...' The Prime Minister, Neville Chamberlain, and his wife Anne carry their gas masks as they walk across Horse Guards Parade for their customary morning walk in St James's Park on 7 September 1939, four days after the outbreak of the Second World War.

worth . . . sandbags . . . £3,000,000 . . . digging trenches across parks and green squares and building refuges . . . at least £2,000,000 in labour and appliances alone'. And then there were the sums individuals spent protecting their families – 600,000 people 'spent an average of £1.10s each on back-garden trenches and on making rooms gas- or splinter-proof. Another million, distrusting either such protection or their own ability to provide it efficiently moved themselves or their families well away from the towns or industrial areas where they lived. Average distance, thirty miles. Average cost, for the week of crisis . . . £3 per head.'

Despite all this emergency expenditure, Britain was woefully ill-prepared to meet the threat of war at the time of the Munich crisis. The Army Chiefs of Staff had warned the Minister for War, Leslie Hore-Belisha, that Germany would overrun Czechoslovakia in a week, and that British intervention would be like 'a man attacking a tiger before he has loaded his gun'. Though an ambitious programme of aircraft construction – 12,000 planes in two years – had been announced after the *Anschluss* in March 1938, the RAF had to rely on a large number of obsolete planes, incapable of effective action in modern warfare: a combined Franco-British air strike would only be able to deliver a third of the bombs the Luftwaffe could, and British fighter planes were considerably slower than the German machines they would have had to intercept. Coastal defences were not able to be deployed to maximum efficiency; the radar chain, warning of the approach of enemy aircraft, was incomplete, giving only partial cover between the Wash and Dungeness; the London balloon barrage was only about a third ready – 142 balloons instead of the 450 needed; the same proportion of the required anti-aircraft guns and searchlights were available, and many of those weren't working properly; and there were only sixty fire pumps in the whole of London. The navy had mobilised but officers' wives had had to turn out to keep the communications systems going. The lack of spares for both aircraft and ships was paralysing, and the government had refused a request from the Air Ministry to draft skilled workers into the munitions industry. As for the army, it had dwindled to five divisions, intended only for home defence and policing the Empire.

Clear moral choice? Political expediency? Pragmatic military necessity? Whatever the reason, Britain was not ready for war, whatever misgivings some might have about the price of peace. 'We don't want this war. No glorification, as Mrs Dean [the blacksmith's wife] remarked: the mouth-piece of the nation, as much as Chamberlain,' wrote Virginia Woolf. 'We cant help being glad of peace. Its human nature. We're made that way.'

But if the foundations of peace had been laid at Munich, it was now time to build the superstructure, as Chamberlain put it. And that would mean rapidly escalating the rearmament programme, with the distortion of the economy and the redeployment of manpower it would necessarily involve. It seemed a contradictory position, as Duff Cooper pointed out. If Chamberlain really believed Hitler's assurances that he had no further territorial ambitions, how could he justify laying the added economic burden on the British people that increased arms production would involve? Furthermore, effective and efficient rearmament would mean the disruption of peacetime industry and commerce and a creeping command economy, with resources, employers and manpower mobilised for war, something Chamberlain was not, as yet, prepared to implement.

Picture Post claimed that Munich had brought home 'to every elector that foreign policy may be as important as street lighting, new housing or the price of milk'. As Oxford and Bridgwater were both obliged to hold parliamentary by-elections in the month after the Agreement, these seemed something of a litmus test of public opinion. Foreign affairs dominated both campaigns, though in those essentially pre-opinion-polling days (although Mass-Observation reported on Oxford) it is hard to be sure exactly what swayed the voters. In both constituencies an anti-appeasement, non-party candidate stood, supported (after some wrangling) by both Labour and the Liberals. In Oxford the campaign between the young Quintin Hogg (later Lord Hailsham), fighting to retain the seat for the Conservatives, and the 'Progressive Independent' candidate, A.D. Lindsay, Master of Balliol, was bitter, fought out in slogans: 'A VOTE FOR HOGG IS A VOTE FOR HITLER' was met by 'HITLER SAYS DON'T DARE TO VOTE FOR LINDSAY'. In the event Hogg won: 'It is not my victory. It is Mr Chamberlain's,' he proclaimed.

> So Thursday came and Oxford went to the polls
> And made its coward vote and the streets resounded
> To the triumphant cheers of the lost souls –
> The profiteers, the dunderheads, the smarties

wrote Louis MacNeice in disgust.

Although Bridgwater, a predominantly agricultural Somerset constituency, was a safe Conservative seat, it had an unemployment rate of over 16 per cent. Yet this hardly figured in the campaign. The candidate who was eventually supported by both the Labour and Liberal parties was a journalist, Vernon Bartlett, who as foreign correspondent for the *News Chronicle* had covered Chamberlain's three visits to Hitler, and whose campaign attacked the government's 'weak and vacillating foreign policy' in meetings in every village and hamlet in the constituency. An unprecedented turnout of over 82 per cent gave Bartlett a resounding victory.

Did these results mean that the country was more pugilistic and eager to stand up for wronged, if faraway, nations than had appeared to be the case only weeks earlier? Did it mean that there was a groundswell in the country in favour of a united front against not only fascism but also against Chamberlain and his search for peace through a policy of appeasement? Probably not. However, the various peace movements, riven with internecine struggles about definition, personnel and tactics, had experienced a falling away of support by 1938, with many people no longer convinced that it was right to meet violence with inaction. The League of Nations Union, which had peaked at 400,000 members in 1931, had 264,000 by 1938; the No More War Movement had considered merging with the Peace Pledge Union. That did not materialise, and membership plummeted; even the PPU never managed to attract many more than the 120,000 members it had achieved in 1937.

Although many on the left argued that a united front with Russia would have avoided the need for the Munich settlement and an arms race, the Labour Party remained divided between a few absolutist pacifists (George Lansbury had lost the party leadership to Attlee over this issue in 1935), those who wished to continue to pursue disarmament and a rather vague notion of collective security through the League of Nations, and those who favoured increased military spending and a more active struggle against fascism, though not in order to save Chamberlain and the British Empire.

Rearmament would always be a particularly thorny issue for the Labour Party, which was accused by some Conservatives of being vociferous in its demands for arms for Spain, while refusing to countenance them for Britain. There was Labour outrage that while the National Government had largely declined to invest in public works to provide work for the unemployed, it was apparently prepared to do so in order to produce weapons. As Attlee charged in February 1937 when Chamberlain proposed to raise £400 million for armaments over five years, 'Do you remember the scream against the Labour party's unorthodox finance in 1931 when they borrowed £100,000,000 for life? . . . *Now we are going to have £400,000,000 for death.*' Money spent on arms would divert resources from housing, schools, roads and other civil projects.

There were still 1,800,000 registered unemployed and a further 200,000 unregistered at the beginning of 1939, and as the *Daily Herald* wrote, 'What national problem compares in importance with unemployment? What evil comes near it in magnitude? . . . We face an international crisis demanding of Britain that she should stand at the peak of efficiency and produce to the maximum. And we have an eighth of our total labour force doing nothing . . . It is intolerable and it should not be tolerated.' While Britain's economy had been gradually recovering since 1932, thanks to new industries, cheaper money, more efficient investment and the housing boom, and unemployment was slowly falling – or rather employment was rising – an export crisis in 1937–38 had seemed to presage another slide into slump. It was largely expenditure on armaments that would cushion this, particularly in the old staple industries of coal, iron, steel and shipbuilding. John Maynard Keynes, speaking in February 1937 in support of the government's five-year defence spending package, argued that 'the sums which the Chancellor of the Exchequer [Chamberlain] proposes to borrow are well within our capacity; particularly if as much of the expenditure as possible is directed to bringing into employment the unused resources of the Special [i.e. depressed] Areas'. Had the government refused to borrow to invest in arms production and defence, unemployment might again have reached three million in 1938.

Within a month the fragility of the Munich Agreement had become apparent. On 9 October Hitler made an aggressive speech at Saarbrücken, not welcoming peace but speaking of the need for Germany to strengthen her fortifications in the West; on 6 November in Weimar he made a derogatory remark about the 'umbrella-carrying bourgeois' Chamberlain, and suggested that the rest of Europe was still hostile towards Germany; on 8 November in the same beer cellar in Munich where he had started the unsuccessful *putsch* of 1923, he threatened that the German people would 'secure for ourselves our rights by another way if we cannot gain them by the normal way'. It hardly sounded like peace for our time.

On 9 November, in retaliation for the shooting of a German embassy official in Paris by a seventeen-year-old Polish Jew protesting against the persecution of Jews in Poland, the Nazis unleashed 'an organised campaign of plunder, destruction and violence' against Jews throughout Germany and Austria. Synagogues were set on fire or dynamited. Shops owned by Jews had their windows smashed and were ransacked, the contents thrown into the street. Jewish offices were broken into and Jews were assaulted and murdered, turned out of their homes and chased through the streets by gangs of Hitler Youth – 'boys of the same age as Boy Scouts in England' – wielding axes and shouting, 'Germany Awake! Perish Judah!'

During these 'spontaneous' acts, 'hardly a policeman was to be seen in the streets other than directing traffic', and none did anything to halt the rampage. Parts of Munich looked as if they had been bombed. Jews were given forty-eight hours to leave the city, and Nuremberg too. The Jewish community was 'fined' the equivalent of nearly £100 million for the destruction it was alleged to have provoked. All insurance for Jews was cancelled, they were thrown out of skilled jobs, banned from places of entertainment and culture and ghettoised, allowed only to walk along certain streets. Thousands were arrested. 'It is not known what is to be done with them,' *The Times* reported ominously. It soon was. Some 30,000 male Jews were despatched to concentration camps that had been built to contain political prisoners. It was, concluded *The Times*, a 'scene of systematic plunder and destruction of which we have seldom seen the equal in a civilized country since the Middle Ages'.

'The disgusting and brutal reprisals in Germany ... render it very difficult to regard the Nazis with any feeling of good will or toleration. Coming as this does when people are trying to thinks of ways of appeasement, it almost makes one despair,' wrote Alan Don on Armistice Day; 'poor Jews, their plight is utterly pitiable'. A letter in *The Times* from Margot Oxford (formerly Asquith), who had formerly applauded Chamberlain's act in 'holding out a hand rather than shaking a fist', agreed: 'We are no longer dealing with a man of Munich whose professions were of peace and goodwill.'

Although Chamberlain rejected the idea of a formal protest to the German government about *Kristallnacht* (the night of broken glass, as the atrocities came to be called), he was prepared to respond to the 'very general and strong desire that something effective should be done to alleviate the terrible fate of the Jews in Germany'. But not by loosening Britain's tight controls on Jewish immigration, which meant that visas were only granted to those refugees who would not become a charge on the state, meaning that not only was an employer prepared to certify his willingness to employ them, but that 'no competent national is available to fill the vacancy'. This economic nationalism in effect meant that almost the only people fleeing Nazi persecution who were allowed into Britain were the wealthy, the distinguished, or women prepared to work as domestics or men who could alleviate the chronic shortage of rural workers. Heartbreaking pleas seeking sponsorship appeared daily in the *Jewish Chronicle*, and those seeking a relaxation in the stringent visa requirements could point to the job opportunities Jews had brought to Britain: in industry in the Midlands for example, or the fur trade in London from furriers evacuating Leipzig. By 1938, seventy-five Jews a day were being admitted – a figure the government was reluctant to disclose, since it feared flak both from those who thought it was too many and those who thought it lamentably few. Between 1933 and 1938 around 11,000 refugees arrived in Britain from Germany and Austria, most admitted on the understanding that they would re-emigrate to the US – of these, 85 to 90 per cent were Jewish.

With thousands of applications being received each day following *Kristallnacht*, the Cabinet discussed 'The Jewish Problem' on 16 November. Chamberlain, who admitted in private that he was no lover of Jews, though he was highly critical of the persecution they were facing, thought that the answer to the increasing exodus from Nazi countries was to resettle them in the Empire. From outside the Cabinet, Winston Churchill suggested that tropical British Guiana might be suitable, but Chamberlain thought 'that would be a long and very expensive business'. The sad discussion petered out.

However, in response to a deputation of Anglo-Jewish leaders on 15 November, Chamberlain did make a limited distinction between a long-term resettlement policy and immediate short-term humanitarian needs, and agreed that unaccompanied Jewish children aged between five and seventeen could be admitted to Britain without needing an individual visa for what was intended to be a transitory stay until they could be shipped on, though this was never clearly specified. There was to be no quota on the number allowed in, but the children were not to cost the British taxpayer anything. Jewish relief agencies were required to post a £50 bond (more than £2,000 today) for each child, and appeals were made both within the Jewish community and beyond for money and accommodation. Earl (Stanley) Baldwin launched an appeal in December 1938 for the victims of 'man's inhumanity to man'. 'Get Them Out Before it's Too Late' urged the posters. The fund raised £500,000.

On 2 December 1938 the first party of the *Kindertransport* (trainloads of children) arrived at Harwich from Vienna. By the end of August 1939, 9,354 children had arrived from Germany and Austria, the vast majority of them Jewish. The heartbreaking task of selection fell largely to the Quakers: they gave priority to orphans (many Jewish orphanages had been burned to the ground on *Kristallnacht*) or to children whose parents were either in concentration camps or had been deprived of their home or the ability to earn a living. Parents were desperate for their children to get away: a few were able to get a visa and to follow, like the mother of the journalist Hella Pick. But most, having selflessly given their children the opportunity of a new life, of survival, would themselves perish in the camps.

At first most of the children were accommodated in a holiday camp at Dovercourt Bay near Harwich, where they stayed for a few weeks learning English. It was a very difficult time for them. Children and young people of all ages and with very different backgrounds were crammed together until they could be found a foster home. There were language difficulties, homesickness, misunderstandings and the ever-present gnawing fear felt by all but the very youngest of what was happening to their families left behind.

Finding suitable foster homes was not easy, though they were only supposed to be temporary until the young people could be sent to the US or 'to help fill up those empty spaces in the Empire', as *Picture Post* put it. Some children from Orthodox homes found it very hard to settle into non-observant households. Rabbi Solomon Schönfeld, who brought 750 children over from Berlin, wrote an impassioned letter on behalf of his fellow London rabbis expressing their dismay that Jewish refugee children had been placed in non-Jewish homes. While acknowledging the spirit of charity in which these offers of accommodation were made, Schönfeld and his colleagues requested 'a definite assurance that children so placed will be transferred to Jewish homes, and that no Jewish children will, in future, be placed in such homes . . . they deem it their sacred duty to call public opinion to this virtual apostasy of Jewish children entrusted to Anglo-Jewry'.

Some children were taken in, as British evacuees would later be, as cheap labour, others were treated cruelly, even abusively, and there were many examples of anti-Semitism shown to both children and adults. But there were many good stories too: the father of the film director John Schlesinger, a doctor at Great Ormond Street Hospital for Sick Children, bought a house in Highgate with some money he had inherited, and housed twelve refugees there and gave work caring for them to others who had fled Nazi persecution. Stella, Lady Reading, widow of a Viceroy of India, was among the many dedicated volunteers who worked tirelessly at Bloomsbury House to help Jewish refugees.

There was heavy snow at Christmas 1938, and it was bitterly cold. Icicles hung for days from the concrete walkway of the penguins' smart new compound at London Zoo. 'It's been a bad year,' Harold Nicolson wrote in his diary on 31 December. 'Chamberlain has destroyed the balance of Power, and Niggs [his son Nigel] got a third. A foul year. Next year will be worse.' 'I have never started a year with more foreboding,' wrote Samuel Rich, a teacher at the Jewish Free School in North London, in his diary on 1 January 1939. 'Doom is in the air.'

In January 1939, although unemployment still stood at around two million, there were no more hunger marches in England or Wales, though in Scotland there had been a march converging on Edinburgh in November 1938. Five hundred had marched along Princes Street to the strains of 'The Internationale', some still wearing the blue berets of the International Brigade, having returned from the fight that was being lost in Spain, fists clenched, demanding work projects including new bridges across the Tay and the Forth, a ship canal and the development of the Highlands.

In London, the tactics organised by the NUWM, were different: spectacles designed to keep the grim facts of unemployment at home in the minds of those whose eyes were now largely focused overseas. In late November two hundred men had marched into the Ritz Grill in one of London's swankiest hotels and demanded tea for tuppence: after much flapping, conferring and confusion, they were served. On 20 December, when the West End was packed with Christmas shoppers, two hundred men lay down in the middle of Oxford Street chanting 'Work or bread' and 'We want extra relief'. On Christmas Day 150 of the unemployed turned up outside the home of the chairman of the Unemployment Assistance Board and serenaded his family with carols: 'Therefore Christian men, be sure, wealth or rank possessing,/Ye who now will bless the poor, shall yourselves find blessing.'

On 30 December a banner was unfurled at the top of the Monument in the City. It read: 'For a Happy New Year the Unemployed Man Must Not Starve'. On New Year's Day, a mock funeral procession wound its way through the streets of London following a black coffin on which the words 'He Did Not Get Winter Relief' (an extra 2s.6d for every unemployed adult, and a shilling for each of their children, to cover the extra fuel and food needed in cold weather) had been painted. Some onlookers bared their heads as a mark of respect, but the police refused to let the procession approach St Paul's Cathedral, fearing this might be regarded as offensive.

The protests continued throughout the spring of 1939. Unemployed men called on expensive restaurants in the West End of London demanding that their hunger should be assuaged too, some invaded Crufts dog show, fifty lay down under unfurled banners at a world conference on recreation and leisure at the Savoy Hotel proclaiming 'Hungry Leisure is No Pleasure', the Lord Privy Seal nearly stumbled across the recumbent bodies of men demanding 'Work for the Unemployed on ARP' at a dinner hosted by the Allied Brewers.

Others chained themselves to railings in front of the home of Ernest Brown, the Minister of Labour, demanding 'Release us from hunger,' and delivered a letter explaining that 'We are compelled to resort to this method of protesting in order to get you to see the justice of our demand for work or bread.' The tactic caught on: soon police with hacksaws were sawing men free from railings outside labour exchanges in Camden, Stepney and Holloway. Men lay down in the snow in Edinburgh, others chained themselves together to protest in Alloa, and banners were flown from churches in Dundee and Kirkintilloch.

Coffins became ubiquitous that winter: they were carried to Downing Street and into the precincts of the House of Commons, and to Victoria station on 10 January as Chamberlain and the Foreign Secretary Lord Halifax left for Rome to meet Mussolini, accompanied by shouts of 'Appease the unemployed – not Mussolini!'

The Rome visit had been agreed at Munich: Chamberlain was always hopeful that Mussolini would prove to be an ally of Britain and a restraint on Hitler. But there were anxieties that the trip would be another round 'in the pursuance of appeasement', and that the Prime Minister and Il Duce would come to some agreement over Spain or Italian intentions towards French colonies. Chamberlain 'would have done better to stay at home', advised the *News Chronicle*, since his 'previous visits have always resulted in his giving away something – something belonging to other people'.

In the event it was a fairly pointless journey. After a round of talking, eating, drinking and opera-going, a communiqué was issued on behalf of both countries which spoke of 'great cordiality', 'a frank and wide exchange of views', and a determination 'to pursue a policy which aims effectively at the maintenance of peace'. Clutching what looked like a new brown umbrella, Chamberlain, after a brief visit to the Pope, got back on the train, was waved off by Mussolini, and returned to London.

On 14 January star-studded concerts had been arranged to raise funds for Baldwin's appeal for Jewish refugees, and all London cinemas gave 10 per cent of their takings that day to the refugees. In Piccadilly a fascist demonstration insisted 'Britain for the British' and queried why there should be a relief fund for 'Czechs, Austrians, Basques and Jews while British unemployed are starving?' The NUWM mounted a counter-demonstration insisting 'The Unemployed are not enemies of Refugees. Help them Both.'

While Chamberlain had been in Italy 'trying to conjure away the danger of war with his diplomatic activity, the work of rearmament had been going on with undiminished vigour'. Sir John Anderson, the Lord Privy Seal, was in charge of civilian defence, and on his return from a skating holiday that was considered rather overlong in the circumstances, he announced that 120,000 tons of steel sheets had been ordered, sufficient to make what would become known as Anderson shelters, backyard air raid refuges intended to protect against bomb splinters and falling debris (but not a direct hit). Local authorities, which had been obliged to submit plans for the protection of their boroughs at the beginning of 1938, were given more resources to do so, and were urged to step up their efforts to recruit and train ARP wardens. On 8 February they were asked to prepare lists of households that would be eligible for free air raid shelters – such households had to have an income of less than £250, and a garden big enough to accommodate a shelter. By April 300,000 'Andersons', sufficient to shelter one and a half million people, had been delivered.

But would some corrugated tin in the garden, or a brick-built shelter in the street, really prove an adequate defence against German heavy bombers? Those who had observed the raids on Barcelona thought not. In a book published just before the Munich crisis, the eminent scientist J.B.S. Haldane claimed that most of the government's precautions were 'the merest amateur trifling'. In his view 'the pressing necessity was to act and act quickly with the resources that are available'. Everyone needed to know exactly what to do in an air raid, and as many people as possible – children, the elderly and infirm 'those whose presence in a vulnerable area serves no imperative national or industrial purpose', which in London might amount to as many as two million people – should be evacuated. A card index of available accommodation within fifty or sixty miles of the areas most at risk was urgently needed, 'and as far as possible billets must be assigned beforehand; on many grounds billeting appears preferable to organising camps for the evacuated'. Haldane believed that, with proper preparation, this mass of people could be moved in less than two days.

For those who had to remain in London, he proposed that a 780-mile system of completely self-contained brick or concrete tunnels, sixty feet under the ground, should be built to hold all 4.4 million residents of the LCC area, at a cost, he reckoned of £11 per head, or £500 million in all. It would take at least eighteen months to construct such a network, which was the time it had taken the Spaniards to dig their deep shelters. Meanwhile – and the meanwhile was to last until 1944, when the first deep shelters in London were opened – other preparations gathered momentum. But Haldane continued to insist that above-ground shelters would give scant protection in an air raid. In February he was photographed fishing for eels in a trench on Hampstead Heath, dug at the time of Munich but which had subsequently filled up with water. 'Bring Anderson to 'eel', read the lame poster, on which Haldane was surrounded by the unemployed, since he argued that the necessary extensive anti-war preparations would provide much-needed work.

On 23 January Chamberlain broadcast to the nation about 'the Government Scheme of Voluntary National Service . . . It is a scheme to make us ready for war. That does not mean that I think that war is coming. You know that I have done, and will continue to do, all I can to preserve peace.' The next evening the campaign was officially launched at the Albert Hall, and this time it was Sir John Anderson who stressed, 'We do not expect war either now nor in the near future.' Within days a forty-five-page booklet was sent to every household in the country outlining the various tasks for which volunteers were needed: younger men could join the Auxiliary Fire Service or the Territorial Army, while under the heading 'Mainly for Older Men' was listed ARP wardens, ambulance drivers and police war reserves, while 'Opportunities for Women' included ARP wardens, the Auxiliary Fire Service, first aid and more.

On the same day a list of reserved (or scheduled) occupations, regarded as essential in wartime, was published. People working in those jobs would not be recruited into war work – at least, not those beyond a specified age. It was a very detailed list, covering some five million workers in a vast range of occupations, from poultry farmers to laundry workers, lighthouse keepers, medical practitioners, prison warders and hundreds of other precisely specified roles – some of which, like *chefs de cuisine*, jewellers, shirt-sleeve makers and ice-cream sellers, seemed hard to justify as being 'essential to the war effort'. This left between six and seven million men between sixteen and sixty-four who were not in reserved occupations, the younger of whom would therefore be available to fight – not that there was any compulsion to join the armed forces as yet. It was made clear that those in reserved occupations would be encouraged to volunteer for civil defence work to fit round their jobs.

In Spain the civil war was coming to a climax. 'Franco at Gates of Barcelona' read the newspaper headlines on 24 January, as the city was bombed and strafed by the Italian air force. The Republican army was exhausted, and starved of weapons and equipment. Attlee charged that the British and French policy of non-intervention meant that the Spanish government was not able to obtain the arms it needed to defend itself from foreign aggressors. Anthony Eden agreed. He had resigned as Foreign Secretary in February 1938, telling Chamberlain that he had become 'increasingly conscious of the differences between us . . . in respect to the international problems of the day and as to the methods we seek to resolve them', though he quit not over objections to Chamberlain's appeasement of Hitler, but over Britain's recognition of the Italian conquest of Abyssinia, arguing that Italy must withdraw most of her troops from Spain first: 'Everyone knows who provides the formidable air power and artillery power . . . How can any of us deny that if Franco wins, his victory will be a foreign victory?'

'Our policy should be to get on the right side of Franco and leave him to rid himself of his Italian and German allies,' thought Cuthbert Headlam, but he recognised that this would be difficult, because 'people in England are so foolishly hostile to Franco'. Some of that 'foolishness' was expressed when, although the Republicans continued to fight for Barcelona, on 28 February Britain and France recognised Franco's regime not as rebels or usurpers, but as representing the legitimate government of Spain. Protesters marched through the streets of London and Liverpool carrying banners and chanting 'Arms for Spain', while Attlee told the crowd in Trafalgar Square that 'By their actions the British government has not only betrayed the Spanish people but democracy throughout the world.' In the House of Commons Chamberlain justified the decision on the grounds that it merely recognised a *fait accompli*, since Franco was in possession of most of Spain. He added an appeasement gloss: 'No one could read accounts of the pitiless procession of wounded men, old men, women and children, without feeling what a terrible thing war is, even in its secondary effects, and how much more it would mean if hostilities were extended.'

On 15 March, German tanks rolled into Prague. It was the end of the fragile independence of Czechoslovakia, the repudiation of the Munich Agreement, and, wrote Cuthbert Headlam, 'the death knell of poor Neville's policy of appeasement, and equally of course all his opponents will say "I told you so!" It is also the end, I should imagine, of any dealings with Hitler – the man henceforth should be treated as outside the pale – and when we are strong enough should be fought.' The *Daily Telegraph* saw that 'a ruthless tyranny is spreading its coil far and wide in Europe. Not one single one of Germany's neighbours is henceforth safe from the deadly embrace . . . The Spirit of Munich is dead and buried, for who can hope to appease a boa constrictor?'

For days the press were 'raging about Hitler; rumours of further "swoops" in Eastern Europe; Tory MPs said to be discontented with Hitler; everyone restless'. The most vulnerable to the boa constrictor was Poland, whose frontier with Germany had been increased by two hundred miles by the occupation of Czechoslovakia. On 21 March Hitler demanded the return of the city of Danzig from Poland; two days later German troops occupied the Baltic seaport of Memel, part of an independent Lithuania, and Hitler declared that though he had no intention of imposing suffering on the rest of the world, the 'new Germany' was 'determined to master and shape its own destiny even if this does not suit the outside world'.

'It's getting harder and harder for the English public,' George Orwell wrote to his friend and fellow writer Jack Common. 'I suppose about 50 per cent of them knew whereabouts Czechoslovakia was, but where is the Ukraine? And where are Memel and Eupen Malmedy, not to mention Russian Subcarpathia? The only people who can really keep up these days are philatelists.' On 31 March Chamberlain announced 'a British guarantee of Polish "independence" (whatever precisely that is) which seems as liable to cause the loss of millions of lives as the similar guarantee of Belgian neutrality which brought us into the War of 1914', despaired the pacifist Vera Brittain.

This commitment hardly seemed to alarm Hitler. Three days later he secretly ordered his generals to prepare for an invasion of Poland anytime after 1 September, and on 28 April he announced that he would no longer be bound by the terms of the Anglo–German Naval Agreement of June 1935, which regulated the size of the *Kriegsmarine* in relation to the Royal Navy. On Good Friday, 7 April, Italy had occupied Albania, which no one had guaranteed to protect, and on 22 May Hitler and Mussolini signed a political and military alliance dubbed a 'Pact of Steel' by Mussolini, who was advised that 'Pact of Blood' might prove unpopular in Italy. 'The terrible inevitability of war has descended upon us,' wrote Chips Channon in his diary.

The Budget, announced on 25 April, allocated £1,322 million to be spent on defence. A few days earlier the government had announced that it would set up a Ministry of Supply, Chamberlain reluctantly conceding that the requirements of war meant that the state had to take control of the allocation of materials, production and eventually labour (though not of the aircraft industry, which had a separate ministry).

Rearmament, the manufacture of guns, bombs, battleships and aircraft, the building of munitions factories and airbases, might – whatever else it indicated – be expected to presage an end to unemployment, new jobs at last in the industries of war. But it was not always that simple. As Chamberlain (then Chancellor of the Exchequer) had explained during his budget speech on 23 April 1936, the government *could* assume the power 'to order any particular industry or firm to cease its commercial work and turn itself to war work . . . there is no doubt that if powers of that kind were taken you could speed up the programme [of rearmament] very materially, but . . . it would mean that you would have to cease from proceeding with a great deal of commercial and industrial work . . . orders would have to be cancelled, would go elsewhere, and in future you might not easily regain the markets which we had set aside'. In his view, by the spring of 1936 the international situation had 'not arrived at that point which would justify the risks necessarily associated with such a step'.

These 'risks' were equally perceived by the unions representing those industries that would be most involved in an escalating armament programme, the building and the engineering industries. Of these it was the Amalgamated Engineering Union (AEU) that most feared a rerun of the post-First World War situation, when thousands of skilled men working in the war industries had been made redundant when the peace came.

The proposal at the time of the mid-1930s international crises to redeploy skilled workers currently in steady commercial work to fuel a short-term (though not as short-term as was thought) armament manufacturing boom was to be resisted lest such workers would again find themselves without work when the arms programme was completed. Moreover, the answer to the shortage of skilled labour unfortunately did not lie with the residue of the long-term unemployed. As Baldwin explained in a debate on the matter in March 1936, 'after a long period of depression this [rearmament demand] has inevitably brought to light . . . a shortage of various classes of skilled operatives. There are obvious reasons for this. Skill has rusted for lack of use, or the skilled man has turned his hand to some other trade. The inflow of apprentices . . . has been reduced.' The experience of firms such as the aircraft manufacturer Vickers-Armstrong bore this out: needing eight hundred skilled workers in January 1938, the firm found that only nineteen of the two hundred men sent by the Labour Exchange had sufficient skill levels.

The solution seemed to be either 'poaching' men from their regular jobs to work in the war industries, or 'redesigning methods of production' – subdividing a skilled job into a number of less skilled tasks; that is, dilution of labour, a practice which was strongly resisted by the unions. As Hitler's tentacles stretched deeper into Europe, government anxiety that it was labour shortages that were the greatest inhibition to rapid rearmament grew, while the AEU continued to protect its members' interests as it saw them, sometimes under the guise of criticising government foreign policy by urging resort to a 'collective security' solution to the problem of German expansion, rather than rearmament.

A Civil Defence Bill was introduced in the Commons, with seventy-four provisions intended to speed up and improve Britain's defences against air attack, organise the 'colossal task' of working out a timetable to evacuate three million children and appoint a command structure of men of 'national standing' who could organise civil defence in London and the provinces should all communication networks be destroyed.

On 27 April Chamberlain, who had pledged that there would never be conscription in peacetime, introduced it. The Compulsory Military Training Bill, 'a departure from our cherished traditions', would require all men aged twenty and twenty-one – some 200,000 – to undertake six months' intensive military training before joining the Territorial Army or special reserves. 'This will raise difficult questions as to Conscientious Objectors etc.,' thought Alan Don, 'but it will surely prove to friend and foe that we mean business.' By August over 4,000 young men had registered as COs – there had been only 1,500 in the First World War – and the tribunals which would hear their objections to military service had already begun the painstaking and imprecise task of looking into their souls and deciding whether their convictions were deeply held or merely opportunistic.

The introduction of military conscription suggested that 'industrial conscription' might be the next compulsion. In August 1939 the AEU agreed to dilution: if there were no skilled men available to do a skilled job, unskilled workers could be employed instead. On 11 September this agreement was extended from 'peacetime emergency conditions' to the duration of 'wartime emergency conditions'.

An alternative strategy to the Anglo-French commitment to defend Poland in the event of a German invasion would have been action through the League of Nations, but that body no longer seemed very credible. Alternatively, a military alliance could have been formed with France, the Soviet Union and Poland, though Poland was reluctant to consider any alliance with Russia. Chamberlain was under considerable pressure from politicians of all parties, most of whom could not see how a guarantee to Poland could function without the support of Russia. The Prime Minister, who was strongly anti-Bolshevik, found it hard to envisage normal relations with a state whose international organisation, the Comintern, he saw as having ambitions to infiltrate Britain's industry and armed forces, thus threatening the nation's social order. Moreover, he distrusted Stalin, had no faith in Soviet military power, and saw such an alliance as fatally altering the European balance of power and slamming the door on any hope of a negotiated peace with Germany. It was not until 23 July that Chamberlain finally agreed to negotiate directly with Russia (there had been some padding round the issue since April, but the British put so many obstacles in the way that no progress was made). Rather than the Prime Minister going himself, or sending the Foreign Secretary, Lord Halifax (who was not at all keen to go), or Anthony Eden (who was, and had been several times before), the implausibly named (and hardly known) Admiral Sir Reginald Aylmer Ranfurly Plunkett-Ernle-Erle-Drax, accompanied by Sir William Strang, a middle-ranking Foreign Office official, set off on their unsuccessful mission on 5 August in a merchant ship bound for Leningrad. It took five days to arrive.

In May *Picture Post* began a series of articles on the subject 'Britain Prepares'. The first was about the Territorial Army; the second, 'The Call for Women', told of the work of the WVS, the Women's Voluntary Services for Civil Defence, set up in the spring of 1938 when Neville Chamberlain asked Stella, Countess of Reading for help in recruiting women as ARP wardens. It had since grown into an efficient organisation with a headquarters staff of 150 (90 per cent of whom were volunteers) and eight hundred branches scattered in towns and villages throughout the country. In London, the WVS supremo was Lady [Montagu] Norman, an LCC councillor and the wife of the Governor of the Bank of England. According to *Picture Post* some 10,000 redoubtable women were enrolling each week (there would be over a million members during the war), proud to wear the bottle-green and beetroot-red uniform, topped by a sensible felt hat, and to work at the myriad exhausting and sometimes dangerous tasks that would mobilise women on the Home Front, the majority of whom had never worked outside the home before.

On 25 May, in a reply to Colonel Josiah Wedgwood, Labour MP for Newcastle under Lyme, who had accused the British of 'washing our hands like Pontius Pilate' of the problem of Jewish refugees, the Home Office revealed that 29,000 had arrived since 1933. There were still half a million Jews in Germany, which continued to advertise its charms in the British press as 'Land of Hospitality', though not for the Jews it wanted to export. Millions more were suffering from anti-Semitism in other European countries, including the 'surplus Jews' of Poland. The burden on the voluntary organisations in Britain was becoming insupportable, with overworked staff and lack of funds. Refugees had been reduced to a trickle of women aged between eighteen and forty-five coming to take up domestic work, those over sixty with funds to support themselves for life, and those with sufficient capital to start a business in Britain. Others arrived without sponsorship, and there were distressing scenes at Croydon airport as they were 'repatriated', often to their death, since no country was providing anything more than a door just ajar: the US took only 65,404 refugees from Germany between 1932 and 1939, and the British administration of Palestine imposed a quota of 10,000 Jews a year.

*   *   *

On 1 June the British submarine *Thetis* left Birkenhead for trials in Liverpool Bay. After an uneventful morning, the submarine descended for a three-hour underwater test. Four hours later she had not surfaced. The *Thetis* was known to carry thirty-six hours' air supply, and the sea was calm, so there was no undue alarm as holidaymakers from Blackpool to Llandudno gathered to watch the rescue operations. At dawn the next day, a destroyer that had been searching all night came across the *Thetis* sixteen miles off Orme Head, four miles from where she had dived, her nose buried on the seabed. As the tide fell, eighteen feet of submarine was exposed, sticking vertically out of the sea. At about 9.30 a.m. two men bobbed to the surface, quickly followed by two more.

Frantic attempts were made to pull the submarine off the seabed, 130 feet below, before the tide rose and covered her again. A cable attached to a tug managed to dislodge her, and six men escaped, but three others drowned before the cable snapped and the *Thetis* slid back under the sea again. Cables were slipped under the submarine in an attempt to float her off the seabed: this failed too. In the late afternoon of 3 June, twenty-five hours after the air supply would have run out, the Admiralty issued a statement regretting that 'all life aboard must now be considered lost. It is now a matter of salvage.' Seven weeks later, on 22 July, the *Thetis* was finally winched from the seabed. Ninety-nine men had drowned or suffocated. The cause of the tragedy was a small piece of aluminium that had obscured the fact that one of the bow caps had been left open, allowing the sea to pour into a torpedo tube. Questions were asked about whether the Admiralty could have done more, and more specifically why oxyacetylene equipment had not been used to tear a hole in the side of the *Thetis* to enable the men to escape during the five hours in which she had been sticking out of the water. The answer appears to have been that 'this was not attempted until matters became desperate in order that the submarine might be damaged as little as possible', since the *Thetis* was a vital and very expensive piece of war equipment.

On 7 June the King and Queen arrived by train at Niagara Falls, where they crossed the border into America after a very successful 7,000-mile tour of Canada. How would the first reigning British monarch to set foot in the United States since the country had fought its way to independence of Britain in 1776 be received? The answer was well. But it was not a foregone conclusion. In some quarters the royal tour was seen as a public-relations exercise to snare America once more into a European 'civil war'. As Franklin Roosevelt's son explained later, 'Father wanted the welcome he planned for the King and Queen of England to act as a symbol of American affinity for a country whose present leadership he did not trust.' Yet in Washington the crowds along Delaware Avenue were even denser than they had been when Charles Lindbergh had paraded in triumph after his transatlantic flight. In New York more than three and a half million people were estimated to have turned out to welcome the royal couple, who took a detour to visit the World's Fair at Flushing Meadow, the scene of a fierce battle between the British redcoats and 'George Washington's ragged Continentals', before eating their first hot dog (at least the King did), which gave the stalls along the Coney Island boardwalk the opportunity to advertise 'By Special Appointment to His Majesty the King'.

Queen Elizabeth was a particularly captivating turn, much admired for her English-rose good looks and warm charm as she tirelessly acknowledged the waving crowds for four exhausting days. 'America is in love with you,' was the pleasing verdict of the American press. But however warm the welcome on a personal level, Roosevelt was unable to get Congress's agreement to amend the Neutrality Act in order to supply the European democracies with the arms and raw materials they would need should war come.

On 29 June the President of Poland made it clear that 'any attempt to change the status quo in the port of Danzig [which he described as "the air and sun of our political life and the basis of our economic and political independence"] either by a move from within or without would be a cause of war'. That same evening, speaking at a dinner at the Royal Institute of International Affairs, the Foreign Secretary Lord Halifax, who but a few weeks earlier had seemed to return to appeasement mode, pledged that 'in the event of further aggression we are resolved to use at once the whole of our strength in fulfilment of our pledges to resist it'. He claimed that the Royal Air Force, 'still undergoing expansion which has outstripped all the expectations of a few months ago, has now nothing to fear from any other. I have no doubt that its personnel, in spirit and in skill, is superior to all others.' The speech was, thought Sir Alexander Cadogan of the FO, 'a moving paraphrase of "we don't want to fight, but by Jingo if we do . . . "'. At about the same time Halifax was speaking, an Institute of British Opinion poll revealed that 57 per cent of those questioned thought the risk of war had decreased since the previous autumn, 30 per cent that it had increased, and 13 per cent didn't know.

On 2 July George Orwell, who was very concerned that opposition to war would soon be illegal, and had written several times to his friend the art critic Herbert Read urging that they ought to procure printing presses and lay in a good supply of paper and 'stickybacks' against the day when they must fight to save England from the fascist state he envisaged it would become in the event of war, took a sheet of paper and headed it 'Diary of Events Leading Up To War'. He took a ruler and divided the page horizontally: above the line he would record events, below it the sources of his information. He then divided the page vertically into five columns, heading them 'Foreign & General', 'Social', 'Party Political', 'Miscellaneous' and 'Remarks'. There would be many empty columns before 1 September when the diary stopped, but since Orwell's main source of information seems to have been the *Daily Telegraph*, a recurring entry in the 'Party Political' column was the call for Winston Churchill to be invited to join the Cabinet, which it was envisaged would 'show Hitler that Britain meant business' – though this did 'not imply strong criticism of Chamberlain'.

In early July Cyril Dunn had noticed that the streets of Hull were 'full of men in uniform, lorries full of them rumble along the streets, hundreds of them are away on training, nearly everyone wears a TA or ARP badge in their buttonhole, through the open window come parade ground shouts and the roar of bombers. "Just like 1914" people say, in much the same indifferent voices as they say, "Nice weather we're having."'

The Marquess of Tavistock, heir to the Duke of Bedford, wrote to *The Times* on 4 July that he wondered if Britain's state of preparedness was not making the country more belligerent, and that in his view 'the withholding from Germany of the mainly German town of Danzig is a quite inadequate reason for a world war', and 'the one thing worse than making a foolish promise is keeping a foolish promise . . . No considerations of honour can justify the slaughter of millions.' That same month Oswald Mosley made a similar point more poisonously at a rally in Earl's Court. 'A million Britons shall not die in your Jews' quarrel,' he had screeched, but the influence of the BU, never very significant, was now even more marginal to the unfolding events.

On 10 July George Orwell scribbled a poignant entry in the 'Social' column of his run-up to war diary. Groups of friends entering the militia, he noted, 'are being split up, sufficiently noticeably for this to call for an explanation by the W[ar] O[ffice]'. The reason apparently was so that there should be no repeat of the 'Pals' Brigade' phenomenon of the First World War, when men from the same town, the same streets, 'all trained together, went into action together, and were almost wiped out in a few moments which concentrated the grief felt at home'.

On 4 August the House of Commons rose for the summer recess. It was planned that it would reassemble three weeks earlier than usual, on 3 October, and a general election, due by 1940, might be called for November. Churchill was outraged. 'It would be a very hard thing,' he said, 'to say to the House: Begone! Run away and play. Take your gas masks with you. Don't worry about public affairs, leave them to experienced Ministers – who so far as defence is concerned landed the country where it was landed last September, and who in foreign policy have guaranteed Poland and Rumania, after having lost Czechoslovakia and without having gained Russia.'

Chamberlain left Downing Street to go fishing in Scotland, promising to keep in touch with London by telephone. The Archbishop of Canterbury infuriated his staff by getting straight into the car that was to take him north without acknowledging their presence by word or glance. 'He might have been going to a meeting at Church House instead of leaving London for two months, during which the world may go up in smoke and Lambeth Palace be reduced to ruins and his devoted staff reduced to smithereens.'

Reports continued to flood in of German troops massing on the Polish border. Preparations for a war that everyone hoped could be avoided continued. The Reserve Fleet had been called up, and the King inspected it on 9 August. That night it had been intended that the South of England would hold a blackout dress rehearsal, but the weather was overcast so it was postponed for twenty-four hours. The exercise revealed how unprepared the capital in particular was, standing out of the stygian gloom like a fire at sea, but perhaps there would be time to get it right.

On 20 August a 'bombshell', as Chamberlain called it, dropped. It had been thought that the talks in Moscow were moving haltingly towards a satisfactory agreement when news of the Nazi–Soviet non-aggression pact broke: the German foreign minister Ribbentrop was on his way to ratify it with Stalin. 'What frauds politicians are!' exclaimed Gladys Langford as she read the newspaper hoardings in Islington. 'Hitler will marry a Jewess next!' For members of the Communist Party it was deeply confusing and disturbing. 'A blow for peace', ventured the *Daily Worker* unconvincingly, but the Central Committee had rallied sufficiently by 2 September to put out a statement about 'a war that need never have taken place. One that could have been avoided . . . had we had a People's Government in Britain.'

In Berlin the British Ambassador, Sir Nevile Henderson, issued a formal warning to Hitler that the British and French guarantees to Poland still pertained. Parliament was recalled. Lord Halifax admitted that the news of the pact came as a surprise to him and the rest of the government, and a Labour MP queried why so much money was being spent on the intelligence services if they hadn't managed to get wind of it. Anthony Eden spoke of the situation as being 'as grave and perilous as any this country has faced at any time in her history', and there were no dissensions in either House on 24 August to the motion to grant the government emergency powers for the Defence of the Realm. The House adjourned: it was planned that it would reassemble on 31 August. Members of the public were reminded that if they were going away for the Bank Holiday, they should remember to take their gas masks with them.

On 25 August, as a plane flew overhead, a bomb exploded in Broadgate, the main shopping area in Coventry. There was wreckage and broken glass all over the street, and when the smoke cleared there were five dead and many more injured. One of those killed was a young woman out shopping for her wedding trousseau, another a boy of twelve. It was discovered that an explosive device had been placed in the basket of an errand boy's bicycle. Later that day bombs went off in Blackpool and Liverpool. These were not the first shots of a European war, but the culmination of a campaign the IRA had been waging on mainland Britain since March, the 'S Plan', or 'Sabotage Campaign'. After a power struggle in the mid-1930s Seán Russell had taken charge of the IRA Army Council and, on the logic that the IRA was the *de jure* legitimate government of Ireland, had declared war on Britain as an occupying power on 12 January 1939, giving the government four days to agree to withdraw British forces from Northern Ireland. When the ultimatum expired, notices started appearing in cities with large Irish communities urging 'in the name of the unconquered dead and the faithful living ... to compel the [English] evacuation of Ireland and to enthrone the Republic of Ireland'.

Since January bombs had exploded at power stations, had damaged electricity cables and been deposited in the left-luggage offices of railway stations with the intention of crippling Britain's power supplies. The government had stepped up police protection of power and communication hubs and government buildings, and searched many people arriving from Ireland by sea. On 4 February two people were seriously injured by a bomb at Leicester Square Underground station. There was an attack on Walton Gaol, where several of the thirty-three suspects who had been rounded up were being held, there were reports of an imminent IRA attack on Buckingham Palace, and explosions at suburban shops. Throughout the spring bombs went off on canal and railway bridges. In June the targets switched, with parcel bombs left in post offices and letterboxes, and attacks on banks. On 26 July there was the first fatality, when a bomb placed in the left luggage office of King's Cross station exploded, wounding one man who subsequently died and seriously wounding two counter assistants. At Victoria station a similar device severely wounded five people and the station was devastated. Then came the atrocity at Coventry, which had already been attacked in February, when balloon bombs (ingenious devices in which nitric acid was stuffed into a balloon; it would burn through the rubber and ignite magnesium, and the bomb would explode) had wrecked department stores.

On 8 February the government of Éire (formerly known as the Irish Free State), which had declared the IRA an illegal organisation in 1936, introduced a Treason Act aimed at curtailing IRA activities within and without Éire, and another that allowed for internment without trial. In Britain the Home Secretary, Sir Samuel Hoare, introduced a Prevention of Terrorism Bill on 24 June that gave the government comprehensive powers to bar immigrants from Ireland, deport those thought undesirable, and extend the requirement for aliens to register with the British police to the Irish. In support of these measures, Hoare told the House that there had been a total of 127 terrorist outrages since January, fifty-seven in London and seventy in the provinces, that sixty-six people had been convicted of terrorist activity, and the police had seized a large quantity of explosive material such as gelignite, potassium chlorate and sulphuric acid.

The five IRA members indicted for the murders in Coventry were tried in Birmingham in December 1939. All pleaded not guilty, but all were found guilty. Peter Barnes, a thirty-two-year old clerk, and James Hewitt, a twenty-nine-year-old labourer whose wife and mother-in-law were also among those on trial, were sentenced to death. Despite a plea from the Irish Taoiseach, Éamon de Valera, for a reprieve, Barnes and Hewitt were hanged on 7 February 1940. The IRA campaign bore no fruit in ridding Ireland of the English, but it provoked a legislative framework that would periodically be extended or revived throughout the continuing 'Troubles' of the twentieth century, and it increased anxiety about Irish intentions in the war with Germany that now seemed unavoidable.

On the day that the IRA bomb exploded in Coventry, the Treaty of Mutual Assistance between Britain and Poland was signed. Sir Nevile Henderson went to see Hitler that afternoon to discuss German demands for Polish territory, and afterwards the Führer announced that the international situation was of sufficient gravity for the Nuremberg Rally planned for 2 September to be cancelled. On the evening of Sunday, 27 August Henderson presented Hitler with the response to his demands over Poland that the FO had worked long and hard on over that weekend.

Cyril Dunn, who was 'drunk in anticipation of an early war', decided on a final fling in London, since 'doing work of any kind seems absurd in these twilight days'. He drove down from Hull with a colleague. It took them ten hours, and 'all night through, along the Great North Road, lorries thundered by, going north with OHMS chalked on them and loads of ammunition in green painted steel trays, and army stores and cylinders of gas for Barrage Balloons. New aerodromes are being built everywhere. Our headlights kept picking out soldiers in steel hats and with fixed bayonets guarding something. The sky was swept with the long slow swordstrokes of searchlights . . . In fact England was an Armed Camp, as the saying is, ready for war.'

On 27 August Chamberlain went to apprise the King of the situation. George VI had returned from Balmoral alone on the twenty-fourth, and arrangements had been made to rent the Earl and Countess of Beauchamp's country house near Worcester in the name of the French ambassador for the royal family. The King repeated an offer he had made to Chamberlain to make a direct appeal to Hitler. Chamberlain again procrastinated, promising to keep the offer in mind.

At 11 o'clock that night, Joseph Kennedy, the US ambassador, who had only arrived in London the previous July with his wife Rose and seven of their nine children, including Katherine (known as 'Kick', who would marry the Duke of Devonshire's heir), John (the future President), Edward and Robert, and who was profoundly sceptical that Britain could win a war against Germany, called on Halifax, who was working late at the Foreign Office, and gave him a lift home, discussing the situation as they went.

The next day, a Bank Holiday, Gladys Langford wrote that 'notices on the walls give details about air raid warnings and signals of gas attacks and children rehearse evacuation. Sand bags obscure windows of big buildings. Everyone talks to everyone else and the heat is intense.' Langford clung to the belief that there would be no war, but that night she dreamed that she was 'sorting rugs swarming with maggots to make shrouds for evacuated children'.

Virginia Woolf stayed out late in her Sussex garden 'to say – what? on this possibly last night of peace. Will the 9 o'clock bulletin end it all? – our lives, oh yes, & everything for the next 50 years? . . . Vita [Sackville-West] says she feels terror and horror early – revives then sinks. For us its like being on a small island. Neither of us has any physical fear. Why should we? But there's a vast calm cold gloom. And the strain. Like waiting a doctor's verdict. And the young – young men smashed up. But the point is one is too numbed to think. London seemed cheery. Most people are numb & have surface optimism . . . No feeling of patriotism. How to go on, through war? – that's the question.'

The Seven Sisters window in York Minster was removed and put into storage, as was the twelfth-century glass from Canterbury Cathedral. Alan Don 'decided to send to Cuddesdon Palace our valuable treasures from [Lambeth Palace], including the Holbein of Warham, Van Dyck's Laud and about a dozen other pictures together with a few bits of furniture'. The Tate Gallery had selected fifty-five out of its collection of 3,000 works to 'ear mark for safety'. These included Turner's *Death of Nelson*, Hogarth's *Marriage à-la-mode* sequence, a Constable, a Whistler and several modern(ish) French paintings by Cézanne, Corot, Degas and Daumier. The National Gallery had a particular problem, since 'every wall . . . is covered with pictures of genius', but seven were singled out, including the Wilton Diptych, Titian's *Bacchus and Ariadne*, a Raphael, a Piero della Francesca, a Bellini and Van Eyck's *The Arnolfini Wedding*. At the Victoria & Albert masterpieces were crated for evacuation, or boarded up *in situ*, and it was the same at the British Museum, 'since the Elgin Marbles, for instance, could not be easily tucked away in a dug-out'. At London Zoo it had been decided that while keepers would be provided with steel shelters, 'all poisonous snakes will be instantly killed, by the simple method of chopping their heads off . . . the giant thirty-foot python is not a danger. If his cage was wrecked, the cold would quickly make him slow and sleepy . . . The deadly spiders – called the Black Widows – are to be extinguished ruthlessly by boiling water . . . ' If any of the 'big fighting animals – the lions, tigers, panthers and so on' – escaped, 'picked men armed with rifles' would take care of them. The elephants were to be taken to Whipsnade, the babies by lorry, but 'the five grown-ups are going to walk all the way. It will take them four days and arrangements have been made for their accommodation each night in farm-houses where the barns are high enough to admit an elephant'. However, 'The Aquarium is, frankly, an impossible problem . . . a bomb dropping anywhere near would certainly smash the glass and nothing could be done to save the fish.'

On Thursday, 24 August Parliament was recalled. The Prime Minister was not able to be very enlightening. Hitler's attitude towards Poland had not changed. Britain still stood by her pledge to Poland (as did France), but was prepared to throw 'our whole influence upon the side of resolving these dangerous issues by negotiation rather than force', Chamberlain announced gravely. 'PM was dignified and calm, but without one word which could inspire anybody. He was exactly like a coroner summing up a case of murder,' wrote Harold Nicolson to his wife Vita Sackville-West. She was at home at Sissinghurst, where she had been asked 'if the Buick would take an eight-foot stretcher or "only sitting cases and corpses". I feel sick with apprehension.'

On the evening of 29 August, a day when Harold Nicolson had found 'the House more cheerful than it has been for weeks and looks at the anti-gas doors being fitted downstairs and the sandbags being heaped on our basement windows with amusement . . . the gloom of anticipation having merged into the gaiety of courage', Gladys Langford found the Maudsley Hospital outpatients' department closed, 'patients evacuated . . . Lots of people carrying cats about in baskets, evidently to be destroyed.'

On Friday, 1 September *The Times* published, without further comment, a map of 'Germany and her neighbours' which showed how deeply embedded at the heart of Europe Germany was, and how many countries shared a border with the Reich. Photographs over the page showed sandbags being filled, City workers whose offices had been moved to a stately home 'somewhere in the country', and a map of nine routes out of London that would be one-way after 7 a.m. to enable a quick getaway.

Late the previous night the order to 'evacuate forthwith' had come, though it was described as a precautionary measure. The Ministry of Health, which was in charge of the operation, insisted that 'No one should conclude that war is inevitable.' Most did, however. The first of the nearly three million children who would leave Britain's vulnerable cities set off for the country – though in some cases that turned out to be not much further than the suburbs. On the morning of 1 September Herbert Morrison, the leader of the LCC, spoke to those evacuating the capital: 'Keep calm. Keep a cheerful British smile on your face . . . Good luck, and a safe return to dear old London.' Armed military police were posted at all railway stations and the public were requested to use neither the roads nor their telephones unless it was absolutely essential, to leave such means of communication clear for the needs of war.

At 6 a.m., a few hours before the child evacuees had converged on the main railway stations, each clutching their gas-mask box, a small suitcase or pillowcase containing their clothes, food for the journey and a single favourite toy, with no preliminary declaration of war thousands of German troops marched into Poland. Polish towns and villages were being strafed and bombed.

Saturday, 2 September was the opening day of the football season, and crowds flocked to watch Arsenal play Bury, Stoke against Portsmouth . . . Individual steel shelters were delivered to Buckingham Palace for the sentries. It was getting all but impossible to find blackout material in the shops since there had been such a rush, though housewives were advised that beige would probably do if it was dense enough. Householders crisscrossed sticky paper tape across their windows to prevent the glass being blown in in case of bomb blast. For weeks advertisements had been appearing in the classified columns of *The Times* with the letters 'ARP' in bold, offering or requiring houses and cottages to rent. By that Saturday they predominated: 'Ladies college (adult) requires large FURNISHED House in the event of national emergency' (the usual euphemism for war); 'Rooms to board for Nannie and one or two children near Reigate'; 'If emergency arises small house required to rent near Bournemouth'; 'In safety zone, only 30 mins. from Waterloo, gentleman's well furnished house'. A house near Leith Hill in Surrey was advertised as having 'no industries, no airports' in the vicinity, thus presumably not being near any potential bomber's target.

The House of Commons met that afternoon, adjourned for an emergency Cabinet meeting and reconvened at 7.30 p.m. The windows of the Palace of Westminster were blacked out, as all premises were supposed to be from that day forward, the streets of London were dark, taxis driving along with sombre blue sidelights, cars and buses with their headlights masked. Chamberlain spoke of 'an apparently aggressive act against Poland', and announced that unless the German troops withdrew, His Majesty's government 'will without hesitation fulfil their obligations towards Poland'. It was a commitment, as Chamberlain himself had said, to 'attack Germany not to save any particular nation, but to pull down a bully'. £5 million was voted for the defence of the realm. The Military Training Act would be extended, making all men aged eighteen to forty-one liable for military service.

A White Paper was hastily published so that MPs could see for themselves the diplomatic parrying that had taken place between Britain and Germany over the past ten days. This time it seemed that Hitler had not been given a definite time limit to withdraw his forces before Britain and France activated their commitment to go to Poland's aid, disturbing some Members with the feeling that 'appeasement had come back'. Arthur Greenwood, standing in for Labour leader Clement Attlee, who was ill, was urged to 'speak for England' in expressing disquiet about 'dragging out what has been dragged out too long . . . Why the delay? We had promised to help Poland "at once". She was being bombed and attacked. We had vacillated for 34 hours. What did this mean?' Alan Don, who had been in the gallery listening to the debate, 'went home sick at heart and hardly slept all night – to add to the gloom a violent thunderstorm with torrential rain burst over London'.

In Hull, at 11.15 that night Cyril Dunn was 'just fixing brown paper round the table lamps and getting bad tempered about it. The smallest thing irritates us after 48 hours of utmost tension.'

At 9 o'clock the next morning, Sunday, 3 September, an ultimatum was delivered to Hitler demanding an assurance that by 11 a.m. that he would withdraw his forces from Poland. No such assurance was received. At 11.15 a.m. the Prime Minister broadcast to the nation:

> We have done all that any country could do to establish peace, but a situation in which no word given by Germany's ruler could be trusted and no people or country could feel themselves safe had become intolerable. And now that we have resolved to finish it, I know that you will all play your part with calmness and courage . . .
>
> May God bless you all . . .

That evening, in her Oxford vicarage, Madge Martin wrote a single word in large letters in her diary. 'WAR'.

ACKNOWLEDGEMENTS

The tentacles of a book such as this stretch wide and deep: it could not have been attempted without the help of a great number of people, nor without the work of numerous scholars, writers, memoirists, diarists and letter-writers on whose work I have drawn. I owe particular thanks to the Society of Authors, whose generous grant made research in provincial archives possible; to my agent Deborah Rogers for her enthusiasm and practical support and to Hannah Westland and Mohsen Shah at Rogers, Coleridge & White; to Arabella Pike at HarperPress who commissioned and encouraged the book, and to her colleagues Robert Lacey, who surpassed his reputation as an exemplary, rigorous and informed editor, and has sharpened the text considerably, John Bond, Helen Ellis, Minna Fry, Sophie Goulden and Martin Redfern; to Douglas Matthews for his scrupulous and imaginative indexing; to Jeffrey Cox, Kenneth Crowhurst, Henry Horwitz, David Kynaston, Peter Mandler, Roger Morgan and Stephanie J. Snow, all of whom read the manuscript in whole or in part and made extremely insightful and helpful comments, and further to David Kynaston for suggestions of recondite thirties material that he discovered in the course of his own research.

I am grateful to Peter Dunn for permission to quote from (and the trusting loan of) the diaries of his father, Cyril Dunn; the Trustees of Lambeth Palace Library for permission to quote from the diaries of the Revd Alan Don; to the Modern Records Centre at the University of Warwick for permission to quote from the diaries of Frank Forster; to Oxfordshire Record Office, Cowley, Oxford, and to Mrs Christine Holland for permission to quote from the diaries of Madge Martin; to Bolton Library, Museum and Archive Service for permission to quote from Robert Heywood Haslam's *Diary of a Journey to Russia* © Bolton Council; to the University of East Anglia for permission to quote from the Solly Zuckerman Archive and the Jack Pritchard papers; to Islington Local History Centre for permission to quote from the diaries of Gladys Langford; and to Sheffield County Libraries Archives and Information for permission to quote from the diaries of Joseph P. Albaya.

ACKNOWLEDGEMENTS

I am also most grateful to the staff at the following libraries and record offices where I consulted material: Bath Central Library; University of Birmingham (Lancelot Hogben and Oswald Mosley papers); Blackpool Local Studies Library; Colin Harris and the staff of the Bodleian Library, Oxford; Bristol Record Office; the staff of the British Library (St Pancras and Colindale); Colchester Record Office; Cornwall Local Studies Library, Redruth; Ealing Record Office; University of Exeter special collections (A.L. Rowse and Jack Clymo papers); Department of Documents, Imperial War Museum; London Metropolitan Archives; Manchester Working Class Movement Library; Mitchell Library, Glasgow; Catherine Bradley, Tom Wharton and the staff of the National Archives; Oldham Local Studies Library; Dr Christopher Lee and the staff of Paisley Museum; National Library of Scotland, Edinburgh; South Wales Miners' Library, University of Wales, Swansea; Local Studies Library, Mass-Observation Archive, University of Sussex; Orwell Papers, University College, London; Wigan Archives Service; and particularly to the unfailingly helpful and friendly staff at the London Library.

The following people have also kindly helped me in various ways: James Alcock of Corruption Films, Penny Aldred of the Angela Thirkell Society, Nicola Beauman and Chris Beauman, Terence Bendixson, Christopher Brewer, Kevin Brownlow, John Christian of Oxford Cockaigne, Ubby Cowan, Jan and Ken Crowhurst, Ann and Mike Dawney, Nicholas Deacon, Margaret Dierden, Taylor Downing of Flashback Television, Lis and Peter Dunn, the late Christopher Elrington and Jean Elrington, the late Jack Gaster, Lucy Gaster, Maureen Gilbertson, Richard Gregory, Sean Haldane, Jill Hale of the English Speaking Union, Corinne Honan and Nicholas Inge, Tem Horwitz, Walter (Wally) Kahn, Susanna Lamb, archivist, Madame Tussaud's, Philippa Lewis and Miles Thistlethwaite, Kate Leys, Deidre McCloskey, Ross McKibben, Imogen Magnus, Alan Powers, Martyn Robertson of Fablevision, Jean Seaton, David and Nicola de Quincy Souden, Gavin Stamp, Stella Tillyard, Gillian Tindall, Jacky Turner, Bruce Watkins, Joan Haldane Watkins, Simon Watson of Worldwide Books, Julie Wheelwright and Robin Woolven. My three children and their partners have been stalwart, forgiving and generous with their interest and time – including a weekend in Suffolk to celebrate completion of this book, many months before it in fact was. And to Henry Horwitz, my thanks.

If, regardless of all this help, errors and omissions remain, they are mine alone.

NOTES

3: seven out of ten children: John Mackie (ed.), *The Edinburgh Cinema Enquiry* (Edinburgh, 1933), 11, quoted in Jeffrey Richards, *The Age of the Dream Palace: Cinema and Society in Britain, 1930–39* (Routledge, 1984), 67

3: Most children spend: Richard Ford, *Children in the Cinema* (Allen & Unwin, 1939), 49

4: uphold the tradition: www.-glencinema.org.uk/history

5: Several people cried out [and following reports]: *The Times*, 1 January 1930

8: in imitation of: Valerie Reilly, *The Official Illustrated History of the Paisley Pattern* (Richard Drew, 1987), 7; see also John Irwin, *The Kashmir Shawl* (HMSO, 1973) and Matthew Blair, *The Paisley Shawl and the Men who Produced It: A Record of an Interesting Epoch in the History of the Town* (A. Gardner, 1904)

9: had employed over 20 per cent: Quoted in T.C. Smout, 'Scotland' in *The Cambridge History of Britain, Vol. I: Regions and Communities* ed.

F.M.L. Thompson (Cambridge University Press, 1990), 211

11: We have: Quoted in Robert Graves and Alan Hodge, *The Long Weekend: A Social History of Great Britain, 1918–39* (Faber, 1940)

11: Gerald Barry: Barry would subsequently edit the *News Chronicle*, and was the brains behind the 1951 Festival of Britain

11: in 1929 we have become: *The Listener*, 8 January 1930

12: 1930 . . . somehow assumes: *The Lady*, 2 January 1930

13: a shilling a week less: Joanna Bourke, *Dismembering the Male: Men's Bodies, Britain and the Great War* (Reaktion, 1996), 65–6

14: Within five days: Ronald Blythe, *The Age of Illusion: England in the Twenties and Thirties, 1919–40* (Hamish Hamilton, 1963), 11

15: under the slogan 'Safety First': Peter Clarke, *Hope and Glory: Britain 1900–90* (Penguin, 1996), 146

15: the revenue raised: ibid., 128

16: large inflow: John Stevenson, *British Society 1914–45* (Penguin, 1984), 103–4

16: its share of world trade: ibid., 104–5

16: from 287 million tons: ibid., 107

17: pound should look: Clarke, 131

17: knave-proof: ibid., 112

18: No one who has: J.K. Galbraith, *The Great Crash, 1929* (Hamish Hamilton, 1955), 121–2

18: Liquidate labor: Herbert Hoover, *Memoirs: Vol. III* (Hollis & Carter, 1953), 30

19: heaving a big: Quoted in Liaquat Ahamed, *Lords of Finance: 1929, the Great Depression and the Bankers Who Broke the World* (William Heinemann, 2009), 369

19: Almost throughout: Quoted in ibid., 383

19: that Cinderella: *The Listener*, 8 January 1930

21: An utterly: *The Collected Poems of Louis MacNeice* ed. E.R. Dodds (Faber, 1960), 105

21: ranking between: Edmund Kemper Broadus, *The Laureateship: A Study of the Office of Poet Laureate in England, with Some Account of the Poets* (Clarendon Press, 1921)

21: The man with: Quoted in Constance Babington Smith, *John Masefield: A Life* (Oxford University Press, 1978), 194, 196

22: long as a street: Neil Potter and Jack Frost, *The Mary: The Inevitable Ship* (Harrap, 1961; Tempus, 1991)

22: great white cliff: *The Times*, 27 September 1934

23: a huge capital sum: I.F. Gibson, 'The Establishment of the Scottish Steel Industry', *Scottish Journal of Political Economy* 5, 1960

23: between December 1918: A. Slaven,
'John Browns of Clydebank, 1919–38' in *Business in the Age of Depression and War* ed. R.P.T. Davenport-Hines (Frank Cass, 1990), 125

23: an order from Cunard: University of Liverpool R/HE945.C9.J61 95

23: Is it wise that: *The Times*, 22 September 1930

23: a particularly raw: Potter and Frost, 25, 34–5

24: announcement proved somewhat: *Daily Telegraph*, 11 December 1931

25: outdid the importunate: David Kirkwood, *My Life of Revolt* (Harrap, 1935), 255

25: fewer ships: *Glasgow Herald Annual Trade Review 1932*, quoted in Lewis Johnman and Hugh Murphy, 'An Overview of the Economic and Social Effects of the Interwar Depression on Clydeside Shipbuilding Communities' in *International Journal of Maritime History* 18, no.1, June 2006, 245

25: The dead on leave: Edwin Muir, *Scottish Journey* (2nd edn Edinburgh, 1979), 137–9

25: A skirl of bagpipes: Howard Johnson, *The Cunard Story* (Whittet Books, 1978), 105

26: if the lambs: Ellen Wilkinson, *The Town that was Murdered: The Life-Story of Jarrow* (Gollancz, 1939), 140

26: Twenty-eight shipyards: Stephen Constantine, *Unemployment in Britain between the Wars* (Longman, 1980), 14

26: Jarrow was utterly: Wilkinson, 191–2

26: 72.6 per cent of its workforce: Quoted in Stephanie Ward, 'The Means Test and the Unemployed in south Wales and the north-east of England, 1931–39' *Labour History Review* 73, no.1, April 2008, 113

26: nearly a third of all coalminers: Stevenson, 270

26: Everybody knows that: *Men Without Work: A Report Made to the Pilgrim Trust* (Cambridge University Press, 1938), xi

27: third England: J.B. Priestley, *English Journey* (Heinemann/ Gollancz, 1934), 397–401, 404

27: claims to be the most: *Men Without Work*, 47

27: depressing monotony: Priestley, 402

27: the national grid: John Stevenson and Chris Cook, *The Slump: Society and Politics During the Depression* (Cape, 1977), 10

27: the length of time: C.H. Feinstein, *Statistical Tables of National Income, Expenditure and Outcome of the United Kingdom, 1855–1965)* (Cambridge University Press, 1972), table 128 (quoted in Johnson, 205)

27: In September 1929: In fact *Men Without Work*. Quoted in Kate Nicholas, *The Social Effects of Unemployment on Teeside, 1919–39* (Manchester University Press, 1986), 32

28: Seebohm Rowntree's survey: B. Seebohm Rowntree, *Poverty and Progress: A Second Survey of York* (Longman, Green, 1941), 46

28: Recovery had failed: *Men Without Work*, 10

28: nearly a quarter of a million: Constantine, 4

28: or 'residual': *Men Without Work*, 223

29: whose burden is: ibid., 45–6

29: Attention has been: ibid., 212

29: across the country: Quoted in Nicholas, 33

29: life in the pits: *Men Without Work*, 73

29: the coal-cutting machines: Kenneth Mahr in Nigel Gray, *The Worst of Times: An Oral History of the Great Depression in Britain* (Wildwood, 1985), 40, 44

30: only half what it would have been: *Men Without Work*, 218, 119

30: I went into a: J. Wolveridge, *Ain't it Grand, or, This was Stepney* (Stepney House, 1976), 56

30: a beautiful place: Charles Graham in Gray, 100–4

31: Donald Kear: ibid., 163

31: went butchering: Jack Shaw in ibid., 84–5

31: I am glad: John Evans in S.P.B. Mais (ed.), *Time to Spare: What Unemployment Really Means* (Allen & Unwin, 1935), 93–4

32: In 1933, 10 per cent: A.D.K. Owen, *A Survey of Juvenile Employment and Welfare in Sheffield* (Sheffield Social Survey Committee, Report no.6, 1933) quoted in John Burnett, *Idle Hands: The Experience of*

Unemployment, 1790–1990 (Routledge, 1994), 207

32: They tell me: *Disinherited Youth: A Report on the 18+ Age Group Enquiry Prepared for the Trustees of the Carnegie United Kingdom Trust* (Constable, 1943), 36

32: large numbers of: *Men Without Work*, 224

32: loss of industrial efficiency: Unemployment Assistance Board, *Report for 1938* 5 quoted in NFR Crafts, 'Long-term Unemployment in Britain in the 1930s' in *Economic History Review* 2nd series, 40, 3, 1987, 424

32: even a short period: E. Wight Bakke, *The Unemployed Man: A Social Study* (Dutton, 1934), 50–1, 72

33: One day I: George Woodcock, 'Worst Journeys' in Keath Fraser (ed.), *Worst Journeys: The Picador Book of Travel* (Picador, 1992), 12–15

34: It was a warm: Edwin Muir, *Scottish Journey* (Heinemann/ Gollancz, 1935), 1–2

35: At the present time: Frank Forster diaries, University of Warwick Modern Records Centre, Mss 364

36: gave the unemployed [and following quotes]: S.P.B. Mais. 74, 159–60, 153, 154

37: thirteen million workers: Timothy J. Hatton and Roy E. Bailey, 'Unemployment Incidence in Interwar London', *Economica* (2002) 69, 633

38: That our present: 16 December 1932, reprinted in *The Listener*, 28 December 1932

38: When a worker's: Bakke, 103

39: unemployment in industry: Fabian Tract, 178, *The War, Women and Unemployment* by the Women's Group Executive (1915), 2

39: although women tended: Keith Laybourn, '"Waking Up to the Fact that there any Unemployed": Women, Unemployment and the Domestic Solution in Britain, 1918–39', *History* 88, 92 (2003), 609

39: in the newer industries: Sally Alexander, 'Men's Fears and Women's Work: Responses to Unemployment in London Between the Wars' in *Gender & History* 12, no.2, July 2000, 408

39: the figure was undoubtedly higher: Cited in Rex Pope, 'Unemployed Women in Inter-War Britain,' *Women's History Review* 9, no.4, 2000, 743–4

40: in return for the dismissal: ibid., 753

40: The procedure: Lettice Cooper, *We Have Come to a Country* (Gollancz, 1935), 149

41: Why can't we be: Walter Greenwood, *Love on the Dole* (Cape, 1933), 12–13, 192–3

41: a woman always had: Quoted in Deirdre Beddoe, *Back to Home and Duty: Women Between the Wars, 1918–39* (Pandora, 1989), 86–7

41: seven such centres: Royal Commission on Unemployment Insurance, *Final Report* (1931), paragraph 629 cited in Laybourn (2003), 618

41: which appear more: *The New Survey of London Life and Labour, Vol. II: London Industries* (1931), 427, 429

41: the London girl has always: ibid., 449

42: while in Preston: Pope, 754–5

42: a live-in housemaid: *The New Survey of London Life and Labour, Vol. II*, 436–7

42: it would only be withdrawn: Pope, 754

42: they knew of women: Deacon 77

43: must have maintained: *Nottingham Guardian*, 18 September 1930. Quoted in Skidelsky, 234

43: Are we to legislate: Quoted in Deacon, 74

43: colourful imagination: Robert Skidelsky, *Politicians and the Slump* (Macmillan, 1970), 266

43: 38 per cent of married women: Deacon, 77 and note 85

43: That month: Pope, 749

43: from £50 million: W.R. Garside, *British Unemployment, 1919–39: A Study in Public Policy* (Cambridge University Press, 1990), 52, 53

44: Such categories included: Deacon, 81

44: We were very poorly: Jill Norris, 'Women's and Men's Unemployment in Macclesfield Between the Wars', *North West Labour History* 9, 9

44: £2 a week: Pope, 750

44: another blow: Alice Foley, *A Bolton Childhood* (Manchester University Extra Mural Department, 1973), 7

45: Doris Bailey's father: Doris M. Bailey, *Children of the Green* (Stepney Books, 1981), 106

45: To qualify for: Sue Bowden and David M. Higgins, C. Price, 'Avoiding Conscription to the Inter-War "Army" of the Unemployed: Short-Time Working in the Iron and Steel Industry', *Labour History Review* 72, no.1, April 2007, 6

46: The favourite trick: Gray, 36

46: The miners were: Clifford Steele in Gray, 129–30

46: at any price: Bowden et al., 14

46: Trade . . . was slack: Norris, 9

47: we know all our men: Cited in Bowden et al., 15–16

47: The Act drove: Kenneth Mahr in Gray, 36

48: Various ruses: John Burnett, *Idle Hands: The Experience of Unemployment, 1790–1990* (Routledge, 1994), 262

48: Stanley Iveson: Quoted in Selina Todd, 'Working-Class Young People in England, 1918–55', *International Review of Social History* 52, 2007, 75

48: meant that everybody: Beatrice Wood, 'Wednesday's Child' in *Struggle or Starve: Women's Lives in the South Wales Valleys Between the Two World Wars* ed. Carol White and Sian Rhiannon Williams (Honno, 1998), 126–7

49: Any family unlucky: Donald Kear in Gray, 164–5

49: It is therefore: G.D.H. and M.I.

Cole, *The Condition of Britain* (Gollancz, 1937), 213–16

49: filled three times: Fenner Brockway, *Hungry England* (Gollancz, 1932), 109

50: County Durham: Stephanie Ward, 'The Means Test and the Unemployed in South Wales and the North-East of England, 1931–39', *Labour History Review* 73, no.1, April 2008, 115

50: We were threatened: Noreen Branson and Margot Heinemann, *Britain in the 1930s* (Weidenfeld & Nicolson, 1971), 27–8

50: If somebody had: Kenneth Mahr in Gray, 36

50: You were only left: Gray, 188–9

51: Suppose I would: Bakke, 161–2

51: It is in many cases: *Rhondda Fach Gazette*, 16 April 1932

51: The government saved: Stevenson and Cook, 69

51: the Means Test has been: *The Listener*, 28 December 1932, 948

52: You were: *Harold Nicolson: Diaries and Letters, 1930–39* ed. Nigel Nicolson (Collins, 1966), 301

52: Southampton to Newcastle: *English Journey*, 397

52: voluptuous, sybaritic: ibid., 3

53: modern historical survey: Richard R. Blewett, *The Village of Saint Day in the Parish of Gwennap, Cornwall*, June 1935, Cornwall Record Office, AD/56/6, 1, 4

53: pocked by mineshafts: Philip Payton, *The Making of Modern Cornwall* (Dyllansow Truran, n.d.), 123, 125, 145

53: towering presence: Sarah Foot, *My Grandfather Isaac Foot* (Bossiney, 1980), 42

54: the prime task: A.L. Rowse, *A Man of the Thirties* (Weidenfeld & Nicolson, 1979), 91. Rowse believed that the only hope for the rejuvenation of Cornwall lay in an 'anti Conservative alliance' of Liberal and Labour.

54: Outside the Duchy: Cicely Hamilton, *Modern England as Seen by an Englishwoman* (J.M. Dent, 1938), 50

54: the need to 'collectivise': John Murray et al., *Devon and Cornwall: A Preliminary Survey* (Exeter: Wheaton, 1947), 159

55: *Trelawney, Tintagel Castle*: John K. Walton, 'Power, Speed and Glamour: The Naming of Steam Locomotives in Inter-War Britain', *Journal of Transport History* 26/2 (2005), 13

55: make North Cornwall: Payton, 128

55: and even: Walton, 13

55: among the fastest: Beverley Nichols, *News of England: Or a Country Without a Hero* (Cape, 1938), 11

55: a thriving Society: Peter Davies, *The St Ives Years: Essays on the Growth of an Artistic Phenomenon* (Wimborne Bookshop, 1984), 10

56: every Cornishman knows: Henry Jenner, *A Handbook of the Cornish Language* (London: David Nutt, 1904), xi–xii

56: If we are quite: Cited in Hugh Miners, *Gorseth Kernow: The First*

Fifty Years (Gorseth Kernow, 1978), 13

57: up again at 3.30 p.m.: F.R. Clymo, *My Memories of St Day* (privately printed, 1987), 31, 27–8

58: a noticeable amount: Blewett, 9

59: the London inquiry: *The New Survey of London Life and Labour, Vol. III: The Eastern Area* (1932), 154

59: never poked his nose: *English Journey*, 406–7, 411–12

59: No words can describe: H.V. Morton, *In Search of England* (Methuen, 1927), 171, 132, cited in C.R. Perry, 'In Search of H.V. Morton: Travel Writing and Cultural Values in the First Age of British Democracy' *Twentieth Century British History* 10, no.4, 1999, 433

59: fact is now the fashion: *Clarion* 19 May 1934, cited in John Baxendale, *Priestley's England: J.B. Priestley and English Culture* (Manchester University Press, 2007), 58

59: magpie picking up: Morton, *In Search of England*, vii

59: deliberately shirked realities: H.V. Morton, *The Call of England* (Methuen, 1931), vii

60: We know no more about: J.L. Hodson, *Our Two Englands* (Michael Joseph, 1936), 284–5

60: those Englishmen cast out: Hamilton, ix, xi, 120

60: differentiate it from: Nichols, 12, 316

60: I have certain: J.B. Priestley writing to Hugh Walpole on 12 July 1936, quoted in Judith Cook, *Priestley* (Bloomsbury, 1997), 151

60: I know there is deep: Priestley, 62

61: figures and statistics: Fenner Brockway, *Hungry England* (Gollancz, 1932), 65

61: the stark reality: Harry Pollitt's introduction to Alan Hutt, *The Condition of the Working Class in Britain* (Martin Lawrence, 1933), xii

61: strange country: George Orwell, *The Road to Wigan Pier* (Gollancz, 1937), 97, 113

61: super sensitive: Introduction to G.A.W. Tomlinson, *Coal Miner* (Hutchinson, 1937)

61: after four years: ibid., 196, 198–9

62: disease of unemployment: Paddy Scannell and David Cardiff, *A Social History of British Broadcasting, Vol. I: 1922–39 – Serving the Nation* (Basil Blackwell, 1991), 58

62: there is not a special: *The Listener*, 13 July 1932

62: subsequently published as a book: *Memoirs of the Unemployed*, introduced and ed. H.L. Beales and R.S. Lambert (Gollancz, 1934)

62: Fifty-seven vivid accounts: M. Jahoda, P.F. Lazarsfeld and H. Zeisel, *Die Arbeitslosen von Marienthal* (Leipzig, 1933), translated as *Marienthal: The Sociology of an Unemployed Community* (Tavistock, 1972)

63: you have never been: S.P.B. Mais in Felix Greene (ed.), *Time to Spare: What Unemployment Really Means* (Allen & Unwin, 1935), 14

63: It's perhaps: *The Listener*, 1 March 1933

63: make yourself known: *The Listener*, 25 January 1933

64: refused to allow: Scannell and Cardiff, 65–6, 61

64: very sordid story: Jeffrey Richards, 'Controlling the Screen: The British Cinema in the 1930s', *History Today* 33, 3, March 1983, 11–17

64: 90 per cent of all: Cyril Connolly, 'Thinness of Materials' in *The Condemned Playground: Essays 1927–44* (Routledge, 1945), 101

65: misfortune to be compelled: Cited in Andy Croft, *Red Letter Days: British Fiction in the 1930s* (Lawrence & Wishart, 1990), 96

65: and was paid £100: On the strength of this, Halward informed the Labour Exchange – and his family – that henceforth he was self-employed, a writer. ibid., 98

65: B.L. Coombes, Miner-Author: Christopher Hilliard, *To Exercise Our Talents: The Democratization of Writing in Britain* (Harvard University Press, 2006), 103

66: the basis for the plot: Croft, 104–5

66: the causes of unemployment: *The Listener*, 11 January 1933

66: clearly passed through: Croft, 108–9

67: O hush: Robin Skelton (ed.), *Poetry of the Thirties* (Penguin, 1964), 113

67: I should call it: James Vernon, *Hunger: A Modern History* (Belknap Press/Harvard University Press, 2007), 119

67: cheapest practical diet: Madeline Mayhew, 'The 1930s Nutrition Controversy', *Journal of Contemporary History* 23, 1988, 449

68: Sir John Boyd Orr: John Boyd Orr, *Food, Health and Income* (Macmillan, 1936), 12

68: an act of God: Political and Economic Planning, *Planning: The Measurement of Need* (St Clements, 1934), 2, quoted in Vernon, 120

68: A table published: Cited in Greene, 152

69: a third of the working class: G. Routh, *Occupation and Pay in Great Britain, 1906–60*, cited in Branson and Heinemann, 347, fig. 10

69: human needs: Burnett (1994), 244

69: In London in 1929: A.L. Bowley and Margaret H. Hogg, *Has Poverty Diminished?: A Sequel to 'Livelihood and Poverty'* (P.S. King, 1925; Garland, 1985)

69: in Sheffield: A.D.K. Owen, *A Report on Unemployment in Sheffield* (Sheffield Social Services Committee, 1932), quoted in Constantine, 27

69: the difference between: *Men Without Work*, 119

70: creative accounting: Vernon, 128–32

70: a sharp fall: Quoted in Margaret Mitchell, 'The Effects of Unemployment on the Social Conditions of Women and Children in the 1930s', *History Workshop Journal* (9), 1985, 115

70: There is no available: Quoted in Webster, 115

71: wanted to know: Lord Boyd Orr,

As I Recall (MacGibbon & Kee, 1966), 115, 117

71: informing the public: Cited in Charles Webster, 'Healthy or Hungry Thirties?', *History Workshop Journal* 13, 1982, 116

71: now ranked ninth: cited ibid.

71: Seventy-six out of every thousand: Branson and Heinemann, 222

71: four times as dangerous: Quoted in Mitchell, 111

71: dull diseases: Margery Spring Rice, *Working Class Wives* (reissued Virago, 1981)

72: It would, indeed: Wal Hannington, *The Problem of the Distressed Areas* (Gollancz, 1937), 58–9

72: a newspaper article: Orwell, *The Road to Wigan Pier*, 85

72: the average weekly rent: Nicholas, 77

72: 44 per cent of the families: Cited in Burnett (1994), 247

72: Rowntree found: *Poverty and Progress*

72: This finding was borne out: G.C.M. M'Gonigle and J. Kirby, *Poverty and Public Health* (London, 1937)

72: I learned the meaning: Max Cohen, *I Was One of the Unemployed* (Gollancz, 1945; EP, 1978), 11–12

73: married with six [and subsequent quotes]: *Memoirs of the Unemployed* introduced and ed. H.L. Beales and R.S. Lambert (Gollancz, 1934), 156, 166–7, 178, 222–3

74: the real secret: Tomlinson, 202

74: about 1 shilling: Beales and Lambert, 256–7

74: had just one attic room: Charles Graham in Gray, 91, 94

75: along with a lot of: John McNamara in ibid., 176

76: the minimum standard: Herbert Tout, *The Standard of Living in Bristol* (1938)

76: been robust: Mrs Pallas in Greene, 26–7, 38, 31, 33–4

77: A woman had: John McNamara in Gray, 176–7

77: It's upon the wives: 'John Evans' in Greene, 89, 90, 94

78: My father didn't: Clifford Steel in Gray, 127–8

78: in almost every street: Charles Graham in ibid., 94–5

78: used to do very well: Joan Crowther quoted in Angus McInnes, 'Surviving the Slump: An Oral History of Stoke-on-Trent Between the Wars' in *Midland History* 18, 1993, 133

78: We are told: Mrs Pallas in Greene, 35

78: I was practically: Marion Watt, 'Aberdeen' in Gray, 158

79: it was a common thing: John McNamara in ibid., 177

79: When our baby: ibid., 193

80: Furthermore, Mr Wellesley: Michael Gilbert, *Fraudsters: Six Against the Law* (Constable, 1986), 133

81: a hodgepodge: Richard Davenport-Hines, *Oxford Dictionary of National Biography* (rather amazingly, there is still no full-length biography of Hatry, though one from David Fanning is long promised. He does, however, figure in various compilations of fraudsters and deceivers.)

81: He also financed: David Kynaston, *The City of London, Vol. III: Illusions of Gold, 1914–45* (Chatto & Windus, 1999), 141

81: a £300,000 finance house: David Fanning, 'Clarence Charles Hatry', *Dictionary of Business Biography*, *Vol. III*, 111

81: This is ruination: Hubert A. Meredith, *The Drama of Money-Making: Tragedy and Comedy of the London Stock Exchange* (Sampson Low, 1931), 309

81: I say he shd: Quoted in Kynaston, 176

82: We want to make: Quoted in H. Montgomery Hyde, *Norman Birkett* (Hamish Hamilton, 1964), 278

82: This Hatry affair: Quoted in Kynaston, 179, 180

83: the Marquess of Winchester: Marquess of Winchester, *Statesmen, Financiers and Felons* (London, 1934), 250, 268, 274

83: Hatry was not: *New Statesman*, 1 February 1930

84: A model prisoner: Clarence Hatry, *The 'Hatry Case': Eight Current Misconceptions* (Pollock, 1938)

84: Hatry was to be found: Fanning, 113

88: One life had been: Sir Peter G. Masefield, *To Ride the Storm: The Story of the Airship R.101* (William Kimber, 1982), 447

88: long-distance overseas voyages:

R.101: The Airship Disaster, 1930 (CD 3825, 1931 abridged edition the Stationery Office, 1999), 15

88: in a few years: Quoted in James Leasor, *The Millionth Chance: The Story of the R101* (Hamish Hamilton, 1957), 54

88: competition in design: *R.101*, 16

88: N.S. Norway: Nevil Shute, *Slide Rule* (Heinemann, 1954), 127–9, 134–5

89: very perfect: Quoted in Leasor, 121

89: this first and successful: Quoted in Masefield, 256

90: You must not: Quoted in Leasor, 131–2

90: nearly £2.5 million: In fact £2, 396, 948 by the time the R101 was launched. Masefield, Appendix 7, 484

90: the total weight: Masefield, 347–8

91: The fifty coffins: *The Diary of Virginia Woolf, Vol. III: 1925–30*, ed. Anne Olivier Bell (Hogarth Press, 1980), 322–3

92: it is clear: *R.101*, 157, 159, 161

92: pots and pans: Leasor, 174

94: We are not: David Marquand, *Ramsay MacDonald* (Cape, 1977), 568–9

95: MacDonaldite slush: letter from Hugh Dalton to G.D.H. Cole 30 May 1932 quoted in Roger Eatwell and Anthony Wright, 'Labour and the Lessons of 1931', *History* (63), 1978, 42

95: more than double: 2,237,501 in October 1930; 2,408, 371 in December 1930 and a peak (or trough) of 2, 811, 615 in September 1931, cited in Neil Riddell, *Labour in Crisis: The Second Labour Government, 1929–31* (Manchester University Press, 1999) 238

95: economic blizzard: Clarke (1996), 158

95: The Labour Party refuses: Quoted in Jim Tomlinson, 'Labour and the Economy' in *Labour's First Century* ed. Duncan Tanner, Pat Thane and Nick Tiratsoo (Cambridge University Press, 2000), 51

95: the unfulfilled task: Elizabeth Durbin, *New Jerusalems: The Labour Party and the Economics of Democratic Socialism* (Routledge, 1985), 13

95: The election of 1929: Philip M. Williams, *Hugh Gaitskell: A Political Biography* (Cape, 1979), 39

96: The capitalist system: Evan Durbin, *The Politics of Democratic Socialism* (Routledge, 1940), 146

97: High Priest: Winston S. Churchill, *Great Contemporaries* (Thornton Butterworth, 1937), 293

97: It is no part: Quoted in Colin Cross, *Philip Snowden* (Barrie & Rockliffe, 1966), 207

97: this was largely the view: Peter Clarke, *The Keynesian Revolution in the Making, 1924–36* (Clarendon Press, 1988), 313

97: Since our return: Thomas Jones, *Whitehall Diary, Vol. II: 1926–30* ed. Keith Middlemass (Oxford University Press, 1969), 23 December 1929, 228

98: to finance rationalised: Kynaston, 190–2

98: better pay the old: Thomas Jones, 15 January 1930, 235

98: a colonising scheme: C.L. Mowat, *Britain Between the Wars, 1918–40* (University of Chicago Press, 1955), 358–9

99: and prophetically warned: John McNair, *James Maxton: The Beloved Rebel* (Allen & Unwin, 1955), 192, 193

99: calculated . . . to promote: Quoted in Marquand, 522

99: never learned to move: Lord Macmillan, *A Man of Law's Tale* (Macmillan, 1952), 196

99: packed in favour [and subsequent quotes]: Clarke (1988), 105, 124, 128

100: Labour is worried: Thomas Jones, 23 December 1929, 229–30

101: If it meets: Quoted in Marquand, 524

101: for all the odds: Riddell, 84

101: he hated woolly: Nicholas Davenport, *Memoirs of a City Radical* (Weidenfeld & Nicolson, 1974), 59

101: an experiment: Susan Howson and Donald Winch, *The Economic Advisory Council, 1930–39: A Study in Economic Advice During Depression and Recovery* (Cambridge University Press, 1977), 1

101: when it was published: Durbin, 64

101: full of overworked: *The Political Diary of Hugh Dalton, 1918–40, 1945–60* ed. Ben Pimlott (Jonathan

Cape/London School of Economics, 1986), 96

102: British equivalent: Quoted in Richard Toye, *The Labour Party and the Planned Economy, 1931–51* (Royal Historical Society/ Boydell Press, 2003), 38

102: as grandiose: *The Diary of Beatrice Webb: Vol. IV, 1924–43, The Wheel of Life*, ed. Norman and Jeanne MacKenzie (Virago/London School of Economics, 1985), 1 March 1931, 240

102: hard dogmatism: Quoted in Marquand, 538

102: a young man's zeal: Webb IV, 29 May 1930, 217

103: not to introduce: C.E.M. Joad, *The Case for a New Party* (1931), quoted in Matthew Worley, 'What was the New Party? Sir Oswald Mosley and Associated Responses to the "Crisis", 1931–32', *History* 92, 2007, 48–9

103: apply scientific method: W.E.D. Allen, *The New Party and Old Toryism* (1931), 2

103: ginger group: 1931 New Party election leaflet quoted in Worley, 49

103: no vision beyond: *New Statesman*, 14 March 1931

103: Parliament itself: Quoted in Worley, 58

104: The most recent: *SSIP Monthly Bulletin*, January 1932, quoted in Eatwell and Wright, 48

104: the ginger group: John Pinder (ed.), *Fifty Years of Political and Economic Planning: Looking Forward, 1931–81* (Heinemann, 1981), 6–7

104: The result was: Toye, 39–40

104: a crusade: Pinder, 17–18

105: it was important that: Riddell, 83

105: as full a development: Quoted in Robert Skidelsky, *Politicians and the Slump: The Labour Government of 1929–31* (Macmillan, 1967: Pelican edition 1970), 258–9

105: so serious . . . that: Alan Bullock, *Ernest Bevin: A Biography* (William Heinemann, 1967; abridged edition Politicos, 2002), 157

105: stagnant swamp: Riddell, 191

105: moribund: Quoted in Durbin, 80

105: diffuse its findings: Riddell, 192

106: the cleverest: Davenport, 97

106: all the claptrap [and subsequent quotes]: ibid., 79, 42–3, 75–6

107: over a City alley: Williams, 47

107: my experts: Durbin, 83

107: over the years: Francis Williams, *Nothing so Strange* (Cassell, 1970), 112

107: or tackling: Clarke (1996), 156

107: Have there ever: Webb, 25 February 1931, 239

108: grow vines: Thomas Jones, 31 October 1930, 276

108: there was no money: Hugh Kenner, *The Pound Era* (Faber, 1972), 301

109: and the power: Canto 38/190:198 (1933), quoted in Kenner, 306–7

109: Another maverick thinker: These paragraphs draw on a number of sources: C.H. Douglas, *Social Credit* (Cecil Palmer, 1924), 215–17; Meghnad Desai, *The Route of All Evil* (Faber, 2006); Hugh Kenner, *The Pound Era* (1972); H.T.N. [Hugh] Gaitskell, *What Everybody Wants to Know About Money* ed. G.D.H. Cole (Gollancz, 1933); T.C. Smout, Introduction to Muir, *Scottish Journey*; Wallace Martin, *The New Age Under Orage: Chapters in English Cultural History* (Manchester University Press, 1967)

110: the age of free trade: *The Times*, 7 April 1930

110: the old Parties: *Daily Express*, 18 February 1930

110: Beaverbrook's plan: Gillian Peele, 'St George's and the Empire Crusade' in Chris Cook and John Ramsden (eds), *By-Elections in British Politics* (UCL Press, 1997), 66

111: under the piecrust: ibid., 75

111: the gloves were off: Lady Diana Cooper, *Autobiography: The Light of Common Day* (Rupert Hart-Davis, 1959), 337

111: open questions: Harold Macmillan, *Winds of Change, 1914–39* (Macmillan, 1966), 249, 250, 263

111: a very able: Skidelsky (1967), 193

112: five clever: Webb, 4 August 1931, 249

112: devilish: Montagu Norman on 29 July 1931, quoted in D.E. Moggridge, *British Monetary Policy, 1924–31: The Norman Conquest of $4.86* (Cambridge University Press, 1972), 195

112: Luxury hotels: Webb, 4 August 1931, 249

112: an unprecedented exodus: Marquand, 608

112: unsoundness: Ross McKibbin, 'The Economic Policy of the Second Labour Government, 1929–31', *Past and Present* 68, 112

112: of no immediate: Macmillan, 268

113: a Commee.: Marquand, 610

113: the only excuse: Webb, 22 August 1931, 251

113: finance . . . was a matter: Memo from US Secretary of State Henry L. Stimson, quoted in Williamson, 777

113: Will the country: Quoted in Kynaston, 236

113: Yes, if we can: ibid., 237

113: terrible gravity: letter from Snowden to MacDonald, 7 August 1931, quoted in Marquand, 613

113: It certainly is: Webb, 23 August 1931, 253

114: drastic action: Marquand, 619

114: a real *dégringolade*: ibid., 621

114: Snowden warned: Quoted in Philip Williamson, 'A "Banker's Ramp"? Financiers and the British Political Crisis of August 1931', *English Historical Review*, 1984, 776

115: quite so desperate: Quoted in Riddell, 202

115: pigs: Webb, 22 August 1931, 252

115: Practically a declaration: Quoted in Riddell, 202

115: MacDonald was disgusted [and subsequent quotes]: Quoted in Marquand, 632, 631, 636–7

116: MacDonald has been: Dalton, 153, 27 August 1931

116: Bankers, it was claimed: Williamson, 770–1, 803

116: I cannot see: *Parliament and Politics in the Age of Baldwin and MacDonald: The Headlam Diaries, 1923–35* ed. Stuart Ball (Historians Press, 1992), 213, 24 August 1931

116: replete with folly: Quoted in Robert Rhodes James, *Bob Boothby: A Portrait* (Hodder & Stoughton, 1991), 133

117: the Scotch minister: Thomas Jones, *A Diary with Letters, 1931–50* (Oxford University Press, 1954), 1 November 1931, 20

117: teachers are: Samuel Morris Rich diaries, University of Southampton Special Collections, Mss168

117: The Labour Party . . . tried: Williams, 40–1

117: adopting some exceptional: Peter Clarke, *The Cripps Version: The Life of Sir Stafford Cripps 1889–1952* (Allen Lane/Penguin Press, 2002), 59

117: The one thing: ibid., 57

118: If Ramsay MacDonald: Rich, December 1931

118: the most astute historian: Clarke (1996), 148–9

119: the beneficial repercussions: R.F. Khan, 'The Relation of Home Investment to Unemployment', *Economic Journal* 41, 1931, 74, quoted in McKibbin, 107

120: What animals: G.A. Tomlinson, *Coalminer* (1937), 105–6

121: Rabbits were: *Hello, Are you Working?: Memories of the Thirties in the North East of England* ed. Keith Armstrong and Huw Benyon (Whitley Bay, Tyne and Wear: Strong Words, 1977), 81

121: every miner's: Hilda Ashby in ibid., 41

121: We used to live: Interview with Harold Wood, Mapperley, Derbyshire, quoted in Colin P. Griffin, 'Survival Strategies of Unemployed East Midland Coalminers in the Inter-War Years: A Guide to Sources and Findings', *East Midland Historian* 6, 1996

121: a contrivance: J.S. Mill, *Principles of Political Economy, Vol. II* (John W. Parker, 1848)

121: the hungry could: David Crouch and Colin Ward, *The Allotment: Its Landscape and Culture* (Faber, 1988), 105

122: new short-sleeved: F.E. Green, 'The Allotment Movement', *The Contemporary Review*, July 1918, quoted in ibid., 71

122: Land Settlement Association: ibid., 74

122: all have gardens: *The Sphere*, 23 April 1932, quoted in Griffin, 5

122: They used to be: Jack Shaw in Gray, 79

123: who had been: Joan Mary Fry, *Friends Lend a Hand* (Friends Book Centre, 1947)

123: Friends stepped in: John Farmer, 'The Growing Years – 1930–80' in *The Gardener's Companion and Diary* (National Society of Leisure Gardeners, 1980), quoted in Crouch and Ward, 107

123: the requisites for: Sheffield

Allotments for Unemployed
Scheme. Fifth Annual Report, 1934

123: We never bought: Herbert Allen in
Gray, 139

124: To get three bags: Will Paynter, *My
Generation* (Allen & Unwin, 1972),
36

124: John Evans: *Time to Spare*, 93

125: Some of them: Brockway, 155

125: Dick Beavis: Armstrong and
Benyon, 20

125: as much as eight shillings:
Tomlinson, 106

125: buying rabbits: Interview with
Connie Mapperley, Derbyshire,
quoted in Griffin, 6

126: did carpentry: Hilda Jennings,
*Brynmawr: A Study of a Distressed
Area* (Allenson, 1934), 139

126: a drink of beer: Interview with Joe
Lively, Griffin 6

126: had to be alive: Interview with
Connie Woods, ibid., 10

126: had pitmen who: Hilda Ashby in
Armstrong and Benyon, 40–1

127: in Durham villages: *The Times*,
cited in Fry, xx

127: getting a clear: Farmer, quoted in
Crouch and Ward, 107

127: worthy woman: Bakke, 141, 95

128: It became quite: Wal Hannington,
*Unemployed Struggles, 1919–36: My
Life and Struggles Among the
Unemployed* (Lawrence & Wishart,
1936)

128: On the main roads: ibid., 181

128: John Brown: John Brown, *I Was a
Tramp* (Selwyn & Blount, 1934),
82–3, 95, 129, 137–8, 150. In the
autumn of 1932 Brown went to

Ruskin College, Oxford, on a TUC
scholarship, taking a cargo boat
from Newcastle to get there. He
gained a diploma in Economics
and Political Science and found
work as a journalist and political
organiser.

129: meat and vegetables: Public
Assistance (Casual Poor) Order of
1931, quoted in Lionel Rose, *Rogues
and Vagabonds: Vagrant Underworld
in Britain, 1815–1985* (Routledge,
1988), 159

129: I tramped: Cohen, 126–9

129: 21 May 1932: Rose, 146

130: It is when: The Rev. Cecil
Northcott, 'Filling the Workless
Day' in Greene, 115

130: Joseph Farrington: 'Manchester' in
Gray, 12

130: Arnold Deane: *Oldham Chronicle*,
22 February 1936

130: felt ill at ease: John Brierley, *In the
Shadow of the Means Test Man:
Memories of a Derbyshire Childhood* (Highedge Historical Society,
1995), 17

130: No man has: T.S. Eliot, *Selected
Poems* (Faber, 1982), 110

131: drunken behaviour: Stephen
G. Jones, *Workers at Play: A
Social and Economic History of
Leisure, 1918–39* (Routledge,
1986), 120

131: the high price: *The Pub and the
People by Mass-Observation* (1943;
Cresset Library, 1987), 31

131: Jack Shaw: Gray, 83

131: You could buy: Donald Kear in
ibid., 165

131: a miner's privilege: Joe Lively, quoted in Griffin, 6

131: Blokes used to: Jack Shaw in Gray, 77

132: the bigger school: Charles Graham in ibid., 113–14

132: marbles – flirting: Joseph Farrington in ibid., 23

132: Jack Shaw: ibid., 77

132: They'd gamble on: Charles Graham in ibid., 114

132: They [the unemployed]: Brockway, 155–6

132: often received: C. Cameron, A.J. Lush and G. Meara (eds), *Disinherited Youth: A Report on the 18+ Age Group Enquiry Prepared for the Trustees of the Carnegie United Kingdom Trust* (Edinburgh, 1943), 108

132: half price: Burnett, 240

132: boxing booths: Quoted in Griffin, 7

133: Some of them: Armstrong and Benyon, 67

133: the pursuits of: Cameron, Lush and Meara, 109

133: one of a gang: *Men Without Work*, 149

133: had no money: Paul Johnson, *The Vanished Landscape: A 1930s Childhood in the Potteries* (Weidenfeld & Nicolson, 2004), 61

133: Thousands used: Brown, 201, 215

134: people were reading: Jack Jones, *Unfinished Journey* (Oxford University Press, 1937), 256–7

134: in Deptford: *Men Without Work*, xx

134: books on Socialism: Bakke, 194–5

134: joined the public: Beales and Lambert, 133

134: brilliantly successful: *Men Without Work*, 282

134: talk[ing] with other: Beales and Lambert, 134, 234

134: Tomlinson read: Tomlinson, 74–7

134: An unemployed miner: *Men Without Work*, 276

135: Donald Kear: Gray, 166

135: DON'T BE DEPRESSED: Robert James, '"A Very Profitable Enterprise": South Wales Miners' Institute Cinemas in the 1930s', *Historical Journal of Film, Radio and Television* 27, March 2007, 31

135: For two and a half hours: Cameron, Lush and Meara, 105

136: 2.6 hours a week: Bakke, 180

136: attendance at cinemas: Cameron, Lush and Meara, 100–9

136: the Rhondda Valley: Peter Miskell, *A Social History of the Cinema in Wales, 1918–51* (University of Wales Press, 2006), 48

136: industrial scenes: James, 30

136: twice nightly: ibid., 33, 41

136: Miners' institutes: Jonathan Rose, *The Intellectual Life of the British Working Classes* (Yale University Press, 2002), 237

137: Miners' libraries were: Chris Baggs, 'The Whole Tragedy of Leisure in Penury: The South Wales Miners' Institute Libraries During the Great Depression', *Libraries and Culture* 39, no. 2, spring 2004, 126

137: Miners' Welfare Fund: Hywel Francis and David Smith, *The Fed:*

A History of the South Wales Miners in the Twentieth Century (Lawrence & Wishart, 1980), 429

137: duty and privilege: *The Other Side of the Miner's Life: A Sketch of Welfare Work in the Mining Industry* (Mining Association of Great Britain, October 1936), 10

137: Tredegar's Workmen's Institute: D.J. Davies, *The Tredegar Workmen's Hall, 1861–1951* (n.p., 1951), 80–93, quoted in Rose, 237

137: *Prifysgol Y Glowyr*: James, 28

138: others in the queue: A.J. Lush, *The Young Adult* (University of Wales Press Board, 1941), 47, 50, 72, 79–82

138: non-existent: Chris Baggs, '"The Whole Tragedy of Leisure in Penury": The South Wales Miners' Institute Libraries During the Depression', *Libraries and Culture* 39, no.2, spring 2004, 126

138: many had bought: Rose, 251

139: single proletarian: Havelock Ellis, *My Confessional: Questions of Our Day* (John Lane, Bodley Head, 1934), 20, 21

139: a surrealist vision: Julian Trevelyan, *Indigo Days* (MacGibbon & Kee, 1957), 82

139: razzing away: Kevin Jackson, *Humphrey Jennings* (Picador, 2004), 213

139: A re-evaluation: Andrzej Olechnowicz, 'Unemployed Workers, "Enforced Leisure" and Education for the "Right Use of Leisure" in Britain in the 1930s', *Labour History Review* 70, no.1, April 2005, 27

139: mistake the desert: Henry Durant, *The Problem of Leisure* (Routledge, 1938), 4

139: various social commentators: See Ross McKibbin, 'The "Social Psychology" of Unemployment in Interwar Britain' in *The Ideologies of Class: Social Relations in Britain, 1880–1950* (Oxford University Press, 1990), 228–58; P. Zawadzki and P.F. Lazarfeld, 'The Psychological Consequences of Unemployment', *Journal of Social Psychology* 6, 1935, 371; and M. Jahod, P.F. Lazarfeld and H. Zeisel, (1972), 54

139: rough progression: Beales and Lambert, 25–6

140: Left to themselves: S.P.B. Mais, Introduction to Greene, 21, 15, 16, 17

140: the glittering prize: Cameron, Lush and Meara, 114–15

141: a national opportunity: Quoted in Ralph H.C. Hayburn, 'The Voluntary Occupational Centre Movement' in *Journal of Contemporary History* 6, no.3, 1971, 158, 159

141: 114 centres: Cameron, Lush and Meara, 109

141: In the Rhondda: *Men Without Work*, 306

141: an orchestra: Hayburn, 160

141: Queen Mary's Hall: Gladys Langford, Diaries 1921–69, Islington Record Office, LHC YX079 LAN, 22 November 1936

142: Many clubs used: Hayburn, 163

142: based on the theory: Cameron, Lush and Meara, 112

142: Hardwick Hall: Olechnowicz (2005), 34

142: Coleg Harlech: Hayburn, 165

142: trying to fob off: Jones (1954), 85

142: on Clydebank: Mais in Greene, 22–3

143: ironically enough: Northcott in ibid., 117–18

143: Spennymoor: www.durham. gov.uk/ miner/projects

144: The Prince of Wales: http:// northumbria.ac.uk/university-gallery/ cornish/

144: Harry Wilson: William Feaver, *Pitmen Painters: The Ashington Group, 1934–84* (Chatto & Windus, 1988), 15

144: didn't last long: Wilson, quoted in ibid., 17, 18

145: a celebrated exercise: ibid., 42–3

145: miners are keen: Janet Adam Smith, *The Listener*, 28 April 1937

145: mining pictures: Peggy Kilbourn, wife of Oliver Kilbourn, one of the Ashington Group artists, in a letter to William Feaver in October 1987, quoted in Feaver, 47

145: suspicion expressed: Ralph Hayburn, 'The National Unemployed Workers' Movement, 1921–36: A Reappraisal', *International Review of Social History* 28, part 3, 1983, 283

146: had never joined: Wal Hannington, *The Problem of the Distressed Areas* (Gollancz, 1937), 194–5, 197

146: the idea behind: Forster, 4 November 1934

146: simply a device: Orwell, (1937), 76–7

146: What we unemployed: letter to the editor: 'Work Centres for the Unemployed', *Spectator*, 3 March 1933, 287, quoted in Olechnowicz (2005), 41

146: physical jerks: 20th Century Society Documentary

147: Wentworth: Catherine Bailey, *Black Diamonds: The Rise and Fall of an English Dynasty* (Viking, 2007), xix, xx

148: the fullest benefits: ibid., 311, 312

148: grimy caryatid[s]: Orwell, *The Road to Wigan Pier*, 18

148: Employment in the coal industry: Chris Williams, *Capitalism, Community and Conflict: The South Wales Coalfield, 1898–1947* (University of Wales Press, 1997), 23

148: Now then, boy: Ralph Boreham quoted in Bailey, 300

148: the Dardanelles pit: Marion Henery in Ian MacDougall (ed.), *Voices from the Hunger Marches: Personal Recollections by Scottish Hunger Marchers of the 1920s and 1930s, Vol. I* (Edinburgh: Polygon, 1990), 55

148: the lab conditions: Clarke (2002), 37–9

149: lethal methane gas: Jonathan Gammond, 'The Real Price of Coal', http://www.bbc.co.uk/ wales/northeast/sires/wrexham/ pages/gresford_colliery

149: While the report: Stanley Williamson, *Gresford: The Anatomy of a Disaster* (Liverpool University Press, 1999), 203

149: Great National Hunger March: Stevenson and Cook, 175–6

149: work or full: Maureen Turnbull, 'Attitude of Government and Administration Towards the "Hunger Marches" of the 1920s and 1930s', *Journal of Social Policy* 2, 1973, 131

149: our future historians: Wal Hannington, *Never on Our Knees* (Lawrence & Wishart, 1967), 246

150: raiding parties: Wal Hannington, *Unemployed Struggles, 1919–36* (Lawrence & Wishart, 1936), 215

150: over thirty: *Manchester Evening News*, 2, 7, 8 October 1931, cited in Stevenson and Cook, 168

150: Articles had started: *Manchester Guardian*, 24 September 1930, 30 November 1936 (Croucher, 107)

151: black-coated proletariat: Hannington (1936), 220

151: might bring the: Rich, 9 and 16 September 1931

151: perfectly absurd: Alan Ereia, *The Invergordon Mutiny* (Routledge, 1981), 44

151: Len Wincott: Anthony Carew, 'The Invergordon Mutiny, 1931: Long-Term Causes, Organisation and Leadership', *International Review of Social History* 3, part 24, 1972, 157–88

151: The words used: Alan Ereia, 'The Hidden Life of the British Sailor', *History Today* 32, 12, December 1982, 27–32

152: Ritchie Calder: Sylvia Scarffardi, *Fire Under the Carpet: Working for Civil Liberties in the 1930s* (Lawrence & Wishart, 1986), 31

152: most of the stokers: Carew, 157

152: portrayed the strike: James Eaden and David Renton, *The Communist Party of Great Britain Since 1920* (Palgrave Macmillan, 2002), 44

152: fourth national march: Peter Kingsford, *The Hunger Marchers in Britain, 1920–40* (Lawrence & Wishart, 1982), 139

153: membership had fallen: G.D.H. Cole and Raymond Postgate, *The Common People, 1746–1946* (1964), 596–7

153: 'strongly' condemning: Ralph Hayburn, 'The National Unemployed Workers' Movement, 1921–36: A Reappraisal', *International Review of Social History* 28, part 3, 1983, 281

153: No illegality: James Allison in *Voices from the Hunger Marches, Vol. I*, 125

153: to stimulate: Report of the 67th Annual Trades Union Congress (1935), cited in Hayburn, 281

153: never to cease: Kingsford, 22

153: resolutions would be passed: Ralph Hayburn, 'The Police and the Hunger Marchers', *International Review of Social History* 17, part 3, 1972, 626 and n2

154: Finlay Hart: *Voices from the Hunger Marches, Vol. I*, 191

154: Harry McShane: ibid., 21

154: Finlay Hart: ibid., 3

154: Isa Porte: ibid., 75

155: Dozens of arrests: Stevenson and Cook, 172–3

155: that much good food: Kingsford, 142–4

156: Coventry Council: ibid., 100, 139–40

156: if we were banned: Harry McShane and Joan Smith, *No Mean Fighter* (Pluto, 1978), 187

156: good big lunch: ibid., 188, 190

156: Flautists: Finlay Hart in *Voices from the Hunger Marches, Vol. I*, 194

156: From Scotland: Frank McCusker in ibid., 33

156: Maryhill Flute Band: Tom Ferns: ibid., 142–3

157: Ramsay [MacDonald]: Ernie Trory, *Between the Wars: Recollections of a Communist Organiser* (Crabtree Press, 1974), 27

157: Oh why are we: Marion Henery in *Voices from the Hunger Marches, Vol. I*, 55

157: a Russian tune: William MacVicar in ibid., 177

157: Emily Swankie: ibid., Vol. II, 237

157: blew his top: Hugh Sloan in ibid., 286

157: there wis many: Michael Beattie in ibid., Vol. I, 115

157: didn't feel: William McVicar in ibid., 177

158: Solidarity not Charity: Trory, 31

158: Hugh Sloan: *Voices from the Hunger Marches, Vol. II*, 285

158: William McVicar: ibid., Vol. I, 5

158: trusting that we: Trory, 31, 34

158: Archie McInnes: *Voices from the Hunger Marches, Vol. I*, 59

158: John Brown: ibid., 45

158: John Lochore: ibid., Vol. II, 320

158: Harry McShane: ibid., Vol. I, 19

159: is calculated to: Quoted in Scaffardi, 33

159: Let the working class: Kingsford, 156

159: The petition was never: McShane and Smith, 192–3

160: If I am to be: Quoted in Kingsford, 162–3

160: The most important: *Time and Tide*, 3 December 1932, quoted in Kingsford, 164

161: Equally, the TUC: Stevenson and Cook, 180

161: Harry McShane: *Voices from the Hunger Marches, Vol. I*, 22

161: Guy Bolton: ibid., Vol. II, 339

161: Hugh Duffy: ibid., 354

161: Local people were: Harry McShane in ibid., Vol. I, 24, 27

162: Archie McInnes: ibid., 45

162: We elected people: Tom Ferns in ibid., 140

162: Finlay Hart: ibid., 192

162: We didnae hae: Michael Beattie in ibid., 11

162: had a place: Tom Ferns in ibid., 144

163: we were loaded: James Allison in ibid., 130

163: over 70,000 men: Stevenson and Cook, 65–6

163: to deal with: Ministry of Labour official to Treasury official, 29 December 1929, quoted in Dave Colledge and John Field, "'To Recondition Human Material . . . ": An Account of a British Labour Camp in the 1930s' in *History*

Workshop Journal 15, spring 1983, 155–6

164: fibre of men: *The Times*, 12 April 1929

164: slave colonies: Colledge and Field, 162

164: once more to: ibid., 157

164: sent to a camp: Len Edmondson in *Hello, Are You Working?*, 66

164: Tom Ferns: *Voices from the Hunger Marches, Vol. I*, 139

165: the outdoor life: Lorraine Walsh and William Kenefick, 'Bread, Water and Hard Labour?: New Perspectives on 1930s Labour Camps', *Scottish Labour History* 34, 1999, 14–33

165: civilian sergeant-majors: *The People*, 11 March 1932, quoted in Colledge and Field 159

165: William Heard: Interview in ibid., 163, 165

165: so much rot: *Oldham Chronicle*, 21 July 1935

165: 83,000 'volunteers': R.C. Davison, *British Unemployment Policy: The Modern Phase Since 1930* (Longman, Green, 1938), 113–22

165: surplus to requirements: Quoted in Ted Rowlands, *Something Must Be Done: South Wales and Whitehall, 1931–51* (Merthyr Tydfil: 2000), 48

166: Special Correspondent: *The Times*, 20, 21, 22 March 1934

166: the importance of: Quoted in Rowlands, 43

166: not a question: Quoted in Miller (1976), 467

166: financial hosepipe [and subsequent quotations]: Rowlands, 55, 67–70

167: neither waste sympathy: Quoted in Frederic Miller, 'The Unemployment Policy of the National Government, 1931–36', *Historical Journal* 19, 2, 1976, 465

167: the people who wish: Quoted in ibid., 469

167: a flea bite: Rowlands, 56, 57

167: *Parturiunt montes*: Quoted in Harold Macmillan, *Winds of Change, 1914–39* (Macmillan, 1966), 300

167: No appreciable reduction: Miller (1976), 469, 472

168: fewer than 50,000: Stevenson and Cook, 65

168: the dead of winter: Quoted in Kingsford, 177

168: old washin' house boiler: Archie McInnes in *Voices from the Hunger Marches, Vol. I*, 44

168: Harry MacShane: ibid., 23

168: Mary Johnston: ibid., Vol. II, 247

169: Emily Swankie: ibid., 235

169: Marion Henery: ibid., Vol. I, 54

170: at Reading: Claude Stamfield mss diary, Swansea University Library, quoted in Stevenson and Cook, 163

170: Frank McCusker: *Voices from the Hunger Marches, Vol. I*, 33

171: the greatest condemnation: David Walter, *The Oxford Union: Playground of Power* (Macdonald, 1984), 78–9

171: Fifteen-year-old: *Out of Bounds: The Education of Giles Romilly and Esmond Romilly* (Hamish Hamilton, 1935), 185

171: Red Menace: Kevin Ingram, *Rebel:*

The Short Life of Esmond Romilly (Weidenfeld & Nicolson, 1985), 6

171: members of the public schools: *Out of Bounds* 1, no.1, March–April 1934, 35–6

171: entire sympathy: *Out of Bounds*, 1935, 242–3

172: a bizarre collection: Anne Chisholm, *Nancy Cunard* (Sidgwick & Jackson, 1979), 243

172: it was at Stamford: letter to Janet Solita quoted in Lois Gordon, *Nancy Cunard: Heiress, Muse, Political Idealist* (Columbia University Press, 2007), 203

172: Eighth day: Joseph P. Albaya, Sheffield Archives 779/F1/1

173: Frank McCusker: *Voices from the Hunger Marches, Vol. I*, 35

173: pulling off a scam: Kingsford, 183

173: rather like: Scaffardi, 47

173: wrapped in mufflers: Claud Cockburn, *In Time of Trouble* (Rupert Hart-Davies, 1956), 228

174: as books about: Mark Lilly, *The National Council for Civil Liberties: The First Fifty Years* (Macmillan, 1984), 2

174: bandits: A.P. Herbert, 'Bandits and Bottles', *The Weekend Review*, 5 August 1933

174: eight flute bands: McShane and Smith, 185

174: got up late: Albaya, Sunday, 25 February 1934

175: Jack Gaster: Interview, 2006

175: not a scuffle: Scaffardi, 46

176: Mary Johnston: *Voices from the Hunger Marches, Vol. II*, 247

176: before they left: Quoted in Kingsford, 196

176: Has anyone: Quoted in Lilly, 9

176: Sir Herbert Samuel: Quoted in Kingsford, 195

177: the 1934 Unemployment Act: Frederic Miller, 'The British Unemployment Crisis of 1935', *Journal of Contemporary History* 14, no.2, April 1979, 332–3

177: as late as 1935: Barry K. Hill, 'Unemployment in Birmingham and South Wales', *Llafur: Journal of Welsh People's History* 8, no.4, 2003, 80

177: Merthyr Tydfil: ibid., 80

177: 10,000 marched: Miller (1979), 343, 338

177: It had been realised: Quoted in ibid., 338

178: showin the authorities [and subsequent quotations]: *Voices from the Hunger Marches*, 9, 35–6, 60, 67, 289, 299

178: participate directly: Quoted in Andrew Thorpe, 'The Membership of the Communist Party of Great Britain, 1920–45' in *Historical Journal* 43, 3, 2000, 779

179: The people's flag: Hugh Sloan in *Voices from the Hunger Marches, Vol. II*, 286

179: NUWM membership: Sam Davies, 'The Membership of the National Unemployed Workers' Movement, 1923–38', *Labour History Review* 57, no.1, spring 1992, 30–1

179: drawing attention: Turnbull, 141–2

179: So successful: Richard Croucher, *We Refuse to Starve in Silence:*

A History of the Unemployed Workers' Movement (Lawrence & Wishart, 1987), 113–14

180: a hive of activity: Tom Ferns in *Voices from the Hunger Marches, Vol. I*, 139

180: Michael Clark: ibid., 363

180: The jiggin': John Lennox in ibid., Vol. II, 375

180: Battery Park: Croucher, 165–6

181: individual members: Thorpe, 779–80, 781, 786–8

181: an opposition party: Stuart MacIntyre, *Little Moscows: Communism and Working-Class Militancy in Inter-War Britain* (Croom Helm, 1980); Willie Thompson, *The Good Old Cause: British Communism, 1920–91* (Pluto, 1992), 48-9

181: three hundred members: Thorpe, 781, 783

181: The chief: *Bolton Journal and Guardian*, 27 January 1933

182: Minority Movement: Henry Pelling, *The British Communist Party: A Historical Profile* (A. & C. Black, 1958), 56–7

182: The Party's: Thorpe, 796

182: Secondly: Anon., *Bromley Communists in the Thirties: A Personal Reminiscence* (Kent and District Committee of the Communist Party, 1983), 2

182: Like practising: Raphael Samuel, *The Lost World of British Communism* (Verso, 2006), 10, 13

182: the pro-Soviet: Eaden and Renton, 38

183: They rambled: Samuel, 13

183: I had become: Trory, 67

183: However, 'sales: *Bromley Communists in the Thirties*, 6

183: Perhaps that was: Kevin Morgan, 'The Communist Party and the *Daily Worker* 1930–56' in Geoff Andrews, Nina Fishman and Kevin Morgan (eds), *Opening the Books: Essays on the Social and Cultural History of British Communism* (Pluto, 1955), 143–6

184: sometimes referred to: quoted in Denis Brogan, 'The Mirage of Moscow', *Fortnightly Review* 135 (new series), May 1934, 524

185: tell us about: C. Day Lewis, *The Buried Day* (Chatto & Windus, 1990), 208–11

186: by the idolisation: Louis MacNeice, *The Strings are False: An Unfinished Autobiography* (Faber, 1965), 145–6

186: Spender did: Stuart Samuels, 'English Intellectuals and Politics in the 1930s' in Philip Rieff (ed.), *On Intellectuals: Theoretical Studies. Case Studies* (Doubleday, 1969), 207

186: thought of as: Charles Rycroft quoted in Miranda Carter, *Anthony Blunt: His Lives* (Macmillan, 2001), 130

186: retired deeper: Philip Toynbee, *Friends Apart: A Memoir of the Thirties* (MacGibbon & Kee, 1954), 60–3

187: these unscrupulous: Robert Stewart quoted in Thorpe, 786

188: Moura Budberg: Andrea Lynn, *Shadow Lovers: The Last Affairs of*

H.G. Wells (Perseus, 2001), 106–11, 186–7

188: H.G. at the centre: Julian Huxley, *Memoirs* (Allen & Unwin, 1970), 171

188: to discuss a magnificent: ibid., 172–3

189: forming a small: Solly Zuckerman, *From Apes to Warlords, 1904–46* (Hamish Hamilton, 1978), 59–60

189: held the key: J.D. Bernal, 'Verantwortung und Verbflichtung der Wissenschaft' in Elga Kern (ed.), *Wegweisser in der Zeitwende: Selbst-zeugnisse bedeutender Menschen lesansgelber* (Munich/Basle, 1955), quoted in Gary P. Werskey, *The Visible College* (Allen Lane, 1978), 71, 75

189: the last man: Ronald Clark, *JBS: The Life and Times of J.B.S. Haldane* (Hodder & Stoughton, 1968), 86

189: primers for an age: Lancelot Hogben, *Mathematics for the Million* (Allen & Unwin, 1936), 9

189: acute mind: Zuckerman, 394–5, 109

190: insist on being: Neal Wood, *Communists and British Intel-lectuals* (Gollancz, 1959), 126, 127–8, 131

190: Obscuration: Edward Conzé, *The Scientific Method of Thinking: An Introduction to Dialectical Mater-ialism* (Chapman Hall, 1935), 35

191: a corporatist state: Julian Huxley, *If I Were Dictator* (Methuen, 1934), 16, 19, 50–3

191: would quantify: John Boyd Orr, *As I Recall* (Macmillan, 1966), 114–20

191: a large proportion: E. McBride, 'Social Control and Birth Control', *Nature* 113, 31 May 1924, 774, quoted in Werskey (1978), 32

191: Jewish scientists: J.G. Crowther, *Fifty Years with Science* (Barrie & Jenkins, 1970), 123–9

191: the university denied him: Jack Morrell, *Science at Oxford 1914–39: Transforming an Arts University* (Clarendon Press, 1997), 375

192: 20 per cent: ibid., 369

192: brains in Germany: Quoted in ibid., 373

192: wandering scholars: Ernest Rutherford, 'The Wandering Scholars: Exiles in British Sanctuary', *The Times*, 3 May 1934

192: greatly enriching: Daniel Snow-man, *The Hitler Émigrés: The Cultural Impact on Britain of Refugees from Nazism* (Chatto & Windus, 2002), 101–5

192: by far the richest: C.P. Snow, 'Chemistry' in H. Wright (ed.), *Cambridge University Studies 1933*, 103, quoted in Werskey (1978), 24

192: of great *value*: T.S. Eliot, 'Euripides and Professor Murray', quoted in Anna K. Mayer, '"A Combative Sense of Duty": Englishness and the Scientists' in Christopher Lawrence and Anna K. Mayer, *Regenerating England: Science, Medicine and Culture in Inter-War Britain* (Amsterdam: Editions Rodopi BV, 2000)

192: moral lag: Sermon reported in *The*

Times (and other newspapers), 5 September 1927, quoted in Lawrence and Mayer, 73

193: efforts of scientists: Solly Zuckerman, 'Science and Society', *New Statesman*, 25 February 1939

193: since scientists: Julian Huxley, *Scientific Research and Social Needs* (Watts, 1934), 15–16, quoted in Gary Werskey, 'British Scientists and "Outsider" Politics, 1931–45', *Science Studies* 1, 1971, 74

193: Bernalism is: Dr John Baker, 'Counterblast to Bernalism', *New Statesman*, 29 July 1939

193: solv[ing] completely: J.D. Bernal, 'Professor Bernal Replies', *New Statesman*, 5 August 1939

194: practically and: Werskey (1978), 210–11

194: would devote: ibid., 71, 76

194: 0.1 per cent: Chris Freeman, 'The Social Function of Science' in *J.D. Bernal: A Life in Science and Politics* ed. Brenda Swann and Francis Aprahamian (Verso, 1999), 110

194: science has ceased: J.D. Bernal, *The Social Function of Science* (Routledge, 1939), xiii

194: though his membership: Brenda Swann, 'Introduction' in Swann and Aprahamian, xxiii

194: During the years: Quoted in Maurice Goldsmith, *Sage: The Life of J.D. Bernal* (Hutchinson, 1980), 67

194: sink of ubiquity: Gary Werskey, 'The Marxist Critique of Science: A History in Three Movements', *Science as Culture* 14, 4, 106

194: In its endeavour: Bernal (1939), 415–16

195: dust and rubble: Frances Donaldson, *Child of the Twenties* (Rupert Hart-Davis, 1959), 154

195: the advanced stages: Innes H. Pearse and Lucy Crocker, *The Peckham Experiment: A Study in the Living Structure of Society* (Allen & Unwin for the Sir Halley Stewart Trust, 1943), 10

195: had been appalled: Alison Stallibrass, *Being Me and Also Us: Lessons from the Peckham Experiment* (Scottish Academic Press, 1989), 9

195: sieve for the detection: Pearse and Crocker, 12

196: health overhauls: Jane Lewis and Barbara Brookes, 'The Peckham Health Centre, "PEP" and the Concept of General Practice During the 1930s and 1940s' in *Medical History* 27, 1983, 152

196: the first survey: PEP Health Group minutes, 16 December 1936, quoted in ibid., 153

196: social self maintenance: A.D. Lindsay, Introduction to Peckham Health Centre's *First Annual Report*, 1926, quoted in Abigail Beach, 'Potential for Partnership: Health Centres and the Idea of Citizenship, c.1920–40' in Lawrence and Mayer, 215

196: scientists hoping: Quoted in Stallibrass, 14

196: vital foods: Albert Howard, *Medical Testament* (1939), quoted in David Matless, *Landscape and Englishness* (Reaktion, 1998), 163

197: strong meat: Donaldson, 159, 165

197: idea was shelved: Charles Webster, 'Medicine and the Welfare State, 1930–70' in Roger Cooter and John Pickstone (eds), *Medicine in the Twentieth Century* (Harwood, 2000), 131

197: a solarium: Fenner Brockway, *Bermondsey Story: The Life of Alfred Salter* (Allen & Unwin, 1949), 168

197: did not rest content: This information is all drawn from Elizabeth Lebas, '"Where Every Street Became a Cinema": The Film Work of Bermondsey Borough Council's Public Health Department, 1923–53', *History Workshop Journal* 39, 1995, 42–66

198: megaphone for health: Peter Coe and Malcolm Reading, *Lubetkin and Tecton: Architecture and Social Commitment* (Arts Council of Great Britain, 1981), 142

198: around 20 million: Noel Whiteside, 'Private Provision and Public Welfare: Health Insurance Between the Wars' in David Gladstone (ed.), *Before Beveridge: Welfare Before the Welfare State* (IEA Health and Welfare Unit, 1999), 29

199: teeth, teeth, teeth: Margery Spring Rice, *Working-Class Wives* (Penguin, 1939; Virago, 1981, 67

199: At least 5,000: Anne Digby and Nick Bosanquet, 'Doctors and Patients in an Era of National Insurance and Private Practice, 1913–38', *Economic History Review* 2nd series, 41, 1, 1988, 81

199: A GP employing: Steven Cherry, 'Medicine and Public Health, 1900–39' in Chris Wrigley (ed.), *A Companion to Early Twentieth-Century Britain* (Blackwell, 2003), 415

199: GPs were expected: Anne Digby, *The Evolution of British General Practice 1850–1948* (Oxford University Press, 1999), 195

199: local cottage hospitals: Julian Tudor Hart, 'Going to the Doctor' in Cooter and Pickstone, 544, 548

199: around 10,000 beds: Cherry, 412

200: a home visit: By 1948, when the NHS became operational, some doctors were still making thirty-eight home visits between the end of morning surgery and evening surgery at 4.30 (and still having time for lunch), though by 1970 this number had dropped to between eight and fifteen per day in most GPs' practices. Tudor Hart in Cooter and Pickstone, 548

200: Dr Cressy would: Eileen Whiteing, *Anyone for Tennis?: Growing up in Wallington Between the Wars* (London Borough of Sutton Libraries and Arts Services, 1979), 41

200: inadequate standards: Quoted in Branson and Heinemann, 225

200: well known to us: George Gladstone Robertson, MD, *Gorbals Doctor* (Jarrolds, 1970), 11–12

200: almost £30 million: Cherry, 411

200: 1939 Cancer Act: Berridge, 235

201: a wandering fire: Quoted in Charles Webster, 'Healthy or Hungry

Thirties?', *History Workshop Journal* 13, 1982, 122

201: struggled on: Spring Rice, 57–63

201: sulphonamide drugs: Hardy, 88

201: But the days: ibid., 83

201: by the end of the decade: Virginia Berridge, 'Health and Medicine' in F.M.L. Thompson (ed.), *The Cambridge Social History of Britain, 1750–1950, Vol. III: Social Agencies and Institutions* (Cambridge University Press, 1990), 229

202: free to all: John Stewart, *The Battle for Health: A Political History of the Socialist Medical Association* (Ashgate, 1999), 1

202: anarchy of capitalism: ibid., 3

202: within the limits: John Stewart, '"For a Healthy London": The Socialist Medical Association and the London County Council in the 1930s', *Medical History* 42, 1997, 427

203: addictive drug: Quoted in Digby, 199

203: new techniques: Anne Hardy, *Health and Medicine in Britain Since 1860* (Palgrave, 2001), 82; Bosanquet and Digby, 91

203: black liquorice: Digby, 188, 198

203: raw liver sandwiches: ibid., 197

203: the significance of vitamins: Cherry, 408–9

204: the dreaded diphtheria: Whiteing, 41–2

204: an out-patient department: Quoted in Bryder, 103

204: radical surgery: Thomas Dormandy, *The White Death: A History of Tuberculosis* (Hambledon, 1999), 249

205: spread throughout the country: ibid., 170

205: more deaths: Bryder, 99

205: folk remedies: Simon Guest, 'Cure, Superstition, Infection and Re-action: Tuberculosis in Ireland 1932–57', *Oral History*, autumn 2004, 67–8

205: the principal: Sir George Newman, Chief Medical Officer to the Ministry of Health, quoted in Linda Bryder, 'Papworth Village Settlement: A Unique Experiment in the Treatment and Care of the Tuberculous?', *Medical History* 28, 1984, 372

205: in isolated locations: Linda Bryder, *Below the Magic Mountain: A Social History of Tuberculosis in Twentieth-Century Britain* (Clarendon Press, 1988), 131. Three instances were reported in 1930 and in 1931 in England, but none in Wales.

205: much appreciated: Quoted in Imogen Magnus, '"Give Him Air. He'll Straight Be Well": Hospitals, Gardens and Grounds for Use in Employment, Therapy, Recreation and Convalescence from the Crimean War to World War II* (unpublished MA dissertation, Birkbeck College, University of London, 2002), 8

206: the model for: Dormandy, 152

206: strict rules: ibid., 171

206: the Royal Sea: Belinda Banham, *Snapshots in Time: Some*

Experiences in Health Care, 1936–91 (Jamieson Library of Women's History, 1991), 7

206: made a ward round: W.A. Murray, *A Life Worth Living: 50 Years in Medicine* (D.J. Croal, n.d.), 33

207: Those children who: Bryder, 148–52

207: The world regards: *Western Mail*, 5 November 1938

207: were actually higher: Bryder, 109

207: a consumptive: Lebas, 60–1

208: suffering from extensive: *British Journal of Tuberculosis* 24, 1931, 175, quoted in Dormandy, 321

208: studying the mechanisms: Varrier-Jones quoted in Bryder (1984), 383

208: We are dealing: ibid., 377

208: not everyone: Rowland Parker, *On the Road: The Papworth Story* (Pendragon Press, 1977), 146

209: turnover was £85,000: Dormandy, 322–4; Bryder, 158–61; Bryder, 'Papworth Village Settlement', 372–90. Papworth Village Settlement ceased treating solely tubercular patients in 1957, and is now a centre for heart transplant surgery.

209: Fresh Air: Ken Worpole, *Here Comes the Sun: Architecture and Public Space in Twentieth-Century European Culture* (Reaktion, 2000), 66–7

209: handed a leaflet: John Welshman, 'Eugenics and Public Health in Britain, 1900–40: Scenes from Provincial Life', *Urban History* 24, part 1, May 1997, 59, 63

210: Life expectancy: *British Social Trends Since 1900: A Guide to the Changing Social Structure of Britain* ed. A.H. Halsey (Macmillan, 1988), 404, Table 11.3

210: death rate was rising: Hardy, 94

210: childhood deaths varied: Mitchell, 111

210: modern estimates: Charles Webster, 'The Health of the School Child During the Depression' in Nicholas Parry and David MacNair (eds), *The Fitness of the Nation: Physical and Health Education in the Nineteenth and Twentieth Centuries* (History of Education Society, 1993), 78–9

211: There is no evidence: Quoted in Bryder, 115

211: Poverty has long: Professor Ralph M.F. Picken quoted in ibid., 114

211: tubercular cows' milk: ibid., 138

211: bad housing: Wilkinson, 236, 240, 241

212: a wise Dictator: *The Listener*, 4 November 1931

212: a compulsory item: *The Listener*, 25 November 1931

212: short-sighted sentimentalism: *The Listener*, 18 November 1931

212: the more suitable races: Francis Galton, *Inquiries into Human Faculty and its Development* (J.M. Dent, 1883), 24–5

213: very distinguished people: G.R. Searle, 'Eugenics and Politics in Britain in the 1930s', *Annals of Science* 36, 1979, 160

213: simple increase: D. Noel Paton and Leonard Findlay, *Poverty, Nutrition and Growth: Studies of Child Life in the Cities and Rural Districts of*

Scotland (1926), quoted in Greta Jones, 'Eugenics and Social Policy Between the Wars', *Historical Journal* 25, 3, 1982, 720–1

213: the fear that: ibid., 726

214: social inefficients: *Eugenics Review* 24, 1932–33, 107

214: standing army: *Eugenics Review* 25, 1933–34, 5, quoted in Searle, 162

214: the proportion of: *Nature* 116, 1925, 456

214: the regular consumption: Quoted in Richard A. Soloway, 'The "Perfect Contraceptive": Eugenics and Birth Control Research in Britain and America in the Interwar Years', *Journal of Contemporary History* 30, 1995, 647

214: even the stupidest: ibid., 639, 640

214: No public assistance: Quoted in Searle, 162

214: Infringement of: Julian Huxley, *What Dare I Think?* (Chatto & Windus, 1931), 88

214: the last resort: E.W. MacBride, 'Sterilisation as a Practical Eugenic Policy', *Nature* 125, 1930, 42

215: mentally defective: King and Hansen, 99

216: the general public: ibid., 100

216: Mostly much impressed: *Inside Stalin's Russia: The diaries of Reader Bullard, 1930–34* ed. Julian Bullard and Margaret Bullard (Day, 2000), 48

216: We saw in the Soviet Union: Margaret Cole, *The Life of G.D.H. Cole* (Macmillan, 1971)

216: An example of: Malcolm Muggeridge, *The Green Stick: Chronicles of a Wasted Time, Vol. I* (Collins, 1972), 228

217: At least he came: Bullard, 118

217: with the relish: Barbara Drake, 'The Webbs and Soviet Communism' in Margaret Cole (ed.), *The Webbs and Their Work* (Frederick Muller, 1949), 227

217: The problem we have: Webb, 7 January 1934, 322, 272–6

217: not find very: Bullard, 6

217: which she found: *The Listener*, 21 November 1934

217: better than anything: Bullard, 192

218: her own invention: Jenni Calder, *The Nine Lives of Naomi Mitchison* (Virago, 1997), 111

218: She'll be pretty: Bullard, 119

218: advocating a revolution: ibid., 193

218: J.D. Bernal: Werskey (1978), 144

218: Julian Huxley, *A Scientist Among Soviets* (Chatto & Windus, 1932), 51

218: a new science: Werskey (1978), 148

219: column after marching: Margaret Gardiner, *A Scatter of Memories* (Free Association, 1988), 247

219: I almost went: *Robert Byron's Letters Home* ed. Lucy Butler (John Murray, 1991), 180, 183

219: increasingly difficult: *Diary of a Journey to Russia by Robert Heywood Haslam 13.8.32 to 25.9.32*, Bolton Archives

220: sold off pretty well: Muggeridge, 227–8

220: a land of hope: Michael Newman, *Harold Laski: A Political Biography* (Macmillan, 1993), 166, 167

220: German town-planning [and subsequent quotes]: Muggeridge, 270, 271–2, 299, 302

225: Land's End of Wales: H.V. Morton, *In Search of Wales* (Methuen, 1932), 119, 122

225: imaginative gesture: Clough Williams-Ellis, *Portmeirion: The Place and its Meaning* (Faber, 1963), 17–18, 19

226: a bath and lavatory: Alwyn W. Turner, 'Portmeirion and its Creator' in *Portmeirion* (Antique Collectors' Club, 2006), 50

226: around one shilling [and subsequent information]: *Portmeirion*, 58, 63–4, 90

227: to rearrange the sheep: *Bucks Free Press*, 27 April 1934

227: By May 1937: Andrew H. Brown and B. Anthony Stewart, 'Beckonscot, England's Toy-Size Town', *National Geographic*, May 1937, 649–61

227: But in 1992: Robin Halstead, Jason Hazeley, Alex Morris and Joel Morris, *Bollocks to Alton Towers: Uncommonly British Days Out* (Michael Joseph, 2005), 217

227: the drab colours: *ICI Trade Talk*, April 1995, 4

228: day was slipping: *The Times*, 1 February 1933

229: preserving England: Margaret Dierden, *More Scenes of Shalford Past* (privately published, 2006), 57

229: a great octopus: Merlin Waterson, *The National Trust: The First Hundred Years* (BBC, 1994), 84

229: flying banner: Clough Williams-Ellis, *England and the Octopus* (Portmeirion Penrhyndeudraeth, 1928; new edn 1975), ix, 1

229: in both Latin and Cornish: Margaret Pollard's obituary by Ann Trevenen Jenkin, *Independent*, 7 December 1996

229: nearly as long: Margaret Pollard's obituary in *The Times*, 2 December 1996

229: donations of £900: Waterson, 88

230: disparate bits: Information from Dierden, 57–9

230: unthinkable that [and subsequent quotes]: Williams-Ellis (1928), 80–5

231: from time to time: Waterson, 109–10

231: planned private enterprise: Cited in John Gaze, *Figures in a Landscape: A History of the National Trust* (Barrie & Jenkins/National Trust, 1988), 121

231: the National Trust could not afford: Paula Weideger, *Gilding the Acorn: Behind the Façade of the National Trust* (Simon & Schuster, 1994), 42–3

231: untrammelled market forces: John K. Walton, 'The National Trust Centenary: Official and Unofficial Histories' in *The Local Historian* 26, no.2, May 1996, 80

232: an aristocrat: Nicolson, 4 February 1934, 164

232: made a vow: James Lees-Milne, *Another Self* (Hamish Hamilton, 1970), 95

232: Times change: Frances, Countess

of Warwick, *Afterthoughts* (Cassell, 1931), 246

233: but as a trustee: A.J.A. Morris, *C.P. Trevelyan, 1870–1958* (Belfast, 1977), quoted in Clare V.J. Griffiths, *Labour and the Countryside: The Politics of Rural Britain, 1918–39* (Oxford University Press, 2007), 297–8

233: thus does Time: *The 1929 Annual Reunions, WTA* (1929), 12, cited in ibid., 297

233: Today unspoiled country [and subsequent quotes]: Williams-Ellis, 65, 24–5, 69, 71, 72–3

234: Houses built haphazardly: Forster, 4 November 1934, 4 June 1937 urban attaque: Patrick Abercrombie, 'The English Countryside', *The Political Quarterly*, April 1930, reprinted in *The Political Quarterly in the Thirties* ed. W.A. Robson (Allen Lane/Penguin Press, 1971), 37 improved locomotion: Williams-Ellis, 15

235: The hut dwellers: S.P.B. Mais, 'The Plain Man Looks at England' in *Britain and the Beast* ed. Clough Williams-Ellis (J.M. Dent, 1937), 213

235: a flimsy bungalow: Clough Williams-Ellis, Introduction to H.H. Peach and N. Carrington, *The Face of the Land* (Allen & Unwin, 1930), 13

235: 755 advertisements: C.E.M. Joad, *The Untutored Townsman's Invasion of the Countryside* (Faber, 1946), Appendix VII, cited in Sean O'Connell, *The Car in British Society: Class, Gender and Motoring, 1896–1939* (Manchester University Press, 1998), 176

235: Letting the great: *The Listener*, 9 April 1930

235: Leave all your troubles: Quoted in Dennis Hardy and Colin Ward, *Arcadia for All: The Legacy of a Makeshift Landscape* (Mansell, 1984), 71

236: a piece of unspoilt: Mais, 'The Plain Man Looks at England' in Williams-Ellis, 216

236: It also riled: Peter Dickens, 'A Disgusting Blot on the Landscape', *New Society*, 17 July 1975

236: as little as £15: Hardy and Ward, 3

236: other thoroughfares designated: Peter Thorold, *The Motoring Age: The Automobile and Britain, 1896–1939* (Profile, 2003), 155

236: jerry-built: Quoted in Hardy and Ward, 7, 172

237: advertised for sale: Colin Ward, *Cotters and Squatters: Housing's Hidden History* (Five Leaves, 2002), 156

237: cheap incongruity: John Lowerson, 'Battles for the Countryside' in *Class, Culture and Structural Change: A New View of the 1930s* ed. Frank Gloversmith (Harvester Press, 1980), 260

237: development of the: *Observer*, 29 September 1929

237: promote suitable: Cited in John Sheail, *Rural Conservation in Inter-War Britain* (Oxford Clarendon Press, 1981), 64

238: what Manchester: Abercrombie, 'The English Countryside', 37

238: towns spilled: ibid., 36

238: tidy-minded wizards: Williams-Ellis (1928), 27

238: It is thus: ibid., 138–9

238: a new direction: *The Face of the Land*, 20

239: the immemorial resort: Williams-Ellis (1928), 66, 144

239: rows of villas: Earl of Crawford, quoted in Sheail, 51

239: England is Stonehenge: Gaze, 110

239: the whole question: Quoted in Sheail, 61

239: of high hopes: *Report of the Committee on Land Utilisation in Rural Areas* (HMSO, 1942), 40

240: 6.7 per cent: Sheail, 21

240: Morris car factory: Arthur Exell, 'Morris Motors in the 1930s. Part I', *History Workshop Journal* 6, 1978, 54

240: no keen observer: *How Labour Will Save Agriculture* (March 1934), 3, cited in Grifffiths, 299–300

241: It was cereal farming: See Alun Howkins, *The Death of Rural England: A Social History of the Countryside Since 1900* (Routledge, 2003) 65, 69–75

242: 50,000 members: Peter Dewey, 'Agriculture, Agrarian Society and the Countryside' in *A Companion to Early Twentieth-Century Britain* ed. Chris Wrigley (Blackwell, 2003), 280

242: Under the system: Steve Humphries and Beverly Hopwood, *Green and Pleasant Land* (Channel Four, 1999), 116

242: It was a sense: Marian Atkinson in ibid., 131–4

242: more than 860,000: Sheail, 22–5

243: In Berkshire: ibid., 32

243: If the village blacksmith: Quoted in Christopher Bailey, 'Rural Industries and the Image of the Countryside' in *The English Countryside Between the Wars: Regeneration or Decline?* ed. Paul Brassley, Jeremy Burchardt and Lynne Thompson (Boydell, 2006), 135

243: Most village garages: Howkins, 103

244: exclusive of stoppages: Trevor Rowley, *The English Landscape in the Twentieth Century* (Continuum, 2006), 21

244: prices were falling: O'Connell, 19–20, Rowley, 26

244: the immediate physical: Patrick Abercrombie, *The Preservation of Rural England* (1926)

244: the AA: O'Connell, 81, 82

245: 3,500 privately owned: W.M. Whiteman, *The History of the Caravan* (Blandford, 1973)

245: Ordnance Survey maps: Malcolm Chase, 'This is no Claptrap: This is Our Heritage' in Christopher Shaw and Malcolm Chase, *The Imagined Past: History and Nostalgia* (Manchester University Press, 1989), 129

245: shuts in: G.K. Chesterton, Introduction to *The Penn Country of Buckinghamshire* (Council for the Preservation of Rural England, 1933), 7–8

246: drive within twenty yards: Dr F.S.

Crowther Smith, *The Countryman*, January 1936, 499–500

246: a glance at: H.V. Morton, *In Search of England* (Methuen, 1927), vii

246: during the Depression: J.A.R. Pimlott, *The Englishman's Holiday* (Faber, 1947), 242

246: despite the advice: Cited in O'Connor, 175

246: Every major: Lowerson, 264; O'Connell, 97

246: Jack Beddington: Ruth Artmonsky, *Jack Beddington: The Footnote Man* (Ruth Artmonsky, 2006), 17–18

247: The proprietors: Patrick Wright, *On Living in an Old Country* (Verso, 1985), 63

247: the Medici: Artmonsky, 35

247: which interest me: Betjeman to Jack Bedddington, 17 August 1933, *Letters: John Betjeman* Vol. 1 ed. Candida Lycett Green (Methuen, 1994), 125

248: the uncritical tripper: John Betjeman, 'A Shell Guide to Typography' in *Typography* 2, 2

248: everything an intelligent: Quoted in Bevis Hillier, *John Betjeman: New Fame, New Love* (John Murray, 2002), 69

248: lived in Cornwall: Betjeman to Beddington, 17 August 1933, Lycett Green, 125

248: who were generally: Wright, 66

248: were the forebears: John Piper in *The Painter's Object* ed. Myfanwy Evans (Gerald Howe, 1937), 118, quoted in David Fraser Jenkins and

Frances Spalding, *John Piper in the 1930s: Abstraction on the Beach* (Merrell, 2003), 38

249: were not expected: John Piper quoted in Hillier, 66

249: large blocks should: Betjeman, *Typography*, 3

249: a man who obviously: C.E.M. Joad, *A Charter for Ramblers* (Hutchinson, 1934), 40

249: to shatter the peace: ibid., 41

250: Central Station: ibid., 12

250: streaming out: *English Journey*, 174–5

251: a gorgeous day: Joad (1946), 116–17

251: Tension between cyclists: O'Connell, 165

251: Over several decades: Joad (1934), 49 (twenty years if the path was over land in absolute ownership and forty years if the use was in any way fettered)

251: In an area: Sheail, 194

252: charged with violent affray: Lowerson, 273–6

252: so often but: C.E.M. Joad, 'The People's Claim' in *Britain and the Beast*, 77

252: took to the hills: Ramsay MacDonald, *Wanderings and Excursions* (Cape, 1925), 63. Perhaps significantly, the book was reprinted in 1932.

252: I am always: Griffiths, 96–7

252: no owner or occupier: Access to Mountains Bill, 11 November 1938, cited in Tom Stephenson, *Forbidden Land: The Struggle for Access to Mountain and Moorland*

(Manchester University Press, 1989), 165

253: such as no access: ibid., 179

253: that grimy visiting-card: *Britain and the Beast*, 72

253: the hordes of hikers: ibid., 78, 80

254: The first President [and subsequent information]: Oliver Coburn, *Youth Hostel Story* (National Council of Social Service, 1950), 3–21, 52, 120–1

255: return to the early: Ernest Westlake, cited in David Prynn, 'The Woodcraft Folk and the Labour Movement, 1925–70', *Journal of Contemporary History* 18, 1983, 80; see also Paul Wilkinson, 'English Youth Movements, 1908–30', *Journal of Contemporary History* 4, no.2, 1969, 3–23

255: proof of great strength: J.L. Finlay, 'John Hargrave, the Green Shirts and Social Credit', *Journal of Contemporary History* 5, no.1, 1970, 55

255: it formed links: ibid., 58–66, Prynn, 82

256: the longing to live: Leslie Paul, *Angry Young Man* (Faber, 1951), 67

256: the physically fit: The Woodcraft Folk continues today, with the aim of 'building a world based on equality, peace, social justice and co-operation', with no uniform but with encouragement to wear 'woodie hoodies' and T-shirts designed by members.

256: your trails: Quoted in Prynn, 91

256: We were socialists: Paul, 69

256: its revival: Bruce Pattison, 'Music

and the Community: Review', *Scrutiny* 11, no.4, March 1934, 400, quoted in Georgina Boyes, *The Imagined Village: Culture, Ideology and the English Folk Revival* (Manchester University Press, 1993), 130

256: They don't know: Beales and Lambert, 190

257: The problem of Leeds: H.V. Morton, *What I Saw in the Slums* (Labour Party, 1933), 37

257: with the object: ibid., 37

258: a communal yard: C.R.A. Martin, *Slums and Slummers: A Sociological Treatise on the Housing Problem* (John Bale, 1935), 56

258: Drip, drip, drip: Mrs Cecil Chesterton, *I Lived in a Slum* (Gollancz, 1936), 250, 267, 95–6

258: had to erect: H.J. Hammerton, *This Turbulent Priest: The Story of Charles Jenkinson, Parish Priest and Housing Reformer* (Lutterworth, 1952), 75

259: carbolic soap: Martin, 70

259: 1909 Town Planning Act: Alison Ravetz, *Model Estate: Planned Housing at Quarry Hill, Leeds* (Croom Helm/Joseph Rowntree Memorial Trust, 1978), 17, 18

259: small private landlords: Morton, 9

259: shortfall of 600,00: Marion Bowley, *Housing and State, 1914–44* (Allen & Unwin, 1945), 12

259: politically inexpedient: John Burnett, *A Social History of Housing, 1815–1985* (Methuen, second edition, 1986), 222

260: 31.5 per cent: M.J. Daunton,

Introduction to *Councillors and Tenants: Local Authority Housing in English Cities, 1919–39* ed. M.J. Daunton (Leicester University Press, 1984), 33

260: possibly the best: *Yorkshire Post*, 17 December 1924, cited in Richard Finnigan, 'Council Housing in Leeds, 1919–39' in *Councillors and Tenants* (1984), 109

260: immensely in advance: *Poverty and Progress*, 213

261: the housing of: *The Times*, 12 April 1919, quoted in Burnett, 219

261: worse than folly: Raymond Unwin, *Cottage Plans and Common Sense*, Fabian Tract 109, 1902, 13

261: a strong aversion: *An Inquiry into People's Homes: A Report Prepared by Mass-Observation for the Advertising Services Guild* (John Murray, 1943), 104–7

262: average council house rents: Burnett, 239

262: the front bedroom: Alan Sillitoe, *Life Without Armour* (Harper Collins, 1995), 7, 8

263: premises known: Jerry White, 'When Every Room was Measured: The Overcrowding Survey of 1935–6 and its Aftermath', *History Workshop Journal* 4, autumn 1977, 88

263: 6,757 families: Alison Ravetz with Richard Turkington, *The Place of Home: English Domestic Environments, 1914–2000* (E. & F.N. Spon, 1995), 68

263: 26,046 people: Morton, 14

263: it was 13.5: Carl Chinn, *Homes for People: Council Housing and Urban Renewal in Birmingham, 1849–1999* (Brewin, 1999), 73

263: No other civilized country: Martin, 29

263: at least a million: *A Policy for the Slums* (Report of the Special Committee of the National Housing and Town Planning Council, 1929), cited in Burnett, 243

263: time capsules: Chris Upton, *Living Back-to-Back* (Philimore, 2005), 147

263: We must look: Morton, 15

263: In Bolton: *Bolton Evening News*, 20 February 1936

263: the St Clements district: Arthur Exell, 'Morris Motors in the 1930s, Part II: Politics and Trade Unionism', *History Workshop Journal* 7, spring 1979, 47

264: Burslem: *Some Housing Conditions in the Potteries: A Report to the North Staffordshire Housing Survey Council,* 1931, 5, 9

264: a kind of shake-down: Morton, 35–6

264: A survey on Merseyside: D. Caradog Jones, *The Social Survey of Merseyside* (Liverpool University Press, 1938)

265: The house: Forster, 27 June 1937

265: In Glasgow: Helen Clark and Elizabeth Carnegie, *She Was Aye Workin': Memories of Tenement Women in Edinburgh and Glasgow* (White Cockade Publishing, 2003), 15–16; John Butt, 'Working-Class Housing in Glasgow, 1900–39' in Ian

McDougall (ed.), *Essays in Scottish Labour History: A Tribute to W.H. Marwick* (John Donald, 1978), 143–69

265: A Sanitary Inspector: Martin, 59–60

266: Joan Conquest: *The Naked Truth: Shocking Revelations About the Slums* (T. Werner Laurie, 1933), 43–4, 51, 57–8, 64

266: candle and toilet-soap works: Sir Hubert Llewellyn Smith, *The New Survey of London Life and Labour* (nine volumes, London School of Economics, 1931–35), *Vol. II*, 394

266: The spread of commerce: Chesterton, 233–4, 235

267: steadily increasing: Jerry White, *London in the Twentieth Century* (Viking, 2001), 22

267: Shoreditch and Bermondsey: Smith, 151

267: worst property: Martin, 28

267: notorious slums: J.H. Forshaw and P. Abercrombie, *County Plan of London* (London County Council, 1943), 21, 28

267: so many unfit: H. Marshall and A. Trevelyan, *Slum* (Heinemann, 1933), 118

267: hopelessly defective: I. Barclay and E. Perry, *Report on a Survey of Housing Conditions in the Metropolitan Borough of Southwark* (1929), quoted in Jim Yelling, 'The Metropolitan Slum' in *Slums* ed. S. Martin Gaskell (Leicester University Press, 1990), 203

267: some districts: Yelling, 191–2

268: The attraction: Chesterton, 205

268: Manchester had: Burnett (1986), 243

268: Manchester had: E.D. Simon and J. Inman, *The Rebuilding of Manchester* (Longman, 1935), 27

268: For all the thousands: Cited in Robert Finnigan, 'Housing Policy in Leeds Between the Wars' in *Housing Policy and the State* ed. Joseph Melling (Croom Helm, 1980), 115

269: a blanket of smog: Martin, 36

269: 8,585 out of 51,000: Morton, 18

269: Smoke upon Stench: *Housing in Stoke on Trent: The Place and the Problem* (Society for Socialist Inquiry and Propaganda, July 1932), 3

269: Ministry of Health: Burnett, 244

269: It was difficult: Robert Finnigan, 'Council Housing in Leeds, 1919–39' in *Councillors and Tenants*, 109–10

269: Reverend Charles Jenkinson: Hammerton, 76, 88n, 91

270: more than 20,000: Finnigan (1984), 107, 113

270: There was evidence: G. M'Gonigle and J. Kirby, *Poverty and Public Health* (Gollancz, 1936), 112–13

270: In Carlisle: Daunton, 23

271: some families: Finnigan, 117

271: In addition: Burnett, 244

272: On what lines: E.D. Simon, 'The Future of Our Great Cities' in *Liverpool and the Housing Problem* (Liverpool Council of Social Care, 1935), 43

272: Town planning of: L.P. Scott, 'A Plan for Stepney: The Practical and the Ideal' in *The Toynbee Outlook* 1, no.3, June 1936, 9

272: crowded together: Simon, 43

272: Unwin travelled: Charles McKean, 'Between the Wars' in *Glasgow: The Forming of a City* ed. Peter Reed (Edinburgh University Press, 1999), 134, 131

272: Removals on so: Quoted in Andrzej Olechnowicz, *Working-Class Housing Between the Wars: The Becontree Estate* (Clarendon Press, 1997), 5

273: more than 90 per cent: A.H. Halsey (ed.), *Trends in British Society since 1900* (1972), 303

273: swaddle: McKean, 132

273: trees and hedges: Sir John Stirling Maxwell quoted in ibid., 131–2

273: One fifth: Chinn, 52

273: Wythenshawe: Burnett, 293

273: a century's progress: Quoted in Manchester Women's History Group, 'Ideology in Bricks and Mortar: Women's Housing in Manchester Between the Wars', *North West Labour History* no.12, 1987, 30, 31

273: very few natural: Olechnowicz (1997), 2

273: larger than: Terence Young, *Becontree and Dagenham: A Report Made for the Pilgrim Trust* (Becontree Social Service Committee, 1934), 98, 106, 118

274: Nothing doing: Chesterton, 237

274: most slum dwellers: Young, 25, 118, 142, 76

275: Out of a total: Quoted in Olechnowicz, 70

275: Lewis Silkin: Quoted in ibid., 67

275: Henry Ford himself: Allan Nevins with the collaboration of Frank Ernest Hill, *Ford, Vol. III: Expansion and Challenge, 1915–33* (Scribner's, 1957), 366

275: a lot of existing: Ted Knightley in *Just Like the Country: Memories of London Families Who Settled the New Cottage Estates, 1919–39* ed. Antonia Rubinstein (Age Exchange, 1991), 59

275: one plant: Chesterton, 271

275: well over 100,000: Olechnowicz (1997), 97

275: Bill Waghorn: *Just Like the Country*, 60

276: During a debate: Cited in Olechnowicz (1997), 51, 99

276: a huge queue: Young, 77

276: daren't have: Alfred Gates in *Just Like the Country*, 27

276: bug van: Ravetz (1978), 38–9

276: Some families ditched: John Hilton, *Rich Man, Poor Man* (Allen & Unwin, 1944), 133

276: Rosina Evans: *Just Like the Country*, 31

277: Roehampton: ibid., 33; *Home Sweet Home: Housing Designed by the London County Council and Greater London Architects 1888–1975* (Greater London Council Department of Architecture and Civic Design, 1975), 32

277: charge per unit: Young, 195

277: St Helier estate: Dorothy Barton in *Just Like the Country*, 35

278: Downham estate: ibid., 43

278: The ceilings: Eric Phillips, Stanley Breeze, Lillian Badger and Phyllis Rhoden in ibid., 45, 47

278: a doctor: Ryan MacMahon, *Tramp Royal: An Autobiography* (John Langdon, n.d.), 111

278: Eric Phillips, May Millbank and Florence Essam: *Just Like the Country*, 44–5

279: Grace Foulkes: Grace Foulkes, *My Life with Reuben* (Shepheard-Walwyn, 1975), 44

279: 'Front parlour' shops: Cited in Olechnowicz (1997), 76

279: pawnshop bus: Young, 76n

279: Despite the cost: *Reminiscences of St Helier Estate* (St Helier Estate Reminiscence Group, 1999), 3; Young, 373–5; *Just Like the Country*, 40

279: 258,126 tenants: The figure is for 1939. *An Inquiry into People's Homes*, 35

279: A Mass-Observation enquiry: ibid., 37

280: uniform town: Leslie Charles Alder in *Just Like the Country*, 60

280: its natural charm: *An Inquiry into People's Homes*, 37, 41, 43, 44

280: the housewife spends: Quoted in Manchester Women's History Group, 36–7, 41

280: the care of which: *An Inquiry into People's Homes*, 163

280: strive to obtain: *Just Like the Country*, 36, 39, 38

281: I like it: *An Inquiry into People's Homes*, 171, 208

281: In Manchester: Simon and Inman, 110

281: a survey of Bermondsey: Greater London Record Office, AR/TP/1/56, *Report on Bermondsey, 3 May 1941*, quoted in J.A. Yelling, *Slums and Redevelopment* (UCL Press, 1992), 172–82

281: the comradeship: G.D.H. Cole, 'The Essentials of Democracy' (1941) reprinted in *Essays in Social Theory* (1950), 109, quoted in Olechnowicz (1997), 228

282: a territorial group: Durant, ix

282: self-contained entity: Abigail Beach and Nick Tiratsoo, 'The Planners and the Public' in Martin Daunton (ed.), *The Cambridge Urban History of Britain, Vol. III: 1840–1950* (Cambridge University Press, 2000)

282: a civic art: S. Meacham, 'Raymond Unwin, 1863–1940: Designing Democracy in Edwardian England' in Susan Pedersen and Peter Mandler (eds), *After the Victorians* (Routledge, 1994), 79–83

282: became for many: Beach and Tiratsoo in Daunton (2000), 537

282: We did not say: H.G. Wells, *Experiment in Autobiography: Discoveries and Conclusions of a Very Ordinary Brain (Since 1866)* (Gollancz/Cresset Press, 1934), 203

283: one shop for every 241: Olechnowicz (1997), 74

283: much missed: *An Inquiry into People's Homes*, 40

283: Watling: Ruth Durant, *Watling: A Survey of Social Life on a New Housing Estate* (P.S. King, 1939), 20–21

283: banished from: George Orwell, *The*

Road to Wigan Pier (Gollancz, 1937), 72

283: perpendicular drinking: Bill Peek, quoted in Gavin Weightman and Steve Humphries, *The Making of Modern London, 1914–39* (Sidgwick & Jackson, 1984), 137–8

283: one medical practitioner: Alan A. Jackson, *Semi-Detached London: Suburban Development, Life and Transport, 1900–39* (Allen & Unwin, 1973), 298, 177

283: probably the most: Cited in Olechnowicz (1997), 74, 87

284: inconvenient: E.D. Simon, 'Housing and Civic Planning' in Harold J Laski, W. Ivor Jennings and William A. Robson (eds), *A Century of Municipal Progress, 1835–1935* (Allen & Unwin, 1938), 207

284: Kingstanding: Chinn, 58

284: a building designed: National Council of Social Services, *Definition of a Community Centre and Community Association* (1938), quoted in Olechnowicz (1997), 163

284: to provide no: Young, 11

284: meagre 'leisure time': See Ravetz (1978), 123

284: Watling estate: Durant, 45, 58, 98–9, 118, 119

285: beyond catering: Olechnowicz (1997), 203

285: people dislike: Rosamond Jevons and John Madge, *Housing Estates: A Study of Bristol Corporation Policy and Practice Between the Wars* (University of Bristol, 1946), 91

285: Sunday school: Young (1934), 222–4

285: All the culture: George Orwell, *England, Your England and Other Essays* (Secker & Warburg, 1953), 196

285: We knew nothing: Foulkes, 38

285: most of the people: *An Inquiry into People's Homes*, xviii, 167

286: a few yards: Durant, 88, 89

286: If Becontree: Young, 23

286: that black and: Chesterton, 8

286: use their baths: Martin, 142

286: pull doors off: Young, 23

286: circuses: ibid., 100

287: Vienna with: Elizabeth Denby, *Europe Re-Housed*, quoted in Lionel Esher, *The Broken Wave: The Rebuilding of England, 1940–80* (Allen Lane, 1981), 28–9

287: dark and dismal: *Liverpool Review*, February 1934, 64

287: The origin of flats: *An Inquiry into People's Homes*, 46

288: *Birmingham Gazette*, 24 May 1930, cited in Anthony Sutcliff, 'A Century of Flats in Birmingham, 1875–1973' in Anthony Sutcliffe (ed.), *Multi-Storey Living: The British Working-Class Experience* (Croom Helm, 1974), 181

288: The Mansions: Chinn, 64, 65

288: The Barracks: *Multi-Storey Living*, 180, 192

288: for the first time: Burnett (1986), 247

288: public policy: *An Inquiry into People's Homes*, 46

288: cost almost double: Burnett (1986), 247–8

288: opposed to the habits: B.S. Townroe, *The Slum Problem* (1928), 61

289: Lord Jersey: Weightman and Humphries, 118

289: until he had studied: Alison Ravetz, 'From Working Class Tenements to Modern Flat: Local Authorities and Multi-Storey Housing Between the Wars' in *Multi-Storey Living*, 133

289: normal family: Finnigan (1984), 128

289: We have nothing: *The Housing Policy in Leeds*, Appendix 21, 86, quoted in Hammerton, 123, 124

290: an impoverished city: Chesterton, 277–8

290: the most squalid: J.G. Lockhart, *Cosmo Gordon Lang* (Hodder & Stoughton, 1949), 96

290: Karl Marx Hof: Ravetz (1978), 51–5,

291: Beachy Head: *Yorkshire Post*, 19 July 1961; Ravetz, (1978), 58

291: refuse container: Ravetz (1978), 63

291: internal green: Alison Ravetz, 'The History of a Housing Estate', *New Society*, 27 May 1971

292: windowboxes: Ravetz (1978), 78

292: Tenants' association: ibid., 125, 126

293: Bishop of Stepney: Branson and Heinemann, 194–9

293: *The Tenant's Guide*: *Picture Post*, 1 April 1939, 54

293: the descent of: Hammerton, 131

293: the most advanced: Ravetz (1978), 64–5

293: blind faith: Ravetz in *Multi-Storey Living*, 137, 138, 141

293: By 1958: Ravetz (1978), 91

294: By 1978: ibid., 223

295: Even during an: Forster, August 1936, 24 October 1935, 7 May 1935

296: around three-quarters of a million: Quoted in Andrew McCulloch, 'A Millstone Round Your Neck? Building Societies in the 1930s and Mortgage Default', *Housing Studies* 5, no.1, 43

296: the vast majority: Esher, 38, 19

297: A striking example: Mark Swenarton and Sandra Taylor, 'The Scale and the Nature of the Growth of Owner-Occupation in Britain Between the Wars', *Economic History Review*, 2nd series, 38, no.3, August 1985, 390

297: It was the same: Annette O'Carroll, 'Tenements to Bungalows: Class and the Growth of Home Ownership Before World War II', *Urban History* 24, 2, 1997, 228

297: In areas where [and subsequent information]: Swenarton and Taylor, 387–90

297: by almost a million: H.W. Richardson and D.H. Aldcroft, *Building in the British Economy Between the Wars* (1968), 302

298: In 1931 nearly: Alan A. Jackson, (1973), 102

298: miles of semi-detached: Priestley, (1934), 401

298: four times more children: *The Listener*, 28 November 1934

299: to provide a reserve: Jackson (1973), 316–17

299: To the East: ibid., 117–20

299: This was where: Paul Vaughan,

Something in Linoleum: A Thirties Education (Sinclair-Stevenson, 1994), 6, 56

300: on the Southern Electric: Alan A. Jackson, *The Railway in Surrey* (Atlantic, 1999), 110, 118, 119

301: Now pioneer: Patrick Abercrombie, *Greater London Plan 1944* (HMSO, 1945), para. 8

301: inviting doorways: Quoted in Christian Barman, *The Man Who Built London Transport: A Biography of Frank Pick* (David & Charles, 1979)

302: Metroland: Christian Wolmar, *The Subterranean Railway* (Atlantic, 2004; revised edn 2005), 221

302: the publicity brochure: *Metro-land*, 1932

302: telly-poem: A.N. Wilson, *Betjeman* (Hutchinson, 2006), 307

302: A regular annual: Swenarton and Taylor, 385

303: key money: Peter Scott, 'Selling Owner-Occupation to the Working Classes in 1930s Britain'

303: Repayment periods: Burnett (1986), 254

304: The builders Laing: ibid., 254; Weightman and Humphries, 112

304: it remained a largely: Burnett (1986), 251, 253

304: something under 35 per cent: Swenarton and Taylor, 376–7, quoting M.J. Daunton, *Coal Metropolis, Cardiff, 1870–1914* (Leicester University Press, 1977), 114, who used figures taken from the Departmental Committee on Valuation for Rates of 1939 taken from returns made between July and December 1938 by the rating authorities of England and Wales, which Swenarton and Taylor have calculated is an overestimate.

304: almost 60 per cent: Ross McKibbin, *Classes and Cultures: England, 1918–51* (Oxford University Press, 1998), 73

304: took in lodgers: Swenarton and Taylor, 378

304: a big signpost: Jane Walsh, *Not Like This* (Lawrence & Wishart, 1953), 55–6

304: a small country village: Foulkes, 59–60, 62–4

306: we are taking on: Quoted in Scott, 27

306: they had vacated: Foulkes, 62–4

306: withheld the mortgage: A.D. McCulloch, 'Owner-Occupiers and Class Struggle: The Mortgage Strikes of 1936–40' (PhD thesis, University of Essex, 1983), 237, 250, quoted in Olechnowicz (1997), 128

307: builders' pool system: Jackson (1986), 197–9; Andrew McCulloch, 'The Mortgage Strikes', *History Today* 51, 6, June 2001; 'The Borders of Insanity', *Picture Post*, 25 March 1939, 56–9; Gavin Stamp, 'Neo-Tudor and its Enemies', *Architectural History* 49 (2006)

307: always having your: *An Inquiry into People's Homes*, 175–6, 177

308: a means of easing: H. Durant, *The Problem of Leisure* (Routledge, 1938), 56; Q.D. Leavis, *Fiction and the Reading Public* (Chatto &

Windus, 1932), 57, cited in Olechnowicz (1997), 148

310: establishing on these: Stephen Taylor, MB MRCP, 'The Suburban Neurosis', *The Lancet*, 26 March 1938, 759–61

310: Painters' estate: Vaughan, 73

310: Dora Gordine: Stuart Durant and Brenda Martin, 'Dorich House, Kingston' in *The Modern House Revisited* (Twentieth Century Society, 1996), 97–100

311: My father settled: Vaughan, 60–1

311: The Farm Estate: Jackson (1999), 137

311: peep up and: Raymond Unwin, *Cottage Plans and Common Sense*, quoted in ibid., 143

311: galleons were very: Paul Oliver, 'The Galleon on the Front Door' in *Dunroamin: The Suburban Semi and its Enemies* ed. Paul Oliver, Ian Davis and Ian Bentley (Barrie & Jenkins, 1981), 161

312: W.D. & H.O. Wills: Stephen Constantine, 'Amateur Gardening and Popular Recreation in the 19th and 20th Centuries', *Journal of Social History* 14, no.3, spring 1981, 398–9

312: Countless new homes: J. Coutts, *All About Gardening* (revised edn 1931), quoted in ibid., 398

313: imitation parquet: Vaughan, 62

314: solid Edwardian oak: Phyllis Wilmott, *Growing Up in a London Village: Family Life Between the Wars* (1970), 133

314: A few bits: *Hire Traders' Record*, April 1936, quoted in Peter Scott, 'The Twilight World of Interwar

British Hire Purchase', *Past and Present* 177, November 2002, 210

315: a telephone: Alan A. Jackson, *The Middle Classes 1900–50* (David St John Thomas, 1991), 101

317: No matter how retrospective: This section draws both on my own interest in and observation of 1930s architecture and design, and also on a number of books and articles including Jackson, *Semi-Detached London*; Davis et al., *Dunroamin*; Vaughan, *Something in Linoleum*; J.M. Richards, *The Castles on the Ground: The Anatomy of Suburbia* (Architectural Press, 1946; 2nd edn John Murray, 1973); Stamp, 'Neo-Tudor and its Enemies', *Little Palaces: House and Home in the Inter-War Suburbs* (MoDA, Middlesex University Press, 2003); Katie Arber, *Thirties Style: Home Decoration and Furnishings from the 1930s* (MoDA, Middlesex University Press, 2003); Helena Bartlett and John Phillips, *Suburban Style: The British Home, 1840–1960* (Macdonald Orbis, 1987); Greg Stevenson, *The 1930s Home* (Shire, 2005)

317: industrial materials: Mark Pinney, 'Architecture' in *Little Palaces*, 27

318: Ideal Home exhibition [and subsequent information]: Jackson (1973), 139

318: a cottage-style semi: Stevenson, 15

318: A man who builds: Anthony Bertram, *The House: A Machine for Living* (1935), 21

319: people cling to: 'Modern Dwellings

for Modern Needs', *The Listener*, 24 May 1933

319: an illusory paradise: Jackson (1973), 40–1

319: If an architect: Osbert Lancaster, *Pillar to Post: English Architecture Without Tears* (John Murray, 1938), 68

319: Come friendly bombs: John Betjeman, 'Slough', *Continual Dew* (John Murray, 1937), reprinted in *The Best of Betjeman* (Penguin, 1978), 24

320: Practically none of: Esher, 27

320: accumulation of: J.M. Richards, Introduction (1973) to *The Castles on the Ground*, 2

320: The miserable sheds: Hilaire Belloc, *Complete Verse* (Nonesuch, 1954), 143

320: represented something: Graham Greene, *A Gun for Sale: An Entertainment* (Heinemann, 1936), 57

320: Gaily into Ruislip Gardens: John Betjeman, 'Middlesex', *A Few Late Chrysanthemums* (1954), 26

321: part of the background: Richards, 16, 20, 19

321: There has been: Sir Leslie Scott, KC, 'Preservation of the Countryside' in *House-Building 1934–39* ed. Ernest Betham (n.d.), 33

322: seven feet tall: Peter Collison, *The Cutteslowe Walls: A Study in Social Class* (Faber, 1963), 13. Most of the subsequent account is based on Collison's excellent book, which is itself based on surveys he made in 1955–56 and 1960, his interest having been aroused by

'one of G.D.H. Cole's sociology seminars [when] the discussion had turned on the difficulties which arose when people of one class found themselves living in close proximity to those of another'; Cole instanced the Cutteslowe walls (13).

323: Led by: Many thanks to Oxford Cockaigne for this information

323: There was this: *Oxford Mail*, 20 May 1935

324: During the Second: *Oxford Mail*, 1 and 3 February 1943

326: stale mixed grill: 'Supplement to the Memorandum on a Proposal to Revise the Typography of *The Times*', 1931, cited in Nicolas Barker, *Stanley Morison* (Macmillan, 1972), 291–2

326: aristocratic type: Oliver Wood and James Bishop, *The Story of The Times* (Michael Joseph, 1983), 240. Alan Hutt pointed out in the *Journal of Typographical Research* that the use of Times New Roman on cheaper paper printed at high speed produced a grey effect.

326: the label on a bottle: Barker, 294

326: but the shock: Note from Barrington-Ward, 27 July 1931, quoted in ibid., 296

327: the old forms: Walter Gropius, *Ja! Stimmen des Arbeitsrates für Kunst in Berlin* (1919), quoted in Christopher Wilk (ed.), *Modernism: Designing a New World* (V&A, 2006), 11

327: proving compelling: Definitions of

modernism – particularly in its wider application – are notoriously slippery: see Christopher Wilk, 'What was Modernism?' in *Modernism: Designing a New World*, 11–21; Deyan Sudic, 'Modernism: The Idea That Just Won't Go Away', *Observer*, 29 January 2006, 10–11

327: no more Chippendale: Quoted in Barker, 270

327: The 'Perpetua' capitals: *The Times*, 27 September 1932

327: Harold Nicolson: *Thirties: British Art and Design Before the War* (Arts Council of Great Britain, 1979), 205

328: In a few weeks: Quoted in the *Illustrated London News*

328: Who *are* Prospero: Fiona MacCarthy, *Eric Gill* (Faber, 1989), 245

328: should be reduced: ibid., 247

328: simian-like creature: Quoted in Edward Lucie-Smith, *Art of the 1930s: The Age of Anxiety* (Weidenfeld & Nicolson, 1985), 170

328: an open insult: Quoted in William Feaver, 'Art at the Time' in *Thirties*, 42

329: lukewarm: Kenneth Clark, 'The Future of Painting', *The Listener*, 2 October 1935

329: only cubist: Andrew Gibbon Williams, *William Roberts: An English Cubist* (Lund Humphries, 2004), 80

329: pedestrian naturalism: Sir James Richards, Foreword to *Unit One:*

Spirit of the 30s, Mayor Gallery exhibition catalogue, 1984, 5

329: the *Daily Mail*: Frances Spalding, *British Art Since 1900* (Thames & Hudson, 1986), 87–8

330: allowed to die: *Architectural Review*, June 1931

330: the expression of: *The Times*, 12 June 1931

330: expelled all artists: Norbert Lynton, *Ben Nicholson* (Phaidon, 2002), 79

330: Nest of Gentle Artists: J.P. Hodin, 'A Study of the Cultural History of Hampstead in the Thirties', *Hampstead in the Thirties: A Committed Decade* (Camden Arts Centre, 1974), 5–6

331: Whether we like it: *Derbyshire Advertiser*, 30 November 1934, quoted in Michael T. Saler, *The Avant-Garde in Interwar England: Medieval Modernism and the London Underground* (Oxford University Press, 1999), 129

331: an aesthetic unity: Herbert Read, *Art Now: An Introduction to the Theory of Modern Painting and Sculpture* (Faber, 1933)

331: preparing the death rites [and subsequent quotations]: David Gascoyne, Hugh Gordon Porteous and Herbert Read, quoted in Lynton, 119–20

332: How many surrealists: David Hopkins, Introduction to *Dada and Surrealism: A Very Short Introduction* (Oxford University Press, 2004)

332: a nation which: *International*

Surrealist Exhibition, New Burlington Galleries catalogue, 1936, 13

332: precipitate revelation: Michel Remy, Surrealism in Britain (Ashgate, 1999), 19

332: wild creature: Eileen Agar (in collaboration with Andrew Lambrith), A Look at Life (Methuen, 1988), 116

332: his mother's house: Trevelyan, 67

333: humming-bird poet: Sharon-Michi Kusunoki, 'Edward James: Architect of Surrealism' in Surreal Things: Surrealism and Design ed. Ghislaine Wood (V&A, 2007)

333: cope with: Neil Bingham, Christopher Nicholson (RIBA Academy Editions, 1996), 44, 45

333: it would be easy: John Lowe, Edward James: A Surrealist Life (Collins, 1991), 127

333: people bathing: Bingham, 69

333: Brighton Pavilion: Lowe, 127

333: tide of careless destruction: Lord Derwent quoted in James Knox, A Biography of Lord Byron (John Murray, 2003), 378

334: the noblest bridge: Quoted in Gavin Stamp, Britain's Lost Cities (Aurum, 2007), 121

334: the Group's supporters: Knox, 380

334: freak house: Kusunoki, 211–12

334: the English contribution: International Surrealist Exhibition, 13

334: and so, overnight: Trevelyan, 66. Trevelyan says three paintings: the catalogue to the exhibition lists five.

334: surrealist phantom: ibid., 72

335: plunging down: Mark Amory, Lord Berners: The Last Eccentric (Chatto & Windus, 1998), 160

335: adapted from Dalí: Remy, 73–81

335: The Water Mug: Surrealist Catalogue, 18

335: powerful biomorphic: Agar, 115

336: lots of little glasses: Trevelyan, 69

336: a strange fascination: Paul Nash, 'Swanage or Seaside Surrealism', Architectural Review LXXIX, April 1936, 151–4, reprinted in Pennie Denton, Seaside Surrealism: Paul Nash in Swanage (Peveril, 2002), 82. Agar continued her fascination with seaside objets trouvés with her famous Ceremonial Hat for Eating Bouillabaisse (1936), fashioned from detritus she had found in the harbour at St Tropez in the south of France.

336: meaninglessness for: Remy, 76

336: Roland [Penrose]'s house: Trevelyan, 72

336: lost much of its: Tevelyan, 80

336: the affair of: Anthony Blunt, 'Art Under Capitalism and Socialism', The Mind in Chains: Socialism and the Cultural Revolution ed. C. Day Lewis (Frederick Muller, 1937), 111

336: aware of social: William Coldstream, 'How I Paint', The Listener, 15 September 1937

336: the slave trade: Bruce Laughton, The Euston Road School: A Study in Objective Painting (Scolar, 1986), 115

336: the influence of Paris: Lynda Morris, 'The Touch of Time' in Making History: Art and Documentary in

Britain from 1929 to Now (Tate, 2006), 28

336: a fund offering: William Townsend, Introduction to *The Euston Road School and Others* (Wakefield City Art Galleries, June 1948), 2, 3

338: training the observation: William Coldstream 'Prospectus', quoted in Laughton, 3

338: to collect: Mass-Observation pamphlet quoted in Judith M. Heimann, *The Most Offending Soul Alive: Tom Harrisson and His Remarkable Life* (Aurum, 2002), 129

339: saw in the: Trevelyan, 82, 84–5

339: honest, unvarnished: Tom Harrisson, 'What They Think in "Worktown"', *The Listener*, 28 August 1938

339: a flat image: Coldstream's depiction now hangs in the National Gallery of Canada in Ottawa.

339: the wider public: Harrisson (1938), 398

339: squalorscape: Quoted in Laughton, 190

339: We're dead: Harrisson (1938), 399

339: (1) The Boltonians: letter from Graham Bell to Oliver Popham, 30 April 1938, quoted in Laughton, 192

339: plain daft: Harrisson (1938), 399

339: the idea of newspapers: Trevelyan, 87–8

340: In art, as in: *Spectator*, 25 March, 1938

340: direct contact: Quoted in Tony Rickaby, 'Artists' International', *History Workshop Journal*, 1978 (6), 155

341: Artists Against Fascism: Spurling (1986), 122–3; Rickaby, 155–68

341: Euston Roaders: Laughton, 94

341: seaside panoramas: Alan Powers, *Eric Ravilious: Imagined Realities* (Imperial War Museum/Philip Wilson, 2003), 15–17

341: The hotel: 'Midland Hotel, Morecambe', *Architectural Review* 74, September 1933, 96–9. The near-derelict hotel, closed in 1998, has been refurbished, and re-opened as a luxury hotel in June 2008.

342: had to repaint: J.M. Richards, *Memoirs of an Unjust Fella* (Weidenfeld & Nicolson, 1980), 99

342: Evelyn Dunbar: Gill Clarke, *Evelyn Dunbar: War and Country* (Sansom, 2006), 23–43

342: received more than: James Steele, *Queen Mary* (Phaidon, 1995), 111

342: Frank Rutter: Agar, 128

343: fashionable shops: Nick Dolan, 'The Susie Cooper Pottery, 1929–66' in *Susie Cooper: A Pioneer of Modern Design* ed. Ann Eatwell and Andrew Casey (Antique Collector's Club, 2002), 48–9

343: The professional artist: Quoted in Fiona MacCarthy, *British Design Since 1800* (Lund Humphries, 1992), 43

343: a talisman: Saler, 123

343: an artistic nation: Quoted in ibid., 124

343: Nikolaus Pevsner: *Inquiry into Industrial Art*, quoted in Alan Powers, 'The Search for a New Morality', *Modern Britain, 1929–39* ed. James Peto and Donna Loveday (Design Museum, 1999), 24–5

343: an oblong: 'Art and Industry', *The Listener*, 1 June 1932

344: go abroad: 'The Prince of Wales Calls for the Recognition of the Artists in Industry', *Studio* 107, January 1934, 3–4

344: Constructivist Fabric [and subsequent material]: Saler, 128–30, 144

345: too 'arty': Anthony Bertram, *Design* (Penguin, 1938), 85

345: It is probably: John Betjeman, 'The Gorell Report', *Architectural Review*, July 1932

345: an itinerary: Richards, 85

345: Frederick Etchells: Dean, 14

345: prejudiced enough: Reginald Blomfield, *Modernismus* (Macmillan, 1934)

346: un-English: Nikolaus Pevsner, 'The Modern Movement in Britain', written for a special issue of *Architectural Review* for 1938–39 but never published. Edited by Bridget Cherry for *British Modern Architecture and Design in the 1930s* ed. Susannah Charlton, Elain Harwood and Alan Powers (Twentieth Century Society, 2007), 17, 33

346: only two examples: Norman Foster, Foreword to *Modern Britain*, 11

346: architects can no: *Architectural Association Journal*, March 1935, cited in David Dean, *The Thirties: Recalling the English Architectural Scene* (Trefoil, 1983), 22

346: a PLANNER: Foreword to the catalogue for an exhibition of International Architecture held in London in 1934. Royal Institute of British Architects, *International Architecture, 1924–34* (London, 1934), 9

346: an architectural solution: Wells Coates, 'Response to Tradition', *Architectural Review*, November 1939

346: We don't want: *The Listener*, 24 May 1933

347: modernist furniture: Alistair Grieve, 'Isokon' in *Modern Britain*, 80

347: All you have to bring: Quoted in Alistair Grieve, *Isokon* (Isokon Plus, 2004), 13

347: Peabody atmosphere: Quoted in ibid., 14. The flats fell into grievous disrepair in the 1950s, and it was not until 2004 that they were fully restored to their original magnificence by the Notting Hill Housing Trust, employing the architectural firm Avanti. In March 2004 eleven of the thirty-two flats were offered for sale, the remainder being reserved for key workers who could buy into a shared ownership scheme.

347: entirely furnished: *View from a Long Chair: The Memoirs of Jack Pritchard* (Routledge, 1984), 92

347: Philip Harben: Paul Levy's entry on Philip Harben in the *Dictionary of National Biography*

348: too large: Pritchard, 91

348: ten shillings: John and Mary Postgate, *A Stomach for Dissent: The Life of Raymond Postgate:*

1896–1971 (Keele University Press, 1994), 201. Pritchard thought five shillings was allowed for wine, and makes no mention of service.

348: middle-sized snakes: ibid., 201, 202

348: scientific relaxation: advertisement for the Long Chair designed by Moholy-Nagy, photography by Philip Harben, reproduced in Grieve (1994), 28. The Long Chair is still in production today.

349: Earl de la Warr: Alastair Fairley, *Bucking the Trend: The Life and Times of the Ninth Earl de la Warr* (Bexhill on Sea: The Pavilion Trust, 2001), 33–40

349: *tecton* being Greek: Peter Coe and Malcolm Reading, *Lubetkin and Tecton: Architecture and Social Commitment, A Critical Study* (Arts Council of Great Britain/University of Bristol, 1981), 69

350: sadly why human: 'A London Health Centre: Employment of a New Architectural Idiom', *Mother and Child*, November 1938, in Coe and Reading, 127

350: at once a scientific: *News Chronicle*, 16 November 1937

350: encouraged children: Nigel Warburton, *The Life of an Architect* (Routledge, 2004), 77

350: Your job does not: Quoted in Robert Elwall, 'New Eyes for Old: Architectural Photography' in *Modern Britain*, 65

350: Elisabeth Benjamin: Lynne Walker, 'Interview with Elisabeth Benjamin' in *The Modern House Revisited*, 75–84

351: On a clear day: Quoted in Sally Beauman, *The Royal Shakespeare Company: A History of Ten Decades* (Oxford University Press, 1982), 111, 112, 113

351: largest windows: Robert Carpenter, *Mr Pink: The Architectural Legacy of W.T. Crittall* (Essex County Council, 2007), 6

351: a village: Joanna Smith, '"Work Collectively and Live Individually": The Bata Housing Estate in East Tilbury' in *Twentieth Century Architecture 9: Housing the Twentieth Century Nation* ed. Elain Harwood and Alan Powers (Twentieth Century Society, 2008), 66

352: given a free hand: Graham Thurgood, 'Silver End Village, 1926–32' in *Thirties Society Journal* 3, 38

352: 'inappropriate' porches: Carpenter, 34. Silver End was designated a Conservation Area in 1983, and the District Council provides advice – but little funding – for those who wish to restore the authenticity of Tait's design.

352: potter about: Quoted in Smith, 58

353: few of their commissions: Highpoint One had originally been intended to provide flats for the working classes, but it was decided this would not be economically viable given the high cost of construction.

353: Sassoon House: Elizabeth Darling,

Re-Forming Britain: Narratives of Modernity Before Reconstruction (Routledge, 2007), 67, 128–34, 141–67; Anthony Bertram, 'Housing the Workers', *The Listener*,18 November 1937, 1007–9

354: a flat roof: Gould, 34–60, a point made by Dean, 22

354: A world of: W.H. Auden, 'Letter to Lord Byron', *Letters from Iceland* (Faber, 1937)

354: many were not white: Elwall, 59

354: very undressed: *Architect & Building News*, 24 June 1932, quoted in Dean, 19

355: an arbitrator: Jackson, 26

355: regular Rolls-Royce: Barbara Tilson, 'The Battle of Bentley Wood', *Thirties Society Journal* 5, 24–31

355: A house which: *Architect's Journal*, 11 March 1937

355: deliberately odd: 'The Ruislip Case: The Full History', *Architect's Journal* 74, 1934

355: allows its more: 'The Ruislip Result', ibid.

356: expressly forbade: Coe and Reading, 153

356: only the Eskimos: *Evening Standard*, 22 December 1937, quoted in Nigel Warburton, *Ernö Goldfinger: The Life of an Architect* (Routledge, 2004)

356: decided in a most: Donaldson, 179

356: impracticable and ugly: Ben Pimlott, *Hugh Dalton* (Macmillan, 1985), 195–6, 197. These two examples are mentioned by Louise Campbell,

'Patrons of the Modern House', *The Modern House Revisited* (Twentieth Century Society, no.2, 1996), 45–6

357: an analysis of: Louise Campbell, 'The MARS Group, 1933–39', *RIBA, Transactions* 8, vol. 4, no.2, 69; 'MARS at Olympia', *Architectural Journal* 80, 1934, 425, quoted in Jackson, 35

357: reactionary forces: Campbell, 72

357: attained one of: MARS Group, 'New Architecture' (London, 1938), 6

357: lyrical appeal: Dean, 114

357: a flat roofs club: Campbell, 76–8; The Design Museum (www.designmuseum.org/design/the-mars-group)

358: was dissolved: Jackson, 60

358: upturned table: Gavin Stamp, 'Battersea Power Station', *Thirties Society Journal* 1, 3–8

358: brick cathedral: *The Listener*, 26 July 1933

358: open, liveable: Elizabeth Darling. 'Wells Coates: His Life and Legacy', *C20: The Magazine of the Twentieth Century Society*, spring 2008, 5

358: the five best: *Architect's Journal*, 25 May 1939

358: remarkable buildings: Royston Foot, 'The Life and Work of Sir Owen Williams', *British Modern Architecture and Design in the 1930s*, 81–8

358: Firestone tyre factory: Joan Skinner, 'The Firestone Factory' in *Twentieth Century Architecture Industrial Design: Journal of the Twentieth Century Society*, summer 1994. Only the Hoover building remains today: the Firestone factory was demolished despite a storm of protest on August Bank Holiday 1980, and the Guinness brewery was torn down in April 2006.

359: leaving age: Stevenson, 249–50

359: Dennis Clarke Hall: Denis Clarke Hall, 'School Design in the 1930s' in *British Modern*, 71–8

359: Village Colleges: Harry Rée, *Educator Extraordinary: The Life and Achievements of Henry Morris, 1889–1961* (Longman, 1973); T. Jeffs, *Henry Morris: Village Colleges, Community Education and the Ideal Order* (Nottingham: Educational Heretics Press, 1998), quoted in M.K. Smith, 'Viewing Impington: The Idea of the Village College', http://www.infed.org/schooling/b-vilcol.htm (2008)

360: if not the best: Nikolaus Pevsner, *Cambridgeshire* (Penguin, 1970)

360: little warriors: Saler, 138–9

360: same broad intentions: Maurice Punch, *Progressive Retreat: A Sociological Study of Dartington Hall School 1926–57 and Some of its Former Pupils* (Cambridge University Press, 1997)

360: the Salem school: Henry L. Breeton, *Gordonstoun: Ancient Estate and Modern School* (Chambers, 1968), 128

360: moral equivalent: J. Swire, *Gordonstoun, 1934–55: A Survey Upon the Occasion of the School's Coming of Age* (Studio Productions, 1955), 9

361: high-minded: Michael Young, *The Elmhirsts of Dartington: The Creation of a Utopian* (Routledge, 1982), 134

361: The sons and daughters: *Punch*, 25

362: Boys' and girls' rooms: Ivan Moffat, 'Dartington Hall School: An Experiment in Education', *Out of Bounds* 1, no.3, winter 1935

362: no Latin: Young (1982), 131

362: On the Library: Moffat, 43

362: kissing club: Young, 148

362: Bertie rather feared: Dora Russell, *The Tamarisk Tree, Vol. II: My School and the Years of War* (Virago, 1981), 7. Beacon Hill later moved to Essex and then Somerset, and closed in 1943.

363: were not very clear: ibid., 16, 26

363: the parents who: *The Autobiography of Bertrand Russell* (Allen & Unwin, 1968), 154

363: visitors who saw: Dora Russell, 27, 66

364: social side [and subsequent quotes]: A.S. Neill, 'Summerhill' in *The Modern Schools Handbook* ed. Trevor Blewitt (Gollancz, 1934), 115–17

364: twenty-five pupils: Dora Russell, 'Beacon Hill' in ibid., 29

364: plating pennies: Blewitt, 119–20

364: how children: ibid., 122–3

365: disappointed feature film-makers: Michael Powell, *A Life in Movies: An Autobiography* (Heinemann, 1986), 241

365: employing the native population: Michael Powell, *200,000 Feet: The Edge of the World* (Dutton, 1958)

366: the necessities of [and subsequent material]: Tom Steel, *The Life and Death of St Kilda* (Collins/Fontana, 1975), 56, 58. This entire account is greatly indebted to Steel's marvellous book.

367: nibbling at socialism: R. Connell, *St Kilda and the Kildans* (1887), quoted in Steel, 189

367: to assist us all: Quoted in Steel, 196–7

368: in the can: Powell (1958), 324

372: by far the greatest: Quoted in Harold Nicolson, *King George the Fifth: His Life and Reign* (Constable, 1952), 524

372: Prince of Sportsmen: Graves and Hodge, 317–18

372: puzzled at: H.G. Wells, *The World of William Clissold: A Novel at a New Angle Vol. III* (Ernest Benn, 1926), 314

373: royal parasites: Stuart Macintyre, *Little Moscows: Communism and Working-Class Militancy in Inter-War Britain* (Croom Helm, 1980), 75, 187

373: There appears: Forster, 3 May 1935, 7 May 1935

373: seemed to be packing: Quoted in Jones (1954), 164

373: a great shock: Madge Martin diaries, Oxfordshire County Record Office, 20 January 1936

373: It is odd: N.J. Crowson (ed.), *Fleet Street, Press Barons and Politics: The Journals of Collin Brooks, 1932–40* (Royal Historical Society, 1998), 150

374: Obvious that: Francis Watson, 'The Death of George V', *History Today* 36, 12, December 1986

374: news given: Vanessa Bell to Julian Bell, Saturday, 25 January 1936, in *Selected Letters of Vanessa Bell* ed. Regina Marler (Bloomsbury, 1993), 403–4

374: The black-bordered press: *The Times*, 21 January 1936; *The Listener*, 22 January 1936; *Spectator*, 24 January 1936; *New Statesman*, 25 January 1936

374: An honest King's: *The Times*, 28 January 1936

374: This man was: Constance Babington Smith, *John Masefield: A Life* (Oxford University Press, 1978), 199

374: most of the men: *The Diary of Virginia Woolf, Vol. V: 1936–41* ed. Anne Olivier Bell (Chatto & Windus/Hogarth Press, 1984; Penguin, 1985), 21 January 1936, 10–11. In fact, at the behest of Edward VIII official mourning was only to last for six months rather than the usual year.

375: I am beginning: Philip Gibbs, *Ordeal in England* (Heinemann, 1938), 12, 14

375: the psychoanalyst Ernest Jones: Ernest Jones, 'The Psychology of Constitutional Monarchy', *New Statesman*, 1 February 1936, 141–2

375: not a republican: letter from Harrison Barrow, *New Statesman*, 15 February 1936

375: had the fecundity: Jones, 165

375: The death of poor: Bell, 25 January 1936, 403

375: watched so many: Lord Dunsany,

'To Rudyard Kipling', *The Times*, 21 January 1936

375: The whole world: *The Times*, 20 January 1936

375: A nation already: *The Times*, 24 January 1934

375: Indians in turbans: Bell, 404

375: unexpectedly lovely: ibid., 405

376: Christ!: Frances Donaldson, *Edward VIII* (Weidenfeld & Nicolson, 1974), 181

376: in a thick long: Jones, 166

376: a most terrible: Nicolson, 23 January 1936, 241

376: the thick felt: Cooper, 160

376: the Underground ran: Piers Brendon and Philip Whitehead, *The Windsors: A Dynasty Revealed 1917–2000* (Hodder & Stoughton, 1994), 68

376: I went almost: Cooper, 160

376: everyone ceased: Asa Briggs, *History of Broadcasting in the United Kingdom, Vol II: The Golden Age of Wireless* (Oxford University Press, 1965), 266

376: had always been: Madge Martin, 21 January 1936

376: comes to the throne: *The Times*, 22 January 1936

377: Unemployed Club: Clarence Huff, *Unbelievable but True* (City of Bradford Metropolitan Council Libraries Division. Local Studies Department. Occasional Publication no.6, n.d.), 27–8

377: The Prince knew: Majorie Brasnett, *Voluntary Social Action* (NCCS, 1969), 76, quoted in Donaldson, 132

377: I am thinking: Quoted in ibid., 133

378: The passing of: Nicolson, 20 January 1936, 239

378: would rise to his: Jones, 164

378: good augury: *The Times*, 22 January 1936

378: uneasy . . . that: Nicolson, 238

378: 'ere we 'ave: ibid., 247

378: it's a tragedy: C.R. Attlee, *As it Happened* (Heinemann, 1954), 89

378: country gentleman: *New Statesman*, 25 January 1936

379: the party conference decided: *The Labour Party Report of the 36th Annual Conference*, 207, 209

379: terrible urgency: *Left Book Club Anthology* ed. Paul Laity (Gollancz, 2001), ix

379: provide an armoury: Graves and Hodge, 334

379: Members had to agree: Betty Reid, 'The Left Book Club in the Thirties' in *Culture and Crisis in Britain in the 30s* ed. Jon Clark, Margot Heinemann, David Margolis and Carole Snee (Lawrence & Wishart, 1979), 194

379: *undertake* to buy: Stuart Samuels, 'The Left Book Club', *Journal of Contemporary History* 1, no.2, 1966, 6

379: It is . . . not too much: *Left Book Review*, June 1936, quoted in Ruth Dudley Edwards, *Victor Gollancz: A Biography* (Gollancz, 1987), 236

380: swollen to 1,200: Ben Pimlott, *Labour and the Left in the 1930s* (Cambridge University Press, 1977), 156

380: from floor to: *The Universe* quoted in Laity, x

380: a total of forty: Neavill, 210

380: walks, tennis, golf: Samuels, 75

380: waking to find: ibid., 86

380: KNOWLEDGE, UNITY: Dudley Edwards, 259

380: intended to become: Forster, 4, 5, 14, 22 March 1938, 12, 29 April 1938

381: white collar workers: Quoted in Samuels, 65

381: The Left Book Clubs: Quoted in Kevin Morgan, *Against the War: Ruptures and Continuities in British Communist Politics, 1935–41* (Manchester University Press, 1989), 257

381: The first titles: Laity, 183

381: dealt with every: Graves and Hodge, 334

381: rooted in fact: John Lewis, *The Left Book Club: An Historical Record* (Gollancz, 1970)

382: For about 15 months: Victor Gollancz, *More for Timothy* (Gollancz, 1953), 357

382: was in broad: Quoted in Michael Newman, *John Strachey* (Manchester University Press, 1989), 48

382: four horsemen: Quoted in Laity, xii

382: only three of: Dudley Edwards, 236, 238

382: a little wooden hut: George Orwell, *Coming Up for Air* (Gollancz, 1939; Penguin Classics, 2000), 515–17

383: astute young social: George Orwell, *The Road to Wigan Pier* (Gollancz,

1937; Penguin Classics, 1989), 147, 151, 169

383: profoundly shocked: Laity, 4

384: Batty Book Club: *The Left News*, March 1938, 719

384: that truth neither: Quoted in Terence Rodgers, 'The Right Book Club: Text Wars, Modernity and Cultural Politics in the Late Thirties', *Literature & History* 12, no.2, autumn 2003, 2

384: difficulty in finding: ibid., 14

384: the most famous: Alistair Cooke, *Six Men* (Bodley Head, 1977), 19

385: The huge factory: Christopher Green, 'The Machine' in Wilk, 111

385: For the Russian: Quoted in Peter Conrad, *Modern Times, Modern Places* (Thames & Hudson, 1998), 437

385: The Rhineland Pact: Rod Miller, 'Britain and the Rhineland Crisis, 7 March 1936: Retreat from Responsibility or Accepting the Inevitable?', *Australian Journal of Politics and History* 33 (1987)

386: Great excitement: Nicolson, 9 March 1936, 248

386: the so-called: Quoted in Keith Middlemass and John Barnes, *Baldwin* (Weidenfeld & Nicolson, 1969), 922

387: in hotels: Letter to the editor of the *Morning Post*, 12 March 1936

387: the actions: House of Commons debate, 26 March 1936, quoted in Ben Pimlott, *Hugh Dalton* (Macmillan, 1985), 233

387: peace with as little: *The Political Diary of Hugh Dalton, 1918–40,*

1945–60 ed. Ben Pimlott (Jonathan Cape/London School of Economics, 1986), 11 March 1936, 198

387: A radio message: Potter and Frost, 131

387: Facilities included: Johnson, 109

387: elegant, romantic: Quoted in ibid., 109–14

388: fight a nomad war: Anthony Mockler, *Haile Selassie's War* (Oxford University Press, 2003), 62

388: Is there another: *The Times*, 2 July 1936

388: Popular with whom?: Donaldson, 200

389: he was allowed to return: Lutz Haber, 'The Emperor Haile Selassie I in Bath, 1936–40' (1992), http://anglo-ethiopian.org /publications/articles. In 1958 Haile Selassie donated his house, Fairfield, to the city of Bath, which converted it into accommodation for the elderly.

388: poor Jim Thomas: Nicolson, letter to Vita Sackville-West, 12 June 1936, 265

389: has fallen victim: Middlemas and Barnes, 934

390: a forlorn, and: Marquand, 783, 789

391: O understand: 'Spain', first published as a pamphlet in 1937, was republished in *Another Time* (Faber, 1940). Auden was continually troubled by some of the implications of the poem, and dropped it from his *Collected Shorter Poems* (Faber, 1966). This and John Cornford's 'Full Moon at Tierz' are both reprinted in Robin Skelton (ed.), *Poetry of the*

Thirties (Penguin, 1964), 133, 137

391: They [the poets: *Poetry of the Thirties*, 36

391: There is no: Jason Gurney, *Crusade in Spain* (Faber, 1974), x

392: the screen: Piers Brendon, *Dark Valley: A Panorama of the 1930s* (Cape, 2000), 307

392: localise the disturbance: Quoted in Tom Buchanan, *Britain and the Spanish Civil War* (Cambridge University Press, 1997), 37

393: Better a leaky: Hugh Thomas, 'The Spanish Civil War' in A.J.P. Taylor (ed.), *History of the Twentieth Century* (Purnell, 1968–69), 1601

393: An elaborate: Winston S. Churchill, *Step by Step, 1936–39* (Macmillan, 1942), 332

393: Rabble against: Douglas Little, *Malevolent Neutrality: The United States, Great Britain and the Origins of the Spanish Civil War* (Cornell University Press, 1985), 241

393: We English hate: Cited in Jill Edwards, *The British Government and the Spanish Civil War, 1936–39* (Macmillan, 1979), 138

393: In April 1937: S.J. Hetherington, *Katherine Atholl: Against the Tide* (Aberdeen University Press, 1989), 183–5. Dame Rachel Crowdy, who had been the League of Nations' Director of Social Welfare, went too.

394: a complete misnomer: Tom Johnston quoted in ibid., 197

394: I have been: D.P.F. Lancien, 'British Left-Wing Attitudes to the Spanish

Civil War' (unpublished B Litt thesis, University of Oxford), quoted in Buchanan, 84

394: Wilfred Roberts: M. Baines 'The Survival of the British Liberal Party, 1932–59' (unpublished DPhil thesis, University of Oxford, 1989), quoted in ibid., 85

394: Clement Attlee: Kenneth Harris, *Attlee* (Weidenfeld & Nicolson, 1982), 138

395: Blackpool and: H.M. Tomlinson, *South to Cadiz* (Heinemann, 1934), 217–20

395: middle-class travellers: Brian Shelmerdine, *British Representations of Spain* (Manchester University Press, 2006), 31

395: the poster world: Kate O'Brien, *Farewell Spain* (Heinemann, 1937; Virago, 1985), 21–5

396: traditionalist Tory: *The Distant Drum: Reflections on the Spanish Civil War* ed. Philip Toynbee (Sidgwick & Jackson, 1976), 67

397: Felicia Browne: Tom Buchanan, 'The Lost Art of Felicia Browne', *History Workshop Journal* 54, autumn 2002, 180–201

397: Esmond Romilly: T.A.R. Hyndman, 'International Brigadier 2' in *The Distant Drum*, 122

397: like a schoolboy: *Daily Express*, 23 November 1936, quoted in Ingram (1985), 136

397: It made me be: Quoted in Jonathan Guinness (with Catherine Guinness), *The House of Mitford* (Hutchinson, 1984), 400

398: cut pictures: Jessica Mitford, *Hons and Rebels: An Autobiography* (Gollancz, 1960), 78, 109

398: running away: *The Mitfords: Letters Between Six Sisters* ed. Charlotte Mosley (Fourth Estate, 2007), Unity Mitford to Jessica, 3 April 1937, 84–5

398: we felt that: Mitford, 132

398: I shall probably: Quoted in Humphrey Carpenter, *W.H. Auden: A Biography* (Allen & Unwin, 1981), 207

398: profoundly shocked: 'Religion and Reality' in *W.H. Auden: A Tribute* ed. Stephen Spender (Weidenfeld & Nicolson, 1975), 89

399: first clenching: Quoted in Valentine Cunningham, *British Writers of the Thirties* (Oxford University Press, 1939), 451

399: waited around: Quoted in Carpenter, 210, 213

399: one of the few: Orwell objected to the line 'The conscious acceptance of guilt in the necessary murder'. Later Auden changed it to 'The conscious acceptance of guilt in the fact of murder,' and eventually discarded the whole poem. George Orwell, *Inside the Whale and Other Essays* (Gollancz, 1940), 169

399: We had a greater: Carpenter, 206

399: no announcements: Laurie Lee, *As I Walked Out One Midsummer Morning* (André Deutsch, 1969; Penguin, 1971), 162

399: He seems: Quoted in Valerie Grove, *Laurie Lee: The Well Loved Stranger* (Viking, 1999)

400: get himself killed: John Sutherland, *Stephen Spender: The Authorized*

Biography (Viking, 2004), 208–9, 315

400: Philipps was wounded: C.V.J. Griffiths, *Dictionary of National Biography*

400: a state of fury: Solita Solano in Hugh Ford (ed.), *Brave Poet, Indomitable Rebel*, 76

400: Franco stands: Chisholm, 251–6

401: Will you please: *The Collected Essays, Journalism and Letters of George Orwell: At An Age Like This, 1920–40* ed. Ian Angus and Sonia Orwell (Secker & Warburg, 1968), 668

401: When 3,000 copies: Gordon, 232

402: In Spain both: Cited in D.J. Taylor, *Orwell: The Life* (Chatto & Windus, 2003), 202

402: Graham Greene: Norman Sherry, *The Life of Graham Greene, Vol. 1: 1904–39* (Cape, 1989), 612–13

402: questioning the certainties: Buchanan (1997), 161

402: John Cornford: Peter Stansky and William Abrahams, *Journey to the Frontier: Two Roads to the Spanish Civil War* (University of Chicago Press, 1966), 313, 316

403: joined the POUM: Cited in Bernard Crick, *George Orwell: A Life* (Secker & Warburg, 1981), 318

403: it is a comic: George Orwell, *Homage to Catalonia* (Secker &Warburg, 1938), 32

403: the war first: Buchanan, 76

404: amateur anarchist: Hugh Purcell, *The Last English Revolutionary: Tom Wintringham, 1898–1949* (Sutton, 2004), 107

404: from 6,500: Buchanan, 69–70

404: in spite of: Charlotte Haldane, *Truth Will Out* (Right Book Club, 1949), 89

404: If every working-class: Quoted in Hywel Francis, *Miners Against Fascism: Wales and the Spanish Civil War* (Lawrence & Wishart, 1984; Warren & Pell, 2004), 71

404: Although the majority: Richard Baxell, *British Volunteers in the Spanish Civil War: The British Battalion in the International Brigades, 1936–39* (Routledge, 2004), 15

405: Misguided stiffs: Cited in ibid., 29

405: Either you were: [and subsequent quotes]: Gurney, 36, 31, 37–8

406: Being a member: *Voices from the Spanish Civil War: Personal Recollections of Scottish Volunteers in Republican Spain 1936–9* ed. Ian MacDougall (Edinburgh: Polygon, 1986), 171

406: tickets for a: ibid., 172

406: Three quarters of those: S.P. MacKenzie, 'The Foreign Enlistment Act and the Spanish Civil War, 1936–39', *Twentieth Century British History* 10, no.1, 1999, 52–66

406: the original eight: Gurney, 38–9

407: by no means all: Haldane, 114, 112

407: limited to the OTC: Gurney, 41

407: The volunteers came: Baxell, 16–20. Baxell points out that the number of volunteers giving their address as London is artificially inflated since many from elsewhere in the British Isles used a 'care-of' address such as the Communist Party offices.

408: a volume of the poetry: Valentine Cunningham (ed.), *Penguin Book of Spanish Civil War Verse* (Penguin, 1980), 33

408: those without work: Tom Wintringham, *English Captain* (Faber, 1939), 330

408: an aliveness: ibid., 66

408: Among the volunteers: Baxell, 21, 26

409: George Green: Paul Preston, *Doves of War: Four Women of Spain* (HarperCollins, 2002), 121–201

410: Death stalked: Quoted in Judith Cook, *Apprentices of Freedom* (Quartet, 1979), 63

410: Despite sensational stories: Baxell, 140

410: a couple of days: Bill Alexander, *British Volunteers for Liberty: Spain 1936–39* (Lawrence & Wishart, 1982), 53–4

410: city-bred: Gurney, 104, 107

410: 68 per cent: MacKenzie, 217 n15, quoting Martin Middlebrook, *The First Day of the Somme: 1 July 1916* (Allen Lane, 1971)

410: There's a valley: Cunningham (1980), 75–7

411: the central experience: Hugh Sloan, *Voices from the Spanish Civil War*, 239

411: Political Affiliation: Bill Alexander, Preface to Colin Williams, Bill Alexander and John Gorman, *Memorials of the Spanish Civil War: The Official Publication of the International Brigade* (Sutton, 1996), xiii

411: at all costs: Wintringham, 258

411: Marx+courage: Michael Jackson, *Fallen Sparrows: The International Brigade in the Spanish Civil War* (American Philosophical Society, 1994), 120

412: I keep talking: Peter Drake, 'Birmingham and the Spanish Civil War' in *Aspects of Birmingham* ed. Brian Hall (Wharncliffe, 2001), 44

412: got a reception: MacDougall, 193

412: On Guard of Freedom: *Daily Worker*, 29 July, 1 August, 17 August 1936

412: the *Worker* managed: Philip M. Taylor, *British Propaganda in the Twentieth Century: Selling Democracy* (Edinburgh University Press, 1999), 102–3

412: the politics had: Cecil King, *Daily Mirror* Advertising Manager, quoted in James Curran and Jean Seaton, *Power Without Responsibility: The Press and Broadcasting in Britain* (Routledge, 1981; 2nd edn 2009), 62

412: although their own: *Daily Herald*, 8 December 1938, cited in L.B. Shelmerdine, 'Britons in an "unBritish" War: Domestic Newspapers and the Participation of UK Nationals in the Spanish Civil War', *North West Labour History* 22, 1997–98

413: the summary execution: *Manchester Guardian*, 20 August 1936, cited in Shelmerdine, 29

413: lazy garden: Anthony Aldgate, *Cinema and History: British Newsreels and the Spanish Civil War* (Scolar, 1979), 106

413: in case I didn't: *Sheffield Daily Independent* (dated June 1938); *Sheffield Star*, 29 January 1964

413: Spain awakening: Kenneth Bradbury, 'Young Oldhamer's Impressions of Spain', *Oldham Standard*, 10 December 1937

414: Poor little things: Eleanor Rathbone, *War Can Be Averted: The Achievability of Collective Security* (Gollancz, 1938), 66

414: except as part: Cited in Buchanan (1997), 94

414: However, it did: Alpert, 428

414: They sent blankets: ibid., 427

414: on the second day: IWM Sound Archive. Accession no.000844/08, 'Isabel Brown: British Involvement in the Spanish Civil War', reel 8

415: Kenneth Sinclair-Loutit: Alpert, 423; Sinclair-Loutit, cited in Buchanan (1997), 102

415: six forward field hospitals: Alpert, 424

415: Fernanda Jacobsen: Jim Fyrth, *The Signal Was Spain: The Aid Spain Movement in Britain, 1936–39* (Lawrence & Wishart, 1986), 190

415: The Committee's intention: Alpert, 430; Buchanan (1997), 119

416: less than one penny: Cited in Shelmerdine, 149

416: This organisation: Buchanan (1997), 99

416: which included £54,000: ibid., 104

416: threepenny milk tokens: Shelmerdine, 152

417: Most towns: Jim Fyrth, 'The Aid Spain Movement in Britain', *History Workshop Journal* 35, November 1993, 155

417: a card index: Isabel Brown, IWM Sound Archive, 13805, reel 3, transcript, 27

417: Robeson was: *The Townsend Journals: An Artist's Record of His Time* (Tate Gallery, 1976), 40

417: We sat for: VW to Janet Case, 26 June 1937, *The Letters of Virginia Woolf, 1936–41, Vol. VI: Leave the Letters Till We're Dead* ed. Nigel Nicolson (Chatto & Windus, 1980), 139

417: If you went: Noreen Branson in Mike Squires, *The Aid to Spain Movement in Battersea, 1936–39* (Elmfield, 1994), 58

418: they gave tins: Celia Baker quoted in Jackson, 57

418: There was always: Interview with Lilian May Price, South Wales Coalfield Collection, University of Wales, Swansea

418: with best wishes: Francis, 50

418: A man came: Beryl Baker IWM Sound Archive 13805, Jackson, 60

418: At a village: Francis, 50, 64

418: the appalling poverty: *Daily Worker*, 16 February 1937

419: Will Lawther: IWM, Brown, reel 8 transcript, 42

419: the unhappy situation: *Girton Review*, Michaelmas term 1937, 33, quoted in Jackson, 63

419: Ackland's offer: Ackland, letter to the *News Chronicle*, 14 September 1936

419: the nearest thing: Claire Harman, *Sylvia Townsend Warner: A Biography* (Chatto & Windus, 1989), 154

419: second visit: Spender and Warner had taken a hearty dislike to each other by the end of the trip: Warner

thought Spender was lightweight
with a youthful tendency to hog the
limelight, while Spender found
Warner's unswerving commitment
to communism as irritating as her
voice, and caricatured her as a
'Communist lady writer [who]
looked like a vicar's wife presiding
over a tea party given on a vicarage
lawn as large as the whole of
Republican Spain'. Stephen
Spender, *World Within World*
(Faber, 1977), 241–3

420: the funniest: Harman, 170–1

420: if we didn't: Branson in Squires, 59

421: The amount: ibid., 11–25, 59

421: There was a need: Patience Edney
(*née* Darton), IWM Sound Archives
8398, quoted in Angela Jackson,
*British Women and the Spanish Civil
War* (Routledge, 2002), 10

421: silly little: Margaret Powell, 'Nurses
There Work in Wards Lit by
Cigarette Lighters', *Daily Worker* 7
January 1938

421: about 80 per cent: MacDougall, 70–1

421: 10,000 *anguilas*: Jackson, 92

422: picking up: Priscilla Scott-Ellis, *The
Chances of Death: A Diary of the
Spanish Civil War* ed. Raymond
Carr (Michael Russell, 1995), 33

422: I know of [and subsequent
quotes]: Quoted in Jackson, 148,
133, 154

422: Most of the nurses: MacDougall, 71

422: recent estimates: Nicholas Rankin, 'A
Case of Crusts', *Times Literary
Supplement*, 6 July 2007

422: George Steer: Paul Preston, 'No
Simple Purveyor of News: George

Steer and Guernica', *History Today*,
May 2007

423: the Holy City: John Patterson,
Guernica (Profile, 2007), 69

423: Euskadi's mines: 'To the Wife of Any
Non-Interventionist Statesman', *Left
Review*, March 1938

423: the perfect opportunity: Cited in
Valentine Cunningham, 'Neutral:
1930s Writers and Taking Sides' in
*Class, Culture and Social Change: A
New Version of the 1930s* ed. Frank
Gloversmith (Harvester, 1980), 61

423: I have spoken: *The Times*, 29 April
1937, cited in Preston (2007), 16

423: his most famous painting: Preston
(2007), 16

424: the limited coterie: Anthony Blunt,
'The Dreams and Lies of Franco',
Spectator, 8 October 1937

424: had wired assurances: Preston
(2007), 14–15

424: *Seven Seas Spray*: *The Times*, 21 April
1937

424: brave lass: Rickword, 'To the Wife of
Any Non-Interventionist States-
man', also reproduced in *Penguin
Book of the Spanish Civil War Verse*,
373–4. However, Rickword
confused Captain Roberts with
another Welshman who ran the
blockade, 'Potato' Jones.

425: match each pound: Adrian Bell, *Only
for Three Months: The Basque
Children in Exile* (Mousehole Press,
1996), 29

425: as soon as: Leah Manning, *A Life for
Education: An Autobiography*
(Gollancz, 1970), 127

425: had been laid: ibid., 131

425: ninety-five women teachers: Fyrth (1986), 224

425: Each child was tagged: H.C. Williams, 'The Arrival of the Basque Children at the Port of Southampton', *British Medical Journal*, 12 June 1937, 1209, cited in Kevin Myers, 'History, Migration and Childhood: Basque Refugee Children in 1930s Britain', *Family and Community History* 3/2, November 2000, 150

425: North Stoneham: Bell, 47

426: but soon came back: Manning, 132

426: Britons Before Basques: *Birmingham Mail*, 23 September 1937, cited in Myers, 153

426: ninety-two private homes and hostels: Dorothy Legarreta, *The Guernica Generation: Basque Refugee Children of the Spanish Civil War* (Nevada University Press, 1984), 347–9

426: reserved for the sons: Fenner Brockway, *Inside the Left* (Allen & Unwin, 1942), 322

426: Aldridge Lodge: Kevin Myers and Ian Grosvenor, 'Generous Help in Hard Times: Basque Refugee Children in the Midlands, 1937–40', *Birmingham Historian* 14, 8–9

427: A long trail: *The Diary of Virginia Woolf, Vol. V*, 23 June 1937, 97

427: Frida Stewart: Frida Stewart (*née* Knight), memoirs quoted in Jackson, 68

428: the great defender: Quoted in Buchanan (1997), 201

428: After the war: Antony Beevor, *The Battle for Spain: The Spanish Civil War 1936–39* (Weidenfeld & Nicolson, 2006), 89

428: And the next day: 'Autumn Journal', *Collected Poems of Louis MacNeice, 112*

429: under the heel: Cited in David Clay Large, *Nazi Games: The Olympics of 1936* (Norton, 2007), 101

429: the blue sky: Cited in Duff Hart-Davis, *Hitler's Games* (Century, 1986), 89

429: mind their own: Cited in Large, 102

430: it would not: Cited in Christopher Hilton, *Hitler's Olympics* (Sutton, 2006), 114

430: rather a good lilt: *Chips: The Diaries of Sir Henry Channon* ed. Robert Rhodes James (Weidenfeld & Nicolson, 1967), 6 August 1936, 106–7

431: Germany to-day: R.H.S. Crossman, 'The Olympic Spirit', *New Statesman*, August 1936

431: private benefactors: Large, 169

431: It is not pleasant: Cited in Hart-Davis, 231, 227

431: no doubt of: *Spectator*, 14 August 1936

432: a black eye: *Illustrated London News*, August 1936

432: a mere toy: *Spectator*, 26 November 1936

432: The blue pennant: Johnson, 122; Potter and Frost, 144–7

433: The Blue Riband always: Frank C. Bowen, 'The Economics of the Queen Mary', *Spectator*, 10 July 1936

433: grey flannel: Nicolson, 21 September 1931, 91

433: pinchbeck candidate: *Manchester Guardian*, 14 April 1934

434: Hurrah for the Blackshirts!: *Daily Mail*, 15 January 1934

435: a better class: Quoted in Stephen Dorrill, *Blackshirt: Sir Oswald Mosley and British Fascism* (Viking, 2006), 276

436: no fundamental difference: *Daily Mail*, 25 April 1934

435: for purposes likely [and subsequent quotes]: Dorrill, 330, 412, 415, 300, 350

436: One must recognise: T.J. O'Connor MP, cited in Martin Pugh, 'The British Union of Fascists and the Olympia Debate', *Historical Journal* 41, 2, 1998, 537

436: he could never: Richard Thurlow, *Fascism in Britain: From Oswald Mosley's Blackshirts to the National Front* (I.B. Tauris, 1998), 72; Dorrill, 309

436: Harry St John Philby: Ferdinand Mount, 'Double-Barrelled Dolts', *London Review of Books*, 6 July 2006

437: the movement swelled: Richard C. Thurlow, 'The Straw that Broke the Camel's Back: Public Order, Civil Liberties and the Battle of Cable Street' in *Remembering Cable Street: Fascism and Anti-Fascism in British Society* ed. Tony Kushner and Nadia Valman (Valentine Mitchell, 2000), 80

437: metallic charm: Quoted in Dorrill, 122

437: manifold activities: John Beckett, *After My Fashion* (unpublished autobiography, c.1940), quoted in Gottlieb (2006), 45

438: The narrow streets: Julie Gottlieb, 'Women and Fascism in the East End' in *Remembering Cable Street*, 37

438: Half the BU's membership: Dorrill, 348

438: Madagascar: *The Fascist*, cited in Colin Cross, *The Fascists in Britain* (Barrie & Rockcliff, 1961), 153

438: Beamish fled: Thurlow, 43–6

438: provoking books: Richard Griffiths, *Fellow Travellers of the Right: British Enthusiasts for Nazi Germany, 1933–9* (Constable, 1980), 61

439: the tsetse fly: The popular writer Nesta Webster, cited in ibid., 63

439: money in furs: T.S. Eliot, 'Burbank with a Baedeker: Bleistein with a Cigar', stanza four, *Poems, 1909–21* (Faber, 1932)

439: Isle of Wight: *Jewish Chronicle*, 9 January 1931, cited in Colin Holmes, *Anti-Semitism in British Society, 1876–1939* (Edward Arnold, 1979), 204

439: fat Jewesses: Ross McKibbin, *Classes and Cultures: England 1918–51* (Oxford University Press, 1998), 56

439: Onward Christian soldiers: *The Crawford Papers: The Journals of David Lindsay, Twenty-Seventh Earl of Crawford and Tenth Earl of Balcarres, 1871–1940, During the Years 1892 to 1940* ed. John Vincent (Manchester University Press, 1984), 3 August 1939, 601

440: Horeb Elisha: Dorrill, 482

440: Is it not a fact: *Hansard*, 24 July 1934, cited in Griffiths, 83

440: Were some of them: *Hansard*, 10 July 1936, cited in ibid., 84

440: a mere dislike: 'Fascism and the Jews', *New Statesman*, 10 October 1936, 496

440: Today he is: Robert Bernays, MP, 'The Future of British Fascism', *Spectator*, 18 December 1936

441: Holbeck Moor: Dorrill, 389–90

441: deliberately played on: William J. Fishman, 'A People's Journey: The Battle of Cable Street' in Frederick Krantz, *History from Below: Studies in Popular Ideology in Honour of George Rudé* (Concordia University, 1987), 385–7

441: night after night: Francis Beckett, *The Rebel Who Lost His Cause: The Tragedy of John Beckett, MP* (London House, 1999), 133

441: 4 October 1936: Cross, 160

442: stay away from: *Their Finest Hour: Ubby Cowan's East End Memories* (unpublished mss)

442: 100,000 signatures: Elaine R. Smith, 'But What Did They Do? Contemporary Jewish Responses to Cable Street' in *Remembering Cable Street*, 52; 77,000 according to Richard C. Thurlow, 'The Straw that Broke the Camel's Back' in the same volume, 83 – but by any reckoning, an impressive number

442: Whether we liked: Joe Jacobs, *Out of the Ghetto: My Life in the East End – Communism and Fascism, 1913–39* (1978; 2nd edn Phoenix Press, 1991), 193

442: bash the fascists: Cited in Elaine R. Smith, *Remembering Cable Street*, 50

443: Leaflets calling for: Jacobs 242, 244–5

443: In those days: Louis Heren, *Growing up Poor in London* (Hamish Hamilton, 1993), 179–80

443: Paris cab drivers: ibid., 181

443: It was the dockers: Bernard Kops, *The World is a Wedding* (MacGibbon & Kee, 1963: Five Leaves, 2007), 38

443: towards the Embankment: Dorrill, 391

443: since I was: Diana Mosley, *A Life of Contrasts* (Hamish Hamilton, 1977), 141

444: Rudolph Valentino: *News Chronicle*, 23 April 1934, cited in Julie Gottlieb, 'The Marketing of Megalomania: Celebrity, Consumption and the Development of Political Technology in the British Union of Fascists' in *Journal of Contemporary History* 41, no.1, 2006, 40

444: around eighty: Dorrill, 392. Again, estimates vary (or rather, perhaps, reports of estimates vary). This is a median figure.

444: His injuries were caused: Cowan, 2

444: Harold Nicolson: Nicolson, 22 September 1931, 92

444: dun ranks: W.E.D. Allen, *BUF: Oswald Mosley and British Fascism* (John Murray, 1934)

444: support was falling off: Martin Pugh, *Hurrah for the Blackshirts!: Fascists and Fascism in Britain Between the Wars* (Cape, 2005), 227–8

444: The best thing: *New Statesman*, October 1936

444: It should not be: Jacobs, 207

444: silly business: Sir John Simon, 16 February 1934, cited in Dorrill, 276

444: a further blow: James and Patience Barnes, 'Oswald Mosley as Entrepreneur' in *History Today* 40, 3, March 1990, 11–16

445: effectively banned: D.S. Lewis, *Illusions of Grandeur: Mosley, Fascism and British Society* (Manchester University Press, 1987), 136

445: probably inhibited: Thurlow in *Remembering Cable Street*, 92

446: tapping their way: Matt Perry, *The Jarrow Crusade: Protest and Legend* (University of Sunderland Press, 2005), 57, 94

446: appliquéd: ibid., ix

446: Conservative mayors: Quoted in Tom Pickard, *Jarrow March* (Allison & Busby, 1982), 117

446: acting as a cartel: Perry, 195–200; *The Times*, 16 July 1936

446: It appears that: *The Times*, 8 July 1936

446: utterly stagnant: Wilkinson, x

446: poverty took its toll: David M. Goodfellow, *Tyneside: The Social Facts* (Co-operative, 1940), 20, 28, 53, 71, 51, cited in Perry, 133

447: Alternative ideas: Pickard, 22–3

447: In every town: *Ripon Gazette and Observer*, 15 October 1936, cited in Perry, 49–50

447: unemployment was falling: *British Labour Statistics*, cited in Andrew Thorpe, *Britain in the Era of the Two World Wars* (Longman, 1994), 88

448: Steel output: Sean Glynn and John Oxborrow, *Interwar Britain: A Social and Economic History* (Allen & Unwin, 1976), 86–114; Stevenson (1984), 108–11; Sue Bowden and David M. Higgins, 'British Industry in the Interwar Years' in *The Cambridge Economic History of Modern Britain, Vol. II: Economic Maturity, 1860–1939* ed. Roderick Floud and Paul Johnson (Cambridge University Press, 2003), 374–80; Dudley Baines, 'Recovery From Depression' in Paul Johnson (ed.), *Twentieth-Century Britain: Economic, Social and Cultural Change* (Longman, 1994), 188–202;

449: icily polite: Wilkinson, 197

449: personally written: Ellen Wilkinson, 'What the Crusade has Achieved', Pickard, 117

449: In one family: ibid., 91

449: The detailed arrangements: ibid., 117

449: in Leeds [and subsequent material]: Perry, 60, 76, 89

450: in Bedford: *The Times*, 27 October 1936

450: ill advised: Perry, 133–4

450: All governments: *The Times*, 26 October 1936

451: Such marches: *The Times*, 18 October 1936

451: may not be: *The Times*, 27 October 1936

451: held up our bus: Langford, 31 October 1936

451: a great reunion: Quoted in Pickard, 110

452: new steel tube works: Wilkinson, 210

452: finally opened: Perry, 160

452: had imagined: Wilkinson, 210

452: No appreciable reduction: Cited in Stevenson and Cook (1977), 65

452: I have not: *News Chronicle*, 5 November 1936

452: that we should: *Northern Echo*, 6 November 1936, cited in Perry, 175

452: The march has: *News Chronicle*, 6 November 1936

452: We got nowt: *Shields Gazette*, Jarrow March supplement, 6 October 1936, cited in Perry, 168

453: waste of time: *News Chronicle*, 6 November 1936

453: the King's car: *Daily Mail*, 19 November 1936, cited in Susan Williams, *The People's King: The True Story of the Abdication* (Allen Lane, 2003; Penguin, 2004), 3

453: brilliant flags [and subsequent material]: *A King's Story: The Memoirs of HRH the Duke of Windsor, KG* (Cassell, 1953), 310–11

454: the slightest interest: Oliver Woods and James Bishop, *The Story of The Times* (Michael Joseph, 1963), 288

454: historical statement: *The Diaries and Letters of Robert Bernays, 1932–39: An Insider's Account of the House of Commons* ed. Nick Smart (Edward Mellen, 1996), 9 and 15 December 1936, 278, 280

454: You may be sure: Quoted in Frances Donaldson, *Edward VIII* (Weidenfeld & Nicolson, 1974), 253

455: in exquisite taste: *A King's Story*, 238

455: the grace of: ibid.

455: not beautiful: Channon, 23 January 1935, 23; 5 April 1935, 30–1; report from Lady Diana Cooper, 7 October

1935, 43; 12 February 1936, 58; 26 and 27 November 1936, 77

456: of London Society: Channon, 4

456: after all: Nicolson, 28 May 1936, 262

456: a child's idea: Cited in John Charmley, *Duff Cooper: The Authorized Biography* (Weidenfeld & Nicolson, 1986), 95

456: What could you: *A King's Story*, 235, 187, 222

456: life aboard: Bernays, 277

456: jigsaw puzzles: *The Duff Cooper Diaries* ed. John Julius Norwich (Weidenfeld & Nicolson, 2005), plate facing 179

457: spick-and-span: Diana Cooper, 175

457: a calamity: Channon, 11 November 1936, 79

457: What is this: Cited in Donaldson, 251–2

457: So far our: The Diaries of the Revd Alan C. Don, Lambeth Palace Library Mss 22864, 28 October 1936

457: the American newspapers: Channon, 11 November 1936, 79

457: all-absorbing: *The Crawford Papers*, 3 November 1936, 573

458: American newspapers: Donaldson, 226

458: the position of: Baldwin speaking in the House of Commons on 10 December 1936, cited in ibid., 247

458: deeply grieved: Middlemas and Barnes, 995

458: grieved beyond words: James Pope Hennessy, *Queen Mary* (Allen & Unwin, 1959), 573

458: the adventuress: Brendon and Whitehead, 81

458: minds terribly: Cited in Philip Ziegler, *Edward VIII: The Official Biography* (Collins, 1990), 324–5

459: King Edward touch: *Daily Mail*, 23 November 1936

459: a permanent wound: Cited in Donaldson, 263

459: sympathy for: C.R. Attlee, *As it Happened* (Heinemann, 1954), 86

459: typical middle-class: Michael Foot, *Aneurin Bevan: A Biography, Vol. I: 1897–1945* (MacGibbon & Kee, 1962: Granada, 1975), 142

460: The country is in: Madge Martin, P5/2J/09

460: aptly named Blunt: Channon, 2 December 1936, 88

460: The Country and: ibid., 89

460: Everybody in England: Madge Martin, 6 December 1936

461: the Chief Whip: Middlemass and Barnes, 1008

461: cutie: Mary Soames (ed.), *Speaking for Themselves: The Personal Letters of Winston and Clementine Churchill* (Doubleday, 1998), 493

461: What is Winston's: Don, 6 December 1936

461: morganatic marriage: Kenneth Harris, *Attlee* (Weidenfeld & Nicolson, 1982), 133

461: the spectacle: Graves and Hodge, 364

461: fascism's ideal King: Robert Skidelsky, *Oswald Mosley* (Macmillan, 1975), 329

462: polite thanks: Dorrill, 403–6

462: cavaliers and roundheads: Channon, 7 December 1936, 94

462: The upper class: Nicolson, 30 November and 3 December 1936, 280, 281–2

462: env[ied] Mrs Simpson: Langford, 3 December 1936

462: at Marble Arch: *Daily Mirror*, 5 December 1936, cited in Williams, 169

462: One two three: Cited in Dorrill, 406

463: marching along: Osbert Sitwell, *Rat Week: An Essay on the Abdication* (Michael Joseph, 1986), 55

463: Woolworths reported: Graves and Hodge, 364

463: other retailers: Donaldson, 285

463: developed a fervent: Anthony Heap diaries, 3 December 1936, LMA Acc. 2243/6/4a

463: the city: *Journals of Collin Brooks*, 182

463: We can't have: *The Diary of Virginia Woolf, Vol. V*, 7 December 1936, 39–40

465: stable and dignified: Sir John Wheeler-Bennett, *George VI: His Life and Reign* (Macmillan, 1958), 298–9

465: He spoke as: *Tribune*, 1 January 1937 cited in Foot, 241–2

465: ran up against: Bernays, 15 December 1936, 280–1

466: Well if he becomes: Wheeler Bennett, 295

466: The King's abdication: 'The King's Decision', *The New Statesman*, 12 December 1936

466: at huge cost: Ziegler, 325–8

466: Thus it has: Don, 10 December 1936

467: backed the wrong: Channon, 11 December 1936, 99

467: The papers full: Madge Martin, 11 December 1936

467: Where are the friends: Sitwell, 59–60

467: We loved him: Donaldson, 199

467: The more one: Don, 12 December 1936

467: second thoughts: Heap, 11 December 1936

467: Noël Coward: Brendon and Whitehead, 85

468: slightly yet perceptibly: *The Diary of Virginia Woolf, Vol. V*, 10 December 1936, 41

468: To combat this: Donaldson, 192

468: He never read: Bernays, 9 and 15 December 1936, 278, 280–1

469: How can I do: Cited in Donaldson, 299

473: heating pipes: J.R. Piggott, *Palace of the People: The Crystal Palace at Sydenham, 1854–1936* (Hurst, 2004), 206

473: Richard Dimbleby: Scannell and Cardiff, 123

473: sinking slowly: Patrick Beaver, *The Crystal Palace, 1851–1936: A Portrait of Victorian Enterprise* (Hugh Evelyn, 1970), 142

473: hundreds of rats: Sydney Legg cited in Piggott, 207

473: missing believed boiled: *The Times*, 1 December 1936

473: Crowds flocked: Piggott, 207

474: found the dark: *Chips*, 30 November 1936, 87–8

474: It really horrified: Heap, 1 December 1936

474: a bright glare: Rich, 30 November 1936

475: 4,000 performers: Christopher Hobhouse, *1851 and the Crystal Palace* (John Murray, 1950), 156

475: just on the point: *New Statesman*, 5 December 1936

476: 30,000 children: Beaver, 146

476: a great glow: David Gascoyne, *Journal 1936–37* (Enitharmon Press, 1980), 9

476: torn up: Beaver, 146

476: it would cost less: J.B.S. Comptor, letter to *The Times*, 4 December 1936

476: Defence expenditure: Cited in J.P.D. Dunbabin, 'British Rearmament in the 1930s: A Chronology and Review', *Historical Journal* 18, 3, 1975

477: number of distinguished: *The Listener*, 16 December 1936

477: What in fact happened: Piggott, 210

477: The same reason: Beaver, 146

478: What a bloody: Quoted in Brendon and Whitehead, 87

478: the coronation mug: Helen Binyon, *Eric Ravilious: Memoir of an Artist* (Lutterworth, 1983), 88–9; *Ravilious and Wedgwood: The Complete Wedgwood Designs of Eric Ravilious* (Dalrymple, 1986), 43; and Alan Powers, *Eric Ravilious: Imagined Realities* (Imperial War Museum/Philip Wilson, 2003), 23–4

479: £524,000: Brendon and Whitehead, 92

479: one of his early biographers: John W. Wheeler-Bennett, *King George VI: His Life and Reign* (Macmillan, 1958), 293

479: Dickie, this is: Philip Ziegler,

Mountbatten: The Official Biography (Collins, 1985), 95

479: There is no more: Mountbatten quoting his father's words to George V in ibid., 95

479: In his first year: Elizabeth Longford, *The Royal House of Windsor* (Weidenfeld & Nicolson, 1974), 139

480: ugly ducking: One of the royal tutors quoted in J.M. Golby and A.W. Purdue, *The Monarchy and the British People: 1760 to the Present* (Batsford, 1988), 111

480: after full consideration: Don, 5 October 1936

480: air being thick: Wheeler-Bennett, 306–7, 324

481: the barriers: *The Times*, 4 May 1937

481: The streets look: *The Diary of Virginia Woolf, Vol. V*, 4 May 1937, 85

481: The strike lasted: Branson and Heinemann, 123–6

481: Quite a lot: *The Lady*, 6 May 1937, 796

482: absolute bedrock: *New Statesman*, 8 May 1937

482: an Indian rajah: Graves and Hodge, 367

482: In the East End: ibid.

482: spirits drooped: Madge Martin, 11 May 1937

482: the best stamps: *New Statesman*, 8 May 1937. Edmund Dulac was a prolific French-born naturalised British illustrator best known for his fine illustrations to *The Arabian Nights*, *The Rubaiyat of Omar Khayyam* and *Sinbad the Sailor*.

482: Camps & latrines: *The Diary of Virginia Woolf, Vol. V*, 30 April 1937, 84

482: The Coronation!: Graves and Hodge, 368

483: faded but not: Diana Cooper, 196–7

483: no possibility: Sarah Bradford, *George VI* (Weidenfeld & Nicolson, 1989), 276

483: a visitor to: Nicolson, 12 May 1937, 300

483: my velvet Court suit: Channon, 12 May 1937, 123–6

484: for long periods: Quoted in ibid., 27 May 1937, 301

484: The Duchess of Hamilton: *Sunday Times*, 6 April 2008

484: George pronounced: Bradford, 278

484: at the Château: ibid., 283

485: were sold off: Graves and Hodge, 369

485: The crowds . . . are: *New Statesman*, 22 May 1937

485: saw and heard: Forster, 23 May 1937

486: if the façade: James Knox, *Robert Byron* (John Murray, 2003), 377

486: the gentle visitor: Robert Byron, 'How We Celebrate the Coronation' *Architectural Review* 81, May 1937, 217

486: long-nosed vampires: ibid., 219

486: for the convenience: Knox, 378

486: barbarian: Byron, 219

486: an Anglican church: *Church Times*, 29 July 1938

487: not [in] congregations: Callum G. Brown, *Religion and Society in Twentieth-Century Britain* (Pearson/Longman, 2006), 141

487: effete establishment: Bishop Hedley Henson cited in Hastings, 252

487: There's a lot: *Puzzled People: A*

Study in Popular Attitudes to Religion, Ethics, Progress and Politics in a London Borough (Prepared for the Ethical Union by Mass-Observation (Gollancz, 1947), 12

487: 60 per cent: McKibbin (1998), 273

487: one person in ten: *Puzzled People*, 51

488: the ratio was: *The Social Survey of Merseyside, Vol. III* ed. D. Caradog Jones (University Press of Liverpool/Hodder & Stoughton, 1934), 326, 334, 338, 341, 330

488: has long been: Priestley, 106–7

488: It is necessary: Mass-Observation, *The Pub and the People: A Worktown Study* (Gollancz, 1943), 162–3

489: Crusaders' movement: Whiteing, 25, 26, 55–6

489: shy of attending: *Men Without Work*, 307

490: dissenters and other: James Obelkevich, 'Religion', *The Cambridge Social History of Britain, 1750–1950, Vol. III* ed. F.M.L. Thompson (Cambridge University Press, 1990), 353

490: Do not forget: Adrian Hastings, *A History of English Christianity, 1920–85* (Collins, 1986), 275

490: Archbishop Bourne: McKibbin (1998), 288

490: Westminster Catholicism: ibid., 286

490: Father Martin D'Arcy: *The Pebbled Shore: The Memoirs of Elizabeth Longford* (Weidenfeld & Nicolson, 1986), 54

491: drawing room apostle: Selina Hastings, *Evelyn Waugh: A Biography* (Sinclair-Stevenson, 1994),

224; Edward Yarnold, 'Martin Cecil D'Arcy', *Dictionary of National Biography*

491: for verification: Hastings, 473

491: He neither wept: Don, 29 January and 9 February 1932

491: more Wolsey: Quoted in J.G. Lockhart, *Cosmo Gordon Lang* (Hodder & Stoughton, 1949), 190

492: the Athenaeum club: Hastings, 274

492: The Gospel contains: William Temple, 'The Conclusion of the Matter' in *Christianity and the Crisis* ed. Percy Dearmer (Gollancz, 1933), 599

492: Jacobin lacquered over: Matthew Grimley, 'Herbert Hensley Henson' *Oxford Dictionary of National Biography*

492: in the category: Norman, 329–30

492: the overcrowded: ibid., 349

493: the best social study: Mowat, 483

493: Christian teachers: F.R. Barry, *The Relevance of Christianity: An Approach to Christian Ethics* (Nisbet, 1931), 284

493: The phoenix: *Christianity and the Social Revolution* ed. John Lewis, Karl Polanyi and Donald K. Kitchen (Gollancz, 1935), 441

494 We have suffered: Church Congress, Bournemouth, October 1935, cited in E.R. Norman, *Church and Society in England, 1770–1970* (Clarendon Press, 1976), 315

494: There was the official: Hastings, 325

494: abstain from: *The Times*, 14 July 1938

495: radical remedies: *The Times*, 15 May 1934

495: The Pilgrimage has: Robert Hughes,

The Red Dean (Churchman, 1987), 87

495: If a system: *Christianity and the Crisis*, 351

495: Social reformers will: Hewlett Johnson, *The Socialist Sixth of the World* (Gollancz, 1939), 40

495: granted a visa: Hewlett Johnson, *Searching for Light: An Autobiography* (Michael Joseph, 1968), 149

495: a massive best-seller: ibid., 155

496: baffling: Hughes, 41

496: Gloomy Dean: So named by the *Daily Mail* after a series of lectures in 1911, and the name stuck, though in fact Inge's writings on politics and economics as well as on religion could be light and witty, and more than twenty years after his death a book entitled *The Wit and Wisdom of Dean Inge* was published.

496: the court-chaplains: The Very Rev. W.R. Inge, *Diary of a Dean: St Paul's 1911–34* (Hutchinson, 1949), August 1930, 150

496: I have made: ibid., 31 December 1930, 153

496: to change the title: ibid., 28 January 1933, 168–9

496: cirrhosis: 'The Realist Dean', 7

496: national importance: E.R. Norman, *Church and Society in England 1770–1970: A Historical Study* (Clarendon Press, 1970), 335–6

496: social prestige: Lecture on 'The Future of the Human Race' to the Royal Institute reported in *The Times*, 30 May 1931

497: Blimp: 'The Realist Dean', *The Times*, 27 February 1954

497: first findings: Richard Hodder-Williams, *Public Opinion Polls and British Politics* (Routledge, 1970), 10; *British Political Opinion, 1937–2000* ed. Anthony King (Politico's, 2001), vii

498: Oxford Pledge: Martin Ceadel, 'The "King and Country" Debate, 1933: Student Politics, Pacifism and the Dictators' in *Historical Journal* 22, 2, 1979, 397

498: quick-witted: Leonard Woolf, *Downhill All the Way: An Autobiography of the Years 1919–39* (Hogarth Press, 1967), 82

498: Children's Hour: *The Times*, 13 February 1933

498: posturers: *Daily Mail*, 11 February 1933

498: There were suggestions: This section draws largely on Ceadel, 'The "King and Country" Debate', 397–422, as well as reports in *Isis* and *Cherwell*.

499: the main issues: C.T. Stannage, 'The East Fulham By-Election, 23 October 1933', *Historical Journal* 14, 1, 1971, 165–200; Richard Heller, 'East Fulham Revisited', *Journal of Contemporary History* 6, no.4, 1971, 172–96

499: peace ballot: Branson and Heinemann, 304

499: compel an aggressor: Cited in Martin Ceadel, 'The First British Referendum: The Peace Ballot, 1934–5' in *English Historical Review* 95, 1980, 820

499: The result: 95.9 per cent for Britain

remaining a Member of the League of Nations and 86.8 per cent in favour of economic sanctions against an aggressor nation compared with 58.7 per cent in favour of 'military measures' against such an aggressor, Branson and Heinemann, 306–7; Martin Ceadel, 'Attitudes to War: Pacifism and Collective Security' in Paul Johnson (ed.), *Twentieth-Century Britain: Economic, Social and Cultural Change* (Longman, 1994), 237

500: Ballot of Blood: *Daily Express*, 23 November 1934

500: now convinced: Hastings, 332

500: 100,000 postcards: Andrew Rigby, 'The Peace Pledge Union, 1936–45' in Peter Brock and Thomas P. Socknat (eds), *Challenge to Mars: Essays on Pacifism from 1918 to 1945* (University of Toronto Press, 1999), 170

501: It sent letters: David C. Lukowitz, 'British Pacifists and Appeasement: The Peace Pledge Union', *Journal of Contemporary History* 9, no.1, January 1974, 117–18

501: the paper did appeal: ibid., 121–2; Rigby, 173–4

501: pacificism: A.J.P. Taylor, *The Trouble Makers: Dissent Over Foreign Policy, 1792–1939* (Hamish Hamilton, 1957), 51n

501: the conference table: Rigby, 171

502: The Devil seems: Vera Brittain, *Testament of Experience: An Autobiographical Account of the Years 1925–50* (Gollancz, 1957), 185–7

502: literally as sheep: Max Plowman cited in Ceadel (1980), 266

502: in excess of 118,000: Rigby, 169

502: a cruel taunt: John Shepherd, *George Lansbury: At the Heart of Old Labour* (Oxford University Press, 2002), 325–8

502: It was very: *The Diary of Virginia Woolf, Vol. IV*, 2 October 1935, 345–6

503: The enthusiasm: Don, 31 July 1935

503: Revival Scenes: *Ruling Passions: The Autobiography of Tom Driberg* (Cape, 1977), 98, 99

503: a polemical book: *The Mystery of Moral Re-armament: A Study of Frank Buchman and his Movement* (Secker & Warburg, 1964)

503: scrupulous shampooed: Harold Begbie, *Life Changers*, cited in Graves and Hodge, 206

503: quiet time: Elizabeth Arweck, 'Frank Nathaniel Daniel Buchman, 1878–1961', *Oxford Dictionary of National Biography*

503: In the summer of 1933: Garth Lean, *Frank Buchman: A Life* (Constable, 1985), 159–61

504: new world order: http://www.stepstudy.org

504: surrendered his or her: Graves and Hodge, 204–5

504: all that business: Nichols

504: He [Buchman] wanted: Lean, 259

504: there is a gift: ibid., 179, 183

504: up and outs: Late-nineteenth-century evangelical preachers, cited in Norman, 337

505: 'house-parties' idea: Lean, 182, 177

505: Driberg (1964), 64

505: God does much: Kingsley Martin, 'God-Control', *New Statesman*, 11 July 1936

506: I thank heaven: Lean, 239

506: It's not an institution: A.J. Russell, *For Sinners Only* (n.p., 1932)

507: Around 70 per cent: McKibbin (1998), 289

507: Many of those: Stuart Mews, 'Religion, 1900–39' in *A Companion to the Early Twentieth Century* ed. Chris Wrigley (Blackwell, 2003), citing Bishop Talbot, 471–2

507: the Boys' Brigade: J. Springhall, B. Fraser and M. Hoare, *Sure and Steadfast: A History of the Boys' Brigade 1883–1983* (Collins, 1983), 129, 132–3

507: *Psychic News*: Jennifer Hazelgrove, 'Spiritualism after the Great War', *Twentieth Century British History* 10, no.4, 1999, 406

507: at least forty: Brown, 141

508: high water mark: Geoffrey Nelson, *Spiritualism and Society* (Routledge, 1969), 161

508: around 100,00: Hazelgrove, 406

508: considerable leakage: ibid., 409

508: too cautious: Cited in ibid., 408

508: look at their stars: *Puzzled People*, 20–2

508: witch balls: Cited in S.C. Williams, *Religious Belief and Popular Culture in Southwark, c.1880–1939* (Oxford University Press, 1999), 70, 71

509: Sundays had consisted: Whiteing, 52

509: The natural reaction: *Church Times*, 2 December 1938, cited in G.T. Machin, *Churches and Social Issues in Twentieth-Century Britain* (Clarendon Press, 1998), 55–6

509: 7 per cent: G.T. Machin, 'British Churches and the Cinema' in Diana Wood (ed.), *The Church and the Arts: Papers Read at the 1990 Summer Meeting and the 1991 Winter Meeting of the Ecclesiastical Society* (Blackwell, 1992), 483

509: the first religious broadcast: Kenneth M. Wolfe, *The Churches and the British Broadcasting Corporation, 1922–56* (SCM, 1984), xxi

509: more anxious: Briggs, 227

510: a large number: ibid., 229–33; Wolfe, 30

510: roughly 45 per cent: ibid., 18

510: the Chief Rabbi: Briggs, 241

510: over 11,000 people: Wolfe, 61

511: parsonical drone: Scannell and Cardiff, 162

511: later series: For example, *God and the World Through Christian Eyes* (1933); Briggs, 235, 239

511: wireless services: Cited in Briggs, 240

511: the engagement: *Church Times*, 27 November 1936, cited in Machin, 84

511: There is at present: *The Listener*, 2 October 1935

511: nearly 5 per cent: Briggs, 54

511: a survey: Wolfe, 127–8

511: the public's money: Scammell and Cardiff, 4

511: 98 per cent: Briggs, 253

511: Adrian Boult: Scannell and Cardiff, 181, 193

511: the performance of: Quoted in Percy Scholes, *The Mirror of Music*, Vol. 2

(Novello/Oxford University Press, 1947), 798

512: the shepherd: *BBC Handbook 1926*, quoted in Scannell and Cardiff, 195

512: We have no desire: *The Times*, 3 October 1936

515: excellent work: Board of Education, *Physical Training and Recreation in Germany* (London, 1937), 73, 75–8, cited in Ina Zweiniger-Bargielowska, 'Building a British Superman: Physical Culture in Interwar Britain', *Journal of Contemporary History* 41, no.4, 2006, 608–9

515: only 14,000 [and following material]: Joanna Bourke, *Dismembering the Male: Men's Bodies, Britain and the Great War* (Reaktion, 1996), 181, 172, 191, 192

516: The Nation's Health: *The Times*, 30 September 1937

516: 100,000 members: Zweiniger-Bargielowska (2006), 601, 607

517: At last our: *Health and Strength*, 24 October 1937, cited in ibid., 607

517: all the troubles: *New Health*, February 1937, cited in Ina Zweiniger-Bargielowska, 'Raising a Nation of "Good Animals": The New Health Society and Health Education Campaigns in Interwar Britain', *Social History of Medicine* 20, no.1, 72, 77

518: over 150 members: Adam Edwards, 'Stark Naked Ambition', *Daily Telegraph*, 10 May 2006

518: should be the same: *The Times*, 18 March 1932

519: bathing reduces: Quoted in Janet Smith, *Liquid Assets: The Lidos and the Open Air Swimming Pools of Britain* (English Heritage, 2005), 19

519: Somehow . . . 'lido': LCC Parks and Open Spaces Committee circular, 1937, cited in Smith, 22

519: first of the decade: Smith, 22–3, 114

519: almost the last: The Oasis, Holborn, had been started in 1937 but was not opened until 1946, Richmond Park pools were opened in 1965. Three other lidos planned before the Second World War – Clissold Park, Stoke Newington; Battersea Park; and Ladywell, near Lewisham in South London – were never built. Smith, 30–1

519: most were demolished: Ken Worpole, *Here Comes the Sun: Architecture and Public Space in Twentieth-Century European Culture* (Reaktion, 2000), 114, 113, 120. So many splendid 1930s lidos have been demolished that in 2008 there were only around 100 open-air pools extant in the whole of Britain, of which eleven were in London.

520: Weston's huge ziggurat construction: The superb Weston diving stage was demolished in 1982. Smith, 134

520: lido at Southport: ibid., 58, 29, 70 After being closed for many years, London Fields lido was refurbished and reopened in July 2007.

521: lost ten thousand pounds: Quoted in Ina Zweiniger-Bargielowska, 'The

Culture of the Abdomen: Obesity and Reducing in Britain, circa 1900–39' *Journal of British Studies* 44, April 2005, 3–4

521: gain two and a half pounds: Graves and Hodge, 189

521: these were regarded: Zweiniger-Bargielowska (2005), 254

521: spring out of bed: Mrs Bagot Stack, *Building the Body Beautiful: The Bagot Stack Stretch and Swing System* (Chapman & Hall, 1931), 70

522: People were enthusiastic: Prunella Stack, *Zest for Life: Mary Bagot Stack and the League of Health and Beauty* (Peter Owen, 1988), 117

522: cultured or uncultured: Cited in Jill Julius Matthews, 'They Had Such a Lot of Fun: The Women's League of Health and Beauty Between the Wars', *History Workshop Journal* 30, autumn 1990, 27

522: business girls: *Zest for Life*, p115

522: In these days: Mrs Bagot Stack, 3

522: fragile crêpe de chine: Cited in Matthews, 35

523: Empire Pageant: *Zest for Life*, 141

523: training the body: Mrs Bagot Stack, 101

523: a Scottish laird: *Zest for Life*, 144. Douglas-Hamilton was killed in the Second World War, as Prunella Stack's father had been in the First.

523: Rational Dress Society: *The Times*, 18 November 1929

524: men should be allowed: Bourke, 200

524: lived all [his] life: Cited in Catherine Horwood, 'Anyone for Tennis?: Male Dress and Decorum on the Tennis Courts in Inter-War Britain', *Costume* 38, 2004, 103

524: funny little boys: H.J. Dion Byngham, 'Better Clothes for Men', *New Health*, May 1930, cited in ibid., 105

524: long shorts: Catherine Horwood, 'Dressing Like a Champion: Women's Tennis Wear in Interwar England' in *The Englishness of English Dress* ed. Christopher Breward, Becky Conekin and Caroline Cox (Berg, 2002)

524: everyone would simply: *The Times*, 30 May 1931

525: The man who: Speech by D. Anthony Bradley in 'Dress Reform Debated', *Tailor and Cutter*, 8 July 1932, 647, cited in Bourke, 207

525: Burton's: E. Sigsworth, *Montague Burton: The Tailor of Taste* (Manchester University Press, 1990), 42–3

525: ready-to-wear: Morrison, 227

525: black-jacket ensemble: *Style Guide* 1935, reproduced in Catherine Horwood, *Keeping up Appearances: Fashion and Class Between the Wars* (Sutton, 2005), 37

525: Austin Reed: Berry Ritchie, *A Touch of Class: The Story of Austin Reed* (James & James, 1990), 44

526: youthful intelligentsia: *The Times*, 30 March 1932

526: those who have: Ethlye Campbell, *Can I Help You, Sir?* (Peter Davis, 1939), 166

526: torso was of [and subsequent

quotes]: Madge Garland, *An Indecisive Decade: The World of Fashion and Entertainment in the Thirties* (MacDonald, 1968), 70, 72–5, 121–3, 126, 92–3

527: Gloves were essential: Georgina Howell, *In Vogue: Six Decades of Fashion* (Allen Lane, 1975)

528: Platinum: Garland, 85–6

528: a slave to whatever: Whiteing, 58

528: well-preserved: Muriel Cox, 'What Price Beauty?', *Good Housekeeping*, 1935, in *Ragtime to Wartime: The Best of Good Housekeeping, 1922–39* (Ebury, 1986), 152–3

528: inner cleanliness: e.g. for Eno's Fruit Salts

528: like bloody talons: St John Ervine, 'Do Women Dress to Please Men?', *Good Housekeeping*, 1931, in *Ragtime to Wartime*, 119–20

529: rumpled pullovers: Garland, 95

529: had not always been: ibid., 104

529: dress agencies: Horwood (2005), 20–2

529: Collect major portion: E.M. Delafield, *Diary of a Provincial Lady* (1930; Virago, 1985), 44–5

530: chain stores: Lawrence Neal, *Retailing and the Public* (Allen & Unwin, 1933), ix

531: a woman of taste: Advertisement in *Good Houskeeping*, 1932, reproduced in *From Ragtime to Wartime*, 136

531: the volume: Scott (2002), 197–8

531: we will: ibid., 215

532: the abuses: ibid., 225

532: On almost every: Jan and Cora Gordon, *The London Roundabout* (Harrap, 1933), 165

534: approximately three million: Claud Cockburn, *The Devil's Decade* (Sidgwick & Jackson, 1973), 85, 101. The correct rendering is F.W. Woolworth or Woolworth's, but many commentators then and now omit the apostrophe and make it Woolworths – and that is how people spoke (and speak) of it.

533: Mr Woolworth's success: Thomas Burke, *London in my Time* (Rich & Cowan, 1934), 132

534: Do you know: Gordon, 104–5

534: In 1931 Rachel Ferguson: Rachel Ferguson, *The Brontës Went to Woolworths* (Ernest Benn, 1931; Virago reprint, 1988); Barbara Comyns, *Our Spoons Came from Woolworths* (Eyre & Spottiswoode, 1950; Virago reprint, 1983), 12–13

534: thirty-four new Woolworths stores: Mr W.L. Stephenson's speech at a meeting of F.W. Woolworth & Co. Ltd, *Time and Tide*, 29 January 1938, 143

535: the thousandth store: 'Boots in the 1930s', Boots Company Archives

535: this commercial giant: Quoted in Goronwy Rees, *St Michael: A History of Marks and Spencer* (Weidenfeld & Nicolson, 1969), 73–4

535: a forest of apparel: Asa Briggs, *Marks and Spencer 1884–1994: A Centenary History* (Octopus, 1984), 54

535: French knickers: Rachel Worth,

Fashion for the People: A History of Clothing at Marks & Spencer (Oxford: Berg, 2007), 33, 31

535: Mrs Goodwife: Briggs (1984), 76–7

536: strong in underwear: Worth, 33

536: not for themselves: Len Cohen, first manager of Marks & Spencer, Marble Arch, cited in Briggs (1984), 76

536: new shops: ibid., 43

536: flagship 'superstore': Rees, 81–2

536: Other stores: Kathryn A. Morrison, *English Shops and Shopping: An Architectural History* (Yale University Press, 2003), 196–8

537: control the whole process: Neal, 24–5

537: frankly modern [and subsequent quotes]: Morrison, 215–16, 222, 226, 234–5. The Halifax store is now a McDonald's restaurant.

538: Peter Jones: Dean, 92–4

538: best modern building: Morrison, 182–3

539: strains of light music: Whiteing, 35

539: Bentall's: Bill Lancaster, *The Department Store: A Social History* (Leicester University Press, 1995), 98–9

539: 'Buy British' campaign: Lindy Woodhead, *Shopping, Seduction and Mr Selfridge* (Profile, 2007), 235

539: Selfridges staff: Gordon Honeycombe, *Selfridges: Seventy-Five Years – The Story of the Store, 1909–84* (Park Lane Press, 1984), 67

540: soundproof room: Woodhead, 235

540: East Ham branch: Morrison, 179

540: Marjory Allen: Lady Allen of Hurtwood, *Memoirs of an Uneducated Lady* (Thames & Hudson, 1975), 99–102

541: growing vegetables: Honeycombe, 164

541: First-hand knowledge: Neal, 10

541: a large drapers: Whiteing, 37–8

542: falling into: Mass-Observation Archive DR 1077, reply to May 1939 directive

543: the grounds on which: S.M. Cretney, 'The Divorce Law and the 1936 Abdication Crisis: A Supplemental Note', *The Law Quarterly Review* 120, 2004, 165

544: the only grounds: Roderick Phillips, *Putting Asunder: A History of Divorce in Western Society* (Cambridge University Press, 1988), 525

544: the King's Proctor: Stephen Cretney, 'Edward, Mrs Simpson and the Divorce Law', *History Today* 53, 9, September 2003, 26–8

545: The captain: Cretney, *Law Quarterly Review*, 168

545: the bounder type: Cretney, *History Today*, 28

546: The previous year: A.P. Herbert, *Holy Deadlock* (Methuen, 1934), 4, 3, 1

546: because I am: 20 November 1936, A.P. Herbert, *Independent Member* (Methuen, 1950), 83

546: the 500,000-strong: Catriona Beaumont, 'Moral Dilemmas and Women's Rights: The Attitude of the Mothers' Union and Catholic Women's League to Divorce, Birth Control and Abortion in England, 1928–39' in *Woman's History Review* 16, no.4, September 2007, 467

547: woman in her forties: *Sunday Pictorial*, 14 February 1937

547: over half: Martin Pugh, *Women and the Women's Movement in Britain* (Basingstoke: Macmillan, 1992), 223

547: almost 60 per cent: Richard L. Morgan. 'The Introduction of Civil Legal Aid in England and Wales, 1914–49', *Twentieth Century British History* 5, no.1, 1994, 48, 49, 52, 53

547: the 1937 Act: Phillips, 529–30

548: considerable social stigma: Morgan, 49

548: less than angelic: Langford, 11 June 1936, 26 December 1937, 31 January 1938

549: just think how many: *Woman*, February 1934, cited in Robin Kent, *Aunt Agony Advises: Problem Pages Through the Ages* (W.H. Allen, 1979), 88, 83

549: Happy and lucky: Cited in Jeffrey Weeks, *Sex, Politics and Society* (Longman, 1981), 205

549: a husband, a cosy home: 'I Am So Happy', *Woman's Own*, 24 December 1932, 373

550: *Live Alone*: Marjorie Hillis, *Live Alone and Like It: A Guide for the Extra Woman* (Duckworth, 1936), 13, 10, x, 11

551: they were charged: Heather Jenner, *Marriages are Made on Earth* (Newton Abbot: David & Charles, 1979), 7, 9, 11, 19; *Daily Mail*, 18 April 1939

551: 750,000: Stevenson, 146

551: around 500,000 girls: Beddoe, 40–1

552: just lived for: Margaret Bondfield, *A Life's Work* (Hutchinson, 1948), 36–7

552: 4,000 women JPs: Women were not appointed as stipendary magistrates (paid justices with legal training and a minimum of seven years' experience as a barrister) until after 1945. Anne Logan, 'Professionalism and the Impact of England's First Women Justices, 1929–50', *Historical Journal* 44, 3, 2006, 841, 846

552: most London hospitals: Lewis, 195

552: extremely rare: Beddoe, 78

552: only the second: Dr Ivy Williams was the first, and Margaret Henderson Kidd was the first woman to be called to the Scottish Bar in 1926. Angela Holdsworth, *Out of the Doll's House: The Story of Women in the Twentieth Century* (BBC, 1988), 71; Beddoe, 78

553: the vast majority: Miriam Glucksmann, *Women Assemble: Women Workers in the New Industries of Inter-War Britain* (Routledge, 1989), 224

553: 84 per cent: Beddoe, 58

553: I don't think: *The Times*, 25 September 1933

553: Men say that: Ellen Wilkinson MP, 'Towards Utopia IV: Can Men and Women be Really Equal?' *The Listener*, 2 April 1930

553: marriage bar: Meta Zimmick, 'Strategies and Stratagems for the Employment of women in the British Civil Service, 1919–39', *Historical Journal* 27, 4, 1984

553: deciding to dismiss: Holdsworth, 71–2

553: Take a regular: Political and Economic Planning, *Women in Top Jobs* (Allen & Unwin, 1971)

554: normal custom: Holdsworth, 74

554: average age at marriage: Clare Langhamer, 'Love and Courtship in Mid-Twentieth Century England', *Historical Journal* 50, 1, 2007, 178

554: a third of women: Jane Lewis, *Women in England, 1870–1950* (Harvester, 1984), 4

554: the Cinderellas: Joan Beauchamp, *Women Who Work* (Lawrence & Wishart, 1937), 27

555: very rarely: Leonora Eyles, *Careers for Women* (Elkins, Matthews & Marrot, 1930), 6, 7, 9

556: 200,000 women teachers: G. Darcy, 'Changes and Problems in Women's Work in England and Wales' (unpublished PhD thesis, University of London, 1984), cited in Beddoe, 77

556: I have not yet: Winifred Holtby, *Women and a Changing Civilisation* (John Lane/Bodley Head, 1934), 130

556: Today there is: *Time and Tide*, May 1935

556: Sapphic Graphic: Emily Hamer, *Britannia's Glory: A History of Twentieth Century Lesbianism* (Cassell, 1996), 76

556: The magazine was: Lesbian History Group, *Not a Passing Phase: Reclaiming Lesbians in History, 1840–1985* (Women's Press, 1989), 146

556: spinster sons: Alison Oram, '"Embittered, Sexless or Homosexual": Attacks on Spinster Teachers, 1918–39' in ibid., 104

557: well-adjusted: *Times Educational Supplement*, 20 July 1935

557: it is a good plan: D.F.P. Hiley, *Pedagogue Pie* (Nicholson & Watson, 1936)

557: fewer than 3,000: G. Darcy, cited in Beddoe, 77

557: Mary Milne: Kevin Brown, 'Milne, Mary Elizabeth Gordon', *Oxford Dictionary of National Biography* online

557: a natural spinster: George Orwell, *Keep the Aspidistra Flying* (Gollancz, 1936; Penguin, 1962), 601, 604

557: waitresses had: Cited in Glucksmann, 124

557: staff competition: 'Nippy', *Picture Post*, 4 March 1939

558: powerful interwar brand: Peter Bird, *The First Food Empire: A History of J.L. Lyons & Co* (Phillimore, 2000), 115, 116, 117

558: ten-hour day: Beddoe, 72

558: close to 400,000: Darcy in ibid., 69

558: small and dirty: Lawrence E. Neal, *Retailing and the Public* (Allen & Unwin, 1932), 198

558: The 1934 Shop Act: Beddoe, 71

559: Marjorie Gardiner: Marjorie Gardiner, *The Other Side of the Counter: The Life of a Shop Girl, 1925–45* (Queenspark), no.17, 18

559: the young and wise: 'Spinsters', *Picture Post*, 8 October 1938

560: The women gathered: D.J. Prickett's unpublished *Biography of Florence White* in Virginia Nicholson, *Singled Out* (Viking/Penguin, 2007), 239–40

560: The committee: Harold L. Smith, 'Gender and the Welfare State: The 1940 Old Age Pensions Acts', *History* 80, no.260, October 1995, 382–99

560: a long trudge: Holdsworth, 96

561: mobile clinics: Kate Fisher, '"Clearing Up Misconceptions": The Campaign to Set up Birth Control Clinics in South Wales Between the Wars' in *Welsh History Review* 19, no.1, June 1998, 118

561: strange filthy things: Beddoe, 107

561: infinitely worse: Brooke quoted in BBC, *Yesterday's Witness*, 21 April 1969, transcript 85

561: tooth and nail: Cited in Fisher (1998), 115

561: one in Belfast: Greta Jones, 'Marie Stopes in Ireland: The Mothers' Clinic in Belfast, 1936–7', *Social History of Medicine* 5, no.2, August 1992, 255–76

562: voluntary clinics: Audrey Leathard, *The Fight for Family Planning: The Development of Family Planning Services in Britain, 1921–74* (Macmillan, 1980), 66

562: its rightful place: Helena Wright, *The Sex Factor in Marriage: A Book for Those who are or are About to be Married with an Introduction by A. Herbert Gray, MA DD* (Williams & Norgate, 1933), 11–12

562: contraceptive intercourse: G.T. Machin, *Churches and Social Issues in Twentieth-Century Britain* (Clarendon Press, 1998), 91, 92, 93

562: safe period: Marie Stopes, *Roman Catholic Methods of Birth Control* (1933), 85, 87

562: only 9 per cent: Lewis, 6

563: thick heavy things: Holdsworth, 96

563: English Rubber Company: Stevenson, 153

563: unisex sheath: Charles & Co., 'combined pessary and sheath', Kate Fisher, *Birth Control, Sex and Marriage in Britain, 1918–60* (Oxford University Press, 2006), 35, 34

563: 40 per cent: Lewis, 18

564: washing your feet: Fisher (2006), 172

564: calculating: Lella Secor Florence, *Birth Control on Trial* (Allen & Unwin, 1930), 68

564: innocence and virtue: Fisher (2006), 66, 68

565: A 1949 report: E. Lewis-Fanning, *Report on an Enquiry into Family Limitation* (1949), 149, cited in ibid., 79

565: most were aware: ibid., 89

565: a particular thrill: Naomi Mitchison, *Comments on Birth Control* (Faber, 1930), 13

565: nearly 30 per cent: Cited in Lesley A. Hall, *Sex, Gender and Social Change in Britain Since 1880* (Macmillan, 2000), 122

565: Our sex-life: Whiteing, 61, 63

566: It makes me wild: Margaret Rae to Marie Stopes, 10 October 1939, cited in Fisher (2006), 149

566: The unlawful side: Florence Gordon to Marie Stopes, 10 December 1937 cited in ibid., 159

567: many mothers seemed: Angus

McLaren, 'Women's Work and the Regulation of Family Size', *History Workshop Journal* no.4, autumn 1977, 75

567: quite justified [and subsequent quotes] Barbara Brookes, *Abortion in England, 1900–67* (Croom Helm, 1988), 117, 110–11, 62

567: Women would get: Lewis, 17

568: Ted Willis: Ted Willis, *Whatever Happened to Tom Mix?: The Story of One of My Lives* (Cassell, 1970), 8–9

568: jar of slippery elm: Cited in Tania McIntosh, '"An Abortionist City": Maternal Mortality, Abortion and Birth Control in Sheffield, 1920–40', *Medical History* 44, 2000, 90

568: It is perfectly possible: Cited in Brookes, 65

569: It costs about: Vita Sackville-West, *The Easter Party* (Michael Joseph, 1953), 93

569: a damned abortionist: A.J. Cronin, *The Citadel* (Gollancz, 1937), 388

569: The Birkett Committee: Cited in McIntosh, 81

569: A midwife working: Cited in Lewis, 18

569: 3,000 Birmingham women: Cited in Elizabeth Roberts, *A Woman's Place: An Oral History of Working Class Women, 1890–1940* (Blackwell, 1984), 97

569: 3.27 women: Thomas and Williams, 304

569: against the law: Hall, 129

570: Dr Aleck Bourne: John Keown, *Abortion, Doctors and the Law:*
Some Aspects of the Legal Regulation of Abortion in England from 1803 to 1982 (Cambridge University Press, 1998), 49–51

571: merely because: Brookes, 66

571: fear of cancer: Cited in Thomas and Williams, 300

571: an ethical question: Cited in Keown, 69, 70

571: It is impossible: Dr John Hannan in *Birth Control News* 16, 1938, 81, cited in Brookes, 108

571: incidence of abortion: Cited in ibid., 108–9; James Thomas and A. Susan Williams, 'Women and Abortion in 1930s Britain: A Survey and its Data', *Social History of Medicine* 1, no.2, 287

571: regarded as: Cited in McIntosh, 75

571: The huge total: A.D.K. Owen, 'A Report on Unemployment in Sheffield', *Sheffield Social Survey Committee*, 1932, cited in ibid., 85

572: deaths due to abortions: S. Szreter, *Fertility, Class and Gender in Britain 1860–1940* (Cambridge University Press, 1996), 426

572: consider what steps [and subsequent quotes]: Brookes, 105, 112, 110, 114, 116, 123

573: necessarily fatal: Cited in Hall, 129–30

573: Birkett Committee's recommendations: Cited in McIntosh, 81

573: The correct name: Marie Stopes, *Enduring Passion* (Hogarth Press, 1928), 29

573: Keep your mind off: Cited in Nicholson, 182

574: I would be bold: Cited in Alkarim Jivani, *It's Not Unusual: A History of Lesbian and Gay Britain in the Twentieth Century* (Michael O'Mara, 1997), 34

574: I am . . . one: Radclyffe Hall, *The Well of Loneliness* (Cape, 1928; Virago, 1985)

575: meritorious and dull: letter from Virginia Woolf to Roger Fry, 16 October 1928, *The Letters of Virginia Woolf, Vol. III: A Change of Perspective*, 523–4

575: very violently: Vita Sackville-West to Virginia Woolf 31 August 1928 in Louise De Salvo and Mitchell A. Leaska (eds), *The Letters of Vita Sackville-West to Virginia Woolf* (Virago, 1992), 296

575: the chief magistrate: Lillian Faderman, *Surpassing the Love of Men: Romantic Friendship and Love Between Women from the Renaissance to the Present* (Junction, 1981), 322

575: a book which; Sir Robert Wallace KC, reported in *The Times*, 15 December 1928

575: Gare du Nord: Jivani, 40–1

575: Oh! The vicarages: Beatrice Gordon Holmes, *In Love with Life: A Pioneer Career Woman's Story* (Hollis & Carter, 1944)

575: It was a revelation: Cited in Jivani, 40–1

576: glorious span: *I'll Stand by You: The Letters of Sylvia Townsend Warner and Valentine Ackland* ed. Susanna Pinney (Pimlico, 1998), 386

576: flooded with happiness: Elizabeth Goudge, *The Joy of Snow* (Hodder & Stoughton, 1974), cited in Nicholson, 185

576: Elizabeth Bowen: Hamer, 101

576: part and parcel: Mary Stocks, *Eleanor Rathbone* (Gollancz, 1949), 7–8

576: Hannah Gluckstein: Hamer, 121

576: she declined to: Hermione Lee, *Virginia Woolf* (Chatto & Windus, 1996), 490

577: Eton crop: Michael Baker, *Our Three Selves: A Life of Radclyffe Hall* (Hamish Hamilton, 1985), 131

577: Morgan [E.M. Forster] said: Virginia Woolf, diary entry for 31 August 1928, quoted in Quentin Bell, *Virginia Woolf, Vol. II* (Hogarth Press, 1979), 273

577: a sodomy club: Jivani, 20

577: really a terrible: Diary, 9 October 1923, quoted in Hugo Vickers, *Cecil Beaton* (Weidenfeld & Nicolson, 1985), 40

577: I propose to: letter to Quentin Bell, 21 December 1933, *The Letters of Virginia Woolf, Vol. V, 1932–35* ed. Nigel Nicolson (Hogarth Press, 1979), 293

578: thirty queer incidents: Matt Houlbrook, *Queer London: Perils and Pleasures in the Sexual Metropolis, 1918–57* (University of Chicago Press, 2005), 53

578: Day after uneventful day: Quentin Crisp, *The Naked Civil Servant* (Fontana, 1977), 28

578: absolute mecca: Michael Davidson, *The World My Flesh* (Arthur Barker,

1962), quoted in Hugh Cecil, *On Queer Street: A Social History of British Homosexuality, 1895–1995* (HarperCollins, 1997), 129

578: Is she so?: Jivani, 14

578: Soho clubs: Houlbrook (2005), 84, 87, 90

578: a 1928 survey: Introduction to *The New Survey of London Life and Labour, Vol. I*, 23

579: map of Ireland: Driberg, 75

579: usherettes were instructed: Houlbrook (2005), 58

579: of such a nature: Police report, 30 August 1933, cited in Matt Houlbrook, 'The Private World of Public Urinals: London 1918–57' *London Journal* 25, 1, 2000, 54

579: More prosperous men: 'A Public Servant's Life' in *Between the Acts: Lives of Homosexual Men, 1885–1967* ed. Kevin Porter and Jeffrey Weeks (Routledge, 1991)

580: In one raid: Crisp, 82

580: I got pretty shrewd: 'An Academic Life' in Porter and Weeks, 61

580: Havelock Ellis: 'A Public Servant's Life' in ibid., 110

580: mums and dads: 'A Remodelled Life' in ibid., 140

580: The difference: *Letters to Christopher: Stephen Spender's Letters to Christopher Isherwood, 1929–39, with 'The Line on the Branch' – Two Thirties Journals* ed. Lee Bartlett (Black Arrow Press, 1980), 45

581: never saw myself: 'A Professional's Life' in Porter and Weeks, 147

581: established homosexual networks: Houlbrook (2005), 9

581: unemployment brought young men: ibid., 47, 176

581: a green dot: *For Your Convenience: A Learned Dialogue Instructive to All Londoners & London Visitors, Overheard in The Theleme Club and Taken down Verbatim by Paul Pry* (Routledge, 1937), 2–3, 9–10, 16

581: Frank Champain: Houlbrook (2005), 57

582: humiliating rituals: Jivani, 14

582: ten arrests: Mrs C. Neville Rolfe, 'Sex Delinquency' in *The New Survey of London Life and Labour, Vol. IX: Life and Leisure* (1935), 322

582: Fancy that: Houlbrook (2005), 244–5. Thirty-five years later the 1967 Homosexual Law Reform Act allowed 'our cult', providing the homosexual acts were between consenting adults aged over twenty-one in private.

582: R.C. Sherriff: *The Fortnight in September* (Gollancz, 1931; Persephone, 2006)

582: like hot cakes: R.C. Sherriff, *No Leading Lady* (Gollancz, 1968), 227–30

584: eight hours' overtime: Stephen G. Jones, *Workers at Play: A Social and Economic History of Leisure 1918–39* (Routledge, 1986), 16

585: entitled to paid holidays: J.A.R. Pimlott, *The Englishman's Holiday: A Social History* (Faber, 1947), 214–15

585: the camel: Herbert G. Kingston,

'Holidays with Pay', *The Listener*, 14 October 1937

585: Roland Robinson: Quoted in Pimlott (1947), 237

586: Sir Walter Citrine: Quoted in ibid., 222

586: We are a town: Quoted in Alistair J. Durie, *Scotland for the Holidays: A History of Tourism in Scotland, 1780–1939* (Tuckwell Press, 2003), 196

586: Barry Island: Nigel J. Morgan and Annette Pritchard, *Power and Politics at the Seaside: The Development of Devon's Resorts in the Twentieth Century* (University of Exeter Press, 1999), 35

587: who prefer their: Nigel Yates, 'Selling Southsea, Promoting Portsmouth', *Portsmouth Papers* 72 (Portsmouth City Council, n.d.), 2

587: Big Wheels: Morgan and Pritchard, 63, 92

587: Lobby Lud: The 'Lobby Lud' seaside promotions continued into the 1960s.

588: each new reader: D.L. LeMahieu, *A Culture for Democracy: Mass Communication and the Cultivated Mind in Britain Between the Wars* (Oxford Clarendon Press, 1988), 255

588: employed more canvassers: Curran and Seaton, 53

588: Dorset, Devonshire: Whiteing, 49

588: 'going off' club: James Walvin, *Beside the Seaside: A Social History of the Popular Seaside Holiday* (Allen Lane, 1978), 109

589: They go back: Charles Graves, *And the Greeks* (Geoffrey Bles, 1930), 189

589: thrift of a sort: Robert Poole, 'Lancashire Wakes Week', *History Today* 34, 8, August 1984, 29

589: by strong determination: *Oldham Chronicle*, 28 August 1931

589: Brixham for example: Walvin, 110

589: Hastings: John K. Walton, *The British Seaside: Holidays and Resorts in the Twentieth Century* (Manchester University Press, 2000), 35, 133

590: some, eccentrically: Stella Davies, *North Country Bred* (Routledge, 1963)

590: Wakes Week: Robert Poole, *The Lancashire Wakes Holidays* (Lancashire County, 1994), 23

590: one town after another: John K. Walton. 'Afterword: Mass-Observation's Blackpool and Some Alternatives' in *Worktowners at Blackpool: Mass-Observation and Popular Leisure in the 1930s* ed. Gary Cross (Routledge, 1990), 229

591: 234 cases: Cited in Gurney, 274–5

591: 2d in Blackpool: Graves, 187–8

591: economy was over-dependent: Terry Potter, *Reflections on Blackpool* (Wilmslow, Cheshire: Sigma Leisure, 1994), 16

591: modernist redesigns: Terry Regan and Alan Hazelhurst, *From Lamp to Laser: The Story of the Blackpool Illuminations* (Skelter, 2004), 48

591: The Big Wheel: Brian Turner and Steve Palmer, *The Blackpool Story* (Blackpool Corporation, 1939), 120

591: This Mecca: *Blackpool: The Holiday*

You Will Never Forget (Blackpool Corporation, 1939)

592: the world's largest: Sue Arthur, 'Crested China, Pineapple Chunks and Cherry Red Velvet: A History of Shopping in Blackpool Town Centre from 1881 to 1958' (MA thesis, Blackpool Borough Libraries, 2003), 47–8

592: a new casino: John K. Walton, *Blackpool* (Edinburgh University Press/Carnegie, 1998), 125

592: one more step: Hugh Casson, 'The Site', *Architectural Review*, June 1939, 26

592: The Blackpool landlady: John Walton, *The Blackpool Landlady: A Social History* (Manchester University Press, 1978), 175–6, 181

593: seven million visitors: J.K. Walton, 'The Seaside Resorts of England and Wales, 1900–50: Growth, Diffusion and New Forms of Coastal Tourism' in G. Shaw and A. Williams (eds), *The Rise and Fall of British Coastal Resorts* (Cassell, 1998), 37, 122

593: 27 miles: Cross, 216–22

593: flowerless town: *Night and Day*, 30 September 1937

593: garish displays: Regan and Hazelhurst, 57–9

593: an outstanding success: Cross, 222

593: three thousand dancing: William Holt, 'Round the Clock with Blackpool's Joy-Seekers, 7 August 1934', cited in Walton (1998), 122–3

594: best-known symbol: Cross, 87, 128

594: Gracie Fields: Jeffrey Richards, *Oxford Dictionary of National Biography*

594: Mae West's Vest: Peter Gurney,

'"Intersex" and "Dirty Girls": Mass-Observation and Working-Class Sexuality in England in the 1930s', *Journal of the History of Sexuality* 8, no.2, 1997, 269

594: Social Mixer: Cross, 105–6, 115

595: 'nude' women: Alison Oram, *Her Husband Was a Woman: Women's Gender-Crossing in Modern British Popular Culture* (Routledge, 2007), 121

595: tattooed women: *Blackpool Gazette and Herald*, 17 September 1932, 21 October 1933

596: The bride too ill: *Blackpool Evening Gazette*, 16 October 1934

596: It is always: *News of the World*, 24 April 1932, cited in Oram, 124

596: I think she's: Gurney, 282–5

596: Harold Davidson: Jonathan Tucker, *The Troublesome Priest: Harold Davidson, Rector of Stiffkey* (Michael Russell, 2007), 26, 145–7

598: Declaring himself: John Hudson, *Wakes Weeks: Memories of Mill Town Holidays* (Alan Sutton, 1992), 68

598: Include Your Wife: *Manchester Evening News*, 9 May 1935, cited in Claire Langhamer, *Women's Leisure in England 1920–60* (Manchester University Press, 2000), 38

598: plain food: Edward Carpenter, *England's Ideal* (Swan Sonnenschein, 1887)

598: middle-class and exclusive: Walton (2000), 38

598: At first visitors: Jill Drower, *Good Clean Fun: The Story of Britain's First Holiday Camp* (Arcadia, 1982)

599: Family-run camps: Colin Ward and Dennis Hardy, *Goodnight Campers!: The History of the British Holiday Camp* (Mansell, 1986), 41

599: Squires Gate: Walton (2000), 131

599: the 1936 Public Health Act [and following quotes]: Ward and Hardy (1986), 31, 41, 40

599: Holiday Fellowship: Rex North, *The Butlin Story* (Jarrolds, 1962)

601: Roll out of bed: Pimlott (1947), 251

601: Included in the cost: Sir Billy Butlin with Peter Dacre, *The Billy Butlin Story: 'A Showman to the End'* (Robson, 1982), 112

601: Please don't get: Pimlott (1947), 252

601: Holidays with pay: North, 66

601: 50,000 visitors: Butlin and Dacre, 125

601: It could house: Piers Brendon, *Thomas Cook: 150 Years of Popular Tourism* (Secker & Warburg, 1991), 273

601: Filey: Ward and Hardy, 68

602: The English Naples: Nigel Yates, 'Selling the Seaside', *History Today* 38, 8, August 1988, 20–7

602: Alternative destinations: Phyllis Hemby, *British Spas from 1815 to the Present: A Social History* (Athlone, 1997), 237, 228, 236

602: aqua cocktail parties: Pimlott, 256

602: owing to the: Durie (2003), 193–5; A.J. Durie, *Water is Best: The Hydros and Health Tourism in Scotland, 1840–1940* (Edinburgh: John Donald, 2006), 134

602: compact home from home: W.M. Whiteman, *The History of the Caravan* (Blandford, 1973), 84

603: most-visited destinations: Clifford O'Neil, '"The Most Magical Corner of England": Tourism, Preservation and the Development of the Lake District, 1919–39' in *Histories of Tourism: Representation. Identity and Conflict* ed. John K. Walton (Channel View, 2005), 232

603: Although from: *Westmoreland Gazette*, 5 April 1919, cited in O'Neil, 233

603: forbidden country: Lawrence du Garde Peach, *Come to Derbyshire* (1934), cited in Melanie Tebbutt, '"In the Midlands But Not of Them": Derbyshire's Dark Peak – An Imagined Northern Landscape' in *Northern Identities: Historical Interpretations of 'The North' and 'Northernness'* ed. Neville Kirk (Ashgate, 2000)

604: Stratford-upon-Avon: Ivor Brown and George Fearon, *A Short History of the Shakespeare Industry* (William Heinemann, 1939) 285–7

604: Colin Ferguson: Glasgow City Archive TD 646/7, July 1933

605: over £31 million: R.G. Pinney, *Britain: Destination of Tourists?* (Travel and Industrial Development Association of Great Britain and Ireland, 1944), 22

605: with its growing: Sir Stephen Tallents, *The Projection of England* (Faber, 1932), 14–15

605: a bell being rung: David Gilbert and Fiona Henderson, 'London and the Tourist Imagination' in *Imagined Londons* ed. Pamela K. Gilbert (State University of New York

Press, 2002), 127; *A Pictorial and Descriptive Guide to London* (Ward, Lock, 53rd edn 1938), 251

607: Hitler arrived: Information from Susanna Lamb, archivist, Madame Tussaud's. In 1942 a ring of pins was found to have been stuck round the Führer's heart.

607: Tussaud's exterior: Information from Susanna Lamb, 1930s catalogues and Pamela Pilbeam, *Madame Tussaud and the History of Waxworks* (Hambledon & London, 2003), 194–9

607: not until 1848: It had been open to Fellows of the Society since 1828.

607: In 1924: J. Barrington-Jones, *The Zoo: The Story of London Zoo* (Robert Hale, 2005), 91

608: solved the problem: Zoological Society of London, Annual Report 1932

608: sensational and: *Architectural Review*, 17–18

608: Pets' Corner: London Zoological Society, Annual Report 1935

608: a report had recognised: P. Chalmers Mitchell, 'The Future of the Zoological Society', *Saturday Review*, 28 August 1909, quoted in *London's Zoo: An Anthology to Celebrate 150 Years of the Zoological Society of London, with the Zoos at Regent's Park in London and Whipsnade in Bedfordshire* compiled by Gwynne Vevers (Bodley Head, 1976), 149

608: Whipsnade's success: Barrington-Jones, 102–3

609: Robert Nichols, *Looking Back at Belle Vue, Manchester* (n.d.)

609: The aquarium: *Manchester Evening News*, 8 April 1936

609: two pandas: *Manchester Guardian*, 27 March 1936

609: a working holiday: Pam Schweitzer, Introduction to *Our Lovely Hops: Memories of Hop-Picking in Kent* ed. Pam Schweitzer with Dianne Hancock (Age Concern Theatre Trust, 1991), 4

609: There is a fairly: *The New Survey of London Life and Labour, Vol. III*, 330

610: tin at first: Kathleen Ash in ibid., 8

610: more basic: Sam Whitbread, Foreword to ibid., 3

610: like sentry boxes: Dennis Freeman, 'Hop Picking in the 1930s', *East London Record* 8, 1985, 27

610: If you wanted: Joan Clarkson, Eileen O'Sullivan and Majorie Balcombe, *Our Lovely Hops*, 12

610: Some families: Freeman, 27

611: Pickers had a bin: Miles Sergeant, 'The Invasion of Kent', 14

611: The laws about: George Orwell, 'Hop–picking', *The Collected Essays, Journalism and Letters of George Orwell, Vol. I: An Age Like This, 1920–40* ed. Sonia Orwell and Ian Angus (Secker & Warburg, 1968), 85

611: some parents would: Vi Lewis, *Our Lovely Hops*, 42

611: That is we were, George Orwell, 'Hop–picking', *New Statesman*, 17 October 1931

611: You never got: *Our Lovely Hops*, 37

612: 'magic lantern' shows: Freeman, 29

612: On the last morning: Orwell, *Collected Essays, Vol. I*, 92

612: *The Golden Bough*: George Frazer, *The Golden Bough: A Study in Magic and Religion*, published in several volumes at the turn of the century

612: The Bull: Sergeant, 14

612: wonder machines: *Kent Messenger*, 1933, reproduced in *Our Lovely Hops*, 104

613: no hut no bathe: Laura Chase, 'Public Beaches and Private Beach Huts: A Case Study of Inter-War Clacton and Frinton, Essex' in Walton, *Histories of Tourism*, 216–17

614: unremitting work: Brendon, 269, 270

614: nearly a million and a half: Sir Frederick Ogilvie, *The Tourist Movement* (P.S. King, 1933), cited in Pimlott, 262

614: Lourdes: Brendon, 271

614: Monte Carlo: Graves, 69–70, 26

614: the Prince of Wales: Pimlott (1947), 265

615: The Land of Dreams: R.G. Studd, *Holiday Story* (Percival Marshall, 1950)

615: less than £37: Pimlott (1947), 262–3

615: Sodom: Brendon, 271

615: alligators, jaguars: 'Escape to the Sun: The Literature of Winter Travel', *Night and Day*, 25 November 1937, 26

616: Every hour: Cited in Pimlott (1947), 265–6

617: Patrick Balfour: Patrick Balfour, *Grand Tour: Diary of an Eastward Journey* (John Long, 1934), vii, 15, 19, 318

617: distressingly like: Evelyn Waugh, *Labels* (Duckworth, 1930)

617: a wretched journey: Selina Hastings, *Evelyn Waugh: A Biography* (Sinclair-Stevenson, 1994), 184–5

617: Mount Etna: Waugh, 169

618: What *Ulysses* is: Paul Fussell, *Abroad: British Literary Travelling Between the Wars* (Oxford University Press, 1980), 95

619: last and finest: *Sunday Times*, 25 April 1937

621: masculine republic: Andrew Davies, *Leisure, Gender and Poverty: Working-Class Culture in Salford and Manchester, 1900–39* (Open University Press, 1992), 30

621: wait for the last: *The Pub and the People*, x

621: Yes, I miss: Bakke, 191–3

621: We always go: Cyril Dunn, unpublished diaries, 5, May 1934, reproduced by kind permission of Peter Dunn

621: over a quarter: *Poverty and Progress*, 351–3; *The New Survey of London Life and Labour, Vol. IX*, 253–4

622: Rowntree estimated: *Poverty and Progress*, 254

622: In 1938 we never: Basil D. Nicholson, 'Introductory Note', *The Pub and the People*, xii

622: The Stoneleigh Hotel: Alan A. Jackson (1973), 280–1

622: dismal sham-Tudor: Orwell, *The Road to Wigan Pier*, xx

622: arterial and by-pass roads: Priestley, 401, 402–3

623: Lady Marguerite Strickland: *Daily Telegraph* obituary of Lady

Marguerite Tangye, 15 October 2002

624: The American-born: Sid Colin and Tony Staveacre, *Al Bowlly* (Elm Tree, 1979), 40

624: a particularly: Scannell and Cardiff, 189

624: Bowlly: Albert McCarthy, *The Dance Band Era: The Dancing Decades from Ragtime to Swing, 1910–50* (Hamlyn, 1974), 87

625: a jazz-minded: Colin and Staveacre, 43

625: the Regent Palace: Jackson (1991), 284

626: middle-class: ibid.

626: Henry Hall: Briggs, 88

627: obliged to continue: Carol Kennedy, 'Give Us Back Our Bad Old World', *The Times Saturday Review*, 30 August–5 September 1986

627: ghastly cubist: Barbara Cartland, *The Isthmus Years* (Hutchinson, 1942), 108–10

628: the prices charged: *Secrets of the 43: Reminiscences by Mrs Meyrick* (John Long, 1933), 267

628: simply a variation: Patrick Balfour, *Society Racket: A Critical Survey of Modern Social Life* (John Long, 1933), 116

628: Queen of Nightclubs: Meyrick, 260

629: part interest: Richard Davenport-Hines, 'Kate Evelyn Meyrick' in *Oxford Dictionary of National Biography*

629: with notebooks like: Blythe, 36

629: melted away: Meyrick, 272–81

629: fairly extensive tour: Maurice Richardson, 'The Bottle-Party Belt', *Night and Day*, 1 July 1937

629: spot of bother: M0OA: MDJ:4/H; 'Night in Soho', *Night and Day*, 14 April 1939

630: The number of 'clubs': Richardson, 23

631: everything Black: Fussell, 186

631: negro folk songs: Thomas Jones (1969), 126

631: junction box: Ian Duffield, 'Blacks in Britain: History and the Historians', *History Today* 31, 9, September 1981, 34

631: new black modernity: Bill Schwarz, 'Black Metropolis, White England' in Mica Nava and Alan O'Shea (eds), *Modern Times: Reflections on a Century of English Modernity* (Routledge, 1996), 180

631: mother Empire: Claude McKay, *A Long Way From Home* (Lee Furman, 1937; reprint Arno Press and the *New York Times*, 1969), 76; *The Passion of Claude McKay: Selected Poetry and Prose, 1912–48* ed. Wayne F. Cooper (Schocken, 1973), 101

631: black entertainers: Cary D. Wintz and Paul Finkleman (eds), *Encyclopedia of the Harlem Renaissance* (Routledge, 2004)

633: the most conscientious [and subsequent quotes]: Nancy Cunard, *Black Man and White Ladyship: An Anniversary* (1931), 4, 2, 9–10

633: had her article printed: Chisholm, 186–7. There is also a biography by Lois Gordon, *Nancy Cunard: Heiress, Muse, Political Idealist* (Columbia University Press, 2007).

633: even Nancy's friends [and subsequent material]: Chisholm, 186–8, 160, 127

634: the 'Colour Bar': In this article Nancy Cunard instanced blatant cases of discrimination. One occurred when a black law student at the Middle Temple was refused service in the Essex tea rooms in The Strand on 10 December 1931, having been invited to take tea there with Isobel Brown. In another, the Hotel Washington in Mayfair refused a room for 'a white wife and a Negro husband' 'as we have so many American visitors, who . . . are so prejudiced against Negroes'. As an addendum A. Ade Ademola told of a Mr Alakija who had reserved a room for ten months at the New Mansion Hotel, Lancaster Gate, London, but when he checked in on 27 August 1931 he was shown the door. Mr Ademola, an Oxford graduate, sued the hotel, which defended its decision on the grounds that Alakija had 'a duty to disclose in the correspondence the fact that he was an African'. As the hotel proprietor 'believed that he was in touch with a European, therefore there was no *consensus as idem*, and therefore no contract'. The judge found against the hotel. There was also the notorious occasion when Paul Robeson was refused entry to the Savoy Hotel when in the company of Lady Colefax in 1929.

634: an American-born: *Negro*, 343

634: libel cases: Ford, xxiii

634: like selling: Chisholm, 208

635: costly exercise: ibid., 220

635: it is Communism: Nancy Cunard, Foreword to *Negro: An Anthology* collected and ed. Nancy Cunard (Lawrence & Wishart, 1931), i

635: damn fine: Chisholm, 221

635: all were destroyed: Hugh Ford, Introduction to *Negro: An Anthology*, xii

635: discriminatory employment practices: In 1930 a Miss M.E. Fletcher, researching the 'colour problem in the ports', wrote to 119 Liverpool firms asking about the employment prospects for 'coloured juveniles': no reply was received from sixty-three and a negative reply from forty-five. Cited in Kenneth Little, *Negroes in Britain: A Study of Racial Relations in English Society* (Routledge, 2nd edn 1972), 92

635: Aliens Act: The Special Restriction (Coloured Alien Seamen) order of 1925 was intended to restrict further alien immigrants to Britain unless they could demonstrate that they could support themselves. It gave the police power to impose various restrictions on aliens, arrest them without a warrant, and to close certain clubs and restaurants. All coloured seamen regardless of nationality or domicile had to register with the police and carry their registration card with them at all times. In Cardiff the police laboured under the misapprehension that every coloured seaman in Cardiff was an alien and zealously pursued them with threats of arrest, imprisonment or deportation, Little, 87–9

635: a new monument: Barbara Bush, 'Blacks in Britain: The 1930s', *History Today* 31, 9, September 1981, 46

636: in all the world: Peter Fryer, *Staying Power: The History of Black People in Britain* (Pluto, 1984), 323–4

636: mounting soapboxes: Schwarz, 178

636: the welfare: Roderick J. MacDonald, 'Dr Harold Arundel Moody and the League of Coloured Peoples, 1931–47: A Retrospective View', *Race* 14, 1972–73, 292

636: Joint Council: Bush, 47

636: the League's membership: Fryer, 327–8

637: you are not: Quoted in Bush, 47

638: poison: Fryer, 340

638: Congolese village: Jeffrey Richards and Anthony Aldgate, *Best of British: Cinema and Society 1930–70* (Basil Blackwell, 1983), 15–26

638: we could not run: Sir Ralph Furse, colonial administrator, quoted in ibid., 18

639: our special English: *Sunday Times*, 7 April 1935

639: So this is: Paul Rotha, *Rotha on Film* (Faber, 1958), 139–40

639: a slanderous attack: *Paul Robeson Speaks* ed. Philip S. Foner (Citadel, 1979), 139–40, 118–19

640: a particular affinity: *Gadewch i Paul Robeson Ganu! Dathlu bywyd Paul Robeson/Let Paul Robeson Sing! Celebrating the Life of Paul Robeson* (National Library of Wales, 2003), 59

640: a great champion: Martin Bauml Duberman, *Paul Robeson* (Bodley Head, 1989), 227–8

640: Workers' Film Association: Bert Hogenkamp, *Deadly Parallels: Film and the Left in Britain* (Lawrence & Wishart, 1986), 176–88

640: Cinema vans: T.J. Hollins, 'The Conservative Party and Film Propaganda Between the Wars', *English Historical Review* 96, no.379, April 1981, 380, 363, 365, 366

641: a number on the left: *The Deadly Parallel*, October 1908, quoted in Hogenkamp, 16–18, 29

641: halting four times: Huntley Carter complaining about a film shown at the Freedom Labour Club, Peckham, South London on 4 May 1931, cited in ibid., 76, 55, 85

642: help of Hugo's: John and Mary Postgate, 173–5

642: Socialist League Film Committee: John Postgate, 'Raymond Postgate and the Socialist Film Council', *Sight and Sound* 60, no.1, winter 1990, 19, 20

644: *March Against Starvation*: Hogen-kamp, 111, 153

644: coordinate the activities: *Daily Worker*, 27 November 1934

644: a title: *Daily Worker*, 20 February 1935. The title was the distinctly unsnappy and not entirely accurate *Mass United Action Beat the UAB*

644: a publicity stunt: *Daily Worker*, 24 September 1935

644: The time has come: Hogenkamp, 124

645: Empire Marketing Board: Juliet Gardiner, 'Candid Culture', *History Today*, April 2006, 5

645: talented film-makers: *The Documentary Film Movement: An Anthology* ed. Ian Aitken (Edinburgh University Press, 1998), 3

646: As far as Grierson: Neil Sinyard, 'Grierson and the Documentary Film' in *The Cambridge Cultural History of Britain, Vol. VIII: Early Twentieth-Century Britain* ed. Boris Ford (Cambridge University Press, 1989), 247

646: this or that: Quoted in *The Documentary Film Movement*, 237

646: It is the task: Basil Wright, 'Documentary Today' in ibid., 237

647: attendance was not: Forster, 4 and 5 March 1938

647: LBC Film Groups: John Lewis (1970), 46–8

647: Workers' Theatre Movement: Raphael Samuel, 'Theatre and Socialism in Britain, 1880–1935' in Raphael Samuel, Ewan MacColl and Stuart Cosgrove, *Theatres of the Left, 1880–1935: Workers' Theatre Movements in Britain and America* (Routledge, 1985), 33

647: great dramatic art: Huntly Carter, 'Workers in the Theatre', *Sunday Worker*, 18 July 1926, cited in ibid., 33

647: Red Megaphones: ibid., 233–7

647: I knew bugger-all: Ewan MacColl, 'Theatre of Action, Manchester' in ibid., 227

648: Tom Thomas: Tom Thomas, 'A Propertyless Theatre for the Propertyless Class' in ibid., 83, 89, 93–5

649: anyone willing: John Allen, *Some Notes on the Formation of Left-Wing Amateur Theatre Groups 1937/8*, cited in Jon Clark, 'Socialist Theatre in the Thirties' in *Culture and Crisis in Britain in the Thirties* ed. Jon Clark, Margot Heinemann, David Margolis and Carole Smee (Lawrence & Wishart, 1979), 223

649: a bevy of: Colin Chambers, *The Story of the Unity Theatre* (Lawrence & Wishart, 1989), 111–13

650: like he's got: Willis, 153

650: performed many times: Review in *New Theatre* cited in Jon Clark, 'Socialist Theatre in the Thirties' in *Culture and Crisis in Britain in the Thirties*, 226–7

650: busmen's strike: Chambers, 66

650: drying up: Duberman, 224

650: turned down: Clark, 227

650: originally written for: Duberman, 223–4

650: the most exciting: Quoted in Clark, 228

650: with 18 people: Forster, 10 March 1938

650: on one occasion: 'Ewan MacColl, 1915–89: A Political Journey', Working Class Movement Library, Salford

651: didactic: Willis, 153

651: rapier of wit: Chambers, 166

651: sob sisters: Branson and Heinemann, 275

651: It slides: *The Townend Journals*, 50

652: light and required: Noël Coward,

Present Indicative (Heinemann, 1937), 229

652: critics were divided: Sheridan Morley, *A Talent to Amuse: A Biography of Noël Coward* (Heinemann, 1969), 197

652: frequently at odds: Philip Hoare, *Noël Coward: A Biography* (Sinclair-Stevenson, 1995), 235–6

653: emotional basis [and subsequent quotes]: Noël Coward, *Autobiography* (Methuen, 1986), 231, 235, 239

654: tawdry: Hoare, 235, 236

654: cash in on my: *Autobiography*, 240

655: aimed at a public: Quoted in Michael Sidnell, *Dances of Death: The Group Theatre of London in the Thirties* (Faber, 1984), 27

655: sweep away: Humphrey Carpenter, *W.H. Auden: A Biography* (Allen & Unwin, 1981), 164–5

655: German cabaret: Richard Davenport-Hines, *Auden* (Heinemann, 1995), 141

655: desiring revolution: *Times Literary Supplement*, 15 March 1934

655: in place of acting: 'The Theatre', *Spectator*, 11 October 1935

655: cockney rhyming slang: Charles Osborne, *W.H. Auden: The Life of a Poet* (Eyre Methuen, 1980), 112

655: run for five years: Carpenter, 191–2

656: meet the crying needs: Lilian Baylis quoted in Felix Barker, *The Oliviers* (Hamish Hamilton, 1953), 117

656: £10 a week: Sheridan Morley, *John G: The Authorised Biography of John Gielgud* (Hodder & Stoughton, 2001), 66, 67

656: pay was cut: Tony Howard, 'Blood on the Bright Young Things: Shakespeare in the 1930s' in *British Theatre Between the Wars, 1918–39* ed. Clive Barker and Maggie B. Gale (Cambridge University Press, 2000), 136

656: no hesitation: Quoted in Morley, 70, 72

656: Sir Henry Irving: Harold Nicolson, 4 October 1930

657: high-profile actors: James Forsyth, *Tyrone Guthrie: A Biography* (Hamish Hamilton, 1976), 131

657: lolling around: Herbert Farjeon, *The Shakespearean Scene* (Hutchinson, 1948), 128

657: the first full-length: Howard, 155

657: to form a ballet company: Elizabeth Schaffer, *Lilian Baylis: A Biography* (University of Hertfordshire Press/Society for Theatre Research, 2006), 217

657: The ballets: Richard Findlater, *Lilian Baylis: The Lady of the Old Vic* (Allen Lane, 1975), 253

658: a pennorth: Schaffer, 219–20

658: When Lilian Baylis died: Findlater, 259

658: seems to have assumed: Gladys Langford diaries, 11 February 1938, Islington Record Office

658: Music was heard: Gavin Weightman, *Bright Lights, Big City: London Entertainment 1830–1950* (Collins & Brown, 1992), 89–90

659: a gypsy wedding: John Snelson, '"We Said We Wouldn't Look Back": British Musical Theatre, 1935–60' in *The Cambridge Companion to the*

Musical ed. William A. Everett and Paul R. Laird (Cambridge University Press, 2nd edn 2008), 129

659: The romantic extravaganza: John Kenrick, *Musical Theatre: A History* (Continuum, 2008), 218

659: *Me and My Girl*: ibid., 219

659: Nine hundred and three million: H.E. Browning and A.A. Sorrell, 'Cinema and Cinemagoing in Great Britain', *Journal of the Royal Statistical Society* 117, 1954, 134, cited in Richards, *The Age of the Dream Palace*

660: The first purpose-built: David Atwell, *Cathedrals of the Movies* (1980), 5

660: around 3,000 cinemas: Mowat, 134

660: between 1932 and 1934: Richards, 12

660: provided three hours: Quoted in Richard Gray, *One Hundred Years of Cinema Architecture* (Lund Humphries, 1996), 63

660: Hello Mr Brown: *Enter the Dream-House: Memories of Cinemas in South London from the Twenties to the Sixties* ed. Margaret O'Brien and Allen Eyles (Museum of the Moving Image, 1993), 39, 106

660: an equal fable: Gray, 63

660: And they used to: *Enter the Dream-House*, 32

661: The Finsbury Park: Richards, 20

661: the Palace: Allen Eyles, *Old Cinemas* (Shire, 2001), 14; Gray, 84

661: The Pyramid [and following material]: Gray, 71, 72, 75, 91–2

662: By 1933 Deutsch: Richards, 38

662: black . . . façade: Gray, 106; Eyles, 21

662: the first family: Richards, 36

663: The third mighty: Gray, 109–12; Eyles, 25, Richards, 38

663: an oblong opening: Elizabeth Bowen in Charles Davy (ed.), *Footnotes to the Film* (Lovat Dickson, 1937), 205

663: But women and: Richard Carr, *World Film News* 1, no.10 (January 1937), 8, cited in Jeffreys, 13

663: the influence: *The New Survey of London Life and Leisure, Vol. IX*, 47

664: go to the cinemas: Quoted in *The Time of Our Lives: Memories of Leisure in the 1920s and 1930s* ed. Pam Schweitzer (Age Exchange, 1986), 34

664: Before they opened: Quoted in *Enter the Dream-House*, 39

664: we queued outside: Quoted in *The Time of Our Lives*, 34

664: a big jelly mould: Quoted in *Enter the Dream-House*, 102

665: one interesting feature: Bakke, 178–9

665: The Laugh and Scratch: Gwyn Thomas, *A Frost on my Frolic* (Gollancz, 1953), ch. vii, quoted in Peter Stead, 'The People and the Pictures: The British Working Class and Film in the 1930s' in Nicholas Pronay and D.W. Spring (eds), *Propaganda, Politics and Film, 1918–45* (Macmillan, 1982), 79

665: a mecca: Leslie Halliwell, *Seats in All Parts: Half a Lifetime at the Movies* (Granada, 1985), 12

665: there was no career: Quoted in *Enter the Dream-House*, 103

665: serving the toughest: Halliwell, 54

666: oddly dark: ibid., 74

666: Its audience was: *Mass-Observation at the Movies* ed. Jeffrey Richards and Dorothy Sheridan (Routledge, 1985), 32–3. The survey, though not published until 1943, was carried out in 1938.

666: Northerners went: McKibbin (1998), 422

666: More Popeyes [and subsequent quotes]: *Mass-Observation at the Movies*, 34–8, 43, 81, 83, 47

667: it is not only: Quoted in Richards, 63

667: quota quickies: Rachel Low, *The History of British Film 1929–39: Film Making in 1930s Britain* (Allen & Unwin, 1985), 33–4

667: cinema owners complaining: ibid., 35, quoting the cinema circuit-owner John Maxwell's report to the Moyne Committee on the effects of the quota system in 1936

667: In 1932 there were [and subsequent information]: Sue Harper, 'A Lower-Middle-Class Taste-Community in the 1930s: Admissions Figures at the Regent Cinema, Portsmouth, UK', *Historical Journal of Film, Radio and Television* 24, no.4, 2004, 565–7, 570

668: superbly acted: Mr G. Harkinson in *Mass-Observation at the Movies*, 84

668: The whole town: Halliwell, 7

668: Talking pictures: Sherriff, 241, 243, 247, 249

669: a bookselling record: Joseph McAleer, *Popular Reading and Publishing in Britain, 1914–50* (Oxford University Press, 1992), 56

669: it was an era: Robert McCrum, *Wodehouse: A Life* (Viking, 2004), 190

670: an omission for which: Cook (1997), 144–6

670: Aldous Huxley, believing: Sybille Bedford, *Aldous Huxley, A Biography, Vol. I: The Apparent Stability* (Collins/Chatto & Windus, 1973), 339–40; David King Dunaway, *Huxley in Hollywood* (Bloomsbury, 1989), 67–126

670: which was reportedly: Nicholas Murray, *Aldous Huxley: An English Intellectual* (Little, Brown, 2002), 306

670: No one's ever gonna: Neal Gabler, *Walt Disney: The Biography* (Aurum, 2007), 92

670: THIS FILM HAS: Halliwell, 25

670: for the next: ibid., 47

671: Seven children: Dr John Mackie (ed.), *The Edinburgh Film Enquiry* (1933), 67, 11; cited in Richards, 70, 18

671: they fidget: British Film Institute, *Report of a Conference on Films for Children*, 20–21 November 1936, 24–6

672: lusty: J.P. Mayer, *Sociology of Film: Studies and Documents* (Faber, 1946), 53

672: for thousands: Sheffield Social Survey Committee and Sheffield Juvenile Organisations Committee: *Survey of Children's Cinema Matinees, Saturday November 29th 1930* (Sheffield Archives MD 1231/60), n.p.

673: What the school: Mayer, 55

673: in the more: Katherine Box, *The*

Cinema and the Public (Central Office of Information Social Surveys Division, 1948), 106, 1946, 12

673: sturdily built: Marcia Landy, 'The Extraordinary Ordinariness of Gracie Fields: The Anatomy of a British Film Star' in *British Stars and Stardom from Alma Taylor to Sean Connery* ed. Bruce Babington (Manchester University Press, 2001), 58

673: bounced off: Basil Dean quoted in Low, 152

674: Listen to her: Priestley, 253

674: the Gracie Fields: Graves and Alan Hodge, 298

674: set the seal: Richards, 188

674: We have an: Paul Rotha and Richard Griffiths, *The Film Till Now* (Spring Books, 1967), 3

674: unemployment can always: *Spectator*, 2 August 1939

674: packed houses: Halliwell, 8

675: she rated third: Richards, 208

676: the *mores* of: Charles Barr, *Ealing Studios* (Cameron & Tayleur, 1977), 26

677: vast canvas: Low, 249–51

678: standing stock still: *The Times*, 10 July 1934

678: 12,000 horse-drawn carriages: *UK Annual Abstract of Statistics, 1924–37*, cited in James Foreman-Peck, 'Death on the Roads: Changing National Responses to Motor Accidents' in *The Economic and Social Effects of the Spread of Motor Vehicles* ed. Theo Barker (Macmillan, 1987), 281

679: 80 per cent: Cited in Ian R. Grimwood, *A Little Chit of a Fellow: A Biography of the Right Hon. Leslie Hore-Belisha* (Book Guild, 2006), 42

679: highest ever number: The number of road deaths in 1934 was not exceeded in peacetime until 1964, when there were five times as many cars on the roads. William Plowden, *The Motor Car and Politics, 1896–1970* (Bodley Head, 1971), 266

679: half the cases: *Golden Milestone: 50 Years of the AA* ed. David Keir and Bryan Morgan (Automobile Association, 1995), 71–2

679: astride a proper: *New Statesman*, 23 August 1930

679: lights controlling traffic: Karl Silex, quoted in Peter Thorold, *The Motoring Age: The Automobile in Britain, 1896–1939* (Profile, 2003), 202

679: was being felled: As was the cyclist: in 1936 two and a half times the number of cyclists were killed or injured on the roads than had been in 1928.

680: Nobody who drives: *The Motor*, 20 October 1931 quoted in Branson and Heinemann, 241

680: Mr Thwale's motor car: 'Haddock v. Thwale: What is a Motor-Car?' in A.P. Herbert, *Uncommon Law* (Methuen, 1935), 124–32

680: Richard Acland: D.E. Butler, *The Electoral System in Britain, 1918–51* (Clarendon Press, 1953)

681: The RAC considered: Plowden, 245–8

681: the 1930 Act: ibid., 259

683: anti-motorist bill: *Hansard*, 10 April 1934

683: wisely experimental: *The Times*, 11 April 1934

683: not a single mile: Thorold, 195

684: consistently denied airtime: Sean O'Connell, *The Car in British Society: Class, Gender and Motoring, 1896–1939* (Manchester University Press, 1998), 129–30

684: blood and tears: Plowden, 282

684: among the most dangerous: EADT, 17 December 1934

684: pampered pedestrians: *The Listener*, 18 August 1937 335

684: preparing for a: Quoted in Thorold, 207

684: He looks: *Journal of Collin Brooks*, 39

685: I went for: Channon, 27 January 1935, 23–4

685: in the following year: Foreman-Peck, 277

685: Government-funded: O'Connell, 133

685: Poole Pottery: MacCarthy (1982), 114

685: look as: Branson and Heinemann, 243

686: attempts to 'sectionalise': Peter Ewer, 'A Gentleman's Club in the Clouds: Reassessing the Empire Air Mail Scheme, 1933–39', *Journal of Transport History* 28, no.1, 2007, 77

686: passengers were able: Gordon Pirie, 'Passenger Traffic in the 1930s on British Imperial Air Routes: Refinement and Revision', *Journal of Transport History* 25, no.1, 2004, 63

686: US planes were: Ewer, 78, 79, 84

686: It is speed: *Oxford Mail*, 2 May 1935

686: passenger traffic: Perkins, 135

686: Empire Flying Boats: Ewer, 90

687: iron turkeys: *Thirties*, 209–10

687: They did not know: Richard Halliburton, *The Flying Carpet*, 139, quoted in Liz Millward, 'The Embodied Aerial Subject. Gendered Mobility in British Inter-War Air Tours', *Journal of Transport History* 29, no.1, 2008, 15

687: a special basin: Millward, 17

687: Moreover, Imperial Airways: Ewer, 79, 88

687: government-subsidised merger: In 1939 British Airways merged with Imperial Airways to form the British Overseas Airways Corporation (BOAC). The company adopted a 'speedbird logo' for their symbol, now the call sign of British Airways.

688: while the number: Perkins, 131–2

688: The 'big four': The railway companies did however invest in road transport, operating buses as feeder transport and for excursions and acquiring the long-distance removal firms of Pickfords and Carter Patersons in 1934. By 1933 the railway companies probably had a stake in about half the buses in Britain. Perkins, 133–4

688: this modernisation: ibid., 133

689: the *Cheltenham Flyer*: Anthony J. Lambert, *Travel in the Twenties and Thirties* (Ian Allan, 1983), 15

689: the *Mallard*: ibid., 17

690: what good was achieved: Charles Jennings, *The Fast Set: Three Extraordinary Men and Their Race for the Land Speed Record* (Little, Brown, 2004), 193

691: Campbell also took: *Speed Machines*, made by Flashback Productions for Channel Four, has informed this section.

692: Hilda Hewlett: Barbara Burman, 'Racing Bodies: Dress and Pioneer Women Aviators and Racing Drivers', *Women's History Review* 9, no.2, 2000, 305

692: In August 1928: Mary S. Lovell, *The Sound of Wings: The Biography of Amelia Earhart* (Hutchinson, 1989)

692: Jean Batten: Ian MacKersey, *Jean Batten: The Garbo of the Skies* (MacDonald, 1991)

693: It was her last: Mary S. Lovell, *Straight on Till Morning: The Biography of Beryl Markham* (Hutchinson, 1987); C.S. Nicholls, 'Beryl Markham', *Oxford Dictionary of National Biography*

693: quite a difficult: Barbara Cartland, *The Isthmus Years* (Hutchinson, 1942), 101

694: That summer: Edward Mole, *Happy Landings* (Airlife, 1984), 53

694: escaped injury: Cartland, 96–7

694: Madam Tussaud's: *Daily Mirror*, 14 March 1932

694: slip of a girl: Robin Higham, 'Amy Johnson', *Oxford Dictionary of National Biography*

694: On 5 May 1930: Midge Gillies, *Amy Johnson: Queen of the Air* (Weidenfeld & Nicolson, 2003), 117

695: unsurveyed desert: Constance Babington Smith, *Amy Johnson* (Collins, 1967); Gillies, 150

696: In 1937 Oxford: R.D. Burnell, *The Oxford and Cambridge Boat Race, 1829–1983* (Oxford University Press, 1954), 94

696: unbroken sequence: Christopher Dodd, *The Oxford and Cambridge Boat Race* (Stanley Paul, 1983). It was suggested that Oxford's failure might be due to the fact that the university's students spent an unseemly amount of time on their academic studies, leaving them insufficient time for rowing practice.

696: everybody who: Richards (1980), 97–8

696: to have a flutter: Derek Birley, *Playing the Game: Sport and British Society, 1910–45* (Manchester University Press, 1995), 199

696: The BBC had been: Mark Pegg, *Broadcasting and Society, 1919–39* Croom Helm, 1983), 7, 22–3, 128, 214

696: both banks: Rudolf Kircher, *Fair Play: The Games of Merrie England* trans. R.N. Bradley (Collins, 1928), 87–9

697: in intermittent dispute: Mike Huggins and Jack Williams, *Sport and the English, 1918–39* (Routledge, 2006), 39–40

697: a diagram: ibid., 37; Pegg, 215

697: It is easier: *Daily Dispatch*, 18 July 1938 cited in Briggs, 121

697: five tracks: *The New Survey of London Life and Labour, Vol. IX*, 55–6

697: fencing, boxing: Briggs, 119

698: nine million households: Scannell and Cardiff, 278–9

698: in the back room: Mark Clapson, *A Bit of a Flutter: Popular Gambling and English Society, c.1823–1961* (Manchester University Press, 1992), 49

699: the majority of: Royal Commission on Lotteries and Betting, quoted in Ross McKibbin, *Ideologies of Class: Social Relations in Britain 1880–1950* (Oxford University Press, 1991), 111

699: The cheapest of all: Orwell, *The Road to Wigan Pier*, 82

699: rather have six: *Poverty and Progress*, 403

699: a new house: John Hilton, *Why I Go in for the Pools . . .* (Allen & Unwin, 1936), 26

699: acquires thereby: *Men Without Work*, 98–100

700: embraced all classes: Mike Huggins, *Horse Racing and the British, 1919–39* (Manchester University Press, 2003), 45, 15

700: £3.1 million: ibid., 19

700: a frequent attender: Wray Vamplew, 'Horse-Racing' in Tony Mason (ed.), *Sport in Britain: A Social History* (Cambridge University Press, 1989), 229

700: forty-three such trains: Huggins (2003), 127, 141

701: the keenest supporters: Mike Huggins, 'Going to the Dogs', *History Today* 56, 5, May 2006, 31–5

701: the abandoned White City: ibid., 32

701: unlicensed or 'flapping': Keith Laybourn, *Working-Class Gambling in Britain c.1906–1960s: The Stages of the Political Debate* (Edward Mellen, 2007), 170

701: Favourite dogs are: Huggins and Williams, 45

701: A certain element: *The New Survey of London Life and Labour, Vol. IX*, 55

702: and in 1931: Laybourn, 174

702: practically unlimited: cited in ibid., 183, 185

702: no more than eight: This was later amended to allow four days a year when this number might be exceeded by up to sixteen races in four hours, and special arrangements were put in place for eight days racing on unlicensed tracks. Laybourn, 184

702: cannot be over-emphasised: cited in Laybourn (2007), 185

703: Twenty-five million: Clapson, 151–2

704: who voted against: The ILP MP James Maxton voted for Davidson's Bill.

704: I believe: *News Chronicle*, 16 November 1936

704: a book on the subject: Hilton (1936)

704: fifty million pounds: Hilton (1944), 166–70

705: two million coupons: Clapson, 162–5

705: Punters predicted: Hilton (1936)

705: The formula: Richard Coopey, Sean O'Connell and Dilwyn Porter, *Mail Order Retailing in Britain: A Business and Social History* (Oxford University Press, 2005) 35–6

705: roughly half: Rowntree, 403

706: three days: *Poverty and Progress*, 403–4

706: drew a fancy: Hilton (1944), 11–12

707: the attempt to stop: ibid., 42, 43

707: when Hitler reoccupied: Orwell, *The Road to Wigan Pier*, 82

708: This appeared to be: Langhamer, 82; Alethea Melling, '"Ray of the Rovers"; the Working-Class Heroine in Popular Football Fiction, 1915–25', *International Journal of the History of Sport* 15, no.1, 1998, 98

708: a Rangers–Celtic game: James Walvin, *The People's Game: The History of Football Revisited* (Mainstream, 1994), 139

708: a Second Division game: Tony Mason, 'Football' in *Sport in Britain*, 152

708: He is a star: *Stoke Evening Sentinel*, 11 December 1938, quoted in Tony Mason, 'Stanley Matthews' in Richard Holt (ed.), *Sport and the Working Class in Modern Britain* (Manchester University Press, 1996), 163

708: the maximum wage: Stephen G. Jones, 44

709: working-class hirelings: Birley, 242; McKibbin (1998), 346

709: striking Art Deco style: Walvin (1994), 123

709: only Allison: McKibbin (1998), 348

709: hooliganism: Richard Holt, *Sport and the British: A Modern History* (Clarendon Press, 1989), 333

709: Sectarian violence: Bill Murray, *The Old Firm: Sectarianism, Sport and Society in Scotland* (Edinburgh: John Donald, 1984), 1; Tom Gallagher, *Glasgow: The Uneasy Peace – Religious Tension in Modern Scotland* (Manchester University Press, 1987), 1

709: They tended to: Andrew Davies, 'Football and Sectarianism in Glasgow During the 1920s and 1930s', *Irish Historical Studies* 35, no.138, November 2006, 202–3

710: Hello, hello: Sung to the tune of 'Marching through Georgia', cited in ibid., 206

710: If it was hazardous: Ibid, 212

710: For some mysterious: Lord Blackburn, Glasgow *Herald*, 26 October 1934

711: the most violent game: Birley, 242

711: the FA vetoed: Peter Beck, 'England v Germany 1938: Football as Propaganda', *History Today* 32, 6, June 1982, 29–34

711: I do not think: Quoted in Walvin (1994), 133; Birley, 275–6

711: It really is important: Quoted in Philip M. Taylor, *The Projection of Britain: British Overseas Publicity and Propaganda 1919–39* (Cambridge University Press, 1981)

712: You do well: Cited in Jack Williams, 'Cricket' in Mason, 126

712: The football public: William Pollock, *The Cream of Cricket* (Methuen, 1934), 70

712: between 1924 and 1934: Williams in Mason, 134; Huggins and Williams, 11

713: broke the record: G. Howat, *Len Hutton: The Biography*, 38–42, quoted in Dave Russell, 'Sport and Identity: The Case of Yorkshire

County Cricket Club, 1890–1930' in *Twentieth Century British History* 7, no.2, 1996, 215–16

713: Hobbs, the son: John Arlott, *Jack Hobbs: Profile of the Master* (John Murray, 1981)

713: The workers settled: John Kay, *A History of County Cricket: Lancashire* (Arthur Barker, 1972), 43

714: Learie Constantine: Hill, 128; Jones, 43

714: fêtes, bazaars: McKibbin (1998), 335

714: Everybody seems: Fred Root, *A Cricket Pro's Lot* (Edward Arnold, 1937), 187, quoted in Jeffrey Hill, 'League Cricket in the North and Midlands, 1900–40' in Holt (1996), 126

714: not, strictly speaking: Patrick F. McDevitt, *May the Best Man Win: Sport, Masculinity and Nationalism in Great Britain and Empire, 1880–1935* (Palgrave, 2004), 80–1

714: menacing fielders: ibid., 82

715: preventable brutality: Graves and Hodge, 295

715: There are two teams: Cited in Mike Cronin and Richard Holt, 'A Gentlemen's Disagreement', *BBC History*, January 2007, 48

715: the chief sentimental: Graves and Hodge, 295

715: a heavy war debt: McDevitt, 85

716: the West Indians: ibid., 90

716: Larwood was never again: Larwood, feeling he had been a victim of the English class system, emigrated to Australia, where he proved very popular.

716: decline of the West: C.L.R. James,

Beyond a Boundary (Hutchinson, 1963; Yellow Jersey, 2005), 187

717: It is impossible: 'Roosevelt Experiment', letter from Frank Darvall, *Time and Tide*, 28 January 1937

717: lurid with: Quoted in John Dizikes, *Britain, Roosevelt and the New Deal: British Opinion, 1932–38* (Garland, 1979), 10

717: The whole world: *News Chronicle*, 1 November 1932

718: magic spell: Hugh Tulloch, *Six Travellers in America, 1919–41* (Edward Mellen, 2000), 314, 321

718: grave defects: *Daily Mail*, 10 November 1932

718: Twilight is fast: *News Chronicle*, 9 November 1932

718: an American renaissance [and subsequent quotes]: Quoted in Dizikes, 34, 53

718: What is all this?: *New Statesman*, 11 March 1933, 279

718: Uncle Sam as: Henry Pelling, *America and the British Left: From Bright to Bevan* (A. & C. Black, 1956), 131

719: Kidnapper headlines: Quoted in *The Landmark*, the journal of the English-Speaking Union, 19, no.8, August 1937

719: murderous country: Tulloch, 135

719: makes a dubious fortune: *The Times*, 8 April 1933

719: The Glass-Steagal Act: David Reynolds, *America, Empire of Liberty: A New History* (Allen Lane, 2009), 346

719: The country needs: 22 May 1932, quoted in ibid., 346

719: I think... President Roosevelt: Quoted in Dizikes, 74

720: We have terminated: *The Times*, 14 July 1933

720: out-of-work actors: D.W. Brogan, 'Uncle Sam's Guides', *Spectator*, 5 August 1938

720: with a passionate suddenness: Daniel T. Rodgers, *Atlantic Crossings: Social Politics in a Progressive Age* (Belknap Press/Harvard University Press, 1998), 424–6

721: impossible not to contrast: *Morning Post*, 26 July 1933, quoted in Dizikes, 126

721: It is an immense: Quoted in ibid., 95

721: You have made: Quoted in R.F. Harrod, *The Life of John Maynard Keynes* (1951)

721: of showing that: *Political Quarterly* 7, 1936, 464

721: Not only the citizens: *Economist*, 5 August 1933

721: real revolution of: Quoted in Rodgers, 411

722: The United States is pursuing: 'A Conversation Between Stalin and Wells', special supplement to the *New Statesman*, 27 October 1934

722: such things as: Ian Horobin, MP, quoted in Dizikes, 133

722: distinctly American: Quoted in Barbara C. Malament, 'British Labour and Roosevelt's New Deal: The Response of the Left and the Unions', *Journal of British Studies* 17, no.2, 1978

723: President Roosevelt will be regarded: Fenner Brockway, *Will Roosevelt Succeed?: A Study of Fascist Tendencies in America* (Routledge, 1934), 245, 248

723: unresolved conflict: Quoted in Jose Harris, *William Beveridge: A Biography* (Clarendon Press, 1977), 326

723: halfway-house: Diary of Beatrice Webb, 23 September 1934, quoted in Dizikes, 181

724: America seems a little: Raymond Burrows, 'American Journey', *Landmark*, 1937

727: Well this was: Unpublished notebook of Cyril Dunn, September 1938–April 1939, 1 October 1938

728: We're learning: ibid., 28 September 1938

729: David Dilkes (ed.), *The Diaries of Sir Alexander Cadogan, 1938–45* (Cassell, 1971), 62–3

729: I shall be called: Nicolson, 28 March 1938, 332–3

729: At this critical: *The Annual Register: A Review of Public Events at Home and Abroad for the Year 1938* ed. M. Epstein (Longman, Green, 1939), 68

730: sort of acting: R.A.C. Parker, *Chamberlain and Appeasement: British Policy and the Coming of the Second World War* (Macmillan, 1993), 4

730: settle the dispute: Quoted in David Faber, *Munich: The 1938 Appeasement Crisis* (Simon & Schuster, 2008), 280

730: a good thing: Charles Madge and Tom Harrisson, *Britain by Mass-Observation* (Penguin, 1939), 65

730: horses left: Quoted in Charmley, 117

730: a certain confidence: Quoted in Faber, 300

730: He has got: *Duff Cooper Diaries*, 24 September 1938, 265

730: the bright faithfulness: Harold Nicolson, *Why Britain is at War* (Penguin, 1939), 106

730: a British working man: *The Political Diary of Hugh Dalton*, 17 September 1938, 240, 256

731: Even if we: Headlam, 25 September 1938, 135. Czechoslovakia was a state created by the Versailles Peace settlement after the First World War.

731: 18 per cent: Madge and Harrisson, 75

731: we had been: Headlam, 25 September 1938, 137

731: a complete surrender: Martin Gilbert, *Winston S. Churchill, Vol. V: Companion Part 3, 'The Coming of War' 1936–39* (Heinemann 1982), 1171–2

731: Stand by: Parker, 167

731: Chamberlain is at: Don, 23 September 1938

732: all the marks: Dunn, 28 September 1938

732: great issues: Overy and Wheatcroft (2nd edn 1999), 102

732: ARP are going: Don, 27 September 1938

732: trenches were dug: *Lancashire and Whitehall: The Diary of Sir Raymond Streat, Vol. I: 1931–39* (Manchester University Press, 1987), 2 October 1938, 588

732: last minute scheme: Dunn, 28 September 1938

732: a quick refuge: Faber, 358–9

733: choice was not: Diana Cooper, 243

733: The masks were: Dunn, 28 September 1938

733: Madge Martin: Madge Martin, 29 September 1938

733: saw long queues: Streat, 2 October 1938, 588

734: What a shave!: *The Diary of Virginia Woolf, Vol. V*, 30 September 1938, 176

735: all this has: Streat, 31 August 1938, 583

735: 40,000 letters: Overy and Wheatcroft say 40,000; R.A.C. Parker (1993) suggests half that number

735: Prayers were said: Andrew Chandler, 'Munich and Morality: The Bishops of the Church of England and Appeasement', *Twentieth Century British History* 5, no.1, 1994, 80, 81, 83

735: a ramshackle republic: W.R. Inge, diary, 24 September 1938, quoted in ibid., 85

735: everybody is glad: Streat, 2 October 1939, 585

736: Other emotions: *The Diary of Virginia Woolf, Vol. V*, 2 October 1938, 178; *Letters of Virginia Woolf, Vol. VI*, letter to Vanessa Bell, 1 October 1938, 278

736: Rayon headscarf: *Wearing Propaganda, 1931–45: Textiles on the Home Front in Japan, Britain, and the United States* ed. Jacqueline M. Atkins (Bard Graduate Center for Studies in the Decorative Arts and Culture, New York/Yale University Press, 2005), 44

736: something that: Don, 6 October 1938

736: After the crisis: *Picture Post*, 15 October 1938

737: man attacking: R.J. Minney (ed.), *The Private Papers of Hore-Belisha* (Collins, 1960), 146

737: five divisions: Basil Collier, *The Defence of the United Kingdom* (HMSO, 1957), 63–70

737: We don't want: *The Diary of Virginia Woolf, Vol. V*, 30 September 1938, 177

738: the superstructure: Parker, 182

738: has brought: 'Crisis By-Election', *Picture Post*, 5 November 1938, 44

738: So Thursday: 'Autumn Journal', *Collected Poems of Louis MacNeice*, 128–9

739: unprecedented turnout: Iain McLean, 'Oxford and Bridgwater' in Cook and Ramsden, 140–63

739: even the PPU: Richard Overy, *The Morbid Age: Britain Between the Wars* (Allen Lane, 2009), 251–2

739: Do you remember: *Manchester Guardian*, 15 February 1937

739: divert resources: Richard Toye, 'The Labour Party and the Economics of Rearmament, 1935–39' *Twentieth Century British History* 12, no.3, 2001, 311

739: What national problem: *Daily Herald*, 1 January 1939, quoted in Robert Kee, *The World We Left Behind: A Chronicle of the Year 1939* (Weidenfeld & Nicolson, 1984), 10

740: employment was rising: G.A. MacDougall, 'General Survey, 1929–37' in *Britain in Recovery: Prepared by a Research Committee of the Economic Science and Statistics Section of the British Association* (Pitman, 1938), 7

740: unemployment might again: R.F. Bretherton, F.A. Burchardt and R.S.G. Rutherford, *Public Investment in the Trade Cycle in Great Britain* (1941), quoted in Thomas, 570–1

740: secure for ourselves: Parker, 188

741: scene of systematic: *The Times*, 11 November 1938

741: The disgusting: Don, 11 November 1938

741: holding out: *The Times*, 14 November 1938

741: very general: Quoted in Louise London, *Whitehall and the Jews, 1933–48* (Cambridge University Press, 2000), 99

741: job opportunities: Sir John Hope Simpson, 'The Refugee Tragedy', *Spectator*, 8 July 1938. Hope Simpson was director of the Royal Institute of International Affairs Refugee Survey. His first study on the problem appeared in the summer of 1938. He urged that it had to be solved by government action, as it was far too large and serious to leave to voluntary organisations.

741: 11,000 refugees: London, 11, 99

742: that would be: ibid., 100

743: to help fill: 'Their First Day in England', *Picture Post*, 17 December 1938

743: a definite assurance: The papers of

Rabbi Solomon Schönfeld, Hartley Library, University of Southampton, Mss 183

743: It's been: Nicolson, 31 December 1938, 384

743: Doom is in: Rich, 1 January 1939

744: We are compelled: Kingsford, 229–30; 'Unemployed! The National Unemployed Workers' Movement', *Picture Post*, 4 February 1939; Kee, 37

745: would have done: *News Chronicle*, 11 January 1939

745: The Unemployed are not: Kee, 49

745: trying to conjure: *The Annual Register for the Year 1939*, 4

746: 300,000 'Andersons': Terence O'Brien, *Civil Defence* (HMSO, 1955), 191

746: Haldane proposed: *New Statesman*, 17 September 1938; 31 December 1938; *Spectator*, 16 September 1938 J.B.S. Haldane, *ARP* (Gollancz, 1938)

746: £11 per head: Robin Woolven, '"Playing Hitler's Game from Fitzroy Road NW1": J.B.S. Haldane in Controversy in WWII', *Camden History Review* 23, 1999, 22, 24

746: Haldane was surrounded: Clark, 126–7; Patricia Fara, 'Looking at J.B.S. Haldane', *Endeavour* 28, no.1, March 2004, 12

747: increasingly conscious: Quoted in Frank McDonough, *Hitler, Chamberlain and Appeasement* (Cambridge University Press, 2002), 56

748: this would be: Headlam, 18 January 1939, 148

748: No one could: Quoted in Kee, 121

748: the death knell: Headlam, 15 March 1939, 151

748: a ruthless tyranny: *Daily Telegraph*, 15 March 1939

748: raging about: *Chronicle of Friendship*, 17 March 1939, 346

748: imposing suffering: Kee, 176

748: I suppose about: *The Complete Works of George Orwell, Vol. II: Facing Unpleasant Facts, 1937–39* ed. Peter Davison (Secker & Warburg, 1998), 12 January 1939, 317–18

749: The terrible inevitability: Channon, 7 April 1939, 193

749: Rearmament: R.A.C. Parker, 'British Rearmament 1936–39: Treasury, Trade Unions and Skilled Labour', *English Historical Review* 96, no.397, April 1981, 306–43

751: This will raise: Don, 27 April 1939

752: a middle-ranking: McDonough, 69

752: some 10,000: *Picture Post*, 13 May 1939

753: the *Thetis*: Tony Booth, *Thetis Down: The Slow Death of a Submarine* (Pen & Sword Maritime, 2008), 33, 89, 201

753: Father wanted: Elliott Roosevelt quoted in Bradford, 373

754: any attempt: Kee, 277

754: a moving paraphrase: Quoted in Andrew Roberts, *The Holy Fox: The Life of Lord Halifax* (Weidenfeld & Nicolson, 1991), 165

754: 57 per cent: Kee, 271

755: show Hitler that: Davison, 361,

755: full of men: Dunn, 3 July 1939

755: the withholding from: *The Times*, 4 July 1939

755: all trained together: Davison, 10

August 1939

756: He might have: Don, 4 August 1939

756: What frauds: Langford, 22 August 1939

756: a war that: Noreen Branson, *A History of the Communist Party of Great Britain, 1927–41* (Lawrence & Wishart, 1985), 263

757: in the name of: Enno Stephan, *Spies in Ireland* (Macdonald, 1963), 15

759: all night through: Dunn, 28 August 1939

759: repeated an offer: Wheeler-Bennett, 402–3

759: called on Halifax: Will Swift, *The Kennedys: Amidst the Gathering Storm – A Thousand Days in London 1938–40* (JR, 2008), 185

759: there would be: Langford, 26–28 August 1939

759: to say – what?: *The Diary of Virginia Woolf, Vol. V*, 28 August 1939, 231

760: The Elgin marbles: A.G. MacDonell, 'Safeguarding Our Art Treasures', *The Listener*, 6 October 1938

760: all poisonous snakes: 'At the Zoo', *The Listener*, 6 October 1938

760: PM was dignified: Nicolson, 24 August 1939, 413

761: the House more: ibid., 29 and 30 August 1939, 414–15

762: attack Germany not: Quoted in James P. Levy, *Appeasement and Rearmament: Britain 1936–39* (Rowan & Littlefield, 2006), 132

762: feeling that appeasement: Nicolson, 2 September 1939, 419

762: went home sick: Don, 2 September 1939

762: was just fixing: Dunn, 2 September 1939

BIBLIOGRAPHY

Published Works

Abercrombie, Patrick, *The Preservation of Rural England* (Liverpool University Press/Hodder & Stoughton, 1926)

Agar, Eileen (in collaboration with Andrew Lambrith), *A Look at Life* (Methuen, 1988)

Agate, James, *Ego: The Autobiography of James Agate* Vols 1–9 (Harrap, 1935–48)

— *Ego: The Selected Diaries of James Agate* ed. Timothy Beaumont (Harrap, 1976)

Ahamed, Liaquat, *Lords of Finance. 1929: The Great Depression and the Bankers Who Broke the World* (William Heinemann, 2009)

Aitken, Ian (ed.), *The Documentary Film Movement: An Anthology* (Edinburgh University Press, 1998)

Aldgate, Anthony, *Cinema and History: British Newsreels and the Spanish Civil War* (Scolar, 1979)

Alexander, Bill, *British Volunteers for Liberty: Spain 1936–39* (Lawrence & Wishart, 1982)

Alexander, Sally, 'Men's Fears and Women's Work: Responses to Unemployment in London Between the Wars' in *Gender & History* 12, no.2, July 2000

Allen, Lady Allen of Hurtwood, *Memoirs of an Uneducated Lady* (Thames & Hudson, 1975)

Allen, W.E.D., *BUF: Oswald Mosley and British Fascism* (John Murray, 1934)

Amory, Mark, *Lord Berners: The Last Eccentric* (Chatto & Windus, 1998)

Arber, Katie, *Thirties Style: Home Decoration and Furnishings from the 1930s* (MoDA, Middlesex University Press, 2003)

Arlott, John, *Jack Hobbs: Profile of the Master* (John Murray, 1981)

Armstrong, Keith and Benyon, Huw (eds), *Hello, Are You Working?: Memories of the Thirties in the North East of England* (Whitley Bay, Tyne and Wear: Strong Words, 1977)

Artmonsky, Ruth, *Jack Beddington: The Footnote Man* (Ruth Artmonsky, 2006)

Attlee, C.R., *As it Happened* (Heinemann, 1954)

Atwell, David, *Cathedrals of the Movies: A History of British Cinemas and Their Audiences* (Architectural Press, 1980)

Auden W.H., *Letters from Iceland* (Faber, 1937)

— *Collected Shorter Poems* (Faber, 1966)

W.H. Auden: A Tribute ed. Stephen Spender (Weidenfeld & Nicolson, 1975)

Babington Smith, Constance, *Amy Johnson* (Collins, 1967)

— *John Masefield: A Life* (Oxford University Press, 1978)

Badger, Anthony, J., *The New Deal: The Depression Years, 1933–40* (New York: Hill & Wang, 1989)

Baggs, Chris, 'The Whole Tragedy of Leisure in Penury: The South Wales Miners' Institute Libraries During the Great Depression', *Libraries and Culture* 39, no.2, spring 2004

Bagwell, Philip S. and Mingay, G.E., *Britain and America: A Study of Economic Change, 1850–1939* (Routledge & Kegan Paul, 1970)

Bailey, Catherine, *Black Diamonds: The Rise and Fall of an English Dynasty* (Viking, 2007)

Bailey, Christopher, 'Rural Industries and the Image of the Countryside' in *The English Countryside Between the Wars: Regeneration or Decline?* ed. Paul Brassley, Jeremy Burchardt and Lynne Thompson (Boydell, 2006)

Bailey, Doris M., *Children of the Green* (Stepney Books, 1981)

Baines, Dudley 'Recovery From Depression' in Paul Johnson (ed.), *Twentieth-Century Britain: Economic, Social and Cultural Change* (Longman, 1994)

Baker, Michael, *Our Three Selves: A Life of Radclyffe Hall* (Hamish Hamilton, 1985)

Bakke, E. Wight, *The Unemployed Man: A Social Study* (Dutton, 1934)

Balfour, Patrick, *Society Racket: A Critical Survey of Modern Social Life* (John Long, 1933)

— *Grand Tour: Diary of an Eastward Journey* (John Long, 1934)

Ball, Stuart, 'The Conservative Party and the Formation of the National Government: August 1931' *Historical Journal* 29, 1986

Banham, Belinda, *Snapshots in Time: Some Experiences in Health Care, 1936–9* (Jamieson Library of Women's History, 1991)

Barker, Felix, *The Oliviers* (Hamish Hamilton, 1953)

Barker, Nicolas, *Stanley Morison* (Macmillan, 1972)

Barman, Christian, *The Man Who Built London Transport: A Biography of Frank Pick* (David & Charles, 1979)

Barnes, James and Patience, 'Oswald Mosley as Entrepreneur' in *History Today* 40, 3, March 1990

Barr, Charles, *Ealing Studios* (Cameron & Tayleur, 1977)

Barrington-Jones, J., *The Zoo: The Story of London Zoo* (Robert Hale, 2005)

Barry, F.R., *The Relevance of Christianity: An Approach to Christian Ethics* (Nisbet, 1931)

Bartlett, Helena and Phillips, John, *Suburban Style: The British Home, 1840–1960* (Macdonald Orbis, 1987)

Baxell, Richard, *British Volunteers in the Spanish Civil War: The British Battalion in the International Brigades, 1936–39* (Routledge, 2004)

Baxendale, John, *Priestley's England: J.B. Priestley and English Culture* (Manchester, 2007)

Baxendale, John and Pawling, Christopher, *Narrating the Thirties: 1930 to the Present* (Macmillan, 1996)

Beach, Abigail and Tiratsoo, Nick, 'The Planners and the Public' in Martin Daunton (ed.), *The Cambridge Urban History of Britain, Vol. III: 1840–1950* (Cambridge University Press, 2000)

Beaton, Cecil, *The Book of Beauty* (Duckworth, 1930)

Beauchamp, Joan, *Women Who Work* (Lawrence & Wishart, 1937)

Beauman, Sally, *The Royal Shakespeare Company: A History of Ten Decades* (Oxford University Press, 1982)

Beaumont, Catriona, 'Moral Dilemmas and Women's Rights: The Attitude of the Mothers' Union and Catholic Women's League to Divorce, Birth Control and Abortion in England, 1928–39' in *Woman's History Review* 16, no.4, September 2007

Beaver, Patrick, *The Crystal Palace, 1851–1936: A Portrait of Victorian Enterprise* (Hugh Evelyn, 1970)

Beck, Peter, 'England v Germany 1938: Football as Propaganda', *History Today* 32, 6, June 1982

Beckett, Francis, *The Rebel Who Lost His Cause: The Tragedy of John Beckett, MP* (London House, 1999)

Beddoe, Deidre, *Back to Home and Duty: Women Between the Wars, 1918–39* (Pandora, 1989)

Bedford, Sybille, *Aldous Huxley, A Biography, Vol. I: The Apparent Stability* (Collins/Chatto & Windus, 1973)

Beevor, Antony, *The Battle for Spain: The Spanish Civil War 1936–39* (Weidenfeld & Nicolson, 2006)

Bell, Adrian, *Only for Three Months: The Basque Children in Exile* (Mousehole Press, 1996)

Bell, Quentin, *Virginia Woolf, Vol. II: Mrs Woolf 1912–1941* (Hogarth Press, 1972)

Bell, Vanessa, *Selected Letters of Vanessa Bell* ed. Regina Marler (Bloomsbury, 1993)

Belloc, Hilaire, *Complete Verse* (Nonesuch Press, 1954)

Bernal, J.D., *The Social Function of Science* (Routledge, 1939)

Bernays, Robert, *The Diaries and Letters of Robert Bernays, 1932–39: An Insider's Account of the House of Commons* ed. Nick Smart (Edward Mellen, 1996)

Berridge, Virginia, 'Health and Medicine' in F.M.L. Thompson (ed.), *The Cambridge Social History of Britain, 1750–1950, Vol. III: Social Agencies and Institutions* (Cambridge University Press, 1990)

Bertram, Anthony, *The House: A Machine for Living* (A. & C. Black, 1935)

Betjeman, John, *Letters, Vol. 1* ed. Candida Lycett Green (Methuen, 1994)

— *Collected Poems* (John Murray, 2001)

Bingham, Neil, *Christopher Nicholson* (RIBA Academy Editions, 1996)

Binyon, Helen, *Eric Ravilious: Memoir of an Artist* (Lutterworth, 1983)

— *Ravilious and Wedgwood: The Complete Wedgwood Designs of Eric Ravilious* (Dalrymple, 1986)

Bird, Peter, *The First Food Empire: A History of J.L. Lyons & Co.* (Phillimore, 2000)

Birley, Derek, *Playing the Game: Sport and British Society, 1910–45* (Manchester University Press, 1995)

Blackpool: The Holiday You Will Never Forget (Blackpool Corporation, 1939)

Blake, George, *The Shipbuilders* (Collins, 1944)

Bloch, Michael, *James Lees-Milne: A Life* (John Murray, 2009)

Blomfield, Sir Reginald, *Modernismus* (Macmillan, 1934)

Blunt, Anthony, 'Art Under Capitalism and Socialism' in *The Mind in Chains: Socialism and the Cultural Revolution* ed. C. Day Lewis (Frederick Muller, 1937)

Blythe, Ronald, *The Age of Illusion: England in the Twenties and Thirties, 1919–40* (Hamish Hamilton, 1963)

Bondfield, Margaret, *A Life's Work* (Hutchinson, 1948)

Bourke, Joanna, *Working-Class Cultures in Britain, 1890–1960: Gender, Class and Ethnicity* (Routledge, 1994)

— *Dismembering the Male: Men's Bodies, Britain and the Great War* (Reaktion, 1996)

Bowden, Sue, Higgins, David M. and Price, C., 'British Industry in the Interwar Years' in *The Cambridge Economic History of Modern Britain, Vol. II: Economic Maturity, 1860–1939* ed. Roderick Floud and Paul Johnson (Cambridge University Press, 2003)

— 'Avoiding Conscription to the Inter-War "Army" of the Unemployed: Short-Time Working in the Iron and Steel Industry', *Labour History Review* 72, no.1, April 2007

Bowker, Gordon, *George Orwell* (Little, Brown 2003)

Bowley, A.L. and Hogg, Margaret H., *Has Poverty Diminished?: A Sequel to 'Livelihood and Poverty'* (P.S. King, 1925; Garland, 1985)

Bowley, Marion, *Housing and State, 1914–44* (Allen & Unwin, 1945)

Box, Katherine, *The Cinema and the Public* (Central Office of Information Social Surveys Division, 1947)

Boyd Orr, John, *Food, Health and Income* (Macmillan, 1936)

— *As I Recall* (MacGibbon & Kee, 1966)

Boyes, Georgina, *The Imagined Village: Culture, Ideology and the English Folk Revival* (Manchester University Press, 1993)

Bradford, Sarah, *George VI* (Weidenfeld & Nicolson, 1989)

Branson, Noreen and Heinemann, Margot, *Britain in the 1930s* (Weidenfeld & Nicolson, 1971)

Brassley, Paul, Burchardt, Jeremy and Thompson, Lynne (eds), *The English Countryside Between the Wars: Regeneration or Decline?* (Boydell, 2006)

Breeton, Henry L., *Gordonstoun: Ancient Estate and Modern School* (Chambers, 1968)

Brendon, Piers, *Thomas Cook: 150 Years of Popular Tourism* (Secker & Warburg, 1991)

— *The Dark Valley: A Panorama of the 1930s* (Cape, 2000)

Brendon, Piers and Whitehead, Philip, *The Windsors: A Dynasty Revealed 1917–2000* (Hodder & Stoughton, 1994)

Brierley, John, *In the Shadow of the Means Test Man: Memories of a Derbyshire Childhood* (Highedge Historical Society, 1995)

Briggs, Asa, *History of Broadcasting in the United Kingdom, Vol. II: The Golden Age of Wireless* (Oxford University Press, 1965)

— *Marks & Spencer 1884–1994: A Centenary History* (Octopus, 1984)

Brittain, Vera, *Testament of Friendship: The Story of Winifred Holtby* (Macmillan, 1940)

— *Testament of Experience: An Autobiographical Account of the Years 1925–50* (Gollancz, 1957)

— *Radclyffe Hall: A Case of Obscenity?* (Femina, 1968)

— *Chronicle of Friendship: Diary of the Thirties* ed. Alan Bishop (Gollancz, 1986)

Brockway, Fenner, *Hungry England* (Gollancz, 1932)

— *Will Roosevelt Succeed?: A Study of Fascist Tendencies in America* (Routledge, 1934)

— *Inside the Left* (Allen & Unwin, 1942)

— *Bermondsey Story: The Life of Alfred Salter* (Allen & Unwin, 1949)

Bromley Communists in the Thirties: A Personal Reminiscence (Kent and District Committee of the Communist Party, 1983)

Brookes, Barbara, *Abortion in England, 1900–67* (Croom Helm, 1988)

Brooks, Collin, *Fleet Street, Press Barons and Politics: The Journals of Collin Brooks, 1932–40* ed. N.J. Crowson (Royal Historical Society, 1998)

Brown, Andrew H. and Stewart, B. Anthony, 'Beckonscot, England's Toy-Size Town', *National Geographic*, May 1937

Brown, Callum G., *Religion and Society in Twentieth-Century Britain* (Pearson/Longman, 2006)

Brown, Ivor and Fearon, George, *A Short History of the Shakespeare Industry* (William Heinemann, 1939)

Brown, John, *I Was a Tramp* (Selwyn & Blount, 1934)

Browning, H.E. and Sorrell, A.A., 'Cinema and Cinema-Going in Great Britain', *Journal of the Royal Statistical Society* 117, 1954

Bryder, Linda, *Below the Magic Mountain: A Social History of Tuberculosis in Twentieth-Century Britain* (Clarendon Press, 1988)

— 'Papworth Village Settlement: A Unique Experiment in the Treatment and Care of the Tuberculous?' *Medical History* 28, 1984

Buchanan, Tom, *Britain and the Spanish Civil War* (Cambridge University Press, 1997)

— 'The Lost Art of Felicia Browne', *History Workshop Journal* 54, autumn 2002

— *The Impact of the Spanish Civil War on Britain: War, Loss and Memory* (Sussex Academic Press, 2007)

Bullard, Julian and Bullard, Margaret (eds), *Inside Stalin's Russia: The Diaries of Reader Bullard, 1930–34* (Day, 2000)

Bullock, Alan, *Ernest Bevin: A Biography* (William Heinemann, 1967; abridged edn Politico's, 2002)

Burke, Thomas, *London in my Time* (Rich & Cowan, 1934)

Burman, Barbara, 'Racing Bodies: Dress and Pioneer Women Aviators and Racing Drivers', *Women's History Review* 9, no.2, 2000

Burnell, R.D., *The Oxford and Cambridge Boat Race, 1829–1983* (Oxford University Press, 1954)

Burnett, John, *A Social History of Housing, 1815–1985* (1978, Methuen; second edn 1986)

— *Plenty and Want: A Social History of Diet in England from 1815 to the Present Day* (Nelson, 1966)

— *Idle Hands: The Experience of Unemployment, 1790–1990* (Routledge, 1994)

Bush, Barbara, 'Blacks in Britain: The 1930s', *History Today* 31, 9, September 1981

Butler, D.E., *The Electoral System in Britain, 1918–51* (Oxford Clarendon Press, 1953)

Butlin, Sir Billy with Peter Dacre, *The Billy Butlin Story: 'A Showman to the End'* (Robson, 1982)

Butt, John, 'Working-Class Housing in Glasgow, 1900–39' in Ian McDougall (ed.), *Essays in Scottish Labour History: A Tribute to W.H. Marwick* (John Donald, 1978)

Robert Byron's Letters Home ed. Lucy Butler (John Murray, 1991)

Calder, Jenni, *The Nine Lives of Naomi Mitchison* (Virago, 1997)

Cameron C., Lush, A.J. and Meara, G. (eds), *Disinherited Youth: A Report on the 18+ Age Group Enquiry Prepared for the Trustees of the Carnegie United Kingdom Trust* (Edinburgh, 1943)

Campbell, Ethlye, *Can I Help You, Sir?* (Peter Davis, 1939)

Campbell, Louise, 'Patrons of the Modern House', *The Modern House Revisited* (Twentieth Century Society, no.2, 1996)

— 'The MARS Group, 1933–39', *RIBA, Transactions* 8, vol. 4, no.2

Carew, Anthony, 'The Invergordon Mutiny, 1931: Long-Term Causes, Organisation and Leadership', *International Review of Social History* 3, 24, 1972

Carey, John, *The Intellectuals and the Masses: Pride and Prejudice Among the Literary Intelligentsia, 1880–1939* (Faber, 1992)

Carpenter, Humphrey, *W.H. Auden: A Biography* (Allen & Unwin, 1981)

Carpenter, Robert, *Mr Pink: The Architectural Legacy of W.T. Crittall* (Essex County Council, 2007)

Carter, Miranda, *Anthony Blunt: His Lives* (Macmillan, 2001)

Cartland, Barbara, *The Isthmus Years* (Hutchinson, 1942)

Caudwell, Christopher, *Studies in a Dying Culture* (Lane, 1938)

Ceadel, Martin, 'The "King and Country" Debate, 1933: Student Politics, Pacifism and the Dictators', *Historical Journal* 22, 2, 1979

— 'The First British Referendum: The Peace Ballot, 1934–5', *English Historical Review* 95, 1980

— 'Attitudes to War: Pacifism and Collective Security' in Paul Johnson (ed.), *Twentieth-Century Britain: Economic, Social and Cultural Change* (Longman, 1994)

Cecil, Hugh, *On Queer Street: A Social History of British Homosexuality, 1895–1995* (HarperCollins, 1997)

Chambers, Colin, *The Story of the Unity Theatre* (Lawrence & Wishart, 1989)

Channon, Henry, *Chips: The Diaries of Sir Henry Channon* ed. Robert Rhodes James (Weidenfeld & Nicolson, 1967)

Charlton, Susannah, Harwood, Elaine and Powers, Alan (eds), *British Modern Architecture and Design in the 1930s* (Twentieth Century Society, 2007)

Charmley, John, *Duff Cooper: The Authorized Biography* (Weidenfeld & Nicolson, 1986)

Chase, Laura, 'Public Beaches and Private Beach Huts: A Case Study of Inter-War Clacton and Frinton, Essex' in John K. Walton (ed.), *Histories of Tourism: Representation, Identity and Conflict* (Channel View, 2005)

Chase, Malcolm, 'This is no Claptrap: This is Our Heritage' in Christopher Shaw and Malcolm Chase, *The Imagined Past: History and Nostalgia* (Manchester University Press, 1989)

Cherry, Steven, 'Medicine and Public Health, 1900–39' in Chris Wrigley (ed.), *A Companion to Early Twentieth-Century Britain* (Blackwell, 2003)

Chesterton, Mrs Cecil, *I Lived in a Slum* (Gollancz, 1936)

Chinn, Carl, *Homes for People: Council Housing and Urban Renewal in Birmingham, 1849–1999* (Brewin, 1999)

Chisholm, Anne, *Nancy Cunard* (Sidgwick & Jackson, 1979)

Churchill, Winston S., *Great Contemporaries* (Thornton Butterworth, 1937)

— *Step by Step, 1936–39* (Macmillan, 1942)

Clapson, Mark, *A Bit of a Flutter: Popular Gambling and English Society, c.1823–1961* (Manchester University Press, 1992)

Clark, Helen and Carnegie, Elizabeth, *'She Was Aye Workin': Memories of Tenement Women in Edinburgh and Glasgow* (White Cockade Publishing, 2003)

Clark, Jon, 'Socialist Theatre in the Thirties' in *Culture and Crisis in Britain in the Thirties* ed. Jon Clark, Margot Heinemann, David Margolis and Carole Smee (Lawrence & Wishart, 1979)

Clark, Ronald, *JBS: The Life and Times of J.B.S. Haldane* (Hodder & Stoughton, 1968)

Clarke, Gill, *Evelyn Dunbar: War and Country* (Sansom, 2006)

Clarke, Peter, *The Keynesian Revolution in the Making, 1924–36* (Clarendon Press, 1988)

— *Hope and Glory: Britain 1900–90* (Penguin, 1996)

— *The Cripps Version: The Life of Sir Stafford Cripps 1889–1952* (Allen Lane/Penguin Press, 2002)

—*Keynes: The Twentieth Century's Most Influential Economist* (Bloomsbury, 2009)

Clymo, F.R., *My Memories of St Day* (privately printed, 1987)

Coburn, Oliver, *Youth Hostel Story* (National Council of Social Service, 1950)

Cockburn, Claud, *In Time of Trouble* (Rupert Hart-Davies, 1956)

— *The Devil's Decade* (Sidgwick & Jackson, 1973)

Coe, Peter and Reading, Malcolm, *Lubetkin and Tecton: Architecture and Social Commitment* (Arts Council of Great Britain, 1981)

Cohen, Max, *I Was One of the Unemployed* (Gollancz, 1945; EP, 1978)

Cole, G.D.H. and M.I., *The Condition of Britain* (Gollancz, 1937)

Cole, Margaret, *The Life of G.D.H. Cole* (Macmillan, 1971)

Colin, Sid and Staveacre, Tony, *Al Bowlly* (Elm Tree, 1979)

Collini, Stefan, *Absent Minds: Intellectuals in Britain* (Oxford University Press, 2006)

Collison, Peter, *The Cutteslowe Walls: A Study in Social Class* (Faber, 1963)

Comyns, Barbara, *Our Spoons Came from Woolworths* (Eyre & Spottiswoode, 1950; Virago, 1983)

Connolly, Cyril, *The Condemned Playground: Essays 1927–44* (Routledge, 1945)

Conquest, Joan, *The Naked Truth: Shocking Revelations About the Slums* (T. Werner Laurie, 1933)

Conrad, Peter, *Modern Times, Modern Places* (Thames & Hudson, 1998)

Constantine, Stephen, *Unemployment in Britain between the Wars* (Longman, 1980)

— 'Amateur Gardening and Popular Recreation in the 19th and 20th Centuries', *Journal of Social History* 14, no.3, spring 1981

Conzé, Edward, *The Scientific Method of Thinking: An Introduction to Dialectical Materialism* (Chapman Hall, 1935)

Cook, Judith, *Apprentices of Freedom* (Quartet, 1979)

— *Priestley* (Bloomsbury, 1997)

Cooke, Alistair, *Six Men* (Bodley Head, 1977)

Cooper, Lady Diana, *Autobiography: The Light of Common Day* (Rupert Hart-Davis, 1959)

Cooper, Duff, *The Duff Cooper Diaries* ed. John Julius Norwich (Weidenfeld & Nicolson, 2005)

Cooper, Lettice, *We Have Come to a Country* (Gollancz, 1935)

Coopey, Richard, O'Connell, Sean and Porter, Dilwyn, *Mail Order Retailing in Britain: A Business and Social History* (Oxford University Press, 2005)

Coutts, J., *All About Gardening* (1931, revised edn Ward Lock, 1955)

Coward, Noël, *Present Indicative* (William Heinemann, 1937)

— *The Noël Coward Diaries* ed. Graham Payne and Sheridan Morley (Weidenfeld & Nicolson, 1982)

— *The Letters of Noël Coward* ed. Barry Day (Methuen Drama, 2007)

Crafts, N.F.R., 'Long-Term Unemployment in Britain in the 1930s', *Economic History Review* 2nd series, 40, 3, 1987

Crawford, Earl of, *The Crawford Papers: The Journals of David Lindsay, Twenty-Seventh Earl of Crawford and Tenth Earl of Balcarres, 1871–1940, During the Years 1892 to 1940* ed. John Vincent (Manchester University Press, 1984)

Cretney, S.M., 'The Divorce Law and the 1936 Abdication Crisis: A Supplemental Note', *The Law Quarterly Review* 120, 2004

— 'Edward, Mrs Simpson and the Divorce Law', *History Today* 53, 9, September 2003

Crick, Bernard, *George Orwell: A Life* (Secker & Warburg, 1981)

Crisp, Quentin. *The Naked Civil Servant* (Cape, 1968)

Croft, Andy, *Red Letter Days: British Fiction in the 1930s* (Lawrence & Wishart, 1990)

Cronin, A.J., *The Citadel* (Gollancz, 1937)

— *The Stars Look Down* (Gollancz, 1941)

Cronin, Mike and Holt, Richard, 'A Gentlemen's Disagreement', *BBC History*, January 2007

Cross, Colin, *The Fascists in Britain* (Barrie & Rockcliffe, 1961)

— *Philip Snowden* (Barrie & Rockliffe, 1966)

Cross, Gary (ed.), *Worktowners at Blackpool: Mass-Observation and Popular Leisure in the 1930s* (Routledge, 1990)

Crouch, David and Ward, Colin, *The Allotment: Its Landscape and Culture* (Faber, 1988)

Crowther, J.G., *Fifty Years with Science* (Barrie & Jenkins, 1970)

Cunard, Nancy, *Black Man and White Ladyship: An Anniversary* (1931)

— *Negro: An Anthology* (Lawrence & Wishart, 1931)

Cunningham, Valentine (ed.), *The Penguin Book of Spanish Civil War Verse* (Penguin, 1980)

— 'Neutral: 1930s Writers and Taking Sides' in *Class, Culture and Social Change: A New Version of the 1930s* ed. Frank Gloversmith (Harvester, 1980)

— *British Writers of the Thirties* (Oxford University Press, 1988)

Curran, James and Seaton, Jean, *Power Without Responsibility: The Press and Broadcasting in Britain* (Routledge, 1981, 7th edn 2009)

Dalton, Hugh, *The Political Diary of Hugh Dalton, 1918–40, 1945–60* ed. Ben Pimlott (Cape/London School of Economics, 1986)

Darling, Elizabeth, *Re-Forming Britain: Narratives of Modernity Before Reconstruction* (Routledge, 2007)

— 'Wells Coates: His Life and Legacy', *C20: The Magazine of the Twentieth Century Society*, spring 2008

Daunton, M.J., *Coal Metropolis: Cardiff, 1870–1914* (Leicester University Press, 1977)

— (ed.), *Councillors and Tenants: Local Authority Housing in English Cities, 1919–39* (Leicester University Press, 1984)

— *Wealth and Welfare: An Economic and Social History of Britain, 1851–1951* (Oxford University Press, 2007)

Davenport, Nicholas, *Memoirs of a City Radical* (Weidenfeld & Nicolson, 1974)

Davenport-Hines, R.P.T. (ed.), *Business in the Age of Depression and War* (Frank Cass, 1990)

Davidson, Michael, *The World my Flesh* (Arthur Barker, 1962)

Davies, Andrew, *Leisure, Gender and Poverty: Working-Class Culture in Salford and Manchester, 1900–39* (Open University Press, 1992)

— 'Football and Sectarianism in Glasgow During the 1920s and 1930s', *Irish Historical Studies* 35, no.138, November 2006

Davies, Peter, *The St Ives Years: Essays on the Growth of an Artistic Phenomenon* (Wimborne Bookshop, 1984)

Davies, Stella, *North Country Bred* (Routledge, 1963)

Davison, R.C., *British Unemployment Policy: The Modern Phase Since 1930* (Longman, Green, 1938)

Davy, Charles (ed.), *Footnotes to the Film* (Lovat Dickson, 1937)

Dean, David, *The Thirties: Recalling the English Architectural Scene* (Trefoil, 1983)

Delafield, E.M., *The Diary of a Provincial Lady* (1930; Virago, 1985)

Dentith, Simon, 'From William Morris to Morris Minor: An Alternative Suburban History' in Roger Webster (ed.), *Expanding Suburbia: Reviewing Suburban Narratives* (Berghahan Books, 2000)

Denton, Pennie, *Seaside Surrealism: Paul Nash in Swanage* (Peveril, 2002)

Desai, Meghnad, *The Route of All Evil* (Faber, 2006)

Dewey, Peter, 'Agriculture, Agrarian Society and the Countryside' in *A Companion to Early Twentieth-Century Britain* ed. Chris Wrigley (Blackwell, 2003)

Dierden, Margaret, *More Scenes of Shalford Past* (privately published, 2006)

Digby, Anne, *The Evolution of British General Practice 1850–1948* (Oxford University Press, 1999)

Digby, Anne and Bosanquet, Nick, 'Doctors and Patients in an Era of National Insurance and Private Practice, 1913–38', *Economic History Review* 2nd series, 41, 1, 1988

Disinherited Youth: A Report on the 18+ Age Group Enquiry Prepared for the Trustees of the Carnegie United Kingdom Trust (Constable, 1943)

Dizikes, John, *Britain, Roosevelt and the New Deal: British Opinion, 1932–38* (Garland, 1979)

Dodd, Christopher, *The Oxford and Cambridge Boat Race* (Stanley Paul, 1983)

Dolan, Nick, 'The Susie Cooper Pottery, 1929–66' in *Susie Cooper: A Pioneer of Modern Design* ed. Ann Eatwell and Andrew Casey (Antique Collector's Club, 2002)

Donaldson, Frances, *Child of the Twenties* (Rupert Hart-Davis, 1959)

— *Edward VIII* (Weidenfeld & Nicolson, 1974)

Dormandy, Thomas, *The White Death: A History of Tuberculosis* (Hambledon, 1999)

Dorrill, Stephen, *Blackshirt: Sir Oswald Mosley and British Fascism* (Viking, 2006)

Douglas, C.H., *Social Credit* (Cecil Palmer, 1924)

Drake, Barbara, 'The Webbs and Soviet Communism' in *The Webbs and Their Work* ed. Margaret Cole (Frederick Muller, 1949)

Drake, Peter, 'Birmingham and the Spanish Civil War' in *Aspects of Birmingham* ed. Brian Hall (Wharncliffe, 2001)

Driberg, Tom, *Ruling Passions: The Autobiography of Tom Driberg* (Cape, 1977)

— *The Mystery of Moral Re-armament: A Study of Frank Buchman and his Movement* (Secker & Warburg, 1964)

Drower, Jill, *Good Clean Fun: The Story of Britain's First Holiday Camp* (Arcadia, 1982)

Duberman, Martin Bauml, *Paul Robeson* (Bodley Head, 1989)

Dudley Edwards, Ruth, *Victor Gollancz: A Biography* (Gollancz, 1987)

Duffield, Ian 'Blacks in Britain: History and the Historians', *History Today* 31

Dunaway, David King, *Huxley in Hollywood* (Bloomsbury, 1989)

Dunbabin, J.P.D., 'British Rearmament in the 1930s: A Chronology and Review', *Historical Journal* 18, 3, 1975

Durant, Henry, *The Problem of Leisure* (Routledge, 1938)

Durant, Ruth, *Watling: A Survey of Social Life on a New Housing Estate* (P.S. King, 1939)

Durant, Stuart and Martin, Brenda, 'Dorich House, Kingston' in *The Modern House Revisited* (Twentieth Century Society, 1996)

Durbin, Elizabeth, *New Jerusalems: The Labour Party and the Economics of Democratic Socialism* (Routledge, 1985)

Durbin, Evan, *The Politics of Democratic Socialism* (Routledge, 1940)

Durie, Alistair J., *Scotland for the Holidays: A History of Tourism in Scotland, 1780–1939* (Tuckwell Press, 2003)

— *Water is Best: The Hydros and Health Tourism in Scotland, 1840–1940* (Edinburgh: John Donald, 2006)

Eaden, James and Renton, David, *The Communist Party of Great Britain Since 1920* (Palgrave Macmillan, 2002)

Eatwell, Roger and Wright, Anthony, 'Labour and the Lessons of 1931', *History* 63, 1978

Edwards, Jill, *The British Government and the Spanish Civil War, 1936–39* (Macmillan, 1979)

Ellis, Havelock, *My Confessional: Questions of Our Day* (John Lane, Bodley Head, 1934)

Ereia, Alan, *The Invergordon Mutiny* (Routledge, 1981)

— 'The Hidden Life of the British Sailor', *History Today* 32, 12, December 1982

Esher, Lionel, *The Broken Wave: The Rebuilding of England, 1940–80* (Allen Lane, 1981)

Ewer, Peter, 'A Gentleman's Club in the Clouds: Reassessing the Empire Air Mail Scheme, 1933–39', *Journal of Transport History* 28, no.1, 2007

Excell, Arthur, 'Morris Motors in the 1930s: Part I', *History Workshop Journal* 6, 1978; 'Part II: Politics and Trade Unionism', *History Workshop Journal* 7, spring 1979

Eyles, Allen, *Old Cinemas* (Shire, 2001)

Eyles, Leonora, *Careers for Women* (Elkins, Matthews & Marrot, 1930)

Faderman, Lillian, *Surpassing the Love of Men: Romantic Friendship and Love Between Women from the Renaissance to the Present* (Junction, 1981)

Fairley, Alastair, *Bucking the Trend: The Life and Times of the Ninth Earl de la Warr* (Bexhill on Sea: The Pavilion Trust, 2001)

Farjeon, Herbert, *The Shakespearean Scene* (Hutchinson, 1948)

Feaver, William, *Pitmen Painters: The Ashington Group, 1934–84* (Chatto & Windus, 1988)

Feinstein C.H., *Statistical Tables of National Income, Expenditure and Outcome of the United Kingdom, 1855–1965* (Cambridge University Press, 1972)

Ferguson, Niall, *The Ascent of Money: A Financial History of the World* (Allen Lane/Penguin Books, 2008)

Ferguson, Rachel, *The Brontës Went to Woolworths* (Ernest Benn, 1931; Virago, 1988)

Fermor, Patrick Leigh, *A Time of Gifts: From the Hook of Holland to the Middle Danube* (John Murray, 1977)

Findlater, Richard, *Lilian Baylis: The Lady of the Old Vic* (Allen Lane, 1975)

Finlay, J.L., 'John Hargrave, the Green Shirts and Social Credit', *Journal of Contemporary History* 5, no.1, 1970

Finnigan, Robert, 'Housing Policy in Leeds Between the Wars' in *Housing Policy and the State* ed. Joseph Melling (Croom Helm, 1980)

— 'Council Housing in Leeds, 1919–39' in *Councillors and Tenants: Local Authority Housing in English Cities, 1919–39* ed. M.J. Daunton (Leicester University Press, 1984)

Fisher, Kate, '"Clearing up Misconceptions": The Campaign to Set up Birth Control Clinics in South Wales Between the Wars', *Welsh History Review* 19, no.1, June 1998

— *Birth Control, Sex and Marriage in Britain, 1918–60* (Oxford University Press, 2006)

Fishman, 'William J., A People's Journey: The Battle of Cable Street' in Frederick Krantz, *History from Below: Studies in Popular Ideology in Honour of George Rudé* (Concordia University, 1987)

Florence, Lella Secor, *Birth Control on Trial* (Allen & Unwin, 1930)

Foley, Alice, *A Bolton Childhood* (Manchester University Extramural Department, 1973)

Foot, Michael, *Aneurin Bevan: A Biography, Vol. I: 1897–1945* (MacGibbon & Kee, 1962)

Foot, Royston, 'The Life and Work of Sir Owen Williams' in *British Modern Architecture and Design in the 1930s* ed. Susannah Charlton, Elain Harwood and Alan Powers (Twentieth Century Society, 2007)

For Your Convenience: A Learned Dialogue Instructive to All Londoners & London Visitors, Overheard in The Theleme Club and Taken down Verbatim by Paul Pry (Routledge, 1937)

Ford, Hugh (ed.), *Brave Poet, Indomitable Rebel (Nancy Cunard)* (Philadelphia: Chilton Book Co., 1968)

Foreman-Peck, James, 'Death on the Roads: Changing National Responses to Motor Accidents' in *The Economic and Social Effects of the Spread of Motor Vehicles* ed. Theo Barker (Macmillan, 1987)

Forshaw, J.H. and Abercrombie P., *County Plan of London* (London County Council, 1943)

Forsyth, James, *Tyrone Guthrie: A Biography* (Hamish Hamilton, 1976)

Foulkes, Grace, *My Life with Reuben* (Shepheard-Walwyn, 1975)

Francis, Hywel, *Miners Against Fascism: Wales and the Spanish Civil War* (Lawrence & Wishart, 1984)

Fraser, Keath (ed.), *Worst Journeys: The Picador Book of Travel* (Picador, 1992)

Freeman, Chris, 'The Social Function of Science' in *J. D. Bernal: A Life in Science and Politics* ed. Brenda Swann and Francis Aprahamian (Verso, 1999)

Freeman, Dennis, 'Hop Picking in the 1930s', *East London Record* 8, 1985

Fry, Joan Mary, *Friends Lend a Hand* (Friends Book Centre, 1947)

Fryer, Peter, *Staying Power: The History of Black People in Britain* (Pluto, 1984)

Fussell, Paul, *Abroad: British Literary Travelling Between the Wars* (Oxford University Press, 1980)

Fyrth, Jim, *The Signal Was Spain: The Aid Spain Movement in Britain, 1936–39* (Lawrence & Wishart, 1986)

— 'The Aid Spain Movement in Britain', *History Workshop Journal* 35, November 1993

Gabler, Neal, *Walt Disney: The Biography* (Aurum, 2007)

Gadewchi Paul Robeson Ganu! Dathlubywyd Paul Robeson (Let Paul Robeson Sing! Celebrating the Life of Paul Robeson) (National Library of Wales, 2003)

Gaitskell, H.T.N. [Hugh], *What Everybody Wants to Know About Money* ed. G.D.H. Cole (Gollancz, 1933)

Galbraith J.K., *The Great Crash, 1929* (Hamish Hamilton, 1955)

Gallacher, William, *The Last Memoirs of William Gallacher* ed. Nan Green (Lawrence & Wishart, 1966)

Gallagher, Tom, *Glasgow: The Uneasy Peace – Religious Tension in Modern Scotland* (Manchester University Press, 1987)

Gardiner, Margaret, *A Scatter of Memories* (Free Association, 1988)

Gardiner, Marjorie, *The Other Side of the Counter: The Life of a Shop Girl, 1925–45* (Queenspark, no.17)

Garland, Madge, *An Indecisive Decade: The World of Fashion and Entertainment in the Thirties* (MacDonald, 1968)

Garside, W.R., *British Unemployment, 1919–39: A Study in Public Policy* (Cambridge University Press, 1990)

Gascoyne, David, *Journal 1936–37* (Enitharmon Press, 1980)

Gaze, John, *Figures in Landscape: A History of the National Trust* (Barrie & Jenkins/National Trust, 1988)

Gibbs, Philip, *Ordeal in England* (Heinemann, 1938)

Gibson, I.F., 'The Establishment of the Scottish Steel Industry', *Scottish Journal of Political Economy* 5, 1960

Gilbert, David and Henderson, Fiona, 'London and the Tourist Imagination' in *Imagined Londons* ed. Pamela K. Gilbert (State University of New York Press, 2002)

Gilbert, Michael, *Fraudsters: Six Against the Law* (Constable, 1986)

Gillies, Midge, *Amy Johnson: Queen of the Air* (Weidenfeld & Nicolson, 2003)

Glucksmann, Miriam, *Women Assemble: Women Workers in the New Industries of Inter-War Britain* (Routledge, 1989)

Glynn, Sean and Oxborrow, John, *Interwar Britain: A Social and Economic History* (Allen & Unwin, 1976)

Golby, J.M. and Purdue, A.W., *The Monarchy and the British People: 1760 to the Present* (Batsford, 1988)

Goldsmith, Maurice, *Sage: The Life of J.D. Bernal* (Hutchinson, 1980)

Gollancz, Victor, *More for Timothy* (Gollancz, 1953)

Goodfellow, David M., *Tyneside: The Social Facts* (Co-operative, 1940)

Gordon, Jan and Cora, *The London Roundabout* (Harrap, 1933)

Gordon, Lois, *Nancy Cunard: Heiress, Muse, Political Idealist* (Columbia University Press, 2007)

Gottlieb, Julie, 'Women and Fascism in the East End' in *Remembering Cable Street: Fascism and Anti-Fascism in British Society* ed. Tony Kushner and Nadia Valman (Valentine Mitchell, 2000)

— 'The Marketing of Megalomania: Celebrity, Consumption and the Development of Political Technology in the British Union of Fascists', *Journal of Contemporary History* 41, no.1, 2006

Graves, Charles, *And the Greeks* (Geoffrey Bles, 1930)

Graves, Robert and Hodges, Alan, *The Long Weekend: A Social History of Great Britain, 1918–39* (Faber, 1940)

Gray, Nigel, *The Worst of Times: An Oral History of the Great Depression in Britain* (Wildwood, 1985)

Gray, Richard, *One Hundred Years of Cinema Architecture* (Lund Humphries, 1996)

Green, Christopher, 'The Machine' in *Modernism: Designing a New World* ed. Christopher Wilk (V& A, 2006)

Green, Martin, *Children of the Sun: A Narrative of Decadence in England after 1918* (Constable, 1976)

Greene, Felix (ed.), *Time to Spare: What Unemployment Really Means* (Allen & Unwin, 1935)

Greene, Graham, *A Gun for Sale: An Entertainment* (Heinemann, 1936)

Greenwood, Walter, *Love on the Dole* (Cape, 1933)

Grieve, Alistair, *Isokon* (Isokon Plus, 2004)

Griffin, Colin P., 'Survival Strategies of Unemployed East Midland Coalminers in the Inter-War Years: A Guide to Sources and Findings', *East Midland Historian* 6, 1996

Griffiths Clare, V.J., *Labour and the Countryside: The Politics of Rural Britain, 1918–39* (Oxford University Press, 2007)

Griffiths, Richard, *Fellow Travellers of the Right: British Enthusiasts for Nazi Germany, 1933–9* (Constable, 1980)

Grimwood, Ian R., *A Little Chit of a Fellow: A Biography of the Right Hon. Leslie Hore-Belisha* (Book Guild, 2006)

Grove, Valerie, *Laurie Lee: The Well Loved Stranger* (Viking, 1999)

Guest, Simon, 'Cure, Superstition, Infection and Reaction: Tuberculosis in Ireland 1932–57', *Oral History*, autumn 2004

Guinness, Jonathan (with Catherine Guinness), *The House of Mitford* (Hutchinson, 1984)

Gurney, Jason, *Crusade in Spain* (Faber, 1974)

Gurney, Peter, '"Intersex" and "Dirty Girls": Mass-Observation and Working-Class Sexuality in England in the 1930s', *Journal of the History of Sexuality* 8, no.2, 1997

Haldane, Charlotte, *Truth Will Out* (Right Book Club, 1949)

Haldane, J.B.S., *ARP* (Gollancz, 1938)

Hall, Carolyn, *The Thirties in Vogue* (Octopus Books, 1984)

Hall, Denis Clarke, 'School Design in the 1930s' in *British Modern Architecture and Design in the 1930s* ed. Susannah Charlton, Elain Harwood and Alan Powers (Twentieth Century Society, 2007)

Hall, Lee, *The Pitmen Painters* (Faber, 2008)

Hall, Lesley A., *Sex, Gender and Social Change in Britain Since 1880* (Macmillan, 2000)

Hall, Radclyffe, *The Well of Loneliness* (Cape, 1928; Virago, 1985)

Halliwell, Leslie, *Seats in All Parts: Half a Lifetime at the Movies* (Granada, 1985)

Halsey, A.H. (ed.), *British Social Trends Since 1900: A Guide to the Changing Social Structure of Britain* (Macmillan, 1988)

Halstead, Robin, Hazeley, Jason, Morris, Alex and Morris, Joel, *Bollocks to Alton Towers: Uncommonly British Days Out* (Michael Joseph, 2005)

Hamer, Emily, *Britannia's Glory: A History of Twentieth Century Lesbianism* (Cassell, 1996)

Hamilton, Cicely, *Modern England as Seen by an Englishwoman* (J.M. Dent, 1938)

Hamilton, Duncan, *Harold Larwood* (Quercus, 2009)

Hamilton, Patrick, *Twenty Thousand Streets Under the Sky* (Constable 1935; Vintage Classics, 2004)

Hammerton, H.J., *This Turbulent Priest: The Story of Charles Jenkinson, Parish Priest and Housing Reformer* (Lutterworth, 1952)

Hannington, Wal, *Never on Our Knees* (Lawrence & Wishart, 1967)

— *The Problem of the Distressed Areas* (Gollancz, 1937)

— *Unemployed Struggles, 1919–36: My Life and Struggles Among the Unemployed* (Lawrence & Wishart, 1936)

Hardy, Anne, *Health and Medicine in Britain Since 1860* (Palgrave, 2001)

Hardy, Dennis and Ward, Colin, *Arcadia for All: The Legacy of a Makeshift Landscape* (Mansell, 1984)

Harman, Claire, *Sylvia Townsend Warner: A Biography* (Chatto & Windus, 1989)

Harper, Sue, 'A Lower-Middle-Class Taste: Community in the 1930s – Admissions Figures at the Regent Cinema, Portsmouth, UK', *Historical Journal of Film, Radio and Television* 24, no.4, 2004

Harris, Jose, *William Beveridge: A Biography* (Clarendon Press, 1977)

Harris, Kenneth, *Attlee* (Weidenfeld & Nicolson, 1982)

Harrod, R.F., *The Life of John Maynard Keynes* (Macmillan, 1951)

Hart-Davis, Duff, *Hitler's Games* (Century, 1986)

Hastings, Adrian, *A History of English Christianity, 1920-85* (Collins, 1986)

Hastings, Selina, *Evelyn Waugh: A Biography* (Sinclair-Stevenson, 1994)

Hattersley, Roy, *Borrowed Time: The Story of Britain Between the Wars* (Little, Brown, 2007)

Hatton, Timothy J. and Bailey, Roy E., 'Unemployment Incidence in Interwar London', *Economica*, 2002

Hayburn, Ralph, 'The National Unemployed Workers' Movement, 1921–36: A Reappraisal', *International Review of Social History* 28, 3, 1983

— 'The Police and the Hunger Marchers', *International Review of Social History* 17, 3, 1972

— 'The Voluntary Occupational Centre Movement', *Journal of Contemporary History* 6, 3, 1971

Hazelgrove, Jennifer, 'Spiritualism After the Great War', *Twentieth Century British History* 10, no.4, 1999

— *Spiritualism and British Society Between the Wars* (Manchester University Press, 2000)

Headlam, Cuthbert, *Parliament and Politics in the Age of Baldwin and MacDonald: The Headlam Diaries, 1923–35* ed. Stuart Ball (Historians Press, 1992)

Heiman, Judith M., *The Most Offending Soul Alive: Tom Harrisson and His Remarkable Life* (Aurum, 2002)

Heller, Richard, 'East Fulham Revisited', *Journal of Contemporary History* 6, no.4, 1971

Hemby, Phyllis, *British Spas from 1815 to the Present: A Social History* (Athlone, 1997)

Herbert, A.P., *Holy Deadlock* (Methuen, 1934)

— *Uncommon Law* (Methuen, 1935)

— *Independent Member* (Methuen, 1950)

Heren, Louis, *Growing up Poor in London* (Hamish Hamilton, 1993)

Hetherington, S.J., *Katherine Atholl: Against the Tide* (Aberdeen University Press, 1989)

Hill, Barry K., 'Unemployment in Birmingham and South Wales', *Llafur: Journal of Welsh People's History* 8, no.4, 2003

Hill, Jeffrey, 'League Cricket in the North and Midlands, 1900–40' in *Sport and the Working Class in Modern Britain* ed. Richard Holt (Manchester University Press, 1996)

Hilliard, Christopher, *To Exercise Our Talents: The Democratization of Writing in Britain* (Harvard University Press, 2006)

Hillier, Bevis, *John Betjeman: New Fame, New Love* (John Murray, 2002)

Hillis, Marjorie, *Live Alone and Like It: A Guide for the Extra Woman* (Duckworth, 1936)

Hilton, Christopher, *Hitler's Olympics* (Sutton, 2006)

Hilton, John, *Why I Go in for the Pools by Tom, Dick and Harry (Also Peggy, Joan and Kate)* (Allen & Unwin, 1936)

— *Rich Man, Poor Man* (Allen & Unwin, 1944)

Hoare, Philip, *Noël Coward: A Biography* (Sinclair-Stevenson, 1995)

Hobhouse, Christopher, *1851 and the Crystal Palace* (John Murray, 1950)

Hodder-Williams, Richard, *Public Opinion Polls and British Politics* (Routledge, 1970)

Hodin, J.P., 'A Study of the Cultural History of Hampstead in the Thirties', *Hampstead in the Thirties: A Committed Decade* (Camden Arts Centre, 1974), 5–6

Hodson, J.L., *Our Two Englands* (Michael Joseph, 1936)

Hogben, Adrian and Anne, *Lancelot Hogben, Scientific Humanist: An Unauthorised Autobiography* (Merlin Press, 1998)

Hogben, Lancelot, *Mathematics for the Million* (Allen & Unwin, 1936)

— *Science for the Citizen* (Allen & Unwin, 1938)

Hogenkamp, Bert, *Deadly Parallels: Film and the Left in Britain* (Lawrence & Wishart, 1986)

Hoggart, Richard, *The Uses of Literacy* (Chatto & Windus, 1957)

Holdsworth, Angela, *Out of the Doll's House: The Story of Women in the Twentieth Century* (BBC, 1988)

Hollins, T.J., 'The Conservative Party and Film Propaganda Between the Wars', *English Historical Review* 96, no.379, April 1981

Holmes, Beatrice Gordon, *In Love with Life: A Pioneer Career Woman's Story* (Hollis & Carter, 1944)

Holmes, Colin, *Anti-Semitism in British Society, 1876–1939* (Edward Arnold, 1979)

Holt, Richard, *Sport and the British: A Modern History* (Clarendon Press, 1989)

— (ed.), *Sport and the Working Class in Modern Britain* (Manchester University Press, 1996)

Holtby, Winifred, *Women and a Changing Civilisation* (John Lane/Bodley Head, 1934)

— *Selected Letters of Winifred Holtby and Vera Brittain, 1920–1935* ed. Geoffrey Handley-Taylor (Brown, 1960)

Home Sweet Home: Housing Designed by the London County Council and Greater London Architects 1888–1975 (Greater London Council Department of Architecture and Civic Design, 1975)

Honeycombe, Gordon, *Selfridges: Seventy-Five Years – The Story of the Store, 1909–84* (Park Lane Press, 1984)

Hopkins, David, *Dada and Surrealism: A Very Short Introduction* (Oxford University Press, 2004)

Horwood, Catherine, 'Anyone for Tennis?: Male Dress and Decorum on the Tennis Courts in Inter-War Britain', *Costume* 38, 2004

— 'Dressing Like a Champion: Women's Tennis Wear in Interwar England' in *The Englishness of English Dress* ed. Christopher Breward, Becky Conekin and Caroline Cox (Berg, 2002)

— *Keeping up Appearances: Fashion and Class Between the Wars* (Sutton, 2005)

Houlbrook, Matt, 'The Private World of Public Urinals: London 1918–57', *London Journal* 25, 1, 2000

— *Queer London: Perils and Pleasures in the Sexual Metropolis, 1918–57* (University of Chicago Press, 2005)

Housing in Stoke on Trent: The Place and the Problem (Society for Socialist Inquiry and Propaganda, July 1932)

Howard, Tony, 'Blood on the Bright Young Things: Shakespeare in the 1930s' in *British Theatre Between the Wars, 1918–39* ed. Clive Barker and Maggie B. Gale (Cambridge University Press, 2000)

Howell, Georgina, *In Vogue: Six Decades of Fashion* (Allen Lane, 1975)

Howkins, Alun, *The Death of Rural England: A Social History of the Countryside* (Routledge, 2003)

Howson, Susan and Winch, Donald, *The Economic Advisory Council, 1930–39: A Study in Economic Advice During Depression and Recovery* (Cambridge University Press, 1977)

Hudson, John, *Wakes Weeks: Memories of Mill Town Holidays* (Stroud: Alan Sutton, 1992)

Huggins, Mike, *Horse Racing and the British, 1919–39* (Manchester University Press, 2003)

— 'Going to the Dogs', *History Today* 56, 5, May 2006

— 'Betting, Sport and the British, 1918–39', *Journal of Social History*, winter 2007

Huggins, Mike and Williams, Jack, *Sport and the English, 1918–39* (Routledge, 2006)

Hughes, Robert, *The Red Dean* (Churchman, 1987)

Humphries, Steve and Hopwood, Beverly, *Green and Pleasant Land* (Channel Four, 1999)

Hutt, Alan, *The Condition of the Working Class in Britain* (Martin Lawrence, 1933)

Huxley, Julian, *What Dare I Think?* (Chatto & Windus, 1931)

— *A Scientist Among Soviets* (Chatto & Windus, 1932)

— *If I Were Dictator* (Methuen, 1934)

— *Memoirs* (Allen & Unwin, 1970)

Hyde, H. Montgomery, *Norman Birkett* (Hamish Hamilton, 1964)

Inge, The Very Rev. W.R., *Diary of a Dean: St Paul's 1911–34* (Hutchinson, 1949)

Ingram, Kevin, *Rebel: The Short Life of Esmond Romilly* (Weidenfeld & Nicolson, 1985)

Isherwood, Christopher, *Christopher and His Kind* (Eyre Methuen, 1977)

— *Letters to Christopher: Stephen Spender's Letters to Christopher Isherwood, 1929–39, with 'The Line on the Branch' – Two Thirties Journals* ed. Lee Bartlett (Black Arrow Press, 1980)

Jackson, Alan A., *The Middle Classes 1900–50* (David St John Thomas, 1991)

— *Semi-Detached London: Suburban Development, Life and Transport, 1900–39* (Allen & Unwin, 1973)

— *The Railway in Surrey* (Atlantic, 1999)

Jackson, Angela, *British Women and the Spanish Civil War* (Routledge, 2002)

Jackson, Kevin, *Humphrey Jennings* (Picador, 2004)

Jackson, Michael, *Fallen Sparrows: The International Brigade in the Spanish Civil War* (American Philosophical Society, 1994)

Jacobs, Joe, *Out of the Ghetto: My Life in the East End – Communism and Fascism, 1913–39* (1978; 2nd edn Phoenix Press, 1991)

James, C.L.R, *Beyond a Boundary* (Hutchinson, 1963; Yellow Jersey, 2005)

James, Robert, '"A Very Profitable Enterprise": South Wales Miners' Institute Cinemas in the 1930s', *Historical Journal of Film, Radio and Television* 27, March 2007

James, Robert Rhodes, *Bob Boothby: A Portrait* (Hodder & Stoughton, 1991)

Jeffs, T., *Henry Morris: Village Colleges, Community Education and the Ideal Order* (Nottingham: Educational Heretics Press, 1998)

Jenkins, Alan, *The Thirties* (Heinemann, 1976)

Jenkins, David Fraser and Spalding, Frances *John Piper in the 1930s: Abstraction on the Beach* (Merrell, 2003)

Jenner, Heather, *Marriages are Made on Earth* (Newton Abbot: David & Charles, 1979)

Jennings, Charles, *The Fast Set: Three Extraordinary Men and Their Race for the Land Speed Record* (Little, Brown, 2004)

Jennings, Hilda, *Brynmawr: A Study of a Distressed Area* (Allenson, 1934)

Jevons, Rosamond and Madge, John, *Housing Estates: A Study of Bristol Corporation Policy and Practice Between the Wars* (University of Bristol, 1946)

Jivani, Alkarim, *It's Not Unusual: A History of Lesbian and Gay Britain in the Twentieth Century* (Michael O'Mara, 1997)

Joad, C.E.M., *A Charter for Ramblers* (Hutchinson, 1934)

— *The Untutored Townsman's Invasion of the Countryside* (Faber, 1946)

Johnman, Lewis and Murphy, Hugh, 'An Overview of the Economic and Social Effects of the Interwar Depression on Clydeside Shipbuilding Communities', *International Journal of Maritime History* 18, no.1, June 2006

Johnson, Hewlett, *The Socialist Sixth of the World* (Gollancz, 1939)

— *Searching for Light: An Autobiography* (Michael Joseph, 1968)

Johnson, Paul, *The Vanished Landscape: A 1930s Childhood in the Potteries* (Weidenfeld & Nicolson, 2004)

Jones, D. Caradog, *The Social Survey of Merseyside* (Liverpool University Press/Hodder & Stoughton, 1934)

Jones, Greta, 'Eugenics and Social Policy Between the Wars', *Historical Journal* 25, 3, 1982

— 'Marie Stopes in Ireland: The Mothers' Clinic in Belfast, 1936–7', *Social History of Medicine* 5, no.2, August 1992

Jones, Jack, *Unfinished Journey* (Oxford University Press, 1937)

Jones, Stephen G., *Workers at Play: A Social and Economic History of Leisure, 1918–39* (Routledge, 1986)

Jones, Thomas, *A Diary with Letters, 1931–50* (Oxford University Press, 1954)

— *Whitehall Diary, Vol. II: 1926–30* ed. Keith Middlemass (Oxford University Press, 1969)

Kay, John, *A History of County Cricket: Lancashire* (Arthur Barker, 1972)

Keir, David and Morgan, Bryan (eds), *Golden Milestone: 50 Years of the AA* (Automobile Association, 1995)

Kenner, Hugh, *The Pound Era* (Faber, 1972)

Kenrick, John, *Musical Theatre: A History* (Continuum, 2008)

Kent, Robin, *Aunt Agony Advises: Problem Pages Through the Ages* (W.H. Allen, 1979)

Keown, John, *Abortion, Doctors and the Law: Some Aspects of the Legal Regulation of Abortion in England from 1803 to 1982* (Cambridge University Press, 1998)

Khan, R.F., 'The Relation of Home Investment to Unemployment', *Economic Journal* 41, 1931

King, Anthony (ed.), *British Political Opinion, 1937–2000* (Politico's, 2001)

Kingsford, Peter, *The Hunger Marchers in Britain, 1920–40* (Lawrence & Wishart, 1982)

Kircher, Rudolf, *Fair Play: The Games of Merrie England* trans. R.N. Bradley (Collins, 1928)

Kirkwood, David, *My Life of Revolt* (Harrap, 1935)

Knox, James, *A Biography of Lord Byron* (John Murray, 2003)

Kops, Bernard, *The World is a Wedding* (MacGibbon & Kee, 1963: Five Leaves, 2007)

Kusunoki, Sharon-Michi, 'Edward James: Architect of Surrealism' in *Surreal Things: Surrealism and Design* ed. Ghislaine Wood (V&A, 2007)

Kynaston, David, *The City of London, Vol. III: Illusions of Gold, 1914–45* (Chatto & Windus, 1999)

Laity, Paul (ed.), *Left Book Club Anthology* (Gollancz, 2001)

Lambert, Anthony J., *Travel in the Twenties and Thirties* (Ian Allan, 1983)

Lancaster, Bill, *The Department Store: A Social History* (Leicester University Press, 1995)

Lancaster, Osbert, *Pillar to Post: English Architecture Without Tears* (John Murray, 1938)

Landy, Marcia, 'The Extraordinary Ordinariness of Gracie Fields: The Anatomy of a British Film Star' in *British Stars and Stardom from Alma Taylor to Sean Connery* ed. Bruce Babington (Manchester University Press, 2001)

Langhamer, Clare, 'Love and Courtship in Mid-Twentieth Century England', *Historical Journal* 50, 1, 2007

— *Women's Leisure in England 1920–60* (Manchester University Press, 2000)

Large, David Clay, *Nazi Games: The Olympics of 1936* (Norton, 2007)

Laughton, Bruce, *The Euston Road School: A Study in Objective Painting* (Scolar, 1986)

Laver, James, *Between the Wars* (Vista Books, 1961)

Laybourn, Keith, '"Waking Up to the Fact That There Are Unemployed": Women, Unemployment and the Domestic Solution in Britain, 1918–39' *History* 88, 292, 2003

— *Working-Class Gambling in Britain c.1906–1960s: The Stages of the Political Debate* (Edward Mellen, 2007)

Lean, Garth, *Frank Buchman: A Life* (Constable, 1985)

Leasor, James, *The Millionth Chance: The Story of the R101* (Hamish Hamilton, 1957)

Leathard, Audrey, *The Fight for Family Planning: The Development of Family Planning Services in Britain, 1921–74* (Macmillan, 1980)

Leavis, Q.D., *Fiction and the Reading Public* (Chatto & Windus, 1932)

Lebas, Elizabeth, '"Where Every Street Became a Cinema": The Film Work of Bermondsey Borough Council's Public Health Department, 1923–53', *History Workshop Journal* 39, 1995

Lee, Hermione, *Virginia Woolf* (Chatto & Windus, 1996)

Lee, Laurie, *As I Walked Out One Midsummer Morning* (André Deutsch, 1969)

Lees-Milne, James, *Another Self* (Hamish Hamilton, 1970)

Legarreta, Dorothy, *The Guernica Generation: Basque Refugee Children of the Spanish Civil War* (Nevada University Press, 1984)

Le Mahieu, D.L., *A Culture for Democracy: Mass Communication and the Cultivated Mind in Britain Between the Wars* (Oxford Clarendon Press, 1988)

Lesbian History Group, *Not a Passing Phase: Reclaiming Lesbians in History, 1840–1985* (Women's Press, 1989)

Lewis, C. Day, *The Buried Day* (Chatto & Windus, 1990)

Lewis, D.S., *Illusions of Grandeur: Mosley, Fascism and British Society* (Manchester University Press, 1987)

Lewis, Jane, *Women in England, 1870–1950* (Harvester, 1984)

Lewis, Jane and Brookes, Barbara, 'The Peckham Health Centre, "PEP" and the Concept of General Practice During the 1930s and 1940s', *Medical History* 27, 1983

Lewis, John, *The Left Book Club: An Historical Record* (Gollancz, 1970)

Lewis, John, Polanyi, Karl and Kitchen, Donald K. (eds), *Christianity and the Social Revolution* (Gollancz, 1935)

Lewis-Fanning, E., *A Study of the Trend of Mortality Rates in Urban Communities of England and Wales, with Special Reference to 'Depressed Areas'* (HMSO, 1938)

Lilly, Mark, *The National Council for Civil Liberties: The First Fifty Years* (Macmillan, 1984)

Little, Douglas, *Malevolent Neutrality: The United States, Great Britain and the Origins of the Spanish Civil War* (Cornell University Press, 1985)

Little, Kenneth, *Negroes in Britain: A Study of Racial Relations in English Society* (Routledge, 2nd edn 1972)

Little Palaces: House and Home in the Inter-War Suburbs (MoDA, Middlesex University Press, 2003)

Llewellyn-Smith, Sir Hubert (ed.), *The New Survey of London Life and Labour, Vols 1–9* (P.S. King, 1931–35)

Lockhart, J.G., *Cosmo Gordon Lang* (Hodder & Stoughton, 1949)

London's Zoo: An Anthology to Celebrate 150 Years of the Zoological Society of London, with the Zoos at Regent's Park in London and Whipsnade in Bedfordshire compiled by Gwynne Vevers (Bodley Head, 1976)

Longford, Elizabeth, *The Royal House of Windsor* (Weidenfeld & Nicolson, 1974)
— *The Pebbled Shore: The Memoirs of Elizabeth Longford* (Weidenfeld & Nicolson, 1986)
Lovell, Mary S., *Straight on Till Morning: The Biography of Beryl Markham* (Hutchinson, 1987)
— *The Sound of Wings: The Biography of Amelia Earhart* (Hutchinson, 1989)
Low, Rachel, *The History of British Film 1929–39: Film Making in 1930s Britain* (Allen & Unwin, 1985)
Lowe, John, *Edward James: A Surrealist Life* (Collins, 1991)
Lowerson, John, 'Battles for the Countryside' in *Class, Culture and Structural Change: A New View of the 1930s* ed. Frank Gloversmith (Harvester Press, 1980)
Lucie-Smith, Edward, *Art of the 1930s: The Age of Anxiety* (Weidenfeld & Nicolson, 1985)
Lukowitz, David C., 'British Pacifists and Appeasement: The Peace Pledge Union', *Journal of Contemporary History* 9, no.1, January 1974
Lynn, Andrea, *Shadow Lovers: The Last Affairs of H.G. Wells* (Perseus, 2001)
Lynton, Norbert, *Ben Nicholson* (Phaidon, 2002)
McAleer, Joseph, *Popular Reading and Publishing in Britain, 1914–50* (Oxford University Press, 1992)
McArthur, Alexander and Long, H. Kingsley, *No Mean City: The Story of the Glasgow Slums* (Longmans Green, 1935)
MacBride, E.W., 'Sterilisation as a Practical Eugenic Policy', *Nature* 125, 1930
McCarthy, Albert, *The Dance Band Era: The Dancing Decades from Ragtime to Swing, 1910–50* (Hamlyn, 1974)
MacCarthy, Fiona, *British Design Since 1800* (Lund Humphries, 1992)
— *Eric Gill* (Faber, 1989)
McCrum. Robert, *Wodehouse: A Life* (Viking, 2004)
McCulloch, Andrew, 'A Millstone Round Your Neck? Building Societies in the 1930s and Mortgage Default', *Housing Studies* 5, no.1, 43
— 'The Mortgage Strikes', *History Today* 51, 6, June 2001
McDevitt, Patrick F., *May the Best Man Win: Sport, Masculinity and Nationalism in Great Britain and Empire, 1880–1935* (Palgrave, 2004)
MacDonald, Roderick J., 'Dr Harold Arundel Moody and the League of Coloured Peoples, 1931–47: A Retrospective View', *Race* 14, 1972–73
MacDougall, Ian (ed.), *Voices from the Hunger Marches: Personal Recollections by Scottish Hunger Marchers of the 1920s and 1930s, Vols 1-2* (Edinburgh: Polygon, 1990)
— (ed.), *Voices from the Spanish Civil War: Personal Recollections of Scottish Volunteers in Republican Spain 1936–9* (Edinburgh: Polygon, 1986)
M'Gonigle, G.C.M. and Kirby, J., *Poverty and Public Health* (Gollancz, 1936)
McInnes, Angus, 'Surviving the Slump: An Oral History of Stoke-on-Trent Between the Wars', *Midland History* 18, 1993
McIntosh, Tania, '"An Abortionist City": Maternal Mortality, Abortion and Birth Control in Sheffield, 1920–40', *Medical History* 44, 2000

MacIntyre, Stuart, *Little Moscows: Communism and Working-Class Militancy in Inter-War Britain* (Croom Helm, 1980)

McKean, Charles, 'Between the Wars' in *Glasgow: The Forming of a City* ed. Peter Reed (Edinburgh University Press, 1999)

MacKenzie, S.P., 'The Foreign Enlistment Act and the Spanish Civil War, 1936–39', *Twentieth Century British History* 10, no.1, 1999

MacKersey, Ian, *Jean Batten: The Garbo of the Skies* (MacDonald, 1991)

McKibbin, Ross, 'The Economic Policy of the Second Labour Government, 1929–31', *Past and Present* 68, 112

— *Ideologies of Class: Social Relations in Britain 1880–1950* (Oxford University Press, 1991)

— *Classes and Cultures: England, 1918–51* (Oxford University Press, 1998)

McLaren, Angus, 'Women's Work and the Regulation of Family Size', *History Workshop Journal* 4, autumn 1977

MacMahon, Ryan, *Tramp Royal: An Autobiography* (John Langdon, n.d.)

Macmillan, Harold, *Winds of Change, 1914–39* (Macmillan, 1966)

Macmillan, Lord, *A Man of Law's Tale* (Macmillan, 1952)

McNair, John, *James Maxton: The Beloved Rebel* (Allen & Unwin, 1955)

MacNeice, Louis, *The Strings are False: An Unfinished Autobiography* (Faber, 1965)

— *Collected Poems of Louis MacNeice* ed. Peter MacDonald (Faber, 2007)

McShane, Harry and Smith, Joan, *No Mean Fighter* (Pluto, 1978)

Machin, G.T., 'British Churches and the Cinema' in Diana Wood (ed.), *The Church and the Arts: Papers Read at the 1990 Summer Meeting and the 1991 Winter Meeting of the Ecclesiastical Society* (Blackwell, 1992)

— *Churches and Social Issues in Twentieth-Century Britain* (Oxford Clarendon Press, 1998)

Mais, S.P.B. (ed.), *Time to Spare: What Unemployment Really Means* (Allen & Unwin, 1935)

— 'The Plain Man Looks at England' in *Britain and the Beast* ed. Clough Williams-Ellis (J.M. Dent, 1937)

Malament, Barbara C., 'British Labour and Roosevelt's New Deal: The Response of the Left and the Unions', *Journal of British Studies* 17, no.2, 1978

— 'Philp Snowden and the Cabinet Deliberations of August 1931', *Bulletin of the Society for the Study of Labour History* 41, 1980

Manchester Women's History Group, 'Ideology in Bricks and Mortar: Women's Housing in Manchester Between the Wars', *North West Labour History* 12, 1987

Manning, Leah, *A Life for Education: An Autobiography* (Gollancz, 1970)

Marquand, David, *Ramsay MacDonald* (Cape, 1977)

Marshall, H. and Trevelyan, A., *Slum* (Heinemann, 1933)

Martin, C.R.A., *Slums and Slummers: A Sociological Treatise on the Housing Problem* (John Bale, 1935)

Martin, Wallace, *The New Age Under Orage: Chapters in English Cultural History* (Manchester University Press, 1967)

Masefield, Sir Peter G., *To Ride the Storm: The Story of the Airship R.101* (William Kimber, 1982)

Mason, Tony, 'Football' in *Sport in Britain: A Social History* ed. Tony Mason (Cambridge University Press, 1989)

Mass-Observation, *An Inquiry into People's Homes: A Report Prepared by Mass-Observation for the Advertising Services Guild* (John Murray, 1943)

— *Puzzled People: A Study in Popular Attitudes to Religion, Ethics, Progress and Politics in a London Borough, Prepared for the Ethical Union by Mass-Observation* (Gollancz, 1947)

— *Mass-Observation at the Movies* ed. Jeffrey Richards and Dorothy Sheridan (Routledge, 1985)

Matthews, Jill Julius, 'They Had Such a Lot of Fun: The Women's League of Health and Beauty Between the Wars', *History Workshop Journal* 30, autumn 1990

Matless, David, *Landscape and Englishness* (Reaktion, 1998)

Mayer, Anna K., '"A Combative Sense of Duty": Englishness and the Scientists' in *Regenerating England: Science, Medicine and Culture in Inter-War Britain* ed. Christopher Lawrence and Anna K. Mayer (Amsterdam: Editions Rodopi BV, 2000)

Mayer, J.P., *Sociology of Film: Studies and Documents* (Faber, 1946)

Mayhew, Madeline, 'The 1930s Nutrition Controversy', *Journal of Contemporary History* 23, 1988

Meacham, S., 'Raymond Unwin, 1863–1940: Designing Democracy in Edwardian England' in *After the Victorians: Private Conscience and Public Duty – Essays in Memory of John Clive* ed. Susan Pedersen and Peter Mandler (Routledge, 1994)

Melling, Alethea, '"Ray of the Rovers"; The Working-Class Heroine in Popular Football Fiction, 1915–25', *International Journal of the History of Sport* 15, no.1, 1998

Memoirs of the Unemployed, introduced and ed. Beales, H.L. and. Lambert, R.S. (Gollancz, 1934)

Men Without Work: A Report Made to the Pilgrim Trust (Cambridge University Press, 1938)

Meredith, Hubert A., *The Drama of Money-Making: Tragedy and Comedy of the London Stock Exchange* (Sampson Low, 1931)

Mews, Stuart, 'Religion, 1900–39' in *A Companion to the Early Twentieth Century* ed. Chris Wrigley (Blackwell, 2003)

Meyrick, Kate, *Secrets of the 43: Reminiscences by Mrs Meyrick* (John Long, 1933)

Middlemas, Keith and Barnes, John, *Baldwin* (Weidenfeld & Nicolson, 1969)

Miller, Frederic, 'The British Unemployment Crisis of 1935', *Journal of Contemporary History* 14, no.2, April 1979

— 'The Unemployment Policy of the National Government, 1931–36', *Historical Journal* 19, 2, 1976

Miller, Rod, 'Britain and the Rhineland Crisis, 7 March 1936: Retreat from

Responsibility or Accepting the Inevitable?', *Australian Journal of Politics and History* 33, 1987

Millward, Liz, 'The Embodied Aerial Subject: Gendered Mobility in British Inter-War Air Tours', *Journal of Transport History* 29, no.1, 2008

Miners, Hugh, *Gorseth Kernow: The First Fifty Years* (Gorseth Kernow, 1978)

Miskell, Peter, *A Social History of the Cinema in Wales, 1918–51* (University of Wales Press, 2006)

Mitchell, Margaret, 'The Effects of Unemployment on the Social Conditions of Women and Children in the 1930s', *History Workshop Journal* 9, 1985

Mitchison, Naomi, *Comments on Birth Control* (Faber, 1930)

Mitford, Jessica, *Hons and Rebels: An Autobiography* (Gollancz, 1960)

The Mitfords: Letters Between Six Sisters ed. Charlotte Mosley (Fourth Estate, 2007)

Mockler, Anthony, *Haile Selassie's War* (Oxford University Press, 2003)

Moggridge, D.E., *British Monetary Policy, 1924–31: The Norman Conquest of $4.86* (Cambridge University Press, 1972)

Mole, Edward, *Happy Landings* (Airlife, 1984)

Morgan, Kevin, *Against the War: Ruptures and Continuities in British Communist Politics, 1935–41* (Manchester University Press, 1989)

— 'The Communist Party and the *Daily Worker* 1930–56' in Geoff Andrews, Nina Fishman and Kevin Morgan (eds), *Opening the Books: Essays on the Social and Cultural History of British Communism* (Pluto, 1995)

Morgan, Nigel J. and Pritchard, Annette, *Power and Politics at the Seaside: The Development of Devon's Resorts in the Twentieth Century* (University of Exeter Press, 1999)

Morgan, Richard L., 'The Introduction of Civil Legal Aid in England and Wales, 1914–49', *Twentieth Century British History* 5, no.1, 1994

Morley, Sheridan, *A Talent to Amuse: A Biography of Noël Coward* (Heinemann, 1969)

— *John G: The Authorised Biography of John Gielgud* (Hodder & Stoughton, 2001)

Morrell, Jack, *Science at Oxford 1914–39: Transforming an Arts University* (Oxford Clarendon Press, 1997)

Morris, Lynda, 'The Touch of Time' in *Making History: Art and Documentary in Britain from 1929 to Now* (Tate, 2006)

Morrison, Kathryn A., *English Shops and Shopping: An Architectural History* (Yale University Press, 2003)

Morton, H.V., *In Search of England* (Methuen, 1927)

— *The Call of England* (Methuen, 1931)

— *In Search of Wales* (Methuen, 1932)

— *What I Saw in the Slums* (Labour Party, 1933)

Mosley, Diana, *A Life of Contrasts* (Hamish Hamilton, 1977)

Mosley, Oswald, *The Greater Britain* (BUF, 1934)

— *My Life* (Thomas Nelson, 1968)

Mowat, C.L., *Britain Between the Wars, 1918–40* (University of Chicago Press, 1955)

Muggeridge, Malcolm, *The Green Stick: Chronicles of a Wasted Time, Vol. I* (Collins, 1972)

Muir, Edwin, *Scottish Journey* (Heinemann/Gollancz, 1935)

Murray, Bill, *The Old Firm: Sectarianism, Sport and Society in Scotland* (Edinburgh: John Donald, 1984)

Murray, Nicholas, *Aldous Huxley: An English Intellectual* (Little, Brown, 2002)

Murray, W.A., *A Life Worth Living: 50 Years in Medicine* (D.J. Croal, n.d.)

Myers, Kevin, 'History, Migration and Childhood: Basque Refugee Children in 1930s Britain', *Family and Community History* 3/2, November 2000

Myers, Kevin and Grosvenor, Ian, 'Generous Help in Hard Times: Basque Refugee Children in the Midlands, 1937–40', *Birmingham Historian* 14

National Council of Social Services, *Definition of a Community Centre and Community Association* (1938)

Neal, Lawrence, *Retailing and the Public* (Allen & Unwin, 1933)

Neill, A.S., 'Summerhill' in *The Modern Schools Handbook* ed. Trevor Blewitt (Gollancz, 1934)

Nelson, Geoffrey, *Spiritualism and Society* (Routledge, 1969)

Newman, Michael, *John Strachey* (Manchester University Press, 1989)

— *Harold Laski: A Political Biography* (Macmillan, 1993)

Nicholas, Kate, *The Social Effects of Unemployment on Teesside, 1919–39* (Manchester University Press, 1986)

Nichols, Beverley, *News of England: Or a Country Without a Hero* (Cape, 1938)

Nicholson, Virginia, *Singled Out* (Viking/Penguin, 2007)

Nicolson, Harold, *King George the Fifth: His Life and Reign* (Constable, 1952)

— *Diaries and Letters, 1930-39* ed. Nigel Nicolson (Collins, 1966)

Norman, E.R., *Church and Society in England, 1770–1970* (Oxford Clarendon Press, 1976)

Norris, Jill, 'Women's and Men's Unemployment in Macclesfield Between the Wars', *North West Labour History* 9

North, Rex, *The Butlin Story* (Jarrolds, 1962)

Nott, James J., *Music for the People: Popular Music and Dance in Interwar Britain* (Oxford University Press, 2002)

Obelkevich, James, 'Religion' in *The Cambridge Social History of Britain, 1750–1950, Vol. III* ed. F.M.L. Thompson (Cambridge University Press, 1990)

O'Brien, Kate, *Farewell Spain* (Heinemann, 1937; Virago, 1985)

O'Brien, Margaret and Eyles, Allen, *Enter the Dream-House: Memories of Cinemas in South London from the Twenties to the Sixties* (Museum of the Moving Image, 1993)

O'Carroll, Annette, 'Tenements to Bungalows: Class and the Growth of Home Ownership Before World War II', *Urban History* 24, 2, 1997

O'Connell, Sean, *The Car in British Society: Class, Gender and Motoring, 1896–1939* (Manchester University Press, 1998)

Olechnowicz, Andrzej, *Working-Class Housing Between the Wars: The Becontree Estate* (Clarendon Press, 1997)

— 'Unemployed Workers, "Enforced Leisure" and Education for the "Right Use of Leisure" in Britain in the 1930s', *Labour History Review* 70, no.1, April 2005

Oliver, Paul, 'The Galleon on the Front Door' in *Dunroamin: The Suburban Semi and its Enemies* ed. Paul Oliver, Ian Davis and Ian Bentley (Barrie & Jenkins, 1981)

O'Neil, Clifford, '"The Most Magical Corner of England": Tourism, Preservation and the Development of the Lake District, 1919–39' in *Histories of Tourism: Representation, Identity and Conflict* ed. John K. Walton (Channel View, 2005)

Oram, Alison, '"Embittered, Sexless or Homosexual": Attacks on Spinster Teachers, 1918–39' in Lesbian History Group, *Not a Passing Phase: Reclaiming Lesbians in History, 1840–1985* (Women's Press, 1989)

— *Her Husband Was a Woman: Women's Gender-Crossing in Modern British Popular Culture* (Routledge, 2007)

Orwell, George, *England, Your England and Other Essays* (Secker & Warburg, 1953)

— *Keep the Aspidistra Flying* (Gollancz, 1936; Penguin, 1962)

— *The Road to Wigan Pier* (Gollancz, 1937; Penguin, 1962)

— *Homage to Catalonia* (Secker & Warburg, 1938)

— *Coming Up for Air* (Gollancz, 1939; Penguin Classics, 2000)

— *Inside the Whale, and Other Essays* (Gollancz, 1940)

— *The Collected Essays, Journalism and Letters of George Orwell: At an Age Like This, 1920–40* ed. Ian Angus and Sonia Orwell (Secker & Warburg, 1968)

— *The Complete Works of George Orwell, Vol. 1: Facing Unpleasant Facts, 1937–1939* ed. Peter Davison assisted by Ian Angus and Sheila Davison (Secker & Warburg, 1998)

— *The Complete Works of George Orwell, Vol. 10: A Kind of Compulsion, 1903–1936* ed. Peter Davison assisted by Ian Angus and Sheila Davison (Secker & Warburg, 1998)

Osborne, Charles, *W.H. Auden: The Life of a Poet* (Eyre Methuen, 1980)

Out of Bounds: The Education of Giles Romilly and Esmond Romilly (Hamish Hamilton, 1935)

Oxford Dictionary of National Biography (online edition)

Parker, Rowland, *On the Road: The Papworth Story* (Pendragon Press, 1977)

Patterson, John, *Guernica* (Profile, 2007)

Paul, Leslie, *Angry Young Man* (Faber, 1951)

Paynter, Will, *My Generation* (Allen & Unwin, 1972)

Peach, H.H. and Carrington, N., *The Face of the Land* (Allen & Unwin, 1930)

Pearse, Innes H. and Crocker, Lucy, *The Peckham Experiment: A Study in the Living Structure of Society* (Allen & Unwin for the Sir Halley Stewart Trust, 1943)

Pedersen, Susan, *Eleanor Rathbone and the Politics of Conscience* (Yale University Press, 2004)

Peele, Gillian, 'St George's and the Empire Crusade' in Chris Cook and John Ramsden (eds), *By-Elections in British Politics* (UCL Press, 1997)

Pegg, Mark, *Broadcasting and Society, 1919–39* (Croom Helm, 1983)

Pelling, Henry, *America and the British Left: From Bright to Bevan* (A. & C. Black, 1956)

— *The British Communist Party: A Historical Profile* (A. & C. Black, 1958)

Perry, C.R., 'In Search of H.V. Morton: Travel Writing and Cultural Values in the First Age of British Democracy', *Twentieth Century British History* 10, no.4, 1999

Perry, Matt, *The Jarrow Crusade: Protest and Legend* (University of Sunderland Press, 2005)

Peto, James and Loveday, Donna (eds), *Modern Britain, 1929–39* (Design Museum, 1999)

Phillips, Roderick, *Putting Asunder: A History of Divorce in Western Society* (Cambridge University Press, 1988)

Pickard, Tom, *Jarrow March* (Allison & Busby, 1982)

Pictorial and Descriptive Guide to London, A (Ward Lock, 53rd edn 1938)

Piggott, J.R., *Palace of the People: The Crystal Palace at Sydenham, 1854–1936* (Hurst, 2004)

Pilbeam, Pamela, *Madame Tussaud and the History of Waxworks* (Hambledon & London, 2003)

Pimlott, Ben, *Hugh Dalton* (Macmillan, 1985)

— *Labour and the Left in the 1930s* (Cambridge University Press, 1977)

Pimlott, J.A.R., *The Englishman's Holiday* (Faber, 1947)

Pinder, John (ed.), *Fifty Years of Political and Economic Planning: Looking Forward, 1931–81* (Heinemann, 1981)

Pinney, Mark, 'Architecture' in *Little Palaces: House and Home in the Inter-War Suburbs* (MoDA, Middlesex University Press, 2003)

Pinney, R.G., *Britain: Destination of Tourists?* (Travel and Industrial Development Association of Great Britain and Ireland, 1944)

Pirie, Gordon, 'Passenger Traffic in the 1930s on British Imperial Air Routes: Refinement and Revision', *Journal of Transport History* 25, no.1, 2004

Plowden, William, *The Motor Car and Politics, 1896–1970* (Bodley Head, 1971)

Political and Economic Planning, *Women in Top Jobs* (Allen & Unwin, 1971)

Pollock, William, *The Cream of Cricket* (Methuen, 1934)

Poole, Robert, 'Lancashire Wakes Week', *History Today* 34, 8, August 1984

— *The Lancashire Wakes Holidays* (Lancashire County, 1994)

Pope, Rex, 'Unemployed Women in Inter-War Britain, *Women's History Review* 9, no.4, 2000

Pope Hennessy, James, *Queen Mary* (Allen & Unwin, 1959)

Porter, Kevin and Weeks, Jeffrey (eds), *Between the Acts: Lives of Homosexual Men, 1885–1967* (Routledge, 1991)

Postgate, John, 'Raymond Postgate and the Socialist Film Council', *Sight and Sound* 60, no.1, winter 1990

Postgate, John and Mary, *A Stomach for Dissent: The Life of Raymond Postgate, 1896–1971* (Keele University Press, 1994)

Potter, Neil and Frost, Jack, *The Mary: The Inevitable Ship* (Harrap, 1961; Tempus, 1991)

Potter, Terry, *Reflections on Blackpool* (Sigma Leisure, 1994)

Powell, Anthony, *The Acceptance World* (Heinemann, 1955)

— *At Lady Molly's* (Heinemann, 1957)

— *Casanova's Chinese Restaurant* (Heinemann, 1960)

— *The Kindly Ones* (Heinemann, 1962)

Powell, Michael, *200,000 Feet: The Edge of the World* (Dutton, 1958)

— *A Life in Movies: An Autobiography* (Heinemann, 1986)

Powers, Alan, *Eric Ravilious: Imagined Realities* (Imperial War Museum/Philip Wilson, 2003)

Preston, Paul, *Doves of War: Four Women of Spain* (HarperCollins, 2002)

— 'No Simple Purveyor of News: George Steer and Guernica', *History Today*, May 2007

Price, David, *Office of Hope: A History of the Employment Service in Great Britain* (Policy Studies Institute, 2000)

Priestley, J.B., *English Journey* (Heinemann/Gollancz, 1934)

Pritchard, Jack, *View from a Long Chair: The Memoirs of Jack Pritchard* (Routledge, 1984)

Prynn, David, 'The Woodcraft Folk and the Labour Movement, 1925–70', *Journal of Contemporary History* 18, 1983

Pub and the People, The, by *Mass-Observation* (1943; Cresset Library, 1987)

Pugh, Martin, 'The British Union of Fascists and the Olympia Debate', *Historical Journal* 41, 2, 1998

— *Women and the Woman's Movement in Britain* (Basingstoke: Macmillan, 1992)

— *Hurrah for the Blackshirts!: Fascists and Fascism in Britain Between the Wars* (Cape, 2005)

— '*We Danced All Night*': A Social History of Britain Between the Wars (The Bodley Head, 2008)

Punch, Maurice, *Progressive Retreat: A Sociological Study of Dartington Hall School 1926–57 and Some of its Former Pupils* (Cambridge University Press, 1997)

Purcell, Hugh, *The Last English Revolutionary: Tom Wintringham, 1898–1949* (Sutton, 2004)

R.101: The Airship Disaster, 1930 (CD3825, 1931; abridged edn The Stationery Office, 1999)

Ragtime to Wartime: The Best of Good Housekeeping, 1922–39 (Ebury, 1986)

Rathbone, Eleanor, *War Can be Averted: The Achievability of Collective Security* (Gollancz, 1938)

Rauchway, Eric, *The Great Depression and the New Deal: A Very Short Introduction* (Oxford University Press, 2008)

Ravetz, Alison, 'From Working Class Tenements to Modern Flat: Local Authorities and Multi-Storey Housing Between the Wars' in Anthony Sutcliffe (ed.), *Multi-Storey Living: The British Working-Class Experience* (Croom Helm, 1974)

— *Model Estate: Planned Housing at Quarry Hill, Leeds* (Croom Helm/Joseph Rowntree Memorial Trust, 1978)

— 'The History of a Housing Estate', *New Society*, 27 May 1971

Ravetz, Alison with Turkington, Richard, *The Place of Home: English Domestic Environments, 1914–2000* (E. & F.N. Spon, 1995)

Read, Herbert, *Art Now: An Introduction to the Theory of Modern Painting and Sculpture* (Faber, 1933)

Rée, Harry, *Educator Extraordinary: The Life and Achievements of Henry Morris, 1889–1961* (Longman, 1973)

Rees, Goronwy, *St Michael: A History of Marks & Spencer* (Weidenfeld & Nicolson, 1969)

Regan, Terry and Hazelhurst, Alan, *From Lamp to Laser: The Story of the Blackpool Illuminations* (Skelter, 2004)

Reid, Betty 'The Left Book Club in the Thirties' in *Culture and Crisis in Britain in the 30s* ed. Jon Clark, Margot Heinemann, David Margolis and Carole Snee (Lawrence & Wishart, 1979)

Reminiscences of St Helier Estate (St Helier Estate Reminiscence Group, 1999)

Remy, Michel, *Surrealism in Britain* (Ashgate, 1999)

Reynolds, David, *America, Empire of Liberty: A New History* (Allen Lane, 2009)

Richards, J.M., *Castles on the Ground: The Anatomy of Suburbia* (Architectural Press, 1946; second edn John Murray, 1973)

— *Memoirs of an Unjust Fella* (Weidenfeld & Nicolson, 1980)

Richards, Jeffrey, *The Age of the Dream Palace: Cinema and Society in Britain, 1930–39* (Routledge, 1984)

— 'Controlling the Screen: The British Cinema in the 1930s', *History Today* 33, 3, March 1983

Richards, Jeffrey and Aldgate, Anthony, *Best of British: Cinema and Society 1930–70* (Basil Blackwell, 1983)

Richardson, H.W. and Aldcroft, D.H., *Building in the British Economy Between the Wars* (1968)

Rickaby, Tony, 'Artists' International', *History Workshop Journal* 6, 1978

Riddell, Neil, *Labour in Crisis: The Second Labour Government, 1929–31* (Manchester University Press, 1999)

Rieff, Philip (ed.), *On Intellectuals: Theoretical Studies; Case Studies* (Doubleday, 1969)

Rigby, Andrew, 'The Peace Pledge Union, 1936–45' in Peter Brock and Thomas P. Socknat (eds), *Challenge to Mars: Essays on Pacifism from 1918 to 1945* (University of Toronto Press, 1999)

Ritchie, Berry, *A Touch of Class: The Story of Austin Reed* (James & James, 1990)

Roberts, Elizabeth, *A Woman's Place: An Oral History of Working Class Women, 1890–1940* (Blackwell, 1984)

Robertson, George Gladstone, MD, *Gorbals Doctor* (Jarrolds, 1970)

Paul Robeson Speaks ed. Philip S. Foner (Citadel, 1979)

Robson, W.A. (ed.), *The Political Quarterly in the Thirties* (Allen Lane/Penguin Press, 1971)

Rodgers, Daniel T., *Atlantic Crossings: Social Politics in a Progressive Age* (Belknap Press/Harvard University Press, 1998)

Rodgers, Terence, 'The Right Book Club: Text Wars, Modernity and Cultural Politics in the Late Thirties', *Literature & History* 12, no.2, autumn 2003

Rolfe, Mrs C. Neville, 'Sex Delinquency' in *The New Survey of London Life and Labour, Vol. IX: Life and Leisure* (P.S. King, 1935)

Rose, Jonathan, *The Intellectual Life of the British Working Classes* (Yale University Press, 2001)

Rose, Lionel, *Rogues and Vagabonds: Vagrant Underworld in Britain, 1815–1985* (Routledge, 1988)

Rotha, Paul, *Rotha on Film* (Faber, 1958)

Rotha, Paul and Griffiths, Richard, *The Film Till Now* (Spring Books, 1967)

Rowlands, Ted, *Something Must be Done: South Wales and Whitehall, 1931–51* (Merthyr Tydfil: 2000)

Rowley, Trevor, *The English Landscape in the Twentieth Century* (Continuum, 2006)

Rowntree, B. Seebohm, *Progress and Poverty: A Second Survey of York* (Longman, Green, 1941)

Rowse, A.L., *A Man of the Thirties* (Weidenfeld & Nicolson, 1979)

Rubinstein, Antonia (ed.), *Just Like the Country: Memories of London Families who Settled the New Cottage Estates, 1919–39* (Age Exchange, 1991)

Russell, Bertrand, *The Autobiography of Bertrand Russell* (Allen & Unwin, 1968)

Russell, Dave, 'Sport and Identity: The Case of Yorkshire County Cricket Club, 1890–1930', *Twentieth Century British History* 7, no.2, 1996

— *Looking North: Northern England and the National Imagination* (Manchester University Press, 2004)

Russell, Dora, 'Beacon Hill' in *The Modern Schools Handbook* ed. Trevor Blewitt (Gollancz, 1934)

— *The Tamarisk Tree, Vol. II: My School and the Years of War* (Virago, 1981)

Sackville-West, Vita, *The Letters of Vita Sackville-West to Virginia Woolf* ed. Louise De Salvo and Mitchell A. Leaska (Virago, 1992)

Saler, Michael T., *The Avant-Garde in Interwar England: Medieval Modernism and the London Underground* (Oxford University Press, 1999)

Samuel, Raphael, 'Theatre and Socialism in Britain, 1880–1935' in Raphael Samuel, Ewan MacColl and Stuart Cosgrove (eds), *Theatres of the Left, 1880–1935: Workers' Theatre Movements in Britain and America* (Routledge, 1985)

— *The Lost World of British Communism* (Verso, 2006)

Samuels, Stuart, 'The Left Book Club', *Journal of Contemporary History* 1, no.2, 1966

Scannell, Paddy and Cardiff, David, *A Social History of British Broadcasting, Vol. I, 1922–39: Serving the Nation* (Basil Blackwell, 1991)

Scarffardi, Sylvia, *Fire Under the Carpet: Working for Civil Liberties in the 1930s* (Lawrence & Wishart, 1986)

Schaffer, Elizabeth, *Lilian Baylis: A Biography* (University of Hertfordshire Press/Society for Theatre Research, 2006)

Scholes, Percy, *The Mirror of Music, Vol. II* (Novello/Oxford University Press, 1947)

Schwarz, Bill, 'Black Metropolis, White England' in Mica Nava and Alan O'Shea (eds), *Modern Times: Reflections on a Century of English Modernity* (Routledge, 1996)

Schweitzer, Pam with Hancock, Dianne (eds), *Our Lovely Hops: Memories of Hop-Picking in Kent* (Age Concern Theatre Trust, 1991)

Scott, L.P., 'A Plan for Stepney: The Practical and the Ideal', *The Toynbee Outlook* 1, no.3, June 1936

Scott, Peter, 'Selling Owner-Occupation to the Working Classes in 1930s Britain –The Twilight World of Interwar British Hire Purchase', *Past and Present* 177, November 2002

— 'Did Owner-Occupation Lead to Smaller Families for Interwar Working-Class Households?' *Economic History Review* 61, 1, 2008

Scott-Ellis, Priscilla, *The Chances of Death: A Diary of the Spanish Civil War* ed. Raymond Carr (Michael Russell, 1995)

Searle, G.R., 'Eugenics and Politics in Britain in the 1930s', *Annals of Science* 36, 1979

Shaw, G. and Williams, A. (eds), *The Rise and Fall of British Coastal Resorts* (Cassell, 1998)

Sheail, John, *Rural Conservation in Inter-War Britain* (Oxford Clarendon Press, 1981)

Shelden, Michael, *Orwell: The Authorised Biography* (William Heinemann, 1991)

Shelmerdine, Brian, *British Representations of Spain* (Manchester University Press, 2006)

Shelmerdine, L.B., 'Britons in an "un British" War: Domestic Newspapers and the Participation of UK Nationals in the Spanish Civil War', *North West Labour History* 22, 1997–98

Shepherd, John, *George Lansbury: At the Heart of Old Labour* (Oxford University Press, 2002)

Sherriff, R.C., *The Fortnight in September* (Gollancz, 1931; Persephone, 2006)

— *No Leading Lady* (Gollancz, 1968)

Sherry, Norman, *The Life of Graham Greene, Vol. 1: 1904–39* (Cape, 1989)

Shute, Nevil, *Ruined City* (Cassell, 1938)

— *Slide Rule* (Heinemann, 1954)

Sidnell, Michael, *Dances of Death: The Group Theatre of London in the Thirties* (Faber, 1984)

Sigsworth, E., *Montague Burton: The Tailor of Taste* (Manchester University Press, 1990)

Sillitoe, Alan, *Life Without Armour* (HarperCollins, 1995)

Simon, E.D., 'The Future of Our Great Cities' in *Liverpool and the Housing Problem* (Liverpool Council of Social Care, 1935)

— 'Housing and Civic Planning' in Harold J Laski, W. Ivor Jennings and William A. Robson (eds), *A Century of Municipal Progress, 1835–1935* (Allen & Unwin, 1938)

Simon, E.D. and Inman, J., *The Rebuilding of Manchester* (Longman, 1935)

Sinyard, Neil, 'Grierson and the Documentary Film' in *The Cambridge Cultural History of Britain, Vol. VIII: Early Twentieth-Century Britain* ed. Boris Ford (Cambridge University Press, 1989)

Sitwell, Osbert, *Rat Week: An Essay on the Abdication* (Michael Joseph, 1986)

Skelton, Robin (ed.), *Poetry of the Thirties* (Penguin, 1964)

Skidelsky, Robert, *Politicians and the Slump: The Labour Government of 1929–31* (Macmillan, 1967)

— *Oswald Mosley* (Macmillan, 1975)

— *John Maynard Keynes: A Biography, Vol. II: The Economist as Saviour, 1930–37* (Macmillan, 1992)

— *John Maynard Keynes: A Biography, Vol. III: Fighting for Britain, 1937–46* (Macmillan, 2000)

Skinner, Joan, 'The Firestone Factory' in *Twentieth Century Architecture and Industrial Design: Journal of the Twentieth Century Society*, summer 1994

Smith, Harold L., 'Gender and the Welfare State: The 1940 Old Age Pensions Acts', *History* 80, no.260, October 1995

Smith, Janet, *Liquid Assets: The Lidos and the Open Air Swimming Pools of Britain* (English Heritage, 2005)

Smith, Joanna, '"Work Collectively and Live Individually": The Bata Housing Estate in East Tilbury' in *Twentieth Century Architecture IX: Housing the Twentieth Century Nation* ed. Elain Harwood and Alan Powers (Twentieth Century Society, 2008)

Snelson, John, '"We Said We Wouldn't Look Back": British Musical Theatre, 1935–60' in *The Cambridge Companion to the Musical* ed. William A. Everett and Paul R. Laird (Cambridge University Press, 2nd edn 2008)

Snowman, Daniel, *The Hitler Émigrés: The Cultural Impact on Britain of Refugees from Nazism* (Chatto & Windus, 2002)

Soames, Mary (ed.), *Speaking for Themselves: The Personal Letters of Winston and Clementine Churchill* (Doubleday, 1998)

Soloway, Richard A., 'The "Perfect Contraceptive": Eugenics and Birth Control Research in Britain and America in the Interwar Years', *Journal of Contemporary History* 30, 1995

Spalding, Frances, *British Art Since 1900* (Thames & Hudson, 1986)

— *John Piper, Myfanwy Piper: Lives in Art* (Oxford University Press, 2009)

Spender, Stephen, *World Within World* (Faber, 1977)

Spring Rice, Margery, *Working Class Wives* (Penguin, 1939; Virago, 1981)

Springhall, J., Fraser, B. and Hoare, M., *Sure and Steadfast: A History of the Boys' Brigade 1883–1983* (Collins, 1983)

Squires, Mike, *The Aid to Spain Movement in Battersea, 1936–39* (Elmfield, 1994)

Stack, Mrs Bagot, *Building the Body Beautiful: The Bagot Stack Stretch and Swing System* (Chapman & Hall, 1931)

Stack, Prunella, *Zest for Life: Mary Bagot Stack and the League of Health and Beauty* (Peter Owen, 1988)

Stallibrass, Alison, *Being Me and Also Us: Lessons from the Peckham Experiment* (Scottish Academic Press, 1989)

Stamp, Gavin, 'Battersea Power Station', *Thirties Society Journal* 1

— 'Neo-Tudor and its Enemies', *Architectural History* 49, 2006

— *Britain's Lost Cities* (Aurum, 2007)

Stannage, C.T., 'The East Fulham By-Election, 23 October 1933', *Historical Journal* 14, 1, 1971

Stansky, Peter and Abrahams, William, *Journey to the Frontier: Two Roads to the Spanish Civil War* (University of Chicago Press, 1966)

Stead, Peter, 'The People and the Pictures: The British Working Class and Film in the 1930s' in Nicholas Pronay and D.W. Spring (eds), *Propaganda, Politics and Film, 1918–45* (Macmillan, 1982)

Steel, Tom, *The Life and Death of St Kilda* (Collins/Fontana, 1975)

Steele, James, *Queen Mary* (Phaidon, 1995)

Stephenson, Tom, *Forbidden Land: The Struggle for Access to Mountain and Moorland* (Manchester University Press, 1989)

Stevenson, Greg, *The 1930s Home* (Shire, 2005)

Stevenson, John, *British Society 1914–45* (Penguin, 1984)

Stewart, John, '"For a Healthy London": The Socialist Medical Association and the London County Council in the 1930s', *Medical History* 42, 1997

— *The Battle for Health: A Political History of the Socialist Medical Association* (Ashgate, 1999)

Stocks, Mary, *Eleanor Rathbone* (Gollancz, 1949)

Stopes, Marie, *Enduring Passion* (Hogarth Press, 1928)

Studd, R.G., *Holiday Story* (Percival Marshall, 1950)

Sutcliffe, Anthony, 'A Century of Flats in Birmingham, 1875–1973' in Anthony Sutcliffe (ed.), *Multi-Storey Living: The British Working-Class Experience* (Croom Helm, 1974)

Sutherland, John, *Stephen Spender: The Authorized Biography* (Viking, 2004)

Swenarton, Mark and Taylor, Sandra, 'The Scale and the Nature of the Growth of Owner-Occupation in Britain Between the Wars', *Economic History Review* 2nd series, 38, no.3, August 1985

Swire, J., *Gordonstoun, 1934–55: A Survey Upon the Occasion of the School's Coming of Age* (Studio Productions, 1955)

Szreter, S., *Fertility, Class and Gender in Britain 1860–1940* (Cambridge University Press, 1996)

Tallents, Sir Stephen, *The Projection of England* (Faber, 1932)

Tanner, Duncan, Thane, Pat and Tiratsoo, Nick (eds), *Labour's First Century* (Cambridge University Press, 2000)

Taylor, A.J.P., *The Trouble Makers: Dissent Over Foreign Policy, 1792–1939* (Hamish Hamilton, 1957)

— *English History, 1914–45* (Oxford Clarendon Press, 1965)

Taylor, D.J., *Orwell: The Life* (Chatto & Windus, 2003)

— *Bright Young People: The Rise and Fall of a Generation 1918–1940* (Chatto & Windus, 2007)

Taylor, Philip M., *The Projection of Britain: British Overseas Publicity and Propaganda 1919–39* (Cambridge University Press, 1981)

— *British Propaganda in the Twentieth Century: Selling Democracy* (Edinburgh University Press, 1999)

Tebbutt, Melanie, *Making Ends Meet: Pawnbroking and Working-Class Credit* (Leicester University Press, 1983)

— '"In the Midlands But Not of Them": Derbyshire's Dark Peak – An Imagined Northern Landscape' in *Northern Identities: Historical Interpretations of 'The North' and 'Northernness'* ed. Neville Kirk (Ashgate, 2000)

Temple, William, 'The Conclusion of the Matter' in *Christianity and the Crisis* ed. Percy Dearmer (Gollancz, 1933)

Thirkell, Angela, *Wild Strawberries* (Hamish Hamilton, 1934)

— *August Folly* (Hamish Hamilton, 1936)

— *Summer Half* (Hamish Hamilton, 1937)

— *Cheerfulness Breaks In* (Hamish Hamilton, 1940)

Thirties: British Art and Design Before the War (Arts Council of Great Britain, 1979)

Thomas, Hugh, 'The Spanish Civil War' in A.J.P. Taylor (ed.), *History of the Twentieth Century* (Purnell, 1968–69)

Thomas, James and Williams, A. Susan, 'Women and Abortion in 1930s Britain: A Survey and its Data', *Social History of Medicine* 1, no.2

Thompson, F.M.L. (ed.), *The Cambridge History of Britain, Vol. I: Regions and Communities* (Cambridge University Press, 1990)

Thompson, Willie, *The Good Old Cause: British Communism, 1920–91* (Pluto, 1992)

Thorold, Peter, *The Motoring Age: The Automobile and Britain, 1896–1939* (Profile, 2003)

Thorpe, Andrew, *Britain in the Era of the Two World Wars* (Longman, 1994)

— 'The Membership of the Communist Party of Great Britain, 1920–45', *Historical Journal* 43, 3, 2000

Thurgood, Graham, 'Silver End Village, 1926–32', *Thirties Society Journal* 3

Thurlow, Richard C., *Fascism in Britain: From Oswald Mosley's Blackshirts to the National Front* (I.B. Tauris, 1998)

— 'The Straw that Broke the Camel's Back: Public Order, Civil Liberties and the Battle of Cable Street' in *Remembering Cable Street: Fascism and Anti-Fascism in British Society* ed. Tony Kushner and Nadia Valman (Valentine Mitchell, 2000)

Tilson, Barbara, 'The Battle of Bentley Wood', *Thirties Society Journal* 5

Todd, Selina, 'Working-Class Young People in England, 1918–55', *International Review of Social History* 52, 2007

Tomlinson, G.A.W., *Coal Miner* (Hutchinson, 1937)

Tomlinson, H.M., *South to Cadiz* (Heinemann, 1934)

Tomlinson, Jim, 'Labour and the Economy' in *Labour's First Century* ed. Duncan Tanner, Pat Thane and Nick Tiratsoo (Cambridge University Press, 2000)

Tout, Herbert, *The Standard of Living in Bristol* (Arrowsmith, 1938)

Townroe, B.S., *The Slum Problem* (Longman, 1928)

Townsend, William, *The Townsend Journals: An Artist's Record of His Time* (Tate Gallery, 1976)

Townsend Warner, Sylvia, *I'll Stand by You: The Letters of Sylvia Townsend Warner and Valentine Ackland* ed. Susanna Pinney (Pimlico, 1998)

Toye, Richard, *The Labour Party and the Planned Economy, 1931–51* (Royal Historical Society/Boydell Press, 2003)

Toynbee, Philip (ed.), *The Distant Drum: Reflections on the Spanish Civil War* (Sidgwick & Jackson, 1976)

— *Friends Apart: A Memoir of the Thirties* (MacGibbon & Kee, 1954)

Trevelyan, Julian, *Indigo Days* (MacGibbon & Kee, 1957)

Trory, Ernie, *Between the Wars: Recollections of a Communist Organiser* (Crabtree Press, 1974)

Tucker, Jonathan, *The Troublesome Priest: Harold Davidson, Rector of Stiffkey* (Michael Russell, 2007)

Tulloch, Hugh, *Six Travellers in America, 1919–41* (Edward Mellen, 2000)

Turnbull, Maureen, 'Attitude of Government and Administration Towards the "Hunger Marches" of the 1920s and 1930s', *Journal of Social Policy* 2, 1973

Turner, Alwyn W., 'Portmeirion and its Creator' in *Portmeirion* (Antique Collectors' Club, 2006)

Turner, Brian and Palmer, Steve, *The Blackpool Story* (Blackpool Corporation, 1939)

Upton, Chris, *Living Back-to-Back* (Phillimore, 2005)

Upward, Edward, *In the Thirties* (Heinemann, 1962)

— *Journey to the Border* (Enitharmon, 1994)

Vaughan, Paul, *Something in Linoleum: A Thirties Education* (Sinclair-Stevenson, 1994)

Vernon, James, *Hunger: A Modern History* (Belknap Press/Harvard University Press, 2007

Vickers, Hugo, *Cecil Beaton* (Weidenfeld & Nicolson, 1985)

Walsh, Jane, *Not Like This* (Lawrence & Wishart, 1953)

Walsh, Lorraine and Kenefick, William, 'Bread, Water and Hard Labour?: New Perspectives on 1930s Labour Camps', *Scottish Labour History* 34, 1999

Walter, David, *The Oxford Union: Playground of Power* (Macdonald, 1984)

Walton, John K., 'Afterword: Mass-Observation's Blackpool and Some Alternatives' in *Worktowners at Blackpool: Mass-Observation and Popular Leisure in the 1930s* ed. Gary Cross (Routledge, 1990)

— *The Blackpool Landlady: A Social History* (Manchester University Press, 1978)

— *The British Seaside: Holidays and Resorts in the Twentieth Century* (Manchester University Press, 2000)

— 'The National Trust Centenary: Official and Unofficial Histories', *The Local Historian* 26, no.2, May 1996

— *Blackpool* (Edinburgh University Press/Carnegie, 1998)

— 'The Seaside Resorts of England and Wales, 1900–50: Growth, Diffusion and New Forms of Coastal Tourism' in G. Shaw and A. Williams (eds), *The Rise and Fall of British Coastal Resorts* (Cassell, 1998)

Walvin, James, *Beside the Seaside: A Social History of the Popular Seaside Holiday* (Allen Lane, 1978)

— *The People's Game: The History of Football Revisited* (Mainstream, 1994)

Warburton, Nigel, *Ernö Goldfinger: The Life of an Architect* (Routledge, 2004)

Ward, Colin, *Cotters and Squatters: Housing's Hidden History* (Five Leaves, 2002)

Ward, Colin and Hardy, Dennis, *Goodnight Campers!: The History of the British Holiday Camp* (Mansell, 1986)

Ward, Stephanie, 'The Means Test and the Unemployed in South Wales and the North-East of England, 1931–39', *Labour History Review* 73, no.1, April 2008

Warwick, Frances, Countess of, *Afterthoughts* (Cassell, 1931)

Waterson, Merlin, *The National Trust: The First Hundred Years* (BBC, 1994)

Watson, Francis, 'The Death of George V', *History Today* 36, 12, December 1986

Waugh, Evelyn, *Labels: A Mediterranean Journey* (Duckworth, 1930)

— *A Handful of Dust* (Chapman & Hall, 1934)

Webb, Beatrice, *The Diary of Beatrice Webb, Vol. IV: 1924–43, The Wheel of Life* ed. Norman and Jeanne MacKenzie (Virago/London School of Economics, 1985)

Webster, Charles, 'Healthy or Hungry Thirties?', *History Workshop Journal* 13, 1982

— 'Medicine and the Welfare State, 1930–70' in Roger Cooter and John Pickstone (eds), *Medicine in the Twentieth Century* (Harwood, 2000)

— 'The Health of the School Child During the Depression' in Nicholas Parry and David MacNair (eds), *The Fitness of the Nation: Physical and Health Education in the Nineteenth and Twentieth Centuries* (History of Education Society, 1993)

Weeks, Jeffrey, *Sex, Politics and Society* (Longman, 1981)

Weideger, Paula, *Gilding the Acorn: Behind the Façade of the National Trust* (Simon & Schuster, 1994)

Weightman, Gavin, *Bright Lights, Big City: London Entertainment 1830–1950* (Collins & Brown, 1992)

Weightman, Gavin and Humphries, Steve, *The Making of Modern London, 1914–39* (Sidgwick & Jackson, 1984)

Wells, H.G., *Experiment in Autobiography: Discoveries and Conclusions of a Very Ordinary Brain (Since 1866)* (Gollancz/Cresset Press, 1934)

Welshman, John, 'Eugenics and Public Health in Britain, 1900–40: Scenes from Provincial Life', *Urban History* 24, part 1, May 1997

Werskey, Gary P., *The Visible College* (Allen Lane, 1978)

— 'The Marxist Critique of Science: A History in Three Movements', *Science as Culture* 14

— 'The Visible College Revisited: Second Opinion on the Red Scientists of the 1930s', *Minerva* 45, 3, 2007

Wheeler-Bennett, Sir John, *George VI: His Life and Reign* (Macmillan, 1958)

Whipple, Dorothy, *They Knew Mr Knight* (John Murray, 1934; Persephone Books, 2000)

White, Carol and Williams, Sian Rhiannon (eds), *Struggle or Starve: Women's Lives in the South Wales Valleys Between the Two World Wars* (Honno, 1998)

White, Jerry, 'When Every Room was Measured: The Overcrowding Survey of 1935–6 and its Aftermath', *History Workshop Journal* 4, autumn 1977

— *London in the Twentieth Century* (Viking, 2001)

Whiteing, Eileen, *Anyone for Tennis?: Growing up in Wallington Between the Wars* (London Borough of Sutton Libraries and Arts Services, 1979)

Whiteman, W.M., *The History of the Caravan* (Blandford, 1973)

Whiteside, Noel, 'Private Provision and Public Welfare: Health Insurance Between the Wars' in David Gladstone (ed.), *Before Beveridge: Welfare Before the Welfare State* (IEA Health and Welfare Unit, 1999)

Wilk, Christopher (ed.), *Modernism: Designing a New World* (V&A, 2006)

Wilkinson, Ellen, *The Town That Was Murdered: The Life-Story of Jarrow* (Gollancz, 1939)

Wilkinson, Paul, 'English Youth Movements, 1908–30', *Journal of Contemporary History* 4, no.2, 1969

Williams, Andrew Gibbon, *William Roberts: An English Cubist* (Lund Humphries, 2004)

Williams, Chris, *Capitalism, Community and Conflict: The South Wales Coalfield, 1898–1947* (University of Wales Press, 1997)

Williams, Colin, Alexander, Bill and Gorman, John, *Memorials of the Spanish Civil War: The Official Publication of the International Brigade* (Sutton, 1996)

Williams, Francis, *Nothing so Strange* (Cassell, 1970)

Williams, Jack, 'Cricket' in Tony Mason (ed.), *Sport in Britain: A Social History* (Cambridge University Press, 1989)

Williams, Philip M., *Hugh Gaitskell: A Political Biography* (Cape, 1979)

Williams, S.C., *Religious Belief and Popular Culture in Southwark, c.1880–1939* (Oxford University Press, 1999)

Williams, Susan, *The People's King: The True Story of the Abdication* (Allen Lane, 2003)

Williams-Ellis, Clough (ed.), *Britain and the Beast* (J.M. Dent, 1937)

— *England and the Octopus* (Portmeirion Penrhyndeudraeth, 1928; new edn 1975)

— *Portmeirion: The Place and its Meaning* (Faber, 1963)

Williamson, Philip, 'A "Banker's Ramp"? Financiers and the British Political Crisis of August 1931', *English Historical Review*, 1984

— 'Financiers, the Gold Standard and British Politics, 1925–1931' in *Businessmen and Politics: Studies of Business Activity in British Politics, 1900–1945* ed. John Turner (Heinemann Educational, 1984)

Williamson, Stanley, *Gresford: The Anatomy of a Disaster* (Liverpool University Press, 1999)

Willis, Ted, *Whatever Happened to Tom Mix?: The Story of One of My Lives* (Cassell, 1970)

Willmott, Phyllis, *Growing Up in a London Village: Family Life Between the Wars* (Peter Owen, 1979)

Wilson, A.N., *Betjeman* (Hutchinson, 2006)

Windsor, Duke of, *A King's Story: The Memoirs of HRH the Duke of Windsor, KG* (Cassell, 1953)

Wintringham, Tom, *English Captain* (Faber, 1939)

Wintz, Cary D. and Finkleman, Paul (eds), *Encyclopedia of the Harlem Renaissance* (Routledge, 2004)

Wolfe, Kenneth M., *The Churches and the British Broadcasting Corporation, 1922–56* (SCM, 1984)

Wolmar, Christian, *The Subterranean Railway* (Atlantic, 2004; revised edn 2005)

Wolveridge, J., *Ain't it Grand, or This was Stepney* (Stepney House, 1976)

Wood, Neal, *Communists and British Intellectuals* (Gollancz, 1959)

Wood, Oliver and Bishop, James, *The Story of The Times* (Michael Joseph, 1983)

Woodhead, Lindy, *Shopping, Seduction and Mr Selfridge* (Profile, 2007)

Woolf, Leonard, *Downhill All the Way: An Autobiography of the Years 1919–39* (Hogarth Press, 1967)

Woolf, Virginia, *The Diary of Virginia Woolf, Vol. III: 1925–30* ed. Anne Olivier Bell (Hogarth Press, 1980)

— *The Diary of Virginia Woolf, Vol. IV: 1930–41* ed. Anne Olivier Bell (Hogarth Press, 1982)

— *The Diary of Virginia Woolf, Vol. V: 1936–1941* ed. Anne Olivier Bell (Hogarth Press, 1984)

— *The Letters of Virginia Woolf, Vol. III: A Change of Perspective, 1923–28* ed. Nigel Nicolson (Hogarth Press, 1978)

— *The Letters of Virginia Woolf, Vol. IV: A Reflection of the Other Person, 1929–31* ed. Nigel Nicolson (Hogarth Press, 1978)

— *The Letters of Virginia Woolf, Vol. V: The Sickle Side of the Moon, 1932–35* ed. Nigel Nicolson (Hogarth Press, 1979)

— *The Letters of Virginia Woolf, Vol. VI: Leave the Letters Till We're Dead, 1936–41* ed. Nigel Nicolson (Hogarth Press, 1980)

Worley, Matthew, 'What was the New Party? Sir Oswald Mosley and Associated Responses to the "Crisis", 1931–32', *History* 92, 2007

Worpole, Ken, *Here Comes the Sun: Architecture and Public Space in Twentieth-Century European Culture* (Reaktion, 2000)

Worth, Rachel, *Fashion for the People: A History of Clothing at Marks & Spencer* (Berg, 2007)

Wrench, David J., '"Cashing in": The Parties and the National Government, August 1931–September 1932', *Journal of British Studies* 23, 2, 1984

Wright, Helena, *The Sex Factor in Marriage: A Book for Those who are or are About to be Married with an Introduction by A. Herbert Gray, MADD* (Williams & Norgate, 1933)

Wright, Patrick, *On Living in an Old Country* (Verso, 1985)

Yates, Nigel, 'Selling Southsea, Promoting Portsmouth', *Portsmouth Papers* 72 (Portsmouth City Council, n.d.)

— 'Selling the Seaside', *History Today* 38, 8, August 1988

Yelling, Jim, 'The Metropolitan Slum' in *Slums* ed. S. Martin Gaskell (Leicester University Press, 1990)

— *Slums and Redevelopment* (UCL Press, 1992)

Young, Michael, *The Elmhirsts of Dartington: The Creation of a Utopian* (Routledge, 1982)

Young, Terence, *Becontree and Dagenham: A Report Made for the Pilgrim Trust* (Becontree Social Service Committee, 1934)

Ziegler, Philip, *Edward VIII: The Official Biography* (Collins, 1990)

— *Mountbatten: The Official Biography* (Collins, 1985)

Zimmick, Meta, 'Strategies and Stratagems for the Employment of Women in the British Civil Service, 1919–39', *Historical Journal* 27, 4, 1984

Zuckerman, Solly, *From Apes to Warlords, 1904–46* (Hamish Hamilton, 1978)

Zweiniger-Bargielowska, Ina, 'Building a British Superman: Physical Culture in Interwar Britain', *Journal of Contemporary History* 41, no.4

— 'The Culture of the Abdomen: Obesity and Reducing in Britain, circa 1900–39' *Journal of British Studies* 44, April 2005

— 'Raising a Nation of "Good Animals": The New Health Society and Health Education Campaigns in Interwar Britain', *Social History of Medicine* 20, no.1

*

Unpublished Works

Albaya, Joseph P., papers, Sheffield Archives, 779/F1/1

Algie, Barbara, Glasgow City Archive, Mitchell Library, TD 671/8

Arthur, Sue, *Crested China, Pineapple Chunks and Cherry Red Velvet: A History of Shopping in Blackpool Town Centre from 1881 to 1958* (unpublished MA thesis, Blackpool Borough Libraries, 2003)

Blewett, Richard, *The Village of Saint Day in the Parish of Gwennap, Cornwall, June 1935*, Cornwall Record Office, Truro, X/97/1

Ubby Cowan's East End Memories (private unpublished papers)

Don, Alan C., *The Diaries of the Reverend Alan C. Don, 1931–46, nos 2286 1–7*, Lambeth Palace Library

Dunn, Cyril, notebooks (diaries), reproduced by kind permission of Peter Dunn

Ferguson, Colin, notebooks, Glasgow City Archive, Mitchell Library, TD 646/7

Forster, Frank, diaries, Modern Records Centre, University of Warwick, Ms 364/1–11

Gaster, Jack (interview in 2007)

Gaster, Jack, Imperial War Museum Department of Sound Records, accession no. 10253/4 (recorded 1988)

Gilbertson, Margaret M., *The Cotton Queens of Great Britain* (University of Lancaster, unpublished dissertation, 2006)

Godlett, Alexnder Kay, *Journal and Daily Log Book: The Years in Ealing, 1934–1940*, Ealing Record Office

Heap, Anthony, diaries, London Metropolitan Archive, Acc. 2243/6/4a

Heywood Haslam, Robert, *Diary of a Journey to Russia 13/8.32 to 25/9.32*, Bolton Archives

Langford, Gladys, diaries, 1921–69, Islington Record Office, LHC YX079 LAN

Magnus, Imogen, *'Give Him Air. He'll Straight Be Well': Hospitals, Gardens and Grounds for Use in Employment, Therapy, Recreation and Convalescence from the Crimean War to World War II* (unpublished MA dissertation, Birkbeck College, University of London, 2002)

Martin, Mrs Madge, diaries, Oxfordshire County Record Office, P5/2J/03–08

Mass-Observation Archive; DR 1077 reply to May 1939 Directive

Pritchard, Jack, papers, University of East Anglia

Rich, Samuel Morris, diaries, University of Southampton Library, Special Collections, Ms 168

Rowse, A.L., diaries, University of Exeter, Ms 113/2/2/29

Schönfeld, Rabbi Solomon, papers, Hartley Library, University of Southampton, Ms 183

Watkins, Bruce and Haldane Watkins, Ruth (interview 2006)

Zuckerman, Solly, archive, University of East Anglia

INDEX